Sam Thayer's

FIELD GUIDE
—| TO |—
Edible Wild Plants

of Eastern & Central
North America

Samuel Thayer

T0243364

Forager's Harvest

FORAGER'S HARVEST PRESS
WEYERHAEUSER, WI

Publisher's Cataloging-in-Publication Data
Names: Thayer, Samuel James, author.
Title: Sam Thayer's field guide to edible wild plants of eastern and central North America /
    Samuel James Thayer.
Description: Weyerhaeuser, WI : Forager's Harvest, 2023. | Includes index.
Identifiers: LCCN 2023900680 (print) | ISBN 978-0-9766266-4-0 (paperback)
Subjects: LCSH: Wild plants, Edible. | Plants, Edible. | Foraging. | Natural foods. | Wilderness
    survival. | Illustrated works. | BISAC: NATURE / Plants / General. | HEALTH & FITNESS /
    Diet & Nutrition / General.
Classification: LCC QK98.5.A1 T53 2023 (print) | LCC QK98.5.A1 (ebook) | DDC 581.8/32--dc23.

ISBN: 978-0-9766266-4-0

Library of Congress Control Number: 2023900680

Book Design by Fiona Raven
Photos by the author except as credited on page 734, which is an extension of the copyright notice on this page. Line drawings © Amy Schmidt. All rights are reserved by the respective artists.

3rd Printing July 2023

Printed in China

Published by
Forager's Harvest
N4623 Pieper Road
Weyerhaeuser, WI 54895
www.foragersharvest.com

 Forager's Harvest

to Melissa

You've supported this endeavor
from beginning to end—
one more good thing (but not the best)
we've built together.

RESPONSIBILITY AND TRUST

I wrote this book to help you gather and eat wild plants. I am responsible for the content. Attorneys get nervous when I write that; taking responsibility is not the American way. But if I propose that you trust my words, I must shoulder the responsibility of making them trustworthy. There is never room to say everything, and no author can be accountable for omitted information. I'm sure this book is imperfect. But I guarantee it to be free of egregious inaccuracies.

I aim to earn your trust through diligent work and honesty. I did not include any plant in this book unless I ate it myself. Where my experiences were minimal or unsuccessful, or I have not eaten certain edible parts of a plant, I usually make this evident. The information in this book is rooted in research of food traditions, but it has grown to its present form through my first-hand experience. With a few noted exceptions, the plant uses described in these pages were included because, after trying them myself, I thought you might want to try them too.

I've had a passionate interest in edible wild plants since early childhood, but there are always new plants and new uses to discover. I don't have all the answers I want, nor even all the questions. But the death of both of my parents in 2019 forced me to reckon with my own mortality and wrap up this project so that it could be turned over to the users. I hope it serves your purpose.

I spent 17,000 hours making this tool for you. Now you must do your part and use the tool correctly. Sometimes it may be hard—especially if you are new to this. It is your responsibility to read and comprehend all the relevant information before consuming any plant. This includes the book's introductory material from pages 11 through 30, and the full account for any edible species you gather. Look carefully and compare reasonably. Be certain of a plant's identity, and that you are eating the correct part prepared in the correct way.

Some plants carry certain inherent risks or are contraindicated by certain medical conditions. I cannot be aware of all such complications, especially regarding wild plants for which little or no research has been done. A person may prove allergic to or intolerant of any new food, wild or domestic. Overindulgence or excessive use of any food or drink will have negative health consequences. Decisions about food consumption are the responsibility of the reader.

I am responsible for my words. You are responsible for your actions. And we trust each other. That's how it's supposed to work. I'm standing by my words. If you can't handle your part, return the book directly to me and I'll give you your money back. Seriously. I won't hold it against you.

Sam Thayer

GRATITUDE

All of us are descended from hunters and gatherers, and we are indebted to our ancestors for our food traditions. Their ingenuity and resourcefulness never cease to amaze me.

I was raised on lands ceded to the United States under unjust circumstances by the Menominee and Chippewa nations. I am humbled by the privilege of having my feet upon this land and these waters in my blood. The knowledge of these and other original peoples of North America has been the single most important source of information for the food uses listed in this book, and I am deeply grateful for that knowledge. I have also drawn heavily upon food traditions from Asia, Europe, Africa, and elsewhere.

My family, my everyday foraging crew, deserves special mention for making this book happen: Myrica, Rebekah, Joshua, and especially Melissa. It has been a perpetual blessing to share a home with you all. Some friends are so helpful that they almost make us forget their services. Almost. This guide has been immensely improved by years of support from Erica Davis, Adam Haritan, Alan Bergo, Joshua Morey, Abe Lloyd, Linda Black Elk, Kim Calhoun, Arthur Haines, Doug Elliott, and Todd Elliott. When I was in middle school, David Black taught me early lessons about prairie plants and fire ecology, that have stuck with me permanently. A long list of people helped me find, use, or identify certain plants: Tim Clemens, John Godar, Josh Vig, Chris Gavin, Demi Pappas, Alexis Nelson, Aaron King, Leda Meredith, Andrew Ozynskas, Brady Wolff, Sarah Haggerty, Russ Lake, Jaye Maxfield, Jesse Bennett, Andy Thompson, Welby Smith, Yanna Fishman, Mark Vorderbruggen, Jeremy Goulet, Marc Williams, Zack Elfers, and that guy I met in Newfoundland who threw up from the spoiled pot roast (not my fault).

I have not forgotten Rose.

I owe a great deal to my graphics and editing crew, not just for excellent work but for being so pleasant through the process: Fiona Raven, Erica Davis, Amy Schmidt, and Gabrielle Ceberville.

There are a number of authors whose works have been immensely helpful to me in learning about edible plants and botany. The list is too long for this space, but many are included in the references section in the back of the book. I would also like to thank the creators and curators of four websites that helped me immensely: illinoiswildflowers.info, minnesotawildflowers.info, bonap.org, and inaturalist.org. The latter two of these expedited finding a number of species in the wild, and were indispensable for creation of the range maps.

Also, a big thanks to everyone who works or volunteers in an herbarium, who submits plant specimens, and who works in ecological research or plant conservation. Thanks to the ethnobotanical workers and collaborators who have shared and preserved so much rich Indigenous knowledge of wild plants and their uses.

Gratitude to the plants that feed us; and for the earth, water, and air from which they are built through the energy of sunlight.

KEY TO THE GROUPS

The first step to identifying a plant with this book is to determine the group to which it belongs. Start at the upper left of the key. Read all the purple options and choose which one pertains to your plant. If it does not belong in groups 1–3, determine if it is **woody** (with tough, perennial, above-ground stems that survive the dormant season, like a tree or bush) or **herbaceous** (all the above-ground growth dies yearly). Go to the woody or herbaceous key and again start with the purple options on the upper left. (They are adjacent or connected by a vertical bar.) After reading *all the purple options*, choose the one that best represents the plant you are trying to identify. You will either find a group number to the right of your choice; or another set of options, indented and coded by a different color, beneath it. Keep choosing until you have arrived at a group number, then page to that group to look for your plant.

If your plant is not edible, it will probably match one of the groups, but it won't be found in this book. There won't be photos of it, and no description will match. Accept this and move on; don't force-fit your plant.

Navigating the group key requires minimal botanical vocabulary, but there are two potentially confusing terms. **Basal leaves** are attached at ground level, *at least sometimes in the absence of an aerial stem.* (A few leaves attached to the stem, incidentally near the base, are not considered basal leaves.) Some plants have obvious basal leaves at all times, but others lose them after the stalk appears. You may have to observe the plant over time to make this determination. **Leafless** means that a stem has no typical leaves—a leafless stem still might have scales, reduced leaves, or bracts.

The woody plant key focuses on the fruiting parts because these are the edible product of a woody plant in the vast majority of cases.

Once you get the knack of this key, navigating it is fast and fun—but if you don't want to use it, you can just read through the descriptions of the plant groups listed in the table of contents and then look up the one that matches your plant.

For more information on identifying plants using this book's system, see page 12.

Fern-like plants, palms, and horsetails.	group 1
Succulent, leafless stems (cacti and glassworts).	group 2
Any plant with fruit composed of many fleshy fruitlets (such as raspberry and mulberry).	group 3
None of the above. Go to the **Woody** or **Herbaceous** key below.	

Woody Plants

Woody grass (bamboo/cane).	group 17
Needle-leaved tree or shrub.	group 4
Broadleaf tree (note—some occasionally fruit when shrub-sized).	
Bearing nuts.	group 5
Bearing large fleshy fruits (over 0.8"/ 2 cm).	group 6
Bearing small fleshy fruit (under 0.8"/ 2 cm).	group 7
Bearing fruit that is dry, wind-borne, or a pod.	group 8
Broadleaf shrub (note—some are tiny, and some occasionally reach tree size).	
Low, trailing, or ground-hugging evergreen mini-shrubs.	group 9
Not as above.	
Bearing nuts.	group 5
Bearing large fleshy fruit (over 0.8"/ 2 cm).	group 6
Bearing small fleshy fruit (berries).	
Berries orange to red.	group 10
Berries not orange to red.	group 11
Bearing dry fruit, nutlets, or pods.	group 12
Woody vine.	group 13

Herbaceous Plants

Aquatic (normally in permanent water).	
or Grass-like emergent leaves, or tubular stems with no apparent leaves.	group 14
Leaves not grass-like (submerged, floating, or emergent).	group 15
Terrestrial (including wetland plants not normally in permanent water).	
Leaves both linear and entire.	
or Onion scented.	group 16
Not onion scented.	group 17
Leaves not both linear and entire.	
Basal leaves present.	
Flowering stems leafless.	
Basal leaves entire.	group 18
or Basal leaves toothed or lobed.	group 19
Basal leaves compound.	group 20
Flowering stems with leaves.	
Stem leaves paired or whorled.	group 21
Stem leaves alternate.	
Leaves simple.	
or Leaves entire (includes arrowhead and heart-shaped).	group 22
Leaf margins toothed.	group 23
or Some leaves lobed or divided.	
Sap milky.	group 24
Sap not milky.	group 25
Leaves compound with distinct leaflets.	
Once-compound.	group 26
or More than once compound.	group 27
Leaves multi-compound with lacy, carrot-like, sometimes indistinct leaflets.	group 28
Basal leaves absent.	
Vine (climbing for support by twining or with tendrils).	group 29
Not a vine (although perhaps trailing along the ground).	
or Leaves whorled.	group 30
Leaves paired.	
Stems squared or 4-sided in cross section.	
or Plants strongly aromatic, minty to basil-like.	group 31
or Plants not distinctly minty-aromatic.	group 32
Stem not squared.	
Leaves simple and entire.	group 33
Leaves toothed, lobed, or compound.	group 34
Leaves alternate.	
Leaves simple.	
Leaves entire.	group 35
or Leaves toothed, not lobed.	group 36
Leaves lobed.	group 37
Leaves compound.	group 38

CONTENTS

List of the Plant Groups

CONTENTS

CONTENTS

INTRODUCTION

The Purpose of This Guide

There has long been an unfulfilled need for a comprehensive field guide to the edible wild plants of eastern and central North America: a book that covers all of the important edible plants of our region, with range maps, clear color photos, thorough descriptions, a reliable system for field identification, and accurate information about the parts used and how to employ them. Here it is. Let this guide be your doorway to the amazing world of plant foraging.

I know, this book is huge—twice the size of most other field guides. It needs to be big, because the topic demands absolute certainty. If a bird on your life list is misidentified, it's not going to require medical attention. But if you eat the wrong plant, the mistake might kill you. A field guide catering to foragers requires an elevated level of certainty and detail. Nevertheless, the bigness of this book is something of an illusion, because no three books could replace it.

Most books on edible wild plants ask the reader to consult multiple references before consuming a plant—but such references can be elusive. The existing edible plant guides ignore a large number of our region's best and most common species, and their descriptions and images are often inadequate. Wildflower guides cover only a portion of a region's plants, depict little besides the flowers, and ignore food uses. Flora manuals may cover all the plants but they are written in a difficult technical jargon. These manuals rarely discuss edibility, and once you decipher their botanical vocabulary, you'll realize that they rarely describe the edible parts or the edible stage of growth. This book solves these dilemmas by combining the color photos you'd expect in a wildflower guide with the botanical detail of a professional flora—but written in the simplest language that clarity allows, and with a focus on the edible parts. It also provides reliable information about food uses. More references are always a good idea, but this book makes them unnecessary.

Much of the edible wild plant literature is based on old historical accounts recorded by smug people who disdained Indigenous foods as the useless knowledge of backward cultures that would soon adopt a European subsistence, rendering their traditional diets obsolete. Such attitudes are not conducive to accurate and careful observation. Even sympathetic ethnographers were not active participants in the food economies they described, so their accounts were susceptible to misinterpretation. Furthermore, Western botany was in its infancy during the Colonial Period, and many plants encountered on the frontier lacked both scientific and English names. Confusion and errors were inevitable.

In compiling this guide I sifted through hundreds of obscure sources. To avoid perpetuating past mistakes, I actually gathered and consumed all the plants in question. This was difficult and time-consuming, but there is no shortcut. In one case I was seriously poisoned by a plant that was listed as edible in a questionable old source. I was the guinea pig so you don't have to be. This book contains a great deal of information that is printed nowhere else, because first-hand experience allowed me to fill some information gaps in the scant literature. I wrote this book to share those insights, and to help you partake of this green miracle that surrounds us.

Why Gather Wild Plants?

Our food traditions make us who we are. They define our relationships to land and each other. We can't throw away four fifths of our food heritage without losing a big part of ourselves. I know you're interested in wild plants, not just because you are reading this, but because you're human. Foraging is the womb that nurtured our species into life, and it fascinates all of us whether we admit it or not. Children pick fruit just like kittens play with mice; the interest is innate.

Some people think of wild food knowledge as insurance against catastrophes such as getting lost, war, or the collapse of civilization. Foraging certainly could be a life-saving skill in such circumstances, but relegating wild food to dire situations is kind of like going naked until you get hypothermia. Unless you forage in your everyday life, you will not be competent to forage in the face of calamity. You might as well start enjoying the benefits of wild food right now.

There is scarcely an ailment—social, mental, or physical—that foraging doesn't help treat or prevent. It exercises our bodies and stimulates the best parts of our minds. In a world beset with diabetes, heart disease, and other ailments of affluence, foraging offers us the optimal human diet. Wild plants are not only high in fiber, they are, on average, much denser in micronutrients than cultivated produce. Ironically, in translating the Mediterranean Diet to American culture, its most essential element—wild leafy greens—was dropped, because gathering was not considered a mainstream activity. This is remiss, like forgetting to mention that breastfeeding infants is an option. Every healthy traditional diet respects the power of wild vegetables, which are brimming with vitamins, minerals, and phytochemicals.

Dietary variety is necessary to achieve nutritional balance, but our modern diets are shockingly simplified versions of what our ancestors ate. I inventoried the largest grocery store within an hour's drive of my house, tallying foods derived from 124 plant and fungi species. (This did not include spices, teas, and food additives like guar gum, but included seasonal items that were unavailable at the time of inventory.) Compare this to the 346 wild species that I regularly or occasionally eat, and which are available within the same distance of my house. Our modern food system wants year-round produce items with a long shelf life, disqualifying the vast majority of our most nutritious fruits and vegetables.

Our bodies crave phytochemically dense foods. This is why we slather sauces, sprinkle spices, put bitters in our beer and botanical aromatics in our sodas. Our modern, domesticated diets want for phytochemicals —so we satisfy that craving with addictive overindulgences laced with botanical flavor signals. These formulas trick our bodies into thinking we are getting the wild greens and berries of our forebears. Mainstream dieticians rarely acknowledge that only gatherers of wild foods have access to nutritionally optimum ancestral diets.

Gathering is an intergenerational activity that appeals to people of all ages. It connects each of us with our heritage—for until recently, all cultures integrated wild plants robustly into their food systems. Foraging inspires us to appreciate other food traditions and the cultures that they belong to—bringing diverse people together over our common need for healthy sustenance. And it's the most delicious food in the world, fresh, not tainted with herbicides: incomparable unique flavors and gourmet ingredients that can't be purchased. Besides that, gathering is really fun, followed by enduring soul satisfaction that reverberates beyond the last morsel of food. Once you start, you will never want to imagine a life without foraging.

But none of these benefits are available unless we can find and identify the things to be gathered. That's what this book is for.

How to Identify Plants Using This Book

Nobody learns "foraging." You learn *one plant at a time*. The process of using this book starts when you find a wild plant and simultaneously ask, "What is this plant called?" and "Can I eat it?" The best plant to start with is a familiar one that you see frequently—something that you *recognize* without knowing its name. Learning which name is attached to it is called *identification*.

For ages humans have learned plants from other people. Grandmother showed you an herb over and over again: identifying big ones, small ones, normal ones, odd ones, dead ones. You'd get to feel the stem, sniff the leaf, flip it over, run it along your cheek, take a nibble—until you recognized it. The fixative power of flavor, scent, location, and a familiar voice would reinforce your memories. Replacing that experience with paper is a tall order. But here you are, trying to recover something of a bygone way of life, holding a book that asks you to identify plants in an entirely different way that might feel a bit unnatural. I know this other way can work, too, because it is how I learned. But you should not expect it to be fast or easy.

Step 1: Find more specimens of the plant. This slows you down, builds and confirms your ability to recognize the plant, reveals its range of variability, and teaches you about its life cycle and habitat. Once you have found multiple specimens, choose a typical individual (preferably one in flower or fruit) as the subject to identify.

Step 2: Determine the group to which your plant belongs. I have divided the plants into 38 groups based on their physical form, such as "Woody plants with nuts," and "Basal leaves present; stem leaves alternate and toothed." Each group contains somewhere between 4 and 40 species. At the outset of the book there is a key where a few simple choices based on the plant's form will determine which group it belongs to. If you don't want to use this key, the groups are also listed in the table of contents.

Step 3: Make a tentative identification. Once you have determined your plant's group, turn to the key on the first page of that group's section. By observing the plant and making a few choices, you can tentatively identify it, but only if it is in the key. *If it is not an edible plant, it won't be in the key.*

If you don't want to use the key you can just page through the group to see if any photos match your plant. *If it is not an edible plant, it won't match any of the photos.* Read the "Quick Check" section at the top of the account to see if it agrees with what you see. If so, you have *tentatively* identified your plant. There are multiple paths to a *tentative* ID, including Uncle Bob, another book, or a phone app. Use any or all of them, *but hold on!* You are not ready to eat the plant. Tentative identification is the beginning, not the end, of the identification process. In all cases you must proceed methodically through step 4.

Step 4: Detailed comparison. Carefully read the description, one detail at a time, and check to see *if* your plant matches. Don't assume that it matches. Compare reasonably—don't delude yourself and make your specimen fit the description just because you really want it to. Your tentative ID might be wrong. It's okay to be wrong now; you're still checking. But you *must* be correct before you eat the plant.

Perhaps you hate reading descriptions and just want to look at the pictures. Too bad. *Read the description.* Many things described are not shown in the photos. Even when they are, you sometimes need words to tell your eyes where to focus. Look back and forth between the text, the photos, and the plant you are trying to identify, again and again, until you confirm or deny each relevant aspect of the description. If your plant is a member of a genus with a group description (such as hickories or sow-thistles), make sure to compare the details in the group description as well.

Step 5: Assess your confidence. If, after carefully, thoroughly, reasonably, slowly, and repeatedly comparing your plant to the photos and description in this book, you are positive that you have correctly identified it, you may consider eating it. But first, ask yourself this question: *Would you bet your life on it?* Because when you swallow it, that's what you are doing. Before eating a plant, you need the same absolute certainty that you would have when eating a banana. Only when you reach this point of instant and confident recognition, what I call "banana confidence," are you ready to collect the plant for consumption. You may need to repeat steps 1–5 multiple times, on other days in other locations, before you achieve banana confidence. That's okay. Nobody said you'd get there today. And if you never get there, you never eat the plant.

▲ To the left are three typical tubers of northern bugleweed (edible). To the right is the tuber of a baby water hemlock plant (deadly poisonous)—much smaller than usual, and atypical in form because it is unbranched and constricted. Gatherers must pay attention to details; these were growing beside each other.

Phone apps for plant ID

Ten years ago these tools were inchoate. Today they are functional, and they will get better, but they are not foolproof. 95% accuracy is helpful, but lags far behind the acceptable success rate of human foragers, who should correctly identify ingested items 100% of the time. Use the software if you wish, then use this book for confirmation until you achieve the absolute certainty required for gathering food.

NOTES ON USING THE KEYS

I know some of you hate keys, or have been intimidated to use them. Please give these keys a shot, even if you have a good phone app for plant ID. Using the key will change the way you think about plant form, and eventually, function.

A key is a written tool by which the reader makes a series of choices based on the observable features of a plant. Each choice narrows down the possibilities until an identification is made. Before making any choice in the key, be sure to read *all options* at that particular level. Then choose the best one. (If none of them seem to fit, your plant is probably not edible.) Most botanical keys are *dichotomous*, meaning that at each level you choose between two options. The keys in this book are not strictly dichotomous; having multiple choices where appropriate makes a key easier to use, makes for shorter and less cumbersome options, and is more space-efficient. The color-coded choices should help any reader quickly grasp this system, which is explained more fully before the Key to Groups at the beginning of the book.

I do not believe that any key should be relied upon as the final answer in plant ID; this would break one of my cardinal rules of plant identification: *Never rely on a single feature*. No key is infallible, and plants are variable—keying errors are made even by professionals. I consider all key results to be tentative—but especially those in this book. First, because food gatherers need a higher level of certainty than botanical collectors. More importantly, these keys *do not contain all the possible plants* in our region, so *some plants just won't fit the given choices*. In this case, don't make it fit; just conclude that the plant is not included because it is not edible. However, **a poisonous or inedible plant that is not covered still might fit the key**. (For example, if your plant is interrupted fern, it will key out as the closely related cinnamon fern.) That's why the key says "Tentative Identification." **You absolutely must verify your identification with the photos and descriptions provided**. This is the only way to be certain: No other plant will match all of those details.

WHAT HAPPENS AFTER IDENTIFICATION?

Identification is only the first part of foraging. After that, the fun begins: gathering, tending, garbling, processing, cooking, and best of all, eating. This book's primary purpose is to help you find and identify edible plants, but it also lists their food uses. My *Forager's Harvest* series (see inside back cover) provides additional details on processing and cooking many of these plants. Recipes are beyond the scope of an identification guide.

The Scope of This Field Guide

THE REGION COVERED

This field guide covers the United States and Canada east of the Rocky Mountains, except for arid and semi-arid western Texas and peninsular Florida. These last two areas have numerous edible plants that are not found in the rest of our region, and covering them would have added hundreds of species to the book. The area covered includes 5 major bioregions: Great Plains, Eastern Deciduous Forest, Southern Evergreen Forest, Boreal Forest, and Tundra. To be as useful as possible to western readers, these plants' western range is also mapped. Plants that occur in our area only in limited, ecologically unique areas are excluded.

THE PLANTS INCLUDED IN THIS BOOK

This guide contains photos and descriptions of 700 edible species, making it by far the most comprehensive edible plant field guide ever produced for this (or any) region. But it still does not include everything. My goal was to cover all of the important edible wild plants in eastern North America—but there is subjectivity in deciding what is important, and what is edible. I considered quality, practicality, abundance, and distribution, giving preference to native plants and those with a strong or interesting cultural history. I left out cultivated plants that rarely form persistent wild populations. There is neither space nor need to cover every member of large, complex edible groups like grasses, hawthorns, or mustards. A few species are left out simply because I have not yet gathered and eaten them. This guide does not cover mushrooms, seaweeds, algae, lichens, or strictly medicinal plants.

On page 677 you will find a list of species that are found somewhere in the edible plant literature but which I have excluded from this field guide for a variety of reasons.

WHAT DOES "EDIBLE" MEAN?

When I say a plant is edible, I don't just mean that you can swallow some without dying. I mean that it is worthy of using as food. Food must meet four criteria.

First, it must be **nutritive**, providing usable energy (macronutrients) or vitamins and minerals (micronutrients) dense enough to warrant its consumption. Second, it must be **digestible**. You have to be able to get the item through your digestive system comfortably, and that system must be able to extract enough of the available nutrients to make it worthwhile. Food also must be **nonpoisonous**. All plants contain chemicals that your body must process and remove because they are not part of your physiology. This is normal and healthy. But when these toxins rise above a level that your liver and excretory pathways can effectively mitigate, they negatively impact your physiological functions. We call that poisonous. Finally, a food must be **rewarding**. It must energetically or nutritionally justify the cost of acquiring and processing it. The world is full of items that are nutritive, nontoxic, and digestible, but which are not used as food simply because they are too small or dispersed to harvest efficiently, or have enclosing material that is too laborious to remove.

EDIBLE VERSUS POISONOUS
Because there is a continuum in each of the characteristics of edibility, there is no clear dichotomy between edible and inedible or poisonous; there is only a complex continuum. "Edible" and "poisonous" or "toxic" are not mutually exclusive categories. Jalapeño peppers are clearly toxic; we eat them primarily because we like their toxicity. (In fact, we like poison so much that phytotoxin dispensaries are a very common and highly regulated form of business.) Plants must be used in reasonable moderation. Toxicity always depends on the dose ingested—"edible" does not mean you can eat something in unlimited quantity. People sometimes die from chronic overconsumption of onions or garlic, but few people dispute their edibility. Nutmeg, cinnamon, and other common spices are actually dangerously toxic in moderate doses (say, an ounce). To be edible, a plant must be chemically safe *in the portion consumed*.

The characteristics of edibility are not immutable: Digestibility can be increased and toxicity reduced through food processing, and new technology can make processing more labor efficient. Such technological advances have been increasing the human food supply for at least 300,000 years.

Many of the species listed as edible in this book can be found listed as poisonous in other sources. This happens for many reasons. Sometimes an edible plant has toxic parts. Sometimes an edible part is toxic without proper preparation or processing. Many plants have earned their reputation as toxic by poisoning livestock—but this is usually irrelevant to humans because livestock are less selective and are often forced to eat large quantities of a single species, which humans would never voluntarily do. Some plants have been labeled as poisonous because of their effects when intentionally abused. Perhaps most importantly, myths of toxicity appear to be universal in human cultures. There are complex reasons for these myths—but the fact that the US Poison Control Centers considers black nightshades of the *Solanum nigrum* complex *deadly poisonous*, despite the fact that these are arguably the most-eaten leafy greens in the world, shows that modern science has done little to quell irrational food xenophobia.

HOW DO WE KNOW THAT A PLANT IS EDIBLE?
I started learning edible wild plants as a child through living traditions—things like black walnuts and raspberries that were common knowledge where I grew up. At the age of ten I began learning additional species from edible wild plant books. These books and traditions are based on knowledge brought from Europe combined with information that European settlers learned from Native Americans. Ethnobotany, the systematic recording of cultural information about plants, was invented in the late 1800s by colonial societies afraid they might lose important practical information held by the cultures they intended to alter or destroy. As an adult I began reading this ethnobotanical literature—which contains much information that has not made its way to the popular foraging books.

However, the unique history of eastern North America leaves a huge gap in our knowledge. Due to the upheaval of European colonization, the loss of Indigenous food traditions in North America, like the loss of languages, was especially severe and rapid. Europeans adopted few traditional plant uses from Native Americans, and colonization in the East happened long before systematic ethnobotany. This resulted in some Indigenous food knowledge going unrecorded before the practices died out. Despite being one of the Earth's richest ecosystems for gathering plant food, the Eastern Woodlands of North America remains the most ethnobotanically unknown region of its size in the world. The accompanying map hints at the extent of our ethnobotanical void.

I have spent much of my life trying to close this gap, ferreting out obscure historical references about edible plants and then trying them myself. Some foods hanging by the scantest thread of knowledge have turned out to be fantastic. Food traditions from other parts of the world are a very important tool in recovering this information. Eurasia especially shares many species with eastern North America. If they eat rattlesnake fern *Botrypus virginianus* in Pakistan, or springwater parsnip *Berula erecta* in Turkey, then I can eat those plants in Wisconsin. Furthermore, many edible Eurasian species have been introduced here.

Foraging traditions are much better recorded in the Old World because there has been a long-standing juxtaposition of hand-to-mouth peasant existence with a literate elite, creating the opportunity to record wild food uses. Also, the economic changes in these societies have been more gradual than the changes that were imposed colonially in North America, and they were largely internally driven. This attached more pride

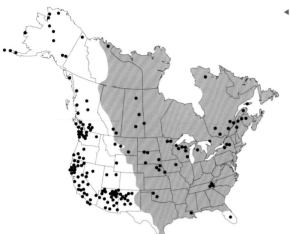

◀ This map is based on Daniel Moerman's *Native American Ethnobotany* (1998), which consolidated information on North American wild food plant uses from 166 published ethnobotanical papers. Each dot represents one reported location (some locations have more than one paper). Although this field guide covers two-thirds of the continent, only 47 of Moerman's reports (28%) pertain to our region, most of these being in the Boreal Forest and the Great Plains. The Eastern Woodlands have only 13 ethnographic reports, all of them located on the periphery or in anomalous locations (infertile sands, mountains, and swamps). There is virtually no relevant ethnobotany from the "American Heartland," despite it being one of the world's richest areas for edible wild plants.

and less stigma to foraging knowledge in the Old World, facilitating more serious attempts at its preservation. Beyond this, Old-World peasants in feudal systems historically suffered more from nutritional stress than Native Americans, and they therefore made greater use of categories of foods, such as leafy greens and mushrooms, that were less emphasized by Indigenous food traditions in North America.

Another source of information on food plants is archeology. There are species for which we have no historical or ethnobotanical record of their use as food, but which archeology shows were once important food sources. Processing techniques have been lost, but experimentation often reveals these plants to be good-tasting and wholesome.

▼ I have found no ethnographic record of the American bellflower *Campanula americana* as food, but its range coincides almost exactly with the ethnographic void described above. Members of this genus are eaten around the world. Did Native Americans eat this one? Of course they did (and perhaps some still do, but nobody I have spoken to keeps this tradition). This species is not only edible, it is delicious, and in my opinion it is the best of an excellent group. I refuse to let the crime of genocide bury such fantastic foods forever.

Sometimes a suggestion of edibility comes from the use of a plant's close relatives in another part of the world. One must be careful about assuming edibility based upon taxonomy, as related plants can differ in toxicity. (The elderberry genus *Sambucus* is an important case in point.) Nevertheless, we often feel comfortable making these edibility assumptions: Nobody asks for historical verification that a *particular species* of blackberry, hawthorn, blueberry, amaranth, acorn, or serviceberry is edible. We just assume these are fine because they belong to a group that is considered edible, and we have a positive and pleasant experience when we eat them. In a genus where edibility varies greatly, the flavor and eating experience also varies greatly. Black nightshade and potato fruits *do not* taste similar. Neither do black and red elderberries, nor lambsquarters and epazote. We wisely and instinctively assume that the edibility of the dissimilar plants is not the same. When a North American plant from the region of ethnographic void has one or more close edible relatives in other regions, with an identical or very similar flavor, and I have repeated positive experiences eating it (especially when this conclusion is independently corroborated by other foragers) I consider the plant edible.

HOW DO WE KNOW THAT A PLANT IS NATIVE?

If the plant is only known from North America it is obviously native here. Species found in both the Old and New Worlds can be problematic, however. Some that were recently introduced, with a spread that has been tracked and documented, are clearly not native. However, for dubious non-scientific reasons, European biologists once declared that no species were native to both Eurasia and the Americas. Because of this belief hundreds of widespread North American species were assumed to have been brought here by European colonizers, even when evidence for this was entirely lacking. Many of these assumptions have been proven false (salient examples being hops, stinging nettle, purslane, black nightshade, yarrow, and chufa), but many others have not been addressed. Readers may be surprised how many plants are of uncertain geographic origin. There are a few species that I list as native in this book because I think the strongest evidence points that way, even though they have customarily been considered introduced. Notable among these are dandelion and wintercress.

Navigating the Individual Plant Accounts

HEADINGS AND NAMES: The plant group's number is embedded in a color-coded banner across the top of the page, along with the group name. A line drawing in the upper right corner represents the group's form. These elements will help you navigate quickly to the appropriate group.

Every plant that appears in the group key is given a number, which appears to the left of its common name. I list only one common name and one Linnaean or "scientific" name at the top of each plant account. Plant names are not standardized the way bird names are; many species have multiple common names in English, while others don't have any. Some common names are misleading. I have tried to use names that will be useful to readers. Note that a hyphen in a plant name means that the plant is not taxonomically what the name suggests. (Hedge-nettle is not a nettle; wood nettle *is* a nettle.) The Linnaean names are also confusing. Most plants have been known by multiple Linnaean names, and there is not necessarily a single "correct" one. Alternative common and Linnaean names are listed in the "Comments" section at the bottom of the plant account, but there is not room to list all possibilities.

Some of the species' names are followed by an abbreviation and page number. These plants are discussed at greater length in one of my previous foraging books, *The Forager's Harvest* (FH), *Nature's Garden* (NG), or *Incredible Wild Edibles* (IWE).

Beside the species name is the family name. Plant families are also subject to change, revision, and disagreement. The family has a latinized name, but there *is no official common family name*. For example, the family *Apiaceae* is often seen listed as the carrot, celery, or parsley family. I list a common name only for a few of the better-known families.

PRODUCE ICONS AND RATINGS: To the right of the plant's common name you will find produce icons representing the kind of edible products that the plant produces. There are 26 icons representing different food products that plants yield. Some of these produce types are familiar to all readers, but others are not represented in the supermarket. Following the icons is a numerical rating, 1–3 (3 being best), of culinary quality for that product. These are based on my own experiences and on my observation of other people's reactions to these foods, but they are subjective. Nevertheless, and I want to give readers realistic expectations. That said, don't count out the low-ranked parts—they might be useful on a hungry hike or in the right recipe, and you might disagree with me.

Seasonings, steeped beverages, saps, and oil are not given ratings. Plant parts needing processing for calcium oxalate raphides (see p. 22) are not given ratings. If other produce icons lack a rating, it means that this edible part is well documented but I have not personally tried it. I have likely failed to list certain edible products because I am unaware of them, but don't assume that you can eat parts that I have not listed unless verified by a trusted source.

Storage roots: Roots thickened to store energy. These may be single taproots (carrots, parsnips), but some species have multiple, enlarged, radiating root branches.

Tubers and corms: A corm is the base of an upright stem enlarged to store food. A tuber is a section of horizontal stem enlarged to store food. Familiar examples include potato (tuber) and taro (corm).

Bulb: A leaf or bud thickened to serve as a food storage organ. (onion, garlic)

Rhizome: A stem, usually horizontal, that stores energy and spreads the plant. These tend to be tougher than other underground vegetables. (ginger)

Lateral shoot: A rapidly forming horizontal rhizome in which the fibers have not yet toughened. No familiar examples.

Shoot: A rapidly expanding young stem in which the fibers have not yet toughened, containing more mass of stem than of leaf. (asparagus, bamboo).

Leafy greens: Leaves and associated tender stems or branch tips (sometimes including flowers and buds), all of which are usually eaten together. (lettuce, spinach)

Petiole: The stem of a leaf, when these are large enough to warrant attention by themselves. (rhubarb, celery)

Peeled shoot: Rapidly growing stems that are tough on the outside but tender in the center. There are no familiar examples (even though several domestic vegetables have edible peeled stalks) because this part has a very short shelf-life.

Heart: The tender inner portion of a cluster of leaves, accessed by peeling away the tougher, mature, outer leaves. This is what a good cook does with a leek, and it is also how one gets a palm heart from a giant cluster of fronds.

Bud: This is the part that will soon open into a flower or leaf. I designate flower buds as a separate produce class only when they are large enough to gather by themselves, either in clusters (like broccoli) or individually.

Flower: If the flower is eaten incidentally with the greens, I don't list it, reserving this icon for large or uniquely flavored flowers that are often used alone without the greens.

Pollen: Collected and used as a flour-like flavor enhancer.

Pod: I use this symbol for any fruit that is typically eaten in the immature, green state. (green beans, okra)

Berry: This symbol refers to all edible fleshy fruits less than 0.8" (2 cm) in the longest dimension, regardless of their structure.

Large fleshy fruit: Any edible fleshy fruit normally larger than 0.8" (2 cm).

Nut: An edible seed large enough to warrant handling individually when collecting, processing, or eating. The lower threshold seems to be about the size of a beech nut.

Seed/grain: Starchy or oily seeds of grasses and other plants.

Cambium: A thin, slushy layer attached to the sapwood, where cell division occurs. (Cambium is not "inner bark.")

Inner bark: The whitish layer found just inside of the corky outer bark and outside of the cambium.

Seasoning: Plants with potent flavors that are used in small amounts as a flavoring rather than a primary ingredient.

Steeped beverage: Plant parts used to brew an infused beverage. (tea, coffee)

Milk-like beverage: Nut milks and similar high-calorie beverages.

Flour: A starch or flour is traditionally extracted. Most seeds or dried roots can be ground into a flour; this category is reserved for plant parts that are commonly eaten that way.

Oil: Seeds, nuts, or tubers that can be pressed or boiled for extracting edible oil.

Sap: Collected by tapping and used for drinking, cooking liquid, or boiling down into syrup. Some other saps are used for chewing gum.

QUICK CHECK: This is one or two lines of bare-bones description to compare against your plant right off the bat. It is meant to slow you down and get you thinking verbally as you look more closely at a few key features. Occasionally the Quick Check will use a word like "oak" or "mint" where that plant group has previously been described. If your plant matches the Quick Check, then begin carefully poring through the full description to check the other details.

ID DIFFICULTY: This numerical rating, on a scale of 1–3, is found after the Quick Check. Plants rated 1 are those that I think are easiest for beginners to identify. Those rated 3 are for gatherers with a high level of confidence. However, nothing in these ratings is meant to imply that it is ever acceptable to eat a plant without positively identifying it. Nor do I mean to discourage or limit what you are comfortable foraging. The identification process is the same regardless of how difficult I have rated the plant, and there are never any shortcuts.

These ratings address how difficult it is to identify a plant to a safe taxonomic level. I don't worry that blackberry species are very hard to tell from each other, because all blackberries are edible. I am concerned, however, when confusing plants are dangerously toxic. The ratings consider the stage of growth at which the plant is eaten—if the flowers are easy to identify, that doesn't mean the shoots are. That said, I am continually surprised by the plants that people find confusing, and I cannot foresee all possibilities. A few tricky plants in the carrot family which look similar to deadly poisonous plants are given a rating of 3+. Don't gather these unless you are highly experienced and adept with plants.

RANGE MAPS: These give a general idea of where the plant is found, but a plant's distribution within the range is patchy and depends on local habitat. Even if you are within a plant's range, it may be hard to find. You can often eliminate a plant from consideration based on geography, but keep in mind that there are occasional outliers that are not mapped. Weedy and introduced plants are especially difficult to map because their occurrence is primarily determined by the idiosyncrasies of human activity. Some weedy species are expanding in range so rapidly that the maps will soon be inaccurate.

DESCRIPTIONS: The descriptions are your primary tool to positively identify the plant. If you go carefully through the text and confirm every described feature, you can identify the plant with certainty. The descriptions in this book are far more detailed than those found in any other wild food field guide, not only allowing you to identify the mature plant, but also the edible parts at their edible stages. *Unusual, diagnostic, or unique features are set off by italics.*

The descriptions in professional manuals are based primarily on dried and pressed herbarium specimens. This results in a predictable set of inaccuracies and omissions. The size of a plant more than double the length of a standard herbarium sheet is usually underreported, because collectors look for specimens small enough to fit the press. The lower portion of larger plants often goes uncollected, and therefore undescribed. Root vegetables are a pain in the press, so they are undercollected and underdescribed. The growth form early in the season, or in a non-flowering year, is rarely described—yet this is often exactly the time to gather it for food. Leaf position, angle, texture, and vein depression all facilitate field recognition of plants, but these features are largely ignored in the botanical literature because they are distorted by pressing. Instead, technical descriptions rely heavily on tiny features requiring a hand lens to observe.

In contrast, the descriptions in this book were based on field observations. I sat next to live, wild plants at the time they are gathered for consumption, examined them, and took notes. The descriptions vary in length based upon necessity; very distinct plants need less description to be identified. Plants with dangerous look-similars or with multiple life phases require longer descriptions. I focus on parts visible to the naked eye (or that can be felt) because I know that most readers will not carry a hand lens.

The descriptions begin with the general aspect of the plant, then proceed from the roots and underground parts to the basal leaves, stems, upper leaves, flowers, and fruits. I try to describe things as they will be perceived by the reader. The leafy tufts in the axils of *Monarda citriodora* really are "short axillary branches," but if I use that phrase to describe them, some readers will be left puzzling. If I say "tufts of leaves," the same readers will say, "Aha, I see that." I'm aiming for the second result. A seed is called a seed even if it is technically also an achene. I sometimes put a more technical term in parentheses afterward, so that if you read about the plant in a manual using technical language you will recognize that we are talking about the same part.

Botanical descriptions often unnecessarily employ lingo that is foreign to the average reader. I avoid technical terms when everyday language is equally clear. There is no good reason to say *plano-convex* when I can say *D-shaped*, or to replace *overlapping* with *imbricate*, *tufted* with *fascicled*, or *hairless* with *glabrous*. However, botanical terms that lack a common English equivalent, such as *raceme*, are necessary. I expect readers to look these up in the glossary if they don't know them already. Important vocabulary pertaining to one group is sometimes also listed in the group introduction above the key.

Botanists have co-opted a few common English words and given them stricter definitions within their jargon, most notably *nut* and *berry*. This unfortunate move confuses and alienates lay readers. Botanists have no authority to change the commonplace definitions of non-technical words that predate their profession. Until they rectify this by coining novel terms for technical use, most English speakers will occasionally suffer pedantic miscorrection about their use of the words *nut* and *berry*. Since this book is written in English, a nut is called a nut and a berry is a berry.

The definitions of some terms used in plant descriptions are not standardized among botanists. Other words, such as entire, and parallel, have special meanings in botany. The glossary clarifies how descriptive terms are used in this text. The descriptions in this book employ some conventions and terminology that may be unfamiliar, even to botanically educated readers. The abbreviation **LYDS** refers to "last year's dead stalk," a feature ignored in most field guides. The abbreviation **USO** means "underground storage organ" and refers to all the things you might call "root vegetables." I use the word "paired" where most books use "opposite" to describe leaf arrangement because my teaching experience has shown that this term results in less confusion. The *base* of a fruit means where it is attached; the end or tip refers to the distal point where it is not attached. I give petiole length as a percentage of leaf blade length. (If the leaf is 2" long and the petiole is 1" long, the petiole is described as "50% of blade length.")

One important identifying feature rarely used in botanical manuals but emphasized here is leaf vein relief. Are the veins slightly depressed, deeply depressed, flat (even with the surface), or slightly raised? When discussing vein relief, unless otherwise specified, I am discussing the upper side of the leaf.

Measurements are given in inches (denoted with ") and feet (') as well as metric units, except that small items under a half inch are usually listed in millimeters only. (There is a millimeter ruler at the top of each page for field comparison.) The measurement ranges given are for typical size, not the occasional aberrations or extremes you may encounter. Measurements refer to length unless otherwise specified. Leaf measurements are for the blade alone, not the petiole; on a compound leaf they refer to the portion after the rachis first divides. These measurements are for generalization, not carpentry; I avoid useless over-precision in metric equivalents.

Some other points to keep in mind as you read the descriptions:

- Assume that a leaf is simple and deciduous unless I tell you that it is compound or evergreen.
- Petals or corolla lobes and sepals normally come in the same number. If a description says a flower has "5 parts," it means 5 petals and 5 sepals.
- With hairs and spines, I use the term *erect* to mean they are standing roughly perpendicular to the surface to which they are attached.
- Some plants are solid in the shoot stage but develop a hollow with maturity.
- Stems that are pithy at maturity are solid in the shoot stage.
- Unless otherwise specified, measurements refer to the long dimensions (length or height).
- When I say that a part is absent, or note what it is not, this usually indicates that there is a reason to expect the part to be present, or to be in the condition that I indicate it is not.
- If a necessary identifying feature of your plant is not available at the moment, you may have to wait to get a positive ID.

PHOTOGRAPHS: I took most of the photos myself. I tried to show the edible parts of each species in their appropriate stage for harvest, as these are the images that are hardest to find in other resources. However, space limitations did not allow me to include every photo that I would have liked. There are important identification features on each plant that are not evident in the photos—*you must* read the description as well. Captions are provided only where I think they are necessary for clarity.

CONFUSING PLANTS: This section is only included for species where I think there is a likely candidate for confusion. That said, I can't predict how other people perceive plants, and the things that people get confused do sometimes amaze me. The species listed here are not the only ones that can be mixed up with the subject plant. A potentially confusing plant is usually not listed under this heading if it is also edible and is covered nearby in the same group. It is listed in **bold red text** if it is poisonous. If the confusing plant is covered elsewhere in this book, only the common name is used, and a page number is given. If it is not covered in this book, a Linnaean name is also given.

HABITAT: The key components of habitat are sunlight, geology, soil composition, topography, moisture, disturbance history, and associated plants. Habitat information will help you find a plant, but don't put much stock in it for identification purposes; plants show up in unexpected locations.

There are two symbols that you might encounter at the end of the habitat section. The bold, red letter **I** indicates an invasive species. These non-native plants outcompete and thereby eliminate native plants. I do not list every introduced plant as invasive—I reserve this symbol for those that have a strong tendency to invade intact native plant communities. Do not plant, promote, or accidentally disseminate these species.

The second symbol you may see is a red flame 🔥. This indicates that fire is an important factor in maintaining this plant's habitat over all or much of its range. Not only does this help a forager find the plant, it raises awareness about species that are likely to decline or disappear due to fire suppression. Most fire-dependent plants in our region have already suffered drastic population reductions.

FOOD USE: In this section I list the edible parts as well as the season and growth stage when they are harvested. I note whether the plant should be eaten raw or cooked, and list any special processing or preparation requirements. This section briefly discusses the season of harvest. Seasons refer to *weather*, not calendar quadrants—which means that summer in Texas is longer than summer in Labrador. Due to space limitations, I provide minimal details on preparation or culinary application.

CONSERVATION RATING: These numbers are listed for native species only, at the end of the "Food use" section. A plant is given up to 3 ratings, each on a scale of 1–3. The different ratings refer to different edible parts: underground parts first, leaves and stems second, and reproductive parts last. The ratings will have slashes between them like this: **3/2/1**. A rating of 1 means that it is difficult to overharvest the part in question; parts rated 3 are more highly susceptible to overharvest.

A rating of 1 is not meant to be a license for irresponsible foraging, nor is a rating of 3 meant to be an injunction against harvest. The ratings indicate a level of prudence, ecological sagacity, and stewardship appropriate for harvesting each food. If you are new to thinking about Nature this way, you may at first want to stick to harvesting the foods rated 1 and 2. *In all cases the guidelines for sustainable harvesting apply* (see p. 25). Keep in mind that these ratings are general. Every plant is rare on the periphery of its range, and in these areas they are often protected. The conservation ratings do not dispute this protection.

RELATED EDIBLES: Sometimes a related plant is discussed with an abbreviated account, to save space by avoiding repetition. You can assume that features not described are identical or substantially similar to those of the first plant under which the related edible is listed. Comparative words like "larger" or "smaller" refer to the first plant listed.

Foraging Safely and Responsibly

Poisonous plants and plant poisonings: Statistically speaking, gathering and eating wild food is one of the safest pastimes you can engage in. The greatest danger associated with foraging—poisoning oneself by mistakenly eating the wrong plant—is an exceedingly rare outcome. Nevertheless, because humans instinctively recoil from unfamiliar foods, the non-foraging population curates a deep and disproportionate fear of the activity. In practice, this fear becomes the caution that keeps rational foragers safe by framing the first rule of gathering: **Never eat something unless you know what it is.** I have yet to encounter a single documented case where an adult was killed or severely poisoned after making a reasonable effort to identify a plant. (Hopeful guesses don't count as "reasonable effort.") Most serious poisonings occur when a person who does not regularly forage decides to eat an unfamiliar plant or mushroom which they have made no attempt to identify. These are not *misidentifications*, they are *non-identifications*. Nothing I can write will fix this irresponsible behavior. Every year some trigger-happy fool shoots a man thinking he's a deer. Don't be the botanical equivalent.

Although plant poisonings are very rare, poisonous plants are easy to find and quite common. A few of the most commonly confused and most toxic plants are included at the end of this book (pp. 656–676). I do not consider learning them to be a priority for new foragers. Just as you don't make friends by identifying enemies, edible plants are never learned through a process of elimination. You learn to forage by learning food plants. Don't get me wrong—it is definitely *good* to recognize toxic plants, but not a necessity. Safe gatherers only eat edible plants that they recognize, so learning poisonous plants will only make you safer if you are already foraging dangerously.

One of the most common causes of poisoning is overdoses of wild plants used for recreational intoxication. Other poisonings result from improperly prepared wild edibles, such as raw poke greens. Don't lump broad taxonomic groups together: "Fern" is not a species, a genus, or even a family—but every year some people are sickened by eating fiddleheads because they consider all ferns to be the same "kind" of plant. "Rules of thumb" regarding which plants are edible should be summarily ignored. Edibility tests are worse than worthless; they are dangerous wastes of time with great potential risk and an imaginary upside. *You must identify a plant before you eat it.*

Don't make it fit. In the Grimm Brothers' version of Cinderella, the evil stepsisters cut off parts of their feet to make them fit the glass slipper. This didn't turn out well for them. If your plant doesn't match the existing description, admit it.

Knowing the species is not enough. Just because a plant is listed as "edible" does not mean you can eat every part of it. You don't make apple pie from the leaves. Sometimes one part is edible, while other parts are poisonous. Even when a part is edible, there is an appropriate season and stage of growth. Some plants are best eaten raw; others must be cooked. A few are poisonous unless processed in specific ways to detoxify them. Seasonings are meant to be consumed only in small quantities. This information will be found in the "Food use" portion of the plant account. Sometimes the species account will direct you to additional information in other parts of the book; carefully read everything that is relevant and follow the instructions.

Beware of pollutants, especially herbicides. Plants can take up toxic chemicals from their environment, so busy roadsides and industrial areas should be avoided. Over the last half century pesticides and herbicides have become perhaps the most dangerous aspect of foraging. *Herbicides are often applied directly to large areas of edible wild vegetation on both public and private lands.* Most agricultural land is sprayed more than once per growing season. Lawns, sidewalk cracks, gardens, ditches, and public parks may also be sprayed. Even native plants in native habitats are sometimes sprayed. Unfortunately there is no simple set of rules to avoid sprayed areas. For starters, never eat a plant with an odd or wilted growth form, and avoid any

▲ Greens of poke, sometimes called "poke salad" or "poke sallet," cannot be eaten raw, despite the name. Every year some people will become ill because they are ignorant of the appropriate preparation of this plant.

plant that appears to have a shiny film or sheen on it. Get to know your local spaces and learn how, and by whom, they are managed.

Use restraint the first time you consume a new species. It is possible that you are allergic to or intolerant of a plant that is normally edible. This is true of both wild and domestic plants. Eat a little bit the first time.

Stop when your body says stop. Just because something is edible does not mean you can eat any quantity of it. Listen to your body. Different plant products are meant to be consumed in different quantities: more potatoes than garlic, more apples than cranberries, more oatmeal than cinnamon. You know how your traditional foods are supposed to go together, but the same may not be true of a new wild plant, so you need to heed your body's "that's enough" signal.

SWALLOWER'S REMORSE
I do not personally know anyone who has had a serious case of poisoning from a foraging misidentification. However, I know many foragers who, after eating a new plant, have experienced the fear of having made a mistake. Swallower's remorse can occur even when there is no rational reason to believe that a mistake has been made. It can result in a cascade of symptoms related to anxiety and hyperventilation, such as tingly arms, hands, or feet and acute nausea, weakness, or dizziness. These might seem to be caused by the plant in question, exacerbating the syndrome and possibly leading to unnecessary medical attention. A key component to this fear-induced reaction is that it tends to be almost instantaneous—a true poisoning is not going to cause symptoms within five seconds of consumption. However, if you have reason to think you have eaten something poisonous, call your Poison Control Center for advice.

RAPHIDES IN PLANT TISSUES
Raphides are needle-like crystals of calcium oxalate monohydrate that are present in the tissues of many plants. These microscopic structures are usually grooved or H-shaped in cross section with one end much sharper than the other. They may be paired, clustered, or barbed. Raphides are often accompanied by small amounts of a protease irritant. When raphide-laden material contacts soft tissues like the mouth, the needles break cell walls and the irritant enters the cells, causing extreme pain and, in severe cases, swelling.

Members of the arum family *Araceae* are protected from herbivory by raphides. But many of them also produce large, starchy USOs. Our hungry and crafty ancestors in many parts of the world came up with ways to circumvent the action of raphides to make this starch edible, such that today several plants containing raphides have become staple foods for hundreds of millions of people. The most important of these is taro *Colocasia esculenta*—however, raphide content has been reduced and changed in cultivated forms.

There are several *Araceae* species in this book that have USOs laden with irritating raphides. This is noted in the "Food Use" section of the species accounts. These plants are not safe to eat unless the raphide-protease synergy has been disrupted. This has traditionally been done by very long baking (many hours or days), fermenting, or roast-drying (again, hours or days). Boiling is only effective after many days. Simple drying may take years. (One batch of sliced skunk cabbage root I collected in 1999 and dried at ambient temperature didn't stop burning until 2015!) I have successfully rendered raphide-containing plants edible on several occasions, and the final product in each case was good—but more often I have been unsuccessful. Scientists are still figuring out the details of how raphides work, and why the traditional processing methods render them harmless. People in many parts of the world have devised reliable means to deal with them, but in the context of specific species or cultivars and technology. It also appears that people who eat raphide-rich food over the long term achieve some level of desensitization.

I don't have solid answers or reliable advice for rendering safe the raphides in the wild North American plants listed. I include them more for historical interest than practical use. Any use of them should be considered tentative, experimental, and done at your own risk. Never consume raphide-protected plant parts raw. Any carefully processed and prepared product should be tested cautiously before consumption: Take a tiny portion onto the tip of your tongue and wait one

▲ This is feral taro, which is loaded with raphides. The domesticated form has had the quantity and/or potency of its raphides greatly reduced, and is rendered safe to eat after brief cooking.

minute to see if a prickling or burning sensation occurs. If so, the material is not fit for consumption. If not, still proceed slowly and in small amounts, in case your batch is not uniformly detoxified.

FURANOCOUMARIN RASHES

These chemicals are found in several plant families, but especially the carrot family *Apiaceae*. The best-known furanocoumarin is psoralen, which has been used in treating psoriasis and other skin conditions, but is also carcinogenic. When exposed to UV light, furanocoumarins can cause cell death. If plant juices containing these compounds get on your skin in the presence of sunlight, it can cause a severe rash or chemical burn known as *phytophotodermatitis*. This may result in painful, weeping blisters and scars that persist for years. Plants known to cause these rashes include parsnip, giant hogweed, cow parsnip, celery, lovage, and angelica—but many (probably most) edible members of the carrot family contain these chemicals. Psoralen has many physiological effects, positive and negative, but the consumption of modest amounts in seasonings and vegetables is attested as safe by their widespread traditional use.

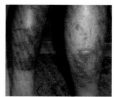

▲ A furanocoumarin rash/burn caused by the juice of parsnip stalks. As you can see, these can be medically serious.

Avoid getting sap from these species on your skin. This normally occurs in early summer when the stalks are at their juiciest stage, and most often affects people cutting them—but dermatitis can also ensue from incidental contact. As the literature frequently mentions, sunlight is required to activate furanocoumarins—but it doesn't seem to require much sunlight. My extensive experiments giving myself furanocoumarin rashes show that sweating is also a very important risk factor. This may be because sweat provides a liquid medium into which psoralen from plant surfaces can readily dissolve and spread; open pores may also give the psoralen-containing liquid a path to penetrate the skin. I have been unable to give myself psoralen rashes through dry-skin contact with dry, unbroken plant surfaces—or at night. I have never experienced rash symptoms on my mouth or lips from eating these plants.

When handling plant parts containing psoralen, such as parsnip, angelica, or hogweed stalks, try to avoid getting the juice on your skin, and immediately wash any exposed skin after contact. Avoid gathering and handling these plants during hot, sunny weather.

PARASITES

Non-foragers sometimes fear that gathering and eating wild plants will infect them with parasites. However, the greatest risk factor for parasites in general is close association with pets and livestock. The two main parasites of concern for foragers are liver fluke and fox tapeworm. These are only a concern when eating raw vegetables—the organisms are destroyed by cooking. Both of these parasites are far more prevalent in Europe than in North America.

Liver fluke *Fasciola hepatica* is a parasitic flatworm with a complex life cycle that most often infects cattle and sheep. Humans can become infected by eating aquatic plant material that has liver fluke larvae encysted on the surface—the most common medium is watercress. Such infections are rare in North America because the preferred intermediate snail host, *Lymnaea truncatula*, is not native here. Liver fluke infections in our region are most common along the Gulf Coast; cold water temperatures limit their occurrence in far northern areas. To avoid consuming liver fluke larvae, do not eat underwater portions of plants raw unless they are peeled. Be especially careful in areas with hoofed livestock.

Fox tapeworm *Echinococcus multilocularis* is actually rather common in wild canines and can be transmitted to domestic dogs and cats. Human infections are very rare, but serious and often fatal. They are primarily caused by contact with wild or domestic carnivores or their feces. It is possible to contract the infection by eating raw greens with excrement on them, so try really hard to avoid this. Never forage in dog kennels or from the immediate vicinity of dead coyotes, cat scat, or things like that.

HUMAN RELATIONSHIPS

Don't trespass to gather plants. Get permission. This may be intimidating, but it is less intimidating than dealing with an angry landowner or law enforcement, and it is much cheaper than buying land. I have developed many great relationships over the years simply through the act of asking for permission to gather plants.

Follow the laws regarding gathering. These vary greatly from one jurisdiction to another, and there are many gray areas. Enforcement officers are often completely unaware of the rules, or don't care. In one wildlife refuge where I frequently forage, the posted signs about harvesting directly contradict the written bylaws. Outdated, obscure, conflicting, and neglected regulations place a large burden on foragers. Is it okay to pick chickweed from the flower garden by the library door? Who would care? Who would you ask? Shoulder the responsibility of gathering as reasonably and respectfully as you can.

NAVIGATING AN ANTI-FORAGING CULTURE

I have been an avid hunter all my life; only occasionally have I been faced with anti-hunting attitudes and never in-the-field harassment. Anti-foraging attitudes and behavior, however, are a constant force that plant gatherers must deal with. They are deeply entrenched, lurking in minds that have no idea they harbor them. Anti-foragers are not organized like anti-hunters, but probably only because they don't have to be. Anti-foraging attitudes are so thoroughly integrated into our existing laws and agencies that organizing would only weaken their power—because acknowledging and naming the philosophy would open it to scrutiny.

The most common anti-foraging arguments are based on conservation, safety, and legality. These are real concerns—but they apply to *any* outdoor activity. Why is foraging so often singled out as "irresponsible?" Because the words *wild* and *foraging* imply "other" food, which is eaten by "other" people, who are perceived as enemies. Deeper examination reveals that the emotions fueling anti-foraging are usually rooted in racial, socio-economic, and political beliefs. Laws against gathering food have been used to control and subjugate people for centuries, especially in Medieval Europe and during colonization of this continent, and they persist today. Modern foragers need to lead the conversation past these attitudes. Our coping strategies may vary between being quiet and unseen, or vocal and well-prepared, depending on the situation—but always our attitude should be positive and our behavior exemplary.

Plant Conservation and Gathering

It is possible to overharvest wild foods, but foraging is the most sustainable relationship to land that humans have ever practiced. The common assertion that there are too many people today for gathering wild plants to be done sustainably is not only false, it is the most dangerous anti-conservation idea that civilization has ever devised to justify its destructive excesses. Eating directly from the wild instills deep awe and gratitude—this is why hunters and gatherers have always been the staunchest conservationists. The people who use a plant are its strongest (and often only) advocates. Our natural resource and land management agencies have largely failed to preserve native plant communities. Without a dispersed legion of wild plant gatherers willing to speak out and work for native plants, to change our failed model of ecosystem stewardship, many species are doomed to disappear from all but a few managed preserves. Gathering wild plants is an ecological responsibility that more people need to take. Here are some conservation practices to guide you:

1. Do not gather protected species. This varies by location; learn what is listed in your gathering area. However, don't count on the government to tell you what's rare—plant populations don't have to become nearly exterminated to be precious.

2. Harvest plants only where they are thriving. Observe until you understand.

3. Never take more than the remaining population can replace. Knowing this requires knowledge of the plant's reproductive strategies and needs, and depends greatly on the part harvested and the local ecology.

4. Become the caretaker. Envision what you can do to help the plants you harvest. Plant seeds. Remove invasive competitors. Return to your harvest location and assess whether or not your gathering has been sustainable. Adjust your practices as necessary.

5. Stop and give thanks. Gratitude leads to longer and deeper thoughts, which lead to greater and better actions.

6. Become an advocate for native plants. Not just the ones you gather—all of them, and all the wildlife that need them. Ally with government agencies, landowners, nonprofit organizations, and Indigenous communities that are doing this work.

SUSTAINABLE GATHERING PRACTICES

These practices are determined by the life cycle of a plant, the parts harvested, and the local conditions. **Introduced plants** are not a conservation concern; collect them as you wish. **Invasive species** are introduced plants that thrive and spread in natural plant communities to the extent that they competitively exclude native plants. Gather as much as you wish and consider spending some additional time removing them. The following categories refer to native species:

Weedy annuals (examples: purslane, black nightshade, amaranth) are heavy seed producers whose populations are limited primarily by the availability of disturbed soil. It is very difficult to overharvest them, but let some go to seed. Consider spreading the seeds to appropriate disturbed locations.

Biennials and monocarpic perennials (examples: evening primrose, American bellflower, thistles) are sometimes weedy, but unlike annuals they often produce root vegetables. Gather less than half of the leaves, stems, or seeds in the population. Disturb the soil if you want to help them spread. Biennials with edible roots actually benefit from a harvest of up to 3/4 of the roots in a population because they require soil disturbance for reproduction. Just be sure to leave healthy adjacent plants spaced to seed the excavated areas, or seed them yourself.

Colonial perennials (examples: common milkweed, stinging nettle, fireweed) spread by rhizomes or other underground structures, sometimes forming large stands. These plants can sustain a rather heavy harvest of shoots or greens, but never take more than a third of the stems once a season unless you are carefully managing or monitoring the colony. If these plants have an edible USO (jerusalem-artichoke, wapato), the soil disturbance of excavation is often highly beneficial to reproduction so long as about a third of the tubers are left to grow.

Stationary perennials with edible shoots or greens (examples: pokeweed, carrion flower) are long-lived plants that spread only by seed. Healthy plants usually have multiple stems and can sustain harvest of less than half of these on a yearly basis.

Stationary perennials with edible USOs (examples: prairie-turnip, camas) are the most susceptible to overharvest, but historically have benefited greatly from the traditional management of Indigenous harvesters. These root vegetables should be dug only where they are truly overcrowded, or by people actively involved in managing them. Planting small trowel-disturbed sites can be highly effective at enhancing reproduction. Many of these species are fire dependent and need landscape-scale management to thrive.

Fruits, berries, and nuts are gifts from the plant in exchange for seed dissemination; you are not harming the plant when you collect them. Planting a few seeds in good growing sites holds up your end of the deal, but be sure to leave a reasonable portion of fruit or nuts for wildlife and other people.

NATIVE PLANT COMMUNITIES FACE FIVE PRIMARY THREATS

Historically, the most important of these is **agriculture**. 18% of the US land surface (415 million acres) has been turned into cropland and has had all native vegetation removed. This was some of the best foraging land in the country. Another 33% is pasture or range land upon which the native vegetation has been dramatically degraded. (These percentages are lower in Canada.) However, the farm acreage has actually declined over the last century, so agriculture poses less risk of additional habitat loss.

Invasive species are an enormous issue in the Eastern Deciduous Forest, and we can reasonably expect a complete overhaul of the wild plant communities of this region over the next few centuries. Native plant communities as we know them will cease to exist except where human intervention maintains them. I cannot imagine

▲ This mesquite savannah in Texas has been sprayed with a broad-leaf herbicide to eliminate hundreds of plant species, increasing the denisity of grasses for beef production. Naturally, the mesquite would be thinned by periodic fires, which maintain a diverse and fertile lanscape supporting numerous wildlife species and edible plants. This is but one example: Tens of millions of acres are being sprayed yearly in similar management systems, with virtually no public outcry or media coverage. Plant gatherers must be instrumental in stopping such abuses.

this happening on any large scale except through the labor of plant gatherers tending their foraging areas. In some other bioregions, especially the boreal forest and tundra, invasive species will be less of a problem.

Herbicide has replaced mechanical control as the primary tool for modulating plant growth. The herbicide revolution is the largest change in the human relationship to Nature since the invention of the internal combustion engine—and possibly since the advent of agriculture itself. Herbicide gives humans a level of control over ecosystems that has never before been possible, and it will economize the destruction of entire biomes. This is already happening in many places. Old-growth herb and shrub communities that have taken hundreds or thousands of years to develop are being wiped out with a few sprayings, and the public remains largely unaware of the problem.

Fire suppression. Fire has been the most important non-human force modulating the Earth's plant communities, many of which developed in relationship to fire. For tens of thousands of years, some Indigenous communities around the world have managed their landscapes with fire. The boreal forest, tallgrass prairie, oak-hickory-walnut savannahs and woodlands, pine barrens, and pine forests were all created and maintained by a periodic mixture of natural and human-ignited fires. None of them will exist in anything like their pre-European form without fires. About a quarter of the native plants in this book (140) depend on fire for their habitat needs in most or all landscapes. All such species have suffered reduced populations from fire suppression—some of them dramatically. If we are going to keep these plants as part of our landscape, we will have to incorporate fire as a management tool.

Development, the removal of native plant communities to create new landscapes to serve humans, affects a small but significant portion of our land. The U.S. has about 46 million acres of lawn and 40 million acres of parking lots and roads, not to mention the millions of acres occupied by buildings. Most new development is carved out of farmland rather than wild land, but nevertheless development is taking a significant toll on native plants.

Only through the practice of foraging will we change the value systems that justify the wholesale destruction of native plant communities that is currently accepted as normal, wholesome, beneficial, and necessary.

Produce and Processing: Turning Plants into Food

The primary reason I want you to identify these plants is so that you can eat them. Some gathered foods can go straight into your mouth without any preparation, but most of our calories are cooked or processed in some way. Since we are accustomed to purchasing our food with the processing already done for us mechanically, and since the dominant American diet incorporates such a tiny variety of produce, some general guidelines and tricks of the trade are offered here.

NUTS

Nuts are large edible seeds. Most are produced by woody plants, but a few are herbaceous. They ripen from late summer to early winter, depending on species. Nuts provide calorie-dense, high-quality food, and they are often easy to gather, but cracking and shelling can be labor-intensive. There are a variety of nutcracking tools available, some species-specific, and none of which work on all nuts. I use a Davebilt nutcracker for acorns, lotus nuts, and hazelnuts. I crack my butternuts and black walnuts with a hammer, and my hickory nuts with a hammer or vise. Nut picks can be very helpful at extracting the meats; I make my own by hammering a nail into the end of a dowel, clipping the head, hammering it for flatness and curvature, then trimming the edges with a file.

Starchy nuts like chestnuts and acorns will keep for a couple weeks at room temperature and several more in refrigeration, but should be dried for longer term storage. Starchy nuts can be eaten whole (raw or cooked) or dried and ground into flour. Acorns generally require leaching to remove tannins before consumption. Oily nuts like walnuts, hickory nuts, and hazelnuts will keep for 4–16 months at room temperature; for longer storage they can be refrigerated or frozen.

Oily wild nuts are excellent for snacking or baking as is most commonly done today, but nut milk and oil were formerly their most important food uses. Oil pressing requires specialized equipment, but nut milks are much easier to make. Add water and process separated nutmeats at high speed in a blender, then (if desired) strain through a rugged jelly-bag or nut-milk bag.

SEEDS may be oily or starchy, and may ripen from late spring to fall. Seeds are the single most important class of plant foods in the world, but harvesting and processing them generally require specialized skills and tools. Seeds are usually gathered by stripping the ripe seed-bearing material from the plant by hand and tossing it into a container, or by beating it off with a paddle or stick.

▼ Wild rice being winnowed in a birchbark tray. You can see the cloud of chaff being pulled out by the snapping movement.

Removing chaff—the inedible fibrous material enclosing or accompanying the seeds—is very important. Chaff is indigestible and often irritating to the mouth and throat. To remove it, the seed material is dried and often parched until brittle. After this it is rubbed vigorously to loosen it from the seeds and break it into small particles. Some seeds can be rubbed between the palms of your hands, but it is more practical to use rubber pads or wear clean rubber boots and rub it with your feet in a barrel. After rubbing, the mixture is winnowed to separate the chaff from the seeds, either by pouring from one container into another in the wind or in front of a fan, or by using a winnowing tray to create air flow that pulls lighter chaff away from heavier seeds. Cleaned seeds can be boiled into mush, and the starchy kinds can be ground into flour. Most seeds, when dry, store well for an extended period of time.

SHOOTS

These are the rapidly growing tender new stems containing relatively little leaf mass. Shoots form mostly on biennial or perennial plants with some sort of storage organ that fuels rapid growth. They are available chiefly in spring or early summer. Some shoots are eaten with the skin on, while others are peeled to reveal a tender interior. Some kinds are excellent raw. Many are great in stir-fry, soup, casseroles, or just steamed and buttered like asparagus. Shoot vegetables can be stored by blanching and freezing, or pressure canning.

LATERALS

On certain colonial plants, rapidly growing horizontal rhizomes form shoots under the soil or water. These are available later in the

season than aerial shoots, often for the duration of summer. Unlike aerial shoots, laterals are pale and nearly colorless. They are exceptionally tender and mildly flavored—excellent raw or cooked.

GREENS

The tender, young leafy portions of plants are the most common edible plant product. Although they are not calorically very important, they are rich in protein and are our most micronutrient-dense class of foods. The peak season for greens of perennials is spring and early summer; annual greens are at their best a few weeks later but are available in lesser quantities all summer. There is a minor resurgence of leafy greens in autumn, extending through the winter in the South.

Most leafy greens can be eaten raw or cooked, but a few kinds must be boiled to be safe. I think the easiest way to use wild food to enhance the healthfulness of our diets is to eat cooked greens. (Why cooked? Because they are more readily digested, and you will eat four times the volume cooked that you would eat raw.) Mild greens can be steamed and served with salt and oil. For bitter or spicy greens, fry in a healthy oil with minced onion or garlic, and season with salt and soy sauce or vinegar. The dish is simple, delicious, versatile, and a nutritional powerhouse that can accompany almost any main course.

Blending mild-flavored greens in a smoothie is another way to make them more digestible and easily incorporate them into your meals.

Greens lose quality rapidly after harvest and should be kept cool and moist and eaten promptly. They can be stored by blanching and freezing, or pressure canning. Some leafy greens also lend themselves well to drying and crumbling, after which they can be added to soups, casseroles, and other dishes.

TEAS AND SEASONINGS

The most common part used for these purposes is the leaf, although seeds and roots are sometimes employed. For storage these parts are generally dried. Most wild teas are not nearly as strong as Oriental tea, so proportionately more herbage is required for steeping. Fermenting fresh leaves before drying enhances the flavor of many herbal teas.

UNDERGROUND STORAGE ORGANS (USOs)

These include taproots, tubers, rhizomes, bulbs, and corms. These parts are collected primarily while the growing parts are dormant and energy has been stored underground. For most species this means from fall through early spring. You can collect these vegetables all winter if the ground isn't frozen, as long as you can recognize the dead tops or small overwintering leaves. You'll probably want a shovel. Hold it vertically to avoid cutting good root vegetables in half. Some smaller USOs are actually easier to gather with a sturdy digging stick (you'll have to make that), a trowel (you can buy that, but get a good one), or a hori hori.

Spring ephemerals die back in early summer, at which time their USOs become full and plump. However, they soon become difficult or impossible to find because the vegetative parts either liquify or blow away. In such cases the best gathering opportunity is that brief period when the mature tops are dying yet still remain visible to indicate plant's location and identity. The taproots of monocarpic plants (those that flower once and then die) are harvested after one or more growing seasons but before a stem is produced; generally this means from fall through spring. When a stem is produced, the energy is drawn out of the root—which thus loses its food value. Storage roots of some polycarpic plants (those that flower in multiple years), especially those adapted to fire, usually have sufficient food reserves to remain edible (though inferior) even at peak growth.

USOs are moderately dense in calories, most of which are in the form of carbohydrate. They are typically eaten cooked, as heat renders them more digestible, but a few are sweet and pleasant raw. Preparation methods can follow those applied for the most physically similar cultivated root vegetables, such as potatoes, carrots, or parsnips. Most root vegetables store very well packed in moist sand in a root cellar or basement. You can keep smaller amounts in the refrigerator if you don't let them desiccate. Some kinds, especially those on the prairie, are customarily dried and often pounded into flour. Others are traditionally lacto-fermented. And you can freeze or pressure can them, like potatoes or carrots.

FRUITS AND BERRIES

These are the most popular foraged foods. Gathering blackberries, raspberries, and blueberries is so "normal" that most people don't even consider them "wild." However, the available variety of wild fruits goes far beyond the few well-known species. Wild berries make the best jams, jellies, pies, cobblers, ice cream, and other desserts. Many kinds are also fantastic for eating by themselves, perhaps embellished with a little milk

or cream. Most wild fruits are quite perishable and should be used or preserved soon after collecting. The best way to store berries for eating out of season is freezing—no pre-cooking is needed, and the half-thawed berries are as good as fresh.

We eat a lot of our wild berries in the form of fruit leather, which is a healthy dried snack with no sugar added. Sweet, pulpy berries such as serviceberry and blueberry make good fruit leather by themselves. More sour or juicy kinds, such as highbush cranberry or raspberry, should be mixed with a base of cooked pear or apple puree, which provides body and texture while also mellowing the flavor. Fruit leather can be dried on metal trays in

the sun in summer weather; be sure to flip the leather over when it is 2/3 dried. It will have to be scraped off with an implement. Or you can use the non-stick sheets in an electric dehydrator such as Excalibur. Store the finished leather in airtight bags or other containers where humidity and meal moths can't wreck it.

Some wild fruits also make good juice by crushing and pressing, boiling and straining, or using a steam-juicer. The product will taste different depending on the method. For crushing and pressing, your primary options are a cider or wine press, or small batches squeezed by hand in a strong jelly bag. You can store the juice by freezing or water-bath canning. You can also use it to make leather, jelly, wine, or vinegar.

I could give you step-by-step instructions on making jams and jellies, but if you don't know how to do this already, it's probably best to buy a packet of commercial pectin mix, such as Sure-Jell or Certo. Inside the package will be excellent instructions and recipes. Most likely they won't mention the specific wild fruit you are using, but by picking the most physically similar fruit from their list, following the correct recipe (jam for whole fruit or pulp, jelly for juice alone), and then doing a ¾ recipe (but using the whole pectin packet), you are all but guaranteed to get a good jell.

Tools and equipment for collecting berries are minimal, but a few things are worth mentioning. For blueberries and a few others, a berry rake can greatly increase your harvest rate. Using one of these is a skill; don't expect to be instantly good at it. The rake does not do the work for you. A blickey (a strap-on berry container that leaves both hands free for picking) is a great time saver for any berry that you pick while standing up. A berry hook (a pole with a hook at the top and a foot-loop at the base) can save a lot of time when picking berries over your head, letting you hold down a branch with both hands free. Finally, a hand-cranked fruit strainer designed for separating apple and tomato seeds and skins from pulp will work for some wild fruits. For fruits with larger seeds, such as persimmons or black haws, you can use a mesh bag or colander and agitate the material by hand.

A discussion of wild fruits would not be complete without mentioning the spotted-wing fruit fly *Drosophila suzuki*. These evil bastards are the worst thing to happen to berry picking in North America at least since European conquest, and perhaps since the last ice age. If this insect hasn't reached you yet, be prepared for the exact opposite of a miracle. For those of you lucky enough to be too hot or dry for this scourge, mark your blessing. Whereas other fruit flies eat overripe, dropped fruit, this one lays its eggs in newly ripening berries. By the time a decent crop ripens, they will usually be spoiled and maggot-filled. In our area blackberry and red raspberry crops have been 75% ruined since about 2010; elderberry losses have been closer to 95%. These flies affect nearly all species of berries. They can't get through thick skins, such as wild plum, but will take advantage of any crack to deposit eggs. The best picking seems to be in areas with only one kind of berry; multiple species ripening in succession allows the fly population to build up over several weeks. Berry picking, for us, has become foremost about avoiding and mitigating this insect. Dry soil helps. Frost kills them. But there is little to be done other than pick individual berries instead of whole clumps, quit if the patch becomes too infested, grumble, and pray for a highly effective predatory wasp to appear.

CAMBIUM

This is not "inner bark" as is so often erroneously stated. Cambium is the layer between the bark and the wood, and when the bark is peeled off, the cambium *adheres to the wood*. The time to eat cambium is late spring and early

summer, when the tree is in its rapid growth phase. At this time the cambium is thick (2-4 mm), slushy, and sweet. After peeling the bark, scrape the cambium off with a spoon, knife, or other implement, and eat it raw. It's surprisingly good. I have never stored it, or even cooked it. It's not good on every tree species, of course— check the Food Use section of the plant account.

▲ On the far left of this fallen slippery elm log I have peeled the outer bark with a draw-knife. After doing this in the center I peeled the inner bark, which is laying crosswise in strips. The cambium remains attached to the wood (but is too thin to collect at this time in early spring).

INNER BARK

Inner bark, which is *not cambium*, is the light-colored inner layer of bark. This is always fibrous, but some tree species store substantial amounts of starch and sugar among the fibers. Trees may use this to fuel an early spring growth spurt, or flowering and fruiting before leaves emerge. Inner bark can be dried or roasted until it is brittle, then pounded or blended into a powder, which can be used as a high-fiber flour. Inner bark can also be boiled to extract the soluble and digestible components and consumed as a beverage or soup broth. Dried strips of bark can be stored for a long time until needed for such purposes.

SAP

Sap can be collected from several tree species in late winter or early spring. It flows out of the light-colored sapwood toward the outside of the tree. Drill a hole of the appropriate size and pound in a spile through which the sap can drip. You can drink sap straight as a beverage, or boil it down to make syrup or sugar. Beware, however, that flowing tapholes will grow a bacteria culture, therefore sap is only safe to drink from freshly tapped holes, especially in warm weather. To make syrup, boil the sap until most of the water is evaporated.

FERMENTATION

What we call fermentation is the partial and controlled decomposition of food, in a way that is not dangerous but beneficial. This has two primary purposes—to extend the storage of food, and to increase its digestibility. Fermentation is integral to most food economies—bread, cheese, beer, and salami, for example, are all fermented. A detailed discussion of these techniques is beyond the scope of this book, but a reminder is in order. Numerous wild vegetables lend themselves well to lacto-fermentation—a great place to start is Sandor Katz's excellent book *Wild Fermentation*. Likewise, most wild fruits can be used for making wine, and hops is not the only flavorful wild herb with a rightful place in brewing.

GROUP 1 FERN-LIKE PLANTS, PALMS, AND HORSETAILS

Plants from four different lineages are grouped here. Ferns and horsetails do not look similar, but they are related and share the feature of reproducing by spores rather than seeds. Neither palms nor coontie are related to the ferns and horsetails, but they share some aspects of their form. Leaf-like structures of these plants are called **fronds**. The stem or petiole of the frond is sometimes called the **stipe**; after the first division it is called the **rachis**. The feather-like leaf divisions attached to the rachis of a fern are called **pinnae** (singular, pinna), and the smaller divisions found on some pinnae are called **pinnules**. Fern spores may be produced on the leafy fronds, or on separate spore fronds. Small clusters of spore cases are visible on the fronds of some species; these are called **sori** (singular, sorus). The young shoots of ferns, unlike those of most plants, uncoil, and these are called **fiddleheads** or croziers. In this stage all of the identification features are not visible, so you may not feel comfortable gathering fiddleheads until you observe them through a whole season.

Unfortunately, many people assume that all fern fiddleheads are equally edible and that the species do not need to be identified. This is not true—you should only eat ferns that have been positively identified to the species level. It is hard to exaggerate the frequency and tenacity of fiddlehead misidentification. The journal *Wilderness and Environmental Medicine*, 2020: 31(2), included an article "Fiddlehead Fern Poisoning: A Case Report" in which the author, S. Bryn Dhir, claimed, "Outdoor enthusiasts are at a high risk of poisonous side effects after ingestion of wild and raw edible fiddlehead ferns, such as the ostrich fern (*Matteucia struthiopteris*) and bracken (*Pteridium* genus) species." The poisoning victim ate two unidentified fiddleheads and later experienced nausea and vomiting. Luckily, she took a photo of the fiddleheads that made her sick, which was published in the article. The photo shows many interrupted fern *Osmunda claytoniana* fiddleheads, as well an opened sensitive fern *Onoclea sensibilis*. There are no ostrich or bracken ferns in the image. Rather than help solve the problem with sound information and reasonable advice, the medical professionals exacerbated it by publishing fear-mongering misinformation. The following information will enable you to make better decisions.

TENTATIVE IDENTIFICATION KEY TO GROUP 1
The key is not your final answer!

or Small, hollow, columnar herbaceous stem with scaly sheaths at ring-like nodes.		1. Field horsetail
Leaves (fronds) fern-like, pinnately or ternately fully divided.		
Fronds single, the stalk directly from the ground.		
or Stalk divides 6–12" above the ground; a grape-like sporangia cluster rises above the blade.		2. Rattlesnake fern
Stalk divides 18–60" above the ground, sporangia on blade.		3. Bracken fern
Fronds clumped, often or always in a whorl or rosette, from a raised or thickened base.		
or Smallest discrete unit (leaflet or pinna) entire.		4. Florida coontie
Smallest discrete unit (leaflet or pinna) with teeth or lobes or both.		
Stem/rachis D-shaped in cross section, not grooved, densely woolly when young.		5. Cinnamon fern
Stem/rachis deeply grooved.		
Surface of stem/rachis with fine powder-like scales; margins lobed.		6. Ostrich fern
Surface of stem/rachis with long, narrow, dark, kinky hair-like scales, margins toothed.		7. Lady fern
Leaves palm or fan-like, a long petiole ending with entire, sword-like segments fused at the base.		
Petiole margins with sharp prickles.		9. Saw palmetto
Petiole margins without prickles.		
Erect trunks to 70' (21 m) tall, blade curled with a long midrib.		8. Cabbage palm
Trunks terminate at or near ground level, blade flat with a short midrib.		10. Dwarf palmetto

1 Field horsetail 1
Equisetum arvense + family *Equisetaceae*

QUICK CHECK: Short, soft, unbranched, tan fertile stem with sheaths of dark scales and a cone-like tip; vegetative stems green with whorls of ascending simple branches. **ID difficulty 1.**

DESCRIPTION: A perennial forming colonies by rhizome, the stems growing singly or occasionally clumped. There are two kinds of stem: fertile and vegetative. **Vegetative stems** to 22" (56 cm) tall, erect, columnar, nearly uniform in thickness, the surface green and finely ridged. In cross section the center has a small hollow, surrounded by a ring of smaller hollow channels. **Nodes** at short intervals, with appressed sheaths cut into sharp teeth that are dark with light margins. Upper nodes produce whorls of 9–12 long, thin, simple, slightly zigzag, ridged, jointed **limbs** with a few sharp teeth at each joint. Limbs are ascending and greatly overlap those above them. **Fertile stems** 6–10" (15–25 cm) tall, appearing for only a short time in spring before dying back. (The vegetative stems will not be visible at this time; they emerge later.) Fertile stems are tan or pinkish with fine vertical ridges, juicy and soft, slightly translucent, hollow, without branches. Sheaths at the nodes are appressed and split halfway to the base, forming sharp teeth. Each stem has 4–6 nodes 1.2–3" (3–8 cm) apart. **Cone** 1–1.5" (2.5–3.5 cm) long, single, at the apex. Before opening, the cone is composed of numerous flat-topped, glossy pentagons or hexagons with an asterisk in the center of a pinkish mica-like surface; after opening they look like whorls of miniature mushrooms on upcurved stalks.

HABITAT: Sunny to somewhat shady moist soil, especially where sandy and disturbed; forest edges, meadows, roadsides, low areas and wetland margins. Native.

FOOD USE: Pick the young, fertile **stems** before or during release of spores, while stems are still tender and juicy. Bite off the sections between the nodes, discarding the bitter nodes along with their scaly sheaths. (Some people cook them whole with the scales attached.) This plant also produces tiny edible tubers on thin rhizomes but these are too small and scattered to warrant collecting. **Conservation 1.**

▲ Infertile (vegetative) stem.

▲ Fertile shoot.

COMMENTS: This is really just a nibble, but certainly a fun and pleasant one that is widely available in spring.

RELATED EDIBLES: Meadow horsetail *E. pratense* has similar (although slightly taller) fertile stems that are nearly as good to eat, but they are not as abundant. After releasing spores they turn green, toughen, and grow branches, but these branches are fewer and thinner than those of field horsetail and spreading rather than ascending. The fertile stems of woodland horsetail *E. sylvaticum* also turn green and toughen after releasing spores, growing branches that divide into many fine branchlets. Its young stems are not as good or tender as those of field horsetail.

2 Rattlesnake fern 3
Botrychium virginianum ✦ family *Ophioglossaceae*

QUICK CHECK: Shin-high to smaller fern with deeply cut, fleshy, triangular, solitary fronds; a grape-cluster-like structure rises above the blade on a long, naked stem. **ID difficulty 2.**

DESCRIPTION: Small fern not spreading by rhizome. **Stipe** (stem) erect but often curvy, single, fleshy, pinkish near the base, roughly D-shaped in cross section but with no sharp corners, the surface smooth, hairless, 4–9" (10–23 cm) tall before dividing. **Frond** deciduous, *triangular in outline*, 4–12" (10–30 cm) long and about equally wide, 2–3 times compound; ternately divided at the base, each of these divisions pinnately divided once or twice, the *divisions sessile*. The ultimate divisions (pinnules) are lanceolate, creased upward along the midvein when young, deeply lobed, the lobes overlapping and ruffled, their *margins toothed*. **Rachis** branches are narrowly winged and have a *raised center ridge* rather than a channel. **Blades** are hairless except that long, very fine and soft hairs may lay sparsely on the surface. They are *fleshy and thick*, *glossy*, light green, held almost horizontally or slightly ascending. **Sporophore** (like a grape cluster) held 6–14" (15–36 cm) above the frond on an erect stalk *arising just below the first frond division*, the surface with scattered, long, appressed woolly hairs and 2 small ridges. The stalk of the sporophore is *as long or longer than the spore-bearing part*, which is branched pinnately 2 or 3 times, the smallest branches bearing tiny, globular, *yellow*, spore-releasing structures that wither by early summer. The early sporophore tip in the shoot stage resembles the rattle of a rattlesnake. The sporophore is not found on all individuals and may be absent at the best young stage for eating.

CONFUSING PLANTS: Other grape ferns (genus *Botrychium*, edibility mostly unknown) have the sporophore stalk attached at or near the base, or have smaller, narrower, and less divided fronds.

HABITAT: Deciduous forests of all types with rich soil and moderate moisture levels. Sometimes also in dry forests, swamps, or openings in conifer forests. Native.

FOOD USE: Fronds as a cooked green. Best in spring when very tender, but unlike most ferns the fronds remain relatively tender through the summer and can be eaten even in autumn after they have been touched with frost, which turns them reddish brown and sweetens them slightly. **Conservation 2.**

COMMENTS: This species is native to North America, South America, Europe, and Asia. It is widely eaten as a traditional potherb in the Himalayas. Interestingly, although it is common and incredibly widespread in North America, I have not found ethnographic reports of its food use here. **AKA** grape fern, *Botrypus virginianus*.

33

3   Bracken fern   2   1
Pteridium aquilinum + family *Dennstaedtiaceae*

QUICK CHECK: Large fern with a triangular frond atop a single, long, straight, vertical stalk. **ID difficulty 1.**

DESCRIPTION: Perennial fern of dry, open country forming extensive colonies by rhizome. Rarely it has a strong almond-extract odor. **Rhizome** about as thick as the erect stalk, black on the outside with hair-like roots; the inside has whitish starch mixed with coarse dark fibers. **Stipe** (stem) single, straight, erect, finely hairy outside and *slimy inside*, 5–10 mm thick, roughly D-shaped with gentle corners near the base, becoming shallowly channeled higher up; it *rises about half the frond's height* before splitting. **Fiddleheads** (croziers) short-woolly with some longer, rusty hairs, the top drooping or curling and each of the 3 main branches coiled separately. There are *2 distinct dark spots where*

the frond first forks, evident on fiddleheads but fading with age. These exude liquid *eaten by ants*, which help protect the bracken from herbivorous insects. **Fronds** 2–6' (60–180 cm) high, the blade held about 45° to the ground, roughly triangular in shape. There are 3 main branches, each twice pinnately compound. **Rachises** have a small channel on top. Proximal **pinnules** are on short stalks but distal ones are sessile. Pinnules taper to a narrow tip and are deeply pinnately lobed, the lobes *cut fully to the midrib*, but *broadly attached and alternating* so the pinnule blade is zigzag-continuous. Lobes are *blunt and mostly entire*, the margins slightly downcurved with a light-colored halo beneath where the spores are produced.

HABITAT: Dry, mostly poor, often acidic soil in full to partial sun: abandoned fields and pastures, roadsides, young or open woods, barrens, forest edges—especially where there is a long-term history of fire. Common under aspen, pine, and white birch. Native. 🔥

FOOD USE: Fiddleheads, collected in spring and early summer, should only be consumed well-cooked; they are carcinogenic when raw. In Asia they are commonly boiled, salted, and dried, then used later in soups or noodle dishes. **Rhizomes** are found 2–8" (5–20 cm) deep and should be cleaned, roasted, and peeled when the tops are dormant; after this the starch can be chewed out of the fibers, but it's only worth the time on the largest plants. **Conservation 1/2.**

COMMENTS: This is one of the most widespread plants on Earth and is probably the most abundant wild edible in North America. Many sources will tell you that bracken fern is deadly

and should never be consumed (see warning below); such statements are deeply ethnocentric. This remains an everyday food item for hundreds of millions of people and can easily be purchased. Its traditional use as food is extensively documented from many regions. Nevertheless, any consumer should *rationally* consider what is known about its chemistry.

WARNING: Always cook thoroughly! Raw bracken fern fiddleheads contain the chemical *ptaquiloside* and have been shown to be **potently carcino-**

genic. Both drying and boiling greatly reduce the content of this carcinogen, but do not fully eliminate it. Some populations have been found to contain no ptaquiloside, and this chemical is also absent from the roots. You may also want to avoid the occasional colonies with almond odor. Mature stems contain ribbon-like structures that can lacerate your hands if you pull on them.

4 Florida coontie
Zamia floridana ◆ *Zamiaceae* (Cycad family)

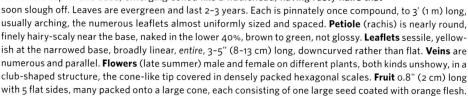

QUICK CHECK: Fern-like leaves in dense clumps, pinnately once compound with long, entire, blunt leaflets; confined to Florida. **ID difficulty 1.**

DESCRIPTION: Perennial evergreen growing from a thick, semi-woody base. **Base** rounded and stump-like, woolly, covered with old hairy petiole bases and scales. **Leaves** form a tuft at the top of this base, emerging coiled like a fiddlehead, having rusty hairs that soon slough off. Leaves are evergreen and last 2–3 years. Each is pinnately once compound, to 3' (1 m) long, usually arching, the numerous leaflets almost uniformly sized and spaced. **Petiole** (rachis) is nearly round, finely hairy-scaly near the base, naked in the lower 40%, brown to green, not glossy. **Leaflets** sessile, yellowish at the narrowed base, broadly linear, *entire*, 3–5" (8–13 cm) long, downcurved rather than flat. **Veins** are numerous and parallel. **Flowers** (late summer) male and female on different plants, both kinds unshowy, in a club-shaped structure, the cone-like tip covered in densely packed hexagonal scales. **Fruit** 0.8" (2 cm) long with 5 flat sides, many packed onto a large cone, each consisting of one large seed coated with orange flesh.

HABITAT: Well-drained sandy soils in full or partial sun, especially over limestone. Forest edges, open woods, abandoned fields, coastal ridges. Native. 🔥

FOOD USE: The enormous **underground storage organ** was once processed on a large scale to extract bland, edible starch, through a detailed process of shredding or pounding, straining, rinsing, fermenting, and drying. I have not eaten this part. Anyone wanting to do this today needs to make sure to obtain the coontie legally (from cultivated plants) and to process the starch so as to render it safe. **WARNING:** Coontie starch is highly toxic before appropriate processing. The ripe fruits are widely considered toxic, although I was introduced to this fruit by a Florida woodsman who called it "the Florida Jolly Rancher." They have a hint of that flavor but are not nearly as sweet, and at this time I'm not comfortable recommending their consumption, although they appear not to be acutely toxic in small quantities. **Conservation 3.**

COMMENTS: The root of this species is not legal to collect from the wild in Florida and is included here only for emergency use or historical interest. This was once a staple food for many people in Florida. Populations were carefully and sustainably managed for thousands of years, but a few decades after European settlers built factories to extract the starch commercially, these old-growth stands were decimated (a real-world analogue to the truffula trees in Dr. Seuss's classic *The Lorax*). Fort Lauderdale was first established to protect white starch harvesters from the attacks of Seminoles defending their livelihoods.

5   Cinnamon fern 🌿 1
Osmunda cinnamomea ✦ family *Osmundaceae*

QUICK CHECK: Large fern of acidic swamps with fronds in a rosette; rachis not grooved, woolly when young; spore fronds separate and cinnamon-colored. **ID difficulty 2.**

DESCRIPTION: Perennial fern from a tussock up to 12" (30 cm) tall, sometimes branching, covered with old roots and the bases of dead fronds. **Stipe/rachis** smooth, D-shaped in cross section, *not grooved*, naked in the lower quarter, to 1 cm thick, *with a tiny tuft of brownish hairs at the base of each pinna.* **Fiddleheads** tightly coiled, *densely covered with white and rusty-colored woolly hairs,* and *not grooved.* **Vegetative fronds** form a funnel-like rosette. They are strongly ascending, 2–5' (60–150 cm) tall and about one fifth as wide, almost straight to gently arching, once pinnately compound, the tips tapered to a point. **Pinnae** half-sessile, touching the rachis on the proximal side only, usually paired on the lower part of the frond and alternate near the tip, spaced so as to rarely touch. Pinnae are often curved, tapered to a point, cut deeply but usually not fully into lobes that often overlap. Lobes are blunt and entire. **Veinlets** fork 1–3 times. **Fertile fronds** fewer, erect and straight, on flimsier stems in the center of the rosette, growing as tall or taller than vegetative fronds, the spore pinnae short and strongly ascending, turning cinnamon-brown before withering in early summer.

CONFUSING PLANTS: Interrupted fern *Osmunda claytoniana* (mildly toxic) is closely related and very similar in appearance, but its rachises lack the tufts of rusty hairs where the pinnae are attached. Fertile fronds of interrupted fern have the leafy portion interrupted by spore-producing pinnae, which are evident even on the fiddleheads.

HABITAT: Full sun to light shade in moist, acidic soil, especially where sandy. Shrub swamps, bog forests, swamp edges, lakeshores, ditches, depressions in sandy country. Look for it especially around tamarack. Native.

FOOD USE: Some people gather the fiddleheads in spring and eat them cooked, but they are quite astringent, and I recommend against it. A small handful in a large stew won't completely ruin the flavor. Some people who eat these collect them by perpetual mistake, but others think wild foods are supposed to taste bad and knowingly insist that cinnamon ferns are the "right" fiddleheads. I include the plant here mostly for their emotional benefit, yet uncertain that this benefit justifies the space. The curved **heart** of the crown in very early spring, before the fiddleheads emerge, sometimes called the "fern banana," tastes slightly better than the fiddleheads, but one must kill the crown to get it. I recommend against eating the fiddleheads, and only feel slightly better about the hearts. **Conservation 3.**

COMMENTS: This species (along with interrupted fern) is often mistakenly mixed with the commercial supply of ostrich fern fiddleheads—despite the fact that they are very easy to tell apart.

WARNING: Eating these fiddleheads raw (or in large quantities, even cooked) makes people sick! Lengthy boiling and draining probably helps prevent this, but not as well as avoiding them.

6 Ostrich fern ▌3 ☐ FH-78
Matteucia struthiopteris ✦ family *Onocleaceae*

QUICK CHECK: Fronds in a funnel-like rosette, with a deep U-shaped groove running the length of the stem; spore fronds separate, dark, stiff, persistent. **ID difficulty 1.**

DESCRIPTION: Spreads by thin rhizomes, often to form large colonies. The base becomes a dark-brown, scaly pedestal or tussock up to 10" (25 cm) high. **Rachis/stipe** straight, deeper than wide, with *a deep, U-shaped channel* (like the groove in a celery stalk) running the entire length. The surface is hairless when mature. **Fiddleheads** tightly coiled with a few loose, broad, light brown papery scales that soon fall; they *do not have a thick woolly coating*. The *deep channel is clearly visible.* **Vegetative fronds** deciduous, 5–9 per rosette, 3–6' (1–2 m) tall and 12–18" (30–46 cm) wide, *widest above the middle* and abruptly narrowing to the tip, strongly ascending to arching, *once compound.* **Pinna** numerous, usually overlapping if laid flat, paired or alternating, sessile or nearly so, 6–9" (15–23 cm) long and 0.6–0.9" (15–23 mm) wide, tapered to the tip, with numerous entire, blunt-tipped pinnate lobes cut more than halfway to the midrib. The lowest pinnae begin near the base and are much reduced; they increase in size gradually going up the rachis. **Midvein** (of pinna) is raised above and shallowly but broadly channeled. **Veinlets** straight, unbranched, depressed, in a herringbone pattern running to the margin. **Fertile fronds** appear in mid to late summer, up to 5 per rosette, vertical, about half as tall as the leafy fronds, the pinna inrolled to form a long, tough, pod-like structure, with the sori hidden in the rolls. These "pods" are first dark green but dry to brown; *fertile fronds become very stiff and persist through the winter.*

CONFUSING PLANTS: Cinnamon fern and interrupted fern *Osmunda claytoniana* (mildly poisonous), are densely woolly as fiddleheads and lack the grooved stem. The fiddleheads of lady fern (p. 8) are smaller, loosely coiled, and wavy with dark, twisted scales and a shallower groove.

HABITAT: Rich disturbed soil in moderate shade to full sun. Needs bare soil to colonize, thus is most common in river floodplains, where it sometimes forms enormous stands. Also ravines, steep slopes, logging trails, roadsides, wooded construction sites. Native.

FOOD USE: Cut or pick the still-tightly-coiled **fiddleheads** *and the attached tender shoots* in spring, taking 2–4 per clump. These may be up to 26" (66 cm) tall on large specimens. You can eat more than the coiled part—please don't waste good food just because it doesn't look like a snail. Steam or boil for 8–10 minutes. **Conservation 2. WARNING:** Do not eat them raw.

COMMENTS: This vegetable is commonly served in restaurants in certain parts of the Northeast and Canada. Raw ostrich fern fiddleheads cause sickness in sufficient quantity. Fiddleheads sold commercially are often misidentified, but the deep groove on the stem makes this species unmistakable to people who pay attention.

▲ Spore fronds persisting from the previous year.

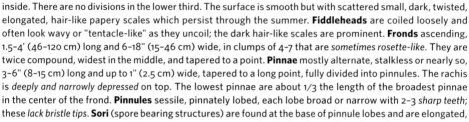

7 Lady fern 2
Athyrium filix-femina ◆ family *Athyriaceae*

QUICK CHECK: Fronds clumped, shallowly grooved with elongated, dark, hair-like scales; fiddleheads coiled loosely and wavy when unfurling. **ID difficulty 1.**

DESCRIPTION: Medium to large fern, sometimes forming small colonies, from a short creeping rootstock at soil level or slightly raised. **Stem/rachis** 4–7 mm thick with a prominent U-shaped groove (but not so deep as the groove in a celery or ostrich fern stalk), usually green but *a purple color phase is common*. When mature there are 2 light green ribbons inside. There are no divisions in the lower third. The surface is smooth but with scattered small, dark, twisted, elongated, hair-like papery scales which persist through the summer. **Fiddleheads** are coiled loosely and often look wavy or "tentacle-like" as they uncoil; the dark hair-like scales are prominent. **Fronds** ascending, 1.5–4' (46–120 cm) long and 6–18" (15–46 cm) wide, in clumps of 4–7 that are *sometimes rosette-like*. They are twice compound, widest in the middle, and tapered to a point. **Pinnae** mostly alternate, stalkless or nearly so, 3–6" (8–15 cm) long and up to 1" (2.5 cm) wide, tapered to a long point, fully divided into pinnules. The rachis is *deeply and narrowly depressed* on top. The lowest pinnae are about 1/3 the length of the broadest pinnae in the center of the frond. **Pinnules** sessile, pinnately lobed, each lobe broad or narrow with 2–3 *sharp teeth*; these *lack bristle tips*. **Sori** (spore bearing structures) are found at the base of pinnule lobes and are elongated, hooked, or horseshoe-shaped.

CONFUSING PLANTS: Many wood ferns (genus *Dryopteris*) are similar, but most species have much larger first (lower) pinnae. The sori of wood ferns are roundish, not elongated or hooked. In the fiddlehead stage the papery scales on the stems of wood ferns are much more prevalent; they are broader, lighter brown, overlapping, and triangular in shape. See also ostrich fern above.

HABITAT: Cool, moist hardwood, conifer, or especially mixed conifer-hardwood forests, in heavy to moderate shade. Also in moist ditches, forest edges, openings, and occasionally meadows. Native.

FOOD USE: Gather a few tender **fiddleheads** per plant when tips are still curled in spring. Use as a cooked vegetable. **Conservation 1.**

COMMENTS: I love the look of these green and purple octopus tentacles that pop up in springtime forests. Although smaller, it is generally more common and widespread than ostrich fern; I find lady fern only slightly inferior in flavor. In the Pacific Northwest it grows larger and seems to taste a little better.

◄ Green and purple color phases.

8 Cabbage palm 🍃3 🍍1
Sabal palmetto ✦ *Arecaceae* (Palm family)

QUICK CHECK: Unbranched palm with down-curled leaves and enormous clusters of tiny flowers and spherical black fruit. **ID difficulty 2.**

DESCRIPTION: Palm tree commonly 12–50' (4–15 m) tall. **Trunk** single, unbranched, proportionately thick, roughened by old leaf scars. Dead petiole bases often persist on the upper trunk below the living leaves, disintegrating after many years; diamond-shaped gaps between them can give the impression of a latticework over the trunk. **Leaves** in a large terminal cluster of 25–40, fan-like, growing at the end of flattened petioles 4.5–7' (140–210 cm) long. **Blades** 5–6' (150–180 cm) long, palmately divided into 40–90 sword-like segments, those near the leaf tip much shorter than the segments near the base. Segments usually have *loose whitish fibers hanging along their margins*. The blade has a prominent **midrib** (costa) extending nearly to the tip; this midrib is *strongly curled downward*. **Inflorescence** an enormous panicle 4–6' (120–180 cm) long spreading from leaf axils, branching into numerous spikes. **Flowers** (early summer) minute and cup-like, 4–6 mm long with 3 off-white, ovate, boat-like petals. **Fruit** spherical, shiny, black, 7–12 mm across, with a thin dryish flesh and a single spherical seed filling most of its volume.

HABITAT: Low sandy areas, especially near ponds and marshes, most abundant near the coast. Native.

FOOD USE: Palm **hearts** are the newly forming leaves and tender leaf bases at the center of the growing tip. These are available all year, especially spring and early summer. A single palm heart is large enough to make a large soup or stir fry and the flavor is fantastic, but you have to kill the tree and cut away all the leaves to get it. Fruit is available in October and November and can be collected in large quantity, but there is little pulp around the large seed, and it doesn't taste very good. **Conservation 3/1.**

COMMENTS: This species has been collected to the point of extermination in many areas for its heart-of-palm. It should only be eaten today in situations where the trees are being taken by development, road building, etc, or have toppled by some natural cause. If you keep your eye out, this actually happens pretty often.

◀ Peeled heart of a cabbage palm.

◀◀ Young trunks hold the bases of old leafstalks.

9 Saw palmetto 🌿 3 🍐 1
Serenoa repens ✦ *Arecaceae* (Palm family)

QUICK CHECK: Miniature palm with fan-like leaves and spiny petioles. **ID difficulty 1.**

DESCRIPTION: Ground-level palm often forming extensive colonies. **Stems** stout, the surface dark and rough-scaly, branching, creeping along the ground (although often hidden by litter), rising sometimes to chest level and leaning or arching. **Leaves** densely clustered near the stem tip, evergreen, 2.5–4' (76–120 cm) across, with 25–30 tightly packed sword-like divisions radiating 320° from one point. *There is no midrib.* **Divisions** conjoined, pleated accordion-like at the base but free and separate distally, 16–26" (41–66 cm) long, tough, folded along the midvein near the base but flatter toward the tip, which is often split. **Petioles** 2–4' (60–120 cm) long, up to 1" (2.5 cm) wide, broadly triangular, not channeled, smooth but for the namesake row of sharp prickles on each edge. **Inflorescence** a branching leafless cluster up to 3' (1 m) long that does not surpass the leaves, the branches light green with contrasting purplish scales. **Flowers** (May–July) small and unshowy, 5–6 mm long, with 3 light-colored reflexed petals. **Fruit** oblong, 0.5–0.9" (13–23 mm) long with a single large seed; ripens to black in autumn.

HABITAT: Pine flatwoods of the coastal plain, coastal scrublands, dunes, high spots in marshes, sandy oak woods close to the water table. Native. 🔥

FOOD USE: The small **palm hearts** can be cut out of the center of the leaf cluster year-round and eaten raw or cooked. Try not to saw up your hands when doing this. Some people grab several petioles close to the tip (with gloves), twist them together, and then yank on this "braid" to pull the heart out. **Fruit** (autumn) has a thin pulp that can be sucked off the hard seeds, dried and ground, or steeped for tea. These are edible but have a strong cheesy vomit flavor that most people don't like. Nevertheless they have been consumed for millennia. **Conservation 3/1.**

The hearts are often very small. ▶

COMMENTS: This is the ubiquitous palmetto of pine flatwoods in the coastal South, especially Florida. The fruit is collected for medicinal use, which has become a multi-million-dollar industry. Due to anti-foraging insanity, it is illegal to collect these berries from your own property without a permit in Florida, but you can destroy all the palmetto plants you want. Collecting the heart kills the crown for a tiny morsel of food, but healthy colonies can spare some, and many acres of palmetto land are developed yearly, offering millions of guilt-free hearts.

Related edible:

10 Dwarf palmetto ◆ *Sabal minor* 3 🍍 2

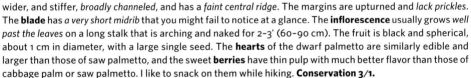

QUICK CHECK: Low palm with a single stem, drooping leaf tips, and long-stemmed clusters of spherical fruit. **ID difficulty 1.**

This species resembles saw palmetto at a glance but is actually more closely related to the cabbage palm. The name can be confusing because it is dwarf in relation to the cabbage palm—but actually larger than the saw palmetto. The **petiole** of dwarf palmetto is longer, wider, and stiffer, *broadly channeled*, and has a *faint central ridge*. The margins are upturned and *lack prickles*. The **blade** has *a very short midrib* that you might fail to notice at a glance. The **inflorescence** usually grows *well past the leaves* on a long stalk that is arching and naked for 2–3' (60–90 cm). The fruit is black and spherical, about 1 cm in diameter, with a large single seed. The **hearts** of the dwarf palmetto are similarly edible and larger than those of saw palmetto, and the sweet **berries** have thin pulp with much better flavor than those of cabbage palm or saw palmetto. I like to snack on them while hiking. **Conservation 3/1.**

GROUP 2   SUCCULENT LEAFLESS STEMS (CACTI AND GLASSWORT)

Cacti and glassworts are not related but share the feature of having thick, fleshy stems and no leaves (or vestigial leaves only). The diversity of edible cacti is much higher west of our region. Because this group contains only a few species, I have left out the key. The **areole** of a cactus is the depression from which a tuft of hairs, glochids, or spines grows. **Glochids** are tiny, stiff, barbed hairs that painfully penetrate skin.

1   Pincushion cactus   🍎 2
Coryphantha missouriensis ✦ *Cactaceae* (Cactus family)

QUICK CHECK: Ground-level cactus with clusters of spines on nipple-like projections; fruits tiny and bright red. **ID difficulty 1.**

DESCRIPTION: Low cactus 2–4" (5–10 cm) wide, barely rising above the soil level with a dome-shaped top, often spreading by basal offshoots to form large clumps of adjacent stems. The surface consists of *numerous nipple-like projections*, each with a flattened cluster of radiating spines at its tip. **Flowers** (spring to early summer) *much larger than the fruit*, 1–2" (2–5 cm) across with numerous narrowly lanceolate, sharp-tipped petals that are dull yellow to greenish-yellow with a darkened, often red-tinted

central stripe. Anthers are yellow and numerous. **Fruit** bright red, egg-shaped, 6–8 mm long, attached in the depressions between nipples, with many small, crunchy, black seeds; ripens the spring after flowering.

CONFUSING PLANTS: *C. vivipara* is an inedible relative with red flowers and fruit that ripens to green.

HABITAT: Well-drained, rocky, sandy, or gravelly prairies. Native.

FOOD USE: The ripe **fruits** are a fun snack with a mild sweet flavor, available from spring through early summer. It can be hard to get them without pricking your fingers. **Conservation 1.**

COMMENTS: This cactus is more common than many people realize—it is just easy to overlook. The fruits or flowers make it easier to spot. **AKA** beehive cactus, *Escobaria missouriensis, Mammillaria missouriensis*.

2 Prickly pear ○ 2 ✿ 2 ╮ 2 ❦ 1 ▭ NG-206
genus *Opuntia* ✦ *Cactaceae* (Cactus family)

QUICK CHECK: Flattened, spiny pads connected to each other; fruits shaped like an egg with the wide end cut off. **ID difficulty 1.**

DESCRIPTION: Medium to large cacti consisting of multiple flattened pads, oval-shaped to nearly round, connected by relatively narrow joints. Some species trail along the ground in chains of connected pads, others rise taller than a person, the pads stacked one upon another. **Pads** flat and smooth, lacking ridges or raised nipple-like structures, the surface with scattered areoles with glochid clusters; some areoles, especially near the margin, bear long, needle-like spines. Young pads from late spring through early summer have vestigial leaves resembling thick fir needles growing from their areoles; these are dropped as they mature. **Flowers** (early to mid summer) borne on the upper rims of pads, with numerous large yellow petals with broad, ragged outer edges. The center has numerous stamens.
Fruit 1–4" (2.5–10 cm) long depending on species, oblong to egg-shaped with the end truncated and slightly depressed, ripening to burgundy, containing numerous semi-hard seeds.

▲ Collective range excluding *O. fragilis*, which is too small to bother with.

SPECIES: The most widespread native species in our region is **eastern prickly pear** *O. humifusa*, which is found in well-drained, sunny, sandy locations, particularly steep south slopes, upper beaches, dunes, and sandstone outcrops. **Plains prickly pear** *O. macrorhiza*, slightly more well-armed, is found on dry soils in the Great Plains. These are both small and mostly ground-hugging, rising no more than 8–16" (20–40 cm). **Desert prickly pear** *O. engelmanii* is a much larger species of the Southwest, up to 6' (2 m) tall, entering our area in the dry prairies of central Texas, but often planted ornamentally outside of its native range.

FOOD USE: Young **pads** that still have vestigial leaves in early summer make a good cooked vegetable; older pads are edible but of lower quality. Pick pads with gloves or tongs in one hand and a knife in the other. The larger spines and the tiny glochids must be cut, burned, or scraped off. I use a copper scratch pad for the latter. Cleaned pads can be cut into strips and fried with other vegetables or added to soups. **Flower petals**, available

in early to mid summer, are easy to collect and innocuous. They make a pleasant nibble or addition to salads or vegetable dishes. **Fruits**, called prickly pears or tunas, ripen in late summer or early autumn. The flavor of some species reminds me of melons, in others of cherries. Remove the glochids by scrubbing and rinsing. Fruits are delicious raw and can be made into juice, jelly, or many other preparations. They store well in a refrigerator. **Seeds** have a tough shell but contain a nutritious kernel; they can be chewed up or pounded for use in gruel. **Conservation 2/1.**

COMMENTS: All parts have a mucilaginous texture. Pads are commonly used in Mexican cooking and can often be found in the produce aisle.

WARNING: Glochids are hard to see and can cause serious discomfort! Also, consuming a large quantity of fruit can cause stomach upset in some people.

◀▼ *O. humifusa.* ▼ *O. engelmanii.*

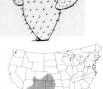

3   Cane cholla   🍎 1
Cylindropuntia imbricata ✦ *Cactaceae* (Cactus family)

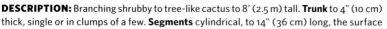

QUICK CHECK: Bush-like cactus with spreading branches covered with high, raised ridges; purple flowers and yellow, ridged fruits. **ID difficulty 1.**

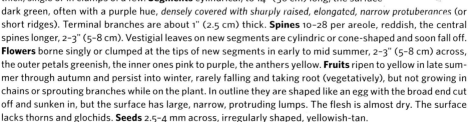

DESCRIPTION: Branching shrubby to tree-like cactus to 8' (2.5 m) tall. **Trunk** to 4" (10 cm) thick, single or in clumps of a few. **Segments** cylindrical, to 14" (36 cm) long, the surface dark green, often with a purple hue, *densely covered with sharply raised, elongated, narrow protuberances* (or short ridges). Terminal branches are about 1" (2.5 cm) thick. **Spines** 10–28 per areole, reddish, the central spines longer, 2–3" (5–8 cm). Vestigial leaves on new segments are cylindric or cone-shaped and soon fall off. **Flowers** borne singly or clumped at the tips of new segments in early to mid summer, 2–3" (5–8 cm) across, the outer petals greenish, the inner ones pink to purple, the anthers yellow. **Fruits** ripen to yellow in late summer through autumn and persist into winter, rarely falling and taking root (vegetatively), but not growing in chains or sprouting branches while on the plant. In outline they are shaped like an egg with the broad end cut off and sunken in, but the surface has large, narrow, protruding lumps. The flesh is almost dry. The surface lacks thorns and glochids. **Seeds** 2.5–4 mm across, irregularly shaped, yellowish-tan.

HABITAT: Well-drained, sunny, gravelly or sandy sites in dry prairies. Native.

FOOD USE: The ripe **fruits** are rather dry and have a bland chalky flavor but they are abundant and not distasteful; you can eat them raw, roasted, or boiled. (This is the only part I have eaten.) The young stems were formerly roasted and rubbed of their spines, then eaten or dried for storage, although they were not highly preferred and are rarely eaten today. I have not heard of the flower buds of this species being roasted and eaten like some of its western relatives, but that does not mean it wasn't done or is impossible. **Conservation 1.**

COMMENTS: The hollow stems with diamond-shaped holes, left when the flesh rots away, are often used as walking sticks and decorations. This plant goes by a huge variety of colloquial names. **AKA** tree cholla, *Opuntia imbricata*.

Related edible:

4   Pencil cholla ✦ *Cylindropuntia leptocaulis*   🌲 2

This cactus often forms thickets of interlocking, narrow stems, the terminal *branches about 1 cm thick or less.* The surface may be almost smooth or have small protuberances. **Spines** few (1–3 per areole) but formidable, widely spaced, erect, up to 2" (5 cm) long. **Flowers** broadly spreading, about 0.8" (2 cm) wide, the petals pale greenish-yellow. **Fruit** 9–14 mm long, egg-shaped, bright red, ripening in late summer and persisting into or through winter. New *green stems sometimes grow from the fruit while it remains attached to the plant.* The fruit lacks large spines but is well armed with glochids. The part eaten is the ripe fruit, and it is much better than that of the cane cholla. **AKA** tesajo cactus, Christmas cholla, *Opuntia leptocaulis.* **Rub the glochids off carefully!**

5 Glasswort ⏐ 3
genus *Salicornia* ✦ family *Amaranthaceae*

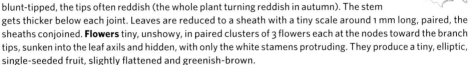

QUICK CHECK: Thick, succulent, erect, jointed stems with paired ascending branches and no apparent leaves. **ID difficulty 1.**

DESCRIPTION: Annual with succulent, erect stems about 5 mm in diameter, to 16" (40 cm) tall, with *paired ascending branches*. **Stems** and branches are hairless, cylindrical, dull green in summer, jointed (the joints much more densely packed toward branch tips), blunt-tipped, the tips often reddish (the whole plant turning reddish in autumn). The stem gets thicker below each joint. Leaves are reduced to a sheath with a tiny scale around 1 mm long, paired, the sheaths conjoined. **Flowers** tiny, unshowy, in paired clusters of 3 flowers each at the nodes toward the branch tips, sunken into the leaf axils and hidden, with only the white stamens protruding. They produce a tiny, elliptic, single-seeded fruit, slightly flattened and greenish-brown.

HABITAT: Salty or brackish wetlands on or near the coast. Occasionally inland in salty depressions. Native.

FOOD USE: Gather **top growth** from spring through fall, going down only as far as the stems are tender. Snack on the beach or use them chopped into salads. The flavor is pleasantly salty and mild, the texture crisp when raw—but it is also good cooked. Stem sections are also sometimes pickled. **Conservation 2.**

SPECIES: The coastal annual glassworts, described above, are sometimes lumped under the name *S. europea*, and sometimes split into multiple species. Plants from the northern Great Plains are often separated as *S. rubra*. Perennial glassworts are known as *S. depressa* or *S. ambigua*. These spread by rhizome to form dense mats. The stems are shorter and unbranched, with segments packed very densely toward the tips. Perennial glassworts are somewhat tougher than the annual species.

COMMENTS: Easy to recognize, simple to gather, and fun to eat. Bring along a child who needs vegetables. Glassworts are sometimes gathered for use in restaurants and go by many names. **AKA** saltwort, sea beans, sea asparagus, samphire, and pickleweed.

GROUP 3 PLANTS WITH FRUIT COMPOSED OF MULTIPLE SMALL FRUITLETS

This is one of the safest groups for beginning foragers—there is nothing dangerous that closely resembles any of these species. The plants in this group may be herbaceous, woody, or semi-woody, but all have multiple tiny one-seeded fruitlets packed together to form a larger berry. All but the mulberries belong to the genus *Rubus*. Most species in this group are *brambles*—long-lived perennials with canes that live only two years. Canes reach their full height the first year without branching (these are called **primocanes**) then harden into semi-woody stems that persist through one winter. The following spring they grow short branches that bear flowers and fruit, after which they die.

Brambles are probably our most popular wild foods, and are collected annually by many millions of people. When fully ripe they spoil quickly and so require rapid freezing or processing. Piling them too deep in your pail will crush them and hasten spoilage. All brambles are delicious for eating out of hand and make superb jams, jellies, pies, and juice. If you want to make fruit leather from any of these species, mix them at the ratio of one-third crushed berry pulp to two-thirds applesauce before drying—this will give your leather some body while retaining the distinct flavor of your bramble berry. All of them store well frozen or canned in a water bath. Seeds can be removed with a Victorio-type fruit strainer. The young tender primocane shoots of the larger brambles are edible in spring; peel off their tough, bitter skin by hand and crunch them raw as a refreshing treat.

TENTATIVE IDENTIFICATION KEY TO GROUP 3
The key is not your final answer!

Trees; fruit with no calyx hangs on a limp stalk.	
or Leaves less than 8" (20 cm) long, smoothish and glossy above, hairs only along major veins below, lobes (if present) blunt.	1. Asian mulberry
Leaves often exceeding 8" (20 cm), sandpapery-rough above, hairs evenly distributed on all veinlets below, lobes (if present) with acuminate tips.	2. American mulberry
Semi-woody canes or prickly/bristly creepers; fruit with a 5-lobed calyx.	
Fruit detaches from the receptacle when ripe, and has a thimble-cavity.	
Leaves simple, lobed.	
or Flowers purple.	3. Purple-flowered raspberry
Flowers white.	4. Thimbleberry
or Leaves compound.	
or Stem and petiole covered with long, stiff bristles, shorter glandular hairs, but no stout prickles. Primocane leaves often with 5 leaflets.	5. Red raspberry
Stem and petiole densely covered with long, gland-tipped hairs and scattered stout prickles. Primocane leaves with 3 leaflets.	6. Wineberry
Stem smooth, hairless, bloom-coated, with scattered broad-based prickles.	7. Black raspberry
Fruits remain attached to the receptacle when ripe; not thimble-like.	
Large upright to arching canes with broad-based prickles.	8. Blackberry
Trailing or limp low canes, armored with small prickles or spines.	9. Dewberry
Herbaceous plants with unarmed stems; fruit with a 5-lobed calyx.	
Leaf simple and lobed, fruit ripens yellowish.	10. Cloudberry
Leaf ternately compound; fruit ripens reddish.	
Leaf tip acute-pointed, flowers white.	11. Plumboy
Leaf-tip obtuse, flowers pink.	12. Nagoonberry

1 **Asian mulberry** 🫐 3 🍃 2 📖 IWE-231
Morus alba ✦ *Moraceae* (Mulberry family)

QUICK CHECK: Tree with glossy, often lobed leaves and hanging blackberry-like fruit. **ID difficulty 1.**

DESCRIPTION: Small to medium-sized tree to 60' (18 m) tall, the trunks sometimes multiple, with densely branched, spreading crowns. **Bark** with numerous fine, shallow, yellowish fissures separated by small gray ridges. **Branches** disorganized and bushy, the twigs medium-sized, minutely hairy when green becoming hairless when older. *Sap milky.* **Leaves** alternate, 1.5–7" (4–18 cm) long, ovate, ranging from deeply lobed to unlobed (more lobed on saplings or shoots in full sun). *Lobes have blunt tips,* and the *sinuses do not have teeth.* Surface somewhat *glossy above,* usually with few to no hairs but sometimes rough-hairy when young; the underside has *hairs only along some of the main veins,* especially in their angles. **Secondary veins** slightly depressed above, two major ones emanating from the base; *veinlets are flat or nearly so.* **Margins** toothed. **Petioles** 15–30% of blade length. **Flowers** (spring) wind-pollinated, the male and female separate, on the same trees or on separate trees, tiny, greenish white, in hanging catkins. **Berry** an elongated cluster of tiny fruitlets packed together, 0.5–1" (13–25 mm), ripening to purple-black (occasionally red, pink, or white) in early to mid summer.

CONFUSING PLANTS: Easy to identify, but because people get confused by its name this is the most mis-identified tree in North America.

HABITAT: A pioneer or weed tree of roadsides, old fields, vacant urban lots, parks, brushy areas, forest edges, and young woods. Thrives on rich soil. Introduced. **I**

FOOD USE: Gather **berries** from the branches by hand or shake them onto a tarp or cloth. They can be dried, eaten fresh, or used in jams, jellies, pies, juice, or ice cream. Young **leaves**, especially on stump sprouts, can be eaten as a cooked green and have been traditionally dried and powdered as a flour additive. Note: the warnings sometimes seen about mulberry sap being hallucinogenic seem overblown and irrelevant to normal food use.

COMMENTS: This is the weedy mulberry familiar to most people, especially in the northern states where it abounds in urban and agricultural landscapes. The ill-conceived names "white mulberry" and *Morus alba* were given based upon aberrant, unpigmented cultivars. The white-fruited feral descendants of these cultivars are sometimes found, but *purple-black is the normal color of the fruit.* This is by far the most abundant invasive tree in our region, but because so many professionals confuse it with the native mulberry it has been largely ignored in the discussion and management of invasive plants. **AKA** white mulberry.

▼ White mulberry fruit normally ripens to dark purple.

▼ Close-up of the midvein underside.

▲ White-fruited abberation of *Morus alba*.

2 American mulberry 🐝 3 🪶 3 📖 IWE-231
Morus rubra ✦ *Moraceae* (Mulberry family)

QUICK CHECK: Tree with large, rough leaves and blackberry-like fruit. **ID difficulty 1.**

DESCRIPTION: Usually a large understory tree but sometimes reaches canopy heights of 90' (27 m). **Bark** in elongated reddish-brown plates, reminiscent of slippery elm. **Branches** are often arranged in flat, horizontal layers. **Twigs** moderately large, sparse, soft-hairy when young, becoming hairless. *Sap milky.* **Leaves** 3–14" (8–36 cm) long, broadly ovate (in sun) to heart-shaped (in shade), *rough-hairy on the upper surface*, finely and *evenly soft-hairy on all veins and veinlets below*, rarely lobed on mature trees but deeply lobed on shoots and saplings. *Major lobes have acuminate tips.* Blades are *highly variable* in size, becoming progressively larger toward the branch tip; flat in shade, smaller and folded in full sun. **Veins,** including the *veinlets, are deeply depressed*, and the blades are often pleated along major veins, which sometimes terminate in an *extra-large, extended tooth.* **Margins** serrated; there are often *large teeth inside the sinuses.* **Petioles** 5–15% of blade length. **Flowers** (spring) wind-pollinated, not showy, male and female separate, sometimes on the same tree, hanging in catkins. **Berry** an elongated cluster of tiny fruitlets packed together, 0.6–1.8" (1.5–4.6 cm) long, often curved, ripening to purple in early to mid summer.

CONFUSING PLANTS: Basswood (p. 119) leaves are hairless and asymmetrical with longer petioles.

HABITAT: Hardwood forests on rich soil, especially small floodplains, valleys, and steep slopes. Highly associated with limestone and pawpaw. More of a generalist in the Deep South. Native.

FOOD USE: Gather ripe **berries** in early summer. These are larger and better tasting than those of Asian mulberry. Tender young **shoots** and **leaves** are excellent raw or cooked. **Conservation 1.**

COMMENTS: American mulberry is strikingly beautiful and elegant, decidedly unlike its weedy cousin. The leaf's astounding resemblance to basswood may partly account for this tree remaining largely unknown (it was actually re-described in a botanical journal as a "newly discovered species" in 2009), but the misapplication of its name to Asian mulberry is the bigger problem. I have seen people confuse *Morus rubra* with basswood and slippery elm, but never with *Morus alba.* Unfortunately the native tree is disappearing in many areas due to genetic swamping by the introduced Asian species. **AKA** red mulberry.

▼ Close-up of midvein underside.

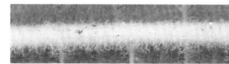

3 Purple-flowered raspberry 🌿 2 🍃 1 📖 IWE-65
Rubus odoratus • Rosaceae (Rose family)

QUICK CHECK: Large, simple, maple-like leaves and a broad, reddish berry that separates from the receptacle; unarmed. **ID difficulty 1.**

DESCRIPTION: Perennial spreading by rhizomes. **Canes** erect to slightly arching, 2-6' (60-180 cm) tall, never rooting at the tips, zigzag, lacking thorns or spines, faintly ridged, the surface glandular-sticky on primocanes becoming gray-brown and exfoliating on older canes. **Leaves** simple, 4-8" (10-20 cm) wide and about equally long, the base deeply notched; 3 or 5 sharp palmate lobes. Both surfaces have at least a few fine, soft hairs but these are denser and longer on the veins beneath. **Veins** and veinlets deeply depressed above. **Margins** finely toothed. **Petioles** 40-70% of blade length, covered with glandular hairs. **Inflorescence** small to large branching

clusters, one or a few blooming at a time. **Flowers** 1.3-1.8" (33-46 mm) across with 5 broad purple petals. **Berry** light orange-red when ripe, *flattened and broad*, 0.5-0.8" (13-20 mm) across, composed of smaller and more numerous fruitlets than other brambles.

HABITAT: Roadsides, forest borders and openings, rocky slopes. Native.

FOOD USE: The **berries** ripen in late summer but are produced sparsely, making them hard to collect in quantity. They are rather dry, but the flavor is still good. Primocane **shoots** in late spring can be peeled and eaten raw. **Conservation 1.**

COMMENTS: Many people call this species "thimbleberry," and some deride the fruit as tasteless, but I think they are secretly just mad they don't get to taste more of it.

Related edible:

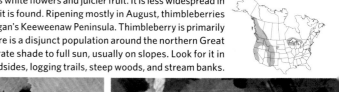

4 Thimbleberry • Rubus parviflorus 🌿 3 🍃 1 📖 IWE-64

This species is nearly identical but has white flowers and juicier fruit. It is less widespread in our region, but gets more love where it is found. Ripening mostly in August, thimbleberries are harvested commercially on Michigan's Keeweenaw Peninsula. Thimbleberry is primarily found in the Mountain West, but there is a disjunct population around the northern Great Lakes. It inhabits moist soil in moderate shade to full sun, usually on slopes. Look for it in clearings and along forest edges, roadsides, logging trails, steep woods, and stream banks.

▲ Thimbleberry fruit—the fruit of purple-flowered raspberry is identical.

5 Red raspberry 🍇 3 🌿 2 ☕ 📖 IWE-62
Rubus idaeus ✦ *Rosaceae* (Rose family)

QUICK CHECK: Canes with stiff bristles but no stout prickles; red fruit detaches from the receptacle. **ID difficulty 1.**

DESCRIPTION: Spreading by rhizomes to form thickets. **Canes** erect or arching but not rooting at the tip, 2–5' (60–150 cm) tall, not angled, the surface sometimes with bloom, *densely covered* with stiff bristles, usually gland-tipped when young. **Leaves** alternate, most often pinnately compound with 5 leaflets on primocanes; 3 leaflets on fruiting canes. The terminal leaflet is slightly larger than the side leaflets. **Petioles** bristly, not channeled, and about the length of the terminal leaflet. **Leaflets** 2–4" (5–10 cm) long, ovate, sometimes lobed, coarsely and irregularly toothed, the *underside whitish* from a dense layer of fine wool. Veins deeply depressed above. **Inflorescence** a short, broad cluster of 3–12, the flowers opening one at a time. **Flowers** (early summer) about 0.5" (13 mm) across, whitish with 5 sharp, triangular, gland-hairy sepals, 5 less conspicuous petals, and numerous stamens. **Berry** juicy, red, about as long as wide, detaching from a soft whitish receptacle.

HABITAT: Forest openings, young woods, swamp margins, roadsides, brush, old fields, recently logged areas. Dry to moist soil of most types, in full sun to light shade. Native.

FOOD USE: Berries ripen over 5–8 weeks in mid to late summer. These make one of the very best jams, and everything else, too. Peeled **shoots** are small but good raw. The leaves can be used fresh or dried for **tea**. **Conservation 1.**

COMMENTS: In our cool northern forests this is often the most abundant wild berry. The stems and leaves are a major food source for hares, rabbits, moose, and deer. Because red raspberries ripen over a long period their crop is less susceptible to weather vagaries. Where their ranges overlap, red and black raspberries frequently hybridize, and these hybrids are just as delicious as they sound.

6 Wineberry 🐌 3 ⚘ 2 📖 IWE-66
Rubus phoenicolasius ✦ *Rosaceae* (Rose family)

QUICK CHECK: Canes with stout prickles and densely covered with sticky red hairs; 3 leaflets; red fruit that detaches from the receptacle. **ID difficulty 1.**

DESCRIPTION: Stems arching, round, purple, to 7' (2.1 m) tall, *densely covered with long, reddish, gland-tipped hairs* and scattered stout prickles. **Leaves** alternate, ternately compound. **Leaflets** 1–4" (2.5–10 cm), the side leaflets ovate; the end leaflet is almost as broad as long and *much larger* than the side leaflets. Blades are sparse-hairy above, wool-coated and silvery beneath; the veins often show red. **Veins** above are strongly depressed.

▲ Rapidly expanding.

Margins coarsely double-toothed, the terminal leaflet often lobed. **Inflorescence** (late spring to early summer) panicles of 8–35, a few blooming at a time. **Flowers** have 5 long, acuminate-pointed sepals, extremely glandular-hairy, cupped, the tips often twisted, wrapped over the developing fruit. **Petals** 5, broad, creased, *folded inward* over the numerous stamens in the center. **Berries** (early to mid summer) juicy and reddish, sticky, without bloom, and detach easily from the *yellow-orange receptacle.*

HABITAT: Well-drained moist soil in partial sun; forest edges, disturbed woods, roadsides. Introduced. **I**

FOOD USE: Berries are excellent for all the uses of blackberries and raspberries, and the large clusters make them easy to collect. The shoots are edible and peel easily.

COMMENTS: Perhaps no exotic invasive plant is so well liked as this delicious berry, always popular with pickers wherever it is found.

7 Black raspberry 🫐 3 ⚓ 3 📖 IWE-63
Rubus occidentalis ✦ *Rosaceae* (Rose family)

QUICK CHECK: Bloom-coated arching stems with scattered prickles, rooting at the tip; black fruit that detaches from the receptacle. **ID difficulty 1.**

DESCRIPTION: Perennial spreading by tip-rooting canes. **Canes** arching, 4–10' (1.2–3 m) long, green or purple with a *thick white bloom*, smooth and hairless between the scattered broad-based prickles. **Leaves** alternate, ternately compound (rarely 5 leaflets on primocanes), the side leaflets sessile but the terminal long-stalked. **Petioles** prickly, not channeled, about equal to blade length. **Leaflets** 1.5–4.5" (3.8–11 cm), roughly ovate with irregularly toothed margins, occasionally lobed, the terminal leaflet largest. Blades *nearly hairless above* with depressed veins, whitish beneath from a fine woolly coating. **Inflorescence** a short, broad cluster of 5–12. **Flowers** with 5 long, pointed, cupped sepals and 5 smaller blunt, oval, white petals. **Berry** black when ripe, bloom-coated, 0.3–0.6" (8–15 mm) across, detaching from the white receptacle.

▲ This map includes the western counterpart, *R. leucodermis.*

HABITAT: Dry or well-drained soil in full to partial sun. Likes sand and dislikes clay. Roadsides, forest edges, savannahs, old fields, fencerows, vacant lots, pastures. Native. 🔥

FOOD USE: Berries ripen more uniformly than red raspberries, and this, coupled with their more clustered nature, makes it possible to collect them faster. They are less acidic than red raspberries, and I think they are better for pie or snacking, but not as good for jam (although still great). The **shoots** peel easier than those of other brambles, and in my opinion taste the best. **Conservation 1.**

COMMENTS: The first jam I ever made, and still one of my favorites. This is possibly the most popular wild berry in North America. Regularly hybridizes with red raspberry. **AKA** black cap.

8 Blackberry 🍇 3 🍴 1 🥄 3 📖 IWE-60
genus *Rubus* (numerous species) + *Rosaceae* (Rose family)

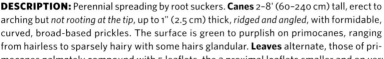

QUICK CHECK: Brambles with ridged stems, wide prickles, palmately compound leaves, and racemes of purple-black berries clinging to the receptacle. **ID difficulty 1.**

DESCRIPTION: Perennial spreading by root suckers. **Canes** 2–8' (60–240 cm) tall, erect to arching but *not rooting at the tip*, up to 1" (2.5 cm) thick, *ridged and angled*, with formidable, curved, broad-based prickles. The surface is green to purplish on primocanes, ranging from hairless to sparsely hairy with some hairs glandular. **Leaves** alternate, those of primocanes palmately compound with 5 leaflets, the 2 proximal leaflets smaller and on very short petioles; the larger distal leaflets 3–6" (8–15 cm) long. Leaves of mature canes usually have 3 leaflets. The upper surface is thinly hairy with depressed secondary veins; lower surface densely *soft-hairy but still green*. **Margins** serrated but not lobed. **Petioles** about equal to the longer leaflets and prickly. **Inflorescence** a panicle of 7–32 flowers, each on a long stalk. **Flowers** (early summer) about 0.7" (18 mm) across, with 5 sharp triangular sepals and 5 broad white petals, with numerous dark-tipped stamens. **Berries** often longer than wide, ripen to purple-black in mid to late summer, and cling to the receptacle.

HABITAT: Open woods, forest edges, old fields, and brushy areas in full to partial sun; on almost any well-drained soil. Native. 🔥

FOOD USE: Berries can be collected faster than any other bramble berry. This is why we like to make juice from them. Their biggest drawback is the large seeds, but these can be removed by straining. **Shoots** are edible but slightly astringent and harder to peel than those of other brambles. **Tufted shoots** are a specialized structure that appears on the common blackberry *Rubus allegheniensis* (and possibly other species) in response to cutting or browsing of the regular shoots in early summer. These are thin, flimsy, and densely packed along the rhizome; they lack prickles and have ternate leaves only. A few weeks after forming they wilt rapidly and die, usually succumbing to an orange blight. They are tender and delicious raw if you get them young enough, lacking the normal astringency of blackberry shoots, and do not need to be peeled. **Conservation 1.**

COMMENTS: This is one of the most popular wild berries in North America. Few humans have noticed that the tufted shoots are delicious—but the deer know all about them. They are a forager's gem.

▲ Tufted blackberry shoots.

9 Dewberry 🐝 3 📖 IWE-61
genus *Rubus* (numerous species) + *Rosaceae* (Rose family)

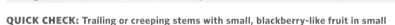

QUICK CHECK: Trailing or creeping stems with small, blackberry-like fruit in small clusters. **ID difficulty 1.**

DESCRIPTION: These are essentially small, low blackberries with trailing, creeping, or decumbent stems that root at the nodes. **Canes** have hairs, spines, or prickles and are variably hairy. **Leaves** of primocanes are ternately compound or palmately compound with 5 leaflets (depending on the species); leaves of mature canes have 3 leaflets. **Leaflets** ovate, obovate, or lanceolate; occasionally lobed, with sharp tips and toothed margins. The surfaces of most species are sparsely hairy. Secondary veins are distinctly depressed above. **Flowers** in clusters of 3–12, with 5 sharp green sepals and 5 broad white petals. **Berries** are like miniature blackberries with fewer fruitlets, clinging to the receptacle when ripe.

HABITAT: Various habitats, mostly in full sun, especially in sandy, moist soils. Native. 🔥

FOOD USE: Berries ripen in summer and are delicious fresh or in various desserts. **Conservation 1.**

COMMENTS: Dewberries generally taste like blackberries and can be used in the same ways, only they are smaller, sparser, and harder to get in quantity. On average the flavor is at least as good. There are dozens of species in our area.

10 **Cloudberry** 🥮 3 📖 IWE-68
Rubus chamaemorus ✦ *Rosaceae* (Rose family)

QUICK CHECK: Low, palmately lobed, ruffled, leathery leaves and large, yellowish berries composed of a few large fruitlets. **ID difficulty 1.**

DESCRIPTION: Low, erect, herbaceous plant spreading by rhizomes. **Stems** 2–12" (5–30 cm) tall, unarmed, smooth and faintly hairy with 1–3 leaves. If the plant has 2 leaves, they usually rise to the same level. **Leaves** alternate, simple, 2–4" (5–10 cm) wide and about equally long, tough and stiff, palmate with 3–7 (usually 5) lobes. The blades are dark green or purplish (the latter especially in full sun, and on the margins), ruffled, folded along the strongly depressed major veins, and cupped or funnel-like—smaller and more ruffled in the sun, larger and more cupped in the shade. The surface is hairless above but hairy along the veins below. **Margins** serrated and finely hairy. **Petioles** 80–100% of blade length. **Flowers** (early summer) borne singly on long pedicels, male and female on separate plants, about 1" (2.5 cm) across with 4 or 5 broad white petals and the same number of ovate, green, nipple-tipped sepals. **Berry** 0.4–0.7" (1–1.8 cm) across, held on an erect stem above the leaves, composed of only 3–18 large fruitlets, *ripening to straw-yellow and very soft* in late summer, easily detaching when ripe but the tiny receptacle remains embedded between the fruitlets.

HABITAT: Acidic soil with high organic content, in full to partial sunlight. Sphagnum moss with black spruce, in muskegs and upland tundra. Native.

FOOD USE: The **berries** get lighter, not darker, as they ripen. They can be used in almost any fruity dessert to great effect. Or just go out in the bog and stuff your face. **Conservation 1.**

COMMENTS: The species name *chamaemorus* means "ground mulberry." This is one of the iconic wild foods of the Far North, found around the globe in forest and tundra regions. Although the berries are sparsely produced, cloudberries are highly esteemed for their unique delicious flavor. **AKA** bakeapple. This name is not a reference to the flavor; it is a corruption of the French *baie q'appelle*, which means "whatchacallit berry."

11 **Plumboy** 🐝 3 📖 IWE-67
Rubus pubescens ♦ Rosaceae (Rose family)

QUICK CHECK: Unarmed trailing bramble with 3-part compound leaves, red fruit not separating from the receptacle. **ID difficulty 1.**

DESCRIPTION: Low herbaceous bramble with two types of stems: long, creeping, thread-like ones by which the plant spreads, and short, erect, fruiting stems arising periodically from nodes along the creeping stem. **Erect stems** to 12" (30 cm) tall, hairy, with no thorns or prickles. **Leaves** alternate, few, ternately compound, on long thin petioles 120% of terminal leaflet length. **Leaflets** sessile or nearly so, light green, 1–3" (2.5–8 cm) long, ovate to lanceolate, sharp-tipped, hairless to faintly hairy on both sides. Major **veins** are deeply depressed above; veinlets scarcely so. Margins are toothed and occasionally lobed. **Inflorescence** single flowers or loose clusters of up to 4, with thin pedicels rising above the leaves. **Flowers** have 5 sharp, lanceolate, reflexed sepals and 5 broad-tipped white petals held almost erect. **Berries** composed of few fruitlets, ripening to burgundy-red and adhering to the receptacle.

CONFUSING PLANTS: Often confused with woodland strawberry (p. 298) when not in fruit, and nagoon-berry when fruiting.

HABITAT: Conifer or broadleaf forests in moderate to light shade, especially where the soil is moist. Often thrives under aspen. Native.

FOOD USE: Berries ripen in early summer and are delicious but hard to collect in quantity. **Conservation 1.**

COMMENTS: This uniquely delicious berry ripens earlier than any other bramble in its range, concurrent with wild strawberry. The plant is often very common but the fruit is produced sparingly. This widespread and abundant berry has no widely accepted common name. **AKA** dwarf raspberry.

12 Nagoonberry 🐝 3 📖 IWE-67
Rubus arcticus + *Rosaceae* (Rose family)

QUICK CHECK: Low, unarmed plant with large purplish flowers and 3 blunt leaflets; red fruit ripening in late summer. **ID difficulty 1.**

DESCRIPTION: Low bramble forming colonies by stolons. **Stems** erect, thin, usually unbranched, herbaceous, 5–12" (13–30 cm), maroon, unarmed, finely hairy. Each stem bears only 1–4 leaves and usually 1 flower or fruit. **Leaves** alternate, ternately compound, on stiff, tough, maroon, hairy petioles 110–180% of the terminal leaflet, deeper than wide with a narrow channel, the lowest petioles scarcely diverging from the stem. **Leaflets** broad with *blunt tips*, occasionally lobed, dark green, scarcely hairy, tough; those in shade are flat and somewhat glossy with depressed veins; those in full sun have *dark purple highlights* and are folded along the midvein and deeply depressed at every major vein to give a *ruffled appearance*. Side leaflets are sessile, asymmetrical, usually with 3 (sometimes 5) lobes. End leaflets are obovate, with petiolules 3–5% of blade length. **Flowers** (summer) single, about 1.5" (4 cm) across, sepals narrow and pointed, the *5–8 petals* elliptic, *pink-purple*, narrow at the base, *often twisted*. **Berries** hemispherical, 9–14 mm in diameter, composed of large, plump fruitlets adhering to the receptacle, ripening to red in late summer, borne above the leaves.

HABITAT: Moist soil in full to partial sun; stream and river banks, muskegs, arctic meadows, swamps.

FOOD USE: Berries ripen in late summer and are slow to gather, but worth it. **Conservation 1.**

COMMENTS: A common and very widespread berry of the North, found also across similar habitats in Eurasia. This berry has good flavor and is among the most coveted treats of the tundra. **AKA** arctic plumboy, arctic raspberry, *Rubus acaulis*.

GROUP 4 NEEDLE-LEAVED TREES AND SHRUBS

Large coniferous trees in our region produce food of several types: cambium, inner bark, tender spring branch tips, and immature cones. The needles of several can also be used to steep a tea. None of our pines produce nuts, however. Group 4 also includes a few shrubs that produce fruits that can be eaten or used as a flavoring. Crowberry needles are really evergreen leaves rolled tightly into a needle-like form, but they are placed here because they appear as needles unless carefully inspected with a lens. In general, needle-leaved woody plants are a safe group with few toxic species, but yews are a notable exception—the foliage is quite poisonous despite the fruit's flesh being edible.

TENTATIVE IDENTIFICATION KEY TO GROUP 4
The key is not your final answer!

Trees.
Needles in wrapped bundles of 2–5.	1. Pine
Needles single, not wrapped in bundles.	
Needles short, overlapping, pointed scales pressed against the twig.	8. Eastern redcedar
Needles square and sharp-tipped, single on a short stub.	2. Spruce
Needles flat, round-tipped, gray-striped below.	
Bark smooth with pitch bubbles; top spire-like, stiff; cones erect.	3. Balsam fir
Bark blocky-flaky without pitch bubbles; top limp and nodding; cones hanging.	4. Hemlock

or

Shrubs.
Seashore shrub with paired, fleshy needles.	5. Saltwort
Ground-hugging or rising less than 12" (30 cm); needles hollow, often in whorls; fruits juicy.	6. Black crowberry
Shrubs with flat needles, rising 1–10' (0.3–3 m) high.	
Needles in whorls of 3, with a stiff, sharp tip and a gray stripe above.	7. Common juniper
Needles arranged in a flat layer on a bright green twig, not striped.	9. Canada yew

1 Pine 🌀1 ✋2 ☕ 🌾3
genus *Pinus* • *Pinaceae* (Pine family)

QUICK CHECK: Conifers with broad crowns not tapered to a point, large cones, and needles in bundles sheathed at the base. ID difficulty 1.

DESCRIPTION: Medium to large trees spreading only by seed. **Trunks** generally straight, erect, and dominant (but on a few species they are forking or crooked). **Crowns** ragged or tufted looking, *widest near or above the middle* and not tapered to a point. **Bark** of mature trees is thick with ridges, plates, or flakes and variable in color. **Needles** up to 18" (46 cm) long on some species; they may be pointed or blunt, flexible or brittle. They are borne in bundles of 2–5, each wrapped in a scaly sheath at the base. **Pollen cones** small and arranged around the base of the new branch shoots. **Seed cones** 1–9" (2.5–23 cm) long with thick, rigid scales that bear a claw-like bristle on some species.

HABITAT: Pines are generally intolerant of shade and dominate in areas of dry soil with low fertility that have been historically prone to fire. They specialize in regenerating in bare mineral soils after burning. Native. 🔥

FOOD USE: Inner bark and **cambium** (p. 30) are edible. Needles can be gathered any time of year and boiled or steeped for **tea**. The flavor is weak unless a great quantity is used; chopping helps the flavor steep out. **Pollen** can be collected in early summer by tapping the male cones over a container. Sift out insects, dry or freeze for storage, and add to various dishes. **Conservation 3/1/1.**

COMMENTS: Pine inner bark is surprisingly sweet, and a single tree can provide enormous amounts. Pine needle tea is a fun winter project for camping children, but unlikely to impress dinner guests. There has lately been much ado about pine pollen as a health supplement *and* a gourmet ingredient. That's a winning combination.

SPECIES: There are 14 native pines in our area and one widespread exotic that is naturalized (Scots pine). All can be used similarly for food although their qualities differ. Three representatives are shown here.

▲ Eastern white pine *P. strobus* is the only species in our region with 5 needles per bundle, elongated cones, and dark, furrowed, non-flaky bark.

▲ Male cones of red pine *P. resinosa*, mature and ready to release pollen.

▲ Longleaf pine *P. palustris*, a stately tree of the Deep South.

▲ Seed (female) cone of red pine *P. resinosa*.

59

2 Spruce 🌿 1 🍃 2 ⎮ 2
genus *Picea* ◆ *Pinaceae* (Pine family)

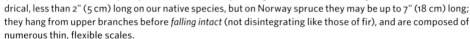

QUICK CHECK: Scaly bark and tapered crown, with short, sharp needles on a pedestal. **ID difficulty 1.**

DESCRIPTION: Medium to large trees. **Trunk** erect, single, dominant, straight, with branches in annual whorls. **Bark** gray, thin, covered in *fine scales.* **Crowns** narrow, broadest at the base and tapered to the top. **Needles** short, less than 1" (2.5 cm) long, *stiff, sharp, 4-sided, borne on short stumps or pedestals on all sides of the twig.* **Seed cones** ovoid to cylindrical, less than 2" (5 cm) long on our native species, but on Norway spruce they may be up to 7" (18 cm) long; they hang from upper branches before *falling intact* (not disintegrating like those of fir), and are composed of numerous thin, flexible scales.

SPECIES: White spruce *P. glauca* is the most abundant and widespread species, co-dominant over much of the boreal forest region. This tree of uplands grows tall and straight with slightly ascending and spreading upper branches. **Red spruce** *P. rubens* is a similar species confined to mountain forests of the Northeast. **Black spruce** *P. mariana* is a slender, small, often crooked tree with an extremely narrow crown that grows primarily in acidic bogs, often in pure stands or associated with white cedar and tamarack. **Norway spruce** *P. abies* is not native but is frequently planted and is locally common as an escape. This spruce has long, often upcurved lower branches with smaller drooping branchlets; the cones are long and curved.

CONFUSING PLANTS: Balsam fir has flat needles, not on pedestals, and not distributed on all sides of the twigs.

FOOD USE: Inner bark and **cambium** (p. 30) can be peeled early in the growing season. **Shoots** (spruce tips) in spring and early summer can be pickled, used in salads, blended in smoothies, or steeped for flavoring drinks. **Conservation 3/1.**

COMMENTS: Spruce tips have become popular in gourmet circles for their tangy and aromatic, but not overpowering flavor. The pitch of black spruce was once mixed with sugar and raw rubber to make chewing gum, and collecting the pitch was a minor industry. What is now called "bubblegum flavor" is an imitation of dried spruce pitch.

▲ White spruce tips.

▲ White spruce.

▲ White spruce.

Black spruce. ▶

3 Balsam fir 🌿 1 ◊ 2
Abies balsamea ✦ Pinaceae (Pine family)

QUICK CHECK: Conifer with a narrow crown tapering to a sharp top; needles flat and blunt. **ID difficulty 1.**

DESCRIPTION: Medium-sized tree with a narrow crown, widest at the base and tapering to a sharp top—the quintessential Christmas tree—to 80' (25 m) tall. **Bark** relatively smooth (not scaly) grayish, with *large resin blisters*; older bark may become irregularly cracked. **Needles** 0.5–1.1" (1.3–2.8 cm) long, straight or curving upward, flattened, blunt, with a *faint groove down the midvein* on the top and a *keel below*; there is a *white-gray strip* on each side of the keel. **Pollen cones** tiny and purplish, clustered around the twigs. **Seed cones** almost cylindrical but rounded on both ends, 1.5–3" (4–8 cm) long, held erect on upper limbs and often crowded, the scales thin, broad, and purplish. After maturing the cones disintegrate in place: The scales and seeds fall down, leaving just a vertical spike on the branch.

CONFUSING PLANTS: Spruce needles are square and sharp-tipped; yew needles have bristle-tips and no whitish lines beneath.

HABITAT: Moist to moderate soil, especially with some clay content; most common in swamp margins, low ground, and valleys. Balsam fir grows in full sun but is extremely shade tolerant. Native.

FOOD USE: Cambium (see p. 30) in early summer. **Immature seed cones** can be gathered in late summer (if you can access the tree tops) and used something like spruce tips for their tangy, piney, aromatic flavor in drinks, confections, or pickles.

COMMENTS: This is the shade-tolerant climax tree of the boreal forest region, and also the most popular Christmas tree in our area, named for its potent scent. Individual needles can persist up to 13 years. The needles are a very important winter food for deer, moose, and snowshoe hares.

◄ This cone is just a little past the tender stage.

4 Eastern hemlock 🪶 1 ☕
Tsuga canadensis ✦ *Pinaceae* (Pine family)

QUICK CHECK: Conifer lacking regular branch whorls, with limp tops, tiny needles, and tiny cones. **ID difficulty 1.**

DESCRIPTION: Tree reproducing only by seed. **Crown** moderately wide, ragged-looking, broadly tapered. **Trunk** single, not as straight as those of pines, firs, and spruces, and more rapidly tapered, 50–120' (15–37 m) tall. **Bark** dark red-brown to gray, divided by fissures into flat-topped plates; *purplish-red inner layers* are visible when cut. **Branches** not produced in distinct annual whorls. The apical shoot leans or droops, and the *twigs are extremely thin.* **Needles** flat with a slightly depressed midvein, round-tipped, thin, 0.3–0.5" (8–13 mm) long, with *tiny (almost invisible) teeth in the distal half* and *a whitish gray line underneath.* They are attached all around the twig on *short petioles,* but these twist so that the *needles lie in flat sprays* on opposite sides of the twig. **Cones** tiny, 0.5–0.8" (13–20 mm) long, hanging individually, maturing in one year, the scales thin and rounded.

RELATED EDIBLE: Carolina hemlock, of limited distribution in the southern Appalachians, is very similar but smaller.

CONFUSING PLANTS: Yew needles lack stripes and have a bristle tip. This tree is unrelated to the herbs called hemlock.

HABITAT: Mature forests with moist to medium soil; associated with beech, yellow birch, sugar and red maple, white pine, and northern red oak. Prefers ravines, north slopes, and the margins of swamp forests.

FOOD USE: Needles can be boiled or steeped for a weakly flavored **tea** at any time—not great, but when backcountry camping, it's better than plain melted snow or boiled lake water. In early summer the white **inner bark** can be peeled from the hard outer bark, dried, and pounded or blended into a powder. This is okay mixed with flour for baking, as an extender for oatmeal or hot cereal, or to drink as a sort of slurry. **Conservation 3/1.**

COMMENTS: Hemlock's inner bark was widely used for food by native peoples of the Pacific Northwest and the Northeast. The tree was formerly decimated in certain regions by the leather tanning industry. Hemlock is slow-growing and in some areas is in danger of extermination from deer browsing and an introduced insect, the hemlock woolly adelgid. You can see vast stands killed by the adelgid in the southern Appalachians. Despite all this, in certain regions it remains among the most prevalent trees.

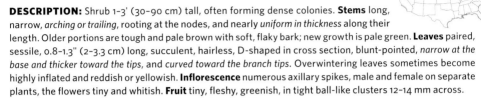

5   Saltwort   3
Batis maritima ✦ family *Bataceae*

QUICK CHECK: Trailing shrub of saltwater shallows with non-tapered light brown or green stems and club-like paired leaves. **ID difficulty 1.**

DESCRIPTION: Shrub 1–3' (30–90 cm) tall, often forming dense colonies. **Stems** long, narrow, *arching or trailing*, rooting at the nodes, and nearly *uniform in thickness* along their length. Older portions are tough and pale brown with soft, flaky bark; new growth is pale green. **Leaves** paired, sessile, 0.8–1.3" (2–3.3 cm) long, succulent, hairless, D-shaped in cross section, blunt-pointed, *narrow at the base and thicker toward the tips*, and *curved toward the branch tips*. Overwintering leaves sometimes become highly inflated and reddish or yellowish. **Inflorescence** numerous axillary spikes, male and female on separate plants, the flowers tiny and whitish. **Fruit** tiny, fleshy, greenish, in tight ball-like clusters 12–14 mm across.

HABITAT: Mucky saltwater shallows, salt marshes, mangrove swamps. Native.

FOOD USE: Tender **leaves** and **branch tips** make a mild salty vegetable, raw or cooked. **Conservation 2.**

COMMENTS: Often very abundant where found. This plant makes that same weird crunchy-squeaky noise as glasswort when you walk through it. **AKA** turtleweed, samphire.

6 Black crowberry 🍓 2
Empetrum nigrum ✦ family *Empetraceae*

QUICK ID: Tiny, needle-like leaves; nearly sessile black berries depressed on both ends. **ID difficulty 1.**

▲ Composite range.

DESCRIPTION: Mat-forming, prostrate shrub. **Stems** creeping, 1–3 mm thick, sparsely branched, the branch tips sweeping upward, sometimes erect where crowded, to 8" (20 cm) high. **Bark** of new growth is pubescent; later it becomes reddish brown and peels. **Leaves** 3–7 mm long, borne mostly in *whorls of 4*, needle-like, blunt-tipped, evergreen, crowded (especially near branch tips). **Margins** *curled so far downward that they join to form a tube* with a *white line underneath* where the margins meet. **Petioles** wide and very short, arising from a peg-like pedestal. **Flowers** nearly stemless, tiny and inconspicuous, pink to purplish, in leaf axils in midsummer. **Berry** roundish, borne singly but often close together, broader than long, 4–6 mm across, dimpled at the end with a little speck of flower remnants, juicy inside with 6–9 hard seeds and no pulp, ripening to black in late summer. Beneath the fruit is a 6-part calyx.

HABITAT: Rocky or gravelly places in full sunlight; open tundra, outcrops, shores, alpine meadows. Native.

FOOD USE: Gather the **berries** by hand or rake in late summer and fall. Eat fresh, use in hot cereal, or make juice. Flavor is mild but pleasant. Sometimes they remain available into winter and the following spring. **Conservation 1.**

COMMENTS: This is an important wild fruit of the arctic, where it is often found in great abundance.

RELATED EDIBLES: Purple crowberry *E. atropurpurea* is very similar but the branch tips rarely stand erect. The fruit is purple and somewhat smaller. It likes drier sites than black crowberry and is often found in rocky or sandy areas along coasts. **Pink crowberry** *E. eamesii* has translucent pink berries depressed in the center; it inhabits dry, rocky or sandy outcroppings and hilltops. The leaves are shorter than those of black crowberry, and clumped at the ends of the numerous short branches. The stems of pink crowberry hug the surface of rocks or sand, the tips scarcely if at all raised above the ground.

◀ Black crowberry.

▲ Pink crowberry.

▲ Purple crowberry.

7 Common juniper
Juniperus communis ✦ *Cupressaceae* (Cypress family)

QUICK CHECK: Waist-high, clump-forming bush with wide-spreading branches sweeping upward, sharp-tipped needles in whorls of 3, and small blue berries. **ID difficulty 1.**

DESCRIPTION: Shrub forming clumps up to 20' (6 m) wide, usually circular, in open areas, the numerous stems growing outward and gently upward, 2–5' (60–150 cm) high and rarely more than 2" (5 cm) thick. **Bark** thin, brown, flaky. **Twigs** hairless, yellowish-green becoming light brown, grooved lengthwise when young. **Needles** 0.3–0.7" (8–18 mm) long and 1–2 mm wide, *in whorls of 3*, narrowed at the base, flattened, depressed in the middle, very sharp-tipped, the upper side (toward the branch tips) with a *broad gray stripe*. **Inflorescence** in the needle axils in late spring, bushes either male or female, not showy; the male cone-like, the female much smaller and green. **Fruit** is a "cone" modified into a berry that takes 2–3 years to ripen, green at first but ripening to blue-black and soft in late summer, the berries sessile, single but crowded, usually containing 3 seeds.

HABITAT: Dry, open sites, usually with poor soil: cliffs, beaches, sandy prairies, rocky outcroppings, old gravel pits, abandoned farmland, roadsides. Native. 🔥

FOOD USE: The **berries** are used as a seasoning in soups, sauerkraut, alcoholic beverages (gin), and many other applications. Tender spring **branch tips** can be used sparingly as a seasoning herb. Needles can also be steeped for **tea. Conservation 1.**

COMMENTS: This may be the most widespread woody species in the world, native to North America and Eurasia. Although the plant is easily killed by fire, it thrives mostly in fire-maintained habitats.

Related edible:

8 Eastern redcedar ✦ *Juniperus virginiana*

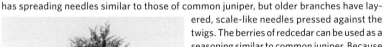

This is a tree-sized juniper that is common and widespread in our region, with trunks that are often furrowed and thin bark that shreds in fibrous, red-brown strips. The young growth has spreading needles similar to those of common juniper, but older branches have layered, scale-like needles pressed against the twigs. The berries of redcedar can be used as a seasoning similar to common juniper. Because there are some known species of juniper with mildly toxic needles, and I am not aware of any food tradition using redcedar needles, I advise against using them for tea or seasoning. 🔥

9 Canada yew 🐾 2
Taxus canadensis ✦ family *Taxaceae*

QUICK CHECK: Shrub with thick, flat needles in flat rows; fleshy red fruit. **ID difficulty 1.**

DESCRIPTION: Shrub often growing in thick colonies, spreading by tip-rooting of branches. **Stems** 2–8' (60–240 cm) tall, typically leaning or decumbent, up to 3" (8 cm) thick. **Bark** light brown with thin, scaly flakes. **Twigs** *uniformly light green* on new growth with a *raised linear ridge* just below each needle; on older branches these ridges remain light green but develop brown bark between them. **Needles** arranged in rows on each side of the twig, reaching 0.8" (2 cm) long; they are thick, soft, flattened, wider than those of other flat-needled conifers in our area, *not striped with light gray underneath*, with a midvein that *protrudes above and below*. The tip is sharp

and bristle-like. **Berry** (an aril) consists of a large elliptic seed surrounded by a soft, red, delicate-skinned flesh that is deeply and neatly indented at both ends, ripening in late summer.

CONFUSING PLANTS: Both hemlock and balsam fir seedlings have blunt-tipped needles with gray-white lines on the underside. There is no confusing fruit in our region.

HABITAT: Mature deciduous and mixed forests; often confined to rugged slopes and islands, persisting elsewhere only where deer numbers are low. Native.

FOOD USE: Gather soft red **berries** and suck the pulp as a snack. **WARNING:** Spit out the seeds; they are toxic, as are the needles and bark. **Conservation 1.**

Comments: The fruits are slimy and very sweet. I have eaten them hundreds of times but have never cooked or stored them. This shrub was formerly extremely abundant in much of the northern US, but since it is preferred above virtually all else as winter browse by white-tailed deer, it has been exterminated from most of its former range.

GROUP 5 TREES AND SHRUBS WITH NUTS

These are woody species with large, edible seeds, which are among the most concentrated wild calorie sources in our region. The oaks can be difficult, but identifying them beyond the three basic acorn types is not vital, so only a few common species are discussed in detail. The various hickories are used differently, so I discuss most species separately. When gathering or processing, remember **THE NUT LAW:** *An unusually adhering husk means a bad nut.* Stop wasting time trying to remove tenaciously clinging valves, cups, or involucres. Just toss the nut. Consider eye protection when cracking hard-shelled nuts.

TENTATIVE IDENTIFICATION KEY TO GROUP 5
The key is not your final answer!

Leaves palmately compound. Buckeye (p. 656).	
or Leaves pinnately compound.	
Flesh surrounding nut a single adhering mass, not splitting in sections.	
or Fruit spherical, not sticky or hairy.	1. Black walnut
Fruit football-shaped, sticky and hairy.	2. Butternut
Flesh surrounding nut loosens in distinct sections.	
Fruit winged or ridged where sections meet.	
Nut elongated, shell smooth, brown.	3. Pecan
or Nut flattened with a dark brown, corrugated, angled shell.	4. Water hickory
Nut broad-based with a smooth, rounded, whitish gray shell.	5. Bitternut
or Fruit grooved but not winged or ridged where sections meet.	
Bark shaggy; fruit not pear shaped.	
or Leaflets 5 (sun) or 7 (shade); nut less than 1.2" (3 cm).	6. Shagbark
Leaflets 7 (sun) or 9 (shade); nut often over 1.2" (3 cm).	7. Shellbark
Bark not shaggy; fruit sometimes pear-shaped.	
Nut with 4 distinct angles, pointed at both ends; shell extremely thick; leaf rachis densely soft-hairy below.	8. Mockernut
Nut smooth or with faint angles, almost rotund; shell very thick.	9. Black hickory
Nut slightly flattened, slightly oblong, smooth or with faint angles; shell moderately thick; fruit oblong and often pear-shaped.	10. Common hickory
Leaves simple.	
Nuts sharply 3-sided, paired in a bristly husk, shells pliable.	11. Beech
or Nuts all or partly rounded, 1–3 in a long-spiny husk; shells pliable.	
Leaves hairless beneath; 4-section bur encloses 1–3 nuts.	12. Chestnut
or Leaves hairy beneath; 2-section bur enclosing 1 nut.	13. Chinkapin
Nuts roundish, shells hard, enclosed singly in clustered leafy husks.	
Husk long and tubular, covered with glochids; nut radially symmetrical.	14. Beaked hazel
or Husk a ruffled clamshell covered with sticky hairs; nut slightly flattened.	15. American hazel
Nuts radially symmetrical with pliable shells and a nipple-tip, held in a cup-like base (oaks).	
Acorns with bright orange flesh.	
Leaves narrow at the base, tapered to a bulging or shallow-lobed tip.	16. Water oak
or Leaves long-elliptic and entire.	17. Shingle oak
Acorns with whitish, creamy, or dull yellow flesh.	
Leaves lobed with 2 or more deep sinuses.	
Lobes with sharp bristle-tips or teeth.	18. Northern red oak
Lobes blunt and rounded, without bristles.	
or Acorns in cups without awns, covering only the base.	19. White oak
Acorns in cups with awns, covering more than half the nut.	20. Bur oak
Leaves regularly toothed but not lobed.	
Bark light gray and flaky; tree of bottomlands.	21. Basket oak
or Bark dark and blocky, never flaky; tree of dry uplands.	22. Chestnut oak
Leaves entire or with a few teeth.	23. Southern live oak

1 Black walnut ⊖ 2 ◊ 1 ⚇
Juglans nigra ◆ *Juglandaceae* (Walnut family)

QUICK CHECK: Tree with pinnately compound leaves and spherical green fruits with flesh not peeling in sections, surrounding a rough-shelled nut. **ID difficulty 1.**

DESCRIPTION: Large tree, the **trunk** single, prominent, generally straight, reaching 100' (30 m) tall, the crown taller than wide. **Bark** dark gray, thick, with deep fissures between blocky ridges. **Twigs** stout, greenish-brown and smooth, finely hairy, with *naked buds*. Pith is wide, tan, and chambered. Leaf scars are heart-shaped, notched at the top, with 3 darkened *bundle scars forming a "monkey face."* **Leaves** up to 2' (60 cm) long, alternate, pinnately compound with 13–21 leaflets, *the end leaflet reduced or absent.* **Petiole/rachis** finely hairy, the *top a narrow ridge*, naked in the proximal quarter. **Leaflets** sessile, 2–6" (5–15 cm) long, lanceolate to ovate, rounded at the base, the tips acuminate, the margins finely serrated, minutely hairy along the midvein above and major veins below. Secondary **veins** numerous, 60–70°, not forking or curving toward tip, flat. **Flowers** wind-pollinated in spring, male and female separate on the same tree. Male flowers are numerous and tiny, in drooping catkins; female flowers are tiny and few in small clusters, each with a naked ovary and two pinkish wing-like projections. **Fruits** nearly spherical, 1.5–3" (3.8–8 cm) in diameter, borne singly or in clusters of 2–3, ripening to green, the flesh not peeling in sections; the aromatic surface is bumpy but not hairy or sticky. **Nut** shell is very thick, and its surface has a corrugated, brain-like texture; the kernel is convoluted.

HABITAT: Wooded slopes and valleys with very rich soil; also colonizes old fields and forest edges. Often planted outside of its natural range and escapes to fencerows. Native.

FOOD USE: Pick **nuts** off the ground in autumn. Soft hulls can be removed by stomping or smashing. (Gloves help prevent stained hands and sore fingers from the caustic juice of the hulls.) Dry the nuts for a few weeks before cracking. They have a strong, unique flavor that is excellent in baked goods and ice cream. **Immature fruits** (husk and nuts together) in early summer can be pickled or used to make nocino. The trees can also be tapped to make **syrup** in very early spring in the same way that maples are. **Conservation 1.**

WARNING: Wear gloves and eye protection while cracking!

COMMENTS: This abundant tree produces one of our most practical wild nuts for home use. Wild black walnuts are commercially harvested and processed and can be purchased in most large grocery stores. The wood is the most valuable in North America.

2 **Butternut** ⊖ 3   ⬩ 1   ⚬   📖 FH-157
Juglans cinerea ✦ *Juglandaceae* (Walnut family)

QUICK CHECK: Tree with pinnately compound leaves and football-shaped sticky green fruits, husks not peeling in sections. **ID difficulty 1.**

DESCRIPTION: Medium to large tree, the **trunks** single or clumped, tall in competition but the crowns of open-grown trees spread wider than tall. **Bark** silver-gray, smooth on young trees, broken by shallow fissures into smooth-topped, almost glossy, interlacing ridges on older trunks. **Twigs** stout, smooth, finely hairy, green at first, turning brown, with wide, dark brown chambered pith, *naked buds,* and *leaf scars with a "monkey face"* that is not notched at the top. **Leaves** alternate, pinnately compound, up to 2' (60 cm) long, with 11–17 leaflets, the *end leaflet similar in size to the side leaflets.* **Rachis/petiole** not channeled, ridged on top, hairy, with some of the hairs topped by sticky glands. **Leaflets** sessile or nearly so, ovate to oblong, 2–5" (5–13 cm) long, rounded at the base, with acuminate tips, hairy on both surfaces but more so below. **Midvein** raised; secondary veins broadly angled, numerous, faintly depressed above. **Margins** finely serrated with wavy, shallow, nipple-tipped teeth. **Flowers** wind-pollinated in spring, male and female separate on the same tree, both tiny. Male flowers hang in catkins; female flowers short-stalked, in clusters, with two curling purplish appendages extending from the ovary. **Fruit** football-shaped, green with a sticky, hairy, aromatic surface, 2–3.5" (5–9 cm) long; this flesh turns brown then black after falling but does not peel in sections. **Nut** has a very thick shell with a *knife-like tip* and a corrugated surface with thin ridges. **Kernel** comes in two *paddle-shaped pieces.*

HABITAT: Rich, well-drained soil, especially sandy loam; with elm, hickory, white ash, sugar maple, and hackberry. Very successful at invading fencerows and abandoned fields. Native.

FOOD USE: Gather the **nuts** as they fall in autumn, or shake them down when ripe. Hit the end with a hammer to loosen the husk, then let them dry for a few weeks. Crack with a hammer by striking either end, not the side. **Immature nuts** can be pickled in their husks. Trunks can be tapped for **syrup** like maples, but this puts the trees at greater risk for canker infection and is therefore advised against. **Conservation 1.**

WARNING: Wear gloves and eye protection while cracking!

COMMENTS: This nut has very soft and delicious meat. However, it is mostly shell, and it takes a pile to get a cupful of nutmeat. Unfortunately, this tree has been decimated by an introduced disease, butternut canker. It survives mainly on forest edges or open areas and has mostly died off in deep woods; introgression with Japanese walnut has imparted disease resistance to some individuals.

HICKORY 📖 IWE-134
genus *Carya* ✦ *Juglandaceae* (Walnut family)

QUICK CHECK: Pinnately compound leaves; fruits with multiple-part peeling husk containing a single nut with a divided interior and convoluted kernel. **ID difficulty 1.**

COLLECTIVE DESCRIPTION: Large trees, the trunks single and erect, dominant, usually straight and taller than wide. **Bark** hard and compact, smooth and very dark gray on saplings, dividing into longitudinal ridges or peeling strips or plates as they age. **Twigs** thick with large terminal buds. **Leaves** alternate and pinnately compound, the leaflets larger toward the end of the leaf. Leaflet counts are important in species identification, but in any one species it is common for the leaves to have one more set of leaflets in shade than in full sun. **Leaflets** paired, sessile, and ovate or obovate to lance-elliptic, the tips pointed. Blades are dark green, tough, and thick with glossy upper surfaces, the margins serrated with shallow teeth. **Midvein** flat to faintly depressed above. **Secondary veins** numerous, broadly angled, straight, flat to faintly depressed above. **Flow-**

ers tiny, wind-pollinated in late spring or early summer, male and female borne separately on the same tree. The male are in catkins, the female single or in small clusters. The fruits (nut and husk together) are 0.7–3" (1.8–8 cm) long, green and smooth on the outside, darkening after falling, *dividing neatly into 2–5 parts* and containing a single nut. **Nuts** have hard, light-colored, smooth or ridged shells. **Kernel** soft, divided, and convoluted.

▲ Typical nuts from four hickory species: mockernut (upper right), bitternut (upper left), shagbark (lower right), and shell-bark (lower left).

FOOD USE: Nuts can be gathered from the ground after they have fallen in autumn or early winter, or you can shake them down. Dry to facilitate cracking and shelling. Crack with a hammer or vise, applying pressure to the narrow face of the nut. Remove nutmeats with a nutpick and small wire cutters. Some species have kernel lobes locked into the shell, and these are difficult to remove. Such nuts are better used to make hickory milk by pounding in a mortar or pulverizing in a blender and then boiling; the mixture is gently stirred so that the shells remain on the bottom but the nutmeat pieces are suspended in the liquid, which is then ladled off and used as a beverage, soup base, or cooking liquid. Some hickories yield very small amounts of sugary sap when tapped. **Conservation 1.**

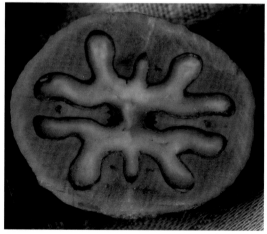

▲ Cross section of a black hickory nut, showing locked lobes that make shelling difficult.

COMMENTS: Hickories are widespread in eastern North America and produce edible nuts that are very popular among wild harvesters. For thousands of years these oil-rich nuts were probably the single most important food in our region. The nuts are frequently infested with weevil larvae (but some regions and species are mostly weevil-free). All are native. As a group the hickories are easy to recognize, but individual species can be tricky and some common names have been systematically misused. Adding to this, hybridization is common between some members. The pecan is our most familiar species of hickory.

3 **Pecan** ⬩ *Carya illinoinensis* ⊖ 3 📖 IWE-134

DESCRIPTION: Our largest hickory, the crown spreading widely, the **bark** dark gray with deep furrows and blocky ridges (reminiscent of black walnut). **Leaflets** narrow, 11–15 per leaf. Fruit elongated, in clusters of up to 10, *husk thin and ridged* along sutures. **Nut** at least twice as long as wide, *not flattened*, the **shell** smooth, brown, thin, without ridges.

HABITAT: Native to the higher parts of river floodplains and rich valleys; commonly associated with black walnut, honey locust, red mulberry, sycamore, shellbark hickory, and swamp chestnut oak. Native.

▲ Often planted outside this range.

COMMENTS: The nuts drop in late fall and can be picked from the ground. They store well and can be easily cracked with a hand-held nutcracker. Pecans yield in great abundance, and a single tree may produce hundreds of pounds. The nuts are also easier to crack and have a much higher kernel proportion than most other species. Pecans are often planted as ornamental or yard trees, expanding collecting opportunities.

4 **Water hickory** ⬩ *Carya aquatica* ◊

DESCRIPTION: Large tree with shaggy bark. **Leaves** have 9–13 leaflets, similar to those of pecan, with which it readily hybridizes. **Nuts** in clusters up to several, *flattened*, in *thin husks* with *raised ridges*. **Shells** *dark and rough*. The kernels are bitter but can be used to make a superb edible oil. **AKA** bitter pecan.

HABITAT: Flat, poorly drained areas, especially with clay soil, and river floodplains, but not the wettest parts.

COMMENTS: The kernels are bitter, but they make an excellent oil. The shell proportion is higher than with bitternut.

5 Bitternut ⋄ *Carya cordiformis* 💧

DESCRIPTION: Bark is smoother than the other species, developing tight crisscross strips with age. **Twigs** thinner than other hickories, the *buds naked and sulphur-yellow*. **Leaves** have 7–11 ovate to lanceolate leaflets. **Husk** *very thin and flexible*, adhering to the nut, with *ridges along the sutures*. **Nuts** *smooth* with *round bases*, elongated *needle-like tips*, and *very thin shells*. Meats have a *highly convoluted "brainlike" surface*.

HABITAT: Hardwood forests with medium levels of soil moisture, especially higher parts of river floodplains and fertile slopes. Associated with sugar maple, elm, white ash, basswood, northern red oak, black walnut, buckeye, and beech.

COMMENTS: Husks must be removed, as they do not fall off. Nuts can be mashed and boiled for a long time, after which oil can be decanted from the top. If you have an adequate press, the delicious oil can be pressed out. It contains none of the kernel's bitterness. This is the best source of vegetable oil native to North America and may have been the most important hickory species in the past. It is the most abundant and widespread hickory and produces the heaviest crops. Most often called "pignut," a name with great confusion attached (see common hickory). Commonly hybridizes with shagbark, pecan, and possibly other species. **AKA** yellowbud hickory, oilnut.

▲ The namesake yellow bud.

6 Shagbark ⋄ *Carya ovata* 🌰 3 ☕ 3 📖 IWE-150

DESCRIPTION: Dark gray **bark** hangs off in *long, thin, shaggy strips*. **Leaflets** 5–7, the terminal 3 much larger. Terminal buds and twigs are very thick. **Husk** 0.2–0.7" (5–18 mm) thick, falling off at maturity. **Nut** ridged, usually somewhat flattened laterally. **Shell** moderately thick, the *kernel lobes not locked* inside them.

HABITAT: Well-drained hardwood forests; most common in hilly areas of limestone-derived soil. Associated with oaks, other hickories, and black cherry.

COMMENTS: This is my favorite nut in the world. Husks should easily loosen from good, ripe nuts. Free lobes make this one of our easier species to shell. Susceptible to weevils. After pecan, this is the most commonly eaten wild hickory nut. In some regions, and in many books before 1960, this tree is called "shellbark."

▲ Shagbark flowers.

◄ The bark is not always this shaggy.

7 Shellbark ◆ *Carya laciniosa* 3 IWE-151

DESCRIPTION: Large tree with shaggy bark (lower trunks of very old trees lose their shagginess). Twigs and buds are very large. **Leaves** to 2' (60 cm) long, usually with 7 (sun) or 9 (shade) leaflets. **Fruits** to 3" (8 cm) long, occasionally more, with extremely thick husks. **Nuts** large, flattened, ridged, with very thick shells.

HABITAT: Rich bottomlands and valleys, high river floodplains. Associated with pecan, swamp chestnut oak, swamp white oak, bur oak, red mulberry, pawpaw, honeylocust, hackberry, black walnut.

COMMENTS: The lobes of the kernels are often slightly locked into the shells, but because of their size they are still one of the easiest to separate—if you can crack them. The flavor is excellent. Not very susceptible to weevils. This uncommon species produces the largest hickory nuts. Unfortunately, because this species prefers extremely fertile soils in flat land, most of its habitat has been destroyed by agriculture. **AKA** kingnut.

◄ Shellbark nuts compared to a black walnut.

8 Mockernut ✦ *Carya tomentosa*   🥜 3   ☕ 3   📖 IWE-153

DESCRIPTION: Large hickory with a narrow crown and *deeply furrowed bark*—but the ridges do not peel or hang off in strips. Twigs and buds are thick. **Leaflets** normally 7, the distal 3 much larger, the undersides and rachis distinguished from other species by *tufts of fine, soft hairs*. Fruits are large and elliptic, the husk moderately to very thick. **Nut** typically elongated and pointed on both ends, its shell *very thick* with prominent angles. **Kernel** proportionately small with locked lobes.

CONFUSING SPECIES: Black hickory tends to be smaller with smaller nuts. Common hickory has thinner bark ridges and smaller nuts. These species are very closely related and hybridize.

HABITAT: Mixed hardwood or pine-hardwood forests on well-drained soil. Native.

COMMENTS: These are difficult to crack, and the lobes of the small kernels are locked into the shell, making them slow and tedious to separate. They are okay for hickory milk, although the shell proportion is very high. Susceptible to weevils. This is the most common hickory in the Deep South. Despite the good flavor and large size, its shelling properties make mockernut one of the least useful species.

◀ Mockernut rachis close up.

9 Black hickory ✦ *Carya texana*   🥜 3   ☕ 3   📖 IWE-157

DESCRIPTION: Small to medium-sized hickory with deeply furrowed bark and medium-thick twigs. **Leaflets** 5–7. **Husks** moderately thick and stiff. **Nuts** almost as broad as long with thick shells, small kernels, and locked lobes.

HABITAT: Most common in dry, hilly country. Associated with post oak, dwarf chinkapin oak, and redcedar. Native.

COMMENTS: The nuts are laborious to shell but store well and are good for hickory milk. Highly susceptible to weevils. Like a drought-adapted cross between common hickory and mockernut, this species can be hard to tell from either one. Over large areas from the Ozarks south and west this is the most common hickory encountered. Sand hickory *C. pallida* is a similar species of dry sandy soils in the Southeast with small leaves and small nuts.

10 **Common hickory** ◆ *Carya glabra* 3 3

DESCRIPTION: Bark *extremely variable*, ranging from almost shaggy to almost smooth. At one extreme it can look like a shagbark, at the other like a bitternut. **Twigs** thinner than shagbark with smaller, more pointed buds. **Leaves** have 5–7 leaflets. **Fruit** often somewhat elongated and *slightly pear-shaped*. **Husks** *stiff*, thin to moderately thick, usually remaining slightly opened but *attached to the nut when ripe*; there are no ridges along the sutures. **Nuts** small and oval with *smooth shells*, lacking sharp angles but sometimes with smooth, faint ridges. **Shells** thick and the kernels locked.

HABITAT: Hardwood forests on well-drained soil, particularly sand.

COMMENTS: Nuts have excellent flavor, but because of their small size, thick shells, and locked lobes they are laborious to shell. However, the nuts keep better than shagbarks and are the best for making hickory milk. Highly susceptible to weevils. Called "pignut hickory" in printed sources, but that name carries insoluble confusion. "Pignut" in spoken American English has always referred to *Carya cordiformis*. Pehr Kalm's writings confirm this was already the case in 1749, and it remains true today. Yet a botanical error well over 100 years ago attached the name "pignut" to *Carya glabra*, and the mistake has since become entrenched in the literature, leading to the erroneous belief that there is a "sweet" and a "bitter" species of pignut. Let me clarify: *C. cordiformis*, which books call "bitternut" or "yellowbud" hickory, but most laypeople call "pignut," has a bitter kernel. *C. glabra*, which most laypeople call "hickory" but books call "pignut," has a sweet kernel. In fact, many people on a taste test will claim it as their favorite hickory nut. Most dendrologists don't eat hickory nuts, so they don't care about this confusion. But for us foragers, it matters. I'm done with the pignut nonsense—this tree is **common hickory** in my book, *and it is delicious*. To add another layer of confusion, botanists have long debated whether *C. glabra* is one highly variable species, or should be split into two. This debate has less relevance to wild nutters; *both forms* have sweet kernels.

11 Beech 🌰 3 💧 🌿 1
Fagus grandifolia • Fagaceae (Beech family)

QUICK CHECK: Small three-sided nuts, usually paired, in bristly husks; smooth, gray bark. **ID difficulty 1.**

DESCRIPTION: Large tree spreading by suckers. **Trunks** large and erect, the crowns broad. **Bark** smooth, gray, very thin with occasional warty nodules. **Twigs** slender, slightly zigzag, hairless, the *buds long and sharp*. **Leaves** alternate, elliptic-ovate to lanceolate with acuminate tips, 2.5–6" (6–15 cm) long, margins sharply but distantly serrated with incurved teeth. The surface is hairless or nearly so above with fine, soft hairs below. Secondary veins are closely spaced, depressed, and run straight to the margins. **Petioles** 2–4% of blade length. Dead leaves often persist through the winter on young trees. **Flowers** (spring) small and unshowy, wind pollinated, with the male and female separate. **Nuts** 11–13 mm long with pliable 3-sided shells, borne in pairs inside a bristly husk that splits open.

HABITAT: Mixed hardwood forests, preferring rich but well-drained soil. Associated with red oak and sugar maple. Native.

FOOD USE: Gather **nuts** as they fall to the ground about the time that the leaves drop in autumn. Crack a few open to check for empties, which are often prevalent. Shell by teeth, with a nutcracker, or between two cutting boards. Store by drying in the shell. Beechnuts make a good snack or addition to hot cereal or baked goods. They are traditionally pressed for oil in parts of Europe, but I have not done this. Young **leaves** are marginally edible in early spring. **Conservation 1.**

COMMENTS: These are delicious nuts; unfortunately they do not often produce heavy crops and are hard to shell due to the small size. This is another native tree being decimated by exotic disease—two of them in fact: beech bark disease and beech leaf disease.

◄ Young beech leaves.

12 **American chestnut** 🌰 3
Castanea dentata ⁺ *Fagaceae* (Beech family)

QUICK CHECK: Lanceolate leaves sharply toothed; smooth-shelled nuts in sharp-spiny husk. **ID difficulty 2.**

DESCRIPTION: Formerly a large, dominant tree, today native chestnuts survive almost exclusively as stump sprouts, which rarely exceed 4" (10 cm) in diameter and 40' (12 m) in height. **Bark** thin, smooth, and dark on sprouts, which usually have *blight scars evident*; separating into broad, flat-topped ridges on older trees. **Twigs** smooth, shiny olive-green to brown with tiny white lenticels, the *pith star-shaped in cross section*. Buds are egg-shaped, tapered to a blunt point. **Leaves** alternate, on petioles about 10% of blade length, lanceolate to narrowly elliptic, 5–9" (13–23 cm) long, acute at the base and tapered to a *very sharp tip*. Blades are hairless with 15–20 closely spaced secondary veins per side, depressed and running straight and unbroken to the margins where they terminate as a bristle. **Margins** have widely spaced, long but narrow teeth, usually oriented toward the tip but hooking in toward the margin, each tooth tip with a thin bristle. **Flowers** (early summer) wind-pollinated, in stiff, semi-erect creamy catkins to 8" (20 cm) long, the male flowers more numerous, the female found near the base of some catkins. **Husk** 1.5–2.5" (4–6 cm) in diameter, densely covered with long, stiff, sharp spines; containing 2–4 **nuts,** these ripening in mid fall, 0.5–0.8" (13–20 mm) wide with thin, smooth, brown, pliable shells, flattened on one or two sides, hairy at the nipple-like tip.

CONFUSING PLANTS: Chinkapins are smaller trees or shrubs with roundish nuts borne one per husk.

HABITAT: Hardwood forests, especially on well-drained lightly acidic slopes and ridges. Native.

FOOD USE: Gather **nuts** in autumn and use like domestic chestnuts. **Conservation 1.**

COMMENTS: This tree once dominated large sections of eastern forests but has been all but exterminated by an introduced disease, chestnut blight, which first began spreading in the early 1900's. In some places extensive stands remain dominated by chestnut stump sprouts, which may produce nuts for a few years before being killed back by the blight. After a century of failure at finding blight-resistant wild trees, the State University of New York's forestry school at Syracuse has recently created a population of fully blight-resistant American chestnuts by adding a single gene from the wheat plant.

Blight scar on a chestnut sprout. ▶

13 Chinkapin ⬬ 3
Castanea pumila ⁘ *Fagaceae* (Beech family)

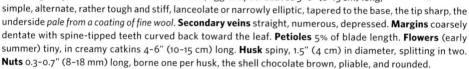

QUICK CHECK: Shrubby tree or bush, narrow leaves with bristle-tipped teeth and single, smooth-shelled nuts in a husk with long, sharp spines. **ID difficulty 2.**

DESCRIPTION: Small tree or large shrub, often with multiple leaning trunks from the base, reaching about 30' (9 m) in height. **Bark** smooth on young stems, gray, eventually becoming flaky with narrow fissures. Buds blunt, egg-shaped. **Leaves** 3–6" (8–15 cm) long, simple, alternate, rather tough and stiff, lanceolate or narrowly elliptic, tapered to the base, the tip sharp, the underside *pale from a coating of fine wool.* **Secondary veins** straight, numerous, depressed. **Margins** coarsely dentate with spine-tipped teeth curved back toward the leaf. **Petioles** 5% of blade length. **Flowers** (early summer) tiny, in creamy catkins 4–6" (10–15 cm) long. **Husk** spiny, 1.5" (4 cm) in diameter, splitting in two. **Nuts** 0.3–0.7" (8–18 mm) long, borne one per husk, the shell chocolate brown, pliable, and rounded.

CONFUSING PLANTS: Chinkapin oak *Quercus muehlenbergii* and dwarf chinkapin oak *Q. prinoides* have similar leaves but their acorns are borne in cups.

HABITAT: Hardwood forests and forest edges in sandy or dry, well-drained soil. Native. 🔥

FOOD USE: Nuts ripen in autumn and can be gathered and used like small chestnuts. **Conservation 2.**

COMMENTS: This species, like its larger cousin the American chestnut, has been decimated by chestnut blight.

RELATED EDIBLE: Ozark chinkapin *C. ozarkensis* is very similar but has shorter leaves.

HAZELNUT 📖 NG-197
genus *Corylus* ✦ *Betulaceae* (Birch family)

QUICK CHECK: Tall clumping shrubs with double-toothed ovate leaves and smooth-shelled nuts wrapped in a leafy husk. **ID difficulty 1.**

DESCRIPTION: Clump-forming shrubs 6–16' (2–5 m) tall, stems 0.6–2" (1.5–5 cm) thick, mostly unbranched near the base. **Bark** thin, grayish brown, slightly roughened. **Leaves** alternate, ovate, rounded to heart-shaped at the base and pointed at the tip, 2.5–4" (6.4–10 cm) long, hairy on both sides (more so below), with double-toothed margins. **Secondary veins** depressed above and protruding below, running straight to the margins where they end in a dominant tooth. **Petioles** 8–15% of blade length. **Flowers** tiny, wind pollinated in very early spring; the male in hanging catkins, the female sessile with a cluster of bright red stigmas protruding from a bud-like set of bracts. **Nuts** borne in ball-like clusters of up to 15, the cluster carrying several aborted nuts. Each nut is wrapped in a leafy involucre. The shells are hard, smooth, and light brown with a lighter zone at the base, the kernel in one mass. We have 2 species, both native.

FOOD USE: Pick the *green* leafy clusters in late summer when the nutshells have turned light brown. (Don't wait for the husks to turn brown!) Wear gloves for collecting beaked hazel. Dry the husks, dance on them in a barrel or gunnysack, then pick the **nuts** out by hand. Before doing this you can singe the glochids off of beaked hazelnuts. Once separated, the nuts can be cracked, shelled, and used like domestic hazelnuts—but they taste better. Wild hazelnuts make a fantastic **nut milk**. They store up to 2 years in the shell, but once cracked should be used within 3–5 months. **Conservation 1.**

COMMENTS: Although the bushes of these two species are extremely similar, the nuts are initially handled quite differently. Beaked hazelnut is more tedious to gather and husk. However, clean nuts and separated kernels are used almost identically.

▲ Beaked hazelnuts in the top row; American hazel below.

14 Beaked hazel ✦ *Corylus cornuta* 🌰 3 ☕

This species inhabits young or open woods and brushy areas, especially with pine, oak, birch, and aspen, on soils ranging from dry to moist. The young *twigs and petioles are not covered with gland-tipped hairs*. The dormant male **catkins** are *nearly sessile* and often rigid.
Nuts ripen 1–2 weeks earlier than American hazel, wrapped tightly in an involucre that is *tubular and extended* (beak-like), *covered with stiff, irritating spines (glochids)*. 🔥

◄ Male catkins of beaked hazel.

15 American hazel + *Corylus americana* 3

This is a species of forest openings, savannahs, and brushy areas, where it may form large, dense thickets. It likes dry, well-drained soil and clay flats. The terminal *twigs and petioles have sticky, gland-tipped hairs.* Dormant male **catkins** *hang on a short stem.* **Nuts** wrapped in a *sticky, aromatic, ruffled involucre densely covered in gland-tipped hairs.* While still abundant in many areas, American hazel has decreased dramatically in much of its range due to fire suppression. 🔥

▼ When the nuts first ripen the husk remains green.

OAK
genus *Quercus* ✦ *Fagaceae* (Beech family)

QUICK CHECK: Nuts with a smooth, pliable shell and nipple-like tip, borne singly in a cup-like structure. **ID difficulty 1.**

COLLECTIVE DESCRIPTION: Trees or shrubs, about 50 species native to our region, with highly variable leaf forms and ecological roles. **Bark** roughened in mature trees by plates, blocks, flakes, or fissures. Twigs moderately thick with *winter buds clustered near the tips*. **Leaves** alternate, simple, borne on short petioles. Blades thick and tough; the variable shapes include deeply pinnately lobed, ovate and toothed, and elliptic and entire. **Veins** pinnate, mostly flat above. **Flowers** wind-pollinated in spring. Male flowers hang in limp catkins, while the female are attached directly to the twigs or on short stalks, singly or in small groups. **Fruit** a spherical to elongated nut (acorn), *radially symmetrical* with a nipple-like tip and a thin, smooth, flexible shell, borne singly in a scaly cup (the scales sometimes supporting hair-like burs). At the bottom of the nut is a wide, light-colored zone of attachment. The nutmeat is creamy, yellowish, or bright orange, divided into two cotyledons (sometimes unequally), the surface smooth or with a few folds or convolutions, covered with a thin skin (testa) that is sometimes hairy.

ECOLOGY: Most oaks are associated with fire and are drought-tolerant, although some are swamp trees. Generally they dominate slightly poorer soils than mesic trees such as maple, ash, elm, buckeye, and basswood. Oaks often occur in association with pines and hickories. All the species listed here are native.

FOOD USE: All acorns are edible but contain tannins which should be leached from the nutmeats before they are eaten in a serving-size quantity. Acorn size has a large impact on labor-efficiency, so the species highlighted here are mostly those with larger acorns. You can shell acorns immediately or dry them first. After shelling they can be **hot-leached** by boiling in several water changes, whole or chopped into smaller pieces. Hot-leached acorns can be used like beans in chili, or they can be dried and ground into a flour that can be mixed with other flours for baking. Acorns can also be **cold-leached** by grinding them into a fine flour and soaking in several changes of cold water or percolating water through them. Cold-leached flour can be baked into a cheese-like food that is hearty and filling. Korean **starch extraction** involves pulverizing fresh acorn meats in a wet blender and percolating cold water through the fine material; the starch granules are then settled by gravity out of the percolated water. Some acorns can also be pressed or boiled to extract **oil**. It is hard to generalize about the use of acorns as food because there are 3 main types or groups of acorns in our region, each with distinct physical and chemical characteristics. Though traditionally lumped together as "acorns," these groups differ far more than many other groups of edible plants that we traditionally split up. **Conservation 1.**

RED (BLACK) OAK GROUP: These 10–12 species have mostly medium-sized acorns (but on two species they are large). They have creamy to yellow flesh, a velvety-hairy inner cup lining, and unequal cotyledons, often with a large convolution, meeting with curved or angled faces. Tannin levels are moderate to high; oil levels moderate. These take two years to develop on the tree and germinate in spring. They dry readily in the shell; once dried they keep for several years. They are ideal for making hot-leached or cold-leached flour.

WHITE OAK GROUP: About 25 species, the acorns small to large, longer than broad, with creamy-colored flesh, having nearly equal cotyledons meeting with flat faces and lacking convolutions; the cup lining is not hairy. Large acorns of this group are more difficult to dry in the shell. When dried they are harder than red oaks acorns. Tannin levels are moderately low to high; oil levels are low. These develop in one season and germinate in autumn; they rancidify after a year or two in storage. They are ideal for hot-leached or cold-leached flour and Korean starch processing.

ORANGE FLESH GROUP: These 12–15 species have small to tiny acorns, as broad or broader than long, mostly with very dark shells. The flesh is *bright orange* (fading to dull yellow-orange when dry). They are high in tannin and much higher in oil (35–55%) than other acorns. Like white oaks, the cotyledons are approximately equal, meet with flat faces, and lack convolutions. Like red oaks, they develop over two seasons, grow from a cup with velvety hairs, and germinate in spring. They are ideal for making oil and can also be leached and eaten. This group is not widely recognized by taxonomists.

16 **Water oak** ✦ *Quercus nigra* ⊖ 1 ◊

DESCRIPTION: Medium-sized oak, erect with a dominant single trunk. **Bark** hard, moderately thick, dark, forming erratic plates or low scaly ridges. **Leaves** 1.5–4" (3.8–10 cm) long and highly variable in shape: often entire, occasionally lobed, but always wide at the tip and tapered to the base. They are tough and semi-evergreen, usually falling slowly over the course of the winter. **Acorns** (orange flesh group) are very small, broad, squat, in shallow cups, the bases nearly flat, the ends rounded, the shell dark brown and often striped, the flesh bright orange.

HABITAT: Most common in high parts of floodplains and woodlots or fencerows on flat land, especially where poorly drained or with clay soil. Common as a yard and park tree.

COMMENTS: The kernels are about 50% oil, which can be extracted by pressing or boiling. The oil is not bitter (tannin is not oil-soluble) and is beautifully orange like the nut's flesh. Here is an untapped native food crop available in enormous quantities. Other high-oil species include *Q. imbricaria* (below), *Q. phellos, Q. hemisphaerica, Q. falcata,* and several others.

17 **Shingle oak** ✦ *Quercus imbricaria* ⊖ 1 ◊

QUICK CHECK: Oak with large, entire leaves that are hairy on the underside; small acorns.

DESCRIPTION: Medium-sized oak with an erect single trunk and narrow crown. **Bark** hard, dark, and covered in low plates. **Leaves** entire and elliptic, 4–7" (10–18 cm) long, the tip with a bristle, hanging on late through the winter. The blade is shiny above with soft brown wool on the underside. **Acorns** (orange flesh group) dark and nearly round, up to 0.7" (1.8 cm) across.

HABITAT: Fertile soils, moderately dry to moist, especially high floodplains, lower slopes, and clay flats.

COMMENTS: This is a good candidate for extracting oil. It is the northernmost of our high-oil acorns and has the largest nuts in the "pumpkin-flesh" group. Of all the entire-leaved oak species in North America, this one has the largest leaves.

18 Northern red oak ✦ *Quercus rubra* 1 2 NG-158

DESCRIPTION: Tall, graceful oak with dark, smooth bark when young, later developing erratic ridges. It sheds its dead lower branches and does not hold its dead leaves in winter. **Leaves** 4–9" (10–23 cm) long with 7–11 point-tipped lobes, the petiole about 40% of blade length. **Acorns** (red oak group) to 1.2" (3 cm) long with flat, shallow cups.

HABITAT: A variety of soils, but most abundant on moderately rich sandy sites, where it often co-dominates with white pine or white oak.

COMMENTS: The large acorns dry readily and are one of the most labor-efficient for shelling. They are good for hot or cold leaching. This is the most common oak in many areas, and in some regions it is the only species. This and the very similar Shumard oak are the only members of the red oak group in eastern North America with large acorns. Several species have leaves with fewer lobes and similar but smaller (and often striped) acorns.

19 White oak ✦ *Quercus alba* 1 2 NG-150

DESCRIPTION: Large tree with a broad crown of spreading or ascending branches. **Bark** light gray, flaky, peeling off in loose, flat strips. **Leaves** 4–7" (10–18 cm) long, hairless or nearly so, with long, narrow, round-tipped lobes. **Acorns** (white oak group) oval or elliptic, to 1" (2.5 cm) long, smooth and brown or purplish brown, in cups covering less than a third of the nut.

HABITAT: Well-drained soil, especially loamy sand and sandstone ridges.

COMMENTS: This is our most prevalent oak. The acorns are medium-sized but often very abundant. They are so eager to germinate that they can sometimes be seen sprouting while still on the tree.

◄ Newly emerging white oak leaves with flower buds.

20 Bur oak + *Quercus macrocarpa*   ⬭ 1   🔥 2   📖 NG-152

DESCRIPTION: Large tree with numerous spreading and ascending branches and a short trunk when grown in the open. **Bark** gray and deeply furrowed, not flaky but often sloughing off at the base. **Leaves** 3–8" (8–20 cm) long with blunt lobes, typically with deep sinuses in the proximal half and shallow sinuses in the broad distal half. The surface is dark green above and light greenish-gray with minute, fine hairs on the underside. **Acorns** (white oak group) broadly elliptic, dull gray-brown, extremely variable in size, from 0.4–1.6" (1–4 cm) long. The cup encloses the nut 60–95% and has a fringe of soft curly awns or "burs."

HABITAT: In prairies and prairie edges; this was the quintessential oak savannah tree. Also scattered in high parts of floodplains or rich hardwood forests, particularly in flat areas of clay soil. 🔥

COMMENTS: In its northernmost range bur oak acorns are quite small, but in the southern US they can be enormous—probably the largest acorn in North America. Bur oak acorns are very resistant to drying. Overcup oak *Q. lyrata* is a similar species of southern floodplains with a bur-less husk completely enclosing the acorn.

21 Basket oak + *Quercus michauxii*   ⬭ 1   🔥 2

DESCRIPTION: Large, straight-growing tree. **Bark** light gray, flaky, resembling white oak. **Leaves** 4–8" (10–20 cm) long, obovate, unlobed but with large, blunt teeth (somewhat resembling chestnut leaves). **Acorns** (white oak group) 0.8–1.5" (2–4 cm) long, longer than wide, dark gray-brown, about half enclosed by the cup.

HABITAT: Bottomlands, upper floodplain forests, flat rich lands. Associated with bur oak, swamp white oak, pecan, honeylocust, silver maple, and sycamore.

COMMENTS: This tree has consistently large acorns that fall from their husks readily, making them among the easiest species to harvest and process—but they are almost never weevil-free. **AKA** swamp chestnut oak. Swamp white oak *Q. bicolor* is a similar species with smaller, long-stalked acorns.

22 Chestnut oak ✦ *Quercus montana* 1 2 NG-154

DESCRIPTION: Large tree with a narrower crown than others in the white oak group. **Bark** dark, deeply furrowed, and blocky (reminiscent of the red oak group). **Leaves** 4–6" (10–15 cm) long, obovate to elliptic, with very large, blunt teeth. **Acorns** (white oak group) oblong, up to 1.3" (33 mm) long, about one-third enclosed by the cup.

HABITAT: Well-drained rocky soil, especially on mountains and hills. Formerly grew with American chestnut, which it has partly replaced on the same sites.

COMMENTS: The acorns are large, high in tannin, and often produced profusely.

23 Southern live oak ✦ *Quercus virginiana* 1 2 NG-158

DESCRIPTION: Short trunk and spreading or leaning form in the open; taller and more erect in the forest. **Bark** dark, with deep, narrow furrows between blocky, slightly flaky ridges. **Leaves** tough and evergreen (dropping in spring), 1.4–4" (3.5–10 cm) long, narrowly elliptic, blunt-tipped. **Margins** entire, sometimes wavy or rarely with a tooth or bump, down-curved. The lower surface is densely pubescent. **Acorns** (white oak group) medium-sized, oblong, dark brown, the cup enclosing half or less of the nut.

HABITAT: Sandy but moist soil, especially along floodplains, borders of coastal wetlands, and other flat areas.

COMMENTS: Live oak can be a prolific acorn producer. It is often the best oak in its area, where most species of acorns are small.

GROUP 6 TREES OR SHRUBS WITH LARGE FLESHY FRUITS (OVER 0.8"/ 2 CM)

Since fruit size varies, any fruit close to the 2 cm threshold may also belong to a plant in group 7, 10, or 11. For all of the species in this group, the fruit is the primary food product.

TENTATIVE IDENTIFICATION KEY TO GROUP 6
The key is not your final answer!

Leaf compound.		
or	Leaf pinnately compound with 7–9 leaflets; fruit smooth and red, ending in a large 5-part calyx.	1. Rugosa rose
	Leaf ternately compound; fruit downy with no end calyx.	2. Trifoliate orange
Leaf simple.		
	Leaf entire.	
	Fruit with a stiff basal calyx almost as wide as the fruit.	
or	Ripe fruit dull orange, skin hairless.	3. Persimmon
or	Ripe fruit black, skin covered with minute wool.	4. Black persimmon
	Fruit with no calyx.	
	Fruit mango to kidney shaped, green, pulpy; dark seeds to 0.8" (2 cm).	5. Pawpaw
	Fruit softball-sized, green and hard, the surface brain-like. Osage orange (not edible).	
	Fruit elongated, spongy, with a single, elongated, woody, ridged seed.	6. Ogeechee tupelo
	Leaf toothed.	
	Fruit firm, with multiple seeds in a core, and a 5-lobed end calyx.	
	Tree thorny; fruit sticky, yellow-green with black spots, less than 2" (5 cm) diameter.	7. American crabapple
or	Tree not thorny; fruit not sticky.	
	Fruit more than 2" (5 cm) and usually less than 7 per umbel.	8. Apple
	Fruit less than 1.5" (4 cm), often more than 8 per umbel.	9. Eurasian crabapple
	Fruit soft when ripe, with no calyx; one large, hard, clam-shaped stone.	10. Wild plum

1 Rugosa rose ✿ 2 🍎 3
Rosa rugosa ✦ *Rosaceae* (Rose family)

QUICK CHECK: Thorny bushes with pinnately compound leaves and toothed leaflets; large shiny red fruit with a prominent calyx at the tip. ID difficulty 1.

DESCRIPTION: Thicket-forming bush spreading by rhizomes. **Stems** and twigs densely covered with straight prickles and fine woolly hairs. **Leaves** alternate, pinnately compound with 7–9 leaflets. **Petioles** finely hairy with a broad stipule attached to the lower part. **Leaflets** sessile or nearly so, ovate to elliptic, blunt pointed, 1–1.8" (2.5–4.5 cm), the margins serrated with blunt teeth. **Midvein**, secondary veins, and veinlets all *strongly depressed above*, resulting in a rough (rugose) surface. **Flowers** 2–4" (5–10 cm) wide, with 5 long, pointed, triangular green sepals and 5 broad, pink petals. **Pedicel** long woolly. **Fruit** a hip up to 2" (5 cm) wide, with smooth, waxy, bright red skin and a prominent calyx at the tip. The hip is pulpy and *hollow in the center*, where the seeds reside mixed with loose, stiff hairs.

▲ Widely planted ornamentally but feral mostly in the mapped area.

HABITAT: Sandy seashore dunes and upper beaches in full sun. Occasional inland. Introduced.

FOOD USE: See p. 142 for a general discussion of roses. The **hips** of this species are among the best in flavor, and their large size makes for labor-efficient pulp separation. The flower **petals** are also large and easy to gather.

COMMENTS: Since this is the largest of our roses it has the easiest hips to use. The flesh has very good flavor. In some seashore areas these hips can be gathered in remarkable abundance. This species is often erroneously called "beach plum."

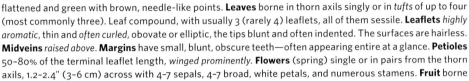

2 **Trifoliate orange** 🍎 2
Citrus trifoliata ✦ family *Rutaceae*

QUICK CHECK: Thick flattened twigs with smooth green bark and large thorns, compound leaves with three leaflets; round, dull, velvety fruit. **ID difficulty 1.**

DESCRIPTION: Large shrub or small tree, branching widely. **Bark** thin, older trunks *striped* with gray-brown and green; branches and twigs uniformly *green and smooth*. **Branches** *zigzag and flattened*, with *numerous thorns* 1–3" (2.5–8 cm) that are long, alternate, flattened and green with brown, needle-like points. **Leaves** borne in thorn axils singly or in *tufts* of up to four (most commonly three). Leaf compound, with usually 3 (rarely 4) leaflets, all of them sessile. **Leaflets** *highly aromatic*, thin and *often curled*, obovate or elliptic, the tips blunt and often indented. The surfaces are hairless. **Midveins** *raised above*. **Margins** have small, blunt, obscure teeth—often appearing entire at a glance. **Petioles** 50–80% of the terminal leaflet length, *winged prominently*. **Flowers** (spring) single or in pairs from the thorn axils, 1.2–2.4" (3–6 cm) across with 4–7 sepals, 4–7 broad, white petals, and numerous stamens. **Fruit** borne on very short, stout pedicels, ripening to a dull yellowish in autumn, with a strong, somewhat rank smell; it is spherical, 1–2" (2.5–5 cm), the surface downy and the rind tough, enclosing many large seeds and juice—there is virtually no pulp.

HABITAT: Full sun to light shade in brushy areas such as fence lines, forest margins, urban waste areas, and parks. Introduced.

FOOD USE: The **oranges** have a very sour juice that can be used like lemon juice, but it definitely has its own twist. It is often derided for not being a real lemon, but I think it makes a really good lemonade or flavoring for carbonated water.

COMMENTS: An exotic, unexpected edible that is locally abundant. Just watch out for those thorns! **AKA** hardy orange, *Poncirus trifoliata*.

3 **Persimmon**   ○ 3   ☕   📖 IWE-253
Diospyros virginiana + Ebenaceae (Persimmon family)

QUICK CHECK: Soft, orange, pumpkin-shaped sessile fruit with a large, tough, 5-pointed calyx. **ID difficulty 1.**

DESCRIPTION: Small to medium-sized pioneer tree. **Trunks** usually single, dominant, 10–70' (3–21 m) tall and 6–14" (15–36 cm) in diameter, the crown narrow even in full sun. **Bark** *very dark* with thick, well-separated blocks. **Twigs** often asymmetrically clustered at the branch tips with several on one side, and may detach easily with the fruit. They are gray to reddish brown with orange pores and closely spaced buds, giving them a "squiggly" appearance; new twigs are hairy. **Leaves** alternate, deciduous, semi-leathery, 3–6" (8–15 cm) long and about half as wide, ovate to elliptic, the tip pointed, margins entire and hairy, the blades flat, often with dark smudges. **Veins** all *flat above*; larger veins protrude below. Secondary veins are light in color, 45–60° to the midvein, breaking up before the margin. **Petioles** reddish, hairy, 1–20% of blade length, faintly channeled. New spring leaves are drooping, shiny, and coppery. **Flowers** male and female on separate trees in late spring, both genders sessile, bell-shaped, about 0.4" (1 cm) across, with 4–5 recurved lobes. Male flowers are greenish-yellow, in small clusters, while female flowers are borne singly and are yellowish to creamy. **Fruit** 0.8–2" (2–5 cm) in diameter, roughly spherical, ripening in autumn to dull orange, often with black or bluish mottling on the *very thin skin* subtended by a *tough, persistent 5-pointed calyx*. Flesh is dull orange and very soft when ripe, pulpy rather than juicy, containing up to 6 flattened, elliptic, brown seeds about 0.6" (1.5 cm) long.

HABITAT: Shade intolerant; found in young or open woods, rocky ridges, fencerows, stream valleys, high parts of river floodplains, old fields, forest edges. Likes well-drained sites. Native.

FOOD USE: Gather the **fruit** from the tree or the ground when it is fully ripe and softened. Allow nearly-ripe fruit to soften after picking. Even slightly unripe persimmons can leave a potent and unpleasant astringency in the mouth. Ripening time varies greatly between trees, from late August to November. Persimmons can be eaten raw, or the pulp can be separated from the seeds and used in baking much like pumpkin. The texture changes dramatically when cooked. Dried or fresh leaves are used for **tea. Conservation 1.**

COMMENTS: Extremely prolific and often available by the bushel, fully ripe persimmons are delicious and versatile. Unripe persimmons can look ripe to the uninitiated, but are an unpleasant experience not easily forgotten. The wild fruit not only tastes better than cultivated persimmons, but is shockingly more nutritionally dense. The leaves of Asian persimmon are sold commercially for tea.

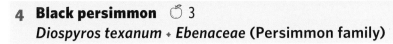

4 Black persimmon 🍎 3
Diospyros texanum ✦ *Ebenaceae* (Persimmon family)

QUICK CHECK: Small scrubby tree with very smooth light-gray bark, ridged wood, and small, entire, leathery leaves; fruit like a black cherry tomato. **ID difficulty 1.**

DESCRIPTION: Small tree (sometimes fruiting at shrub size) to 40' (12 m) tall, often multi-trunked, scrubby and twisted, dense with stiff branches at broad angles. **Bark** *very smooth and thin*, light gray, flaking off in paper-thin layers, the wood ridged or "muscly." **Twigs** red-brown to grayish with light lenticels, the new twigs finely hairy. Twigs are rougher and darker than older trunks—opposite the situation on most trees. **Leaves** alternate, persisting at least into early winter, *crowded at twig tips,* mostly *ascending,* leathery, 0.7–2" (1.8–5 cm) long. Blades entire, obovate or spoon-shaped with blunt tips that are rounded or occasionally notched, narrowed at the base, the margins rolled downward. **Surface** sparsely hairy and dark above, the veinlets slightly depressed; densely woolly and lighter green on the underside. Secondary veins are scarcely evident. **Petioles** extremely short. **Flowers** (spring to early summer) male and female on separate trees, solitary or in small clusters. A calyx of 5 broad, thick lobes persists through fruiting. **Corolla** urn-shaped, greenish white, soft-hairy, 1 cm long with 5 spreading lobes often notched at the tip. **Fruit** spherical or slightly compressed, 0.7–1" (18–25 mm) across, green at first ripening suddenly to black, pulpy and juicy, the surface covered with minute wool, subtended by a 5–6 lobed calyx. **Seeds** 3–8, red-brown, semi-hard, 5–9 mm long, shaped like a lentil bulged on one side.

HABITAT: Rocky, hilly, well-drained, sunny sites, especially on limestone-derived soils. Native.

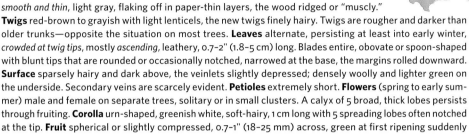

FOOD USE: Ripe fruit (late summer to early autumn) can be eaten right off the tree or the pulp used in baking or for fruit leather. It can also be used to make wine. **Conservation 1.**

COMMENTS: Delicious, large, coal-black berries with black juice—this sounds like something a child would make up. But it's real. The heartwood is almost black, the pale bark clay-smooth. Interesting that our two persimmons have utterly opposite bark characteristics. The first time I encountered black persimmon I thought I was seeing dead, sun-bleached wood. This fruit seems to lack the astringent fake-ripe phase of common persimmon. **AKA** Texas persimmon.

5   Pawpaw   ◌ 3   📖 IWE-243
Asimina triloba ✦ family *Annonaceae*

QUICK CHECK: Very large entire leaves, wider toward the tip; large, kidney-shaped fruit. **ID difficulty 1.**

DESCRIPTION: Large shrub or small tree, forming colonies by suckering. **Trunks** single, erect, 8–35' (2.4–11 m) tall and up to 10" (25 cm) in diameter. **Bark** smooth or with faint bumps, almost uniform gray, thin. **Branches** few and twigs large, with *silky-pubescent, dark brown buds*. **Leaves** 8–18" (20–46 cm) long, wider toward the tip, with entire margins. Numerous **secondary veins** (10–15 per side) 45° to the midvein, curling forward and splitting just before the margin. Midvein protrudes prominently below. Ripped leaves have a *potent, unpleasant odor*. **Petioles** 2–3% of blade length, slightly winged with a dense patch of dark rusty hairs on top. **Flowers** (mid spring) 1.5" (3.8 cm) wide with 3 hairy green-maroon sepals and 6 petals (of 2 different sizes, the inner 3 much smaller), green at first but turning dark maroon, the *petals with deeply depressed veins*. **Fruit** 2–8" (5–20 cm) long, often slightly curved or kidney-shaped; skin thin, green with black areas; flesh pale yellow, becoming very soft upon ripening. **Seeds** numerous, flattened, oblong, about 0.8" (2 cm) long, dark brown.

HABITAT: Hardwood forests on rich soil, especially floodplains and valleys. Often with pecan, bitternut, hackberry, sycamore, elm, ash, red mulberry. Most common at forest edges or where the overhead canopy is sparse. Native.

FOOD USE: Gather ripe **fruit** from the tree or from the ground in late summer or early autumn, well before the leaves fall. Smacking the trunk will often bring down a few ripe pawpaws (watch your head). The fruit is notoriously hard to see, as it is the same color as the leaves. Pawpaws can be eaten fresh or used in many desserts. **Conservation 1.**

COMMENTS: The largest edible fruit native to North America. In good pawpaw groves the fruit can sometimes be gathered very easily. I prefer them soft but with the skin still green. The flavor and smell are strong and disagreeable to some people—but it reminds me of a delicious cross between bananas and mangos. Interestingly, a single flower can produce a cluster of pawpaws.

WARNING: A fairly large percentage of people experience nausea, sometimes severe, after eating pawpaws. An even larger percentage of people experience diarrhea after eating them underripe.

RELATED EDIBLES? There are 6 additional species of pawpaw in North America, mostly confined to Florida (although one species, *A. parviflora*, is found as far north as Virginia). All of the others have much smaller fruit. I have not eaten any of these other pawpaws, nor have I spoken to anyone who has, so I can't recommend them as food.

6 Ogeechee lime 🍎 1
Nyssa ogeche • *Cornaceae* (Dogwood family)

QUICK CHECK: Swamp tree with alternate, entire, oblanceolate leaves and elliptic dull fruit with a single elongated seed. **ID difficulty 1.**

DESCRIPTION: Small to medium-sized, often multiple-trunked tree to 60' (18 m) tall. **Trunks** with enlarged, buttressed bases, the bark gray with shallow furrows, the ridges broken into many small blocks. **Twigs** thick and sparse, light brown, faintly hairy, smooth. **Leaves** alternate, clustered at twig tips, entire, 3–7" (8–18 cm) long and less than half as wide, elliptic to oblanceolate, the tips abruptly narrowed to a sharp point or sometimes blunt, the bases acute. The surface is downy on both sides but more so below. **Midvein** depressed above; secondary veins are about 45° to the midvein, flat to raised and brownish; all veins protrude below. **Petioles** about 15% of blade length, downy, usually downcurved, channeled faintly if at all. **Flowers** male and female on separate trees. Both kinds are tiny, unshowy, and greenish-white. Male flowers lack petals, looking like little stamen balls on a drooping stem; female flowers are short-stalked with petals and an obvious ovary. **Fruit** elliptic, about 1" (2.5 cm) long, hanging on a hairy pedicel about the same length, the surface rippled, smooth and waxy, with a nipple-like tip, green at first becoming tawny blushing pink to red when ripe. Flesh is slightly juicy, pale to pinkish *with air pockets* (it disperses by flotation), *divided inside with papery wings*, enclosing a single long, woody, ridged seed almost as long as the fruit.

CONFUSING PLANTS: Water tupelo *N. aquatica* is a close relative of similar habitat and some range overlap, but its leaves often have scattered large teeth and its smaller fruit ripens to blue-black.

HABITAT: Swamp forests, often in standing water. Native.

FOOD USE: The **fruits** are very sour and can be used in juice mixes, jams, jellies, or other situations where this quality is desired. **Conservation 1.**

COMMENTS: This tree is usually easy to spot because its leaves tend to be much larger than those of the trees around it. **AKA** ogeechee tupelo.

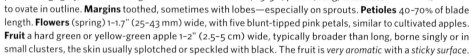

7   Native crabapples 🍎 1
genus *Malus* (in part) ◆ *Rosaceae* (Rose family)

QUICK CHECK: Apple-shaped fruit 1–2" in diameter; green, hard, and sticky when ripe. **ID difficulty 1.**

DESCRIPTION: Small trees up to 30' (9 m) tall and 16" (40 cm) in diameter, with a broad, spreading crown and single trunk. **Bark** reddish brown to gray with small, peeling, scaly plates. **Twigs** gray, often with rough thorns. **Leaves** alternate, 1.5–3" (4–8 cm) long, lanceolate to ovate in outline. **Margins** toothed, sometimes with lobes—especially on sprouts. **Petioles** 40–70% of blade length. **Flowers** (spring) 1–1.7" (25–43 mm) wide, with five blunt-tipped pink petals, similar to cultivated apples. **Fruit** a hard green or yellow-green apple 1–2" (2.5–5 cm) wide, typically broader than long, borne singly or in small clusters, the skin usually splotched or speckled with black. The fruit is *very aromatic* with a *sticky surface*.

SPECIES: There are three similar native wild apples in our region, with ranges that barely overlap. **Prairie crabapple** *Malus ioensis* is found in the lower Midwest mostly west of Lake Michigan; its leaves are downy beneath. *M. coronaria* (**sweet crabapple**, a very misleading name) is found east of Lake Michigan and has leaves that are mostly hairless underneath. Southern crabapple *M. angustifolia* has narrower leaves with less prominent teeth; it is found through most of the South.

CONFUSING PLANTS: Hawthorns (genus *Crataegus*) are similar in appearance but tend to have denser crowns with smoother thorns. Their fruit is much smaller and ripens to red. Eurasian crabapples usually have smaller fruit with many per cluster, ripening to some combination of red, yellow, or orange. Feral apples are larger and softer. None of these have the green and black mottled sticky skin.

HABITAT: Forest edges, young forests and thickets, old fields, river and stream valleys. Native. 🔥

FOOD USE: These ripen in mid to late autumn as or after the leaves fall and can be picked from the tree or the ground. They can be simmered to make a sour, high-pectin juice to mix with milder fruits like elderberry for making jelly. They can also be canned or made into an extremely sour sauce or fruit leather. Children might enjoy nibbling them raw, as I used to. They remain hard for months at room temperature. **Conservation 1.**

COMMENTS: Native crabapples do not look, feel, smell, or taste like feral apples or introduced Eurasian crabapples. Occasional trees produce a bumper crop. Confusion is rampant about which crabapples are native: At the time of this writing most Inaturalist photos, and every photo on the Ohio Department of Natural Resources web page for *Malus coronaria*, were of quite dissimilar non-native species.

▲ *Malus ioensis* flowers, (inset) fruit.

▲ *Malus coronaria* (top) leaf, (bottom) fruit.

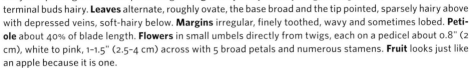

8 Apple ⚹ 3
Malus domestica ✦ *Rosaceae* (Rose family)

QUICK CHECK: Large fruit 1.5-5" in diameter with 5-pointed calyx on a depressed end and the stem attached in depressed base; leaves erratically toothed, alternate. **ID difficulty 1.**

DESCRIPTION: Trees to 50' (15 m) tall and 2' (60 cm) diameter with a single trunk, widely branching and spreading in full sun, leaning in shade. **Bark** smooth at first becoming flaky and peeling in short strips with age. **Twigs** finely hairy when young, *lacking thorns*; terminal buds hairy. **Leaves** alternate, roughly ovate, the base broad and the tip pointed, sparsely hairy above with depressed veins, soft-hairy below. **Margins** irregular, finely toothed, wavy and sometimes lobed. **Petiole** about 40% of blade length. **Flowers** in small umbels directly from twigs, each on a pedicel about 0.8" (2 cm), white to pink, 1-1.5" (2.5-4 cm) across with 5 broad petals and numerous stamens. **Fruit** looks just like an apple because it is one.

CONFUSING PLANTS: Hawthorns (genus *Crataegus*) and native crabapples (genus *Malus*), grow on similar-looking trees, but have thorns and smaller fruit.

HABITAT: roadsides, old home sites, pastures, abandoned fields, forest edges, young second-growth woods. Introduced.

FOOD USE: Wild apples can be used in the same ways as cultivated apples, but you must be selective about the fruit. Some trees have excellent flavor.

COMMENTS: This escape from cultivation is abundant in many regions and is one of our most useful wild fruits; millions of bushels are gathered and used annually. Some wild trees have fabulous fruit.

Related edible:
9 **Eurasian crabapples** ✦ *genus Malus* ⚹ 2

These have gone feral, especially around urban areas, in much of our region. This is not a single species, but an assortment of several species and hybrids. A crabapple is not just any small apple—these are entirely separate species, but they do frequently hybridize with apples. Eurasian crabapples have flowers and fruits in umbels of 5-20, the fruits structured like an apple but ranging from 0.2-1.5" (5-38 mm) in length. The branches lack thorns. Eurasian crabapples are high in pectin and make excellent jelly, alone or mixed with other fruits. They can be pickled or used in ciders or vinegar, sauces, leather, or pie.

◄ Fruit size and color are highly variable.

93

10 Wild plum ○ 3 ◊ 📖 NG-305
genus *Prunus* (in part) ◆ *Rosaceae* (Rose family)

QUICK CHECK: Small trees or shrubs with toothed, alternate leaves and smooth-skinned fruit with a single, large, hard, clam-shaped stone. **ID difficulty 1.**

DESCRIPTION: Large shrubs or small trees 5–40' (1.5–12 m) tall and 1–12" (2.5–30 cm) in diameter, often forming thickets by root suckers but the stems are not clumped. The trunks are crooked and the crowns spread broadly with stiff and thorny branches. **Bark** smooth and dark brown on young stems with prominent light lenticels; with age the bark peels sideways to form flakes or scales. **Leaves** alternate, 2–5" (5–13 cm) long, ovate to lanceolate with toothed margins and acuminate tips. The upper surface is reticulated by *depressed veinlets*, often diseased with pinkish phallic growths; surfaces variably hairy. **Petioles** about 15% of blade length. **Flowers** (early spring) bisexual, in umbels of 2–5 from twigs and spurs, appearing with or before the leaves, 0.6–0.9" (15–23 mm) across, symmetrical, with 5 round-tipped white petals (sometimes turning pink with age), and numerous protruding stamens. **Fruit** spherical to oblong with no calyx or attached flower parts when ripe, slightly if at all depressed on the stem end, 0.6–1.6" (1.5–4 cm) in diameter, ripening to yellow, pink, reddish, or bluish and becoming soft inside. **Pedicel** 50–100% of fruit length. The *skin is smooth with a coating of bloom* and the fruit contains a *single, large, hard, clam-shaped stone*. In some regions plums are frequently afflicted with diseases that ruin the fruit.

▲ Composite range.

FOOD USE: Gather **ripe** fruit from the twigs by hand, or shake it onto a sheet or tarp. If one acts promptly, good fruit can sometimes be picked up from the ground. Mash ripe fruit and strain to remove seeds and skins; the puree can be used for excellent jam or fruit leather. Whole plums can be canned like peaches in a light sugar syrup. You can split them in half, remove the pits, and dehydrate. For juice or jelly, crush very-ripe plums and then let the juice strain through a cloth by gravity, or use a steam juicer. An excellent **oil** can be pressed from the pits. **Conservation 1.**

COMMENTS: In many areas wild plums are available in incredible quantities. All species produce edible fruit, but the quality varies. Four of the best-known species are pictured below. 🔥

AMERICAN PLUM: *P. americana* is our most common and widespread species and may also have the largest fruit. It often forms large thickets along streams and in old fields and fence-rows. The plums ripen in late summer or early autumn, ripening yellow-orange to reddish, with a thick, astringent skin and a sweet, juicy interior.

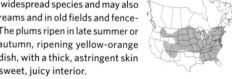

◄ ▲ American plum.

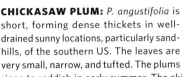

CHICKASAW PLUM: *P. angustifolia* is short, forming dense thickets in well-drained sunny locations, particularly sand-hills, of the southern US. The leaves are very small, narrow, and tufted. The plums ripen to reddish in early summer. The skins are thin and the pulp very juicy. In my opinion, this is our best wild plum, and the best one for canning whole.

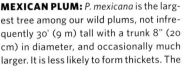

MEXICAN PLUM: *P. mexicana* is the largest tree among our wild plums, not infrequently 30' (9 m) tall with a trunk 8" (20 cm) in diameter, and occasionally much larger. It is less likely to form thickets. The fruit, dull yellow-orange to reddish and coated with a heavy bloom, is small, sour, and less juicy than our other species, but still makes good food when fully ripe in late summer to fall. **AKA** big tree plum.

▲ Chickasaw plum.

▲ Mexican plum.

▲ Mexican plums fallen.

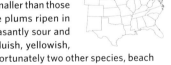

BEACH PLUM: *Prunus maritima* is a straggling shrub of infertile, sandy coastal areas. The leaves and fruit are smaller than those of other wild plums. The plums ripen in late summer and are pleasantly sour and astringent, ripening to bluish, yellowish, or colors in between. Unfortunately two other species, beach sandcherry *Prunus pumila* (p. 162) and rugosa rose *Rosa rugosa* (p. 86) are also frequently called "beach plum."

◄▲ Beach plum.

95

GROUP 7 BROADLEAF TREES WITH SMALL FLESHY FRUITS (LESS THAN 0.8" / 2 CM)

For all of the species in this group except devil's walking stick, sassafras, and red bay, the primary edible part is the fruit. Because fruit size varies between individuals, a plant with fruit near the 2 cm threshold may belong in group 6 or 7. Some shrubby species that occasionally grow to tree size might also key here (check groups 10 and 11). The key below includes a few commonly encountered inedible tree fruits.

TENTATIVE IDENTIFICATION KEY TO GROUP 7
The key is not your final answer!

Leaves compound.

Leaves once pinnately compound, stem not spiny, fruit orange, in a compact, flat-topped cluster 3-7" (8-18 cm) wide. — **1. Mountain-ash**

Leaves 2-3 times compound, stem spiny, purple fruit in a loose panicle to 40" (100 cm). — **2. Devil's walking stick**

Leaves simple.

Fruit with a single seed.

Leaf margin toothed.

Fruit elliptic, in a flat-topped cluster, seed flat. Black haw (see group 11).

Seed and fruit roundish, not in a flat-topped cluster.

Fruit ripens in autumn with semi-hard, sticky flesh. — **3. Hackberry**

Fruit ripens from summer to autumn with soft, juicy flesh.

Fruit purple-black, in racemes.

Fruit with ragged 5-lobed calyx at the base. — **5. Black cherry**

Fruit with no calyx at the base. Chokecherry (see group 11).

Fruit red, in umbels.

Fruit smaller than 8 mm; blades lanceolate, smooth above. — **6. Pin cherry**

Fruit larger than 12 mm; blades broadly elliptic, rough above. — **7. Sweet cherry**

Leaf margin not toothed.

Fruit spherical or nearly so.

Skin blue-black, pulp greenish and soft. — **8. Red Bay**

Skin brownish to orange, pulp brownish. — **4. Sugarberry**

Fruit elliptic to egg-shaped.

Fruit grayish and dryish with a flaky surface; silvery leaves. — **9. Russian-olive**

Fruit bright red with a smooth surface and juicy flesh. — **10. Cornelian-cherry**

Fruit dark blue-purple-black.

Fruit in a branched cluster, the red pedicel thickened at the tip. — **11. Sassafras**

Fruit on grayish pedicels about as long as the fruit, in umbels directly from the twig. — **12. Woolly bumelia**

Pedicels/peduncles many times longetr than the fruit, which is single or in sessile clusters of 2-3. Black gum (not edible).

Fruit with multiple seeds.

Fruit with a 5-part calyx at the tip.

Ripe fruit dark purple, in racemes; seeds soft; tree not thorny. — **13. Serviceberry**

Ripe fruit red to yellow, in umbels, seeds soft; tree not thorny. Eurasian crabapple (see group 6).

Ripe fruit red, orange, or yellow, in umbels, seeds hard; tree thorny.

Fruit ripens late summer to fall. — **14. Hawthorn**

Fruit ripens late spring to early summer. — **15. Mayhaw**

Fruit with no calyx at the tip.

Fruit bright red, on pedicels less than the diameter of the fruit, persisting into winter. Holly (various species, berries not edible).

Fruit purple-black, on pedicels greater than the fruit diameter. Buckthorns (mostly not edible, see pp. 660-661).

1 Mountain-ash 🍇 1
genus *Sorbus* ✦ *Rosaceae* (Rose family)

QUICK ID: Small trees with pinnately compound leaves and orange fruit in large flat-topped clusters. **ID difficulty 1.**

DESCRIPTION: Small trees 10–50' (3–15 m) tall, often with multiple trunks 4–16" (10–40 cm) in diameter, but not spreading to form thickets. The crown is narrow and rounded. **Bark** thin and smooth at first with *large lenticels*, brownish or silvery gray; on older trees breaking into plates or strips and eventually peeling horizontally. **Twigs** dull green to brown, moderately thick, with a bitter almond smell when broken. **Leaves** alternate, pinnately compound, with 11–19 *sessile leaflets*, the rachis channeled. **Leaflets** narrowly lanceolate to oblong, 1–3" (2.5–8 cm) long, with toothed margins. Surfaces are variably hairy. **Midvein** depressed; secondary veins numerous, depressed, straight, at angles greater than 45°. **Inflorescence** a showy, rounded to flat-topped cluster 3–8" (8–20 cm) across with dozens of flowers. **Flowers** (early to mid summer) 5–12 mm across, with a 5-lobed calyx, 5 rounded white petals, and numerous light stamens. **Fruit** roughly spherical, shaped like a miniature apple 5–8 mm in diameter, with an indented or crimped end bearing a 5-part calyx, ripening to orange and soft, containing multiple soft seeds.

SPECIES: Showy mountain-ash *S. decora* and **American mountain-ash** *S. americana* are both native; **European mountain-ash** *S. aucuparia* is introduced from Eurasia but has naturalized over a broad area. All of these species are similar in appearance and food use.

HABITAT: Dry or moist sunny sites, often poor soil. Forest edges and openings, rocky ridges and hillsides, abandoned industrial sites, lakeshores, dunes, riverbanks, fencerows, shrub swamps. Native and introduced.

FOOD USE: Pick **fruit** after it fully ripens in autumn. Some sources say that frosts sweeten and mellow the flavor; I have not observed this despite testing it many times. The fruit can be used to make jams or preserves, or crushed and dried for future use. **Conservation 1.**

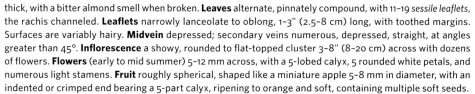

COMMENTS: These berries are easy to pick in enormous quantities by grabbing whole clusters. The drawback is that their flavor is bitter and, for the most part, terrible. A few people like preserves made from this fruit. Without a generous dose of sugar or dilution by other ingredients, practically nobody would eat them.

▲ Fruit of *Sorbus aucuparia*.

2 Devil's walking stick 2
Aralia spinosa ✦ *Araliaceae* (Ginseng family)

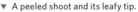

QUICK ID: Enormous, very thick twigs and prickly bark; leaves very large and multi-compound; flowers and fruit in large clusters with numerous umbels. **ID difficulty 1.**

DESCRIPTION: Large shrub or small tree, 10-35' (3-11 m) tall and up to 6" (15 cm) in diameter, often spreading by root suckers to form colonies. The crowns are open with few branches. **Bark** smooth and gray with broad-based prickles. **Twigs** *extremely thick*—probably the thickest in our region, *prickly*, with thick pith, orange lenticels, enormous U-shaped leaf scars wrapping almost fully around the twig, and a very large terminal bud. **Leaves** alternate, *2 or 3 times pinnately compound*, 2-5' (60-150 cm) long including the thick petiole, 2-3' (60-90 cm) wide, the rachis spiny and bulged at junctures. **Leaflets** numerous, paired, sessile or nearly so, 2-5" (5-13 cm) long, flat, ovate with a sharp and sometimes acuminate tip. Surfaces are sparsely hairy, with *spines on the midveins*. Veins are nearly flat above. Margins are finely toothed. **Inflorescence** a large, branching terminal cluster to 4' (1.2 m) long and equally broad, composed of numerous umbels. **Flowers** (mid to late summer) white, 3-4 mm across, with 5 regular parts. **Fruit** oblong, 3-4 mm, juicy, with 5 bulges, 5 seeds, and persistent styles protruding from the tip, ripening to purple-black in fall.

HABITAT: Young woods, forest edges, or disturbed areas within older forests. Native.

FOOD USE: The **shoots** in spring can be eaten cooked or raw while they are still tender, before any prickles have become hard. They have an aromatic, slightly fruity flavor and are best peeled, as the skin tastes strong and unpleasant. **Conservation 2.**

COMMENTS: This is one of the most distinct woody plants of our region. A close and nearly identical relative, *A. elata*, is eaten in Japan and often grows feral here. I am not aware of the berries of either species being edible or toxic, but they are distasteful.

▼ A peeled shoot and its leafy tip.

▲ Spring growth.

3 Hackberry 🍄 2 🍓/⊖ 3 (fruit/nut combo) 📖 NG-123
Celtis occidentalis ✦ *Ulmaceae* **(Elm family)**

QUICK ID: Warty-barked tree with simple, alternate leaves and pea-sized spherical fruit. **ID difficulty 1.**

DESCRIPTION: Medium to large tree to 90' (27 m) tall. **Trunks** dominant, single, straight, with a moderately spreading crown. **Bark** with variably spaced *corky bumps, ridges, or thick peeling plates* and a *layered appearance*, sometimes described as "Grand Canyon bark." Bark between the ridges is smooth and gray. **Twigs** thin, reddish brown in winter, zigzag, often *clustered near branch tips.* **Buds** 3–6 mm long and half as wide, brown, appressed to the twigs. **Leaves** 2.5–6" (6.4–15 cm) long, ovate with blunt, *asymmetrical bases* and long-pointed or acuminate tips, often with warty growths (nipple galls). The upper surface may be nearly hairless or have short, stiff hairs; the underside has finer hairs along the major veins. **Veins** and veinlets are prominently depressed above, the veinlets perpendicular to the secondary veins, forming a net-like pattern. **Margins** coarsely serrated except near the base. **Petiole** hairy, 7–10% of blade length. **Flowers** (spring) unisexual, male and female separate on the same tree, both tiny and unshowy; the male with 5 lobes, hanging in tiny clusters; the female single with a split and recurved pistil. **Fruit** spherical, smooth, 7–11 mm, with a single large stone, ripening to orange-brown or purple-brown in early autumn and often persisting through the winter.

HABITAT: Primarily higher parts of flood-plain forests, but also well-drained upland hardwood forests, particularly on rich sandy soil. Common as a street tree in some regions. Native. (Continued on the next page.)

◄ Hackberry bark close-up.

▼ Hackberry nipple galls often form on the leaf underside.

3   Hackberry (continued)

FOOD USE: Gather **fruit** from the branches, or by knocking them down onto a sheet or tarp. They are ripe if the pulp is sweet, from early fall onward. Mash whole fruits (pulverizing the seedshells) and then eat as-is, or mix with other nuts or dried berries. Mashed fruit can also be boiled and then strained to make "hackberry milk," a rich, filling drink or soup base. The **cambium** can be eaten in early summer. **Conservation 1.**

COMMENTS: Hackberry is a dry, sweet fruit, like a date, with a thin-shelled oily seed. Combined, the two make a wholesome and filling food, but there is no practical way to remove the thin seedshell. Just learn to like the odd texture. There is archaeological evidence of humans eating hackberries for more than 500,000 years.

RELATED EDIBLE: Dwarf hackberry *Celtis tenuifolia* is a large shrub or small tree with fruit that can be eaten in the same ways.

Related edible:

4   **Sugarberry** ✦ *Celtis laevigata*   2   / 3   📖 NG-123

This tree is similar to hackberry but is on average a slightly smaller tree with a more southerly distribution. The leaves are entire or have a few scattered teeth, the bark is smoother with fewer warty projections, and the fruit averages slightly smaller. Sugarberry can be used similarly for food. The seeds are a bit harder and the fruit tastes more "fruity."

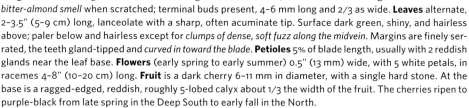

5 Black cherry 🍇 2 📖 NG-293
Prunus serotina ⁕ *Rosaceae* (Rose family)

QUICK ID: Dark scaly bark on mature trees; smooth, purple-black cherries in racemes. **ID difficulty 2.**

DESCRIPTION: Can become a large forest tree to 100' (30 m) tall, but in open areas tends to be short and widely spreading. **Bark** smooth, shiny, and dark with many horizontal white lenticels when young; at maturity covered with thin, peeling, black *"burnt potato chips."* **Twigs** smooth, thin, green in summer turning to reddish-brown, the bark with a strong *bitter-almond smell* when scratched; terminal buds present, 4–6 mm long and 2/3 as wide. **Leaves** alternate, 2–3.5" (5–9 cm) long, lanceolate with a sharp, often acuminate tip. Surface dark green, shiny, and hairless above; paler below and hairless except for *clumps of dense, soft fuzz along the midvein.* Margins are finely serrated, the teeth gland-tipped and *curved in toward the blade.* **Petioles** 5% of blade length, usually with 2 reddish glands near the leaf base. **Flowers** (early spring to early summer) 0.5" (13 mm) wide, with 5 white petals, in racemes 4–8" (10–20 cm) long. **Fruit** is a dark cherry 6–11 mm in diameter, with a single hard stone. At the base is a ragged-edged, reddish, roughly 5-lobed calyx about 1/3 the width of the fruit. The cherries ripen to purple-black from late spring in the Deep South to early fall in the North.

CONFUSING PLANTS: Chokecherry leaves are broader, obovate, sharp-toothed, and not shiny above; the fruit is more crowded on the raceme and lacks the calyx.

HABITAT: Full sun and well-drained soil, especially sand; hardwood forests, old fields, fence rows, oak and pine barrens. The best trees for picking are typically in open areas, where the branches may spread close to the ground. Native. 🔥

FOOD USE: Strip **cherries** from clusters; ripe ones will detach easily. They may be eaten raw, but more commonly are cooked. You can separate pulp from seeds in a food mill for jams and desserts. Dried pulp will turn out thick and sticky like prunes. For juice, use a steam-juicer or simmer fruit and then strain through a jelly cloth. **Conservation 1.**

WARNING: Do not crush and eat the seeds. They have a stronger flavor than those of chokecherry and I can find no ethnographic record of their use as food.

COMMENTS: Black cherries are remarkably variable in flavor from tree to tree and region to region. Some are detestable, while others are delicious out of hand. This is a major food source for songbirds, bears, and raccoons. The fruit can be collected in great quantity. This is the largest native cherry tree, and a very important lumber source.

6 Pin cherry 🍇 2 📖 FH-221
Prunus pensylvanica ✦ *Rosaceae* (Rose Family)

QUICK ID: Tiny red cherries borne on long stems in small umbels. **ID difficulty 1.**

DESCRIPTION: Large shrub to small tree, forming clones by root suckers, to 60' (18 m) tall and 12" (30 cm) in diameter, the crown tall and narrow even in the open. **Bark** smooth and dark reddish, metallic-shiny with numerous large, horizontal, brown lenticels when young; black on older trees, often peeling in horizontal strips. **Twigs** very thin, shiny, reddish to brown, usually hairless with a thin exfoliating layer, almond-scented when scratched. **Buds** 2–3 mm, plump, often clustered at the tip. **Leaves** alternate, 1.5–4" (4–10 cm), light green, very thin, ovate to lanceolate, the base blunt and the tip pointed to acuminate. Surface shiny and hairless above; the underside sparsely hairy, especially along the main veins. **Midvein** and secondary veins slightly depressed above; veinlets flat. **Margins** finely serrated with forward-pointing, irregularly sized, gland-tipped teeth. **Petioles** about 10% of blade length, with glands near the leaf base. **Flowers** (early spring) bisexual, 6–11 mm across with 5 white petals, in umbels of 3–7 from a short stub. **Fruit** on thin pedicels about 0.8" (2 cm) long, spherical, 5–8 mm in diameter, ripening to bright red and slightly translucent in mid to late summer, with a single hard stone inside.

HABITAT: Pioneer tree of dry, sunny sites, especially with poor rocky or sandy soils: forest edges, rocky slopes, pine barrens, riverbanks. Thrives after fires or logging, or on old mine sites, gravel pits, razed building sites, abandoned farmland, and highway shoulders. Native. 🔥

FOOD USE: Ripe **fruit** is juicy and detaches easily from stems. It can be strained or juiced to make superb jam or jelly. Cherries can also be eaten fresh from the tree. **Conservation 1.**

WARNING: Do not crush and eat the seeds. They have a potent bitter flavor and seem far more toxic than chokecherry or black cherry pits.

COMMENTS: For most palates pin cherries are usually too sour to snack on, but occasional trees have milder fruit. They make one of my favorite jams. Pin cherry seeds can remain viable in the soil for at least 50 years, waiting for a disturbance to stimulate germination. In fire-prone boreal forests this seed bank strategy is very effective. **AKA** fire cherry.

7 Sweet cherry 🍇 3
Prunus avium ✦ *Rosaceae* (Rose family)

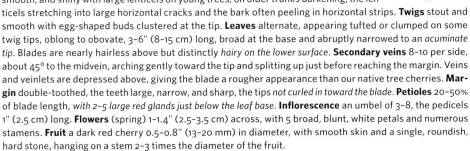

QUICK ID: Tree with alternate, simple, oblong, toothed, pointed leaves; bark dark, shiny, and peeling horizontally; fruit a small red cherry. **ID difficulty 1.**

DESCRIPTION: Small to medium-sized tree to 60' (18 m) tall and 24" (60 cm) thick with single or few erect to leaning trunks, the crown narrow to spreading. **Bark** grayish red, smooth, and shiny with large lenticels on young trees; on older trunks darkening, the lenticels stretching into large horizontal cracks and the bark often peeling in horizontal strips. **Twigs** stout and smooth with egg-shaped buds clustered at the tip. **Leaves** alternate, appearing tufted or clumped on some twig tips, oblong to obovate, 3–6" (8–15 cm) long, broad at the base and abruptly narrowed to an *acuminate tip*. Blades are nearly hairless above but distinctly *hairy on the lower surface*. **Secondary veins** 8–10 per side, about 45° to the midvein, arching gently toward the tip and splitting up just before reaching the margin. Veins and veinlets are depressed above, giving the blade a rougher appearance than our native tree cherries. **Margin** double-toothed, the teeth large, narrow, and sharp, the tips *not curled in toward the blade*. **Petioles** 20–50% of blade length, *with 2–5 large red glands just below the leaf base*. **Inflorescence** an umbel of 3–8, the pedicels 1" (2.5 cm) long. **Flowers** (spring) 1–1.4" (2.5–3.5 cm) across, with 5 broad, blunt, white petals and numerous stamens. **Fruit** a dark red cherry 0.5–0.8" (13–20 mm) in diameter, with smooth skin and a single, roundish, hard stone, hanging on a stem 2–3 times the diameter of the fruit.

HABITAT: Forest edges, disturbed woodlots, fence lines, roadsides—most often in rich, well-drained soil. Introduced and sporadic in occurrence, most common in hilly farm country and urban areas.

FOOD USE: The **cherries** of feral trees are smaller than those of our domestic cultivars but are similar and delicious and can be used in all the same ways.

COMMENTS: This is one non-native tree I don't mind encountering. Birds usually pick them clean, but occasionally I get a few mouthfuls. **AKA** mazzard.

RELATED EDIBLE: Sour cherry *Prunus cerasus* is also sometimes found escaped from cultivation. It is juicier and more sour but makes delicious juice, pie, jam, and leather.

◄ Sour cherry fruit.

8 Red bay & swamp bay
Persea borbonia & *P. palustris* ✦ *Lauraceae* (Laurel family)

QUICK ID: Small tree with large, flat, entire evergreen leaves and pea-sized spherical fruit with a large roundish seed. **ID difficulty 2.**

DESCRIPTION: Large shrubs or small to medium-sized trees 10–50′ (3–15 m) tall with a narrow crown of stout branches. **Bark** thin with vertical fissures revealing red-brown beneath, the ridges becoming thicker on old trees. **Twigs** thick and sparse, dark and finely woolly, with terminal buds 0.2–0.3″ (5–8 mm) long. **Leaves** evergreen, aromatic, *clustered at branch tips*, close together, 2–6″ (5–15 cm) long, but *the proximal ones often miniature*. Blades are flat, stiff and leathery, entire, broadly to narrowly elliptic, acute at the base, blunt-pointed or sometimes rounded or notched at the tip, sometimes curved to the side. The surface is shiny and hairless above. **Midvein** *flat above except near the base, where it is raised*. **Secondary veins** 5–6 per side at a 50–75° angle to the midvein, usually unbranched, the ends curving toward the tip; they are nearly flat above. **Petioles** 10% of blade length, dark and densely woolly, round in cross section, not channeled. **Inflorescence** short, widely branching clusters of 3–12 from leaf axils of the new year's growth, the pedicels about 1″ (2.5 cm) long. **Flowers** (summer) 3–5 mm across, whitish to pale pink or yellow, cup-like with 3 ovate sepals and 3 smaller, hard-to-see petals inside. **Fruits** few, single or in small clusters from leaf axils, spherical, 8–13 mm, with smooth black skin (later wrinkling) and very thin green flesh around *a large, spherical, blackish, pea-sized seed with a purplish kernel*.

CONFUSING SPECIES: Sweet bay magnolia *Magnolia virginiana* shares the habitat and much of its distribution and also has aromatic leaves, but the flowers are much larger, 2–3″ (5–8 cm) across, and the fruit is a cone with bright red seeds. When these parts are absent the sweet bay magnolia can be told apart by the silver-hairy underside of its leaf and the much larger terminal bud about 2 cm long.

HABITAT: Low, moist, sandy, open woods, especially where acidic; swamp and pond margins. Native.

FOOD USE: Leaves make an excellent **seasoning** like bay or avocado leaf and can be collected at any season and used fresh or dried. Powder the young leaves and mix them with sassafras for a gumbo filé *par excellence*. **Conservation 1.**

COMMENTS: Green flesh. Dark skin. Single seed. This is in the same genus as avocado, but there isn't much flesh to the fruit. Many taxonomists divide this into two species. Red bay *P. borbonia* is somewhat larger and grows on slightly richer soil. Its twigs and leaf undersides are hairless (the latter even glaucous). Swamp bay *P. palustris* is a smaller tree or shrub characteristic of acidic low-lands in pine barrens. It is differentiated by dense hairs on the twigs, petioles, and lower leaf surfaces. In my limited experience swamp bay seems to have the stronger flavor and more mucilaginous leaf.

9 Russian-olive 1 NG-326
Elaeagnus angustifolia ◆ family *Elaeagnaceae*

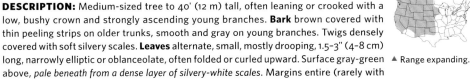

QUICK ID: Low, bushy tree with narrow, silvery leaves and olive-shaped, gray-green fruit. **ID difficulty 1.**

▲ Range expanding.

DESCRIPTION: Medium-sized tree to 40' (12 m) tall, often leaning or crooked with a low, bushy crown and strongly ascending young branches. **Bark** brown covered with thin peeling strips on older trunks, smooth and gray on young branches. Twigs densely covered with soft silvery scales. **Leaves** alternate, small, mostly drooping, 1.5–3" (4–8 cm) long, narrowly elliptic or oblanceolate, often folded or curled upward. Surface gray-green above, *pale beneath from a dense layer of silvery-white scales.* Margins entire (rarely with a few teeth). **Veins** flat above and mostly obscure; secondary veins protrude slightly below. **Petioles** silvery, 10–15% of blade length. **Flowers** (late spring) single on short pedicels from leaf axils, about 1 cm across, bell-like with 4 triangular lobes, each with a ridge in the center, yellow inside and silver-gray outside. **Fruit** elliptic, olive-shaped, 11–13 mm long, hanging on a silvery pedicel about 1/3 the length of the fruit, often crowded on twig sections that drop their leaves and thus resemble a raceme. The surface is gray-green, covered in soft scales, blushing faintly yellow or reddish upon ripening in fall, the flesh dryish and powdery-pulpy. Each berry contains a single elliptic *leathery seed pointed at both ends.*

HABITAT: Dry soil in full sun. Tolerates cold, heat, and drought. A common escape around urban areas and in shelterbelts and stream bottoms of the Great Plains. Introduced. **I**

FOOD USE: Gather ripe **fruit** by hand. Nibble raw, or boil and then strain to separate pulp from seeds for fruit leather, baked goods, and spreads.

COMMENTS: Russian-olive is a unique fruit poorly suited for jams and jellies. It is often dry and astringent but has a sweet overtone, like a floury mixture of dates and chokecherries. The flavor is highly variable, so taste around for good trees. Seeds are tough but the kernel inside has good flavor. Russian-olive is not related to olives, but is so named for the resemblance of its elongated green fruit. This tree is related to autumnberry (p. 139) and silverberry (p. 155).

10 Cornelian-cherry 🍐 2
Cornus mas ✦ *Cornaceae* (Dogwood family)

QUICK ID: Small tree with scaly bark; entire leaves with prominent veins reconverging at the leaf tip; umbels of yellow flowers, and oblong shiny red fruit. **ID difficulty 2.**

DESCRIPTION: Large shrub to small tree, often with multiple trunks, to 30' (9 m) tall. **Trunks** crooked, to 10" (25 cm) thick, the bark at maturity covered with thin gray-brown flakes. **Twigs** greenish to reddish and hairy at first, becoming brownish with a thin exfoliating layer when older, the terminal buds bulging and ridged. **Leaves** paired, ovate, entire, 2.5–5" (6.4–13 cm) long, often curled, with broadly acute to obtuse bases and abruptly pointed tips. The surface is finely hairy on both sides. **Midvein** depressed, offset by yellowish color. There are 3–5 prominent **secondary veins** per side emanating in the lower half of the leaf, *strongly depressed above* and protruding below, that *arch out and back toward the tip.* Veinlets are flat above. **Petioles** about 5% of blade length. **Inflorescence** an umbel of 14–24 at the end of a short stub, the pedicels all about the same length, each umbel with *4 broad, cupped, hairy bracts behind it.* **Flowers** (early spring before the leaves) *yellow in all parts,* 5–9 mm across, with 4 ovate, pointed, recurved petals; 4 curved, projecting stamens; and a single pistil with a broad disk around the base. **Fruit** oblong, olive- or slightly pear-shaped, 0.6–0.8" (15–20 mm), with a small dimple on each end but otherwise smooth, bright red when ripe in fall, containing a single elongated, hard stone that is not flattened. **Pedicel** about 70% of fruit length.

HABITAT: Old farmsteads, brushy areas, parks, roadsides, disturbed woods, urban areas, forest edges. Introduced.

FOOD USE: Fruit matures in early fall and is best when very ripe—you may want to let them sit to ripen further after picking. They are very sour but delicious in jams, jellies, pies, fruit leather, etc.—or just to snack on, if you're into sour fruit.

COMMENTS: Cornelian-cherry has been extensively planted in some areas for wildlife, and like Eurasian crabapples it has gone feral in moderate numbers but has not yet become a problematic invasive plant.

11 Sassafras 🪶 2 🔲 ☕ 📖 IWE-328
Sassafras albidum ✦ *Lauraceae* (Laurel family)

QUICK ID: Twigs green and lemony-aromatic; leaves toothless, ovate or lobed. **ID difficulty 2.**

DESCRIPTION: Medium-sized tree suckering to form clones, the crown narrow and the trunk often crooked. All above-ground parts of the tree have a strong, pleasant, lemony aroma. Root bark is *rusty-brown with a root beer scent.* **Bark** dark gray and deeply furrowed on mature trees. **Branches** of saplings are sometimes whorled. **Twigs** bright green and smooth, aromatic when scratched. Terminal buds are large, green, finely and densely pubescent. **Leaves** alternate, concentrated (almost tufted) near branch tips, 3–6" (8–15 cm) long, tapered at the base, blunt at the tip, usually hairless above but finely pubescent below, with a pair of prominent secondary veins near but not at the base. The blades come in three shapes: ovate and unlobed (most common on mature trees), mitten-shaped, or 3-lobed (most common on young trees in full sun). Young spring leaves are finely downy. **Petioles** 10–30% of blade length. **Shoots** have whitish bloom and elongated purple spots. **Inflorescence** loose racemes of 8–14, with multiple racemes from the same bud, the stems with very soft hairs. **Flowers** in spring, male and female on different trees, 1 cm wide, with 6 narrow, spreading, light yellowish sepals. **Fruit** (early fall) an oblong purple drupe about 1 cm long, held upright on a distinct red stalk that enlarges to form a cup-like, 6-lobed base. The seed is single and smooth.

HABITAT: Young or disturbed woods; most prevalent on well-drained sand, gravel, or other poor soil. Common invader of old fields, pastures, and roadsides. Native. 🔥

FOOD USE: Gather young **leaves** just after emerging; they can be used in salad or soup, or dried and powdered to make gumbo filé. Dig up roots (easiest on small saplings), wash, and boil to make **tea**. (With larger roots, just use the bark.) Dry bark or roots for use later. Roots can be boiled multiple times. The liquid can be drunk sweetened or not, or brewed into root beer. **Conservation 2, 1.**

COMMENTS: This plant produces two of the most potent and distinct flavors of any in North America; the flavor of the root is completely different from that of the leaves, flowers, and twigs. Sassafras is the primary root that flavors traditional "root beer," which is now rarely sold. Food or drink containing sassafras root was banned (sort of, but not explicitly) due to research concluding that one of its components, safrole, caused cancer in rats when fed to them in enormous quantities. However, safrole is dissipated by drying and destroyed by boiling and so may not even be present in traditional sassafras drinks. Gumbo filé is still commercially made from sassafras leaves—which contain no safrole.

12 Woolly bumelia 1
Sideroxylon lanuginosum + family *Sapotaceae*

QUICK ID: Short tree with a bushy crown, entire, blunt-tipped, tufted leaves that are felty below, milky sap, tiny summer flowers, and black fruit in early fall. **ID difficulty 2.**

DESCRIPTION: Shrub or small tree to 40' (12 m) tall, with *milky sap*, the trunk usually single and erect. Trees may be unarmed or have thorn-tipped spur branches or naked thorns to 0.8" (2 cm). **Bark** furrowed with narrow, flaky, reddish to chocolate brown ridges on older trunks. New shoots are densely pubescent. **Branches** consist of slow-growing spurs and fast-growing shoots, yielding an odd, crooked crown. **Twigs** thick, sparse, and strongly zigzag. New growth is red-brown and woolly with alternate leaves; older twigs are hairless with white lenticels and tufted leaves. On still older branches the leaf tufts are borne on stout, scar-roughened spurs. **Leaves** 0.5–4" (1.3–10 cm) long—much smaller on old spurs, tardily deciduous (nearly evergreen in the Deep South), often drooping. Blades simple, entire, leathery, oblanceolate or obovate to elliptic, often wavy or wrinkled, the tips blunt to rounded or notched, tapered to a narrow base, the margins downcurved. **Surface** pubescent above only at first; the underside remains densely woolly. Secondary veins and veinlets are flat above. **Petiole** 2–5% of blade length, reddish, channeled, hairy. **Inflorescence** a sessile umbel of 8–40 flowers, from leaf axils. **Flowers** (summer) sweet-fragrant, 4 mm wide, bell-shaped, the calyx light greenish brown with 5 lobes, the corolla white and 5-lobed, each lobe split at the tip into 3 parts. Inside the corolla is a whorl of false petals. **Fruit** ovoid to elliptic, 6–12 mm long, on a drooping pedicel about as long, usually with a sharp beak protruding, milky when immature, ripening in September or October to shiny and black, the skin smooth and glossy, the *flesh green and thin with lengthwise lines*. It has a small, light-brown calyx of 6 blunt lobes at the base. **Seed** single, large, oblong, smooth, brown, with a light zone near the base and a thin, brittle shell over an oily whitish kernel.

HABITAT: Well-drained sandy woodlands, old fields, sandy coastal scrub, open rocky slopes, fence lines, forest edges, streamsides in arid areas. Native. 🔥

FOOD USE: The **fruit** tastes like a cross between dates and buckthorn berries—sweet but bitter. The skins are thick and annoying but not tough. I like to nibble them while hiking but probably won't be making a bumelia pie. **Conservation 1.**

COMMENTS: A common tree in much of the South, the fruits of which are an important food for many birds. Other species of bumelia (genus *Sideroxylon*) are safe to eat but not choice. **AKA** buckthorn bully, gum bully, gum bumelia, chittamwood, *Bumelia lanuginosa*.

13 **Serviceberry** 🍇 3 📖 FH-209
genus *Amelanchier* + *Rosaceae* (Rose family)

QUICK ID: Smooth-barked, thornless trees with ovate simple leaves and clusters of soft fruit with a 5-part calyx. **ID difficulty 1.**

DESCRIPTION: Clump-forming shrub or small tree, typically 10–40' (3–12 m) tall and 1.5–8" (4–20 cm) in diameter. **Trunks** curvy with smooth, gray bark. Branches almost never have a sharp angle and taper gently to thin twigs. **Leaves** alternate, ovate to oblong or elliptic, 1–3" (2.5–8 cm) long, often finely hairy below, with evenly toothed margins. **Midvein** depressed above, but secondary veins and veinlets are flat. **Inflorescence** loose, drooping racemes of 3–12, the pedicels long and unequal with the *lowest being much longer*. **Flowers** (spring) 0.6–1.5" (1.5–4 cm) across with 5 elongated white petals that are narrowed toward the base, blunt-tipped, often curvy or cupped; there are 5 sharp-triangular sepals and multiple stamens. **Fruit** ripens from late spring to late summer depending on species and location; round to slightly oblong, soft, juicy, red-purple, with delicate skin and a persistent 5-part calyx on the end. **Seeds** 5–10, chewy.

SPECIES: Serviceberries as a group are easy to recognize but the species are difficult to distinguish and often hybridize. Such technicalities are ignored here.

HABITAT: Usually well-drained, sunny sites. Roadsides, old fields, fencerows, steep slopes, cutovers, young woods, streambanks, ridge tops, barrens. Most common in areas of poor soil. Native. 🔥

FOOD USE: The **berries** soften before fully darkening and developing their best flavor, but in many areas birds remove them before they ripen. Serviceberries are very soft and spoil quickly, so they must be used or stored immediately after picking. You can strain out the seeds, but some people like them. Serviceberries make good pie, jam, or juice; they are superb for eating fresh and delicious dried. **Conservation 1.**

COMMENTS: This berry is common, underappreciated, and variable in quality. Despite the prevalent etymological myth, the name "serviceberry" has nothing to do with church services. Until about 1900 this berry was called "sarviss" in English—a name derived from the Latin *sorbus* for another fruiting tree, possibly mountain-ash. Today, serviceberries are grown commercially—mostly in Saskatchewan, under the name "saskatoon." **AKA** juneberry, shadbush.

14 Hawthorn 🍓 1-3
genus *Crataegus* ✦ *Rosaceae* (Rose family)

QUICK ID: Small, scrubby trees with broad, irregularly double-toothed leaves, formidable thorns, and red fruit with a 5-part calyx. **ID difficulty 1.**

DESCRIPTION: Small trees up to 12" (30 cm) in diameter and 30' (9 m) tall with short, stout trunks and wide, spreading crowns of *nearly horizontal grayish branches*. **Twigs** strongly zigzag, characterized by strong, smooth, *very sharp thorns*—simple or branched, depending on species. **Bark** of mature trees peels in long, thin, gray strips. Bare trees in winter can be told from a great distance by their distinctive silver-gray hue. **Leaves** alternate on new growth but *clustered at the tips of spurs on older wood*, 1-4" (2.5-10 cm) long and almost as broad, the blades broadly ovate or elliptic to obovate in outline. **Margins** entire near the base and sharply serrated distally, usually double toothed or with small lobes. **Midvein** and secondary veins *deeply and narrowly* depressed above on most species, protruding below; veinlets depressed above. **Petioles** channeled, ranging from 20-60% of blade length. **Inflorescence** branching flat-topped clusters of 5-25. **Flowers** (late spring) showy, 0.5-1" (13-25 mm) across, white to pink, with 5 triangular sepals, 5 petals, and many stamens. **Fruit** spherical to slightly oblong, 0.2-0.8" (5-20 mm), in small clusters; ripening to red, with calyx lobes and dried styles protruding from the end, the flesh pale yellowish to pink, usually containing 2-5 hard, whitish, asymmetrical seeds.

IMPORTANT SPECIES: There are numerous hawthorn species, and taxonomists famously disagree over their classification. All are edible, so just taste test the fruit from prospective trees.

HABITAT: Moist to dry soils after disturbance such as fire, windstorms, and human activity. Common in floodplains, often invading old fields, pastures, roadsides, forest edges, and fence lines. Native. 🔥

FOOD USE: The earliest hawthorns will ripen in late summer; others not until late fall. Taste the **fruit** to see if it is worth collecting; the best taste like a cross between pears and strawberries. The fruit can be eaten fresh or strained to remove the seeds and then used in fruit sauce or leather. A rare few are even tangy enough to make jam. The pulp can also be mixed in quick bread batter. **Conservation 1.**

COMMENTS: The vexing problem with hawthorns is that they are almost always heavily infested with grubs. This problem is so prevalent that it can be nearly impossible to find wholesome fruit in many areas.

15 Mayhaw 🐝 3
Crataegus aestivalis, C. opaca + Rosaceae (Rose family)

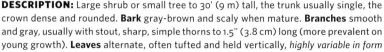

Quick ID: Broad, bushy-topped, thorny little tree growing in or near water, with toothed leaves and bright red fruit ripening in spring. **ID difficulty 1.**

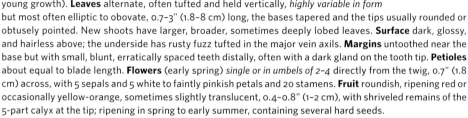

DESCRIPTION: Large shrub or small tree to 30' (9 m) tall, the trunk usually single, the crown dense and rounded. **Bark** gray-brown and scaly when mature. **Branches** smooth and gray, usually with stout, sharp, simple thorns to 1.5" (3.8 cm) long (more prevalent on young growth). **Leaves** alternate, often tufted and held vertically, *highly variable in form* but most often elliptic to obovate, 0.7–3" (1.8–8 cm) long, the bases tapered and the tips usually rounded or obtusely pointed. New shoots have larger, broader, sometimes deeply lobed leaves. **Surface** dark, glossy, and hairless above; the underside has rusty fuzz tufted in the major vein axils. **Margins** untoothed near the base but with small, blunt, erratically spaced teeth distally, often with a dark gland on the tooth tip. **Petioles** about equal to blade length. **Flowers** (early spring) *single or in umbels of 2–4* directly from the twig, 0.7" (1.8 cm) across, with 5 sepals and 5 white to faintly pinkish petals and 20 stamens. **Fruit** roundish, ripening red or occasionally yellow-orange, sometimes slightly translucent, 0.4–0.8" (1–2 cm), with shriveled remains of the 5-part calyx at the tip; ripening in spring to early summer, containing several hard seeds.

SPECIES: The two listed are very similar and some taxonomists do not separate them. The biggest difference is that the western mayhaw *C. opaca* ripens somewhat later, into early summer.

HABITAT: Pond and slough margins, forest depressions, swamps, floodplains, clay flats, often standing in shallow water. Prefers moderate to full sun. Native.

FOOD USE: The ripe, pectin-rich **haws** are a good nibble and make excellent jelly, jam, juice, etc. They can often be gathered in great quantity from a single tree. Traditionally they were harvested by shaking branches over the water and collecting them with a net.

COMMENTS: This exceptional, early-ripening hawthorn is an almost-legendary wild edible in its range. There are even a few mayhaw festivals, a breeding program at Louisiana State University, and a small network of commercial growers. Not to be confused with may*apple*. The fruit is said by many to be "too sour" to eat as-is, but I like them a lot, and so do my children.

▲ Mayhaw in typical floodplain habitat.

GROUP 8 BROADLEAF TREES; FRUIT SMALL AND DRY, WIND-BORNE, OR A POD

For most of the woody plants covered in this book, the fruit or seed is the primary or only edible part. Group 8 is a significant exception to this pattern. In keeping with the format of the other woody plant groups, this key relies heavily on fruit characteristics even though many different parts of these trees are edible, and the fruits or seeds are of primary interest in only five cases. Read carefully—Do not assume the fruits are edible just because the key refers to them. Specialized vocabulary pertaining to legume flowers can be found on page 681.

TENTATIVE IDENTIFICATION KEY TO GROUP 8
The key is not your final answer!

Fruit a bean-like pod.
  Leaf simple, heart-shaped.
    or Pods flat, less than 6" (15 cm) long. | 1. Redbud
       Pods plump and round, more than 8" long. Catalpa (not edible).
  or or Leaf compound, usually or always lacking end leaflets; pod with pulp inside.
       Pods stiff, at least 0.6" (15 mm) thick and 1.5" (3.8 cm) wide; seeds 0.7" (18 mm); leaflets pointed and ovate. | 2. Kentucky coffeetree
       Pods about 1 cm wide, plump, constricted between seeds; leaflets linear. | 3. Honey mesquite
       Pods flattened, flexible, more than 6" (15 cm) long; seeds less than 1 cm. | 4. Honey locust
    Leaf compound, with end leaflets; pods without pulp inside (genus *Robinia*).
       Flowers white with a yellow banner. | 5. Black locust
       Flowers pink to purple.
         Twigs and inflorescence covered with sticky glands. | 6. Clammy locust
         Twigs and inflorescence covered with long, stiff, reddish hairs. | 7. Bristly locust
         Twigs and inflorescence not covered with sticky glands or long reddish hairs. | 8. New Mexican locust
or Fruit spherical with leathery-shelled seeds in winged clusters. | 9. Basswood
Fruit wind-borne with attached fluff or wings.
  or Fluffy parachuted seed; bark white, at least on upper branches. | 10. Quaking aspen
  Tiny winged fruit less than 3 mm wide; leaves of older branches borne on spurs (birches).
    Broken twigs do not smell like wintergreen.
      or Bark whitish to coppery, peeling in papery sheets. | 11. Paper birch
    or Bark multicolored, breaking into many thin chips or plates. | 12. River birch
    Broken twigs smell like wintergreen.
       Bark yellow to silvery, peeling into papery sheets or scales. | 13. Yellow birch
       Bark dark, almost black, breaking into shiny ridges or plates. | 14. Sweet birch
  Fruits paired and fused, each with a single asymmetrical wing more than 1 cm (maples).
    Leaf simple, palmately lobed.
       Leaf margin with just a few large, blunt teeth. | 15. Sugar maple
    or or Leaf margin with numerous sharp teeth.
         Samaras less than 1" (2.5 cm), twigs red, leaf pale below. | 16. Red maple
         Samaras more than 1.5" (3.8 cm), twigs brown, leaf silvery below. | 17. Silver maple
    Leaf compound. | 18. Boxelder
Fruit a disk-like wing around a flattened seed (elms).
    Leaf 4" (10 cm) or more, folded along midvein, sandpapery-rough above. | 19. Slippery elm
    Leaf less than 4" (10 cm), not folded or sandpapery on top. | 20. Siberian elm

1 Redbud ✿ 2 ◗ 2
Cercis canadensis ◆ *Fabaceae* (Bean family)

QUICK CHECK: Small tree with entire, heart-shaped leaves, irregular pink flowers borne directly from older branches, and small, thin pods. **ID difficulty 1.**

DESCRIPTION: Small understory tree up to 30' (9 m) tall, with a spreading crown. **Bark** with thin, short, narrow, peeling gray strips, revealing orange-brown beneath. **Twigs** smooth, brown at first becoming dark gray, the buds *tiny*, 1–1.5 mm; flower buds 2–3 mm and plump, *red with dark scales*. **Leaves** simple, alternate, thin, 3–5" (8–13 cm) long, heart-shaped, with pointed tips, shallow basal lobes, and entire margins. Blades are hairless, grayish below, with *7 main veins from the base* that are slightly depressed to flat. **New leaves** reddish and cupped with wavy margins. **Petioles** stiff and straight, often angled above the twig, rounded with no channel, *bulged at both ends*, 40–70% of blade length and out of plane with it. **Flowers** (spring) 9–12 mm across, pink-purple, pea-like with 5 unequal petals, borne in short-stalked clusters of 4–8 *on older wood*. The location of flower clusters is highly unusual—they often come directly out of medium to large branches or trunks. **Pods** 2–4" (5–10 cm) long, 0.4–0.7" (10–18 mm) wide, flat, thin, pointed at both ends, dark brown at maturity, often persisting into winter, the surface veiny, *the top with a wing rising above a ridge on each side*. Pedicel 9–15 mm in fruit. **Seeds** several, flat, 4–5 mm long, turning dark red and then brown.

HABITAT: Hardwood forests with rich soil, especially slopes, valleys, and forest edges. Native.

FOOD USE: Gather **flowers** in spring, preferably unopened or recently opened. Use as a garnish, in salads, or as a snack. They can be steeped in hot water to make a drink or jelly. Newly formed **young pods** can be eaten raw or cooked. (Do not eat mature pods or seeds.) **Conservation 1.**

COMMENTS: An abundant understory tree over much of our region, blooming redbuds are a beautiful feature of spring landscapes. The flowers make a delightful addition to seasonal dishes.

▲ Immature redbud pods.

2 Kentucky coffeetree ⬤ 1 ⬤ 3 (immature) ☕ 📖 IWE-178
Gymnocladus dioicus ✦ Fabaceae **(Bean family)**

QUICK CHECK: Doubly compound leaves with ovate leaflets and stout pods; seeds more than 0.6" (1.5 cm) wide. **ID difficulty 1.**

DESCRIPTION: Tree spreading by suckers to form colonies, the trunk straight and dominant, to 100' (30 m) tall, with a loose, narrow crown. **Bark** of mature trees thin, covered with dark brown scales or chips curling sideways. **Twigs** *very thick*, blunt, at first densely covered with short reddish hairs but later peeling with a thin crust. Terminal buds absent; side buds are tiny, placed above enormous concave leaf scars. **Leaves** enormous, alternate, doubly-compound, up to 38" (1 m) long; they are among the last to emerge in spring and the first to fall in autumn. **Petiole** thick, rounded, hairless, often reddish, with a light bloom, bearing 6–10 rachis divisions, each with 6–15 pinnately arranged leaflets, the *end leaflet absent*. **Leaflets**, 1.5–3" (4–8 cm) long, elliptic or ovate with pointed tips, hairless, the margins entire or minutely toothed. Midvein and secondary veins are faintly depressed above. **Inflorescence** male and female usually on separate trees, the male in clusters 3–4" (8–10 cm) long, the female clusters 9–12" (23–30 cm). **Flowers** (early summer) 10–12 mm across with a hairy tube widening into 5 linear, keeled, whitish petals alternating with 5 narrower sepals. **Pod** 4–9" (10–23 cm) long, 1.5–2.2" (3.8–5.5 cm) wide, and at least 0.6" (15 mm) thick, ripening to dark brown and often persisting into winter. **Seeds** 4–7, dark, flattened, lentil-shaped, very hard with a thick shell, about 0.7" (18 mm) across, embedded in *sticky greenish pulp*.

CONFUSING PLANTS: Honeylocust has thinner twigs, smaller leaflets, and thinner, longer, twisted pods.

HABITAT: Rich soils of lower slopes, river floodplains, and valleys, but above the regularly flooded zone. Also commonly planted as an ornamental. Native.

FOOD USE: Gather ripe pods from fall through winter, extract the **seeds**, and roast at 350°F for 20 minutes or until the shells are brittle, then crack them with a nutcracker. Remove kernel from the shell and roast at 350 until dark brown, then grind and **brew** like coffee. Seeds roasted less dark can also be eaten boiled or ground into flour to mix sparingly into baked goods. **Immature seeds**, gathered when the pods are still pinkish to yellow in mid to late summer, can be cut with a knife, peeled, boiled, and used like fava beans. **Conservation 1.**

COMMENTS: Of the many coffee substitutes touted in the wild food literature, this one is perhaps the best. The immature beans are excellent, versatile, and easy to gather. This common street tree is a great find for urban foragers.

WARNING: Seeds should not be eaten or brewed raw.

▲ The green, unripe seeds are like fava beans.

3 Honey mesquite 🗯 2
Prosopis glandulosa ✦ *Fabaceae* (Bean family)

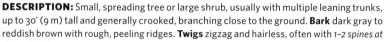

QUICK CHECK: Scrubby, multi-trunked tree with thorns; twice compound leaves with 2 pinnate divisions and linear leaflets; long, narrow, roundish pods. **ID difficulty 1.**

DESCRIPTION: Small, spreading tree or large shrub, usually with multiple leaning trunks, up to 30' (9 m) tall and generally crooked, branching close to the ground. **Bark** dark gray to reddish brown with rough, peeling ridges. **Twigs** zigzag and hairless, often with *1–2 spines at the nodes*, the spines up to 2" (5 cm) long. **Leaves** alternate on new growth but *clustered* on older branches. They are twice compound; the petiole *forks into two main divisions* (occasionally 4), each of which is 3–7" (8–18 cm) long and pinnately compound. There is a soft spine where the rachis forks. **Petioles** 30–70 % of the length of the leaf divisions, with 2 ridges on the upper side, these often with a row of sparse hair. **Leaflets** 12–36, sessile, paired, *well-spaced* (not touching), held 90° to the rachis (except near the ends). There is *no end leaflet*. **Blades** linear, entire, rounded or abruptly pointed at the base and tip, 0.8–2" (2–5 cm) long and about 10% as wide. Both surfaces are hairless and smooth. Secondary veins are obscure and faintly raised above. **Inflorescence** a drooping, crowded, catkin-like cluster 2–5" (5–13 cm) long, bearing numerous tiny pale yellowish flowers, each with a 5-lobed calyx, 5 linear petals, and 10 long, protruding stamens. Honey mesquite may flower any time from spring through late summer when moisture is ideal, but the heaviest flowering occurs in spring and early summer. **Pods** 3–9" (8–23 cm) long and about 1 cm wide, nearly straight, plump, constricted between the several seeds, containing spongy-crumbly, sweet pulp. **Seeds** oblong, slightly flattened, shiny brown.

HABITAT: Semi-arid flat lands and hill country, especially where sandy. Native.

FOOD USE: Pulverize and sift dry pods to make a sweet **flour** from the pulp that can be added to baked goods or hot cereal. Or just grab a pod and chew on it. Avoid moldy, fallen pods. **Conservation 1.**

COMMENTS: Mesquite flour has been a staple food for many people in its range and is still widely harvested and available commercially. Mesquite is better known as a dense wood good for smoking meats and as a "weed tree" of Texas range lands. In a quiet ecocide ignored by the media, millions of acres of mesquite lands are being aerially sprayed with herbicide, destroying most of the native plant community.

4   Honeylocust   🗡 1   🌿
Gleditsia triacanthos ✦ *Fabaceae* (Bean family)

QUICK CHECK: Long, flat, spiraled or curling pods; pinnately compound leaves. ID difficulty 2.

DESCRIPTION: Tree with a single erect trunk and spreading crown. **Bark** rather smooth when young, but on older trees peels into plates, chips, or curved ridges. Most wild trees have scattered bunches of branching *antler-like thorns* up to 7" (18 cm) long. (Street trees are thornless cultivars.) **Twigs** zigzag, shiny, red-brown at first turning gray, with reddish thorns (usually branched but sometimes simple) and tiny, often clumped buds. **Leaves** alternate and *once or twice pinnately compound* (twice compound more common on vigorous shoots). Once-compound leaves are 5–6" (13–15 cm) long with 14–30 leaflets, the leaflets paired or offset. Twice compound leaves have 6–12 pinnate divisions, each of which averages slightly smaller than a once-compound leaf. The petiole and rachises are faintly hairy. End leaflets are usually absent but occasionally present. **Leaflets** 0.6–1.6" (1.5–4 cm) long, sessile or nearly so, thin, narrowly ovate or elliptic with a blunt tip and a bristle. Surface smooth, semi-glossy, hairless or nearly so above but with minute hairs on the lighter undersurface. Major veins are *faintly raised above.* **Margins** entire or with tiny rounded teeth. **Inflorescence** crowded, hanging, compact racemes 2–4" (5–10 cm) long. **Flowers** (early summer) tiny, light yellow-green, fragrant, with 3–5 hairy sepals and 3–5 petals. **Pods** flattened, about 1" (2.5 cm) wide and 8–14" (20–36 cm) long, burgundy-brown when ripe in autumn, filled with sticky pulp and several hard, flattened, oval seeds about 1 cm long.

CONFUSING PLANTS: Water locust *G. aquatica* is similar in appearance and inhabits swamps in much of the South; however, its pods are extremely short and typically contain just one seed.

HABITAT: River floodplain forests and rich valleys. Also scattered invading pastures and disturbed sites. Native, but frequently planted as an ornamental well beyond its natural range.

FOOD USE: The **pulp** in ripe pods is very sweet with a variably bitter aftertaste and a slight irritating quality. Every now and then I chew on this pulp until it bothers my throat. Crushed pods can be steeped to make a drink. I have heard reliable reports of the **seeds** being soaked and boiled like beans, but I have not tried this. **Conservation 1.**

COMMENTS: The thorns are almost terrifying. The pods are produced so copiously that I fantasize about finding some way to get good food out of them. At least the deer love them.

5 Black locust ✿3 🌿2 ▭ FH-246
Robinia pseudoacacia ✦ *Fabaceae* (Bean family)

QUICK CHECK: Pinnately compound leaves with blunt, entire leaflets, drooping clusters of fragrant white flowers, and small, flat pods with proportionately small seeds. **ID difficulty 2.**

DESCRIPTION: Medium-sized tree spreading by root suckers to form clones. **Trunks** 30–80' (9–25 m) tall and up to 26" (66 cm) in diameter, erect but crooked, taller than wide even in full sun. **Bark** grayish, thick, and *deeply furrowed.* **Twigs** moderately thick, smooth and hairless, with short, stout, curved, laterally flattened, *very sharp* thorns to 13 mm long—or 2" (5 cm) on vigorous shoots. *Mature trees often become thornless.* **Leaves** alternate, once pinnately compound, 8–17" (20–44 cm) long, with 9–27 leaflets, the *end leaflet present.* **Rachis** enlarged at the base with 2 tiny appendages sometimes enlarged into thorns, hairless or with minute hairs, with a broad, shallow channel. **Leaflets** entire, elliptic, rounded at the base, the tips rounded or indented but usually with a tiny extended bristle 1–2.8" (2.5–7 cm) long. Blade flat and hairless, the midvein slightly depressed above but other veins flat. Petiolules 5% of blade length. **Inflorescence** a hanging crowded raceme 5–8" (13–20 cm) long containing 8–26 flowers, the pedicels 9–12 mm. **Flowers** (spring to early summer) 0.7–1" (18–25 mm) long, pea-like (with 2 wings, a keel in the middle, and a large banner petal above), white with a yellow spot on the banner when first open, fading as they age. **Pods** 3–4" (8–10 cm) long and about 0.6" (15 mm) wide, ripening in late summer; each contains 4–8 flattened, slightly oblong seeds 4–5 mm long.

▲ Inner area shows what is believed to be the original range.

CONFUSING PLANTS: Eve's necklace *Sophora affinis* ranges south from Arkansas and Oklahoma. This large shrub has no spines; the leaflets are glossy, pointed, and widely spaced. Flowers resemble those of black locust but are widely spaced and the keel and sometimes the wings are purple. The fruit is a jet-black pod fully constricted to a thin rod between the seeds. No part should be eaten.

HABITAT: Native to slopes in the Appalachian and Ozark regions, possibly elsewhere. Has been planted widely in most of the US and southern Canada, often escaping to roadsides, pastures, woodlots, and old fields. Thrives on very poor soil due to its ability to fix nitrogen. (Continued on the next page.)

5 Black locust (continued)

FOOD USE: Gather **flowers** soon after or just before they open—before the yellow spot fades or the edges wilt. They are delicious raw or cooked in almost any dish you can imagine, from ice cream to chicken soup. Most often I just eat them raw by the cluster or in salads. In mid to late summer while the pods are still green, split them open and strip out the small **beans**. These must be cooked before eating. Their flavor is good but shelling is laborious. Dried seeds can be gathered later and eaten after thorough boiling, but they seem to take forever to soften. **Conservation 1.**

COMMENTS: These magnificent-smelling and delicious flowers are very easy to use and available in huge quantities. You can smell blooming trees from a block away. This seriously might be the best edible flower in the world—but you will be disappointed if they are too old.

RELATED EDIBLES: Three native locusts are similar in appearance to black locust but smaller—typically large shrubs or small trees (but with larger flowers). All are planted and naturalized widely outside their regions of origin and have excellent edible flowers—although none are quite as delicious as black locust. Note: I have not eaten the beans of any of these.

6 Clammy locust ✦ *Robinia viscosa* ✿ 3

This small tree is native to scattered locations in the Southeast. The thorns are smaller and weaker; the twigs, peduncles, pedicels, calyces, and pods are covered with short, sticky, glandular hairs, and the leaflets are hairy on the underside. The flowers are light pink.

7 Bristly locust ✦ *Robinia hispida* ✿ 3

▲▼ Mostly introduced.

Native to the southern Appalachians, this is a shrub or rarely a small tree with gorgeous pink-purple flowers to 1.2" (3 cm) long, blooming later in the season than black locust and for a much longer time. The twigs, petioles, and inflorescence are all densely covered in long, reddish, bristly hairs.

8 New Mexican locust ✦ *Robinia neomexicana* ✿ 3

The natural distribution of this large shrub or small tree barely comes into our region, but like the others it is planted and escapes outside of its native range. The flowers are dull pinkish and slightly larger than those of black locust. The racemes are sometimes compound and the pods are hairy.

▲ Bristly locust.

▲ Clammy locust.

▲ New Mexican locust.

9 Basswood 🌿3 ✂1 🌱3 ☕ 📖 FH-269
Tilia americana + *Malvaceae* (Mallow family)

QUICK CHECK: Large, heart-shaped, toothed, alternate leaves; flowers and fruit in clusters attached to a long, tongue-like bract. **ID difficulty 1.**

DESCRIPTION: Large tree to 120' (37 m), much taller than wide even in the open, trunks *often clumped* or with a ring of sprouts surrounding the original center trunk. **Bark** gray, moderately thick, with many narrow fissures and narrow flat ridges. **Twigs** stout, smooth, hairless, gray, zigzag. **Buds** egg-shaped, blunt, smooth and shiny, covered by 2 large green to red scales. **Leaves** large, alternate, heart-shaped, *distinctly asymmetrical*, 5–9" (13–23 cm) long, *hairless on both sides*, with sharply toothed margins. Veins nearly flat above. **Petioles** 20% of blade length. **Inflorescence** a cluster of 5–12 *attached to the middle of a light yellow-green tongue-like bract* that serves as a wing for wind-dispersal of the whole cluster. **Flowers** (midsummer) bisexual, 11–13 mm wide with 5 downy sepals, 5 creamy petals, and a prominent stigma with a 5-lobed tip. **Fruit** spherical, 6 mm, the flesh leathery, the large nut-like seed woody, ripening in autumn and often persisting into winter.

CONFUSING PLANTS: American mulberry (p. 48) has remarkably similar leaves, but they are more symmetrical, have depressed secondary veins, and are hairy on both sides.

HABITAT: Mixed deciduous forests, preferring rich soil. Native.

FOOD USE: The **young leaves** are best immediately after the buds open in spring, when the leaves are still curled; they remain edible until they reach their full size. You can cook them, but I like them best raw. In winter you can nibble the **buds** for a slimy snack. **Cambium** is thick and sweet in early summer. **Flowers** can be steeped for tea, either dried or fresh. The **seeds** have tasty kernels that are impractical to extract; they can be roasted whole to make a chocolate-like flavoring.

COMMENTS: Linden flower tea is a popular bedtime drink. Basswood leaves are not as well known, but in my opinion are the native tree's most important edible part. **AKA** linden, lime—but these names more often refer to Eurasian species.

10 Quaking aspen 🦌 2
Populus tremuloides ✦ *Salicaceae* (Willow family)

QUICK CHECK: White, powdery bark that does not peel; small broad leaves on vertically flattened petioles. **ID difficulty 1.**

DESCRIPTION: Tree spreading by root suckers to form large clones, trunks 50–80' (15–25 m) tall with an open, narrow crown. **Bark** white, smooth, and powdery (sometimes green on branches), becoming dark gray-black, blocky, and furrowed on lower parts of older trunks. Branch bases are often black even where trunks are white. **Twigs** thin, brittle, reddish brown and shiny in the first year, after that becoming grayer, dull, and hairless. **Buds** scaly, pointed, brown, shiny, not sticky. **Leaves** alternate, 1.5–3" (4–8 cm) long and about as wide, widest near the roundish base and quickly tapering to a point, the blades flat, hairless on both surfaces. **Veins** flat above and offset by light color; there are 2 secondary veins from the base. **Margins** have small, rounded, wavy teeth and scattered hair. **Petioles** 70–100% of blade length, *vertically flattened*, which makes the leaf shake in the slightest wind. **Flowers** (late winter to early spring) in catkins, unshowy. **Fruit** a pointed capsule 6 mm long, opening in early summer to release tiny parachuted seeds.

CONFUSING PLANTS: White birch bark peels; aspen bark does not. Bigtooth aspen *P. grandidentata* has larger teeth on its leaves and yellowish bark. Other poplars have rougher bark with the smooth part not as white; the leaf shapes are different, and the petioles are not laterally flattened. None are poisonous. Chinese tallow tree *Triadica sebifera* does not share the distribution of quaking aspen but has smooth bark and a remarkably similar leaf shape—however, the margins are entire and the sap is milky.

HABITAT: Young forests after disturbance by fire, wind, or logging. In boreal regions it inhabits better, well-drained soils of nearly any parent material. Native.

FOOD USE: In early summer the **cambium** can be harvested (p. 30). Sometimes it is bitter, but at its best it is surprisingly sweet. **Conservation 2.**

COMMENTS: In the not-so-olden days when people peeled pulpwood logs by hand, woods workers knew that an aspen cut at the right time and peeled fresh could provide a slushy treat slurped right off the spud. Harvesting cambium weakens or kills the tree, so except in emergencies it should be done only when they are being cut for some other purpose. Clones of this tree can live for tens of thousands of years.

BIRCH
genus *Betula* ✦ *Betulaceae* (Birch family)

QUICK CHECK: Trees with simple, toothed, alternate leaves, thin twigs and branches, shiny or papery bark, and tiny winged seeds. **ID difficulty 1.**

DESCRIPTION: Erect to leaning trees, trunks single or clumped, the branches thin, delicate-looking, and often crowded at the tip. **Bark** smooth and often shiny when young with elongated horizontal lenticels; eventually peeling horizontally into thin papery flakes or sheets or breaking into smooth-topped plates. **Twigs** thin with narrowly egg-shaped, pointed buds. (Buds on older spurs are blunt on some species.) Smaller branches bear *short spurs, roughened by the ridges of many crowded leaf scars.* **Leaves** alternate on twigs, paired or in sets of 3 on spurs. **Blades** small and thin, 2.5–5" (6–13 cm) long, ovate, the margins double-toothed, the surfaces variably fine-hairy or hairless, *secondary veins slightly depressed above.* **Petioles** 5–30% of blade length. **Flowers** tiny, inconspicuous, wind-pollinated in early spring, the male and female separate on the same tree, both hanging in catkins. **Seeds** tiny, elliptic, 1–2 mm long with a papery wing on each side, released along with tiny bracts that are shaped either like the silhouette of a bird in flight, or like a bird track.

FOOD USE: Birches can be tapped like maples for their sap; the season partly overlaps but runs later. Birch sap runs do not require freezing. Fresh sap can be drunk like water, or it can be boiled down to make **syrup**. It takes 80–120 gallons of white birch sap to make one gallon of syrup, and even more for yellow birch. Birch syrup burns more easily than maple; it should be finished *rapidly at a rolling boil or with constant stirring* to avoid excess time exposed to heat. Yellow and especially sweet birch contain oil of wintergreen in the bark. This can be extracted in alcohol as a **flavoring**. The twigs and inner bark can be used to brew **tea** or **birch beer**. Syrup from these trees, however, *does not* have a wintergreen flavor. The **cambium** is edible, with good flavor, but the trees are hard to peel. I have seen reports of the inner bark being eaten but have had no success with this.

COMMENTS: We tap 300–400 birches, mostly white and a few yellow, immediately after we pull our maple taps out. Maples yield more syrup for the same effort, and most people prefer its flavor over that of birch. However, I enjoy the distinct flavors of both, and birch is a nutritional powerhouse. Once you start to recognize birch bracts you will notice them littering the forest floor or speckling snowbanks by the millions.

IMPORTANT SPECIES: There are many birches in our region, and all can be tapped, but the following are most commonly used. All are native.

11 **White birch** ✦ *Betula papyrifera* 1

This is the widespread, iconic species of the Far North, growing in poor to moderately rich soils. The trunks are sometimes clumped, especially after logging, and may grow to 80' (25 m) tall and 2' (60 cm) in diameter. Leaves are broadly ovate with doubly toothed margins. Seeds ripen in late summer, and the bracts are bird-in-flight-shaped. Due to its sheer abundance, this is the species most often used for syrup. Another species, heart-leaved birch *B. cordifolia*, is sometimes recognized. At a glance people often confuse white birch with quaking aspen, but this should never happen when you are close enough to touch (i.e. eat) any part of the tree. **AKA** paper birch.

12   River birch ✦ *Betula nigra*

This is a tree of sandy floodplains that often grows in clumps, the trunks typically leaning, sometimes very large. The multicolored bark peels into irregular plates or papery flakes, exposing lighter and smoother bark beneath, creating a combination of silvery, yellowish, pinkish, rusty, and dark gray. The leaves are broad, very coarsely double-toothed, and finely woolly below; the new growth is also woolly. The seeds are released in spring, with bracts shaped like a bird foot. **AKA** water birch, red birch, black birch. I have not made syrup from this tree but two friends have done so.

13   Yellow birch ✦ *Betula alleghaniensis*

A long-lived forest dominant that may exceed 100' (30 m) in height and 3' (1 m) in diameter. The bark may peel in thin, papery shreds or large, thick plates; it ranges from bright bronze-yellow to silvery, sometimes with dark brown areas. The leaves are narrower than those of white birch with more numerous and more closely spaced secondary veins. The margins are more evenly toothed and the petioles proportionately shorter. The twigs and bark have a mild scent of wintergreen. Seeds fall in winter, the bracts shaped like a bird foot. Yellow birch is found on rich, moist soil, often associated with hemlock. **AKA** silver birch, *B. lutea*.

▲ River birch.

14   Sweet birch ✦ *Betula lenta*

This birch has smooth, reddish-brown bark when young, and dark scaly bark when older. In either form it somewhat resembles cherry bark, and the leaves show similarity as well—but cherries never have a wintergreen odor. The leaves are narrower than those of other birches—ovate to lanceolate—and have smaller teeth. The twigs and bark have a strong wintergreen odor—the bark is the commercial source of natural wintergreen flavoring. Seeds ripen in fall and the bracts look like a bird foot. It is found primarily on rich, moist, rocky slopes. **AKA** cherry birch, black birch.

MAPLE 📖 IWE-187
genus *Acer* ✦ family *Sapindaceae*

QUICK CHECK: Leaves in opposing pairs, palmately lobed or pinnately compound; fruit a fused pair of winged keys splitting apart at maturity. **ID difficulty 1.**

DESCRIPTION: The species featured here are medium to large trees with rough furrowed or scaly bark at maturity. **Leaves** paired, on petioles 60–110% of blade length, the blades palmately lobed or pinnately compound. **Flowers** (early spring) primarily wind-pollinated, lacking petals, with a 5-lobed calyx that may be red, yellow, or greenish. **Fruit** *a pair of conjoined samaras* (known as "keys"), borne at the end of a single pedicel, splitting apart neatly at an abscission line, each with one soft seed and an *asymmetrical, one-sided*, propeller-like wing 0.6–2.4" (1.5–6 cm) long.

FOOD USE: Sap can be used to make syrup, vinegar, or sugar. Drill holes about 1.2" (3 cm) into maple sapwood in late winter when the days get warm enough for some thawing to occur (generally over 40 degrees F). In warmer areas, you'll be waiting for a midwinter freeze, not a spring thaw. Drive in a wooden or metal spout and hang a bucket or other container to collect dripping sap. Trees under 10" in diameter produce little. Sap generally runs from the first thaws until just before the leaf buds open, but requires fluctuation between freezing and thawing temperatures. Sap should be boiled down soon after collection to avoid spoilage. A typical ratio for sugar/black maple is 38 gallons of sap for one gallon of syrup; other species are usually a little less sweet. Boil until the syrup reaches 7° F above the boiling point. Filter while still hot, then reheat and bottle the syrup. You can boil the syrup down further to make maple sugar.

CONFUSING PLANTS: The few other large trees in our region with palmately lobed leaves bear them alternately. No other trees in our region have a double samara with asymmetrical wings.

COMMENTS: Most commercial production is from sugar/black and red maple respectively, but boxelder and silver maple are also tapped commercially and are perfectly suitable for personal production.

IMPORTANT SPECIES: All are native:

15 **Sugar maple** ✦ *Acer saccharum*

Here I am including three very similar trees sometimes separated from sugar maple: black maple *A. nigrum*, southern sugar maple *A. barbatum*, and chalk maple *A. leucoderme*. These species are collectively called "hard maple" and the first two are the primary maples used to make syrup. Sugar maples are large, erect, *single-trunked*, long-lived, shade-tolerant trees with rugged and variable bark. The leaves are 4–6" (10–15 cm) long with 3 major and 2 minor lobes, the *sinuses between lobes rounded at the base*. There are a *few large, blunt teeth* on some of the lobes, but otherwise the leaf *margins are smooth*. The samaras are about 1" (2.5 cm) long and ripen in early autumn. Sugar maple dominates many forests in the northeastern

US and southeastern Canada. It prefers well-drained but moist, rich soil, especially on rocky slopes and ridges or glacial till. This tree is bad for carbon emissions because of all the miles people drive to see its brilliant yellow-or-ange-red leaves on autumn color tours.

123

16 Red maple + *Acer rubrum*

Also called soft maple, this large, upright tree has smooth bark when young that becomes furrowed, scaly, or shaggy when older. The trunks are often clumped, and the *winter twigs are reddish*. Leaves are 3–5" (8–13 cm) long with 3 major lobes, not as deeply cut as those of silver maple but also with *toothed margins and a gray underside*. Female flowers, although small, are bright red and showy in early spring. The samaras are about 1" (2.5 cm) long and ripen in late spring or early summer. Red maple grows in most forest types but tends to be most prevalent in slightly dry or slightly wet soils, and less prevalent on mesic soils where sugar maple and beech dominate. It is increasing in abundance throughout much of our region. Red maples on rich soil produce almost equally to sugar maples, although the minimum tapping size is somewhat larger.

17 Silver maple + *Acer saccharinum* 1

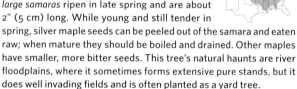

This is a large, spreading, fast-growing tree with *smooth gray bark* when young, breaking into *shaggy strips* when older. Trunks are often clumped. The leaves are 3–6" (8–15 cm) long with 3–5 *deeply cut lobes* and *several shallower lobes*, the margins with sharp teeth. Blades are *silvery on the underside*. The *large samaras* ripen in late spring and are about 2" (5 cm) long. While young and still tender in spring, silver maple seeds can be peeled out of the samara and eaten raw; when mature they should be boiled and drained. Other maples have smaller, more bitter seeds. This tree's natural haunts are river floodplains, where it sometimes forms extensive pure stands, but it does well invading fields and is often planted as a yard tree.

18 Boxelder + *Acer negundo*

This maple has leaning, crooked, often clumped trunks that can reach fairly large diameters. The bark is light brown with shallow furrows; it never shags or peels. The leaves are *compound* and have 3 or 5 leaflets, all stalked, each 3–4" (8–10 cm) long with large teeth or erratic small lobes. Twigs have *smooth green bark coated with bloom*. The samaras are about 1.4" (3.5 cm) long, the *seeds elongated* and the keys *acutely angled*, forming in spring but not ripening until fall and often persisting through winter. Boxelder's wild habitat is river floodplains but it colonizes disturbed ground in both urban and agricultural areas and has become one of our most common "weed" trees. Boxelder is commercially tapped in Manitoba and should not be ignored by backyard sugarmakers, especially since it is found on the Plains where other maples are absent. **AKA** ash-leaf maple, Manitoba maple.

19 **Slippery elm** 🌿 3 🍃 2 🌀 3 🍄 3
Ulmus rubra ✦ *Ulmaceae* (Elm family)

QUICK CHECK: Sandpapery-rough, toothed, alternate leaves folded along the midvein when growing in full sun; fruit a green papery disk. **ID difficulty 2.**

Description: Medium-sized tree, tall and lanky in the woods but spreading widely in the open. **Bark** reddish-brown, peeling in narrow strips, sometimes loosening sideways. If you cut into the outer bark, it will show *alternating layers of reddish brown and darker reddish brown*. **Twigs** medium thick, pubescent and green at first, becoming gray. **Buds** blunt, 4–6 mm, with several scales, the ends *covered in rusty fuzz*. **Leaves** alternate, ovate to elliptic, 4–8" (10–20 cm) long, the base narrow but rounded, the tip pointed, often acuminate, *creased along the midvein in full sun*, sometimes dramatically. Surface hairy on both sides: *sandpapery rough* from stiff hairs above, the hairs softer below. Midvein deeply depressed above. **Secondary veins** numerous, *closely spaced, nearly straight*, 45°, *deeply depressed* above; veinlets also depressed. Margins double toothed. **Petioles** about 5% of blade length. **Flowers** (late winter or very early spring) small, unshowy, wind-pollinated. **Fruit** a disc-like samara 0.6–0.7" (15–18 mm) across, ripening as the leaves emerge; round to slightly oblong, green turning brown, the wing hairless and ruffled, with a tiny notch in the end. **Seed** single, flattened, in the samara center, the *seed bulge hairy*.

Confusing plants: American elm *U. americana* has smaller, smoother, flatter leaves, more pointed and hairless buds, smaller and hairy-winged samaras, and outer bark with whitish-gray layers.

Habitat: Hardwood forests with well-drained but rich soil, especially limestone; mostly on slopes or high floodplains. Native.

Food use: **Inner bark** can be harvested all year; it contains much embedded starch. Fresh or dried, the bark can be boiled to extract the starch in a drinkable water solution that is pleasant lightly sweetened. Dried bark can be ground in a blender and then sifted to remove the fibers. This elm flour can be dissolved in water as a drink or mixed with other flours for cooking. **Cambium** can be scraped off the wood in spring or early summer (p. 30). Unripe **samaras** are excellent as a salad green or cooked. Ripe **seeds** can be rubbed out of the dried samaras and cooked like oatmeal.

Comments: Perhaps one of our strangest wild foods, slippery elm bark flour is also one of the few that is commercially available. When dried, slippery elm bark has a sweet odor remarkably like maple syrup. **AKA** red elm. PS, I have no relationship to the company selling slippery elm lozenges.

▲ When sliced the outer bark of slippery elm shows all brown layers.

▲ The sliced outer bark of American elm has brown and whitish-gray layers.

Related edible:

20 Siberian elm + *Ulmus pumila* 3 2 2 3 📖 FH-165

This introduced weedy tree has a crooked trunk, blocky dark gray bark, and a spreading crown of silver-gray branches. The twigs are more zigzag and winter buds are less fuzzy. Leaves are much smaller, 1–3" (2.5–8 cm) long, ovate to lanceolate, and flat rather than folded; the upper surface lacks the stiff, sandpapery hairs. The samaras are slightly smaller than those of slippery elm, rounder, and the seed bulge is not hairy. Siberian elm is often erroneously called Chinese elm, but that species, *Ulmus parvifolia*, has leathery, semi-evergreen leaves and lacy bark. Siberian elm invades open, human-disturbed habitats in full sun: roadsides, empty urban lots, old fields. It is tolerant of heat, drought, and cold and thrives on the Great Plains where it often forms nearly pure stands. All parts can be used like those of slippery elm. The samaras are smaller, but also tend to be produced in larger quantities that are easier to reach. The two species readily hybridize, and in some regions these hybrids are crowding out native slippery elm populations.

9 LOW OR TRAILING SHRUBS OR VINES WITH LEATHERY, EVERGREEN LEAVES

The free-standing branches of these species never rise more than 12" (30 cm), and most of the time are much shorter—although they may creep horizontally for long distances. This life form is an adaptation to poor soil and long, cold winters under the protection of snow, so most of the species have a decidedly northern distribution. The arctic and alpine bearberries are placed here even though their leaves are semi-deciduous because their growth form otherwise matches the pattern of this group. All but one of the species in this group are members of the heath family *Ericaceae*. The primary edible part of all but one species is the fruit; one species is also commonly used for tea. This is a very safe group; I am aware of no plants with this life form producing dangerous berries. *Nevertheless, you still need to identify everything you eat!*

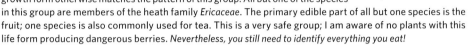

TENTATIVE IDENTIFICATION KEY TO GROUP 9
The key is not your final answer!

Leaves tiny, often whorled, the sides scrolled downward into a needle-like tube. Crowberries (p. 64).	
or Leaves not rolled into a tube, entire or with a few tiny teeth, thick and leathery.	
Fruit a dry, hairy, seed-filled capsule; some leaves over 2" (5 cm).	1. Trailing arbutus
Fruit fleshy, mealy, or juicy; leaves less than 2" (5 cm) long.	
Stems limp, thread-like, 2 mm thick or less.	
Leaves paired, red fruit with 2 depressions at the end.	2. Partridgeberry
or Leaves alternate; white fruit on a short pedicel.	3. Creeping snowberry
Leaves alternate; reddish fruit on a long, thread-like pedicel.	
or Leaves blunt, margins slightly downturned.	4. Large cranberry
Leaves pointed, margins strongly scrolled downward.	5. Small cranberry
Some stems over 2 mm thick; leafy branches erect and rigid.	
Fruit single with a large 5-point indent at the end.	7. Wintergreen
Fruit clustered, not indented at the end.	
Seeds soft, leaves slightly creased along the midvein.	6. Lingonberry
Seeds hard, leaves not creased along the midvein.	8. Bearberry
Leaves flat, serrated, thin, the surface roughened above by deeply depressed veinlets.	
Fruit red.	9. Arctic bearberry
Fruit black.	10. Black bearberry

1 Trailing arbutus 2
Epigaea repens ✦ *Ericaceae* (Heath family)

QUICK CHECK: Blunt, leathery, ground-hugging leaves with heart-shaped bases, a rough surface, and clusters of tubular, 5-lobed flowers. **ID difficulty 1.**

DESCRIPTION: Stems vine-like, 6–20" (15–50 cm) long, about 2 mm thick, creeping, green to reddish, often hidden under leaf litter, with only the ground-hugging leaves visible. New growth has white hair; old growth has prominent, erect, red-brown hairs. **Leaves** alternate, 1.2–2.7" (3–7 cm) long, leathery, elliptic to ovate with a heart-shaped base, rounded

or indented at the tip, often with a tiny nipple. The blade has long red-brown hairs below, and is roughened above by scattered, short, stiff hairs. **Veins** and veinlets are all deeply depressed above, rendering a rough texture. Midvein and secondary veins protrude below, but veinlets do not (they are faintly depressed and darkened). **Margins** entire with scattered long, stiff hairs. **Petioles** about 40% of blade length, hairy, with a very narrow channel. (Continued on the next page.)

1 Trailing arbutus (continued)

Inflorescence (early to mid spring) a compact terminal clusters of 3–15, partly to fully hidden under the leaves. **Flower** has a tubular, white corolla 5–10 mm long abruptly spreading at the tip, about 13 mm wide, with 5 white to faintly pink triangular lobes. The throat and tube are densely woolly, and a single pistil protrudes. The calyx is symmetrical, the 5 sepals long-triangular and sharply pointed, creamy to very light green; behind these are 3 hairy, cupped, pointed bracts, one smaller than the other two. **Fruit** a spherical, hairy, 5-chambered capsule ripening in late summer and holding numerous tiny brown seeds.

HABITAT: Dry, sandy, acidic soil in full to partial sun, usually under some combination of pine, oak, and white birch, especially near lakes. Native. 🔥

FOOD USE: The part eaten is the flower, which reminds me of lilac but is less bitter with a nice persistent aftertaste. **Conservation 1.**

COMMENTS: The flowers make a fun snack or attractive garnish, and searching for them under dead leaves in the drab woods of early spring is like a magical treasure hunt.

2 Partridgeberry 🍓 1
Mitchella repens ◆ family *Rubiaceae*

QUICK CHECK: Small, paired leaves with white midveins; 2-eyed red fruit with a white interior. **ID difficulty 1.**

DESCRIPTION: Small, trailing evergreen, the wiry stems branching sparsely, to 20" (50 cm) long, rooting at the nodes. **Leaves** paired, 0.5–0.8" (13–20 mm) long and as wide or wider, broadly ovate to round, rounded at the tip and shallowly heart-shaped to rounded at the base, the margins entire. Surface dark and hairless above, the *midvein and sometimes other major veins offset by pale color*; veins essentially flat. **Petioles** 30–90% of blade length, grooved, with 2 lines of fine hairs. **Flowers** (summer) borne in terminal pairs, each from a cup-like lobed calyx, the corolla a tapered pink tube 8–11 mm long before spreading widely into 3–7 (most often 4) lobes, white and *very densely hairy on the inside*. The sexual parts come in two separate arrangements, both arrangements bisexual. **Berry** ripens in late summer and persists through winter; bright red and waxy outside, white inside. It is actually two adjacent fruits grown together, and two depressed calyx lobes can be seen on the terminal end.

HABITAT: Forests in moderate shade. Widely tolerant; under conifers and hardwoods, from moist to dry soil of nearly all types. Native.

FOOD USE: The **berries** are available almost any time there is not snow on the ground. They are too sparse to pick in quantity and have little flavor, but there is nevertheless some joy in any jewel-like forest nibble. **Conservation 1.**

COMMENTS: Though rarely abundant, this plant inhabits almost every forest type in our region.

3 Creeping snowberry 3
Gaultheria hispidula ◆ Ericaceae (Heath family)

QUICK CHECK: Tiny evergreen vine with white berries and wintergreen odor. **ID difficulty 1.**

DESCRIPTION: Miniature creeping woody vine often forming mats over stumps, logs, or rocks. **Stems** less than 1 mm thick and up to 16" (40 cm) long, prostrate, leafy for most of their length, the leaves nearly touching to overlapped at the stem tip. **Bark** has appressed brown hair when young; later shredding. Branches are few and scattered. **Leaves** tiny, evergreen, alternate, broadly elliptic, blunt-pointed at both ends, 3-5 mm long, arched, the upper surface shiny green and hairless, the lower surface pale with a few large, scale-like, appressed brown hairs. Midveins and secondary veins are faintly depressed above. **Margins** entire and downcurved. **Petioles** 2-5% of blade length. **Flowers** on short stalks from leaf axils in early summer; tiny, 4-lobed, white. **Berry** elliptic, white, 5-9 mm, growing on a thick, curved, green pedicel 15-20% of its length with 2 ovate bracts beneath the fruit. The end is dimpled with a 4-lobed soft calyx and has a protruding style. The surface has scattered brown hairs and the inside is juicy with small, soft seeds.

HABITAT: Bogs and mossy acidic uplands, generally under conifers in partial shade. Native.

FOOD USE: The small **berries** ripen in late summer; they are often hidden in the moss and hard to collect in quantity. They can be eaten fresh and make delightful jams or desserts. They seem to fruit better on rocks and logs than in bogs. **Conservation 1.**

COMMENTS: This berry is one of the most precious in all our flora: juicy and acid like a good wild strawberry, but with a burst of crisp wintergreen. You won't often find enough to bring home, and you may not want to share, but if you do it'll be memorable. **AKA** moxie plum.

CRANBERRY 📖 NG-266
genus *Vaccinium* (in part) ◆ Ericaceae (Heath family)

QUICK CHECK: Tiny evergreen vines with small leaves and smooth, round to slightly elongated cranberries. **ID difficulty 1.**

COMBINED DESCRIPTION: Small, creeping, woody vines with thin, wiry stems rooting at the nodes; where growing densely they may stand erect up to 10" (25 cm). **Leaves** alternate, evergreen, 0.2–0.6" (5–15 mm), elliptic to ovate, entire, dark green above and pale beneath, on very short petioles. **Flowers** (early to midsummer) single or in loose clusters of up to 6, each on a *long, thin pedicel*, nodding like a shooting star (*Dodecatheon*), with 4 long, pink, reflexed petals behind a tight protruding cluster of stamens that has been fancied to resemble a crane's beak (hence *crane-berry*). **Berry** spherical to elliptic, 0.3–0.9" (8–23 mm) long, on a thread-like pedicel with 2 tiny bracts, ripening in fall to red or a mottled mixture of red, light green, and cream.

CONFUSING PLANTS: Lingonberry *V. vitis-idaea* has thicker, stiffer, shorter stems, blunter leaves, and fruit in tight clusters. Creeping snowberry vines have brown hairs and a wintergreen smell.

HABITAT: Sunny bogs with sphagnum moss, with or without standing water. Native.

FOOD USE: Gather ripe fruit from the moss by hand; if the vines stand erect you can use a rake. Use like cultivated cranberries. Soft but unspoiled "bletted" berries (this happens after freezing and thawing) have a different flavor that you cannot get from store-bought cranberries. **Conservation 1.**

COMMENTS: Cranberries are more abundant than many people realize, because people rarely venture into bogs. Large cranberries are cultivated in artificial bogs in New England, New Jersey, and the Great Lakes region. Most cultivars are selected directly from wild plants, which can still provide huge crops of fruit. We have two species:

4   Large cranberry ◆ *Vaccinium macrocarpon* 3

This species has larger leaves than small cranberry, *almost flat* (the margins scarcely downcurved) and the *tips rounded*. The vines are longer and more likely to climb other vegetation or stand erect. The fruit averages larger, 0.4–0.9" (10–23 mm) and may be spherical or elongated. The bracts on the pedicel are close to the fruit. Large cranberry grows further south than small cranberry and inhabits wet, floating bogs or the boggy margins of open water—although it can tolerate dry conditions. It is usually much faster to collect.

5   Small cranberry ◆ *Vaccinium oxycoccus* 3

This has slightly smaller fruit (5–13 mm) that is usually spherical and often paler when ripe. The 2 bracts are close to the middle of the pedicel. The leaves, like everything else, average smaller: 7–10 mm. They are more silvery beneath, have *pointed tips*, and the margins are *strongly down-curved*. Small cranberry grows in floating bogs or muskegs that may be seasonally dry. The flavor is perhaps superior, but the berries take longer to collect.

6 Lingonberry 🍍 3 📖 NG-266
Vaccinium vitis-idaea ✦ *Ericaceae* (Heath family)

QUICK CHECK: Erect mini-shrub with tiny, evergreen, spoon-shaped leaves and clusters of spherical red berries. **ID difficulty 2.**

DESCRIPTION: Low, trailing, mat-forming mini-shrub, the erect branches to 6" (15 cm) tall. **Stems** branching, at first with curly white hairs, older stems becoming dark brown to black and peeling. **Leaves** 0.2–0.8" (5–20 mm) long, evergreen, leathery, alternate, oval to elliptic, the tips rounded or indented, the base tapered. The surface is dark, glossy, and hairless above; paler below with black dots. **Midvein** depressed above and the blade slightly creased; other veins are faint. **Margins** entire and rolled downward, hairy near the leaf base. **Petioles** hairy, 10–20% of blade length. **Inflorescence** a one-sided terminal raceme of up to 10, each pedicel with 2 tiny bracts. **Flowers** (summer) white to light pink, the calyx bell-like with four lobes, the style protruding beyond the opening. **Berries** spherical, 8–10 mm, dark red, with a visible end calyx, containing several soft seeds. They ripen in late summer but often persist through the winter.

CONFUSING PLANTS: Bearberry *Arctostaphylos uva-ursi* has larger leaves and the midvein is only faintly depressed. Its fruits are larger and dry inside with hard seeds and a calyx at the base.

HABITAT: Full sun. Open rocky slopes, alpine meadows, tundra, bog edges. Native.

FOOD USE: Gather ripe **berries** by hand or with a berry rake beginning in late summer, continuing until snow cover and sometimes again the following spring. They are most often canned with sugar and eaten like cranberry sauce. They do not need additional pectin to thicken. They can also be used for juice, in breads, or any other way you'd use cranberries. **Conservation 1.**

COMMENTS: Lingonberries are circumboreal in distribution and are abundant in Scandinavia, where they are still commonly eaten. Canned wild lingonberries of several brands are imported to North America from Sweden and are available in most grocery stores. This is one of the most abundant wild berries of northern Canada and Alaska. **AKA** cowberry, partridgeberry, lowbush cranberry.

7 Wintergreen 🫐 2 ☕ ⚱
Gaultheria procumbens ✦ *Ericaceae* (Heath family)

QUICK CHECK: Tiny evergreen shrub 2–7" (5–18 cm) tall with broad leaves, waxy pink berries with a depressed end, and a wintergreen odor. **ID difficulty 1.**

DESCRIPTION: Very small shrub in colonies that spread by rhizome. **Stems** erect, 2–7" (5–18 cm) tall, red and minutely downy at the top, each bearing 3–7 alternate leaves *crowded near the top*. **Leaves** evergreen, tough and leathery, broadly elliptic to nearly round, 0.8–1.7" (2–4.3 cm) long, rounded to blunt-pointed at the tip and angled at the base, dark green or red tinted and glossy above, pale green below, hairless on both sides. Major **veins** are flat to etched. **Margins** are slightly down-curved, nearly entire but with *tiny, widely-spaced teeth*, each with a *bristle hugging the margin*. **Petiole** downy, 5–10% of blade length. **Flowers** single, on nodding pedicels from leaf axils in mid to late summer, with a small 5-lobed calyx and a white, barrel-shaped corolla that is constricted at the tip with 5 recurved lobes. **Berries** 1–5 per plant, hanging beneath the leaves, spherical to slightly elongated, bright red, *with a 5-pointed star depressed into the end* and a persistent style. The flesh is white and spongy, not juicy, with a dry chamber inside containing numerous light brown seeds, maturing in late summer to early autumn but overwintering—they seem to reach their best size and development late the following spring.

HABITAT: Dry or well-drained northern forests with acidic soil, especially under mixtures of birch, oak, and pine. Most common in sandy soil in sunny areas at forest edges. Native. 🔥

FOOD USE: Berries are a pleasant nibble, good in desserts or smoothies raw. Do not eat a large quantity. Leaves can be collected at any time and nibbled for their wintergreen flavor, and they can be used to brew a surprisingly weak **tea.** A **flavoring** can be extracted with alcohol.

COMMENTS: This well-known and much loved Northwoods plant is dear to many, although it is more of a flavoring than a food. The year-round availability is appreciated. **AKA** teaberry.

8 Bearberry 1
Arctastaphylos uva-ursi ✦ *Ericaceae* (Heath family)

QUICK CHECK: Short erect branches and spoon-shaped leaves; round, red, mealy fruit on a short, thick pedicel. **ID difficulty 1.**

DESCRIPTION: Trailing stem lying flat on the ground, often hidden by litter, sending up numerous erect branches to 6" (15 cm), forming a dense mat. New branches are rusty brown and finely hairy; older branches have peeling papery skin. **Leaves** alternate, 0.5–1" (13–25 mm) long, oblong to obovate with rounded tips and a tapered base, the leaf often arching. Blades are leathery, hairless and semi-glossy above, paler and faintly hairy below, not creased along the midvein, with the veins only faintly depressed. **Margins** entire, curled down and hairy. **Petioles** 10–15% of blade length, often appressed to the stem. **Inflorescence** a compact terminal drooping cluster of 3–7, with a triangular bract at the base of each pedicel. **Flowers** (late spring) 5–7 mm long, on very short pedicels, hanging like an overturned vase, broadest at the whitish base and tapering to a pinkish opening with 5 tiny lobes. **Berries** in small clusters, spherical, 7–12 mm, with a tiny 5-lobed calyx pressed to the base, the flesh whitish, nearly dry, mealy, containing up to 5 hard seeds. They ripen to red at the end of summer but often persist through winter.

CONFUSING PLANTS: Lingonberries have smaller leaves, smaller fruits lacking hard seeds, and leaves slightly creased on the midvein.

HABITAT: Sunny sites on the poorest dry soil: pine barrens, rocky ridges, tundra, steep slopes, sand dunes. Native. 🔥

FOOD USE: Berries ripen in late summer and are typically available through the following spring. You can eat them raw or cooked, but they are hardly good in either case. The flavor is supposedly better after hard frosts. Due to the astringency, large quantities can cause stomach upset. The Iñupiat of Alaska eat them preserved in animal fat, which is said to soften and sweeten the berries while lending a good flavor to the fat.

Conservation 1.

COMMENTS: In some places these can be gathered in great quantities. While they are well-known among northern edibles, they are not highly esteemed. The leaves are used to make an infusion to fight urinary tract infections. (Consult a health care provider for details.)

9 Arctic bearberry 🫐 1
Arctous rubra ✦ *Ericaceae* (Heath family)

QUICK CHECK: Trailing tundra shrub with deeply depressed leaf veins and bright red, translucent, soft, juicy, spherical fruit. **ID difficulty 1.**

DESCRIPTION: Trailing vine with stems resting directly on the ground, although the tips may be raised slightly. **Stems** to 2' (60 cm) long and 5 mm thick, but the thicker portions are usually covered with litter, leaving little more than the leafy branch tips visible. Branches numerous, at broad angles, bearing leaves only in the terminal 3–5" (8–13 cm). **Bark** brown with a shredding papery layer—on older stems this layer turns black, rotting as it sloughs off. New twigs are light brown, made angular by papery bark ridges. **Buds** large, about 5 mm, red, pointed, with fine, soft hairs on the scale margins. **Leaves** alternate, tardily deciduous to semi-evergreen (turning bright red in fall, dying but remaining attached into winter, but most eventually dropping), 1–1.6" (2.5–4 cm) long, obovate or spoon-shaped with a blunt tip, tapered to the base, hairless, sometimes with a reddish cast. Blades are flat and thin, the margins not downturned. **Veins** *net-like and deeply depressed above* to create a rough texture. **Margins** evenly *toothed*, the teeth blunt and pointing distally. **Petiole** flat and red, channeled, 20–30% of blade length, gently tapering into the leaf base. **Inflorescence** small clusters of up to 3 on short pedicels in early summer. **Flowers** urn-shaped, 4–5 mm long, 5-lobed, white to pink. **Berries** spherical, 6–10 mm, with a tiny calyx underneath. The skin is thin, semi-translucent, and dull red; the inside very juicy with 5 seeds. Ripens in mid to late summer.

HABITAT: Tundra, especially where rocky or gravelly, but occasionally in bogs. Native.

FOOD USE: The red **berries** usually rest directly on the ground. Their flavor is not particularly sweet nor sour, but the texture is pleasant and juicy. I like to suck on them while chewing gently and then spit out the seeds, but I don't think they'd make great pie or jelly.

COMMENTS: This fruit and the next species were traditionally eaten as last resorts, mixed with other berries to extend the food supply. A few botanists lump these two *Arctous* species together, but if you collect them they sure look, feel, and taste like different plants. **AKA** red alpine bearberry, *Arctostaphylos rubra*.

Related edible:

10 Black bearberry ✦ *Arctous alpina* 🫐 1

This is very similar to the red arctic bearberry, but it is characteristic of dry tundra and rock outcroppings at slightly higher elevations. The leaves are somewhat smaller on average, with *long hairs on the margins, especially near the base*. The blades are somewhat narrower,

more gently tapered into the petiole, less rounded at the tip, thicker and more deeply depressed by veinlets, which are *distinctly darkened* on the underside, forming a net-like pattern. The leaves are somewhere between deciduous and evergreen—they die in winter but remain attached, disintegrating in place. The fruit is slightly larger, ripens to black, and is less juicy than arctic bearberry. The flavor is boring, with a faint unpleasant aftertaste. **AKA** alpine bearberry, *Arctostaphylos alpina*.

GROUP 10 BROADLEAF SHRUBS WITH ORANGE TO RED BERRIES

The plants in this group represent a variety of families. All but one have edible berries; a few also provide edible greens, flowers, or teas. Some of our smaller trees with red berries will key here if they begin fruiting at an unusually small size. Likewise, unusually large specimens of some of these shrubs may key as trees. Berries are defined here as edible fleshy or juicy fruits less than 0.8" (2 cm) in the greatest dimension.

TENTATIVE IDENTIFICATION KEY TO GROUP 10
The key is not your final answer!

Leaves in opposing pairs.
  or Leaf compound, leaflets toothed. — **1. Red elderberry**
  Leaf simple, entire.
    Berries paired, pressed together, with multiple seeds. Honeysuckle (not edible, p. 657).
    or Berries single or in clusters of up to 7, seeds single.
      Bush thorny, leaves 3–4 x longer than wide, secondary veins obscure. — **2. Silver buffaloberry**
      Bush thornless, leaves less than twice as long as wide, secondary veins evident and depressed. — **3. Canada buffaloberry**
  Leaf simple, palmately lobed and toothed.
    Shrub over 8' (2.4 m) tall, berry clusters over 3" (8 cm) across, terminal leaves lobed. — **5. Highbush cranberry**
    Shrub under 6' (2 m) tall, berry clusters less than 2" (5 cm) across, terminal leaves not lobed. — **6. Squashberry**
or Leaves alternate.
  Leaves compound.
    or Pinnately compound with 5–9 serrated leaflets. — **7. Roses**
    Ternately compound, leaves stiff and evergreen with sharp points. — **8. Agarita**
  Leaves simple.
    Leaf margins smooth with no lobes or teeth.
      Berry with multiple seeds.
        Berry with an expanded pedicel and a 3–5-part calyx at the base.
          or or Leaves thin and deciduous; inland. — **9. Goji berry**
          Leaves semi-evergreen and succulent; coastal. — **10. Christmas berry**
        or Berry without a 5-part calyx at the base. — **12. Japanese barberry**
      Berry with a single seed.
        Berry covered with silvery scales, seed ridged, pointed at both ends. — **4. Autumnberry**
        Berry smooth and shiny; seed smooth with blunt ends. — **13. Spicebush**
    Leaves palmately lobed, margins toothed.
      or Berries smooth and hairless, on a drooping raceme. — **14. Red currant**
      Berries in an erect raceme, covered with musky gland-tipped hairs. — **15. Skunk currant**
    Leaves not lobed, margins toothed.
      Stems trailing along the ground in tundra. Arctic bearberry (p. 134).
      Stems standing upright.
        Berries in flat-topped clusters of 12–40. — **16. Red aronia**
        Berries in small umbels from twigs on long individual stems. Pin cherry (p. 102).
        Berries in drooping racemes; stems with 3-part thorns. — **11. European barberry**
        Berries single or in very short-stalked clusters from twigs.
          Leaves less than 1.5" (4 cm), tough, evergreen. — **17. Yaupon (berries not edible)**
          Leaves mostly over 2" (5 cm), thin, deciduous. Winterberry (not edible).

1   **Red elderberry**   🍇 1   ☕   📖 NG-410
Sambucus racemosa ✦ family *Adoxaceae*

QUICK CHECK: Arching shrub with pinnately compound leaves and large clusters of tiny red berries ripening in early summer. **ID difficulty 1.**

DESCRIPTION: Medium to large multi-stemmed shrub spreading by root suckers. **Stems** arching, up to 4" (10 cm) thick, often producing new shoots near the base. **Bark** smooth and light gray-brown with frequent large, warty lenticels. Bark on oldest trunks becomes furrowed with narrow plate-like or flaky ridges. **Twigs** very thick, the first-year growth greenish-brown with short hairs. **Buds** sometimes tiny and inconspicuous, but the *flower buds are large and almost spherical*, to 1 cm. They bulge away from the twig and have brown outer scales and green and purple inner scales. **Leaves** paired, pinnately compound, usually with 5 leaflets (occasionally 7). **Leaflets** lanceolate to ovate with acuminate tips and mostly asymmetrical bases. Side leaflets are almost sessile, but the terminal leaflet has a distinct petiolule. Both surfaces are hairy, but the lower is more so—especially along major veins. **Midvein** light in color and depressed above; secondary veins are slightly depressed, breaking up before reaching the margin. **Margins** sharply and finely serrated, the claw-tipped teeth pointing forward. **Petiole** 30–70 % of blade length, purplish, the petiole/rachis channeled and densely covered in short, soft hairs. **Inflorescence** an elongated to ball-like crowded panicle of usually well over 100, the branches often at right angles. **Flowers** (spring) 4–6 mm across with 5 tiny sepals and 5 blunt white petals strongly recurved to surround the ovary; 5 radiating filaments hold large yellow anthers. **Berries** (early summer) spherical, 3–6 mm, bright red, smooth and glossy, yellowish inside, containing 3–5 seeds.

CONFUSING SPECIES: Black elderberry (p. 163) is easy to tell apart in flower or fruit; the rest of the year it can be differentiated by its darker, glossier leaflets with longer petiolules and few to no hairs, the more deeply channeled hairless rachis, and the lack of bulging flower buds.

HABITAT: Disturbed forests, forest edges, brushy areas, young woods, steep slopes, usually on moderately rich soil. It does exceptionally well in the understory of pine plantations in locations that would normally not support pine, and in collapsed buildings. Native.

FOOD USE: The cooked **berries** can be eaten in sauces and soups or mixed with other fruit. The juice is a traditional marinade for salmon on the Northwest Coast. **Flowers** can be steeped for tea.

WARNING! Raw berries cause nausea; some people may be sensitive to them even cooked.

COMMENTS: Common opinion (mine included) does not hold these berries very palatable, but they were once an important food on the Northwest Coast, where they were stored in huge quantities by drying, and are still used to a lesser extent today. The flavor is not fruity like one might expect—it is more like a cross between tomatoes and squash, and the pulp is yellowish. There is a black-fruited form of this species, but I am not aware of it being found in our region.

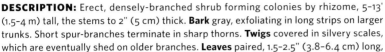

2 Silver buffaloberry 🍇 2
Shepherdia argentea ◆ family *Elaeagnaceae*

QUICK CHECK: Thorny shrub with narrow, blunt-tipped, silvery, entire leaves, tiny flowers, and small, orange-red, single-seeded berries. **ID difficulty 1.**

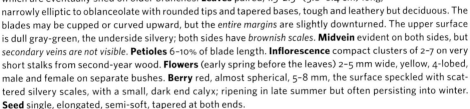

DESCRIPTION: Erect, densely-branched shrub forming colonies by rhizome, 5–13' (1.5–4 m) tall, the stems to 2" (5 cm) thick. **Bark** gray, exfoliating in long strips on larger trunks. Short spur-branches terminate in sharp thorns. **Twigs** covered in silvery scales, which are eventually shed on older branches. **Leaves** paired, 1.5–2.5" (3.8–6.4 cm) long, narrowly elliptic to oblanceolate with rounded tips and tapered bases, tough and leathery but deciduous. The blades may be cupped or curved upward, but the *entire margins* are slightly downturned. The upper surface is dull gray-green, the underside silvery; both sides have *brownish scales*. **Midvein** evident on both sides, but *secondary veins are not visible*. **Petioles** 6–10% of blade length. **Inflorescence** compact clusters of 2–7 on very short stalks from second-year wood. **Flowers** (early spring before the leaves) 2–5 mm wide, yellow, 4-lobed, male and female on separate bushes. **Berry** red, almost spherical, 5–8 mm, the surface speckled with scattered silvery scales, with a small, dark end calyx; ripening in late summer but often persisting into winter. **Seed** single, elongated, semi-soft, tapered at both ends.

CONFUSING PLANTS: Autumnberry has broader, larger, alternate leaves with more pointed tips and elongated fruit; the distribution scarcely overlaps.

HABITAT: Dry, well-drained soil in full sunlight. Typically found in ravines and on slopes and roadsides in prairie areas. Native.

FOOD USE: Ripe **fruit** can be collected by hand or, more efficiently, by shaking branches over a drop cloth. The flavor is better if the fruit sits on the bush red for a while. Buffaloberries can be eaten fresh or made into juice. After straining seeds out, the pulp is great for jams, jellies, pie, or fruit leather. **Conservation 1.**

COMMENTS: This is the Great Plains' answer to autumn-olives, only native. The fruit is often produced in great quantity, and the flavor is far superior to that of Canada buffaloberry.

3 Canada buffaloberry 🌿 1
Shepherdia canadensis + family *Elaeagnaceae*

QUICK CHECK: Thornless shrub with broad, entire leaves mottled with brownish scales, tiny flowers, and red, single-seeded fruits. **ID difficulty 1.**

DESCRIPTION: Medium-sized thornless shrub forming loose thickets 2–7' (0.6–2 m) tall, the stems leaning or arching. **Bark** dark gray-brown and rather smooth but minutely peeling. **Twigs** gray-green, mottled with rusty brown scales. *Where branches fork, the stem is bulged and appears jointed.* **Buds** small, often clustered, and covered with rusty scales. **Leaves** paired, broadly ovate or elliptic with rounded bases and blunt tips, 1–4" (2.5–10 cm) long, green above dotted with silvery scales, the underside with many rusty brown scales. Midvein and secondary veins are evident and slightly depressed above. Margins are entire and *the blade is slightly downcurved*, as is the tip. **Petioles** 5–15% of blade length, channeled, *nearly appressed to the stem*, the leaf blade diverging at an angle to the petiole. **Inflorescence** a short, compact spike of 4–12 from second-year wood, the pedicels very short. **Flowers** (spring) 3–5 mm across, light dull yellow, 4-lobed, the male and female on separate bushes. **Berry** almost spherical, 4–7 mm long, bright red with scattered brown scales, the skin thin, flesh juicy, with a small persisting end calyx; ripens in late summer. **Seed** single, *grooved, elongated, semi-soft*.

HABITAT: Well-drained sites, rocky or gravelly areas, in full to partial sunlight, typically in sparse woods or forest edges, especially along steep slopes, banks, rock outcroppings. Native.

FOOD USE: Gather **berries** when ripe in late summer and fall, use for juice or confections. **Conservation 1.**

COMMENTS: Canada buffaloberries are very bitter and most people who did not grow up eating them find them quite distasteful. Nevertheless, like many bitter foods this is an acquired taste—Canada buffaloberries have long been enjoyed by many Native American cultures and are traditionally beaten with oil to make a frothy dessert, aided by the high saponin content of the juice.

4 Autumnberry 3 📖 NG-321
Elaeagnus umbellata ✦ family *Elaeagnaceae*

QUICK CHECK: Entire, lanceolate, alternate leaves and elliptic red berries with silvery flakes on the surface, containing a single leathery seed. **ID difficulty 2.**

DESCRIPTION: Medium to large shrub with arching, clumped stems 6–16' (2–4 m) tall and up to 4" (10 cm) thick, typically forming dense thickets. **Bark** gray and nearly smooth on older stems. **Twigs** covered densely with soft red-brown scales, as are the small, blunt buds. Vigorous shoots may have large thorns, but many branches are thornless.
Leaves alternate, elliptic to lanceolate, angled at the base and blunt-pointed at the tip (smaller leaves may have rounded tips), tough and semi-leathery but deciduous, 1.5–4" (4–10 cm) long. **Blades** dark, dull green on top, hairless, and *silvery beneath, densely covered with soft scales*. **Midvein** and secondary veins are flat above and protruding below; *veinlets obscure* on both sides. **Margins** slightly downcurved, entire but often wavy. **Petioles** about 10% of blade length. **Inflorescence** (mid spring), despite the Latin name, is a short, compact, drooping *raceme* of 5–10, the pedicels unequal. **Flowers** dull creamy yellow, funnel-shaped, 5–8 mm long, abruptly spreading 5–7 mm wide into 4 triangular lobes. They have a cloyingly sweet smell. **Berries** ripen in late summer and fall, becoming orange or red spangled with silvery flakes. They are oblong (like an olive), 5–8 mm long, and indented at the tip. The juicy pulp contains a single grooved, leathery seed that is pointed at both ends.

CONFUSING PLANTS: Silver buffaloberry has narrower, blunt-tipped, paired leaves and more spherical berries.

HABITAT: well-drained disturbed ground such as old pastures, roadsides, gravel pits. Also does very well on poor, dry soils in full sun or partial shade, including in oak and pine woodlands. **I**

FOOD USE: Gather **berries** when fully ripe and soft; they may turn red well before developing their best flavor. They are highly variable in quality and timing from one tree to the next, but in general the flavor is tart but delicious when fresh. After straining the seeds, the pulp can be used for pie or jam, and also makes fantastic fruit leather. If the pulp is allowed to sit, the solids will naturally coagulate and separate from the juice, which is almost totally clear and can be excellent.

COMMENTS: This invasive shrub has taken over vast areas of the eastern U.S. and in many regions is the most abundant wild fruit. Single bushes may produce several gallons in a good year. Autumnberry has the ability to symbiotically fix nitrogen, giving it a competitive advantage on degraded sites. The fruit is remarkably high in lycopene, a phytonutrient that is believed to promote prostate health. **AKA** autumn-olive.

5 Highbush cranberry 🦫 2 📖 FH-318
Viburnum trilobum + family *Adoxaceae*

QUICK CHECK: Clusters of juicy red berries with a single flat seed; palmately lobed leaves. **ID difficulty 2.**

DESCRIPTION: Clump-forming shrub sometimes spreading by layering. **Stems** to 3" (8 cm) thick and 18' (5.5 m) tall, lanky in the shade. **Bark** relatively smooth and *light gray*. **Twigs** hairless, green at first turning pale gray, the buds large, plump, blunt, hairless, and shiny red or green. **Leaves** paired, 2–5" (5–13 cm) long, palmate with 3 main lobes, hairless or nearly so above and hairy below, mostly on the main veins. **Veins** *strongly depressed* above. **Margins** have large, blunt, irregularly spaced teethed. **Petioles** *red*, channeled, 20–30% of blade length, with large glands near the base of the leaf. **Inflorescence** a flat-topped, branching cluster (cyme) 2.5–5" (6–13 cm) across. The outer rim of the cluster has flat, sterile, "pretend" flowers 0.8" (2 cm) wide. The fertile flowers in the center are much smaller (3–6 mm), all of them crammed together. **Flowers** of both kinds are white and 5-lobed, the pistils and stamens protruding on fertile ones. **Berry** spherical to slightly elliptic, 8–12 mm, red, hard at first becoming soft and juicy, containing a *single, large, flat seed*. Ripens in late summer but persists through autumn.

▲ The southern edge of the range is uncertain because most taxonomists don't care anymore.

CONFUSING PLANTS: European guelder-rose *V. opulus* is sometimes considered the same species, but to foragers it certainly is not. The keyable difference is that the glands on the petiole of *V. opulus* are broader than tall and concave, while those of *V. trilobum* are taller than broad and not concave. When ripe you can just taste them; the American species tastes like cranberry, while the European is extremely bitter.

HABITAT: Moist, rich soil in full sun to moderate shade. Most common in river floodplains, shrub swamps, wetland margins, or young woods and field edges where the soil is moist. Native.

FOOD USE: The **berries** can be gathered quickly due to the large size and clustering habit. You can pick them as soon as they are red (even if still hard), and this is when the flavor is best. The berries occasionally remain until winter, but they will soften and shrink. They can be used to make jelly, juice, wine, or sauce. **Conservation 1.**

COMMENTS: The taste is reminiscent of bog cranberries. The flavor difference between the American and European plants is extreme and unmistakable. The latter commonly escapes from cultivation and predominates near most populated areas. Unfortunately, if you try to buy this shrub from the nursery trade, you are likely to get the European species mislabeled as the American.

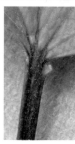

▲ Comparison of the leaf glands of American (right) and European (left) highbush cranberry.

6 Squashberry 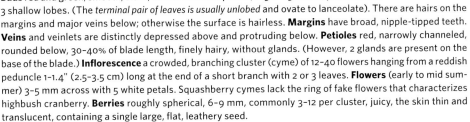 2
Viburnum edule + family *Adoxaceae*

QUICK CHECK: Waist to chest-high bush of rocky slopes with paired maple-like leaves and small clusters of red berries. **ID difficulty 1.**

DESCRIPTION: Mid-size shrub, not forming dense thickets. **Stems** one to few, erect to leaning, sometimes lying flat, 2–6' (0.6–2 m) long or tall, to 0.6" (15 mm) thick. **Bark** moderately smooth and light gray with occasional raised lenticels. **Twigs** green, smooth, hairless. **Buds** red and green, smooth, blunt, hairless. **Leaves** paired, 2–3.2" (5–8 cm), palmate with 3 shallow lobes. (The *terminal pair of leaves is usually unlobed* and ovate to lanceolate). There are hairs on the margins and major veins below; otherwise the surface is hairless. **Margins** have broad, nipple-tipped teeth. **Veins** and veinlets are distinctly depressed above and protruding below. **Petioles** red, narrowly channeled, rounded below, 30–40% of blade length, finely hairy, without glands. (However, 2 glands are present on the base of the blade.) **Inflorescence** a crowded, branching cluster (cyme) of 12–40 flowers hanging from a reddish peduncle 1–1.4" (2.5–3.5 cm) long at the end of a short branch with 2 or 3 leaves. **Flowers** (early to mid summer) 3–5 mm across with 5 white petals. Squashberry cymes lack the ring of fake flowers that characterizes highbush cranberry. **Berries** roughly spherical, 6–9 mm, commonly 3–12 per cluster, juicy, the skin thin and translucent, containing a single large, flat, leathery seed.

CONFUSING PLANTS: Maple-leaf viburnum *Viburnum acerifolium* has similarly shaped leaves, but the bark is darker and the bitter fruit ripens to blackish.

HABITAT: Open or semi-open bouldery or rocky slopes in or near boreal forest. Native.

FOOD USE: The **berries** can be eaten raw or cooked in jams, jellies, juice, or other preparations. Tastes very similar to highbush cranberry.

COMMENTS: This is our northernmost viburnum. **AKA** highbush cranberry, lowbush cranberry. (This seems like a contradiction; the first name lumps it with *V. trilobum* and compares it to bog cranberries, while the second name compares it to *V. trilobum*, which is taller.) Also pembina, mooseberry.

7   Rose   🍂 2   🌸 2   ☕   📖 IWE-319
genus *Rosa* ◆ *Rosaceae* (Rose family)

QUICK CHECK: Prickly shrubs with pinnately compound leaves and toothed leaflets; flowers with 5 broad petals; smooth-skinned, mealy, red fruit with a hollow, hairy center. **ID difficulty 1.**

COLLECTIVE DESCRIPTION: Small to medium-sized clone-forming shrubs spreading by suckers or stolons. **Stems** prickly or bristly, reddish or green, almost always less than 0.8" (2 cm) in diameter, with thin bark. **Leaves** alternate, pinnately compound with 3–11 leaflets (mostly 5–9), with conspicuous *wing-like stipules* attached along the base of the rachis. **Leaflets** lanceolate, ovate, or elliptic, with coarsely sharp-toothed margins. Side leaflets are sessile or nearly so. **Midveins** deeply depressed above; secondary veins are depressed, several, and straight. **Inflorescence** usually a branching cluster (although a few species have roses sometimes borne singly), each flower on a long pedicel. **Flowers** showy, fragrant, most often pink, with 5 narrowly tri-angular, long-pointed sepals and 5 broad-tipped petals that are separate at the base but usually overlapping. Stamens are numerous. **Fruits** (hips) spherical to ovoid or elliptic, the skin smooth and reddish, the flesh mealy or pulpy, usually in a thin layer. The center of the hip is hollow, where the several seeds are found mixed with hairs. Many hips have constricted, nipple-like ends and retain their 5-part calyces. They ripen in late summer to fall.

SPECIES: There are about 2 dozen species of wild roses in our region—too many to list here. They vary greatly in the quality of their fruits and flowers. I pro-vide photos of a few representatives so you can rec-ognize the group, and you can try out those in your area. The highly invasive Multiflora rose *R. multiflora* is unusual: The flowers are much smaller than those of our native roses and white. The hips are also small. While there is little pulp to be had from them, they have a nice tangy flavor. This shrub's long, arching stems have formidable prickles and often form impenetrable thickets. Rugosa rose *R. rugosa* has very large hips and keys out into group 6.

▲ Hips of smooth wild rose.

▲ Flower of a typical wild rose.

▲ Multiflora rose has small white flowers.

HABITAT: Disturbed open or semi-open sites ranging from dry sands to swamps, depending on species. Roadsides, ditches, stream edges, old fields, forest clearings and trails, lakeshores, swamp openings, beach dunes. Most species native.

FOOD USE: Flower **petals**, collected in early summer, can be used as a garnish or flavoring. Pulp of ripe **hips** can be used in breads, fruit leather, pies, jam, or the hips can be eaten fresh. Some people complain of the

hairs inside the hips irritating the digestive tract. This problem appears to depend on the species, the person, and the preparation. Larger hips can be cut in half and have the inner hairy portion scooped out. Flavorful hips can be steeped for a tea rich in vitamin C, or simmered and strained to make rose hip jelly. The young leaves, when dried, make a decent **tea**. **Conservation 1.**

COMMENTS: Most rose hips are bland and mealy. A few natives have good tasting hips, but the best-tasting species all seem to be introduced from Eurasia. However, all species are safe and wholesome, so feel free to try any rose flowers or hips you encounter.

◀ Tiny hips of multiflora rose.

▲ Wild rose leaves are pinnately compound.

◀ *Rosa canina*, our best tasting rose hip, is a European introduction.

8 Agarita 🍇 3
Mahonia trifoliata ✦ *Berberidaceae* (Barberry family)

QUICK CHECK: Evergreen shrub with compound leaves of 3 sessile leaflets, the lobe tips stiff with needle points; yellow flowers and bright red berries. **ID difficulty 1.**

DESCRIPTION: Shrub to 10' (3 m) tall. **Bark** gray to red brown on older stems, covered with small, thin scales. **Branches** stiff; twigs are smooth, red or green at first turning brown or gray. The wood is yellow. **Leaves** evergreen, alternate, compound with 3 sessile leaflets, on a reddish-green hairless petiole about equal to leaflet length. **Leaflets** 1–2.5" (2.5–6.4 cm) long, very stiff and tough, lanceolate in outline with 3–7 lobes, each lobe acuminate with a stiff, needle-like point. **Surface** hairless with *flat whitish veins* above, the lower surface paler. **Inflorescence** multiple short racemes of a few flowers borne at the same node, the pedicels 0.3–0.7" (8–18 mm). **Flowers** (February–April) bisexual, 9–12 mm across, with 6 sepals and 6 petals, alternating smaller and larger, all of them bright yellow and cupped with broad rounded tips and narrowed bases. The sepals are distant, while the petals overlap, and the two layers do not touch each other when open. One stamen is pressed against the center of each petal. **Fruit** oval to rounded, 7–10 mm, bright red, shiny, aromatic, containing several elliptic, crunchy seeds, ripening from mid April to early June.

HABITAT: Rocky, hilly, sunny, well-drained open woods or brushy country. Native. 🔥

FOOD USE: Ripe **berries** make an intensely sour but excellent juice that can be drunk diluted, used to make wine or jelly, or mixed with mild fruits to make leather.

COMMENTS: These can often be collected in great quantity, for the bushes are abundant and can yield heavily. Agarita is a very common shrub in the Texas Hill Country and is occasionally grown as a hedge. It is closely related to Oregon grape and contains berberine, for which it has been used medicinally in a similar fashion. A yellow dye can be made from the wood, especially of the root. **AKA** algerita, agarito, palo amarillo, and many other names.

9 **Goji berry** 2 2
Lycium barbarum ◆ *Solanaceae* (Nightshade family)

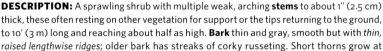

QUICK CHECK: Arching thorny shrub with clumped or alternate entire leaves of highly variable size; long red berries with many small seeds. **ID difficulty 2.**

DESCRIPTION: A sprawling shrub with multiple weak, arching **stems** to about 1" (2.5 cm) thick, these often resting on other vegetation for support or the tips returning to the ground, to 10' (3 m) long and reaching about half as high. **Bark** thin and gray, smooth but with *thin, raised lengthwise ridges*; older bark has streaks of corky russeting. Short thorns grow at scattered nodes but are not particularly sharp or stiff. **Leaves** 0.3-0.8" (8-20 mm) long on older wood, but may be up to 3" (8 cm) on new shoots. They are borne alternately on young shoots, and in clumps on older wood, the outer leaves of the clump much smaller than the central leaf. **Blades** thin, brittle, smooth, hairless, entire, elliptic to lanceolate or oblanceolate, the tips blunt-pointed or rounded. **Midvein** and secondary veins are slightly depressed above, protruding below; secondary veins are few and do not reach the margins. **Petioles** 10-20% of blade length, winged, the wing gradually widening into the leaf base. **Inflorescence** single or in clusters of up to 7 from leaf axils. **Flowers** (late spring through fall) 7-9 mm wide, the corolla tube-like with usually 5 (occasionally 4) spreading, light purple lobes. **Berry** elliptic, 0.3-0.7" (8-18 mm) long with smooth, bright-red skin, narrowed at both ends and *nipple-like at the base,* juicy inside with many small, flattened, whitish seeds. It hangs on a green pedicel about 0.8" (2 cm) long that *expands toward the tip* into an *irregular calyx with 3-5 unequal lobes.*

CONFUSING PLANTS: Barberries have no calyx at the base and have larger, harder seeds.

HABITAT: Disturbed wooded and brushy areas in partial shade: roadsides, old homesteads, urban woodlots, forest and road edges, brushy floodplains. Introduced.

FOOD USE: Gather the ripe **berries** from late summer to autumn and eat fresh or dried. Young **leaves** also make a decent raw green or potherb.

COMMENTS: Goji berries are popular as a health food and can be easily purchased in the dried form. They have long been used as food in their native China and have a reputation for promoting health and longevity. Long ago this berry was a popular ornamental here; it escaped from cultivation and has become locally common. **AKA** matrimony vine.

10 Christmas berry 🍇 2 🍃 2
Lycium carolinianum ✦ *Solanaceae* (Nightshade family)

QUICK CHECK: Sprawling thorny coastal shrub with arching pale branches, fleshy, almost needle-shaped leaves, and hanging glossy-red berries with numerous tiny seeds. **ID difficulty 1.**

DESCRIPTION: Shrub 4–10' (1.2–3 m) tall, the major branches large, often forking dichotomously, arching and sprawling, supporting scattered, short, thorn-tipped spur branches. **Stems** grow straight and vertical, shoot-like, with very short side branches, before arching over. Twigs are *very bumpy.* **Bark** smooth and light chalky gray. **Leaves** mostly *tufted* on older growth, alternate on shoots, evergreen or nearly so, sessile, *fleshy and succulent,* 0.2–1.2" (0.5–3 cm) long. Blades are linear or narrowly oblanceolate to club-shaped or almost needle-shaped, wider near the blunt tip and tapered to the base, with entire margins. **Midvein** flat to faintly depressed above; other veins not evident. **Flowers** (summer to winter, but mostly fall) bisexual, solitary from the leaf axils on drooping pedicels, tubular, the calyx and corolla both split into 4 (occasionally more) lobes. **Corolla** pale purplish-blue (fading to yellow), spreading 8–12 mm wide, the tube hairy inside, one stamen protruding at each cleft between lobes. **Fruit** shiny, red, 0.3–0.7" (8–18 mm) long, ovoid to elliptic, juicy, soft, ripening nearly year-round but mostly fall to midwinter, containing dozens of tiny seeds.

HABITAT: Full sun on beaches, margins of coastal wetlands (or ridges or mounds within them), shell mounds, ditches; occasionally on salt flats inland. Native.

FOOD USE: Ripe **fruit** can be eaten fresh or dried. Succulent salty **leaves** can be nibbled year-round.

COMMENTS: This close relative of the goji berry is even better and makes fun foraging at a time when few berries are ripe.

11 European barberry 🍇 3 🌿 1 ☕
Berberis vulgaris ✦ family *Berberidaceae*

QUICK CHECK: Thorny shrub with arching stems, clumped leaves with spiny margins, and small red fruit in hanging clusters. **ID difficulty 2.**

DESCRIPTION: Stems multiple, 4–9' (1.2–3 m) long; new stems straight and erect, older ones arching with drooping branches. **Bark** light green at first, becoming gray with a darker brown latticework of low, papery ridges. **Twigs** grooved, bearing scattered thorns in sets of 3, each 5–10 mm long, flattened, and broad at the base. There are 3 ridges *running down from each node onto the twig.* **Leaves** 0.3–2" (0.8–5 cm) long, alternate on new shoots but *borne in clumps of 2–9 on older wood,* each clump associated with a thorn and containing *leaves of varying size.* **Blades** broadly obovate to elliptic (narrower on older growth), hairless on both sides, slightly downcurved, the base tapered, the tip rounded but with a tiny extending bristle. **Midvein** slightly depressed; smaller veins mostly obscure or minutely depressed. **Margins** usually entire on the leaves of green shoots but leaves on older growth have *scattered bristle-teeth pointing forward.* **Petioles** wide and up to 100% of blade length—it is hard to say where the petiole ends and the leaf begins, and some leaves could be construed as sessile. **Inflorescence** a drooping raceme 1–2" (2.5–5 cm) long of up to 19 flowers on thin pedicels. **Flowers** (spring) 4–5 mm across, with 6 sepals and 6 blunt petals, all bright yellow. Stamens are hidden, pressed against the petals, and there is one large pistil. **Berry** elongated, almost cylindrical, often broader toward the black tip, 0.5–0.7" (13–18 mm) long, bright red, juicy when ripe in fall, borne on a very thin pedicel 4–7 mm long. **Seeds** dark, elongated, slightly curved, flat on one side, soft, one to a few per fruit.

▲ This plant has been eradicated from many areas and was once more widespread.

HABITAT: Old fields, forest edges, pastures, woodlots. Introduced. **I**

FOOD USE: Use the very sour **fruit** to make jam, jelly, or juice. The **leaves** are also sour and can be nibbled or steeped to brew a tart drink.

COMMENTS: Barberry was formerly cultivated for its tangy fruit. Thoreau (2002) reported gathering and selling bushel baskets of this berry in Massachusetts. After it was discovered that barberry was an alternate host for wheat stem rust, a concerted effort was made to eradicate it, especially in wheat-growing regions, but it remains rather common in some areas. Appalachian barberry *B. canadensis* is a similar native species confined to the southern Appalachians. It is shorter, has toothed leaves, and bears smaller clusters of less juicy fruit.

Related edible:

12 Japanese barberry ✦ *Berberis thunbergii* 1 🪴 1 ☕

This is a shorter bush, rarely more than chest-high. The stems more arching and less erect, and the thorn at each node is single. The leaves are entire, to 1.2" (3 cm) long. Flowers are produced in small umbel-like clusters of 1–4. The fruit is 7–9 mm long and mealy rather than juicy—not nearly as good as European barberry—but the tangy leaves are similar. Because Japanese barberry cannot serve as an alternate host for wheat stem rust, it has not been subject to eradication efforts. **I**

13 Spicebush 🏮 ☕
Lindera benzoin ✦ *Lauraceae* (Laurel family)

QUICK CHECK: Alternate, entire, aromatic leaves and red berries with yellowish flesh and a single dark seed. **ID difficulty 2.**

DESCRIPTION: Large shrub 4–12' (1.2–3.7 m) tall. **Bark** of trunks has no ridges or scales but many small raised bumps. Trunks tend to be crooked, and the branch angles wide. **Twigs** aromatic, thin and gray, hairless, conspicuously dotted with raised lenticels, with small rounded flower buds clustered around the nodes; new growth is green and hairy. **Leaves** alternate, entire, 2–7" (5–18 cm) long, thin and delicate, obovate to oval, acute at both ends, with soft hairs along the margin and main veins below. **Midvein** slightly depressed above; secondary veins few, broadly angled, and slightly depressed above; veinlets flat. **Petioles** 5–8% of blade length, finely hairy, grooved. **Flowers** in short-stalked clusters of 3–6 in early spring, each tiny and yellow with 3 *petals*. **Berries** oval, 8–10 mm long, hanging on short pedicels, the skin smooth, ripening to bright red on the outside, yellowish to pink inside, the flesh aromatic. **Seed** single, dark, elongated, smooth.

HABITAT: Moist, rich soil in moderate shade: hardwood forests, especially in valleys and on high river floodplains, or near lakes and ponds. Native.

FOOD USE: Gather ripe **fruits** from late summer through fall to use as a seasoning fresh or dried. I like the pulp better than the seed, so I separate them. Twigs can be collected at any time of year and steeped in hot water for **tea**. The **leaves** can also be used for tea, and the young ones can be chopped into dishes in small amounts for their distinct flavor. **Conservation 2/1.**

COMMENTS: Spicebush is a member of the laurel family, a group rife with aromatic oils. Other members of this family include cinnamon, sassafras, bay leaf, and avocado. Southern spicebush *Lindera melissifolia* is a rare species scattered in the Deep South. It may be similarly edible but it is protected and I have not tried it.

14 Red currant 🍓 3
Ribes triste ✦ *Grossulariaceae* (Gooseberry family)

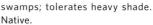

QUICK CHECK: Small shrub with maple-like leaves and hanging clusters of juicy, spherical red berries with multiple tiny seeds. **ID difficulty 1.**

DESCRIPTION: Low, spreading, unarmed shrub, rooting at branch tips and growing scattered or in loose colonies. **Stems** to 3' (1 m) tall, thin with few branches, dark red-brown and hairless; twigs faintly ridged, gray, and hairless. **Leaves** alternate, 1–3" (2.5–8 cm) long, palmate with 3 major lobes. The upper surface is sparsely hairy with all veins deeply depressed; the lower surface is moderately hairy. **Margins** finely hairy and double-serrated, the teeth blunt to rounded with light claw-tips. **Petioles** straight, 40–70% of blade length, often hairy. **Inflorescence** a *drooping raceme* of 6–20, often hidden under leaves, 1–2.5" (2.5–6 cm) long. **Flowers** appear almost flat, 3–5 mm across, *pinkish to purple-mottled*, with 5 narrow spreading petals (almost too small to see) and 5 much larger, broad, reflexed sepals (which at a glance appear to be the petals). The stamens are very short. **Berries** spherical, 5–9 mm, in clusters of 4–9, *smooth*, ripening to *translucent red*, containing several soft seeds. This is our only red-fruited currant with smooth skin.

HABITAT: Low, wet hardwood or conifer forests. Especially common on banks of small streams and in shrub swamps; tolerates heavy shade. Native.

FOOD USE: Eat fresh **berries** whole in midsummer, or juice them for drinking or making desserts. **Conservation 1.**

COMMENTS: The flavor of these is very similar to that of cultivated red currants, but wild red currants are smaller and grow on smaller bushes, usually widely scattered in small clusters. If you can manage to get any quantity, they make superb jam or jelly.

15 Skunk currant 1
Ribes glandulosum ⬩ *Grossulariaceae* (Gooseberry family)

QUICK CHECK: Low shrub, the leaves with pointed palmate lobes and depressed veins; strong musky smell and racemes of red berries with gland-tipped hairs. **ID difficulty 1.**

DESCRIPTION: Low unarmed shrub, the branches resting on the ground or weakly elevated, rooting at the nodes. **Bark** of older stems is smooth and blackish, often with exfoliating sections. Branches are hairless and the twigs are ridged or angled. A *musky odor* is released when leaves or bark are rubbed. **Leaves** alternate, 1–3.5" (2.5–9 cm) long, palmate, with 5–7 *pointed lobes*, the base heart-shaped. **Surface** dark green and hairless above with all *veins deeply depressed*; paler beneath with fine hairs, especially along the veins. **Margins** double toothed, the teeth large and blunt with nipple tips. **Petioles** about equal to blade length, not grooved, with fine hairs, the base expanded and sheath-like with a few glandular hairs. **Inflorescence** an *upright raceme* of 4–10, the rachis and pedicels with gland-tipped hairs. **Flowers** (late spring) bowl-shaped, to 5 mm across, the outer margin with an *alternating ring* of 5 pink petals and 5 much larger whitish-green sepals, both wider toward the tip and sometimes shallowly 3-lobed. **Fruit** a spherical red berry 6 mm in diameter, soft, translucent, and covered with *long glandular hairs*, ripening in mid to late summer, containing multiple soft seeds.

HABITAT: Shaded to partly sunny sites with thin, mossy soil, often over rock. Edges of boreal forests on rocky soil. Native.

FOOD USE: Ripe **berries** can be eaten raw or cooked. **Conservation 1.**

COMMENTS: This currant has a unique sour and musky flavor that many find disagreeable at first, but some develop a taste for it.

RELATED EDIBLES: Northern black currant *R. hudsonianum* has similar leaves and erect flower clusters, but the fruit ripens to purple-black. This species is found mostly in conifer swamps and, like skunk currant, is edible but not choice.

16 **Red aronia** 🐝 1
Aronia arbutifolia + *Rosaceae* (Rose family)

QUICK CHECK: Erect, lanky, colonial bog shrub with toothed simple leaves and clusters of red fruit in fall. **ID difficulty 2.**

DESCRIPTION: Shrub forming colonies by root suckers. **Stems** erect, thin and lanky with few *ascending branches*, 4–16' (1.2–5 m) tall, the bark dark gray. **Twigs** gray and woolly with large, pointed, red-tipped buds. **Leaves** alternate, 1.5–4" (4–10 cm) long, elliptic to obovate or oblanceolate, the base tapered and the tip abruptly pointed or blunt. Blades are glossy and hairless above, the underside *coated with fine wool.* **Midvein** depressed above, with a row of *tiny, dark-purple, raised gland-dots.* Secondary veins and veinlets are also depressed above. **Margins** serrated with small, blunt, purplish *gland-tipped* teeth. **Petioles** about 10% of blade length, covered in fine wool, with narrow, soft stipules attached at the base (often falling late in the season). **Inflorescence** a flat-topped, spreading, compact terminal cluster of 8–30, the stems densely woolly. **Flowers** (spring) with a 5-lobed calyx. The corolla is 9–12 mm across with 5 broad petals that are narrowed and fully separated at the base, pink becoming white. There are 5 pistils, and numerous stamens. **Berries** spherical, 7–9 mm, red, the surface with *fine wool*, the end with a *5-point dimple and a persistent calyx.* The flesh of somewhat dry pulp contains several soft seeds, ripening in fall but often persisting into winter.

HABITAT: Acidic moist ground in full to partial sun. Pond and lake margins, bogs, low spots in flatwoods, swamp openings, ditches. Native.

FOOD USE: The **fruits** are rather dry and astringent but can be good when mixed with blander fruits for leather, jelly, juice, or in baked goods. **Conservation 1.**

COMMENTS: This attractive shrub is often planted outside of it natural habitat as a landscape element. In such places it tends to grow faster and larger than in its natural boggy haunts. Unfortunately the fruit is not as juicy nor quite as flavorful as its dark-fruited cousin (p. 169). There is also a purple aronia, somewhere between the red and black aronia in most characteristics—and indeed, many taxonomists recognize it as no more than a hybrid between them. **AKA** red chokeberry. The chokeberries are placed in the genera *Photinia, Aronia, Sorbus,* and *Pyrus* by various taxonomists.

17 Yaupon
Ilex vomitoria ✦ *Aquifoliaceae* (Holly family)

QUICK CHECK: Evergreen holly with tiny, blunt-toothed, non-prickly, alternate leaves and red berries. **ID difficulty 3.**

DESCRIPTION: Large shrub or small tree 7–25' (2–8 m) tall, usually with multiple stems from the base and a dense crown of often twisted branches, often forming thickets. **Bark** is pale gray and smooth. Branches spread at broad angles, about 80°. **Twigs** very stiff, hairy at first but with age becoming hairless and slightly rough with a waxy feel. **Leaves** *almost evenly distributed along the twigs* and smallest branches for 14–20" (36–50 cm) back from the tip. They are alternate, not in plane, 0.5–1.6" (1.3–4 cm) long, elliptic, blunt at the base and tip. Blades are thick and tough, smooth, flat to slightly wavy, paler below, generally hairless (except along the top of the midvein when young). **Veins** *protrude* above and below. **Margins** down-rolled with a few, widely spaced, forward-pointing teeth, each tooth blunt with a tiny bristle. **Petioles** reddish, 3–5% of blade length, not channeled. **Flowers** (late spring) on short pedicels directly from the twigs, 4–6 mm across with a 4–5 lobed calyx and 4–5 united petals, whitish green to creamy. **Berry** spherical, 4–6 mm, bright red with yellow-orange pulp (**not edible!**) containing multiple seeds, borne singly but sometimes densely, directly from twigs on a stiff stem about 1/3 of its diameter. **Seeds** usually 4, shaped like a broken crescent, tan and faintly striped.

CONFUSING PLANTS: Other hollies either have pointed teeth or no teeth.

HABITAT: Coastal dunes, low woods, flatwoods, roadsides; dry, open hill country in Texas. 🔥

FOOD USE: Gather and dry the leaves and brew like green **tea. Conservation 1.**

COMMENTS: This is one of the few plants native to North America that contains caffeine. It is closely related to maté, a popular drink in South America. There are a few commercial enterprises selling wild-harvested yaupon leaves. Despite the Latin name, you can drink it in normal quantities without vomiting.

▲ Yaupon berries are not edible!

GROUP 11 BROADLEAF SHRUBS WITH BERRIES—NOT ORANGE TO RED

Berries are here defined as fleshy or juicy fruits less than 0.8" (2 cm) in the largest dimension. For all but one of the shrubs in this group the primary edible part is the fruit. Several of these species may occasionally grow to tree size and would then key into group 7.

TENTATIVE IDENTIFICATION KEY TO GROUP 11
The key is not your final answer!

Fruit ripens greenish.	1. Deerberry
Fruit ripens silver-gray.	2. Silverberry
Fruit ripens white.	3. Red-osier dogwood
Fruit ripens blue, purple, or black.	
Seed single.	
Seed somewhat to very flattened.	
Leaves ovate, elliptic, obovate, or lanceolate, not velvety; seeds very flattened.	4. Black haws
Leaves heart-shaped to nearly round, velvety; seeds somewhat flattened.	5. Hobblebush
Seed spherical to roughly oval.	
Leaves entire, evergreen. Red bay (see group 7).	
Leaves toothed, deciduous.	
Fruit in drooping racemes.	6. Chokecherry
Fruit hanging directly from branches in clusters.	7. Sandcherry
Seeds multiple.	
Leaves pinnately compound.	8. Black elderberry
Leaves simple, palmately lobed, alternate and tufted.	
Stems with sharp spines or bristles; fruit single or in umbels.	9. Gooseberry
Stems unarmed; fruit in hanging racemes.	
Leaves hairless, veins not depressed above.	10. Buffalo currant
Leaves hairy, veins strongly depressed above.	11. American black currant
Leaves simple, not lobed.	
Leaves paired.	
Leaves entire, fruit elongated and blue.	12. Blue honeysuckle
Leaves toothed.	
Leaves broadly elliptic, fruit black. Common buckthorn (not edible, p. 660).	
Leaves lanceolate, fruit bright pink-purple.	13. Beautyberry
Leaves alternate.	
Leaves with prominent gland-tipped teeth.	14. Black aronia
Leaves entire or with tiny teeth.	
Fruit lacking a calyx, in tiny umbels, with 3 large seeds; leaves with deeply depressed secondary veins reaching margins.	15. Carolina buckthorn
Fruit with calyx lobes or a ring at the tip, in racemes; seeds tiny; secondary veins less depressed, breaking up before the margins.	
Leaf underside dotted with small, yellow, resinous glands; seeds crunchy.	
Compact raceme without bracts.	16. Black huckleberry
Loose, dangling raceme with bracts.	17. Dangleberry
Leaf underside not dotted with resinous glands.	
Leaf tough and leathery, seeds crunchy.	18. Farkleberry
Leaf not leathery, seeds soft.	
Fruit thick-skinned, musky-scented.	1. Deerberry
Fruit thin-skinned, not musky.	
Bush taller than 4' (1.2 m).	19. Highbush blueberry
Bush shorter than 4'.	
Leaves much longer than fruit diameter.	20. Lowbush blueberry
Leaves about as long as fruit diameter.	
Fruit black, ripens May–June; leaves pointed.	21. Mayberry
Fruit blue, ripens July–August; leaves blunt.	22. Bilberry

1 Deerberry 🦌 2
Vaccinium stamineum ✦ *Ericaceae* (Heath family)

QUICK CHECK: Branchy erect shrub with alternate, entire, blunt leaves; dangling spherical greenish fruit in clusters with miniature leaves. **ID difficulty 1.**

DESCRIPTION: Spreading to leaning, much branched shrub 3-8' (1-2.5 m) tall, the branches almost horizontal. Bark of older stems peels in thin brown strips. **Twigs** very thin, *minutely hairy*, the buds of flowering branches notably plumper than the buds of leafy shoots. **Leaves** alternate, thin but leathery, bluish-white beneath, entire (rarely with a few teeth near the base), broadly elliptic to obovate, the base heart-shaped to rounded, the tips blunt-pointed to rounded. On branch tips the leaves are up to 3" (8 cm) long, but *at the base of new branches there are 2-4 miniature leaves*. The blades are hairless above except on the midvein, hairy on the margins, and hairy below, especially on major veins. **Veins** (including the midvein) lightly depressed above; secondary veins are angled 50-70°. **Petioles** 2-5% of blade length, broadly channeled, minutely hairy. **Inflorescence** a raceme of 3-8, *interrupted by tiny leaves*; there may also be single flowers hanging from the axils of larger leaves on flowering branches. **Flowers** bell-like, drooping, 5 mm across, with a small green 5-lobed calyx, 5 spreading triangular corolla lobes, and 10 *protruding dull orange stamens tightly packed around a style protruding twice as far*. **Berry** roughly spherical, 5-13 mm in diameter with a calyx at the end, hanging on a thin pedicel slightly longer than the fruit's diameter. It ripens to green, yellow, or occasionally reddish in late summer and develops an odd musky odor. The skin is thick and tough with nearly colorless pulp inside, containing many soft seeds. Some populations in the Deep South have purple-black fruit on much taller bushes.

▲ Despite being green, these deerberries are ripe.

HABITAT: Dry woods in moderate shade, especially under hickory, oak, and pine. Common on rock outcrops and poor soil. Native. 🔥

FOOD USE: Gather **berries** in late summer or autumn by hand. They can be eaten fresh or dried, and used in jams, pies, and preserves. The skins are tougher than blueberry skins, so you may want to run these through a fruit strainer. **Conservation 1.**

COMMENTS: This common and widespread berry is often disdained because it is not like the blueberries to which it is closely related—but some people enjoy its unique flavor. This plant is highly variable in size, pubescence, and fruit color across its range and has been given a number of names and divided into several subspecies. It is so different from other blueberries that some have placed it in its own genus, *Polycodium*. **AKA** squaw huckleberry in older literature.

2 Silverberry 🍓 1
Elaeagnus commutata ✦ family *Elaeagnaceae*

QUICK CHECK: Colonial thornless shrub with alternate, entire leaves covered with silvery scales; fruits silver-green. **ID difficulty 1.**

DESCRIPTION: Shrub 3–8' (1–2.5 m) tall, spreading by suckers to form loose but often extensive colonies that appear *silver-gray from a distance*. **Stems** not clumped, erect, generally less than 1" (2.5 cm) thick. The form is taller than wide with a narrow crown, the branches short. **Bark** gray-brown and generally smooth but peeling erratically with random stretch marks and scattered transverse lenticels. **Twigs** red-brown, densely *covered with shiny, darker brown scales* that fade to gray in the second year. **Leaves** simple, alternate, hairless, highly variable in size, 0.6–3.5" (1.5–9 cm) long—the smaller leaves are elliptic and blunt, the larger ones ovate and pointed. The surface is soft, almost velvety below, *covered with reflective scales* that are silvery above, silver and reddish on the underside. **Margins** entire and *downcurved*. **Midvein** slightly depressed above; secondary veins flat to slightly raised above. **Petioles** 5% of blade length, broadly and shallowly channeled. **Inflorescence** small clusters from leaf axils. **Flowers** (early summer) with a tubular base 7–9 mm long and four yellow sepal lobes (which look like petals). **Fruit** (late summer) slightly oblong to spherical, 12–14 mm long, dimpled at both ends, *dull gray-green*, the sides sometimes ridged, on a pedicel 20% of its length. The surface is slightly bumpy and not glossy; *flesh is dry, powdery-spongy, and greenish*. **Seed** single, large, leathery, *football-shaped, ridged and striped lengthwise*.

CONFUSING PLANTS: Russian-olive (p. 105) has much narrower leaves and grows to tree size; the fruit is smaller but similar.

HABITAT: Forest edges, stream banks, meadows, thickets, sparse woods, brushy prairies, and other sunny situations. Native. 🔥

FOOD USE: The **berries** ripen in late summer or early fall and are dry, mealy, and somewhat astringent, much like those of Russian-olive. They can be eaten raw but few people find them appealing; they are better cooked, strained, and mixed with other fruit. **Conservation 1.**

COMMENTS: Not well known, not well liked, but often available in great quantity for anybody who wants a bland mealy fruit almost as good as a Russian-olive. The seeds are sometimes dried and used for necklace beads or pea-shooter projectiles. **AKA** wolfberry.

▲ The silvery foliage stands out at a distance.

155

3   Red-osier dogwood 🍇 1
Cornus stolonifera ✦ family *Cornaceae*

QUICK CHECK: Clump-forming shrub with paired, entire leaves, reddish or green bark, and clusters of soft white berries. **ID difficulty 2.**

DESCRIPTION: Clumping shrub 5-12' (1.5-4 m) tall, sometimes spreading by layering. Stems 0.5-2" (1.3-5 cm) in diameter, erect. **Bark** smooth, yellow to green in summer, *bright red in winter*, with scattered, light-colored, raised corky lenticels. New growth is green or red, densely covered with short hair, often angled. **Leaves** simple, paired, entire, ovate to elliptic, 2-4" (5-10 cm) long, the bases angled and the tips pointed, both surfaces with fine appressed hairs. **Veins** strongly depressed above and protruding below; secondary veins arch toward the tip, running just inside the margin. **Petioles** 18-25% of blade length, reddish, channeled, fine-hairy. **Inflorescence** a dense, flat-topped to rounded cluster (cyme) of 30-140. This shrub blooms twice per growing season—once in spring and once in midsummer as the fruit from the first flowers is ripening. **Flowers** 5 mm across with 4 sharp-tipped, ovate, white petals and 4 protruding stamens. **Berries** spherical, 5-8 mm, white, smooth-skinned, with a remnant protruding style. The juicy flesh contains one seed. Ripens in both mid summer and fall.

CONFUSING PLANTS: Silky dogwood *C. amomum* often has reddish stems, but it has less glossy bark and its berries ripen to blue.

HABITAT: Low, wet, or poorly drained ground in full to partial sun, such as shrub swamps, lake edges, marshes, ditches, sunny streamsides, and flat areas of clay soil. Native.

FOOD USE: The **berries** ripen in mid to late summer and can be eaten fresh but are bitter. **Conservation 1.**

COMMENTS: This is one of the most widespread and abundant shrubs in North America, being especially common in the North. Like Canada buffaloberry, the fruit is bitter and unpalatable to most who try it. After having nibbled these occasionally over the years I have grown to enjoy them in small quantities. Like beer, it is an acquired taste; unlike beer, there are no country songs about it.

4 Black haws 🐝 2 📖 FH-311
genus *Viburnum* (in part) ✦ family *Adoxaceae*

▲ Composite range.

QUICK CHECK: Paired, unlobed leaves and cymes of elliptic, black, pulpy (not juicy) fruit with a single flattened seed. **ID difficulty 2.**

DESCRIPTION: Large shrubs forming thickets, or small trees to 25' (8 m) tall, with multiple erect trunks, often spreading by suckers. When invading sunny locations these plants are often shrubby; in moderate competition they are more likely to have single trunks and be tree-like. **Bark** of young stems dark brown and smooth with a thin, peeling cuticle and scattered brown lenticels; older bark composed of small dark gray plates or blocks separated by narrow fissures. **Leaves** paired, simple, unlobed, broadly elliptic to lanceolate or obovate, smooth above, the margins finely toothed. **Petioles** 5-20% of blade length, often with a *winged or bumpy margin*. **Inflorescence** (late spring or early summer) a flat-topped crowded cluster (cyme) of 12-40 flowers 2-5" (5-13 cm) across. **Flowers** 5 mm across, bell-like, white, with 5 triangular lobes, 5 protruding stamens, and a single 3-lobed stigma. **Fruit** slightly oblong to nearly spherical, 0.3-0.6" (8-15 mm) long, black when ripe, sometimes coated with bloom, smooth at first but *soon becoming wrinkly*, the flesh *pulpy but not juicy*, containing a single large, flattened, leathery, oval seed (like a watermelon seed). The berries ripen in fall, in drooping clusters with reddish pedicels.

CONFUSING PLANTS: Arrowwoods (closely related) are smaller shrubs with smaller, extremely bitter fruit in smaller clusters. Their teeth are larger and more prominent and have secondary veins terminating in them. You will not be harmed by tasting an arrowwood berry, but stop there.

HABITAT: Open woods, forest edges, swamp margins, brushy areas, river floodplains, steep slopes—in a variety of soil conditions. See individual species for specifics. All species are native.

FOOD USE: Gather **berries** in fall when they are black and soft; the clusters make them easy to pick in quantity. They can be eaten raw, or they can be simmered in a small amount of water and run through a strainer to separate the pulp from the seeds. The flavor is uniquely sweet and reminiscent of a mixture of prunes and bananas. The pulp can be dried as fruit leather or used in quick breads like mashed banana. It can also be used as the base for non-jelled fruit spreads.

COMMENTS: All of these have good fruit that is similar but not identical in flavor. The group is easy to identify, but the species can be somewhat tricky. It is not vital to know which kind of black haw you are eating. These berries often crop heavily in full sun. Black haws are among the last wild berries to ripen. They are easy to grow and well worth planting or encouraging for wildlife and human food.

Species:

Nannyberry ✦ *Viburnum lentago*

This plant has ovate leaves 2.5-5" (6-13 cm) long, hairless on both sides, the tips pointed, the margins finely toothed, the teeth with extended nipple tips. The petioles are conspicuously but irregularly winged. The buds are elongated like a bird's beak. Nannyberry likes moist to mesic rich soil and is most common on river floodplains, shrubby wetland margins, forest edges, old fields, fence rows, and roadsides. It has the largest leaves, fruit, and fruit clusters of the black haw group.   ▼ Flower bud.

157

4 Black haws (continued)

Wild raisin ◆ *Viburnum cassinoides* and *Viburnum nudum*

These two are sometimes considered separate species, and sometimes lumped together. Both have elliptic to obovate leaves 2–5" (5–13 cm) long with margins that are entire or wavy-toothed. These species inhabit wet, acidic soils in shrub swamps, lake edges, and bog margins—*V. cassinoides* in the North and *V. nudum* in the South. **AKA** withe-rod, possum-haw.

Common black haw ◆ *Viburnum prunifolium*

This species has ovate elliptic leaves 1–2.8" (2.5–7 cm) long and hairless on both sides. The stems tend to be more densely clumped than those of nannyberry. Petioles are scarcely if at all winged, and the buds are pointed but shorter than those of nannyberry. The fruit averages slightly smaller and is borne in slightly smaller clusters. Common black haw likes disturbed habitats and young woods on dry, well-drained sites; it is characteristic of oak-hickory forests and savannahs. 🔥

Rusty black haw ✦ *Viburnum rufidulum*

Grows in upper floodplains and dry, disturbed, rocky or sloped woods of the Southeast. Its small leaves are 1.5–2.5" (4–6 cm), shiny, thick, and much broader than those of other blackhaws, sometimes nearly round, yet with the tip abruptly pointed. Veins are nearly flat above. The petioles are broad and rusty-hairy, as are the buds. The fruit is large with prominent bloom. 🔥

Dwarf black haw ✦ *Viburnum obovatum*

A small species with small, nearly entire, obovate to spoon-shaped or narrowly elliptic, hairless leaves 0.8–2" (2–5 cm) long, evergreen or semi-evergreen. The petioles are extremely short. Both the fruits and the clusters are small. This species inhabits floodplains, wetland margins, and moist depressions in the extreme Southeast. It is listed by a broad assortment of common names.

5   Hobblebush 🦫 2
Viburnum alnifolium ◆ family *Adoxaceae*

QUICK CHECK: Shrub with very large, nearly round, paired leaves with prominently depressed veins; dark fruit in clusters on pink stems. **ID difficulty 1.**

DESCRIPTION: Shrub 2–12' (0.6–3.7 m) tall, scattered or forming loose thickets. **Stems** to 1.5" (4 cm) thick, not clumped, standing erect or leaning and nearly prostrate, often *rooting where the branches touch the ground*. **Bark** thin, purplish-gray to brown, russet-cracked with scattered lenticels, especially below—the larger of these raised as bumps. **Twigs** sparse and thick, dark purple-green, with scattered clumps of dense, cinnamon-brown hairs. **Buds** large, *naked*, terminal, sometimes 2 or 3 clustered at the twig tips, woolly, yellowish to orange-brown, 0.5–1" (13–25 mm) long; *parallel grooves* from secondary veins are already visible in the bud. **Leaves** paired, conspicuously large, 4–10" (10–25 cm) long and nearly as wide, broadly ovate to nearly rounded with an abruptly-pointed tip and a symmetrical, heart-shaped base. Both surfaces are soft-hairy at first, but the top eventually becomes hairless. **Margins** finely toothed. **Petioles** 6–12% of blade length, rounded, not channeled, with short, clumpy, glandular hairs extending onto the midvein. **Veins** depressed above and protruding below; the secondary veins are numerous and prominent. **Inflorescence** (late spring) a flat-topped cluster (cyme) 3–5" (8–13 cm) across with 20–60 flowers, the *outer ones larger and showy but lacking sexual parts*. **Flowers** 3–4 mm wide, white with 5 petals. **Fruit** oval, 6–9 mm long, smooth and shiny, red at first, ripening to black and very soft with black pulp; pedicels woolly and pinkish. **Seed** somewhat flattened with a light groove and dark line down each face—plumper than other viburnum seeds.

HABITAT: Wooded ravines and moist rocky slopes. Native.

FOOD USE: Collect **berries** in late summer to early autumn. The whole cluster does not ripen at once. These are softer and juicier than black haws but harder to collect in quantity. **Conservation 1.**

COMMENTS: This is one of our most distinctive and attractive shrubs. It is sometimes called moosewood. Because striped maple is also sometimes called moosewood, and because striped maple and hobblebush often grow together, some people have come up with the cockamamie idea that they are two genders of the same plant. Um, no.

6 Chokecherry 🥀 2 📖 FH-214
Prunus virginiana ✦ Rosaceae (Rose family)

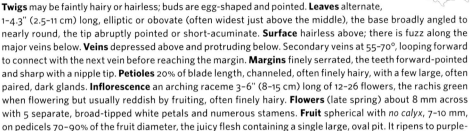

QUICK CHECK: Shrub or small tree with purple-black, single-stone fruit in racemes. **ID difficulty 2.**

DESCRIPTION: Large thornless shrub or small tree, often cloning by root suckers to form small colonies. **Trunks** commonly 6–16' (2–5 m) tall but occasionally much larger. **Bark** dark gray with reddish brown lenticels, becoming shallowly grooved on older trees. **Twigs** may be faintly hairy or hairless; buds are egg-shaped and pointed. **Leaves** alternate, 1–4.3" (2.5–11 cm) long, elliptic or obovate (often widest just above the middle), the base broadly angled to nearly round, the tip abruptly pointed or short-acuminate. **Surface** hairless above; there is fuzz along the major veins below. **Veins** depressed above and protruding below. Secondary veins at 55–70°, looping forward to connect with the next vein before reaching the margin. **Margins** finely serrated, the teeth forward-pointed and sharp with a nipple tip. **Petioles** 20% of blade length, channeled, often finely hairy, with a few large, often paired, dark glands. **Inflorescence** an arching raceme 3–6" (8–15 cm) long of 12–26 flowers, the rachis green when flowering but usually reddish by fruiting, often finely hairy. **Flowers** (late spring) about 8 mm across with 5 separate, broad-tipped white petals and numerous stamens. **Fruit** spherical with *no calyx*, 7–10 mm, on pedicels 70–90% of the fruit diameter, the juicy flesh containing a single large, oval pit. It ripens to purple-black (occasionally red) in late summer to fall.

CONFUSING PLANTS: Glossy buckthorn (p. 661) has entire leaf margins and fruit hanging directly from branches, with 2–3 seeds. **Common buckthorn** (p. 660) has thorns, and fruit like glossy buckthorn. Black cherry (p. 101) has narrower, shinier leaves with flat veins above and fruit with a tiny calyx at the base.

HABITAT: Young woods, forest edges, open woodlands, fencerows, floodplains, roadsides. Native. 🔥

FOOD USE: Fully ripe **fruit** is black and detaches easily from its stem. These can be boiled and strained to make juice or jelly. They can also be strained raw to remove the seeds and the pulp used for jam or fruit leather. Chokecherries are traditionally pounded with the pits included and then fermented, cooked, or sun-dried before eating. Raw kernels should not be eaten in large quantities.

COMMENTS: This is the most widespread North American tree or shrub producing edible fruit. The cherries are often remarkably abundant and have been a staple food in some regions. As traditionally eaten, many of the calories come from the oil-rich pits. Many white authors, without adequate evidence, warn against this traditional use—but clearly Native Americans figured out how to make the seeds a wholesome part of their food supply.

7. Sandcherry 🍇 2 📖 NG-299
Prunus pumila, P. susquehanae + Rosaceae (Rose family)

QUICK CHECK: Shrub with small, narrow leaves and purple-black fruit with a single hard stone. **ID difficulty 1.**

DESCRIPTION: Low shrubs 1–6' (30–180 cm) tall, smaller plants often laying prostrate or decumbent, larger stems weakly erect to leaning, the branches rather sparse. **Bark** dark with light-colored, transverse, elongated lenticels, covered with a thin, light-colored cuticle that eventually flakes off. **Leaves** alternate, 1–2.2" (2.5–5.5 cm) long, oblanceolate to elliptic, tapered to the base and usually broader toward the tip, the blades often somewhat folded along the midvein, hairless on both sides. **Veins** and veinlets nearly flat above. **Margins** have small, widely spaced, non-glandular teeth (but the proximal quarter lacks teeth). **Petioles** channeled, reddish, 10–30% of blade length. **Inflorescence** an umbel of 2–4 attached directly to the twig, usually at the base of a short, spur-like branch. **Flowers** (late spring) 9–12 mm across with 5 broad, separate white petals, narrowed at the base, with numerous stamens. **Fruit** spherical to slightly oblong, 0.3–0.7" (8–18 mm) long, ripening to dark purple-black, with a single, large, hard stone.

SPECIES: There are two very similar species. *P. pumila* grows larger and has narrower leaves; the cherries are larger and taste better. It grows primarily on sandy prairies or savannahs and beaches. *P. susquehanae* rarely exceeds knee-high and has broader leaves and smaller cherries that usually do not taste as good. It can be found in pine barrens but is also characteristic of sterile rocky slopes and hilltops. *P. susquehanae* has minutely hairy twigs; *P. pumila* has hairless twigs.

HABITAT: Beaches, sand dunes, sandy prairies, pine and oak barrens. Native. 🔥

FOOD USE: Gather **cherries** when they are dark purple-black and soft. They can be eaten fresh, pitted and dried, or made into jam, jelly, juice, or pie. **Conservation 1.**

COMMENTS: This has the largest fruit of our wild cherries, but it is the smallest plant. The flavor is highly variable from one bush to another—the best ones are delicious, but some are quite astringent.

8 Black elderberry 🦌 2
Sambucus canadensis • family *Adoxaceae*

QUICK CHECK: Shrub with pinnately compound leaves and broad cymes of numerous small 5-petaled flowers followed by tiny, dark berries. **ID difficulty 2.**

DESCRIPTION: Multi-stemmed shrub suckering to form colonies. **Stems** 4–15' (1.2–4.5 m) tall (occasionally taller in the South), weak, erect, with few branches. **Twigs** very thick and hairless with thick white pith. **Buds** tiny—especially in proportion to the twigs. **Bark** thin and gray with scattered, raised, wart-like lenticels. **Leaves** paired, pinnately compound, 14–22" (36–56 cm) long, with 5–9 (usually 7) leaflets. Leaves are occasionally twice compound, with a few rachis branches that divide into 3 leaflets. **Leaflets** lanceolate to ovate, 2–5" (5–13 cm) long, the bases rounded and the tips long-pointed, often folded along the midvein, sessile or on short petiolules up to 10% of blade length. The upper surface is nearly hairless; the underside usually has sparse hair along major veins. **Midvein** raised in a gentle valley above, protruding below. Secondary veins 45°, arching toward the tip, faintly depressed above. **Margins** serrated with sharp, forward-pointing, claw-tipped teeth. **Petiole** channeled and *green*, the channel becoming narrower distally. **Inflorescence** a flat-topped cluster (cyme) 4–10" (10–25 cm) across containing dozens to a few hundred flowers. **Flowers** (early to mid summer) 4–7 mm across, with a tiny calyx, 5 recurved white petals joined at the base, and 5 spreading stamens. **Berries** spherical, 5–6 mm, purple-black, containing several small seeds, ripening mid to late summer.

CONFUSING PLANTS: Water hemlock (p. 668) could be confused in flower, but has a compound umbel rather than a cyme. *Sambucus ebulus*, a possibly toxic European elder that has been found at a very few sites in North America, is herbaceous, typically just a few feet high, and has clusters of black berries pointing skyward rather than drooping.

HABITAT: Rich, moist soil in full to partial sun. Common in ditches, fencerows, streamsides, floodplains, pond margins, and barnyards. Native.

FOOD USE: Pick whole clusters of **berries** and remove from the stems with fingers or a fork, or by freezing the whole clusters and smacking them inside a bucket. For juice, a steam juicer yields better flavor than boiling. Drying whole fruit greatly improves the flavor. Elderberry is also a popular wine. **Flowers** are steeped to make tea or thrown into fritters or other baked goods. Both flowers and fruit should be removed from the stems, although small amounts of stem are harmless.

COMMENTS: Some botanists consider this to be the same species as the European black elder *S. nigra*. In my opinion the fresh fruit is only mediocre in flavor, but its abundance makes it an attractive foraging option. Some studies have shown elderberries reducing the symptoms of influenza. **AKA** American elder.

WARNING: Elderberries cause gastric upset in some individuals, particularly when raw and if the seeds are ingested.

9   Gooseberry 🍓 3 📖 IWE-129
genus *Ribes* (in part) ◆
Grossulariaceae (Gooseberry family)

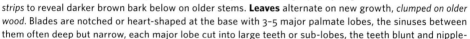

QUICK GROUP ID: Thorny shrubs with alternate or tufted, palmately lobed leaves; dangling spherical berries contain numerous small, soft seeds. **ID difficulty 1.**

GROUP DESCRIPTION: Multi-stemmed, clump-forming shrubs 2.5–8' (75–245 cm) tall, the **stems** with scattered *needle-like bristles* and *stout spines at the nodes.* Main stems are dominant and the branches short; new stems are erect but outer, older stems *arch* and sometimes root at the tips. **Bark** light and thin on new growth, peeling in *papery lengthwise strips* to reveal darker brown bark below on older stems. **Leaves** alternate on new growth, *clumped on older wood.* Blades are notched or heart-shaped at the base with 3–5 major palmate lobes, the sinuses between them often deep but narrow, each major lobe cut into large teeth or sub-lobes, the teeth blunt and nipple-tipped. **Surfaces** hairy on both sides (but variably so); *major veins are strongly depressed above* and protrude below. **Petioles** 60–100% of blade length, grooved or channeled. **Flowers** (late spring to early summer) 5–10 mm long, single or in small, short-stalked umbels of up to 3, with a pair of tiny bracts on each pedicel. **Calyx** tubular, splitting at the end into 5 greenish-white *reflexed lobes.* **Petals** 5, smaller and hard to see, whitish, projecting forward. In the center is a *cluster of parallel stamens, not spreading,* and projecting at least slightly past the petals. **Berries** spherical, 0.3–0.6" (8–15 mm), the skin tough and often partly translucent, lined lengthwise, with beak-like dried flower remnants projecting from the end; pulpy-juicy and faintly purplish to dark purple, containing numerous small seeds and not detaching readily from the pedicel when ripe in mid to late summer.

HABITAT: Forest openings, swamps, rocky slopes, brushy areas, pastures. All species native.

FOOD USE: Gather **berries** when soft and purple and eat them fresh or cooked. The stems, skins, and dried flower parts are tough and best strained out. Clean pulp is great for pies, jam, or fruit leather, and combines well with milder fruits. Nearly-ripe green fruit can be mixed with water, blended, and strained to make a lemonade-like drink. **Conservation 1.**

Missouri gooseberry *R. missouriense.* ▲ ▼

COMMENTS: Gooseberries are common and all species have good flavor—they are not nearly as variable as their cousins the currants. Because gooseberries are alternate hosts of white pine blister rust there was a concerted effort for several decades to eliminate them, resulting in the destruction of millions of bushes. They have been exterminated from some large sections of public forest land. Later it was realized that this didn't do much to help the white pines because the spores can travel long distances on the wind. A few of the more common species are photographed here.

▲ Northern gooseberry *R. oxyacanthoides.*
Prickly gooseberry *R. cynosbati.* ▶

10 American black currant 🌳 2
Ribes americanum ✦
Grossulariaceae (Gooseberry family)

QUICK CHECK: Unarmed chest-high shrub with palmately lobed leaves and hanging clusters of dark fruit. **ID difficulty 1.**

DESCRIPTION: Multi-stemmed, clump-forming shrub to 5' (1.5 m) tall. **Stems** erect at first, often leaning or arching later, unarmed, bearing few branches, with *3-angled* and finely hairy twigs. **Bark** smooth red-brown with light brown papery ridges. **Leaves** alternate on new shoots, tufted on older growth, 0.6–2.8" (1.5–7 cm) long, palmately 3 or 5 lobed, the lobes pointed. Blades nearly hairless above and sparsely hairy below, the hairs concentrated in major vein axils; there are *numerous yellow gland-dots, especially on the underside*. **Veins** strongly depressed above and protruding below. **Margins** doubly toothed; leaves on new growth have ciliate margins. **Petioles** 80–100% of blade length and channeled. Petioles of the *smaller leaves in each tuft have broad sheaths with ciliate margins*. **Inflorescence** a drooping raceme of 5–9, the pedicels shorter than the flowers, each with a lanceolate bract. **Flowers** bell-shaped, 7–9 mm long, light yellow, with 5 reflexed sepals and 5 smaller, overlapping, forward-pointing petals. **Berries** spherical, 6–9 mm, black, with a smooth, glossy surface except for the dried calyx at the end, each containing multiple soft seeds, ripening mid to late summer.

HABITAT: Moist soil in full to partial sun; stream banks, lakeshores, moist meadows, clearings, fencerows, low spots in woods. More common in rich agricultural soil than other currants. Native.

FOOD USE: Berries can be eaten fresh, strained and used for fruit leather or jam (best mixed with milder fruit), or made into juice or jelly. **Conservation 1.**

COMMENTS: Easier to gather than many other currants, but not the best in flavor, tending somewhat too tart for most palates. The leaves of American black currant lack the powerful musky scent that characterizes its European counterpart.

RELATED EDIBLES: Northern black currant *R. hudsonianum* tends to be shorter and has musky-smelling leaves. It is found through the boreal forest region, preferring moist soil, and is usually associated with conifers. Bristly black currant *R. lacustre* is a small species of boreal forests. Unlike other currants it has very bristly stems. The fruit is covered with glandular hairs.

11 Buffalo currant 🍇 3
Ribes odoratum ✦ *Grossulariaceae* (Gooseberry family)

QUICK CHECK: Unarmed, clumped shrub with alternate or tufted, shiny, palmately lobed leaves and hanging racemes of spherical black berries. **ID difficulty 1.**

DESCRIPTION: Clumped, unarmed shrub 3–6' (1–2 m) tall, often forming thickets. **Stems** straight and erect at first, leaning to arching with age. New twigs are light yellow-brown and finely hairy; older branches and stems become ridged and eventually hairless from peeling bark, finally becoming dark gray. **Leaves** alternate on new growth, but on older wood they are *tufted on short spurs*. **Blades** tough, broadly fan-shaped with 3 palmate lobes separated by deep, narrow sinuses, each lobe with a few large blunt teeth (or small sub-lobes) toward the end, but otherwise not toothed along most of the margin. **Surfaces** of new leaves may be faintly hairy, but *mature leaves are hairless*, the top glossy dark green, the bottom pale green—either side may be copiously gland-dotted or not at all. **Veins** *flat to slightly raised above*, slightly protruding below. **Petioles** 80–100% of blade length, narrow and faintly hairy. **Inflorescence** a compact raceme (that looks like an umbel) of 5–11, interspersed with reduced leaves. **Flowers** (spring) brilliant yellow and highly fragrant, the thin tubular base twice the length of the 5 rounded calyx lobes, the petal tips in the center yellow at first *turning bright red*. Stamens are shorter than the petals and hidden. The raceme lengthens in fruit and becomes no longer umbel-like. **Berry** spherical, 7–12 mm, glossy and smooth, lined lengthwise when almost ripe, with a long beak of persistent flower parts at the tip, ripening in mid to late summer to purple-black and juicy with several soft seeds.

HABITAT: Open, dry sites such as forest edges, prairies, and hillsides. Native, but often planted as an ornamental for its remarkable flowers.

FOOD USE: Gather these **currants** by the handful and eat fresh or use to make pies, jellies, jams, juice, or wine. They can also be dried, and are traditionally stored this way. It's best to strain them to get rid of the thick skins and flower remnants.

COMMENTS: This is perhaps the best of North America's wild currants: large, juicy, prolific, easy to collect, and with excellent flavor. It is sometimes considered the same species as the golden currant (*R. aureum*) of the Rocky Mountains, which may have red, orange, yellow, or black fruit when ripe.

12 Blue honeysuckle 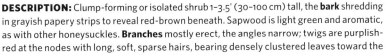 3
Lonicera caerulaea ✦ family *Caprifoliaceae*

QUICK CHECK: Knee-high shrub of bogs with paired, entire leaves and "two-eyed" blue berries. **ID difficulty 1.**

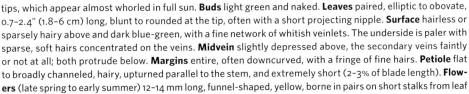

DESCRIPTION: Clump-forming or isolated shrub 1–3.5' (30–100 cm) tall, the **bark** shredding in grayish papery strips to reveal red-brown beneath. Sapwood is light green and aromatic, as with other honeysuckles. **Branches** mostly erect, the angles narrow; twigs are purplish-red at the nodes with long, soft, sparse hairs, bearing densely clustered leaves toward the tips, which appear almost whorled in full sun. **Buds** light green and naked. **Leaves** paired, elliptic to obovate, 0.7–2.4" (1.8–6 cm) long, blunt to rounded at the tip, often with a short projecting nipple. **Surface** hairless or sparsely hairy above and dark blue-green, with a fine network of whitish veinlets. The underside is paler with sparse, soft hairs concentrated on the veins. **Midvein** slightly depressed above, the secondary veins faintly or not at all; both protrude below. **Margins** entire, often downcurved, with a fringe of fine hairs. **Petiole** flat to broadly channeled, hairy, upturned parallel to the stem, and extremely short (2–3% of blade length). **Flowers** (late spring to early summer) 12–14 mm long, funnel-shaped, yellow, borne in pairs on short stalks from leaf axils. The two flowers have joined ovaries that grow together into a single berry with *2 small linear bracts underneath*. **Berry** 5–8 mm long, oval, the skin smooth and bloom-coated, ripening to purple-blue in mid summer, the flesh soft and juicy with a few semi-soft seeds inside, the end with a small *double-dimple with protruding flower remnants*.

HABITAT: Conifer or alder swamps, especially with cedar; mossy uplands, fens, and lakeshores, usually with calcareous soil. Found in shade but only fruits well in sunny sites. Native.

FOOD USE: Ripe **berries** can be eaten raw or cooked. The flavor is good, but they are usually hard to collect in quantity. **Conservation 1.**

COMMENTS: This little-known berry is an unusual gem of the northern swamps. Those from Eurasian populations have been bred for larger fruit and heavy bearing, giving us what the nursery trade calls haskaps or honeyberries. **AKA** waterberry, *Lonicera villosa.*

13 Beautyberry 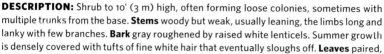 1
Callicarpa americana ✦ *Lamiaciae* (Mint family)

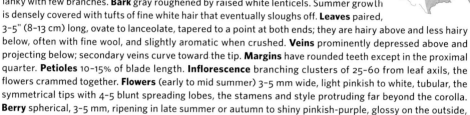

QUICK CHECK: Head-high shrub with paired leaves and tight, showy clusters of bright purple berries encircling the stem at each node. **ID difficulty 1.**

DESCRIPTION: Shrub to 10' (3 m) high, often forming loose colonies, sometimes with multiple trunks from the base. **Stems** woody but weak, usually leaning, the limbs long and lanky with few branches. **Bark** gray roughened by raised white lenticels. Summer growth is densely covered with tufts of fine white hair that eventually sloughs off. **Leaves** paired, 3–5" (8–13 cm) long, ovate to lanceolate, tapered to a point at both ends; they are hairy above and less hairy below, often with fine wool, and slightly aromatic when crushed. **Veins** prominently depressed above and projecting below; secondary veins curve toward the tip. **Margins** have rounded teeth except in the proximal quarter. **Petioles** 10–15% of blade length. **Inflorescence** branching clusters of 25–60 from leaf axils, the flowers crammed together. **Flowers** (early to mid summer) 3–5 mm wide, light pinkish to white, tubular, the symmetrical tips with 4–5 blunt spreading lobes, the stamens and style protruding far beyond the corolla. **Berry** spherical, 3–5 mm, ripening in late summer or autumn to shiny pinkish-purple, glossy on the outside, the whitish flesh inside containing four small seeds. The fruit cluster is packed so tightly around the stem as to give the impression of an aggregate (hence the name, French mulberry).

HABITAT: Disturbed woodlands, forest borders, and forests with thin canopies. Often prevalent in pine plantations. More common on poor soils, moist or dry. It can persist in shady woods but rarely fruits well there. Native. 🔥

FOOD USE: Ripe **berries** are boring but beautiful raw. Cooked into jam/jelly or fruit leather they are much better. They often sit on the bushes for months after ripening. **Conservation 1.**

COMMENTS: This is one of the only woody plants in our region belonging to the mint family, and it is one of the most attractive and distinctive shrubs of the South. The raw berries are bland, but some people rave about the jelly. **AKA** French mulberry.

14 Black aronia 2 NG-314
Aronia melanocarpa ◆ *Rosaceae* (Rose family)

QUICK CHECK: Shrub with alternate, finely serrated leaves and clusters of black fruit with a dimpled end and a 5-part end calyx. **ID difficulty 2.**

DESCRIPTION: Medium-sized shrub forming loose clumps of limber stems 3-8' (1-2.5 m) tall. **Leaves** alternate, ovate to obovate, slightly folded along the midvein, 1-3" (2.5-8 cm) long, the base acute to tapered and the tip abruptly pointed to acuminate. There are small elliptic to lanceolate stipules at the base. The surface is glassy and hairless above, but may be soft-hairy below. **Midvein** flat or slightly depressed above, offset by light green color, with tiny, *dark purplish gland-hairs.* Secondary veins are 4-5 per side, *arching toward the leaf tip,* flat or faintly depressed above. **Margins** evenly serrated with small, gland-tipped, blunt teeth. **Petioles** 5-8% of blade length, hairless, flattened to faintly channeled on top. **Inflorescence** a branching flat-topped cluster of 8-20. **Flowers** (late spring) 0.5-0.8" (13-20 mm) across, with 5 triangular sepals, 5 broad, separate white petals, and numerous stamens. **Berry** spherical, 6-10 mm, with a distinct 5-point indent or *crimp on the end* along with a 5-lobed calyx. The flesh is juicy with many soft seeds, ripening to blue-black.

CONFUSING PLANTS: In landscape plantings it is sometimes confused with various species of *Cotoneaster,* but these do not have similarly clustered fruits.

HABITAT: Shrubby borders of swamps and bogs, lakeshores in full to partial sun, and occasionally on dry

hilltops and cliffs. Most common in sandy soil. Often cultivated as an ornamental, in which case it will tolerate almost any sunny site regardless of drainage. Native.

FOOD USE: The **berries** are astringent even when fully ripe. While they can be used whole, they are best diluted by milder flavors. However, little of the fruit's astringency is imparted to raw, cold-pressed juice. Boiling or steaming to get juice will make it more astringent. **Conservation 1.**

COMMENTS: Russian agronomists identified this North American shrub as a potential crop in the late 1800s and began a breeding program. It is now an important juice crop in much of eastern Europe—the cultivars incorporating some genetics of mountain ash to increase fruit size—but aronia is mostly ignored as a food in its native

hemisphere. However, it has become a popular shrub for landscape plantings and can often be collected by urban foragers, and the cultivars planted are better than the average wild fruit. *A. arbutifolia* (red chokeberry) is a close relative with red fruit (p. 151). **AKA** black chokeberry. Because of the similar names, people often confuse choke-Berry with chokeCherry. **WARNING:** The juice can be a strong laxative for some people.

15 Carolina buckthorn  1
Rhamnus caroliniana +
Rhamnaceae (Buckthorn family)

QUICK CHECK: Large shrub with alternate, faintly-toothed leaves and dark, round fruit with 3 hard seeds. **ID difficulty 2.**

DESCRIPTION: A large shrub or small tree 8–32' (2.5–10 m) tall, thornless, taller than wide, sometimes forming loose thickets. **Bark** gray, smooth or faintly furrowed. Twigs have a small amount of fine woolly hair but older branches lose this. **Buds** naked; side buds are tiny while terminal buds are long and pointed. **Leaves** alternate, 2–5" (5–13 cm) long, oblanceolate to long-elliptic, the tips abruptly pointed to blunt, the bases rounded to obtuse. The upper surface is dark green, shiny, and essentially hairless; the lower surface is pale and may be woolly, especially along the main veins. **Midvein** depressed. Secondary veins are conspicuous, depressed above, straight or arching but curving gently forward just before reaching the margin. **Margins** at a glance appear entire, but a closer look reveals very short, wide, blunt teeth. **Petioles** 7–10% of blade length, not channeled, with fine wool. **Inflorescence** a small, few-flowered, short-stalked umbel. **Flowers** (late spring) 4–6 mm across with 5 sepals, 5 smaller whitish to light yellow petals, 5 stamens, and a 3-forked style. **Berry** spherical with a tiny disk at the base, first turning scarlet, then black, containing 3 large, hard seeds. The flesh is mealy to slightly juicy but not dark inside when ripe in fall.

CONFUSING PLANTS: Glossy buckthorn (p. 661) has 2 seeds and toothless leaves. Lance-leaf buckthorn *R. lanceolata* has blunt, rounded, scale-covered buds and 2 seeds per fruit. These species are reputed to be mildly poisonous.

HABITAT: Dry, open woods and forest edges, especially on limestone soils. Native. 🔥

FOOD USE: Berries can be eaten raw or cooked, but are not very good. **Conservation 1.**

COMMENTS: This berry is slightly sweet and bland. Edible, but nothing anybody gets excited over. In fact, I am so unexcited that I had trouble deciding to include it in this book. I feel pretty certain that eaten in any substantial quantity these would give you diarrhea. That said, I have eaten a palmful many times without incident, and they weren't bad enough to prevent me from doing it again.

16 Black huckleberry 🍇 3 📖 NG-275
Gaylussacia baccata ✦ *Ericaceae* (Heath family)

QUICK CHECK: Knee to chest-high bush with elliptic, entire, gland-dotted leaves and small, spherical blue-black berries with crunchy seeds. **ID difficulty 1.**

DESCRIPTION: Erect shrub 2–5' (60–150 cm) tall with a widely branching top, spreading underground to form loose colonies. **Twigs** very thin, brownish and minutely hairy at first but eventually losing their pubescence. Older stems are dark purple-gray, often with peeling papery bark. **Buds** very small and blunt. **Leaves** alternate, 0.8–2.5" (2–6 cm) long, distinctly larger toward twig tips, elliptic or oblong to ovate, tapered at the base and abruptly pointed or blunt at the tip. **Surface** with yellowish resinous dots, especially below, and fine, soft hairs along the midvein above. **Secondary veins** 3–5 per side, slightly depressed; the veinlets minutely depressed. **Margins** entire with fine hairs. **Petiole** 2–5% of blade length. **Inflorescence** a small raceme of 3–9, to 0.7" (18 mm) long, usually one-sided, on twigs of the previous year. **Flowers** (late spring) 4–6 mm long, the corolla bell or urn-shaped, dull red, drooping, with 5 recurved lobes at the tip and a 5-lobed green calyx about 1/3 its length. **Berry** spherical, 5–8 mm with a tiny calyx at the tip, ripening to blue-black, the surface with little to no bloom, containing 10 hard, crunchy seeds. There are no mini-leaves (bracts) in the fruiting raceme.

HABITAT: Poor, acidic, dry or moist soils in full sun to light shade. Common in sandstone hills under mixed oak and pine and also in glacial outwash sand plains. Native. 🔥

FOOD USE: Ripe **berries** are delicious fresh despite the crunchy seeds. They make excellent pie and fruit leather. **Conservation 1.**

COMMENTS: This species is not the same as what is called black huckleberry in the West. By flavor I prefer it over any blueberry. The deep, spreading root system easily survives litter fires. There are several other members of this genus, all with edible fruit.

Related edible:

17 **Dangleberry** ✦
Gaylussacia frondosa 🍇 3

This is a shrub of moist, sandy, acidic soil in places like swamp margins, low spots in sandy woods, and boggy flatwoods. It averages somewhat taller than black huckleberry, reaching 7' (2.1 m). The leaves are larger, up to 4" (10 cm) long, whitish and *downy on the underside*, and only the lower surface has resinous dots. The fruit *clusters are much longer and drooping*, containing *tiny leaves* (bracts), most of which fall upon ripening. The berries are on long individual stems. The skin is coated with bloom. This species is as good as black huckleberry. **AKA** tall huckleberry.

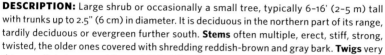

18 Farkleberry   2
Vaccinium arboreum ✦ *Ericaceae* (Heath family)

QUICK CHECK: Large shrub with blunt-tipped leaves and very small, dryish black berries without a powdery coating, drooping on thin pedicels. **ID difficulty 2.**

DESCRIPTION: Large shrub or occasionally a small tree, typically 6–16' (2–5 m) tall with trunks up to 2.5" (6 cm) in diameter. It is deciduous in the northern part of its range, tardily deciduous or evergreen further south. **Stems** often multiple, erect, stiff, strong, twisted, the older ones covered with shredding reddish-brown and gray bark. **Twigs** very thin, usually hairy, greenish or reddish at first, becoming gray. **Leaves** alternate, thick and leathery, extremely variable in size, 0.8–2.5" (2–6 cm) long, obovate to broadly elliptic, the base acute, the tip blunt or rounded with a downturned nipple or claw-like point. **Surface** above shiny and hairless except along the midvein; duller below and often hairy, especially along the major veins. **Midvein** slightly depressed above; secondary veins flat or slightly raised and net-like. **Margins** curled downward, entire but with minute, widely-spaced waves and glands. **Petioles** 3–5% of blade length. **Inflo-**

rescence a short raceme 1–3" (2.5–8 cm) long with miniature leaves (bracts) and up to 7 flowers, the pedicels long and arching. **Flowers** (May–July) 3–5 mm across, bell-shaped, *all parts snow-white*, the tips with 5 *strongly re-curled lobes*. **Berry** 3–7 mm across, spherical, almost hard, mealy rather than juicy, ripening to purple-black, shiny, with tiny crunchy seeds and a small 5-lobed calyx at the tip. Ripens from late summer to fall on an arching to drooping pedicel longer than the fruit's diameter.

CONFUSING PLANTS: Gallberries (*Ilex glabra* and *I. coriacea*) have thicker, fully evergreen leaves with sparsely-toothed margins and bark that does not become flaky with age. The fruit has no calyx at the end and has a projecting bristle; it is on a shorter, stiffer pedicel that does not droop.

HABITAT: Dry, open woods, forest edges, bluff tops, swamp margins on poor soil. Likes acidic soil in full sun. Native. 🔥

FOOD USE: Gather ripe **berries** in autumn as a nibble. Mix with bland or mild fruits for a tart, huckleberry-like flavor, or throw a few in hot cereal. **Conservation 1.**

COMMENTS: Although often dismissed as worthless, I think farkle-berries have a strong, tart, pleasant taste. They are somewhat dry and should not be compared to blueberries. My family raves about the farkleberry-apple pie I once made at a cabin in the Ozarks. "Farkleberry" is also a term used to mock politicians in Arkansas, apparently because a popular cartoonist thought one Governor's ability to identify native woody plants warranted derision. **AKA** sparkleberry.

19 Highbush blueberry 🫐 3 📖 NG-256
Vaccinium corymbosum • *Ericaceae* (Heath family)

QUICK CHECK: Tall shrub with alternate, entire leaves and blue berries with a 5-part calyx. **ID difficulty 1.**

DESCRIPTION: Large shrub typically 6–14' (1.8–4 m) tall. **Stems** 0.6–2" (1.5–5 cm) thick and crooked. **Twigs** green and faintly angled at first, eventually having a peeling red-brown cuticle; the oldest trunks are gray. **Leaves** alternate, ovate to lanceolate, entire or occasionally with a few tiny teeth, 1–3" (2.5–8 cm) long, thin, pointed at both ends, mostly hairless but downy on the main veins below, the margins sometimes slightly downcurved. **Petioles** 2–5% of blade length. **Inflorescence** an umbel-like raceme (corymb) of 5–15. **Flowers** bell-like, 7–11 mm long, with 5 spreading, white to pinkish lobes. **Fruit** the familiar blueberry, rotund with a 5-part calyx on the end, dark blue and usually glaucous, 6–12 mm.

HABITAT: Low, wet, acidic soils, especially on sandy or rocky soil, usually in light shade. Stream, bog, and lake margins, swamps, low ground in sandy woods. Native. 🔥

FOOD USE: Fruit ripens in mid summer (early summer in the South). Pick **berries** by hand or with a rake; because the bushes are tall a blickey can often be used. **Conservation 1.**

COMMENTS: This is the ancestor of the cultivated blueberry and sometimes produces in great abundance.

Cultivated varieties have been selected for smaller bushes, as the wild ones can often grow out of reach. The highbush blueberry has been split by some taxonomists into separate species, but here we are sticking with one.

20 **Lowbush blueberry** 3 ☐ NG-256
genus *Vaccinium* (in part) + *Ericaceae* (Heath family)

QUICK CHECK: Low shrubs with tiny, pointed, alternate leaves, thin green twigs, and blue-black berries with a 5-part calyx. **ID difficulty 1.**

COLLECTIVE DESCRIPTION: Small shrubs 8–40" (20–100 cm) tall, spreading by rhizomes to form colonies. **Stems** upright but the branches are crooked and often spread wider than tall. **Bark** smooth and grayish on older growth. **Twigs** extremely fine and often ridged or angled, *green* or occasionally reddish. **Buds** miniscule, egg-shaped with a point. **Leaves** alternate, 0.3–1.5" (8–38 mm) long, lanceolate, elliptic, or obovate, pointed at both ends, sessile or nearly so. Veins and veinlets are depressed. **Margins** entire or very finely toothed. **Inflorescence** a crowded raceme of up to 15. **Flowers** (spring) bell or urn-shaped, mostly hanging, with five short lobes at the tip, whitish (often with pink highlights), 4–7 mm long, the stamens not projecting past the opening. **Fruit** spherical with a calyx of 5 triangular lobes on the end, blue-black, 5–12 mm, often glaucous, ripening in mid to late summer.

▲ Composite range of all species.

SPECIES: There are many species of lowbush blueberries; two representatives are shown here.

HABITAT: Poor acidic soils, especially sand or gravel, in full to partial sun, wet or dry. Rocky wooded hillsides, boreal forests, pine lands, clearings, bog edges, young forests that cast light shade—proliferating after logging and fire. 🔥

FOOD USE: Pick the ripe fruit by hand or with a blueberry rake. Eat fresh or use to make pies or other desserts. Store by freezing, canning, or drying. **Conservation 1.**

COMMENTS: These are among the most popular wild foods in North America, and deservedly so. Millions of pounds are collected annually, both commercially and for personal use. Lowbush blueberries are classic fire-adapted species: although fire destroys the aboveground stems, it also destroys the competition and releases mineral nutrients, resulting in bumper crops usually 2 years after the blaze. In the absence of fire blueberries lose ground to taller woody plants. Native people traditionally managed millions of acres of blueberries with fire; picking has deteriorated greatly where fires have been suppressed.

▼ *Vaccinium myrtilloides.*

▲ *Vaccinium angustifolium.*   ▲ *Vaccinium angustifolium.*

Related edible:

21 **Mayberry** ✦ *Vaccinium elliottii* 3

This low blueberry species of sandy pine woods in the Deep South blooms in February or March and ripens in late May to early June. The leaves are very small—only slightly longer than the berry—and the small berries ripen to black, usually without bloom. The flavor is superb. 🔥

22 **Bilberry** 🍇 3 📖 NG-256
Vaccinium uliginosum ✦ *Ericaceae* (Heath family)

QUICK CHECK: Very low shrub with tiny oval leaves and blueberry-like fruit. **ID difficulty 1.**

DESCRIPTION: Tiny deciduous shrub 2–10" (5–25 cm) tall, branching profusely with very thin twigs, often forming colonies or mats by long, prostrate stems creeping under the duff. **Bark** light brownish-orange with a thin, peeling, gray outer layer. New twigs are greenish and minutely hairy. **Buds** small but plump, blunt, reddish, conspicuous at branch tips when the fruit is ripe. **Leaves** alternate, sessile, 0.2–0.8" (5–20 mm) long, broadly oval to nearly round, blunt or rounded at both ends, the tip often with a dark nipple, the surfaces hairless and the margins entire. **Veins** *depressed above* and protruding below, in a net-like pattern. **Flowers** pink, bell-like or urn-shaped, hanging, 4–5 mm long, with 4–5 tiny blunt lobes at the opening, borne singly or in pairs from leaf axils. **Fruit** hangs on a pedicel 30% of its length, spherical to slightly oval, 6–8 mm, ripening to light blue with a bloom (occasionally blackish and without bloom). There is a *single protruding style that persists* within the 5-lobed end calyx, the lobes blunt and turned inward (not spreading as in blueberries). Seeds are tiny and hard to notice.

CONFUSING PLANTS: Told from lowbush blueberries by its small size, broad, blunt leaves, fruit borne mostly singly, the protruding style on the fruit, and the lack of a spreading calyx.

HABITAT: Rocky places with poor soil in full sun: tundra, exposed hilltops, coastal balds, occasionally bogs. Native.

FOOD USE: Gather **berries** in late summer through early fall. Delicious like an intensely flavored blueberry, but harder to collect in quantity. **Conservation 1.**

RELATED EDIBLE: Another bilberry, *V. cespitosum*, is characteristic of poor sands or gravels in the boreal region. The leaves are obovate with blunt teeth and less depressed veins, and the flowers are white and more constricted with a vase-like opening.

GROUP 12 **BROADLEAF SHRUBS WITH DRY FRUIT, NUTLETS, OR PODS**

Highly aromatic shrubs tend to have dry, non-fleshy fruits that are not dispersed by animal feeding. Another ecological trend you may notice in this group is their adaptation to some combination of poor soil (whether wet or dry) and heavy disturbance. The primary use of every plant in this group is as a drink or flavoring. Because the leaves are the part most often used, the key uses leaf features where possible. Large specimens of the red sumacs and prickly ash may key as trees.

TENTATIVE IDENTIFICATION KEY TO GROUP 12
The key is not your final answer!

or Leaf ternately compound; fruit red.	4. Fragrant sumac
Leaf pinnately compound.	
Branches prickly; red fruit held close to the branches.	5. Prickly-ash
Branches not prickly; fruit in erect spikes or panicles.	
Fruit red, spherical to oval.	
or Leaf rachises with a wing between leaflets.	1. Winged sumac
Leaf rachises not winged between leaflets.	
New growth densely covered with soft erect hairs.	2. Staghorn sumac
New growth smooth and bloom-coated.	3. Smooth sumac
Fruit a tiny green to brown pod; leaves densely covered in whitish wool.	6. Leadplant
Leaf simple.	
or Leaf margins deeply pinnately lobed; leaf long and narrow.	7. Sweet fern
Leaf margins toothed; leaves deciduous.	
Margins regularly serrated; 2 major depressed secondary veins arise at leaf base.	
or Inflorescence at the end of a naked stem from a leaf axil.	8. Large New Jersey tea
Inflorescence at the end of a normal leafy branch.	9. Small New Jersey tea
Margins with teeth in the distal half only; no major secondary veins from the base.	
Fruit pointed, packed into a tight spike.	10. Sweet gale
Fruit a tiny ball covered with grayish waxy gobs.	11. Bayberry
Leaf margins not toothed; blades tough and evergreen.	
Margin strongly scrolled downward; leaf very densely woolly underneath.	12. Labrador tea
Margin slightly downcurved; leaf not woolly underneath.	13. Leatherleaf

RED SUMACS ▢ FH-252
genus *Rhus* (in part) ◆ *Anacardiaceae* (Cashew family)

QUICK CHECK: Thick-twigged shrubs with pinnately compound leaves and erect, compact clusters of numerous small, red fruit. **ID difficulty 2.**

DESCRIPTION: Shrubs or small trees, not clumped but forming clones by rhizome. *Sap milky.* **Stems** erect, to 25' (8 m) tall, rarely branching near the ground, the crown spreading widely with sparse branches. **Bark** smooth, gray, with prominent *raised transverse brown lenticels* on older trunks. **Twigs** *thick and sparse with thick pith.* **Buds** tiny, squat, blunt, cradled by the horseshoe-shaped leaf scar. **Leaves** alternate, concentrated in dense, palm-like *tufts near the branch tips,* pinnately compound, 7–20" (18–51 cm) long with 7–23 leaflets. **Petiole/rachis** purplish, not channeled. **Leaflets** sessile, ovate to lanceolate, 1–5" (2.5–13 cm) long, the tips sharp and the bases angled to rounded. Secondary veins are widely angled and numerous. **Inflorescence** a *crowded terminal panicle* 2–8" (5–20 cm) long, widest at the base and roughly tapered to the tip, with dozens to hundreds of flowers on short pedicels. **Flowers** (early to mid summer) tiny and pale greenish-yellow with 5 sepals and 5 petals, male and female on separate trees. **Fruit** spherical to slightly oblong and slightly flattened, 3–5 mm, dry or with a thin outer pulp when first ripe, *hairy or often coated with white sticky exudate,* containing a single seed that constitutes most of its volume.

CONFUSING PLANTS: Shoots can resemble ailanthus or walnut, both of which lack the milky sap and have highly aromatic leaves. **Poison sumac** (p. 659) has shiny leaflets lacking teeth, but the rachis is never winged, and the whitish fruit droops in grape-like clusters—plus it grows in swamps.

FOOD USE: Pick **shoots** in late spring when they snap easily and do not yet have a white pith. Peel off bitter outer bark and eat the interior of the shoot raw. Staghorn is best for this because the shoots are larger. **Berries** can be steeped to make a lemonade-like drink. Taste the berries to make sure they are very sour; if not they will make a weak and inferior brew. Pick clusters and steep in cold water for half an hour or so (remove berries from stems if you want to steep hot), then strain through a cloth. Rains eventually wash out the flavor. A **seasoning** can be made from the dried fruits (see fragrant sumac, next). **Conservation 1.**

COMMENTS: Sumac-ade will disappoint if you collect flavorless berry clusters or steep the bitter stems with boiling water. If you pay careful attention to detail, the drink can be excellent.

WARNING: Sumacs are related to cashews, mangoes, and poison ivy. Rare individuals are also highly allergic to the edible red sumacs.

IMPORTANT SPECIES: The three common and widespread species in our region are listed. All are native.

1 Winged sumac ◆ *Rhus coppalina*   2

Winged (shining) sumac is easily distinguished by the *wings along the rachis* between the shiny, *entire leaflets*. The fruit is hairless. This drought-tolerant sumac likes dry, sunny sites such as sandy openings and rocky ridges. 🔥

2 Staghorn sumac ◆ *Rhus typhina*   2

Staghorn sumac has twigs and fruit *densely covered with soft hairs*.  The leaves are hairy below and faintly so above. The secondary veins are slightly depressed, the margins serrated with large, forward-pointing teeth. This species is found in disturbed, well-drained soil in forested regions. 🔥 (Images continued on the next page.)

2 Staghorn sumac (continued)

◀ Staghorn sumac shoot at the stage for peeling.

▼ Staghorn sumac, ripe fruit cluster.

3 Smooth sumac ◆ *Rhus glabra* 2

Smooth sumac has hairless twigs and fruit, the new growth *covered with bloom*. Leaves are nearly hairless, the secondary veins slightly depressed, and the margins serrated. This is a species of dry, open habitats, more typical of prairies and savannahs. The ripe berries often develop a thick white coating of sour paste.

Smooth sumac flowers. ▶

4 Fragrant sumac ☕ 🏛
Rhus aromatica ✦ *Anacardiaceae* (Cashew family)

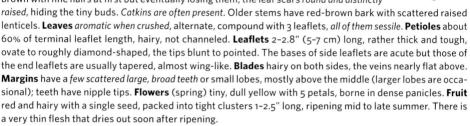

QUICK CHECK: Belly-high shrub with 3-part compound leaves and small clusters of dry red fruit. **ID difficulty 2.**

DESCRIPTION: Widely-branching, sprawling to upright shrub 2–5' (60–150 cm) tall, often forming thickets in full sun. **Twigs** much thinner than those of other sumacs, reddish-brown with fine hairs at first but eventually losing them, the leaf scars *round and distinctly raised*, hiding the tiny buds. *Catkins are often present.* Older stems have red-brown bark with scattered raised lenticels. **Leaves** *aromatic when crushed*, alternate, compound with 3 leaflets, *all of them sessile*. **Petioles** about 60% of terminal leaflet length, hairy, not channeled. **Leaflets** 2–2.8" (5–7 cm) long, rather thick and tough, ovate to roughly diamond-shaped, the tips blunt to pointed. The bases of side leaflets are acute but those of the end leaflets are usually tapered, almost wing-like. **Blades** hairy on both sides, the veins nearly flat above. **Margins** have a *few scattered large, broad teeth* or small lobes, mostly above the middle (larger lobes are occasional); teeth have nipple tips. **Flowers** (spring) tiny, dull yellow with 5 petals, borne in dense panicles. **Fruit** red and hairy with a single seed, packed into tight clusters 1–2.5" long, ripening mid to late summer. There is a very thin flesh that dries out soon after ripening.

CONFUSING PLANTS: Often mistaken for **poison ivy** (p. 658) when not in fruit—the two are related, their leaf textures are similar, and they often grow near each other. Poison ivy has larger leaves; its terminal leaflet is long-stalked and the petiole of the whole leaf is longer than the leaflets.

HABITAT: Dry, sandy soil or rocky outcrops in full sun to moderate shade. Native. 🔥

FOOD USE: Mature berries can be steeped to make a **beverage** as with other red sumacs, but the shoots are too small to be peeled and eaten. The berries can be dried and then rubbed to loosen the outer coating; after the seeds are sifted out, this powder can be used as a **seasoning** like the sumac powder in za'atar traditionally used

in Middle Eastern cooking. (This can also be done with the fruit of other sumacs.) **Conservation 1.**

COMMENTS: Not as well-known as the larger sumacs, this species is separated here because of its distinct form. Fragrant sumac's berries have a unique peppery hint. This species is frequently planted as a landscape shrub and can likely be found in the parking lot of your local Walmart or McDonald's.

WARNING: Rare individuals are allergic to the edible sumacs, which are related to cashews, poison ivy, and mangoes.

5 Prickly-ash
Zanthoxylum americanum ◆ family *Rutaceae*

QUICK CHECK: Thicket-forming large shrub with light gray bark, stout spines, pinnately compound leaves, and short-stemmed clusters of red fruit. **ID difficulty 1.**

DESCRIPTION: Large shrub, not clumped but often spreading by rhizomes to form thickets. **Stems** erect, 6–20' (2–6 m) tall and up to 3" (8 cm) in diameter, the bark thin, finely bumpy, *gray blotched with lighter gray.* Branches have paired, *wide-bottomed spines about 1 cm long* at the nodes. New growth is green; twigs are dark purple-brown and hairless or nearly so. **Leaves** alternate, pinnately compound, 3–8" (8–20 cm) long, with mostly 7–13 leaflets, highly aromatic. **Rachis** dark purple-brown and grooved with occasional small spines. **Leaflets** 1.5–3" (4–8 cm) long, ovate to elliptic, the bottom broadly angled to rounded, the tip blunt-pointed and *notched*. Side leaflets are sessile but the terminal one has a stalk about 25% of its length. The surfaces are hairy, more so below. **Midvein** strongly depressed, secondary veins irregularly depressed, and veinlets slightly depressed, giving a rough texture to the upper surface. **Margins** hairy, not toothed *but notched*. **Flowers** (spring) tiny and greenish, the male and female on separate plants, in short-stalked, compact axillary clusters. **Fruit** bumpy, red, oily, roundish, highly aromatic, 4–6 mm, borne on red pedicels, splitting open at maturity in late summer to release a single shiny, black seed.

HABITAT: Dry slopes, savannahs, forest edges, and upper parts of floodplains, especially on soil that is sandy but moderately rich. Prefers full sun and is very effective at invading abandoned fields. Native. 🔥

FOOD USE: The dried fruit can be used as a **seasoning**, especially after roasting. The leaves can be used as well. Both parts have a potent citrusy flavor as well as a numbing quality. **Conservation 1.**

COMMENTS: This spice is easy to overuse: I've had a few dishes where it was distinctly overemployed. Sichuan pepper is a prickly-ash, and the fruit of many species from this genus are traditionally used as a seasoning. Because of its dependence on fire, prickly-ash has a spotty distribution in the eastern part of its range. There are other members of this genus in the US, but I have not had the occasion to try them.

6 Leadplant ☕
Amorpha canescens ♦ *Fabaceae* (Bean family)

QUICK CHECK: Small shrub with pinnately compound leaves composed of tiny leaflets; large clusters of purple flowers. **ID difficulty 1.**

DESCRIPTION: Semi-woody shrub (upper branches die back in winter, but thicker branches and main stems usually persist) spreading by root suckers, forming clumps but not thickets. **Stems** erect or leaning, to 40" (1 m) tall, branches few. **Bark** gray-brown on older stems, hairless, with *lenticel bumps of the same color.* New growth is green, straight, unbranched, roundish with fine ridges, *densely covered with short, fine, curly gray hair.* **Leaves** alternate, 2–4" (5–10 cm) long, pinnately compound with 13–47 crowded, overlapping leaflets beginning at or near the base of the rachis. **Rachis** nearly straight, thin, woolly, channeled. **Leaflets** nearly sessile, often held out of plane, 0.4–0.8" (1–1.5 cm) long, ovate to elliptic (terminal leaflet broadly obovate), the bases broad to rounded and the tips blunt to angled with a *projecting bristle.* The blades are entire and gray-green from a dense coating of minute, soft, silvery wool on both sides (but denser below). **Midvein** depressed above and protruding below; secondary veins are broadly angled but *nearly invisible.* **Inflorescence** a cluster of dense racemes at the branch tip, 3–7" (8–18 cm) long, holding numerous flowers on very short pedicels. **Flowers** (early to mid summer) have a densely hairy, glandular calyx tube 3–4 mm long with 5 sharp lobes; the corolla is a *single, curved, purple petal* sheathing bright *yellow-orange protruding stamens.* **Fruit** a small, hard, up-curved, woolly pod usually holding one seed, ripening in late summer to fall.

HABITAT: Dry prairies in well-drained, sunny areas, especially steep slopes or sandy soil. Native. 🔥

FOOD USE: Gather the leaves any time and use fresh or dried for **tea**; the flavor is best in early summer. The tea is best boiled to extract the most flavor. **Conservation 2.**

COMMENTS: This attractive shrub is an indicator of native prairie ecosystems and is an important food for mule deer and other hoofed mammals. It is closely related to the prairie clovers (p. 647). When cut to the

ground it resprouts vigorously and appears herbaceous; it is occasionally used as a wonderful-smelling hay crop. Leadplant is so named for the grayish color of the leaves, not for an association with lead in the soil. This popular tea is still available to purchase on some of the Great Plains Indian reservations. It is one of my favorites.

7 Sweet-fern
Comptonia peregrina ◆ family *Myricaceae*

QUICK CHECK: Knee-high shrub with linear, blunt-lobed, ruffled, aromatic leaves. ID difficulty 1.

DESCRIPTION: Highly aromatic shrub forming colonies by rhizome. **Stems** erect to leaning, to 40" (1 m) tall, branching sparsely, the new growth reddish to brown with long, soft hairs, the older bark brown and becoming hairless. Buds are blunt and almost rounded. **Leaves** alternate, sessile or with short petioles, with *small linear stipules* that are odd shaped, cupped, and *much larger on vigorous new shoots*. **Blades** 1.5–5" (4–13 cm) long, linear, tapered to a blunt tip, with many *short, blunt lobes cut fully or almost to the midvein*, the lobes mostly alternate, with little space between them, and cupped downward. **Surfaces** usually hairy on both sides (especially along the midvein) and *rippled or wavy* along the depressed secondary veins. **Flowers** (spring) in catkins, the male drooping and green; the female small, erect, and red from protruding stigmas. **Fruit** a green bur-like structure 0.4–0.8" (1–2 cm) across with 5–15 embedded shiny nutlets, egg-shaped with a point, 5–6 mm long.

HABITAT: Dry, poor, sandy or gravelly soils in full sun. Native.

FOOD USE: Leaves are used for **tea** or occasionally a seasoning. The nutlets are sometimes reported as edible, but they are almost always empty, and the kernels are so small that there is really no practical way to use them as food. **Conservation 1.**

COMMENTS: This shrub has nitrogen-fixing bacteria on its roots, which helps it thrive in extremely poor soil. The seeds can remain dormant in the soil for 70 years, waiting for fire or another disturbance to stimulate germination. A hot summer day when the sun hits sweet-fern under red pines generates a scent that embeds itself forever in your memory.

NEW JERSEY TEA 📖 NG-280
genus *Ceanothus* (in part) ✦ *Rhamnaceae* (Buckthorn family)

QUICK CHECK: Low shrubs with alternate toothed leaves on very short petioles, with 3 prominent veins from the leaf base. **ID difficulty 2.**

DESCRIPTION: Knee to waist-high shrubs from a large root mass, spreading only by seed. **Stems** clumped, the new growth green and covered with fine hairs; older stems turn red-brown, then gray, eventually becoming hairless. The bushes are *semi-woody*; the lower portion persists through the winter, but most of the thin, straight, erect branchlets die back and fall off. **Leaves** alternate, 1.2–3.5" (3–9 cm) long, ovate to lanceolate, sparsely hairy above and hairier below, especially on the main veins. **Midvein** and major veins are strongly depressed above and protruding below; there are *3 major veins from the base*, arching toward the leaf tip. **Margins** serrated with small, blunt, claw or gland-tipped teeth. **Petioles** 5–10% of blade length, fine-hairy, not channeled. **Inflorescence** a dense elongated or ball-like cluster of dozens to hundreds of flowers, consisting of many *stalkless mini-umbels* packed near each other along a central rachis, sometimes branched, the *pedicels long, straight, extremely thin, and white.* **Flowers** (early to mid summer) 3 mm across, with 5 white triangular sepals curved in toward the center and 5 *petals shaped like a folded or cupped hood at the end of a thin, curved, stalk-like base.* **Fruit** is a dry, brown, rounded, 3-lobed capsule about 5 mm across, attached to a flat, saucer-like base. The fruits or their bases often persist for many months, aiding identification.

FOOD USE: Gather leaves and dry them out of direct sunlight; young leaves of early summer are best. Brew **tea** by boiling leaves until the water turns golden or reddish (depending on your preference). Use a large volume of leaves (enough to loosely fill the boiling vessel). Fermenting them like tea leaves will increase the potency of the flavor. The species can be used almost interchangeably—the flavors are not exactly the same, but close. **Conservation 2.**

COMMENTS: The two species of New Jersey tea are among the better and more popular wild teas. They were widely used during the Revolutionary War when Oriental tea supplies were cut off.

8 Large New Jersey tea ✦ *Ceanothus americanus*

This species is larger in all respects. The leaves are ovate with rounded bases, and they are usually densely hairy underneath. The inflorescence is at the end of a long, naked, straight stalk arising from a leaf axil, and it blooms about 3 weeks later than the smaller species. Large NJ tea is more characteristic of rich, dry soils in prairies, rock outcroppings, and oak savannahs. 🔥

9 Small New Jersey tea ✦ *Ceanothus herbaceus*

This plant is shorter with smaller, narrower leaves, typically lanceolate or elliptic with tapered or narrowly angled bases. The blades are less hairy. The inflorescence is borne at the end of a normal leafy branchlet. Small NJ tea is characteristic of poor, dry soils, such as are found in pine and oak barrens and sand prairies. 🔥

10 Sweet gale ☕ 🕯
Myrica gale ✦ family *Myricaceae*

QUICK CHECK: waist-high shoreline shrub with narrow, dark blue-green, ascending leaves crowded at branch tips. **ID difficulty 2.**

DESCRIPTION: Shrub often forming clumps, layering and suckering for short distances. **Stems** erect to leaning, 2–5' (60–150 cm) tall, the branches ascending. **Bark** red-brown with whitish lenticels. Twigs hairy with plump, squat buds. **Leaves** alternate, crowded at branch tips, ascending, sessile or on extremely short petioles. They are much larger on new shoots and near the tips (to 3.5"/9 cm). Lower leaves on older growth may be as small as 3 mm, but the average size is 1.5–2.2" (4–6 cm). **Blades** oblanceolate, with blunt tips and a tapered base, nearly flat, but the margins are slightly and minutely downcurved, especially near the base. **Surface** hairless; new leaves have golden speckles above, while all leaves have larger *golden speckles below.* **Midvein** *light green, protruding*

slightly above, significantly below. Secondary veins are numerous but faint, at broad angles. **Margins** *toothed only in the terminal 40%;* teeth have a light dot at the tip. **Inflorescence** (spring) ascending catkins: the male with broad purple scales, their tips acuminate and dark; the female with a tuft of long purple stigmas. **Fruit** tiny, yellow-green, sessile, egg-shaped, with a tooth-like tip and dark, thread-like flower remnants, highly aromatic, in a cone-like spike 1 cm long, ripening in late summer, exuding a yellow-orange wax (visible if pressed on paper).

HABITAT: Shorelines in full sun, especially with infertile rock, gravel, or sand; often on thin peat or muck over such material, but rarely in floating bogs. Native.

FOOD USE: Leaves can be used to brew a **tea** or as a **seasoning** in broths, like bay leaf. Flower buds and fruits can be used similarly and are more aromatic. **Conservation 1.**

COMMENTS: Often extremely abundant in Northwoods lake country, perfuming the shoreline breeze on hot summer days.

11 Bayberry
Myrica pensylvanica ◆ family *Myricaceae*

QUICK CHECK: Waist-high aromatic bush with nearly entire oblanceolate leaves crowded at the twig tips; small, round, waxy, gray berries clustered on naked stems below the leaves. **ID difficulty 2.**

DESCRIPTION: Bushy aromatic shrub to 6' (2 m) tall with stiff ascending branches. **Twigs** usually hairy and resinous with small, plump, reddish-brown to whitish buds; older bark has longitudinal cracks. **Leaves** alternate, crowded and overlapping at the twig tips, often twisted sideways, tough but not evergreen, although falling late. Blades obovate or oblanceolate, 1.5–4" (4–10 cm) long, tapered to a narrow, wedge-shaped base, blunt-pointed at the tip. **Surface** dark, dull green and hairless or slightly hairy above; the underside is downy with small resin globs. **Margins** entire or with a few small teeth in the distal half. **Flowers** (May–July) tiny and wind-pollinated, male and female on separate bushes, from naked stem sections below the leaves. Male catkins are 0.3–0.6" (8–15 mm) long. Female catkins are in dense clumps close to the stem. **Fruit** aromatic, spherical, 3–5 mm, in small, stiff clusters with very short pedicels, coated with lumps of light grayish wax, containing a single large seed, ripening in late summer and often persisting through winter.

HABITAT: Sandy coastal areas slightly above water level. Native.

FOOD USE: Leaves can be used as a **seasoning** in soups, like bay leaf. **Conservation 1.**

COMMENTS: The berries are sometimes gathered and boiled to extract the fragrant wax coating—the source of bay wax candles.

RELATED EDIBLE: Wax myrtle *Myrica cerifera* is a closely related shrub or small tree with a more southerly distribution. It can be used similarly as a flavoring (and for wax-making) but the flavor is weaker.

▲ Wax myrtle.

185

12 Labrador tea
Ledum groenlandicum ◆ *Ericaceae* (Heath family)

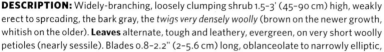

QUICK CHECK: Evergreen bog shrub; leathery aromatic leaves with downcurved edges and profuse wool underneath. **ID difficulty 1.**

DESCRIPTION: Widely-branching, loosely clumping shrub 1.5–3' (45–90 cm) high, weakly erect to spreading, the bark gray, the *twigs very densely woolly* (brown on the newer growth, whitish on the older). **Leaves** alternate, tough and leathery, evergreen, on very short woolly petioles (nearly sessile). Blades 0.8–2.2" (2–5.6 cm) long, oblanceolate to narrowly elliptic, tapered to a blunt point on both ends. **Surface** dark green and hairless above except along the depressed midvein; *rippled from depressions of the faintly visible secondary veins*. Underneath they are aromatic and *densely matted with wool*—white at first but reddish-brown on older leaves. **Margins** entire, *strongly downcurved*. **Inflorescence** a crowded, terminal, umbel-like, rounded cluster of up to 40, the radiating green pedicels 0.4–0.9" (1–2.3 cm) long. **Flowers** about 1 cm across with 5 separate, spreading, elongated, blunt-tipped, white petals and 5–7 strongly protruding stamens. **Fruit** a brown capsule of 5 parts, *splitting from the base* rather than the tip and drooping like a shooting star or cranberry flower.

HABITAT: Moist, acidic sites in full sun to partial shade: sphagnum bogs, muskegs, boggy margins of lakes, rivers, and wetlands. Often persisting but never thriving in dense shade as the canopy closes. Occasionally on thin-soiled rocky slopes and ledges. Native.

FOOD USE: Use leaves fresh or dried for **tea**. Due to small amounts of the toxin *ledol* in the leaves, some anti-foraging authorities advise not to boil them—although many people do, and I have never heard of this having any ill effect. Boiling is fine as long as the tea is not drunk in excessive amounts. This is a very well-established traditional drink. **Conservation 1.**

COMMENTS: Despite the strong, distinctive, and pleasant aroma of the leaves, the flavor they impart is weak. To make a tea with any strength requires a lot of leaves and steeping time. Despite the weakness, this has long been a popular tea across the North Country.

13 Leatherleaf ☕
Chamaedaphne calyculata ✦ *Ericaceae* (Heath family)

QUICK CHECK: Waist-high bush of boggy shores with tough, evergreen, elliptic, entire leaves. **ID difficulty 2.**

DESCRIPTION: Shrub spreading by rhizomes to form colonies. **Stems** in dense clumps, to 4' (1.2 m) tall and 0.6" (15 mm) thick, curved and crooked but *the new growth erect*. The wood is light green. **Bark** finely shredding, reddish and smooth beneath the papery layer. **Twigs** slightly zigzag, hairy in the first year. **Leaf buds** tiny; flower buds much larger and pointed, on short stalks. **Leaves** elliptic with a blunt point at both ends, up to 1.6" (4 cm) but *drastically and progressively reduced in size toward the tips of flowering branches* (some as small as 2 mm), held *vertically or nearly appressed to the twig*, often *recurved*. **Blades** hairless on both sides, green and glossy above dotted with sparse silvery scales; densely covered with red-brown or pale gray scales below. **Margins** hairless, *downcurved*, entire or with *tiny irregular bump-teeth*, mostly toward the tip. **Midvein** slightly depressed above, slightly protruding below; secondary veins faint but several, 55–70°. The *petiole and lower midvein are maroon on new leaves*. **Petioles** 10% of blade length. **Flowers** borne singly on drooping pedicels from the axils of reduced terminal leaves, the corolla white and urn-shaped, the opening with 5 small lobes and a slightly protruding style, the base hugged by 5 triangular brown sepals about one third the length of the corolla. **Fruit** a 5-part capsule, the end somewhat flattened, the sepals and long style persistent, ripening in fall.

HABITAT: Acidic bogs and boggy shorelines in full sun. Native.

FOOD USE: Leaves can be used for **tea**, fresh or dried. Collect at any time of year. **Conservation 1.**

COMMENTS: This abundant bog shrub usually grows with the much better-known Labrador tea. Of the two, I think leatherleaf makes a better beverage. When boiling, it gives off a similar scent but imparts more flavor.

GROUP 13 WOODY VINES AND CREEPERS

The foods produced by the plants in this group are variable: fleshy fruits, flowers, roots, leafy greens, shoots, and inner bark. Read the specific accounts carefully to determine the edible part or parts of each plant. This group contains two large, complex genera: the greenbriers (*Smilax*) and the grapes (*Vitis*). Treating these is problematic due to the large number of similar species and the varying quality of their edible parts. I have tried to discuss the average while also illustrating some of the standouts. Since I have not eaten every species in these groups, surely some good ones have been left out. The key includes a number of common non-edible vines that are confusing or dangerous.

TENTATIVE IDENTIFICATION KEY TO GROUP 13
The key is not your final answer!

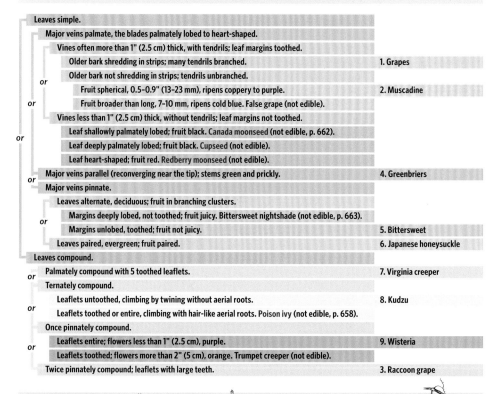

Leaves simple.
 Major veins palmate, the blades palmately lobed to heart-shaped.
  Vines often more than 1" (2.5 cm) thick, with tendrils; leaf margins toothed.
   Older bark shredding in strips; many tendrils branched. — **1. Grapes**
   or Older bark not shredding in strips; tendrils unbranched.
    Fruit spherical, 0.5–0.9" (13–23 mm), ripens coppery to purple. — **2. Muscadine**
   or Fruit broader than long, 7–10 mm, ripens cold blue. False grape (not edible).
  or Vines less than 1" (2.5 cm) thick, without tendrils; leaf margins not toothed.
   Leaf shallowly palmately lobed; fruit black. Canada moonseed (not edible, p. 662).
   Leaf deeply palmately lobed; fruit black. Cupseed (not edible).
   Leaf heart-shaped; fruit red. Redberry moonseed (not edible).
 or Major veins parallel (reconverging near the tip); stems green and prickly. — **4. Greenbriers**
 Major veins pinnate.
  Leaves alternate, deciduous; fruit in branching clusters.
   or Margins deeply lobed, not toothed; fruit juicy. Bittersweet nightshade (not edible, p. 663).
   Margins unlobed, toothed; fruit not juicy. — **5. Bittersweet**
  Leaves paired, evergreen; fruit paired. — **6. Japanese honeysuckle**
Leaves compound.
 or Palmately compound with 5 toothed leaflets. — **7. Virginia creeper**
 Ternately compound.
  Leaflets untoothed, climbing by twining without aerial roots. — **8. Kudzu**
  or Leaflets toothed or entire, climbing with hair-like aerial roots. Poison ivy (not edible, p. 658).
 Once pinnately compound.
  or Leaflets entire; flowers less than 1" (2.5 cm), purple. — **9. Wisteria**
  Leaflets toothed; flowers more than 2" (5 cm), orange. Trumpet creeper (not edible).
 Twice pinnately compound; leaflets with large teeth. — **3. Raccoon grape**

1 **Wild grape** 🍇 1–3 🌿 1–2 🍴 2 📖 FH 260
genus *Vitis* ✦ *Vitaceae* (Grape family)

QUICK CHECK: Shaggy bark, no aerial roots, branching tendrils, rounded or palmately lobed leaves, and grape-like fruit. ID difficulty 3.

DESCRIPTION: Large woody vines to 100' (30 m) long and 10" (25 cm) diameter (but usually much smaller). **Bark** brown, *peeling in long strips* on older stems. **Tendrils** usually 2–3 branched, borne at nodes opposite a leaf. **Leaves** alternate (paired with a tendril) on grooved petioles 40–100% of blade length. Blades 3–10" (8–25 cm) long, about equally broad, palmately lobed or heart-shaped, the base heart-shaped, the tip pointed to acuminate. All major veins are depressed above. **Margins** sometimes lobed, always with nipple-tipped

▲ Composite range of wild grapes.

teeth—varying from small to very large depending on species. **Inflorescence** an elongated panicle with a dominant central axis (like a domestic grape cluster) borne opposite a leaf. **Flowers** (early summer) small and unshowy, male and female on different vines, with 5 petals fused at the tip to form a cap that drops off as the flower opens. **Fruit** spherical, 0.2–0.7" (5–18 mm), with thick, deep purple skin often heavily coated with bloom, the inside juicy, containing 1–4 large, ovoid, semi-hard seeds, ripening in late summer to fall.

CONFUSING PLANTS: Several woody vines have similar fruit—and these are frequently found growing in the same habitat. Virginia creeper and woodbine have palmately *compound* leaves, non-shaggy stems, and sparser fruit clusters. On woodbine, the fruit stems are bright pink. These species have acrid juice that tastes unpleasant and leaves a burning sensation in the mouth, but they are not particularly dangerous. **Canada moonseed** (poisonous, p. 662) contain a single crescent-shaped seed. Moonseed vines spiral around their supports (grape vines do not) and are much thinner than grape vines, greenish, and never shaggy. Moonseed leaves lack teeth on their margins. False grape *Ampelopsis cordata* has leaves much like those of wild grape, but it has very few tendrils. The fruit grows in a wide, dichotomously forked cluster; it ripens to turquoise blue with raised corky dots on the skin and is never quite spherical. This fruit is unpalatable but not dangerous.

HABITAT: River floodplains, roadsides, empty urban lots, fences, forest edges, steep slopes, and other disturbed, sunny locations. Sometimes found in the canopies of mature hardwood forests. Native.

FOOD USE: Young **tendrils** and growing tips make a tangy snack in spring and early summer, popular with children. Young **leaves** can be used as wraps for stuffed grape leaves (dolmades). For this purpose they are best when nearly full-sized but still tender. The **fruit** can be used to make pie, juice, jelly, jam, or wine—the quality varies greatly by species. Some wild grapes are tiny and very sour with little pulp. If the flavor is too strong wild grape juice can be mixed with a milder fruit, such as apple, to make superior jelly. **Conservation 1.**

CAUTION: Many of the smaller wild grapes are high in tartrate and calcium oxalate, which should be removed before use. (It will make jam or jelly gritty, and in juice it will irritate your mouth and throat). Tartrate settles to the bottom of a container of juice as a grayish sludge after a day or two; the good juice can be poured off the top.

COMMENTS: Wild grapes are widespread and abundant in most of the East, and can make superb products even though many are too sour to enjoy raw.

SPECIES: Several in our area: A few representatives are pictured here and on the next page.

◄ (left) Grape vines have shredding bark. (right) Wild grape panicle in flower.

▼ (left) False grape (genus *Ampelopsis*). (right) Wild grape tendrils.

NOT EDIBLE

1 **Wild grape** (continued)

▲ Summer grape *V. aestivalis* leaves and fruit—this
◀ might be the best-tasting of our small grapes. Note the
whitish leaf underside.

▲ Mustang grape *V. mustangensis*. This species is very
common in Texas and has cupped leaves that are
densely woolly on the underside. The grapes are
large with good flavor.

▲ *V. labrusca*. This large-fruited species is an ancestor of
Concord, and is one of our best wild grapes. It is often
called fox grape, but unfortunately this name is also
applied to the very different *V. vulpina*.

▲ Riverside grape *V. riparia*. This is our most widespread species. It has small grapes with potent but
good flavor. ▶

2 Muscadine 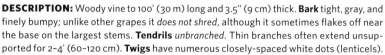 3
Vitis rotundifolia ◆ *Vitaceae* (Grape family)

QUICK CHECK: Bark not shaggy; roundish leaves with large teeth; small clusters of large, tough-skinned grapes. **ID difficulty 2.**

DESCRIPTION: Woody vine to 100' (30 m) long and 3.5" (9 cm) thick. **Bark** tight, gray, and finely bumpy; unlike other grapes it *does not shred*, although it sometimes flakes off near the base on the largest stems. **Tendrils** *unbranched*. Thin branches often extend unsupported for 2–4' (60–120 cm). **Twigs** have numerous closely-spaced white dots (lenticels).
Leaves alternate, 2–4" (5–10 cm) long, round in outline with heart-shaped bases and abruptly pointed tips, the margins not lobed, with large, broad teeth. **Surface** hairless or nearly so above and below. Major **veins** nearly flat to faintly protruding above. **Petioles** 90–120% of blade length. **Flowers** resemble those of other grapes (see above). **Grapes** large, 0.6–1" (15–25 mm), greenish to purple or occasionally bronze colored when ripe, the skins very *thick with tiny warts*, in small, not elongated *clusters of less than 12* (usually 3–7), ripening in fall, the grapes *dropping once they ripen*.

CONFUSING PLANTS: The false grape *Ampelopsis cordata* has very few tendrils and leaves that are more finely toothed and tapered to a sharp tip. The fruits are smaller and more numerous per cluster.

HABITAT: Open young woods, forest edges; also sometimes in forest interiors. Native. 🔥

FOOD USE: Pluck the **fruit** from the vine or pick them up off the ground (their thick skins protect them from damage). You can do all of the things with muscadines that are done with smaller grapes: eat them fresh, or make superb jelly, wine, or juice. The flavor is milder and sweeter than that of smaller grapes, and the juice contains less tartrate/calcium oxalate. Muscadines also lend themselves to uses that are impractical with smaller grapes: They are delicious dried after the skins have been removed, and they can also be made into pie. **Conservation 1.**

COMMENTS: This has the largest fruit of our native grapes and several cultivars have been bred. It is the most genetically distinct of our grapes and is placed in its own genus by some taxonomists. I separate it from other grapes here due to its many unique features.

▲ (above) Ripe muscadines.
▲ (top) Muscadine stems are not shaggy.
◄ Unripe muscadines, showing small clusters.

191

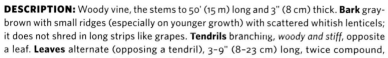

3 Raccoon grape 🖌 1
Ampelopsis arborea ✦ *Vitaceae* (Grape family)

QUICK CHECK: Bark without shaggy strips, leaves twice compound; half-inch, purple, grape-like fruit in small clusters. **ID difficulty 2.**

DESCRIPTION: Woody vine, the stems to 50' (15 m) long and 3" (8 cm) thick. **Bark** gray-brown with small ridges (especially on younger growth) with scattered whitish lenticels; it does not shred in long strips like grapes. **Tendrils** branching, *woody and stiff*, opposite a leaf. **Leaves** alternate (opposing a tendril), 3–9" (8–23 cm) long, twice compound, pinnate or ternate at each division, with 9–33 leaflets. Rachises are hairy, especially toward the leaflets. **Petioles** deeper than wide, channeled faintly or not at all, sparsely hairy, 20–120% of the blade length. **Leaflets** 0.6–2.4" (15–24 mm) long, sessile or on very short petiolules, ovate in outline with a few lobes or very large teeth. Hairs scattered beneath, mostly on major veins. **Veins** depressed above and protruding below. **Inflorescence** a cluster of 3–28, much shorter than the leaves, *widely forking* at first but the final branches densely-packed and umbel-like (but not really an umbel). **Flowers** (early summer) tiny, off-white, with 5 petals and 5 stamens. In fruit the *cluster stems are green*. **Berries** black, almost spherical but slightly broader than long, usually touching in the cluster, the skin *shiny with tiny whitish spots*. The inside is juicy with reticulate flesh, the liquid almost clear but faintly purple. **Seeds** 3, greenish, about 4 mm long and nearly as wide, flat on one or two faces and rounded on the outer face.

HABITAT: In full to partial sun where well drained: young forests, open woodlands, forest edges, fence lines, roadsides, brushy areas. Native.

FOOD USE: Collect **fruit** when ripe and use like wild grapes. The flesh is faintly irritating to the mouth, which can be alleviated in juice by letting it sit overnight in the fridge and then decanting the sludge-free liquid on top (as with wild grapes). **Conservation 1.**

COMMENTS: These are like lame, bland grapes—edible but not very exciting. Despite being usually reported as inedible, they are better than the worse species of wild grapes and taste much better than our other species of *Ampelopsis*. **AKA** pepper vine—I have no idea why it is called this, or why it has the species name *arborea* (tree-like).

4 Greenbrier 1-3
genus *Smilax* (in part) +
Smilacaceae (formerly *Liliaceae*, Lily family)

QUICK CHECK: Green stems with thorns or spines, tendrils, and entire leaves with parallel veins; flowers or fruit in umbels. **ID difficulty 1.**

DESCRIPTION: Medium-sized woody vines often forming dense thickets over brush, variably armed with short spines or long needles, depending on species. **Stems** to 40' (12 m) long, usually less than 0.8" (2 cm) thick, scarcely tapering, angled on some species and rounded on others. Bark bright green or glaucous-green at first, often darkening to nearly black with age, not shredded or peeling, sometimes with protruding white lenticels.

▲ Composite range.

Shoots to 0.6" (15 mm) thick and often several feet long with large tendrils but only tiny leaves or scales. **Leaves** simple, alternate, often evergreen or semi-evergreen, mostly ovate to heart-shaped or rounded but on a few species they are long-elliptic, linear, or bulging at the base. Blades are glossy when young, tough when mature, and mostly hairless. **Midvein** and major veins are depressed above and strongly protruding below, but *smaller veins are flat to faintly raised above*. There are 1–3 *prominent parallel veins* on each side of the midvein, arching out from the base and converging at the tip. **Margins** entire but occasionally spiny. **Petioles** 5–15% of blade length, grooved and sheathed, with *stipules or tendrils attached to the sides*. **Inflorescence** a tight spherical umbel of 6–30 at the end of a peduncle from a leaf axil, the cluster 1–2" (2.5–5 cm)

across. **Flowers** (early summer) male and female on different plants, very small and yellow-green, with 6 tepals arranged in two layers, the male flowers with 6 stamens. **Fruit** spherical or nearly so, 4–10 mm, smooth-skinned, ripening dark blue-black, the flesh pulpy to mealy with one to several large seeds.

SPECIES: There are many species in our region; a few representatives are pictured here and on the next page.

CONFUSING PLANTS: Carrion flowers (p. 494) are herbaceous members of the same genus. They have proportionately much thicker stems and lack thorns, and are similarly edible.

HABITAT: Edges of fields, roadsides, thickets, fencerows, young or open woods, streamsides. Native.

▲ Greenbrier fruits.

FOOD USE: The rhizomes or **tubers** of some species have been used to make a nourishing drink. For this they were apparently pounded, after which the starch was settled out in water, then boiled to make the reddish drink. These details are nebulous, and it is not fully clear which species were used or preferred. My experiments with this have so far been unsuccessful—the tubers I have unearthed were shockingly hard and woody. **Shoots** and young **greens** can be eaten raw or cooked from spring to early summer and occasionally later. These vary in flavor from slightly bitter to pleasantly tangy. **Conservation 3/1.**

COMMENTS: Greenbriers can be tricky to identify to species, but are easy to recognize as a group: there are no other vines in our region with tendrils and green stems, and there are no other climbing vines that are prickly. One species, *S. walteri*, has red berries. (Images continued on the next page.)

▲ Tubers from *S. laurifolia* and *S. glauca* (I forget which is which). I had no luck extracting starch from either one. ▲

4 Greenbrier (continued)

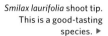

Smilax laurifolia shoot tip. This is a good-tasting species. ▶

▼ *Smilax bona-nox* shoots. These are excellent.

Smilax hispida, our most widespread species, but the shoots are low in quality. ▶

▼ *Smilax glauca* leaves.

▲ *Smilax rotundifolia*, a common greenbrier with good shoots.

▲ *Smilax laurifolia* leaves.

5 Bittersweet 🌀1 | 1
Celastrus scandens ✦ family *Celastraceae*

QUICK CHECK: Curvy, smooth-barked vine without tendrils, the leaves simple and unlobed; fruit orange, splitting open to reveal a red interior. **ID difficulty 2.**

DESCRIPTION: Vine or mound-forming shrub. **Stems** sinuous, curving gently, climbing without tendrils, to 60' (18 m) long and 2" (5 cm) thick. **Bark** gray-brown and smooth on older stems; the bark of new growth is smoother, hairless, and green to greenish-brown with brown lenticels. Inner bark is fibrous and green. When broken, *young stems are hollow with air chambers* separated erratically by soft pithy membranes. Leaf scars are D-shaped to roughly triangular. **Leaves** alternate, 2–4" (5–10 cm) long, ovate to obovate or broadly oval, with a long, acuminate tip and a broad, short-acuminate, or tapered base that is *folded*. **Surfaces** hairless, the veins depressed above and protruding below. **Margins** have small, regular, blunt, often down-curved teeth with a dark glandular tip. **Petioles** curved, 10% of blade length, with a shallow wing-channel. **Inflorescence** a terminal cluster of 10–24, slightly longer than wide. **Flowers** (late spring and early summer) 5–6 mm across with 5 spreading, pale greenish-yellow petals. **Fruit** spherical to slightly oblong, 7–12 mm, the skin smooth, turning bright orange in late summer, with a dark-tipped beak. Later, *the outer flesh peels back in 3 lobes to reveal a red interior* that encloses 2 elongated whitish seeds. **Pedicels** 90–140% of fruit diameter, widening and turning orange distally, the end with a 5-pointed calyx pressed against the base of the fruit.

HABITAT: Sunny woods, forest margins, oak savannahs, fence lines, steep hillsides, rocky areas and cliffs, floodplain forests, young brushy woods. Native. 🔥

FOOD USE: After peeling the outer bark (all year, but especially winter), the **inner bark** can be scraped off and chewed—it tastes pretty good, but the fibers must be spit out—or it can be boiled as a base for soups. The tender **shoots** (spring and early summer) can be eaten raw or cooked. **Conservation 2.**

COMMENTS: The inner bark has served as a winter famine food. The taste is better than I expected, and it is fun to have something to collect in winter, but the shoots are more practical.

RELATED EDIBLE: Asian bittersweet *Celastrus orbiculatus* is a common invasive species, and in much of our region it is far more common than the native. It is eliminating/diluting the native bittersweet through genetic swamping and the two species are likely to converge over time. Asian bittersweet has rounder leaves and the fruit is borne in smaller clusters from many leaf axils. The food uses are identical. **I**

▲ Bittersweet (native) with ripe berries.

▲ Asian bittersweet shoots.

▲ Asian bittersweet with unripe fruit. **195**

6 Japanese honeysuckle ❀ 2
Lonicera japonica ◆ family *Caprifoliaceae*

QUICK CHECK: No tendrils; paired, entire leaves; large, paired, fragrant white flowers with a tubular base splitting into 2 asymmetrical lips; black berries. **ID difficulty 2.**

DESCRIPTION: Twining woody vine lacking tendrils, to 26' (8 m) long and 4" (10 cm) thick, forming dense tangles on the ground or climbing. **Twigs** hairy, green at first, turning red-brown. **Bark** light colored, peeling off in narrow flaky strips on older trunks. **Leaves** paired but never fused, tough and *mostly evergreen* (tardily deciduous in its northern range), ovate to oblong, 1–3" (2.5–8 cm) long, obtuse at the base and abruptly pointed at the tip. **Margins** hairy and entire—except on *shoots, which often have leaves with large teeth or lobes.* **Surface** hairless above except along the midvein; moderately soft-hairy below, especially along the veins. Veins are nearly flat above. **Petioles** broader than deep, nearly sessile to 8% of blade length. **Flowers** (late spring to early summer) tubular, 1.2–2" (3–5 cm) long, highly fragrant, in pairs directly from the leaf axils or at the end of a short peduncle, white at first but fading to dull yellow. **Corolla** a long, narrow, hairy tube suddenly diverging into 2 lips; one lip is narrow, recurved, wider toward the tip; the other lip is much broader with the tip split into 4 lobes. The pistil and stamens protrude prominently. There is a pair of reduced leaves beneath each pair of flowers, and a pair of tiny, broad bracts at the base of each individual flower. Unopened flower buds are long, thin, club-like, light green, and hairy. **Fruit** paired, spherical, about 5 mm, ripening to black in late summer or fall, containing several black, shiny seeds.

CONFUSING PLANTS: Other vining honeysuckles have smaller flowers and fruit that does not ripen black.

HABITAT: Sunny to moderately shady well-drained soil, especially where fertile. Disturbed woodlots, fences, forest edges, vacant lots, brushy areas, young or semi-open woods, steep banks, streamsides. It survives but is less dominant in shady mature forests. Introduced. **I**

FOOD USE: Pluck mature white **flowers**, bite off the bottom, and suck the nectar from the base. Flowers can also be eaten in salads, chopped up and soaked for a drink, or dried for tea.

COMMENTS: Over much of our region this is the most ecologically significant invasive plant. This is one of the most accessible of all wild edibles, but its culinary applications are limited. The fruits are not edible. This is a good nectar flower for hummingbirds, and the scent of a blooming colony on a hot June evening is amazing.

▲ Japanese honeysuckle young leaves.

7 Virginia creeper, woodbine 1 1
Parthenocissus quinquefolia and *P. vitacea* ♦
Vitaceae (Grape family)

QUICK CHECK: Palmately compound leaf with 5 toothed leaflets; non-shaggy bark. ID difficulty 2.

▲ Composite range.

DESCRIPTION: Woody vine or creeper, stems to 100' (30 m) long and 5" (13 cm) thick, climbing high in trees, creeping along the ground, or sprawling over boulders, brush, and fences. **Bark** gray when young, roughened by lenticels and small fissures, becoming rough but never shaggy. **Tendrils** branched, growing opposite a leaf. **Leaves** alternate, palmately compound with 5 leaflets. **Petioles** long and shallowly channeled. **Leaflets** 2.5–5" (6–13 cm) long, elliptic to obovate, pointed at both ends, variably hairy, turning red in fall. **Midvein** raised in a shallow valley above; secondary veins depressed. **Margins** toothless near the base, otherwise with large, sharp, forward-pointing teeth with claw-like tips. **Inflorescence** a branching cluster of 25–80. **Flowers** (mid summer) 5–6 mm across with 5 light green, recurved and boat-shaped petals. **Berry** nearly spherical, 4–10 mm, ripening to blue-black in late summer or early fall, juicy, with 3–4 seeds.

SPECIES: Both are commonly called Virginia creeper, although some people insist that this name only applies to *P. quinquefolia* and that the proper name for *P. vitacea* is woodbine. *P. vitacea* has fruit clusters with a wide, dichotomous-branching shape, the pedicels hot pink. The stems lack climbing roots. The bark of old vines becomes deeply furrowed and blocky. The tendrils usually lack enlarged tips. *P. quinquefolia* has slightly smaller fruit in an elongated cluster with a dominant central axis and green pedicels. The stems often have aerial climbing roots and the tendrils have enlarged, pad-like tips.

HABITAT: Most wooded or brushy situations: mature forests, roadsides, fences, abandoned farms and orchards. Ranges from dry to moist sites. Native.

FOOD USE: Gather thick sections of stem any time of year, cut into manageable lengths, then peel the outer bark. A thick, soft layer of **inner bark** then can be peeled off the woody core. Boil for at least 40 minutes, after which it can be used like a starchy vegetable in stews or soup. **Shoots** are slightly tangy and can be eaten in spring or early summer—they are better cooked. **Conservation 2.**

COMMENTS: If you've ever wanted to eat a stick, here's your chance. It's not as bad as it sounds. Being available in the dead of winter, and often in great quantity, this is an excellent survival food, in case you ever want to survive. Eaten raw or undercooked, the bark has the same unpleasant irritating quality of the fruit, but this is destroyed by prolonged cooking.

WARNING: The berries of these plants are not edible! They are acrid and cause discomfort in the mouth and throat if ingested. A few sources list them as edible, but I have tried them many times and recommend against it.

P. vitaceae, showing layers of the peeled stem. ▶

▲ Virginia creeper shoot.   ▲ *P. vitacea* fruit.   ▲ *P. vitacea* leaf.

8 Kudzu 1 2
Pueraria lobata ⁕ Fabaceae (Bean family)

QUICK CHECK: Tight bark; compound leaves with 3 broad, entire leaflets, purple pea-like flowers, and hairy pods. **ID difficulty 1.**

DESCRIPTION: Large, sprawling or climbing vine from an enlarged root, with stems up to 100' (30 m) long, the older portions becoming woody and up to 3" (8 cm) thick, the younger growth thinner and herbaceous. Woody portions are light gray-brown with scattered raised lenticels, the bark not shredding or flaky. **Shoots** or rapidly growing tips have *long internodes* 9-14" (23-36 cm). They bear tiny new leaves and are covered with *fine black specks* and *dense, long, stiff, straight hairs that lean toward the base*; there are *dark scales at the nodes*. **Leaves** alternate and compound with three leaflets. **Petioles** enlarged at the base, to 20" (50 cm) long, not tapered, nearly round but slightly deeper than wide, with a small channel. **Stipules** 2-lobed, each lobe long, thin, and pointed. **Leaflets** 3-8" (8-20 cm) long, often drooping, broadly ovate to diamond-shaped (almost as broad as long) or bulging at the base with rounded lobes, acuminate, the side leaflets lopsided on short petiolules with their own mini-stipules. The surface is faintly hairy above, with dense appressed hairs below. **Secondary veins** 45° to the midvein, *raised above* and much protruding below. Veinlets 90° to the secondary veins, often running unbroken between them. **Inflorescence** a crowded, erect axillary spike-like raceme up to 10" (25 cm) long, the empty lower rachis bumpy from the stubs of dropped pedicels. **Flowers** (late summer) pea-like, 0.5-0.8" (13-20 mm) long, purple with a yellow portion on the interior of the largest lobe, fragrant with a grape-like scent. **Fruit** a flattened, brownish pod up to 2" long, the *surface with very long hairs*, containing 1-7 seeds.

HABITAT: Roadsides, steep slopes, streambanks, forest edges; it likes ample sun and is usually found on erodible or disturbed sites—rarely in intact native vegetative communities. Introduced. **I**

FOOD USE: The enormous **rootstocks** can be dug all year but will contain the most food value when the top is dormant. Clean, shred (easiest in a powerful blender), and then strain through a cloth to separate the starch. Seek smaller vines; the roots of large vines are simply too big to dig. Commercially extracted in Asia, kudzu starch is nutritious and tasty and has many uses. In spring, the **shoots** and tender young leaves can be eaten raw or cooked and have a mild, slightly green bean-like flavor. **Flowers** and **flower buds** can also be eaten as a vegetable.

COMMENTS: This is the well-known "weed that ate the South." The dense tangles that it forms as it smothers second-growth trees and shrubs are familiar to most who live within its range. It was introduced intentionally from Asia in the early 1900s to reduce soil erosion.

▼ Small kudzu root.

▲ Kudzu shoots.

9 **Wisteria** 2
genus *Wisteria* ◆ *Fabaceae* (Bean family)

QUICK CHECK: No tendrils, tight bark, pinnately compound leaves with entire leaflets, and large racemes of purple pea-like flowers. **ID difficulty 1.**

DESCRIPTION: Woody vines with stems to 60' (18 m) long and up to 8" (20 cm) thick, but often much smaller. New growth is pubescent, the buds silky and the stems with notable bumps beside old leaf scars; older bark is gray-brown and bumpy but smoothish and not shaggy or scaly. Tendrils absent. **Leaves** alternate, pinnately compound, 4–16" (10–40 cm) long, the leaflets typically not in plane with the rachis. **Rachis** thin, grooved, and often arching. **Leaflets** 7–15 (terminal leaflet present), ovate, entire, pointed, 1.5–3" (4–8 cm) long, dark green and somewhat glossy, finely hairy at first, becoming nearly hairless, on

▲ Composite range.

very short, hairy petiolules 2–3% of blade length. **Inflorescence** a drooping raceme 4–14" (10–36 cm) long, the rachis, pedicels, and calyces densely hairy. **Flowers** (spring) 0.6–0.9" (15–23 mm) long, with a broad, rounded banner like a canopy over two drooping wings hiding a keel, these parts light purple except for a yellow-green zone at the base of the banner. **Fruit** a bean-like pod up to 6" (15 cm) long, somewhat flattened, often constricted between the large, brown seeds, ripening to brown in fall.

FOOD USE: Gather **flowers** when freshly opened in spring; strip whole clusters after shaking out any insects. The flowers can be eaten raw or cooked in a variety of dishes, where they impart a pea-like flavor with a floral note. They can be steeped to brew tea or even wine. **Conservation 2** (*frutescens*).

COMMENTS: Wisteria produces an abundance of food and beauty. Flowering vines are hard to miss in springtime. The flavor of the flowers is akin to black locust, only without the sweetness and touch of vanilla.

SPECIES: American wisteria *W. frutescens* is a native plant of rich forest edges and river and stream valleys. The vines rarely exceed 1.5" (4 cm) thick. The inflorescence and calyces have a dense covering of thick-tipped glandular hairs, but the pod is hairless. This species flowers after the leaves are fully formed. The raceme is 4–9" (10–23 cm) long. Flowers at the base of the raceme open long before those at the tip. **Chinese wisteria** *W. sinensis* is an introduced invasive plant of disturbed woods, roadsides, vacant lots, and urban areas. It is very similar to the native wisteria in appearance, but is larger in most respects—the stems grow much thicker, the flower clusters are 7–16" (18–40 cm) long, and the pod is hairy. The flowers open as the leaves emerge, and the whole cluster ripens almost in unison. Chinese wisteria is generally more common than the native species. **I**

▲ American wisteria.

▲ Chinese wisteria.

GROUP 14 AQUATICS WITH GRASS-LIKE LEAVES OR TUBULAR LEAFLESS STEMS

Here I include plants that would typically be found growing in standing water. Plants that usually grow in moist soil are placed in group 17. Since water levels fluctuate, some of these plants may be found away from open water, and moist soil plants may sometimes be found in standing water. Check both groups if necessary.

Freshwater marshes are the most biologically productive ecosystems on Earth, and to dominate under such ideal growing conditions requires what I call the "biomass warfare" strategy: occupying all available space to exclude competitors. This puts a premium on productivity and leaves little energy for the production of toxins. Thus the plants in this group tend to be incredibly prolific and also mild in flavor. (But this is Nature, so of course there are exceptions.)

There are hundreds of potential edibles in this group that are not covered here. The tender parts of almost every sedge, rush, and grass are nontoxic and usually tasty. However, most of these are impractical to use because of their small size. Labor efficiency is one of the most important determinants of food traditions. Here I cover the larger aquatic grass-like plants that people have found practical to eat.

TENTATIVE IDENTIFICATION KEY TO GROUP 14
The key is not your final answer!

Plant with a tubular stem and no apparent leaves.	1. Soft-stem bulrush
or Leaves few, sheathing, borne at bulging nodes on a hollow stem.	
or Stem flattened; panicle branches drooping; seeds egg-shaped.	2. Rice cutgrass
Stem roundish; panicle branches ascending; seeds linear.	3. Wild rice
or Leaves not basal, distributed evenly along a spongy-solid triangular stalk.	4. Sweet bulb-rush
or Leaves all or mostly basal.	
Leaves all basal, never keeled.	
or Leaves not flattened or sharp-edged, channeled near the base, less than 1 cm wide. Seaside arrow-grass (see group 17).	
Leaves flattened on one side, sharp-edged, never channeled, more than 2 cm wide.	5. Cattail
Leaves mostly basal but one or a few are borne on the stem; possibly keeled.	
Leaf bundle not flattened; leaves keeled below, not side-slotted.	6. Great bur-reed
Leaves in a flattened bundle with sharp edges, one blade inserted into the slotted side of an adjacent leaf. Leaves weakly keeled on both sides or not at all.	
Flowers and fruits tiny, packed on a penis-like spike; leaves sweet-fragrant.	7. Calamus
Flowers large and showy; fruit a large pod; leaves not aromatic. Iris (not edible, p. 664).	

1 Soft-stem bulrush ⌐1 🌿3 ⚘2 🌾1
Scirpus validus ✦ *Cyperaceae* (Sedge family)

QUICK CHECK: Leafless plant with a round vertical stem and a cluster of flowers drooping to one side at the top. **ID difficulty 1.**

DESCRIPTION: Perennial from a network of tough rhizomes, often growing in dense colonies. **Rhizome** 0.4–0.8" (1–2 cm) thick, hard and stiff, almost woody, crooked, light orange-brown with numerous transverse rings and attached roots, the core fibrous. **Stems** 3–8' (1–2.5 m) tall and up to 0.6" (15 mm) thick at the base, round in cross section, spongy with 2–4 air chambers in the upper stem, soft (easily crushed by hand), tapered very gently, the surface smooth, hairless, glaucous gray-green, with no leaves. There is a single, erect, pointed leaf (bract) at the top, which appears to be an extension of the stem. **Inflorescence** a single, drooping cluster of several compound branches emanating from the same point and hanging to one side near the apex of the stem. **Flowers** (early to late summer) wind-pollinated and inconspicuous, peeking out from the reddish-brown scales. **Seeds** (achenes) tiny, brown, flat on one side and convex on the other.

HABITAT: Margins of lakes, rivers, and other open water, occasionally to 3' (1 m) deep. Usually found in less fertile sites where the bottom is sand, gravel, or otherwise firm. Native.

FOOD USE: Rhizome tips (summer) are good raw or cooked, but small. Break off the tender, smooth-skinned, white terminal portion that has not yet produced roots. Mature rhizomes are much too tough to eat. Tender **stem bases** (spring or early summer) can be eaten raw or cooked; pull or cut the soft, whitish bottom part. **Pollen** is collected by leaning flowering heads over a container and tapping or shaking; after sifting out impurities it can be used as flour. **Seeds** (late summer) can be eaten as a hot cereal or flour after labor-intensive processing. **Conservation 2/2/1.**

COMMENTS: In England the common name "bulrush" often refers to the plant that we normally call "cattail" in North America, so many accounts confound the two plants. The edible properties of the cattail (*Typha*) are often erroneously attributed to the bulrush (*Scirpus*) in the American literature. The uses of the plants are similar in many ways, except that for most uses cattail has larger edible parts. Mature bulrush rhizomes are not a good source of starch because they are extremely tough. **AKA** *Schoenoplectus validus.*

RELATED EDIBLES: All bulrushes are theoretically edible, but this is the big one that is most worth your time.

▲ *Young bulrush rhizomes have small, tender, white tips.*

▲ *Mature bulrush rhizomes are tough and semi-woody.*

▲ *Bulrush heart, so tender it broke as I peeled it.*

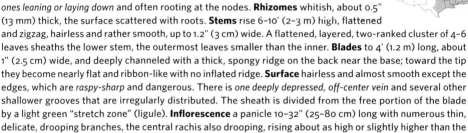

2 Rice cutgrass ✎ 2 ⌐→2 ❦ 2
Zizaniopsis miliaceae ✦ *Poaceae* (Grass family)

QUICK CHECK: Very large clumping grass with flattened stems and sharp-edged leaves, leaning at the edge of the clump; large drooping seedheads. **ID difficulty 1.**

DESCRIPTION: Perennial grass forming dense clumps, the center stems erect, the *outer ones leaning or laying down* and often rooting at the nodes. **Rhizomes** whitish, about 0.5" (13 mm) thick, the surface scattered with roots. **Stems** rise 6–10' (2–3 m) high, flattened and zigzag, hairless and rather smooth, up to 1.2" (3 cm) wide. A flattened, layered, two-ranked cluster of 4–6 leaves sheaths the lower stem, the outermost leaves smaller than the inner. **Blades** to 4' (1.2 m) long, about 1" (2.5 cm) wide, and deeply channeled with a thick, spongy ridge on the back near the base; toward the tip they become nearly flat and ribbon-like with no inflated ridge. **Surface** hairless and almost smooth except the edges, which are *raspy-sharp and dangerous*. There is *one deeply depressed, off-center vein* and several other shallower grooves that are irregularly distributed. The sheath is divided from the free portion of the blade by a light green "stretch zone" (ligule). **Inflorescence** a panicle 10–32" (25–80 cm) long with numerous thin, delicate, drooping branches, the central rachis also drooping, rising about as high or slightly higher than the tallest leaves. **Flowers** (mostly April–June) tiny and inconspicuous. **Seeds** egg-shaped, about 2 mm long, enclosed in chaff with a short awn, ripening mostly May–July.

HABITAT: Shallow, mucky areas: pond and lake edges, marshes, and riverine wetlands, especially near the coast, in fresh or brackish water. Often in shade but only fruits well in full sun. Native.

FOOD USE: Tender **stem bases** (spring and early summer) can be peeled and eaten raw or cooked. **Lateral shoots** of fast-growing rhizomes (summer) are tender and delicious. **Seeds** (late spring or early summer) can be harvested by beating, like wild rice, and processed by rubbing and winnowing. **Conservation 1.**

COMMENTS: If I lived in the South I would adapt the techniques used for wild rice and make this one of my staple foods. **AKA** giant cutgrass or southern wild rice, but the latter name is better reserved for *Zizania aquatica*.

3 Wild rice 🌿 3 📖 FH-117
Zizania palustris, Z. aquatica + *Poaceae* (Grass family)

QUICK CHECK: Large grass with large rod-like seeds in raspy husks with awns longer than the kernels. **ID difficulty 1.**

DESCRIPTION: Annual grass that grows in water up to 4' (1.2 m) deep, or on mudflats if the water level has dropped. Seedlings emerge first as submerged aquatic leaves. After reaching the surface these float for several weeks before the stems stand erect. **Erect stems** 2–13' (0.6–4 m) tall, unbranched, clumped (up to 70 per plant where competition is low) 0.2–0.9" (5–23 mm) thick, roundish, hollow, smooth and hairless, enlarged above each node. There are usually only 2–4 leaves per stem. **Leaves** 0.7–3" (18–80 mm) wide and 10–42" (25–110 cm) long with a sharp tip. **Midvein** prominent, depressed above, enlarged, *spongy, stiffening the leaf* (especially proximally); there are 4–6 prominent veins evenly spaced on each side. **Surface** hairless and smooth except near the margins, which are very rough when rubbed from tip to base, *rougher on one edge than the other.* **Inflorescence** an erect, Christmas-tree-shaped panicle 10–30" (25–75 cm) long with a dominant central rachis, often rising far above the leaves on a naked stem; it may be spread wide or have all the upper branches folded in tightly. Panicle branches are whorled or alternate and up to 7" (18 cm) long. The lower branches are male and spreading, the upper female and ascending. Female **flowers** are inconspicuous; the male drooping and showy (for a grass), up to 1 cm long. **Seed** rod-like, 0.3–1.1" (8–28 mm) long and 1.5–3 mm wide, borne in a 2-part husk that has stiff, raspy hairs, especially on the ridges, and a *barbed awn much longer than the kernel.*

SPECIES: Northern wild rice *Z. palustris* has larger kernels but its vegetative parts tend to be smaller. **Southern wild rice** *Z. aquatica* is a larger plant with smaller kernels that tends to grow in shallower water. Southern rice has copious amounts of very slick, aromatic, sour-lemony lubricant on the panicle stems, which is reduced or absent in northern rice. The female portion of the panicles of southern rice are always spread open when the seeds are ripe; on northern they often stay closed or spread only slightly.

HABITAT: Shallow areas of lakes with inlets and outlets, and rivers. Wild rice needs very soft muck over a sand or gravel bottom and is very sensitive to boat traffic and similar disturbance. Native.

FOOD USE: Harvest **seeds** in late summer to early autumn when the kernels fall upon being struck gently. Propel a small watercraft through the rice with a paddle or pole and knock the rice into the boat with sticks. Wild rice needs to be dried, parched, rubbed, and winnowed before cooking (see p. 27). **Conservation 1.**

WARNING: Rice awns are tiny and barbed and may penetrate eyes, mouth, nose, ears, armpits and other crevices; they burrow under finger and toe nails. Never put fresh green wild rice into your mouth—the hulls must be removed.

COMMENTS: One of the iconic wild foods of North America, this is an excellent starchy staple, but the great majority of wild rice on the market is cultivated. Although wild rice is widespread, it is most abundant in Minnesota, Wisconsin, Michigan, Saskatchewan, and Ontario. Both species can be used similarly, but northern wild rice is generally more efficient to harvest. Indigenous peoples developed a rich body of techniques and knowledge that makes practical use of this food possible. All foragers need to join them in protecting this and other native plant foods.

▲ (top left) Northern wild rice flowering.
(top right) Northern wild rice, ripe grain.

◀ Wild rice, floating stage.

4 Sweet bulb-rush ⟨💧⟩ 3 ⟜2 🌿 2
Bolboschoenus fluviatilis ◆ *Cyperaceae* (Sedge family)

QUICK CHECK: In colonies; large, smooth, 3-sided leafy stem; leaves grass-like, grooved, borne on the stem rather than at the base. **ID difficulty 1.**

DESCRIPTION: Robust perennial spreading by rhizome to form large and often pure colonies. **Rhizomes** 8–13 mm thick, white inside with a spongy outer layer and a tough cord in the middle; new ones are light on the outside, but older ones become very dark brown to black. **Tuber** (or corm, but not a bulb as the name suggests) 0.6–1.1" (15–28 mm) in diameter, white and soft when young, dark and wooden-hard when older; *occurring in chains on older rhizomes.* A scaly sheath attaches to a ring around the tuber; there is a bud at the end, and a few attached roots. **Stems** 3–6' (1–2 m) tall, erect, never branching, dark purple-brown at the bottom but green higher up, triangular (but the leaf clusters may be squared), smooth and hairless, up to 0.8" (2 cm) thick. **LYDS** persistent. **Leaves** *not basal, distributed evenly to the top of the stem,* alternate, ascending with drooping tips, spongy inside, sheathing at the base, rough but not tough, hairless, 14–24" (36–60 cm) long, tapered to a very thin tip. Blades have a sharp keel below and are gently arched on each side, creating a cross section like a depressed lowercase M. New **leaf clusters** in spring have the lower sheaths fused at the base; these clusters are 3-sided and the tender inner parts stain dark gray when broken. Upper leaves often surpass the inflorescence, which has 3–6 spreading bracts at its base. **Inflorescence** an umbel-like cluster of 10–20 spikelets on stalks of varying lengths up to 3" (8 cm). **Flowers** (early to mid summer) tiny, inconspicuous, and *not commonly produced.* **Seeds** (achenes) 3-sided, 3.5–5 mm, pointed at both ends, with 6 toothed, linear bracts beneath them.

CONFUSING PLANTS: Several other closely related bulrushes (*Scirpus atrovirens, S. robustus,* most notably) are similar in appearance; all are similarly edible, just with smaller parts.

HABITAT: Muddy lakeshores and river banks, marshes. Full sun to moderate shade. Often forms large, pure stands along the backwaters of flood-prone rivers. Native.

◀ Shoot ready for peeling.

◀ This shows the form of a mature stalk, but they typically grow in dense colonies.

◄◄ (left) Base of shoot and young corm.

◄ (right) The same corm after peeling. Older ones become woody.

FOOD USE: Young corms forming at stem bases, while still soft and white (from late spring to mid summer), have a sugarcane flavor and are delicious raw or cooked. **Lateral shoot** tips (summer) are good but small and hard to gather. In spring, young **stem bases** can be pulled from the mud and peeled to reveal the tender, white interior. This makes a good vegetable raw or cooked. **Conservation 2.**

COMMENTS: This plant is extremely prolific and can easily withstand human harvest—just as it does with muskrats, who relish the same parts. The immature tubers are an unsung delicacy. **AKA** river bulrush, thee-square, *Scirpus fluviatilis.*

5 Cattail 〰2 ⟿3 🌱3 ⫯2 ⬇2 📖 FH-87
genus *Typha* ✦ *Typhaceae* (Cattail family)

QUICK CHECK: Smooth, vertical, sword-like leaves with hollow chambers in a round-based cluster; sausage-shaped seedhead at the stem's apex. **ID difficulty 1.**

DESCRIPTION: Perennial plant spreading by rhizome to form large colonies. **Rhizomes** 0.7-1.2" (18-30 mm) thick and very long, not branching between stem bases, the surface tan to reddish brown with occasional rings and scattered white roots on all sides, the outer layer soft and spongy, the center firm and stringy. **Leaves** basal, two-ranked, in a tight rounded bundle, erect to strongly ascending, linear, sword-like, 3-8' (1-2.4 m) tall and 0.7-1.3" (18-33 mm) wide, spongy inside, the surface smooth and hairless with *no depressions or ridges.* **Stalk** straight, erect, unbranched, solid, mostly hidden by leaves and only exposed in the upper part, which is 5-9 mm in diameter. **Inflorescence** a densely-packed spike of numerous tiny yellow flowers (male above, female below) at the stalk's apex. These ripen into a 4-8" (10-20 cm) hot-dog like head of densely packed seeds, each with a fluffy parachute.

CONFUSING PLANTS: Irises (p. 664) have proportionately broader leaves that are less erect; their leaf clusters are flattened rather than rounded at the base, and their rhizomes are short, stout, and firmer.

SPECIES: Common cattail *T. latifolia* is a more robust native plant with the male and female portions of the spike nearly touching. Native. **Narrow-leaf cattail** *T. angustifolia* has narrower leaves, stalks, and rhizomes, and the male and female portions of the spike are widely separated. This species is native near the coast but has been spreading to interior wetlands. Hybrids between the two species are common.

HABITAT: Freshwater marshes, ditches, wet depressions; margins of lakes, ponds, or rivers. (Continued on the next page.)

◄ Cattail spikes, the left ready for eating the flower buds, the right ready for collecting pollen.

5 Cattail (continued)

FOOD USE: Peel off the outer spongy layer of the **rhizome** and chew on the core raw, sucking out the starch and spitting out the fiber. Roasting sweetens the rhizomes. Cores can be dried and ground into flour, after which the fibers can be sifted out. **Lateral shoots** are sweet and delicious eaten raw or cooked. The **heart** at the base of the leaf cluster in spring and early summer is mild in flavor but when eaten raw often causes mild irritation in the throat; it is great cooked. In early summer while the leafy sheath still encloses the immature **green flower spike**, you can boil or steam the whole spikes and nibble off the flower buds, or scrape them off to mix with grain or vegetables. The male flowers (top section of the spike) are better than the female; this part snaps off easily by hand. **Pollen** can be collected by leaning the flowering spikes over a pail or bag and tapping. It should be dried to prevent spoilage, then sifted to remove insects and debris. Use pollen mixed with other flours to give baked foods a nice golden color and pleasant flavor. **Conservation 2/2/1**

COMMENTS: This is one of our most versatile, productive, abundant, and delicious wild food plants.

▲ (top) Forming cattail rhizomes with lateral shoot tips.
(middle) Mature cattail rhizome. (bottom) Cattail hearts.

6 Great bur-reed 🐿1 ↙2 ✏2 |2 🍃2
Sparganium eurycarpum ◆ *Typhaceae* (Cattail family)

QUICK CHECK: Leaves basal and on the stem, in non-flattened bundles, with keeled bottoms; stem zigzags between round flower clusters or spiky fruit balls. **ID difficulty 2.**

DESCRIPTION: Perennial spreading by rhizome to form sometimes large colonies. **Roots** 2–3 mm thick, radiating from the base. **Rhizomes** usually less than 12" (30 cm) long and 8 mm thick, the surface smooth with brown leafy sheaths, widening toward the end, producing a small, semi-hard terminal tuber with a sheath at the base and an upturned bud at the tip. **Leaves** sword-like, to 4' (120 cm) long and 0.3–0.8" (8–20 mm) wide, both basal and on the stem (stem leaves shorter), strongly ascending, the tips sharp and not drooping. Basal leaf bundles are rounded to roughly 4-sided. The lower part of the leaf is thick and folded, with some purple coloration. There is a V-groove on the inside and a high, sharp ridge on the back. Distally the leaves are nearly flat and ribbon-like, without the groove but still with a small keel. **Stems** *strongly tapered, very zigzag,* spongy-solid, rounded, rarely branched, shorter than the tallest leaves. **Flowers** greenish to white, tiny, borne in *tight round balls* at intervals along the zigzag stems, with female flowers near the base and male ones near the top. **Fruit** pointed, pyramid-shaped, green, each with a tough spike or "bur" at the end, *packed tightly into a distinctive, hard, spiky ball like a mace head* 1–1.5" (2.5–4 cm) across.

CONFUSING PLANTS: Sweet flag *Acorus calamus* has a distinctive sweet odor and side-slotted leaves. Cattail has no keel running the length of the leaf.

HABITAT: Shallows of permanent water with a rich mucky bottom in full sun. Native.

FOOD USE: Tubers can be eaten while they remain tender, but are quite small and soon toughen. **Lateral shoots** can be eaten throughout summer, but they are small. The **heart** at the base of the leaf clusters can be pulled in spring or early summer and eaten raw or cooked. In early to mid summer the tender flower spike **shoot** (well before the flowers appear) can be cooked as a vegetable. The immature **flower bud clusters** are also edible raw or cooked. **Conservation 2.** (Continued on the next page.)

6 Great bur-reed (continued)

COMMENTS: A surprisingly good and versatile food plant that is largely ignored among the multitude of wetland vegetables.

RELATED EDIBLES: Other bur-reeds are similarly edible, but smaller.

▲ Bur-reed base and peeled heart.

▲ Bur-reed tuber and rhizome.

7 Calamus 🌿 2 🍶 3 🏮 📖 IWE-73
genus *Acorus* ✦ family *Acoraceae*

QUICK CHECK: Erect, sword-like, yellow-green leaves in a flattened bundle with a sausage-like flower cluster projecting near the middle of the leaf-like stem; highly aromatic. **ID difficulty 1.**

DESCRIPTION: Perennial forming colonies by rhizome, the above-ground parts very aromatic with a sweet odor. **Rhizome** white on older parts, pink to dark purple on newer growth, 0.5–1" (13–25 mm) thick, erratically constricted, wider than deep, with many feathery scales or leaf remains. Numerous *roots are attached on the bottom half only, oriented downward.* Rhizome aromatic but not sweet-scented like the top. **Leaf bundle** *flattened at the base with 2 sharp edges,* each blade *fitting into a slot in the margin of the adjacent leaf.* The slot may be more than half the blade's width near the base, but decreases in depth going up the leaf; *the margin is indented just above the spot where the slot ends.* **Leaves** sword-like, 1–4' (30–120 cm) long and up to 1" (2.5 cm) wide, erect to ascending, spongy, flattened, hairless and smooth with a *gentle ridge* down the middle and a sharp tip. Hidden parts of leaf bases are *white and pink.* **Stems** *flattened, with one sharp edge, the other edge thicker with a deep channel.* A single spike is borne

▲ The area in purple is inhabited exclusively by introduced calamus.

near the midpoint of the plant; above this the stem turns leafy with both edges sharp. **Spike** green, penis-like, 1.5–3.5" (4–9 cm) long and up to 0.7" (18 mm) wide, nearly erect, tapering gently to a blunt tip, packed tightly with hundreds of tiny flowers or fruits forming a continuous surface. **Flowers** tiny, white, and inconspicuous. **Fruits** tiny, pale brown, angled, containing 1–6 seeds.

SPECIES: *A. americanus* is native; its leaves thicken gradually to a gentle midvein ridge, and the heads produce viable seed. *A. calamus* is introduced from Europe; its leaves have a sharp, abrupt midvein ridge and are often rippled, and the heads generally do not produce viable seed. The two are very similar and not separated by all botanists.

CONFUSING PLANTS: Only irises (p. 664) have similarly side-slotted leaves, but iris leaves have no prominent keel and are not sweet-aromatic. The flowers and fruits are very different.

HABITAT: Lakeshores, river edges, reservoirs, estuaries; in shallow, often slow-moving drainage waters that fluctuate in depth, where the bottom is shallow mud over gravel or sand.

FOOD USE: Rhizomes can be collected all year; they are used medicinally or as a flavoring for candy or syrup. Their taste is extremely potent and they should be used in moderation. Tender **hearts** of leaf cluster bases can be eaten raw or cooked. Young **spikes** of immature flower buds are fragrant, tasty, and mucilaginous. **Conservation 2/ 2/ 1.**

▲ *A. americanus* leaf cross section.

COMMENTS: Calamus candy, made from the rhizomes, was formerly sold commercially. This plant is found across the northern hemisphere and has long been appreciated for its fabulous aroma. Studies have shown a constituent of the rhizomes of the old-world species to be carcinogenic under lab conditions. The leaves, and the native North American species, are not known to contain the carcinogenic compound. **AKA** sweet flag.

▲ *A. calamus* leaf cross section.

▲ Young *A. americanus* plants.

▲ *A. americanus* rhizome.

▲ *A. americanus* peeled heart.

▲ Immature flower spike.

GROUP 15   AQUATICS—NOT GRASS-LIKE OR TUBULAR

This group includes some easily identified plants—but it also includes some tricky species with deadly poisonous look-similars. The edible parts include leafy greens, shoots, lateral shoots, seeds, pods, and storage organs. I have included here plants that are typically found in standing water at normal or average water levels. Since water levels fluctuate, aquatic plants will occasionally be found on land adjacent to water, and terrestrial plants will sometimes be flooded. Some plants are regularly found both in standing water and on moist uplands nearby; I have tried to place such plants where they are most common and thrive best. When in doubt about any plant found near water, check it in both the aquatic and terrestrial groups. **CAUTION:** I advise cooking aquatic plant parts, unless they are peeled or carefully scrubbed and washed, to avoid ingesting parasites such as liver flukes or snail larvae.

TENTATIVE IDENTIFICATION KEY TO GROUP 15
The key is not your final answer!

Leaves tape-like, the edges clear; fruit a cylinder.	1. American eelgrass
Leaves compound.	
Without basal rosettes.	2. Watercress
With basal rosettes.	
Leaves more than once compound.	
Leaflets lanceolate to ovate, no bulblets in leaf axils. Javan water celery (group 27, p. 443).	
Leaflets linear, bulblets in upper leaf axils. Bulblet water hemlock (deadly, p. 670).	
Leaves once compound.	
Upper leaves lanceolate, serrated but not lobed.	3. Water parsnip
Upper leaves variably, sometimes deeply, lobed.	4. Springwater parsnip
Leaves simple, not tape-like.	
Leaves paired, all on stem.	
Stem hairless, roundish; leaves toothed; midvein flat to depressed above.	5. Brooklime
Stem with 2 hairy grooves; leaves usually entire; midvein raised above.	6. Alligator weed
Leaves not paired (all basal or alternate).	
Leaves toothed or notched.	
Leaves diamond-shaped to triangular, in a floating rosette.	7. Water-chestnut
Leaves roundish, on long stalks in shallow water.	8. Water pennywort
Leaves not toothed or notched.	
Sap milky.	
Leaf arrowhead-shaped.	9. Wapato
Leaf elliptic.	
Petiole 2–5 x longer than blade; fruits directly on scape.	10. Spoon-leaved wapato
Petiole less than 2 x blade length; fruits on panicle branches.	11. Water-plantain
Sap not milky.	
Leaf sometimes or always floating on a limp petiole—a "lily pad."	
Pad (leaf) with no lobe, cutout, or sinus.	
Leaf oblong, less than 6" (15 cm), never emergent, with a thick gel layer below.	12. Water shield
Leaf round, more than 12" (30 cm), often emergent, without gel.	13. American lotus
Pad (leaf) with a cut or sinus at the base, resulting in 2 lobes.	
Pad oblong, lobes rounded, flowers yellow.	14. Yellow pond-lily
Pad round, lobes with a sharp corner, flowers white. White water-lily (p. 677).	
Leaf emergent on a rigid petiole—not a "lily pad."	
Leaf arrowhead-shaped with two pointed, divergent, backward lobes.	
Petiole attached at or very near the edge of the blade.	15. Arrow arum
Petiole attached 0.8" (2 cm) or more from the edge of the blade.	16. Wild taro
Leaf blunt; if lobed the lobes are rounded, not pointed.	
Petiole with a large balloon-like inflation.	17. Water hyacinth
No balloon-like inflation on the petiole.	18. Pickerelweed

1 American eelgrass ◊ 2
Vallisneria americana + family *Hydrocharitaceae*

QUICK CHECK: Submerged, ribbon-like leaves with translucent edges and a darker center stripe; tubular fruits at the end of thin, coiled stems. **ID difficulty 1.**

DESCRIPTION: Despite the name this is not a grass. Submerged perennial, spreading by thin rhizomes and often forming colonies. **Leaves** mostly in basal rosettes or clumps of several, each clump associated with a tuft of fibrous roots—although this arrangement may not be evident from the surface. **Blades** flat and ribbon-like, 5–10 mm wide, of rather uniform width, thin and fragile, 2–7' (60–210 cm) long, sometimes reaching the surface. They have a dull green stripe in the center and *translucent edges*. Margins are entire and the tips rounded. Plants are male or female. Male stems are short and unlikely to be noticed, rising only 1–6" (2.5–15 cm) from the base, and bear a cluster of tiny flowers enclosed in a spathe. **Female stems** very thin and leafless, about 2 mm in diameter, 2–10' (5–25 cm) long, reaching the surface, rounded, smooth, *string-like and coiled*, inflating at the end. **Flower** single, tiny, terminal, white, with 3 petals and 3 sepals, in mid to late summer. **Fruit** (late summer) cylindric, 2–6" (5–15 cm) long and 4–6 mm wide, curving slightly, dull gray-green and smooth outside, the inside holding numerous elongated seeds embedded in a gelatinous material.

HABITAT: Water of permanent lakes, ponds, sloughs, and slow-moving rivers, 1–8' (30–240 cm) deep, usually with a mucky bottom. Native.

FOOD USE: The **fruits**, ripe or unripe, can be gathered from the water surface in late summer or early fall. They are mild flavored and can be cooked as a vegetable. (I don't eat them raw lest they have parasitic mollusk larvae on the surface.) The mucilaginous texture makes them good in soup. **Leaves** are traditionally eaten raw in East Asian cuisine, but I have not tried them. **Conservation 1.**

COMMENTS: This fascinating plant's tiny male flowers separate at maturity and float to the surface, where they drift around like bachelors at a beach, hoping to meet a female. The coiled female stems retract to pull the mature fruit underwater. Eelgrass fruits are an important waterfowl food, especially for the canvasback *Aythya vallisneria*, which was named for the plant. It is said to give canvasback meat a superb flavor. American eelgrass is widespread and very common, often fruiting in great abundance. **AKA** water-celery.

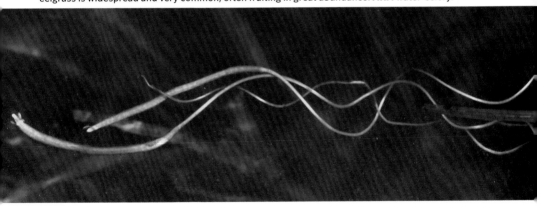

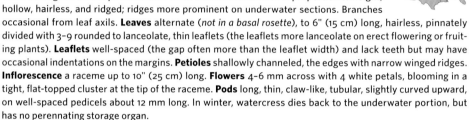

2 Watercress 🖊 3 📖 IWE-381
Nasturtium officinale ✦ *Brassicaceae* (Mustard family)

QUICK CHECK: Decumbent herb of spring water with pinnately divided leaves, rooting from the stems. **ID difficulty 1.**

DESCRIPTION: Perennial with weak trailing or creeping stems that often float and form dense, thick mats. The tips stand erect up to 18" (46 cm) in summer. Thin, thread-like, white roots grow in clumps from underwater nodes. **Stems** thick in proportion to height, hollow, hairless, and ridged; ridges more prominent on underwater sections. Branches occasional from leaf axils. **Leaves** alternate (*not in a basal rosette*), to 6" (15 cm) long, hairless, pinnately divided with 3–9 rounded to lanceolate, thin leaflets (the leaflets more lanceolate on erect flowering or fruiting plants). **Leaflets** well-spaced (the gap often more than the leaflet width) and lack teeth but may have occasional indentations on the margins. **Petioles** shallowly channeled, the edges with narrow winged ridges. **Inflorescence** a raceme up to 10" (25 cm) long. **Flowers** 4–6 mm across with 4 white petals, blooming in a tight, flat-topped cluster at the tip of the raceme. **Pods** long, thin, claw-like, tubular, slightly curved upward, on well-spaced pedicels about 12 mm long. In winter, watercress dies back to the underwater portion, but has no perennating storage organ.

CONFUSING PLANTS: Pennsylvania cress (p. 431) has leaves in a basal rosette.

HABITAT: Springs and spring-fed streams high in calcium. Tolerates shade but thrives in full sun. Often grows without any connection to soil. Introduced. **I**

FOOD USE: Gather **greens** from late winter through late fall (but especially spring) and use raw in salads or on sandwiches. They can also be fried or used in soup or casserole.

COMMENTS: This is another wild vegetable that is identical to the cultivated form sold at high prices in grocery stores. Watercress has a strong pungency that can be overpowering when used in too great a quan-

tity, but wonderful when used appropriately. The spicy flavor is greatly reduced by cooking. There are actually two very similar species of watercress. *N. officinale* is the larger and more common of the two; the smaller species is one-row watercress *N. microphyllum*, so named because the seeds in the pod are found in a single row as opposed to the two of common watercress. Both are used similarly.

CAUTION: Watercress may have larvae of parasitic snails or liver flukes on its surface. This is most likely in warmer regions and in areas where livestock are pastured. To avoid infection, cook all watercress from suspect areas, and never eat underwater portions raw. See p. 24.

3 Water parsnip 🌿 3 | 3 ✐ 2 📖 IWE-388
Sium suave ✦ *Apiaciae* **(Carrot family)**

QUICK CHECK: Pinnately compound leaf with long-lanceolate leaflets; a single, angled stem; scattered umbels of small white flowers. **ID difficulty 3+.**

DESCRIPTION: Perennial from clustered roots, the aerial parts with variable morphology based on season and water levels. **Roots** multiple, usually 12–30, in a *radiating cluster*, white inside and outside, with many depressions but no ring-like constrictions, 5–12" (13–30 cm) long and 4–10 mm thick, limp and flexible but brittle, unbranched, widest near the middle, tapering gently toward both ends. Occasional roots are shorter and widest near the tip. **Rosettes** have 4–9 leaves. **Typical basal leaves** pinnately once-compound, 6–12" (15–30 cm) long with 15–21 leaflets. If the leaf is upright, the plane of the leaflets is perpendicular to the leaf, forming "ladder leaves" like those of parsnip. Basal leaves may come up as **spear-like shoots**: long, straight, tapered, with *unopened leaflets wrapped into a pointed tip*. **Leaflets** flat, sessile, neatly paired, lanceolate, 1.5–3.5" (4–9 cm) long, with needle-like tips. Occasional leaflets are deeply lobed, especially near the base of the leaf. **Margins** have low, claw-tipped, forward-pointing teeth. **Midvein** *flat to raised* above. **Secondary veins** numerous but not straight and none very prominent, 20–35° to the midvein, roughly flat above, breaking into veinlets before reaching the margins. Veinlets terminate mostly in teeth. **Underwater leaves** (and often the earliest spring leaves of terrestrial plants) have feathery leaflets *deeply pinnately cut into many thin, lacy divisions. Neither the leaflets nor the lacy divisions are stalked.* **Petioles** hollow, thin-walled, strongly tapered, not channeled, *with one or a few purple-brown rings and an internal septum below the first leaflets.* After the first leaflets, the rachis is ridged on top. **Stems** usually single, 16–64" (40–160 cm) tall and 0.4–1" (1–2.5 cm) thick, hollow, whitish inside, jointed, erect, hairless, green except for a small amount of purple sometimes near the base. The surface is *ridged with 7–9 angles* which become sharper toward the top; it also has fine, light green grooves. Portions of *stems that develop underwater are thick-walled*

and spongy with visible air channels and may root at the nodes. Internodes are 4–6" (10–15 cm) long (closer near the stem base). **Branches** few, only in the upper 2/3, ascending. **Stem leaves** alternate, once-compound with 3–13 leaflets (fewer toward the top), on petioles usually less than half the blade length, shorter toward the top. Upper leaves are sessile or have the sheath extending to the first leaflets. **Petioles** of stem leaves are sheathing, broad, flat, and thin with a tiny, crescent-shaped hollow, fine grooves, and papery margins. After the first leaflet the rachis abruptly narrows and becomes rounded and hollow with a small groove above that soon tapers away. *Flooded plants delay flowering.* **Inflorescence** flat-topped compound umbels 1.3–2" (3.3–5 cm) across, at branch tips and from upper leaf axils. **Rays** 13–19, ridged, each 0.4–1.4" (1–3.5 cm) long (longer in fruit). Beneath the first umbel division, as well as each umbellet, is a whorl of 3–11 linear to lanceolate **bracts**, entire with thin whitish margins, 3–12 mm long, reflexed against the peduncle or ray. There are minute hairs on and around these bracts. **Umbellets** only occasionally touch each other, but the flowers within them are often touching, on pedicels 3–5 mm long. **Flowers** 3 mm across, 5 white petals with the tips folded in. **Fruit** 2–3 mm long, broadly oval, slightly flattened, hairless, with 3 prominent ridges on each broad side and one on each edge (for a total of 8). In fruit the umbels are sometimes covered with a powdery mildew, giving them a hoary look. (Continued on the next page.)

3 Water parsnip (continued)

CONFUSING PLANTS: Misidentifications with **water hemlock** (pp. 668-670) have resulted in death! Water hemlock leaves are 2–3 times compound, splitting 3 ways at the first division. The stems are not angled. Water hemlock roots are 1–5" (2.5–13 cm) long and much stouter (about 20% as thick as long), widest in the middle, stiff, yellowish or straw-colored outside, often with yellow lines inside. **Bulblet water hemlock** (p. 670) has multiple thin roots that taper from the top. The leaves are 2–3 times compound, splitting 3 ways at the first division, with the leaflets very thin and lobed, the smallest divisions linear. The stems are not angled. When mature, the bulblets in the leaf axils are diagnostic. *Oxypolis rigidior* (p. 424) is similar to water parsnip in form, but the leaflets are entire or with a few scattered, large teeth toward the end of the leaflet. Its roots are clustered and white with spherical enlargements toward the end. *Berula erecta* (see next) is another member of the carrot family that also goes by the common name "water parsnip." This is a smaller plant; its leaves are shorter and broader than those of *Sium suave*, and coarsely toothed. The upper leaves have large teeth or deeply cut lobes.

HABITAT: Marshes, lakeshores, ditches, ponds, hardwood swamps, river oxbows. Especially likes rich muck and thrives with water level fluctuations. Native.

FOOD USE: Exercise extreme care in identifying this plant. The **roots** can be collected from fall through spring and eaten raw or cooked. Dig up plants gingerly so that roots don't snap. Break off the larger roots and replant the crown. Young **stems**, **leaves**, and **leaf shoots** can be eaten raw or cooked in spring and early summer. **Conservation 3/2.**

COMMENTS: Due to the danger of misidentification, this vegetable is rarely used or written about. One of the few documented deaths from plant misidentification that I have been able to find resulted from mistaking western water hemlock for water parsnip. However, water parsnip's roots are a highly esteemed food in many Native American cultures. Skirret (*Sium sisarum*), a closely related plant with nearly identical flavor, has been cultivated as a root and stem vegetable in Asia for thousands of years. It is still available from some seed catalogs in the US.

▲ Typical leaflet close up.
▶ (middle) Young basal leaves and leaf shoots emerging in summer after flood recession. (right) Water parsnip stems are strongly angled or ridged, unlike those of water hemlock.

▲ Lacy early spring leaves.

4 Springwater parsnip 3
Berula erecta • *Apiaciae* (Carrot family)

QUICK CHECK: Mat-forming plant of springwater with pinnately compound leaves, the leaflets with large teeth; small umbels of tiny white flowers. **ID difficulty 3+.**

DESCRIPTION: Perennial forming dense mats like watercress, spreading by creeping horizontal stems with *no storage organ*; these are round with whorls of thread-like white roots at the nodes. **Basal leaves** in a rosette, pinnately once-compound with 14–21 leaflets, the lowest leaflets much reduced, the terminal leaflet occasionally conjoined to those adjacent. **Submerged rosettes** tend to be smaller and often form dense mats on the bottom of spring pools. **Leaflets** *all sessile*, slightly clasping, attached to the top of the rachis rather than the sides, sometimes strongly out of plane, hairless, very thin, ovate, to 2" (5 cm) long, shallowly lobed or with large, blunt teeth. **Midvein** and secondary veins are faint and *not depressed*. **Petiole/rachis** leafy for half or more of its length; *viewed from the side it appears scalloped or wavy*, rising at each node. Petioles are hollow, finely ridged with a small channel on top, brittle, green with fine stripes, smooth, hairless, ringed only where leaflets attach. **Aerial stems** weak, to 28" (70 cm) long and 0.6" (15 mm) thick, sometimes erect but more often leaning or decumbent. They are hollow, juicy, often sinuous, hairless, jointed, roundish in cross section with fine lines and faint ridges near the base but the *upper part is distinctly angled*. Branches are spreading or ascending. **Stem leaves** alternate with a small sheath near the base, pinnately compound with 7–11 leaflets. Uppermost leaves are reduced to a few widely spaced leaflets, narrower and *deeply cut with large teeth or small lobes*. **Inflorescence** a compound umbel (occasionally thrice compound) 1–2" (2.5–5 cm) across, with a *whorl of several entire, linear bracts* to 12 mm at the base of the great umbel; there are bracts beneath each umbellet about as long as the rays. **Umbellets** 8–12 mm across, mostly not touching each other; the flowers within them do not touch either. **Flowers** tiny and white with 5 petals curved in at the tip. **Fruit** tiny, oval, slightly flattened, seldom maturing.

CONFUSING PLANTS: Often confused with the larger, more erect relative that is also called water parsnip (*Sium suave*, see previous), but *Berula erecta* is much smaller, less erect, mat-forming, and roots from the nodes of prostrate stems. Javan water celery has twice compound leaves with depressed veins. Also compare with **water hemlocks** (deadly poisonous, p. 668).

HABITAT: Open to shaded spring water in pools, marshes, streamsides, and fens, in alkaline soil. Native. This plant is being widely displaced and outcompeted by non-native watercress.

FOOD USE: The tender **greens** (early spring to autumn) are good raw or cooked. They have a strong celery-parsley-parsnip flavor, much like *Sium suave*, and are used in salads, soups, casseroles, etc. **Conservation 2.**

COMMENTS: This little-known edible (which, like many edible members of the carrot family, is often erroneously reported as toxic) is remarkably widespread—it is found in Asia, Europe, Africa, Australia, and North America. Its ecology is much like that of watercress, which crowds it out and is the greatest threat to its survival. Despite the name, there is not an edible root—springwater parsnip has no taproot at all. **AKA** water parsnip, small water parsnip, water celery, *Berula pusilla*. See liver fluke caution p. 24.

▲ Rosettes are often permanently under water.

◄ Springwater parsnip floating rosettes growing beside watercress.

5 Brooklime 1
Veronica americana + family *Scrophulariaceae*

QUICK CHECK: In spring water; fleshy stems and thick, paired, shallowly-toothed leaves. **ID difficulty 2.**

DESCRIPTION: Perennial herb growing in water, sometimes with underwater leaves, often in dense colonies, 6–30" (15–75 cm) tall. **Stems** leaning, trailing, decumbent, or erect; smooth, hairless, often reddish (especially at nodes), round, hollow, succulent, up to 0.9" (23 mm) thick, rooting at lower nodes, branching infrequently at angles of 45–60°. **Leaves** paired, hairless, thick, succulent, brittle, ovate, folded or cupped; the underside has tiny, dark dots. **Major veins** faintly depressed above, but veinlets are hardly evident. **Margins** have small, widely-spaced, blunt teeth. **Petioles** short, broad, winged, shallowly channeled, about 5% of blade length; upper leaves on flowering plants may be clasping.

▲ Composite range of native and introduced populations.

Inflorescence racemes 3–4" (8–10 cm) long with 12–50 flowers, from leaf axils on peduncles much thinner than the main stem, held at about the same angle as the branches, the flowers not touching, on very thin pedicels 13 mm long, each with a lanceolate bract at the base. **Flowers** (late spring to fall) 5–6 mm across with 4 sepals and 4 petals, the latter purple with darker purple streaks, a few blooming at once. **Fruit** a 2-part capsule that retains its protruding pistil and the 4-part calyx underneath.

CONFUSING PLANTS: A close relative, water speedwell *V. anagallis arvensis* also grows in water, but it has thinner leaves that are more lanceolate, and the upper ones are sessile with clasping bases. This plant is marginally edible, so there is no danger.

HABITAT: Springs, fens, small brooks and their edges, in full to partial sunlight—often growing right in the water like watercress. Native.

FOOD USE: Gather the tender **growing tips** from spring through early fall. (For raw use, pick only the portion well above the water to eliminate the risk of liver flukes.) Best raw in salads or sandwiches. **Conservation 2.**

WARNING: See liver fluke caution (p. 24) before eating any aquatic plant raw.

COMMENTS: Populations of this plant are scattered due to its habitat requirements, but it can be locally prolific. In many areas it has been outcompeted and displaced by watercress. Although the greens are tender, they are rather bitter and astringent and are best used sparingly. Based upon taxonomic technicalities this plant's family name has been changed to *Plantaginaceae* in newer sources. There has long been debate over whether this species should be separated from the very similar Old-World *V. beccabunga*.

6 Alligator weed 2
Alternanthera philoxeroides ✦ family *Amaranthaceae*

QUICK CHECK: Mat-forming plant with thin hollow stems and narrow, paired, entire, sessile leaves; flowers in spiky whitish balls. **ID difficulty 2.**

DESCRIPTION: Mat-forming perennial that may be rooted in mud or floating—it also sometimes grows well away from the water. **Stems** creep laterally, rooting at the nodes then turning weakly erect to 16" (40 cm) high and 10–14 mm thick, tapering little. They are smooth, light green distally but often reddish near the lower nodes, spongy-walled, hollow, hairless except at the nodes, and slightly squared. There are 2 shallow grooves on opposite sides, along which there is sometimes *a faint line of fine hairs.* The *lower stem is distinctly bulged above each node,* but there is little to no bulge at the upper nodes. *At each node there is a collar around the stem, which in aerial parts is fringed with fine hairs.* **Branches** infrequent but major. **Leaves** paired, elliptic to obovate or oblanceolate, 1.25–4" (3.2–10 cm) long, thick and rather succulent, tapered to the base, the tips rounded on lower leaves, blunt-pointed on upper. Blades are flat and hairless or have scattered appressed hairs on both sides that point toward the tip. **Margins** entire or with a few scattered, tiny teeth; bristly on upper leaves. **Midvein** light in color, *protruding above* and below. **Secondary veins** several, 60–90° to the midvein, flat above and protruding slightly below. **Petioles** to 100% of blade length in aquatic parts; leaves in aerial parts are sessile. **Inflorescence** a tight *ball-like white cluster* 1 cm wide, borne at the end of a straight, faintly hairy peduncle

▲ Rapidly expanding.

2–4" (5–10 cm) long, terminal or from leaf axils. **Flowers** (summer through fall) *dry and chaffy* with 5 stiff-pointed, ovate tepals that scarcely spread open; they are so jammed together that the parts are hard to count. The small fruits are dry and bladder-like.

HABITAT: Ponds, ditches, marshes, canals, lake edges; or muddy ground nearby. Does best in full sun but tolerates some shade. Introduced. **I**

FOOD USE: Young **leaves** and **stem tips** can be gathered through the growing season, but are best in spring and early summer. They are mild in flavor and can be eaten raw but are much better cooked.

COMMENTS: This amaranth relative is extremely abundant in some waterways of the South and is rapidly spreading. Indeed, alligators often lurk in clumps of it.

▲ Small leaves on winter growth.

219

7 Water-chestnut ⬭ 3
Trapa natans ◆ *Lythraceae* (Loosestrife family)

QUICK CHECK: Floating rosettes of small, diamond shaped, sharply toothed leaves; rope-like underwater stem; nuts with 4 sharp points. **ID difficulty 1.**

DESCRIPTION: Aquatic annual forming large mats over water. **Stems** fully submerged, long and rope-like, mostly unbranched, tapering, *thinner toward the base*, 3–10 mm thick, with nodes every 2–4" (5–10 cm), each node with a *raised scar on one side*. **Underwater leaves** in an offset pair, *feathery and finely dissected*. At the surface the stem enlarges and forms a crowded rosette. **Surface leaves** diamond or fan shaped, 1–2" (2.5–5 cm) wide, broader than long, glossy, flat, hairless above. **Veins** scarcely depressed above, the midvein hardly evident, but all veins protrude below. **Margins** not toothed near the base, but toward the tip they are serrated with broad, regular, bristle-tipped teeth. **Petioles** thick, round, hairy (especially below), 1–6 times the blade length, with an *inflated float* in the outer half. **Flowers** 4–7 mm across, borne singly on thick pedicels among the leaves; they have 4 obovate, veiny white petals with wavy edges. **Fruit** odd-shaped, 1–1.5" (2.5–4 cm) wide, dark brown, with 4 large, very sharp spikes, enclosing a single, white-fleshed, asymmetric starchy kernel of uniform texture.

▲ Range expanding.

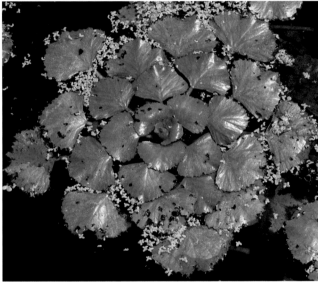

HABITAT: Slow-moving water up to 10 feet (3 m) deep, in full to partial sun. Introduced. **I**

FOOD USE: Flip rosettes in late summer and pick the larger **nuts** from beneath—one or a few may be ripe at a time. Nuts can be dried whole and then cracked with a hammer, or cut in half before drying. Kernels can be steamed, fried, boiled in soups, or ground into flour.

COMMENTS: An excellent edible locally available in huge quantities. Beware of the sharp spines while harvesting—nuts may sink to the bottom and get stepped on. The rosettes can have shockingly attractive symmetry. This plant is extremely invasive; do not put the nuts anywhere they might be able to grow. In some areas the seeds are illegal to transport. But if you eat them, I won't tell on you. **AKA** water caltrop, bull nut, bat nut.

▲ Ripe nuts sliced in half.

▲ Nuts attached on the rosette underside.

8 Water pennywort 🖋 1
Hydrocotyle umbellata ✦ *Araliaceae* (Ginseng family)

QUICK CHECK: Dense colonies of small, round, shiny, peltate leaves with rounded teeth and umbels of tiny white flowers; growing in shallow water. **ID difficulty 1.**

DESCRIPTION: Emergent aquatic perennial to 9" (23 cm) tall, forming dome-like clumps of overlapping leaves in full sun. Spreads by **rhizome**; these are about 3 mm thick, whitish, smooth, and produce a cluster of thread-like roots at each node, where a single petiole is attached. **Petioles** erect, straight, *round*, with no channels or grooves of any kind, smooth and hairless, spongy inside, light green, to 9" (23 cm) long. **Blades** peltate (the petiole connected to the center), at a right angle to the petiole, nearly rounded but usually slightly wider than long, 1.2–2.1" (3–5 cm) wide, thick and fleshy, *glossy and hairless on both sides*. **Margins** have broad, shallow, rounded lobes, each with a few small notches. Light **veins** radiate from the leaf center and run almost straight to the margins; they are depressed scarcely if at all above and do not protrude below. **Inflorescence** a simple umbel about 0.8" (2 cm) across with short, straight pedicels containing 3–6 dozen crowded flowers, atop a straight, erect scape that is slightly shorter and proportionately thinner than the petioles, often red-tinted, smooth, and hairless. **Flowers** tiny, the corolla with 5 pointed, ovate, white petals, each with a prominent central vein. **Fruit** flattened, kidney-shaped, wider than long.

HABITAT: Shallow permanent waterways with relatively stable water levels, in full to partial sun. Native.

FOOD USE: Tender **leaves** and **stems** can be eaten raw or cooked throughout the growing season, but are most prevalent in early summer. **Conservation 2.**

COMMENTS: The leaves are slightly aromatic with a pleasant flavor that is mildly bitter. The petioles and scapes taste milder than the leaves. This green is remarkable for its very long season of availability. The ginseng family is closely related to the carrot family and is sometimes classed with it.

RELATED EDIBLES: The members of this genus are generally edible, and there are several others in our area (p. 288, 620).

▲ Water pennywort spreading by rhizomes.

9 **Wapato** 🐟3 ✏️2 ⏳2 ⟼2 📖 FH-101
Sagittaria latifolia ✦ family *Alismataceae*

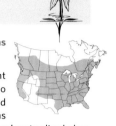

QUICK CHECK: Emergent leaves with two backward-pointing lobes about as long as the main blade. **ID difficulty 2.**

DESCRIPTION: Transient perennial sprouting from tubers distant from the parent plant. *Sap milky.* **Leaves** all basal, in rosettes, rising 1–5' (30–150 cm) high, with two *backward-pointing lobes about as long as the blade.* **Blades** 8–32" (20–80 cm) long and 0.6–20" (1.5–50 cm) wide, *broad with a rounded tip or very narrow and pointed*—both forms may be present on the same plant. The lobes are always pointed. Major **veins** flat above and protruding below, radiating in a spider-like pattern from the leaf base and *terminating in the leaf and lobe tips.* **Margins** have no teeth. **Petioles** usually much longer than the blade, tapered, spongy with air-filled tubes, rounded except for a small flat face on the upper/inside surface, smooth and hairless, the lower fifth with broad, thin, tapered wings forming a deep channel. **Stalk** simple, naked, thick, spongy, angled, hairless, to 28" (70 cm) tall and 0.9" (23 mm) thick. **Inflorescence** a raceme at the stalk's apex, the flowers in 3–9 widely spaced whorls of 3, each on an ascending, thick pedicel 0.5–1.5" (13–38 mm) long, with a single bract. **Flowers** have three waxy white, nearly round or faintly notched petals and a fuzzy-looking greenish mound of numerous sexual parts in the center. **Fruit** flattened, dry, winged seeds (achenes) with a hook at the end, borne hundreds together in a ball-like cluster. **Tuber** 1–3.5" (2.5–9 cm) long, egg-shaped to occasionally flattened, with ringed sections, dead leafy veils, and a pointed, curved, fang-like bud projecting from the end. The smooth skin is creamy, purple, rusty, or brown in color; the white to creamy-yellow flesh is crisp and not fibrous. Tubers are borne singly at the end of long, unbranched, spongy rhizomes up to 5' (1.5 m) long and 1" (2.5 cm) thick.

CONFUSING PLANTS: The backward-pointing lobes of pickerelweed leaves are blunt rather than pointed, and the veins follow the contour of the lobes without terminating there. Arrow arum lobes are proportionately smaller and point more outward; see the photos for venation differences. Neither of these plants has any underground part that even remotely resembles a wapato.

HABITAT: Lakeshores, river edges, ponds, ditches, marshes. Grows best with a clay-mud bottom and randomly fluctuating water levels. Native.

FOOD USE: Gather **tubers** either by following rhizomes from the plant base to their ends, or by digging in the mud in thick colonies. Where there is standing water, stomp systematically to break up the mud; released

◀▲ Leaf shape is highly variable. At far left is a newly emerging leaf shoot at the stage for eating.

tubers will float to the surface. Tubers can be baked, fried, or boiled and mashed like potatoes. After cooking they can also be dried and ground into hot cereal or flour. They are preferable peeled and unpalatable raw. **Lateral shoots** are okay raw but best cooked. **Leaves**, when young and tender, are excellent after boiling and then draining. Flower spike **shoots**, well before any flowers open, can also be boiled. (If steamed or fried the grapefruit peel flavor is strong.) **Conservation 2/1.**

COMMENTS: The tubers make one of the best starchy wild foods and their potato-sweet corn-grapefruit flavor is liked by most who try them; they were formerly a staple food in some regions. Wapato often grows in enormous pure stands, especially along the Mississippi River. Wapato is cultivated in China. The greens and shoots are less well known but also make good vegetables. All parts have a grapefruit peel flavor when raw. **AKA** arrowhead. All members of this genus are edible. Annual species have edible greens but no tubers.

10 **Spoon-leaved wapato** ✦ *Sagittaria rigida*

Spoon-leaved wapato has smaller leaf blades that lack lobes (and thus are not arrowhead-shaped). Wider leaves of this species resemble those of water-plantain, but *S. rigida* grows in much deeper water and has a petiole many times longer than the leaf. The edible uses are the same as wapato, but all parts are smaller. Even when the leaves have wilted this plant can be identified by the seed balls clinging directly to the stem (sessile), and the stem's odd tendency to curve dramatically just above those seed balls. The tubers of this species are harder, tawny colored, spherical, and not quite as tasty.

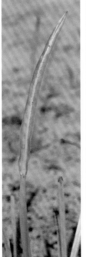

11   **Water-plantain**   1   2   2
Alisma plantago-aquatica ✦ family *Alismataceae*

QUICK CHECK: Rosette of entire, elliptic, parallel-veined leaves on long petioles; Christmas-tree like inflorescence of compound whorls. **ID difficulty 2.**

DESCRIPTION: Perennial. **Corms** stout, amorphous, hard, the outside with numerous tough, dark, thin, hairlike roots; the inside light yellowish. *Sap milky.* **Leaves** 9–14, all in a basal rosette, may be submerged, floating, or emerged, but the most prominent leaves emerge. Blades are elliptic to nearly round, entire, 3–9" (8–23 cm) long, neither end tapered, occasionally with a heart-shaped base, *hairless.* **Midvein** and secondary veins not depressed above. There are 2 prominent pairs of secondary veins diverging near the base, and another pair just below the middle; all of these converge near the leaf tip. **Veinlets** numerous, prominent, running *straight, parallel, and unbroken between the midvein and secondary veins.* **Petioles** *spongy,* hairless, thick, *not channeled,* D-shaped in cross section and 0.8–3 times the blade length (shorter on early leaves). **Stalk** single and leafless, to 45" (114 cm) tall, unbranched in the lower third, the surface smooth, glaucous, often red-tinted, the center spongy-hollow; cross section with 3 or more gentle, smooth-topped ridges. **Inflorescence** a large branching panicle wider at the base (Christmas-tree shaped), the branches in whorls of up to 6, each with whorls of smaller branches bearing umbels or compound umbels, the pedicels very thin. There are 3 sheathing lanceolate bracts beneath inflorescence junctures. **Flowers** (midsummer) 6–8 mm across with 3 thin white petals alternating with 3 green sepals half as long. **Fruit** (fall) tiny, flattened, oval, and dry with a central groove; many of these are pressed together to form a doughnut-shaped mass.

CONFUSING PLANTS: Some species of wapato with unlobed leaves are similar, but they have proportionally longer petioles.

HABITAT: Muddy shores, pond margins, vernal pools, seasonal puddles or wet depressions—prefers full or partial sun. Native.

FOOD USE: Gather **corms** from fall through spring by grabbing them just below the base of the plant and pulling them out of the muck. Rinse and detach the hair-like roots. Corms are hard and unpalatable raw, better cooked. They are best used sparingly, more as a seasoning. Tender **young leaves** and **shoots**, collected in spring and early summer, can be used as potherbs—the flavor resembles that of its close relative, wapato. Conservation 3/2.

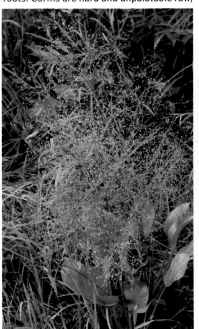

COMMENTS: I call the corms "Pine-Sol potatoes" because of their smell. The plant is killed when the corms are harvested, so gather sparingly. The shoots are super tender and excellent cooked. Other species in this genus are presumably edible, but this is the only one I've tried.

12 Water shield 🌱 1
Brasenia schreberi ✦ family *Cabombaceae*

QUICK CHECK: Oblong lily pads smaller than your hand, with a slimy underside. **ID difficulty 1.**

DESCRIPTION: Perennial spreading by creeping rootstocks 6–8 mm thick. *All underwater parts are coated with a thick layer of jelly-slime.* **Stems** roughly rounded, 6–8 mm thick, rope-like, to 9' (3 m) long. **Leaves** alternate, 2–5" (5–13 cm) long, elliptic, peltate with the long petiole attached near the center, entire, the blade rather thin if you don't count the slime. **Flower** (early summer to fall) single on a stout peduncle up to 6" (15 cm) long, arising from a leaf axil; 0.4–0.6" (1–1.5 cm) across with 6 recurved, lanceolate, unequal tepals, the inside surface dull purple, with 12–18 long-protruding stamens. **Fruit** a club-shaped leathery pod 4–8 mm long, not splitting open, that floats for dispersal and contains 1 or 2 seeds.

HABITAT: Shallows of lakes, slow rivers, and ponds. Native.

FOOD USE: Young **leaves**, still coiled, are traditionally used in soups in East Asia. Chop fine to avoid eating a giant slime gob. I have also heard of eating them raw, but I worry about parasites on raw aquatic vegetables directly in contact with water. **Conservation 2.**

COMMENTS: Some sources refer to edible tubers on this plant. I wish. This grows all over the lakes near me. I have dug the rhizomes many times and have never found a tuber, or anything tuber-like. Besides North America, this fascinating plant is native in Asia, parts of Africa, and also Australia. It might be the single most unmistakable species in this book—no other plant in our region is similarly slime-coated.

13 American lotus 🐾 2 🌰 3 🖊 1 📖 NG-99
Nelumbo lutea ✦ family *Nelumbonaceae*

QUICK CHECK: Large pads, floating or emergent, with no slit; enormous flowers and flat seedheads. **ID difficulty 1.**

DESCRIPTION: Perennial from tubers, forming large colonies of "lily pads" by fast-growing, smooth rhizomes. **Tubers** are about the size and shape of a banana, ranging from off-white to dull yellow or brown, with distinct symmetrical air chambers inside. **Leaves** floating or emergent, round, up to 34" (86 cm) across, with no slit or cut-out, borne singly and widely spaced on the rhizomes. Pad edges are upturned. Floating leaves are flat but emergent leaves are broadly funnel-shaped. **Petiole** rigid, up to 7' (2.1 m) long, erect, rough, attached at the center of the leaf. Flower stalks, petioles, rhizomes, and tubers have hollow air channels running lengthwise, and when broken have *fine, elastic, silk-like threads trailing from them.* **Inflorescence** borne singly atop an unbranched erect scape essentially identical to the petiole, rising directly from the rhizome to the water's surface or several feet above it. **Flowers** creamy yellow, 6–9" (15–23 cm) across, with numerous ovate petals and a funnel-like yellow receptacle in the center. **Receptacle** becomes more broadly funnel-shaped, growing 4–9" (10–23 cm) wide, first green then brown, holding 12–30 nuts about 90% enclosed. **Nuts** acorn-like with a thin, flexible shell and a single mass inside, about 0.7" (18 mm) long at ripening, drying and shrinking to about 0.5" (13 mm) and becoming very hard.

CONFUSING PLANTS: Water lilies (*Nymphaea*) and pond lilies (*Nuphar*) have smaller, oblong leaves with a slit-like sinus.

HABITAT: Rivers, ponds, lakes, sloughs. Prefers solid bottom of sand or clay. In the North it is confined to large lakes and river systems; further south is more of a generalist. Native.

FOOD USE: Gather **tubers** from late summer through spring. Dig along the rhizomes, usually 1–6' (30–180 cm) from the petiole base. Young, tender tubers can be peeled and sliced for eating raw, or used in stir-fry with other vegetables. Older tubers are firm and starchy and should be well cooked. **Nuts** ripen from late summer through fall. Ripe seedheads detach from the stem easily. Soft, moist nuts can be eaten raw or roasted. Dried nuts will keep for a lifetime with no loss in quality; they can be cracked and boiled or ground for flour or meal. Newly emerging **leaves** are also eaten, especially as a wrap for vegetables and rice.

Conservation 2/1/1

COMMENTS: One of the best wild staple foods in North America, lotus is productive and delicious. It is also hated as a "weed" by many boaters and fishermen.

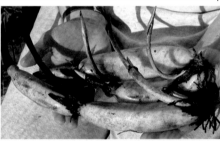

14 Yellow pond-lily 🦷 1 🌿 2
genus *Nuphar* ✦ family *Nymphaeaceae*

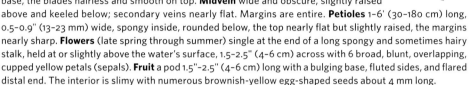

QUICK CHECK: Elliptic lily pads with a slit at one end; yellow flowers. **ID difficulty 1.**

DESCRIPTION: Aquatic perennial with large floating or slightly emergent leaves. **Rhizomes** several feet long and up to 5" (13 cm) thick, roughened like a palm trunk by old leaf scars, variously yellow, green, or brown. They kind of look like giant underwater snakes. **Leaves** *elliptic*, to 24" (60 cm) long, with two rounded and often overlapping lobes at the base, the blades hairless and smooth on top. **Midvein** wide and obscure, slightly raised above and keeled below; secondary veins nearly flat. Margins are entire. **Petioles** 1-6' (30-180 cm) long, 0.5-0.9" (13-23 mm) wide, spongy inside, rounded below, the top nearly flat but slightly raised, the margins nearly sharp. **Flowers** (late spring through summer) single at the end of a long spongy and sometimes hairy stalk, held at or slightly above the water's surface, 1.5-2.5" (4-6 cm) across with 6 broad, blunt, overlapping, cupped yellow petals (sepals). **Fruit** a pod 1.5"-2.5" (4-6 cm) long with a bulging base, fluted sides, and flared distal end. The interior is slimy with numerous brownish-yellow egg-shaped seeds about 4 mm long.

CONFUSING PLANTS: White water lilies (genus *Nymphaea*) have rounded rather than elliptic leaves.

HABITAT: Warm lakes, ponds, sloughs, and slow-moving rivers with muck bottoms, in water 1-6' (30-180 cm) deep. Native.

FOOD USE: Rhizomes can be peeled and boiled in several changes of water, after which they are marginally edible—fresh they are exceptionally bitter. Gather ripe pods from early summer through early fall, from a canoe or by wading. Let them sit in water for a few days to soften, then mash them and strain the **seeds** from the pulp. Soak, rub, and rinse the seeds to get rid of the bitter flavor of the pulp residue. After this they can be eaten popped, boiled, or ground into flour. **Conservation 3, 1.**

COMMENTS: I advise ignoring the many reports that the rhizomes of these plants are edible. Simply cooked,

they taste terrible and have made many people ill. Through numerous changes of water you can make them marginally edible. The seeds, however, are definitely edible, and have been an important food source in several regions of the world.

15 Arrow arum
Peltandra virginica ✦ *Araceae* (Arum family)

QUICK CHECK: Arrowhead-shaped leaves with round-tipped lobes and no milky sap; flowers on a club wrapped inside a greenish spathe. **ID difficulty 2.**

DESCRIPTION: Perennial with a *thick, vertical rootstock.* **Leaves** all basal, the blades 8–22" (20–56 cm) long, arrowhead-shaped, the tip pointed or rounded, the lobes *shorter than the forward-pointing leaf portion,* each with a *rounded point* (look closely!). Surfaces are hairless. **Midvein** flat or broadly depressed above, protruding and rounded below. There is a *prominent, straight vein from the base to the tip of each lobe.* **Secondary veins** numerous, flat above, *whitish and closely spaced,* running mostly unbranched and straight from the midvein *almost to* the margin, at broad angles; a few of them are more prominent, and may be slightly depressed or have a lighter green halo. Just inside the margin is a vein or two *running parallel to the edge;* this is where the secondary veins stop. Margins are entire. **Petioles** 1.2–3 times the blade length, *attached at the edge,* thick and spongy, the outer ones with a sheath at the base wrapping around adjacent leaves; above the sheath the petiole is channeled progressively less, finally becoming nearly round. **Stalk** a thick leafless scape, erect and shorter than the leaves when in bloom, curving downward or falling limp in fruit. **Inflorescence** a long, narrow spike, white at first, later yellow-orange, the flowers tiny, without petals. The spike is partially hidden in a scrolled, pointed, erect spathe 4–8" (10–20 cm) long with light, wavy margins. The lower part of the spathe persists pod-like around the **fruit,** which is a cluster of tapered berries embedded in slime, each pointed at the base, 7–12 mm long, green turning shiny purple-brown, containing 1–3 seeds.

CONFUSING PLANTS: Taro petioles are not attached at the leaf edge. Wapato has milky sap and multiple major veins running onto each lobe.

HABITAT: Mucky shallow water along rivers, lakes, and ponds, in full to partial sun. Native.

FOOD USE: The **rootstock** can be eaten after baking for an exceptionally long time. I've done this once. **Conservation 3.**

WARNING: Contains calcium oxalate raphides (p. 22). This plant cannot be eaten without careful processing!

COMMENTS: There are old historical accounts suggesting that this was once an important staple food in the mid-Atlantic region—although the identity has been questioned. I am aware of no Indigenous people practicing this tradition today. Before processing the rootstocks taste nearly identical to those of its relative, wild taro—which is to say, so horribly painful in the mouth that if there is any flavor, you are not going to notice it. Perhaps, after several thousand years of cultivation, this might be turned into a fantastic vegetable like taro. As it now stands, arrow arum is not a practical food plant for modern foragers, but it is included here for historical interest. **AKA** tuckahoe. Note that there is also a fungus, *Wolfiporia,* which produces a sclerotium that goes by the name "tuckahoe." This is basically a loaf of bread that grows underground, excellent and sustaining raw or roasted. Confusing the two could be a painful experience.

16 **Wild taro** 🐾
Colocasia esculenta ✦ *Araceae* (Arum family)

QUICK CHECK: Tall basal leaves, arrow-shaped with blunt lobes, not cut all the way to the petiole. **ID difficulty 2.**

DESCRIPTION: Aquatic perennial forming dense colonies of basal rosettes growing from a 2-4" (5-10 cm) corm with numerous attached roots. **Blade** smooth and hairless, 9-24" (23-60 cm) long, held about 80° to the petiole, thin, with two blunt, back-pointing lobes, *the blade not cut all the way to the petiole between the lobes* (peltate). The leaf tip has a boat-like projection 3-4 mm long. *Sap is not milky.* **Midvein** and secondary veins *protrude above* and more so below. Secondary veins are wide and prominent, most running straight to the edges; 4-6 emanate where the petiole is attached, these only branching in the lobes. Major veins have faint, light, lengthwise lines on the surface. *A double vein runs just inside the leaf margin on its entire perimeter; all interior veins stop here.* **Veinlets** between secondary veins are numerous, faintly *raised above*, and flat below. Veinlets originate at a secondary vein, almost at a right angle to it, but each one then curves out toward the margin. **Margins** entire but wavy. **Petioles** straight, erect, tough, smooth, hairless, solid, not channeled, *juicy inside*, oxidizing brown in a few minutes, to 4.5' (1.4 m) tall. **Inflorescence** a single, large, erect spathe atop a thick stem much shorter than the leaves, the hood green at the base and dull orange above, scrolled so the top is pointed; there is an opening near the bottom by which the spike is revealed. Flowers are rarely produced, and I've never seen the fruit.

CONFUSING PLANTS: Wapato and arrow arum both have similarly shaped leaves but they are not peltate and the vein patterns differ. Wapato has milky sap.

HABITAT: Shallow water along lakes and slow streams, ditches, and ponds, in full sun to moderate shade. Introduced. Scattered but widespread; abundant where found. **I**

FOOD USE: The **corms** can be long-roasted as a starchy vegetable.

WARNING: Wild taro cannot be treated like domesticated taro! It must be more extensively processed for its raphides (p. 22).

COMMENTS: This species is a major staple in many tropical parts of the world; however, the domesticated form has undergone thousands of years of selection to increase the corm size and, more importantly, reduce the concentration of raphides to only a tiny fraction of that found in wild plants. Wild taro requires much more careful preparation than the domestic form to make it safe. Tasting fresh wild taro (don't do it!) makes me marvel that people ever figured out that these could be detoxified; it also makes one appreciate the improvements made through domestication.

17 Water hyacinth 🪶 2
Eichhornia crassipes ✦ family *Pontederiaceae*

QUICK CHECK: Rosettes in mudflats or open water, with inflated petioles and entire blades that are broader than long; spike of showy purple flowers. **ID difficulty 1.**

DESCRIPTION: Perennial with rosettes; spreading by smooth, unbranched rhizomes about 6 mm thick. **Roots** in soft mud near the surface, numerous and *feathery with very fine hair-like rootlets*. **Leaves** 2–4" (5–10 cm) wide, curled, wider than long, not lobed, the margins entire and the tip rounded. Both surfaces are smooth and hairless. **Veins** begin at the base, fan out, and curve back toward the tip; there is no evident midvein on younger leaves, but older ones may have the midvein and a few other veins raised on the upper surface. New leaves are wrapped tightly around the inflated petiole of a neighboring leaf. **Petioles** spongy, about

▲ Rapidly expanding.

1 cm thick at the base, then *inflating to a bladder-like structure* before narrowing again; outer petioles are *strongly curved back* toward the center. **Inflorescence** a single spike of 7–18 flowers on a thick unbranched stem rising 8–20" (20–60 cm) from the center of the rosette. The stem is smooth, hairless, round with a pinhole hollow, spongy inside with spiderweb-like fibers when broken. There are two overlapping sheaths near the top, one of which has a miniature leaf at its tip. The rachis of the spike is densely covered in fine, curvy, soft hairs. **Flowers** light purple with 4 petals 1–1.3" (25–33 mm) long, the upper petal largest with a yellow spot in the center surrounded by blue. The bases are tubular, green, and curved outward. **Fruit** a 3-part capsule 1 cm long containing numerous tiny winged seeds.

HABITAT: Warm, stagnant or slow-moving water, especially with a muddy bottom or shoreline; thrives in full sun. Introduced. **I**

FOOD USE: Tender young **leaves** can be used as a potherb. The newest leaves are extremely tender but slightly irritating if eaten raw.

COMMENTS: Considered one of the worst invasive plants of the South, water hyacinth has become abundant over extensive areas and is spreading northward. Some people have reported an itchy rear end after eating this plant. I haven't checked this out. **AKA** *Pontedaria crassipes*.

18 Pickerelweed 🌱 1 🌱 1 🌿 2
Pontederia cordata ✦ family *Pontederiaceae*

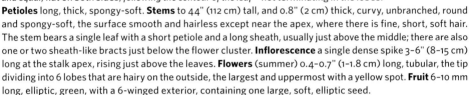

QUICK CHECK: Emergent aquatic leaves with arrowhead to heart-shaped, blunt-lobed bases and no prominent veins other than the midvein. **ID difficulty 1.**

DESCRIPTION: Emergent aquatic perennial from thick rhizomes, rooted firmly in the bottom, forming dense colonies. **Leaves** mostly basal, elongated-heart-shaped or arrowhead-shaped with blunt lobes, 4–10" (10–25 cm) long, standing 10–38" (25–95 cm) above the water, the blade thick and spongy-fleshy, hairless with entire margins. **Veins** *numerous and equal,* flat on both sides, *following the contour of the leaf*—not terminating in the lobes. **Petioles** long, thick, spongy-soft. **Stems** to 44" (112 cm) tall, and 0.8" (2 cm) thick, curvy, unbranched, round and spongy-soft, the surface smooth and hairless except near the apex, where there is fine, short, soft hair. The stem bears a single leaf with a short petiole and a long sheath, usually just above the middle; there are also one or two sheath-like bracts just below the flower cluster. **Inflorescence** a single dense spike 3–6" (8–15 cm) long at the stalk apex, rising just above the leaves. **Flowers** (summer) 0.4–0.7" (1–1.8 cm) long, tubular, the tip dividing into 6 lobes that are hairy on the outside, the largest and uppermost with a yellow spot. **Fruit** 6–10 mm long, elliptic, green, with a 6-winged exterior, containing one large, soft, elliptic seed.

CONFUSING PLANTS: Wapato and arrow arum have sharper-tipped lobes in which major veins terminate.

HABITAT: Shallow waters of lakes, slow-moving rivers, and ponds, especially where the bottom is soft muck. Native.

FOOD USE: The flower cluster **shoot**, still wrapped in a sheath in early summer, is okay raw or cooked. The **fruit** ripens in late summer and breaks easily from the cluster. The semi-soft green flesh is rather bitter with a poor aftertaste but also has a hint of tropical fruitiness; it's worth a curious nibble. The **seed** is soft and oily with good flavor, but hard to effectively separate from the flesh. **Conservation 2/1.**

COMMENTS: Although widespread and often very abundant, this species is barely worth including. If I knew of an effective way to separate the seeds from their green flesh, my assessment might change. Several sources mention the young, tender leaves as a potherb, but this appears to be based on Fernald and Kinsey (1943), who only suggest that the leaves *might* be edible because a loosely related Asian species is eaten. Pickerelweed's leaves are formed deep underwater, then the petiole is extended to the surface. The tender stage is tiny and takes place where it is almost inaccessible. I have gathered them on several occasions and have found neither the flavor nor texture appealing.

GROUP 16 LINEAR, ENTIRE, ONION-SCENTED LEAVES

All of these plants are in the genus *Allium* along with cultivated onion, leek, garlic, and chive. Although cultivated alliums frequently escape and numerous non-native species can occasionally be found growing feral, I have only included the three most common introduced species. Alliums can be distinguished by their distinctive onion odor, which makes them one of the easiest and safest groups to identify if your sense of smell is functioning. However, some species can be hard to tell from each other. Since most are just called "wild onion," the names contrived for field guides are repetitive and confusing. Although there is no danger in confounding the various species, they do have slightly different culinary applications.

genus *Allium* ✦ family *Alliaciae* (formerly part of the greater lily family, *Liliaceae*)

DESCRIPTION: Perennials with layered bulbs and a radiating cluster of thin, white roots. **Leaves** linear, hollow or not, hairless, with no prominent veins, all basal but sometimes wrapped around the stalk for some distance. (When we speak of stem leaves on some species, we mean the sheath wraps far up the stalk before the blade diverges from it.) **Stalk** (scape) single per bulb, erect, unbranched, leafless (or with leaves sheathing it), hairless. **Inflorescence** a terminal umbel with thin, broad bracts beneath it, enveloping the whole umbel in a balloon-like sac before it opens. **Flowers** have 6 tepals arranged in 2 layers that are similar in size and color, with 6 stamens and a single pistil. In some species some or all of the flowers may be replaced by bulblets. **Fruit** a 3-lobed capsule containing 3 black seeds.

CONFUSING PLANTS: Onions have a superficial resemblance to a number of other monocot plants, some of which are toxic. **Death camas** (p. 665) has a leaf or two on the stem, and its flowers are in racemes. **Star-of-Bethlehem** (p. 666), has mucilaginous leaves, flowers in a raceme, and green leaf bases extending through the center of the bulb. **Atamasco lily** *Zephyranthes atamasca* has broader, thicker, blunt leaves with many more per rosette; the flowers are large and showy and grow singly. All of these toxic look-similars lack the allium scent, which is a good distinguishing feature, but where they grow beside wild onions the smell from broken alliums can confuse the nose of the gatherer.

FOOD USE: All parts of these alliums are edible: the bulbs, leaves, scapes, buds, and flowers. They can be used as seasoning vegetables just like their cultivated relatives. In the species accounts I do not list food uses that are possible but seem largely impractical.

CONSERVATION NOTE: All onions are perennials and potentially long-lived. When harvesting any native clump-forming onion, be sure to leave behind at least two intact, healthy bulbs from each clump of 6 or less, three healthy bulbs from clumps of 6-20, or 5 healthy bulbs from clumps over 20. For non-clumping species leave at least 3 bulbs within a hand-spread from any bulb you collect. Greens should also be collected sparingly.

TENTATIVE IDENTIFICATION KEY TO THE GENUS ALLIUM
The key is not your final answer!

Leaves flat, 1-3.5" (2.5-9 cm) wide.	1. Ramp
Leaves round, tubular.	
Bulblets present in umbel; underground bulbs oblong to spherical.	2. Field garlic
No bulblets in umbel; underground bulbs long and narrow.	3. Chive
Leaves deeply folded at the base, with a rough keel below, to 1.2" (3 cm) wide.	4. Feral garlic
Leaves flat, angled, or channeled; not tubular and less than 1 cm wide.	
Flowering spring to early summer.	
Bulblets often present in umbel; 2 leaves diverge several inches up the stem.	5. American garlic
Bulblets not present in umbel; all leaves basal.	
Flowers white; bulb with a thick fibrous sheath.	6. Textile onion
Flowers pink or white; bulb with a thinner fibrous sheath.	7. Prairie onion
Flowering late summer to fall.	
Flowers white to faint pink, scape nodding in bloom.	8. Nodding onion
Flowers pink, scape erect in bloom.	9. Tall pink onion

1   **Ramp** 🧅 3 🌿 3 ▐ 3 📖 FH-144
Allium tricoccum, A. burdickii ⁘ family *Alliaciae*

QUICK CHECK: Onion with 2–4 large, broad, flat, elliptic leaves. **ID difficulty 1.**

DESCRIPTION: Spring ephemeral forming dense colonies by offsets. **Bulb** white, to 1" (2.5 cm) wide and 2.2" (5.5 cm) long, tapered to the top, the outer layers moist and membranous, with a stout *vertical rhizome* at the base. **Leaves** 2–4, flat, delicate, limp, creased slightly in the middle but with no prominent veins, up to 4" (10 cm) wide and 12" (30 cm) long, elliptic, tapered to a distinct petiole with a sheath 1–2.4" (2.5–6 cm) long at the base. Sheaths are maroon or green. Leaves appear in very early spring, dying and disappearing by early summer. **Scape** solid, smooth, round, hairless, straight, reddish to dull green, 7–16" (18–40 cm) tall and 3–4 mm thick, emerging as or after the leaves die. **Umbel** of 14–50, spherical, 1–1.5" (25–38 mm) across. **Flowers** (early to mid summer) bell-like, 4–7 mm long, white, none forming bulblets. **Capsule** bulging, opening to reveal shiny, round, black seeds in late summer.

CONFUSING PLANTS: False hellebores (p. 674) tend to have much broader leaves. *V. parviflorum* and perhaps other species in the young stage may have narrower, ramp-like leaves, but they have numerous depressed veins and folds or ridges, which ramps lack. *Clintonia* (p. 268) leaves are much thicker and tougher and not ephemeral. Both of these lack the onion odor.

SPECIES: The narrow-leaved ramp *A. burdickii* has narrower leaves that always have green petioles, while those of *A. tricoccum* are *usually* (not always, as some people claim) red. The narrow-leaved ramp has a milder flavor and flowers about a month earlier—the flowering stem is well developed (although unopened) before the leaves die back. It seems to prefer more clayey soils, but the two are sometimes found together, and in such cases often hybridize, especially in the northern part of their range. The insistence by many that sheath/petiole color definitively distinguishes these species has led to great confusion; there are many clear distinctions which are not very "keyable." (Continued on the next page.)

1 Ramp (continued)

HABITAT: Hardwood forests and high floodplains with rich soil, especially those dominated by sugar maple, bitternut hickory, and elm. In southern parts of its range it prefers north slopes. Native.

FOOD USE: Gather **bulbs** preferentially from late spring through early summer; later the quality deteriorates. **Greens** are available only in spring and are much better before fully grown; by the time the bulbs reach full size, the leaves have passed their prime. Ramps are excellent in soup, stir fry, casserole, salad, and many other dishes. The leaves can be dried and crumbled for use as a seasoning; bulbs can be pickled, canned, or dried. Any tender parts, including **scapes**, flower buds, and green pods, are edible. Narrow-leaved ramp has a milder flavor. **Conservation 3/2** (see note before key).

COMMENTS: Considered by many to be our best wild onion, this species is collected commercially, sold at farmer's markets, and served in fine restaurants. There are some unscrupulous harvesters who overcollect these. There is also a great deal of unnecessary ramp-shaming online and in the media. Although some people claim that the plant is endangered, or that it is always irresponsible to harvest the bulbs, these claims are based primarily upon one ill-conceived anti-foraging paper reporting on research designed to underrepresent the plant's reproductive potential. Ramp conservation problems are highly localized. In fact, populations have been generally increasing nationwide for about a century, and these species are faring far better than most of our native onions. It is entirely possible to harvest ramp bulbs or leaves sustainably and ethically. **AKA** wild leek, but that name is also used for feral leeks.

▲ Ramp seedheads in fall.

▲ *Allium burdickii*. Note the green scapes, fully elongated while the leaves are still green.

2 Field garlic ◊ 2 🌾 2 📖 IWE-121
Allium vineale ✦ family *Alliaciae*

QUICK CHECK: Onion with hollow, rounded leaves; a leaf often sheathing the base of the stem; umbel with bulblets, most germinating on the plant. **ID difficulty 1.**

DESCRIPTION: Winter perennial, the tops dormant from early summer to early fall. Small plants often form dense, grass-like clumps where bulblet-heads have fallen. **Bulbs** of older plants form clusters to 1.3" (33 mm) long and almost as wide, with one or more offset or "daughter" bulbs on the side. Clusters contain 3 kinds of bulbs: small offsets, which are wrapped in thick sheaths and can remain dormant for years; large offsets, which form new plants beside the mother bulb; and central bulbs, which regenerate the existing plant. Young plants have a single bulb. **Leaves** 3–4, basal or attached to the lower part of the stem, separated by 2–5" (5–13 cm), each leaf sheathing those above it. Blades are narrow, *hollow*, tubular (but often still channeled), up to 34" (86 cm) long but often much shorter—especially in lawns. Young leaves may have *twisting, curly tops*, which are much thinner and tougher than *Allium canadense* leaves. The lowest leaf withers long before the upper, and the tips turn dry and brown by flowering. The uppermost leaf is erect, diverging slightly from the flower scape and usually a bit taller. **Scapes** to 30" (75 cm) tall. The flower cluster bud is long and narrow, not inflated, and maroon at the base. **Umbel** may have up to 50 small, densely packed purple flowers in late spring—but mostly it *bears bulblets* instead, which are about the size of a grain of wheat and will *sprout leaves while still attached*. The weight of the growing bulblets makes the stem lean down to the ground.

HABITAT: Open or semi-open areas with a history of soil disturbance: old fields, roadsides, lawns, parks, empty lots. Most often in urban areas or near agriculture. Introduced. **I**

FOOD USE: Bulbs are available from late spring through summer. The central bulbs are best; hard offsets are hardly worth your time. Once the tops have died back it becomes harder to find them, so early summer is a good time to gather them. Young **leaves** can be used like chives or scallions but are tougher than our native onions; gather them from late winter through spring. Older, tough leaves can still be bundled and boiled for their flavor in soup stock, then removed. (Continued on the next page.)

▲ Curly winter leaves.

2   Field garlic (continued)

COMMENTS: This is probably the *Allium* most readily available to the greatest number of people in North America, since it is remarkably abundant in the lawns and parks of many urban areas, as well as being a pervasive agricultural weed in many regions. Since it is non-native and weedy, harvest to your heart's content.

Allium vineale, grasslike clump. ▶

3   Chive ◊ 2 🌿 3 ✿ 3
Allium schoenophrasum ✦ family *Alliaciae*

QUICK CHECK: Densely clumped, very narrow, erect stems and tightly packed umbels. **ID difficulty 1.**

DESCRIPTION: Densely clustered onion. **Bulbs** long and narrow, covered by a papery coating, typically bearing 3 leaves each. **Leaves** erect at first but often leaning with age, *hollow, round in cross section*, 10–24" (25–60 cm) tall and very narrow (2–4 mm wide). Leaves completely encircle the scape for 4–5" (10–13 cm) at the base, then split open to allow the stem through; above this they form a tube again and have a thin membrane blocking off entry to their inside. **Scapes** erect to leaning, hollow, rounded, smooth, green, 10–22" (25–56 cm) tall. Each scape has a large leaf almost equal to its height, a smaller leaf, and a third leaf soon withering at the base. **Umbel** compact, *spherical*, about 1.2" (3 cm) wide, with numerous flowers on pedicels 5–10 mm, the scape turned toward one side but not nodding. **Flowers** (early to mid summer) 12–14 mm long, the tepals not spreading (bell-like), light purple with a darker purple central vein, the tips curved outward with a tiny, sharp point. Flowers are *not replaced by bulblets*.

HABITAT: Rocky river banks and shoreline outcrops; open, moist, rocky ground. Garden escapes persist in sunny spots around old homesteads and often spread to roadsides. Native, but with many introduced populations.

FOOD USE: Bulbs can be eaten at any time, but they're best when the tops are dormant. Gather tender **leaves** from spring through early summer and use as a seasoning exactly as cultivated chives. A new flush of good leaves is produced again in fall. **Flowers** make a nice garnish or addition to salads. **Conservation 3, 2, 1**

COMMENTS: Wild chives are native and widespread in the boreal forest region of North America. Our native chives are of the variety *sibiricum*, which is *larger* than the typical cultivated chive, and has leaves that are usually shorter than the scape. Cultivated chives are a different variety of the same species, originating in Asia, and can be found as an occasional garden escape through much of the region south of the native chive's range.

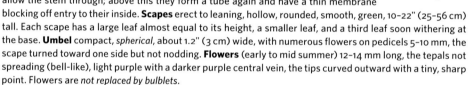

Native chive clump. ▶

4 Feral garlic 🧅 3 🌿 2 ⫙ 3
Allium sativum + family *Alliaciae*

QUICK CHECK: Leaves deeply folded near the base, clasping and layered in the lower third of the stem. **ID difficulty 2.**

DESCRIPTION: This is a smaller version of cultivated garlic, but wild plants are usually found in dense clumps, so the bulbs flower and divide less frequently (also depending on the genetics of origin). **Bulbs** usually long and narrow, gently tapered to a scarcely thickened base, but mature ones ready to flower will be enlarged and nearly spherical. Bulbs are covered with a papery sheath, purplish except for the very bottom. Offsets are tiny with one or more flat sides, but in crowded wild clumps are infrequently produced. **Leaves** 3-4 per plant, rising 14-28" (36-70 cm), fully clasping the lower stem or leaf cluster for 3-9" (8-23 cm) with a long, pale-green sheath before becoming free. Blades are folded into a V in cross section (more so when young), with a small, sharp, *rough keel* on the bottom and a tiny hood at the tip. They are up to 1.2" (3 cm) wide, faintly glaucous, the *tips drooping with maturity*. **Margins** *roughened by tiny membranous teeth* (usually not visible without magnification, but you can feel them). **Scapes** solid, to 32" (80 cm) tall and 4-8 mm thick. **Umbel** (May-July) spherical with numerous pedicels, mostly bearing bulblets with a long beak. Beneath the umbel is a *single bract with a long beak*. **Flowers** bell-shaped, greenish-white to pink, 3-4 mm long; these generally do not ripen into fruits—instead forming bulblets.

HABITAT: Disturbed and usually forested areas with rich, moist soil, especially on roadsides and around old homesteads. Introduced.

FOOD USE: Bulbs like cultivated garlic. Since fewer offsets (cloves) are produced in wild populations, don't forget that you can use the young **greens** and **scapes**. This has the strongest, hottest flavor of any of our wild onions.

COMMENTS: At a glance, you might pass these over as just another clump of daffodils or daylilies, with which they often grow. The growth pattern suggests that the clumps are very long-lived, and garlic has spread and gone truly feral in many areas, yet I have never seen it become invasive.

5   American garlic 💧 3 🌿 3
Allium canadense ✦ family *Alliaciae*

QUICK CHECK: Narrow, channeled leaves, not hollow, clasping the lower scape; umbel with bulblets and/or flowers. **ID difficulty 2.**

DESCRIPTION: Spring ephemeral sometimes forming lawn-like carpets. **Bulbs** single, stout, broadly egg to teardrop-shaped, 0.3–0.8" (8–20 mm) long, symmetrical, not producing offsets. **Leaves** solid, 2–5 mm wide, to 20" (50 cm) tall, gently U-shaped in cross section, becoming flatter toward the tip, often with a faint off-center keel below. Young leaves are limp and weakly erect with a pointed tip. With maturity they taper to an extremely thin tip, which is often wilted even before blooming. Each flowering plant has 3 leaves sheathing the stem for 2–8" (5–20 cm), the top 2 often nearly paired where diverging. **Scapes** 18–32" (46–80 cm) tall, erect, pithy inside, not nodding in bloom. **Umbel** usually has a cluster of several tightly-packed, sessile, blunt-pointed bulblets 5–11 mm long, along with a few flowers on pedicels 0.3–1.2" (8–30 mm) long. In some areas, however, plants with all flowers and no bulblets predominate. **Flowers** white to pink, usually with a purple stripe down the center of each tepal, blooming in late spring. **Seeds** rarely produced, triangular.

CONFUSING PLANTS: Field garlic has hollow leaves. False garlic (p. 259) has fewer and much larger flowers, and mostly lacks the onion scent.

HABITAT: Moist, rich soil in forests, open woodlands, forest edges, clearings, meadows. Tolerates more shade than nodding and prairie onion. Native.

FOOD USE: In summer, dig up the shallow **bulbs**—if you can remember where they are. Use the **greens** as a seasoning in early to mid spring, like mild chives or scallions. The bulblets can also be collected in mid to late summer—use some and plant some. **Conservation 3/2/2.**

COMMENTS: This native onion is still abundant in many rich woods and meadows, but in many places the non-native and culinarily inferior *A. vineale* is outcompeting it.

▼ Umbel with bulblets.

▲ Early spring leaves.

▼ Dormant bulbs.

▼ Harvested plants just before blooming.

6 Textile onion ◗ 3 🌿 2
Allium textile ✦ family *Alliaciae*

QUICK CHECK: Short onion with erect umbels of white flowers in spring. **ID difficulty 2.**

DESCRIPTION: Onion growing singly or in small clumps. **Bulb** egg-shaped, pro-portionately large, *wrapped in many layers of coarse, burlap-like sheath.* **Leaves** 1–3 per bulb, all basal, 5–12" (13–30 cm) long, often wavy, 2–4 mm wide, sheathed together for about 1.5" (4 cm), not hollow, the larger leaves U-channeled, the smaller leaves an-gled and not channeled. Leaves begin to die back shortly after flowering be-gins. **Scape** single, 7–12" (18–30 cm) tall, round. **Umbels** of 8–30, hemi-spherical or with all the pedicels as-cending. **Flowers** (late spring to early summer) erect, not opening widely, the tepals white, often with a green stripe down the center.

HABITAT: Sandy or rocky prairies. Native.

FOOD USE: Use **bulbs** and **leaves** like domestic alliums. **Conservation 3/2.**

COMMENTS: The most common and widespread onion on the Great Plains, this one has a large bulb for its size and good flavor.

7 Prairie onion ◐ 3 🌿 2
Allium drummondii + family *Alliaceae*

QUICK CHECK: Short onion with erect umbels of pink or white flowers in spring. **ID difficulty 1.**

DESCRIPTION: Small onion, the bulbs usually clumped. **Bulb** egg-shaped, 8–13 mm long, with a fibrous coating. **Leaves** all basal, 2–3 per bulb (occasionally more), 4–12" (10–30 cm) long and 1–4 mm wide, tapered to a very narrow tip, channeled. **Scape** usually single, rounded, 5–11" (13–28 cm) tall. **Umbel** of 9–25, erect, the pedicels 1–2.5 times the length of the flower. The 2–3 thin, papery bracts under the umbel are sharp-tipped with a *single prominent central vein*. The pedicels lengthen in fruit and become wavy and stiff. **Flowers** bell-like (in shape, but not hanging), 6–9 mm long, the tepals pink (occasionally white) with a darker vein down the center. Bulblets only rarely form in the umbel.

HABITAT: Dry prairies, especially on rich but thin limestone soils. Native.

FOOD USE: Dig **bulbs** when you can find them, never taking a whole clump. (If there is only one plant, leave it.) Eat **greens** very early—well before flowering. **Conservation 3/2.**

COMMENTS: Great flavor, but tiny, and oh so pretty. The flowers are variable in color: usually pinkish but often white and sometimes yellowish.

RELATED EDIBLE: The fragrant onion *A. perdulce* is the smallest onion in our region, the blooming scapes only 5–8" (13–20 cm) tall, but it has proportionately large pink-purple flowers with a strong, pleasant smell entirely unlike that of our other species. The bulbs and greens have just the faintest onion flavor and odor. This spring-blooming species is found in prairies with poor soil.

◀ These flowers are deeper purple than usual.

8 Nodding onion ◐ 2 🌿 2
Allium cernuum + family *Alliaceae*

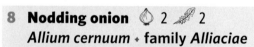

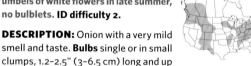

QUICK CHECK: Leaves solid; nodding umbels of white flowers in late summer, no bulblets. **ID difficulty 2.**

DESCRIPTION: Onion with a very mild smell and taste. **Bulbs** single or in small clumps, 1.2–2.5" (3–6.5 cm) long and up to 0.8" (2 cm) thick, slender and *tapering gradually, pinkish,* surrounded by several layers of papery sheath. **Leaves** 3–9, erect, very narrow, sometimes twisted, shorter than the flower stalk, 4–17" (10–43 cm) long and 3–8 mm wide, *shallowly U-channeled* except near the top, which is flat. Leaves sheath the stem for 2–5" (5–13 cm), the sheath thin and papery. Some leaves are withered at blooming. **Scapes** 8–32" (20–80 cm) tall, glaucous, tough by flowering, *somewhat flattened with 1 or 2 sharp edges,* with a minute hollow in the center. **Umbels** of 11–35, the scape tip *nodding in bloom,* producing no bulblets. **Flowers** (mid to late summer) white to pink-purple, 4–6 mm across, pedicels 0.6–1.2" (15–30 mm) long. *After blooming, the pedicels turn and point vertically.* **Capsule** 3–4 mm long with 3 blunt lobes and black, triangular seeds.

HABITAT: Likes full sun and rich soil in meadows, open woods, roadsides, lightly used pastures, rocky outcrops, and savannahs. Mostly in dry soil, but occasionally in moist prairies, even marsh and fen edges. Native. 🔥

FOOD USE: Bulbs are best when the top is mostly dormant. **Leaves** have a long season of availability, as they are not ephemeral. **Conservation 3, 2.**

COMMENTS: This species grows much larger, on average, in the eastern states than it does in the Rocky Mountains, but it is less common. Under ideal conditions the bulbs can grow quite large, but usually they are small. The flavor of all parts in mild.

Related edible:

9 Tall pink onion + *Allium stellatum* 2 ✦ 2

QUICK CHECK: Leaves solid; pink flowers blooming late summer to fall, no bulblets.

ID difficulty 1.

This species is very similar to nodding onion but slightly smaller, reaching 12–20" (30–50 cm). **Bulbs** somewhat plumper than those of nodding onion and have a papery sheath. **Leaves** triangular near the base, sometimes with a shallow groove in the center; distally they are shallowly U-channeled. **Flowers** (mid summer to fall) light pink-purple and borne in an erect cluster (although the cluster nods before the flowers open). Tall pink onion is found in dry, sunny sites, such as oak savannahs, limestone glades, and sandy prairies. **AKA** tall prairie onion. 🔥

GROUP 17 LINEAR, ENTIRE LEAVES— NOT ONION-SCENTED

Most of these are grasses, sedges, or lily relatives. Several lily relatives are dangerously toxic, while grasses and sedges are among the safest groups of plants. Nearly all grasses have edible starchy seeds; labor efficiency has been the primary factor determining which species are eaten. Harvesting and processing grass seeds requires a specialized skill and tool set (see p. 27).

TENTATIVE IDENTIFICATION KEY TO GROUP 17
The key is not your final answer!

Leaf distinctly folded in a V or M shape, with a keel underneath.

Sap milky; leaves in a radiating rosette.

or
    All leaves basal. — **1. Prairie false dandelion**

    Erect leafy stem 3-6' (1-2 m) tall. — **2. Salsify**

or Sap slimy; leaves 2-ranked. — **3. Spiderwort**

or Sap neither milky nor slimy.

    Leaves 2-ranked; flowers orange, in branching clusters. — **4. Day lily**

or   Leaves not 2-ranked.

        Stem not triangular, no whorl at the top; showy flowers in racemes.

        or   Stem with 1-3 leaves; flowers white. Death camas (poisonous, p. 665).

           Stem without leaves; flowers pale blue to purple. — **20. Camas**

        Stem triangular with an unequal whorl at the top; flowers chaffy and unshowy.

           Spikes yellow-brown; tubers single at the end of thread-like rhizomes. — **5. Chufa**

           Spikes purplish; tubers multiple along thicker, crooked rhizomes. — **6. Purple nutsedge**

Leaf not folded and keeled: flat (with at most a midvein ridge), inflated, curled, or U-channeled.

or Stem absent; flowers directly from root crown; leaf semi-fleshy. — **7. Prairie star lily**

or Stem hollow with bulging, ringed, solid nodes (grasses).

    Stems taller than waist-high, tough and strong.

    or   Evergreen 4-30' (1.2-9 m) tall, rarely seen with seedheads. — **8. River cane**

        Not evergreen; seedheads present in the colony each fall. — **9. Phragmites reed**

or   Stems shorter than waist-high, easily broken.

    Inflorescence a widely-spreading loose panicle. — **10. Western rice-grass**

    Inflorescence a compact head.

        Chaffy, scaly heads without awns. — **11. Maygrass**

        Heads with many long, straight, vertical awns. — **12. Little barley**

Stem without ringed nodes (not grasses).

    Stems erect, with numerous typical leaves; flowerheads purple. — **13. Small blazing star**

    Stems with 1-3 leaves; flowers with 6 white tepals spotted near the base. Death camas (p. 665).

    Stems absent or leafless (may have vestigial leaves or bracts).

        Leaves very thick, fleshy, brittle, not spongy nor slimy. — **14. Seaside plantain**

        Leaves tough, sharp-tipped, more than 16" (40 cm) long and 14 mm wide, in rosettes of more than 12. — **15. Yucca**

        Leaves not as above.

           Flowers in an umbel. — **16. False garlic**

           Flowers in a spike or raceme.

               Leaves 2-ranked, spongy, long-sheathed at the base. — **17. Seaside arrow-grass**

               Leaves not 2-ranked, spongy, or long-sheathed

                  Flowers urn-shaped, without petals (tepals), hanging, purple. — **18. Grape hyacinth**

                  Flowers with 6 distinct petals (tepals), not hanging.

                      Flowers white, opening skyward; raceme short and broad. Star-of-Bethlehem (p. 666)

                      Flowers blue, opening to the side; raceme elongated. — **19. Camas**

1 Prairie false dandelion 〰 2 〰 2 〰 2 〰 2
Nothocalais cuspidata ◆ Asteraceae (Composite family)

QUICK CHECK: Basal rosette of grass-like leaves with a white midvein; dandelion-like yellow flowers on a short, naked stem. **ID difficulty 2.**

DESCRIPTION: Perennial. **Root** large and thick, often flattened or irregular in cross section, sometimes multi-crowned, narrowed at the top. Flesh is light, slightly opaque, very brittle, and tender. **Basal rosette** radiating with numerous linear leaves 4–6" (10–15 cm) long. **Leaves** gently tapered to a narrow white base, V-folded, with a pointed tip and wavy margins. The midvein is *broad and nearly white* but not depressed above; it is rounded below. Secondary veins are parallel. The blades are glossy, but the margins have much fine, soft, long hair. **Sap** *milky* but not profuse. **Scapes** 6–8" (15–20 cm) tall, thin, hollow, woolly, twisted, lined and finely ribbed lengthwise, each bearing a single flower head. **Heads** yellow, 1.2–2" (3–5 cm) across. The bracts are lanceolate, withering, yellow-green, often with a dark central stripe, the tips acuminate and brown. **Rays** yellow and truncated, the tip with 5 lobes, the center of each outer ray purple-brown near the bottom. **Seed** (achene) bullet-shaped with a white pappus. The plant blooms in mid to late spring, often producing multiple scapes in succession.

HABITAT: Medium to dry prairie in full sun, especially where sloped and sandy or rocky. Native. 🔥

FOOD USE: Roots are hard to dig up, but large and tender. They are slightly bitter raw, but milder after being steamed or boiled. Young **leaves**, **flowers**, and **flower stalks** can be eaten raw or cooked. **Conservation 3/2.**

COMMENTS: This attractive prairie plant is still rather common in some areas, as it thrives on soils too dry and poor for farming. It is in most ways similar to dandelion, but the flavor is less bitter. The root is proportionately large. The flowers smell like sunflowers.

2 Salsify 〰 3 〰 3 〰 2 〰 3 📖 NG-471
genus Tragopogon ◆ Asteraceae (Composite family)

QUICK CHECK: Long grass-like leaves, milky sap, and tall branching stems with dandelion-like flowers. **ID difficulty 2.**

DESCRIPTION: Biennials. **Taproot** thick, fleshy, light brown, rapidly tapered, usually lacking major branches, with *milky sap*. Rosette single. **Basal leaves** several, 7–12" (18–30 cm) long and up to 0.6" (15 mm) wide, without petioles, grass-like, deeply folded, hairless, widest at the base and tapered to a thin, sharp tip, *arranged radially* rather than 2 or 3-ranked. Margins

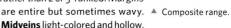
▲ Composite range.

are entire but sometimes wavy. **Midveins** light-colored and hollow, slightly depressed above and protruding below. Secondary veins are light, parallel, flat above and below, all emanating from the base. **Stems** 2.5–5' (75–150 cm) tall and 0.4–0.8" (1–2 cm) thick, erect, straight, roundish, thick-walled with a small hollow, hairless at maturity— but leaves and stems of young plants have scattered gobs of *loose, unattached wool*, especially toward the inflorescence. **Branches** many but absent in the lower third, simple or compound, strongly ascending to erect. (Continued on the next page.)

◀◀ Salsify flower bud and peduncle at the right stage for eating (*T. pratensis*).

◀ Salsify shoot at the right stage for peeling (*T. dubius*).

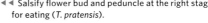

243

2 Salsify (continued)

Stem leaves alternate, numerous and overlapping at first, similar to the basal leaves but shorter and clasping; *broad at the base, abruptly narrowing to a long, tapered tip.* **Flowers** single composite heads 1.2–1.8" (3–4.6 cm) across at the end of a long peduncle, composed of ray florets only; yellow or purple. There are several long, pointed, keeled bracts on the outside of each head. After flowering this ripens into the familiar "giant dandelion" seedhead, with a spherical cluster of long, thin, seeds with a golden parachute on the end (which looks white from a distance).

SPECIES: There are 3, all introduced, all excellent. *T. dubius* has yellow flowerheads with an inflated, hollow peduncle. The rays are broader toward the tip and the bracts are longer than the rays. It prefers slightly drier soil. *T. pratensis* has yellow flowerheads with a less inflated peduncle. The rays are almost uniform in width, and longer than the bracts. This slightly smaller species is more common in moist soils. *T. porrifolius* has purple flowers and rays tapered to the tip. It is locally common in rich disturbed soil.

CONFUSING PLANTS: Nonflowering plants may be hard to tell from grasses, sedges, or spiderworts (none of which are poisonous) at a glance, but all of these have ranked rather than radiating rosettes, and none produce latex. Spiderworts have slimy sap, and the stalks are fully solid.

HABITAT: Sunny open areas with ample moisture: roadsides, fields, open slopes, building sites, vacant lots. Often near pavement edges, especially in semi-arid regions where it takes advantage of runoff. Not common in pastures because livestock relish it. Introduced.

FOOD USE: Roots should be dug in fall or early spring from plants without stalks, and are best cooked. All tender green parts are edible raw or cooked: upright **leaves** at the center of the cluster in spring, **shoots** in late spring, and **flower buds** and their **peduncles** in summer.

COMMENTS: Salsify is one of our best vegetables: versatile with several delicious edible parts available over much of the year. Certainly this plant would be more commonly eaten if it were not so hard to tell from grasses at a glance. In my opinion, young stalks harvested at just the right stage, peeled of their lower leaves and steamed until tender, are among the finest vegetables in existence.

▲ *T. dubius.*   ▲ *T. porrifolius.*   ▲ *T. pratensis.*

3 Spiderwort 2 2 2 2
genus *Tradescantia* ⬩ family *Commelinaceae*

QUICK CHECK: Thick, succulent, grass-like leaves with slimy sap, a jointed stem, and purple flowers with 3 petals. **ID difficulty 1.**

GENUS DESCRIPTION: Perennial herbs with grass-like leaves, the roots fibrous, sometimes thickened and fleshy, the *sap slimy*. **Stems** single or clumped, simple or sparely forking, erect to leaning, zigzag, up to 40" (1 m) tall and 0.6" (15 mm) thick, *solid*, roundish in cross section, succulent and juicy (remaining moist even as the leaves wither), jointed. **Leaves** sessile, *2-ranked*, linear, narrow, entire, semi-succulent, deeply to slightly folded (at least near the base), with parallel veins, the margins entire. Stem leaves are alternate and clasp with a sheath. **Inflorescence** an umbel of 4–50, terminal or axillary, with one or two leaves beneath it. Only 1–3 flowers per cluster bloom at once, facing skyward; the spent flowers and unopened buds *hang on limp pedicels*. **Flowers** (late spring through summer) are radially symmetrical, 0.7–1.4" (18–36 mm) across with 3, separate, ovate, green sepals. **Petals** 3, broadly ovate, separate, *alike in size* (unlike dayflowers, where one is reduced), not constricted to a stalk-like base, usually blue or purple but sometimes pink and rarely white. There are 6 stamens with *thick blue-purple filaments* and yellow anthers, arising from *a tuft of kinky blue threads* around the single pistil. **Fruit** an egg-shaped, 3-part capsule 4–8 mm long, holding 3–6 seeds. Some species die back in early to mid summer as the soil desiccates.

CONFUSING PLANTS: Resembles salsify but lacks latex. Told from grasses and sedges by its thick, mucilaginous sap. Dayflowers have a bract folded over the inflorescence and one smaller petal.

SPECIES: There are a dozen or so in our region, all edible.

HABITAT: Mostly open, sunny, dry locations. All species native. 🔥

FOOD USE: All tender parts are edible raw or cooked. The young **leaves** and **hearts** of young leaf clusters are gathered in spring or early summer. **Stems** are good when young, but older stems, even late in the growing season, can sometimes be eaten after peeling the tough rind. In summer you can pick the **flowers** and **flower buds**. **Conservation 2.**

COMMENTS: The texture is mucilaginous, but the flavor is mild and pleasant. These highly attractive plants are great for edible native landscaping, especially in dry sand.

▲ Ohio spiderwort *T. ohiensis* has two-ranked basal leaf clumps and hairless, forking stems. This species is common in dry, sandy, sunny soil. This is probably our best spiderwort for eating.

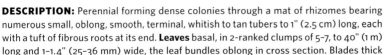

4 Day lily 🐛2 🥬2 🌿2 🌼3
Hemerocallis fulva ◆ family *Asphodelaceae*

QUICK CHECK: Dense colonies of long, narrow, basal leaves; naked stems bearing large orange flowers with 6 long tepals. **ID difficulty 1.**

DESCRIPTION: Perennial forming dense colonies through a mat of rhizomes bearing numerous small, oblong, smooth, terminal, whitish to tan tubers to 1" (2.5 cm) long, each with a tuft of fibrous roots at its end. **Leaves** basal, in 2-ranked clumps of 5–7, to 40" (1 m) long and 1–1.4" (25–36 mm) wide, the leaf bundles oblong in cross section. Blades thick and spongy, hairless, with no prominent veins. Near the tip they are broadly V-shaped, but near the base they are deeply folded, with thin, membranous edges that often overlap and fully encircle the inner leaves. *The tips of young leaves are turned into a keel.* **Stems** 36–60" (90–150 cm) tall, smooth, glaucous, round, hairless, hollow, unbranched except in the flowering top (and then only sparely), leafless except for an occasional bract. **Inflorescence** usually has 2 major branches, each spike-like or raceme-like with few to several flowers. **Flowers** 3–4" (8–10 cm) across, with 6 tepals that are orange-red except for a yellow zone at the base, the inner 3 larger and veiny with ruffled margins and a light central stripe, recurved when open—which lasts just one day. Stamens 6, with long curvy filaments, the anthers long and narrow, one side black and one side orange. **Flower buds** cylindrical and up to 3.5" (9 cm) long. Fruit a leathery 3-sided capsule that is rarely produced.

CONFUSING PLANTS: There are other species and hybrids of day lily, the safety of which are questionable (even more than this one.)

HABITAT: Full sun to moderate shade in a wide variety of soils, but not waterlogged or exceedingly dry. Introduced, spreading from cultivation and often persisting after homes have disappeared. Most common in old fields, forest edges, abandoned home sites, or along roadsides. **I**

FOOD USE: Tubers can be used as a vegetable—I recommend only using firm ones and cooking them. The whitish **heart** of the leaf cluster in spring, and the **shoots** in early summer, can be eaten raw or cooked. **Flower buds** and **flowers** gathered in summer and eaten cooked; petals are traditionally stored by drying and then reconstituted for cooking.

COMMENTS: This is one of the best-known wild edibles, and it produces lots of food in a small area. Where found it is often way too abundant, and you'd do the woods a favor by getting rid of some.

WARNING: Many people experience gastric discomfort after eating this plant—explosive diarrhea and sometimes vomiting. For some people the flower buds cause an uncomfortable burning in the throat. Additional serious symptoms have been reported. Adverse reactions are not rare. Although much is written in the foraging literature about this plant, I no longer allow people to eat it in my foraging classes. Eat at your own risk.

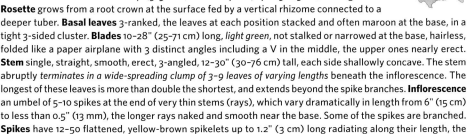

5 **Chufa** 🍠 2 🥛 2 🗋 3 ◊ 📖 IWE-98
Cyperus esculentus ✦ *Cyperaceae* (Sedge family)

QUICK CHECK: Light yellow-green, short sedge with a straight stalk bearing a spreading whorl of unequal leaves on top, and an unequal umbel of yellowish spikelets. **ID difficulty 2.**

DESCRIPTION: Perennial sedge spreading by tubers and seeds. **Tubers** spherical to flattened or asymmetric, hard, 0.2–0.7" (5–18 mm), light orange-brown, produced only at the end of thread-thin rhizomes 2–14" (5–36 cm) from the plant, up to 5" (13 cm) underground. **Rosette** grows from a root crown at the surface fed by a vertical rhizome connected to a deeper tuber. **Basal leaves** 3-ranked, the leaves at each position stacked and often maroon at the base, in a tight 3-sided cluster. **Blades** 10–28" (25–71 cm) long, *light green*, not stalked or narrowed at the base, hairless, folded like a paper airplane with 3 distinct angles including a V in the middle, the upper ones nearly erect. **Stem** single, straight, smooth, erect, 3-angled, 12–30" (30–76 cm) tall, each side shallowly concave. The stem abruptly *terminates in a wide-spreading clump of 3–9 leaves of varying lengths* beneath the inflorescence. The longest of these leaves is more than double the shortest, and extends beyond the spike branches. **Inflorescence** an umbel of 5–10 spikes at the end of very thin stems (rays), which vary dramatically in length from 6" (15 cm) to less than 0.5" (13 mm), the longer rays naked and smooth near the base. Some of the spikes are branched. **Spikes** have 12–50 flattened, yellow-brown spikelets up to 1.2" (3 cm) long radiating along their length, the spikelets not touching each other at the base. Tiny curving filaments protrude from beneath the scales of blooming spikelets. **Fruit** a tiny, 3-sided brown seed (achene).

CONFUSING PLANTS: Other sedges in the genus Cyperus—none are dangerous, but you can waste a lot of time digging the wrong plants. *C. strigosus*, what I call "false chufa," has more crowded and pointed spikelets; to verify your ID, dig and check for tubers.

HABITAT: River floodplains, sandbars, mudflats, banks, lakeshores, disturbed wet meadows. It spreads in moist disturbed soil and agricultural fields and is often a common weed in clay-rich farmland. Native.

FOOD USE: From fall through spring, dig around the plants and pick out the **tubers**. They can be refrigerated for long periods or dried. Traditionally dried (sometimes roasted) and ground into a flour or paste that is used in breads or mixed with water to make a drink (horchata). You can put the fresh tubers in a blender with water, then strain through a cloth to get a **milky liquid** for hot cereal or gravy. They are also dried and pressed for **oil** (which I've purchased but never made.) **Conservation 1.**

COMMENTS: This widespread plant was domesticated in Egypt where it has been eaten for tens of thousands of years. It has also been an important cultivated food of the Owens Valley Paiute of California. Wild tubers are smaller, sparser, and more fibrous than the cultivated form, but still very good. **AKA** yellow nutsedge, earth-almond.

6 Purple nutsedge 🖐️ 1 ◊
Cyperus rotundus ✦ *Cyperaceae* (Sedge family)

QUICK CHECK: Dark-leaved short sedge with a whorl of unequal leaves on top and an unequal umbel of purple-brown spikelets. **ID difficulty 1.**

DESCRIPTION: Similar to chufa (previous) but the base grows directly from a parent tuber near the surface, which sends out zero to a few wiry, crooked **rhizomes** 1–2 mm thick covered with dark brown sheaths. These are persistent and much thicker and tougher than chufa rhizomes, bearing tubers at their ends and often periodically *along their length, connected in chains.* **Tubers** roundish to elongated or flattened, often amorphous or irregular-knobby in shape, 0.2–0.9" (5–23 mm) long, the surface dark brownish-purple when mature (white when forming), covered with bristly, chaffy scales, with one or sometimes more claw-like buds; the flesh white and semi-hard. **Leaves** smaller than those of chufa, strongly creased, dark blue-green, and the sheathed bundle at the base tends to be taller, appearing almost stalk-like. **Stems** to 24" (60 cm) tall. **Inflorescence** has typically 3–7 rays, and the bracts beneath the umbel are shorter than those of chufa, none extending beyond the longest spike. **Spikelets** *sparse*, 5–14 per spike, often curvy, *dark brownish-purple*, with the light-colored *twisty filaments very evident* against the dark scales.

HABITAT: Disturbed rich soil in full sun, especially agricultural fields, lawns, roadsides, ditches. Introduced.

FOOD USE: Tubers have been pounded and boiled or pressed for their oil, sometimes on a large scale (I have not done this). They have a strong, unique flavor and I like to chew on them whole, especially the young ones. I would like to try a horchata from these, but haven't had the chance yet.

COMMENTS: This plant has been given the title "worst weed in the world" by some agronomists but it is most pernicious in tropical and subtropical crop fields. The tubers were being intensively processed 19,000 years ago along the Nile in Egypt. They are slightly bitter and quite oily with the classic spicy-sedge aroma. Do you know the "spicy-sedge aroma"? Stand downwind from a big sedge meadow on a 90-degree July afternoon and you will. That's one of my favorite smells in the world. I'm tickled by the fact that Nature has encapsulated it in a vegetable, but I'm not yet sure of the best way to eat that aroma.

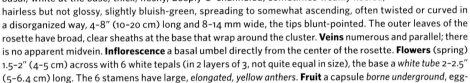

7 Prairie star lily   1   2
Leucocrinum montanum ⬩
Asparagaceae (Asparagus family)

QUICK CHECK: Low rosettes of short, fleshy, linear leaves; large white 6-petaled flowers from a basal umbel in the center of the rosette. **ID difficulty 1.**

DESCRIPTION: Perennial. **Roots** (there is no bulb) in a radiating cluster, whitish, semi-fleshy, gently tapered, 3–4 mm thick at the base. Rosettes are solitary or multiple. **Leaves** all basal, white at the base, thick, fleshy, deeply U-channeled, sometimes weakly keeled, hairless but not glossy, slightly bluish-green, spreading to somewhat ascending, often twisted or curved in a disorganized way, 4–8" (10–20 cm) long and 8–14 mm wide, the tips blunt-pointed. The outer leaves of the rosette have broad, clear sheaths at the base that wrap around the cluster. **Veins** numerous and parallel; there is no apparent midvein. **Inflorescence** a basal umbel directly from the center of the rosette. **Flowers** (spring) 1.5–2" (4–5 cm) across with 6 white tepals (in 2 layers of 3, not quite equal in size), the base a *white tube* 2–2.5" (5–6.4 cm) long. The 6 stamens have large, *elongated, yellow anthers*. **Fruit** a capsule *borne underground*, egg-shaped, the tip broader than the base, 6–8 mm long, 3-sided, breaking open when ripe to release shiny, black, angular seeds.

HABITAT: Dry, often sandy prairies, especially on slopes and with disturbance. Native.

FOOD USE: The small **roots** can be eaten cooked, and taste something like day lily tubers. The **flowers** are edible raw or cooked. **Conservation 3/1.**

COMMENTS: Only a botanical Grinch could dislike this eye-candy. Considering that this long-lived plant must be killed to eat its small, mediocre roots, they shouldn't be high on anyone's gathering list. A few flowers, however, can be taken without harming the plant. **AKA** sand lily, mountain lily.

8 River cane   1   2
Arundinaria gigantea ⬩ *Poaceae* (Grass family)

QUICK CHECK: Large evergreen perennial grass with hard, rigid stems (our only native bamboo). **ID difficulty 1.**

DESCRIPTION: Perennial woody grass (bamboo), typically in dense colonies (canebrakes) spreading by rhizomes. **Stems** 4–30' (1.2–9 m) tall but often leaning or arching, up to 1" (2.5 cm) thick, rounded in cross section (not with a flat side above each node as in golden bamboo), with conspicuous ringed *nodes that usually have multiple branches, many forked near the base and all very small compared to the stem.* **Branches** purplish, weakly to strongly ascending, and covered with dead, brown sheaths with hairy margins. (Continued on the next page.)

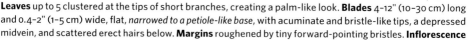

8   River cane (continued)

Leaves up to 5 clustered at the tips of short branches, creating a palm-like look. **Blades** 4–12" (10–30 cm) long and 0.4–2" (1–5 cm) wide, flat, *narrowed to a petiole-like base*, with acuminate and bristle-like tips, a depressed midvein, and scattered erect hairs below. **Margins** roughened by tiny forward-pointing bristles. **Inflorescence**

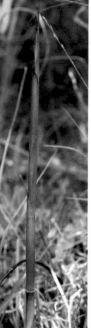

▲ Ripe rivercane seedheads.

(April–May, but rarely produced) a loose terminal panicle with the male and female flowers separate, unshowy, the branches drooping in fruit. **Seeds** 0.4–0.6" (10–15 mm) long, broadest in the middle and tapered to both ends, encased in chaff without awns.

HABITAT: Wetlands, floodplains, moist slopes and ravines with rich soil—often in light shade but more robust in full sun. Native.

FOOD USE: Gather **shoots** in spring or early summer, peel off the leaves, and eat cooked or raw. If you are lucky enough to encounter a fruiting colony, it is a foraging bonanza. When ripe (look for brown chaff) the **seeds** can be harvested by leaning the plants over a large container such as a wheelbarrow or sled and knocking the heads with a stick, which will dislodge ripe grains easily from the panicle. After harvest, dry, parch, rub, and winnow (see p. 27). The grain can be boiled into mush or ground into flour. **Conservation 1/1.**

COMMENTS: A colony may grow for decades or centuries before flowering, after which it dies. This is perhaps the largest grass seed native to our continent, and would be among the premiere starchy foods of North America if it produced consistently. The only drawback is a tough strip down the side of each grain that makes it less pleasant to eat. River cane has suffered due to fire suppression and its preference for the most fertile sites, which have been largely taken for farmland. Some botanists consider all of our forms to be variation within a single species, while others recognize three similar species of native cane.

Related edibles:

Bamboo ◆ (multiple species and genera)   2

Several non-native bamboos are grown ornamentally and sometimes escape. The shoots are generally edible but vary in quality and should be boiled and drained before eating. The most common feral Asian bamboo in our region is golden bamboo *Phyllostachys aurea*, which grows 12–30' (3.5–9 m) tall and has stems that often turn yellow when exposed to sunlight. These have a flat area on one side above each node, and the stem nodes near the base are often densely packed and bulging. The sheath scars are fringed with whitish hairs.

▲ Peeled bamboo shoot.

Bamboo shoot, species uncertain. ▶

Golden bamboo colony. ▶ ▶

9 Phragmites reed   1 ⬭ 2
Phragmites communis ✦ *Poaceae* (Grass family)

QUICK CHECK: Very tall grass forming dense colonies with stiff hollow stems and large plumes at the top. **ID difficulty 1.**

DESCRIPTION: Perennial grass spreading by rhizomes to form dense and often extensive colonies. **Stems** not clumped, 6–14' (2–4 m) tall, rounded, smooth, purple or green, hollow, straight, erect, up to 0.7" (18 mm) thick. On **shoots**, leaf sheaths encircle the stems, overlapping vertically, the edges also overlapping around the stem; there is cottony stuff inside the shoot. **Leaves** *2-ranked*, sometimes arranged primarily on one side of the stem, 1–2' (30–60 cm) long and 1–2" (2.5–5 cm) wide, arising from sheaths, the *blades flat, not keeled*, broadest in the lower quarter then long-tapered to a very thin tip, lightly crimped in two spots roughly marking thirds of its length. **Surfaces** not hairy or raspy, but the margins are rough with minute teeth and have fine hairs. Sheath margins are thin and purplish; there is a tuft of hair where a fully formed leaf joins the sheath. **Inflorescence** (summer to early fall) a large, purplish, plume-like terminal panicle 6–16" (15–40 cm) long, with numerous slender ascending branches, the branch tips and top nodding slightly. The panicle turns brown as the seeds ripen, and the branches may become all disposed toward one side. **Spikelets** have 3–6 flowers with long, silky hairs between them. The chaff has long-pointed tips but no extending awn. **Seeds** 2–3 mm long but not often forming.

CONFUSING PLANTS: River cane and giant reed *Arundo donax* are both evergreen and have thicker, stiffer stems.

HABITAT: Moist soil, marshes, wetland borders, ditches. Primarily in full sun, and especially common where disturbed or degraded. There are native and non-native populations—the non-native ones are highly invasive. **I**

FOOD USE: Shoots are edible raw or cooked. Rhizome shoots (**laterals**) can be gathered and peeled in summer, but getting them out is only practical at the edges of colonies. Other food uses have been listed, but I have not had success with them. **Conservation 1** (native subspecies).

COMMENTS: There are clearly distinguishable native and introduced forms of this plant, usually considered separate subspecies. The native reed is smaller with sparser inflorescences and grows less densely; it blooms and dies earlier in the growing season. The lower stem is purple and smooth (on the introduced reed it is green and slightly ridged). Native *Phragmites* is a normal part of wetland communities, but the introduced populations aggressively take over vast expanses to the virtual exclusion of all other vegetation, and such monocultures may be seen near many urban areas in our region. Also, be careful not to step on a reed sprout while barefoot—they are *sharp!*

◀ Phragmites reed shoots.

10 Western rice grass 🌾 2
Oryzopsis hymenoides ✦ *Poaceae* (Grass family)

QUICK CHECK: Knee-high clumped grass with thin wiry leaves and loose, spreading panicles of stout, dark seeds with an attached tuft of hair. **ID difficulty 1.**

DESCRIPTION: A "bunchgrass"—each plant has several stems, and multiple adjacent plants often form large clumps with dozens or hundreds of stems each. **Basal leaves** numerous, cold-hardy and emerging early among the persistent remains of last year's growth, the central ones erect but the outer ones spreading or limp. **Blades** 7–12" (18–30 cm) long and extremely thin (1–3 mm), the margins often *strongly rolled inward making it almost needle or wire-like*. Most basal leaves are brown by the time seeds ripen. **Stems** erect, 12–22" (30–56 cm) tall, about 2 mm thick, hairless. Each stem usually has 2 leaves sheathing it for a few inches before the free portion narrows abruptly. **Panicles** 6–11" (15–28 mm) long, taller than wide and very loose, the branches usually *spreading dichotomously at angles of 110–170°*, the *spikelets widely separated* and the pedicels thread-thin and wavy. Upon ripening, the two enclosing bracts spread open to release the chaff-covered seeds, which have a *wavy awn* 4–7 mm long and are *embedded in a whitish downy tuft* that catches the wind for dispersal. **Grains** *dark brown to black*, oval, 2–3 mm long, pointed, with a thick seedcoat.

HABITAT: Dry, sunny sites in prairies, especially slopes and sandy areas or where disturbed; often common on roadsides. Native.

FOOD USE: The **grain** is gathered in early to mid summer by beating the heads into a bin or basket, or by stripping the tops by hand. Dark, plump seeds are good; empties are smaller and light brown. Parch to burn off the fluff, then rub and winnow to purify the seed (see p. 27). **Conservation 1.**

COMMENTS: This was formerly a staple Indigenous food in the High Plains and Intermountain West. It often grows in large populations and the seeds are moderately large and easier to harvest and winnow than those of most other grasses. Unfortunately, the seed has a thick coat that is hard to remove. It is possible to eat it without removal if the seed is ground or pounded, but this adds a lot of roughage. Western rice grass has been the subject of much selection, research, breeding, and (gulp) even some genetic engineering. For a while in the 2000's one variety was commercially grown in Montana as a cereal crop. This is one of the most important livestock range plants of the semi-arid West, and it is the state grass of both Nevada and Utah. **AKA** Indian rice grass, sandgrass, *Stipa hymenoides*, *Eriocoma hymenoides*, *Achnatherum hymenoides*.

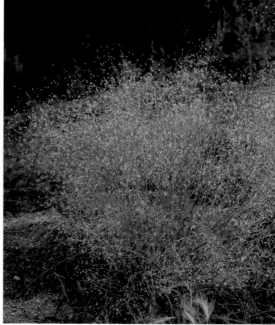

11 Maygrass ❧ 2
Phalaris caroliniana ✦ *Poaceae* (Grass family)

QUICK CHECK: Waist-high grass with short, plump, fluffy heads lacking awns, atop a thin, nearly naked stem; falling seeds tiny and teardrop-shaped. **ID difficulty 1.**

DESCRIPTION: Annual grass 12–40" (30–100 cm) tall, single or forming tufts. **Stems** erect, 1–3.5 mm thick, hairless, sparingly branched in the lower part. **Leaves** to 8" (20 cm) long, few and sparse, the free portions of blades not overlapping on the upper half of the stem. **Blade** flat, smooth, hairless, 2–9 mm wide; it feels smooth when rubbed from bottom to top but minutely raspy when rubbed from tip to base. Leaf sheath 1.5–2.5" (4–6 cm) long, rounded and smooth on the back. **Inflorescence** an oblong panicle 0.8–2.4" (2–6 cm) long, narrowed at both ends, oriented vertically, bushy and dense, the branches not evident unless you take the panicle apart. It is borne at the top of a naked section of stem 4–12" (10–30 cm) long and 1 mm thick. **Grains** borne between two ovate scales (glumes) 5–6 mm long, with a scabrous keel (hard to see with the naked eye), and a sharp boat-like tip, but *no awn*. These glumes have a lanceolate-shaped window of clear or whitish material in the center and on one edge, giving them a *snow-on-the-mountain look*. The unit that falls free (grain wrapped in thin chaff) is 3–5 mm long and teardrop-shaped with an acuminate tip; the surface has minute appressed hairs that are hard to see. The separated grains are egg-shaped and 2–3 mm long.

HABITAT: Old fields, disturbed moist ground, floodplain forests, alluvial soil near creeks—especially loamy sand. Likes full sun. Native.

FOOD USE: Gather **grain** in late spring, parch, rub, and winnow (see p. 27). **Conservation 1.**

COMMENTS: Archeobotany indicates that this grass was formerly much harvested and probably cultivated in parts of the South, although this tradition has been dead for hundreds of years. Although the seeds and heads are small, their tall and exposed position on the plant, lack of attached awns, ease of separation, low chaff percentage, and the presence of large pure stands, must have all contributed to the practicality of using this grain. It often grows mixed with little barley and sumpweed, two other important ancient seeds, and I suspect that the entire community was managed with fire.

12 Little barley 2
Hordeum pusillum ✦ *Poaceae* (Grass family)

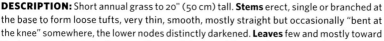

QUICK CHECK: Short grass of disturbed soil with proportionately large vertical heads, the seeds with long awns ripening in late spring. **ID difficulty 1.**

DESCRIPTION: Short annual grass to 20" (50 cm) tall. **Stems** erect, single or branched at the base to form loose tufts, very thin, smooth, mostly straight but occasionally "bent at the knee" somewhere, the lower nodes distinctly darkened. **Leaves** few and mostly toward the base, erect or strongly ascending, 2–4" (5–10 cm) long and 3–6 mm wide, narrowing rather abruptly to a point, the blades flat at first, the edges later inrolled or boat-like, especially at the tip and when brown. **Inflorescence** a single, erect, slightly flattened spike 1–3" (2.5–8 cm) long, the spikelets and awns also erect and never spreading. Each seed-bearing spikelet is surrounded by shorter sterile spikelets, so the "disarticulating unit" (the thing that breaks off with a grain in it) has a long awn surrounded by several shorter awns. *Dry, ripe spikelets jump like grasshoppers.* **Seeds** are narrow and 2–3 mm long.

HABITAT: Well-drained, disturbed soil in full sun. Roadsides, farm fields, construction sites, pastures, sunny clearings in floodplains. Commonly seen lining interstates in spring. Native.

FOOD USE: Used as a **grain** like barley. (See grain processing, p. 27.) Seeds ripen in late spring or early summer. Beat them into a basket, or cut sheafs and dry them, then thresh out the spikelets. My experience is limited, but this one is tricky to de-hull, and the chaff percentage is very high. Parching to burn off the dangerous awns is especially important when processing this cereal. **Conservation 1.**

COMMENTS: There are very few plants that you can identify by the name, but if you know what domestic barley looks like, you will easily recognize this relative, which looks like a miniature version. This grass was once gathered in great quantities and probably cultivated thousands of years ago; it is a regular find in archeological sites of the South. When you collect it, fully ripe spikelets seem to jump off the top of the plant at the slightest touch; in doing so they embed in clothing or fur. I do not know if this results from the kinetic energy of contact being some-

how channeled to the spikelet, or if there is tension built into the rachis that is released (like an exploding jewelweed pod) by touch. Either way, walking through it gives you the feeling that hundreds of tiny grasshoppers are jumping from the tops of the grain heads.

13 **Small blazing star** 2
Liatris punctata / mucronata +
Asteraceae (Composite family)

QUICK CHECK: Shin-high plant with clumped stems and very narrow, sharp, tough, pointed leaves; purple flower heads small, crowded, erect, and narrow. **ID difficulty 3.**

DESCRIPTION: Perennial from an enlarged root. **Roots** may be elongated and carrot-like or short and bulbous; they are firm with *alternating light and dark layers when sliced* (a characteristic shared by all *Liatris* I have checked). **Basal leaves** mostly wither by flowering and are similar to the stem leaves, only somewhat larger with the base narrowed to a petiole. **Stems** usually clumped, 2–15 per plant, 12–26" (30–66 cm) tall and 2–5 mm thick, erect or leaning, stiff, often curved, *unbranched*. **Stem leaves** alternate, 2–5" (5–13 cm) long and *very narrow*, 3–7 mm wide, linear, sessile, numerous, overlapping, *crowded*, strongly ascending, tough and stiff, the tips darkened but with a light-colored needle-point. The surface has tiny darkened, depressed dots on both sides; it is hairless except on the **margins**, which are entire, often whitish and papery, with scattered short, stiff hairs. **Midvein** protrudes slightly above and below; other veins not evident. **Inflorescence** a leafy spike of numerous small heads nearly *appressed to the rachis*, moderately crowded and somewhat overlapping, encompassing the upper third of the stem. **Heads** longer than wide with only *3–8 florets*. **Bracts** appressed, overlapping, triangular, with a purple midvein, an acuminate claw-like bristle at the tip, and the margins ciliate and purple. **Florets** purple with 5 spreading, curled, lanceolate lobes, the column in the center *very dark purple* near the base. **Fruit** a dry seed (achene) with a feathery pappus.

CONFUSING RELATED EDIBLES: *Liatris* is an easy genus to recognize, but the members can be confusing to differentiate. None are dangerous, but the roots of most are too woody to be food. *L. aspera* also has an enlarged bulbous root—but it has a strong soapy flavor and can only be eaten sparingly. *L. aspera* averages slightly taller and has larger, broader leaves; the flowerheads are larger and less crowded. *L. squarrosa* also has a roundish root; it has sparser leaves, grows on poor soil, and has more than 10 florets per head.

HABITAT: Dry prairies in rich or sandy soil. Native.

FOOD USE: The **roots** are reported as food from several Native peoples on the Great Plains, although they are not commonly eaten today. The elongated taproots are tough and woody. However, some round, enlarged **roots** are less tough, and they have a mild pleasant flavor that is good in stews. **Conservation 3.**

COMMENTS: Neither the taxonomy nor the ethnobotany of these plants is sorted out. Most botanists recognize a single species of *Liatris punctata*, but some have split this into two closely related species with nearly identical above-ground parts, but quite different underground parts. If they are separated, those with woody taproots are *L. punctata* and those with semi-hard roundish roots are *L. mucronata*. By this scheme, the flowering stems pictured here are *L. punctata* from rich soil in Minnesota and the bulbous taproot is *L. mucronata* from sandy soil in Oklahoma. I ate the root pictured and liked it, but the elongated roots I've tried have been very woody.

14 Seaside Plantain 3 2
Plantago maritima + family *Plantaginaceae*

QUICK CHECK: Dense rosette of numerous elongated fleshy leaves with a midvein groove; leafless spikes packed with unshowy flowers. **ID difficulty 1.**

DESCRIPTION: Perennial from a thick taproot, older ones producing multiple adjacent rosettes. **Leaves** numerous, all basal, erect to leaning or spreading, linear, 4–7" (10–18 cm) long and 0.4–0.6" (10–15 mm) wide, *very thick and fleshy*, hairless, brittle, folded or curved into a trough, with a slight groove down the center. **Midvein** slightly lighter green, as is the one faintly visible vein on each side. The tips are pointed and darkened; the bases are not sheathed. **Margins** sometimes minutely hairy, entire or with *widely scattered tiny teeth*. **Scape** single, unbranched, leafless, 4–10" (10–25 cm) long, erect to leaning or spreading, often wavy, soft-hairy (especially on the upper part), round, often reddish. **Inflorescence** a spike on the upper third of the stem, the flowers densely packed and touching. **Flowers** (June–September) tiny, greenish white, with a tube spreading into 4 lobes at the end. **Fruit** an egg-shaped capsule that separates around the middle when ripe to release multiple dark seeds.

CONFUSING PLANTS: Seaside arrow-grass has longer, thinner leaves and taller stalks with less densely flowered spikes; its leaves are distinctly sheathed at the base.

HABITAT: Rocky slopes, cliffs, tidal marshes, upper edges of beaches, and occasionally salty highway shoulders, in full sun. Native.

FOOD USE: Leaves can be gathered at any time during the growing season and eaten raw or cooked. They are mildly salty, tender, and delicious. Young **flower stalks** can also be eaten. **Conservation 2.**

COMMENTS: This is a common plant, excellent for eating, with a long season of availability. When it grows on roadsides away from the coast it is less salty and more astringent. **AKA** Goose tongue, *P. oliganthos, P. juncoides.*

15 Yucca 🌱 2 🌸 2
genus *Yucca* ✦ *Asparagaceae* (Asparagus family)

▲ Composite range.

QUICK CHECK: A dense cluster of numerous long, sharp-tipped, tough leaves and a single leafless flower stalk with large drooping flowers. **ID difficulty 1.**

DESCRIPTION: Perennials with a tough, semi-woody base that occasionally becomes a short trunk on certain species. **Leaves** all basal (or in a whorl at the stem tip), several dozen, linear, 16–30" (40–75 cm) long and up to 2" (5 cm) wide, tough and stringy (often with loose fibers attached to the margins), evergreen, sharp-tipped, with no prominent veins and no petioles. **Stem** single from the rosette center, erect (sometimes leaning later), 2–9' (60–275 cm) tall and 0.8–1.6" (2–4 cm) thick, round, solid, bearing only reduced, scale-like leaves. **Inflorescence** a large panicle or raceme at the apex of this stalk. **Flowers** (early to mid summer) numerous and large, 1.5–3.5" (4–9 cm) across, drooping or nodding, white to greenish off-white, with 6 separate tepals; there are six stout stamens with the tips cocked outward surrounding a stout stigma. **Fruit** (late summer to fall) a large, oblong, 3-part green capsule that turns brown and splits open upon drying, containing numerous black seeds.

HABITAT: Sunny sites on sand, gravel, or rocky soil. Outside of the Great Plains, yuccas are mostly found on dunes, sunny slopes, outcrops, barrens, roadsides, or disturbed forest edges. Native, but also widely cultivated and escaped outside of their natural ranges.

FOOD USE: The flower stalk **shoot** in late spring or early summer can be used as a cooked vegetable. Peel the outer skin for the best dining experience. Eat **flower petals** raw or cooked in midsummer. (Some people find them slightly irritating raw.) The **fruit** of some species is cooked and eaten, sometimes dried for storage, although I have not eaten the fruit of any yuccas in our region. **Conservation 2/1.**

COMMENTS: "Yucca" is pronounced with a short u sound and should not be confused with the tropical root crop yuca (pronounced with a long U sound), also called manioc or cassava, often misspelled by grocery stores and produce distributors, creating endless confusion. The two plants are unrelated and utterly dissimilar. Yuca has edible roots; yucca does not!

SPECIES: There are 8–10 yuccas native to our area, depending on who's doing the counting, and all are edible. I'm featuring the two most common and widespread here:

Great Plains yucca *Y. glauca* is widespread on the prairies. It has stiff, broadly U-channeled leaves 8–12 mm wide with needle-like tips. The inflorescence is a raceme standing less than 5' (1.5 m) high, bearing its lowest flowers beneath the height of the leaves. Nearly identical yuccas further south on the Plains are sometimes called *Y. arkansana*, differentiated by having leaves about twice as wide.

(Continued on the next page.)

▲ *Y. glauca.*

15 Yucca (continued)

Common yucca *Y. filamentosa* is the common species of the Southeast, which has also been widely introduced in sandy areas north of its native range. The leaves are up to 2" (5 cm) wide, flatter, and sharp but not needle-like at the tip. Common yucca has a branched cluster (panicle) of flowers that reaches 6–9' (2–3 m) in height, and the lowest flowers are borne well above the top of the leaves. The panicle stems often arch under the weight of flowers. Common yucca has smaller pods and seeds than Great Plains yucca. The plants with less stiff leaves and hairy panicles are sometimes separated as *Y. flaccida*, but the food uses are the same. 🔥

▲ (top left) *Y. glauca* fruit. (top right) *Y. filamentosa* shoot. (bottom) *Y. filamentosa.*

16 False garlic ◐ 2
Nothoscordum bivalve ✦ *Alliaceae* (Onion family)

QUICK CHECK: All leaves basal; a single scape bearing an umbel of attractive white flowers with 6 petals. **ID difficulty 2.**

DESCRIPTION: Polycarpic perennial. **Bulbs** globular or egg-shaped to amorphous and bulging, especially when large, 0.3–0.9" (8–23 mm) wide, the larger ones with small, scale-like offset bulbs. **Leaves** 3–7, all basal, wrapped in a sheath for 1–2" (2.5–5 cm) above the bulb, the blades to 15" (38 cm) long and 2–5 mm wide, shallowly U-channeled, not hollow, the tips blunt and thin. **Scapes** 6–16" (15–40 cm) tall, single, erect, straight, solid, smooth, hairless, round to slightly angled. **Inflorescence** a single terminal umbel of 5–12 with 2 brown, papery, triangular, pointed bracts beneath it, the pedicels ascending and unequal, 1.5–2.2" (3.8–5.6 cm) long. **Flowers** (mostly spring but occasionally through summer and often in fall) have 6 long-elliptic, blunt pointed, white tepals 9–13 mm long arranged in 2 layers of 3, each with a prominent center vein (on the outside this vein is yellow-green at the base but often purplish toward the tip); stamens 6. **Fruit** a 3-part capsule, egg-shaped, wider at the tip (which is sometimes flattened), 3–5 mm wide and 6–10 mm long, turning light brown upon drying and splitting into boat-shaped valves holding angular, rough, black seeds.

CONFUSING PLANTS: Star-of-Bethlehem (p. 666) is shorter with very slimy sap. The leaves have a whitish center stripe and the flowers are in a short raceme.

HABITAT: Full to partial sun with moderately rich soil of medium moisture, especially where disturbed. Lawns, roadsides, parks, meadows, high floodplains, savannahs, sparse forests and edges. Native. ◗

FOOD USE: Bulbs can be collected at any time and eaten cooked. They have a faint garlic flavor. **Conservation 3.**

COMMENTS: At the moment of writing I have eaten these bulbs on four occasions, in greater quantity each time (in the last instance a quarter cup). Archeological evidence suggests that false garlic was once an important food in some regions. This species was formerly classified in the genus *Allium*, and the differences by which it is separated are minor. The garlic flavor is faint but evident when you eat the bulbs. Though common in lawns, this plant is much smaller there than in unmowed grassy areas. **AKA** crow poison, but you won't have much luck poisoning crows with it. The name "crow poison" is thrown at a number of remotely similar plants, such as *Amianthium muscitoxicum*, which is actually poisonous.

17 Seaside arrow-grass 🌿 3 🥄 3
Triglochin maritima ✦ family *Juncaginaceae*

QUICK CHECK: Clumps of thick, narrow, erect leaves with a long sheath at the base; unbranched scape with a spike-like top. **ID difficulty 2.**

DESCRIPTION: Perennial forming clumps from a thick root crown. In bogs, fens, and marshes it is taller and grows singly or in small clumps; in open coastal habitats it is shorter but often grows in dense clumps. **Leaves** all basal, two-ranked, 8–22" (20–56 cm) long, erect to leaning, thick and spongy-fleshy, hairless, very narrow with pointed tips, mostly plump, *spongy inside* with thin outer walls, shallowly channeled in the lower part but near the top they are not channeled and may be almost rounded. The leaves are not visibly veined and have a conspicuous *sheath on the lower third to half* clasping the inner adjacent leaves of the cluster. **Stems** 10–38" (25–97 cm) tall, erect, thin and unbranched, *hollow, slightly flattened on one side,* often curvy. (Stem shoots are solid at first.) **Inflorescence** a spike-like raceme comprising the upper 35–50% of the scape, with numerous small, unshowy flowers on pedicels 2–5 mm, the space between them decreasing toward the top. There is a narrow ridge along the rachis below each pedicel. **Flowers** 3–4 mm across, green, with 6 tiny tepals and purple stigmas. **Fruit** a cylindrical or urn-shaped capsule with 3–6 fuzzy, outward-pointing *lobes at the tip and base.*

CONFUSING PLANTS: Marsh arrow-grass *T. palustre* (edibility unknown) is much smaller with a 3-lobed fruit. Seaside plantain has shorter and broader leaves that are brittle and flat or channeled (but not rounded); it flowers in a true spike that is much shorter and more crowded.

HABITAT: Most abundant in coastal wetlands. Also found on lakeshores, river banks, pond margins, calcareous bogs and fens, brackish wetlands; in full sun. Needs dissolved mineral salts. Native.

FOOD USE: In spring or early summer, pull up the leaf cluster and eat the tender, inner, white **heart** enclosed by sheaths. **Shoots** of flower stalks are also edible. Nibble these parts raw or add them to salads, tacos, salsa, or vegetable dishes. The pleasant taste reminds me of cilantro, but is better because it lacks the soapy flavor. Seeds are reported as edible, but are tiny and hard to separate; I've had no success. **Conservation 2.**

COMMENTS: In large quantities this plant is known to have toxic effects on livestock, but this seems irrelevant to human culinary use. The leaf bases are traditionally eaten and relished by several Indigenous groups.

▶ (top left) Spring shoot of a bog specimen.
(top middle) Tall spike of a bog specimen.

▶ (below right) Growing on a rocky sea beach.

▼ Hearts.

18 Grape hyacinth ◊ 1 ✿ 1 ☕
genus *Muscari* ✦ *Asparagaceae* (Asparagus family)

QUICK ID: Short spring ephemeral with linear leaves and dense racemes of drooping, roundish, purple flowers. **ID difficulty 2.**

DESCRIPTION: Perennial. **Bulb** to 1" (2.5 cm) long, teardrop-shaped, symmetrical, smooth with a papery, light-brown skin, whitish inside. **Leaves** all basal, 5–8 on flowering specimens, to 14" (36 cm) long and 11 mm wide, thick, semi-succulent and somewhat slimy, broadly U-shaped in cross section, whitish and channeled at the base. The underside has numerous small ridges, but the top is smooth and lacks these. The surface is hairless with a faint bloom on the surface. **Scape** 6–14" (15–36 cm) tall and 2–4 mm thick (thicker toward the top), round, solid, smooth, hairless, not ridged, strictly leafless (no bracts or scales). **Inflorescence** a dense terminal raceme 1–3" (2.5–8 cm) long, of 20–40 flowers, the pedicels 6–9 mm, each with a tiny bristle underneath. **Flowers** nodding, urn or egg-shaped, 4–7 mm long, purple, with a constricted, often whitish opening at the end with 6 tiny recurved lobes. The surface is hairless, smooth while blooming but becoming grooved or pleated before falling off. There is a faint grape-like smell. The sexual parts are hidden deep inside the urn; the inside often appears star-like. **Fruit** a 3-part capsule containing 6 seeds.

SPECIES: The genus is easy to recognize, but the species are hard to differentiate. The most common feral species in our region are *M. botryoides*, *M. armeniacum*, and *M. neglectum*. The differences are subtle, and the food uses similar.

HABITAT: Moist, rich soil in full sun to moderate shade. Lawns, meadows, waste areas, forest edges and woodlots in urban areas or near old homesteads. Introduced.

CONFUSING PLANTS: This plant is hard to tell from **Star-of-Bethlehem** (p. 666) unless in bloom, and the two often grow together, but the SOB has slimier, narrower leaves. Flowering grape hyacinth is unmistakable.

FOOD USE: Bulbs are extremely bitter and somewhat toxic when raw. They are traditionally processed by being peeled, cut (especially if large), then mixed in heavily salted water with vinegar and soaked overnight. After this they can be cooked or pickled *if they no longer taste bitter*. If they are still bitter they should be boiled and drained. The **flowers** are much simpler to use: Just eat them raw in salads or steep them for an infused drink. They are pretty but don't taste very good either.

COMMENTS: The fresh bulbs are terrible, but hungry European peasants long ago figured out how to make them palatable. The plant is remarkably widespread because it is grown ornamentally; although persisting after escape, it spreads slowly and rarely becomes a problematic invasive.

19 Camas ◊ 3 | 3 ✎ 2
genus *Camassia* ✦ *Asparagaceae* (Asparagus family)

QUICK CHECK: Long, thin leaves, basal only, keeled in the lower part; leafless scape with a long raceme of blue to whitish-blue flowers with 6 petals. **ID difficulty 3.**

DESCRIPTION: Perennial spring ephemeral. **Bulbs** 2–5" (5–13 cm) deep, symmetrical, spherical to slightly teardrop-shaped, 0.5–1.7" (13–43 mm) in diameter, layered, the flesh whitish, hard, and smooth but covered with a thin, dark, papery, layered skin. **Leaves** 3–14, all basal, hairless, erect to ascending with the tips limp, scrolled near the base becoming channeled with reflexed edges, flat to weakly keeled in the distal third, faintly to strongly keeled in the proximal part. They are often flipped *upside-down*. Blades 0.2–0.7" (5–18 mm) wide and 9–20" (23–50 cm) long, linear, tough, thick, slightly fleshy, faintly glaucous with numerous small parallel veins, the tips long-tapered, sharp, often brown. Torn leaves show *faint threads*. **Scapes** 12–40" (30–100 cm) tall, thin for their height, 2–5 mm in diameter, smooth, hairless, glaucous (especially near the base), erect, unbranched, round in cross section but often with one flat spot, solid, rigid, the sap slimy. **Shoots** have cone-like clusters of *flower buds with long, whiskery bracts pressed over them*. **Inflorescence** a long raceme of 12–80 flowers in spring to early summer, most pedicels slightly ascending, 30–40% of flower length. Beneath the pedicel there may be a bract roughly equal

to its length, broad at the base but abruptly narrowing to thread-like. **Flowers** 0.4–0.9" (10–23 mm) across, blue or sometimes nearly white, with 6 tepals that are elliptic and blunt or abruptly pointed. At bloom, tepals are about 3 times as long as wide, but the edges soon dry and curl inward, making them appear much narrower. The ovary is elongated and yellow. **Fruit** a triangular or 3-part capsule 0.4–0.7" (10–18 mm) long, containing many black seeds.

SPECIES: Two in our region, both native: thriving in rich, mildly disturbed soil. 🔥

Eastern camas *C. scilloides* inhabits woodlands, nut savannahs, and prairies, especially on slopes, upper floodplains, and rocky hilltops. The leaves are typically more keeled, the flowers are paler, and there are few bracts in the inflorescence. **AKA** Atlantic camas, wild hyacinth. 🔥

▲ Western camas in blue; Eastern and prairie camas in purple; Eastern camas only in green.

▲ Eastern camas: (top left) Shoot. (top middle) In a prairie area, just beginning to flower. (top right) Pods. (bottom) In wooded habitat.

Prairie camas *C. angusta* is a tallgrass prairie species, larger in all respects, with flatter leaves and darker blue flowers bearing many bracts in the inflorescence and blooming about a month later. This plant is rare and protected in most of its range and should not be gathered under normal circumstances. 🔥

CONFUSING PLANTS: Death camasses (p. 665) have a few stem leaves (but only on plants with a stem!), white flowers, and always have keeled or deeply V-folded leaves. Death camas bulbs have a strong bitter flavor, giving you one last chance to spit out your mistake if you somehow mess up.

FOOD USE: Bulbs can be dug any time, but it is best to do so just after flowering in early summer so the plant can be identified more readily. Bulbs should be baked or steamed for a prolonged period (preferably 12 hours or longer) to break their undigestible starches down into simple sugars—this renders them sweet and delicious, like a cross between cooked persimmon and sweet potatoes. **Shoots** and **greens** can be eaten as a vegetable raw or cooked in spring. **Conservation 3/2.**

COMMENTS: Our camasses were probably once managed staple crops just like their western relatives. The eastern species is ideal for growing in the herbaceous layer of a nut forest managed by fire. Because they inhabit rich soils camasses have lost most of their haunts to agriculture (and most of the rest to fire suppression).

▲ Prairie camas (top) and eastern camas (lower left) bulbs.

▲ Eastern camas in forest, with tender young leaves that have been nipped by deer.

◀◀ (left) Prairie camas rosette.

◀ (right) Prairie camas.

GROUP 18 FLOWERING STEM LEAFLESS, BASAL LEAVES ENTIRE

A few of these plants may occasionally have tiny vestigial leaves on the scape. The absence of the scapes (or leaves) during part of the year may complicate identification, but I have tried to provide sufficient detail to identify these plants when only the leaves are present. Otherwise this group is rather easy to navigate.

TENTATIVE IDENTIFICATION KEY TO GROUP 18
The key is not your final answer!

Leaf always single.	
Leaf with 50-60 prominent whitish veins above.	1. Puttyroot
Leaf with 5-7 prominent dark veins above.	2. Cranefly orchid
Leaves always paired, on densely hairy petioles directly from the rhizome.	3. Wild ginger
Leaves 1-3 per plant.	
Leaves usually mottled, ephemeral, never hairy; single flower per scape.	4. Trout lily
Leaves not mottled, not ephemeral, margins hairy when young; flowers multiple.	5. Bluebead lily
Leaves in rosettes of usually 5 or more.	
Most leaves over 14" (36 cm) long, stinky when broken, veins white below.	6. Skunk cabbage
Leaves generally less than 14" long, not stinky.	
Major veins palmate and depressed above.	7. Mountain sorrel
Major veins flat or raised above.	
Veins mostly raised; scape minutely woolly or smooth, solid.	8. Shooting star
Veins flat; scape hollow, densely covered with erect hairs. Swamp saxifrage (p. 284).	
Major veins parallel and depressed above.	
Blade blunt-tipped, 60-90% as broad as long.	9. Common plantain
Blade pointed, 15-30% as broad as long.	10. Narrow-leaf plantain

1 Puttyroot 2
Aplectrum hyemale ✦ *Orchidaceae* (Orchid family)

QUICK CHECK: A single, dry, broadly elliptic, pleated leaf with numerous silver-white parallel veins; no leaf at flowering time. **ID difficulty 1.**

DESCRIPTION: *Winter perennial* with a single leaf from fall through spring. **Corm** nearly spherical, about 1" (2.5 cm) across, white, hard, smooth except for 2 circular scars, one in the middle and one near the base. There is an old, dry sheath attached to the base and each scar, but not encircling the corm. A bud about 1.4" (3.5 cm) long is present when the stalk is absent. The pervious year's spent corm is often attached, or next year's new corm is forming. **Leaf** 5-8" (13-20 cm) long, broadly elliptic, tough and dry, wrinkly, hairless, green above with a faint purple tint below. The midvein and 5 other prominent veins protrude on the underside; the leaf is keeled or folded along each of these. The *upper surface has numerous (about 60) whitish, raised, parallel veins.* **Petiole** about 50% of blade length, thick, *roughly triangular but with 4 unequal grooves*, the largest one in the center of the top side. The edges of the lower blade curl in and meet to form an *enclosed channel*; these edges fuse to create a hollow petiole. There is a distinct ring where the leaf base attaches to the petiole. The petiole is whitish near the base, purple distally. **Stalks** are produced in late spring or early summer, when leaves are absent. They are unbranched, erect, 12-22" (30-56 cm) tall and 5-7 mm thick, rounded, hairless, the lower portion covered by a long leafy sheath. **Inflorescence** a sparse raceme of 4-16, the rachis wavy or zigzag, the pedicels 8-12 mm, arched, strongly grooved, twisted. **Flowers** (summer) about 1 cm long, irregular in form, with 2 arching petals and a white lip, plus 3 spreading sepals; the floral parts a mixture of green,

yellow, and red-brown. **Pods** about 0.8" (2 cm) long, narrow at both ends, formed by 6 sections of 2 different sizes, drooping from the stem beginning in late summer.

HABITAT: Rich hardwood forests. Native.

FOOD USE: The **corms** can be eaten cooked or raw. The flavor is mild, starchy, and pleasant, but the texture is very pasty and sticky (like Elmer's paste without the minty flavor). **Conservation 3.**

COMMENTS: This plant has an unusual life cycle: It has a single leaf through the fall, winter, and spring, which takes advantage of the long season of available sunlight while the forest canopy lacks leaves. The plant stores this energy in its bulb, which fuels flowering in summer when the leaf has withered away. This long-lived perennial reproduces slowly and is killed when the bulb is dug; it should be collected sparingly and judiciously if at all. **AKA** Adam-and-Eve.

2 Cranefly orchid 🐷🐷 2
Tipularia discolor ✦ *Orchidaceae* (Orchid family)

QUICK CHECK: Single, broadly ovate leaf, folded along several prominent parallel veins, dark purple underneath; long raceme of cranefly-like flowers. **ID difficulty 1.**

DESCRIPTION: Winter perennial with a single basal leaf withering in spring. **Tubers** in chains of 3–5, each about 1" (2.5 cm) long, white, with little to no rhizome between them. The surface is smooth except for 1 or 2 ring-like scars and an occasional bud or bud scar. The most recent tuber is the largest and firmest, while those behind it are progressively softer. Roots are borne only at the narrow points between tubers. **Leaf** 2.5–4" (6–10 cm) long, leathery, broadly ovate to heart-shaped with a pointed tip, entire, with the margins curled near the base. The veins are parallel, with the midvein very prominent. There are *2 prominent veins on each side of the midvein, and the blade is creased along them.* The upper surface is green with small, *dark, raised blotches; the lower surface is deep purple.* **Petiole** roughly equal to the blade, finely mottled with purple, hairless, and triangular with sharp corners. It is not channeled at the base, but is in the upper third—becoming deeply and narrowly so just below the blade. **Stems** erect, rounded, hairless, thin, 10–26" (25–66 cm) tall, unbranched, appearing in midsummer. **LYDS** often prominent with drooping fruit still attached (see photo). **Inflorescence** a raceme 5–9" (13–23 cm) long, containing 16–40 purple-green to dull yellow-orange flowers, the rachis finely ridged, the pedicels flattened, ridged, twisted. **Flowers** 0.7" (18 cm) across, a mixture of light mottled maroon and yellowish; they are said to resemble a cranefly, with 5 long, narrow, petal-like parts, plus a lip petal with 3 lobes, the middle one elongated; the lip has a long, tubular spur extending backward from it. **Fruit** a hanging, elliptic capsule 10–12 mm long.

HABITAT: Dry to moderately dry oak, hickory, and pine forests. Native. 🔥

FOOD USE: Harder **tubers** can be cooked and eaten, but this should be done sparingly, as the plant reproduces slowly. **Conservation 3.**

COMMENTS: The tubers taste like Solomon's seal rhizomes, but milder and better.

3 Wild ginger
Asarum canadense ◆ family Aristolochiaceae

QUICK CHECK: Large, paired, heart-shaped leaves on thick, very hairy petioles from a surface rhizome. **ID difficulty 2.**

DESCRIPTION: Low growing perennial herb, often forming dense colonies by rhizome. **Rhizomes** 7–9 mm thick, dull green, roundish but sometimes with a slight ridge, creeping directly on or just below the soil surface. **Leaves** in pairs from the rhizome, 3–6" (8–15 cm) long and about equally wide, heart to kidney-shaped, the base with 2 large rounded lobes and a deep sinus. The upper surface is very dark green and covered with scattered stiff hair; the underside is lighter green and hairier. **Veins** palmate, deeply depressed above and protruding below, looping together well before reaching the margins, sometimes *highlighted by white hairs on top*. **Petioles** stout, channeled, straight, erect, typically slightly longer than the blade, densely covered with long white hairs that *lean toward the base*. **Inflorescence** (spring) single flowers borne on a peduncle 0.5–2" (1.3–5 cm) long directly from the rhizome between the leaves and often well hidden. **Flowers** bell or urn-like, to 0.8" (2 cm) long, the inside *white with a maroon pentagon*. There are *3 densely hairy, recurved, long-pointed lobes* spreading 1–1.5" (25–38 mm) wide, greenish on the back and *maroon from the front*. **Fruit** a fleshy capsule with a calyx at the end.

CONFUSING PLANTS: Members of the related genus *Hexastylis*, common in similar habitats of the Southeast, look similar but lack the long, spreading lobes on the flower. These plants are used by some people as wild ginger is used, but I advise against this (see warning). Certain asters are sometimes confused with wild ginger, but their leaves are longer than wide, thinner, and typically grow in rosettes. Asters lack the thick surface rhizome and have very different flowers.

HABITAT: Hardwood forests with rich soil, especially slopes. Native.

FOOD USE: The **rhizomes** can be used sparingly as a seasoning any time of year. Strong flavor resembles ginger but also suggests cardamom. It is slow growing and easily overharvested, so gather with care. **Conservation 3.**

WARNING: This plant contains aristolochic acid, a renal toxin and potential carcinogen. If used, it should be ingested occasionally and in small amounts.

COMMENTS: This attractive herb is well known to wildcrafters and naturalists. It often grows on steep slopes where you could fall down and ginger yourself. It is not related to cultivated ginger.

4 Trout lily 🔹 3 🔹 2 📖 NG-75
genus *Erythronium* ✦ *Liliaceae* (Lily family)

QUICK CHECK: 1-3 entire, broad, hairless, mottled leaves; single nodding flower with 6 long petals on a short scape. **ID difficulty 1.**

DESCRIPTION: Perennials. **Bulbs** teardrop-shaped, not layered inside, whitish, up to 0.6" (1.5 cm) long, with roots in a tuft at the bottom. Non-flowering bulbs sometimes plant clonal bulbs nearby through a worm-like structure called a "dropper." **Leaves** 1-3, all basal, 3-7" (8-18 cm) long and about 1/3 as wide, long-elliptic to obovate, tapered at the base and pointed at the tip, *hairless* with entire margins. There are no conspicuous veins, but the blade is gently creased along the middle. Leaves are *mottled* with green and maroon when they first appear; this fades with age but usually not completely. **Scape** 4-8" (10-20 cm) tall and 2-3 mm thick, hairless, unbranched, nodding at the apex with a *single flower*, present on only a minority of plants. **Flowers** 1.2-2" (3-5 cm) across, nodding to drooping, with 6 separate lanceolate tepals, yellow or white, recurved when open. There is a single pistil and 6 stamens with long, dark anthers. Flowers close at night or when cloudy. **Fruit** a green, 3-part, elliptic to egg-shaped pod 0.4-0.9" (10-23 mm) long, with a thin beak almost as long as the fruit.

▲ Collective range of the genus *Erythronium*.

SPECIES: *E. americanum* and *E. rostratum* both have yellow flowers and are found in hardwood forests with rich soil. *E. albidum* has white flowers and somewhat smaller leaves; it grows in rich soil in forests and upper floodplains. *E. mesochoreum* 🔥 has white flowers and much narrower unmottled or scarcely mottled leaves. It lives in prairies or savannahs with moderately moist soils. The bulbs of this species are larger than those of our others. All species native.

FOOD USE: Bulbs can be eaten at any time. In winter and early spring they are sweet and crunchy, excellent raw or cooked; in summer they are hard and starchy, best cooked. Bulbs are found 1-5" below the surface—large ones deeper than small ones. Young **leaves** are nibbled raw or mixed with other cooked greens. **Conservation 3/2.**

COMMENTS: Trout lily bulbs are delicious but unfortunately very labor-intensive to gather due to their small size, which prevented them from becoming staple foods like *E. grandiflorum* of the Mountain West. The leaves are not ethnographically documented as a food source but are popular with some foragers today. Eating flowers gives some people an unpleasant burning in the mouth. Trout lily seeds contain an oily chunk of stuff on the outside, called an elaiosome, which ants eat, dispersing the seeds. **AKA** fawn lily, dogtooth violet.

▲ (top left) White trout lily. (top middle) Yellow trout lily flowers. (top right) Prairie trout lily leaf.

◄◄ (left) Trout lily self-planting stem (dropper).

◄ (right) Yellow trout lily bulbs.

5 Bluebead lily 1
Clintonia borealis ✦ *Liliaceae* (Lily family)

QUICK CHECK: Glossy, rubbery, entire leaves with finely hairy margins; new leaves tightly rolled; blue berries. **ID difficulty 2.**

DESCRIPTION: Perennial spreading by rhizomes to form colonies. **Leaves** all basal, 2–3 per rosette, 4–10" (10–25 cm) long, elliptic or obovate with the tip short-acuminate or blunt with a nipple, the base narrowed but lacking a petiole. **Blades** thick and rather tough at maturity, dark green, depressed in the center (less so toward the tip), the surfaces smooth and hairless. Upon emerging they are lighter green, rubbery, erect, and *rolled tightly*. Young leaves squeak when rubbed together. **Veins** parallel, scarcely visible, flat to faintly depressed above, flat below. **Margins** entire, at first with a *fringe of long hairs* but these are lost with age. **Scape** 6–20" (15–50 cm) tall, 3–4 mm thick, erect (often leaning in fruit), the surface usually downy when young, bearing 3–15 flowers in a terminal umbel, occasionally accompanied by other pedicels lower on the scape. **Flowers** (late spring to early summer) 0.8–1.3" (2–3.3 cm) across, open skyward or nodding, on pedicels as long as the flower, the 6 tepals narrowly elliptic to almost strap-like, tapered toward both ends but not sharp-tipped, recurved, light creamy-yellow; the stamens and pistil as long as or longer than the petals. **Fruit** a smooth, waxy-looking, glossy, roundish blue berry about 1 cm, maturing late summer, not edible.

CONFUSING PLANTS: Lily-of-the-valley *Convallaria majalis* (toxic) has 2 leaves on the stem, which is D-shaped in cross section with sharp edges.

HABITAT: Moderate shade in conifer or mixed conifer-hardwood forests with moist, usually somewhat acidic soil. Does especially well under white birch. Native.

FOOD USE: Gather young **leaves** in early spring, preferably while still curled, and eat raw in salads or on sandwiches. **Conservation 2.**

COMMENTS: The flavor of this spring green is cucumbery but bitter. The bitterness only seems to be accentuated by boiling. I am not personally fond of these greens, but know some people who are.

RELATED EDIBLE? *C. umbellulata* is a very similar species endemic to the Appalachians. It may be edible in the same way but I have not tried it.

Bluebead lily leaves furled in spring. ▶

6 Skunk cabbage
Symplocarpus foetidus ✦ *Araceae* (Arum family)

QUICK CHECK: Rosettes of huge, entire, stinky, ovate leaves on long, sturdy petioles; large, curved, maroon flowers come directly out of the mud. **ID difficulty 1.**

DESCRIPTION: Perennial from a thick, short, unbranched taproot with numerous small, fibrous roots, the whole plant with a *strong musky scent*, all parts *hairless*. **Leaves** in a rosette of 4–7, ascending to erect (not ground-hugging), squeaky when manipulated, the new ones tightly scrolled. Blades ovate with abrupt, blunt tips, to 2' (60 cm) long, very thin for their size, glossy, heart-shaped with the lobes curled. **Margins** entire but often with tooth-like folds or waves. **Veins** and veinlets are depressed above and protruding below. *Major veins have a prominent white halo below.* Secondary veins are numerous, spreading toward the margins at first, then gently curving toward the tip and approaching the margin gradually over a long path nearly parallel to it. **Petioles** about 80% of blade length, to 1" (2.5 cm) thick and spongy, not hollow but with numerous tiny air-filled tubes and string-like fibers distributed throughout, broadly U-channeled with paper-thin upper edges, gently rounded below. **Flowers** emerge in very early spring directly out of the root crown at mud level and consist of a curving maroon hood about 3" (8 cm) long covering a bumpy club-like structure. This club matures into an egg-shaped cluster of roundish bean-like seeds 7–11 mm long in autumn.

HABITAT: Mucky swamps and wetland margins with rich soil, especially with spring water seepage, and especially in high-calcium soils. Native.

WARNING: All parts contain calcium oxalate raphides and cannot be eaten before processing (see p. 22).

FOOD USE: The large, starchy **roots** can be long-dried (weeks to years) or baked (many hours to several days) and then eaten. The youngest **leaves** can be eaten after similar processing. **Conservation 3/2.**

COMMENTS: With a few thousand years of selective breeding to increase the size and eliminate the raphides, this might become a popular vegetable like taro.

7 Mountain sorrel 2
Oxyria digyna + Polygonaceae (Buckwheat family)

QUICK CHECK: Alpine plant with clumps of small, broad leaves with heart-shaped bases, on long petioles; flowers tiny, clustered, numerous. **ID difficulty 2.**

DESCRIPTION: Perennial herb spreading by rhizomes to establish new crowns, all parts *hairless*. **Leaves** in a basal rosette, heart-shaped at the base, rounded at the tip, 1–2" (2.5–5 cm) across, slightly broader than long, succulent and very tender. **Major veins** palmate, depressed above and protruding below. **Margins** wavy but toothless. **Petioles** mostly erect, about 3 times blade length, rising 4–6" (10–15 cm), 1.5–2.5 mm thick, elliptic in cross section (wider than deep), mostly green (sometimes reddish near the base), smooth but for a faint channel, out of plane with the blade. **Stems** 1–4 per rosette, to 12" (30 cm) tall and 5 mm thick, roundish, hollow, smooth; they may have one or two reduced leaves. There is a broad, clear, membrane-like sheath at the nodes and inflorescence branches. **Inflorescence** a panicle, its branches raceme-like and densely packed. **Flowers** tiny, greenish with 4 blunt, cupped tepals and red sexual parts in the center. These ripen into 3-sided seeds (achenes) surrounded by broad papery wings, light colored but eventually turning red. The mature red panicles are highly visible in summer.

HABITAT: Alpine and arctic tundra, especially on slopes nestled among boulders. Native.

FOOD USE: The **leaves** can be eaten raw or cooked and are best when young and green. They are tender and sour at first, becoming tougher, more astringent, and often reddish with age. **Conservation 2.**

COMMENTS: This tangy edible is better known from the Rocky Mountains, but like many alpine plants, it is also widespread in the Far North.

8 Shooting star 2 2
genus *Dodecatheon* ✦ *Primulaceae* (Primrose family)

QUICK CHECK: Elliptic, entire basal leaves; leafless stem bearing a cluster of flowers with 5 spiraled, reflexed petals, and stamens in a beak-like cluster. **ID difficulty 1.**

DESCRIPTION: Perennial. **Leaves** elliptic or oblanceolate with rounded tips, 4–11" (10–28 cm) long, tapered at the base, lying flat where exposed but ascending where crowded. Blades soft, hairless, rather thick, sparkling in sunlight. **Midvein** slightly depressed above, gently keeled below. **Secondary veins** at acute angles, *raised above and depressed below*; veinlets are also raised above. **Margins** entire but often wavy and may have a few scat-tered tooth-like formations. **Petioles** absent or to 30% of blade length, light in color, flat to broadly channeled. (Because of the tapered, winged edges, it is impossible to say where the petiole starts, or often, if there even is one.) **Scapes** single, erect, smooth, reddish, rounded, solid in the shoot stage, minutely woolly, up to 24" (60 cm) tall. **LYDS** sometimes persistent and still holding capsules. **Inflorescence** a terminal umbel of 5–75, or an umbel with one or more whorls beneath it. There is a whorl of overlapping triangular bracts beneath the inflorescence. Pedicels are long, curving, and unequal in length. **Flowers** (mid to late spring) *drooping*, the petals 0.6–0.9" (15–23 mm) long, spiraling and swept back so far as to often touch each other. 5 stamens with yellow anthers point forward and are pressed together to form a "beak." **Fruit** a 5-part, oblong, vase-like capsule 0.3–0.7" (8–18 mm) long, pointing skyward.

▲ Collective range of the 2 species listed.

SPECIES: *D. meadia*, of the Eastern Woodlands, is larger in all respects. Its flowers are always in an umbel and have white or pink petals. *D. pulchellum,* of the Western Plains is a somewhat smaller plant with narrower leaves, fewer flowers per umbel, and purple petals.

CONFUSING PLANTS: Similarly sized saxifrages have hairy leaves and more toothed margins.

HABITAT: Rich wooded slopes and ridgetops, especially in sunny spots; oak and pine savannahs on rich soil, clearings and meadows. Native.

FOOD USE: Gather **greens** and **shoots** in spring; eat them raw or cooked. They have a slight wintergreen flavor with a faint bitter aftertaste, and are very tender when young. **Conservation 2.**

COMMENTS: These are excellent greens cooked, not as good raw. The leaves taste better than the scapes. Especially in the East, shooting stars have declined dramatically due to fire suppression and agricultural development.

▲ *D. meadia* flowers.

◄ *D. pulchellum* flowers.

▶ Young leaves and shoot of *D. meadia*.

9   Common plantain   🌿 1   ⚱ 1   🌾 2
Plantago major, P. rugelii ◆
Plantaginaceae (Plantain family)

QUICK CHECK: Broad basal leaves, the main veins parallel; leafless spikes of unshowy flowers. **ID difficulty 1.**

DESCRIPTION: Perennial with a fibrous root system. **Leaves** in rosettes of 5–11, hugging the ground where vegetation is absent or short but ascending where crowded, the blades broadly elliptic or ovate to nearly round, sometimes cupped, often ruffled, to 11" (28 cm) long, tapered at the base and blunt-tipped. **Margins** irregularly bumpy or wavy, often with a few features that could be called very low, broad teeth, but they are never serrated. **Major veins** parallel, depressed above and protruding below. **Petioles** 40–140 % of blade length, ridged below, broad and flat to slightly channeled above, the petiole margins sharp. The blade and petiole are hairless or have small, sparse hairs. **Scape** erect, leafless, often curved near the base, round, solid, smooth, tough, finely hairy, 8–30" (20-76 cm) tall and 2–3 mm thick. **Inflorescence** (mid to late summer) a densely packed spike to 20" (50 cm) long, bearing tiny, unshowy, 4-part flowers and occupying the upper half or more of the scape. **Fruit** ascending capsules 2–3 mm long, shaped like elongated eggs, turning brown when ripe and breaking in two near or below the middle to release several angled brown or black seeds.

SPECIES: The two listed are nearly identical and foragers need not differentiate them, but the native *P. rugelii* has the purple petiole.

HABITAT: Lawns, fields, roadsides, trails—almost any sunny or partly sunny ground with soil disturbed within the last 20 years or so. Native and introduced.

FOOD USE: The youngest, light green **leaves** can be eaten raw or cooked. The best use I've tried is baked like kale chips. Immature **spikes** with small flower buds (throughout summer) can be eaten raw or cooked—I like them roasted in a campfire for 30 seconds. Ripe, brown pods (late summer through fall) can be stripped from the spikes easily by hand; after separating the **seeds** from their capsules they can be cooked in porridge. **Conservation 1.**

COMMENTS: Because it grows in almost everyone's lawn, plantain is usually one of the first plants that a forager learns. While edible, it usually disappoints. The leaves are stringy and have an odd, mediocre flavor. The roasted immature spikes taste better but are insubstantial, and mostly roughage. The seeds seem promising, but are very hard to separate from the chaff.

Related edible:

10 Narrow-leaf plantain ◆ *Plantago lanceolata* 1   1

An introduced plant of lawns, roadsides, and disturbed open areas. It has mostly erect, pointed, narrowly elliptic to lanceolate leaves to 16" (40 cm) long, the surfaces with erect hairs and the margins entire or with scattered tiny teeth (glandular bumps). The major veins are deeply depressed above and strongly protruding below. The leaf base tapers gradually into a broad, channeled, green petiole—it is hard to say where the petiole ends and the blade begins. The scape is tough, 5-*angled*, rough-hairy in the upper part, 14–32" (36–80 cm) tall. Flower spikes are less than 5" (13 cm) long, *occupying a small portion of the scape.* The young leaves and flower spikes can be eaten like those of common plantain, but the seeds are too small to mess with. **AKA** English plantain.

GROUP 19 FLOWERING STEM LEAFLESS, BASAL LEAVES TOOTHED OR LOBED

Some of these plants have reduced, modified leaves on the stalk below the inflorescence. What their stems lack are typical, full-sized, "normal" leaves. This creates the possibility for a gray area, but most often we will come to the same conclusions regarding what is or is not a "leafless" stem (known as a *scape*). When in doubt, check your plant in all potential groups.

TENTATIVE IDENTIFICATION KEY TO GROUP 19
The key is not your final answer!

Single, five-petaled, asymmetric flowers at the end of a long, hooked, very thin scape with an offset pair of tiny bracts. (Stemless violets.)

or

     Blade heart-shaped, teeth curled toward leaf tip like a cresting wave. — **1. Blue violet**

     Blade elongated, the base somewhat arrowhead-lobed, with large teeth. — **2. Arrowhead violet**

     Blade very deeply palmately lobed, the lobes narrow. — **3. Birdfoot violet**

Not as above. (Everything but stemless violets.)

     Leaves distinctly longer than wide; veins pinnate (if evident).

         Sap milky.

             Scape with a single head, never branched.

                 Scape smooth, multiple per rosette. — **4. Dandelion**

                 Scape with fine ridges; one per rosette.

or

                     Lobes few to none. — **5. Potato dandelion**

                     Lobes several on each leaf. — **6. Tuberous false dandelion**

or

             Scapes branched, with multiple heads.

                 Leaves with dense erect hairs on both sides. — **7. Hairy cat's ear**

                 Leaves sparsely hairy or hairless. — **8. Fall dandelion**

         Sap not milky.

             Flowers directly from the base (no stalk). — **9. Gumbo-lily**

             Stalk solid, less than 8" (20 cm) tall with a single head. — **10. English daisy**

             Stalk hollow, more than 10" (25 cm) tall, with a panicle of numerous small flowers.

                 Leaves thick with blunt wavy teeth and no clear petiole. — **11. Swamp saxifrage**

                 Leaves thin with sharp teeth and a distinct winged petiole. — **12. Brook saxifrage**

     Leaves about as broad as long; veins palmate.

         Blades densely woolly-whitish below and often more than 6" (15 cm) long.

or

             Leaves shallowly lobed or double-toothed. — **13. Coltsfoot**

             Leaves deeply palmately lobed. — **14. Northern coltsfoot**

         Leaves not densely wooly-whitish beneath.

             Petiole attached to the underside (not the edge) of the blade. — **15. Beach pennywort**

             Petiole attached to blade edge at a cut-out base. — **16. Coinleaf**

STEMLESS VIOLETS   2   2   IWE-372
genus *Voila* (in part) ◆ family *Violaceae*

Stemless violets are a group of many species with highly variable leaf shape. For the sake of brevity I list three species that are widespread, common, and taste good. However, all violets of the genus *Viola* are edible, and several good species are not listed. Violets, as a group, are very easy to identify when flowering, but harder with only the leaves present. Familiarize yourself deeply with violet leaves while they are flowering, and then you can collect them any time.

COLLECTIVE DESCRIPTION: To avoid repetition, note that all the stemless violets share these characteristics: **Leaves** arranged in rosettes or clumps of rosettes, with stipules packed at the base. **Petioles** long and thin. **Peduncles** individual from the base but several to many per plant; they are long, thin, green, solid, fleshy (not tough), erect, *hooked at the top*, with an *offset pair of tiny bracts partway up the stalk*. **Flowers** have 5 separate sepals and a corolla of 5 separate, unequal petals, not radially symmetrical, arranged like an upside-down person: a close pair for the legs, an opposing pair for the arms, and a single large petal with an enlarged, rounded spur for the head. **Fruit** a small capsule.

1 Common blue violet ✦ *Viola sororia* 2 2

QUICK CHECK: Long-stalked, curled, heart-shaped clustered leaves; irregular 5-petaled blue flower borne singly at the end of a long, thin, nodding stem. **ID difficulty 2.**

DESCRIPTION: Perennial herb growing from a stout horizontal rhizome. **Leaves** 2–6" (5–15 cm) long, held at a sharp angle to the petiole, heart to kidney-shaped, often wider than long, the blunt *basal lobes often curled upward*, the tips blunt-pointed to rounded. **Surface** occasionally hairless but more often finely hairy on both sides. **Midvein** flat above, becoming *raised distally*. There are 4–6 major secondary veins from the base (usually only 2 arising farther along the midvein). Secondary and smaller veins are slightly depressed, or raised in a valley. **Margins** have blunt teeth, each slightly raised, with nipple-tips *turned toward the leaf tip like a cresting wave*. **Petiole** 4–20" (10–50 cm) long, ascending when growing in the open but much taller and erect in competition, solid, D-shaped with a wing-channel that often widens toward the blade, the margin hairy; the other surfaces hairless or densely coated in fine hairs, especially when young. **Stipules** linear, sharp-tipped, often twisted, whitish, the edges membranous with soft bristles. **Peduncle** about as tall or taller than the leaves. **Flowers** 0.4–0.8" (10–20 mm) long, purple (rarely white) with a greenish-white throat and darker veins. Sepals are triangular, 4–7 mm long. Side petals are hairy at the base. Stamens are hidden. There are also *hidden, self-fertilizing, unshowy flowers produced in summer on stems that stay at ground level.* **Fruit** an ovoid capsule 10–12 mm long, dark green, containing dark brown seeds 2 mm long.

HABITAT: Moderate soil moisture, moderate to high fertility, in full sun to fairly heavy shade, especially where frequently but not severely disturbed. Lightly used pastures, forest edges, lawns, weedy areas, hayfields, ditches, floodplain forests, swamp margins. Native.

FOOD USE: Tender **greens** are most abundant in spring and early summer, but a few good ones can be found most of the growing season. They can be eaten raw, but I much prefer them cooked. **Flowers** and **peduncles**, available at the same time, are also edible. The flowers are sometimes candied. **Conservation 1/1.**

COMMENTS: This is one of the most common and widely available edible greens in our area. Nutritional tests have shown blue violet greens to be extremely high in vitamins C and A. There has long been taxonomic uncertainty with blue violets, with botanists recognizing one to several similar species. Regardless, if they fit this general description, they are worth eating.

2 Arrowhead violet 🌿 2 ❀ 2
Viola sagittata ✦ family *Violaceae*

QUICK CHECK: Short violet with elongated leaves, the bases lobed or flared outward, with enlarged teeth; flowers blue. **ID difficulty 2.**

DESCRIPTION: Perennial from short rhizomes. **Leaves** 1.2–4" (3–10 cm) long, (but rarely that large during early bloom when they are best) lanceolate to long-triangular or narrowly heart-shaped, the tip blunt. The base is broad, lobed backward (arrowhead-like) and often flared outward as well; the lobes are curled up, often enough to meet. Surfaces may be glossy and hairless to densely hairy. **Midvein** *raised above*, protruding below. Secondary veins 4–6 per side, narrowly angled, *raised above*. **Margins** have low, blunt, forward-pointing teeth or waves, except on the *basal lobes*, which *have enlarged, sharper teeth*. Stipules are lanceolate. **Petiole** erect, 60–110% of blade length, with a broad, deep wing-channel. **Peduncle** 3–6" (8–15 cm) tall, somewhat flattened and grooved, rising about to the level of the leaves. **Flowers** 0.7–0.9" (18–23 mm) long, the petals crammed together (spreading less than most violets), purple (the bases white with purple veins). Side petals are hairy at the base. The nectary spur is prominent, pale, and laterally flattened.

HABITAT: Oak-hickory-pine forests, forest edges, roadsides, clearings—moist to dry. Native.

FOOD USE: Young **leaves**, **peduncles**, and **flowers** are all good, but they are on the small side for collecting in quantity. **Conservation 2/1.**

COMMENTS: This is one of the better-tasting violets. Botanists split this into two forms: a hairless one mainly in the South, and a hairy one mainly in the North. My experience and the photos here pertain to the southern form. Other botanists separate these into two species.

3 Birdfoot violet 🌿 2 ❀ 2
Viola pedata ✦ family *Violaceae*

QUICK CHECK: Low plant with clusters of leaves that have long, thin lobes; large, flat-faced violet flowers rise above the leaves. **ID difficulty 3.**

DESCRIPTION: Perennial from a short horizontal rhizome, forming small clumps or colonies. **Leaves** numerous, clustered, overlapping, deeply palmately lobed (almost fully divided), the lobes usually narrowly oblanceolate, blunt-tipped (never clawed), often cupped slightly upward, mostly entire but occasionally with a large tooth or two. **Surfaces** shiny and hairless. **Major veins** (down the center of each lobe) slightly *raised above* and *flat below*; smaller veins not evident. **Petiole** thin, erect, 2–5" (5–13 cm) tall, broadly V-channeled with *a raised line down the center*. **Stipules** long-pointed, often hidden near the ground, with *cilia on the margins*. **Peduncles** grooved, rising above the leaves. **Flowers** (late spring) to 1" (2.5 cm) across, the sepals long and tapered, the petals blue-violet, none of them hairy at the base, the largest one white at the base with darker blue veins. The corolla appears like it has been flattened.

CONFUSING PLANTS: Various species of **larkspurs** (*Delphinium*) and **monkshood** (*Aconitum*) (both dangerously toxic) have leaves of a similar shape which taste bitter or acrid. These species have most of their leaves on the stem, and the lobes of basal leaves are broader with more teeth than those of birdfoot violet. Basal leaves of our most common larkspurs (*D. tricorne* and *D. carolinianum*) have pointed lobes, depressed veins, and hairy petioles and margins. Monkshood leaves are hairless or nearly so, but the lobes and teeth, if not pointed, are nipple or claw-like. If you are not deeply familiar with birdfoot violet leaves, eat them only when the flowers are present to confirm identification.

HABITAT: Dry, usually sandy soil in full sun: prairies, pine or oak barrens, rock outcrops. Native. 🔥

FOOD USE: The young **leaves**, **flowers**, and **flower stalks** are all good raw or cooked. The leaves are mucilaginous and remain rather tender at maturity even late into the growing season. **Conservation 2/1.**

COMMENTS: This is reported to be the only North American violet species that lacks hidden self-pollinated flowers. It is perhaps the most impressive of all our species in bloom, and is also an excellent edible.

4 Dandelion 👤 1 🌿 3 🍃 3 🌾 1 ⚜ 2 ☕ 📖 NG-453
Taraxacum officinale ✦ *Asteraceae* (Composite family)

QUICK CHECK: Leaves with large teeth or lobes pointing toward the base; multiple hollow scapes, each with a single broad, yellow flowerhead. **ID difficulty 2.**

DESCRIPTION: Perennial from an enlarged taproot, often forked at the top into multiple crowns, without rhizomes. All parts with milky sap. **Leaves** in a dense basal rosette, 3–20" (8–50 cm) long, *wider toward the tips,* which are blunt or broadly pointed. The blade is ruffled, with sparse scurfy hairs above. **Midvein** low and almost flat above, rounded beneath, often woolly but never with erect hairs. Secondary veins 70–80° to the midvein, faint, nearly flat above and protruding below. **Margins** often entire near the tip, but otherwise usually have large teeth or lobes, sometimes with very *long, needle-like tips;* lobes tend to point back toward the center of the rosette. *Leaf shape is highly variable.* It's hard to say where the leaf ends and the petiole begins—if there is a petiole it has a toothed wing. **Scapes** may be single but are usually clumped, 2–25 per rosette, hollow and thin-walled, unbranched, 4–32" (10–80 cm) tall and 4–11 mm wide, light tawny or green to reddish, often woolly (especially when young). **Flowers** composite, each head borne singly at the scape's apex, 1.5–2" (3.8–5 cm) across, composed of bright yellow 5-toothed ray florets, the head subtended by numerous long bracts. **Seeds** (achenes) elongated with a thin beak terminating in a parachute (pappus), these forming a fluffy, whitish-gray spherical head.

CONFUSING PLANTS: Many plants have similar leaf shape and milky sap, but they either have leaves on the stems, branched stems, or both. In the rosette stage most of these species can be told from dandelion by having either keeled midveins below, erect hairs, or both. Luckily, most confusing species are related edibles.

HABITAT: From moist to dry soil on disturbed ground; thrives in full sun and partial shade. Fields, lawns, trails, yards, etc. Probably native.

FOOD USE: Roots of young plants have a nice texture and flavor but are somewhat bitter; they are best boiled and drained. Roots of any age can be dried, roasted until brown and brittle, then used to brew a coffee-like **beverage**. The **heart** is the young center leaves and embryonic flower parts clustered above the root crown in early spring. I gouge them out of the ground with a stiff teaspoon and steam or fry them. **Leaves** are best in spring before flowers open, but edible all year. **Flower stalks** are quite bitter but for some reason I love them. **Flowers** can be nibbled raw, used as a garnish, cooked, or brewed in tea either fresh or dried. They are also the flavoring for the famed dandelion wine. **Conservation 1.**

COMMENTS: Among our best-known weeds and most popular wild edibles, dandelion greens are excellent when gathered and used according to tradition. Try the spring leaves, before flowering, fried with bacon and onions. Despite it being "common knowledge" that dandelions were introduced from Europe, I have seen no good evidence or sound argument that *Taraxacum officinale* is not also native to North America.

5 Potato dandelion 🐷 2 🌿 2 🌸 2
Krigia dandelion ✦ *Asteraceae* (Composite family)

QUICK CHECK: Dandelion-like herb with a single scape; leaves entire or nearly so. ID difficulty 2.

DESCRIPTION: Colony-forming perennial herb spreading by rhizomes and forming **tubers,** pea to grape-sized, roughly rounded and often knobby. Sap milky. **Leaves** all basal (there is occasionally a pair just above the base), 2–8 per crown, narrow, oblanceolate to lin-

ear, 2–8" (5–20 cm) long and generally less than 1" (2.5 cm) wide, thin and delicate; a careful look reveals scattered minute hairs. **Midvein** light in color, wide at the base, slightly depressed above; secondary veins few and faintly depressed. **Margins** finely and sparsely hairy, entire or with a few *very widely spaced* teeth or lobes. The *lobes are blunt* with a tiny nipple. (Continued on the next page.)

279

5 Potato dandelion (continued)

Scape *solitary*, 5–22" (13–56 cm) tall and 2–4 mm wide, proportionately much *thinner than that of dandelion*, with a very small hollow in the center, *finely ridged*, glaucous, hairless except right under the flowerhead. **Inflorescence** (spring to early summer) a single, yellow, terminal head 1–1.5" (25–38 mm) across, with ray florets only, the outer rays much larger than the inner. The sides of rays are parallel and the tip truncated with 5 deeply cut teeth. Under the stress of shade or mowing the plants are stunted and may rarely flower. **Seed** columnar, reddish brown, with an attached parachute.

CONFUSING SPECIES: A close relative, *Krigia virginica*, is safe but *very* bitter.

HABITAT: Roadsides, old fields, forest borders, prairies, savannahs and open woods with medium-moisture, medium to rich soil, sandy or clay-loam. Native. 🔥

FOOD USE: Dig the small **tubers** at any time and use as a cooked vegetable; they are good but mildly bitter. The **greens** can be used raw or cooked whenever present, but are best in early spring; the small size hampers gathering in quantity. **Flowers** and scapes are edible too but tiny. **Conservation 2/1.**

COMMENTS: I bet you never knew there was such a plant. It surprised me, too.

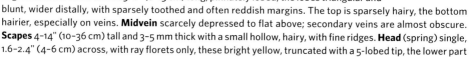

6 Tuberous false dandelion 🥔 1 🌿 1 ⚗ 1
Pyrrhopappus grandiflorus ✦
Asteraceae (Composite family)

QUICK CHECK: Small rosette of blunt-lobed, dandelion-like leaves with a single stalk bearing a single large yellow flower. **ID difficulty 2.**

DESCRIPTION: Perennial spring ephemeral from a spherical to elliptic **tuber** to 1" (2.5 cm) long, with brown skin and white flesh, the roots attached mostly at the top and bottom but not the sides. Above this tuber is a vertical white stem to 3" (8 cm) terminating in a rosette at ground level. **Basal leaves** 3–6" (8–15 cm) long, pinnately lobed, the lobes triangular and blunt, wider distally, with sparsely toothed and often reddish margins. The top is sparsely hairy, the bottom hairier, especially on veins. **Midvein** scarcely depressed to flat above; secondary veins are almost obscure. **Scapes** 4–14" (10–36 cm) tall and 3–5 mm thick with a small hollow, hairy, with fine ridges. **Head** (spring) single, 1.6–2.4" (4–6 cm) across, with ray florets only, these bright yellow, truncated with a 5-lobed tip, the lower part of the column dark. **Seeds** elongated with a thread-like attachment ending in a broad parachute, forming a rounded head.

HABITAT: Dry, sunny, well-drained prairies, especially where sandy or disturbed. Native. 🔥

FOOD USE: Tubers can be eaten cooked—they are best when the tops are dormant. Young **leaves** and **scapes** can be eaten raw or cooked; they are rather bitter. **Conservation 3/2.**

COMMENTS: This beautiful sunburst seems too big a flower for its little rosette. To get the tubers you need to remember where the flowers were in spring.

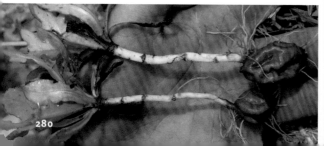

7 Hairy cat's ear ✒ 2 ⌇ 2
Hypochaeris radicata ✦ Asteraceae (Composite family)

QUICK CHECK: Very hairy dandelion-like rosette leaves; yellow composite flowerheads on a branched stalk. **ID difficulty 1.**

DESCRIPTION: Weedy perennial, the rosette often tightly hugging the ground. **Leaves** basal, without petioles, 3–7" (8–18 cm) long and 0.9–1.6" (23–40 cm) across, with numerous blunt lobes at a right angle to the midvein, the sinuses shallow. Curving, *erect hairs grow from raised bumps* evenly distributed over both sides. **Midvein** slightly convex above, hairy, often with dark bumps, and rounded below. There are *no evident secondary veins above.* **Stalks** 8–20" (20–50 cm) tall, 2–4 mm thick, *solid, faintly ridged,* hairless except sometimes near the base, sparsely branched (often near the base), spreading or leaning to

▲ Occasional outside mapped area.

erect. There are a few tiny reduced leaves less than 1 cm scattered on the stalk. **Inflorescence** composite heads at branch tips, yellow, about 1" (2.5 cm) across (resembling small dandelions), with ray florets only, the tips 5-toothed. Outer rays are gray-green in the center and stalked at the base (they must be pulled out to see this). **Seeds** (achenes) narrow, beaked, parachuted, in a round gray head like that of dandelion but smaller and with a ragged appearance.

HABITAT: Primarily lawns, but also in other sunny, disturbed sites. Introduced.

FOOD USE: Collect the tenderest, lushest, and cleanest **leaves** you can find, from robust, healthy plants; best in late spring and early summer. Edible raw in salads but better as a cooked green. Flower stalk **shoots**, picked when short and before they branch, are good boiled or steamed.

COMMENTS: This plant is a less-touted relative of the common dandelion that is almost as good. While common locally in the eastern U.S., it is not nearly so prevalent here as it is in the Pacific Northwest, where it is often a dominant lawn weed.

8 Fall dandelion 1
Leontodon autumnalis + *Asteraceae* (Composite family)

QUICK CHECK: Rosette of narrow leaves with a long narrow tip, bearing widely-spaced narrow lobes; wavy branching stem with a few yellow flowerheads. **ID difficulty 2.**

DESCRIPTION: Perennial with a rosette, or multiple rosettes from a forking root crown. **Leaves** nearly linear, tapered at both ends, to 8" (20 cm) long, pinnately lobed, the tip long and narrow. The lobes are well-spaced, narrow but blunt, pointing perpendicular to the midvein or slightly forward. The sinuses are of uniform depth and do not come close to the midvein, giving the appearance of a narrow leaf with lobes added to the exterior rather than a wide leaf with sinuses cut into it. The blades may be hairless or have scattered, long hairs. Petioles are absent, or winged, depending on how you think of it. **Midvein** light, narrow, flat to raised above and rounded below. *Other veins are obscure.* Margins have lobes but *no teeth.* **Stems** 1-several per rosette, 6–24" (15–60 cm)

tall, 2–4 mm thick, often curved at the base, mostly hairless, *finely ridged,* hollow, few-branched or unbranched. The stem may bear *a few reduced, narrow, entire leaves.* **Inflorescence** a cluster of a few heads on long peduncles that are enlarged and hollow just before the flowerhead, the involucre hairy. **Heads** about 1" (2.5 cm) across, yellow and dandelion-like but with fewer rays, blooming in late summer and fall. The ball of fluffy parachuted seeds is smaller than that of dandelion and irregular in form.

CONFUSING PLANTS: Leaves are narrower than those of hairy cat's ear and not as hairy. The related *Leontodon saxitilis* is edible but even worse; it has densely hairy leaves with shorter, blunter lobes.

HABITAT: Sunny, open areas under long-term disturbance: lawns, parks, pastures, fields, roadsides. Introduced.

FOOD USE: Gather **leaves** when young and tender, from spring through fall. They can be used in salads or fried.

COMMENTS: This is perhaps the most bitter of the dandelion-like leaves I've covered here. Use them sparingly or in some way that alleviates that bitterness.

9 Gumbo-lily 🧍 1 🌿 1 🍃 2 🌸 2
Oenothera caespitosa ✦
Onagraceae (Evening primrose family)

QUICK CHECK: Rosettes of coarsely, irregularly toothed leaves on open clay; large white to pink 4-petaled flowers attached directly to the crown. **ID difficulty 1.**

DESCRIPTION: Perennial from a taproot, older plants with multiple crowns. **Root** thick at the crown, tapering downward for 2-3" (5-8 cm), thickening again where the root branches meet, then tapering and branching again, 0.6-1" (15-25 mm) wide at its thickest point. Root skin peels in a distinct layer; inside is white flesh in two layers. **Rosettes** of numerous leaves, often adjacent and overlapping, the crowns sometimes raised slightly above the soil surface on short branches, these with 2 faint ridges. **Leaves** 3-6" (8-15 mm) long, semi-succulent, elliptic to narrowly elliptic, the tips blunt or pointed, the bases gently tapered, the surface with fine, short, appressed hair, especially above. **Margins** may be entire but more often have large scattered teeth or small lobes; a few will have larger lobes. **Midvein** light, not depressed, protruding below but not keeled. Secondary veins about 40°, 3-4 per side, not depressed. **Petioles** about 30% of blade length, D-shaped, flat above with short, sparse hairs, *winged nearly to base* (it is hard to say where the petiole ends and the blade begins). **Flowers** (early to mid summer, blooming mostly at night) are attached directly to the crown by a narrow tube 2-2.5" (5-6.5 cm) long, widening toward the flower. There are 5 narrow, pointed sepals about 1.2" (3 cm) long, finely hairy on the back. Petals 1" (2.5 cm) long, whitish becoming dull pink, narrow at the base, the tips broad, overlapping, and bluntly 2-lobed. There are 8 protruding yellow stamens 1" (2.5 cm) long. **Fruit** is a tapering cylindrical pod about 1" (2.5 cm) long with a blunt, depressed tip, the base angled by bumpy ridges, enclosing many small, slightly curved seeds.

HABITAT: Dry, bare clay in full sun, generally with little competition. These sites are often created by erosion: badlands, steep slopes, roadbanks, river banks, clay flats. Native.

FOOD USE: Roots are best when the plants are dormant, much better cooked (and still not very good). Young **leaves** are marginally edible. **Flowers** and **flower buds** are also edible. This species tastes similar to the com-

mon evening primrose but its leaves are stronger and its roots are milder but tougher. **Conservation 3/1/1.**

COMMENTS: Because this plant is long-lived and its root is marginal food, think carefully before digging one up. This is not a lily. The name refers not to soup, but to its occurrence on sticky "gumbo" clay. This is one of the many amazing wildflowers you will likely see if you visit Yellowstone in early summer. **AKA** desert evening primrose, tufted evening primrose.

10 English daisy 🌿 1 🌸 1
Bellis perennis ✦ *Asteraceae* (Composite family)

QUICK CHECK: A single flowerhead with white rays and a yellow disk on a short leafless stalk with spoon-shaped basal leaves. **ID difficulty 1.**

DESCRIPTION: Low perennial herb with fibrous roots spreading by rhizome to form colonies in lawns and pastures. **Leaves** all basal, 1–3" (2.5–8 cm) long, blunt-tipped, spoon shaped, tapering to the base, with scattered hairs or hairless, thick and semi-succulent, rosettes mostly ground-hugging. **Midvein** may be gently and broadly depressed but other veins are flat above. **Margins** have scattered long hairs; occasionally they are entire but more often they have a few teeth tipped with white nipples. **Petioles** broad, flat, green to reddish, 50–80% of blade length. **Scapes** usually multiple, finely hairy, 2–8" (5–20 cm) tall, not round in cross section (erratically angled with a tiny, angled hollow). **Inflorescence** a *single flat flowerhead* about 0.8" (2 cm) wide. The rays are several times longer than wide, broader at the tip (which is rounded to truncated), white except for a tinge of purple on the back near the tip; the disk is convex and yellow. **Seeds** dark, flat, *lacking a parachute*.

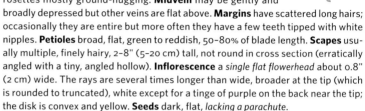

HABITAT: Primarily lawns. Occasionally pastures, meadows, roadsides, gardens. Introduced.

FOOD USE: Gather tender **leaves** any time during the growing season, the **flowers** in spring and early summer. Eat these sparingly raw or cooked as the flavor is rather strong.

COMMENTS: This plant is more of a seasoning than a vegetable, as it is highly aromatic like ox-eye daisy—which has similar but much larger flowers. It is highly sporadic in occurrence and, while locally abundant, is not particularly common.

11 Swamp saxifrage 🌿 1 🕯 3 📖 FH-205
Saxifraga pensylvanica ✦ family *Saxifragaceae*

QUICK CHECK: Large, broad, thick leaves; a single thick, hollow, hairy stalk. **ID difficulty 1.**

DESCRIPTION: Perennial, the taproot often splitting to form multiple adjacent crowns but not spreading by rhizome. **Leaves** basal, in a rosette, ovate or usually broadly elliptic, to 12" (30 cm) long, blunt-tipped, often hugging the ground, thick but not leathery, often wavy or ruffled, sometimes nearly hairless but usually with long erect hairs on both sides. Leaves are narrowed to the base but there is no clear place where the blade ends and the petiole begins; if there is a petiole it is short and broadly winged. **Midvein** above is light in color, prominent, broadly and shallowly depressed; secondary veins are *crowded near the base of the blade* at low angles, nearly flat on both sides. **Margins** often entire on the first spring leaves but wavy or shallowly toothed on larger leaves, the tooth tips darkened and nipple-like. **Stalk** erect, single, up to 4' (1.2 m) tall and 0.2–0.8" (5–20 mm) thick, *hollow with thin walls*, rounded, green, brittle, *densely and uniformly covered with long, slightly sticky hairs*. There is a linear bract under each branch of the inflorescence, but these are not always evident on shoots. **Inflorescence** a panicle, wider than tall, that commences blooming when still rather densely packed; at maturity the individual branches are widely spaced, each with a crowded bunch

of flowers at the tip. **Flowers** 3–5 mm across with green centers and 5 whitish to occasionally reddish, narrowly elliptic or lanceolate petals, remote from each other, spreading, the stamens with yellow to orange anthers, also widely spreading. **Fruit** a small capsule of tiny seeds.

HABITAT: Wooded swamps, ravines, stream edges, and other low areas where soil is disturbed, mostly in light shade. Commonly associated with marsh-marigold. Native.

FOOD USE: Gather flower stalk **shoots** in mid spring before the inflorescence has begun to branch; later they will be tough and bitter (the tops are always bitter). Shoots can be eaten cooked but are especially good raw. The young **leaves** are supposedly edible but are tough and astringent. **Conservation 2.**

COMMENTS: These flower stalk shoots are an ephemeral springtime treat for foragers, so crisp they croak when picked, so juicy you can sometimes drink from the hollow stem if you pinch the base when you pick it. Luckily I have thousands growing in the ditch near my cabin. **AKA** *Micranthes pensylvanica.*

Related edible:

12 Brook saxifrage ♦ *Saxifraga micranthidifolia* 1 3

QUICK CHECK: Along mountain brooks and seeps; narrow leaves with sharp teeth at right angles to the margin; thin, erect, hairy stalk. **ID difficulty 1.**

DESCRIPTION: Leaves 3–12" (8–30 cm) long, light green, erect to ascending, narrower than swamp saxifrage, tapered to the base, *very thin*, the surfaces *hairless*. The midvein is more strongly depressed but the veinlets are raised above. **Margins** hairy with *prominent sharp teeth oriented perpendicular to the margin* and abruptly constricted to sharp points. **Petiole** flat, broadly winged, 15–70% of blade length. **Stem** 12–32" (30–80 cm) tall and 6–9 mm wide, also densely hairy. The slightly smaller panicles bloom earlier in spring; the petals are white with a small yellow spot near the base.

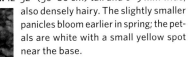

HABITAT: In the Appalachians along rocky springs, seepages, swamps, and brooks in wooded environments. Native.

FOOD USE: Tender spring **greens** are astringent and best boiled and drained, or fried. The **shoots** are milder in flavor and are pleasant raw. **Conservation 2.**

COMMENTS: Lettuce saxifrage leaves are bitter like those of swamp saxifrage but thinner and more tender; they can be realistically rendered enjoyable. The plant is limited in distribution but often very abundant within its limited habitat. **AKA** *Micranthes micranthidifolia,* brook lettuce, deer tongue.

13 Coltsfoot   1   2
Tussilago farfara ♦ *Asteraceae* (Composite family)

QUICK CHECK: Thick, scaly flower stalk with a single yellow flowerhead before any leaves appear; large-toothed leaves shaped roughly like a horse's hoof. **ID difficulty 1.**

DESCRIPTION: Perennial forming colonies by thin white rhizomes. **Leaves** basal or borne on a short, raised, purplish stub. **Blades** 3–8" (8–20 cm) long and about equally wide, roughly shaped like a horse's hoof (hence the name) but with a heart-shaped base and many angles or short lobes, ruffled at first with light wool above, the veins flat above. With age, leaves become flatter (but never totally flat) with veins depressed above. Surfaces of mature leaves have small, scattered, erect hairs above; *below they are whitish and densely woolly* with prominently protruding veins. **Midvein** dark purple at the base, this color sometimes extending up the major veins a short distance. Besides the midvein there are 4–6 major veins from the base, plus two more shortly distal to them; these run straight at first but after their first major fork zigzag to the margins where they end in a lobe tip. **Margins** have irregularly sized, broad, nipple-tipped, outward-pointing teeth; on young leaves they are *downcurved and purple*. First **spring leaves** are usually paired, appearing as the seedheads are going to fluff. **Petioles** 100–140% of blade length, out of plane with it, leaning, solid, D-shaped (shallowly depressed or channeled on the flat side), reddish (especially the channel ridges), flared at base, with soft hairs and multiple cords inside. The petiole of one leaf in a pair clasps the other. **Stems** hollow, unbranched, often clumped, emerging from the ground at a location separate from the leaves, 4–10" (10–25 cm) tall, 4–7 mm thick, wavy, with short gland-tipped hairs and a *cobwebby coating*; finely ridged, the ridges often purple, with numerous triangular, *clasping, scale-leaves* about 0.8" (2 cm) long. *Sap is clear.* **Heads** borne singly (early spring, before or as the leaves emerge), about 1" (2.5 cm) across, with numerous purple bracts. Heads droop before going to gray fluff. **Florets** bright yellow, the rays very narrow; there are some disk florets with 5 spreading lobes in the center.

HABITAT: Moist but often well-drained soil that has been disturbed—especially rocky areas of high-calcium stone. In shade or full sun. Common along railroad tracks and roads. Introduced.

FOOD USE: Flower stalk **shoots** before or during blooming in early spring can be eaten raw or cooked. They are tender, mildly sweet, slightly astringent, and better with the scale-leaves stripped off. Later in spring, pick young **leaves** only, boil and drain before eating. Leaves are best when young but not super young—wait until after the wool becomes less prominent on the *upper* surface.

COMMENTS: This plant is unusual in that its flowers appear on a stem separately from the leaves. Coltsfoot is well known and highly regarded as a medicinal herb, but as a food it is just mediocre.

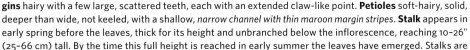

14 Northern coltsfoot 1 2
Petasites frigidus ✦ *Asteraceae* (Composite family)

QUICK CHECK: Single, large, deeply palmately lobed leaf; stout, unbranched flower stem with multiple white heads on top. **ID difficulty 1.**

DESCRIPTION: Leaves single or paired, wider than long, 4–12" (10–30 cm) across, deeply palmately lobed with 7–9 major lobes, these pointed, widest in the middle, with occasional sub-lobes. **Surface** light green with fine, soft hairs on top; finely woolly below. **Veins** radiate from the base, the larger ones strongly depressed above and protruding below. **Margins** hairy with a few large, scattered teeth, each with an extended claw-like point. **Petioles** soft-hairy, solid, deeper than wide, not keeled, with a shallow, *narrow channel with thin maroon margin stripes.* **Stalk** appears in early spring before the leaves, thick for its height and unbranched below the inflorescence, reaching 10–26" (25–66 cm) tall. By the time this full height is reached in early summer the leaves have emerged. Stalks are

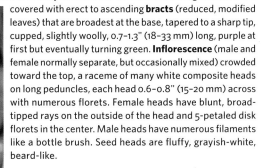

covered with erect to ascending **bracts** (reduced, modified leaves) that are broadest at the base, tapered to a sharp tip, cupped, slightly woolly, 0.7–1.3" (18–33 mm) long, purple at first but eventually turning green. **Inflorescence** (male and female normally separate, but occasionally mixed) crowded toward the top, a raceme of many white composite heads on long peduncles, each head 0.6–0.8" (15–20 mm) across with numerous florets. Female heads have blunt, broad-tipped rays on the outside of the head and 5-petaled disk florets in the center. Male heads have numerous filaments like a bottle brush. Seed heads are fluffy, grayish-white, beard-like.

HABITAT: Canopy openings in boreal forest, especially under birch and aspen, and especially on rocky soils. Native.

FOOD USE: Young **leaves** are barely edible. They were reportedly burned and used as a salt substitute—I have not tried this. The flower stalk **shoots** in early spring, before the peduncles elongate and the heads open, are tender but have an aromatic, sweet but almost soapy flavor. **Conservation 2.**

COMMENTS: I have not yet found a really good way to prepare these due to the strong flavor, but there must be one. The plant can live for decades before flowering.

15 Beach pennywort 🪶 1 ☕
Hydrocotyle bonariensis ✦ *Araliaceae* (Ginseng family)

QUICK CHECK: Flat, shiny, scallop-edged leaves in ground-hugging colonies; tiny white flowers in a compound umbel. **ID difficulty 1.**

DESCRIPTION: Ground-hugging perennial that creeps by rhizomes. **Leaves** single, on petioles directly from the rhizome, the blades flat, thick, *very glossy*, roundish to slightly oblong, 1–5" (2.5–13 cm) across, hairless, with a light spot in the center. **Veins** radiate from the center, straight, *faintly raised above and flat below*. **Margins** wavy with blunt, rounded teeth on the waves. **Petioles** 2–14" (5–36 cm) long (much taller in competition), smooth, hairless, solid, 2–4 mm thick, rounded with no grooves or ridges, erect or decumbent, *attached in the middle of the blade*. **Inflorescence** a compound umbel, at first looking like a small, simple umbel but branching into a large *multi-compound structure*, the scape rounded and solid. **Flowers** 2–3 mm across with a green center and 5 triangular white petals. **Fruit** flattened, larger than the flowers.

Hydrocotyle verticillata has stacked umbels. ▶

▼ *Hydrocotyle bonariensis* compound umbel, just beginning to expand.

HABITAT: Sunny, moist, disturbed, often sandy soil. Lawns, beaches, pond edges, roadsides. Native.

FOOD USE: **Leaves** and their petioles can be eaten raw in salad, cooked in many ways, blended in smoothies, or used to make a **tea**. New leaves are best but older leaves are serviceable, and are available all year. **Conservation 1.**

COMMENTS: The flavor is faintly celery-like. This is one of the most ubiquitous wild edibles of the Gulf Coast region, often abundant in urban areas.

RELATED EDIBLES: Other members of the genus *Hydrocotyle* look and taste similar and can also be used; because of their differences in form and habitat, they may be found in groups 15 and 37 (p. 221 and p. 620). Similar to beach pennywort is **whorled pennywort** *H. verticillata*, which has smaller leaves and is more common inland, and has stacked umbels or whorls rather than compound umbels.

▲ Beach pennywort, young leaves.　　▲ *Hydrocotyle verticillata* leaf.

16 Coinleaf 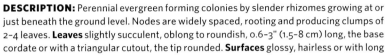 2
Centella erecta • *Apiaceae* (Carrot family)

QUICK CHECK: Small rosette of a few broad, toothed leaves on long petioles forming carpets over the ground; flowers in tiny umbels near the ground. **ID difficulty 1.**

DESCRIPTION: Perennial evergreen forming colonies by slender rhizomes growing at or just beneath the ground level. Nodes are widely spaced, rooting and producing clumps of 2–4 leaves. **Leaves** slightly succulent, oblong to roundish, 0.6–3" (1.5–8 cm) long, the base cordate or with a triangular cutout, the tip rounded. **Surfaces** glossy, hairless or with long soft hairs mostly near the margins. All major **veins** emanate from the base, faintly depressed above; only the midvein is strongly protruding below, occasionally darkened maroon. **Margins** sometimes maroon, wavy or with a few shallow, blunt, widely spaced teeth, these usually with a light-colored nipple. **Petioles** reddish, fleshy with a narrow channel, erect to leaning, attached at the edge of the blade (not peltate), hairy, 60% of blade length on lawn plants but much longer in unmowed vegetation, sometimes reaching 14" (36 cm) in crowded wetland margins. **Inflorescence** a tiny crowded umbel of 3–9 on a straight, erect, solitary, hairy peduncle 1–4" (2.5–10 cm) tall, growing directly from the rhizome at a node and not rising above the leaves. The pedicels are extremely short and there is a pair of thick, short bracts beneath the umbel. **Flowers** (summer) 2 mm across with 5 narrow petals, whitish tinted with green or pink, *incurved at the tip.* Sepals absent. **Fruit** flattened with conspicuous ridges, not fleshy.

HABITAT: Sunny to partly shaded areas with moist soil and little tall herbaceous cover, often disturbed. Lawns (especially along waterways), edges of waterways and marshes, swamps, fens, seepage areas, interdune swales, beaver meadows, ditches, low spots in pine flatwoods. Native.

FOOD USE: Tender new **leaves** can be nibbled raw or used in salads. More commonly used in smoothies or the leaves steeped for **tea. Conservation 1.**

COMMENTS: This is sometimes considered the same species as the gotu kola of East Asia; the North American populations are only subtly different. Gotu kola is used in herbal medicine to promote wound healing (especially burns), vascular health, and also as a memory enhancer or brain tonic. **AKA** spadeleaf, *Centella asiatica.*

GROUP 20 BASAL LEAVES COMPOUND, FLOWERING STEM LEAFLESS

This physical form is largely an adaptation to full sun. Group 20 contains plants from five different families with a variety of edible parts, but 8 of the 12 produce root vegetables. The hardest species to identify here are plants 3–6, the carrot family (*Apiaceae*) members. Despite the reputation of this family for difficulty and danger, none of these resembles any dangerous species when in bloom or fruit—the tricky part is differentiating the various edibles from each other. (The very young rosettes of poison hemlock (p. 671) can resemble these *Apiaceae* plants when not in bloom.) Note that plants 3–6 do not have functional common names in English—the names you see in books are highly variable and usually not helpful. There are two different genera with soft edible roots (*Lomatium* and *Cymopterus*) that I am calling *biscuitroot*, reflecting the fact that foragers tend to think of them together. Also, plant #6 is included here despite normally having a stem, because the stem is so short that most people will not notice it.

TENTATIVE IDENTIFICATION KEY TO GROUP 20
The key is not your final answer!

Leaves single, more than 12" (30 cm) long, widely spaced, 2 or 3 times compound with distinct ovate or obovate leaflets.	1. Wild sarsaparilla
Leaves single, less than 1" (2.5 cm) long, closely spaced along a rhizome, carpet-forming, ternately compound, with tiny teeth and chevron markings.	2. White clover
Leaves in rosettes or clumps.	
Leaves multi-compound and lacy with indistinct divisions.	
Flowers yellow; fruit ribbed or ridged but not broadly winged.	
Lobe tips rounded or abruptly pointed, petiole not channeled.	3. Yellow prairie biscuitroot
Lobes thread-like with sharp tips; petiole broadly channeled.	4. Thread-leaf musineon
Flowers white; fruit prominently winged.	
Leaves shiny.	5. Small winged biscuitroot
Leaves dull grayish.	6. Large winged biscuitroot
Leaves once pinnately compound with toothed leaflets of 2 distinct alternating sizes.	7. Silverweed
Leaves ternately compound.	
Leaflets elliptic or obovate, sharply toothed with depressed veins.	
Fruit heart-shaped with the seeds in a pitted surface.	8. Common strawberry
Fruit pointed with the seeds in a non-pitted surface.	9. Woodland strawberry
Leaflets entire, creased and shaped like a paper heart.	10. Violet wood sorrel
Leaves palmately compound with 3–8 leaflets.	
Leaves with 3–5 leaflets, densely hairy on top.	11. Small prairie-turnip
Leaves with 5–8 leaflets, hairless to sparsely hairy on top.	12. Nashville breadroot

1 Wild sarsaparilla
Aralia nudicaulis ✦ *Araliaceae* (Ginseng family)

QUICK CHECK: Single compound leaf with 3 main pinnate branches; flowering umbel on long, naked stem separate from leaves. **ID difficulty 2.**

DESCRIPTION: Perennial forming large, well-spaced colonies by rhizome. **Leaves** single, twice or occasionally thrice compound, 12–20" (30–50 cm) long with three primary divisions, each with typically 3–7 (most often 5) leaflets. The rachis is dark purple where leaflets attach. **Leaflets** mostly sessile, some (especially terminal ones) stalked or *half-sessile*, borne in plane roughly parallel to the ground, 2–7" (5–18 cm) long, ovate to elliptic, the tip acuminate. **Surfaces** have scattered short hair on both sides. Major veins and veinlets are depressed above and protruding below. **Margins** densely serrated with long, narrow, sharp teeth pointing toward the tip. **Petioles** erect, rising from a *woody base* that may stick slightly above the ground, smooth, not channeled, red-purple, *solid*, 4–6 mm thick and up to 28" (70 cm) tall, with a small sheath at the base (that withers by maturity). **Leaf shoot** covered with *fine wool*, the folded leaf cluster at the shoot's top *hairy on all parts*. **Scapes** single, erect, solid, straight, borne on a woody base beside a petiole but somewhat shorter, the surface smooth and soft-hairy. **Inflorescence** 1–3 tight, ball-like umbels about 1.4" (3.5 cm) in diameter. **Flowers** (early summer) numerous, white, 2–3 mm across, with stamens radiating far beyond the five petals. **Berry** spherical, 3–4 mm, with calyx remnants at the tip, ripening to purple-black in mid summer, containing several seeds.

CONFUSING PLANTS: Young shoots can be confused with those of **red baneberry** (p. 676), which sometimes grow beside it and emerge at about the same time. **This may be the most difficult distinction between a poisonous and edible plant in our region!** Baneberry shoots (the stem part) are glaucous and hairless with a pinhole hollow in the center; the folded leaf clusters are slightly hairy, with the hair on the bottom of the blades only. Flowering shoots show a cluster of flower buds on a small branch borne below the primary leaf division. Baneberry does not emanate from a woody base. Sarsaparilla is often mistaken for ginseng, to which it is related, but the flowers of ginseng are borne on the same stem as the leaves.

HABITAT: Dry or young forests that cast light to moderate shade, especially pine, oak, birch, or aspen. Becomes more common after logging or fire. Native. 🔥

FOOD USE: Rhizomes can be collected at any time and boiled to make a weak-flavored drink. Young **shoots** of petioles, before the leaves open up, make a good raw snack with unique flavor. **Berries** can be nibbled only in limited quantity due to the strong spicy, soapy flavor. Some people make wine or jelly from them; I've tried both and liked neither. **Conservation 3/2/1.**

COMMENTS: This is one of the most abundant forest herbs in some regions. While the drink from boiled rhizomes is the best-known way to use this plant, it's not as exciting as the exotic name suggests.

2 White clover  1 2
Trifolium repens ◆ *Fabaceae* (Bean family)

QUICK CHECK: Ground-cover with three-part compound leaves on long, erect petioles, leaflets all sessile, bearing chevrons; flowers white. **ID difficulty 1.**

DESCRIPTION: This is the common clover of lawns, with perennial stems creeping along the ground and rooting at the nodes every 0.8–2" (2–5 cm). Both petioles and pedicels are borne on the side of the stem, then turn to rise erect, up to 28" (70 cm) tall—but *much* shorter where mowed. **Petioles** long and thin, broadly and shallowly channeled, often curvy. **Leaves** ternately compound. **Leaflets** sessile, broadly elliptic to obovate, the tips blunt with a small notch, the surface with a light chevron. **Midvein** slightly depressed; secondary veins tiny, numerous, and straight. **Margins** have tiny needle-teeth (so small you might overlook them and call the margin entire). **Inflorescence** a tight, round bundle of tiny, ascending to erect flowers (the whole cluster often mistakenly considered a single flower). The peduncle is *very strongly ridged*—and not symmetrically; one groove is much deeper than the others. **Flowers** irregular, narrowly pea-like, generally white but sometimes pinkish, especially toward the bottom of the cluster. **Fruit** a tiny pod.

HABITAT: Open, sunny, disturbed ground with short vegetation, mostly lawns and roadsides. Introduced.

FOOD USE: Tender young **leaves** can be nibbled anytime, but are best in spring. The **flowers** are a sweet snack and can be used for garnish, salads, or in cooked vegetable dishes. They can also be used fresh or dried for tea.

COMMENTS: I wonder what would have happened if I had found a four-leaf clover while writing this description.

RELATED EDIBLE: Strawberry clover *T. fragiferum* is a creeping plant nearly identical to white clover, but its flowers are mostly pink and its leaves lack chevrons.

3 Yellow prairie biscuitroot 3 3 3
Lomatium foeniculaceum ◆ *Apiaceae* (Carrot family)

QUICK CHECK: Low herb with multi-compound leaves that have tiny, lacy divisions; naked stalk with a compound umbel, the umbellets yellow and tightly packed. **ID difficulty 1.**

DESCRIPTION: Perennial. **Taproots** vertical, unbranched, thickest in the middle or toward the end, the larger ones to 0.9" (23 mm) wide, abruptly narrowed near the top. Some plants develop multi-headed crowns. The enlarged portion is 5–8" (13–20 cm) long. The root is brown outside with a thick, 2-layer waxy skin, smoothish but broken by scattered shallow fissures and a few raised bumps; lacks encircling constrictions. **Flesh** white, starchy, scarcely fibrous, with a non-woody, cream-colored core. The root does not reach the surface; there is a *short underground stem layered with many encircling sheaths*. This species is usually covered with fine, soft, curly hair—but southern populations may be hairless or nearly so, and these have sometimes been recognized as a separate species, *L. daucifolium*. **Basal leaves** in a rosette of 4–8, each

3–8" (8–20 cm) long, resting on the ground in the open but ascending under competition, very ruffled or fluffy in appearance. The leaves are 2–3 times compound and once deeply lobed or divided. The first division is ternate, the next 1–2 divisions pinnate. Ultimate lobes are linear and minute, flat, and out of plane with each other, with a *rounded or abruptly-pointed tip*. **Petioles** about 60% of blade length, 2–4 mm thick with thin purple lines, not channeled, with an abruptly widening, fleshy, purplish sheath at the base. **Rachis** has a long naked section after its first division; its branches are narrowly channeled. **Scapes** 1–3 per rosette, rounded with fine ridges, solid at first, becoming hollow, leaning to decumbent in the open but often erect in competition, 3–16" (8–40 cm) long, proportionately stout (4–9 mm thick), typically curved. **Inflorescence** a flat-topped compound umbel that is closely packed and ball-like with 8–30 extremely short rays when first flowering; the rays elongate up to 3.5" (9 cm) in fruit, at which time the umbellets do not touch. There are *no bracts* beneath the great umbel, but under the umbellets there are numerous overlapping, hairy bracts equaling the rays and *arranged in a lopsided whorl*. **Umbellets** are tightly packed (and remain so even in fruit) with 9–14 rays. **Flowers** (early to mid spring) *tiny*, with 5 yellow petals that *curl inward so their tips touch*; stamens protrude by about the length of the flower. **Fruits** 6–7 mm long, flattened, ovate to oblong, light brown with prominent reddish-brown tubes.

HABITAT: Prairies, savannahs, roadsides, lightly used pastures—especially where steep and rocky or lightly disturbed, on limestone-derived, clay-rich soils. Native. 🔥

FOOD USE: The **roots** are sweet with a slightly aromatic aftertaste, and have a nice texture. You can eat them raw but they are better cooked. Tender young **leaves**, **stems**, and **flowers** can be used as a vegetable or seasoning, raw or cooked. These are only available in spring or early summer. **Conservation 3/2.**

COMMENTS: This fantastic edible is an early spring wildflower that is locally abundant but has suffered greatly from habitat loss. The Latin species name means "fennel-like" in reference to the look rather than the flavor. This plant does not taste like parsley—the flavor is very strong, like celery or lovage. The roots are traditionally dried and pounded into flour or cakes by Indigenous people. **AKA** prairie parsley.

RELATED EDIBLES: A few additional edible species of this large genus are occasionally found at the western edge of our region, including *L. macrorhizus* and *L. cous*. Also see white prairie biscuitroot (p. 468).

4 Thread-leaf musineon 1 1
Musineon tenuifolium ⁎ *Apiaceae* (Carrot family)

QUICK CHECK: Small plant with tufted, erect stems and lacy leaves and tiny, bright yellow 5-petaled flowers in compound umbels above the leaves. **ID difficulty 1.**

DESCRIPTION: Perennial spring ephemeral growing in dense clumps from a multi-headed root crown. All parts are hairless. **Taproot** long, narrow, tapered, fibrous with a woody core. **Leaves** all basal, *erect*, in rosettes, to 9" (23 cm) high, 2–3 times compound or divided, finely dissected with *the ultimate divisions very narrow*, about 1 mm wide and linear, with *needle-like tips*. **Petioles** 1.5–2.5 mm thick, *erect*, broadly V-channeled, with a wide but inrolled papery sheath at the base. Many dead petiole bases persist attached to the crown from earlier years. **Scape** 7–12" (18–30 cm) tall and 3–5 mm thick, rounded, faintly ridged, scarcely tapered, rising slightly above the leaves, sometimes hairy just below the umbel but otherwise usually hairless. **Inflorescence** a small compound umbel up to 1.2" (3 cm) across, usually lacking bracts under the great umbel, but with a whorl of 5–10 linear, *pointed bracts under the umbellet* usually *surpassing the flowers*. **Flowers** yellow, tiny, the 5 petals curled in strongly, touching in the center. **Fruit** 2–4 mm long, egg-shaped to oblong and flattened, prominently ribbed.

HABITAT: Dry, rocky, sunny hillsides. Native. 🔥

FOOD USE: Leaves can be chopped and used as a seasoning. **Roots** have a carroty flavor and can be eaten cooked but are rather small and tough. **Conservation 3/2.**

COMMENTS: This delicate member of the carrot family often makes incredible displays on rocky prairie hillsides in spring. Foodwise it is the least useful of our small carrot-family prairie plants with edible roots. This species appears to hybridize with *M. divaricatum* (p. 467) in some areas, resulting in lacy-leaved plants with erect, forked, leafy stems.

5 Small winged biscuitroot 🥕 2 🌿 2 ⚱
Cymopterus acaulis ◆ *Apiaceae* (Carrot family)

QUICK CHECK: Small, shiny, carrot-like rosette with a scape bearing a tightly-packed compound umbel of white flowers and broadly-winged fruits. **ID difficulty 2.**

DESCRIPTION: Low perennial from a taproot that does not reach the surface; a short stem rises about 1" (2.5 cm) to the surface, where it produces a rosette of leaves and one or more scapes. **Taproot** thin, tapering, to 0.6" (15 mm) thick and 6–9" (15–23 mm) long, the exterior skin thick but tender, brownish, the surface of the flesh beneath often *tinted yellow-orange* after peeling. **Leaves** several in a rosette, the blades 1.2–2" (3–5 cm) long, pinnately once compound, with each division again pinnately compound or divided. The divisions are widely spaced and rarely overlapping, the lobes blunt with light tips.

Surfaces *glossy, hairless*, nearly flat. **Major veins** *depressed below*, not above. **Petioles** 90–140% of blade length, roughly triangular, *shallowly channeled*. **Scape** rises about as high as the leaves, 1–3" (2.5–8 cm) long, and may be twisted or have maroon lines. **Inflorescence** a compound umbel to 1.6" (4 cm) across that is packed so tightly that it forms one *ball-like mass of flowers and fruits*. The primary rays lack bracts (or the bracts very reduced); umbellets have unequal lanceolate **bracts** *on the outer side only, connected at the base*, green with a sharp, whitish tip and a dark central vein. **Flowers** (spring) tiny with 5 white petals, their tips in-curled; anthers are white to brown.

Fruits flattened, oval, 3 mm long, with 6–9 *conspicuous wings on all sides*, often purplish, becoming *white and sometimes wavy* with age, on pedicels about 1 mm.

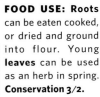

HABITAT: Dry prairies, especially where rocky or sandy, often on hillsides. Native. 🔥

FOOD USE: Roots can be eaten cooked, or dried and ground into flour. Young **leaves** can be used as an herb in spring. **Conservation 3/2.**

COMMENTS: The roots are good tasting but small; the leaves have a pleasant lemon-parsley flavor. This tiny plant is easy to overlook, but once you look closely, it is hard to forget. The fruits are amazing under magnification, as are the shimmery leaves. **AKA** *Cymopterus glomeratus*, plains spring parsley.

6   Large winged biscuitroot   3   1
Cymopterus montanus ✦ *Apiaceae* (Carrot family)

QUICK CHECK: Small ground-hugging rosette of lacy grayish leaves with twisted divisions and a very short flowering stalk with dull flowers and winged fruits. **ID difficulty 2.**

DESCRIPTION: Perennial spring ephemeral, low and ground-hugging. **Taproot** to 8" (20 cm) long and 1.5" (4 cm) thick, widest near the middle, the skin light brown, bumpy, and rough, the flesh white and soft, very tender and easily broken. It terminates below ground, where it produces 1–4 **underground stems** 1.5–3" (4–8 cm) long, that are smooth, whitish, solid, tough, and widening toward the soil surface where they form a crown that bears the basal leaves and branches. (The branches are so short that most people will see the leaves as basal.) **Basal leaves** in a pair, 3–5" long, 2–3 times pinnately compound, the ultimate divisions deeply lobed, the lobes numerous, *upturned*, blunt, mucronate, *extremely crowded and overlapping*. **Surfaces** whitish-gray but not visibly hairy. **Petioles** of basal leave are *broad and flat* with thin edges, channeled slightly if at all, 120% of the blade length; the rachis is also flat. **Stems** few to several (if present), *extremely short*, spreading, to 1 cm long. (This is not a typo—they are *that short!*) **Stem leaves** very crowded and usually paired (but may appear basal); their petioles are narrower than those of basal leaves and broadly U-channeled. **Inflorescence** compound umbel to 1.4" (3.5 cm) across with up to 8 primary rays, some without bracts, others with a few ovate to linear bracts of variable size. **Scapes** (or peduncles) 1–3" (2.5–8 cm) long and 3 mm thick, fleshy with a pinhole center, the surface finely ridged and having longer, stiffer hairs than other parts. **Umbellets** well-spaced, *not touching even early in bloom*—but the flowers and fruit *within* the umbellet are always tightly packed on very short pedicels. Beneath the umbellet is a ring of several broad, *overlapping bracts*, green in the central third with a darker green central nerve, the outer parts white and papery and often broken. **Flowers** tiny, white, often pink tinted, with 5 crowded, nearly uncountable petals. **Fruit** egg-shaped with *prominent wings on all sides*, turning purple with age.

CONFUSING PLANTS: *Cymopterus acaulis* (previous) and *Lomatium orientale* (p. 468) are both similar (but also edible). Look for the dull gray leaves and flat basal petioles on *Cymopterus montanus*.

HABITAT: Dry shortgrass prairies or semi-arid brushlands in full sun, sometimes with mixed junipers or pines. Usually not on pure sand or clay. It can thrive with disturbance such as mowing, and is therefore often most abundant on road shoulders. Native. 🔥

FOOD USE: Roots are large, starchy, and mild—good raw, hearty and excellent cooked. They can be baked or dried or made into flour. The **leaves** don't taste very good. **Conservation 3/1.**

COMMENTS: The root of this plant is shockingly large in relation to the size of the above-ground portion. Similar to prairie-turnip, it is one of the best root vegetables of its plant community and can be eaten heartily in a pinch without cooking.

RELATED EDIBLES: The very similar *Cymopterus macrorhizus* grows in Texas and Oklahoma; I have not yet eaten it.

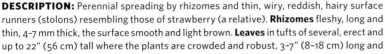

7 Silverweed 🌿 2
Potentilla anserina ✦ *Rosaceae* (Rose family)

QUICK CHECK: Low shoreland plant spreading by runners; tufted pinnately compound leaves with silver undersides; 5-petaled yellow flowers on leafless stems. **ID difficulty 1.**

DESCRIPTION: Perennial spreading by rhizomes and thin, wiry, reddish, hairy surface runners (stolons) resembling those of strawberry (a relative). **Rhizomes** fleshy, long and thin, 4–7 mm thick, the surface smooth and light brown. **Leaves** in tufts of several, erect and up to 22" (56 cm) tall where the plants are crowded and robust, 3–7" (8–18 cm) long and prostrate or slightly ascending where leaf clumps are sparse, pinnately compound. **Rachis/petiole** channeled, leafy almost to the base. **Leaflets** increase in size toward the leaf tip; *miniature leaflets are located between the typical leaflets.* **Leaflet blades** sessile, up to 2" (5 cm) long, elliptic to oblanceolate with *prominent, sharp teeth.* (Miniature leaflets may be entire). **Surfaces:** the upper dark green, glossy and hairless or slightly hairy; the lower covered with *dense, fine, silvery wool,* making the leaflets distinctly bicolored. **Secondary veins** straight, literally parallel, and deeply depressed. Stolons, leaf rachises, and flower pedicels are all *softly hairy.* **Flowers** about 0.7" (18 mm) across, bright yellow, with 5 separate petals, borne singly on a long, slender pedicel from the stolon. **Fruits** in a cluster surrounded by bracts—appearing like a dry, reddish to brown strawberry composed of spherical fruitlets.

HABITAT: Shores of large bodies of water, primarily the Ocean and Great Lakes. Occasionally found inland in open, disturbed soil such as road shoulders and gravel pits. It needs full sun and will form large colonies on sand, rock, or gravel, but grows larger and better in rich, soft mud. Native.

FOOD USE: Dig **rhizomes** from fall through spring. Wash, then eat them boiled, steamed, or roasted. Look for large, lush plants on mudflats; the tiny, crooked rhizomes of stunted plants on gravel shores are hard to dig, and hardly worth eating if you dig them. **Conservation 2.**

COMMENTS: For a perennial, silverweed varies enormously in its robustness. It is more commonly large and lush in the Pacific Northwest, as well as in northern Europe, both places where it was traditionally used as food. The rhizomes are tender and sweet but also astringent. A coastal form found in our region along the Atlantic coast from Labrador south to Long Island is sometimes considered a separate species, *P. pacifica.* Some botanists place silverweeds in their own genus, *Anserina.*

STRAWBERRY 📖 NG-286
genus *Fragaria* ✦ *Rosaceae* (Rose family)

QUICK CHECK: Three hairy, toothed leaflets and a miniature strawberry. **ID difficulty 2.**

DESCRIPTION: Low perennial herbs spreading by stolons. **Leaves** basal, ternately compound. **Leaflets** almost sessile, on petiolules 1–3 mm long, the blades elliptic to obovate, 1–3" (2.5–8 cm) long, finely hairy on both sides. **Midvein** and secondary veins strongly depressed above; secondary veins about 45°, running straight and literally parallel for most of their length, then usually forking shortly before the margins. **Margins** evenly serrated with large, sharp teeth. **Petioles** straight, thin, solid, with a faint channel, evenly covered with long, erect hairs. At the base are reddish, triangular stipules with bristle tips. **Inflorescence** of 3–11, umbel-like or forking into 2 or more umbel-like clusters, the scape with long hairs, and hairy bristle-toothed bracts beneath the junctures. **Flowers** 0.5–0.8" (13–20 mm) across with 5 broad, blunt, separate white petals, usually not overlapping, narrowed at the base. In the center is a yellow mound from which numerous stamens radiate. There are usually 10 lanceolate, sharp-tipped, occasionally lobed, green, hairy sepals. **Fruit** like a cultivated strawberry in miniature—a red fleshy structure, narrowed at the base, the surface holding numerous scattered seeds (achenes).

CONFUSING PLANTS: Certain cinquefoils, especially *Potentilla norvegica*, are often confused with wild strawberry, but their fruits are not similar. Barren strawberry *Waldsteinia fragarioides* is another relative with dry, inedible fruit. The bland but edible false strawberry (p. 434) is so similar that it has fooled millions.

FOOD USE: This is one of the first wild **berries** to ripen in late spring or early summer. While tedious to gather, they are astoundingly delicious. All strawberry recipes are immensely better when made with wild fruit. The leaves can be used for a moderately astringent **tea. Conservation 1.**

COMMENTS: Technically, the fleshy part is the receptacle, and the seeds on its surface are the actual fruits. I'm warning you so you are ready for the next techno-botanical correctobot you encounter.

8   Common wild strawberry ✦ *Fragaria virginiana*   3

This species has its seeds embedded in pits in the heart-shaped fruit's surface. It likes full sun and moist but well-drained fields and roadsides, often thriving in very poor soil. Native.

9   Woodland strawberry ✦ *Fragaria vesca*   3

The woodland strawberry has more pointed fruit, with the seeds not in pits; it is less intensely flavored. This species is characteristic of woodlands, especially young, open forests and forest edges. Native.

10 **Violet wood sorrel** 2 2 3 NG-338
Oxalis violacea ◆ family *Oxalidaceae*

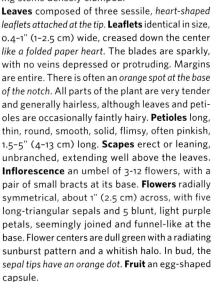

QUICK CHECK: Low, clumped plant with three-part compound leaves and leaflets like a paper heart; purple flowers with green centers on thin leafless stalks. **ID difficulty 1.**

DESCRIPTION: A perennial spring ephemeral growing from a cluster of bulblets with leafy sheaths on the outside, the numerous leaves and flowering stems densely clumped.

Leaves composed of three sessile, *heart-shaped leaflets attached at the tip.* **Leaflets** identical in size, 0.4–1" (1–2.5 cm) wide, creased down the center *like a folded paper heart.* The blades are sparkly, with no veins depressed or protruding. Margins are entire. There is often an *orange spot at the base of the notch.* All parts of the plant are very tender and generally hairless, although leaves and petioles are occasionally faintly hairy. **Petioles** long, thin, round, smooth, solid, flimsy, often pinkish, 1.5–5" (4–13 cm) long. **Scapes** erect or leaning, unbranched, extending well above the leaves. **Inflorescence** an umbel of 3-12 flowers, with a pair of small bracts at its base. **Flowers** radially symmetrical, about 1" (2.5 cm) across, with five long-triangular sepals and 5 blunt, light purple petals, seemingly joined and funnel-like at the base. Flower centers are dull green with a radiating sunburst pattern and a whitish halo. In bud, the *sepal tips have an orange dot.* **Fruit** an egg-shaped capsule.

HABITAT: Dry, open prairies, rocky hillsides, open woods. Native.

FOOD USE: Bulbs are edible, with a pleasant, slightly tangy flavor. Beneath the bulb is a thickened **taproot** that is tender and delicious—but both of these underground parts are small. All **above-ground parts** are edible, tender, sour, and delicious—but they are available only during the spring. They are good in salads, soups, or as a trailside nibble. **Conservation 3/2.**

COMMENTS: I think this strikingly beautiful plant is the best tasting of our many wood sorrels. The presence of bulbs is unusual for a dicot. To preserve the population, I suggest not collecting underground parts. Laura Ingalls Wilder wrote of collecting and eating this plant on the prairies of Minnesota and South Dakota.

RELATED EDIBLE: Mountain wood sorrel *O. montana* is a stemless, hairy species of low, cool, coniferous forests. It has beautiful pink and white flowers somewhat like those of spring beauty. The leaves are evergreen and edible, but not very attractive as food because they are tough.

◀ *Oxalis montana.*

11 Small prairie-turnip  3 📖 IWE-282
Pediomelum hypogaeum ✦ *Fabaceae* (Bean family)

QUICK CHECK: Small ground-hugging plant with hairy stems and palmately compound leaves with 5 entire leaflets; dense cluster of bluish, pea-like flowers. **ID difficulty 2.**

DESCRIPTION: Perennial with a short vertical underground stem terminating at or near the surface—occasionally extending 1–2" (2.5–5 cm) above the ground. Green parts (especially bracts) have a *strong turpentine-like smell*. **Root** enlarged, turnip-like to elliptic, 2–4" (5–10 cm) underground, the enlarged portion 0.7–1.3" (18–33 mm) long and 30–80% as thick, narrowing suddenly at the base to a thin, tough, unbranched taproot. **Leaves** palmately compound, all basal or packed onto the very short stem, decumbent or reclining, *layered with densely hairy, narrowly triangular, greenish to papery stipules* 9–16 mm long. **Petioles** 3–6" (8–15 mm) long, hollow, *densely covered with long, white hairs that are appressed, leaning, and erect*. **Leaflets** 3–5, all sessile, 0.7–1.3" (18–33 mm) long, entire, obovate, acute at the base and blunt to rounded at the tip, indented or nipple-tipped, *densely hairy on both sides* and especially the margins, the hairs *very long, soft, and mostly appressed*. **Midvein** slightly depressed above and protruding below; other veins not evident. **Peduncles** usually multiple, curved and decumbent, hollow, tough, 2.5–4.5" (6–11 cm) long, densely covered with long, soft, erect and leaning hairs. **Inflorescence** a dense, compact, spike-like raceme 1–2.5" (2.5–6 cm) long, each pedicel with an ovate, dark green-purple, bristle-tipped bract beneath it, almost as long as the corolla. **Flowers** pea-like, 10–14 mm long, the banner broad, white to pale blue with darker blue veins. The wings equal the banner in length, are deeply cupped, and much darker purple. The keel is hidden, much shorter, and dark purple-brown. The corolla fades to pale straw-yellow. **Pods** tiny and hidden.

CONFUSING PLANTS: Prairie-turnip (p. 652) is larger in all respects with an erect stem; the upper surface of the leaves is hairless or nearly so. Some lupines (genus *Lupinus*) look similar; confirm the hairiness, flowers, and root form.

HABITAT: Prairies and savannahs, especially where soil is sandy or otherwise poor. This short plant does best where grazing, trampling, mowing, or poor soil reduce the competition. Native. 🔥

FOOD USE: Roots can be dug whenever the plants are visible, then peeled and eaten raw or cooked in many ways. They dry readily, can be ground into flour or meal, and are very good dehydrated. **Conservation 3.**

COMMENTS: This plant is like a miniature, ground-hugging, dry-soil version of its larger cousin the prairie-turnip, and the root tastes essentially identical.

▲ Small prairie-turnip in blue; Nashville bread-root in purple.

Related edible:

12 Nashville breadroot 𝄃 3
Pediomelum subacaule ✦ Fabaceae **(Bean family)**

QUICK CHECK: Ground-hugging plant with hairy stems and dark green, palmately compound leaves; brilliant purple flowers rising above the leaves; Nashville area. **ID difficulty 1.**

This species is also ground-hugging, but somewhat larger. The **roots** are larger and lumpy or amorphous. **Leaves** have 5–8 oblanceolate leaflets with blunt tips. There are dense, long, white hairs below, especially on the midvein and margins, but *few to no hairs on the upper surface.* **Peduncles** usually multiple, decumbent or ascending, to 9" (23 cm) tall, hollow, densely covered with erect hairs. **Raceme** 1–4" (2.5–10 cm) long, rising *well above the leaves.* **Flowers** with a short-lobed, dark purple calyx (the tube 3–4 times longer than the lobes). **Corolla** uniformly deep purple-blue, the banner narrow and slightly recurved.

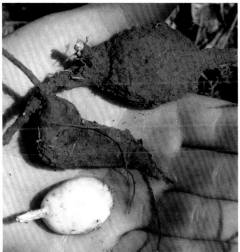

HABITAT: Well-drained sunny sites on thin soil over limestone: roadsides, power-line cuts, cedar glades, and field edges. It is occasionally abundant in lawns, which it turns brilliant purple in April. Native. ◢ Range map on previous page.

FOOD USE: The **root** is slightly bitter raw but still tasty with a faint coconut flavor. The bitterness can easily be leached out by boiling and draining one time.

COMMENTS: Confined mostly to the Nashville Basin, where it is locally abundant. This species has lost much habitat to development and even more to fire suppression. This has the most limited distribution of any plant in this book. It desperately needs foragers raising their voices about its value, for there are many hundreds of square miles of potential habitat—if only different land management choices were being made. Indeed, it has been eliminated from much public land due to bureaucratic disinterest.

GROUP 21 BASAL LEAVES PRESENT, STEM LEAVES PAIRED OR WHORLED

This group contains a rather erratic assortment of species with a variety of edible parts. Some of them lose their basal leaves very early, or have leaves that might be argued as "not really basal, just stem leaves crammed at the base," or in one case, "not really paired, just alternate leaves crammed together." With certain colonial plants in this group you can expect to see fertile leafy stems near to but separate from infertile basal leaves. Such plants may be hard to place in the key based upon a single flowering stem. This trouble-some group of oddballs was the hardest to fit into this guide's organizational scheme.

TENTATIVE IDENTIFICATION KEY TO GROUP 21
The key is not your final answer!

Basal leaves attached at the bottom of or adjacent to leafy, flowering stems.

  Stem leaves whorled.

    or   Some or all leaves compound. — **1. Rue anemone**

        All leaves entire. — **2. Carpetweed**

  Stem leaves paired.

    Stem leaves both paired and alternate.

      or   Paired leaves unequal, entire; sap milky. — **3. Common dwarf dandelion**

        Paired leaves not distinctly unequal, toothed; sap not milky. Scurvy-grass (p. 341).

    Stem leaves all paired.

      or   Leaves pinnately lobed, hairy; stem squared with few leaves. — **4. Lyre-leaf sage**

        Leaves simple, toothed but not lobed.

        or   Large, irregular teeth along the leaf margin. — **5. Cup plant**

          Teeth few, mostly near leaf base. — **6. Cornsalad**

      Leaves entire.

        Leaves thick and fleshy, one pair per stalk. — **7. Spring beauty**

        Leaves not thick and fleshy, more than one pair per stalk.

          Stem erect with 2 grooves. — **8. Heal-all**

          Stem limp and leaning or spreading, not grooved.

            Blade hairless on both sides (may have hairy margin). — **9. Bladder campion**

            Blades densely soft-hairy on both sides. — **10. White campion**

Basal leaves not attached at the bottom of leafy flowering stems; they are borne separately.

  Leaves deeply palmately lobed and more than 8" (20 cm) across; flowers single. — **11. Mayapple**

  Leaves compound; 4-petal flowers in a raceme.

    Leaves multi-compound and fern-like.

      or   Divisions elliptic, lanceolate, or lobed. — **12. Cut-leaf toothwort**

        Divisions thread-like. — **13. Thread-leaf toothwort**

    Leaves ternately compound.

      Blades lanceolate or oblanceolate, erratically toothed to lobed. — **14. Slender toothwort**

      Blades ovate and regularly toothed. — **15. Broad-leaved toothwort**

1 Rue anemone 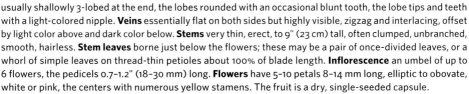 1
Anemonella thalictroides ✦
Ranunculaceae (Buttercup family)

QUICK CHECK: Short plant with compound leaves, the leaflets rounded with large blunt teeth; flowers with variable numbers of white to pink petals, in umbels. **ID difficulty 3.**

DESCRIPTION: Delicate perennial spring ephemeral, 6–10" (15–25 cm) tall, from root system with multiple small, pointed, straw-colored tubers. **Basal leaves** several on long, very thin petioles, usually ternately divided 2 times, resulting in 9 leaflets. **Leaflets** round to broadly ovate in outline, very thin, hairless, *pale below*, often heart-shaped at the base, usually shallowly 3-lobed at the end, the lobes rounded with an occasional blunt tooth, the lobe tips and teeth with a light-colored nipple. **Veins** essentially flat on both sides but highly visible, zigzag and interlacing, offset by light color above and dark color below. **Stems** very thin, erect, to 9" (23 cm) tall, often clumped, unbranched, smooth, hairless. **Stem leaves** borne just below the flowers; these may be a pair of once-divided leaves, or a whorl of simple leaves on thread-thin petioles about 100% of blade length. **Inflorescence** an umbel of up to 6 flowers, the pedicels 0.7–1.2" (18–30 mm) long. **Flowers** have 5–10 petals 8–14 mm long, elliptic to obovate, white or pink, the centers with numerous yellow stamens. The fruit is a dry, single-seeded capsule.

CONFUSING PLANTS: False rue anemone *Enemion (Isopyrum) biternatum* is a larger plant of rich-soiled valleys, up to 13" (33 cm) tall, with more deeply lobed leaflets. The 5-petaled flowers are always white, the petals broader and more rounded. The flowers are usually single (occasionally 2 or 3 together) from leaf axils. The roots of this plant may be toxic.

HABITAT: Hardwood forests, especially those with lots of oak and hickory. Native. 🔥

FOOD USE: The root system produces tiny **tubers.** These are terrible and probably mildly toxic when raw, passable after boiling and draining—but I wouldn't eat a large quantity. **Conservation 3.**

COMMENTS: This beautiful and abundant wildflower has tubers that are scarcely good enough to call edible. Their obscurity in the foraging literature, despite their widespread availability, is a testament to their mediocrity. **AKA** *Thalictrum thalictroides.*

2   **Carpetweed**   2
Mollugo verticillata ✦ family *Molluginaceae*

QUICK CHECK: Small plant with thin stems creeping over the ground, forming mats; entire leaves of unequal size in whorls of usually 6. **ID difficulty 1.**

DESCRIPTION: Prostrate, spreading annual, usually hugging the ground, growing from a whitish taproot. **Basal rosette** of about 12 oblanceolate to spoon-shaped leaves of *highly unequal size*, the largest to 1.6" (4 cm), tapering to a sessile base, the tip abruptly and obtusely pointed. Blades are light green, entire, hairless, glossy or sparkly in full sun, very tender, succulent but not thickened. **Stems** several, radiating from the crown, their *bases much enlarged and often reddish*; stems beyond the enlarged portion are about 1 mm thick, slightly angled, smooth, solid. Stems may branch at whorls; these branches also have enlarged bases. **Stem leaves** are in well-spaced whorls, usually of 6, the *leaves of highly dissimilar size*, oblanceolate, sessile, sometimes folded along the midvein, similar to the basal leaves but narrower. Leaves hug the ground in full sun. **Midvein** faintly depressed above, protruding below. *Secondary veins are obscure above, but the veinlets are faintly raised.* **Flowers** 2–5, borne on thin, straight pedicels to 1 cm long from the center of the whorl. They are inconspicuous, tiny, with 5 ovate, cupped petals, whitish inside and light greenish-yellow outside, with prominent, darker green veins.

HABITAT: Disturbed, moist soil in full sun to moderate shade. Yards, trails, vacant lots, forest openings, construction sites. Often appears after windstorms and logging. Native.

FOOD USE: Tender leaves can be eaten raw or cooked. They stay succulent often well into flowering, but are often too small to bother with. **Conservation 1.**

COMMENTS: This plant tastes like raw button mushrooms, and would be eaten more if it were larger and didn't hug the dirt.

3 Common dwarf dandelion  2
Krigia caespitosa ◆ *Asteraceae* (Composite family)

QUICK CHECK: Hairless little plant with linear leaves paired at forks in the stem; milky sap and tiny dandelion-like flowers. **ID difficulty 1.**

DESCRIPTION: Winter annual from a root that is thickened and corm-like at the top with small radiating roots underneath. The overwintering rosette withers in spring as flowering commences. *Sap milky.* **Basal leaves** 2–6" (5–15 cm) long, long-lanceolate to nearly linear, entire, sessile, tapered to the base, hairless, glaucous. **Stems** multiple from the base, erect to leaning, to 18" (46 cm) tall and 2–4 mm thick, solid, often slightly angled near the base but round above, covered with a light bloom, forking. Occasionally the *branches are in whorls of 3–5* with a vertical stem in the center, each branch with *a leaf wrapped around its lower portion.* **Stem leaves** *alternate and paired*—the paired leaves are smaller, unequal, usually slightly offset, and associated with a branch or inflorescence. All stem

leaves are sessile, long-lanceolate, entire but for occasional obscure teeth or rarely a lobe, strongly folded, keeled below. **Midvein** scarcely evident, slightly depressed above or in the form of a wide trough. The largest stem leaves sometimes have a pair of prominent parallel secondary veins on the underside; otherwise the veins are obscure. **Inflorescence** one or a few heads at the end of thin, erect to occasionally spreading peduncles to 1.6" (4 cm) long, arising from a leaf pair, the peduncle round and smooth, often with a few hairs just below the head. Before blooming the heads are bulbous and squat. **Flower heads** 9–13 mm across, yellow, with only ray florets, each about twice as long as wide, cupped when fully open, the tip truncated and 5-lobed. The outside of the head has a single row of broad, triangular to ovate bracts. **Seed** ridged crosswise with no parachute attached.

HABITAT: Full sun in moist to moderate soil where disturbed. Fields, roadsides, lawns, ditches. Native.

FOOD USE: The tender **leaves and stems** can be eaten raw or cooked like those of dandelions, lettuce, and other relatives. **Conservation 1.**

COMMENTS: Not well known but widespread and abundant, this cute dandeliony thing would be a lot more popular if only it were larger, because the leaves are pretty good.

4 Lyre-leaf sage   1
Salvia lyrata ✦ *Lamiaceae* (Mint family)

QUICK CHECK: Ground-hugging basal rosette of hairy, pinnately-lobed leaves, often with purple zones; square stem and a raceme of irregular tubular flowers. **ID difficulty 1.**

DESCRIPTION: Perennial from a short rhizome with fibrous roots. **Basal leaves** 6–15 in a rosette, usually hugging the ground, 4–8" (10–20 cm) long, deeply pinnately lobed with a very large terminal section, the lobes blunt, sometimes cut fully to the midvein, strongly ruffled, with no space between them. Both surfaces are densely hairy. **Veins** very deeply depressed above, with the depressed parts dark purple (especially in winter). **Margins** often purple with widely spaced, broad, nipple-tipped teeth. **Petiole** short, deeply channeled or broadly winged. The midrib is whitish, contrasting sharply with the dark blade.

Stem to 26" (66 cm) tall and 5 mm thick, usually single and erect (sometimes there are a few small, leaning stems beside the main one), solid, not tapered, squared, the corners ridged, the surface densely covered with down-curved hair. Branches are absent or paired. **Stem leaves** sometimes absent, but usually there is at least one pair, greatly reduced in size, deeply pinnately lobed, with very long hair on the midvein below. **Inflorescence** a raceme at the apex, 4–12" (10–30 cm) long, with spaced whorls usually of 6 flowers in the axils of ovate bracts, drooping on short pedicels. **Flowers** (spring) 0.7–1.2" (18–30 mm) long, the calyx dark purple-green with 5 hairy, pointed lobes. The corolla is hairy, tubular, light blue, much longer than the calyx, the 2-lobed lower lip extending well beyond the upper. **Seeds** dark brown, about 2 mm long.

HABITAT: Open areas with little ground vegetation: roadsides, lawns, forest clearings, especially on poor soil. Native.

FOOD USE: The basal leaves have a strange and terrible flavor, and they are sandy. But the tender **shoots** are just barely good enough to eat on purpose. Try them in spring well before they bloom. **Conservation 1.**

COMMENTS: This is a really neat-looking plant even if it's not the best to eat, and it is remarkably common. It is better known as a medicinal than an edible. **AKA** cancer weed.

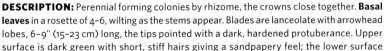

5 **Cup plant** 2 2 1
Silphium perfoliatum ✦ *Asteraceae* (Composite family)

QUICK CHECK: Large, clump-forming herb with squared, ridged stems and large-toothed, lanceolate leaves with petioles forming a cup at the base. **ID difficulty 1.**

DESCRIPTION: Perennial forming colonies by rhizome, the crowns close together. **Basal leaves** in a rosette of 4-6, wilting as the stems appear. Blades are lanceolate with arrowhead lobes, 6-9" (15-23 cm) long, the tips pointed with a dark, hardened protuberance. Upper surface is dark green with short, stiff hairs giving a sandpapery feel; the lower surface is pale green and rubbery with sparse, softer hairs confined to major veins. Secondary veins are depressed above and protrude below. **Margins** with irregular, very large, obtuse, abruptly pointed teeth with hardened tips. **Petioles** 100-140% of blade length, solid, with scattered hairs, broadly V-channeled, the channel pinkish, margins with green wings. **Stems** one per rosette, sometimes purplish at the base when young, straight, unbranched, erect, 5-8' (1.5-2.5 m) tall, to 0.7" (18 mm) thick, glossy and hairless; in cross section they are solid and *squared*, each angle with a prominent ridge. There are bulges or ridges crosswise at each node. **LYDS** prominent, squared. **Stem leaves** paired, similar to basal but on shorter petioles. *The petiole wings enlarge at the base and fuse with those of the opposing leaf to form a cup that may hold water.* **Inflorescence** a loose, spreading cluster of heads widely spaced on smooth peduncles 3-4 mm thick and 2-4" (5-10 cm) long, with cupped conjoined bracts below each juncture. **Flower heads** sunflower-like, 2.5-3.5" (6.5-9 cm) across, the rays long and narrow, in a single ring, *not touching at the base.* Disk florets 3 mm across, yellow with a brown column in the center. Bracts behind the head are layered, hairless, glossy, and broadly ovate.

HABITAT: Full to partial sunlight in rich, moist soil. Field edges, roadsides and ditches, forest openings, moist prairies, especially in floodplains. Native.

FOOD USE: Young **shoots**, generally a foot or less in height, can be peeled and eaten raw or cooked. Young **petioles** can also be used and need not be peeled. The **leaves** themselves are edible when very young but have a strong, bitter flavor. **Conservation 2/1.**

COMMENTS: The petioles taste milder than the leaves, and the peeled shoots are pretty good. This is a very attractive plant, often grown ornamentally, and is easy to grow in almost any soil. A colony you plant is likely to outlive you. Treefrogs like to sit on the leaves next to the little water pools.

6 Cornsalad 2
genus *Valerianella* • family *Caprifoliaceae*

QUICK CHECK: Short herb with forked, angled stems and blunt, paired, clasping leaves with a few large teeth; tiny tightly-clustered flowers. **ID difficulty 1.**

DESCRIPTION: Winter annual herbs, with rosette leaves withering around flowering time. **Basal leaves** (and lowest stem leaves) are spoon-shaped, 1–2" (2.5–5 cm) long, broadest near the rounded tip and tapered to the sessile base, usually entire. Blades are light green, delicate, hairless or with very fine hairs on top, but the margins are usually hairy. **Stems** to 28" (70 cm) tall, proportionately thick, Y-forking near the top or bottom, sparsely branched, hollow, *angled with winged ridges*, usually hairy on the angles. **Stem leaves** 1–2.5" (25–65 mm) long, paired, clasping, slightly broader near the base and tapering to a blunt tip, the margins with short hairs and *a few prominent teeth*, often only *near the base*. Nodes are widely spaced—up to 5" (13 cm). **Midvein** and secondary veins depressed above; 2 major secondary veins arise near the base and arc toward the tip before becoming obscure. Veinlets above are flat to faintly raised. **Inflorescence** a dense terminal cluster of 16–25 with a *nearly flat layer of many overlapping bracts underneath*. **Flowers** white to very pale blue, 1–2 mm across, tubular at the base with 5 petal-like spreading lobes at the tip. **Fruits** brown, egg-shaped, angled, 2 mm long.

SPECIES: There are several, native and introduced, which can be hard to tell apart. All are edible.

HABITAT: Moist, rich, disturbed soil in full sun to partial shade.

FOOD USE: Gather **tender growth** in spring and eat raw or cooked. **Conservation 1.**

COMMENTS: This green is often abundant but overlooked. The greens are tender and the flavor ranges from very good to mediocre. *V. locusta*, our most common exotic species, is cultivated and can be found in many seed catalogs. **AKA** lamb's-lettuce, mache.

7 Spring beauty ⏳ 3 🖋 2 📖 FH-193
genus *Claytonia* ✦ family *Montiaceae*

QUICK CHECK: Single pair of thick, succulent leaves on each stem; clustered pinkish flowers with 5 petals, leaning to one side. **ID difficulty 1.**

DESCRIPTION: Low, succulent, perennial spring ephemeral, all parts hairless. **Basal leaves** range from linear to broadly ovate. They are thick and hairless with entire margins, pointed at the tip and tapered at the base. **Midvein** lightly incised; a few secondary veins may be faintly visible—otherwise the veins are obscure. **Petioles** 60–100% of blade length, channeled. **Stems** in clumps of 3–12 (occasionally more), 3–5" (8–13 cm) long and 2–3 mm thick, solid, roundish, weakly erect to leaning or prostrate. Each stem bears one pair of leaves. **Stem** leaves similar to basal, but the petioles are much shorter. **Inflorescence** a raceme of 5–12 (at first appearing like an umbel before the rachis lengthens), each flower on a long pedicel, these *oriented to one side*, the mature raceme 4–6" (10–15 cm) long. The pedicels of unopened flowers droop. **Flowers** (early spring) 0.5–0.6" across with 2 blunt, overlapping sepals and 5 obovate petals, narrowed to a stalk-like base, pink or white with darker pink or purple veins. There are 5 stamens with bright pink anthers. The flowers close at night and on cloudy days. **Fruit** is a tiny egg-shaped to round capsule containing a few seeds.

▲ Virginia spring beauty.

▲ Carolina spring beauty.

SPECIES: **Virginia spring beauty** *C. virginica* is widespread in eastern woodlands. The leaves are narrow and linear, with no veins visible but the midvein. **Carolina spring beauty** *C. caroliniana* is found in rocky or mountainous forests. The leaves are elliptic to ovate and have a few secondary veins faintly visible.

HABITAT: Rich hardwood forests, especially those dominated by sugar maple, elm, basswood, bitternut hickory, and white ash. Native.

▲ *Claytonia virginica* tubers.

▲ *Claytonia virginica* flowers.

▲ *Claytonia virginica*.

FOOD USE: Dig up **tubers** with a small trowel or digging stick. To find larger tubers, look for dense clusters of stems emanating from the same spot. Tubers are best when the plants are dormant, but this is when they are hard to find. They may irritate the mouth when eaten raw; cooked they are like miniature potatoes, but softer and sweeter. The **greens** (all above-ground parts) are easy to harvest and mild in flavor; they are best eaten raw as a nibble or in salad. **Conservation 3/2.**

COMMENTS: These ephemerals are visible for only four to nine weeks in spring, then wither for the summer. In some areas they are remarkably abundant. Both species make equally excellent food. People like to debate whether the USO is a tuber, corm, or root. It is.

◄ *Claytonia caroliniana*.

309

8 Heal-all  1
Prunella vulgaris ✦ *Lamiaceae* (Mint family)

QUICK CHECK: Low, non-aromatic mint with hairy petiole margins, mostly toothless leaves, and flowers in a single large, dense, terminal spike. **ID difficulty 3.**

DESCRIPTION: Perennial spreading by rhizomes and creeping stems; it overwinters as an evergreen rosette that disappears by flowering. Non-aromatic. **Basal leaves** entire, sparsely hairy, on petioles about equal to blade length, the midvein and secondary veins depressed but veinlets faint and flat. **Stems** often multiple (or branched near the base of the erect portion), to 14" (36 cm) tall, usually unbranched, solid, squared in a modified way: 2 opposite sides are larger, convex, and rounded, while the other 2 sides are smaller and depressed into a groove. The position of the groove alternates between nodes. The lower stem is hairless or has sparse, soft hairs—especially on the angles; the upper stem is hairier and squarer. **Leaves** paired, 1.5–3" (4–8 cm) long, ovate, entire or scarcely and bluntly toothed. **Surface** has scattered, leaning hairs growing from small bumps on top; the undersides are hairy mostly on the veins. **Petioles** channeled, hairy, the margins with a thin leafy wing; 60–120% of blade length near the plant's base, but short and almost sessile on the upper stem. **Inflorescence** a proportionately large, cylindrical, terminal spike of densely-packed flowers layered with rounded bracts, each bract with a bristle tip. **Flowers** irregular, tubular, with 2 lips; the upper lip is longer and purple, while the lower lip is light purple to white and has 3 lobes, the middle one with long teeth.

CONFUSING PLANTS: When young may be easily confused with fringed loosestrife *Lysimachia ciliata* (edibility unknown but it sure doesn't taste good). Fringed loosestrife emerges earlier and has single stems, without rosettes, that do not creep at the base. The stem is squared with blunt angles but lacks the grooves of heal-all, and has a small hollow in the center. The leaves are typically coppery-purple when young. The petioles lack leafy wings and have more and longer hairs on the margins. Otherwise the plant is nearly hairless.

HABITAT: Full to partial sunlight on moist soil of almost any type; well drained to mucky or clay. Abundant in fields, meadows, forest edges, and along trails and forest roads. Native.

FOOD USE: Gather tender young **leaves** in spring or early summer. They can be eaten raw but are better cooked—indeed, better when boiled with one water poured off. **Conservation 1.**

COMMENTS: This herb is better known as a medicinal. It is among the poorer leafy greens included in this book, only worth mentioning as food because it is so ubiquitous. To be worth eating, the leaves must be collected at their tenderest, from the top of robust stems in spring. **AKA** self-heal.

▲ Winter rosette.

▲ Spring greens.

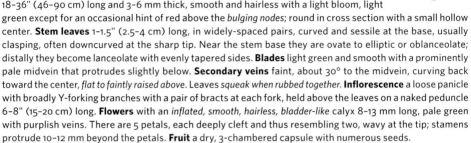

9 Bladder campion 🌿 3 📖 IWE-51
Silene vulgaris and *S. cserii* ✦ *Caryophyllaceae* (Pink family)

QUICK CHECK: Hairless plant with clumped stems and sessile paired leaves; white flowers with a bladder-like base. **ID difficulty 2.**

DESCRIPTION: Perennial. **Basal leaves** (withered by flowering) 1–4" (2.5–10 cm) long, broadly ovate, glaucous, entire, hairless except for very fine hair on the margins, the midvein below keeled proximally. **Stems** clumped, weakly erect to leaning or decumbent, 18–36" (46–90 cm) long and 3–6 mm thick, smooth and hairless with a light bloom, light green except for an occasional hint of red above the *bulging nodes*; round in cross section with a small hollow center. **Stem leaves** 1–1.5" (2.5–4 cm) long, in widely-spaced pairs, curved and sessile at the base, usually clasping, often downcurved at the sharp tip. Near the stem base they are ovate to elliptic or oblanceolate; distally they become lanceolate with evenly tapered sides. **Blades** light green and smooth with a prominently pale midvein that protrudes slightly below. **Secondary veins** faint, about 30° to the midvein, curving back toward the center, *flat to faintly raised above*. Leaves *squeak when rubbed together*. **Inflorescence** a loose panicle with broadly Y-forking branches with a pair of bracts at each fork, held above the leaves on a naked peduncle 6–8" (15–20 cm) long. **Flowers** with an *inflated, smooth, hairless, bladder-like* calyx 8–13 mm long, pale green with purplish veins. There are 5 petals, each deeply cleft and thus resembling two, wavy at the tip; stamens protrude 10–12 mm beyond the petals. **Fruit** a dry, 3-chambered capsule with numerous seeds.

CONFUSING PLANTS: Soapwort or bouncing bet *Saponaria officinalis* (not edible) has depressed secondary veins that arch back to the leaf tip; it is a larger, erect plant forming colonies by rhizome.

HABITAT: Full sun in dry, rocky or sandy, disturbed soil. Common on roadsides, yards, building sites, abandoned farmland, waste places. Introduced.

FOOD USE: Collect the tender young **leaves and stems** in spring and early summer, before the plant flowers. Tender tips with flower buds are good through mid summer. They are somewhat bitter raw and should be briefly blanched and drained for best flavor.

COMMENTS: This beautiful and abundant weed is not well known as a wild edible but the delightful greens certainly deserve more attention. It is a very popular foraged green in the Mediterranean region. **AKA** *Silene cucubalis*.

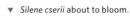
▼ Older shoot.

▼ *Silene cserii* about to bloom.   ▼ Very young shoot.

10 White campion 🌿 1 📖 IWE-54
Silene alba ✦ *Caryophyllaceae* (Pink family)

QUICK CHECK: Thigh-high, limp, fuzzy-stemmed weedy plant with entire, hairy, paired leaves and showy, bladder-like white flowers. **ID difficulty 2.**

DESCRIPTION: Short-lived perennial. **Basal leaves** similar to stem leaves but larger and broader; they wither by flowering. **Secondary veins** few, diverging from the midvein in the lower half of the leaf and gently curving back to converge at the tip. **Stems** multiple, spreading or leaning, to 40" (1 m) long and 0.6" (15 mm) thick, round with a thick-walled hollow, *densely covered with long, soft, curvy hair,* enlarged and lighter green above each node, repeatedly branching or forking at 35–40°. The top half of the plant has very few leaves and long, straight internodes. **Stem**

leaves tapered to the base with a broadly winged petiole, V-channeled and keeled below. They are ovate to elliptic, entire, acute-pointed at the tip, the lower ones 2–5" (5–13 cm) long, very hairy on both sides and the margin, often with a pair of smaller leaves in the axil (a branch bud waiting to grow). Each fork in the upper half has a pair of reduced, ovate to lanceolate, acuminate leaves, often with purple margins. **Midvein** and *secondary veins are deeply depressed above* and protruding below. **Inflorescence** a cluster of 3–15 at branch tips, branching widely, the pedicels hairy. **Flowers** with ovate bracts and a bladder-like calyx 0.5–1" (13–25 mm) long, hairy and ridged, the ridges purplish, sometimes with white streaks between them. **Corolla** 0.6–1" (15–25 mm) across, the 5 white petals spreading abruptly, each cut deeply into 2 rounded, blunt-tipped lobes. **Fruit** a broadly egg-shaped dry rattly capsule containing numerous tiny seeds.

HABITAT: Sunny, disturbed sites with moderate soil moisture. Hayfields, backyards, meadows, roadsides, pastures, ditches. Introduced.

FOOD USE: The tender young **leaves** can be eaten cooked. (Raw their flavor is rather strong.) Pick them in spring well in advance of flowering.

COMMENTS: This is one of our most abundant and widespread weeds. Many people call white campion "bladder campion," which has led to much confusion in discussing these edibles, because white campion's flavor and texture are distinctly inferior to bladder campion. **AKA** *Silene latifolia, Lychnis alba.*

11 Mayapple ◌ 3 📖 NG-116
Podophyllum peltatum ✦ family *Berberidaceae*

QUICK CHECK: 2 large, palmately lobed leaves bearing a single flower or fruit where the petioles diverge. **ID difficulty 1.**

DESCRIPTION: Perennial herb forming often extensive colonies by rhizome. **Basal leaves** single, to 16" (40 cm) across, roundish in outline, with 5-10 primary lobes radiating from a *whitish center spot*, the sinuses cut almost to the leaf center, the lobes drooping and often sub-lobed or notched at the end, abruptly pointed. Leaves are thin and delicate for their size. **Surface** hairless above, gray-green and sparsely hairy on the underside (hairier on veins) and margins. **Major veins** strongly depressed above and protruding below; veinlets scarcely depressed above and flat below. **Margins** have scattered, erratic teeth with light-colored, claw-like projections. **Petioles** erect, smooth, round, hollow, hairless, proportionally thick, 14-26" (36-66 cm) tall, *attached at the leaf center.* **Stems** to 34" (86 cm) tall and 0.4-0.7" (10-18 mm) thick, smooth, round, hairless, forking and supporting two leaves, rising slightly higher than the basal leaves. **Stem leaves** attached toward the side and have 4-7 primary lobes. **Flowers** (mid spring) *always single*, hidden by leaves, nodding on a 1-1.5" (2.5-3.8 cm) pedicel from the fork in the stem, 1.2-2" (3-5 cm) across with 6-9 waxy, broad, white petals, the stamens dull yellow and not extending past the *very thick* creamy pistil/ovary. **Fruits** egg or kiwi-shaped, 1-2.5" (25-64 mm) long, dull yellow when ripe, smooth at first but eventually becoming brown and dimpled or wrinkly. The interior is soft and pulpy with numerous seeds 4-5 mm long.

HABITAT: Hardwood forests with rich, well-drained soil and light to moderate shade; wooded pastures, forest edges, clearings, roadsides in forested regions. Native. 🔥

FOOD USE: Mayapples do not ripen in May. Gather them from early summer (in the South) to late summer (in the North) when they are dull yellow or straw-colored and the pulp is very soft. At this time, the plants may be wilting or broken over. Suck out the pulp for a delicious snack, but spit out the somewhat toxic seeds. Mayapple pulp also makes excellent jam, jelly, juice, or pie. The skins are bitter. **Unripe fruit is toxic and** tastes terrible. **Conservation 1.**

COMMENTS: This delicious, interesting fruit is highly regarded among foragers, and with good reason. Fruiting is highly variable and erratic. Large colonies may go years producing little to no fruit—this often happens when they are on the decline due to increasing shade or deer depredation. The most productive colonies have large plants and grow in sunny spots.

12 Cut-leaf toothwort 🪶 2 📖 NG-244
Dentaria laciniata ◆ *Brassicaceae* (Mustard family)

QUICK CHECK: Short, fern-like mustard with 3 deeply divided, palmate leaves on the flowering stems; racemes of 4-petal white to pink flowers. **ID difficulty 2.**

DESCRIPTION: Spring ephemeral forming colonies from tubers connected weakly in chains. **Tubers** 0.4-1" (1-2.5 cm) long, greenish, yellow, or white, constricted into short tooth-like sections touching at the tip and breaking apart easily, the surface smooth except for a few "eyes." Non-flowering plants produce a single **basal leaf** to 6" (15 cm) across and about equally long; these are 3 times compound/divided, the final divisions/leaflets sessile or with a very short wing-channeled petiolule. **Leaflets** deeply lobed to divided, often fully to the midvein on one side but not the other, with long, narrow, erratic teeth or small lobes of variable size, with nipple tips. The upper surface and margins are faintly hairy. **Major veins** slightly depressed above and protruding below; smaller veins flat. **Petioles** erect, solid, 6-12" (15-30 cm) tall, with sparse, soft, fine hairs; D-shaped in cross section, becoming shallowly channeled in the upper part, with *a scar about halfway between the base and the blade.* **Stems** smooth, hairless to faintly hairy, solid, roughly triangular in cross section, straight and unbranched, to 16" (40 cm) tall. **Stem leaves** similar in form to the basal leaves but arranged in a whorl-like set of 3 (often offset), on broadly wing-channeled petioles about 15% of blade length. **Inflorescence** a single raceme of 5-20 rising 4-8" (10-20 cm) above the leaves on a soft-hairy peduncle, the pedicels 0.6-0.9" (15-23 mm). **Flowers** 11-14 mm long, white to pinkish, with four petals about twice as long as the sepals. **Fruit** a narrow pod about an inch long, normally held horizontally upon ripening.

HABITAT: Hardwood forests with rich soil. Native.

FOOD USE: Tubers, found just beneath the surface, have a strong flavor of horseradish and can be used similarly as a seasoning. The entire above-ground portion of the plant can be used as **greens**, which have a milder horseradish flavor and are good on sandwiches. **Conservation 2/1.**

COMMENTS: A good plant to know if you like horseradish. Toothwort greens are available for only a short time; this is one of the earliest spring ephemerals to die back. The long-standing taxonomic debate regarding toothworts is whether or not to lump them together with the bittercresses in the genus *Cardamine*. I keep toothworts separate due to their distinct form. Some people claim they are called "tooth" worts because the leaves are toothed (like 6,000 other plants in North America). Others claim that the bumps on the rhizomes of certain species are "teeth." (I doubt it.) Maybe it's because the tubers look *almost exactly like canine teeth.* **AKA** *Cardamine concatenata.*

Related edibles (both with rhizomes breaking into tooth-like sections):

13 **Thread-leaf toothwort** ✦ *Dentaria multifida*

This species has 2–4 stem leaves. Basal and stem leaves both have fine, thread-like divisions. The whole plant is hairless. The greens are mild with only a faint horseradish flavor. This species grows in high floodplains and other rich sites in the center of the Eastern Woodlands region. **AKA** *Cardamine dissecta*.

14 **Slender toothwort** ✦ *Dentaria heterophylla*

The basal leaves have 3 lanceolate to ovate leaflets, the margins erratically cut with large teeth or small lobes. The stem has 2 or 3 leaves that are paired, whorled, or slightly offset, each with 3 leaflets, much smaller and narrower than those of basal leaves. This species is found in rich floodplain soils of the lower Midwest and Southeast. The flavor of the greens is milder and less horseradishy than cut-leaf or broad-leaf toothwort. **AKA** *Cardamine angustata*.

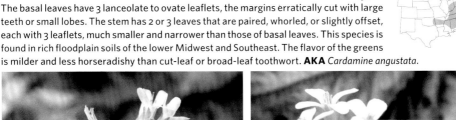

▲ (top left) Slender toothwort *Dentaria heterophylla.*

▲ (top right) Thread-leaf toothwort *Dentaria multifida.*

◀ (bottom) These are the tubers of cut-leaf toothwort *D. laciniata* (previous page), but both *D. multifida* and *D. heterophylla* have similar tooth-shaped tubers.

15 Broad-leaved toothwort  2
Dentaria diphylla + *Brassicaceae* (Mustard family)

QUICK CHECK: Low, colonial herb with 3 coarsely toothed leaflets per leaf; 4-petal white to pink flowers on a raceme rising well above the leaves. **ID difficulty 2.**

DESCRIPTION: Perennial forming colonies by **rhizome**, these 3–8 mm thick, whitish, irregularly constricted and knobby with many old scars. **Basal leaves** *absent on flowering stems*—they are borne separately and singly. They are compound with 3 broadly ovate leaflets 2–3.5" (5–9 cm) long, the side leaflets asymmetrical, each leaflet on a short, winged, petiolule up to 20% of blade length. There are 2–4 major **secondary veins** emanating near the base of the leaflet, *light colored*, slightly *raised above* and protruding below. **Margins** have large, sparse, round-tipped teeth with a light-colored nipple. **Petioles** rounded with a faint channel, rising 3–8" (8–20 cm) high. **Stems** 6–16" (15–40 cm) tall, solid, roundish, smooth, hairless, never branched, bearing *only two leaves in an offset pair about an inch apart.* **Stem leaves** smaller than the basal leaves with *all leaflets sessile*; the blades have tiny, scarcely visible hairs and the veins may be slightly depressed above. **Petioles** of stem leaves about 2" (5 cm) long, ascending, wing-channeled, rounded below. **Inflorescence** a raceme of 8–15, erect above the leaves, the peduncle naked for about 5" (13 cm), the pedicels about 1" (2.5 cm). **Flowers** 0.6" (15 mm) across with 4 blunt, white petals aging faintly pinkish. There are 4 green sepals with the tips curled in; the stamens are green. **Fruit** a thin cylindrical pod.

HABITAT: Mature hardwood forests with well-drained, rich soil. Native.

FOOD USE: Rhizomes can be used as a horseradish-like seasoning. **Greens** can be eaten in salads, sandwiches, etc., for their spicy flavor. **Conservation 2/1.**

COMMENTS: This doesn't look much like cut-leaf toothwort at a glance, but the flavor is nearly identical. **AKA** *Cardamine diphylla.*

0 mm 1 cm

GROUP 22 BASAL LEAVES PRESENT, STEM LEAVES ALTERNATE, ENTIRE

I consider heart or arrowhead-shaped leaves, or those with only 2 basal flares or lobes, to be entire. The burdocks are placed here, but their leaf margins are variable and would sometimes be interpreted as having small, broad teeth. Most of the species in group 22 have edible leafy greens; a few produce stalk or root vegetables.

TENTATIVE IDENTIFICATION KEY TO GROUP 22
The key is not your final answer!

Leaves hairless.	
Leaf with pointed basal lobes.	
Lobes oriented outward; blades constricted after lobes and widest in the middle.	
Stems less than 30" (75 cm); valves about as long as the seeds.	1. Sheep sorrel
Stems often over 30" (75 cm); valves much longer than seeds.	2. Southern sheep sorrel
Lobes oriented backward; blade not narrowed after lobes, broadest near base.	3. Sorrel
Leaves without pointed basal lobes.	
Stem with a sheath at each node.	
Inflorescence a single flower at the end of a long peduncle.	4. Lesser celandine
Inflorescence a single spike, mostly producing egg-shaped bulblets.	5. Alpine bistort
Inflorescence a branched panicle producing triangular seeds surrounded by papery valves.	
Leaves elongated, narrow, and sometimes wavy or "crisped."	
Leaves often exceed 10" (25 cm), valves not bristly.	
Leaves strongly crisped; tubercles (on valves) in different sizes.	6. Curly dock
Leaves merely wavy; tubercles absent.	7. Yard dock
Leaves flat, glossy, not crisped or wavy; tubercles all large. Willow dock (p. 587).	
Leaves less than 10" (25 cm), very smooth with faint veins; valves with long bristles.	8. Golden dock
Leaves ovate to heart-shaped.	
5-8' (1.5-2.4 m) tall with bright purple stems and rounded valves.	9. Patience dock
2-4' (60-120 cm) tall with dull stems, the valves with long teeth.	10. Bitter dock
Stem not sheathed.	
Blades broadly elliptic, the tips abruptly pointed or blunt to rounded.	
Erect woodland ephemeral with thin, delicate leaves.	11. Virginia bluebells
Trailing stems forming mats on sea beaches; leaves succulent.	13. Seaside bluebells
Blades narrowly elliptic or lanceolate, sharp-tipped, 2-ranked; petioles nested and deeply V-channeled.	14. Seaside goldenrod
Leaves with hairs or wool.	
Leaves frequently more than 10" (25 cm) long.	
Blades lanceolate, sharp-pointed, deeply folded; hairs stiff.	15. Comfrey
Blades ovate to triangular or heart-shaped, blunt, not folded, soft-woolly (burdocks).	
Burs not woolly, each on a pedicel more than 1" (2.5 cm) long.	16. Great burdock
Burs not woolly, some on very short pedicels less than 5 mm.	17. Common burdock
Burs densely woolly-cobwebby.	18. Woolly burdock
Leaves less than 9" (23 cm) long.	
Leaves all sessile.	
Stem ridged, hollow, 2-4 mm thick. *Castilleja indivisa* (p. 380).	
Stem not ridged, solid, 4-8 mm thick.	19. New England aster
Leaves (at least the lower ones) with a distinct petiole.	
Petioles channeled.	12. Northern bluebells
Petioles not channeled.	
Secondary veins numerous and strongly evident. Evening primrose (p. 351).	
Secondary veins scarcely evident.	20. Hoary alyssum

317

1   Sheep sorrel 🍃 3
Rumex acetosella ◆ *Polygonaceae* (Buckwheat family)

QUICK CHECK: Smooth, spoon shaped leaves with 2 small, right-angle lobes at the base. **ID difficulty 1.**

DESCRIPTION: Small perennial herb spreading by root suckers. **Basal leaves** in a rosette, 0.5–3" (1.3–8 cm) long, spoon-shaped to ovate with rounded, blunt, or abruptly pointed tips and two blunt ear-like lobes jutting outward at the base, usually out of plane with the main portion of the blade. (Smaller leaves lack these lobes.) Blades are often red-tinted in dry or cold conditions. The surface is hairless and sparkles when held up in sunlight. **Midvein** faint and slightly depressed above, protruding below. Four **secondary veins** arise near the base (2 running into the lobes, 2 running forward); these are flat above and protrude for a short distance on the underside. Veinlets are few, obscure, faintly *raised above* and flat below. **Margins** entire. **Petioles** 70–140% of blade length, hairless, V-channeled, the channel becoming deeper and winged toward the blade. **Stems** usually multiple; tough, wiry, solid, up to 20" (50 cm) tall and 2–4 mm thick, ridged, hairless, zigzag, jointed at the nodes with a ring that is often purple, with a small sheath (often withering and falling off). **Stem leaves** alternate, much smaller and narrower than basal leaves and on shorter petioles. **Inflorescence** a panicle encompassing the upper 35–50% of the plant, each branch a raceme containing numerous flowers in small whorls. **Flowers** (early summer) with 6 green, yellow, pink, or purple tepals. **Seed** (achene) 3-sided, 1–1.5 mm long, surrounded by valves about equally long.

HABITAT: Well-drained poor soil in full sun, especially sand or gravel. Sometimes also on rich, disturbed sites, where it grows larger. Possibly introduced.

FOOD USE: Tender **leaves**, especially in spring and fall, can be used raw or cooked as an addition to salads, soups, or sandwiches, or pureed into an excellent sauce or soup base. In poor soil the plants may be small and coarse; leaves are best for eating on non-flowering plants with no red coloration, where the soil is moist and rich. *High in oxalic acid.*

COMMENTS: This tenacious little plant is especially popular with children, who relish its sour flavor and often teach each other to eat it.

▲ Sheep sorrel flowers range from greenish to deep red. ▲   (Images continued on the next page.)

▲ Sheep sorrel leaves. ▲

Related edible:

2 Southern sheep sorrel ✦ *Rumex hastatalus*

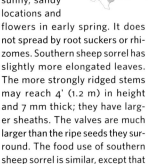

This is a larger species native to the Southeast, where it is common in sunny, sandy locations and flowers in early spring. It does not spread by root suckers or rhizomes. Southern sheep sorrel has slightly more elongated leaves. The more strongly ridged stems may reach 4' (1.2 m) in height and 7 mm thick; they have larger sheaths. The valves are much larger than the ripe seeds they surround. The food use of southern sheep sorrel is similar, except that its shoots are larger and have good flavor (those of common sheep sorrel are usually astringent).

◄◄ (left) Shoot of southern sheep sorrel.

◄ (right) Southern sheep sorrel in fruit.

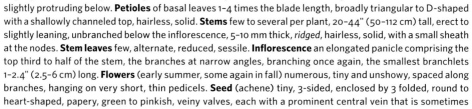

3 Sorrel 🌿 3
Rumex acetosa + *Polygonaceae* (Buckwheat family)

QUICK CHECK: Brittle, tender, hairless leaves with flat to raised veins and two reflexed lobes on the leaf bases; large panicles of tiny red-green flowers. **ID difficulty 1.**

DESCRIPTION: Perennial. **Basal leaves** in a rosette, long-lanceolate, 3–8" (8–20 cm) long and 1–2.4" (2.5–6 cm) wide, blunt-pointed at the tip, thick, tender, brittle, hairless, *many leaves with 2 pointed, backward lobes at the base.* Margins are entire. **Midvein** flat to slightly raised above, protruding below. Secondary veins flat above, scarcely evident, slightly protruding below. **Petioles** of basal leaves 1–4 times the blade length, broadly triangular to D-shaped with a shallowly channeled top, hairless, solid. **Stems** few to several per plant, 20–44" (50–112 cm) tall, erect to slightly leaning, unbranched below the inflorescence, 5–10 mm thick, *ridged*, hairless, solid, with a small sheath at the nodes. **Stem leaves** few, alternate, reduced, sessile. **Inflorescence** an elongated panicle comprising the top third to half of the stem, the branches at narrow angles, branching once again, the smallest branchlets 1–2.4" (2.5–6 cm) long. **Flowers** (early summer, some again in fall) numerous, tiny and unshowy, spaced along branches, hanging on very short, thin pedicels. **Seed** (achene) tiny, 3-sided, enclosed by 3 folded, round to heart-shaped, papery, green to pinkish, veiny valves, each with a prominent central vein that is sometimes inflated near the base.

HABITAT: Disturbed, sunny soil, especially sand or gravel. Mostly roadsides and fields. Native, but most populations encountered are outside the native range and introduced (as with chives).

FOOD USE: Tender **leaves** are excellent in salad, soup, or stir fry. Basal leaves are best, and are available in spring or early summer, then again in late summer or autumn. *High in oxalic acid.* **Conservation 1.**

COMMENTS: This is the same species as garden sorrel. It is like a giant and better version of sheep sorrel. Delicious but erratic in occurrence, it is locally abundant in some regions, including near Bemidji, Minnesota and the city of Quebec.

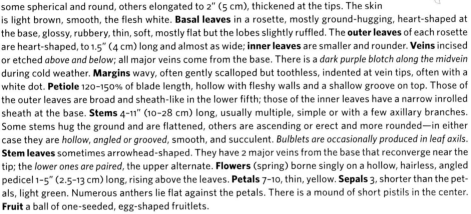

4 Lesser celandine 🐾 2 🌿 1
Ficaria verna ✦ *Ranunculaceae* (Buttercup family)

QUICK CHECK: A spring carpet of small, heart-shaped hairless leaves with a dark blotch; bright yellow flowers rise above the leaves. **ID difficulty 1.**

DESCRIPTION: Perennial winter/spring ephemeral often forming carpets over the ground, all parts hairless. **Tubers** one to several per plant, attached directly to the rosette base, some spherical and round, others elongated to 2" (5 cm), thickened at the tips. The skin is light brown, smooth, the flesh white. **Basal leaves** in a rosette, mostly ground-hugging, heart-shaped at the base, glossy, rubbery, thin, soft, mostly flat but the lobes slightly ruffled. The **outer leaves** of each rosette are heart-shaped, to 1.5" (4 cm) long and almost as wide; **inner leaves** are smaller and rounder. **Veins** incised or etched *above and below*; all major veins come from the base. There is a *dark purple blotch along the midvein* during cold weather. **Margins** wavy, often gently scalloped but toothless, indented at vein tips, often with a white dot. **Petiole** 120–150% of blade length, hollow with fleshy walls and a shallow groove on top. Those of the outer leaves are broad and sheath-like in the lower fifth; those of the inner leaves have a narrow inrolled sheath at the base. **Stems** 4–11" (10–28 cm) long, usually multiple, simple or with a few axillary branches. Some stems hug the ground and are flattened, others are ascending or erect and more rounded—in either case they are *hollow, angled or grooved*, smooth, and succulent. *Bulblets are occasionally produced in leaf axils.* **Stem leaves** sometimes arrowhead-shaped. They have 2 major veins from the base that reconverge near the tip; the *lower ones are paired*, the upper alternate. **Flowers** (spring) borne singly on a hollow, hairless, angled pedicel 1–5" (2.5–13 cm) long, rising above the leaves. **Petals** 7–10, thin, yellow. **Sepals** 3, shorter than the petals, light green. Numerous anthers lie flat against the petals. There is a mound of short pistils in the center. **Fruit** a ball of one-seeded, egg-shaped fruitlets.

HABITAT: Moist, rich soil in moderate shade. Mostly in urban parks, lawn margins, woodlots, especially in floodplains. Introduced. **I**

FOOD USE: The **tubers** are small but abundant and can be eaten cooked. They are best collected when the tops are dormant from late summer through winter. The young **leaves** can be eaten in spring but are slightly acrid and should also be boiled and drained.

COMMENTS: This plant is highly invasive in rich, moist, high floodplains—our most edible-rich herbaceous native plant communities. While it is edible, its food value doesn't come even remotely close to that of the 20–40 edible species it displaces in any given woodland. Lesser celandine is abundant in some of our major urban areas.

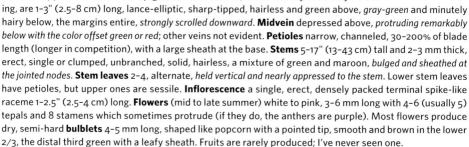

5   Alpine bistort 🐛1 🌿2 🍃2
Bistorta vivipara ◆ *Polygonaceae* (Buckwheat family)

QUICK CHECK: Erect, unbranched, shin-high herb with entire, long-lanceolate leaves and a single spike of tiny white flowers or bulblets. **ID difficulty 1.**

DESCRIPTION: Perennial herb. **Rhizome** 7–10 mm thick and 0.6–1.5" (15–38 mm) long, curved into a J or U shape, dark brown and rough on the outside, covered with layers of old, dark, papery sheaths; whitish inside. The back end of the rhizome is truncated and black—it appears to die as the tip grows. **Basal leaves**, which mostly wither by flowering, are 1–3" (2.5–8 cm) long, lance-elliptic, sharp-tipped, hairless and green above, *gray-green* and minutely hairy below, the margins entire, *strongly scrolled downward*. **Midvein** depressed above, *protruding remarkably below with the color offset green or red*; other veins not evident. **Petioles** narrow, channeled, 30–200% of blade length (longer in competition), with a large sheath at the base. **Stems** 5–17" (13–43 cm) tall and 2–3 mm thick, erect, single or clumped, unbranched, solid, hairless, a mixture of green and maroon, *bulged and sheathed at the jointed nodes*. **Stem leaves** 2–4, alternate, *held vertical and nearly appressed to the stem*. Lower stem leaves have petioles, but upper ones are sessile. **Inflorescence** a single, erect, densely packed terminal spike-like raceme 1–2.5" (2.5–4 cm) long. **Flowers** (mid to late summer) white to pink, 3–6 mm long with 4–6 (usually 5) tepals and 8 stamens which sometimes protrude (if they do, the anthers are purple). Most flowers produce dry, semi-hard **bulblets** 4–5 mm long, shaped like popcorn with a pointed tip, smooth and brown in the lower 2/3, the distal third green with a leafy sheath. Fruits are rarely produced; I've never seen one.

HABITAT: Moist tundra and alpine meadows. Native.

FOOD USE: The **rhizomes** can be eaten after boiling but are rather astringent. The young, tender **leaves** are slightly tangy and taste good raw or cooked. Mature **bulblets** can be stripped off by hand in late summer and eaten raw, parched and ground into meal, fried, or toasted; they are starchy with a pleasant nutty flavor. **Conservation 3/1/1.**

COMMENTS: One of the best edible plants to know in the Far North, with multiple edible parts. The bulblets are an important food for ptarmigan. **AKA** *Polygonum viviparum, Persicaria vivipara.*

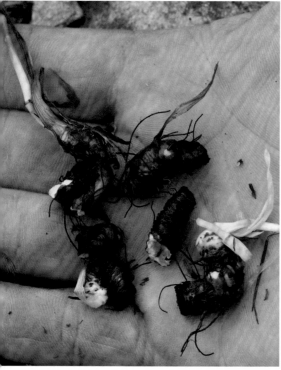

DOCK 📖 NG-226
genus *Rumex* (in part) ✦ *Polygonaceae* (Buckwheat family)

QUICK CHECK: Rosette of large entire leaves; stems jointed and sheathed at the nodes; large clusters of unshowy flowers and brown papery valves enclosing 3-sided fruits. **ID difficulty 1.**

COLLECTIVE DESCRIPTION: Perennials from taproots, the mature form taller than wide. **Basal leaves** several, heart-shaped to lanceolate or almost linear, 4–20" (10–50 cm) long, *hairless*, often *ruffled or wavy* like lasagna noodles (crisped). **Midvein** thick, *not depressed*, lined lengthwise, usually with a small *raised ridge down the center*. **Secondary veins** pinnate, numerous, broadly angled, variably depressed, arching forward or breaking up before reaching the margin. **Margins** often minutely wavy but *not toothed*. **Petioles** 15–70% of blade length, *solid*, hairless in most species, D-shaped in cross section, the top *flat and not channeled*, lined lengthwise. *The petiole base is wrapped in a large sheath* (ocrea), that is thin and membrane-like, partly translucent and holding slime when young; older sheaths dry and become papery-brittle. **Stems** multiple, zigzag, ridged, mostly hairless, *jointed at the nodes* with an encircling ring and usually a bulge, *wrapped in a papery or membrane-like sheath above each node*, solid, *unbranched except for strongly ascending inflorescence branches*. **Stem leaves** alternate, similar to basal leaves but progressively smaller with shorter petioles. **Inflorescence** a large branched cluster of hundreds of flowers hanging from thread-thin pedicels in numerous tiny whorls in the upper half of the plant, sometimes with reduced leaves interspersed. **Flowers** (early summer) tiny with 6 tepals of 2 different sizes, reddish or green. **Seed** (achene) three-sided (like buckwheat), surrounded by three papery wings called valves. The middle of each valve on many species holds a small rounded or teardrop-shaped growth called a **tubercle**. Tubercle and valve features help distinguish the species. The valves and fruits turn dark brown and are very noticeable in early summer.

CONFUSING PLANTS: Horseradish (p. 344) and prairie-dock (p. 353) leaves resemble dock's at a glance, but both have small teeth; the flowering parts are very different.

HABITAT: Moist soil in sunny or lightly shaded, disturbed localities: agricultural fields, roadsides, gardens, empty lots, barnyards. Some species are found in alpine meadows, marshes, floodplains, and woodland openings. There are native and introduced species.

FOOD USE: Young **leaves** are best cooked. They should still be scrolled up or folded, or have obvious creases where they have just unfolded. Young **petioles** can be used as a vegetable like rhubarb, and the milder ones are good raw. Peel young **stems** to reveal a tender interior that is good raw or cooked. Mature **seeds** can also be separated from their chaff and used as a grain, but generally they are too bitter to be palatable and must be leached.

COMMENTS: Docks are common and have several edible parts. Their flavor is tangy and somewhat astringent; it is variable from one plant to another even within species. Some people report eating dock roots, but I have found them too strong to be food. In foraging circles it is common to eat dock chaff, but this is not a food—it is added roughage like bran that modifies flavor and texture but reduces food value.

SPECIES: Docks are easy to identify as a group but can be hard to tell from one another. One common species, willow-leaved dock *R. triangulivalvis*, lacks a basal rosette and can be found in group 35. I have included bitter dock here, despite its low food quality, because it is so commonly encountered and is sometimes eaten. There are additional good, edible docks in our region, but our large wetland species tend to be quite bitter.

6 Curly dock ✦ *Rumex crispus*

This very common, weedy, introduced dock is the most abundant species in many areas. It likes disturbed ground and moist soil in full to partial sun. Its leaves are long and narrow with crisped edges (sometimes very much so). The stems stand 3–5' (1–1.5 m) tall. Valves are smooth-edged with tubercles in 3 different sizes on each fruit. This is the most commonly eaten dock. (Continued on the next page.)

▲ Curly dock fruit.
◄ Young, tender curly dock leaves.

7 **Yard dock** + *Rumex longifolius* 1 1 1 1

This widespread and abundant species resembles curly dock in size, habit, and form, and is thus frequently confused with it. Yard dock inhabits the same disturbed habitats and tends to replace curly dock in cooler regions. Its leaves are slightly broader than those of curly dock and less prominently crisped (if at all). It can be easily and positively distinguished by its broad valves with no tubercles. Yard dock is somewhat bitter, making it a frequent source of disappointment among foragers. **AKA** *R. domesticus.*

◄ Yard dock in fruit.

8 Golden dock ◆ *Rumex fueginus* 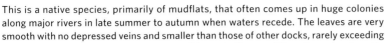 3

This is a native species, primarily of mudflats, that often comes up in huge colonies along major rivers in late summer to autumn when waters recede. The leaves are very smooth with no depressed veins and smaller than those of other docks, rarely exceeding 9" (23 cm). They are thin, extremely crisped in full sun and flat in competition. The petioles are faintly hairy. Basal leaves disappear by flowering. Stems are usually single. The flowers are golden in the center. The valves consist of 3–5 long bristles, each one with a claw-like tubercle. The tender leaves of this dock are among the best eating, and they occur at a time when other docks are long past their edible stage. The stems, however, are too small to bother with. **AKA** *R. maritimus.*

9 Patience dock ◆ *Rumex patientia* 3 3 3 1

This species is also called monk's rhubarb. It was formerly cultivated as a vegetable and is the premiere dock for eating. Widespread but sporadic in occurrence, it is very abundant in some areas. It likes well-drained rich soil in full to partial sun. Patience dock has broader and much larger leaves than most docks and is typically 5–8' (1.5–2.5 m) tall at maturity, with deep purple stems. The valves are broad and rounded with just one small tubercle. I also often encounter "false patience dock" with similarly broad but slightly smaller and rougher leaves, and more than one tubercle. These may be hybrids between patience dock and curly dock, or they may be *R. cristata*, which is so similar to patience dock that it is often lumped with it in herbarium collections. These impostors are edible, just not as good as the real thing.

▲ Young patience dock greens.

▲ Patience dock fruiting.

10 Bitter dock ◆ *Rumex obtusifolius* 1 1

This species has broad, heart-shaped basal leaves reticulated with a network of depressed veins. Stem leaves are narrower than basal ones but still broader than those of most other docks. The valves have long teeth and narrow tubercles. This introduced species is very common, especially in moist, wooded situations along forest roads and trails. The leaves and stems are usually very bitter; occasionally they are mild enough for me to almost like them. **AKA** broad-leaf dock.

◀ Bitter dock rosette.

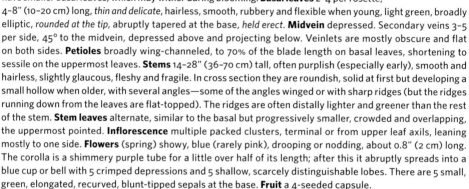

11 Virginia bluebells 2
Mertensia virginica ✦ *Boraginaceae* (Borage family)

QUICK CHECK: Delicate, elliptic, erect leaves with rounded tips, all parts smooth and hairless; clusters of bell-like blue flowers with a tubular base, mostly leaning to one side. **ID difficulty 1.**

DESCRIPTION: Perennial spring ephemeral often growing in multi-crowned clumps and *large colonies*. Non-flowering plants have rosettes of several large leaves; flowering plants have smaller basal leaves, which may wither during blooming. **Basal leaves** 2–4 per rosette, 4–8" (10–20 cm) long, *thin and delicate*, hairless, smooth, rubbery and flexible when young, light green, broadly elliptic, *rounded at the tip*, abruptly tapered at the base, *held erect*. **Midvein** depressed. Secondary veins 3–5 per side, 45° to the midvein, depressed above and projecting below. Veinlets are mostly obscure and flat on both sides. **Petioles** broadly wing-channeled, to 70% of the blade length on basal leaves, shortening to sessile on the uppermost leaves. **Stems** 14–28" (36–70 cm) tall, often purplish (especially early), smooth and hairless, slightly glaucous, fleshy and fragile. In cross section they are roundish, solid at first but developing a small hollow when older, with several angles—some of the angles winged or with sharp ridges (but the ridges running down from the leaves are flat-topped). The ridges are often distally lighter and greener than the rest of the stem. **Stem leaves** alternate, similar to the basal but progressively smaller, crowded and overlapping, the uppermost pointed. **Inflorescence** multiple packed clusters, terminal or from upper leaf axils, leaning mostly to one side. **Flowers** (spring) showy, blue (rarely pink), drooping or nodding, about 0.8" (2 cm) long. The corolla is a shimmery purple tube for a little over half of its length; after this it abruptly spreads into a blue cup or bell with 5 crimped depressions and 5 shallow, scarcely distinguishable lobes. There are 5 small, green, elongated, recurved, blunt-tipped sepals at the base. **Fruit** a 4-seeded capsule.

HABITAT: Moist, rich soil in hardwood forests, especially in valleys and floodplains. Native.

FOOD USE: Gather the young **leaves** in spring before the plants flower, or just as they are beginning to flower. Eat raw or cooked; they are extremely tender but somewhat bitter. **Conservation 2.**

COMMENTS: This is one of our most beloved spring wildflowers, and it is often planted ornamentally inside and outside of its natural distribution, but the flavor is mediocre in my opinion.

12 Northern bluebells 2
Mertensia paniculata • *Boraginaceae* (Borage family)

QUICK CHECK: Hairy, large, entire leaves with depressed veins and pointed tips; drooping panicles of blue, bell-like flowers. **ID difficulty 3.**

DESCRIPTION: Perennial, *not ephemeral*, with one to several stems from the base. **Basal leaves** up to 8" (20 cm) long, broadly ovate, entire, the tip pointed, the base heart-shaped to abruptly angled. Blades are rough-hairy below; the upper surface is bumpy and has smaller hairs pointing toward the tip. **Midvein** light colored and very deeply depressed above, protruding below. Secondary veins few, arching toward the leaf tip, deeply depressed above. **Veinlets** depressed to flat. **Petioles** about equal to the blade, broad, thin, shallowly U-channeled with a bubbly or blistered look inside the channel; they can be hairy (especially on the margins) to nearly hairless. **Stems** one to several per clump, 22–42" (56–107 cm) tall, unbranched below the inflorescence, erect to leaning, sparsely hairy, with a small hollow in the center, the surface with double ridges running down from the nodes. **Stem leaves** alternate, narrower, up to 6" (15 cm) long. The petioles are winged and get shorter going up the stem; uppermost leaves are sessile. There are small, *paired leaves in the upper branches* near the flowers. **Inflorescence** a drooping panicle of 3–18 at the top of the stem, the branches repeatedly forking. **Flowers** about 0.6" (1.5 cm) long with a blue, bell-like corolla with 5 *shallow lobes*. The calyx has 5 long, pointed, hairy lobes much shorter than the corolla. Flower buds are pinkish. **Fruit** a 4-seeded capsule.

CONFUSING PLANTS: Northern wild comfrey *Cynoglossum boreale* has blunt-tipped lower leaves, often with down-curled edges, and the upper ones clasp the stem. The secondary veins are more broadly angled and less depressed. There are no leaves in the inflorescence or on the upper stalk, and the flower tubes are shorter and spread more widely.

HABITAT: Lightly shaded, moist slopes in boreal forests, especially under birches where rocky. Native.

FOOD USE: The tender spring **greens** make a nice salad green or potherb. Leaves persisting through summer remain tender enough to eat. **Conservation 2.**

COMMENTS: The taste of northern bluebell's greens is a little better than that of Virginia bluebell, and they are available for much longer. This species is more characteristic of the Mountain West. **AKA** chiming bells, mountain bluebells, tall lungwort, tall bluebells.

13 Seaside bluebells 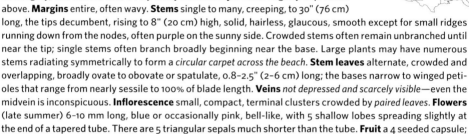 2
Mertensia maritima ∙ *Boraginaceae* (Borage family)

QUICK CHECK: Creeping bluish-gray plant of seashores with broad, smooth, entire, hairless, succulent leaves and small, blue, bell-like flowers. **ID difficulty 1.**

DESCRIPTION: Perennial, not spreading by rhizome. Rosettes are only evident on young plants with small or no stems. **Basal leaves** ovate to broadly elliptic, 2.5-4" (6-10 cm) long, the tip abruptly pointed and often downturned. The blades are thick, soft and succulent, smooth, hairless with *scattered dark gland-dots* above, bluish gray, and coated with a *very heavy bloom.* **Major veins** slightly depressed above. **Margins** entire, often wavy. **Stems** single to many, creeping, to 30" (76 cm) long, the tips decumbent, rising to 8" (20 cm) high, solid, hairless, glaucous, smooth except for small ridges running down from the nodes, often purple on the sunny side. Crowded stems often remain unbranched until near the tip; single stems often branch broadly beginning near the base. Large plants may have numerous stems radiating symmetrically to form a *circular carpet across the beach.* **Stem leaves** alternate, crowded and overlapping, broadly ovate to obovate or spatulate, 0.8-2.5" (2-6 cm) long; the bases narrow to winged petioles that range from nearly sessile to 100% of blade length. **Veins** *not depressed and scarcely visible*—even the midvein is inconspicuous. **Inflorescence** small, compact, terminal clusters crowded by *paired leaves.* **Flowers** (late summer) 6-10 mm long, blue or occasionally pink, bell-like, with 5 shallow lobes spreading slightly at the end of a tapered tube. There are 5 triangular sepals much shorter than the tube. **Fruit** a 4 seeded capsule; pedicels get much longer in fruit.

HABITAT: Gravelly, sandy, or pebbly ocean shores. Native.

FOOD USE: Tender **leaves** and stem tips can be eaten raw or cooked. **Conservation 2.**

COMMENTS: This wild arctic delicacy unfortunately comes south only to northern New England. In Alaska and Canada it is well-known and highly appreciated among foragers. It is traditionally chopped and fermented with other seashore vegetables for winter storage. **AKA** oyster leaf. This name refers to the rich, satisfying flavor of the greens, which some people liken to that of oysters. (I find the comparison a stretch.) The flavor is actually very similar to Virginia bluebells, but milder and a bit salty.

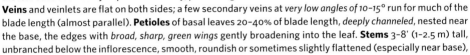

14 Seaside goldenrod 🌿 1 ✂ 1
Solidago sempervirens + *Asteraceae* (Composite family)

QUICK CHECK: Large, narrow, entire, erect, evergreen leaves crowded near the base of tall, erect stems with lanceolate leaves; clusters of small yellow flower heads. **ID difficulty 2.**

DESCRIPTION: Perennial evergreen spreading by short rhizomes to form *multiple adjacent crowns*. **Basal leaves** in *two-ranked clumps*, to 14" (36 cm) long, erect or ascending, linear-lanceolate with a tapered tip and base. **Blades** glossy, smooth, *thick, hairless, flat*, entire, silvery below when mature. **Midvein** offset by light color, deeply depressed above near the leaf base but weakly depressed distally, protruding with a blunt keel on the underside. **Veins** and veinlets are flat on both sides; a few secondary veins at *very low angles of 10–15°* run for much of the blade length (almost parallel). **Petioles** of basal leaves 20–40% of blade length, *deeply channeled*, nested near the base, the edges with *broad, sharp, green wings* gently broadening into the leaf. **Stems** 3-8' (1-2.5 m) tall, unbranched below the inflorescence, smooth, roundish or sometimes slightly flattened (especially near base), faintly ridged, hairless or with faint hairs following the ridges. **Stem leaves** somewhat smaller than the basal (much smaller in the inflorescence), alternate, tapered and deeply folded at the base, without a clear petiole; their broad bases clasp the stem. **Inflorescence** a terminal panicle with many raceme-like branches, the branches erect, scarcely diverging from the main stalk, the heads numerous, crowded, tending toward one side. **Heads** yellow, 1 cm or more long, with ray and disk florets. **LYDS** prominent and stiff.

HABITAT: Sunny, disturbed areas along the ocean (occasionally inland), especially where organic matter and moisture collect, ranging from dunes to marsh edges. Native.

FOOD USE: Tender young **leaves**, and the **shoots** after peeling, can be eaten raw or cooked. The season of availability is long, especially in the South. Leaves can be used for tea. They are aromatic like other goldenrods but much more substantial and not as strong. **Conservation 2.**

COMMENTS: I'm not keen on eating goldenrod greens, but this is perhaps the best of a mediocre group, if for no reason other than it's size, succulence, and faint saltiness. Seaside goldenrod is divided into two species by some taxonomists, in which case the southern form, more characteristic of marshes and having smaller flower heads, is called *S. mexicana*. I have eaten both, but not enough to develop an opinion on culinary differences. In warm climates seaside goldenrod may bloom from May through January.

15 Comfrey 🌿 2 🍃 2 ❀ 2
Symphtum officinale ✦ *Boraginaceae* (Borage family)

QUICK CHECK: Basal leaves large, pointed, folded along the midvein, on long petioles covered with stiff hairs; coiled flower clusters. **ID difficulty 2.**

DESCRIPTION: Polycarpic perennial from a large taproot, the *sap slimy.* **Basal leaves** in a rosette, 8–14" (20–36 cm) long, lanceolate with entire margins, arched, conspicuously folded along the midvein, the tip acute-pointed, the base abruptly broadening, both sides *densely covered with long, stiff hairs.* **Midvein** light in color, deeply depressed above and protruding below. Secondary veins 6–8 per side, 40–60°, arching forward, breaking up, and forming a scalloped pattern well before the margins. Secondary veins and veinlets are *deeply depressed above and strongly protruding below.* **Petioles** 60–80% of the blade length, deeper than wide, keeled below, with a deep V-channel with sharp margins, covered with stiff erect to leaning hairs. **Stems** 2.5–4.5' (75–135 cm) tall, clumped, mostly leaning, hairy, roundish, solid, tough, with wings extending downward from each node. **Branches** in the upper third, short and strongly ascending. **Stem leaves** alternate, similar in shape but smaller, sessile or with a broadly winged petiole. **Inflorescence** a branching terminal cluster coiled to one side. **Flowers** with a calyx of 5 sharp, triangular lobes, the corolla with an elongated bell shape, 0.6" (15 mm) long, purple to white, the tip with 5 very short lobes curled outward; *2 thin, spear-like, white styles lengthen and persist after the corolla falls away.*

CONFUSING PLANTS: Foxglove (p. 667) has smaller, toothed leaves and a velvety texture from fine, soft hairs; the flowers are very different.

HABITAT: Full sun to moderate shade in rich but well-drained soil. Roadsides, old fields, orchards, old homesteads. Introduced.

FOOD USE: Gather the young, tender **leaves** in spring and use as greens raw or cooked. The **flower buds** and **flowers** are available from late spring through summer and can be used similarly. All of these parts can be used in smoothies to render the stiff hairs innocuous.

COMMENTS: This has been one of the most popular plants in temperate herb gardens for millennia. Once established, colonies can live for centuries, so it inevitably persists after escape.

WARNING: Comfrey contains pyrrolizidine alkaloids, which are liver toxins—the greens much less than the roots. While the greens have been eaten for thousands of years, chronic consumption of large amounts has resulted in serious medical issues. However, most comfrey-related problems have resulted from persistent medicinal use of comfrey root tea or extracts.

BURDOCK 2 2 2 FH-324
genus *Arctium* ◆ *Asteraceae* (Composite family)

QUICK CHECK: Rosettes of huge broad leaves on long petioles, woolly beneath; Velcro-like burs. **ID difficulty 1.**

DESCRIPTION: Massive monocarpic perennials 4-7' (1.2-2.1 m) tall and spreading almost as wide. **Roots** massive, up to 3" (8 cm) thick and 40" (1 m) long, fleshy, light grayish inside, vertical with few side branches, rough and dark near the top, with a single crown. **Basal leaves** 3-9 in a radiating rosette, 10-28" (25-70 cm) long, ovate to wedge-shaped, ruffled or wavy, the tip blunt to rounded, the base heart-shaped. The upper surface is finely hairy. **Major veins** light in color and flat or nearly so; veinlets are depressed. The underside has protruding veins and is *densely covered with fine whitish-gray wool.* **Margins** wavy or irregular, not sharply or regularly toothed, but there may be nipple-like projections. (I wouldn't disagree if you called some of them toothed, but most people at a glance consider the leaf entire.) **Petioles** about equal to the blade, up to 1" (2.5 cm) thick, the surface woolly, ridged on all sides, with a channel on top. **Stems** solid, stout, 1-2.3" (2.5-6 cm) thick at the base, often purple in the lower parts, heavily tapered, the surface with *round-topped ridges.* **Branches** ascending, usually only in the upper 2/3. **Stem leaves** alternate, progressively smaller, with shorter petioles. **Inflorescence** a panicle of several heads at branch tips. **Heads** spherical, 0.8-1.6" (2-4 cm) in diameter, subtended by hooked bracts; the numerous thin florets are purple and white, giving the appearance of an old-fashioned shaving brush. These ripen into the familiar vexatious burs.

CONFUSING PLANTS: Often confused with rhubarb, but rhubarb leaves are smoother and glossy, not woolly beneath, and the petioles have no hollow parts.

HABITAT: Disturbed areas with moderate to rich soil, well-drained, in full sun: roadsides, barnyards, old fields and pastures, forest edges, fencerows, river floodplains. All species introduced.

FOOD USE: Roots can be collected all year from plants without stems. They grow very deep and require extensive excavation, but are often large enough to be worth it. Make a deep hole beside the root, then carefully loosen it sideways. The top of the root is tough; the good part is the lower 2/3. Use roots in pot roast or stew, boiled, or sliced and fried. Cut **stalks** at the base when less than 1/3 of their final height and still vigorously growing (in late spring or early summer, well before any branches appear), then peel the outer rind. Cut the peeled stalk into sections and use like potatoes. The whiter lower part of the stalk takes much longer to cook than the greenish upper part. **Petioles** can also be used before they have reached full size. The outer surface is bitter and should be peeled or scraped off, then rinsed. After this they can be used in soups or stew; the texture (but not the flavor) is reminiscent of celery.

COMMENTS: Burdocks are easy to recognize as a group, but the individual species can be hard to tell apart. These are amazingly useful and labor-efficient food plants. Common burdock's roots account for much culinary disappointment; it is best to seek great burdock for this use. The young stalks of all species are good, and are the easiest part to use. I advise you to ignore the sources claiming that the leaves themselves are edible. Handling burdock stems and leaves (especially common burdock) will put an extremely bitter substance on your fingers that should be washed off carefully lest you ruin the next food you touch. (Continued on the next page.)

◀ Great burdock root (see next page).

Burdock species:

16 Great burdock ✦ *Arctium lappa*

This is the species widely cultivated in Japan, and it is the best one to use for food.

The roots are larger, sweeter, and more tender, and the stems and petioles are thicker. Distinguished by its broad, heart-shaped leaves without nipple-like projections on the margin, petioles with only a small hollow vessel, and larger burs borne on long stems in spreading clusters.

17 Common burdock ✦ *Arctium minus*

Common burdock has triangular leaves and channeled petioles that have a larger hollow in the center; the burs are smaller and borne in tight clusters on short stems. This species is similar to great burdock but of slightly lesser quality as a vegetable, with narrower, woodier roots.

▼ (below left and right) Peeled and unpeeled shoots of common burdock.

18 Woolly burdock ✦ *Arctium tomentosa*

Woolly burdock is similar to great burdock in form but the flowerheads are covered with a spiderweb-like wool, and the leaf margins have nipple-like projections.

19 New England aster 3
Aster novae-angliae ✦ *Asteraceae* (Aster/Composite family)

QUICK CHECK: Rosette of narrow, hairy, sessile leaves; stem hairy with crowded clasping leaves; large purple flowerheads in autumn. **ID difficulty 1.**

DESCRIPTION: Perennial from a short rhizome, usually with multiple clumped stems. Old plants produce several rosettes in proximity. **Rosette leaves** crowded, sessile, hairy, flat, evenly tapered, the tips sharp but not acuminate, 3–5" (8–13 cm) long, the bases with two broad lobes. The surfaces have scattered, stiff, erect hairs—denser above. **Midvein** straight and nearly white, scarcely depressed above and protruding below, *broadening dramatically* at the base. Secondary veins are thin, clear, depressed, arising near the base. *Rosettes disappear by flowering.* **Stems** 2–6' (60–180 cm) tall, erect at first but often leaning in bloom, 4–8 mm thick, round with a few fine grooves, solid, hardly tapered, stiff, straight, evenly and densely covered with stiff, erect hairs—often glandular, especially above. **Branches** straight, simple, strongly ascending, only in the upper third. **Stem leaves** sessile and clasping, closely spaced and overlapping, the base with two backward-pointing, slightly downcurved, blunt lobes. Blades are 1.2–3" (3–8 cm) long, often twisted, broadest near the base and tapered to the sharp tip, shallowly folded near the base but flattening in the distal half. The upper surface is finely hairy and rough with a network of fine veinlets; the bottom is hairless. **Margins** entire, finely hairy, slightly downturned. **Inflorescence** (late summer through fall) a leafy panicle with densely glandular branches bearing many composite heads subtended by numerous long, narrow bracts. **Heads** 1.2–1.8" (3–4.6 cm) wide, with 40–50 rays, typically purple but sometimes reddish or pink (rarely white). Disk florets are yellow with a strong sunflower smell.

HABITAT: Sunny, open areas, moist or dry: old fields, prairies, meadows, roadsides, lightly used pastures, marsh edges, weedy areas near lakeshores. Native, but widely planted. 🔥

FOOD USE: Tender young **leaves** and **stem tips** are a nice green; I prefer them raw. **Conservation 2.**

COMMENTS: This is the large, strikingly beautiful purple aster that livens up roadsides in autumn, and for that reason it is widely planted as an ornamental—several cultivars have been developed. It is not so bold or easily spotted in spring or early summer when the greens are eaten. Asters have a distinctive, aromatic, almost piney flavor, but this species is one of the mildest and best—the youngest leaves taste like sunflower microgreens. **AKA** *Symphyotrichum novae-angliae.*

RELATED EDIBLES: All of our asters (genus *Aster* or *Symphyotrichum*) are edible or nontoxic. Most are too small, tough, or strong-flavored to be worth seeking, but a few others are quite good.

333

20 Hoary alyssum 2
Berteroa incana ✦ *Brassicaceae* (Mustard family)

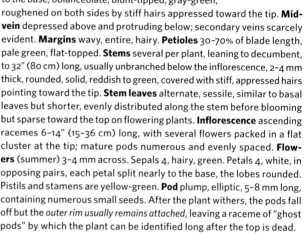

QUICK CHECK: Low, gray-green mustard of dry, sunny sites, the leaves rough and mostly basal; racemes of small white flowers with 4 petals in opposing pairs. **ID difficulty 1.**

DESCRIPTION: Biennial or short-lived perennial from a stout root with multiple crowns. **Basal leaves** numerous, usually wilting before flowering, in a rosette or multiple rosettes packed together, 3–6" (8–15 cm) long, tapered gently to the base, oblanceolate, blunt-tipped, gray-green, roughened on both sides by stiff hairs appressed toward the tip. **Midvein** depressed above and protruding below; secondary veins scarcely evident. **Margins** wavy, entire, hairy. **Petioles** 30–70% of blade length, pale green, flat-topped. **Stems** several per plant, leaning to decumbent, to 32" (80 cm) long, usually unbranched below the inflorescence, 2–4 mm thick, rounded, solid, reddish to green, covered with stiff, appressed hairs pointing toward the tip. **Stem leaves** alternate, sessile, similar to basal leaves but shorter, evenly distributed along the stem before blooming but sparse toward the top on flowering plants. **Inflorescence** ascending racemes 6–14" (15–36 cm) long, with several flowers packed in a flat cluster at the tip; mature pods numerous and evenly spaced. **Flowers** (summer) 3–4 mm across. Sepals 4, hairy, green. Petals 4, white, in opposing pairs, each petal split nearly to the base, the lobes rounded. Pistils and stamens are yellow-green. **Pod** plump, elliptic, 5–8 mm long, containing numerous small seeds. After the plant withers, the pods fall off but the *outer rim usually remains attached*, leaving a raceme of "ghost pods" by which the plant can be identified long after the top is dead.

HABITAT: Dry, disturbed, sunny ground, especially with poor, sandy soil. Common along roadsides, railroads, beaches, gravel pits, parking lots, fallow fields, sandy meadows, lawn edges. Introduced.

FOOD USE: The thin **shoots** can be eaten raw or cooked. Get them before they become tough and raspy with stiff hairs. I usually discard most of the young leaves, which roughen before the stems. The seeds can be used sparingly as a seasoning.

COMMENTS: The edible part is too small to be an important vegetable, but the taste is easy to describe: hot cabbage.

GROUP 23 BASAL LEAVES PRESENT, STEM LEAVES ALTERNATE, TOOTHED

The plants in this group belong to several families, of which the mustard family (*Brassicaceae*) is the most important. All plants in group 23 provide leafy greens or stems (for many it is both). Six species produce an edible underground storage organ—but none of them qualify as staple root vegetables. One species makes an edible fleshy fruit. The plants in this group are not particularly tricky, and there are few dangerous look-similars.

Burdock and lesser celandine are placed in group 22 but might key here because their leaf margins are faintly toothed or wavy, and interpretations of toothiness vary.

TENTATIVE IDENTIFICATION KEY TO GROUP 23
The key is not your final answer!

Sap milky; flowers bluish with 5 petals.	
Basal leaves mostly roundish and soon withering.	
Stem leaves narrow and linear, hairless; stem ridges hairless.	1. Harebell
Stem leaves lanceolate, hairy; stem ridges hairy.	2. American bellflower
Basal leaves mostly heart-shaped; some persist to flowering.	3. Creeping bellflower
Sap not milky.	
Leaf surfaces generally hairless (rarely the midvein or margin may have hairs).	
Basal leaves roundish to heart or kidney-shaped.	
Stems hollow, flowers with 5–10 yellow petals.	
Forms carpets; stems to 7 mm thick; leaves less than 2" (5 cm) across, often with purple centers. Lesser celandine (p. 321).	
Forms clumps; stems often over 11 mm thick; leaves over 2" (5 cm) across, never with purple centers.	4. Marsh-marigold
Stems solid; flowers with 4 white petals.	
Seashore annual with stout, spreading stems and bulbous pods.	5. Scurvy-grass
Moist-soil perennial with thin, erect stems and long, thin pods.	6. Bulbous bittercress
Basal leaves elliptic to obovate with a blunt, rounded tip.	
Stem with faint wing-ridges, hairless; pods 9–17 mm, flat.	7. Field pennycress
Stem not ridged, hairy in the lower half; pods 5–8 mm, half-inflated.	8. Garlic pennycress
Basal leaves long-elliptic, long-lanceolate, to linear with a pointed tip.	
Teeth rounded; larger veins white.	9. Horseradish
Teeth bristle-like; veins not white.	
Leaves less than 10" (25 cm) long; flowers in racemes.	10. Smooth rock cress
Leaves often over 14" (36 cm); flowers in ball-like umbels.	14. Rattlesnake master
Basal leaves triangular to arrowhead-shaped.	15. Strawberry spinach
At least one leaf surface (check both!) has sparse or dense hairs distributed across it.	
Blades of basal and lower leaves taper gradually; it is hard to say where the petiole begins.	
Basal leaves mostly ground-hugging, rippled between prominent lateral veins; teeth faint and blunt; hairs soft.	16. Evening primrose
Basal leaves mostly erect, not rippled; teeth prominent and erratic; hairs stiff.	11. Dame's rocket
The change from petiole to blade is more sudden on basal and lower leaves.	
Leaves commonly exceed 12" (30 cm) in length.	
Blade soft-woolly below, veins depressed above. Burdock (p. 331).	
Blade rough-hairy below, veins flat or protruding above.	17. Prairie-dock
Leaves less than 10" (25 cm) long.	
Flowers with 4 petals and arranged in a raceme.	
Leaf gray-woolly; upper leaves appressed and clasping.	12. Whitetop
Leaf not woolly; upper leaves not appressed or clasping.	13. Garlic mustard
Flowers with numerous petals (ray florets) arranged in a panicle.	18. Bigleaf aster
Flowers with 5 unequal petals, individual at the end of a long, hooked stalk.	
Petals white with a yellow base; leaf moderately hairy to hairless.	19. Canada violet
Petals yellow; leaf densely soft-hairy.	20. Common yellow violet

1 **Harebell** 🐛1 🍃3 ❀2 ❘3
Campanula rotundifolia ♦ family *Campanulaceae*

QUICK CHECK: Thin, wiry, erect stems with linear leaves and nodding, bell-like blue flowers; basal leaves rounded or elongated; sap milky. **ID difficulty 1.**

DESCRIPTION: Perennial from a rhizome, sometimes forming small, dense colonies. **Rhizomes** whitish, knobby, crooked, branching, erratic in thickness but generally less than 8 mm in diameter. Sap milky. Rosettes are present in spring but only rarely do a few leaves persist to flowering. **Basal leaves** roundish, with a deep sinus or ear-like lobes at the base, 0.6–1.5" (1.5–4 cm) across, hairless, the margins with scattered blunt teeth or notched, the notches often white-dotted. Some basal leaves are elongated and blunt-tipped. All major veins arise from the base and are not depressed. **Petioles** very thin, longer than the blade, out of plane with it, channeled, purple or green. **Stems** usually clumped, erect, 12–22" (30–56 cm) tall, unbranched or sparsely branched near the top, purple-brown near the base but green higher up, mostly hairless but faintly hairy near the base. Cross section round but with a small double-ridge coming down from each node. **Stem leaves** *utterly different from basal leaves*: alternate, linear, sessile, long-tapered to the base, overlapping, strongly ascending to erect. Lower stem leaves are wider toward the tip and may have a few teeth; upper leaves are entire. **Inflorescence** a loose, branching cluster (or flowers single) with thread-like leaves, the pedicels thread-thin, nodding to the side in bloom. **Flowers** (summer) blue, 0.5–0.8" (13–20 mm) long, the corolla bell-like, fused for more than half its length, then spreading into 5 abruptly pointed lobes. **Calyx** has 5 linear, pointed, spreading lobes. The pistil has a purple style and white stigma split into 3 recurved parts; there are coiled stamens in the base of the flower.

HABITAT: Dry, sunny, poor, well-drained soil. Pine barrens, cliffs and ledges, steep banks, gravel pits, shore-lines, rocky or sandy prairies. Native. 🔥

FOOD USE: Rhizomes taste okay but are small and rather tough. Young **leaves** and **shoots** can be eaten raw or cooked. **Flowers** make an attractive, mildly-flavored garnish or nibble. **Conservation 3/2/1.**

COMMENTS: The basal and stem leaves are so different that it is hard to reconcile their production by the same plant. The new shoots in late spring are a superb, little-known vegetable.

▲ Basal leaves (including the narrow ones).

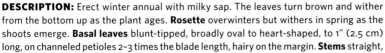

2 American bellflower ⌇ 3 🌿 3 🌼 2 🍃 2
Campanula americana ✦ family *Campanulaceae*

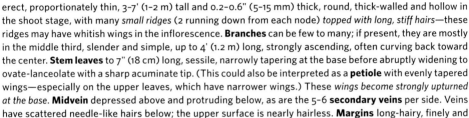

QUICK CHECK: Tall, straight, thin stem with well-spaced, long-lanceolate leaves; sap milky; 5-lobed blue flowers with long, protruding, upturned style. **ID difficulty 2.**

DESCRIPTION: Erect winter annual with milky sap. The leaves turn brown and wither from the bottom up as the plant ages. **Rosette** overwinters but withers in spring as the shoots emerge. **Basal leaves** blunt-tipped, broadly oval to heart-shaped, to 1" (2.5 cm) long, on channeled petioles 2-3 times the blade length, hairy on the margin. **Stems** straight, erect, proportionately thin, 3-7' (1-2 m) tall and 0.2-0.6" (5-15 mm) thick, round, thick-walled and hollow in the shoot stage, with many *small ridges* (2 running down from each node) *topped with long, stiff hairs*—these ridges may have whitish wings in the inflorescence. **Branches** can be few to many; if present, they are mostly in the middle third, slender and simple, up to 4' (1.2 m) long, strongly ascending, often curving back toward the center. **Stem leaves** to 7" (18 cm) long, sessile, narrowly tapering at the base before abruptly widening to ovate-lanceolate with a sharp acuminate tip. (This could also be interpreted as a **petiole** with evenly tapered wings—especially on the upper leaves, which have narrower wings.) These *wings become strongly upturned at the base*. **Midvein** depressed above and protruding below, as are the 5-6 **secondary veins** per side. Veins have scattered needle-like hairs below; the upper surface is nearly hairless. **Margins** long-hairy, finely and remotely serrated, the teeth *pointing forward and curving inward like a rolling wave* with a light-colored claw at the tip. Upper leaves are shorter and droop; they often have a dimple near the base. **Inflorescence** loose, terminal, spike-like racemes 10-40" (25-100 cm) long. The lower part has

▲ Basal leaves.   (Continued on the next page.)

2   American bellflower (continued)

▲ Shoot at the ideal stage for eating.

typical leaves, while the upper raceme has a single linear, pointed, downcurved bract, with a prominent light midvein, beneath each flower. Short pedicels are borne in clusters at leaf nodes. Flower buds are strongly ridged, purple, and white at the base. **Flowers** (mid to late summer) about 0.9" (23 mm) across, the corolla blue with a short tube that spreads widely into 5 pointed, hooked lobes. Sepals are fused at the base, then wide-spreading and linear. The *style protrudes conspicuously and usually curves upward*, terminating in a stigma that splits into 3 or 4 parts. **Fruit** a small, many-seeded capsule.

HABITAT: Well-drained, rich soil in moderately disturbed hardwood forests, such as steep slopes, high floodplains, recently logged forests, forest edges, and dirt road margins. Native. 🔥

FOOD USE: Young **shoots** and **leaves** can be eaten raw or cooked, and at the ideal stage are extremely tender and mild. **Flower buds** and **flowers** are also edible. **Conservation 2/1.**

COMMENTS: American bellflower greens have a peculiar flavor—almost fishy, slightly sweet, but very good, especially when cooked. This nearly-unknown edible would be more popular if it were more distinct when young. It is the best of the bellflowers, and remains one of the best kept foraging secrets in our region. **AKA** *Campanulastrum americanum.*

3   Creeping bellflower   🌱 3 🥬 3 │ 3 🌿 2 🌸 2 📖 IWE-107
Campanula rapunculoides ✦ family *Campanulaceae*

QUICK CHECK: Heart-shaped hairy basal leaves, becoming lanceolate on an unbranched stem with drooping blue-purple flowers on one side. **ID difficulty 2.**

DESCRIPTION: Perennial forming colonies by thin rhizomes that send down enlarged vertical **taproots**, *usually clustered*, light brown and smooth outside with whitish flesh. *Sap milky.* **Basal leaves** heart-shaped, 2–6" (5–15 cm) long, densely soft-hairy on both sides (longer on the veins below). Basal leaves are present at flowering—but *not those at the*

base of a stalk. **Veins** and midvein deeply depressed above and protruding below; there are 4 major secondary veins from the base. **Margins** have broad, rounded, closely-spaced teeth with a *tiny tan nipple on the distal side*. **Petioles** 1.5–3 times the blade length with a *sharp-edged, dark-green channel* that is *wider at both ends*, with erect hairs especially on channel edges and the underside. **Stems** 24–38" (60–100 cm) tall and 4–6 mm thick, single or in small clumps, erect when young, usually gently arched or leaning when mature, *unbranched*, round, solid, the surface green to purplish, smooth with faint ridges running down from each node, *hairy on the ridges* when young, sometimes becoming hairless with age. **Stem leaves** alternate, the lower ones similar to the basal leaves; upward they decrease in size to about 1" (2.5 cm) and become lanceolate to triangular, hairy only on the main veins below. Petioles also decrease; upper leaves are sessile. **Inflorescence** a terminal raceme up to half the stem's length, the flowers single, paired, or in small clusters on curved and drooping pedicels tending to one side. Occasionally there are small raceme branches. **Flowers** (mid to late summer) 0.8–1.4" (2–3.5 cm) long. **Corolla** blue-purple, bell-like, divided halfway to the base into 5 triangular, spreading lobes. **Calyx** 5 green, narrowly triangular, sharp, spreading to reflexed lobes about 20% of petal length. **Fruit** a round 5–8 mm capsule that dries to release its seeds through multiple openings.

CONFUSING PLANTS: Basal leaves may be told from those of violets or asters by the milky sap.

HABITAT: Escaped from cultivation and persistent. Most commonly seen near old home sites, also spreading to roadsides, meadows, and fields. Likes light shade but sometimes grows in full sun.

FOOD USE: Dig the **roots** at the base of the plant at any time of year; they are best from fall through spring. They are branched and usually thin near the surface; the enlarged section begins a few inches deep. Eat them cooked. Young **leaves** and **shoots** can be gathered when tender in spring and early summer and are good raw or cooked, although their texture is hairy. **Flowers** and **flower buds** are edible raw or cooked.

COMMENTS: This is one of our best cooked root vegetables, with a mild and sweet flavor. The leaves have the slightly fishy taste characteristic of this genus; they are one of my favorite fried greens. This was once a popular plant of perennial gardens but has now fallen so far out of favor that it has been made illegal to grow in many jurisdictions, despite minimal invasive tendencies.

4 Marsh-marigold 🌿 1 📖 FH-200
Caltha palustris ✦ *Ranunculaceae* (Buttercup family)

QUICK CHECK: Short, clumped, stout, multi-stemmed, glossy herb with rounded or kidney-shaped basal leaves on long petioles. **ID difficulty 2.**

DESCRIPTION: Perennial from a stout root system, often with several adjacent crowns. **Basal leaves** 3–6 per rosette, broader than long, kidney-shaped to roundish with a deep sinus where the petiole attaches, 2–8" (5–20 cm) across, hairless, glossy, thin and rubbery. All major veins arise from the base; these and veinlets are *lightly etched above*. **Margins** have broad, shallow, rounded teeth, often with whitish nipple-tips when mature. **Petioles** 2–3 times the blade, 4–10 mm thick with a pinhole hollow, D-shaped in cross section, nearly flat on top but with a *shallow double groove*. **Stems** typically several per plant, the outer ones leaning, stout, to 22" (56 cm) tall and 0.7" (18 mm) thick, hairless, thick-walled and spongy with a small hollow in the center, shallowly furrowed, zigzag, usually with a few large branches. Nodes have small papery sheaths. **Stem leaves** reduced in size with shorter petioles (the uppermost sessile). At harvest time the plant shows many leaves huddled close together and the stems extending scarcely if at all beyond them, with clumps of spherical, hairless, pea-sized flower buds pressed against a leaf. **Inflorescence** single or in clusters up to 7 from the leaf axils, each flower on a thick, ridged pedicel. **Flowers** (early to mid spring) bright yellow, up to 2" (5 cm) across with 5–9 overlapping petals (sepals), dozens of stamens, and several pistils. **Fruit** a green, star-like cluster of elongated, beaked, claw-like pods, splitting open when ripe to release the seeds.

CONFUSING PLANTS: Lesser celandine (p. 321) has much smaller leaves and flowers.

HABITAT: Hardwood swamps, shaded or semi-shaded wet ground, ditches, and occasionally in open marshland. Native.

FOOD USE: Collect **young growth** before the flowers open in early spring. I usually pluck whole stems with attached leaves and flower buds. To rid the greens of their bitterness, boil in voluminous water for 20 minutes or more, changing water if desired, then drain. **Conservation 1.**

COMMENTS: In many areas marsh-marigold can be collected easily in huge quantity and is a popular spring green. It is rather bitter but can be made very mild through long cooking, after which you'll have a pile of super-soft "green pudding." **AKA** cowslip.

WARNING: Should not be eaten raw, as it is mildly toxic and quite acrid tasting in this state.

▲ Marsh-marigold seedpod.

▲ Young plants at the right stage for eating.

5 Scurvy-grass 3
genus *Cochlearia* ♦ *Brassicaceae* (Mustard family)

QUICK CHECK: Tiny plant with small, broad, succulent basal leaves on long petioles; branching stems with small, blunt leaves and 4-petaled flowers. **ID difficulty 2.**

DESCRIPTION: Small, short-lived perennial or winter annual. **Basal leaves** in a rosette, fleshy, hairless, almost veinless, 0.3–0.8" (8–20 mm) long and about as broad, the blade widening abruptly at the base, triangular to broadly ovate, obovate, or heart-shaped, blunt-tipped. **Margins** usually entire but sometimes wavy or slightly toothed. **Petioles** thin, channeled, 0.4–4.5" (1–11 cm) long (longest where they must reach past rocks for sunlight). Basal leaves wither as flowering approaches. **Stems** usually multiple, 2–12" long, erect to prostrate or decumbent, stiff and tough at maturity, green with purplish highlights, *strongly ridged* with *internodes often much longer than the leaves.* Central stems are often erect but shorter with many spreading branches, often in imperfect whorls or offset pairs. **Stem leaves** borne mostly toward the tips of the branches or stems; they are nominally alternate but *usually in offset pairs.* The blades are sessile or nearly so, tapered to the base, usually narrower than basal leaves, with a few blunt teeth in erratic locations. **Inflorescence** *with many small leaves packed behind it*; a short, crowded, terminal raceme to 1" (2.5 cm) long. **Flowers** (June–August) 4–5 mm across with 4 blunt, obovate white petals, not touching each other. **Pod** plump, about 5 mm broad and almost equally long, with a seam down the center, turning from green to yellow-brown, containing several rounded seeds.

SPECIES: *C. groenlandica* and *C. tridactylites* are very similar and used identically.

HABITAT: Open areas near the sea: beaches, tidal flats, rocky shores and slopes, sometimes tundra or stream banks. Likes high nitrogen levels and therefore is more common where dead seaweeds get caught behind rocks, or near seabird colonies. Native.

FOOD USE: Tender **leaves** and **stems** are eaten raw or cooked. They are excellent—like a slightly salty, slightly hot cabbage. **Conservation 2.**

COMMENTS: This dainty herb is credited with saving many sailors of yore from scurvy. It has been sometimes cultivated as a vegetable. The genus name means "ear-shaped" in reference to the leaf. Leaf, stem, and pod shape is highly variable. While the taxonomy within this genus remains unsettled, the group is very easy to recognize. The association with seabird colonies is dramatic—in some regions it is found nowhere except the heavy bird turd zones, and it grows much larger in these locations.

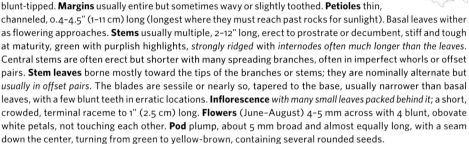

6 Bulbous bittercress 🖋 2 🏮
Cardamine bulbosa ✦ *Brassicaceae* (Mustard family)

QUICK CHECK: Small plant with erect, unbranched stem and broad lower leaves; upper leaves narrow, sessile, with large teeth; 4-petaled white flowers in racemes. **ID difficulty 2.**

DESCRIPTION: Perennial herb from a white, amorphous, knobby **tuber** 8–15 mm across, with roots on all sides, sometimes connected in short chains. **Basal leaves** appear in fall and persist through the winter, disappearing with flowering. They are 0.5–1.5" (13–38 mm) wide, hairless or nearly so, entire but with gentle indents where veins meet the margin. **Veins** mostly obscure and flat on the upper surface. **Petioles** about twice the blade length, erect, thin, channeled, with scattered minute hairs. **Stems** often clustered (from adjacent tubers), 12–24" (30–60 cm) tall, 1.5–3 mm thick, the bases usually purple with very fine hairs; above that hairs are fewer and finer. The lower stem is roundish, becoming angled higher up, with a flat area running down from each leaf axil. **Branches** rare; if present they are strongly ascending. **Stem leaves** 4–8, widely spaced, 1.2–2.4" (3–6 cm) long, on short petioles (becoming sessile upward), ovate to lanceolate, the veins mostly obscure (visible ones are faintly depressed), the margins with 0–3 widely spaced teeth per side. Uppermost leaves are smaller, narrower, sessile, with larger teeth or small lobes. **Inflorescence** terminal racemes 2–7" (5–18 cm) long, the flowers in a round-topped bunch, the pedicels ascending. Much smaller racemes may grow on very low branches. **Flowers** (spring to early summer) with 4 petals, white or rarely pink, 0.6–0.8" (15–20 mm) across. **Pods** ascending, thin and rod-like, about 1" (2.5 cm) long, on a pedicel about the same length.

HABITAT: Low, muddy areas in shade or sun: edges of temporary pools in floodplain forests and low, rich woods, swamps, seeps, fens, marshes, pond margins. Native.

FOOD USE: The **tuber** resides close to the surface and can be unearthed by hand. All **tender parts** above ground can be eaten raw or cooked. All parts have a horseradish flavor. **Conservation 3/2.**

COMMENTS: This might be the showiest of our bittercresses. It thrives in cool weather and grows larger and lusher in the South where winters are mild and spring lasts longer.

RELATED EDIBLES: Other members of the genus *Cardamine* are edible and spicy, with a horseradish flavor; a few strongly resemble this one.

7 Field pennycress 🌿 1 ⬚ 2 🍃 1 ⬚
Thlaspi arvense ✦ *Brassicaceae* (Mustard family)

QUICK CHECK: Tall, narrow, strong-smelling, spring-blooming mustard with tiny white flowers, unlobed stem leaves, and large, flat seed pods. **ID difficulty 2.**

DESCRIPTION: Erect winter annual with a slightly unpleasant smell. **Basal leaves** in dense rosettes that wither by flowering, the blades 1–3.5" (2.5–9 cm) long, obovate or elliptic to nearly round, *hairless*, the tips rounded, entire or with a few shallow, blunt, often whitish nipple-teeth. **Midvein** and major veins are slightly depressed above. **Petioles** winged, gradually widening into the blade. **Stems** single or branching at the base, to 40" (1 m) tall and 1 cm thick, straight, erect, roundish with numerous *wing-ridges*, 3 of them running down from each node, *hairless*. **Branches** rare below the flowering top; form is taller than wide. **Stem leaves** alternate, ascending, overlapping, 1.5–3" (4–8 cm) long, lanceolate, *clasping* with pointed, ear-like lobes at the base, hairless. **Secondary veins** *flat or nearly so*; the midvein is depressed. **Margins** curve downward with a few large, blunt teeth. Uppermost leaves are scattered, smaller, and more pointed with larger teeth. **Inflorescence** ascending racemes at the apex, the rachis ridged; flowers in a tight cluster at the tip. **Flowers** tiny with four elliptic white petals that scarcely spread open. **Pod** *broad, flattened, almost round, winged, nearly the size of a dime* (10–17 mm), notched at the tip, held ascending on a slightly ascending pedicel 1–2 times its length.

HABITAT: Rich disturbed ground, especially on heavy soil, with lots of sun. Most commonly seen in agricultural fields, on roadsides, and in building sites. Introduced.

FOOD USE: All tender parts are edible, but the **leaves** and **flower buds** have a very strong flavor; I remove them before cooking shoots. **Seeds** can be used as a seasoning.

COMMENTS: I consider this a second-rate mustard.

Related edible:
8 Garlic pennycress ✦ *Thlaspi alliaceum*

This is a recently established exotic weed that is rapidly spreading; in many parts of our region it is now far more common than field pennycress. **Stems** more slender and typically 10–30" (25–75 cm) tall. They are round, without wing-ridges; near the base they have long, soft, sparse hairs (as do the leaves) but the upper stem and leaves are hairless. **Pods** much smaller than those of field pennycress (4–7 mm), and inflated. **AKA** *Mummenhoffia alliacea.*

▲ Rapidly expanding.

9 Horseradish 2 2
Armoracia rusticana ◆ *Brassicaceae* (Mustard family)

QUICK CHECK: Thick clumps of large, erect, irregularly toothed or scalloped, dock-like leaves on long petioles; tall stalk with racemes of white flowers. **ID difficulty 1.**

DESCRIPTION: Perennial plant from a large multi-crowned taproot or taproot cluster, with multiple adjacent rosettes. **Basal leaves** 8-30" (20-90 cm) long, hairless, ovate to oblong or narrowly oblanceolate, often curly (with much longer waves than dock leaves), the tip rounded or blunt, the base gently tapered into the petiole. **Midvein** broad, white, and flat above, protruding and rounded below. Secondary veins numerous, prominent, white, 65-85° to the midvein, flat or raised above and protruding below, running straight halfway to the edge, then forking, the branches looping to meet the next vein. **Margins** scalloped with irregularly sized, rounded teeth. *Some basal or lower stem leaves are deeply pinnately lobed with very thin lobes.* **Petioles** 70-110% of blade length, solid, hairless, broadly and shallowly channeled. **Stalks** 2-5' (60-150 cm) tall and 0.4-0.8" (1-2 cm) thick, single or multiple, erect, solid, roundish but ridged, hairless, thick, branched only in the inflorescence; usually *emanating where rosette leaves are small or absent.* **Stem leaves** similar to the basal but narrower; the uppermost and those in the inflorescence are linear and often nearly entire. **Inflorescence** a large panicle of numerous ascending racemes, the flowers crowded at the tip. **Flowers** 11-13 mm across with 4 blunt, white petals, wrinkly and overlapping at the base. **Pods** tiny, 2-3 mm long, plump, slightly flattened, on a thin, almost appressed pedicel—the fruit often falling off and not maturing.

CONFUSING PLANTS: Dock (p. 323) leaves lack teeth and their veins are not white.

HABITAT: An escape from cultivation persisting and spreading on roadsides and in old fields; usually near old homesteads. Intolerant of shade.

FOOD USE: Young **leaves** and **shoots** in spring and early summer can be eaten raw or used as a potherb. More often, sections of **root** are peeled and blended or grated as a seasoning. The root can be collected at any time, but is best when the plant is dormant.

COMMENTS: This is exactly the same as cultivated horseradish. While not generally abundant, horseradish survives and spreads at homestead sites and is found as scattered robust colonies or individual plants. To the untrained eye, a patch of horseradish looks like an overgrown dock colony.

10 Smooth rock cress 🌿 2 | 3 🥬 2
Boechera laevigata ✦ *Brassicaceae* (Mustard family)

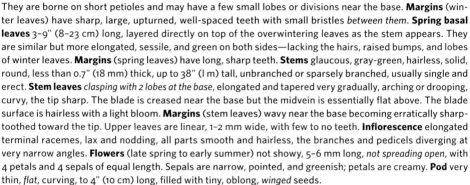

QUICK CHECK: Basal rosette of tough, dark green, lance-elliptic leaves with large, sharp teeth; stem leaves similar but thinner, sessile, and light green. Pods long and narrow. **ID difficulty 2.**

DESCRIPTION: Biennial mustard with a basal rosette producing 2 leaf forms. **Overwintering leaves** *evergreen*, narrowly elliptic, tough and leathery, glossy, 1.5-6" (4-15 cm) long, dark-green with short hairs from raised bumps on the upper surface, often purplish below. They are borne on short petioles and may have a few small lobes or divisions near the base. **Margins** (winter leaves) have sharp, large, upturned, well-spaced teeth with small bristles *between them*. **Spring basal leaves** 3-9" (8-23 cm) long, layered directly on top of the overwintering leaves as the stem appears. They are similar but more elongated, sessile, and green on both sides—lacking the hairs, raised bumps, and lobes of winter leaves. **Margins** (spring leaves) have long, sharp teeth. **Stems** glaucous, gray-green, hairless, solid, round, less than 0.7" (18 mm) thick, up to 38" (1 m) tall, unbranched or sparsely branched, usually single and erect. **Stem leaves** *clasping with 2 lobes at the base*, elongated and tapered very gradually, arching or drooping, curvy, the tip sharp. The blade is creased near the base but the midvein is essentially flat above. The blade surface is hairless with a light bloom. **Margins** (stem leaves) wavy near the base becoming erratically sharp-toothed toward the tip. Upper leaves are linear, 1-2 mm wide, with few to no teeth. **Inflorescence** elongated terminal racemes, lax and nodding, all parts smooth and hairless, the branches and pedicels diverging at very narrow angles. **Flowers** (late spring to early summer) not showy, 5-6 mm long, *not spreading open*, with 4 petals and 4 sepals of equal length. Sepals are narrow, pointed, and greenish; petals are creamy. **Pod** very thin, *flat*, curving, to 4" (10 cm) long, filled with tiny, oblong, *winged* seeds.

HABITAT: Well-drained hardwood forests with canopy openings and disturbances such as logging, windthrow, flood, or construction. More common in hilly, mountainous, or rocky terrain, or poor sandy soil—often on trails or roadsides. Native.

FOOD USE: Tender spring **leaves**, **shoots**, and **flower buds** can be eaten raw or cooked. **Conservation 2.**

COMMENTS: This is a good, mild-flavored, native mustard that is hardly known as a food plant. The overwintering rosette is attractive and unmistakable, but the evergreen basal leaves are hardly worth eating. However, the new spring rosette leaves are good, and sometimes very hot. **AKA** *Arabis laevigata*.

RELATED EDIBLES: Other members of the genus *Boechera* are edible. *B. canadensis* is very similar in appearance but has longer, drooping pods and non-clasping leaves. *B. missouriense* has leaves with much more prominent teeth that are more numerous on the stem. There are several more in our area.

11 Dame's rocket 🌿 2 ⎸ 3 🌿 2 ✿ 3
Hesperis matronalis ✦ *Brassicaceae* (Mustard family)

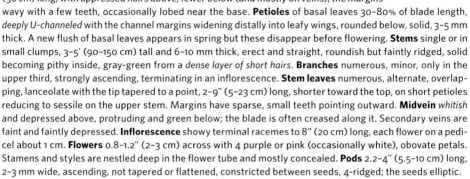

QUICK CHECK: Colonial herb with erect, chest-high stems unbranched below the top, toothed hairy leaves, racemes of 4-petaled pink-purple flowers and long, thin pods. **ID difficulty 2.**

DESCRIPTION: Perennial herb spreading by rhizomes. **Basal rosettes** prominent in autumn and winter, the leaves *mostly erect*, long-elliptic, tapered at the base, blunt-tipped, to 12" (30 cm) long, with appressed hairs above, fewer below (and mostly on veins), the margins wavy with a few teeth, occasionally lobed near the base. **Petioles** of basal leaves 30–80% of blade length, *deeply U-channeled* with the channel margins widening distally into leafy wings, rounded below, solid, 3–5 mm thick. A new flush of basal leaves appears in spring but these disappear before flowering. **Stems** single or in small clumps, 3–5' (90–150 cm) tall and 6–10 mm thick, erect and straight, roundish but faintly ridged, solid becoming pithy inside, gray-green from a *dense layer of short hairs*. **Branches** numerous, minor, only in the upper third, strongly ascending, terminating in an inflorescence. **Stem leaves** numerous, alternate, overlapping, lanceolate with the tip tapered to a point, 2–9" (5–23 cm) long, shorter toward the top, on short petioles reducing to sessile on the upper stem. Margins have sparse, small teeth pointing outward. **Midvein** whitish and depressed above, protruding and green below; the blade is often creased along it. Secondary veins are faint and faintly depressed. **Inflorescence** showy terminal racemes to 8" (20 cm) long, each flower on a pedicel about 1 cm. **Flowers** 0.8–1.2" (2–3 cm) across with 4 purple or pink (occasionally white), obovate petals. Stamens and styles are nestled deep in the flower tube and mostly concealed. **Pods** 2.2–4" (5.5–10 cm) long, 2–3 mm wide, ascending, not tapered or flattened, constricted between seeds, 4-ridged; the seeds elliptic.

CONFUSING PLANTS: Phloxes have 5 petals and paired leaves with no teeth.

HABITAT: Forest borders, roadsides, old homesteads, woodlots, open woods—generally in rich but well-drained soil in full sun to moderate shade. Introduced. **I**

FOOD USE: The large **winter leaves** persist through hard frost and make a nice potherb when few are available, but they are not as good as the **spring leaves**. In late spring the **shoots** make an okay vegetable raw and an excellent one cooked. Use any tender **greens** at the shoot top before flowering. **Flower buds** are okay; **flowers** have a slightly sweet-hot flavor and add beautiful color to food.

COMMENTS: A common, attractive, invasive flower of open areas and forest margins, this plant was introduced in flower gardens and has escaped widely. Although not much touted in the wild food literature, it is a good mustard for eating, with a surprisingly mild flavor.

12 **Whitetop** 2 1 1
Cardaria draba ✦ *Brassicaceae* (Mustard family)

QUICK CHECK: Hairy colonial mustard with grayish leaves and stems, flat-topped clusters of white flowers in spring, and plump, heart-shaped pods. **ID difficulty 2.**

DESCRIPTION: Perennial from a root system that spreads laterally to form colonies. **Basal leaves** and lower stem leaves are elliptic to obovate, 1–3" (2.5–8 cm) long, flat, fleshy, entire, acute at the base, blunt and often indented at the tip, both sides *densely coated with soft hair*. They wither about flowering time. **Veins** offset by light color, flat or scarcely depressed above and flat or scarcely protruding below. **Petioles** of lower leaves up to 150% of blade length, broad and nearly flat on top, D-shaped below. **Stems** erect and single with competition; multiple and leaning without, 12–28" (30–70 cm) tall and 7–11 mm thick, solid, roundish but slightly angled, the color uniform gray-green, *densely soft-hairy*, branched only in the upper part. **Stem leaves** alternate, held erect and appressed on progressively shorter petioles—sessile and clasping near the top. Upper leaves are elliptic with blunt tips and scattered blunt teeth, with the veins more strongly depressed above and protruding below. **Inflorescence** multiple racemes, at first compact with flowers crowded at the tip, the several adjacent clusters about the same level, giving a flat-topped appearance in bloom. The white flowers often show even in the bud stage. During and after flowering the racemes lengthen a little and the right-angled, straight pedicels lengthen a lot (ultimately becoming 3–5 times as long as the flower), resulting in a gangly, crowded cluster where the members of adjacent racemes mingle. **Flowers** 6–10 mm across with four blunt, obovate, widely spaced, white petals, not held at right angles to each other. **Pods** short, plump, *lopsided*

▲ Much more abundant westward.

heart-shaped, with a line dividing them into two unequal "halves."

HABITAT: Disturbed sunny areas with well-drained soil; fields, roadsides, vacant lots, pastures. Introduced.

FOOD USE: Tender new **shoots**, **leafy tops**, and **flower bud clusters** (spring) can be used raw or cooked like a strong broccoli.

COMMENTS: One of the most common weedy mustards of urban areas in the High Plains, whitetop can often be collected in great quantity with little effort. Some other mustards are also sometimes called "whitetop." **AKA** *Lepidium draba*, hoary cress, heart-pod hoary cress.

13 Garlic mustard Ⅰ 3 ✦ 1 Ⅰ 1 📖 NG-250
Alliaria petiolata ✦ *Brassicaceae* (Mustard family)

QUICK CHECK: Deeply toothed, triangular stem leaves with hairy petioles and garlic odor; broad, kidney-shaped basal leaves. **ID difficulty 2.**

DESCRIPTION: Biennial from a small, branching, whitish taproot. The scent of vegetative parts is pungent with an overtone of garlic. **Basal leaves** in a rosette of 3-7, kidney-shaped to rounded with overlapping basal lobes, 1.5-3.5" (4-9 cm) wide, hairless above with long, soft, sparse hairs below. There are 4-6 major secondary veins from the base. **Veins** and veinlets form a network that is deeply and narrowly depressed above and protruding below. **Margins** have *long but rounded, outward-pointing teeth,* each with a light, *downcurved tip.* **Petioles** reddish to green, up to four times as long as the leaf on basal and lower stem leaves, shallowly channeled, hairy along the upper channel margin. **Stems** single or multiple, straight, purple at the base, erect, 18-40" (0.5-1 m) tall and 5-10 mm thick, round in cross section, solid when young (pithy at maturity), smooth with a light bloom and long, scattered, soft, erect hairs toward the base. **Branches** only near the apex, ascending, terminating in an inflorescence. **Stem leaves** alternate, heart-shaped to triangular with an elongated tip, on progressively shorter petioles, the teeth becoming larger and more pointed on upper leaves. **Inflorescence** multiple terminal racemes, at first crowded with flowers and buds at the tip, later elongating to 8-12" (20-30 cm) with well-spaced pedicels. **Flowers** 6-8 mm across with 4 blunt, white, spreading petals. **Pods** 1-2.3" (2.5-6 cm) long, rod-like, curving upward, on short pedicels of equal thickness.

HABITAT: Hardwood forests with rich soil, especially in human-altered landscapes. **I**

FOOD USE: Roots are horseradishy but small and tough. Tender **leaves** can be used at any time, but more for seasoning than bulk. **Shoots**, before the flowers have opened in mid spring, are the mildest part of the plant and can be used raw in salads, cooked in soups or stir-fry, or steamed like asparagus.

COMMENTS: This weed is one of the most destructive invasive plants in eastern North America. It sometimes takes over woodlands and kills off 90% of all other herbaceous plants, forming a near monoculture through competitive exclusion and allelopathic chemicals. According to Dr. John Kallas, it is also one of the most nutrient-dense foods known.

▼ Shoot at the optimum stage for eating.

14 Rattlesnake master 2
Eryngium yuccifolium + Apiaceae (Carrot family)

QUICK CHECK: Long, stiff, sharp-tipped, yucca-like leaves with spiny-toothed margins; ball-like clusters of tiny pale flowers. **ID difficulty 1.**

DESCRIPTION: Perennial from a multi-headed knobby root mass. **Basal leaves** strap-like, resembling grass or yucca leaves, linear, stiff and leathery, often U-channeled but not keeled or folded, erect to ascending, 1–3' (30–90 cm) long and 0.6–1.5" (1.5–4 cm) wide, sessile, needle-tipped, the surface hairless and strongly glaucous. **Veins** parallel and flat or nearly so on both sides. **Margins** have *widely spaced, long, sharp, semi-stiff bristle teeth.* **Stems** single per crown but often crowded because crowns are usually packed together, 2–5' (60–150 cm) tall and 0.3–0.6" (8–15 mm) thick, erect, round, hollow with thick walls, jointed, simple or few-branched in the upper third, the surface hairless, smooth, and glaucous. **Stem leaves** alternate, clasping, few per stalk and

widely spaced, vertical, similar to basal leaves but progressively smaller upward. **Inflorescence** few to several densely packed heads (compact umbels) in an irregularly forking or umbel-like cluster at the apex. **Heads** 0.4–1" (1–2.5 cm) long, ball or egg-shaped, pale, containing numerous flowers, spiky from a stiff bract beneath each flower. There are long, stiff bracts at the inflorescence junctures, and a whorl of 5–10 smaller bracts beneath most heads. **Flowers** (mid to late summer) 2–3 mm wide with 5 white to faintly greenish, oblong, blunt petals, not spreading widely; sexual parts protrude well beyond the petals. **Fruit** an angled schizocarp 5–7 mm long that splits in two at maturity.

HABITAT: Tallgrass prairies and rich-soiled savannahs; now mostly on roadsides and rocky ridges or slopes. Often planted ornamentally. Native.

FOOD USE: The tender bases of young **shoots** can be eaten in late spring, raw or cooked. You may want to peel them. **Conservation 3.**

COMMENTS: This plant has been used medicinally for many purposes—including as a snakebite remedy, hence the name. The genus contains many species, some of which are traditional vegetables or flavorings in various parts of the world. While our other species are *probably* safe, this is the only one that I have eaten on multiple occasions. Like other tallgrass prairie plants, it has suffered greatly from habitat loss. A relative, *E. leavenworthii*, lacks a common name despite being arguably the most strikingly beautiful North American plant. Check it out.

349

15 Strawberry spinach 🌿 3 🍓 3 📖 IWE-357
Chenopodium capitatum • family *Amaranthaceae*

QUICK CHECK: Triangular or arrowhead-shaped basal leaves on long, flimsy petioles; fleshy, red, glob-like clusters of fruit. **ID difficulty 1.**

DESCRIPTION: Weedy annual or winter annual. **Basal leaves** in a rosette of 7–15, laying on the ground or weakly ascending, 2–5" (5–13 cm) long, triangular or arrowhead shaped, somewhat ruffled, light green, thin, hairless, smooth but not glossy, the tip pointed but not sharp. **Midvein** and major veins lightly depressed above and protruding below; veinlets are mostly obscure. **Margins** entire on smaller leaves, the larger ones wavy or with a few large, scattered, outward-pointing teeth. **Petioles** *long, thin, flimsy, shallowly channeled,* 100–180% of blade length. **Stems** erect, leaning, or prostrate, branching mostly at the base, solid, hairless, ridged, zigzag, 12–28" (30–70 cm) tall. **Stem leaves** alternate, on shorter petioles, otherwise similar to basal. **Inflorescence** terminal interrupted spikes of dense, ball-like clusters. **Flowers** (mid summer to fall) tiny and unshowy with no petals, the parts hard to distinguish. As they mature, the *sepals expand and become juicy and deep red,* crowding together. The seeds ripen inside of these red, **strawberry-like balls,** which are the plant's most distinctive feature—while fruiting it is virtually unmistakable. The stems droop under their weight.

CONFUSING PLANTS: Maple-leaved goosefoot (p. 634) lacks basal leaves.

HABITAT: Forests on poor soil that have been disturbed through logging, fire, flood, windstorms, or construction. Also, clearings and roadsides in such forests. Occasionally becomes an agricultural weed. Native. 🔥

FOOD USE: From early summer through early fall the **greens** can be used raw or cooked. The juicy, red **fruit/flower clusters** are mildly sweet and make an attractive addition to salads or cooked vegetable dishes, or a fun snack. They can be eaten raw or cooked—the taste is like sweet, juicy beets. **Conservation 1.**

COMMENTS: This is an iconic yet exotic wild edible of our northern forests. The red "berries" are often dismissed as "flavorless" because they don't taste like strawberries, but I think they're delicious. The seeds can remain dormant for centuries in the soil, only germinating after a fire or other catastrophe, making its abundance fleeting. This species is sometimes sold in seed catalogs. **AKA** strawberry blite.

16 Evening primrose ✿ 2 ❙ 2 ✑ 1 ✿ 2 ✿ 2 ❀ 2
Oenothera biennis ✦ family *Onagraceae*   📖 FH-274

QUICK CHECK: Numerous long-lanceolate leaves with whitish midveins; the stem tall, unbranched, and erect; raceme of large 4-petaled yellow flowers. **ID difficulty 2.**

DESCRIPTION: Biennial with a rosette of numerous layered leaves, often hugging the ground, that disappear by flowering. **Basal leaves** narrowly elliptic to oblanceolate, up to 9" (23 cm) long, decurrent or tapered to the base, the tip abruptly blunt-pointed, with soft, straight, erect hairs on both sides. **Midvein** *prominently offset* by whitish or light red color, flat to slightly raised above and protruding below. Major secondary veins 11–15 per side, often whitish, 60° to the midvein, arching toward the tip, almost reaching the margin, each vein flat at the bottom of a broad valley on the upper side (the blade is raised between them giving a rippled look). **Margins** sometimes wavy, entire or with widely scattered, broad, shallow, nipple-tipped teeth. **Petioles** winged, 10–40% of blade length (but it is hard to say where the petiole ends and the blade begins), broadly and shallowly channeled, the underside bluntly keeled. **Stems** single, erect, stiff, straight, round, solid at first becoming pithy, *unbranched*, 4–7' (1.2–2.1 m) tall and 0.4–0.7" (10–18 mm) thick, sparsely coated with long, straight, erect hairs, some of them growing from *red bumps*. **Stem leaves** alternate, numerous, 3–6" (8–15 cm) long, on short petioles near the base, sessile near the top. **Inflorescence** a terminal spike to 28" (70 cm) long, the rachis angled, flowers borne singly in the axil of a bract.

Flowers (mid summer to early fall) with an enlarged green base 0.6" (15 mm) long, narrowing to a yellow tube 3–4 mm wide and 1.5–2" (4–5 cm) long. At the end of the tube are 4 linear, canoe-shaped, recurved, claw-tipped, dull yellow sepals about 1" (2.5 cm) long. **Petals** 4, broad-tipped, shallowly notched, bright yellow, overlapping scarcely if at all when fully open and spread about 1.5" (4 cm) wide. There are 8 stamens and the pistils split into 4 parts; the sexual parts are all yellow. Flowers open in the evening and close the following morning. **Fruit** an ascending, cylindrical, slightly tapered, 4-section pod 0.8" (2 cm) long, the tip truncated and depressed, splitting open after maturity with recurved lobes to release numerous tiny, brown, elongated seeds. (Continued on the next page.)

▲ Fall rosette.

16 Evening primrose (continued)

RELATED EDIBLES: There are many species of evening primrose in North America. All are safe to try but many are too tough or strong to be food.

HABITAT: Sunny, well-drained, disturbed soil: farm fields, pastures, building sites, gravel pits, beaches, roadsides, riverbanks, sloped prairies. Native.

FOOD USE: Dig **roots** from fall through spring from rosettes that lack a stem; cook them before eating. Tender, erect **leaves** from second-year plants in spring, just before the stem bolts, make a decent potherb. In late spring **shoots** can be eaten after peeling and cooking. **Flower buds** (located *above* the open flowers) are eaten raw or cooked. **Flowers** make a pleasant nibble or cooked vegetable. The **seeds** from ripe, dry pods can be ground and used in hot cereal or breads. **Conservation 2/1/1.**

COMMENTS: A common and versatile plant, sometimes subdivided into multiple species. All parts but the flowers and seeds are slightly irritating to the mouth and throat, especially when raw.

17 Prairie-dock 🕭 2
Silphium terebinthinaceum ✦
Asteraceae (Composite family)

QUICK CHECK: Enormous basal leaves held erect on long petioles; very tall stems with alternate, reduced leaves and large, yellow, composite heads. **ID difficulty 1.**

DESCRIPTION: Perennial, the larger plants with multiple rosettes from a multi-headed crown. **Basal leaves** 10–22" (25–56 cm) long, elliptic to ovate, thick, tough, *flat except small curls on the basal lobes,* bumpy, *rough-hairy below, hairless above.* **Veins** *raised on both sides;* secondary veins numerous and prominent, 65–90° to the midvein. **Margins** hairy, usually with broad nipple-tipped teeth (occasionally they are lobed or entire). **Petioles** erect, straight, stiff, 80–350% of blade length, solid, roundish, not channeled or keeled, roughened by scattered short, stiff, hairs oriented downward, with a small sheath at the base. **Stem leaves** on the lower third (often hidden by basal leaves) are similarly shaped but *greatly reduced,* widely spaced on short petioles; above this are *curled, clasping, sheath- or boat-like leaves* 1–3" (2.5–7 cm), often with maroon veins. **Stems** single to few, 6–9' (2–3 m) tall, 0.5–0.8" (13–20 mm) thick, with scattered bumps but nearly hairless, round, rigid, solid, erect, branching only in the upper half, the branches long, naked, and strongly ascending. **Inflorescence** consists of 5–35 widely-spaced, sunflower-like heads at the ends of thin, smooth, hairless peduncles 1.5–9" (4–23 cm) long. **Flower heads** (mid summer to early autumn) composite, to 3.5" (9 cm) wide, backed by smooth, layered bracts. **Ray florets** long, narrow, notched at the tip, grooved, bright yellow. **Disk florets** yellow with 5 triangular lobes, but the base of the column is dark brown.

CONFUSING PLANTS: Elecampane *Inula helenium* has narrower leaves with more pointed tips, and the stem leaves are more prominent.

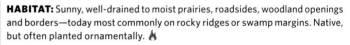

HABITAT: Sunny, well-drained to moist prairies, roadsides, woodland openings and borders—today most commonly on rocky ridges or swamp margins. Native, but often planted ornamentally. 🔥

FOOD USE: The tender young **shoots** of the flower stalks, appearing in mid-summer, can be peeled and eaten raw or cooked. They are mild, tender, and slightly sweet. **Conservation 2.**

COMMENTS: This is an absolutely striking and unforgettable plant, one of our largest herbs. It has lost much habitat due to fire suppression and agriculture, and should be considered for native restorations and ornamental plantings. Eating one shoot will not harm a healthy plant, but let most stalks go to bloom.

▲ Tender shoot. Notice the entire leaf margins on this plant. **353**

18 Bigleaf aster 1
Aster macrophyllus ◆ *Asteraceae* (Composite family)

QUICK CHECK: Large, rough, hairy, heart-shaped leaves forming a forest ground cover. **ID difficulty 2.**

DESCRIPTION: Perennial spreading by rhizomes, forming dense colonies with numerous rosettes of 2–6 leaves from a *semi-woody, often raised base.* Leaves are pleasantly aromatic when crushed. **Basal leaves** have an elongated heart shape, the tips sharp-pointed and the lobes overlapped. **Blades** 4–10" (10–25 cm) long with erect hairs all over—denser below, shorter and stiffer on top. Tender young leaves are scrolled, *glossy on top,* and upright. **Midvein** depressed; secondary veins slightly depressed and also offset by color and dense hair. The underside is gray-green with protruding veins. **Margins** serrated with large, broad, forward-pointed teeth with extending bristles. **Petioles** 80–160% of blade length, hairy all over, deeply U-channeled with sharp margins, the channel narrowing toward the top so the edges nearly touch. **Stems** (infrequently produced) erect, zigzag, to 34" (86 cm) high and 6 mm thick, branching only in the upper part, solid, tough, gently angled, burgundy, covered with long erect hairs. **Stem leaves** alternate, smaller with the *broadly winged* petioles becoming shorter upward; uppermost leaves are ovate and sessile. **Inflorescence** a spreading panicle of 12–80 heads, the branches very zigzag and forked dichotomously. **Flower heads** (mid summer to early fall) 0.6–1.1" (15–28 mm) across, with 9–18 long-elliptic, white to pink-purple rays and yellow disk florets in the center.

CONFUSING PLANTS: Wild ginger (p. 266) has a thick surface rhizome, paired leaves, and no teeth. Creeping bellflower (p. 338) has softer hairs and milky sap.

HABITAT: Dry, sunny woods; forest borders and clearings. Especially common under broadleaf trees that cast light shade, such as aspen, oak, and birch. Native.

FOOD USE: The young, tender **leaves**, before they have unfurled, make an aromatic nibble that can be added sparingly to salads or cooked greens. **Conservation 1.**

COMMENTS: This species has larger basal leaves than other asters. This trait, along with its remarkable abundance in many regions, makes it the most practical aster to gather. The plants may live for many decades without flowering, and few are seen blooming in most years—although logging often stimulates mass flowering. **AKA** *Eurybia macrophylla.*

RELATED EDIBLES: Tender young leaves of other asters are safe to try, and a few are quite good.

Young leaves for eating. ▶

19 **Canada violet** 3 IWE-375
Viola canadensis + family *Violaceae*

QUICK CHECK: Short herb with broad, toothed leaves on long petioles with stipules; each 5-petaled irregular flower at the end of a nodding stem. **ID difficulty 2.**

DESCRIPTION: Short perennial herb from a thin, semi-woody rhizome. Hairiness of the vegetative parts is highly variable—some populations are almost completely hairless, while others are densely hairy. **Basal leaves** light green, 3–6" (8–15 cm) long, heart-shaped, the tips blunt to acuminate. **Veins** semi-palmate, with 2 or 4 major veins from the base, then another nearby pair arching toward the tip. Veins and veinlets are depressed above and protrude below.

Margins have widely spaced, white-tipped teeth, shaped like a wave cresting toward the leaf tip. **Petioles** thin, channeled, green, 1–4 times the blade length. **Stem** to 13" (33 cm) tall and 2–3 mm thick, zigzag, light green, round, smooth, solid, the internodes long. **Stem leaves** alternate, smaller and narrower with shorter petioles and long-acuminate tips. **Stipules** narrow, entire, 0.5–0.6" (13–15 mm) long. **Flowers** single on long, erect, hooked pedicels from upper leaf axils. Pedicels have an offset pair of tiny bracts, and each flower has a calyx of 5 separate, pointed, linear sepals shorter than the petals. **Corolla** 5 petals of unequal size, the largest (head) pointing down and spurred at the base, one pair (arms) spreading, and another pair (legs) pointing back toward the stem. **Petals** white with a yellow base, the lower 3 with darkened purple veins, the "arm" petals with "hairy armpits." Petal backs are light violet. Hidden, self-fertile flowers are occasionally produced in the axils of upper leaves after the showy flowers are done. **Pod** round to elliptic, 5–12 mm long.

HABITAT: Rich-soiled but usually rocky deciduous forests, especially on slopes. Native.

FOOD USE: Tender young **leaves** in spring, raw or cooked. **Conservation 2.**

COMMENTS: This is my favorite violet to eat. The leaves are tender, large, and mild-tasting with an exotic hint of wintergreen. Occurrence of this species can be hard to predict, but it is locally abundant. Because of its great regional variation it has been divided into a number of forms or subspecies. All true violets (in the genus *Viola*) are safe. There are many stemmed species with a variety of leaf shapes. (Stemless violets are in group 19.)

Related edible:

20 Common yellow violet + *Viola pubescens* 1

This is a common, widespread, stemmed violet with large leaves that grows in forests, but it is more characteristic of sandy or loamy, less rocky soils than Canada violet. It may have from one to a few basal leaves, although occasionally basal leaves are absent. **Leaves** 1–3.2" (2.5–8 cm) long, broadly triangular to heart-shaped; the tips may be abruptly pointed or blunt. **Margins** have widely spaced, blunt teeth, and usually a fringe of hairs. **Surfaces** range from densely soft-hairy (especially below) to nearly hairless. **Stipules** ovate

and sometimes notched. **Flowers** 0.5–0.7" (13–18 mm) across with yellow petals, the lower one (sometimes 3) with dark purple-brown veins. The side petals have a yellow "beard" at the base.

COMMENTS: This species is not as good-tasting as Canada violet, and it lacks the wintergreen flavor, but it is easy to collect. Some sources claim that yellow-flowered violets are not edible, but I have been unable to find any basis for this claim. I have eaten this particular species hundreds of times, both raw and cooked, although never more than a handful or two, because it's rather low on my preference list. It may actually be two species: Some taxonomists recognize *V. pubescens* as a species with fewer basal leaves and stems and blades that are always densely hairy (downy yellow violet). Plants that have more numerous basal leaves that are nearly hairless, and stems that are hairless or have the hair concentrated in a few narrow lines, are separated as *V. eriocarpa*. If you pay attention you may eventually notice these differences, but you can eat either form.

GROUP 24 BASAL LEAVES PRESENT, STEM LEAVES ALTERNATE, LOBED OR DIVIDED, SAP MILKY

All members of this group belong to the family *Asteraceae*, making it among the safest groups in the book. Several edible thistles in the genus *Cirsium* are not included in the text or key. Thistles and nipplewort have only slightly milky sap and could key to group 25 if this is not noticed.

TENTATIVE IDENTIFICATION KEY TO GROUP 24
The key is not your final answer!

Leaves arrowhead-like, 3-lobed, or erratically palmately lobed.	1. Prenanthes
Leaves linear, some unlobed; lobes often linear when present.	
Leaves less than 1 cm wide; flowers blue.	2. Texas skeletonplant
Leaves often more than 1 cm wide; flowers yellow.	3. Scorzonera
Leaves longer than wide, not linear, and pinnately lobed.	
Leaves with sharp, hard, needle-like spines on the outer edge.	
Leaves and stems whitish-gray on all surfaces.	9. Scotch thistle
Leaves with prominent white veins and veinlets.	11. Milk thistle
Leaves whitish only on the underside from dense wool.	
Basal leaves deeply pinnately lobed.	4. Pasture thistle
Basal leaves broadly elliptic and unlobed.	5. Tall thistle
Leaves gray to green on the underside, variably hairy.	
Spring-blooming, florets a mixture of pale yellow and purple, with a dense whorl of leaves beneath the heads.	6. Spring thistle
Summer-blooming, the florets purple to pink; no dense leaf whorl beneath heads.	
Thorny, leafy wings on stems; basal leaves not compound-lobed.	
Leaves densely hairy, not silvery; heads orient skyward.	7. Bull thistle
Leaves sparsely hairy, silvery-edged; heads nodding.	10. Nodding thistle
Stems without thorny, leafy wings; basal leaves with compound lobes.	8. Swamp thistle
Leaves without sharp, hard, needle-like spines (although they may be prickle-toothed).	
Leaves with hairs across the upper surface.	
Petiole/rachis keeled below.	23. Bitter lettuce
Petiole/rachis rounded below.	
Lower leaves with very small, fully separated divisions near the base; heads small.	
Blade has a large, unlobed terminal section; stem usually single, erect.	12. Nipplewort
Terminal section of blade lobed; stems multiple, leaning.	13. Japanese hawksbeard
Lower leaves lack fully separated divisions; heads large—over 1" (2.5 cm) wide.	
Less than 24" (60 cm) tall; flowers yellow.	15. False dandelion
Often over 30" (75 cm) tall; flowers blue.	16. Chicory
Upper leaf surface hairless or nearly so, or with hairs confined to the margins or midvein.	
Midvein rounded below.	14. Carolina dandelion
Midvein keeled below.	
Keel naked, without hairs or spines.	
Margins always toothed, often lobed.	
Margins gently prickle-toothed, lobes deep, auricles pointed.	17. Common sow-thistle
Margins painfully stiff-prickly, lobes shallow, auricles rounded.	18. Prickly sow-thistle
Margins gently prickle-toothed, lobes shallow, auricles rounded.	19. Perennial sow-thistle
Margins toothless, sometimes lobed; upper leaves mostly entire.	24. Blue lettuce
Keel with hairs.	
Latex browning rapidly; leaf tips narrow; flowers yellow.	20. Good lettuce
Latex turning slowly light brown; leaf tips not arrowhead-shaped; flowers orange-red.	21. Hairy lettuce
Latex remains white; leaf tips arrowhead-shaped; flowers bluish.	22. Woodland lettuce
Keel with prickles or spines.	See key next page.

(Continued on next page.)

(Continued from previous page.)

Keel with prickles or spines.

Stem leaves clasping with 2 small, pointed lobes at the base, tapered to a point, nearly entire.	25. Willow-leaf lettuce
Stem leaves toothed, often lobed, but lacking pointed basal lobes.	
Prickles long, dense; stem prickly and latex white.	26. Prickly lettuce
Prickles short, sparse; stem not prickly; latex turns brown.	27. Prairie lettuce

1 Prenanthes 2 1 📖 NG-447
Prenanthes alba ✦ *Asteraceae* (Composite family)

▲ Composite range of eastern *Prenanthes*.

QUICK CHECK: Broad, arrowhead-shaped basal leaves on long petioles; tall stalk with drooping flower heads. **ID difficulty 1.**

DESCRIPTION: Monocarpic perennial with latex turning brown. For most of its life it has 1-3 **basal leaves** 1-10" (2.5-25 cm) long, almost unbelievably variable in shape: at first arrowhead-shaped with smooth edges, becoming more prominently toothed as they get larger, eventually developing multiple lobes, sometimes deep and complex. **Surfaces** hairless above, hairy below (especially on main veins). **Midvein** nearly flat above, often reddish; veinlets are slightly depressed above and protruding below. **Margins** have scattered, large, mucronate teeth. **Petioles** rounded with a small channel, hollow, about 120% of blade length, generally hairless, with a double-wing ridge on top that starts at the blade and tapers toward the base. **Stalks** single, 2-7' (0.6-2.1 m) tall and 0.4-0.8" (1-2 cm) thick, straight, unbranched, rounded, hollow, the surface smooth except for scattered dark, raised bumps. **Stem leaves** alternate, deeply 3-lobed or pinnately lobed, on broad-based, winged petioles that become shorter going up the stalk. **Inflorescence** crowded panicles of drooping heads at the tips of ascending branches. **Heads** *cylindrical, not bulged at the base*, 0.4-0.6" (10-15 mm) long, the bracts purplish with lighter margins, opening bell-like but not broadly. Florets whitish, truncated with 5-lobed tips, the seeds 5-6 mm long with a reddish-brown parachute.

HABITAT: Hardwood or mixed hardwood-conifer forests in almost all soil types. Rarely abundant but found in almost every woodlot or forest within its range. Most common under a light canopy (such as oak, aspen, and pine) on hillsides; often proliferates after logging or windstorms. Native.

FOOD USE: Tender **leaves** in spring or early summer can be eaten raw or cooked. Just prior to bolting, the leaves (even meristematic ones) usually become more bitter. The **shoot** is bitter but can be eaten steamed or boiled, and is very tender when young. **Conservation 2.**

COMMENTS: Prenanthes is not particularly well known as an edible green but is abundant, widespread, and pretty good. **AKA** *Nabalus albus*, white lettuce, rattlesnake root, lion's foot.

RELATED EDIBLES: There are several species of *Prenanthes*, all of which are edible and can be used similarly, although some of them are quite bitter. *P. altissima* is large and lush and equally good. *P. trifoliata* has lower leaves that are often divided into 3 fully separate sections.

▼ Variable shape of basal leaves.

0 mm   1 cm

2 Texas skeletonplant 🌿 3 | 3 🍃 3
Lygodesmia texana ♦ *Asteraceae* (Composite family)

QUICK CHECK: Thin, lanky, lax stems with a few linear leaves and widely spaced, broad heads of light purple florets. **ID difficulty 1.**

DESCRIPTION: Perennial from a tough taproot, also spreading by rhizome. Latex white. **Basal leaves** 4-8" (10-20 cm) long, very narrow (less than 1 cm), linear, with widely-spaced, very narrow, short, linear lobes. Blades are hairless, the major veins parallel but obscure above and faintly visible below. *Rosette eventually disappears during flowering.* **Stems** lanky and weakly erect to leaning or lax, often supported by surrounding vegetation, to 28" (70 cm) tall and 4-5 mm thick, single or few, roundish, smooth to minutely roughened, hairless, faintly angled. **Branches** sparse and widely spreading. **Stem leaves** alternate, widely spaced, sessile, to 6" (15 cm) long and 6 mm wide, linear (only occasionally with a short, outward-pointing tooth or lobe), long-tapered to the base and the sharp tip, the blade broadly V-channeled. **Flower heads** (May-Sept.) few and widely spaced, the involucres 0.8" (2 cm) long and 5-7 mm wide, cylindrical, with long, ridged, hairless bracts, *appearing conjoined; free only near the sharp recurved tips.* **Florets** 8-12 per head, rays only, the open head spreading 1.1-1.5" (28-38 mm) across. Sexual columns in the center are long, purple, and curvy. The seed is small with attached bristles but no parachute.

HABITAT: Dry, sunny locations: Open forests and savannahs, roadsides, prairies, fields. Native. 🔥

FOOD USE: Every tender part above ground is edible and excellent: leaves, stems, peduncles, and flower buds. These are most abundant in early summer but new tender growth appears in small amounts any time the plants are flowering. **Conservation 2.**

COMMENTS: Because of the small volume embodied in this plant it is probably easier to overharvest than most members of this group, especially when harvesting shoots. If you eat it, curate it; plant ripe seeds in small disturbances to help propagation.

RELATED EDIBLES: *L. juncea* is much more widespread but also much smaller; it has no basal leaves. Rose-rush *L. aphylla* is found in sandy pine woodlands and savannahs mostly in Florida; it is almost identical to Texas skeletonplant, but the stems are leafless. It has declined greatly due to fire suppression.

▲ Flower bud and tender stem.

▲ No lobes are visible here because they are mostly confined to basal leaves.

3 Scorzonera ⅃ 2 🌿 3 ⅃ 3 🌿 2
Scorzonera laciniata ✦ *Asteraceae* (Composite family)

QUICK CHECK: Basal leaves with long, narrow lobes but no teeth; shin-high, branching stalks with dandelion-like yellow flowerheads. **ID difficulty 2.**

▲ Rapidly expanding.

DESCRIPTION: Winter annual or biennial with white latex. **Taproots** fleshy but not thicker than the leafy crown, long, tapering, not much branched, *dark-skinned*, with milky sap. **Rosette leaves** numerous, hugging the ground without competition but erect where vegetation is dense, sometimes growing thick like lawn grass, to 16" (40 cm) long, the blades occasionally entire but usually with long, narrow lobes. The leaf tips are often deeply folded. The blade is finely scurfy, especially on the margin. **Lobes** or segments are usually *few, long and projecting, widely separated and out of plane with the rachis*, long-lanceolate to linear, the tip thin and the base often slightly narrowed. **Margins** *not toothed*. The rachis has upturned wings/blade between the lobes. On low-competition rosettes the terminal lobe often widens toward the blunt tip. **Petioles** 40-70% of blade length, narrow, deeper than wide, hollow, densely to sparsely hairy and wing-channeled, the channel silvery. **Stem leaves** alternate, smaller, and *usually entire*. **Stems** single or multiple, prostrate (without competition) to erect, up to 16" (40 cm) tall, and 8 mm thick, rounded, solid at first becoming hollow with age, often purple near the base, the surface with fine ridges that are more pronounced toward the top. Branches are few. Leaves and stems may have scattered clumps of woolly hair when young but are hairless with age. **Inflorescence** (spring) a few apical flowerheads on peduncles to 8" (20 cm) long, single or in small clusters. Buds have layered, triangular bracts that are strongly keeled along the central vein, the tip margins purple-brown. **Heads** 1-2.5 cm (0.4-1") across with yellow rays, opening in the morning and soon closing, tapered to a point when closed. **Seeds** parachuted, elongated, borne in small dandelion-like heads.

HABITAT: Well-drained, sunny, disturbed soil of the higher and drier parts of the Great Plains. Adapted to salty conditions and thus thriving and spreading on the sides of major highways. Introduced.

FOOD USE: The **roots** can be dug in fall, winter, or spring from plants that have not yet produced a stalk, and can be eaten cooked. The flavor is rich and hearty like salsify, but the root is small and has a tough core. The young, tender **leaves**, **shoots**, and **flower buds** can be collected in spring or early summer and eaten raw or cooked. Their flavor is mild and excellent.

COMMENTS: This is a close relative of the cultivated scorzonera *S. hispanica*. It was first discovered as a weed in the US near Boulder, Colorado in the 1950s and has spread through much of the western Great Plains. Distribution is erratic, but the plant is locally abundant, and is expanding its range. **AKA** false salsify, viper root.

THISTLE ▢ FH-333
genera *Cirsium, Carduus, Onopordum, Silybum* ⬩
Asteraceae (Composite family)

QUICK CHECK: Erect herbs, leaves woolly below and toothed or lobed, with sharp spines on the margins; brush-like heads of numerous thin, radiating florets. **ID difficulty 1.**

COLLECTIVE DESCRIPTION: Biennials or perennials, most species with large taproots (although a few have fibrous or spreading roots). *Sap is faintly milky.* **Basal leaves** numerous, 8–22" (20–56 cm) long, mostly pinnately lobed and ruffled or wavy, several times longer than wide. **Surfaces** hairy or tomentose at least on the underside. **Midribs** broadly triangular, flat above and keeled below. **Margins** toothed and armed with long, sharp spines, especially on the lobe tips. **Stems** 2–7' (60–210 cm) tall and 0.7–1.5" (18–38 mm) thick, straight, erect, usually unbranched below the middle, hairy, often spiny and winged below the nodes, roundish but angled, thick-walled but hollow. **Stem leaves** alternate, sessile, similar to the basal but becoming progressively smaller. **Flower heads** 1–2" (2.5–5 cm) wide, the involucre roundish to elongated, covered by numerous *spine-tipped bracts with a thickened midvein*, constricted at the tip. **Florets** spread moderately like the bristles of a shaving brush, light purple or pink in most species, occasionally yellow or white, appearing thread-like, consisting of a long, thin tube divided into 5 long, slender lobes. **Seeds** (achenes) flattened, with parachutes.

FOOD USE: (This is a generalized account; some uses are not applicable to certain species.) **Taproots** (fall through spring) of most species can be eaten raw or cooked. **Shoots** (late spring to early summer) can be eaten raw or cooked after they have been carefully peeled. I start by removing the leaves and spines in the field with a knife, then peeling the thick skin. **Midribs** (spring through fall) of the leaves can be eaten raw or cooked after removing the leafy sides and accompanying spines; they are crisp, juicy, and a bit stringy, like celery. **Flower buds** (early to mid summer) can be peeled, and the tender centers eaten like artichoke hearts, but on most species they are too small and difficult to bother.

COMMENTS: Thistles are one of the best and easiest groups of edible plants for a forager to learn. They are abundant throughout our region, especially in human-disturbed landscapes. They are great for converting wild food skeptics—if you learn the nuances of selecting them at the right time. The peeled stalks are usually the best produce from a thistle, but the taproots of some species are also superb.

SPECIES: I am lumping four closely related genera together here, since their food uses are similar. All species are edible, but the quality varies. There are many *Cirsium* thistles not listed, including some excellent ones.

▲ *Bull thistle shoots, before and after peeling.* ▲

4 Pasture thistle ⬩ *Cirsium discolor* 🕯 2 🍁 2 🔪 3

Common in meadows and fields, this native thistle grows 4–6' (1.2–1.8 m) tall. The leaves have narrow lobes and are silvery-white on the underside. The florets are pale purple. Full-grown pasture thistle has large, tender, sweet roots. The stalks and midribs are also good, especially as cooked vegetables. **Conservation 3/2.** 🔥 (Continued on the next page.)

4 Pasture thistle (continued)

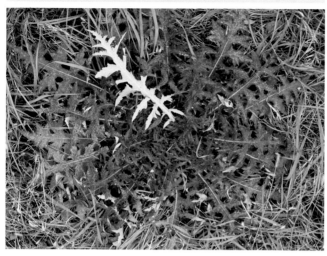

5 Tall thistle ✦ *Cirsium altissimum* 3 🍂 2 🥕 3

An elegant native thistle typically 6–10' (2–3 m) tall, inhabiting open woodlands and forest margins on rich soil. The basal leaves are lightly armed, scarcely lobed or unlobed, and silvery-white beneath. Stem leaves may be lobed or entire. Florets are light

purple. The roots are large, tender, and sweet—good even raw. The stalks and midribs are also larger and more tender than most species, and are less thorny to handle. **AKA** woodland thistle. **Conservation 3/2.** 🔥

6 Spring thistle ✦ *Cirsium horridulum* 🥕 3 🍂 3 🔪 3

A native species with yellow to purple flowers that blooms in spring, much earlier than other thistles in the same area. The stems reach 2–5' (60–150 cm) tall and are proportionately very thick. The leaves are exceptionally spiny and there is a dense whorl of leaves directly beneath the flower heads. The petioles are the tenderest of any thistle I've tried, and the peeled shoot is delicious raw, with a flavor reminiscent of honeydew melon. Don't believe me? Go try it. I have not eaten the root. It might be really good.

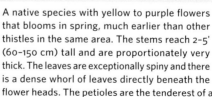

◀ Spring thistle, beginning to bloom but the stem is still tender.

7 **Bull thistle** ✦ *Cirsium vulgare*

Abundant, non-native, weedy species reaching 4–7' (1.2–2.1 m) in height. The stem is hairy and robust, branching widely in full sun, with purple flowerheads. The leaves are not silvery on the underside, and they have a thorny wing that runs down onto the stem below. This is one of our most heavily-armed thistles, and it is the only species in our area with spines lying flat on the upper leaf surface. Shoots make a good cooked vegetable, and the leaf midribs are large enough to be worth peeling. The roots are tough and less preferable.

◄ Bull thistle shoot at the stage for peeling and eating.

8 **Swamp thistle** ✦ *Cirsium muticum*

This native thistle reaches 6–9' (1.8–2.7 m) tall, the stalks ridged and proportionately thinner than our other species. The leaves are long, with long, narrow lobes cut close to the midvein,

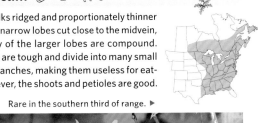

and many of the larger lobes are compound. The roots are tough and divide into many small fibrous branches, making them useless for eating. However, the shoots and petioles are good.

Rare in the southern third of range. ►

9 **Scotch thistle** ✦ *Onopordum acanthium*

Biennial 4–9' (1.2–2.7 m) tall. All parts are covered with wool in varying density—at the extreme it gives the plant a ghostly *whitish-gray appearance*. The basal leaves are large and deeply ruffled but shallowly lobed; stem leaves are less ruffled. *Broad, spiny, leafy wings run down the stem* from each node, often obscuring it. Flower heads are usually in small clusters, held upright, with purple florets. Once you get past the spiny wings, this species has respectable flavor, but I've only eaten the stems.

10 Nodding thistle ◆ *Carduus nutans*   3   2   3

Biennial 5–8' (1.5–2.4 m) tall. Basal leaves are 8–12" (20–30 cm) long and *almost hairless*, the edges *strongly ruffled and silvery*, the midribs light and hairless above. Stems are covered with leafy, spiny, ruffled wings that extend down from the leaf axils. The peduncle is *long, ascending, almost naked*, without leafy wings, not spiny, slightly hairy, with a single large, *nodding, purple flowerhead* 1.3–2.5" (33–65 mm) across at the end. The spiny bracts of the involucre are 4–10 mm wide (very wide compared to other thistles) and the *outer ones are reflexed*. The seeds (achenes) have no parachute at the end. This species is introduced and inhabits dry, well-drained, sunny areas with disturbed soil. The roots are tough and fibrous. The midribs are of middling quality among thistles. If you are going to peel thistle flower buds, as with artichoke hearts, this species has the largest in our region. The shoots are among our best and are sweet and pleasant to eat even raw. The closely related *Carduus acanthoides* is much smaller. While edible, its parts are hardly worth peeling. Both *Carduus* species are invasive. **I**

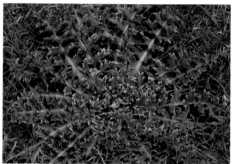

Carduus acanthoides rosette. ▶

11 Milk thistle ◆ *Silybum marianum*   2

This biennial species is sparsely distributed in our area, where it occasionally escapes from cultivation for medicinal uses. It is readily recognized by its variegated, shiny green leaves with *bright white veins*. The florets are purple, and beneath the head there is a whorl of long, stiff, spine-tipped, U-channeled bracts. The stems are grooved and usually have sparse,

fine wool on the surface. The leaf blades/petioles/ midribs, young stalks, and roots are all edible—although I have only eaten the leaves.

12 Nipplewort 2 2
Lapsana communis ✦ *Asteraceae* (Composite family)

QUICK CHECK: Hairy lobed leaves with depressed veins, almost all surface area in a large, triangular, coarsely toothed, terminal lobe; tiny heads of yellow flowers. **ID difficulty 2.**

DESCRIPTION: Winter annual with milky sap. **Rosette leaves** 3-7" (8-18 cm) long with a winged whitish midrib that has a few small, blunt, widely spaced lobes, and a much larger terminal lobe containing most of the surface area. Lobe margins are hairy with large, irregular, obtuse teeth tipped with white nipples. Blades are hairy on both surfaces with deeply depressed veins on top; they are thin and velvety to the touch. **Midrib** D-shaped or bluntly triangular in cross section, not channeled, decreasing in length up the stem, densely covered with long, erect hairs. **Stems** erect, hollow, thin, roundish with very minor angles (especially in the lower part), 2-6' (60-180 cm) tall and 3-9 mm thick, soft-hairy, branching in the upper half, which is sparsely leafed. **Stem leaves** become progressively smaller, the petioles shorter, the terminal lobe more triangular. Their teeth have mucronate tips. Uppermost leaves may be entire and nearly sessile. **Inflorescence** a loose, terminal panicle, the heads on long, thin, straight, naked peduncles. **Heads** cylindrical, 5-8 mm long with 8-15 yellow ray florets spreading 7-11 mm across. The seeds *have no parachute* (pappus). They are *borne inside a capsule-like enclosure formed by dry bracts*, which persist on dead stalks.

HABITAT: Moist, rich, disturbed soil in full to partial shade. Pastures, backyards, gardens, and especially dirt roads or trails through wooded areas. Introduced.

FOOD USE: Gather young **leaves** from robust rosettes, especially where crowding keeps them off the ground, as their texture can hold dirt. These are available mostly in spring, less so in summer and fall. Use in salads or as a potherb. Tender **shoots** with attached leaves, in late spring or early summer, also make a nice cooked vegetable.

COMMENTS: This weed is widespread and sporadically abundant in much of our region. It is better known and more appreciated by foragers in Europe, where it is native.

365

13 Japanese hawksbeard 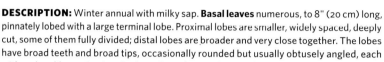 1 1
Youngia japonica ✦ *Asteraceae* (Composite family)

QUICK CHECK: Deeply lobed basal leaves with a large terminal lobe; the stem thin and wavy, hairy and leafy near base; tight clusters of elongated heads that are orange when closed. **ID difficulty 2.**

DESCRIPTION: Winter annual with milky sap. **Basal leaves** numerous, to 8" (20 cm) long, pinnately lobed with a large terminal lobe. Proximal lobes are smaller, widely spaced, deeply cut, some of them fully divided; distal lobes are broader and very close together. The lobes have broad teeth and broad tips, occasionally rounded but usually obtusely angled, each with a claw-like projection. Both surfaces have *soft, erect hairs*. **Midvein** slightly depressed above and very hairy. The few evident smaller veins are also depressed above and protrude below. **Petioles** especially hairy, 10–60% of blade length, deeper than wide, rounded below, not channeled. **Stems** one to several per plant, erect, thin, *leafy only in the lower third*, purplish near the base, rounded with many fine ridges, hollow, not stiff, usually curvy, 12–30" (30–76 cm) tall and 3–7 mm thick, *dense with long hairs near the base but becoming almost hairless upward*. Very small stalks are often present at the base of large ones. **Branches** minor and only in the inflorescence. **Stem leaves** alternate, few, only near the base. **Inflorescence** a *tight panicle* of small composite

▲ Rapidly expanding.

heads on very short pedicels, many sessile or nearly so. The heads are 3–5 mm across with ray florets that are yellow when spread open, orange when closed (the latter being more typical); the involucres are longer than wide and purplish at the tip. **Seed** has a parachute.

HABITAT: Disturbed ground, often at least partly shaded and moist. Gardens, clearings, fields, dirt roads, trails, yards, construction sites, disturbed woods. Introduced.

FOOD USE: Use the young **stems** and tender **leaves** (if they are clean, which is rare) raw or cooked.

COMMENTS: Another of the many bitter greens in the lettuce tribe of the aster family. This herb is spreading quickly in the Southeast, where it is already an abundant weed in many locations. **AKA** Asiatic false hawksbeard, *Crepis japonica*.

14 Carolina dandelion 1
Pyrrhopappus carolinianus + Asteraceae (Composite family)

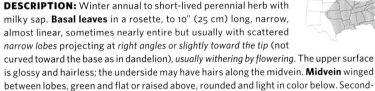

QUICK CHECK: Rosette of narrow dandelion-like leaves; multiple branching stems with a few leaves; showy yellow flowerheads. **ID difficulty 2.**

DESCRIPTION: Winter annual to short-lived perennial herb with milky sap. **Basal leaves** in a rosette, to 10" (25 cm) long, narrow, almost linear, sometimes nearly entire but usually with scattered *narrow lobes* projecting at *right angles or slightly toward the tip* (not curved toward the base as in dandelion), *usually withering by flowering*. The upper surface is glossy and hairless; the underside may have hairs along the midvein. **Midvein** winged between lobes, green and flat or raised above, rounded and light in color below. Second-

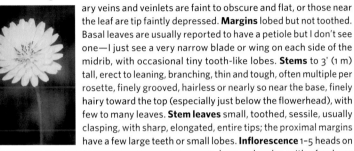

ary veins and veinlets are faint to obscure and flat, or those near the leaf are tip faintly depressed. **Margins** lobed but not toothed. Basal leaves are usually reported to have a petiole but I don't see one—I just see a very narrow blade or wing on each side of the midrib, with occasional tiny tooth-like lobes. **Stems** to 3' (1 m) tall, erect to leaning, branching, thin and tough, often multiple per rosette, finely grooved, hairless or nearly so near the base, finely hairy toward the top (especially just below the flowerhead), with few to many leaves. **Stem leaves** small, toothed, sessile, usually clasping, with sharp, elongated, entire tips; the proximal margins have a few large teeth or small lobes. **Inflorescence** 1-5 heads on long peduncles, with a few long, thin bracts behind the involu-cre. **Heads** 1-1.8" (2.5-4.6 cm) across when open, bright yellow, with ray flowers only, *the columns blackish*. **Seeds** small, elongated, with a parachute, forming a round fluffy head.

HABITAT: Well-drained sunny sites: fields, roadsides, pastures, sunny slopes, dunes. Native.

FOOD USE: Another of the dandelion-like bitter greens, the young **leaves** are edible raw or cooked. **Conservation 1.**

COMMENTS: Looks and tastes a lot like a dandelion, but not as good.

Related edible:
15 False dandelion + *Pyrrhopappus multicaulis*

False dandelion has broader basal leaves with lobes that are much longer and closer together, persisting through flowering. The stem leaves are larger and widely lobed, the uppermost are small but often have long, very thin lobes. This species is generally shorter and stouter than *P. carolinianus*. Despite the name, there are usually only 1-2 stems per crown, these growing 10-20" (25-50 cm) tall and 6-12 mm thick, ridged, maroon, zigzag, nearly solid with a pinhole hollow, soft-hairy near the base. The flavor of the greens is similar—bitter and dandelion-like.

16 Chicory 2 1
Cichorium intybus • *Asteraceae* (Composite family)

QUICK CHECK: Dandelion-like leaves with erect hairs on the midvein; bright blue flowerheads on nearly leafless stalks. **ID difficulty 2.**

DESCRIPTION: Perennial from a fleshy, light brown taproot, on larger plants developing multiple crowns. Latex white but dilute. **Basal leaves** persist almost to flowering, 5–14" (13–36 cm) long and 1.5–4" (4–10 cm) wide, broadest near the tip and tapered to the base, deeply lobed in the proximal 2/3, the lobes curving back toward the base. Lobes and unlobed margins have scattered teeth. The upper surface has erect hair; the underside has more. **Lateral veins** numerous, at broad angles, nearly flat on top and slightly protruding below. **Midrib** flat above and gently rounded below, strongly offset by color, usually whitish but often purple, with *dense, erect hair on both sides*, winged or leafy to the base, where the wings are strongly upturned. **Stem** to 5' (1.5 m) tall and 12 mm thick, usually single per crown, erect, zigzag, the upper part widely branching, roundish with angles or ridges (often purple-topped), the surface green, densely to sparsely coated with erect hairs (more near the base); cross section with a small, non-round hollow. **Stem leaves** alternate, sessile, *clasping*; they are large, crowded, and lobed near the base but become much smaller, sparser, and unlobed toward the top. Upper branches are naked except for small, lanceolate bracts with sharp purple tips under each head. **Flowerheads** widely scattered along stem and branches, sessile, in groups of up to 3, not opening simultaneously, 1.5–2.5" (4–6 cm) across with ray florets only, these light blue with a ragged 5-toothed tip. Seeds have a tiny hair tuft but no parachute.

CONFUSING PLANTS: Dandelion leaves lack the erect hairs on the midrib.

HABITAT: Roadsides, pastures, old fields, yards. Introduced.

FOOD USE: Roots of first-year plants can be eaten cooked, but older ones become much tougher. Young or old roots can be dried and roasted until brown, then ground and used to brew a coffee-like **beverage**. Young spring **leaves** can be used raw or cooked as a potherb. Aim for clean ones because the hairs make them hard to wash.

COMMENTS: The bitterness of the leaves is sometimes intense but varies greatly. Large, lush leaves just before the stem bolts, especially on rich soil, are best. Chicory has long been a popular wild vegetable, and a variety of milder cultivated forms have been developed for their roots and leaves. Roasted chicory root is available commercially.

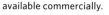

SOW-THISTLE 📖 NG-439
genus *Sonchus* ✦ *Asteraceae* (Composite family)

QUICK CHECK: Erect herbs with sharply pointed teeth or spines on the leaf margins; dandelion-like yellow flowerheads in terminal clusters of 3–12. **ID difficulty 1.**

COLLECTIVE DESCRIPTION: Erect herbs to 6' (2 m) tall, with white milky sap. Form always taller than wide. **Basal leaves** to 12" (30 cm) long and 4" (10 cm) wide, wider toward the tip and tapered to the base, usually pinnately lobed, the lobes broad-based and triangular. The surfaces are hairless or faintly hairy below. Secondary veins and veinlets are depressed above. **Margins** erratically *toothed along the full length*, the teeth pointing outward rather than forward, terminating in a sharp point with a *bristle or spine*. **Midvein** *strongly keeled below*, without hairs or spines. **Stems** thick-walled, hollow, to 0.8" (2 cm) thick, hairless, rarely branching below the inflorescence. **Stem leaves** alternate, similar to the basal but smaller, the *bases clasping the stem* with lobes (called auricles). **Inflorescence** one or more panicles in the upper part of the plant, with 3–16 heads on hollow peduncles with *gland-tipped hairs*. **Heads** 0.6–2" (1.5–5 cm) wide, *bulging at the base*, with many narrow overlapping scales, containing 40–250 bright yellow ray florets, ripening to a flattened seed shaped like an elongated teardrop with a white parachute at the end.

CONFUSING PLANTS: Wild lettuces (genus *Lactuca*) tend to have smaller heads in much greater number, each with fewer florets, and not all species have bright yellow flowers. Lettuces usually have hairs or spines on the bottom of the midvein, and many species have untoothed sections of leaf margin.

17 Common sow-thistle ✦ *Sonchus oleraceus* 🌿 3 🪝 2

QUICK CHECK: Stout-stemmed sow-thistle with small heads; deeply lobed leaves with an arrowhead tip; clasping lobes triangular.

DESCRIPTION: Annual or winter annual 8–80" (20–200 cm) tall. **Leaves** *deeply pinnately lobed*, the side lobes often long and narrow, the *terminal lobe large, broad, and arrowhead-shaped*. Sparsely hairy below. **Teeth** sharp and faintly stiff. **Midribs** mostly greenish to purple. Clasping basal lobes (auricles) are pointed and triangular. Upper leaves are shorter but usually *proportionately wider*. **Stem** 0.1–1" (2–25 mm) thick, fleshy, hollow, strongly ridged, purplish, hairless with light bloom, leafy, rarely branching in the lower half. **Inflorescence** an umbel-like cluster (sometimes compound) of 3–16 heads on peduncles of variable length, the open heads 0.6–0.9" (15–23 mm) across.

HABITAT: Disturbed, rich soil; yards, gardens, city lots, crop fields, roadsides. Introduced.

FOOD USE: Tender **leaves** can be gathered from spring through summer (most abundant in early summer) and eaten raw or cooked. Tender **stems**, primarily available in early summer, can be peeled and used as a vegetable.

COMMENTS: This is the best of our three sow-thistles. It grows largest in warm climates during mild winters. Where it is both large and abundant, it is one of the best greens to know.

18 Prickly sow-thistle • *Sonchus asper* 1 2

QUICK CHECK: Thick-stemmed sow-thistle with small heads, shallow lobes, stiff prickles, and rounded auricles where the leaves meet the stem.

DESCRIPTION: Erect annual or winter annual growing 2–5' (60–150 cm) high. **Leaves** mostly *shallowly lobed*, faintly hairy below, with *wavy, downcurved margins*, especially under the *hard spines*. The clasping leaf base (auricle) is *curled downward and rounded*. **Midribs** mostly white. **Stem** 0.4–1" (1–2.5 cm) thick, hairless, hollow, angled with usually 6 flat sides, often tinged reddish. **Inflorescence** an umbel-like cluster (sometimes compound) of 3–16 heads, the peduncles of varying lengths, the open heads 0.6–0.9" (15–23 cm) across.

HABITAT: Disturbed soil such as gardens, roadsides, building sites, and crop fields. Introduced.

FOOD USE: The **peeled stalk** of vigorously growing young plants in spring or early summer is good raw or cooked. It is crisp, mild, and sweet, but many specimens are too small to bother with. The **leaves** can be eaten raw or cooked when they are very young and tender. Cooking reduces the prickliness, and blending in a smoothie eliminates it.

COMMENTS: This is the only sow-thistle that has armor worth worrying about. If you need gloves to pull it from your garden, it's this species.

19 Perennial sow-thistle • *Sonchus arvensis* 2

QUICK CHECK: Sow-thistle with thin stems sparsely leafed near the top; lower leaves long-tapered at the base, teeth not prickly; wide-spreading inflorescence and large heads.

DESCRIPTION: Perennial spreading by rhizome to form colonies. **Basal leaves** erect in heavy competition, long and narrow with a few shallow lobes, long-tapered at the base, the tips mostly blunt, the midribs mostly whitish. **Margins** with fine, sharp, but not prickly teeth. **Stems** 2–6' (60–180 cm) tall and 5–11 mm thick, unbranched until the top, smooth, rounded, mostly hairless below the inflorescence. **Stem leaves** smaller, few and reduced in the upper part. **Inflorescence** a large, loose panicle with slender branches and long peduncles, usually gland-hairy. **Heads** *broad, dandelion-like*, 1.2–2" (3–5 cm) across.

HABITAT: Disturbed areas in full sun with moist to moderately dry soil: fields, meadows, pastures, roadsides, vacant lots, gardens, seashores. Introduced.

FOOD USE: Tender **leaves** in spring through early summer can be eaten raw or cooked. I especially like them fried.

COMMENTS: This is usually the most abundant of the sow thistles in rural areas and fields. It is the one most commonly seen blooming along highways in the summer. Some have argued that it is native. **AKA** field sow-thistle.

WILD LETTUCE 📖 NG-429
genus *Lactuca* ⊹ *Asteraceae* (Composite family)

QUICK CHECK: Dandelion-like leaves and milky sap; midvein below is keeled with erect hairs or prickles; tall stalk with a panicle of numerous small flowerheads. **ID difficulty 2.**

COLLECTIVE DESCRIPTION: Biennials or perennials with milky sap, at maturity much taller than wide. **Basal leaves** in a rosette, much longer than wide and thicker toward the tips, the margins erratically toothed and/or lobed, sessile or with a winged petiole. **Midribs** prominent and offset by color but scarcely depressed above; *sharply keeled below, the keel usually with erect hairs or spines.* **Secondary veins** few, soon branching into a net-work of slightly depressed veinlets. **Stems** erect, rounded, mostly hollow, *not ridged or angled,* hairless, leafy, unbranched except in the inflorescence. **Stem leaves** sessile or on a winged petiole, alternate, deeply lobed to entire. **Inflorescence** a terminal panicle above the leaves with several to numerous heads. **Heads** (early to late summer) 5–12 mm across when open (except for blue lettuce, which has heads about 25 mm), with only strap-like ray florets. **Fruit** a flattened seed (achene), narrowed and beak-like at the tip, with an attached parachute.

CONFUSING PLANTS: There are no obvious macro-features that clearly differentiate all lettuces from all sow-thistles. All of our lettuces normally have less than 50 florets in a head (and some average 10–15), while our sow-thistles all average more than 80. (But nobody wants to count florets!) The seeds of lettuces are beak-like at the tip, while those of sow-thistles are not. Luckily, both groups are edible.

FOOD USE: Tender **leaves** can be eaten raw or cooked in spring. The best are found in the upright cluster of new leaves in the center of the rosette just before the stem elongates (bolts); this is analogous to a "head" of domestic lettuce. **Shoots** can also be eaten in early summer. The flavor is highly variable among the species, but those with browning latex tend to taste better.

COMMENTS: This genus includes some of the most common (and tallest!) herbaceous plants in our region. The flavor of lettuces is highly variable, so differentiating the species is important for culinary reasons. I have included the most common and widespread species here, but there are others. Technical manuals usually require mature seeds (cypselae) for ID, but I don't focus on that feature because mature lettuces are not good eating. This group contains the ancestor of domestic lettuce (*L. serriola*) but some other species are actually better. Members of this genus contain sedatives in various amounts, so maybe don't drive after your big salad. **WARNING:** A Eurasian species, *L. virosa,* has high enough concentrations of sedatives that it is used medicinally and as an intoxicant. It is dangerous in large quantities and is occasionally found as an escape in North America. I have eaten every species covered here without any notable effect.

20 **Good lettuce** ⊹ *Lactuca canadensis* 3 3

QUICK CHECK: Leaves with long, thin lobes and few to no teeth on the margins; yellow flowers; latex turns brown.

DESCRIPTION: Biennial. Latex rapidly turns *brown.* **Rosette leaves** long and narrow, usu-ally with widely spaced, long, narrow, pointed lobes with few teeth. (The youngest rosette leaves are broader with more teeth.) The terminal section of the leaf is also long, narrow, and pointed. The blade is hairless. Veins above are flat to faintly depressed. The midrib usually has scattered long, soft, wavy hairs on top and on the keel. **Stem** 6–10' (2–3 m) tall, solid or with a small hollow, hairless, bloom-coated, often purplish, with leaves distributed nearly evenly from top to bottom. **Stem leaves** alternate, typically 5–12" (13–30 cm) long and deeply lobed with *few teeth* and *narrow, elongated tips.* The lobes decrease in number upward; on some plants upper leaves are unlobed and nearly entire with scattered bristles. Blades are often *deeply folded.* **Inflorescence** of many strongly ascending branches forming a broom-like top, each branch with a panicle of numerous *small yellow heads.* The seeds have the parachute attached by a *needle-like beak.* (Continued on the next page.)

◄ Good lettuce rosette just before bolting.

20 Good lettuce (continued)

HABITAT: Forest borders, fields, roadsides, prairies, logging sites; disturbed ground in full sun to light shade. Native.

COMMENTS: This is the best tasting wild lettuce—in fact I prefer it over any cultivated leaf lettuce. **Conservation 2. AKA** Canada lettuce, yellow wild lettuce.

▲ Good lettuce can be identified by its long, narrow leaf tips and the rapidly browning latex. The flowers are bright yellow, much like those of prickly lettuce (plant 26).

21 Hairy lettuce ⋆ *Lactuca hirsuta* 2 2

This plant is similar but averages shorter than *L. canadensis*. The leaves have long, narrow lobes with large teeth, and are less pointed than the lobes of good lettuce. The midrib has long, thin hairs on both sides, and the stem is also usually hairy and often reddish. Hairy lettuce has larger flower heads than good lettuce and the florets are usually orange. The latex turns faintly brown, often slowly.

HABITAT: Disturbed dry forests and savannahs, especially rocky slopes. 🔥

COMMENTS: The flavor is almost as good as that of its taller cousin. **Conservation 2.**

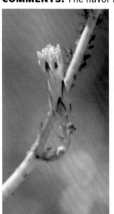

22 Woodland lettuce♦ *Lactuca floridana* 1 1

QUICK CHECK: Tall lettuce, the leaves with a few broad, blunt lobes, toothed margins, and broad, spearhead-like tips; small flowerheads with bluish flowers.

DESCRIPTION: Biennial with white latex. **Rosette leaves** to 12" (30 cm) long with *a winged petiole* that is sparsely hairy below, especially on the midvein. The midvein above is flat; smaller veins are flat or faintly depressed. **Stem** 5–13' (1.5–4 m) tall, straight, unbranched, smooth and round, hollow with thin walls, usually reddish, hairless. **Stem leaves** typically have a *winged petiole* and a few broad-spreading lobes with small teeth along the margins. Sometimes a pair of triangular lobes at the leaf base clasps the stem, but usually these are lacking. **Inflorescence** a panicle with numerous small heads, the rays purplish to light blue, similar to bitter lettuce but darker and with the heads more widely spaced. The seed has a whitish parachute directly attached to a narrowed tip.

HABITAT: Most common on well-drained rich soils in partial sun. Likes forest edges, roadsides, and disturbed openings in oak-hickory forests and savannahs. Native.

COMMENTS: At maturity this must be the lankiest, flimsiest thing in the woods, like if you wanted to build the tallest plant possible using the smallest amount of cellulose. This species largely replaces *L. biennis* in the southern US, but tastes only slightly better. **Conservation 2.**

23 **Bitter lettuce** ◆ *Lactuca biennis* 🖋 1 🗋 1

QUICK CHECK: Very tall lettuce with white milk and bluish-white flowers; leaves hairy below with broad, spearhead-shaped tips.

DESCRIPTION: Biennial with white latex. **Basal leaves** with several broad lobes per side, the lobes toothed, the *leaf tips broadly spearhead-shaped*. The upper surface has scattered short hairs; the *underside has longer erect hairs on the veins*. **Midvein** green to purplish (not white as in many lettuces), flat above. **Veinlets** *depressed above*—more so than any of our other species. **Stems** extremely tall, 6–13' (2–4 m), rounded, hollow, the walls thin, the surface bloom-coated and mostly hairless. **Stem leaves** alternate and sessile, similar to the basal leaves except the uppermost often become linear and entire. **Inflorescence** an enormous panicle, taller than wide, with numerous small heads, the florets light blue to nearly white or faintly yellowish-blue. The seed (achene) has a light brown parachute. (In some parts of its range, especially the Ohio River Valley, one finds "form *integrifolia*," which has unlobed leaves and often yellowish flowers. At a glance this will appear to be another species altogether—and maybe it is, but it tastes the same.)

HABITAT: Disturbed areas in full sun to shade, especially openings in forests caused by construction, logging, or wind storms. Native.

COMMENTS: This is our largest wild lettuce—I once measured a specimen 16' 4" tall, and 9' is about average. The greens are usually extremely bitter, but they can be boiled and drained, or fried, to alleviate the bitterness. The shoots can be very tender but have an odd bitter-metallic flavor. To enjoy them you need to boil and drain the water. **Conservation 1. AKA** tall blue lettuce.

Lactuca biennis tall plant. ▶

24 Blue lettuce + *Lactuca pulchella* 🖋 1

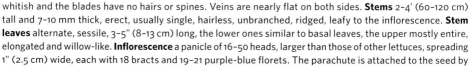

QUICK CHECK: Belly-high lettuce with white latex, spreading by rhizome; the leaves entire in the terminal third; heads large and purple-blue.

DESCRIPTION: Perennial spreading by deep rhizomes to form loose colonies; latex white. Rosettes wither by flowering. **Basal leaves** gently tapered at the base, 6–8" (15–20 cm) long, narrow with the tip pointed. **Margins** have erratic large teeth or narrow, pointed lobes that curve toward the base—but *the terminal third or so is entire.* The midvein is distinctly whitish and the blades have no hairs or spines. Veins are nearly flat on both sides. **Stems** 2–4' (60–120 cm) tall and 7–10 mm thick, erect, usually single, hairless, unbranched, ridged, leafy to the inflorescence. **Stem leaves** alternate, sessile, 3–5" (8–13 cm) long, the lower ones similar to basal leaves, the upper mostly entire, elongated and willow-like. **Inflorescence** a panicle of 16–50 heads, larger than those of other lettuces, spreading 1" (2.5 cm) wide, each with 18 bracts and 19–21 purple-blue florets. The parachute is attached to the seed by a stout but elongated beak.

HABITAT: Full sun in fertile soil with medium soil moisture. Common in meadows and roadsides in the Great Plains, especially along waterways. Native; adventive further east. (Its ecology is similar to perennial sow thistle, with which it is often found.)

Comments This is our only lettuce that is a long-lived perennial spreading by rhizome. It is one of the more bitter species. **Conservation 1. AKA** *Lactuca tatarica.*

25 Willow-leaf lettuce + *Lactuca saligna* 🖋 1

QUICK CHECK: Short lettuce with long, narrow leaves with arrow-like bases; small yellow heads in spike-like clusters.

DESCRIPTION: Winter annual with white latex. **Basal leaves** and lower stem leaves to 6" (15 cm) long, pinnately lobed, the lobes long, narrow, and widely spaced, the margins with a few prickle-like teeth. The surface is hairless and the veins flat above and below. **Midvein** *whitish,* flat above, the underside protruding and keeled, usually with scattered prickles. **Stem** to 34" (85 cm) tall and 12 mm thick, single or clumped (branched at the base), erect to strongly leaning, hairless, round, with light bloom, the plant young but *often becoming branchy* at maturity. **Stem leaves** *held almost vertically or appressed,* clasping with two *small, pointed lobes at the base;* above the base the blades are often narrow, elongated, and entire or nearly so. Uppermost leaves are very small. **Inflorescence** a panicle with long, spike-like branches, the heads small, 8–10 mm across in bloom, usually with less than 18 yellow florets. Seeds have a long thread-like beak about twice as long as the body.

HABITAT: Disturbed, dry, sunny sites with low fertility such as roadsides, vacant lots, pavement cracks, etc. Introduced.

COMMENTS: Willow lettuce is often too small to bother with, except under better growing conditions where it is robust—and even then the food quality is mediocre.

26 Prickly lettuce + *Lactuca serriola* 2

QUICK CHECK: Chest-high weedy lettuce with spiny leaves that turn to optimize sunlight; numerous small heads of yellow flowers.

DESCRIPTION: Biennial or winter annual with white latex. This species has the peculiar habit of twisting the bases of its leaves to optimize the leaf blades' exposure to the sun, sometimes making the whole plant look laterally flattened on a sunny day. **Basal leaves** shallowly lobed or unlobed, wider toward the blunt tip, the margins toothed, with *reddish spines on the bottom of the midvein and the leaf margins* (longer and denser than those on prairie lettuce but not as stiff). **Stem** bloom-coated, hairless, round, hollow, 3–6' (1–2 m) tall, *with spines, especially in the upper part*. **Stem leaves** alternate, clasping, the lobes longer but still broad. **Inflorescence** a panicle of numerous small heads, the heads drooping before opening; florets yellow. The seed is attached to the parachute by a long thread-like extension.

CONFUSING PLANTS: Often mistaken for a sow-thistle, but note the row of soft spines on the bottom of the lettuce leaf's midvein.

HABITAT: Disturbed, well-drained soil in sunny locations: roadsides, vacant lots, gardens, crop fields. Introduced.

COMMENTS: Believed to be the ancestor of cultivated lettuce, which gives one an appreciation for how much we have altered the flavor and form of plants through domestication. The youngest spring greens of this incredibly common weed are rather mild and are especially good cooked, but they soon get quite bitter.

27 **Prairie lettuce** ✦ *Lactuca ludoviciana* 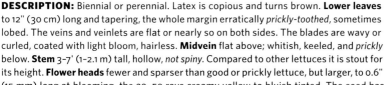 2   2

QUICK CHECK: Lettuce with brown latex, the leaves with prickly midveins and margins, the heads medium-sized and yellowish or bluish.

DESCRIPTION: Biennial or perennial. Latex is copious and turns brown. **Lower leaves** to 12" (30 cm) long and tapering, the whole margin erratically *prickly-toothed*, sometimes lobed. The veins and veinlets are flat or nearly so on both sides. The blades are wavy or curled, coated with light bloom, hairless. **Midvein** flat above; whitish, keeled, and *prickly* below. **Stem** 3–7' (1–2.1 m) tall, hollow, *not spiny*. Compared to other lettuces it is stout for ▲ Rare outside the its height. **Flower heads** fewer and sparser than good or prickly lettuce, but larger, to 0.6" Great Plains and (15 mm) long at blooming, the 20–50 rays creamy yellow to bluish tinted. The seed has a long, needle-like beak with the parachute at the end.

▲ Rare outside the Great Plains and south-central.

HABITAT: Prairies and meadows (especially where sloping), roadsides, river floodplains, generally in full sun in rich soil with moderate moisture levels, benefitting from recurring small soil disturbances. Native. 🔥

COMMENTS: This is one of our best wild lettuces for eating but it is uncommon in most regions. At a glance it can be hard to tell from prickly lettuce but it is larger, has larger heads, and does not have a spiny stem. If you have some in your area, disturb a patch of ground and spread the seeds. **Conservation 2. AKA** western lettuce.

GROUP 25 BASAL LEAVES PRESENT, LEAVES ALTERNATE, LOBED OR DIVIDED, SAP NOT MILKY

Some plants in this group lose their basal leaves by the time of flowering. A few of the summer-blooming annual mustards I placed here have basal leaves for only a fleeting period after germination. Their dead remains are sometimes visible, and their former presence is indicated by leaf scars. The leaf form referred to in the key, unless specified otherwise, generally refers to the leaves from mid-stem downward. (Upper leaves are often drastically different.) This is the largest group in the book partly because the lobed and divided leaves are lumped together. This was necessary because many of the plants have highly variable leaf form (even on the same individual).

Thistles will key here if you do not notice the faint milky sap.

Most members of group 25 belong to the mallow family (p. 688) or the mustard family (p. 682). Most members of both families are edible—and none are dangerously toxic. Since many of these species are eaten as leafy greens before the flowers appear, I used leaf features in the key to the extent possible—but I was forced to use flower features toward the end. Because mustard leaves usually vary dramatically in shape from the top to the bottom of the plant, I often employ leaf hairiness and vein depression, which are more consistent across leaf shapes, as distinguishing criteria. This is not trouble-free either: A few plants toe the line between the categories. If your plant seems on the fence regarding any feature, check it both ways in the key.

TENTATIVE IDENTIFICATION KEY TO GROUP 25
The key is not your final answer!

or — Leaves spiny on the margin. Thistles (see group 24; these have milky sap, which is easy to miss).

or — Leaves not spiny; basal leaves entire (only the upper leaves are lobed). → **1. Scarlet paintbrush**

Leaves not spiny; basal leaves toothed, lobed, or divided (upper leaves may not be lobed/divided).

  Leaves 3-lobed or ternately divided.

    or — Deeply lobed or divided, the terminal division 3-lobed, toothed; stem erect. → **2. Sochan**

    Leaf with 2 small side lobes, otherwise entire; stem prostrate. → **3. Poverty weed**

  Leaves palmately lobed or divided, or with a large palmate terminal division.

    Leaves with stipules; sap slimy; basal leaves palmately lobed and always lacking watermarks.

      Major veins essentially flat above.

        or — Stems limp, rising less than 14" (36 cm); flowers single or in small groups. → **4. Purple poppy-mallow**

        Stems stiff, usually rising more than 24" (60 cm); flowers in a large, loose panicle. → **5. Fringed poppy-mallow**

      Major veins depressed above.

        or — Creeping or decumbent, mostly ground-hugging plant, <20" (50 cm) tall. → **6. Common mallow**

        All or some stems erect, often >20" (50 cm) tall.

        or — Stems <5' (1.5 m) tall; leaves <5" (13 cm) long; flowers >0.8" (2 cm) wide, pink to purple.

          or — Leaves deeply cut; flowers pale pink. → **7. Musk mallow**

          Leaves shallowly lobed; flowers deep pink with purple streaks. → **8. High mallow**

        Stems >5' (1.5 m) tall, leaves >8" (20 cm) long, flowers <13 mm across, white. → **9. Glade mallow**

    Leaves without stipules; sap not slimy; first spring leaves with whitish watermarks.

      Largest watermarks more contiguous and clearly follow the main lateral veins; flowers bluish, borne above the leaves. → **10. Biennial waterleaf**

      Largest watermarks blotchy, not or only loosely following main lateral veins; flowers white, borne below the leaves. → **11. Broad waterleaf**

  Leaves pinnately lobed or divided—the blade usually longer than wide with 4 or more side lobes or divisions. → See key next page.

(Continued on next page.)

(Continued from previous page.)

Leaves pinnately lobed or divided—the blade usually longer than wide with 4 or more side lobes or divisions.

Leaves in sets of 3, 2 of which are really enlarged stipules, and only these are lobed.	14. Pansy
Leaves enormous, oriented vertically, with sinuous, blunt lobes all in plane.	15. Compass plant
Leaves fern-like, densely and evenly lobed, each lobe with rounded sub-lobes.	16. Lousewort

Not as above.

Blade surface hairless; if any hairs present, they are confined to the major veins and margins.

Blade shallowly lobed, the lobes erratic and angled toward the leaf tip.

or Leaf margin hairless; stem erect with soft hairs and ridged.	17. Ox-eye daisy
Leaf margin hairy; stems spreading with stiff hairs, not ridged.	19. Annual wall rocket

Blade deeply lobed or divided, the lobes right-angled to the rachis.

or Lobes or divisions not ruffled, blunt-pointed with several large, pointed teeth.

or Lobes closely spaced; erect stem more than 24" (60 cm).	20. Marsh yellow cress
Divisions widely spaced; decumbent stem less than 12" (30 cm).	21. Creeping yellowcress

Lobes or divisions ruffled, rounded, entire or with a few waves or blunt teeth.

2–8 side lobes; much larger terminal lobe is most of the leaf's blade.	22. Wintercress
14–22 side lobes; large terminal lobe not most of the blade.	23. Southern wintercress

Blade sparsely to densely hairy across one or both surfaces.

or Flowers single from upper leaf axils, with a long, tubular base.	18. Cut-leaf evening primrose

Inflorescence a one-sided panicle, coiled when emerging; flowers with 5 parts.

or Leaves with 5-7 major lobes.	12. Virginia waterleaf
Leaves with 9-13 major lobes.	13. Large waterleaf

Inflorescence a raceme, not coiled or one-sided, flowers with 4 parts.

or Flowers blue-purple; only robust basal leaves are lobed (others are lanceolate).	24. Blue mustard

Flowers with tiny (<2 mm) whitish to pink petals, or petals absent.

Pods roughly triangular.	25. Shepherd's purse
or Pods round to broadly elliptic or slightly heart-shaped.	
Stem leaves clasping and appressed.	26. Field pepperweed
Stem leaves not clasping, tapered to the base.	27. Common pepperweed

Flowers with pale creamy to bright yellow petals 3 mm or longer.

Stem smooth and hairless (perhaps a few hairs near the base).

or Stem leaves entire, appressed; veins flat and obscure.	28. Tower mustard
Stem leaves not appressed, mostly lobed and ruffled; veinlets depressed.	29. Field mustard

Stem with scattered to dense hairs (upper parts sometimes nearly hairless).

Pods nearly spherical.

or Upper stem smooth; pedicels appressed.	30. Bastard cabbage
Upper stem bumpy; pedicels ascending.	31. Hill mustard

Pods elongated, appressed to the rachis or nearly so.

or 5-8' (1.5-2.5 m) tall; upper leaves narrowly elliptic and toothed; uppermost leaves drooping and entire.	32. Black mustard
2-5' (60-150 cm) tall; upper leaves lobed; uppermost toothed, not drooping.	34. Hedge mustard
1-3' (30-90 cm) tall; uppermost leaves unlobed, toothed.	39. Charlock mustard

Pods elongated, not appressed to the rachis.

or Upper leaves with thread-like lobes.	36. Tumble mustard

Upper leaves with pointed side lobes at least 3 times as long as wide.

Lobes broad at the base, tapered to a point.	35. Tall hedge mustard
or Lobes linear or slightly narrowed at the base, broadest in the middle, the tips abruptly pointed.	37. Highway mustard

Upper leaves with blunt side lobes less than 3 times as long as wide.

or Raceme with a lobed bract at the base of each pedicel.	38. French rocket
Pods with a halo of white hairs near the base.	33. White mustard

Upper leaves toothed but without side lobes.

Pod slightly bulged around seeds, nearly appressed, 3 mm thick or less.	39. Charlock mustard
Pod distinctly bulged, 3-6 mm thick; long-tapered beak.	40. Wild radish

1 Scarlet paintbrush ✎ 2 ❀ 2
Castilleja coccinea ✦ family *Orobanchaceae*

QUICK CHECK: Shin-high herb with leaning scarlet tops in spring; lower leaves linear and pointed, upper leaves with three lobes. **ID difficulty 1.**

DESCRIPTION: Biennial or winter annual. **Basal leaves** in a rosette, small and clasping, 1–2" (2.5–5 cm) long, narrowly elliptic, abruptly pointed, folded along the midvein. **Stems** single or clustered, 8–24" (20–60 cm) tall and 2–4 mm thick, purple with fine darker purple ridges, hollow, densely hairy, erect, unbranched. **Stem leaves** alternate, clasping, 2–3" (5–8 cm), almost linear, the tops often curled. Lower leaves are entire, but *upper leaves have one or two long, pointed lobes on each side*. Small leaves are tucked into the axils. Blades have one *prominent parallel vein on each side of the midvein*—all three of these strongly depressed above and protruding below. Both sides are densely covered with long hairs. **Flowers** in packed terminal spikes, each with a bract beneath it. The bracts of lower flowers resemble the regular leaves, but *those below upper flowers have scarlet tips*, as does the *2-lobed tube* from which the corolla, anthers, and pistil scarcely protrude. The corolla tube is *almost colorless* and has *an opening near the middle from which 3 small claw-like appendages protrude*.

HABITAT: Sunny, disturbed soil, often on slopes. Native. 🔥

FOOD USE: The **tender tops**, including the flowers, can be eaten raw or cooked. **Conservation 2.**

COMMENTS: This species is partially parasitic and has a mild and slightly sweet version of the "parasitic plant flavor."

RELATED EDIBLE: In Texas, Oklahoma, and Louisiana this species is replaced by the equally edible *C. indivisa*, which is similar but has unlobed upper leaves (so it would key into group 22).

WARNING: These parasitic plants are suspected of absorbing toxins from host plants and should not be eaten when growing beside poisonous species.

2 Sochan ✎ 2 ⚘ 2 📖 IWE-346
Rudbeckia laciniata ✦ Asteraceae (Composite family)

QUICK CHECK: Tall plant with large, deeply cut leaves with 3 main lobes or divisions, sunflower-like flowers with a bulging center, and drooping yellow rays. **ID difficulty 3.**

DESCRIPTION: Perennial herb from short rhizomes with many crowns. Hairiness is variable between individuals. **Basal leaves** single or in rosettes, to 13" (33 cm) long, with 3 main divisions, fully or almost fully separated, the middle division again deeply (occasionally fully) cut again. Early **spring leaves** start out purple; these and fall leaves tend to have narrower, deeper lobes. A new flush may appear in late summer after flowering; these have fewer, broader, blunter, shallower lobes and a smoother texture. **Upper surface** has short, erect hairs, which become stiff on older leaves. **Underside** has longer hairs on the major veins. **Margins** have irregular, large, acute to obtuse, claw-tipped teeth. **Major veins** nearly flat above and protruding below, *offset by yellowish color*. Veinlets are etched above on new leaves but less so as they expand. **Petioles** 80–120% of blade length, ascending to erect, usually light green (sometimes maroon, especially in the channel), hairless or with erect hairs, solid, the cross section a blunt-bottomed V with 2 small grooves on the outside and a *deep, narrow channel* with winged margins. The petiole base becomes broadly channeled and sheath-like but remains fleshy (not papery). **Stems** multiple, erect, 3–8' (1–2.4 m) tall, 0.3–0.8" (8–20 mm) thick, solid, smooth, lightly bloom-coated, somewhat angular,

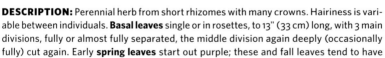

branching only in the inflorescence. **Stem leaves** alternate, the lower ones with long, narrow, pointed lobes; upward they become progressively smaller, and the petioles shorter. Uppermost leaves are sessile. Reduced leaves of the inflorescence are entire or merely toothed. **Inflorescence** loose with many long, ascending branches terminating in solitary heads atop long, *vertical, grooved pedicels*. **Flowerheads** (mid to late summer) subtended by about a dozen ovate-lanceolate, entire bracts about 0.6" (15 mm) long. The head consists of a *yellow-green button or tall mound* of disk florets in the center, surrounded by 6–16 *drooping yellow rays* 1.5–2" (4–5 cm) long. **Seeds** like miniature sunflower seeds.

CONFUSING PLANTS: Bristly buttercup *Ranunculus hispidus* often grows in the same areas and is mildly toxic. This and most other buttercups have petioles with a small channel and a hollow center, leaf sheaths with papery margins, and secondary veins that are deeply depressed and not offset by color.

HABITAT: Rich, moist soil in partial shade to full sun. Most commonly in floodplains, valleys, shrub swamps, forest margins. Native.

FOOD USE: The young **leaves** can be eaten raw or cooked. In late spring or early summer, the **shoots** can be peeled and eaten raw or cooked. New tender leaves occasionally appear throughout the growing season, especially after mowing. Sochan greens are traditionally fried in pork fat. **Conservation 1.**

COMMENTS: This vegetable has a somewhat aromatic, faintly resinous flavor reminiscent of goldenrods and asters. "Sochan" is a Cherokee name. The plant does not have a generally accepted common name in English, despite the fact that it is among the most common and widespread plants on our continent and has been eaten for thousands of years. **AKA** tall coneflower, green-headed coneflower, cut-leaf coneflower, golden glow.

▲ (top left) Shoots at the stage for peeling.

▲ (top right) Early spring leaves.

◄ (bottom) New flush of leaves in late summer, broader and blunter than the spring leaves.

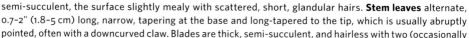

3 Povertyweed 🌿 2
Monolepis nuttalliana ◦ family *Amaranthaceae*

QUICK CHECK: Small sprawling plant with semi-succulent leaves, lobed at the base with an elongated toothless tip; tiny, unshowy flowers and fruits. **ID difficulty 1.**

DESCRIPTION: Weedy annual or winter annual, rosettes present in spring but later withering; rosette leaves similar to lower stem leaves. **Stems** multiple from the base (or branching widely at the base), spreading to decumbent or ascending, sometimes branching above, to 12" (30 cm) long and 4 mm thick, roundish with gentle troughs, solid, semi-succulent, the surface slightly mealy with scattered, short, glandular hairs. **Stem leaves** alternate, 0.7-2" (1.8-5 cm) long, narrow, tapering at the base and long-tapered to the tip, which is usually abruptly pointed, often with a downcurved claw. Blades are thick, semi-succulent, and hairless with two (occasionally

4) spreading, pointed, triangular lobes in the lower third; otherwise they are entire. **Surfaces** hairless but minutely granular. **Midvein** depressed; the only evident secondary veins are faint and run to the lobe tips. **Petioles** 70-90% of the blade length on lower leaves; upper leaves are reduced in size, on much shorter petioles. **Flowers** tiny and unshowy, sessile, borne in small, tight clusters in the upper leaf axils, accompanied by several linear, often curved, fleshy bracts. **Fruit** a tiny, plump disk containing one seed.

HABITAT: Disturbed and compacted soil with high salt content, moist more often than dry, in full sun. Roadsides, crop fields, floodplains, waste areas. Native.

FOOD USE: Young, tender **stems** and **leaves** can be eaten raw or cooked. **Conservation 1.**

COMMENTS: Like miniature succulent lambsquarters with dirt on it. Luckily, dirt can be washed off the hairless leaves.

4 Purple poppy mallow 🌿 2 🌿 1 ❀ 1 ◊ 1 📖 IWE-300
Callirhoe involucrata ◦ *Malvaceae* (Mallow family)

QUICK CHECK: Low, trailing, multi-stemmed, hairy herb with palmately lobed leaves; showy purple 5-petal flowers on long, erect pedicels. **ID difficulty 2.**

DESCRIPTION: Low perennial herb spreading only by seed. **Enlarged taproot** to 1.3" (33 mm) thick and 7" (18 cm) long, not branching, thickest in the middle, narrowed abruptly to the crown and short-tapered below to a narrow taproot. **Basal leaves** 1-3" (2.5-8 cm) long and about as wide, palmately lobed with 3-5 primary lobes, cut deeply or shallowly, with a few large teeth or smaller lobes toward the tip—otherwise toothless. Lobe tips are mostly blunt. **Surfaces** *finely hairy on both sides* but denser below, the hairs pointing distally. **Veins** palmate; the major veins and veinlets flat to faintly etched above. **Petioles** hairy, not (or faintly) channeled, 3–4 times the blade length. **Stems** multiple, spreading, ground hugging at first but the tips later decumbent, to 30" (75 cm) long and rising about 12" (30 cm), solid, with scattered long hairs. Flowering stems die back in early to mid summer; new rosettes appear in autumn. **Stem leaves** alternate, similar to basal but with narrower and more pointed lobes, on progressively shorter petioles, with clasping **stipules** about 13 mm long and equally wide, with sharp acuminate tips. **Inflorescence** a single flower atop a long, erect, hairy, pedicel up to 8" (20 cm) long, rising above the leaves. **Flowers** have 5 hairy, lanceolate sepals about 0.7" (18 mm) long, fused at the base; immediately below these are 3 long, narrow, sepal-like bracts. **Corollas** 2–3" (5–8 cm) across, cup-shaped, showy, with 5 rose to purple petals that are overlapped but not fused at the whitish base and wider toward the wavy tip. The central column and stamens are whitish. **Fruits** flattened, wheel-like, 1 cm wide, composed of 14–20 sections.

CONFUSING PLANTS: Buttercups may have similar leaves but the petioles are thicker, the flowers are very different, and the roots fibrous. **Prairie larkspur** *Delphinium carolinianum* leaves have longer, narrower lobes.

HABITAT: Dry, open areas: prairies, roadsides, lightly used pastures, meadows—especially where sandy. Native. 🔥

FOOD USE: Roots are best from late summer through early spring when the plant is fully or partially dormant. They are eaten cooked as a vegetable. Young **leaves** can be eaten raw or cooked, or used as a soup thickener. The **flowers** make an attractive garnish. **Immature fruits** can be eaten like those of common mallow. **Conservation 3/1.**

COMMENTS: This is one of the most practical root vegetables native to North America. It is large, tastes good, and is easy to harvest, clean, and store. All of the edible parts are mucilaginous, as is characteristic of the mallow family. The common name is sort of silly, because most species of poppy-mallow have flowers about the same color. The members of this genus depend on soil disturbance for propagation, and a forager can increase their abundance by spreading seeds into small excavations. **AKA** winecup, prairie winecup.

RELATED EDIBLES: Other poppy-mallows have edible roots, fruits, flowers, and leaves, but I have not tried all the species. Some are rare and protected.

5 Fringed poppy mallow 🌱 2 🏺 2 🍃 2 🌿 2
Callirhoe pedata + *Malvaceae* (Mallow family)

QUICK CHECK: Knee-high plant with a loose, spreading cluster of bright pink-purple flowers on long pedicels, held well above the palmately compound leaves. **ID difficulty 2.**

DESCRIPTION: Perennial from a **taproot** with a medium-sized, turnip-shaped enlargement and thin, smooth, light-colored skin, and slightly fibrous flesh. **Basal leaves** 2–4" (5–10 cm) long, deeply palmately lobed with the lobes long and narrow. **Petioles** 2–4 times the blade length, with a whitish, winged, sheath-like base and a wing toward the distal end. The blades are mostly hairless above but slightly hairy below. **Stems** one to several, erect or spreading and then sweeping upward, reaching 30" (75 cm) tall and 3–6 mm thick, thin for their height, appearing delicate but actually rather stiff, the *upper portion leafless*, round, sometimes furrowed near the base but smooth above, usually hairless but sometimes stiff-hairy, coated gray-green. **Stem leaves** alternate, confined to the lower stem, deeply cut with very narrow, almost lacy lobes. **Inflorescence** usually a loose raceme, the pedicels to 6" (15 cm) long, thin, almost hairless, ascending. **Flowers** (mostly spring) have a calyx of 5 triangular to ovate, acuminate lobes, fused near the base, with 3–5 *keel or wrinkle-like veins protruding on the outside*. **Petals** purple (rarely pink or white) with a minute fringe at their tips. The column is whitish. **Fruits** small, wheel-like, composed of many sections.

CONFUSING PLANTS: Prairie larkspur *Delphinium carolinianum* has hairier leaves with depressed veins.

HABITAT: Shortgrass or mixed prairies, especially where rocky. Native. 🔥

FOOD USE: The small thickened **root** is excellent when cooked. Young **leaves**, **shoots**, and **flower buds** are all better than those of purple poppy-mallow. **Conservation 3/2.**

COMMENTS: If I lived in Oklahoma or North Texas I'd be sure to have this elegant wildflower growing all around my property. This species is sometimes considered a smaller southern form of *C. digitata*, a plant of tallgrass prairies just to the north. *C. digitata* is the tallest and showiest species in this genus, and ethnography suggests that it may have had the most preferred root for eating, but it is rare and should not be collected from wild populations.

6 Common mallow 1 2
Malva neglecta + *Malvaceae* (Mallow family)

QUICK CHECK: Creeping herb with very long petioles and shallowly lobed, roundish leaves; fruit a flattened "wheel" divided into sections. **ID difficulty 1.**

DESCRIPTION: Weedy annual to short-lived perennial. Sap slimy. **Basal leaves** sometimes absent, especially on smaller plants—and rosettes without stems are rarely seen. Leaves are roundish in outline with a cutout at the base, the lobes usually not overlapped. **Blades** ruffled, 1–3" (2.5–8 cm) across, with 5–7 shallow lobes, sparsely hairy on both sides, the margins with blunt teeth. **Veins** palmate, *all major veins running straight to lobe tips*, depressed on top and protruding below. **Petioles** 1.5–4 times the blade length, 1.5–2.5 mm thick, one side flattened to faintly channeled, hairy. **Stems** multiple on larger plants, leaning or decumbent to prostrate (rarely weakly erect), to 28" (70 cm) long and 7 mm thick, branched occasionally (including near the base), solid, purplish or green, finely pubescent, roundish to slightly angled. **Stem leaves** alternate with small triangular stipules, otherwise like the basal leaves. **Inflorescence** axillary tufts of 1–4 flowers on pedicels 0.5–1.5" (1–4 mm) long. **Flowers** (April–October) 9–15 mm across with 5 broad, sharp, triangular sepals. **Petals** 5, with broad, notched tips, white with light purplish veins. **Fruit** flattened and wheel-like, green turning brown, consisting of *12–15 "pie-slice" carpels around a circular middle*, with 5 calyx lobes wrapped around it.

HABITAT: Moist soil in full sun to light shade. Likes yard edges, gardens, building foundations, weedy areas. Introduced.

FOOD USE: Gather young **leaves** and tender **stem tips** from late spring through summer; they are edible raw but better as a potherb or soup thickener. **Immature fruits**, called cheeses, can be cooked as a vegetable.

COMMENTS: Mallow cheeses are unique in appearance with an excellent, mild flavor. It's too bad that it takes so long to collect a cupful.

RELATED EDIBLE: *M. pusilla* is nearly identical, though slightly smaller, and is used in the same ways.

7 **Musk mallow** 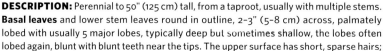 2   2
Malva moschata ◆ *Malvaceae* (Mallow family)

QUICK CHECK: Waist-high stalk; leaves deeply palmately lobed; flowers large and pink with 5 petals. **ID difficulty 1.**

DESCRIPTION: Perennial to 50" (125 cm) tall, from a taproot, usually with multiple stems. **Basal leaves** and lower stem leaves round in outline, 2–3" (5–8 cm) across, palmately lobed with usually 5 major lobes, typically deep but sometimes shallow, the lobes often lobed again, blunt with blunt teeth near the tips. The upper surface has short, sparse hairs; there are longer hairs below and on the margins. **Major veins** palmate and depressed above. **Petioles** 2–3 times blade length, hollow, hairy, rounded beneath, channeled on top, sparsely covered with *long* erect hairs. **Stems** erect to slightly leaning, rounded, 5–12 mm thick, gently zigzag, solid or pithy inside, green, sparsely coated with stiff hairs. **Branches** minor, ascending from upper leaf axils. **Stem leaves** alternate, on progressively shorter petioles, similar to basal leaves but larger, with narrower and more deeply cut lobes, the 3 or 5 main sections cut nearly to the base and deeply lobed themselves. **Stipules** triangular, 3–9 mm long, entire or with 1–2 teeth. **Inflorescence** a compact terminal cluster of about a dozen, the pedicels 8–10 mm, hairy, with a linear bract that is sometimes toothed at the base. **Flower buds** have raised ridges where the edges of the 5 hairy, triangular sepals meet. **Flowers** subtended by 2–3 linear, ciliate bracts. **Corolla** 2–2.3" (5–6 cm) across with 5 thin, pink (occasionally white) veiny petals narrowed at the base, where the sides are fuzzy; the tip is shallowly but broadly notched (like a fish tail). **Fruit** a flattened wheel surrounded loosely by papery sepals; upon maturity the carpels break apart and rattle loose within them. **LYDS** nearly black, moderately stiff, sometimes standing.

HABITAT: Disturbed ground in sun to moderate shade; forest edges, open woods, brushy areas, vacant lots, trailsides, ditches. Introduced.

FOOD USE: All the tender parts are edible, but the young **leaves** and **flower bud clusters** are best.

COMMENTS: Despite the name, I don't find this plant very musky. This attractive non-native is not very invasive; though widespread it is usually not abundant. It is not quite as good as some of the other mallows, mostly because the parts get tough sooner, but if it grows near you it is worth adding to your foraging repertoire.

8 High mallow 🌿 2 ❀ 2 🍃 2 ◊ 2
Malva sylvestris ✦ *Malvaceae* (Mallow family)

QUICK CHECK: Leaves palmate with blunt lobes and long petioles, stems almost smooth and often erect, flowers pinkish with purple highlights. **ID difficulty 1.**

DESCRIPTION: Biennial from a taproot. **Rosette leaves** numerous, 1–4" (2.5–10 cm) long, nearly rounded to kidney-shaped with 3–7 blunt, shallow lobes; often slightly ruffled. There is usually a deep *maroon area where the petiole attaches*. The surface is hairless or nearly so and rather glossy above, usually with sparse and tiny hairs below. **Veins** and veinlets are depressed above and protrude below. **Margins** have blunt or wavy teeth. **Petioles** several times blade length, rounded below and flat to faintly channeled above, often with *a narrow line of hairs running along the top*. **Stems** 1.5–5' (45–150 cm) tall, usually clumped, mostly erect (especially in competition) but may be leaning or decumbent without competition, solid, roundish but faintly angled, branched (but not at the base, and the branches of erect stems remain short). The surface is hairless to sparsely hairy, occasionally roughened. **Stem leaves** 2–6" (5–15 cm) long, alternate, more deeply lobed than basal leaves, with sharper teeth and lobes, the blades more ruffled, and the petioles shorter. **Stipules** linear to triangular, 4–9 mm. **Inflorescence** axillary clusters of 3–22 on pedicels and peduncles ranging from almost sessile to 2" (5 cm) long. **Flower** (summer and fall) 0.9–1.9" (23–48 mm) across with 3 elliptic to lanceolate bracts just behind the calyx of 5 broadly triangular sepals. **Petals** 5, longer than wide, *widest at the tip with a rounded notch* like a fishtail; long and narrow proximally with dense, short hairs near the base, pink to pale purple *with darker streaks along the veins*. The column is pink-purple but the anthers white. **Fruit** wheel-shaped, 7–10 mm wide and 3 mm thick, pale green at first drying to brown, composed of 10–12 parts (carpels), the back roughened by raised veins. The calyx persists and wraps around the fruit.

▲ Rare in mapped area. Occasional elsewhere.

HABITAT: Weedy edges of yards and parks, disturbed forests. Introduced.

FOOD USE: The **greens** can be eaten raw or cooked almost all growing season, but are best when new and tender in spring and early summer. Older leaves can still be used as a soup thickener. **Flowers** and **buds** are edible, the former making a pretty garnish. Immature **fruits**, while still green, make a fun nibble or vegetable.

COMMENTS: This species is common and well-known in Europe. In North America it is often grown in flower gardens but only rarely does it escape and persist. Young plants, especially when growing along the ground, look much like common mallow *M. neglecta*—but once they stand up or flower the differences become obvious. Since it is cultivated the genetics are especially diverse, making the form and size highly variable. Adding confusion, this species is also often called "common mallow."

9 Glade mallow 🌱 2 🍁 3 🌿 2 ✂ 3 🍃 2
Napaea dioica ◆ *Malvaceae* (Mallow family)

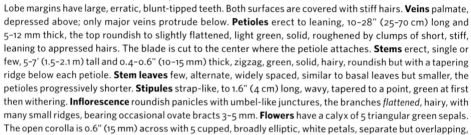

QUICK CHECK: Very large palmately lobed leaves; thin stems reach over your head; large clusters of relatively small white flowers with five petals. **ID difficulty 1.**

DESCRIPTION: Perennial from a large, long, often hollow, sometimes multi-crowned **taproot** with whitish, semi-fibrous flesh. **Basal leaves** 8-20" (20-50 cm) across, round in outline, with 7-9 major lobes radiating almost symmetrically, the sinuses cut nearly to the center; each lobe in turn is pinnately lobed, and some of these lobes are lobed further. Lobe margins have large, erratic, blunt-tipped teeth. Both surfaces are covered with stiff hairs. **Veins** palmate, depressed above; only major veins protrude below. **Petioles** erect to leaning, 10-28" (25-70 cm) long and 5-12 mm thick, the top roundish to slightly flattened, light green, solid, roughened by clumps of short, stiff, leaning to appressed hairs. The blade is cut to the center where the petiole attaches. **Stems** erect, single or few, 5-7' (1.5-2.1 m) tall and 0.4-0.6" (10-15 mm) thick, zigzag, green, solid, hairy, roundish but with a tapering ridge below each petiole. **Stem leaves** few, alternate, widely spaced, similar to basal leaves but smaller, the petioles progressively shorter. **Stipules** strap-like, to 1.6" (4 cm) long, wavy, tapered to a point, green at first then withering. **Inflorescence** roundish panicles with umbel-like junctures, the branches *flattened*, hairy, with many small ridges, bearing occasional ovate bracts 3-5 mm. **Flowers** have a calyx of 5 triangular green sepals. The open corolla is 0.6" (15 mm) across with 5 cupped, broadly elliptic, white petals, separate but overlapping,

each with a narrow, hairy, stalked base. A white column protrudes in the center. **Fruit** wheel-like, 8-10 mm across.

HABITAT: Moist prairies and meadows, oak savannahs, streamside openings. Locations with very rich soil, much sun, and soil disturbance. Native.

FOOD USE: The **roots** are large and only slightly stringy, with excellent flavor. Young **petioles** and **peeled shoots** are large and excellent. **Leaves** are tender at first but become slightly coarse even while still ruffled; after this they should be cooked or used in a smoothie. **Flowers** and **flower buds** are also good. All these parts are slimy, and make a good soup thickener. **Conservation 3/2.**

COMMENTS: A giant mallow with mild-flavored greens—what more could a mallow muncher ask for? This unique plant is the only member of its genus. Its distribution is limited and it has lost most of its habitat to agriculture. If you have an appropriate location, plant a glade mallow that will provide food and beauty beyond your lifetime. The only roots I have eaten were those damaged in transplanting—wild plants are too precious to kill for the root.

10 Biennial waterleaf  2 ❘ 3
Hydrophyllum appendiculatum ✦ family *Hydrophyllaceae*

QUICK CHECK: Maple-like, hairy stem leaves; basal leaves watermarked in spring, pinnately divided with a broad, palmate, terminal lobe. **ID difficulty 2.**

DESCRIPTION: Biennial or short-lived perennial herb from a root cluster. **Basal leaves** 5–8" (13–20 cm) long, *several in a rosette*, pinnately divided with 3–7 major divisions, the terminal one much larger with 3 major lobes. The *blade center and tooth-sinus bases are prominently watermarked in spring*. The watermark of side lobes or divisions is *elongated, often triangular, and follows the midvein*. The upper surface has long, soft hairs. **Veins** depressed above. **Teeth** *blunt to rounded on mature leaves*. **Petioles** flat-topped with a sharp, winged edge near the base. **Stems** 14–22" (36–56 cm) tall and up to 0.6" (15 mm) thick, often multiple, erect to leaning, light green, slightly zigzag, solid, the lower part diamond-shaped in cross-section with 2 opposite ridges, the surface covered with erect to base-leaning hairs that upon close examination can be seen to have two distinct lengths. **Stem leaves** alternate, on petioles 30–40% of blade length, the blades 3–6" (8–25 cm) long, *not divided nor cut close to the midvein*, 5–7 lobed in a strange way that is *between palmate and pinnate*, the lobe tips elongated and sharp, the teeth few, wide, angled or rounded, with claw-tips. **Inflorescence** a dichotomously branching, broad, one-sided cluster 2–3.5" (5–9 cm) wide containing several flowers that extend above the leaves. **Flowers** 0.6–0.8" (15–20 mm) across with a calyx of 5 narrow, hairy, pointed, triangular lobes and a corolla of 5 broad, irregular-rimmed, light-purple petals fused at the base, the stamens and pistils extending beyond the petals (but not as far as with other waterleafs). The fruit is a 3–4 mm capsule with a few seeds.

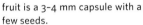

HABITAT: Hardwood forests with very rich, moist soil, typically in deep shade; lower slopes, valleys, and small floodplains. Native.

FOOD USE: The **leaves**, best when young in spring and to a lesser extent again in fall, can be eaten raw or cooked. The young **shoots**, available in mid to late spring, are sweeter and more tender than those of Virginia waterleaf and make a delicious nibble—leave some on each plant to go to seed. **Conservation 2.**

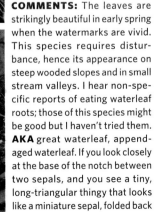

COMMENTS: The leaves are strikingly beautiful in early spring when the watermarks are vivid. This species requires disturbance, hence its appearance on steep wooded slopes and in small stream valleys. I hear non-specific reports of eating waterleaf roots; those of this species might be good but I haven't tried them. **AKA** great waterleaf, appendaged waterleaf. If you look closely at the base of the notch between two sepals, and you see a tiny, long-triangular thingy that looks like a miniature sepal, folded back away from the flower, you have found the namesake appendage.

Related edible:

11 Broad waterleaf ♦ *Hydrophyllum canadense* 2 2

Perennial spreading by rhizomes, the basal leaves borne singly or in clumps of a few. **Basal leaves** have a large terminal division comprising almost all of the blade; it is deeply cut into 5–7 major lobes, each with smaller lobes or large, rounded teeth. There are only 1–4 much smaller, fully separated side divisions, often widely spaced from the terminal. The watermarks are splotchy and amorphous (not distinctly following the midvein of lateral lobes). **Stems** shorter and less robust than those of our other waterleafs. The later basal leaves and **stem leaves** lack watermarks and are palmately lobed, not divided, with sharp, elongated lobe tips and sharp teeth. The two kinds of lower leaves are about the same size and often intermingle, and because the coloration, shape, tooth shape, and vein depth all differ, it may appear that two different species are present. The petioles are nearly hairless on stem leaves. **Flowers** white, not spreading open, the clusters hidden under the leaves rather than rising above them. Broad waterleaf likes moist, rich soil in deep shade. The best part to eat is the new, glossy, still-folded leaf. **Conservation 2.**

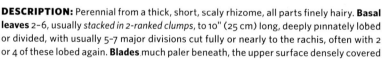

12 Virginia waterleaf 1 2 📖 FH-306
Hydrophyllum virginianum ♦ family *Hydrophyllaceae*

QUICK CHECK: Short, finely hairy herb with pinnately divided leaves bearing gray watermarks in spring; purplish 5-petal flowers with protruding stamens. ID difficulty 2.

DESCRIPTION: Perennial from a thick, short, scaly rhizome, all parts finely hairy. **Basal leaves** 2–6, usually *stacked in 2-ranked clumps*, to 10" (25 cm) long, deeply pinnately lobed or divided, with usually 5–7 major divisions cut fully or nearly to the rachis, often with 2 or 4 of these lobed again. **Blades** much paler beneath, the upper surface densely covered with stiff appressed hairs. **Major veins** deeply depressed (less so when young). The **first leaves** of spring, as well as some autumn leaves, have distinct *gray-white watermarks at the base of the sinuses between lobes and sometimes teeth*; summer leaves lack them. **Margins** dark, hairy, and irregularly toothed, the teeth large, *acute, and sharp* with claw tips. **Petioles** broadly but shallowly channeled, sometimes recurved, often reddish, 120–150% of blade length on lower leaves. The petiole base is flared and sheath-like, often lined with long, rusty wool on young leaves. **Stems** usually multiple, often forked near the base and again near the top but rarely in middle, up to 16" (40 cm) tall, *roughly diamond-shaped* in cross-section, solid, with 2 wings on opposite sides running down from petiole margins; purple at the base, green with scattered purple streaks above that. **Stem leaves** few, smaller, on shorter petioles. Clusters of unopened **flower buds** form hairy balls, sometimes nearly wrapped in one or two leaves. **Inflorescence** a branched, crowded, one-sided cluster. **Flowers** bell-like with numerous kinky threads inside, 11–14 mm long. **Petals** 5, fused at the base, light purple (occasionally nearly white), each with a keel on the outside, spreading slightly, blunt-tipped. Stamens and style are much longer than the petals, the anthers dark and long. **Fruit** a roundish capsule 3–4 mm long containing 2–4 seeds.

CONFUSING PLANTS: Purple phacelia (p. 437) has compound leaves and flowers with wide spreading petals. Young leaves of sochan (p. 380) are more rigid, less hairy, not as deeply divided nor as sharply toothed; they have fewer lobes and lack watermarks.

HABITAT: Hardwood forests with rich soil, especially slopes and floodplains. Native.

FOOD USE: Young **leaves** in spring, while still small and water-marked, can be eaten raw or cooked. A few tender leaves appear again in fall and can be nibbled until winter. **Shoots** are tender and juicy, sweet with a slight astringency; I like them raw. **Conservation 1.**

COMMENTS: The greens are not fantastic but are often extremely abundant and have a long season of availability. Virginia waterleaf is what I call an "optional ephemeral"—most leaves die back in summer, but some of those with more sunlight persist.

Related edible:

13 Large waterleaf ◆ *Hydrophyllum macrophyllum* 1 ⌸ 1

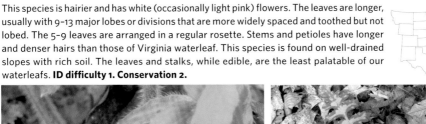

This species is hairier and has white (occasionally light pink) flowers. The leaves are longer, usually with 9–13 major lobes or divisions that are more widely spaced and toothed but not lobed. The 5–9 leaves are arranged in a regular rosette. Stems and petioles have longer and denser hairs than those of Virginia waterleaf. This species is found on well-drained slopes with rich soil. The leaves and stalks, while edible, are the least palatable of our waterleafs. **ID difficulty 1. Conservation 2.**

14 Pansy 2
Viola bicolor ✦ family *Violaceae*

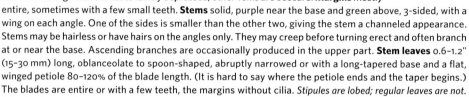

QUICK CHECK: Short herb appearing to have 3 leaves per node, two of them lobed; two-toned, violet-shaped flowers on nodding stems. **ID difficulty 1.**

DESCRIPTION: Annual to 18" (46 cm) tall, with a wintergreen odor, especially in the roots. **Basal leaves** 0.4–0.8" (1–2 cm) long, on petioles 1.5–3 times the blade length, broadly ovate to nearly rounded, not lobed, the surface hairless or with sparse, minute hairs; withering late in flowering. **Midvein** flat to faintly depressed; other veins are obscure. **Margins** mostly entire, sometimes with a few small teeth. **Stems** solid, purple near the base and green above, 3-sided, with a wing on each angle. One of the sides is smaller than the other two, giving the stem a channeled appearance. Stems may be hairless or have hairs on the angles only. They may creep before turning erect and often branch at or near the base. Ascending branches are occasionally produced in the upper part. **Stem leaves** 0.6–1.2" (15–30 mm) long, oblanceolate to spoon-shaped, abruptly narrowed or with a long-tapered base and a flat, winged petiole 80–120% of the blade length. (It is hard to say where the petiole ends and the taper begins.) The blades are entire or with a few teeth, the margins without cilia. *Stipules are lobed; regular leaves are not.*

Stipules *large, clasping, and deeply lobed near the base*, the lobes long and finger-like; stipules become more prominent at the upper nodes, sometimes equal to the leaf in size, giving the *appearance of 3 leaves at a node.* **Flowers** borne singly on long, thin, nodding stems. Sepals 5, pointed, *ear-like at the base*, making for a crown-like structure on the drooping flower bud. **Corolla** 7–9 mm long, bluish or white with blue veins, the center yellow, consisting of 5 petals arranged asymmetrically, the side petals with "hairy armpits." **Fruit** an ovoid capsule 4–7 mm long, breaking into sections.

HABITAT: Fields, pastures, meadows, lawns, open grassy woods. Native.

FOOD USE: Eat **all tender parts**, including the flowers, in spring. They are pleasant raw as a nibble or in salads, with an interesting wintergreen flavor. **Conservation 1.**

COMMENTS: This is an excellent "gateway edible" from the front lawn. The leaf-and-stipule clusters are diagnostic, and the wintergreen flavor begs you to bite.

RELATED EDIBLE: *Viola arvensis*, the European field pansy, is a close relative that has escaped from gardens and is widely established in much of the same range as our native species. Most parts are larger and the upper leaves are more toothed. It can be used similarly for food.

15 **Compass plant** ⋔ 2 ⚲
Silphium laciniatum ✦ *Asteraceae* (Composite family)

QUICK CHECK: Enormous, deeply-lobed, erect, flattened basal leaves and thick, tall stems with yellow sunflower-like heads. **ID difficulty 1.**

DESCRIPTION: Perennial from a large root. **Basal leaves** several but not always in clear rosettes, *enormous, vertical, twisting into one plane to optimize sunlight exposure*, the blade to 32" (80 cm) long and 18" (46 cm) wide. Blades are very rough, leathery, *stiff-hairy on both sides*, deeply cut into many long, narrow lobes, these lobed again, mostly blunt-pointed; the margins with stiff hairs but not toothed. **Veins** wide, flat and protruding above (although it's hard to say which side is which on a vertical leaf), rounded and protruding below, offset from the blade by pale green color (the midvein sometimes reddish). Veinlets are rough-reticulate on both sides. **Petioles** erect with a sheath at the base, 6–16" (15–40 cm) tall and up to 0.7" (18 mm) thick, not channeled, rounded, solid, with scattered stiff hairs. **Stems** single or clumped, erect, *unbranched*, to 0.8" (2 cm) thick and 8' (2.4 m) tall, round, solid, light green or reddish, roughened with stiff, curvy or kinked hairs. **Stem leaves** have a sheath wrapped around the stem; they are similar to the basal leaves but smaller, often erect and appressed to the stem. Petioles progressively shorten; uppermost leaves are sessile. **Inflorescence** a raceme-like cluster of a few to a dozen heads, widely spaced (or in widely-spaced sets of 2–3), the peduncles 1–2" (2.5–5 cm) long, often twisting to one side, each pedicel with a pinnately cut bract at its base. **Heads** (mid summer to early fall) 2.5–4" (6.5–10 cm) across with ray and disk florets. Rays are yellow and notched at the tip. Disk flowers are tubular, yellow, and 5-lobed. Heads are subtended by large, stiff, hairy, layered bracts, the tips long and narrow with inrolled margins.

HABITAT: Rich, well-drained soil in full sun: tallgrass prairies, mixed prairies, rocky outcroppings, roadsides, oak savannahs. Native. 🔥

FOOD USE: The **shoots** can be peeled and eaten raw or cooked. They are slightly astringent and aromatic. The cut stems exude a **gum** that some people like to chew. **Conservation 3.**

COMMENTS: This is one of our most striking and unmistakable plants, and it is often used in landscaping for its giant, unique leaves and gorgeous flowers. In the wild, compass plant has suffered enormously from habitat loss—but robust plants can handle losing an occasional shoot. The plants can live for hundreds of years—so plant and tend a few for your grandchildren to enjoy.

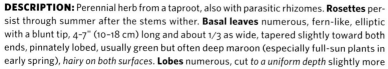

16 Lifelong Lousewort 2 | 2
Pedicularis canadensis ◆ family *Orobanchaceae*

QUICK CHECK: Low, hairy, stout-stemmed herb with numerous fern-like basal leaves; irregular yellow flowers in a densely clustered spike. **ID difficulty 1.**

DESCRIPTION: Perennial herb from a taproot, also with parasitic rhizomes. **Rosettes** persist through summer after the stems wither. **Basal leaves** numerous, fern-like, elliptic with a blunt tip, 4–7" (10–18 cm) long and about 1/3 as wide, tapered slightly toward both ends, pinnately lobed, usually green but often deep maroon (especially full-sun plants in early spring), hairy on both surfaces. **Lobes** numerous, cut *to a uniform depth* slightly more than halfway to the middle, *twisted to give the leaf a ruffled appearance* (especially in full sun and early spring), the lobes *closely and evenly spaced*, their tips rounded. The lobes have shallow, rounded mini-lobes covered with rounded teeth. **Midveins** and secondary veins are *strongly depressed above*, protruding and rounded below. **Petioles** 60–120% of blade length, solid, sparsely hairy, rounded below, deeper than wide, the top flat with a double-wing ridge. **Stems** often clumped, erect to leaning or decumbent, 6–16" (15–40 cm) tall, proportionately stout, hollow, never branched, densely covered with long, straight hairs, the surface usually green but sometimes maroon (especially early in the season), with *many*

short wings. **Stem leaves** crowded on the lower stem and sparse above that, alternate (although upper ones may be almost paired), similar to the basal leaves but smaller, 1.2–2.5" (3–6 cm), on petioles 15–20% of blade length. **Inflorescence** a densely hairy terminal spike-like raceme 1.5–2.2" (38–56 mm) long in bloom, tightly packed with flowers and lobed leafy bracts—expanding up to 7" (18 cm) long in fruit. **Flowers** 0.6–1" (15–25 mm) long, irregularly shaped, *tubular at the base, broadening into an upper and lower lip*, the upper lip longer and hood-like, hooked over the lower. **Corolla** dull yellow to maroon, often bicolored with the upper lip darker. *Flowers are all curved clockwise, giving the spike a distinct look from the top, like a twirling yellow torch.*

HABITAT: Sunny open forests, forest edges and openings, beaver cuttings, prairies, fields near woods, on poor or rich soil. Native. 🔥

FOOD USE: The young **shoots** and attached **leaves** in early spring are eaten raw or cooked—more commonly cooked. **Conservation 2.**

COMMENTS: Before it could be a popular vegetable, this plant probably

needs a new name. The flavor is hard to explain—not unpleasant when you're accustomed to it, but definitely odd, exemplifying what I call the "parasitic plant flavor." You'll have to try it to find out. **AKA** wood betony.

WARNING: These parasitic plants are known to absorb chemicals from their host plants and should not be eaten when growing beside poisonous species.

17 Ox-eye daisy 🌿 2 📖 NG-423
Chrysanthemum leucanthemum ✦
Asteraceae (Composite family)

QUICK CHECK: Small hairless leaves, wider toward the tip, with large blunt teeth; broad, flat, yellow disk with large white rays. **ID difficulty 2.**

DESCRIPTION: Erect perennial herb. **Basal leaves** 2–6" (5–15 cm) long, in rosettes, blunt and spoon-like in outline, tapered at the base, dark green and glossy above, slightly fleshy, smooth, *hairless*. **Margins** irregularly and deeply toothed or shallowly lobed, the teeth mostly rounded. **Midvein** whitish, flat; secondary veins mostly obscure and flat. **Petiole** 40–80% of blade length, channeled, winged, keeled near the base, bearing occasional tiny lobes widely separated from the main blade. **Stems** usually multiple, 18–34" (45–85 cm) tall and 4–6 mm thick, angled, with 3 ridges running down from each petiole, hairless or with sparse, fine hairs. Ascending branches arise from some axils, but the plant is always taller than wide. **Stem leaves** alternate, becoming much smaller, sessile, and clasping on the upper

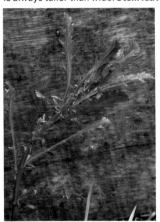

stem. **Flowerheads** (summer) solitary at the end of long, grooved peduncles 1.5–2.5" (4–6 cm) across, with a flat yellow disk surrounded by long white ray florets.

CONFUSING PLANTS: Daisy fleabanes (genus *Erigeron*, greens not edible) have a similar leaf shape and share the habitat; however, the leaves are thinner and hairy with more prominent secondary veins, and the flowerheads are much smaller.

HABITAT: Roadsides, pastures, meadows; any open area with poor, well-drained soil and sufficient moisture. Introduced.

FOOD USE: Leaves and tender **stem tips** make a nice addition to salads or can be eaten as a snack. Their strong, unique flavor is best appreciated raw.

COMMENTS: This cold-hardy nibble is often available late into fall or winter, and again in very early spring. Where they grow large and lush in unusually fertile conditions the leaves are especially good.

18 Cut-leaf evening primrose 🌿 1 🌿 2 🌿 2
Oenothera laciniata ✦ family *Onagraceae*

QUICK CHECK: Creeping to spreading with many lobed but not toothed leaves; veins flat above; large yellow 4-petal flowers at the end of a long tube. **ID difficulty 1.**

DESCRIPTION: Biennial, the rosette persisting at least to early flowering. **Basal leaves** elliptic in outline, slightly to moderately soft-hairy, 2–6" (5–15 cm) long, sometimes entire but usually deeply pinnately lobed with up to 6 lobes per side, the lobes longer than wide, similar in length, ruffled-wavy, blunt-tipped, entire or with a few blunt teeth. The distal portion of the leaf is often unlobed; the tip is blunt or rounded. The base of the blade tapers along the upper petiole. **Midvein** offset by light color, flat above; *secondary veins are flat or faintly raised* above. **Petioles** 40–70% of blade length, solid, flat-topped with a keel below, wider than deep, with short, soft hairs on both sides, only winged distally. **Stems** multiple; the central ones may be erect but the outer ones are leaning, prostrate, or decumbent, to 30" (75 cm) long and 7 mm thick, solid, unbranched or with a few major branches, roundish in cross section, covered with soft hairs. **Stem leaves** 1–4" (2.5–10 cm) long, shorter distally, sessile except for the lowest ones, commonly in offset pairs on the lower stem but the upper leaves are clearly alternate. **Blades** elliptic to lanceolate, the major veins whitish and flat above, protruding slightly but flat-bottomed below; lobes tend to be shorter on stem leaves, sometimes reduced to large teeth. **Flowers** (spring and summer) borne singly from leaf axils along the distal stems, appearing to have long hairy pedicels. (The "fake pedicel" consists of a long, striped, cylindric ovary that later becomes the fruit, and an elongated calyx tube of differing color and texture.) At the end of the tube are 4 hairy triangular lobes 7–13 mm long, folded back away from the flower. **Corolla** spreads 0.9–1.5" (23–38 mm) wide with 4 broad yellow petals (fading to orange), each notched and rippled inward. The sexual parts are all yellow. **Pod** tubular, curved, in 4 sections, drying to release many tiny seeds.

HABITAT: Well-drained, disturbed soil in full sun, especially sand and gravel. Common on roadsides and steep field edges. Native.

FOOD USE: Tender **leafy stem tips** in spring or early summer should be cooked to reduce the slightly irritating quality. **Flowers** and **flower buds** can be collected from spring through summer, sometimes later. I have not eaten the root of this species. **Conservation 1.**

COMMENTS: Unlike its taller cousin, this species' flowers are open all day, not just revealing themselves in the evening. On road shoulders, mowing has selected to favor more prostrate growth forms, but in more natural habitats it is sometimes thigh high. You'll probably never eat a bunch of this plant, but the flowers are an abundant and easy nibble.

19 Annual wall rocket 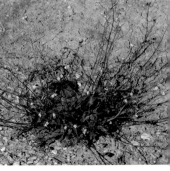 2
Diplotaxis muralis + *Brassicaceae* (Mustard family)

QUICK CHECK: Small-leaved, ground-hugging, aromatic mustard with small leaves and nearly naked stems bearing yellow flowers and long pods in widely spaced racemes. **ID difficulty 1.**

DESCRIPTION: Annual to short-lived perennial, often with multiple rosettes crowded on a multi-crowned taproot, which is white and tough with a very hot flavor. **Basal leaves** 8–14 per rosette, *thick and fleshy*, with a *strong aroma*, the blades 1.5–3" (4–8 cm) long, oblanceolate in outline, blunt-pointed at the tip and wedge-like at the base. **Margins** have erratic, large, blunt, triangular teeth or shallow pinnate lobes. Surfaces are *hairless except for sparse needle-hairs on the margin.* **Midvein** whit-ish and slightly *raised above.* **Secondary veins** scarcely evident and faintly depressed. **Petioles** winged, about 20% of blade length. **Stems** multiple (or branched at the base), decumbent to leaning or sprawling, 2–3 mm thick, tough, purple-green, round, solid or with a pinhole hollow, with scattered needle-like hairs, especially toward the base. **Stem leaves** few, alternate, mostly near the base, similar to basal leaves. **Inflorescence** a terminal raceme with a few flowers or buds packed at the tip, but lengthening greatly in fruit so the *pods are very widely spaced*—sometimes more than 2" (5 cm) apart. **Flowers** (summer to fall) 5–8 mm across with 4 broad-tipped yellow petals (sometimes purple tinted on the outside), opening in the morning, the sepals about half the petal length. **Pods** to 1.3" (33 mm) long and rod-like, roundish to slightly triangular or flattened in cross section, the tip with a broad, blunt beak falling off at maturity, on spreading to ascending pedicels 40–100% of pod length.

HABITAT: Disturbed, well-drained, often poor soils in full sun—hot and dry conditions. Construction sites, yards, beaches, road shoulders. Introduced.

FOOD USE: The succulent **leaves** remain tender even to maturity. They make an unexpected nibble or addition to salads, tasting like a hot, aromatic arugula. The flavor reminds me of blue mustard (p. 402). Just take care to wash off the dirt. The roots are too tough to use as a vegetable.

COMMENTS: This mustard tastes even stranger than it looks, and the leaves make an exotic garnish that nobody will have tasted before. This plant uses a mixture of C3 and C4 photosynthesis strategies.

20 Marsh yellowcress 2 | 2
Rorippa palustris ◆ *Brassicaceae* (Mustard family)

QUICK CHECK: Basal leaves with numerous deep lobes, flowers tiny and yellow, pods short and stout. **ID difficulty 2.**

DESCRIPTION: Annual or winter annual, the rosettes persisting through flowering. **Basal leaves** numerous, 3–10" (8–25 cm) long, deeply pinnately lobed starting at the base or nearly so. Sinuses extend almost to the midvein, which has at least a thin wing along all parts. The lobes are *evenly spaced* and gradually larger toward the tip, widest at the base, pointed, with scattered, tiny whitish nipple-tipped teeth, the surfaces *hairless or finely hairy*. **Midvein** flat to slightly protruding above and widely keeled to rounded below, usually with scattered hair on both sides. Veins are flat to slightly protruding above and protruding below. **Stems** 1–4' (30–120 cm) tall, usually multiple per crown, zigzag, angled, hollow, hairless or finely hairy, unbranched at first but with small ascending branches at flowering, the overall shape taller than wide. Center stem is erect; if multiple, the outer stems tend to lean strongly or spread, especially in full sun. **Stem leaves** strongly ascending, less deeply lobed than the lower ones, and less neatly pinnate; they are usually clasping with auricles. **Inflorescence** racemes, terminal and in upper leaf axils. **Flowers** tiny, yellow, 2 mm wide, with 4 elliptic petals. **Pods** 3–6 mm long, cylindrical, beaked, often slightly curved and oriented toward the tip, borne on pedicels 3–6 mm long, about 90° to the rachis.

HABITAT: Margins of waterways and wetlands in full to partial sun, preferring mucky soil. Also in wet roadsides and trails, dried up ponds or puddles in late summer, and moist agricultural fields. Occasionally in random, disturbed, dry places. Native.

FOOD USE: Gather the **leaves** and **shoots** and use them raw or cooked. Makes a good vegetable steamed like broccoli. The best time to collect this plant is in spring, but occasionally the greens are tender in summer, and it sometimes germinates in late fall where ponds dry up. **Conservation 1.**

COMMENTS: This common native mustard has a good, mild flavor but is largely overlooked. It is often found in wild areas and natural habitats where other weedy mustards are usually absent. All members of the genus *Rorippa* are edible.

21 Creeping yellowcress 🖋 2
Rorippa sylvestris + *Brassicaceae* (Mustard family)

QUICK CHECK: Small, low rosettes of pinnately divided leaves forming a dense, overlapping lawn cover, mostly in flood-prone areas. **ID difficulty 2.**

DESCRIPTION: Perennial spreading by short lateral rhizomes, forming dense colonies of numerous adjacent and partly overlapping rosettes, these often raised slightly by short vertical rhizomes. **Basal leaves** 5–8" (13–20 cm) long, deeply pinnately divided, the divisions narrowed at the base (some leaves appearing almost compound with sessile leaflets). The lowest divisions are often long-elliptic, tiny, and widely spaced. Upper divisions are more crowded, up to 1.2" (3 cm) long, lanceolate, with deep and erratic pinnate lobes that are blunt-pointed with light-colored nipple-tips. Minute hairs are sometimes found on the lower part of the rachis; *otherwise all surfaces are hairless.* **Midrib** deeply D-shaped, *not channeled* (flat or slightly convex above), naked in the lower 20–40%, winged its entire length, but the wing narrower toward the base. **Stems** wavy or zigzag, 5–14" (13–36 cm) tall, slightly angled in cross-section, faintly hairy. **Stem leaves** much smaller, with the lower portion of the petiole naked but faintly winged, the base *not clasping*. **Inflorescence** small crowded racemes, the pedicels 6–9 mm, ascending. **Flowers** 3–7 mm across with 4 yellow petals. **Pods** angled toward the raceme tip, to 14 mm long, 1–2 mm wide, cylindrical, usually seedless.

HABITAT: Moist, low, flat ground, especially flood-prone sites with rich alluvial soil, in full sun to partial shade. Abundant along many major river systems in parks and lawns, and occasionally in disturbed forests. Introduced.

FOOD USE: Tender **greens** are good raw or cooked and remain available into late fall or early winter.

COMMENTS: This is one of our mildest mustards, but unfortunately the leaves are often coated in mud after floods. If you get a mouthful of leaves you may notice a hint of strawberry. (I thought this was my imagination the first five times I ate it.)

22 Wintercress ✏ 2   ❘ 2 ✐ 2   📖 IWE-423
Barbarea vulgaris ✦ *Brassicaceae* (Mustard family)

QUICK CHECK: Rosette leaves pinnately divided, hairless, with a large, blunt terminal division and much smaller side divisions; stem angular; yellow flowers in spring. **ID difficulty 3.**

DESCRIPTION: Winter annual or biennial. **Basal leaves** in a rosette, 4–9" (10–23 cm) long and 2–3" (5–8 cm) wide, pinnately lobed or divided with 3–9 lobes, both surfaces hairless. The terminal lobe composes most of the blade; it is blunt and ovate to rotund, usually with 2 *curled, ear-like sections* at the base, the margins with *light spots at the vein tips*. Side lobes are small and blunt, one pair very close to the terminal lobe but the rest well-spaced; some have a narrowed, stalk-like base. **Major veins** *depressed faintly, veinlets not at all.* **Midrib** long and hairless with a broad, shallow channel edged distally with a thin leafy wing, bluntly keeled beneath. Basal leaves are wilting but present at flowering. **Stems** multiple, to 3' (1 m) tall and 0.7" (18 mm) thick, solid or with a tiny hollow, green, *strongly angled and grooved in an asymmetric fashion*, hairless, with ascending simple branches in the upper half. **Stem leaves** clasping, flared at the base with 2 ear-like lobes, shorter than basal leaves. They have *a few long hairs on the rachis wings, especially near the base*—these are the only hairs on the plant. The terminal divisions are narrower and often lobed. Uppermost leaves, associated with the inflorescence, have large, blunt teeth. **Inflorescence** terminal and axillary racemes, the peduncles long and naked for 3–9" (8–23 cm). Flower buds green with yellow, spiky tips. **Flowers** (late spring) have 4 bright yellow petals, 1 cm across when open, maturing into long, narrow seedpods.

CONFUSING PLANTS: Often confused with watercress (p. 212) because of the name. Watercress has compound leaves with more and larger lateral leaflets, hollow stems, white flowers, no basal rosette, and is aquatic. **Butterweed** *Packera glabella* grows in similar habitats and resembles wintercress in spring before flowering. It can be told apart by teeth on the lobes or divisions, more lobes per leaf, and the fact that the uppermost leaves are pinnately divided (they are only lobed in wintercress). A silvery sheen follows butterweed veins on the upper surface; the stems have a large hollow and bright purple ridges.

HABITAT: Moist, disturbed ground, in full to partial sun. Agricultural fields, gardens, yards, parks, roadsides, riverbanks, lakeshores, dried puddles, construction sites, meadows, trails through low woods. Native.

FOOD USE: Gather the **shoots** and tops while still meristematic in early to mid spring, when **flower buds** are visible but have yet to open; use like a strong-flavored broccoli. Basal **leaves** are best collected in late autumn, winter, or very early spring, when their flavor is mildest. **Conservation 1.**

◄ Butterweed *Packera glabella* may be confused with either species of wintercress.

COMMENTS: Like beer, wintercress has a strong flavor and is an acquired taste. People who have long eaten it crave it. Many botanists separate the native North American populations into a separate species, *B. orthoceras*, but nobody seems able to explain clear or consistent differences between them. I think the distinction lies somewhere between insignificant and bogus. **AKA** yellow rocket.

Related edible:

23 Southern wintercress + *Barbarea verna* 🌿 3 | 3 🥄 3 🌱

A smaller plant with a rosette that persists through blooming. **Basal leaves** are pinnately divided with 15–23 lobes (plus mini-lobes between them), crowded and getting progressively larger toward the tip. The side lobes or divisions are about twice as long as wide, blunt with scattered nipple-teeth, 20–40% as large as the terminal lobe. **Midribs** have hairs along the channel and near the base. **Stems** multiple, branched, even more angled than common wintercress, often nearly triangular. The flowering and fruiting parts are similar but smaller. **ID difficulty 2.**

HABITAT: Disturbed, rich soil (less moist and mucky, on average, than common wintercress, but they sometimes occur together). This plant largely replaces common wintercress in the Southeast. Introduced.

FOOD USE: The flavor is hotter than that of common wintercress, but lacks the bitter overtone—it tastes nearly identical to watercress. Cooking greatly reduces the hotness.

COMMENTS: This is a popular wild green and is grown commercially to a limited extent. It is sometimes differentiated from wintercress by calling it "early" or "spring" wintercress—names which are contradictory, since winter is earlier than spring. It is also called "creasy greens."

24 Blue mustard  3
Chorispora tenella ✦ *Brassicaceae* (Mustard family)

QUICK CHECK: Small, sticky-haired mustard with lanceolate, sparsely-toothed leaves and loose racemes of light blue flowers with 4 petals. **ID difficulty 1.**

DESCRIPTION: Annual or winter annual. **Basal leaves** to 6" (15 cm) long, often persisting to early flowering, especially on robust plants. They are long-elliptic, tapered to both ends, and may be toothed or deeply pinnately lobed—if lobed, there is usually a crimped-up wing between the lobes. **Petioles** shallowly channeled, 15–25% of blade length on basal leaves, 5–12% on stem leaves. **Stems** erect to spreading or prostrate, sometimes branched from the base, 3–22" (8–56 cm) tall and 3–13 mm thick, round, hollow on large specimens, covered with gland-tipped hairs and scattered needle-hairs. **Branches** prominent, strongly ascending in competition, wide-spreading in full sun. **Stem leaves** progressively shorter toward the top; they are erratically alternate, sometimes 2 on one side, *the first two on each branch borne close together in an offset pair. Under full sun and moisture stress, leaves point vertically and twist to optimize sun exposure, so that all leaves on each branch are in plane.* The surface has gland-tipped hairs and bumps or spots on both sides. **Midvein** nearly flat above and light in color. **Secondary veins** *depressed slightly or not at all.* **Margins** sparsely but almost regularly toothed, the points sharp, often purple, oriented outward. **Inflorescence** a sparse terminal raceme, the pedicels ascending and slightly shorter than the flower. **Flowers** (spring) have an elongated, narrow base with 4 purplish sepals. The 4 narrow, blue-purple petals are darker and wavy or crimped at the base, wider toward their rounded tips, and spread 9–12 mm. **Pods** 1.2–1.8" (3–4.6 cm) long, rounded in cross section, thin, hairy, *curved, ascending, with a long, thin, tapering, needle-like tip.* The short, stout pedicel widens to meet the pod's base. At maturity the pods break into 2-seeded sections.

HABITAT: Sunny, well-drained, disturbed soil, especially sandy; likes fallow crop fields, roadsides, construction sites, and vacant lots. Introduced.

FOOD USE: Young, tender **stems** and **leaves** can be eaten raw or cooked. They are moderately radishy-hot. Individual leaves often remain tender well into flowering when stems have toughened. Beware: The sticky hairs can hold wind-blown soil.

COMMENTS: This mustard has a distinct, unique flavor that is odd and unforgettable but pleasant and slightly sweet. It is short, blooms at the same time as henbit, has flowers of similar color, and the two are often intermingled. You might be overlooking it. **AKA** musk mustard, purple mustard, crossflower.

25 Shepherd's purse ⚹ 2 ⏐ 3 ✦ 3 ▭ IWE-339
Capsella bursa-pastoris ✦ *Brassicaceae* (Mustard family)

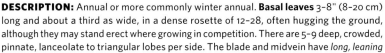

QUICK CHECK: Dense rosette of dandelion-like leaves; stem leaves few and sparse; tiny white flowers and triangular seedpods. **ID difficulty 2.**

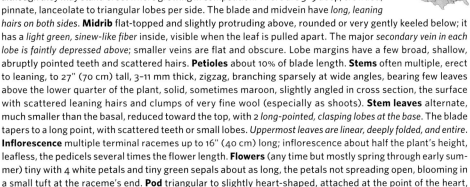

DESCRIPTION: Annual or more commonly winter annual. **Basal leaves** 3–8" (8–20 cm) long and about a third as wide, in a dense rosette of 12–28, often hugging the ground, although they may stand erect where growing in competition. There are 5–9 deep, crowded, pinnate, lanceolate to triangular lobes per side. The blade and midvein have *long, leaning hairs on both sides*. **Midrib** flat-topped and slightly protruding above, rounded or very gently keeled below; it has a *light green, sinew-like fiber* inside, visible when the leaf is pulled apart. The major *secondary vein in each lobe is faintly depressed above*; smaller veins are flat and obscure. Lobe margins have a few broad, shallow, abruptly pointed teeth and scattered hairs. **Petioles** about 10% of blade length. **Stems** often multiple, erect to leaning, to 27" (70 cm) tall, 3–11 mm thick, zigzag, branching sparsely at wide angles, bearing few leaves above the lower quarter of the plant, solid, sometimes maroon, slightly angled in cross section, the surface with scattered leaning hairs and clumps of very fine wool (especially as shoots). **Stem leaves** alternate, much smaller than the basal, reduced toward the top, with 2 *long-pointed, clasping lobes at the base*. The blade tapers to a long point, with scattered teeth or small lobes. *Uppermost leaves are linear, deeply folded, and entire.* **Inflorescence** multiple terminal racemes up to 16" (40 cm) long; inflorescence about half the plant's height, leafless, the pedicels several times the flower length. **Flowers** (any time but mostly spring through early summer) tiny with 4 white petals and tiny green sepals about as long, the petals not spreading open, blooming in a small tuft at the raceme's end. **Pod** triangular to slightly heart-shaped, attached at the point of the heart, with a line down the middle, on a pedicel twice the pod's length.

HABITAT: Disturbed ground in rich, drained soil; gardens, yards, construction sites, crop fields. Usually reported as introduced but I have seen no evidence presented—it's probably native.

FOOD USE: Roots are good, but usually small and fiddly to clean. Gather robust, tender **leaves** mostly in spring and fall in the North, winter in the South. They can be eaten raw in salads or cooked as a potherb. **Shoots** are available primarily in winter (South) or spring (North). The flavor is good raw and superb cooked.

COMMENTS: Supposedly the seedpods resemble purses that shepherds carry. It's been a while since I've seen that. This is my favorite mustard. The tender young stems are one of the world's finest vegetables. Young leaves are very good, too—especially when they stand erect on rich soil. When old and tough and easy to spot, this plant is not good eating. Reports that the root can be used as a seasoning like ginger are based on inattentive copying of information (see Kallas 2010) and should be ignored.

26 Field pepperweed 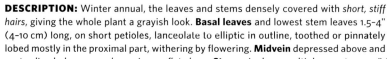 2
Lepidium campestre ✦ Brassicaceae (Mustard family)

QUICK CHECK: Small, lobed basal leaves and clasping, entire stem leaves; all parts hairy; tiny disc-like seed pods with a notched tip. **ID difficulty 1.**

DESCRIPTION: Winter annual, the leaves and stems densely covered with *short, stiff hairs*, giving the whole plant a grayish look. **Basal leaves** and lowest stem leaves 1.5–4" (4–10 cm) long, on short petioles, lanceolate to elliptic in outline, toothed or pinnately lobed mostly in the proximal part, withering by flowering. **Midvein** depressed above and protruding below; *secondary veins are flat above*. **Stems** single or multiple, erect, 10–24" (25–60 cm) tall and 3–5 mm thick, tough, roundish but finely ridged. **Branches** mostly in the upper half, simple, ascending. **Stem leaves** alternate, 1–2" (2.5–5 cm) long, sessile, becoming shorter and *clasping with a lobed base*, crowded and overlapping, lanceolate, the blades cupped downward. **Margins** may be entire but more often have sparse, small, nipple-like, light-tipped teeth. **Inflorescence** dense terminal racemes up to 9" (23 cm) long. **Flowers** tiny, inconspicuous, with barely visible (sometimes absent) petals, obovate to elliptic, widely separated, white to pinkish. **Pod** circular to heart-shaped, about 3 mm across, divided in half by a prominent suture line, cupped upward, winged on the edges, notched at the tip, on a pedicel slightly longer than its diameter.

HABITAT: Disturbed soil such as gardens, crop fields, sidewalk cracks, vacant lots, construction sites, road shoulders. Introduced.

FOOD USE: The young **leaves** and **stem tips** can be collected while tender and eaten raw or cooked (they're better cooked). The flavor is moderately strong. The seedpods and **seeds** have a hot, peppery flavor. You can use them when just formed, or when mature.

COMMENTS: This mustard has good flavor and in some areas is a prevalent agricultural weed. Unfortunately the plant is inconspicuous in its ideal eating stage.

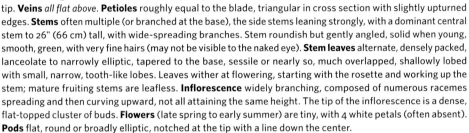

27 Common pepperweed 🌿 2 ⫿ 3 ⌂
Lepidium virginicum and *L. densiflorum* ✦ *Brassicaceae* (Mustard family)

QUICK CHECK: Shin-high plant with crowded, pinnately lobed basal leaves and a broad, spreading top with numerous racemes, tiny flowers, and disc-like pods. **ID difficulty 2.**

DESCRIPTION: Annual or winter annual, at first with a dense basal rosette. **Basal leaves** numerous, the blade tapering from a narrow base, widest at the tip, with several forward-pointing lobes. Sinuses may be deep near the leaf base with fully divided sections; distal sinuses get shallower. Blades *minutely hairy on both sides*, the hairs leaning toward the tip. **Veins** *all flat above.* **Petioles** roughly equal to the blade, triangular in cross section with slightly upturned edges. **Stems** often multiple (or branched at the base), the side stems leaning strongly, with a dominant central stem to 26" (66 cm) tall, with wide-spreading branches. Stem roundish but gently angled, solid when young, smooth, green, with very fine hairs (may not be visible to the naked eye). **Stem leaves** alternate, densely packed, lanceolate to narrowly elliptic, tapered to the base, sessile or nearly so, much overlapped, shallowly lobed with small, narrow, tooth-like lobes. Leaves wither at flowering, starting with the rosette and working up the stem; mature fruiting stems are leafless. **Inflorescence** widely branching, composed of numerous racemes spreading and then curving upward, not all attaining the same height. The tip of the inflorescence is a dense, flat-topped cluster of buds. **Flowers** (late spring to early summer) are tiny, with 4 white petals (often absent). **Pods** flat, round or broadly elliptic, notched at the tip with a line down the center.

Species: *L. densiflorum* is shorter, often bushy and wider than tall, especially in the open where decumbent branches give it a tumbleweed form. The flower petals are tiny or absent. *L. virginicum* is usually slightly taller than wide and is less branchy, and the flowers normally have petals.

CONFUSING PLANTS: Ox-eye daisy leaves (also edible, p. 395) are glossier, darker, and thicker.

HABITAT: Dry, disturbed soil; roadsides, yards, sidewalk cracks, vacant lots, railroads, edges of parking lots, beaches, crop fields, construction sites. Native.

FOOD USE: The tender **leaves** and leafy **shoots** can be eaten cooked or raw in late spring; they are mild to average among mustards as far as hotness. The tender tip of each growing **inflorescence** (about half an inch) can be used as a hot seasoning. Mature **seed pods** can be gathered and ground as "pepper" but are not as peppery as the flower buds. **Conservation 1.**

COMMENTS: This is a common weed that everyone has seen, even in the largest urban areas. It is distinct at maturity, but harder to recognize early in the season when it is best for eating. The two species covered here are nearly identical when young.

▲ *Lepidium virginicum* flowering.
◄ (left top and bottom) *L. densiflorum.*

405

28 Tower mustard 🖊 1 🍶 3
Arabis glabra + *Brassicaceae* (Mustard family)

QUICK CHECK: Straight, unbranched mustard, all parts pointing vertically; entire, narrow, clasping stem leaves, often purple. **ID difficulty 1.**

DESCRIPTION: Winter annual. **Basal leaves** to 7" (18 cm) long and 1.2" (3 cm) wide, with pointed lobes 90° to the midrib, the sinuses between them wide and cut nearly to the midrib, especially on proximal lobes. The distal third of the blade may be entire. The upper surface has *hairy bumps* and *flat veins*. The midrib is hairy underneath. **Stems** single, 2–6' (60–180 cm) tall, *strictly erect, straight, unbranched below the inflorescence, hairless*, solid, round, *heavily coated with white bloom*, smooth except for very faint ridges descending from the nodes. **Stem leaves** alternate, 1–5" (2.5–13 cm) long (the lowermost twice that long), spaced regularly up the stem, *pointing skyward and almost appressed*, lanceolate or tapered to the pointed tip, broadest at the base, clasping with 2 narrow, round-tipped lobes. The blades are hairless except that low to mid-stem leaves have a line of hairs on the midvein below. **Midvein** *in a deep valley*, projecting below but not sharply keeled; other veins are *flat and obscure above*, giving the leaf a *very smooth surface*. Lower leaves are purple on the underside; those on young plants often *dark purple on both sides*. **Inflorescence** branching but the branches almost pressed together, all pointing up; multiple racemes to 24" (60 cm) long, the flowers blooming in an elongated cluster at the tip. **Flowers** 5–7 mm wide, the 4 elliptic petals creamy to pale yellow, on short pedicels. **Pods** to 3" (8 cm) long, rod-like and very narrow, crowded, overlapping, and appressed.

HABITAT: Sandy fields, dry meadows, barrens, and roadsides. Native. 🔥

FOOD USE: The **shoots** make a good vegetable in spring; raw they are acceptable, but steamed or briefly boiled they are excellent. Older growth quickly becomes too tough to eat. **Leaves** may remain tender even on flowering plants but are usually strong and bitter in flavor. **Conservation 2.**

COMMENTS: At maturity this is one of the easiest herbaceous plants in our region to recognize. The shoots are not well known, but excellent if you can identify them at that stage. **AKA** *Turritis glabra*.

29 Field mustard 🌿 2 ⎸ 3 🦋 3
Brassica rapa + *Brassicaceae* (Mustard family)

QUICK CHECK: Large, spring-blooming mustard with yellow flowers and a smooth stem; lower leaves lobed, upper stem leaves clasping and entire. **ID difficulty 1.**

DESCRIPTION: Annual or winter annual. **Basal leaves** in a rosette, up to 18" (46 cm) long, deeply pinnately lobed or divided, the lobes/divisions usually alternate and sometimes twisted, the terminal lobe containing most of the leaf's surface area. The blades are ruffled, with *scattered hairs* growing from light-colored bumps on the upper surface and on the midrib below. **Midrib** whitish in color with thin, continuous wings of varying width, essentially flat; *smaller veins slightly depressed to flat.* **Margins** irregularly wavy and toothed, sometimes shallowly lobed, with scattered hairs. **Stems** 2–5' (60–150 cm) tall, solid when young but sometimes with a small hollow when older, *smooth,* gently ridged, with *few to no hairs,* usually covered by a *whitish bloom.* **Stem leaves** clasping; lower ones pinnately lobed with proximal lobes pointing back toward the stem; going up the stem they become progressively smaller and less lobed. **Uppermost leaves** much smaller, elongated, unlobed, with pointed tips and entire or sparsely toothed margins, *the bases clasping with overlapping rounded lobes.* **Inflorescence** a

▲ Sparse over much of this range but locally abundant.

terminal raceme of more than 12, the pedicels about 1" (2.5 cm) long, 90° to the rachis. **Flowers** (spring) 9–11 mm across with 4 obovate yellow petals, not veiny. **Pods** 1–2" long, thin, curved toward the tip, round in cross section, containing numerous tiny, dark seeds.

CONFUSING PLANTS: Black mustard, charlock mustard, and wild radish all bloom later in the season; they have hairy stems and their upper leaves are not clasping. The differences listed in many technical manuals to separate the closely related *B. napus* often do not work in the field. The two are so similar that foragers need not worry over the distinction.

HABITAT: Disturbed soil, especially farmland, roadsides, and construction sites. Introduced.

FOOD USE: Gather any tender growth. **Greens** can be used raw or cooked like cultivated mustard or turnip greens. **Flower bud clusters** are like miniature, superior broccoli. **Shoot tips** are very mild in flavor and are good raw or briefly steamed. Field mustard is most prevalent in spring, although occasionally one can get greens from it later in summer or autumn.

COMMENTS: This locally abundant plant is the wild ancestor/descendant of the cultivated turnip. The flavor is mild, and it is one of our best wild mustards.

30 Bastard cabbage 🌿 1 🌱 2
Rapistrum rugosum ✦ *Brassicaceae* (Mustard family)

QUICK CHECK: Mustard blooming yellow in cool seasons, with rough, hairy, blunt-tipped, mostly basal leaves; stems almost naked; tiny round pods. **ID difficulty 1.**

DESCRIPTION: Annual or winter annual with a rosette that persists at least through early flowering. **Basal leaves** (and lowest stem leaves) 6–10" (15–25 cm) long, *rounded at the tip*, oblanceolate or elliptic in outline with some small but deeply cut lobes near the base; the distal majority is merely toothed or wavy-edged. The blade is *thick, almost succulent*, both surfaces with scattered, stiff, leaning, whitish hairs, those on top growing from *light-colored bumps*. **Midrib** pale or purple, depressed above and protruding below. **Secondary veins** at broad angles, *deeply depressed above* and protruding below. **Petiole** 5–10 % of blade length, slightly triangular with a *deep, narrow groove on top* (becoming flat where the blade starts).

▲ Widespread but scarce outside mapped area.

Stems 2–5' (60–150 cm) tall but often first blooming when much shorter; erect, zigzag, solid, somewhat grooved or *flattened*, very hairy at first and near the base but *almost hairless in the upper parts*. Stems branch widely on robust plants but smaller ones may be simple and spire-like. **Stem leaves** alternate, few, on petioles, reduced in size upward, often deeply folded and ascending, the underside hairy but the *top almost hairless*. **Inflorescence** long, wiry terminal racemes to 20" (50 cm). **Flowers** 6–9 mm across with 4 nearly round, bright-yellow, stalked petals and 4 narrow yellow sepals. **Pods** *ball-like*, the round part 2–3 mm, grooved lengthwise, *beaked at the base and the tip*, on an *appressed pedicel* 4–6 mm long, containing 1–2 seeds.

HABITAT: Disturbed soil in full sun. Yards, construction sites, agricultural fields, vacant lots, weedy areas. Introduced.

FOOD USE: Leaves can be eaten raw or cooked—mostly in winter and spring. They are hairy and rough, so they hold dirt easily and are better when softened by cooking. Tender **tops** and **shoots** of robust plants taste better and are less likely to be dirty. The flavor is cabbage-like—not very hot.

COMMENTS: This mustard is extremely common in the east half of Texas; in this area it should be one of the first mustards you learn. Outside of Texas and southern Oklahoma it is sparse or absent. No other mustard can be more easily recognized by its pods. **AKA** turnipweed, ball mustard.

31 Hill mustard 3 2 2
Bunias orientalis ✦ *Brassicaceae* (Mustard family)

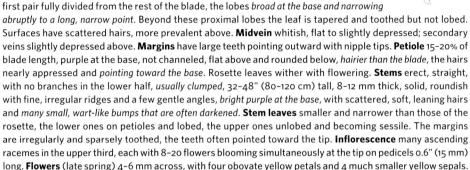

QUICK CHECK: Erect mustard with yellow flowers in early summer; leaves pointed, toothed or lobed; stems warty; pods nearly rotund. **ID difficulty 1.**

DESCRIPTION: Perennial mustard with a mild but distinct scent reminiscent of blue mustard (p. 402), producing multiple adjacent rosettes from branching root crowns. **Rosette leaves** 7-12" (18-30 cm) long, lanceolate, usually with *4 side lobes near the base*, the first pair fully divided from the rest of the blade, the lobes *broad at the base and narrowing abruptly to a long, narrow point*. Beyond these proximal lobes the leaf is tapered and toothed but not lobed. Surfaces have scattered hairs, more prevalent above. **Midvein** whitish, flat to slightly depressed; secondary veins slightly depressed above. **Margins** have large teeth pointing outward with nipple tips. **Petiole** 15-20% of blade length, purple at the base, not channeled, flat above and rounded below, *hairier than the blade*, the hairs nearly appressed and *pointing toward the base*. Rosette leaves wither with flowering. **Stems** erect, straight, with no branches in the lower half, *usually clumped*, 32-48" (80-120 cm) tall, 8-12 mm thick, solid, roundish with fine, irregular ridges and a few gentle angles, *bright purple at the base*, with scattered, soft, leaning hairs and *many small, wart-like bumps that are often darkened*. **Stem leaves** smaller and narrower than those of the rosette, the lower ones on petioles and lobed, the upper ones unlobed and becoming sessile. The margins are irregularly and sparsely toothed, the teeth often pointed toward the tip. **Inflorescence** many ascending racemes in the upper third, each with 8-20 flowers blooming simultaneously at the tip on pedicels 0.6" (15 mm) long. **Flowers** (late spring) 4-6 mm across, with four obovate yellow petals and 4 much smaller yellow sepals. **Pods** nearly rotund with a beak-like tip, 5-9 mm long.

HABITAT: Sunny, open areas with well-drained rich soil: roadsides, meadows, pastures. Introduced. **I**

FOOD USE: Young **leaves**, tender **shoots**, and **flower bud clusters** can all be used as a vegetable, raw or cooked, in spring.

COMMENTS: This mustard is sometimes cultivated; it is currently very local in North America, but where found it is often extremely abundant. It is allelopathic, releasing chemicals that inhibit the growth of competing plants, so that it forms large, pure stands to the exclusion of native vegetation. Hill mustard should NOT be spread intentionally. **AKA** Turkish cabbage, Turkish rocket, warty cabbage.

409

32 Black mustard 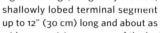 3 ⏐ 3 🏺 📖 IWE-45
Brassica nigra ✦ *Brassicaceae* (Mustard family)

QUICK CHECK: Mustard with yellow flowers above your head in midsummer; lower leaves with a large terminal segment; long overlapping pods held against the stem. **ID difficulty 1.**

DESCRIPTION: Annual with a *short-lived rosette*, the basal leaves soon disappearing as the stem emerges. **Lower leaves** to 18" (46 cm) long with a large, irregularly toothed, shallowly lobed terminal segment up to 12" (30 cm) long and about as wide, comprising 90–95% of the leaf surface. Lower on the rachis are 2–4 much smaller, usually fully separated segments. **Blades** ruffled, with sparse needle-hairs growing from bumps above; hairier underneath, especially on the veins. **Veins** and veinlets depressed above and protruding below. **Margins** have obtuse, light, nipple-tipped teeth. **Petiole** deeper than wide, bluntly keeled, scarcely channeled except near the base (which is more deeply channeled), the rachis with a faint, close, double wing along the top. **Stems** single, erect, to 8' (2.4 m) tall and 0.9" (23 mm) thick, smooth, green to purple, faintly ridged, solid, bloom-coated, with large but scattered needle-hairs near the base, decreasing to few or none on the upper stems. Upper **stem leaves** are coarsely and irregularly toothed but not lobed. *Uppermost leaves at bloom are entire, elongated, tapered at both ends, and drooping on long petioles.* **Inflorescence** lanky, nearly leafless, sparse, with many long, *twisting, curvy, or leaning racemes,* rising 1–3' (30–90 cm) above the leafy zone of the plant; open flowers are crowded at the tip. **Flowers** (mid to late

summer) 9–13 mm across with four fan-shaped yellow petals, each with a long stalked base; the 4 linear sepals are also yellow. **Pods** long and narrow, roundish with 4 ridges, narrowed and beak-like at the tip, *overlapping and nearly appressed.* **Seeds** spherical and light brown to reddish-brown or dark gray.

HABITAT: Disturbed soil, especially where very rich and hilly. Commonly found in gardens, agricultural fields, building sites, compost heaps. Introduced.

FOOD USE: Young plants are found mostly from early to mid summer. **Leaves** and **tender tips** are excellent raw or cooked—those near the inflorescence are much hotter than lower parts. Leaves are more pungent than

the stems. Ripe **seeds** can be collected by stripping the dry pods or beating the mature tops, then winnowing (see p. 27). Black mustard is grown commercially for its hot seeds.

COMMENTS: This giant mustard is locally abundant in rich soil. The flavor is great if you can handle the heat. (The uppermost greens are fire-in-the-sinus hot.) The seeds make my favorite wild mustard.

Related edible:

33 **White mustard** ✦ *Sinapis alba*

A belly-high, yellow-flowered, summer-blooming weedy mustard with short, broad leaves with a few large lobes. The pods are curved and tapered with a *halo of white hairs around the base.* The tender greens can be collected from early summer through autumn, and the seeds can be used to make a condiment. This mustard is extremely easy to recognize in fruit. It is pure nose-burning hot, without any horseradish flavor or bitterness—one of the best hot greens.

▲ Widespread but sporadic.

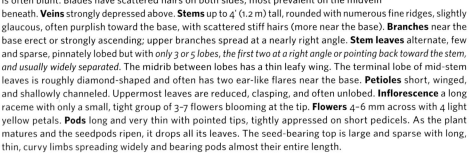

34 Hedge mustard 🌿 2
Sisymbrium officinale ✦ *Brassicaceae* (Mustard family)

QUICK CHECK: Stem leaves with a few widely spaced lobes; plant loses its leaves when bearing seed; tiny, tightly clumped yellow flowers; pods pressed against the stem. **ID difficulty 1.**

DESCRIPTION: Annual with a sparse, airy look. **Basal leaves** pinnately lobed almost to the midvein, with 8–12 narrow side lobes (the first of which are linear); the terminal lobe is often blunt. Blades have scattered hairs on both sides, most prevalent on the midvein beneath. **Veins** strongly depressed above. **Stems** up to 4' (1.2 m) tall, rounded with numerous fine ridges, slightly glaucous, often purplish toward the base, with scattered stiff hairs (more near the base). **Branches** near the base erect or strongly ascending; upper branches spread at a nearly right angle. **Stem leaves** alternate, few and sparse, pinnately lobed but with *only 3 or 5 lobes, the first two at a right angle or pointing back toward the stem, and usually widely separated.* The midrib between lobes has a thin leafy wing. The terminal lobe of mid-stem leaves is roughly diamond-shaped and often has two ear-like flares near the base. **Petioles** short, winged, and shallowly channeled. Uppermost leaves are reduced, clasping, and often unlobed. **Inflorescence** a long raceme with only a small, tight group of 3–7 flowers blooming at the tip. **Flowers** 4–6 mm across with 4 light yellow petals. **Pods** long and very thin with pointed tips, tightly appressed on short pedicels. As the plant matures and the seedpods ripen, it drops all its leaves. The seed-bearing top is large and sparse with long, thin, curvy limbs spreading widely and bearing pods almost their entire length.

HABITAT: Disturbed rich soil in full to partial sunlight, usually around human habitation. This common weed seems to like growing along building foundations and large objects (such as water tanks, junked cars, or lumber piles). Introduced.

FOOD USE: Young **leaves** and **stems** are prime in early summer. The youngest plants are tender but dainty, with small leaves; you can cut the whole thing for greens. Slightly later, as flowering begins, the tender stem tips are thin with few leaves and little volume; at this time it is easiest to pick the largest leaves from further down the stalk rather than mess with the spindly top.

COMMENTS: This is one of our hottest mustards, with a horseradish-like flavor. Greens in or near the young inflorescence are especially potent.

▲ Mid-stem leaf.   ▲ Lower leaf.

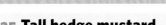

35 Tall hedge mustard ✍ 2 ▯ 2
Sisymbrium loeselii ✦ *Brassicaceae* (Mustard family)

QUICK CHECK: Tall, hairy mustard with long racemes of yellow flowers blooming in late spring; the leaves are deeply lobed. **ID difficulty 1.**

DESCRIPTION: Winter annual (usually) or annual. The stem, petioles, and leaf blades all have *long, erect, stiff hairs*. **Basal leaves** in rosettes, withering during flowering, to 10" (25 cm) long and 2–3" (5–8 cm) wide, deeply pinnately lobed, the lobes pointed, often *toothed and twisted*, hairy on both sides. **Veins** strongly depressed above. **Stem** 3–5.5' (1–1.7 m) tall and 9–15 mm thick, roundish with a small hollow in the center, densely covered with long, erect, needle-like hairs. The upper stem has fine ridges, but the lower stem does not. The shoot first grows tall and straight before producing many long, strongly ascending branches. **Stem leaves** have 2–4 lobes per side, shortening toward the top; these lobes are much narrower than those of basal leaves and pointed, and the first set is angled back toward the stem. **Inflorescence** racemes held erect, to 26" (66 cm) long, the pedicels ascending. **Flowers** (late spring to early summer) 6–7 mm across with 4 nearly round yellow petals. **Pods** 1–2" (2–5 cm) long, thin, cylindrical, nearly straight, longer and thicker than the pedicels.

HABITAT: Dry, sunny, disturbed sites; roadsides, railroads, vacant lots, crop field margins. Introduced.

FOOD USE: Basal **leaves** in early spring are *very* mild and can be used as a salad green or potherb. Once the stems begin to grow this plant's flavor changes dramatically; the **stem tips** and stem leaves are then horseradish-hot and similar to hedge mustard.

COMMENTS: This weed is one of the most abundant mustards in the eastern Plains and western Midwest, but it seems to be a newcomer, for it is way more common than herbarium records suggest. The flavor change with age is astounding, perhaps the greatest that I am aware of for any plant. The biggest drawback to this green is the stiff hairs, which detract from the mouth-feel.

413

36 Tumble mustard 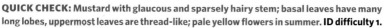 2 | 1
Sisymbrium altissimum ✦ *Brassicaceae* (Mustard family)

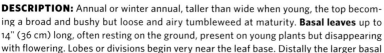

QUICK CHECK: Mustard with glaucous and sparsely hairy stem; basal leaves have many long lobes, uppermost leaves are thread-like; pale yellow flowers in summer. **ID difficulty 1.**

DESCRIPTION: Annual or winter annual, taller than wide when young, the top becoming a broad and bushy but loose and airy tumbleweed at maturity. **Basal leaves** up to 14" (36 cm) long, often resting on the ground, present on young plants but disappearing with flowering. Lobes or divisions begin very near the leaf base. Distally the larger basal leaves are deeply pinnately lobed, with the lobes long, narrow, and well-spaced; proximally they are divided fully to the midrib. Smaller basal leaves may have triangular lobes with large teeth; these lobes often have *one sub-lobe on the proximal side pointing toward the base.* Surfaces have erect hairs on both sides. *The midrib is round, hollow, not channeled even at the base; the proximal portion has a small double-wing ridge on its top, with both wings oriented vertically.* **Stem** to 5' (1.5 m) tall, single, erect, solid, light gray-green, zigzag, smooth and glaucous but also with scattered long, thin, wavy hairs (these densest near the base and in the inflorescence). **Branches** many and ascending; in fruit these grow longer and branch or curve inward and downward to fill out the tumbleweed form. Each branch juncture has a dark line forming a raised scar. **Stem leaves** become progressively more divided, the divisions longer and narrower with fewer teeth. Many *lobes point vertically.* Uppermost leaves have *extremely thin, deeply folded, mostly entire, thread-like lobes* up to 3" (8 cm) long. **Inflorescence** many long racemes; at bloom the flowers are crowded at the tip, but in fruit the rachis elongates and the pods from adjacent racemes intermingle in a giant tangle. **Flowers** pale yellow to almost white, 8–13 mm across, with 4 petals in 2 pairs (not at right angles to each other). **Pods** up to 4" (10 cm) long, very stiff, the same thickness as the pedicels but 6–10 times longer, and not angled at the juncture—making the pod look like a leafless branch.

HABITAT: Disturbed, sunny, dry sites; roadsides, railroad banks, vacant lots, crop fields, ditch banks. Introduced.

FOOD USE: All young, **tender growth** is edible: leaves, flower buds, and stems. Gather these mostly in spring. Basal leaves are mild, but when the stems appear a hotness and a less desirable strong flavor soon develops, especially in the inflorescence. Use these parts in moderation.

COMMENTS: This is one of many "tumbleweeds" on the Great Plains; the dead plants break from their roots and tumble in the wind to disperse the seeds. Although the scientific species name means "the tallest," this species tends to be shorter than *S. loeselii.* The pods are remarkably long and stiff, but one of my favorite books says they grow up to *four feet* long. Even my uncle wouldn't exaggerate that bad, so it must be a typo.

37 Highway mustard 🖋 3
Coincya monensis ✦ *Brassicaceae* (Mustard family)

QUICK CHECK: Lanky mustard, much branched near the base, with sparse leaves and large yellow flowers in early summer. **ID difficulty 1.**

DESCRIPTION: Annual or winter annual from a taproot, all vegetative parts with scattered, stiff, needle-like hairs. **Basal leaves** in a rosette, to 10" (25 cm) long, pinnately lobed or divided with 15–19 lobes, these well-spaced and longer than wide, the proximal ones entire and broadest near the base, the distal ones broadest near the tip and shallowly lobed or with a few large, blunt teeth. **Surfaces** rough-hairy on both sides with depressed major veins. Rosette usually withers by flowering. **Rachis** often purple, flat to wing-channeled above. **Stems** single or few, often much branched at or near the base (with few branches above that), the branches nearly equal to the stem in height. Stems reach 2.5–4' (75–120 cm) tall and 12 mm thick, weakly ridged and angled, coated with bloom. **Stem leaves** alternate, sparse (especially upward), deeply pinnately lobed/divided, with a continuous wing and occasional extensions along the rachis. **Major veins** more deeply depressed than on basal leaves. Toward the top of the plant lobes get progressively fewer, longer, narrower, and more fully divided with few to no teeth; side lobes are right angled to the midrib. Lobes are often deeply folded. **Petiole/midrib** has a shallow groove that is *offset by light color.* **Inflorescence** racemes 10–14" (25–36 cm) long, the tips crowded and umbel-like, with evenly spaced pedicels at maturity. **Flowers** (late spring to early summer) to 0.7" (18 mm) across, with 4 bright yellow petals with *distinct veins, especially beneath.* The *base is a tubular calyx* with 4 stiff-hairy triangular lobes at the tip. **Pods** long and narrow, curved, roundish, to 3" (8 cm) long with a flattened beak, spreading 90° to the rachis on pedicels to 8 mm long.

HABITAT: Disturbed, sunny, gravelly soil; especially roadsides. Introduced.

FOOD USE: All the **tender parts** can be eaten raw or cooked, from spring through early summer. This is one of the milder-flavored mustards.

COMMENTS: This enigmatic species is abundant in Pennsylvania but is almost never found anywhere else. However, since its spread in PA has been rapid, I'm assuming it will soon

spread outside of that state. This is perhaps the most attractive of our weedy mustards, and one of the best for eating, too. It doesn't have a common name here, but in the UK it goes by the eloquently beautiful (read with sarcasm) "Isle-of-Man Cabbage." I made up "highway mustard," which is not only accurate, but conveniently shorter than "Pennsylvania-railroad-right-of-way cabbage."

38 French rocket 2
Erucastrum gallicum + *Brassicaceae* (Mustard family)

QUICK CHECK: Knee-high mustard with long, pinnately compound-lobed leaves; yellow flowers and loose racemes of very thin pods. **ID difficulty 1.**

DESCRIPTION: Annual or winter annual. **Basal leaves** in a rosette of 3–7, persisting until early bloom, 4–7" (10–18 cm) long with 9–17 deeply cut pinnate lobes, ruffled. **Lobes** blunt-tipped, longer distally, with large blunt teeth; longer lobes are *pinnately lobed again*. Sinuses become deeper proximally, and near the base of the rachis there are a few small, simple lobes fully divided. The upper surface has scattered, *stiff, appressed hairs* and *depressed major veins*. **Midribs** often purplish. **Stems** 12–28" (30–70 cm) long, 3–5 mm thick, often leaning, *densely covered with appressed hairs*, roundish to slightly angled, with a few widely-spreading, ascending branches. **Stem leaves** become smaller toward the top with fewer lobes, but these are

▲ Distribution very sporadic.

proportionally longer and more deeply cut. **Inflorescence** a long raceme rising well above the leaves, the open flowers clustered tightly at the tip, lengthening greatly in fruit so the pods are widely spaced. There is *a tiny, pinnately-lobed leaf at the base of most pedicels*. **Flowers** (summer to fall) 6–9 mm wide with 4 yellow to white petals, the base narrow and stalk-like, the spreading tips fan-like or obovate. The 4 narrow sepals are purple at the base shading to yellow at the tip. **Pods** uniform in thickness, 1–1.3" (25–33 mm) long, rod-like, with a beaked tip, ascending but not pressed to the rachis, on pedicels 30% of their length. **Seeds** oval and red-brown.

HABITAT: Disturbed, dry, sunny ground: crop fields, roadsides, construction sites, lakeshores, waste areas. Introduced.

FOOD USE: Tender **leaves** and **stem tips** can be eaten raw or cooked; they are moderately hot.

COMMENTS: At a glance this looks like a *Brassica*, but the tiny lobed leaves subtending the pedicels distinguish it from all other mustards in our area. This mustard is pretty good, but being short and hairy makes it prone to being dirty. **AKA** dog mustard, hairy rocket.

39 Charlock mustard 2
Sinapis arvensis ✦ *Brassicaceae* (Mustard family)

QUICK CHECK: Knee-high, bushy mustard with yellow flowers in summer; basal leaves pinnate with dominant terminal lobe, uppermost leaves not lobed. **ID difficulty 1.**

DESCRIPTION: Annual with large leaves concentrated at or near the base, some of them held through flowering. **Basal leaves** (and lowest stem leaves) 7–11" (18–28 cm) long and about half as broad, with 2–3 small divisions near the base. The bulk of the leaf is an elliptic to ovate terminal section 5–8" (13–20 cm) long. The blade has scattered needle-hairs, especially on the underside of the veins. The surface above is corrugated by depressed veins and veinlets.

Margins have broad, blunt, irregular teeth and shallow lobes. **Midrib** has a small channel on top and is bluntly keeled below. **Stems** erect, 2–3' (60–90 cm) tall, roundish but grooved, usually hollow, densely covered with downward-pointing needle-hairs at the base (becoming sparser toward the top). **Branches** spreading widely, sweeping upward, with purplish coloration at the junctures. **Upper leaves** broadly triangular, coarsely toothed but not lobed, sessile. **Inflorescence** a branching cluster of racemes, open flowers equaling or exceeding the unopened buds. **Flowers** (summer) 10–12 mm across, the petals yellow, not touching, narrowed at the base, nearly round. **Pods** 1–2" (2.5–5 cm) long and up to 3 mm thick, rod-like, with *tapered beaks about 40% of their length*, at maturity slightly constricted between the dozen or so seeds, the pods leaning strongly toward the rachis but not appressed, on pedicels 10% of pod length.

CONFUSING PLANTS: Wild radish has thicker pods with larger seed bulges.

HABITAT: Gardens, agricultural fields, building sites, other disturbed soil. Probably introduced.

FOOD USE: Gather all **tender parts**—young leaves, stem tips, and flower bud clusters—in spring or early summer (occasionally fall). All parts can be eaten raw or cooked, and have a pungent flavor.

COMMENTS: A common weed in many areas, not quite as mild as field mustard in flavor, nor as hot as black mustard, but also good. **AKA** *Brassica kaber*.

40 **Wild radish**   2   3   IWE-415
Raphanus raphanistrum ✦ *Brassicaceae* (Mustard family)

QUICK CHECK: Summer-blooming mustard with light yellow flowers; leaning stems with needle-like hairs; pods deeply constricted between seeds. **ID difficulty 1.**

DESCRIPTION: Annual, the rosette persisting to flowering. **Basal leaves** up to 10" (25 cm) long with pinnate lobes, the lower ones smaller and nearly or fully divided, increasing in size toward the end of the leaf, with a large terminal lobe that is longer than wide. Both surfaces have scattered, stiff, *needle-like hairs*. **Veins** and veinlets are strongly depressed above. **Petioles** 20–40% of blade length, channeled and winged. **Stems** typically multiple, spreading from the base, leaning, to 32" (80 cm), with scattered needle-like hairs and faint ridges, the surface bloom-coated. Branches are few and at broad angles. Lower **stem leaves** have fewer lobes, with almost all the volume contained in the terminal segment. Upper stem leaves are elongated and pointed with scattered large teeth but typically no lobes. **Inflorescence** long, sparse, terminal racemes. **Flowers** (summer) 0.6–0.7" (15–18 mm) across with 4 green sepals and 4 veiny yellow petals that are widest at the tip, on pedicels 0.5–1" (13–25 mm) long. **Pods** 2–3" (5–8 cm) long and 4–6 mm wide, curved, deeply constricted between the seeds, the tips forming long, tapered beaks. The pods do not split open at maturity: The constrictions become more pronounced and the surface becomes ridged, and when dry they break into sections containing one elliptic, light brown seed 3 mm long.

HABITAT: Agricultural fields, gardens, disturbed ground. Introduced.

FOOD USE: Eat the **tender parts** of clean, vigorous plants from late spring to mid summer, raw or cooked. They have a hot, radish-like flavor. The immature **pods** make a nice vegetable for salads or stir fry.

COMMENTS: The needle-like hairs of this species are among the most formidable on any of our mustards. Literature and herbarium records regarding this species are unreliable due to frequent confusion with **feral radish** *R. sativus*, which is much less common in our region and has purple or purple-veined petals and shorter, stouter pods. I have not found enlarged roots on either species, but in some climates this is reported to occur.

▲ Pods of *R. sativus.*
    Flowers of *R. sativus.* ▶

GROUP 26 BASAL LEAVES PRESENT, LEAVES ALTERNATE, ONCE COMPOUND WITH DISTINCT LEAFLETS

Group 26 includes two good root vegetables, and the rest are leaf and stem vegetables. There are 7 plants here from the carrot family *Apiaceae*, of which a few are very easy to identify. Members of this family can be distinguished from other members of group 26 by their *jointed stems*. However, Cherokee swamp potato is one of the trickiest edibles in North America and is certainly not for beginners. Some aquatic plants will key here if their water has dried up; check group 15 if in doubt. The 5 members of the mustard family *Brassicaceae* can be a little tricky to tell from each other, but there are no dangerous plants in this family. I would rather have included false strawberry next to the true wild strawberries, but in keeping with the premise of the book I had to place it where its physical form indicated.

TENTATIVE IDENTIFICATION KEY TO GROUP 26
The key is not your final answer!

Basal leaves with 3 leaflets.	
Leaflets more than 12" (30 cm) long, deeply and erratically lobed.	
Stem lacking raised purple dots; no ring of hairs at the nodes.	1. Cow parsnip
Stem with raised purple dots; a ring of hairs at the nodes.	2. Giant hogweed
Leaflets less than 5" long.	
Leaflets erratically needle-toothed and lobed, hairless; major veins flat above.	3. Mitsuba
Leaflets unlobed, hairy, broad-toothed; veins depressed; stems trailing.	13. False strawberry
Leaflets unlobed, faintly hairy, entire to minutely toothed; the petiole base has wing-like stipules.	14. Red clover
Basal leaves palmately compound with 3-7 sessile, hairless leaflets.	4. Sanicle (5 species)
Basal leaves pinnately compound, some with more than 3 leaflets.	
All leaflets distinctly less than 1" (2.5 cm) long.	
Petiole long, sinuous, mostly naked with ridiculously widely spaced leaflets.	8. Cuckoo flower
Petiole just normal and mostly straight, with non-ridiculous leaflet spacing.	
Leaflets sharp-pointed, entire, with stiff, leaning hairs.	15. Small-flower phacelia
Leaflets of basal leaves blunt to rounded, never deeply lobed; hairless or soft-hairy.	
Plant of uplands; leaf margins faintly hairy; vertical pods shoot seeds.	9. Shotweed
Plant of wetlands; leaves hairless; erect pods not exploding.	10. Pennsylvania cress
Leaflets of basal leaves often or usually deeply lobed.	
Stems erect, usually more than 14" (36 cm) tall.	11. Narrow-leaf bittercress
Stems prostrate to decumbent, less than 14" (36 cm).	12. Twin cress
Most leaflets clearly larger than 1" (2.5 cm) long.	
Some side leaflets much, much smaller than the terminal one(s).	17. Chocolate root
Side leaflets almost as large as the terminal leaflet.	
Leaves hairless; leaflets lanceolate with no teeth or a few large ones.	5. Cherokee swamp potato
Leaves hairy, at least lightly (check leaf underside); leaflets erratically toothed/lobed.	
Leaflet always deeply lobed, dark-speckled when young; young stem purplish and densely long-hairy.	16. Purple phacelia
Leaflet sometimes deeply lobed, lobes blunt; stem sparsely soft-short-hairy, strongly ridged/angled.	6. Parsnip
Leaflet (basal) toothed but not lobed (upper deeply lobed); stem finely ridged and densely stiff-short-hairy.	7. Burnet-saxifrage

1 Cow parsnip 〰 1 ⚘ 3 🍂 2 🌿 2 🍃 1 ⌂ 📖 NG-365
Heracleum lanatum ✦ *Apiaceae* (Carrot family)

QUICK CHECK: Enormous hairy herb with stout stems and giant 3-part compound leaves, each leaflet deeply lobed; broad, flat-topped umbels of white flowers. **ID difficulty 1.**

DESCRIPTION: Very large perennial. **Basal leaves** compound with *3 leaflets, none sessile*, each 12–20" (30–50 cm) long, ruffled, hairy, deeply palmately lobed, the margins irregularly toothed and lobed, the teeth broad with sharp tips. **Veins** and veinlets deeply depressed above, giving a corrugated appearance. When young the leaves are *deeply folded or pleated*. **Petiole** to 28" (70 cm) long and 1.2" (3 cm) thick, *hollow, round, faintly ridged and lined lengthwise*, hairy in varying density, but the *hair always stiff and erect*; the base is a large sheath. **Stems** 4–8' (1.2–2.4 m) tall and 0.7–1.8" (18–46 mm) thick, round, hollow, jointed, erect-hairy, with few branches (and these only toward the top). Both stems and petioles have *skin that is green, purple, or a mixture of the two*. **Stem leaves** alternate, few, smaller toward the top, on progressively shorter petioles—the uppermost have no petiole beyond the very large sheath. **Inflorescence** *flat-topped compound umbels* up to 10" (25 cm) across, the rays and pedicels ridged, hollow, and hairy; the umbellets not touching but the flowers within them crowded. **Flowers** (late spring to early summer) 5–7 mm across with 5 white, *2-lobed, asymmetrical petals of varying size, the largest petal many times bigger than the smallest*. **Fruit** thin, flat, 5–9 mm long, ripening to light brown with 4 darker brown streaks, oval with the tip notched and the edges sharp, splitting into 2 flat sections each with one seed; highly aromatic.

HABITAT: Moist, rich soil in full sun to partial shade. Roadside ditches, wet forest edges, clearings, swamps, lakeshores, streamsides, and especially floodplain forests. Native.

FOOD USE: Roots can be collected when the tops are dormant; they are powerfully spicy and most people find them too strong except as a seasoning. Gather tender, young **stalks** and **petioles** in spring or early summer before fully formed (well before flowering). Peel and eat raw or cooked like celery in stew. Young **leaves** (early to mid spring) can be cooked or fermented. **Flower bud clusters**, along with their enclosing sheath (late spring) can be used sparingly in salads or to flavor various cooked dishes. The **fruits/seeds** can be gathered from mid to late summer to use as a seasoning. **Conservation 2.**

WARNING: Phototoxic juice—do not get it on your skin! (See p. 23.) (Continued on the next page.)

COMMENTS: The flavor of all parts of this plant are strong and distinct. Many close relatives have been traditionally used as food throughout Europe and Asia. The Russian word *borscht*, now used more generally for vegetable soups, originally referred to a soup made from the fermented leaves of European hogweed. Our native cow parsnip is in serious decline from herbicide spraying by people who think that anything looking remotely like giant hogweed must die. European hogweed *H. sphondylium* is occasionally found as an escape in our region. The leaves usually have 5 leaflets rather than 3. The leaves and petioles are not as tender as our native species, but are similarly edible.

Related edible:

2 Giant hogweed + *Heracleum mantegazzianum*

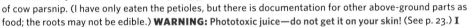

An exotic invasive that has been subject to intense eradication efforts, this plant has received much media attention for its phototoxic juice. It is similar to cow parsnip but larger in all respects, the stems reaching 14' (4 m) tall and the leaves 5' (1.5 m) across. **Stems** have *numerous maroon dots or blotches* and are encircled by a *thick beard of stiff whitish hairs at each node*. **Leaflets** *deeply incised*, in places fully or almost to the midrib (especially in the terminal leaflet) and the *narrow lobes have long, tapered points*. The blades are *glossy and hairless or nearly so underneath*. Tender young growth of this species can be eaten like that of cow parsnip. (I have only eaten the petioles, but there is documentation for other above-ground parts as food; the roots may not be edible.) **WARNING:** Phototoxic juice—do not get it on your skin! (See p. 23.) **I**

◄ Close up of giant hogwed petiole showing narrow ridge, purple spots, and needle-hairs.

3 Mitsuba 2 2 3
Cryptotaenia canadensis ◆ Apiaceae (Carrot family)

QUICK CHECK: Plant hairless, leaves ternately compound; channeled petiole widens at the base to wrap around the stem; flowers tiny, white, on very unequal pedicels. **ID difficulty 3.**

DESCRIPTION: Perennial herb, all parts hairless, the roots thin and whitish with major branches. **Basal leaves** 3–11, ternately compound, the side leaflets normally sessile, the terminal often on a short petiolule with upturned, tapering wings. **Leaflets** 2–4" (5–10 cm) long, narrowed at the base and broad toward the tip. Terminal leaflets usually have 3 major lobes; side leaflets usually have 2. Lobes are abruptly pointed. Sinuses are sometimes cut fully to the midvein on one side. **Midvein** and secondary veins are *raised above*; the *veinlets are slightly depressed above* (scarcely so on the youngest leaves). All veins protrude on the *glossy underside*. **Margins** double-toothed and have small lobes; the teeth are *very sharp*, claw-tipped, and point forward. **Petioles** 1.5–3 times the length of the terminal leaflet, the lower third or so with a broad, glossy, translucent-edged sheath; above that the petiole is *not channeled*, deeper than wide, with a small hollow. **Stems** usually single, to 40" (1 m) tall and 11 mm thick, solid or with a pinhole hollow, jointed, the surface smooth, hairless, and light green, with fine lines. **Stem leaves** alternate, sparser toward the top, with wings extending far up the petiole. Terminal leaflets are sessile, the base decurrent and saw-toothed. Upper leaves have much narrower ovate to lanceolate leaflets with few to no lobes, narrower teeth, and long-pointed tips. **Inflorescence** terminal compound umbels with 3–5 unequal rays at the first juncture and 5–11 unequal and narrowly spreading pedicels in the second, with no bracts at either level. **Flowers** (early summer) 3–4 mm across with 5 white petals. **Fruit** shaped like a tiny, stout banana, turning brown and splitting in two in late summer.

CONFUSING PLANTS: Sanicle leaves are usually more palmate with all leaflets sessile and often cut fully to the base; major veins of mature leaves are more depressed. In flower or fruit, differences are quite evident. Most buttercup leaves are either hairy, have blunt teeth, or have depressed major veins.

HABITAT: Rich, lightly disturbed soil in full to partial shade; mostly hardwood forests, especially in valleys or floodplains and on lower slopes. Native.

FOOD USE: Roots are good but tiny. **Leaves** can be cooked as a potherb or used to flavor vegetable broth; they are best in spring and fall. The spring **shoots** make a delectable vegetable and can be steamed or boiled by themselves and served like asparagus, or they can be eaten raw. They make a superb ingredient in soups and casseroles. **Conservation 2/1.**

COMMENTS: This abundant native herb is not as popular as it deserves to be, partly because it is one of our trickier plants to recognize. It is well worth the effort—and the most confusing species, the sanicles, are related and similarly edible. This species or a very close relative (taxonomists disagree) is native to eastern Asia. In Japan it is a popular cultivated vegetable; the name *mitsuba* means "three leaves" in Japanese. **AKA** honewort, wild chervil.

4 Sanicle 2 2
genus *Sanicula* + Apiaceae (Carrot family)

QUICK CHECK: Smooth, hairless knee-high plants with palmately compound leaves of 3–7 leaflets; compound umbels with few rays, the tiny umbellets packed with sessile burs. **ID difficulty 3.**

DESCRIPTION: Perennials or biennials with little scent, all parts *hairless and without bloom,* often with multiple root crowns in close proximity. **Basal leaves** in clumps or rosettes, often gone by blooming, palmately divided into 3–7 *sessile leaflets* (the outer sometimes not fully divided). Older leaves are dark, dull, and flat; new leaves are light green, glossy, and

▲ Collective range.

ruffled. **Leaflets** lanceolate or oblanceolate, tapered to both ends, pointed, coarsely and irregularly toothed and occasionally lobed, with acuminate, bristle-tipped, forward-pointing teeth. (Sometimes the first spring leaves are obovate or fan-like.) **Veins** and veinlets are lightly depressed above and protrude below—even more so on new leaves. **Petioles** long and narrow, limp or rigid, 2–3 mm thick, erect or ascending, solid, several times longer than the blades, maroon near the base, green above, channeled and sheathing in the lower 2" (5 cm) or so, (the outer ones more broadly so). Above the sheath, the cross section is channeled or round with a small flat area on top and 2 tiny wings. **Stems** one to few per rosette, solid, round, hairless, jointed, erect or leaning, 12–30" (30–75 cm) tall and 4–8 mm thick, almost smooth, but with numerous faint ridges becoming more prominent toward the top, *forking at about 70°* a few times in the upper half, with long, straight sections between forks. **Stem leaves** reduced in size upward, with very short sheathing petioles, borne mostly at forks in the stem. **Inflorescence** a few compound umbels, terminal or from upper leaf axils. The primary rays are *few* (usually 2–3) and often unequal in length; the *umbellets are compact, forming dense heads,* often with two forms of flower. There are commonly 3 sessile, bisexual bur-flowers, and a few to several much smaller, non-bristly, male flowers on pedicels. **Flowers** 2–3 mm across with 5 white or dull yellowish petals and 5 pointed sepals. **Fruit** is a compact bur 3–6 mm long, covered with hooked bristles.

SPECIES: There are 5 similar species in our region: *S. canadensis, S. marilandica, S. odorata (gregaria), S. trifoliata,* and *S. smallii.* They taste similar (but not identical) and differentiating them when not in bloom is difficult, so I will lump them together for discussion here.

CONFUSING PLANTS: All species are easily confused with honewort *Cryptotaenia canadensis* (also edible), especially *S. trifoliata.* The best differences are the two tiny wings on the sanicle petiole, and its more deeply depressed veins.

HABITAT: Well-drained hardwood forests and savannahs, sunny openings, slopes, borders, and trailsides. Native. 🔥

FOOD USE: The young **greens** and **shoots** can be used as a vegetable raw or cooked, mostly in spring and early summer. The flavor varies between the species but is generally like mitsuba with a hint of cilantro and sometimes a slight bitterness. **Conservation 2.**
(Continued on the next page.)

4 Sanicle (continued)

COMMENTS: These plants are abundant and easy to find in most of eastern North America; the group is easy to identify in bloom or fruit. They are often erroneously reported as poisonous. Worldwide there are about 45 species in this tightly-related genus. Many are traditionally eaten as leafy greens in Europe, Asia, and western North America, and they have been widely used for medicinal purposes by Native Americans in our region. I interpret the lack of ethnographically reported food uses in our region as a failure of the record, not evidence of toxicity. The Latin name is derived from *sanus* for "healthy." I have eaten all five species on multiple occasions; they taste similar to each other and to ethnographically documented food species in the West. **AKA** black snakeroot.

5 Cherokee swamp potato ⓌⒸⒹ 3
Oxypolis rigidior ✦ Apiaceae (Carrot family)

QUICK CHECK: Wetland plant with once-pinnately compound leaves, the leaflets entire or with a few teeth; tall stalk with compound umbels. **ID difficulty 3+.**

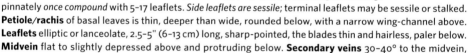

DESCRIPTION: Polycarpic perennial, sometimes spreading by rhizomes. **Roots** clustered, radiating, *white, thin, flexible,* unbranched, terminating in hard, smooth, spherical to elliptic *whitish* tubers 0.4-1" (1-2.5 cm) across and up to 2.5" (6 cm) long. There is no dominant taproot. **Basal leaves** in a rosette, absent by blooming, 8-14" (20-36 cm) long, ascending, pinnately *once compound* with 5-17 leaflets. *Side leaflets are sessile;* terminal leaflets may be sessile or stalked. **Petiole/rachis** of basal leaves is thin, deeper than wide, rounded below, with a narrow wing-channel above. **Leaflets** elliptic or lanceolate, 2.5-5" (6-13 cm) long, sharp-pointed, the blades thin and hairless, paler below. **Midvein** flat to slightly depressed above and protruding below. **Secondary veins** 30-40° to the midvein, soon splitting and conjoining in a net-like pattern, flat to slightly depressed above. **Margins** often purple, entire or with *a few teeth per side, only in the distal 2/3.* The teeth *may be very large* if there are only 1-2 per side, or small, if there are 4 or more. Teeth often curve out away from the margin. **Stem** single, erect but sometimes weak and leaning in shade, 2-6' (60-180 cm) tall and 0.4-0.8" (1-2 cm) thick, round with minute ridges, hollow, jointed, the inside white at maturity. The surface is smooth, usually hairless but sometimes with short, stiff hairs (especially near the base when young), intermittently glaucous, green striped with lighter green. **Stem leaves** alternate, similar to basal but shorter with fewer leaflets. Their petioles consist entirely of *a scrolled sheath* up to 7" (18 cm) long. Side

leaflets occasionally have short petiolules. Leaflets are often highly asymmetric, with less blade at the base on the distal side. *Midveins are not depressed*. The rachis is deeper than wide and channeled. **Inflorescence** compound umbels, one to a few, terminal or from upper branches in axils of reduced leaves with a clasping petiole, the peduncle round, smooth, thin, to 9" (23 cm) long. **Great umbels** 3–8" (8–20 cm) across, may be nearly flat-topped in shade but become hemispheric in full sun, the rays rounded, 1.5–5" (4–13 cm) long, subtended by 0–2 linear, drooping, needle-tipped bracts with inrolled margins. **Umbellets** 7–21, 0.5–0.8" (13–20 mm) across, mostly well separated, subtended by 1–5 tiny, short, thread-thin bracts (hard to see). **Flowers** (late summer to early fall) on thread-thin curved pedicels, not touching, 4 mm across, green in the center with 5 white petals, the sharp petal tips incurved making them look short and blunt. Petals are roughly equal in size and barely or almost touch each other. **Fruit** dry upon maturity, 3–4 mm long, oval, flattened, sharp-edged.

CONFUSING SPECIES: Common water hemlock *Cicuta maculata* (p. 668) may share its habitat, and appears similar at a glance, but has regularly serrated leaf margins and multi-compound leaves with smaller leaflets, and far more of them. The secondary veins are numerous, straight at first, and deeply depressed. The roots of water hemlock are entirely dissimilar. **Bulblet water hemlock** *Cicuta bulbifera* (p. 670) is mostly aquatic and has multi-compound leaves with exclusively narrow leaflets, and bulblets in upper leaf axils. Also check springwater parsnip (p. 216) and water parsnip (p. 213), both edible.

HABITAT: Seepages, ponds margins, marshes, wet meadows and stream edges, in rich, high-calcium soil. Grows in shade to full sun, but larger in sun. Native.

WARNING: This is one of the three plants in this book that I consider the most likely for deadly misidentification. Proceed with great caution!

FOOD USE: The **tubers** can be used as a potato-like vegetable, best gathered from fall through spring. They are fantastic in any way you'd use a potato. Take a couple and replant the crown. **Conservation 3.**

COMMENTS: Probably my favorite root vegetable: like a potato with a faint hint of carrot, but with a better texture and flavor than either. Widely and erroneously reported as poisonous to livestock; the name results from confusion with water hemlock. This vegetable, almost completely unknown to modern foragers, was eaten by the Cherokee (and probably many Native nations in our region) but its food tradition has been hanging by a thread for a century. Although you will find it listed as deadly poisonous in many sources, this is nonsense. I grow this vegetable, eat it as often as I can, and feed it to my guests, who have universally found it excellent. This is what the colonial destruction of food knowledge looks like. I have not listed the shoots or greens as edible due to the lack of ethnographic information, but they are not poisonous. There are other species in this genus, the edibility of which are unknown to me. **AKA** stiff cowbane, pig potato.

▲ Leaflets may be entire or toothed.

425

6 Parsnip 🧍 3 🍃 3 🏮 📖 FH-281
Pastinaca sativa ⬦ *Apiaceae* (Carrot family)

QUICK CHECK: Long basal leaves with 11–13 ruffled, erratically toothed or lobed, paired leaflets out of plane with the rachis; stem deeply ridged; flowers yellow. **ID difficulty 2.**

DESCRIPTION: Biennial, taller than wide. **Basal leaves** in rosettes of 3–7, pinnately compound, 8–22" (20–56 cm) long with 11–13 leaflets, which are often out of plane with the rachis in full sun. **Rachis** narrowly channeled, deeper than wide, gently ridged, solid, usually purplish, hairy or hairless, naked in the lower 40–70%, with a short sheath at the base and a faint bulging ring where each set of leaflets is attached. **Leaflets** 1–3" (2.5–8 cm) long, paired (not offset), mostly sessile but occasionally with short petiolules, roughly ovate, coarsely and irregularly toothed and/or lobed, usually ruffled, the teeth large and blunt with a nipple tip. The surface is semi-glossy above, variably hairy but more so below. **Veins** and veinlets are *flat or nearly so above* and protruding below. **Stem** single, erect, with few leaves toward the top, branched in the upper third, 4–6' (1.2–2 m) tall, thick-walled with a small, irregular hollow, jointed. the surface finely hairy with numerous prominent, sharp ridges. **Stem leaves** alternate, the lower ones up to 30" (75 cm) long on robust plants and sometimes partly to fully double-compound; the upper ones shorter with fewer leaflets and no petiole beyond the broad, tapered sheath. **Inflorescence** *flat-topped* compound umbels (may be 3 times compound) up to 7" (18 cm) wide near the top of the plant, the rays ridged, with no bracts at the junctures. **Flowers** (early to mid summer) yellow, tiny, with 5 petals barely extending past the yellow-green ovary and hooking back to the center, the outer flowers in the umbellet larger, the center flowers crowded and touching. **Fruit** flattened, oblong, 5–8 mm, smooth, held erect, very aromatic, ripening to brown in mid to late summer, drying and splitting in two.

CONFUSING PLANTS: Butterweed *Packera glabella* blooms in spring and the stalk has a large hollow.

HABITAT: Rich, well-drained soil in full sun. Needs disturbance, although not yearly. Roadsides, pastures, old fields, forest edges, meadows. Introduced. **I**

FOOD USE: Dig **taproots** from fall through early spring and use them exactly like cultivated parsnips (they are the same plant): mashed, fried, baked, grated into casseroles, in soup, or just boiled and served with butter.

Roots in mowed areas tend to be of poor quality. Tender young **shoots** in late spring and early summer can be peeled and eaten raw or cooked. Be careful of juice (see below).

COMMENTS: On rich soil wild parsnips can be as large as those from a garden, and taste as good, if not better. In the areas where it is found, parsnip is often available by the ton—and most landowners would be glad to get rid of it. Few wild vegetables can be collected as easily. Although reviled as invasive, it rarely invades native habitats.

◄ Parsnip shoot at the stage for peeling.

CAUTION: The juice from aboveground parts of parsnip plants (domestic or wild) can cause severe burns and blisters if it gets on the skin! (See p. 23.) Be especially careful if gathering stalks, which are very juicy. Most people who get the rash contract it in early summer when the flowering stalks are tall but still soft, easily bruising to release liquid. If you get the juice on your skin, wash it off as soon as possible.

7   Burnet-saxifrage 🌿 1
Pimpinella saxifraga ✦ *Apiaceae* (Carrot family)

QUICK CHECK: Parsnip-like leaves, the leaflets with large teeth; stem leaves few and small with narrow lobes; stems widely branching, thigh-high, with white umbels. **ID difficulty 2.**

DESCRIPTION: Polycarpic perennial from a tough, white taproot; older plants have multiple crowns. **Basal leaves** (usually gone by flowering, but present on nearby non-flowering plants) once pinnately compound, 7–14" (18–36 cm) long, with 7–11 leaf-

▲ Rapidly expanding.

lets crowded in the distal half, the terminal 3 sometimes conjoined or 3-lobed; leaflets nearly in plane. **Rachis** 2.5–3.5 mm thick, naked in the lower half, rounded below, slightly deeper than wide, with many small grooves, a narrow channel on top, and a very short sheath at the base, which is often reddish. **Leaflets** 1.1–2.3" (28–58 mm) long, with blunt tips and broadly angled bases (120–160°), ovate or broadly elliptic, sessile, attached above rather than at the side of the rachis. Blades have very short hairs on both sides. **Veins** *depressed above* and protruding below. **Margins** have large, blunt, deeply cut teeth, irregular in size with abruptly pointed tips; occasional leaflets have shallow lobes. **Stems** single or few from the base, erect, to 30" (75 cm) tall and 6 mm thick, branching widely, rigid and tough, round but with numerous fine ridges, pithy inside with a pinhole hollow, jointed. The surface is *roughened by very short, stiff hairs*, these less prominent in the inflorescence. (Continued on the next page.)

427

7 Burnet-saxifrage (continued)

Stem leaves are few, smaller with fewer leaflets, widely spaced, reduced toward the top, with a finely ridged sheath fully encircling the stem for 1.2–2" (3–5 cm), with little to no petiole beyond the sheath. The leaflets are long, narrow, deeply lobed, with few teeth; uppermost leaves tiny with 1–3 narrow pointed lobes. **Inflorescence** is a nearly flat-topped compound umbel 2–3.2" (5–8 cm) wide in bloom, to 4.5" (11 cm) in fruit, with 14–28 umbellets. **Umbellets** are spaced from each other, but the 9–28 flowers within are tightly packed and touching. Rays are smooth and hairless. There is usually no bract beneath the primary umbel, but occasionally there is one pointed, linear, sheathing bract; umbellets lack bracts. **Flowers** (mid to late summer) 4–5 mm across with 5 unequal white petals, the tips curled back toward the center. **Fruit** triangular to heart-shaped, ribbed, 3–4 mm long, slightly flattened, breaking in two.

HABITAT: Dry roadsides, fields, meadows, hayfields, forest edges, especially where limy and sandy. Full sun. Introduced. **I**

FOOD USE: The **tender tops** of stems and their associated leaves, before flowering, have a taste strongly reminiscent of cilantro but hotter, less soapy, with a fruity aftertaste and an unpleasant texture. They can be used sparingly as a seasoning herb.

COMMENTS: This plant is neither a burnet nor a saxifrage. It is a close relative of the commercial anise (*Pimpinella anisum*), and it has been grown as a fodder crop on poor soils in northern Europe. It occurs sporadically and is locally abundant in some regions—for example, it is perhaps the most common roadside plant around Hayward, Wisconsin. Expect its population to explode in the coming decades. The plant is better known as a medicinal than a food.

▲ (bottom left) Upper stem leaf. (top right) Basal leaf.
(bottom right) Tender tip. ▶

8 Cuckoo flower 2
Cardamine pratensis ✦ *Brassicaceae* (Mustard family)

QUICK CHECK: Small, delicate mustard of wetlands and moist soil, the basal petioles thread-like and sinuous, the flowers light purple. **ID difficulty 1.**

DESCRIPTION: Short, delicate perennial from a small knobby rhizome. **Basal leaves** with a very long, *thread-like, sinuous rachis/petiole*, often *naked until near the tip*, with a small, shallow channel. **Leaflets** 1–7, mostly entire and nearly rounded, 0.2–0.7" (5–18 mm) long, in *remote pairs*, the terminal leaflet larger. Veins are mostly obscure. **Stems** sinuous, flimsy, resting on other plants, hairless or nearly so, roundish, to 18" (46 cm) long and 3 mm thick. **Stem leaves** similar to basal but upward the petioles become shorter and the leaflets less remote. Leaflets are entire (except that the terminal may be shallowly lobed), nipple-tipped, narrowed at the base, almost hairless. **Inflorescence** a terminal raceme of 6–12, the pedicels 8–14 mm. **Flowers** 0.4–0.8" (1–2 cm) wide when open, with 4 sepals 3–4 mm long and 4 much larger petals, light purple with darker veins. **Fruit** a thin pod 1–2 mm wide and 0.7–1.5" (18–38 mm) long with comparatively large, light brown seeds.

HABITAT: Low, wet, calcium-rich soil in shade or sun. Damp openings in low woods, streamside wetlands, fens, marsh edges, beaver meadows. Native.

FOOD USE: The **tubers** are edible raw or cooked but are really too small to mess with. **Vegetative parts** can be eaten raw or cooked and have a mild horseradish flavor. **Conservation 3/2.**

COMMENTS: I spent years looking for this pretty little mustard because it was in the Peterson field guide. When I finally gave up and went camping with some friends, I found it.

9   Shotweed   2
Cardamine hirsuta ✦ *Brassicaceae* (Mustard family)

QUICK CHECK: Very small mustard with vertical exploding pods and few stem leaves; rosette leaves pinnately compound with almost-round leaflets. **ID difficulty 1.**

DESCRIPTION: Small annual or winter annual. **Basal leaves** *numerous, 16–90 per rosette,* 2–4" (5–10 cm) long, pinnately compound with 7–11 leaflets. **Rachis** *winged, hairy on the margin (especially near the base),* naked for 30–60% of its length. **Leaflets** 5–13 mm long, out of plane, hairless to soft-hairy above, nearly hairless below, the margins hairy with occasional blunt teeth. Lateral leaflets are broadly elliptic to nearly round (proximal leaflets often narrower), abruptly widening at the base, with a few large, blunt teeth, on petiolules 10% of their length. The terminal leaflet is much larger, to 1" (2.5 cm) wide, broader than long. **Veins** mostly obscure, only the largest visible, these all coming from the base and faintly depressed above. **Stems** multiple, spreading to erect, often leaning out then curving back in, 6–14" (15–36 cm) tall and 2–4 mm thick, ridged, hairless or nearly so, simple or with strongly ascending branches. **Stem leaves** alternate, few, concentrated in the lower portion, with the petioles shorter and the wing wider. The leaflets are fewer and narrower, occasionally lobed, and tapered to the base. **Inflorescence** a dense, erect, terminal raceme to 5" (13 cm) long, the pedicels strongly ascending. **Flowers** (fall, winter, or early spring) tiny and white, the 4 broad petals (sometimes absent) hardly spreading, often *overtopped by pods from below.* **Pods** 0.6–1" (15–25 mm) long and about 1 mm thick, hairless, nearly cylindrical, vertical; *when ripe they explode upon contact, spraying numerous tiny brown seeds high enough to hit your face.*

HABITAT: Rich, moist, disturbed soil, sunny or moderately shady. Often abundant in sidewalk cracks, gardens, yards, and flower planters. Introduced.

FOOD USE: Gather the tender **greens** in fall, winter, or spring and use like watercress in salads, sandwiches, mixed potherbs, soups, or casseroles.

COMMENTS: This common, often overlooked weed has a flavor like mild watercress. It grows in cool weather. Children rarely forget this plant after the pods explode and shoot seeds into their eyes. Despite the Linnaean name, the few hairs are not one of the features first or readily noticed. Interestingly, the flowers of this species have 4 stamens, unlike the 6 normally found in the mustard family—but this is not something that you are likely to notice without a hand lens and very steady fingers. **AKA** hairy bittercress.

RELATED EDIBLES: There are several similar edible species in this genus, such as *C. parviflora* and *C. flexuosa.*

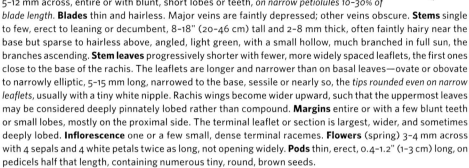

10 **Pennsylvania cress** 2
Cardamine pensylvanica ✦ *Brassicaceae* (Mustard family)

QUICK CHECK: Small mustard of mucky wetlands with tiny white flowers and compound leaves with tiny blunt leaflets. **ID difficulty 1.**

DESCRIPTION: Annual or winter annual. **Basal leaves** several to numerous, 2–6" (5–15 cm) long, pinnately compound with 7–13 scarcely touching leaflets. **Rachis** flat above, naked in the lower quarter or third, and narrowly winged between leaflets. **Leaflets** lumpy-rounded, 5–12 mm across, entire or with blunt, short lobes or teeth, *on narrow petiolules 10–30% of blade length.* **Blades** thin and hairless. Major veins are faintly depressed; other veins obscure. **Stems** single to few, erect to leaning or decumbent, 8–18" (20–46 cm) tall and 2–8 mm thick, often faintly hairy near the base but sparse to hairless above, angled, light green, with a small hollow, much branched in full sun, the branches ascending. **Stem leaves** progressively shorter with fewer, more widely spaced leaflets, the first ones close to the base of the rachis. The leaflets are longer and narrower than on basal leaves—ovate or obovate to narrowly elliptic, 5–15 mm long, narrowed to the base, sessile or nearly so, the *tips rounded even on narrow leaflets*, usually with a tiny white nipple. Rachis wings become wider upward, such that the uppermost leaves may be considered deeply pinnately lobed rather than compound. **Margins** entire or with a few blunt teeth or small lobes, mostly on the proximal side. The terminal leaflet or section is largest, wider, and sometimes deeply lobed. **Inflorescence** one or a few small, dense terminal racemes. **Flowers** (spring) 3–4 mm across with 4 sepals and 4 white petals twice as long, not opening widely. **Pods** thin, erect, 0.4–1.2" (1–3 cm) long, on pedicels half that length, containing numerous tiny, round, brown seeds.

HABITAT: Shady areas with bare or disturbed mud, but usually not flood-scoured. Marshes, swamps, flood-plain puddles, drying pond margins, ditches, springs and seepage areas. Native.

FOOD USE: Tender **greens** are slightly hot, between horseradish and watercress, and can be used raw or cooked. The rosette leaves are often abundant in late fall; the tender leafy stems appear in spring. **Conservation 1.**

COMMENTS: I like this plant. It's not just in Pennsylvania. We find lots of it in the Mississippi floodplain from wapato time until snow cover. The biggest drawback of this common and widespread native mustard is that it is small, although occasional plants in full sun on rich muck might get as thick as a small person's pinkie. Some people call this "American watercress"—a great way to add confusion where none needs to exist. The usual book name "Pennsylvania bittercress" is equally bad in a different way, because the plant is hot rather than bitter.

431

11 Narrow-leaf bittercress 🗡 2
Cardamine impatiens ✦ *Brassicaceae* (Mustard family)

QUICK CHECK: Shin-high mustard with angled stems, leaves with numerous small leaflets about the same size; flowers tiny, pods thin. **ID difficulty 1.**

DESCRIPTION: Mostly winter annual, sometimes annual or biennial. **Basal leaves** numerous, prevalent in cold weather but gone by blooming, long and thin, often sinuous, with usually 13–21 small *leaflets of similar size distributed evenly* and almost to the base. **Rachis** proportionately very narrow, purple when cold, green later, wing-channeled, mostly hairless. **Leaflets** 8–12 mm long and about as wide, often ruffled, moderately to deeply lobed in a palmate or compact-pinnate pattern, *lopsided* (more blade on the proximal side of the leaflet), on *petiolules* 5–20% of the blade length. The surface has scattered, almost appressed hairs; the margin is hairier. Lobes are blunt with a nipple or claw tip. **Major veins** above are usually offset by light color, flat or faintly raised at the bottom of a broad valley. **Stems** usually single but sometimes multiple, erect, *strongly angled or ridged*, mostly unbranched, to 28" (70 cm) tall, hairless. **Stem leaves** alternate, 4–6" (10–15 cm) long, ascending, *the base with a long, narrow, scrolled, curved, entire auricle wrapping around the stem*, with long hairs on the margins. **Rachis** has a shallow wing-channel with occasional long hairs on the margin. **Leaflets** 13–17, narrower than on basal leaves, *lanceolate*, to 0.7" (18 mm) long, inequilateral, the tips blunt-pointed with a nipple, margins entire or with a few large, erratic teeth or small lobes (more on the proximal side); becoming almost sessile and less lobed upward. Major veins are in valleys. **Inflorescence** terminal racemes to 7" (18 cm) long, crowded. **Flowers** tiny with 4 long-elliptic white petals *or the petals absent*. **Pods** numerous, 1" (2.5 cm) long, thin, straight, sharp-pointed, strongly ascending, flattened laterally, the edges dark, on pedicels 1/3 their length.

▲ Rapidly expanding.

HABITAT: Rich soil in shade; disturbed hardwood forests, especially floodplains. **I**

FOOD USE: Tender parts can be eaten raw or cooked, mostly in spring or early summer.

COMMENTS: A common invasive weed rapidly spreading in floodplains of the East. The basal leaflets are shaped very differently from those on the stem.

▼ Stem leaf.

12 Twin cress 🌿 2
Lepidium didymum ✦ *Brassicaceae* (Mustard family)

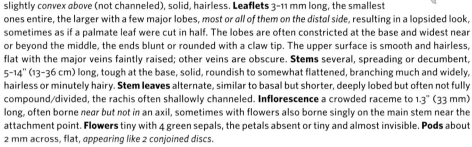

QUICK CHECK: Tiny, ground-hugging mustard with decumbent stems and compound leaves with tiny leaflets and tiny flowers. **ID difficulty 2.**

DESCRIPTION: Winter annual with basal rosettes. **Basal leaves** many, 2-5" (5-13 cm) long, pinnately compound with numerous tiny, sessile or very short-stalked leaflets. **Rachis** naked for 20-50% of its length, proportionately very wide, gently rounded below, slightly *convex above* (not channeled), solid, hairless. **Leaflets** 3-11 mm long, the smallest ones entire, the larger with a few major lobes, *most or all of them on the distal side*, resulting in a lopsided look, sometimes as if a palmate leaf were cut in half. The lobes are often constricted at the base and widest near or beyond the middle, the ends blunt or rounded with a claw tip. The upper surface is smooth and hairless, flat with the major veins faintly raised; other veins are obscure. **Stems** several, spreading or decumbent, 5-14" (13-36 cm) long, tough at the base, solid, roundish to somewhat flattened, branching much and widely, hairless or minutely hairy. **Stem leaves** alternate, similar to basal but shorter, deeply lobed but often not fully compound/divided, the rachis often shallowly channeled. **Inflorescence** a crowded raceme to 1.3" (33 mm) long, often borne *near but not in* an axil, sometimes with flowers also borne singly on the main stem near the attachment point. **Flowers** tiny with 4 green sepals, the petals absent or tiny and almost invisible. **Pods** about 2 mm across, flat, *appearing like 2 conjoined discs.*

HABITAT: Disturbed soil, usually rich, in full sun to moderate shade. Probably native but possibly introduced or adventive from South America.

FOOD USE: All the **tender parts**, especially leaves and stem tips, can be eaten raw or cooked. The flavor is strong, aromatic, a bit strange, but pleasant. Not particularly hot. The best time is late winter or early spring. It can be hard to find clean plants. **Conservation 1.**

COMMENTS: This tiny mustard is quite abundant but easy to overlook. It has one of the more peculiar flavors of our mustards. The common and Linnaean names come from the unique form of the seedpods. **AKA** lesser swine cress, wart cress.

13 False strawberry  1
Duchesnea indica ✦ *Rosaceae* (Rose family)

QUICK CHECK: Low plant with 3-part compound leaves, strawberry-like fruit, and yellow flowers with 5 petals. **ID difficulty 1.**

DESCRIPTION: Trailing perennial herb from a rhizome, spreading by stolons (runners) to form colonies. **Basal leaves** in a rosette, compound with 3 leaflets, on petiolules 2–3 mm long. **Leaflets** ovate to elliptic, 0.7–1" (18–25 mm) long, hairy on both sides, the margins with large, blunt, often dark purple teeth. Midvein and secondary veins depressed above. **Petioles** 2–3" (5–8 cm) long, hairy, channeled. **Stipules** hairy, bristle-tipped, partly attached to the petiole base. **Stems** multiple, radiating from the base, creeping, 2–3 mm thick, roundish with appressed to leaning soft hairs. **Stem leaves** alternate, similar to basal but the leaflets are sessile or nearly so and the petioles shorter; stipules are ovate or triangular. **Flowers** single, on long, thin peduncles from leaf axils, the corolla 0.5–0.7" (13–18 mm) wide with 5 yellow petals, their tips broad and slightly notched. The calyx has 5 triangular, hairy, acuminate-pointed sepals about as long as the petals. Behind these are 5 green, 3-lobed bracts. Sexual parts in the center are numerous. **Fruit** strawberry-like, to 0.8" (2 cm) across, an enlarged, red, juicy receptacle constricted at the base with numerous red seeds embedded in the surface—these rub off in your hand when you collect them. The inside is whitish and spongy.

HABITAT: Moist, semi-shaded to shady disturbed soil, especially around homes, porches, parks, yards, etc. Introduced.

FOOD USE: The **berries** can be collected from summer to fall and eaten raw or cooked.

COMMENTS: Edible, juicy, but with hardly any flavor. These have fooled many into thinking that "wild strawberries" are lame and flavorless. They are closely related to strawberries, but far from the real thing.

14 Red clover 🌿 1 🌸 2
Trifolium pratense ✦ *Fabaceae* (Legume family)

QUICK CHECK: 3-part compound leaves with sessile leaflets; numerous tiny flowers in a tightly-packed, rounded cluster. **ID difficulty 1.**

DESCRIPTION: Perennial herb. **Basal leaves** in a rosette, usually mixed with stems, on shallowly channeled, hairy, *hollow* petioles 3–6" (8–15 cm) long, with 3 sessile leaflets marked with a whitish chevron (broad V). **Leaflets** 0.6–1.2" (15–30 cm) long, ovate to elliptic with blunt tips that may have a tiny notch. The lower surface and margins have long, soft hairs; the upper surface has fewer or none. The margins are entire or very minutely toothed. **Midvein** slightly depressed or flat in a valley; secondary veins numerous, close together, very thin, branched, flat to slightly raised above. **Stems** to 52" (132 cm) long and 3–6 mm thick, creeping or decumbent to weakly erect, uniformly green, round with fine ridges and scattered long hairs. The internodes are very long, branches few. **Stem leaves** alternate, similar to basal but the leaflets narrower, the petioles becoming progressively shorter toward the top. Petioles have a *broad, unusual sheath at the base formed by two conjoined stipules, nearly transparent but with green veins*, with 2 tapering needle-like appendages; the sheath is often split, the two parts converging to form the petiole. **Inflorescence** a tightly-packed round head (actually a condensed raceme) 1–2" (2.5–5 cm) across, at the end of a grooved peduncle 2–5" (5–13 cm) long, containing 20–200 flowers. (Many people mistakenly see this whole cluster as a single flower.) Right *under each head is a pair of leaves* with stipules forming a broad, *butterfly-like, veiny sheath*. **Flowers** tiny and pink-tipped to wholly purple-red, with 5 irregular parts, the banner extending far beyond the wings and keel.

HABITAT: Sunny to partially sunny situations in man-made habitats such as meadows, pastures, hayfields, and roadsides. It can thrive in low-nitrogen and poorly drained soil. Introduced.

FOOD USE: Flowers have a nice flavor to nibble raw as a snack. They can also be used in tea mixtures, and they can be ground or blended and used in baked goods. Tender young **leaves** and **stem tips** can be eaten raw or cooked. They are mediocre and should be eaten in limited quantity due to their low digestibility. Young leaves of red clover, eaten raw, cause an unpleasant burning sensation in my mouth.

COMMENTS: The most commonly used part is the flower. Literature often mentions the edibility of the roots of various clovers, but I know of no one who eats those of our common weedy species.

RELATED EDIBLES: Alsike clover *T. hybridum* is clump-forming like red clover but smaller, and the stems are reclining or decumbent. The flowers are both pink and red, in smaller clusters that are not subtended by leaves. Its leaves lack chevrons and have tiny, sharp teeth on the margins. Crimson clover *T. incarnatum* is an annual introduced species common in the southern states, with elongated heads of bold red flowers. It does not taste nearly as good as red clover.

▲ Alsike clover.   ▲ Red clover.

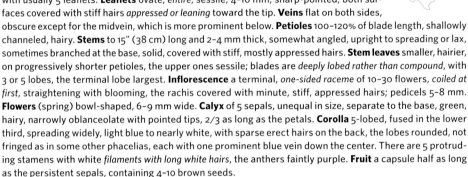

15 Small-flower phacelia 1
Phacelia dubia ✦ *Boraginaceae* (Borage family)

QUICK CHECK: Small plant with pinnately lobed or compound leaves with no teeth, covered with stiff appressed hairs; light bluish 5-petaled flowers in coiled clusters in spring. **ID difficulty 2.**

DESCRIPTION: Winter annual. **Basal leaves** few, to 2" (5 cm) long, pinnately compound with usually 5 leaflets. **Leaflets** ovate, *entire*, sessile, 4–10 mm, sharp-pointed, both surfaces covered with stiff hairs *appressed or leaning* toward the tip. **Veins** flat on both sides, obscure except for the midvein, which is more prominent below. **Petioles** 100–120% of blade length, shallowly channeled, hairy. **Stems** to 15" (38 cm) long and 2–4 mm thick, somewhat angled, upright to spreading or lax, sometimes branched at the base, solid, covered with stiff, mostly appressed hairs. **Stem leaves** smaller, hairier, on progressively shorter petioles, the upper ones sessile; blades are *deeply lobed rather than compound*, with 3 or 5 lobes, the terminal lobe largest. **Inflorescence** a terminal, *one-sided raceme* of 10–30 flowers, *coiled at first*, straightening with blooming, the rachis covered with minute, stiff, appressed hairs; pedicels 5–8 mm. **Flowers** (spring) bowl-shaped, 6–9 mm wide. **Calyx** of 5 sepals, unequal in size, separate to the base, green, hairy, narrowly oblanceolate with pointed tips, 2/3 as long as the petals. **Corolla** 5-lobed, fused in the lower third, spreading widely, light blue to nearly white, with sparse erect hairs on the back, the lobes rounded, not fringed as in some other phacelias, each with one prominent blue vein down the center. There are 5 protruding stamens with white *filaments with long white hairs*, the anthers faintly purple. **Fruit** a capsule half as long as the persistent sepals, containing 4–10 brown seeds.

HABITAT: Full sun to moderate shade on well-drained but rich soil. Roadsides, fields, infrequently mowed lawns, pastures, woodlands (especially where rocky), cedar glades. Native.

FOOD USE: Tender young **greens** can be eaten raw or cooked. Due to the rough texture they are better cooked. **Conservation 2.**

COMMENTS: The greens of this plant are recorded as a traditional Cherokee food, but they are pretty bland, very small, and have a mediocre texture. **AKA** Appalachian phacelia.

RELATED EDIBLES: Many phacelias are ethnographically documented as food. *Phacelia gilioides* is a very similar species that has at times been classified as a variety of *P. dubia*, and can be used similarly.

16 Purple phacelia ✎ 2 ⎸ 2
Phacelia bipinnatifida ✦ *Boraginaceae* (Borage family)

QUICK CHECK: Low, hairy herb with pinnately compound leaves, the leaflets lobed, silver-splotched when young; showy purple 5-petaled flowers in a coiled raceme. **ID difficulty 2.**

DESCRIPTION: Biennial. **Basal leaves** pinnately compound with 3–5 leaflets, the rachis hairy and deeply V-channeled with a small groove in the bottom of the V. **Petiole** about twice the blade length, widened at the base, solid, with erect hairs. **Leaflets** deeply lobed and sometimes divided, highly asymmetrical, with irregular large teeth, ovate to lanceolate in outline. Proximal leaflets usually have short petiolules while distal ones are sessile. **Surface** hairy above, green, with silvery blotches near sinus bases in spring; the underside is less hairy and all silvery. Major veins are depressed above. **Stems** single to several, 8–32" (20–80 cm) tall and 6–15 mm thick, erect to leaning or decumbent, purple when young, branched dichotomously at the base or above, zigzag, solid or thick-walled with a small hollow, covered with straight, erect, minutely gland-tipped hairs. **Stem leaves** similar to basal with a shorter petiole and a deeper groove in the rachis. **Inflorescence** (spring) a terminal raceme, one-sided, coiled at first but straightening at maturity and lengthening in fruit. The rachis is densely covered with hairs of 2 lengths, some gland-tipped, the pedicels 7–10 mm long. **Calyx** has 5 narrow, pointed, green, hairy lobes. **Corolla** purple with a white star in the center, 0.5–0.8" (13–20 mm) across, 5-lobed, the lobes broad with minutely wavy margins, cut only about 2/3 to the base, the outer surface minutely hairy. *Each lobe has a bulging white nectary at its base*, visible even before opening. **Filaments** *purple with erect white hairs of two lengths, protruding far beyond the corolla*, tipped with orange-brown anthers. **Fruit** an ovoid capsule with 2–4 seeds, each seed 3–4 mm, finely ridged or pitted, black.

CONFUSING SPECIES: Told from other *Phacelias* by the combination of purple flowers with entire petals and compound leaves. Told from Virginia and large waterleafs (pp. 390–391) by the silvery blotches being less distinctly bordered, and the presence of some clearly separated, stalked leaflets.

HABITAT: Rich, moist soil in moderate shade, especially where leaf litter accumulates on or near mossy boulders. Moist woods, creek borders, rocky slopes, road banks, cliff bases. Native.

FOOD USE: Young **leaves** and **shoots** can be eaten raw or cooked. **Conservation 2.**

COMMENTS: This flower is gorgeous. Not a well-known edible, purple phacelia tastes like a good waterleaf in my opinion, and it is common and widespread.

RELATED EDIBLES: There are many *Phacelia* species in our region, and I know of none that are dangerous, but this one tastes the best of those I have tried.

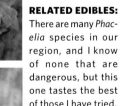

◀ Purple phacelia has leaflets that are sometimes fully divided.

17 Chocolate root ☕
Geum rivale ✦ *Rosaceae* (Rose family)

QUICK CHECK: Rosettes in wet, shaded soil, the terminal leaflets 20–100 times larger than the side leaflets and extremely variable in shape. **ID difficulty 2.**

DESCRIPTION: Perennial. **Rhizome** 8–13 mm thick, curved, branching at constricted joints on larger plants and often multi-headed, the exterior scaly, dark purple-brown with many small roots. The flesh is whitish inside with purple veins. **Basal rosette** of 3–9 leaves, to 22" (56 cm) long (including the petiole), limp to ascending, pinnately compound with several *tiny, sessile side leaflets;* terminating with one or three *much larger* leaflets, the terminal of which is largest. **Rachis** 2–4 mm wide, scarcely tapered, deeply and broadly V-channeled, green with scattered long hairs, *naked in the lower half,* with a *sheath at the base.* **Leaflets** sessile or nearly so; they have two extremely different shapes, often on the same plant. Sometimes the terminal leaflet is broader than long, nearly rounded or kidney-shaped, unlobed or with very shallow lobes and blunt teeth, less hairy than other leaflets and glossier above. Other leaves have 3 large leaflets at the tip, slightly narrower, each with more prominent lobes, pointed and with sharper teeth. **Veins** on all leaflets *very deeply depressed* above, with scattered long hairs on both surfaces, but more below. Teeth are light in color. **Stems** 20–40" (50–100 cm) tall, often leaning or broken, one to few per plant, 2–4 mm thick, round, solid, slightly curvy, *unbranched below the inflorescence,* the surface slightly rough, with long, curving hairs. **Stem leaves** alternate, widely spaced, 4–7" long, much reduced, with 1–3 major leaflets and ovate stipule-like lobes at the base. **Inflorescence** a small, lone panicle of up to 7 flowers, widely spread on long, *nodding, hairy pedicels.* **Flowers** (early to mid summer) 11–14 mm wide with 5 triangular-ovate hairy sepals 5–7 mm long, brownish purple with darker veins, their tips sharp to acuminate. Between these sepals are 5 tiny, linear, recurved sepal lobes about 1/3 the length of the main sepals. **Petals** (almost hidden) whitish to dull yellow with purplish blotches and veins, narrow at the base with a broad fan-like tip. Stamens and pistils are numerous. Each style is *twisted and jointed* about 90° and *appears to have a tiny feather* attached loosely to its tip. Shortly after flowering, while the sepals remain purple, this "feather" falls off. **Fruit** is a sticktight ball, each seed with a single hook-tipped barb.

HABITAT: Wet soil high in organic matter, not too acidic, in partial shade: ash, cedar, or shrub swamps, depressions in woods, wooded wetland margins. Native.

FOOD USE: The **rhizomes** can be gathered at any time and boiled fresh or roasted to make a drink that is supposedly "chocolate-like." **Conservation 3.**

COMMENTS: With a name like "chocolate root" this must be great. Right? Well, like chocolate, it's bitter. Few people will find this drink pleasant unless it is sweetened. Then it's rather good, in my opinion. The tradition of making a drink from avens "root" is ancient, widespread, and applies to multiple species. This is the one most commonly mentioned in North American literature, and it is the only one I've tried. **AKA** water avens, purple avens.

GROUP 27 BASAL LEAVES PRESENT, LEAVES ALTERNATE, MULTI-COMPOUND WITH DISTINCT LEAFLETS

All but one of the plants in this group belong to the carrot family, *Apiaceae*. Members of the carrot family have fruits called *schizocarps* that dry out and split into two seed units (mericarps) upon maturity. Probably the most toxic plant in our region, common water hemlock *Cicuta maculata*—is a carrot family member that will key to this group. For this reason, some of the plants in group 27 are considered highly difficult to identify and should be used only by well-seasoned foragers who are highly confident in their identification skills. However, there are other plants in this group, such as columbine and yellow pimpernel, that cannot be confused with water hemlock by anyone applying reasonable attention to details. It would be a shame to shy away from *everything* in the carrot family because a few members are very poisonous.

Prairie parsnip and the members of the genus *Osmorhiza* have leaflets that are deeply cut, and some might reasonably key them into group 28—but they are on the fence, and I had to put them somewhere. Note that all of the species which normally have unlobed leaflets will occasionally have a leaflet that is incompletely separated, resulting in an oddly-lobed leaf. In the key I ignore this aberrant minority and focus on the shape of typical leaflets even though abnormal leaflets are to be expected. Two species are placed twice in the key because the hairiness of their parts is variable.

TENTATIVE IDENTIFICATION KEY TO GROUP 27
The key is not your final answer!

Leaflets hairless on both sides.	
or Leaflet margins entire.	1. Yellow pimpernel
Leaflet margins regularly toothed but usually not lobed.	
Leaflets narrowly lanceolate, toothed near the base; stems usually branched with leaf sheaths clasping the larger branches; umbels twice compound. Water hemlock (poisonous, p. 668).	
Leaflets ovate with broad, untoothed bases; stems usually unbranched, leaf sheaths not clasping branches if present; larger umbels thrice compound.	2. American lovage
or Leaflets typically or frequently lobed.	
Lobes and teeth rounded with the tip indented; veinlets flat above.	13. Red columbine
Lobes and teeth pointed with a projecting claw; veinlets depressed above.	
Bracts beneath the umbellet far exceeding the rays.	3. Javan water celery
Bracts beneath the umbellet shorter than or roughly equal to the rays.	
Leaflet margins not toothed in the proximal third.	4. Sea lovage
Leaflet margins toothed very close to the base.	5. Seaside angelica
Leaflets with hairs on one or both sides. (Check underside and veins carefully.)	
Main stem hairless (there may be hairs on stems in the inflorescence).	
Petioles commonly more than 0.5" (13 mm) thick.	
or Blooming in late spring; umbels spherical or hemispherical.	6. Purple angelica
Blooming in late summer; umbels flat-topped.	7. Mountain angelica
or Petioles less than 0.2" (5 mm) thick.	
Fringe of long hairs present on sheaths and at nodes.	11. Aniseroot
No fringe of hairs on sheaths or at nodes.	
Margins double-toothed; 15 or fewer leaflets.	9. Goutweed
Margins simple-toothed; large leaves with 22+ leaflets.	2. American lovage
Main stem with hairs (may be hairless at the base).	
Hairs very short; major veins on leaflets flat or faintly raised above.	
or Leaflets lobed, deeply incised; basal leaves held close to the ground.	10. Prairie parsnip
Leaflets toothed but not lobed; basal leaves held well off the ground.	8. Hairy angelica
Hairs long; major veins on leaflets depressed above.	
Stem maroon and faintly to moderately hairy; anise-scented.	11. Aniseroot
Stem green and very hairy, lacking anise scent.	12. Sweet cicely

1 Yellow pimpernel 🌱 2 🥕 3 🌿 3 🏺
Taenidia integerrima ✦ *Apiaceae* (Carrot family)

QUICK CHECK: Very thin stems, elliptic entire leaflets with veins not prominent, and tiny yellow flowers in tight umbellets widely spaced from each other. **ID difficulty 1.**

DESCRIPTION: Perennial, the only member of the carrot family in our region with yellow flowers and entire leaflets. **Roots** thickened and branched, the outside brown, tough, and bumpy with a thick skin that peels readily from a semi-fibrous inside. **Basal leaves** usually 1-4, mostly withered by flowering on fertile plants, typically 3 times compound, each time ternately divided, resulting in 27 leaflets. **Rachises** *not channeled at any level* but distally may be flat on top. **Leaflets** entire, ovate to elliptic, 0.6-1.3" (15-33 mm) long, flat, blunt at the base, blunt to abruptly pointed at the tip, hairless, very thin. **Veins** flat above, giving a smooth appearance; veinlets offset by light color. Side leaflets are sessile; end leaflets may have a short stalk. Leaflets are sometimes incompletely separated. **Stems** 18-45" (46-115 cm) tall and 3-7 mm thick, usually clumped, proportionately thin and delicate-looking, thick-walled but hollow, jointed, roundish, reddish or dull green, often with darker lines, smooth, hairless, bloom-coated, zigzag. **Branches** few to none, wide spreading if present. **Stem leaves** widely spaced, alternate, with broad, clasping sheaths that encircle the stem; the lower ones on very long petioles. *Upper leaves are held vertically, appressed to the stem, and folded around it.* **Inflorescence** a hemispherical compound umbel 2.5-4" (6-10 cm) across, borne at the top of a long, straight, very thin peduncle. There are no bracts in the inflorescence. Great umbels have 7-16 widely spreading, thin rays. Umbellets are widely spaced with 14-30 crowded flowers on thread-like pedicels. **Flowers** (late spring to early summer) tiny, yellow, with 5 petals curved inward so the tips meet. **Fruit** a schizocarp 3-5 mm long, slightly less wide, plump but somewhat flattened.

HABITAT: Dry, open, often rocky woodlands and savannahs with calcium-rich soil, often with oak and hickory; especially the edges of such woods along trails, clearings, and roads. Native. 🔥

FOOD USE: The **roots** are mild, sweet, and pleasant, although rather tough and small; they should be left to conserve the plants. The **leaves** and **shoots** have a strong but pleasant flavor much like cultivated lovage or celery leaf. The flavor and texture are best in spring. **Seeds** make an excellent soup seasoning, like celery seed. **Conservation 3/2/1.**

COMMENTS: This is the only member of the carrot family with a lovage-celery flavor native to the Eastern Woodlands bioregion. I think it is one of our best native culinary herbs—a fantastic addition to a venison stew. Although widespread, easy to identify, superb, and locally common, it is hardly known as a wild edible. The population has greatly diminished due to fire suppression. The seeds are the secret seasoning in my chicken gumbo. *T. montana* is a close relative, rare in the Appalachians, reportedly less tasty.

2 American lovage   🌱 2 🍃 3   🥄 3
Ligusticum canadense ✦ *Apiaceae* (Carrot family)

QUICK CHECK: Tall herb with hairless, glaucous, thin stems and paired or whorled upper branches; leaves with 3 main divisions, leaflets toothed; umbels 2-4 times compound. **ID difficulty 3.**

DESCRIPTION: Perennial herb from thickened roots, multi-crowned on older plants. **Basal leaves** 3-4 times compound, often single (especially in the shade)—clumps or rosettes are more common at the base of flowering stalks; leaflet form varies between single leaves, rosette leaves, and sun or shade. Lone leaves of non-flowering plants in shade are balanced on vertical petioles up to 30" (75 cm) tall, solid as shoots but becoming hollow. **Petioles** on flowering plants or those in full sun are usually shorter and leaning. **Rachis** divides 3 ways at first, the branches spreading widely; after the first division they are hollow with a rounded bottom and slightly ridged top. After the second division the rachis branches are solid with a small groove on top, which deepens after the final division and continues onto the top of the leaflet's midvein. There may be sparse, fine hairs near divisions of the rachis, especially when young. Flowering plants may have few or no basal leaves; in this case there is a large leaf hugging the lower stem and nearly balanced on all sides of it. **Leaflets** 1.2-4.5" (3-11 cm) long, sessile or on stalks to 25% of blade length, lanceolate to ovate or elliptic with a pointed tip, angled at the base and often inequilateral, the blades flat and hairless above, sometimes faintly hairy on the midvein below. **Midvein** above may be incised (in shade) to flat (in sun). Secondary veins are incised to flat above, about 45°, running almost straight and *mostly to tooth tips.* Veinlets are flat to raised above. **Margins** sharply serrated with moderately large, claw-tipped teeth, but *the proximal 20-30% of the blade is toothless.* Occasional leaflets are deeply lobed or incompletely separated. **Stems** usually single per crown, *tall, straight, and lanky,* erect and hollow but thick-walled, jointed, 2-6' (60-180 cm) tall and 8-14 mm thick, hairless below, smooth, round, blotchy-glaucous, mostly green (purplish near the base) with fine stripes. **Branches** widely-spaced, *thin, naked, spreading or ascending, in pairs or whorls,* often subtended by elongated simple leaves. **Stem leaves** few and widely spaced, greatly reduced upward, the *petioles vertical, appressed, and broadly sheathing.* **Inflorescence** a series of branch whorls on the upper stalk; the smaller bear twice-compound umbels but most bear *thrice-compound umbels;* robust stalks terminate in an *umbel 4-times compound.* Thrice compound umbels have 3-8 rays at the first juncture, each 4-8" (10-20 cm) long, subtended by lanceolate to linear (occasionally lobed) bracts (lacking on smaller umbels). Rays may have sparse hairs. Secondary rays are 1-1.5" (2.5-4 cm) long and ridged. Twice compound umbels are roundish and consist of 8-13 widely spaced umbellets, each densely packed with 8-22 flowers. **Flowers** 2-3 mm across with 5 broad, widely separated white petals with a sharp tip folded in toward the center, attached to a light green, disk-like pistil. **Fruit** elliptic, slightly flattened, ribbed schizocarps 3.5-7 mm long.

CONFUSING PLANTS: Water hemlock (p. 668) does not grow in the same habitat, and the flowering stem has a very different form. Water hemlock's leaflets are much narrower, toothed to the base, and have veins terminating in the notch between teeth. **Baneberries** (p. 676) have smaller, more numerous teeth and erratically lobed leaves. (Continued on the next page.)

▲ Basal leaf in sun.

▲ Isolated shade leaf.

2 American lovage (continued)

HABITAT: Thin-canopy hardwood forests and savannahs, especially over limestone soils in mountainous or hilly country. Native. 🔥

FOOD USE: The **root** has a strong but not overpowering flavor that is nice in soup. Young **greens** and **stems** can be eaten raw or cooked. **Conservation 3/2.**

COMMENTS: Technical descriptions in many floras incorrectly describe the inflorescence of this plant, probably because it is so unusual. Although ignored in the wild food literature, this distinctive herb has been a prized vegetable and medicinal for ages, and the root is still collected commercially. There are many places named for it (such as Jellico, Tennessee). Despite the name, it does not taste like lovage. **AKA** nondo, jellico, angelico.

3   Javan water celery 🌿 2 🥄 3
Oenanthe javanica ✦ *Apiaceae* (Carrot family)

QUICK CHECK: Mat-forming plant with once and twice-compound leaves and slender knee-high stems with compound umbels of white flowers. **ID difficulty 3+.**

DESCRIPTION: Perennial from a fibrous root system, spreading by rhizomes/stolons and rooting at nodes to form mats, all parts hairless. **Rhizomes** 3 mm thick, red to white, semi-hollow, the thin skin containing usually *4 separate vascular bundles surrounded by air space.* **Basal leaves** in rosettes, 3–8" (8–20 cm) long (including the petiole), pinnately *once or twice* compound with 5–23 leaflets, withering by blooming on flowering stalks. **Leaflets** 0.4–0.8" (1–2 cm) long, blunt and roughly ovate, the smallest leaflets appearing palmately veined, the base broadly angled and often inequilateral; sessile or with very short petiolules; the terminal leaflet long–stalked or sessile. **Surface** hairless, glossy below. **Margins** often purple, with a few large, blunt, nipple–tipped teeth. Major **veins** are depressed above and *flat to faintly depressed below,* running to tooth tips. **Petioles** green, hollow, thin, with several small ridges, the top with a hairline groove, the lower third with a wide, often reddish sheath. Rachis is hollow, more strongly grooved than the petiole. **Stems** 10–40" (25–102 cm) tall and 5–11 mm thick, juicy inside, jointed, purple and nearly solid at the base but green above and developing a small, *non-round, off-center hollow.* Cross section is angled, often *almost diamond-shaped;* increasingly so toward the top, with the uppermost angles becoming sharp and winged. The surface is hairless with fine vertical lines, branched, erect to leaning or decumbent. **Stem leaves** alternate, on long internodes, twice pinnately compound, the rachis branches few, most with 3–5 leaflets per branch, the blade 8–12" (20–30 cm) long with a total of 20–40 leaflets. **Leaflets** of stem leaves are 1–2" (2.5–5 cm) long, ovate to lanceolate, pointed, coarsely toothed and occasionally lobed, the teeth sharp, the veins more depressed—otherwise similar to basal. **Petioles** of stem leaves with narrow sheaths, often long and nearly vertical, the walls thin and *sharply angled* (especially on uppermost leaves), the hollow also not centered. **Rachises** of upper leaves are *flattened with sharp, clear-winged edges,* a ridge below, and a narrow groove above. **Inflorescence** flat-topped compound umbels 1.5–2.5" (3.8–6.4 cm) across at the end of a *ridged peduncle,* the ridges sharp-winged, bearing 8–14 *crowded* umbellets, each 10–13 mm wide with 12–22 flowers. Rays are 0.7–1.5" (18–64 mm) long, *distinctly ridged or angled.* There is a whorl of several long, linear, green bracts beneath each umbellet, often *surpassing the outer flowers;* there are usually no bracts beneath the great umbel, but occasionally 1–2 are present. **Flowers** 2–3 mm across, with 5 white petals of roughly equal size, the tips folded in toward the center, and 5 stamens. The calyx is light green and cup-like. **Fruit** slightly compressed, broadly elliptic, hairless, ribbed, the ribs with *corky wings.*

▲ Rapidly expanding.

CONFUSING PLANTS: Springwater parsnip (p. 216) has once-compound leaves with the veins not depressed. **Water hemlock** (deadly poisonous, p. 668) is much larger with narrower leaflets and round stems with a round hollow; it lacks rhizomes (among many other differences).

HABITAT: Rich, mucky soil near streams, rivers, ponds, and lakes, usually in shade. Introduced.

FOOD USE: Young **shoots** and **leaves** and can be used like tender celery, all growing season but especially in spring and early summer. (Continued on the next page.)

3 Javan water celery (continued)

COMMENTS: This plant is widely cultivated as a vegetable and an ornamental, and there are some named cultivars. Because it is introduced and easily overlooked, this species is far more common than official records indicate. It is not in most floras and is included in no field guides. Expect it to spread and be added to more invasive plant lists. Do not transplant it or spread the seeds. Interestingly, some other members of this genus are extremely poisonous—*Oenanthe crocata*, for example, is perhaps the most feared wild plant in Europe. Because of the loose resemblance to our native water hemlocks, proceed with due caution.

▲ Spring basal leaves.

4 Sea lovage 2 ⬤ 2 ✎ 2
Ligusticum scoticum ✦ *Apiaceae* (Carrot family)

QUICK CHECK: Coastal herb, knee to thigh high, with basal leaves on long, erect, reddish, round petioles; leaves twice divided in three; umbels flat-topped. **ID difficulty 3.**

DESCRIPTION: Perennial herb. **Roots** long and slender, smooth, gently tapering, nearly white; many of them are often adjacent under robust plants. **Basal leaves** clumped, numerous, 3 times compound, the rachis dividing into 3 branches, each with 3 leaflets. Most side leaflets are sessile; most terminal leaflets stalked. **Leaflets**, especially terminal ones, may be deeply cut. The blades are thick, broadly ovate to diamond-shaped, 1.2–3" (3–8 cm) long, shiny, hairless, the top with a network of depressed veinlets. **Midveins** flat to faintly depressed above. **Margins** sharply and coarsely toothed but not near the base, the teeth with light claw tips. **Petioles** long and straight, to 14" (36 cm) long and 3–9 mm thick, reddish at least at the base, erect in competition or leaning in full sun, sheathed and channeled in the lower 2–4" (5–10 cm). Above the tapered, wavy-edged sheath the petioles are round, hairless, nearly smooth (finely ridged), *solid or with a pinhole hollow*, 3–8 mm in diameter, sometimes slightly grooved near the top. **Rachis** branches are shallowly channeled. **Stems** to 32" (80 cm) tall and 0.6" (15 mm) thick, about twice the height of the basal leaves, hollow, hairless, usually erect, not glaucous, purplish at the base (and sometimes all over), with

fine ridges, often purple striped. Branches are few, strongly ascending to nearly vertical. **Stem leaves** alternate, with a short sheath at the base, often clasping a branch, the petiole often purple striped. Upper stem leaves divide immediately beyond the sheath. **Inflorescence** compound umbels 2–2.6" (5–7 cm) across, flat-topped or slightly convex in flower (may be slightly concave in fruit), on a long, thick peduncle above the leaves, each with 14–26 rays 1–2" (2.5–5 cm) long. The umbellets are crowded and touching, as are the flowers within them. Under each umbellet is a whorl of linear bracts, which wither at flowering. Flowers 6–7 mm across with 5 white petals of uniform size, hooked inward so strongly the tips often touch the petal near the base. Anthers are purple at the tips of spreading filaments. **Fruit** a slightly flattened schizocarp with prominent ridges.

HABITAT: Rocky seashores and occasionally high spots in salt marshes. Native.

FOOD USE: The **roots** can be used as a parsnip-like vegetable, especially when tops are dormant. Gather young, tender **stems** and **greens** in spring and early summer and use like celery in soups, casseroles, etc. The leaves can be dried and used as a seasoning much like cultivated parsley or lovage. **Conservation 3/2.**

COMMENTS: This herb has excellent flavor, but it doesn't taste like lovage. It's more like a strong, lemony celery. Those who live near its haunts should check it out. **AKA** Scotch lovage.

445

5 Seaside angelica 🎋 2 🌿 1 🌱 1 🗼
Angelica lucida ❖ *Apiaceae* (Carrot family)

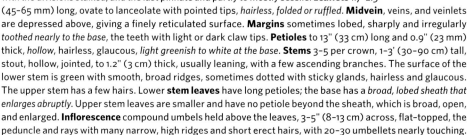

QUICK CHECK: Coastal herb with ground-hugging basal leaves 3-4 times compound, thick stems and petioles, and flat-topped compound umbels. **ID difficulty 3.**

DESCRIPTION: Perennial from a stout taproot. *Sap milky* (at least later in the season). **Basal leaves** in a rosette of 3-5, often hugging the ground, 3-4 times compound with 25-45 leaflets; the first division ternate with the branches long-stalked, the second pinnate with the divisions stalked, and the last pinnate and partly to mostly sessile. **Leaflets** 1.7-2.5" (45-65 mm) long, ovate to lanceolate with pointed tips, *hairless, folded or ruffled.* **Midvein**, veins, and veinlets are depressed above, giving a finely reticulated surface. **Margins** sometimes lobed, sharply and irregularly *toothed nearly to the base*, the teeth with light or dark claw tips. **Petioles** to 13" (33 cm) long and 0.9" (23 mm) thick, *hollow*, hairless, glaucous, *light greenish to white at the base.* **Stems** 3-5 per crown, 1-3' (30-90 cm) tall, stout, hollow, jointed, to 1.2" (3 cm) thick, usually leaning, with a few ascending branches. The surface of the lower stem is green with smooth, broad ridges, sometimes dotted with sticky glands, hairless and glaucous. The upper stem has a few hairs. Lower **stem leaves** have long petioles; the base has a *broad, lobed sheath that enlarges abruptly.* Upper stem leaves are smaller and have no petiole beyond the sheath, which is broad, open, and enlarged. **Inflorescence** compound umbels held above the leaves, 3-5" (8-13 cm) across, flat-topped, the peduncle and rays with many narrow, high ridges and short erect hairs, with 20-30 umbellets nearly touching.

There are numerous purple-tipped linear bracts under the umbellet in bloom, which wither as the fruit ripens. Great umbels in fruit often have a single large bract. Flowers within the umbellets are densely packed. **Flowers** (June-Sept.) 3-4 mm across with 5 white, hooked petals, adjacent to slightly overlapped at the base. **Fruits** 6-10 mm, oblong, very densely packed, plump, with prominent ridges and *corky wings.*

HABITAT: Rocky coasts and upper beaches, especially near boulders. Native.

FOOD USE: Young **leaves** and **petioles** can be used like celery, but sparingly. **Shoots** are peeled and eaten. **Seeds** can be used as a seasoning.

COMMENTS: This plant tastes about the same as purple angelica; it's just a shorter, salt-tolerant version. **AKA** seawatch.

6 Purple angelica 🌿 2 🍂 1 🌱 1 ⚱

Angelica atropurpurea • *Apiaceae* (Carrot family)

QUICK CHECK: Enormous herb, the stems and petioles large, hollow, hairless, purple; flowers in early summer, the clusters large and spherical. **ID difficulty 3+.**

DESCRIPTION: Very large perennial or biennial herb reaching 5-8' (1.5-2.4 m) tall, with a strong soapy scent when broken. The *taproot is large and fleshy.* **Basal leaves** 2-3 times pinnately compound, up to 32" (80 cm) long and about equally wide, composed of 20-80 leaflets, *close together and often overlapping.* **Leaflets** 1.5-3.5" (4-9 cm) long, lanceolate to ovate, occasionally lobed or incompletely divided, the bases obtuse to tapered (especially the terminal leaflet); tips are pointed. **Surfaces** hairless or nearly so above, the *underside densely coated in very fine, soft hairs.* **Veins** and *veinlets are depressed above* and protrude below, giving the leaf a *finely reticulate textured* surface. *Major secondary veins end in a tooth.* **Margins** irregularly serrated with small teeth (9-14 per inch), the tooth tips with a *white claw or nipple.* **Petioles** of basal leaves 60-90% of the blade length and at an angle to it, hollow, rounded, not channeled, smooth, up to 1.5" (4 cm) thick. **Rachis** hollow with a ridge on top and a tiny groove on top of this ridge, the rachis branches much deeper than wide with a narrow, sharp-edged channel. Most leaflets are sessile but some have short stalks. **Stems** usually single, 1-2" (2.5-5 cm) thick at the base, smooth, covered with bloom, some combination of purple and green (but purple predominates), slightly zigzag between nodes, hollow, jointed, sparingly branched and only in the upper half. **Stem leaves** alternate, mostly near the base, the petioles with a broad, ridged sheath around the stem. Uppermost leaves have a disproportionately large, open, boat-like sheath bearing a tiny leaf (or blade absent). **Inflorescence** a few large, almost spherical compound umbels 5-9" (13-23 cm) in diameter, the 18-40 primary rays strongly ridged. Umbellets do not touch but the 18-40 flowers within them are crowded into balls. There are *no bracts* beneath the great umbel or the umbellet. **Flowers** 3-5 mm across with 5 tiny, pale greenish, triangular petals with the tips curved back toward the center; stamens wide-spreading. **Fruit** an oblong schizocarp 5-6 mm long with prominent sharp ridges.

CONFUSING PLANTS: Water hemlock (p. 668) is less robust with flat umbels and hairless leaves with secondary veins ending in notches between the teeth.

HABITAT: Streamsides, lakeshores, marshes, shrub swamps, ditches, fens, springs. Needs rich, wet soil with lots of organic matter and full to partial sun. Native. (Continued on the next page.)

6 Purple angelica (continued)

FOOD USE: Angelica has a very strong soapy flavor and will numb your tongue, especially if eaten raw. For this reason it is typically used in moderation, more as a **seasoning** than a vegetable. However, the **heart** in spring, pale and wrapped in sheaths when 4-9" (10-23 cm) tall, is not so soapy and can be used in soups or casseroles like celery. Young **stalks** and **petioles** are strong but can be used as a flavoring and have been traditionally candied. **Seeds** have also been used as a seasoning. Conservation 2/1.

WARNING: The juice is phototoxic to the skin (see p. 23).

COMMENTS: My friends at Prairie Moon Nursery aptly call them "stately sentinels along stream beds." Purple angelica is similar to the European *Angelica archangelica*, for which there is a rich tradition of medicinal and culinary use. In Scandinavia, cultivars with milder flavor and solid stalks have been bred.

7 Mountain angelica ⸱ 2 ⸱ 2 ⸱ 2 ⸱
Angelica triquinata ⸱ *Apiaceae* (Carrot family)

QUICK CHECK: Large herb with thick stems and large basal leaves; stems smooth, purple, with bloom; umbels flat-topped, blooming in late summer. **ID difficulty 3+.**

DESCRIPTION: Perennial herb spreading by seed only, with usually 1–2 basal leaves per plant, whether flowering or not. **Basal leaves** thrice compound, usually splitting 3 ways, 3 ways again, and the final division 5 ways. Lone basal leaves are on erect **petioles** to 0.6" (15 mm) thick and 18" (46 cm) high. The petioles are straight, smooth, round, hollow, hairless, dark purple, with bloom; they are not channeled, but rachises usually have a tiny groove above. **Leaflets** ovate, 1.5–4.5" (4–11 cm) long, mostly sessile except the terminal leaflets, obtuse to abruptly tapered at the base. **Blades** flat, minutely hairy on the veins above; hairs are sparser below but larger and stiffer. **Margins** minutely hairy, often lobed, with large, irregular teeth tipped with a whitish claw. **Midvein** essentially flat above; secondary veins flat to *raised above and protruding below*, straight, rarely splitting, 45° to the midvein, running to the claw of a larger tooth. **Stems** to 5' (1.5 m) high and 1" (2.5 cm) thick, round, smooth, without ridges or grooves, hollow, jointed, dark purple. Basal leaves persist through blooming. **Stem leaves** few, large in the lower third but greatly reduced above. **Inflorescence** several flat-topped compound umbels to 5" (13 cm) across in the upper branches; reduced inflorescences are also borne in lower axils. **Peduncle** has numerous small ridges, sparsely covered with minute hairs, the hairs becoming dense near the umbel. Primary rays have a small channel with minute hairs along the rim; there are no bracts beneath them. Beneath the umbellet there is a whorl of about a dozen tiny, linear, very sharp bracts, usually recurved in bloom. **Flowers** (mid August to mid Sept.) tiny, with 5 curled creamy petals. **Fruit** a schizocarp 4–6 mm long with 8–10 wings, a longer pair with white margins on each side.

CONFUSING PLANTS: Water hemlock (deadly poisonous, p. 668) has smaller, narrower leaflets with depressed secondary veins; the entire plant lacks hairs.

HABITAT: Moist, rich, disturbed soil in moderate shade at higher elevations. Along mountain streams, roadsides, eroding banks, wet areas along cliffs and rock slides, swamp edges, seeps. Native.

(Continued on the next page.)

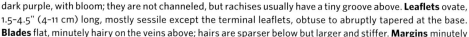

7 Mountain angelica (continued)

FOOD USE: Tender young **leaves** can be used as a vegetable raw or cooked, as can peeled **petioles** and **stems**. The seeds can be used as a seasoning. **Conservation 2/1.**

WARNING: Juice is probably phototoxic to the skin (see p. 23).

COMMENTS: This species is much milder tasting than purple or seacoast angelica. For use as a celery-like soup vegetable it is the best of the angelicas in our region. **AKA** Appalachian angelica, filmy angelica.

▲ (top) Mature fruits.
(bottom) Early spring leaf.

8 Hairy angelica 2 2
Angelica venenosa ◆ *Apiaceae* (Carrot family)

QUICK CHECK: Plant of dry forests bearing leaves with numerous small leaflets and flat-topped umbels in late summer; stiff stems, densely hairy in the upper parts. **ID difficulty 3.**

DESCRIPTION: Polycarpic perennial spreading only by seed. **Basal leaves** often single on non-flowering plants, the petiole rising nearly erect for 8-16" (20-40 cm) before splitting 3 ways. Other non-flowering plants have 3-5 small basal leaves. Flowering plants lose the basal leaves late in maturity. Blades of larger leaves are up to 15" (38 cm) long and 3-4 times compound with 55-81 leaflets. **Petioles** straight, scarcely tapered, maroon, to 5 mm in diameter, finely striated with purple lines and faint ridges, hairless or nearly so, with a small channel distally. They are *pithy—not hollow.* **Leaflets** 0.5-1.6" (13-41 mm) long, narrowly ovate, occasionally lobed or incompletely separated, the tips acute with a short, light claw. There are often wings between leaflets on the smaller rachises. Distally the rachises become faintly hairy. **Blades** hairless to faintly and minutely hairy above, fine-hairy below, especially on veins. **Midvein** in a slight depression but protruding above; *veins and veinlets raised on the upper surface,* nearly flat below. **Margins** regularly toothed, the teeth small, broad, forward-pointed with a light claw-tip. **Stems** smooth, roundish, and hairless on the lower parts, becoming more ridged and striated toward the top, with *short hairs becoming prevalent on ridges of the upper stem.* The stem is *pithy inside with*

◀ Young spring leaves.

only a pinhole hollow, reaching 28–40" (70–102 cm) in height and 12 mm thick. **Stem leaves** few and widely spaced, alternate, progressively smaller on shorter petioles, the sheaths enlarged, thick, stiff, and brittle. **Inflorescence** a nearly flat compound umbel to 4.5" (11 cm) wide with 18–30 channeled, hairy, primary rays; umbellets not touching in bloom. Rays of the umbellet are very short—flowers and fruit both crowded. The primary umbel lacks bracts; *umbellets have 5–6 pointed, linear bracts on the outer side only, clustered like fingers.* **Flowers** (early to late summer) tiny, with petals nearly invisible. **Fruits** multi-ridged, plump, hairy schizocarps.

CONFUSING PLANTS: Water hemlock (p. 668) grows in very different habitat; it has depressed veins, pointed leaflets, and hairless stems.

▼ Upper stem and leaf.

HABITAT: Dry, open woodlands and forest margins, especially where the soil is sandy or thin; associated with oaks, pines, black cherry, and sassafras. Native. 🔥

FOOD USE: Young, tender **leaves** in spring can be used like parsley. Tender **shoots** before blooming (often drooping) can be used as a cooked vegetable— but the flower buds are strongly flavored and I avoid them. **Conservation 2.**

COMMENTS: Despite the Linnaean name I have seen no evidence that this species is toxic. I have eaten it several times and have received reliable reports from other people who have eaten it, none with any ill effect. In fact, it is much milder than purple angelica, and I think the greens are far better. Some sources report that the root is the toxic part; I do not eat, nor recommend eating, the roots of any angelica. **AKA** woodland angelica.

▲ Shoot.

9 Goutweed 2 3 2
Aegopodium podagraria ◆ Apiaceae (Carrot family)

QUICK CHECK: Basal leaves form thick ground cover, blades ovate, hairless above, with deeply depressed veins; knee-high white flowers in compound umbels in early summer. **ID difficulty 2.**

DESCRIPTION: Perennial spreading by rhizome. **Basal leaves** of spring are twice compound; first ternately divided into 3 branches, each of which bears 2-5 stalked or sessile leaflets. Summer leaves are usually *once compound* with only 3 leaflets, each stalked. **Petioles** to 16" (40 cm), nearly erect, straight, solid, hairless, triangular in cross-section, the top shallowly but broadly channeled. **Leaflets** ovate to lanceolate, 1-3" (2.5-8 cm) long, usually pointed but sometimes blunt, often inequilateral at the base, occasionally lobed. **Surface** hairless above, corrugated by depressed veinlets. The underside has minute hairs along the veins. Cultivated clones of this plant are commonly seen with variegated green and white leaves; feral plants have a plain green leaf. **Midvein** strongly depressed above and protruding below, as are secondary veins, which are 45° to the midvein, most running straight and unbroken to a tooth tip. **Margins** serrated, often double-toothed, the teeth rounded with a sharp claw tip. **Petiolules** proportionately narrower and deeper than the rachis with thin, upturned, wing-like margins. **Stems** 1.5-3' (45-90 cm) tall, erect to leaning, hollow, jointed, hairless, light green, 4-6 mm thick at the base, round in the lower part but with straw-colored ridges in the upper; zigzag, the internodes straight and 8-15" (20-38 cm) long; branches few to none. *Shoots turn faintly purple inside when broken.* **Stem leaves** few, reduced to once compound with 3 narrow leaflets near the top, the petioles with a broad, lobed sheath to 1.5" (4 cm) long. Uppermost leaves are sessile. **Inflorescence** terminal compound umbels 2.5-5" (6-10 cm) across, with 15-20 curved rays, the umbellets not touching but flowers within them tightly packed. **Flowers** (early summer), 4-5 mm across with 5 white petals incurved at the tip. **Fruit** a schizocarp shaped like two cylinders connected on the long side, with a 2-humped yellowish tip.

HABITAT: Well-drained rich soil in full to partial shade. Forest edges, trails, roadsides, and especially old homesteads. Introduced.

FOOD USE: Collect young **leaves** at any time, but mostly in spring. Use as a vegetable raw or cooked; they are mild with a hint of celery or parsley. They can be simmered like nettles or honewort (or with them) to make a nice vegetable soup base. The **shoots** and **petioles** are pleasant raw or cooked.

COMMENTS: The all-green feral form of this herb is harder to recognize than the variegated forms under cultivation, but it is locally abundant. Of course, the cultivated plants are edible, too. I don't know if it really cures gout, but there's no harm in trying. **AKA** ground-elder, bishop's weed.

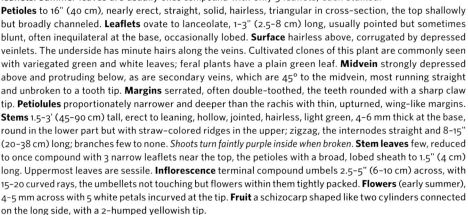

▼ Variegated leaf of a domestic cultivar.

10 Prairie parsnip ⟨ 1 ⟩ 2 ✎ 1
Polytaenia nuttallii/texanum ✦ *Apiaceae* (Carrot family)

QUICK CHECK: Dark green compound leaves tri-forked at first, leaflets lobed; erect zigzag stem with large umbels of tiny yellow flowers in late spring. **ID difficulty 2.**

DESCRIPTION: Perennial 2-6' (60-180 cm) tall, the form taller than wide. **Taproot** parsnip-like, to 1.5" (4 cm) thick, brown and bumpy on the outside, rarely branched, the flesh semi-fibrous and gray-white, weakly aromatic. Stems, petioles, rachises, and inflorescence are all *covered with dense but short, erect, very fine, semi-soft hairs* (especially when young).
Basal leaves twice compound, in a rosette of 5-9, persisting to early flowering, 6-12" (15-30 cm) long. **Petiole** has a short sheath at the base, beyond which it is hollow, not channeled, deeper than wide, faintly lined, 4-8" (10-20 cm) long before forking ternately and *widely*. Rachis branches divide again, the distal parts with a small channel on top. **Leaflets** sessile and *flat*, *dark* green, widening toward the tips with spreading lobes cut to varying depth. Lobe tips have large teeth with whitish nipples; margins are otherwise nearly toothless. Side leaflets are broadly attached and abruptly widening; terminal leaflets are tapered to a narrow base. **Major veins** *raised above*, bearing short, fine hairs—otherwise the surfaces are *hairless or nearly so*. Veinlets are flat. **Stems** erect, zigzag, to 0.8" (2 cm) thick with a small hollow or almost solid, jointed, roundish but gently ridged, the surface light green. **Branches** ascending, mostly in the upper half. **Stem leaves** alternate, widely spaced, reduced in size and becoming sessile upward. **Inflorescence** compound umbels 2-5" (5-13 cm) wide, convex, on finely ridged peduncles. **Umbellets** 12-20 mm across, densely packed with 12-35 flowers. The great umbel has no bracts; umbellets have a whorl of tiny, thread-like linear bracts. **Flowers** (late spring to early summer) 2 mm across with 5 greenish-yellow petals strongly curled inward, the stamens protruding through the gaps. **Fruit** a schizocarp 5-11 mm long, somewhat flattened, ribbed, the larger side ribs with corky wings.

CONFUSING PLANTS: From a distance it resembles parsnip but the leaf details are very different.

HABITAT: Well-drained or rocky parts of tallgrass prairies or moist pockets in shortgrass prairies, especially where sandy, high in calcium, and disturbed. Mostly on slopes, including roadsides. Native. 🔥

FOOD USE: The **roots** are large and parsnip-like but rather fibrous and strong-flavored, although sliced thin they work in a stew. **Peeled shoots** are tender and have good flavor. The **leaves** are tough and lame. **Seeds** can be used as a seasoning. **Conservation 3/2/1.**

COMMENTS: This is most commonly separated into two species based on subtle differences, but to the untrained eye they are identical, and the food uses are similar. The species or subspecies *texanum* predominates in Texas and southern Oklahoma, where it is abundant on roadsides. In much of its range the plant is rare due to habitat loss. **AKA** prairie parsley, but I think the comparison to parsnip is much more apt.

This root broke off at a rock. ▶

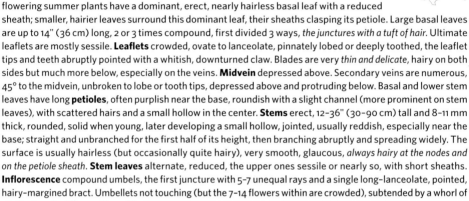

11 Aniseroot 🌱 2 🏺 3 🌿 2 📖 IWE-363
Osmorhiza longistylis ♦ Apiaceae (Carrot family)

QUICK CHECK: Knee to thigh-high herb with straight, erect stem branching widely and suddenly in the upper half, hairy at the nodes; compound umbels with unequal rays. **ID difficulty 2.**

DESCRIPTION: Perennial. **Taproot** small, thin, forking, whitish, aromatic. **Basal leaves** that overwinter are small with a broad whitish sheath at the base; these die back in spring. Non-flowering summer plants have a dominant, erect, nearly hairless basal leaf with a reduced sheath; smaller, hairier leaves surround this dominant leaf, their sheaths clasping its petiole. Large basal leaves are up to 14" (36 cm) long, 2 or 3 times compound, first divided 3 ways, *the junctures with a tuft of hair*. Ultimate leaflets are mostly sessile. **Leaflets** crowded, ovate to lanceolate, pinnately lobed or deeply toothed, the leaflet tips and teeth abruptly pointed with a whitish, downturned claw. Blades are very *thin and delicate*, hairy on both sides but much more below, especially on the veins. **Midvein** depressed above. Secondary veins are numerous, 45° to the midvein, unbroken to lobe or tooth tips, depressed above and protruding below. Basal and lower stem leaves have long **petioles**, often purplish near the base, roundish with a slight channel (more prominent on stem leaves), with scattered hairs and a small hollow in the center. **Stems** erect, 12–36" (30–90 cm) tall and 8–11 mm thick, rounded, solid when young, later developing a small hollow, jointed, usually reddish, especially near the base; straight and unbranched for the first half of its height, then branching abruptly and spreading widely. The surface is usually hairless (but occasionally quite hairy), very smooth, glaucous, *always hairy at the nodes and on the petiole sheath*. **Stem leaves** alternate, reduced, the upper ones sessile or nearly so, with short sheaths. **Inflorescence** compound umbels, the first juncture with 5–7 unequal rays and a single long-lanceolate, pointed, hairy-margined bract. Umbellets not touching (but the 7–14 flowers within are crowded), subtended by a whorl of

similar bracts. **Flowers** tiny with 5 white petals, the tips curled in. **Fruits** dark, almost banana-shaped schizocarps, each half with a barbed awn making it cling to clothing; persisting through fall, winter, and into the following spring attached to **LYDS**.

HABITAT: Rich, moist, but well drained soil in forests; more common under hardwoods. Native.

FOOD USE: Roots are small but highly flavored and make a pleasant nibble. All aerial parts are edible when tender. The best part is the **shoot** in mid spring; it can be eaten raw as a sweet, refreshing snack, or added to soups. **Leaves** can be eaten throughout the growing season. **Conservation 3/2.**

COMMENTS: I hate black licorice, but I love aniseroot stalks; they are one of my favorite spring vegetables. They often grow luxuriantly along with wood nettle, mitsuba, cleavers, and waterleafs in rich wooded valleys, especially thriving under black walnut. **AKA** sweetroot. *Osmorhiza chilensis (berteroi)* is a smaller and less common species scattered across the northern Great Lakes region and northern Appalachians.

Related Edibles:

12 Sweet Cicely ✦ *Osmorhiza claytonii* 📖 IWE-363

Very similar to aniseroot and many people lump the two together, but sweet cicely is almost uniformly light green and much hairier. The lower **stems** may be hairy or nearly hairless; upper stems and petioles are uniformly and densely covered with long, straight, erect, whitish hairs. The **leaflets** are narrower and more crowded, with the margins deeply pinnately incised into many small lobes with little to no space between them. The teeth are rounded, but the leaf divisions are more pointed and long-tapered. Sweet cicely inhabits most of the same hardwood forests as aniseroot, but also does well in some sandier soils where the latter is absent. Its stems are sweet but lack the anise flavor.

13 Red columbine ❀ 3
Aquilegia canadensis ❖ *Ranunculaceae* (Buttercup family)

QUICK CHECK: Thin stems; compound leaves divided in threes, the leaflet lobes rounded; flowers with 5 long spurs that have enlarged nectar cavities at the end. **ID difficulty 1.**

DESCRIPTION: Perennial. **Basal leaves** 3–10, twice compound, divided 3 ways each time, the rachises purple, hairless or with scattered very fine hairs, not channeled. **Leaflets** may be stalked or sessile, the blades very thin and delicate, 1–2.5" (2.5–6 cm) long, close together, smooth, hairless, rounded to broadly angled at the base with *3 main lobes, each often divided again into more lobes or large teeth*. Lobes and teeth are rounded, sometimes slightly indented, with a nipple tip. **Margins** entire near the leaflet base. **Major veins** palmate; veinlets are net-like and not depressed. **Petioles** delicate, 6–12" (15–30 cm) long and 2–3 mm thick, purple, not channeled. **Stem** purple-brown, thin but stiff and hard, naked for about 1/3 of its height, finely angled, faintly hairy toward the top. **Stem leaves** have a small, *stiff* sheath at the base. The first stem leaves are twice compound; upper ones are once compound or divided, the leaflets usually sessile. **Inflorescence** a loose cluster of widely-spaced flowers on long, *very thin, nodding pedicels*. **Flowers** (late spring to early summer) distinct: about 1.5" (4 cm) long, they have 5 yellow petals largely hidden by five reddish sepals, and 5 *long, backward-pointing spurs that terminate in an enlarged, rounded nectar cavity*. A dense cluster of numerous yellow stamens protrudes well beyond the petals. **Fruit** is a capsule or pod of 5 compartments, these fused at the base but splitting at the end and curving outward, each with a long bristle-like tip and containing numerous small seeds.

HABITAT: Woods and forest edges or clearings, especially where steep, rocky, or disturbed. Native.

FOOD USE: The **flowers** are a delicious snack or garnish enjoyed by many. Some people bite off just the 5 nectaries at the end of the spurs, but hungrier people like me eat the entire flower. Other parts of the plant are reported as toxic. **Conservation 1.**

COMMENTS: This plant, while rarely abundant, is very widespread and inhabits most forests. It is especially common around cliffs and rock outcroppings, which it seems able to find from miles away. Harvesting the flowers does not harm this long-lived perennial, but leave some for the hummingbirds. **The flowers are the only edible part.**

GROUP 28   BASAL LEAVES PRESENT, LEAVES ALTERNATE, MULTI-COMPOUND, FERN-LIKE OR LACY

Most of the plants in this group belong to the carrot family (*Apiaceae*). This family also includes some very poisonous species that will key to group 28—**poison hemlock** and **bulblet water hemlock**. Pay special attention to your identification.

Group 28 includes some culturally important root vegetables as well as flavorings, teas, leafy greens, and shoots. These plants are mostly spring ephemerals or they are adapted to open, sunny habitats. Since the difference between groups 27 and 28 is a judgment call, and plant form varies between individuals, you might want to check group 27 if your plant is not found here.

TENTATIVE IDENTIFICATION KEY TO GROUP 28
The key is not your final answer!

Blades and rachises hairless.	
Lower leaves divide immediately at the base.	**1. Pineapple weed**
Lower leaves have a naked petiole section before the first division.	
Petioles of typical lower leaves (the tiniest may differ) hollow with no channel on top.	
Petiole hollow proportionately small; stem solid; leaf divisions thread-like.	**2. Fennel**
Petiole and stem thin-walled with a large hollow, purple spots, and thick bloom; leaf divisions regularly pinnately toothed or lobed. Poison hemlock (poisonous, p. 671).	
Aquatic; petiole and stem thin-walled, hollow; bloom faint; leaf divisions not regularly toothed or lobed; upper leaf axils with bulblets. Bulblet water hemlock (poisonous, p. 670).	
Petioles of typical lower leaves hollow with a channel on top.	**3. Hemlock parsley**
Petioles of lower leaves solid, ribbon-like becoming broadly V-channeled.	**4. Caraway**
Petioles of lower leaves solid or with a tiny hollow, channeled on top.	
Basal leaves usually 3; stalks 3–5' (1–1.5 m), blooming in summer.	**5. Eastern yampa**
Basal leaves 1 or 2, stalks <8" (20 cm), blooming in spring.	**6. Harbinger of spring**
Blades and rachises with only minute woolly to scurfy hairs.	
Leaves glossy.	**7. Broad-leaf musineon**
Leaves dull to grayish, not glossy.	
Stems leaning or spreading, 1–5" (2.5–13 cm) long.	**8. White prairie biscuitroot**
Stems erect, 1–4' (30–120 cm) tall.	
Pods shorter and much thicker than the pedicels, the tip slightly thickened.	**14. Western tansy mustard**
Pods longer than and only slightly thicker than the pedicels; thickness uniform.	**15. European tansy mustard**
Blades and rachises with relatively straight, typical, visible, erect to appressed hairs.	
Hairs on lower stem distinctly pressed downward.	
Mid-stem thick-walled hollow, with 12–20 flat-topped ridges.	**9. Cow parsley**
Mid-stem solid with fine ridges.	**10. Erect hedge parsley**
Stem hairs more or less erect (right angle to the surface).	
Stem very smooth, nearly hairless or with soft hairs. Aniseroot and sweet cicely (group 27).	
Stem very finely ridged and/or with stiff hairs.	
Flowers pink-purple; fruit needle-like, pointing vertically.	**16. Alfilaria**
Flowers white; fruit variably shaped schizocarps.	
3–6' (1–2 m) tall; stalked compound umbels with 30–90 rays (summer).	**11. Wild carrot**
Less than 3' (1 m) tall; tiny umbels of less than 10 flowers (spring).	
18–30" (45–75 cm) tall; umbels compound or in clumps of 3–5.	**12. Southern chervil**
4–16" (10–40 cm) tall; umbels mostly simple and single.	**13. Spreading chervil**

1 Pineapple weed 🌿 1 🌸 1 ☕
Matricaria matricarioides ◆ *Asteraceae* (Aster family)

QUICK CHECK: Very short; lacy divided leaves; aromatic, yellow, cone-like heads with no rays. **ID difficulty 1.**

DESCRIPTION: Low annual or winter annual. Rosette present on early spring plants, withering by maturity. **Basal leaves** 1.5–4" (4–10 cm) long, hairless, broad at the base, deeply divided 1–3 times into numerous, *thin, lacy segments*, the ultimate lobes linear, pointed, and often curved. There are *no distinct petioles or petiolules within the leaf*; subdivision always begins at the base of each structure. The first divisions are pinnate, but smaller divisions are palmate or nearly so. **Stems** erect if single (when multiple or branched at the base, the outer stems lean), to 12" (30 cm) tall, proportionately thick, solid, hairless to faintly hairy, roundish but somewhat angled with ridges running down from each node, often with profuse ascending compound branches. **Stem leaves** alternate, similar to basal, dividing immediately with *lobes crowded at the broad and nearly clasping base*. **Rachis** flat and broad, not channeled, slightly keeled below, the same color as leaf divisions. **Inflorescence** (late spring to early summer) composite heads 5–8 mm across, solitary and terminal on long peduncles from upper branches, light greenish yellow, rounded at first becoming bluntly conical, composed of disk florets only.

CONFUSING PLANTS: Chamomile *M. chamomilla* is a larger species that has ray and disk florets.

HABITAT: Disturbed, moist ground, especially in poor soil. Common in driveways, parking areas, road shoulders, sidewalks, vacant lots. Reportedly introduced from Asia but this conclusion is suspect; probably native here as well.

FOOD USE: The young **greens** and **flowerheads** can be eaten as a nibble or garnish, and can also be used to steep a pleasant tea reminiscent of chamomile. Primarily available from late spring through early summer; sometimes found later, but usually dying with dry weather.

COMMENTS: The name is derived from a supposed similarity between the flavor of this plant's flowers and pineapple. Often mistakenly called "wild chamomile," although the tea is similar in flavor. Pineapple weed has been used as a traditional mosquito repellent, and research has verified the effectiveness and isolated the active chemicals. **AKA** *Matricaria discoidea.*

2 **Fennel** ⋔ 3 ✏ 2 ⚘ 2 ⌂ 📖 IWE-113
Foeniculum vulgare ✦ **Apiaceae (Carrot family)**

QUICK CHECK: Tall, smooth, glaucous herb with thread-like leaves and compound umbels of yellow flowers; aromatic. **ID difficulty 2.**

DESCRIPTION: Perennial forming large, multi-crowned clumps, all parts hairless and highly aromatic with the same scent as cultivated fennel. **Basal leaves** rosette-like and often ground-hugging on plants that lack stems, but on plants with stems they are erect and *two-ranked*. They wither by flowering. Larger leaves are 3–4 times pinnately compound, the ultimate divisions *thread-like*, not in plane, and folded or channeled. In early spring the outer leaf in the cluster has a broad sheath 3–10" (8–25 cm) long, the edges overlapping, with a blunt upturned lobe at the top; this sheath encircles a cluster of inner leaves and stems. **Petioles** elliptic in cross section with a small elliptic hollow but no channel; they are deeper than wide, smooth but with many fine ridges. **Rachis** becomes more distinctly ridged after the first division; rachis branches are channeled. *Branching in the rachis is out of plane.* **Stem leaves** similar to basal leaves but smaller, with wide, clasping sheaths, often much lighter in color than the stems. **Stems** 4–7' (1.2–2.1 m) tall and 0.6–0.9" (18–23 mm) thick, rigid, green when young (darkening with age), glaucous, solid when young but sometimes developing a small hollow, jointed, roundish with minor ridges. **Branches** in the upper half, these minor and strongly ascending—the form always taller than wide. **Inflorescence** flat-topped compound umbels with 24–38 primary rays, these not ridged. Great umbels and umbellets lack bracts. Umbellets are not touching (except those in the center), but the flowers are packed tightly together. **Flowers** tiny with all parts yellow. The 5 petals do not touch and are curled inward; spreading stamens extend well beyond them. **Fruit** a ribbed, elliptic schizocarp 2.5–3.5 mm long.

HABITAT: Disturbed, dry, rocky or gravelly ground, mostly roadsides and waste areas. Introduced.

FOOD USE: All tender parts are edible. The **peeled shoots** are a first-rate vegetable raw or cooked. Clusters of young **leaves** and **flower buds** are also good as a flavoring herb. The **seeds** can be gathered late in the growing season and used as a seasoning like commercial fennel seed. (Continued on the next page.)

2   Fennel (continued)

COMMENTS: This is the feral version of the domestic vegetable. Wild fennel lacks the enlarged leaf sheaths for which the cultivated plant has been bred—but the tender stalks are even better, and plenty large enough to make good use of your time. Fennel is widespread near the Atlantic coast and grows sporadically inland, but it is much more prevalent on the West Coast. Finely sliced fennel stems salted and dipped in hickory oil is a much-loved delicacy in our house.

3   Hemlock parsley   2
Conioselinum chinense ✦ *Apiaceae* (Carrot family)

QUICK CHECK: Delicate hairless herb with lacy carrot-like leaves, thin stalks and petioles, and umbels of tiny white flowers in late summer. **ID difficulty 3+.**

DESCRIPTION: Perennial from a whitish taproot, stems and leaves hairless. **Basal leaves** 3-4 times compound/divided and *persisting through flowering*, few in shade but numerous in sun, the leafy part 8-18" (20-46 cm) long, triangular in outline. **Petiole** 80-160% of blade length, twice and sometimes thrice pinnately divided. Petiole and rachises are *hollow with a U-channel above* that is *whitish in the bottom*. **Leaflets** deeply lobed, the lobe tips sharp and white, the surface slightly glossy, the major veins *flat to faintly depressed or the blade slightly creased along the vein*. **Stems** thin and lanky, to 5' (1.5 m) tall in shade, or stout and robust and much shorter in sun, 6-12 mm thick, smooth, hairless, faintly to strongly striated, sometimes lightly coated with bloom (especially in shade), round, hollow, jointed, with very long internodes, purple near the base but green above and *not purple spotted*. **Stem leaves** alternate, reduced, the sheaths of the upper ones enlarged, open and boat-like, 1-2.2" (25-56 mm) long; lower sheaths are less prominent. **Inflorescence** a few compound umbels 2-5" (5-13 cm) across on the upper third of the stem, each with 8-20 primary rays, these distinctly channeled, curving upward, the umbel with a slightly rounded top. The rays have minute, stiff hairs. There are *no bracts under the primary rays*, but there is a whorl of several sharp-tipped linear bracts beneath each umbellet. Umbellets are few and widely spaced in shade, but many, crowded, and touching in full sun. **Flowers** (late summer to early fall) 16-34 per umbellet, tiny with 5 white petals, the tips strongly curved inward. **Fruit** an oblong, brown, somewhat flattened schizocarp 3-5 mm long, the edges winged, with 3 prominent ridges in the middle of each side.

CONFUSING SPECIES: Looks quite like **poison hemlock** (p. 671), and was named for this resemblance, but hemlock parsley blooms in late summer through fall and has only a few umbels per stem. Poison hemlock rachises lack the white-bottomed channel of hemlock parsley and the boat-like, open upper sheaths. Poison hemlock has bracts under the great umbels.

HABITAT: Two distinct habitats: open limestone ledges, slopes, pebbles, or gravel near the coast; and calcium-rich fens and swamps inland, especially with cedar. Native.

FOOD USE: Roots (fall) can be used as a cooked vegetable. They are fibrous but like a cross between a strong wild carrot and celery root in flavor. Tender **greens** can also be used as a seasoning like parsley. I have eaten both parts, but in limited amounts. **Conservation 3/2.**

COMMENTS: This plant has two distinct growth forms in its different habitats; you would hardly suspect they are the same plant. Coastal plants are shorter, stouter, and leafier. Inland populations are sparse and rare and should generally not be gathered. Coastal plants are robust and may be abundant; on the Pacific coast they were formerly managed by Indigenous people as a root crop. Some botanists say this plant is found in eastern Asia. Others claim that despite the name, it is not found in China, and was named for Linnaeus' misreading of *Genesee* (New York) on a specimen label, and the plants found in China are just a close relative. In any case, it looks remarkably similar to **poison hemlock**. This is the trickiest "look-alike" in North America. Be darn sure and then some before you eat it!

▲ (top right) Small root. I ate the tip before taking the photo.
  (bottom right) In full sun on rocky seashore.

◄ (bottom left) Tall, lanky plant of a shady inland bog.

4 Caraway ⚡ 2 🍃 3 ✏ 2 ⚱ 📖 IWE-84
Carum carvi ✦ *Apiaceae* (Carrot family)

QUICK CHECK: Hairless plant with finely-cut, multi-compound leaves with linear lobes, the leaves full and fluffy; white flowers in compound umbels. **ID difficulty 3.**

DESCRIPTION: Biennial, *all parts hairless.* **Taproot** thick, strongly tapered, with a dominant central root, whitish outside and inside, the surface bumpy, aromatic. **Basal leaves** 6-13, in a rosette, 5-9" (13-23 cm) long and less than half as wide. There are no widened sections to the leaf—all leaflets, lobes, and divisions are thin and linear. Most leaves are twice compound and once deeply lobed, the final divisions creased down the center. **Main veins** of each lobe are depressed. The leaf has a full and fluffy look, not being flattened in any dimension since the rachises and leaflets are out of plane with each other. Leaf undersides are tinted silver-gray. Basal leaves wither by fruiting. **Petioles** *solid, V-channeled,* not winged on the margin, light green, 80-130% of the blade length on lower leaves. Rachis and rachis branches are also deeply channeled. **Stems** solid or with a thin hollow in the center of the upper stem, 18-32" (45-80 cm) tall and 9-13 mm thick, jointed, zigzag, branching widely in the upper half, the mature form almost as wide as tall. Stem surface is light green, faintly bloom-coated, finely ridged, and striped with darker green. Cross section of shoot shows 3 color zones alternating light and dark green. **Stem leaves** alternate, the lower ones with a semi-translucent sheath at the base, *flat, broad, and ribbon-like, the flat part nearly white inside* with prominent ridged veins. Upper leaves are greatly reduced. **Inflorescence** several flat-topped compound umbels 2-2.8" (5-7 cm) wide, the umbellets 0.5-0.7" (13-18 mm) across, usually not touching except sometimes in the center. The great umbel has a whorl of linear bracts at the first junction, often hidden by being pressed against the rays. **Flowers** (early summer) tiny, often not touching, the center dull yellow-green or brown. The 5 white petals are almost equal in size and have claw-like tips curved back toward the center. **Fruit** elliptic schizocarps 2-3 mm long with darkened ridges, brown when mature (identical to cultivated caraway).

CONFUSING PLANTS: Wild carrot is hairy and taller, less branched, and has fruits with hooked hairs; it has less of a clasping sheath at the leaf base. Cow parsley has hairy stems and leaves. **Poison hemlock** (p. 671) is much taller with a hollow stem, very heavy bloom, and purple spots.

HABITAT: Fields, pastures, and roadsides in full sun, with moist soil. Introduced.

FOOD USE: Dig **roots** during the dormant season (fall through spring), wash, and use like carrots or parsnips.

Use tender spring **shoots** as a vegetable raw or cooked, and the chopped young **leaves** as an herb like parsley. **Seeds** can be gathered in mid-summer and used as a seasoning identical to cultivated caraway seed.

COMMENTS: Caraway resembles wild carrot but is shorter and hairless. The root is generally larger than that of wild carrot, at least in proportion to the size of the plant; it is also more tender and has better form. It makes a nice vegetable with a sweet, aromatic flavor, although there is a faint bitter aftertaste. Caraway likes cool climates; in parts of the northern US and much of Canada it is among the most common roadside weeds. This plant is the same as the cultivated caraway; all culinary uses besides the seeds have been nearly forgotten.

5 Eastern yampa 3 3
Perideridia americana + *Apiaceae* (Carrot family)

QUICK CHECK: Hairless, glaucous, delicate plant with deeply cut leaves and compound umbels of white flowers. **ID difficulty 3+.**

DESCRIPTION: Perennial *dying back by midsummer*, all parts hairless. *Tubers usually in a pair, 2–4" (5–10 cm) underground*, shaped like a tooth or elongated teardrop, 1–1.7" (25–43 mm) long, pointed at the tip, with a cracked brown papery coating that rubs off to reveal a white surface with horizontal lenticels. There is a faint ring of yellow channels inside the flesh, which is *brittle, starchy, white*, and carroty-aromatic. *A ring of small roots radiates at the stem base near the top of these tubers—roots do not emanate from the tuber sides or tip.* **Basal leaves** usually 3 per crown, appearing in early spring but *wilting as the stem appears*, attached 2–4" (5–10 cm) underground, wrapped together in a whitish bundle with broad sheaths (the outer of which are free and not attached to leaves) then spreading at the surface. The blade is 4–10" (10–25 cm) long, twice compound and then once deeply lobed/divided. Ultimate divisions or lobes are 2–8 mm wide and linear, *not toothed*, blunt, ending in a faint straw-colored nipple tip. The major vein of each lobe is flat to faintly depressed. **Petioles** 25–40% of blade length, broadly sheathed/winged underground but tapering quickly to a channeled top above ground, *solid*. **Stems** thin and lanky, 1.5–5' (45–150 cm) tall and 5–8 mm thick, round, hollow, single, erect, jointed, with long internodes of 10–15" (25–38 cm), *unbranched below the inflorescence*. The surface is *uniformly green*, very smooth, and glaucous with notable white powder. **Stem leaves** alternate, the petioles equal in length to the blades on lower leaves, reduced upward to sessile or nearly so, the sheath margins overlapping and incurved to form a tapered scroll before *uniting to form a hollow petiole*. Uppermost leaves near the inflorescence branches are tiny and 3-lobed or linear. **Inflorescence** 3–5 *round-topped, symmetrical compound umbels* on broadly spreading branches at the top of the stem, the umbellets not touching in bloom. **Rays** 6–20, 0.8–1.8" (20–45 mm) long in bloom, longer in fruit. **Great umbels** 1.8–2.8" (45–70 mm) across in bloom, 4–7" (10–18 cm) across in fruit. Peduncles and pedicels are very thin. There are usually 2 tiny linear bracts below the great umbel; these are shed as the fruit matures. **Umbellets** have a whorl of 8–14 tiny linear bracts and are tightly packed with 14–26 flowers. **Flowers** (early summer) about 2 mm across, white with 5 petals, these narrowed abruptly to needle-like tips that are strongly incurved. **Fruit** a 3–5 mm elliptic schizocarp, smooth and hairless, flattened, with no wing on the outside.

CONFUSING PLANTS: Poison hemlock (p. 671) is much larger with numerous umbels per plant; it has leaf divisions

without linear lobes, and the lobes or teeth are sharp-tipped. The stem is purple-spotted with a very heavy coating of white bloom, and the underground portion is a large taproot. Small specimens of **common water hemlock** (p. 668) can have similar tubers, but water hemlock tubers have roots upon them, and the leaves are very different. Yampa is usually wilting and dead before water hemlock blooms. **Bulblet water hemlock** (p. 670) is aquatic, has toothed leaves, and bulblets in upper leaf axils; its roots are enlarged but have no tubers.

HABITAT: Open woodlands, blufftops, prairies, glades, forest edges, meadows, roadsides; in rich but well-drained calcium-rich soils. Native. 🔥

FOOD USE: From early summer to autumn the **roots** can be gathered and used as a cooked vegetable. Because the plant is killed by harvest, always scatter seeds from nearby mature plants on the excavation holes, and replant any small rootlets. Young **greens** in spring taste remarkably like parsley but are super tender. **Conservation 3/2.**

COMMENTS: This obscure edible is a relative of the better known and more common yampa *Perideridia gairdneri* of the Rocky Mountains. A lover of the best farm soils, this plant has been eliminated from most of its range by agriculture, and in many areas is rare and protected; harvest is only responsible when you are propagating and managing it. This superb native food plant is worthy of broad use as an edible ground cover in yards, orchards, and nut groves. **AKA** thicket parsley.

▲ (top left) Stem leaves. (bottom) Early spring rosette.

6 Harbinger of spring 3 2
Erigenia bulbosa ✦ Apiaceae (Carrot family)

QUICK CHECK: Tiny forest herb with carrot-like, hairless leaves and umbels of 5-petaled white flowers in early spring. **ID difficulty 3.**

DESCRIPTION: Very small spring ephemeral from an enlarged, roundish **root** 9–14 mm in diameter. **Basal leaves** usually 1 on flowering plants, 2 on non-flowering plants. They are hairless, 3–7" (8–18 cm) long and about as wide, the rachis first dividing 3 ways, each branch again dividing 3 ways; after this they are palmately or pinnately divided once or twice. **Blade** smooth, hairless, glossy, the major veins flat or faintly raised above, the lobe tips blunt or pointed with a tiny nipple. **Petiole** usually maroon (at least at the base) shallowly and broadly U-channeled, solid or with a tiny hollow; rachis branches are similar but distally become more broadly channeled. **Stems** up to 3 per plant, 2–5" (5–13 cm) tall, unbranched, faintly ridged, hairless. **Stem leaf** single, *much smaller, double-pinnate,* borne just beneath the great umbel. **Inflorescence** a small compound umbel with 3 (rarely 4) rays at the first juncture. **Umbellets** each have 3–8 tiny flowers on very short pedicels; beneath these are usually 1–2 oblanceolate bracts. **Flowers** (early spring) have 5 white, obovate petals, not curled in toward the center, that contrast with the *large purple-brown anthers.* **Fruit** a schizocarp, broader than long, flattened, notched, with 2 white "whiskers" curling around the edge.

CONFUSING PLANTS: Dutchman's breeches and squirrel's corn (genus *Dicentra,* probably poisonous) may share the habitat. *Dicentra* leaves are more palmately divided, balanced on more erect petioles; the surfaces have a bloom giving them a grayish cast, especially below. The flowers and USOs are entirely different. Spreading chervil (p. 475) has hairy petioles.

HABITAT: Rich, moist deciduous forests with diverse spring ephemerals, especially small floodplains and lower slopes. Native.

FOOD USE: The rounded, enlarged **root** tastes like carrot or parsnip. Usually close to the surface, it can be eaten at any time but is easiest to find in spring when the plant is up. The **greens** have a pleasant parsley-like flavor. **Conservation 3/2.**

COMMENTS: Harbinger of spring is easily over-harvested and is protected in many areas; collect only where abundant and do so judiciously and sparingly. This sweet little vegetable reminds me of dwarf ginseng (p. 511) but is far better. **AKA** pepper-and-salt.

0 mm   1 cm

7 Broad-leaf musineon 1 1
Musineon divaricatum ✦ *Apiaceae* (Carrot family)

QUICK CHECK: Low plant with thick, broad, shiny, divided basal leaves and packed compound umbels of tiny yellow flowers. **ID difficulty 2.**

DESCRIPTION: Low perennial spring ephemeral from a taproot. There is a *subterranean vertical stem starting a few inches underground that rises to the surface where it bears leaves.* **Taproot** rather fibrous, somewhat enlarged, the surface brown. **Basal leaves** 4–6" (10–15 cm) long, long-triangular in outline, hugging the ground, first pinnately divided, then deeply pinnately lobed or divided again. The broadest divisions are 3–8 mm across—much wider than those of other short prairie ephemerals in the carrot family. **Blades** *glossy, thick,* hairless (or nearly so) on both sides with a few large, blunt teeth with light-colored nipple tips. **Veins** offset by color, with occasional hairs; they are flat to *raised above* and *depressed below.* **Petiole** about as long as the blade, has scattered stiff hairs; the base is a sheath, fleshy rather than papery, tapering to a broad U-channel. Rachis sections are winged. **Stems** often multiple, *very short,* 1–4" (2.5–10 cm) long, spreading to ascending, *often splitting into 2 equal forks,* with low, lined ridges, almost solid with a pinhole hollow, the surface with scattered stiff hairs. Some plants appear stemless. **Stem leaves** smaller, alternate or so close as to appear paired; the petioles are deeper than wide and deeply

channeled. **Inflorescence** a compound umbel on a solid peduncle that may be prostrate or upright (but curved), 1–5" (2.5–13 cm) long, with fine ridges. *One of the outer primary rays is sometimes widened and slightly winged.* There are *no bracts* under the great umbel, but under the umbellets they are *numerous and linear.* The umbellets and florets are packed. **Flowers** tiny, about 1 mm across, with 5 yellow petals curled in to meet in the center (looking almost like an unopened bud), and yellow anthers and filaments. **Fruit** a somewhat flattened, strongly ridged schizocarp.

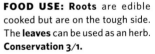

HABITAT: Dry prairies on soil that is not too sandy. Native.

FOOD USE: Roots are edible cooked but are on the tough side. The **leaves** can be used as an herb. **Conservation 3/1.**

COMMENTS: This beautiful little plant is easy to recognize, with its shiny, plastic-looking leaves. It sometimes turns hillsides yellow in spring. You might encounter plants that seem intermediate between this and its close relative, *Musineon tenuifolium* (p. 294). Both species are too strong (leaves) and tough (roots) to be used in quantity, but are pleasant when used sparingly. This plant doesn't really have a common name, but is sometimes **AKA** leafy musineon or leafy wildparsley.

467

8   White prairie biscuitroot   2   2
Lomatium orientale ♦ Apiaceae (Carrot family)

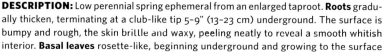

QUICK CHECK: Low carroty plant made gray from fine white hairs; leaves crowded on lower stem; crowded umbels of white flowers with dark maroon centers. **ID difficulty 2.**

DESCRIPTION: Low perennial spring ephemeral from an enlarged taproot. **Roots** gradually thicken, terminating at a club-like tip 5–9" (13–23 cm) underground. The surface is bumpy and rough, the skin brittle and waxy, peeling neatly to reveal a smooth whitish interior. **Basal leaves** rosette-like, beginning underground and growing to the surface before spreading, ground-hugging or ascending, 3–7" (8–18 cm) long, long-elliptic in outline; first pinnately compound with the divisions often widely spaced, then deeply pinnately lobed (distally) or fully divided (proximally), the final divisions with long lobes often curling upward, the tips abruptly pointed to blunt. The surface is covered with *fine, soft, dense, whitish hair giving a dull grayish appearance.* **Rachis** naked for half its length; at the base it has a long, broad, tapered sheath with papery edges and purple highlights and veins. Beyond the sheath it is *deeply channeled*. **Stems** usually multiple, beginning slightly underground, extending 1–5" (5–13 cm) above the soil, 3–4 mm thick, erect (in competition) or sometimes ground-hugging (without), hollow, faintly ridged and lined, minutely soft-hairy. **Stem leaves** few and much smaller, alternate, with the sheath margins folded upward and touching or nearly so; there is usually a small axillary inflorescence wrapped in this sheath. **Inflorescence** crowded compound umbels to 1.5" (4 cm) wide, with no bracts underneath, at the end of a proportionately thick, naked peduncle 2–5" (5–13 cm) long, grooved more deeply than the stem. Reduced axillary clusters are also often present. **Umbellets** small and crowded with a whorl of narrowly lanceolate tapered bracts with whitish margins behind the rays. **Flowers** 2 mm wide with 5 white petals strongly curled inward and meeting in the center; maroon anthers give it a bicolored look. **Fruit** an elliptic and only slightly flattened schizocarp.

CONFUSING PLANTS: *Cymopterus montanus* (p. 296) has the same grayish look but is even smaller and has no stem above ground. The leaves are more compact and ruffled, and less woolly. Its umbellets are almost enveloped by papery bracts, and the fruit has broad wings.

HABITAT: Dry prairies with sandy or gravelly soil. Native.

FOOD USE: Although the **roots** are rather small and hard to dig, they are starchy and have good flavor.

Greens make a good parsley/lovage type herb. **Conservation 3/2.**

COMMENTS: This species is more common than its relative *L. foeniculaceum* because it inhabits poorer soils not put to the plow. It can do well in light grazing, but disappears under heavy use. Gather judiciously and spread seeds to avoid overharvest. **AKA** white prairie parsley.

9 Cow parsley ⚘ 1 🌿 1 ⚘ 2
Anthriscus sylvestris ◆ *Apiaceae* (Carrot family)

QUICK CHECK: Chest-high with carrot-like leaves and tiny white flowers in flattish umbels; stem ridged and hairy at the base. **ID difficulty 3.**

DESCRIPTION: Perennial spreading by forming new adjacent root crowns, the herbage very dark green. *Sap milky.* **Taproots** white inside and outside, carroty-scented, 8–14" (20–36 cm) long and up to 1.2" (3 cm) thick, often branching near the top. **Basal leaves** 5–7 per rosette, wedge-shaped in outline, 8–20" (20–50 cm) long, 2–3 times pinnately compound, the divisions often widely spaced and much smaller toward the tip. At the first and second levels the divisions are stalked proximally, becoming sessile distally; 3rd level divisions are

▲ Rapidly expanding.

always sessile. The first two large segments are out of plane with the rest of the blade. Ultimate leaflets are deeply pinnately lobed. Blades are scarcely hairy above but are *hairy on the margins and below*; rachises are also hairy. **Midveins** and main veins of each lobe are depressed. **Petioles** 100–180% of blade length, sheath-like and purplish at the base, thick-walled and hollow except near the base (which is solid). The surface is *stiff-hairy*, the hairs pointing toward the base—especially on the sheath. Petioles have a smooth-bottomed channel that is glossy and bubbly looking, weakly keeled beneath, with many small ridges. **Stems** 2–4.5' (60–140 cm) tall, often multiple, branching widely, zigzag, jointed, enlarging slightly below each node, with a *small, hollow center near the base of the shoot.* This hollow enlarges upward and with age. The surface is green (sometimes reddish near the base or nodes) with *12–20 flat-topped ridges*, often with smaller ridges between them. *Near the base, stems have many short, stiff hairs pointing downward*; these become sparser going up the stalk. Upper branches are nearly hairless. Stems die back in mid summer. **Stem leaves** similar to basal but smaller and less hairy, with petioles reduced. **Inflorescence** widely branching with *multiple umbel-like junctures of 3 or more branches, each juncture with a reduced but still compound leaf*, the branches hairless except at sheaths, terminating in flat-topped compound umbels 2–3" (5–8 cm) wide with up to 18 rays. **Umbellets** slightly spaced, but the 10–20 flowers within them are densely packed. There are no bracts under the great umbel, but each umbellet has a whorl of 5–8 small, hairy, ovate bracts with a sharp acuminate tip. A lone compound umbel often arises from a lower branch juncture; these open first. **Flowers** (late spring to early summer) 2–3 mm across, white, with five asymmetrical petals (those on the outside of the umbellet much larger than those on the inside). Petals are broad at the tip and often notched, but *not folded or curled inward*. (Continued on the next page.)

9 Cow parsley (continued)

Fruit hairless (except very minutely on the beaks), held vertical, looking like 2 tubes fused on the long edge, slightly wider at the base and narrowed to a double beak-like tip. After dying and drying they turn blackish and the 2 halves hang together loosely by the tip.

CONFUSING PLANTS: Wild carrot has larger, more crowded compound umbels subtended by many long bracts, and the leaves are much smaller. **Poison hemlock** (p. 671) has leaves of similar shape but is hairless with a smooth, hollow stem coated in bloom, and is much taller.

HABITAT: Roadsides, pastures, open woods, forest edges. An invasive from Europe that is spreading rapidly in some areas, this plant has a disjunct and spotty distribution but is locally very abundant. **I**

FOOD USE: Roots are remotely carroty but the flavor is very strong and they are tough—not recommended. If you eat them do it sparingly and well-cooked. Tender **greens** in spring can be used as an herb in soups, casseroles, etc., as one would use parsley. **Shoots** can be used as a vegetable raw or cooked after the skin is peeled.

COMMENTS: This is a very close relative to the cultivated chervil *Anthriscus cerefolium*. Well known among foragers in England where it is native and abundant, this species is rapidly increasing in some parts of North America. The leaves resemble those of poison hemlock—but the ridged, hairy stems are distinctive. **WARNING:** The juice is probably phototoxic. (See p. 23.)

10 Erect hedge parsley 🌿 1 🌿 1
Torilis japonica ✦ Apiaceae (Carrot family)

QUICK CHECK: Knee to thigh-high carrot-like plant with leaves and stems roughened by stiff hairs; flowers white, clusters small, fruits stick-tights. **ID difficulty 3.**

DESCRIPTION: Winter annual. **Rosette** leaves few, 2–6" (5–15 cm) long, twice pinnately compound and once deeply pinnately lobed; these leaves wither by flowering. **Stem** erect, jointed, strongly zigzag when young, lanky at maturity, 2–4.5' (60–140 cm) tall and 6–14 mm thick, *solid*, round with numerous *fine ridges*, these becoming narrower but more prominent on the upper stem. Stems are covered with short, *stiff hairs appressed toward the base* in the lower part. **Branches** large and often several at or near the base, fewer above, strongly ascending. The upper internodes are long and naked. **Stem leaves** near the base are much larger than rosette leaves, to 12" (30 cm) long. They have sheaths up to 0.8" (2 cm) wide, inrolled, very thin and transparent near the edge, gradually transforming into a petiole that is solid and deeply channeled. **Petioles** may be as long as the blade but get shorter going up the stem. After the first division the rachis branches are channeled less deeply. Petioles and rachises have short, stiff hairs appressed toward the tip. **Blade** triangular in outline with a gap after the first division, then leaflets crowded toward the rachis branch ends, which are often drooping. The terminal division is deeply pinnately incised, gradually tapered to a long, narrow tip—especially on the uppermost leaves. **Leaflets/divisions** mostly in plane, very dark green, covered on both sides with stiff hairs that are appressed toward the tip. The lobes and teeth are sharp and point distally, tipped with light-colored claws. **Major veins** deeply depressed above. **Inflorescence** compound

▲ Composite range of *T. arvensis* and *T. japonica*.

umbels about 1.2" (3 cm) across with 5–10 rays, at the end of a peduncle that may be very short or up to 8" (20 cm) long. **Umbellets** 6–8 mm across, densely packed with 5–10 flowers, *sometimes unequal*. There are several pointed, linear bracts under the umbels and umbellets, shorter than the rays and usually pressed against them. **Flowers** (early to mid summer) tiny with 5 white petals, *notched* at the tip but *not folded* or curled inward. Stamens spread widely; the tiny anthers of newly opened flowers are purplish. **Fruit** an egg-shaped sticktight schizocarp 2–4 mm long, the spines leaning toward the tip and curved slightly but not hooked; these are bunched together into a head-like mass when ripe.

CONFUSING PLANTS: Wild carrot *Daucus carota* also has sticktight fruits, but is a much larger plant with sparser, softer, erect hairs. **Poison hemlock** (p. 671) is hairless and much taller; it has a hollow stalk and is covered in white powder.

HABITAT: Forest openings and edges, paths, roadsides, forests of moderate shade; on rich soils. Introduced and highly invasive. **I**

FOOD USE: Tender young **stems**, after peeling, can be eaten raw or cooked. Youngest **greens** can be chopped like parsley or chervil, but are best when softened by cooking.

COMMENTS: The flavor is okay, but the stems are first too small and then too rough. This plant has been so consistently confused with another introduced hedge parsley, *Torilis arvensis*, even by professionals, that very little written about its distribution is reliable. Both species are edible and very similar. *T. arvensis* has only 1–2 bracts under the great umbel, and the rays are often much longer. Another introduced species, *T. nodosa*, is common in the South but I have not tried it.

11 **Wild carrot** 2 3 🖋 1 📖 NG-351
Daucus carota ✦ *Apiaceae* (Carrot family)

QUICK CHECK: Leaves 2–4 times compound; whole plant with erect hairs; a dark purple flower in the center of a large, dense umbel of many white ones. **ID difficulty 3.**

DESCRIPTION: Biennial, leafy parts with a carroty scent. **Taproots** thick, strongly tapered, rarely branched, white inside and outside, with a potent, pleasant, carroty scent when broken. **Rosette** with 9–12 leaves, the leafy portion 6–16" (15–40 cm) long, much longer than wide, twice pinnately compound and once deeply pinnately lobed (nearly divided). The first division is usually stalked; the second division is almost always sessile. The lobes are linear and pointed with a claw tip. Blades have scattered, long, straight hairs leaning toward the tip. Secondary veins and veinlets are *flat above* and flat to faintly protruding below. Leaf divisions are ruffled, often folded, and out of plane. **Petioles** to 12" (30 cm) long with a hairy-margined whitish sheath at the base, narrow, not hollow or inflated, broadly U-channeled with a winged margin; the channel becomes narrower in the rachis, but all *rachis branches remain channeled.* **Stems** 3–6' (1–2 m) tall, usually single but sometimes branched at the base, round, solid, jointed, with fine and usually lined vertical ridges, the surface green to reddish with *scattered to dense erect hairs.* **Branches** few and strongly ascending, the form taller than wide. **Stem leaves** alternate, decreasing in size and frequency toward the top, the leaf divisions fewer, more linear, and more widely spaced. Sheaths long, thick, tapered, green with white papery margins—although it is hard to say where the sheath turns to a channeled petiole. Uppermost leaves have short sheaths and begin dividing immediately thereafter. **Inflorescence** few to several flat-topped compound umbels 2.5–6" (6–15 cm) across at the top of *very long, finely ridged, erect peduncles* to 16" (40 cm) long. **Great umbel** has 30–90 ridged rays. Beneath is a *whorl of 9–14 bracts* up to 3" (8 cm) long, these *pinnately lobed, the lobes paired, linear, widely spaced,* and sharp-tipped, the edges of the proximal part with a *wide, white, papery wing.* **Umbellets** 0.3–0.6" (8–15 mm) across, crowded, mostly touching, subtended by a smaller but similar whorl of bracts, the flowers within them *crammed together.* **Flowers** (late spring in the Deep South to mid summer in the North) 2–4 mm across, unequal in size (those in the umbellet center smaller), with 5 white petals. **Petals** equal in size on central flowers but *extremely unequal*

on outer flowers (largest petals may be 10 times larger than the smallest). Large outer petals are often *not folded inward*, or they may have an erratic crease; those of some smaller central flowers are strongly curled and creased. There is usually a *small central umbellet of dark brownish-purple flowers*, or a single such flower. At maturity the umbel curls into a "bird's nest." **Fruit** an egg-shaped sticktight schizocarp 3–4 mm long, densely covered with stiff, hook-tipped hairs.

CONFUSING PLANTS: Southern chervil flowers in spring and has very small umbels. Caraway and hemlock parsley are hairless. Hedge parsley is a smaller plant with smaller umbels with shorter, stiffer hairs. Cow parsley is stouter and blooms much earlier. *Daucus pusillus* is a native relative of the southern states that does not taste good. **Poison hemlock** (p. 671) is hairless and has smooth, hollow stems with purple spots or streaks; it is coated with profuse white bloom and has hollow petioles.

HABITAT: Disturbed soil, from heavy clay to loose sand or gravel, with lots of sun: old hayfields and pastures, empty lots, roadsides, weedy locations. Introduced.

FOOD USE: Dig **taproots** from fall through early spring on plants with no stalk, wash thoroughly, chop cross-wise, and use cooked like carrots or parsnips. They may be eaten raw but are somewhat stringy. **Peeled shoots** should be harvested in late spring while still tender. Young **leaves** can be chopped fine and used as a seasoning.

COMMENTS: This excellent, widespread edible is the same species as the cultivated carrot, but the root is tougher and white. The flavor and scent are similar—but wild carrot is stronger. The stalks are less well known but may actually be the better vegetable, as they are easier to collect and are typically larger and more tender. Wild carrot resembles the deadly poison hemlock, but careful observation allows for positive identification. **AKA** Queen Anne's lace.

12 Southern wild chervil 🌿 2 | 2
Chaerophyllum tainturieri ◆ *Apiaceae* (Carrot family)

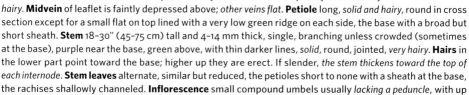

QUICK CHECK: Short, spreading, hairy, carrot-like herb with white flowers in small compound umbels in spring. **ID difficulty 3.**

DESCRIPTION: Winter annual, dying back in early summer, often in very crowded colonies on roadsides or steep banks. **Basal leaves** in a rosette, triangular in outline, slightly longer than wide, 2–3 times ternately or pinnately compound, then the final leaflets deeply lobed or divided. Lobes have rounded to blunt tips with a tiny claw. The blade is *sparsely to moderately hairy*. **Midvein** of leaflet is faintly depressed above; *other veins flat*. **Petiole** long, *solid and hairy*, round in cross section except for a small flat on top lined with a very low green ridge on each side, the base with a broad but short sheath. **Stem** 18–30" (45–75 cm) tall and 4–14 mm thick, single, branching unless crowded (sometimes at the base), purple near the base, green above, with thin darker lines, *solid*, round, jointed, *very hairy*. **Hairs** in the lower part point toward the base; higher up they are erect. If slender, *the stem thickens toward the top of each internode*. **Stem leaves** alternate, similar but reduced, the petioles short to none with a sheath at the base, the rachises shallowly channeled. **Inflorescence** small compound umbels usually *lacking a peduncle*, with up

to 5 primary rays of unequal length spreading directly from the stem or axil, the longer about 1" (2.5 cm) in bloom (lengthening in fruit). **Umbellets** have 3–10 flowers, closely packed, on pedicels of differing length, the *ovary elongated and enlarged while the flower blooms* (looking like a thickened pedicel). Under the umbellet is a *symmetrical whorl of 5 ovate bracts* 3–5 mm long. **Flowers** (spring) 2 mm across with 5 obovate, white petals, the tips often abruptly narrowed to a nipple but *not folded or curved inward* like most members of the carrot family. **Fruit** is a narrow schizocarp, dark purple-brown when ripe, 5 mm long, shaped like 2 cylinders fused at the side, with a beaked tip.

CONFUSING PLANTS: Wild carrot is much taller and flowers much later, with larger clusters. Hedge parsley flowers later and has larger umbellets and stiffer hairs. **Poison hemlock** (p. 671) is hairless in all parts, the leaves with sharper lobes tipped with a white claw, each lobe with a depressed central vein; otherwise, overwintering seedlings can be easily confused.

HABITAT: Full sun to light shade in disturbed areas with moist soil, especially on sandy soil. Fields, roadsides, parks, clearings, disturbed woods. Native.

FOOD USE: Tender **greens** and **shoots** have a pleasant, mild flavor and can be eaten raw or cooked. **Conservation 1.**

COMMENTS: I hate to call any plant "wild chervil" since the name has been used for several different genera; but unfortunately, there is no other common name applied to this group. This is a very common plant that has been totally ignored in foraging literature. **AKA** American chervil, hairy wild chervil.

Related edible:

13 **Spreading chervil** ✦ *Chaerophyllum procumbens* 2

This species is much smaller, typically 4–12" (10–30 cm) tall, with lax stems often resting on the ground for a few inches before standing weakly erect or spreading. **Stems** faintly ridged and not as bulged at nodes, with scattered hair (less than *C. tainturieri*), sometimes on only one side of the upper stem. There are usually 2–4 major branches at or near the base. Leaf sheath margins, petioles, rachises, and blade margins are also sparsely hairy. Stem leaves are mostly borne close to the base. **Inflorescence** stalkless compound umbels with 3 or fewer rays, each terminating in a small umbellet of 3–7 flowers—but sometimes the umbels are not compound. **Petals** ovate and cupped but not folded or curled inward. **Fruits** smaller, less tapered, and less pointed. As with its larger cousin, the seeds germinate in autumn and form small rosettes with typical compound leaves as well as *entire, elongated cotyledon leaves* that resemble those of Virginia spring beauty. This species inhabits rich soil of river floodplains and valleys, usually growing in shade, and is found further north than its larger cousin. Although smaller and thus harder to gather in quantity, I prefer its flavor. **ID difficulty 3.**

CONFUSING PLANTS: These seedlings are edible at a time of year when leafy greens are few, but they very much resemble the overwintering seedlings of the deadly **poison hemlock** (p. 671). If you are going to eat them, examine them carefully for hairs and scent (poison hemlock has a nasty rank smell), as other features are absent on such small specimens. Seedlings of spreading chervil are often confused with harbinger of spring, which shares its habitat. However, that plant has hairless leaves and petioles and is dormant in early winter.

▲ Winter seedlings showing cotyledon leaves.

14 Western tansy mustard 2 2 2
Descurainia pinnata ✦ *Brassicaceae* (Mustard family)

QUICK CHECK: Leaves pinnately multi-lobed, fern-like; long, loose racemes with yellow flowers; the pods ascending but not appressed. **ID difficulty 3.**

DESCRIPTION: Winter annual. **Basal leaves** 3–6" (8–15 cm) long, much longer than wide, first pinnately compound, then pinnately deeply lobed to nearly divided. Rachis is shallowly channeled, covered with clumped woolly whitish hairs (giving a grayish look), the lower third or so not leafy. Ultimate lobes are linear to obovate, blunt-tipped, curled and cupped. Basal leaves disappear by flowering. **Stems** 12–40" (30–102 cm) tall, usually straight and erect, solid, covered with short, soft hairs, usually branching but the branches short; form much taller than wide. **Stem leaves** at first larger than the basal, then smaller; upper ones may be sessile, dividing immediately at the base. The blades become less hairy toward the top of the plant. Stem leaves also drop at maturity, from the bottom up. **Inflorescence** a very long, rather loose but evenly spaced, naked terminal raceme, up to 18" (46 cm) long, with only the crowded tip blooming. **Flowers** yellow, sometimes whitish- or rose-tinged, tiny, with 4 obovate petals narrowed at the base. **Fruit** an elongated pod slightly thicker toward the end, usually angled upward from the pedicel and often curving slightly. **Pedicels** slightly ascending or at a right angle to the rachis, about equal to or longer than the pods. **Seeds** numerous, tiny, oblong, somewhat flattened, light yellowish-brown to reddish-brown.

▲ Scarce in the eastern range.

CONFUSING PLANTS: Poison hemlock (p. 671) has hairless, hollow petioles and hollow stalks covered with bloom.

HABITAT: Dry, sunny, disturbed soil such as pastures, roadsides, vacant lots, crop fields, prairie washes, floodplains. Native.

FOOD USE: Young **greens** and **stems** can be eaten raw or cooked, but are strong and should be used sparingly. The dry **seeds** can be gathered winnowed, and used to make a mild-tasting gruel. **Conservation 2/1.**

COMMENTS: Most mustard seeds are hot, but these are not. There are many species of tansy mustard, all of which are edible. Here I am just covering the two most common.

▲ Tansy mustard rosette. I'm not actually certain which species—they are very similar at this stage.

Related edible:

15 European tansy mustard ✦ *Descurainia sophia* 2

This is a similar but introduced species, more common as an agricultural and yard weed than western tansy mustard. The leaves are more divided—the larger ones twice pinnately compound and once divided. The ultimate lobes are narrower and more pointed, at least on upper stems. The pods are much longer and thinner, held almost vertically, and are much longer than their pedicels. The seeds are not as mild tasting as those of western tansy mustard. The greens from the upper stem have a very strong flavor and should be used sparingly. **AKA** flixweed.

▲ Scarce in the eastern range.

16 Alfilaria 2
Erodium cicutarium ✦ Geraniaceae (Geranium family)

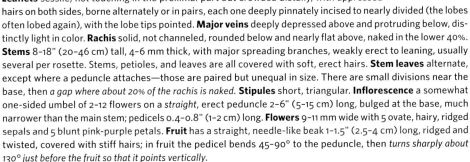

QUICK CHECK: Short, hairy herb with pinnately compound leaves and pinnately lobed leaflets; one-sided umbel with beak-like fruit on a bent stem. **ID difficulty 3.**

DESCRIPTION: Short biennial or winter annual. **Basal leaves** numerous and dense but disappearing by maturity, to 8" (20 cm) long and 1–1.7" (25–43 mm) wide, the lowest leaves longest, often hugging the ground, pinnately compound with a thick but not stiff rachis. **Leaflets** sessile, not touching in the proximal part but crowded distally, with appressed hairs on both sides, borne alternately or in pairs, each one deeply pinnately incised to nearly divided (the lobes often lobed again), with the lobe tips pointed. **Major veins** deeply depressed above and protruding below, distinctly light in color. **Rachis** solid, not channeled, rounded below and nearly flat above, naked in the lower 40%. **Stems** 8–18" (20–46 cm) tall, 4–6 mm thick, with major spreading branches, weakly erect to leaning, usually several per rosette. Stems, petioles, and leaves are all covered with soft, erect hairs. **Stem leaves** alternate, except where a peduncle attaches—those are paired but unequal in size. There are small divisions near the base, then *a gap where about 20% of the rachis is naked.* **Stipules** short, triangular. **Inflorescence** a somewhat one-sided umbel of 2–12 flowers on a *straight*, erect peduncle 2–6" (5–15 cm) long, bulged at the base, much narrower than the main stem; pedicels 0.4–0.8" (1–2 cm) long. **Flowers** 9–11 mm wide with 5 ovate, hairy, ridged sepals and 5 blunt pink-purple petals. **Fruit** has a straight, needle-like beak 1–1.5" (2.5–4 cm) long, ridged and twisted, covered with stiff hairs; in fruit the pedicel bends 45–90° to the peduncle, then *turns sharply about 130° just before the fruit so that it points vertically.*

CONFUSING PLANTS: The specific name of the plant, *cicutarium,* refers to the leaves' resemblance to hemlock—

suggesting a potentially deadly mistake. (Although the name suggests water hemlock in particular, alfilaria more closely resembles **poison hemlock**, p. 671.) However, all parts of alfilaria are hairy, and the petioles are solid.

HABITAT: Disturbed, often dry and compacted soil in full sun. Yards, parks, gardens, roadsides, fields. Introduced.

FOOD USE: Gather tender young **leaves** in spring or summer, and sometimes again in fall. Chop into short sections and use in salads or as a cooked vegetable, or nibble the whole thing raw. Go for the leaves in the center of the rosette, as these are younger and less likely to be in contact with dirt.

COMMENTS: The leaves are more tender than they look, growing among so much coarse, dry vegetation. The flavor reminds me of bellflower leaves, mild and faintly fishy. **AKA** filaree, storksbill.

GROUP 29 HERBACEOUS VINES

I consider a plant a vine if it climbs by wrapping itself around other vegetation or by using tendrils to grasp objects for support. Plants that simply lean on other plants or trail along the ground are not placed here. Herbaceous vines produce a great variety of food types: root vegetables, seeds, greens, shoots, flowers, buds, and fruits. Although there are many species here, most can be readily identified by obvious features, and few dangerously toxic plants have this life form. Observe stems carefully, as many woody vines have very long tender tips that can look herbaceous.

TENTATIVE IDENTIFICATION KEY TO GROUP 29
The key is not your final answer!

or Leaf twice compound.	1. Balloon vine
Leaf once compound.	
Leaf with two leaflets.	
Stem angles distinctly winged.	
or or Stipules 5–12 mm wide.	2. Everlasting pea
Stipules less than 4 mm wide.	3. Narrow-leaved vetchling
Stem angles with wings absent or less than 0.5 mm.	4. Tuber vetchling
Leaf with 3 leaflets.	
Vines 1–1.5 mm thick with long erect hairs; pods brittle, hairy on edges; 3 flat, gray-mottled seeds.	9. Ground bean
or Vines 2–7 mm thick with short erect hairs; pods stiff, hairless; 3–5 flat, dark seeds.	10. Wild bean
Vines 2–3 mm thick with hairs pressed toward the base; seeds elongated, plump, straight-sided, blackish, embedded in cottony fuzz.	11. Fuzzy bean
Leaf with more than 3 leaflets.	
Leaflets broadly elliptic to ovate, often more than 1.4" (3.5 cm) long.	
Vine without tendrils.	12. Hopniss
Vine with tendrils.	
Corolla pale creamy to white.	5. Pale vetchling
or or Corolla pink to purple.	
Leaves with 4–6 leaflets; flowers pale pink; stipules toothed.	6. Marsh pea
Leaves with 7–12 leaflets; flowers purple; stipules not toothed.	7. Veiny pea
Leaves with 8–16 leaflets; flowers purple; stipules toothed.	8. Beach pea
Leaflets narrowly elliptic to lanceolate or linear, less than 1.4" long.	
Flowers 1 or 2 directly from the leaf axil.	13. Common vetch
Flowers in a one-sided raceme.	
Flowers pale creamy to white.	14. Carolina vetch
Flowers purple.	
Raceme with 2–9 flowers; leaf veins evident.	15. American vetch
Raceme with 15–40 flowers; leaf veins obscure.	
Upturned banner half as long as the straight base of the flower; lower (longest) calyx lobes almost bristle-like.	16. Hairy vetch
Upturned banner equal to the straight base of the flower; lower (longest) calyx lobes narrowly triangular.	17. Tufted vetch
Leaf simple.	
Leaf entire.	
All major veins arise at the base; at least the innermost reconverge at the tip.	
Stem 5–20 mm thick, with tendrils; inflorescence an umbel.	18. Carrion flower
or Stems 1–3 mm thick, without tendrils; inflorescence a spike.	
or Aerial tubers present.	19. Air potato
Aerial tubers absent. American wild yam (p. 678).	
Some major veins arise beyond the base, none reconverging at the tip.	
Stem with a small sheath at each node; flowers tiny; fruit 3-sided.	20. Black bindweed
Stem lacking sheaths; flowers large, showy; fruit egg-shaped.	21. Bigroot morning glory
Leaf lobed.	See key next page.

(Continued on next page.)

(Continued from previous page.)

Leaf lobed.
- Leaf margin toothed.
  - Stem 10-18 mm thick; leaves 4-10" (10-25 cm) long; lobe tips (if present) obtuse, blunt.
    - *or*
      - Leaves usually triangular; gourds spherical, drying straw-yellow. — **22. Buffalo gourd**
      - Leaves usually lobed; gourds teardrop-shaped, drying whitish gray. — **23. Ozark gourd**
  - *or*
    - Stem 3-7 mm thick; leaves 4-6" long, the lobe tips acute and sharp.
      - Stem with raspy ridges; leaf teeth sharp; lacks tendrils.
        - *or*
          - Midvein below hairy but not prickly; cone bracts appressed. — **25. Hops**
          - Midvein prickly below; cone bracts spread outward. Japanese hops (see Hops).
      - Stem rounded, soft-hairy; leaf teeth blunt; climbs with tendrils. — **26. Maypop**
- Leaf margin not toothed.
  - Leaf surface smooth and hairless. — **27. Yellow passion flower**
  - Leaf surface roughened by short, stiff hairs. — **24. Melonette**

1 Balloon vine 1
Cardiospermum halicacabum ◆ family *Sapindaceae*

QUICK CHECK: Vine with twice-compound leaves, the leaflets with pointed lobes and long teeth; fruit a three-part inflated pod with round bicolored seeds. **ID difficulty 1.**

DESCRIPTION: Perennial vine from an elongated rootstock, the stem dividing near the base into several major branches; each of these with minor branches. **Stems** thin, tough, wiry, 4-8' (1.2-2.4 m) long and 2-3 mm thick, minutely grooved, and essentially hairless. **Branches** alternate, in a leaf axil with a tendril and/or inflorescence, *all three parts borne on the same side but often one or two of them reflexed to the other side*. **Leaves** 2-4" (5-10 cm) long, usually *twice ternately compound with 9 total leaflets*. Leaflets of the second division are sessile. **Leaflets** longer than wide, pointed, the terminal leaflet with the tip often greatly elongated, with large pointed lobes and several large teeth. **Blades** flat and hairless with the midvein and major *veins slightly protruding above and below*. **Petiole** thin, about 20% of blade length, minutely channeled; *rachises are winged*. **Inflorescence** a few-flowered cluster on a thread-like stem 2-3" (5-8 cm) long, with a pair of small, coiled tendrils just below the cluster. **Flowers** 6-8 mm across, with a disorganized, asymmetrical shape. There are 2 elliptic, *strongly cupped, light purplish sepals* and 4 shorter, broad white petals—plus various other parts. (You'll see what I mean.) **Fruit** an inflated, balloon-like capsule with papery skin 0.9-1.2" (23-30 mm) long, with 3 equidistant, thin wing-ridges and 3 grooves on the outside. The interior has 3 membranous divisions, each bearing a *smooth, shiny, spherical seed* 4-6 mm in diameter. The seed is green with a *whitish, kidney to crescent shaped "scar"* wrapped halfway around it. The

balloons are green to reddish, drying to brown; dry seeds turn nearly black with a white scar.

HABITAT: Full sun to moderate shade in soils of medium moisture, especially where disturbed. Forest edges, ditches, thickets, ravines, floodplain forests. Introduced. **I**

FOOD USE: Young **greens** (mostly spring and early summer, but occasionally later) can be eaten raw or cooked.

COMMENTS: A very common invasive weed of the South, this plant has seeds that are beautiful and unmistakable. The odd flavor of the greens requires getting used to. Interestingly, this plant is related to maples.

2 Everlasting pea   🌿 3 🍃 3 🌸 3 🫛 2 🌿 2
Lathyrus latifolius • Fabaceae (Bean family)

QUICK CHECK: Pea-like vine with broadly winged stems and petioles, only two leaflets, and one tendril per leaf; flowers large, in clusters on long peduncles. **ID difficulty 1.**

DESCRIPTION: Trailing or climbing perennial, often forming dense clumps or mats, all parts hairless. **Stems** 3-7' (1-2 m) long, glaucous, hairless, occasionally branched, ridged with *2 broad wings* 3-5 mm wide. **Leaves** alternate, tendril-tipped, compound with only *2 leaflets*, these *overlapping at the base*. **Tendril** large, about twice the leaflet length, branched ternately and proximally flat. **Petioles** about equal to a leaflet, very *broadly winged*. **Stipules** *entire*, pointing forward and back, 0.8-1.5" (2-4 cm) long and 5-12 mm wide. **Leaflets** ovate to elliptic, sessile, entire, hairless, flat, angled at the base, angled or rounded at the tip, with a bristle. **Midveins** and major veins flat above, offset by light color, protruding below. Two prominent veins from the base run for most of the leaf's length; secondary veins angle strongly toward the tip and terminate near these prominent veins. **Veinlets** fine, net-like, flat above. **Inflorescence** a raceme of 4-12 from a leaf axil. **Peduncle** vertical, 6-10" (15-25 cm) long, roundish with gentle angles; pedicels 0.6-0.8" (15-20 mm) long. **Flowers** about 1" (2.5 cm) long, pink to purple (occasionally almost white), pea-like, the calyx lobes unequal with sharp, acuminate tips. The banner is folded up and much wider than the rest of the flower; the wings overlap. **Pods** smooth, pea-like, 2-4" (5-10 cm) long with 10-15 seeds.

HABITAT: Rich, moist, disturbed soil in full sun to moderate shade. Found occasionally along roadsides and forest edges, in parks, old homesteads, etc. Introduced.

FOOD USE: All young, tender parts are edible raw or cooked: **shoots** and **greens** from spring through mid summer; **flowers** later. Young **pods** are a bit tough but the flavor is good. Plump **green seeds** are excellent eaten like green peas. Mature **seeds** should be cooked—after drying they will take very long cooking.

COMMENTS: Planted mostly as an ornamental, this plant sometimes escapes and thrives, especially in coastal areas with cool summers. If you find a patch it will provide excellent food for a long season.

▼ (left) The leaflet has a broadly winged petiole and only two leaflets. (right) Tender shoot.

Related edible:

3 Narrow-leaved vetchling ⚬ *Lathyrus sylvestris* ⎮ 2 🌿 2 ❀ 3 ⎮ 2

This introduced plant is very similar, but everything about it is more slender. **Stems** thinner with wings less than 3 mm wide. **Branches** several but mostly short. **Leaflets** almost sessile, long-elliptic to almost linear with a bristle-tip. The midvein is depressed above and protruding below—as are the 2 prominent *basal veins on each side near the margin. Veinlets are raised above.* **Stipules** less than 4 mm wide. **Inflorescence** a much smaller raceme of about 6 flowers on a straight, stiff, angled peduncle 4–9" (10–23 cm) long. **Flowers** smaller, 0.7" (18 mm) wide, the wings much darker than the banner and the keel pale. **Pods** nearly straight, about 2.5" (6.5 cm) long, with about 8 tightly packed, uniformly pea-green seeds 5 mm in diameter when fresh. This species likes sunny to lightly shaded disturbed ground, similar to everlasting pea, but perhaps tolerating drier conditions. It has similar food uses and is almost as good. **ID difficulty 2.**

4 Tuber vetchling ⏳ 3
Lathyrus tuberosus ✦ *Fabaceae* (Bean family)

QUICK CHECK: Tangle-forming vine with thin, 4-angled stems, 2 leaflets and a tendril per leaf, and bright red-purple flowers. **ID difficulty 2.**

DESCRIPTION: Small perennial vine forming dense clumps. **Tubers** 0.7–1.4" (18–36 mm) long, roughly egg-shaped, the surface rough with thick, leathery, dark brown-black skin, the flesh whitish and firm, borne 2–7" (5–18 cm) underground along thin, rough but brittle rhizomes that are not easily traced to the stem. **Stems** to 40" (1 m) tall and 2 mm thick, tough, hairless, smooth, thinner at the base than the middle, *4-angled (diamond-shaped)*, 2 corners sometimes with a tiny wing; often branching profusely. **Leaves** alternate with *only 2 leaflets,* usually *drastically folded* upward, *terminated by a tendril*. **Tendrils** simple or ternately branched. **Petioles** 25–30% of leaflet length, flat or broadly channeled above, weakly keeled below, not winged. **Stipules** lanceolate to linear, sharp, 4–11 mm long, the fore lobe larger than the back lobe; one right-angle tooth is sometimes present near the attachment point. **Leaflets** elliptic to obovate, almost sessile, entire, flat and smooth, hairless, glaucous (especially below), blunt-tipped with an extending bristle. Leaflets 0.4–1.2" (1–3 cm) long, in two distinct sizes—those on the main stems are much larger than those on the minor branches. **Veins** flat on both sides; secondary veins arching and intersecting. **Inflorescence** a crowded raceme of 3–6 on a stiff, angled peduncle 2.5–3.5" (6–9 cm) long. Pedicels 4–8 mm, each with a tiny linear bract. **Flowers** (early to mid summer) bright red-purple, with a broad, rounded, 2-lobed, creased banner about 0.8" (2 cm) across. The much smaller wings meet over an upturned keel. The calyx is hairless with 5 sharp lobes. **Pod** small, hairless, narrow, about 1.2" (3 cm), holding up to 5 light brown seeds.

HABITAT: Moist, disturbed soil in full sun. Roadsides, meadows, fields, ditches. Introduced and sporadic, but often in great abundance where found.

FOOD USE: The small, hard **tubers** are sweet and can be eaten cooked.

COMMENTS: Considered a weed, this is a forager's treasure: a delicacy that long ago was collected commercially in Europe. Maybe I'm just paranoid because it looks like hopniss, but I'm afraid to eat it raw. I do not know of any other edible parts besides the tuber—the flowers don't taste pleasant like those of other members of this genus.

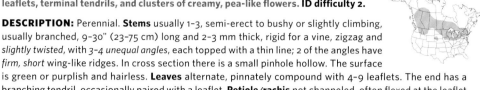

5 Pale vetchling 🌿 3 🌸 3 🍃 2 🌱 2
Lathyrus ochroleucus ✦ *Fabaceae* (Bean family)

QUICK CHECK: Short, semi-erect vine with pinnately compound leaves, blunt veiny leaflets, terminal tendrils, and clusters of creamy, pea-like flowers. **ID difficulty 2.**

DESCRIPTION: Perennial. **Stems** usually 1–3, semi-erect to bushy or slightly climbing, usually branched, 9–30" (23–75 cm) long and 2–3 mm thick, rigid for a vine, zigzag and *slightly twisted*, with *3–4 unequal angles*, each topped with a thin line; 2 of the angles have *firm, short* wing-like ridges. In cross section there is a small pinhole hollow. The surface is green or purplish and hairless. **Leaves** alternate, pinnately compound with 4–9 leaflets. The end has a branching tendril, occasionally paired with a leaflet. **Petiole/rachis** not channeled, often flexed at the leaflet junctures, not bearing leaflets at its base. **Stipules** *butterfly-like*, 0.5–0.8" (13–20 mm) long, the fore lobe pointed and entire, the back lobe blunter with a few *broad, shallow teeth near the base*. Petiolules extremely short, light-colored, upturned. **Leaflets** egg-shaped, 1–2" (2.5–5 cm) long, entire, *flat*, broadly angled at the base. The tips are blunt with a tiny downcurved claw. The blades are smooth and hairless on both sides, pale below, appearing glaucous but with little to no bloom. **Veins** *above are strongly offset by light color, but none are depressed.* **Inflorescence** a one-sided axillary raceme of 4–9 pea-like flowers, each on a pedicel about 25% of their length. **Flowers** 0.6–0.8" (15–20 mm) long, creamy white, boot-shaped, becoming dull yellow with age. The banner is deeply creased in the center, sharply reflexed at bloom. The wings are small and meet over the keel tip. The calyx is creamy with light green veins and 5 sharp, unequal, lanceolate lobes. **Pods** 2–2.5" (5–6.5 cm) long, flattened, relatively broad, green turning dark brown, containing several seeds.

HABITAT: Dry, sandy or rocky, semi-open woods or savannah, mostly with oak or pine. Native. 🔥

FOOD USE: Tender **stem tips** can be eaten raw or cooked. The **flowers**, available in late spring and early summer, make a sweet snack raw, and can be added to salads or cooked dishes. Young **pods** and ripe **seeds** can also be eaten cooked (early to late summer). The literature reports roots or tubers eaten from this plant, but all I find are slightly enlarged rhizome tips and tiny tuber-like nodules on the finer roots—both have good flavor, but are much too small to bother with.

COMMENTS: The delicious flowers of this widespread plant taste a bit like those of black locust, but aren't quite as sweet or aromatic. **AKA** creamy pea, creamy vetchling.

◀ The large, distinctive "butterfly stipule."

483

Related edibles:

6   Marsh pea • *Lathyrus palustris* 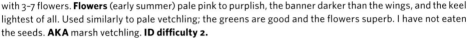 3   3

This native perennial grows in marsh edges or streamside meadows, especially where sandy, usually among sedges; its habit is more vine-like than pale vetchling. The entire plant is hairless. **Stems** 2–3' (60–90 cm) long with few to no branches, angled, with wings about 1 mm. **Leaves** have 4–6 leaflets, the terminal one often off-center and opposite a tendril. **Leaflets** 1–2.5" (25–64 cm) long, elliptic to narrowly elliptic, flat, often strongly out of plane with each other. **Stipules** similar to those of pale vetchling but narrower and the fore lobe much longer than the back lobe. Peduncles are 3–4" (8–10 cm) long, the raceme with 3–7 flowers. **Flowers** (early summer) pale pink to purplish, the banner darker than the wings, and the keel lightest of all. Used similarly to pale vetchling; the greens are good and the flowers superb. I have not eaten the seeds. **AKA** marsh vetchling. **ID difficulty 2.**

7   Veiny pea • *Lathyrus venosus*  2   2

This is a slightly larger plant of sandy prairies and savannahs, up to 42" (1.1 m) tall, with more of an erect, bushy form. **Stem** rigid, ridged but not winged, fine-hairy, often twisted, widely branched. **Leaves** have 7–12 leaflets, small tendrils, and a channeled rachis. **Leaflets** elliptic to ovate or lanceolate, 1.2–2.5" (3–6 cm) long, flat and nipple-tipped with fine hairs. Secondary veins are faintly depressed above and protruding below, 20–40° to the midvein. **Stipules** narrow, pointed at both ends, 4–10 mm long, not toothed. **Flowers** blue-purple, 0.5–0.8" (13–20 mm) long, in racemes of 8–18. The calyx is hairy. The flowers and young greens are edible. 🔥 **ID difficulty 2.**

8 **Beach pea** 🝆 1 🌿 2
Lathyrus japonicus ✦ *Fabaceae* **(Bean family)**

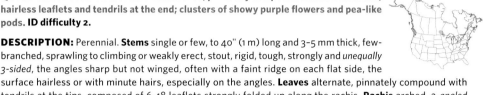

QUICK CHECK: Short beach vine with arched, pinnately compound leaves with broad, hairless leaflets and tendrils at the end; clusters of showy purple flowers and pea-like pods. **ID difficulty 2.**

DESCRIPTION: Perennial. **Stems** single or few, to 40" (1 m) long and 3–5 mm thick, few-branched, sprawling to climbing or weakly erect, stout, rigid, tough, strongly and *unequally 3-sided*, the angles sharp but not winged, often with a faint ridge on each flat side, the surface hairless or with minute hairs, especially on the angles. **Leaves** alternate, pinnately compound with tendrils at the tips, composed of 6–18 leaflets strongly folded up along the rachis. **Rachis** arched, *3-angled* like the stem, the first leaflets attached near the base. **Stipules** clasping with one lobe pointing forward and two backward; the forward lobe is entire and sharp-pointed, the backward lobes usually downcurved with 1–3 large teeth. **Leaflets** paired or alternate on the rachis, nearly sessile, 1.2–2.3" (3–6 mm) long, ovate to broadly elliptic, entire, the bases blunt, the tips blunt and occasionally indented with a downturned claw. The blade is flat and smooth, rather thick, and bloom-coated. Beach peas along the Great Lakes are normally hairless, while those on the seacoast are often soft-hairy on the pedicels and lower leaf surface. **Veins** set off by light color, flat to slightly raised on *both sides*. Secondary veins several, 45° to the midvein, breaking up before the margins. **Inflorescence** a crowded raceme of 4–12 hanging mostly to one side at the end of a straight, finely hairy peduncle 2.5–3.5" (6.5–9 cm) long, the pedicels 5 mm. **Calyx** smooth, hairless, with dark, often purple veins and 5 sharp triangular lobes. **Corolla** 0.5–0.7" (12–18 mm) across, blue-purple, the banner large, broad, folded back, with darkened veins; wings and keel lighter in color and much smaller. **Pods** purplish at first, turning green at full size, then plump like a miniature garden pea pod 2" (5 cm) long, containing several small roundish peas.

HABITAT: Beaches along the shores of the Great Lakes and oceans. Native.

FOOD USE: Young **pods** can be eaten raw or cooked. For **peas**, gather pods when they are full sized but preferably still soft, moist, and green. At maturity the peas become less sweet, dry out, and turn brown. Cook and use like domestic peas. **Conservation 2/1.**

COMMENTS: Beach peas are not as sweet as domestic peas. In times of famine when these peas have been eaten as the primary source of calories for weeks on end, they have caused a paralysis condition known as lathyrism. Much is made of this fact in the literature, to the great satisfaction of alarmist anti-foragers. However, this concern is irrelevant to non-starving people with alternative subsistence options.

9 Ground bean 🌿 3/2 📖 FH-226
Amphicarpaea bracteata ◆ *Fabaceae* **(Bean family)**

QUICK CHECK: Very thin hairy stem; leaves with three leaflets and no tendrils forming dense mats on or just above the ground. **ID difficulty 2.**

DESCRIPTION: An annual that reproduces by aerial seed in full sunlight but in shade acts like a perennial, replanting itself in the form of a large, cloned, asexual seed. **Stems** thread-like, up to 8' (2.4 m) long but only 1 mm thick, roundish, with *long, fine hairs*, the surface green or reddish, sprawling over the ground or climbing low vegetation by twining; *lacks tendrils.* **Young plants** up to about 14" (36 cm) tall often stand erect, with slightly thicker stems, before producing thinner vining stems. At each node a long, pointed, sheath-like **stipule**, split at the tip, wraps around the stem. **Leaves** ternately compound. Side leaflets are nearly sessile, while the slightly larger terminal leaflet is often out of plane and has a petiolule 25–30% of its length. **Leaflets** entire, broadly ovate, flat, 1–2.5" (2.5–6 cm) long, faintly fine-hairy above and more so below. **Midvein** and secondary veins (of which there are 2 from the base) are nearly flat above. **Petioles** 120% of terminal leaflet length, growing from an enlarged, darkened pedestal. **Aerial flowers** (summer) pea-like, light pinkish to nearly white, in long-stalked, dense racemes of 5–13. **Aerial pods** about 1" (2.5 cm) long, each containing three flattened, mottled, lentil-like seeds 4–5 mm across. **Underground seeds** plump to slightly flattened, 5–14 mm across, wrapped individually in a thin skin. Rarely produces single flat seeds with a tough green skin on the soil surface.

CONFUSING PLANTS: Fuzzy bean and wild bean are larger with thicker stems; the leaflets are thicker and tougher and some-times flared at the base. Neither species produces underground seeds. Some tick trefoils (genus *Desmodium*) are also very similar, but the stems are thicker, stiffer, and less hairy, and the pods are constricted between the seeds.

HABITAT: Well-drained hardwood forests and floodplains in light to moderate shade, especially with sandy soil. Native. 🔥

FOOD USE: Gather **underground beans** by loosening the soil to 2" (5 cm) under a thick clump of vines (that lack aerial beans) and picking out the beans. Boil until tender and use like domestic beans; they have a distinctly sweet flavor. They can be dried easily and store indefinitely in that state. Gather **aerial beans** from fall into winter, dry the pods, then rub and winnow. Boil the seeds for a long time until tender. **Con-servation 2/1.**

COMMENTS: This often abundant plant is a very important food source for turkeys, mice, chipmunks, and other wildlife. The beans are traditionally collected by raid-ing the caches where rodents store them, trading corn for beans. If I had better skill finding these caches, I would eat ground beans as a staple—they are the best bean I've ever eaten. **AKA** hog-peanut.

▼ (top left) Underground beans. (top right) Aerial beans. ▼

10 **Wild bean** 🌱 2
Phaseolus polystachios ✦ *Fabaceae* (Bean family)

QUICK CHECK: Thin vine with 3 leaflets, no tendrils, and very long internodes; small, curved, pointed, stiff pods with 3-5 seeds like miniature lima beans. **ID difficulty 2.**

DESCRIPTION: Perennial from a large tuberous root. **Stems** many on older crowns, 5-35' (1.5-11 m) long and 2-7 mm in diameter, rounded, sparsely covered with short, fine hairs, climbing by twining (without tendrils), branching infrequently. **Leaves** alternate, pinnately compound with 3 leaflets of similar size. Side leaflets are sessile, but the terminal one is stalked. **Petiole** about 80% of terminal leaflet length, grooved. **Leaflets** broadly ovate, pointed, the tips downcurved, entire, 2-4" (5-10 cm) long, blades hairless to faintly hairy (especially on margins). **Midvein** slightly raised above and sometimes minutely hairy. **Stipules** triangular, 3 mm long, sharp but not stiff, *turning dark brown* after maturity; leaflets have similar tiny stipules. **Inflorescence** a raceme 1-6" (2.5-15 cm) long of 4-24 flowers, from leaf axils. **Flowers** light purple (greenish white at the base), 7-9 mm long, irregular and pea-like with 5 lobes, on very short pedicels. *The lower petal (keel) is spiraled; the wing petals are widely spread, incurved, and rotated*; the upper petal (banner) is strongly cupped. The calyx is green with maroon speckles; the lobes are very short. **Pods** *hanging*, 1.8-3.5" (45-90 mm) long, somewhat flattened, turning *light brown and stiff* and inflating slightly when dry, with long, *sharp tips*. **Beans** 3-5, flattened and broad, about 0.2" long, *shaped like lima beans*; light greenish at first but drying to dark brownish-black with fine mottling.

▼ Hopniss beans on upper left, wild beans on upper right, fuzzy beans below.

CONFUSING PLANTS: Ground bean pods are not stiff or pointed when dry, the beans are much smaller, and there are only 3 per pod. The stems of ground bean are thinner, hairier, and less tough. Fuzzy bean has longer, narrower, plumper pods that dry to blackish; they are straight and do not hang but are held stiffly.

HABITAT: Rich or sandy soil of floodplains, stream banks, forest edges, savannahs, clearings, sunny or disturbed woods, especially along rock outcrops or cliffs. Native. 🔥

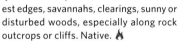

FOOD USE: Gather ripe **beans** in late summer or autumn and use like domestic beans. The root is reported edible, but I have not tried it, and doing so would be irresponsible under normal circumstances, as it would kill a long-lived, declining, uncommon plant. **Conservation 2.**

COMMENTS: This is a close relative of the cultivated common bean (*P. vulgaris*) and lima bean (*P. lunatus*). Its remains have been widely found in archeological sites in our region. Wild bean has suffered dramatically, first from farmland clearing, then fire suppression, and now the spraying of roadside herbicides. There is another form (variety *sinuatus*) with leaves that are bulged at the base and often two toned—this variety is common in sunny pine woods of the Deep South and looks like a different species altogether. **AKA** thicket bean, wild kidney bean.

11 Fuzzy bean 🖊 3 🌿 2
Strophostyles helvola ✦ *Fabaceae* (Bean family)

QUICK CHECK: Vine with no tendrils and straight, stiffly-held beans in small clusters, ripening to black; 3 leaflets, with some bulged or lobed at the base. **ID difficulty 2.**

DESCRIPTION: Annual. **Stems** to 7' (2.1 m) long and 2–3 mm thick, rounded, twisty, faintly grooved, with hairs pointing toward the base. *Tendrils absent.* **Leaves** alternate, compound with 3 leaflets, the terminal leaflet sometimes drastically out of plane, on grooved petioles 70–100% of terminal leaflet length. **Leaflets** 0.8–1.8" (2–4.5 cm) long, ovate to diamond-shaped with entire margins but often *bulged or lobed laterally at the base.* Blades are hairless above but have scattered, stiff, appressed hairs below. **Veins** flat above. There are small stipules at the base of the leaflets. **Inflorescence** *a tight cluster of 2–10 sessile flowers at the end of a stiff, ridged peduncle 3–5" (8–13 cm) long.* Only 1–2 bloom at a time, and new flowers may be in the same cluster with ripe pods. **Flowers** very pale pink to light purple, 10–13 mm across with a broad, flat banner, 2 small wings, and the keel—*from which a narrow, darkened, claw-like, usually curled appendage rises toward the center of the banner.* **Pods** sessile, single or in a radiating cluster of usually 5 or fewer, *straight, cylindrical,* 2–5" (5–13 cm) long, green at first, becoming *dark blackish-brown* at maturity, abruptly tapered at both ends, with a claw-like point at the tip. In clusters they *do not droop but are held rigidly* at *wide angles.* **Beans** up to 5 per pod, *straight* and almost rectangular, 9–11 mm long and 1/3 as wide, packed tightly end to end, green mottled with dark purple, with *a white bar where attached,* and surrounded by a cottony substance. Upon drying the pods split open and the halves coil up; the beans turn nearly black.

HABITAT: Sunny, disturbed soil, especially where sloped and sandy. Most common in floodplain openings. Native.

FOOD USE: Young **pods** can be eaten raw or cooked like garden beans. When mature in autumn, the **beans** inside can be eaten after cooking. They become very dark, almost black, and the skins are a bit thick, but the flavor is good. **Conservation 2.**

COMMENTS: These are pretty good beans, and easy to collect; it makes me happy when I find a *helvola* of them. **AKA** wild bean, trailing bean.

RELATED EDIBLES: Other members of the genus *Strophostyles* are presumably also edible, although smaller. I have also eaten the beans of *S. leiosperma*.

Leaflets may be bulged or lobed at the base. ▶

12 Hopniss 2 2 2 FH-234
Apios americana • *Fabaceae* (Bean family)

QUICK CHECK: Thin stem, no tendrils, pinnately compound leaves with 5-7 leaflets, tubers strung together by a thin rhizome; flowers purple-brown, beans milky when green. **ID difficulty 2.**

DESCRIPTION: Perennial herbaceous vine to 17' (5 m) long, often with multiple stems, forming tangled mats over shrubs and herbs. *Sap milky.* **Tubers** 1-3" (2.5-8 cm) long and almost as wide, scattered *on long rhizomes like beads on a string*, light brown, smooth with buds at first, becoming rougher and developing knobs when older. **Stems** 2-3 mm thick, roundish, not tapered, usually with sparse hairs leaning toward the base, climbing *without tendrils*, by twining. **Leaves** alternate and pinnately compound, on petioles about equal to the rachis. **Leaflets** 5-7 (occasionally 3 or 9), ovate to lanceolate, rounded at the base, entire, pointed, 1-3" (2.5-8 cm) long, the surface sparsely hairy. **Midvein** raised above; secondary veins are flat to faintly depressed. The rachis has a narrow, shallow channel on top. The terminal leaflet has a stalk 30-40% of its length; side leaflets are nearly sessile. **Inflorescence** a short, dense raceme of about a dozen flowers, borne on 1-2" (2.5-5 cm) hairy stems from leaf axils. **Flowers** *brownish purple*, about 0.6" (15 mm) long, with irregular pea-like form, fragrant. **Pod** much like a garden bean, 2-5" (5-13 cm) long and 8-11 mm wide, round in cross section, the surface glossy and hairless, the walls thick and fleshy when the pod is green, hanging on pedicels 5 mm long. **Beans** 4-6 per pod, stout, drying *wrinkly* and light brown.

CONFUSING PLANTS: Ground bean, wild bean, and fuzzy bean are similar but smaller vines with only 3 leaflets; none of them has a chain of underground tubers.

HABITAT: Sandy, rich soil in full to partial sunlight; wet to dry sites. Most common in river floodplains, along roadsides, near springs, and along lakeshores. Native.

FOOD USE: Dig **tubers** preferably when the vines are dormant and cook thoroughly. The flavor is like a cross between boiled peanuts and potatoes. The tubers store very well in a refrigerator or root cellar. Immature **pods** (late summer to autumn) can be cooked like green beans. Mature **seeds** can be cooked fresh or dried; they look more like peas but taste more like beans. **Conservation 2/1.**

COMMENTS: This iconic wild edible is a traditional food for most Native people within its extensive range. The vines often grow densely and can produce an enormous quantity of food. Hopniss was also widely used by European settlers. The tubers are relatively high in protein, and its amino acids complement those of grass seeds to form a "complete" protein. **AKA** groundnut. Traveler's delight *A. priceana* is a larger vine that bears a single, large, edible tuber. This rare species is confined to the southern Midwest and upper South and is federally protected.

WARNING: There is a high incidence of serious allergic or intolerance reactions to hopniss. Such people experience diarrhea, nausea, or vomiting 1-4 hours after eating it. To reduce the chances of such adverse reactions, I advise following the preparation traditions of Native Americans: always eat hopniss very well-cooked, such as in a stew or pot roast. If you react negatively, do not eat it again.

VETCHES
genus *Vicia* ✦ *Fabaceae* (Bean family)

QUICK GROUP CHECK: Small vines with angled stems; pinnately compound leaves with many small, narrow leaflets and a terminal tendril; small, narrow flowers on short pedicels. **ID difficulty 2.**

COLLECTIVE DESCRIPTION: Small herbaceous vines, rather stiff and usually somewhat self-standing at first, the stems trailing and bushy later or climbing with tendrils. **Stems** 1–5' (30–150 cm) long and 2–4 mm thick with a small hollow, *angled or ridged (often roughly squared) but not quite winged*, sometimes hairy, usually branched. **Leaves** alternate, pinnately compound with 8–40 leaflets, the *rachis ridged*, bearing leaflets near the base, with a branching or simple tendril at the end. There are small stipules 2–10 mm long at the base. **Petiole** very short to none before the first leaflet; rachis channeled above and ridged on the sides. **Leaflets** long-elliptic to nearly linear, 0.4–1.3" (10–33 mm) long, entire, on very short petiolules. **Midvein** faintly depressed above and protruding below. Secondary veins are *flat to raised above*; if visible, they are *closely spaced and distinctly pinnate* (not net-veined). **Inflorescence** variable; all the species covered here have *very short pedicels, 3 mm or less*. **Flowers** (spring to early summer) have tubular pea-like corollas 0.3–1" (8–25 mm) long, *much longer than wide*, extending far beyond the calyx. **Pods** 0.7–2" (18–50 mm) long, pointed, containing 4–14 seeds ranging from nearly spherical to somewhat flattened.

FOOD USE: For the vetches listed, tender **shoots, leafy tips**, and **flowers** can be eaten raw or cooked. Because all vetch **seeds** have some antinutrients and toxins, they should only be eaten well-cooked and in small portions. Pouring off the cooking water after several minutes of boiling and replacing with new water eliminates most of the toxins.

COMMENTS: Five abundant species are covered here—2 native and 3 introduced. The literature often vaguely suggests that this is a dangerous group for unspecified reasons. However, many true vetches of the genus *Vicia* have a robust history of food use around the world. Like *all legumes* they should be eaten in moderation. **NOTE: Crown vetch** (p. 673) is not a true vetch and should not be eaten.

13 **Common vetch** ✦ *Vicia sativa* 2 1

QUICK CHECK: Vetch with one or two bluish flowers or long, dark pods per node.

DESCRIPTION: Annual. **Stems** angled, faintly soft-hairy. **Leaves** have 6–14 leaflets and a branching tendril. **Leaflets** elliptic, 0.6–1.1" (15–28 mm) long, the tips blunt but with an extended bristle. Secondary veins are visible, 35–45°. **Stipules** 5–7 mm long with 2–3 sharp-tipped lobes and often a dark nectary on the underside. **Flowers** borne *1–2 per node*, not in a raceme, the corolla purplish to blue, the calyx with straight linear lobes almost as long as the tube. **Pods** 1–2" (2.5–5 cm) long, ripening to *black*, *plump (nearly round in cross section)*, and not hanging but *diverging widely*. Inside are 7–12 nearly spherical seeds, 2–3 mm, finely mottled with dark and light gray to nearly black.

HABITAT: Weedy areas, roadsides, fields. Introduced.

COMMENTS: The cooked seeds have been eaten for thousands of years in western Asia and Europe. Today it is mostly grown as livestock feed. The taste has a hint of vanilla. **AKA** blackpod vetch, narrow-leaf vetch.

14 Carolina vetch 2 3
Vicia caroliniana + Fabaceae (Bean family)

QUICK CHECK: Vetch with very narrow, widely spaced leaflets and long racemes of small pale flowers.

DESCRIPTION: Perennial, the stems very thin and up to 3' (1 m) high, hairless or nearly so. **Leaves** with 8–16 leaflets and a tendril that is usually unbranched. **Leaflets** narrowly elliptic, sometimes almost linear, 0.4–1.1" (10–28 mm) long, often deeply folded along the midvein, usually bristle-tipped, the surface with very fine hair. Secondary veins are visible on the bottom but obscure on the top; often at very low angles. **Stipules** 3–4 mm long, lanceolate, *entire or with one lobe at the base.* **Inflorescence** a one-sided raceme of 8–20 flowers on a long, faintly hairy peduncle. **Flowers** 8–12 mm long, very narrow, the corolla white with purple veins in the center. **Pods** 0.6–1.2" (15–30 mm), somewhat flattened, containing 4–9 seeds.

HABITAT: Dry forests or savannahs of oak and pine, roadsides, forest margins, especially where sandy and mildly acidic. Native. **Conservation 2/1.**

COMMENTS: A tasty and attractive wildflower, this species is very easy to recognize. I have not eaten the seeds. **AKA** pale wood vetch.

15 American vetch + *Vicia americana*  2 3 1

QUICK CHECK: Vetch with purple flowers in short, one-sided racemes.

DESCRIPTION: Perennial. **Stems** to 52" (132 cm) long, strongly angled, hairless or nearly so, green or purple. **Leaves** have 8–16 hairless leaflets and a branching tendril. **Stipules** with a fore and back lobe, 8–10 mm long, *toothed, resembling a bat or dragon wing.* **Leaflets** 0.6–1.4" (15–36 mm), elliptic, often blunt-tipped, the end bristled, with visible veins about 45°, hairless. **Inflorescence** a loose, one-sided raceme of 2–9 on a peduncle 3–4" (8–10 cm) long. **Flowers** 0.6–1" (15–25 mm) long, the calyx often purple with short lobes, the corolla purple-blue with many darker veins; the wing tips and keel are whitish. **Pods** 1–1.4" (25–36 mm) long, light brown and thin-walled at maturity, somewhat flattened, with 7–14 brown, roundish seeds.

HABITAT: Dry or rocky open woodlands, forest edges and openings, roadsides, rocky outcrops, streambanks. Native. **Conservation 2/1.** (Continued on the next page.)

15 **American vetch** (continued)

COMMENTS: This species has the largest flowers among the vetches covered here. It is not well known as an edible, and is largely ignored in the foraging literature despite being easy to collect, pleasant to eat, common, extremely widespread, and having a robust ethnographic record of food use in many Native traditions. Its habits are weedy enough that you might think it's invasive. **AKA** purple vetch.

16 **Hairy vetch** + *Vicia villosa*

QUICK CHECK: Weedy vetch of fields and roadsides; large crowded clusters of purple-blue flowers in one-sided racemes.

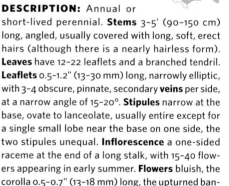

DESCRIPTION: Annual or short-lived perennial. **Stems** 3–5' (90–150 cm) long, angled, usually covered with long, soft, erect hairs (although there is a nearly hairless form). **Leaves** have 12–22 leaflets and a branched tendril. **Leaflets** 0.5–1.2" (13–30 mm) long, narrowly elliptic, with 3–4 obscure, pinnate, secondary **veins** per side, at a narrow angle of 15–20°. **Stipules** narrow at the base, ovate to lanceolate, usually entire except for a single small lobe near the base on one side, the two stipules unequal. **Inflorescence** a one-sided raceme at the end of a long stalk, with 15–40 flowers appearing in early summer. **Flowers** bluish, the corolla 0.5–0.7" (13–18 mm) long, the upturned banner shorter than the straight base of the corolla. The wings are enlarged at the tip and light in color, sometimes white. The pedicel is attached on the side of the flowers just in front of the base. The calyx has bristle-like lobes, two of which are much longer and wrap slightly around the tube. **Pods** flatter and broader than those of other vetches, with 3–7 seeds.

HABITAT: Full sun and disturbance: roadsides, field margins, meadows. Introduced.

COMMENTS: The tender growing tips are not as palatable as those of American vetch, but the flowers are good raw or cooked. Over a broad region this is the most common weedy vetch, a pretty sight when blooming on roadsides in early summer. It looks much like tufted vetch, but the flowers are more elongated and the pedicels connected more to the side.

17 Tufted vetch + *Vicia cracca* 1 2 1

QUICK CHECK: Upright, bushy vetch with numerous bluish flowers in erect racemes.

DESCRIPTION: Perennial. **Stems** bushy, 3–4' (90–120 cm) tall, sharply angled with 3–4 prominent ridges, covered with fine, curvy to nearly appressed hairs. **Leaves** have 14–22 leaflets and a branching tendril. **Leaflets** narrowly elliptic, to 1.3" (33 mm) long, covered with appressed hairs, the tips bristled. There are two major secondary **veins** from the base, and 5–6 total pairs of secondary veins, at very low angles of 5–10°. **Stipules** narrow and pointed, the lower ones with a back lobe. **Inflorescence** a long, crowded, *vertical*, one-sided raceme of 15–30 flowers on a long, naked peduncle. **Flowers** 9–13 mm long, purple-blue, the upturned banner about the same length as the straight base of the corolla. The wings are not enlarged at the end. The calyx is short with unequal triangular lobes. The pedicel is attached slightly off-center at the end. **Pods** hairless, up to 1.3" (33 mm) long, ripening to brown and becoming very stiff and slightly flattened, containing 2–7 pea-like seeds, these nearly spherical, dark brown-black at maturity.

HABITAT: Sunny ground, mostly roadsides and vacant lots, especially where rocky. Introduced.

COMMENTS: The ripe seeds can be quickly stripped from the clusters by hand; get them just before they split open and separate seeds in a colander, then winnow out the husk pieces. **AKA** bird vetch, cow vetch.

18 Carrion flower ▌3 🍓 1 📖 FH-151
genus *Smilax* (in part) ✦ family *Smilacaceae*

QUICK CHECK: Thick-stemmed, unarmed herbaceous vine, free standing at first, with entire, alternate leaves and tendrils; umbels of greenish flowers and dark blue berries. ID difficulty 2.

COLLECTIVE DESCRIPTION: Perennial from a rootstock. **Stem** thick, to 0.8" (2 cm), strongly tapering for a vine, to 13' (4 m) long, roundish to gently angled, occasionally with a shallow groove or flat side, solid, *sap slimy*, branched sparingly and not near the base, the surface hairless and thornless, coated with a light bloom, green to purplish-brown (often a mottled mixture of the two). **Shoot** very tall, sometimes to 7' (2.1 m), straight, and freestanding; later leaning or falling to the side and grabbing nearby vegetation for

▲ Composite range.

support, the tops then climbing as vines. Shoots have pale sheaths to 1.5" (4 cm) long at the nodes, the end of the sheath with a tendril on each side and a third tendril or reduced leaf between them; higher up typical leaves appear. Larger shoots have ball-like flower bud clusters. **Leaves** alternate, 2–5" (5–13 cm) long, tough at maturity, broadly lanceolate or heart-shaped to nearly round, entire, the bases broad and rounded, the tips abruptly pointed to rounded. **Surface** hairless above, rather glossy, with 5–7 major veins from the base, these depressed and arching to reconverge at the tip. The underside may be hairless or hairy (especially on the veins). **Stipules** extended, fused, broad and sheath-like, bearing tendrils at their tips. **Petioles** 60–90% of blade length. **Tendrils** unbranched. **Inflorescence** a compact, spherical umbel 1–1.5" (2.5–4 cm) across, of 10–90 flowers, on a long, straight, naked peduncle from a leaf axil. **Flowers** (late spring) green, 3–8 mm across, with 6 distant tepals; sometimes foul-smelling. **Fruit** (fall) in compact rounded clusters, dark blue with bloom, roundish, 4–10 mm, mealy to pulpy, containing a few seeds.

SPECIES: There are many herbaceous species in the genus *Smilax*, including: *herbacea, lasioneura, pulverulenta, pseudochina, ecirrata,* and *illinoensis.*

CONFUSING PLANTS: Greenbriers (p. 193) are thorny and woody. Wild yams (*Dioscorea*) have similarly shaped leaves but much thinner stems.

HABITAT: Rich, moist, sandy soil in full to partial sun: river floodplains, ditches, forest borders, fencerows, lake and pond margins, open woodlands. Native. 🔥

FOOD USE: Gather the **shoots** and **tender leafy tips** in spring and early summer and eat raw or cooked. Easily overharvested, so collect in moderation. Plants in full sun come up 2–3 weeks later than those growing in shade. The roots of *S. pseudochina* reportedly contain good-tasting starch that can be extracted in water, but I have not had the chance to try this. **Berries** are bland but sweet and make a pleasant nibble on a hungry hike. **Conservation 2/1.**

COMMENTS: Similar in flavor and texture to asparagus. No, really. I know they always say that, but this time it's true. This is one of our best shoot vegetables. All of our species taste good. *S. ecirrata* is an erect herb with whorled leaves rather than a vine—its shoots are quite small.

19 Air potato 2 2
Dioscorea polystachya + family *Dioscoreaceae*

QUICK CHECK: Thin vine with no tendrils; simple leaves, unusually broad at the base with parallel veins; many tiny tubers on the stem. **ID difficulty 2.**

DESCRIPTION: Thin-stemmed perennial herbaceous vine from an enlarged **root** that is broad and blunt at the bottom, irregular in shape, not smooth, and nearly white. Each season the vine grows a new yam and aborts the old one, thus it is often found with a Y at the base. **Stems** up to 13' (4 m) long and 2–5 mm thick, often several wrapped around each other, scarcely tapering, twisted, climbing *without tendrils* by twining. The surface is finely ridged, solid, hairless, a mix of green and deep purple, *the interior of new vines slimy.* Stems produce tiny potato-like **aerial tubers** 8–12 mm long, attached directly, often in pairs, at leaf axils. These tubers have large wart-like bumps and are slimy inside, especially when young; at maturity their skin becomes tough. **Leaves** may *be paired, alternate, or occasionally in whorls* of 3. They are 1–4" (2.5–10 cm) long (those on tightly coiled vine tips smallest) with entire margins. **Blades** hairless, *purple at the base,* heart-shaped—but the lobes are extended or bulging and the tip is elongated, needle-pointed, lightened, and often downturned. All major **veins** (usually 7) emanate from the base—*the middle three reconverging at the tip.* Veins are depressed above, strongly protruding below. **Petioles** 70–85% of blade length, usually at a nearly right angle to the leaf and sharply upturned from the stem, *with an enlarged pedestal at the base, which is twisted, kinked, and shallowly channeled.* The main petiole is shallowly wing-channeled, the wings often purple. *Wings enlarge just before the leaf, becoming wavy and often touching.* **Inflorescence** a small spike. **Flowers** white, inconspicuous, with a cinnamon-like scent. **Fruit** (rarely produced) is a 3-winged pod.

CONFUSING PLANTS: American wild yam (p. 678) leaves normally have 9 major veins from the base and lack the purple zone, the wavy wing at the top of the petiole, and the elongated leaf tip. They have no tubers, aerial or underground, and frequently produce fruit. Bigroot morning glory also has similar leaves.

HABITAT: Fencerows, roadsides, floodplains, disturbed forest edges. **I**

FOOD USE: The large **underground tubers** are the more practical food source; eat them cooked. They contain more food value when the tops are dormant. Large roots, even cooked, may cause a mild burning from raphides (p. 22). **Aerial tubers** may be collected from midsummer to autumn by shaking the vines over a tarp or wide container; cook them also.

COMMENTS: This introduced vine is closely related to cultivated yams (not to sweet potatoes). It has become a troublesome weed in many areas and is available in great quantity. Tender young roots are delicious. **AKA** Chinese yam, cinnamon vine, *Dioscorea oppositifolia.* Other invasive edible yams are sometimes found, especially in Florida.

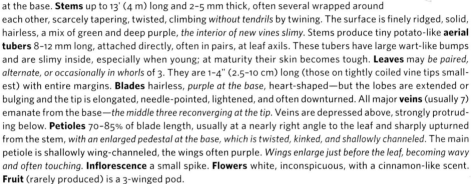

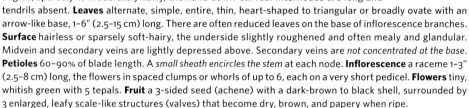

20 **Black bindweed** ❦ 1 galls 2 🌿 2
genus *Fallopia* (in part) ◆ *Polygonaceae* (Buckwheat family)

QUICK CHECK: Thin herbaceous vines without tendrils; simple entire leaves with lobed bases; racemes of tiny flowers becoming 3-sided shiny black seeds in a papery husk. **ID difficulty 2.**

DESCRIPTION: Thin herbaceous vines to 16' (5 m) long, often forming dense tangles or mats. **Stems** 2–3 mm thick, branching occasionally, reddish, slightly rough and sometimes angled, sparsely to moderately hairy, the hairs down-curved. Internodes are long and tendrils absent. **Leaves** alternate, simple, entire, thin, heart-shaped to triangular or broadly ovate with an arrow-like base, 1–6" (2.5–15 cm) long. There are often reduced leaves on the base of inflorescence branches. **Surface** hairless or sparsely soft-hairy, the underside slightly roughened and often mealy and glandular. Midvein and secondary veins are lightly depressed above. Secondary veins are *not concentrated at the base.* **Petioles** 60–90% of blade length. A *small sheath encircles the stem* at each node. **Inflorescence** a raceme 1–3" (2.5–8 cm) long, the flowers in spaced clumps or whorls of up to 6, each on a very short pedicel. **Flowers** tiny, whitish green with 5 tepals. **Fruit** a 3-sided seed (achene) with a dark-brown to black shell, surrounded by 3 enlarged, leafy scale-like structures (valves) that become dry, brown, and papery when ripe.

SPECIES: *F. convolvulus* is an introduced annual. The leaf tips are longer and more pointed, and the upper leaves have arrowhead lobes at the base. The valves are about as long as the seed, and the seed surface is dull and rough. *F. scandens* is a native perennial that grows larger than the other species and has strongly angled stems. The valves are much longer than the ripe seed and have the midvein enlarged into a broad wing. The seed surface is black and shiny. *F. clinodis* is a native perennial with smaller seeds and soft-hairy leaves. It can be distinguished by the fringe of backward-pointing hairs at the nodes. Veins and veinlets are more deeply depressed and the midvein is often red.

CONFUSING PLANTS: Redvine *Brunnichia ovata* (edibility unknown) is a related native of the South distinguished by its elongated leaves and fruit, and the presence of tendrils.

HABITAT: Disturbed, sunny places, especially with rich, moist soil. Lake shores, river floodplains, steep banks, fence lines, roadsides, forest edges, disturbed woods, weedy lots.

FOOD USE: Shoots (spring) of the *perennial* species can be eaten cooked; they are astringent and sour like dock greens. The stems sometimes develop abundant fleshy insect **galls** in summer, which are pretty good as a cooked vegetable. **Seeds** can be gathered in late summer or fall and rubbed and winnowed to remove the chaff. After this the shells must be cracked and winnowed off. The resulting grain is like buckwheat and can be used similarly. (*F. clinodis* seeds are inferior.) **Conservation 1** (native species).

COMMENTS: The seeds of black bindweed have been collected since ancient times in Europe and have served as an important food, even being cultivated. **AKA** climbing false buckwheat.

▲ (top left) *Fallopia scandens* ripe fruit. (top right) *Fallopia scandens* ripe seeds. (bottom right) *Fallopia clinodis* leaves. ▶

21 Bigroot morning glory 1
Ipomoea pandurata • family Convolvulaceae

QUICK CHECK: Thin vine with entire, heart-shaped leaves and no tendrils; large white flowers with purple centers. **ID difficulty 2.**

DESCRIPTION: Perennial. **Roots** elongated and fleshy, usually curved, smooth-skinned, with a thick rind, becoming very large with age. **Stems** to 15' (4.5 m) long, 2–5 mm thick, branching occasionally (sometimes at the base), trailing along the ground or climbing low vegetation *without tendrils* by twining. Stems are roundish, finely grooved or ridged, hairless or faintly hairy but minutely roughened, maroon or light green. *Sap is milky.* **Leaves** alternate, but those on the lower side of the stem are curved upward so that all leaves are roughly in plane. Blades are 1–6" (2.5–15 cm) long, rather tough, heart-shaped, with the lobes and tips sometimes elongated. The tips are acuminate, but *minutely rounded or blunt, ending abruptly in a downturned tooth*, the tip often minutely folded. The blades are pale below with scattered hairs and protruding veins. **Margins** entire and wavy. (Rarely a lobe is pointed or has a tooth). There are 5–6 *secondary veins crowded near the base of the leaf*, and a few more distally, arching toward the tip. Major veins are raised in a gentle valley, but minor veins are depressed or have the leaf raised between them to give a rippled look. **Petioles** about 100% of blade length, rounded with a small channel, at a nearly right angle to the blade. **Inflorescence:** single flowers or small clusters from leaf axils near branch tips, the peduncle 1.3" (33 cm), curved, and thickening toward the tip. **Flowers** (mid to late summer) 2–4" (5–10 cm) wide, white with purple centers, hairless. **Corolla** forms a broad funnel of 5 fused petals, the funnel narrow and purplish inside for about 1.2" (3 cm), then abruptly spreading. Each petal has a faint keel down the center and a jagged outer edge. There are 5 narrow triangles where the petals overlap, each with a groove on both long edges. There are 5 layered sepals of unequal size, blunt-tipped, bulging at the base, with longitudinal ridges. **Fruit** an egg-shaped capsule 10–15 mm long containing a few seeds.

CONFUSING PLANTS: Other members of the genus *Ipomoea* (morning glories), but none have the large white flowers with purple centers. Air potato has wings on the petiole margin, a distinctly enlarged pedestal at the petiole's base, and all major veins emanating from the leaf base.

HABITAT: Sunny, well-drained sites such as fields, forest edges, fencerows, roadsides, open woods, and dry meadows. Native.

FOOD USE: Although the **roots** can grow enormous, you want to dig them from small plants, as older roots become tough and bitter. You can dig them at any time of year, but they are better when dormant. They are marginally edible raw, much better cooked (but still not great). **Conservation 3.**

COMMENTS: This species seems to interest the imagination more than the palate. It is a close relative of the cultivated sweet potato, and has a very large root, but there is limited evidence of its use as food. The youngest roots are fairly sweet and acceptably tender, but older roots are terrible. Some other vines in this genus may have edible roots, but I have not confirmed this.

22 Buffalo gourd 🍼 🌾 1 🌼 2 💧
Cucurbita foetidissima ⁘ *Cucurbitaceae* (Cucumber family)

QUICK CHECK: Large, thick-stemmed vine with raspy leaves and stems, large squash-like yellow-orange flowers, and smooth, round gourds. **ID difficulty 1.**

DESCRIPTION: Perennial from an enlarged root. **Stems** multiple on large plants, trailing along the ground to 30' (9 m) long and 0.7" (18 mm) thick, solid, deeply grooved, raspy-hairy. **Leaves** alternate, 4–10" (10–25 cm) long, thick, densely stiff-hairy on both sides, ruffled, triangular to ovate with heart-shaped bases, sometimes 3 or 5-lobed, with tapered tips. The underside is light gray-green. **Veins** and veinlets are depressed above and strongly protrude below. **Margins** wavy with tiny, widely spaced, outward-pointing teeth. **Petiole** 25% of blade length, *often thicker than the stems they are attached to,* raspy, deeply grooved on all sides. **Tendril** attached at the node. **Flowers** (mid to late summer) yellow-orange, normally solitary, on short pedicels from leaf axils, 3–4" (8–10 cm) across with 5 petals fused in the lower half, much like squash flowers. **Fruit** a nearly spherical, smooth-skinned gourd 2.5–4" (6–10 cm) in diameter, ripening to a mixture of greenish and orange fading to dull straw yellow when dry. The gooey, partly air-filled insides hold numerous flat seeds that resemble pumpkin seeds in miniature.

▲ Rare in the eastern third.

HABITAT: Sand or gravel in full sun, at low points where water drains into coarse soil such as ditches, vacant lots, streambanks, washes, gullies, and lower hillsides. Native.

FOOD USE: Seeds can be gathered from ripe fruit. They need to be rubbed and soaked in several changes of water to remove the taint of the bitter juice, after which can be used like pumpkinseeds (including pressing for oil). A faint bitterness always remains. The enormous root is too bitter to eat as a vegetable, but starch for culinary purposes can supposedly be extracted from it (I have not done this). **Flowers** can be eaten like squash blossoms. Some people report eating the baby fruit cooked. **Conservation 3/1.**

COMMENTS: This is closely related to the ancestors of domestic squashes, which were grown for their edible seeds rather than pulp for the first few thousand years. There have been experiments with growing buffalo gourd as a starch-root crop, but growth is slow and the processing costly.

Related edible:

23 Ozark gourd ⁘ *Cucurbita pepo* variety *ozarkana/texana/ovifera*

This gourd is naturally distributed along river systems in the southern states, where it colonizes driftwood and flotsam piles; it has spread widely to disturbed habitats. The leaves are deeply lobed, and the gourds ripen to pale whitish-gray. The seeds and blossoms can be used similarly to buffalo gourd. This plant is the ancestor of some domestic squashes, but today populations may also cross with domestic squashes. The flesh contains perhaps the bitterest substance known—just taste the tiniest bit to amaze yourself.

24 Melonette ○ 3
Melothria pendula ✦ *Cucurbitaceae* (Cucumber family)

QUICK CHECK: Thin vine with blunt-tipped palmate leaves and fruits dangling singly like tiny, smooth cucumbers before turning black. **ID difficulty 1.**

DESCRIPTION: Perennial, branching widely. **Stems** 8-16' (2.4-5 m) long and 2-4 mm thick, grooved lengthwise, smooth and hairless, green. **Leaves** alternate, each with an opposing unbranched **tendril**, the latter coiling very tightly and lacking pads at the tip. **Blades** 2-3.5" (5-9 cm) long and about equally wide, palmately but shallowly lobed, the lobe tips blunt. Surface dark green above and roughened by short, stiff hairs; below it is gray-green and less hairy. **Major veins** above are raised proximally, but distally they become slightly depressed; below they protrude. **Margins** wavy but lack teeth. **Petioles** about 60% of blade length, *as thick or thicker than the adjacent stem*; they have a small but distinct channel, and *contrast with the stem by having raspy hairs*. Stipules absent. **Inflorescence** male and

female separate; the male in small clusters from the leaf axils, the female solitary. **Flowers** *tiny, 2.5-4 mm across,* yellow, symmetrical, the corolla joined at the base with 5 spreading, square-tipped lobes, the calyx with 5 tiny pointed lobes. **Fruits** broadly elliptic, 0.6-0.9" (15-23 mm) long, solitary, green with whitish mottling, with 8 faint lines running lengthwise. The flesh is partly translucent with cucumber-like seeds, *ripening to black and soft.* **WARNING:** When ripe the fruit is reported to be a strong laxative and should not be eaten.

HABITAT: Forest margins and openings, fence rows, brushy areas, streamside woods. Native. 🔥

FOOD USE: The **underripe fruit** tastes like a cucumber, but in my opinion, better. Fully ripe fruit gets a sour, musky flavor that is disagreeable. Use the fruits as you would cucumbers. **Conservation 1.**

COMMENTS: This little-known fruit looks like a miniature watermelon; it is common, easy to harvest, and delicious. A close relative, *M. scabra*, is native to Mexico and sold in seed catalogs. **AKA** creeping cucumber.

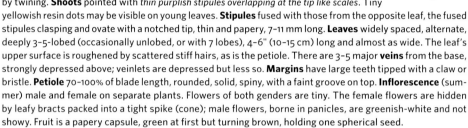

25 Hops ⬦ 3 ⬦ 📖 IWE-165
Humulus lupulus ✦ *Cannabaceae* (Hemp family)

QUICK CHECK: Herbaceous vine with deeply lobed simple leaves, no tendrils, thin raspy stems, and cone-like clusters of fragrant papery fruits. **ID difficulty 2.**

DESCRIPTION: Thin perennial herbaceous vine from a thick rootstock. **Stem** 8–30' (2.4–9 m) long and 3–6 mm thick, unbranched, uniformly green, round in cross section with *6 small ridges roughened by short spurs pointing toward the base. Lacks tendrils*; climbs by twining. **Shoots** pointed with *thin purplish stipules overlapping at the tip like scales.* Tiny yellowish resin dots may be visible on young leaves. **Stipules** fused with those from the opposite leaf, the fused stipules clasping and ovate with a notched tip, thin and papery, 7–11 mm long. **Leaves** widely spaced, alternate, deeply 3–5-lobed (occasionally unlobed, or with 7 lobes), 4–6" (10–15 cm) long and almost as wide. The leaf's upper surface is roughened by scattered stiff hairs, as is the petiole. There are 3–5 major **veins** from the base, strongly depressed above; veinlets are depressed but less so. **Margins** have large teeth tipped with a claw or bristle. **Petiole** 70–100% of blade length, rounded, solid, spiny, with a faint groove on top. **Inflorescence** (summer) male and female on separate plants. Flowers of both genders are tiny. The female flowers are hidden by leafy bracts packed into a tight spike (cone); male flowers, borne in panicles, are greenish-white and not showy. Fruit is a papery capsule, green at first but turning brown, holding one spherical seed.

HABITAT: Rich, moist soil, especially sandy, usually in partial shade but sometimes full sun. Principally floodplains and streamsides, spreading to forest edges, fence lines, and other brushy areas. Native.

FOOD USE: The **shoots** or rapidly growing vine tips (spring through early summer) are good (but raspy) raw and excellent cooked. Papery fruit clusters are used to **flavor** beer. For this purpose they are harvested in late summer and then dried. **Conservation 2/1.**

COMMENTS: Long cultivated and well known as an ingredient in beer, hops is native and widespread in North America. Feral populations of cultivated hops also occur but are uncommon. **Japanese hops** *H. japonicus* is an invasive annual species that is locally abundant, thriving in disturbed riparian zones with rich soil. The leaves usually have 5–7 lobes with deep sinuses between them, and the lobes are broadened near the tip. The tender vine tips are raspy but marginally edible.

Japanese hops.

26 Maypop 🍎 3 🌿 2 🌸 2 📖 NG-238
Passiflora incarnata ✦ family *Passifloraceae*

QUICK CHECK: Herbaceous vine with deeply lobed, small-toothed leaves and egg-shaped, egg-sized, green to yellow fruit. **ID difficulty 1.**

DESCRIPTION: Perennial. **Stems** 10-25' (3-8 m) long, roundish, slightly hairy (more so when young), green, 3-7 mm thick, climbing with long, *coiling tendrils*. **Leaves** alternate, 4-5" (10-13 cm) long, deeply 3-lobed, heart-shaped at the base with the rounded lobes upturned, the lobe tips acuminate-pointed. Sinuses are rounded. The surface is faintly hairy above at first, becoming hairless or nearly so; hairless to densely fine-hairy below. **Veins** and veinlets are depressed above; secondary veins are angled broadly, not forking, arching toward the tip. **Margins** have small, blunt teeth oriented toward the tip. **Petioles** stout, 25-40% of blade length, *with a pair of large, breast-like glands on the upper side near the blade*. There are small thread-like stipules that fall early in the growing season. **Inflorescence** single flowers on long, rounded, finely hairy pedicels 2.5-4" (6-10 cm) long, from the axils. **Flower buds** large and inflated, about 1.2" (3 cm) long, oval, green, with 5 fused sepals, each with a spur near the tip. **Flowers** 2-3" (5-8 cm) across and *highly distinctive*. The 5 petals are light bluish to white. Above them is a whorl of numerous zigzag or twisted white and purple threads. There is an erect central column supporting 5 thick stamens, green with purple speckles, the anthers drooping at full bloom. The tip of the column has 3-4 widely spreading style branches. **Fruit** 1.2-3" (3-8 cm) long, hanging on a long pedicel that is *double-jointed near the end*, spherical to oval, with a tough outer skin, at first smooth and green, becoming straw-yellow and wrinkly, surrounding numerous crunchy seeds 3-4 mm long, each encased in a teardrop-shaped sack of pale to yellowish pulp.

HABITAT: Sunny, well-drained, disturbed sites. Likes vacant lots, forest edges, roadsides, fence lines, brushy areas, high ground along stream banks. Native. 🔥

FOOD USE: Gather the **fruit** in late summer to fall when the insides are soft and juicy—usually after the skin becomes slightly wrinkly. You can rip them open and suck out the pulp to eat raw, or you can cook the pulp and run through a strainer to get pulp for pies, jam, or other desserts. Maypops store well, even at room temperature, and can often be gathered by the bucketload. Tender new **leaves and stem tips** can be eaten raw or cooked in spring and early summer. **Flower buds** are also edible.

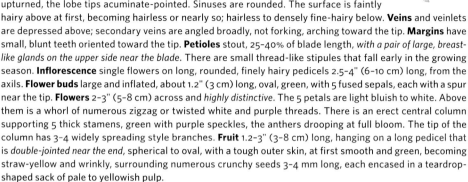

COMMENTS: This is one of the most unexpected fruits native to North America—a close relative of the tropical passionfruit sold commercially. Easy to identify and gather, it is popular with foragers across the South. The greens have a distinctive flavor that some relish and others do not.

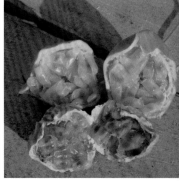

27 **Yellow passion flower** 🍍 1 🍃 2 🌿 2
Passiflora lutea + family *Passifloraceae*

QUICK CHECK: Very thin vine with flat leaves of 3 rounded lobes, complex yellow-green flowers, black spherical fruit, and thin tendrils often coiled like a spring. **ID difficulty 1.**

DESCRIPTION: Perennial. **Stems** 6–12' (2–3 m) long and 2–3 mm thick, gently ridged, hairless, often twisted, mostly green but dark purple near the nodes. **Leaves** alternate, 2–2.5" (5–6.5 cm) long and about as broad, 3-lobed, the lobes *gently rounded* and toothless, the blade hairless and *remarkably flat*. **Veins** all flat above and gently protruding below, the secondary veins 75° to the major veins, straight at first then curving and breaking up before reaching the margin. **Petioles** not channeled, purplish near the base, 40–60% of blade length and at a right angle to it. **Stipules** light yellow-green, 3–4 mm, claw-like, wrapping around the stem. **Tendrils** long and thread-like, unbranched, often *densely coiled like a spring*. **Flower buds** to 0.7" (18 mm) long, blunt, cylindrical, yellow-green, slightly bulged at the base, *paired at nodes* on *thread-like pedicels* to 1.3" (33 mm) long. **Flowers** about 1" (2.5 cm) across, composed of 5 narrow, yellow-green petals alternating with broader, blunt sepals of the same color but about 50% longer. There is a ring of numerous *wavy, yellow-green, thread-like appendages* and another *ring of numerous short filaments* around a *5-part pistil*. **Fruit** is nearly spherical, black, soft, about 0.6" (15 mm) across, the several *seeds zebra-striped* lengthwise.

HABITAT: Fertile brushy areas, usually in partial sun; floodplains, roadsides, forest margins, near lakes and wetlands. Native. 🔥

FOOD USE: Tender young **leaves**, **vine tips**, and **flower buds** can be eaten raw or cooked from late spring through midsummer. Ripe **fruit** (late summer to fall) can also be eaten. **Conservation 2/1.**

COMMENTS: The fruit is lame—scarcely worth mentioning as edible. However, the tender tips are quite good, and I enjoy eating them raw. The flower is not nearly so large and showy as that of most passion flowers, but a close look reveals the same unusual and complex form. This is the northernmost species of passion flower.

▲ Tender tip.

GROUP 30 BASAL LEAVES ABSENT, LEAVES WHORLED

The plants in this group come from several families and are quite dissimilar in appearance; there are few generalizations to be made about them. The most problematic plant in this group is the Swedish bunchberry, which has leaves in both whorls and pairs.

TENTATIVE IDENTIFICATION KEY TO GROUP 30
The key is not your final answer!

Leaves entire.

  or Plant with a single whorl of 3 leaves. | 1. Trillium

  Plant with 1 or 2 whorls, at least one of them with more than 3 leaves.

    or A lower whorl of 6–11 leaves; flowering plants with an upper whorl of 3; stem woolly. | 3. Cucumber root

    A single whorl of 4 or 6 leaves (6 when flowering); clustered red berries. | 4. Bunchberry

  Plant with many whorls of leaves along the stem.

or   Leaves thick and succulent.

      or Stems creeping; leaves narrow and pointed, all oriented upward. | 6. Whorled stonecrop

      Stems weakly erect; leaves spoon-shaped, in flat whorls. | 7. Woodland stonecrop

    or Leaves not thick and succulent.

      Stem strictly erect, 6–15 mm thick and rounded; flowers 2–6" (5–15 cm) wide. | 2. Lily

      Stem creeping, reclining, or leaning, 2–3 mm thick, squared; flowers tiny. | 8. Cleavers

  Plant with whorls only at branch tips; lower leaves paired. | 5. Swedish bunchberry

Leaves compound.

  Leaflets entire. Point-leaf tick trefoil (p. 645).

  Leaflets toothed.

    Stems to 9" (23 cm) tall; leaflets sessile, about twice as long as wide; fruits yellow-green, ripening in late spring. | 9. Dwarf ginseng

    Stems to 22" (56 cm) tall; leaflets on petiolules, the blades almost as broad as long; fruits red, ripening in early fall. | 10. American ginseng

---

1 Trillium 2
genus *Trillium* ✦
family *Melanthiaceae* (formerly in *Liliaceae*)

QUICK CHECK: Three entire leaves atop a smooth, unbranched stem; single large, 3-petaled flower. **ID difficulty 3.**

DESCRIPTION: Perennial herbs from a stout, short rhizome. **Stem** single, erect, 6–24" (20–60 cm) high and stout for its height, up to 12 mm thick; unbranched, round, smooth, hairless, green or maroon or a mottled mixture of the two, terminating in a single whorl of 3 leaves. In the shoot stage it has three leaves *folded upward*, scrolled together at first; *there is no sheath around the lower stem*. **Leaves** sessile, ovate to elliptic (often very broadly), angled at the base and sharp at the tip, entire, 2–7" (5–18 cm) long, hairless above but sometimes soft-hairy below. Prominent **veins** arise at the base and reconverge at the tip; these may have branches also arching toward the tip, and always have pinnate veins between them. Veins are strongly depressed, the blade raised between them. **Flower** (spring) single, sessile or on a pedicel. **Sepals** 3, green and leafy, about as long as the petals, pointed. **Petals** 3, larger than the sepals, colored white, yellow, or maroon, elliptic with pointed or angled ends, the surface veiny, with larger veins depressed. **Fruit** fleshy, white or greenish to red, broad at the base, pointed at the tip, with 6 angles; contains many small, hard-shelled seeds.

CONFUSING PLANTS: At maturity jack-in-the-pulpit (p. 569) is forked with two ternately compound leaves, but young plants have a single leaf. At emergence (about when trilliums begin to flower) JITP has a sheath at the base; one leaflet points upward and the other two are folded downward. When unfurled, the leaf venation is different; JITP leaves, like those of other arums, have a prominent central vein with pinnate secondary veins that terminate at a marginal vein running just inside of the blade's edge.

HABITAT: Hardwood forests on well-drained soil. Native. (Continued on the next page.)

1   Trillium (continued)

FOOD USE: The young shoots, while the leaves are drooping or folded, can be eaten raw or cooked. I think the stems taste better than the leaves. **Conservation 3.**

COMMENTS: The shoots are okay, not excellent. There are numerous species of trillium in our area. Most are not common enough to justify collection, and in different jurisdictions various species are protected. However, certain species are abundant in some regions, and a few of these are noted below. Eating a trillium shoot does not generally kill the plant, but it will grow back much smaller—and repeated cutting will eventually kill it. Trillium populations have been severely reduced in most of our region in the last 50 years by high deer numbers—there are few plants that deer like more.

Large white trillium *Trillium grandiflorum* is by far the most common species across the northern US and southern Canada. The stems reach 24" (60 cm) tall; shoots usually emerge green. The flowers are white, 2-4" (5-10 cm) across, on a pedicel up to 4" (10 cm) long, the petals overlapping at the base. The fruits are small, strongly ridged, and whitish.

▲ *Trillium grandiflorum.*

▲ *Trillium grandiflorum* shoots.

Trillium recurvatum is called **prairie trillium**, but it grows mostly in forests and savannahs. It is one of our taller species, reaching 18" (46 cm). The stems are mottled maroon and green. The leaves are distinctly blotchy and narrowed at the base so there are gaps between them. The maroon petals are narrowed at the base,

held erect, arching with the tips usually remaining in contact; the sepals are strongly reflexed, hanging downward between the leaves. This species has the best young trillium stems I have eaten.

▲ *Trillium recurvatum* before flowering, with tender stem.

▲ *Trillium recurvatum.*

Nodding trillium *Trillium cernuum* is a tall species with smaller white flowers hanging below the leaves. I have eaten the shoots, but the large red fruits, which ripen in late summer, are a little-known delicacy that can be harvested without harming the plant. Suck the tasty juice and pulp and then spit out the distasteful seeds to disseminate them.

◄ *Trillium cernuum,* ripe fruit.

2 Lily ◊ 2
genus *Lilium* ✦ *Liliaceae* (Lily family)

QUICK CHECK: Straight, erect, unbranched stem with whorls of narrow, entire leaves and large flowers with 6 spotted petals. **ID difficulty 2.**

DESCRIPTION: Perennials from a bulb that is surrounded by white bulblets or bulb-scales. **Stems** erect, single, hairless, glaucous, rounded, sometimes faintly ridged, unbranched, 1–6' (30–180 cm) tall and 6–15 mm thick. **Leaves** in whorls of 4–11, occasionally with scattered alternate leaves between them. (All leaves are alternate in *L. lancifolium*.) They are hairless, sessile, 2–7" (5–18 cm) long, narrowly lanceolate or elliptic (almost linear), with pointed tips and entire margins. **Veins** parallel, the major ones deeply depressed above. **Inflorescence** a single flower or cluster, at the apex or from upper leaf axils, the pedicels long, often nodding, and often with a single bract. Flower buds 1–2" (2.5–5 cm) long, much longer than wide. **Flowers** (summer) showy, 2–6" (5–15 cm) wide, with 6 petals, recurved slightly to drastically, mostly reddish to orange or yellow with spots at least near the base. There are 6 long stamens, the thick filaments usually curving away from the central style. **Fruit** an elongated 3-part capsule containing many seeds.

▲ Turk's cap lily.

FOOD USE: Bulblets at the base (underground) are sweet and starchy and can be eaten raw or cooked, but are better cooked. **Conservation 3.**

▲ Wood lily.

COMMENTS: Lilies are wildflowers of striking beauty that are easy to spot and recognize. Long-lived and rarely abundant, they are destroyed when collected, and should generally only be gathered in true emergencies, or where development is about to claim their habitat. The edible part is small in proportion to the size of the plant. The two species I have eaten are shown here.

Turk's cap lily is a group of species that has been classed as one in the past, and is now divided into *L. michiganense, L. canadense,* and *L. superbum*. These similar species are found in openings in forests with moist, rich soil—especially floodplains. In some regions they colonize roadside ditches. The flowers are on drooping pedicels in whorls, or in the case of *L. superbum,* in a large raceme at the top.

Wood Lily *L. philadelphicum* is a shorter species of dry, open areas such as pine barrens and oak savannahs. The flowers are few in number in a terminal cluster, turned skyward rather than nodding in bloom; the petals are narrowed to a stalk-like base. 🔥

▲ This small *Lilium michiganense* plant has a few white bulblets at the base.

▲ (above) *Lilium philadelphicum*. (right) *Lilium michiganense*. ▶

3 Cucumber root 〈🌱〉 3
Medeola virginiana ✦ *Liliaceae* (Lily family)

QUICK CHECK: Erect, thin, single stem with one whorl of 5–11 narrow, pointed leaves, plus a second whorl of 3 on flowering plants. **ID difficulty 2.**

DESCRIPTION: Small perennial herb from a white **tuber** to 2" (5 cm) long and 0.6" (15 mm) thick, positioned horizontally to one side of the stem immediately at the base, the surface smooth but with bumps where roots attach. **Stems** single, erect, rounded, straight, solid or with a pinhole hollow, stiff, smooth, unbranched, to 22" (56 cm) tall and 1–2.5 mm thick; very fine wool lays on the surface when young, persisting longer near the base and the leaves. There may be a few whitish papery sheaths near the stem base. **Leaves** whorled; most often there is a single whorl of 6 on non-flowering specimens, and an additional whorl of 3 on flowering plants—but there may occasionally be more whorls containing up to 11. The center of the whorl on nonflowering plants is maroon on top. **Blades** linear-lanceolate, pointed at the tip and tapered to the base, entire, sessile, 1.5–4" (4–10 cm) long, curved upward, glossy, smooth. The leaf underside has fine wool, sparse near the tip but thicker near the base; it may wear off late in the season. **Veins** depressed above and protruding below. There is one prominent vein on each side of the midvein, converging at the tip. **Inflorescence** a terminal umbel of 3–10, borne just above the upper whorl of leaves and often hanging below them. **Flowers** (summer) about 0.9" (23 cm) across, greenish to light yellow with 6 *recurved tepals*. **Fruit** a globose berry 5–7 mm in diameter, ripening to dark blue-black.

CONFUSING PLANTS: Starflower *Trientalis borealis* is similar in appearance and often shares the habitat of cucumber root, but is shorter with narrower leaves in a single whorl. It has a small, tough rhizome. The whorled pogonias (genus *Isotria*) have only one or two flowers, and these have 3 petals and 3 long sepals; when not flowering they can be told from cucumber root by the hollow stems lacking wool, and by the tendency to have fewer and broader leaves in each whorl. Several lilies (genus *Lilium*) also have whorls, and when very young may resemble cucumber root, but they are not woolly, have longer leaves, and have bulblet clusters rather than tubers.

HABITAT: Moist, organic, usually mildly acidic soil in hardwood or mixed conifer-hardwood forests, in moderate to heavy shade. Native.

FOOD USE: Dig **tubers** at any time of year (best when the top is dormant), clean and eat raw or cooked. They can be pickled, used in salads, or served as a cooked vegetable. **Conservation 3.**

COMMENTS: The rhizomes are delicious—much better than cucumbers. However, they are easy to overharvest and should be reserved for an occasional treat.

4 Bunchberry 🍓 2 📖 NG-333
Cornus canadensis ◆ *Cornaceae* (Dogwood family)

QUICK CHECK: Short herb with tough entire leaves in whorls of 6 and a single tight cluster of red berries. **ID difficulty 1.**

DESCRIPTION: Perennial herb from creeping woody rhizomes. **Stems** single, thin, unbranched, 4–8" (10–20 cm) tall and 1–2 mm thick, with a single whorl of 4 or 6 leaves. Fruiting plants have 6 leaves, and 2 of them are usually much smaller than the others. **Leaves** sessile, 1.5–3" (4–8 cm) long, elliptic, entire, pointed at both ends, *evergreen*, rather stiff (but not thick or stiff for an evergreen leaf). The upper side has scattered stiff hairs pressed against the surface. There are *2–3 major secondary veins per side*, all arising in the proximal third of the blade, *arching and reconverging near the tip*; these and the midvein are *very deeply depressed above*. Smaller veins are obscure. **Inflorescence** a tightly packed umbel subtended by a set of *4 white bracts that look like petals*, giving the whole cluster the appearance of one large, 4-petaled flower. The actual **flowers** are tiny with 4 square-tipped, white, petals and a blackish pistil. **Berries** ripen to bright orange-red but have whitish flesh; each contains a single, hard seed.

HABITAT: Moist, organic, acidic soil in partial sun. Coniferous and mixed forests, low woods, bog margins. Native.

FOOD USE: Ripe **berries** can be collected in late summer and sometimes into fall. They have a weak but pleasant flavor and make a nice trail nibble. The seeds stick to the pulp and are thus hard to spit out, but can be harmlessly swallowed. Whole berries, seed and all, can be mashed or blended and eaten as a kind of sauce or pudding. This fruit is better raw than cooked. **Conservation 1.**

COMMENTS: One of the iconic wild plants of the Northwoods, the ubiquitous and beautiful bunchberry seems to be the most popular photography subject in the boreal forest. **AKA** crackerberry, because the seeds are often crunched to eat the fruit.

Related edible:
5 Bunchberry ◆ *Cornus suecica* 🍓 2

This is a taller plant than the common bunchberry, but has smaller, *mostly paired* leaves only 0.6–1.4" (15–35 mm) long. The topmost leaves are often whorled (or in pairs so crowded as to appear whorled). The stem is often branched at 45° from the axils of upper leaves, these branches ending in a whorl of leaves. The tiny flowers are *dark purple*. The berries

are darker red and slightly larger than those of bunchberry, but borne in smaller clusters. Swedish bunchberry grows in open, moist areas in the Far North, especially meadows and coastal tundra. The berries have a somewhat more intense and fruitier flavor than bunchberries—but more importantly, the seed shells are thinner and easier to chew. In some locations they can be collected in great quantities.

6 Whorled stonecrop ✐ 2
Sedum sarmentosum ✦ family *Crassulaceae*

QUICK CHECK: Mat-forming, prostrate plant with thick, fleshy, narrow leaves in sets of three, all oriented toward the upper side. **ID difficulty 1.**

DESCRIPTION: Perennial creeping along the ground and forming mats. **Stems** to 10" (25 cm) long, thinner than the leaves, smooth and round, pale brownish, branching occasionally. **Leaves** sessile, *in sets of three* but all are oriented toward the upper side. **Blades** 0.2–0.9" (5–23 mm) long, light green, elliptic, hairless, tapered to both ends, with pointed tips; they are thick and fleshy but flat on both sides. Leaves get smaller toward the branch tips. **Inflorescence** a widely-spreading cluster of a few zigzag spikes held 3–6" (8–15 cm) above the leaves, the flowers borne with reduced leaves. **Flowers** (late spring to early summer) 12–14 mm across, sessile, oriented skyward. **Sepals** 5, lanceolate, fleshy, green. **Petals** 5, lanceolate, yellow, sharp-pointed, depressed in the center, slightly longer than the sepals. At the center are 5 yellow pistils in a star-like cluster, and dark anthers at the end of long filaments. **Fruit** a cluster of 5 tiny united pods (follicles).

CONFUSING PLANTS: At a glance it looks sort of like the commonly cultivated *Sedum acre*, which is bitter and inedible, but that plant has shorter and stouter leaves not in whorls.

HABITAT: Rocky or sandy well-drained sunny areas: ledges, cliffs, and bluffs. Introduced.

FOOD USE: The leaves have a mild, slightly tangy flavor and can be eaten raw or cooked from spring through early fall, but they are best in spring and early summer.

COMMENTS: Easy to identify, easy to use, beautiful in bloom. This is one of our most widespread and best tasting introduced sedums. **AKA** stringy stonecrop.

7 Woodland stonecrop 2
Sedum ternatum • family *Crassulaceae*

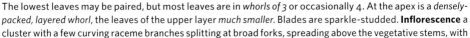

QUICK CHECK: Tiny, succulent, evergreen, hairless forest plant with thick, spoon-shaped leaves in whorls. **ID difficulty 1.**

DESCRIPTION: Low, evergreen perennial often forming mats or clumps. *All parts hairless.* **Stems** reddish green, solid, creeping under litter and rooting at the nodes, then turning weakly erect to about 7" (18 cm) tall, the aerial parts not branched. **Leaves** to 0.7" (18 mm) long, thick and succulent, broadly spoon-shaped, flat, and sessile with entire margins. The lowest leaves may be paired, but most leaves are in *whorls of 3* or occasionally 4. At the apex is a *densely-packed, layered whorl*, the leaves of the upper layer *much smaller*. Blades are sparkle-studded. **Inflorescence** a cluster with a few curving raceme branches splitting at broad forks, spreading above the vegetative stems, with

slightly overlapping flowers rather evenly spaced on very short pedicels, oriented skyward when open. **Flowers** 9–11 mm across, usually with 4 narrow, pointed, white petals, creased along a central vein. Between these are 4 shorter green sepals. Dark anthers give the flowers a peppered look. **Fruit** composed of 5 fused pods (follicles).

HABITAT: Rich hardwood forests on rocks, logs, or moist soil. Most common on rocky slopes in heavy shade. Native.

FOOD USE: Tender **leaves** and **stem tips** can be eaten raw or cooked any time of year, but especially spring and early summer. **Conservation 2.**

COMMENTS: This common and widespread edible makes a fun nibble. The leaves are not acrid or astringent like those of many sedums. **AKA** mountain stonecrop, whorled stonecrop, 3-leaved stonecrop.

▲ (top) Summer leaves. (bottom left) Tender spring leaves.

8 Cleavers 🌿 1 ☕
Galium aparine ✦ family *Rubiaceae*

QUICK CHECK: Reclining or weakly erect plant with raspy, clinging stems and whorls of linear leaves. **ID difficulty 1.**

DESCRIPTION: Annual prostrate or trailing herb. **Stems** to 4' (1.2 m) long and 2–3 mm thick, usually several per plant, erect in dense vegetation but eventually falling over, square with a small round hollow, the angles with narrow *wings, hairs, and bristles*. **Leaves** in whorls of 6–9, entire, sessile, tapered at the base, very narrow but wider toward the abrupt, blunt, bristly tip. The upper surface is minutely bumpy and hairy. Margins are incurved and bristly. **Midvein** depressed above and sharply keeled with spines below; other veins

▲ Very sparse in the dry West.

are not evident, except that from below there appears to be a faint wavy vein running the length of the leaf. **Inflorescence** small stalked whorl-like clusters of 1–5 growing from leaf axils or branch tips. **Flowers** 1–2 mm across with 4 ovate white petals with nipple tips and 4 stamens. **Fruit** tiny, spherical, covered with tiny spines by which they cling weakly to clothing; they turn light brown and separate into two parts at maturity, releasing a single seed that composes most of its volume.

HABITAT: Moist, rich soil high in organic matter, typically in half shade. Often found in disturbed woodlots, forest edges, wooded pastures, brushy areas. Native.

FOOD USE: The tender **spring growth** can be eaten raw or cooked—before it gets raspy enough to be irritating. Because of the coarse texture it is best cooked, or used in a smoothie. Dry **seeds** can be roasted and ground to make a coffee-like drink. **Conservation 1.**

COMMENTS: There are many species in this genus; *Galium aparine* is perhaps the most abundant and also one of the largest, often growing in thick colonies. It is actually in the same botanical family as coffee, although one would never guess by glancing at the two plants. Cleavers "coffee" is frequently mentioned in the wild food literature but few people actually try it, probably because the seeds are tedious to collect and winnow. However, the flavor is pleasantly reminiscent of coffee. The presence of caffeine is widely reported in the literature, but I have not seen a primary source for this claim.

RELATED EDIBLES: Other species of *Galium* are safe, but some are bitter or tough.

Fragrant bedstraw *Galium triflorum* is a forest plant that grows to about 3' (1 m) long, the stems raspy especially near the base, spreading or leaning on other plants. Leaves are ovate to elliptic, in whorls of 6, raspy mostly just on the midvein below. Flowers are in groups of 3 from leaf axils. The leaves have a strong vanilla flavor when dried and can be infused as a flavoring.

Smooth bedstraw *G. mollugo* is an introduced plant of fields. It is not raspy. The leaves are very narrowly elliptic and are borne in whorls of mostly 8. The inflorescence is a large branching cluster held above the leaves. Smooth bedstraw has tender stems and leaves in spring.

▼ (bottom left) *G. triflorum*. (right) *G. mollugo*, young shoots. ▶
The other photos show *G. aparine*.

9 **Dwarf ginseng** 2
Panax trifolius ◆ Araliaceae (Ginseng family)

QUICK CHECK: Small herb with a single whorl of 3 compound leaves, each with 3–5 sessile leaflets; one central umbel of tiny white flowers. **ID difficulty 1.**

DESCRIPTION: Perennial *spring ephemeral* from an enlarged spherical **tuber** 0.2–0.6" (5–15 mm) in diameter, typically 2–4" (5–10 cm) underground. **Stems** 3–9" (8–23 cm) tall and 1–3 mm thick, single, erect, unbranched, rounded, smooth, and hairless. **Leaves** in a single whorl of 3 (rarely 4), each palmately compound with 3–5 (more often 3) sessile leaflets. **Petioles** reddish, channeled, 60–80% of the terminal leaflet's length. **Leaflets** 0.5–2.5" (13–65 mm) long, elliptic or oval to lanceolate, hairless (occasionally with a few appressed hairs along the veins), coarsely toothed, occasionally lobed at the base. **Midvein** slightly depressed above but smaller veins are nearly flat. **Inflorescence** a single, long-stalked *spherical umbel* of 12–22, reaching 1–4" (2.5–10 cm) above the leaves, *the pedicels white*. **Flowers** (spring) white, 4 mm wide, with 5 blunt-tipped, long-elliptic petals and protruding stamens. **Fruit** a yellow-green 3-angled pod 5 mm wide, the surface with several ridges.

HABITAT: Rich, moist soil in hardwood or mixed conifer-hardwood forests, especially with white cedar, black ash, balsam fir, red maple, or yellow birch. Often on the margins of swamps, in depressions in wooded areas, or at the base of tree trunks. Native.

FOOD USE: In a dense colony select a few of the larger **roots**. These are available all year but are easiest to find when the tops are present. They are slightly sweet, aromatic, and pleasant to nibble raw but better cooked. **Conservation 3.**

COMMENTS: This beautiful and delicate plant has thus far been spared the fate of its close relatives in North America and Asia; hopefully it will never develop a reputation as a medicinal. Dwarf ginseng's root is very different in form than the commercial ginsengs and is also much smaller.

10 American ginseng 🌱 1
Panax quinquefolia ✦ *Araliaceae* (Ginseng family)

QUICK CHECK: Shin-high, single-stemmed herb with a single whorl of palmately compound leaves and an umbel rising out of the center; berries red. **ID difficulty 2.**

DESCRIPTION: Perennial. **Taproot** enlarged, often forked, whitish inside and out. **Stem** single, erect, to 22" (56 cm) tall and 5 mm thick, round, smooth, solid, hairless. **Leaves** in a whorl of usually 3 or 4, each palmately compound with 5 leaflets, 2 of them very small, the center leaflet largest. **Petioles** channeled, up to 1.5" (4 cm) long; leaflets are on short petiolules 2–12% of blade length. **Leaflets** 1.5–6" (4–15 cm) long, obovate with acuminate tips and rounded bases, the blades flat, thin, hairless, with a metallic gray sheen below; the margins regularly toothed. **Veins** depressed above and protruding below, not offset by color; secondary veins at 35–45°. **Inflorescence** a spherical, compact umbel of 8–40 flowers that rises from the center of the whorl on an erect peduncle but usually *does not overtop the leaves*. **Flowers** (early to mid summer) 2–3 mm across with 5 petals, whitish or yellowish green. **Fruit** (late summer) elliptic but slightly flattened laterally, ripening to red (when green they are faintly ribbed and much more flattened), to 8 mm in the widest dimension, usually containing 2 seeds. The pedicel is attached to the flat edge on a longer side.

CONFUSING PLANTS: Wild sarsaparilla *Aralia nudicaulis* (p. 290) is related and looks remarkably similar but the flowers and fruit are on a separate, leafless stem and the berries ripen to black.

HABITAT: Mixed hardwood forests with well-drained but rich soil, especially oak-hickory stands casting only moderate shade. Native. 🔥

FOOD USE: Roots can be eaten raw or cooked; gather in autumn. **Conservation 3.**

COMMENTS: Many wild populations of ginseng have been exterminated by commercial collectors, and most remaining populations are planted and tended by harvesters. Collecting generally requires a license and practices are regulated. The primary use is medicinal, but the roots can also be eaten in moderation as a food. They are rather bitter, but not terrible.

GROUP 31 BASAL LEAVES ABSENT, LEAVES PAIRED, STEMS SQUARED, MINTY-AROMATIC

The plants in group 31 all belong to the mint family, *Lamiaceae*. Their repertoire of food uses is small—primarily as flavorings—but mints are well-known and popular among foragers. Many species are cultivated. This is one of the easiest and safest groups for beginners.

The most problematic part of this key is that variable leaf form occasionally results in an atypical specimen having toothed or entire leaves in defiance of its species' norm.

TENTATIVE IDENTIFICATION KEY TO GROUP 31
The key is not your final answer!

Most leaves entire or nearly so (margins may be wavy or gland-dotted).

  Leaves narrowly lanceolate to almost linear.

    or Ankle to shin-high; a few purple flowers in most leaf axils. — **1. Calamint**

    Thigh to waist high; small terminal clusters of whitish flowers. — **2. Virginia mountain mint**

  or Leaves lanceolate or broader; definitely not linear.

    Generally less than 18" (45 cm) tall; calyces green.

      or Flowers in most axils; leaf hairless above, finely dotted. — **4. American pennyroyal**

      Flowers in a few axils; leaf soft-hairy above, not dotted. — **5. Wild basil**

    2–4' (60–120 cm) tall; terminal flower clusters with purple bracts and calyces. — **6. Oregano**

Most leaves distinctly toothed (although the teeth may be few and distant or rounded).

  Stem erect and woody at the base; shrub-like. — **7. Dittany**

  Stem creeping with overlapping, leathery, evergreen leaves. — **1. Calamint**

  Stem erect and herbaceous.

    Stem hairless.

      or Flowers almost regular with 4 nearly equal lobes. — **8. Anise hyssop**

      Flowers clearly irregular, with 4 very unequal lobes or diverging lips. — **12. Mint**

    Stem hairy (although the hairs may be tiny, woolly, or confined to the corners).

      Leaf very rough-corrugated by many deeply depressed veinlets.

        or Flowers in rounded clusters above drooping pairs of stem leaves. — **9. Horehound**

        Flowers in terminal spike- or panicle-like clusters. — **10. Catnip**

      Leaf with secondary veins depressed but veinlets less so or not at all.

        Stem corners rounded; all 4 sides deeply and narrowly grooved. — **11. Shiso**

        Stem corners not rounded; sides flat, convex, or concave but not deeply 4-grooved.

          Flowers almost regular with 4 nearly equal lobes. — **12. Mint**

          Flowers clearly irregular, with 4 very unequal lobes or 2 diverging lips.

            or Flowers in one-sided clusters of a few from leaf axils. — **14. Creeping charlie**

            Flowers in dense, stacked clusters of many.

              or Clusters separated, with whorls of many bracts longer than the flowers; flowers 15–30 mm long. — **15. Horsemint**

              Clusters mostly crammed together, with whorls of bracts shorter than the flowers; flowers 8–12 mm long. — **13. Tall woodmint**

          Flowers mostly or only in dense terminal clusters.

            Flowers 4–8 mm long with 4 unequal lobes. — **3. Broad-leaved mountain mint**

            Flowers 20–40 mm long with 2 long, narrow, diverging lips. — **16. Bergamot**

1 Calamint
Calamintha arkansana + Lamiaceae (Mint family)

QUICK CHECK: Intensely aromatic mint, creeping or short and bushy, with thin stems and very small, tough leaves. **ID difficulty 1.**

DESCRIPTION: Low perennial mint with distinctly different flowering and non-flowering stems, forming colonies. **Non-flowering stems** form in late summer and are evergreen, creeping along the ground, 4–7" (10–18 cm) long, squared and rooting at the nodes, with few to no branches and the leaves crowded and often overlapping. **Leaves** (of creeping stems) evergreen, paired, nearly sessile, thick and fleshy or slightly tough but *flexible*, 3–10 mm long, broadly oval to obovate with blunt to rounded tips, the blades slightly creased along the midvein, both sides hairless and finely dotted, often purplish above, light in color below. **Margins** entire or with a few teeth in the distal quarter. **Midvein** depressed above and flat below; secondary veins obscure. **Petioles** 40–100% of blade length. **Flowering stems** form in spring, usually multiple, erect or ascending, 4–14" (10–36 cm) tall and 1–2 mm thick, *branchy*,

squared, the angles faintly winged, hairless except sometimes at the nodes. **Leaves** (of flowering stems) paired, sessile or nearly so, 8–12 mm long, often with a tuft of smaller leaves in the axil, hairless, linear to narrowly oblanceolate, tapered to the base, entire (rarely with a few teeth), the tip usually blunt, with *no prominent secondary veins*. **Inflorescence** small clusters of 1–7 per leaf axil, the pedicels 2–10 mm long. **Flowers** (summer) 1 cm long, tubular, the 5-lobed calyx almost symmetrical. **Corolla** whitish to pink-purple, hairy, tubular, much longer than the calyx, with 4 lobes of about equal length, the upper one broader, shallowly notched, and recurved.

HABITAT: Harsh, sunny, rocky sites with poor, thin, limestone-derived soil—especially where rock prevents water percolation. Ridges and ledges, dry glades and hilltop openings, open shores of large lakes. Spottily distributed due to very specific habitat needs, but locally abundant.

FOOD USE: The **leaves** can be used as a tea or seasoning, fresh or dried. The overwintering leaves are too tough for food, but the sprouts of the erect stems in spring are tender. **Conservation 2.**

COMMENTS: This remarkably potent herb is our strongest smelling mint and has caused many hikers to pause and look under their feet. Calamint is probably my favorite mint for tea. The taxonomy of these plants is very confusing; they are considered two species or one, depending on the authority, and can go by several scientific names besides the one listed in the heading. **AKA** *Clinopodium arkansanum, Satureja arkansana, Satureja glabella, Clinopodium glabellum.*

▼ Creeping winter stem.

2 Virginia mountain mint
Pycnanthemum virginianum ✦ *Lamiaceae* (Mint family)

QUICK CHECK: Aromatic mint with very narrow, entire, sessile leaves and stems with hairy ridges; flowers packed into terminal clusters. **ID difficulty 1.**

DESCRIPTION: Clumped perennial herb from short rhizomes, the form much taller than wide. **Stems** 1.5–3.5' (45–110 cm) tall and 3–5 mm thick, *hairy primarily on the angles*, the sides not concave, becoming *tough and rigid and very dark at maturity*, with ascending branches in the upper part. **LYDS** prominent, top clusters retaining some scent. **Leaves** sparse, on mature plants clustered near branch tips, sessile or on very short, upturned petioles. The blades are *entire*, long-elliptic to nearly linear, 0.8–2.5" (2–6 cm) long, sharp-pointed, hairless above but hairy on the veins beneath; dark dots are visible on both sides. **Midvein** depressed above and protruding below. Secondary veins few, *nearly parallel*, light in color, depressed or flat above. **Margins** entire, strongly downcurved. **Inflorescence** terminal with multiple levels of 3-way branching, ending in dense clusters 10–12 mm wide subtended by a whorl of numerous very hairy bracts, with only a few of the flowers open at any time—these oriented skyward. **Flowers** (summer) 5 mm long, the corolla white with purple speckles, 2-lipped, the lower lip with 3 lobes.

HABITAT: Sunny areas, both moist and dry. Marsh edges, wet meadows, prairies, bases of limestone bluffs. Native. 🔥

FOOD USE: Gather **leaves** and young stems throughout the growing season to use fresh or dried for tea or as a flavoring. **Conservation 2.**

COMMENTS: This widespread species apparently has 2 chemotypes: some populations taste like mint, and others like bergamot. Narrow-leaf mountain mint *P. tenuifolia* is very similar in appearance, with even narrower leaves, but it has little minty scent.

◀ Shoot.

3 Broad-leaved mountain mints
genus *Pycnanthemum* (in part) ✦ *Lamiaceae* (Mint family)

QUICK CHECK: Waist to chest-high colonial, erect, branchy mints with sparsely-toothed, often whitish leaves and tiny irregular flowers in packed terminal clusters. **ID difficulty 1.**

DESCRIPTION: Perennials in colonies spreading by rhizome. Scent minty or monarda-like. **Stems** erect, 2.5–6' (75–180 cm) tall, thin in proportion to their height, branchy. **Leaves** paired, sessile or nearly so, ovate to narrowly lanceolate, tapered to an acute tip, 2–3.5" (5–9 cm) long, the *upper leaves often silvery-white*. Surfaces faintly to strongly hairy, not glossy. **Midvein** depressed; secondary veins less so. **Margins** with scattered, widely-spaced, small, blunt teeth (occasionally entire). **Petioles** 10–30% of blade length, flat above to faintly channeled. (Continued on the next page.)

3 Broad-leaved mountain mints (continued)

Inflorescence dense terminal clusters (also sometimes in the uppermost axils), round-topped to flat—never elongated or spike-like—with reduced leaves beneath the cluster. **Flowers** (summer) very small, 4–8 mm long, with 4 protruding stamens. The calyx has 4 pointed lobes. **Corolla** whitish with purple to pinkish spots, protruding well beyond the calyx, irregular with 4 lobes, the top one usually strongly recurved.

HABITAT: Mostly open or young forests, savannahs, and forest edges. All species native. 🔥

FOOD USE: Used like other mints for **tea** or **seasoning**, fresh or dried. **Conservation 2.**

▲ Collective range of broad-leaved mountain mints.

COMMENTS: Mountain mints are not as well-known as the mints of the genus *Mentha*; however, many are highly aromatic and good for the same uses. There are several similar species in our area that I have lumped together for discussion, but they do not all taste the same—some are more like mint or like bergamot. A few examples are pictured below.

▲ (above) *Pycnanthemum muticum* has broad leaves with the veins flat on the upper surface and tends to grow in dense colonies. (right) *Pycnanthemum incanum* has lanceolate leaves, the upper ones whitened. ▶

▲ (above) *Pycnanthemum verticillatum* flowers.
◀ (left) *Pycnanthemum verticillatum* has lanceolate leaves and small heads of small flowers; the upper leaves are not whitened.

4 American pennyroyal
Hedeoma pulegioides ◆ *Lamiaceae* (Mint family)

QUICK CHECK: Low, tiny mint with small, well-spaced leaves, entire or with a few large teeth, and tiny flowers in most axils. **ID difficulty 1.**

DESCRIPTION: Small annual. **Stems** single, erect or leaning, 6-15" (15-38 cm) tall and 1-3 mm thick, squared, densely covered with fine hair, unbranched or with a few ascending branches mostly in the middle third. **Leaves** in well-spaced pairs, often with a tuft of smaller leaves in the axil, *the members of the pair often unequal in size*, lanceolate to elliptic, 0.3-0.8" (8-20 mm) long, acute at both ends, the tip often blunt. **Blade** flat, *dotted*, hairless on top but with sparse, fine hairs below. A few major veins are depressed above and protruding below, but veinlets are obscure. **Margins** entire or with a few scattered, large teeth. **Petioles** 20% of blade length. **Inflorescence** clusters of 2-12 in most or all leaf axils, each cluster with a pair of miniature leaves beneath it. The pedicel is about half the length of the calyx. **Flowers** (summer) irregular, 5-7 mm long. **Calyx** *highly irregular*, bulged on the bottom, a curved green tube with *prominent raised ridges* supporting a row of stiff, hooked hairs. The tip is 5-lobed; the top 3 lobes are recurved, triangular, and sharp, while the bottom 2 are narrower, curved upward with stiff bristles—like a pair of pinchers on a beetle. **Corolla** whitish to light blue or purple (usually a mottled mixture of these colors), about as long as the calyx, tubular, the end 2-lipped, the lower lip smaller with 3 broad lobes. **Seeds** four, brown, in the base of the calyx tube.

HABITAT: Open or semi-open sites with a long-term trend of, but not necessarily immediate, disturbance. Dry or open woods, savannahs, forest openings, pastures, hillside prairies, roadsides, trails through woods. Mostly on limestone. Native. 🔥

FOOD USE: Collect **leaves** and use dry or fresh for tea. **Conservation 2.**

COMMENTS: One of our strongest mints, this species has been grown commercially for the flavoring extracted from it. The present species is not the same as the true pennyroyal *Mentha pulegium*, an Old-World mint. **AKA** false pennyroyal. *Hedeoma hispida* is a close relative with long, narrow, entire leaves and a raspier texture; it has little scent. It is native to dry fields and barrens with poor, sandy soil.

5 Wild basil
Satureja vulgaris ✦ *Lamiaceae* (Mint family)

QUICK CHECK: Short, clumped mint, soft-hairy all over, with ovate, blunt-tipped leaves with wavy edges. **ID difficulty 1.**

DESCRIPTION: Perennial from creeping, rooting, semi-woody stems on the surface, the erect stems usually in small groups. **Stems** 6–20" (15–50 cm) tall and 1–2 mm wide, erect but weak, often leaning on other plants, simple or with a few branches, squared, the surface covered with fine, soft hair. There is often a long naked section between the miniature lower leaves and the upper ones. **Leaves** paired, 0.7–2.5" (18–64 mm) long (tiny on the lower stem), ovate to elliptic, the bases rounded, the tips blunt to rounded, acutely angled (at least on larger leaves). Blades are thin and delicate, soft-hairy on both sides (denser below). **Midvein** deeply depressed above. Secondary veins 4–6 per side, arching, deeply depressed above; veinlets mostly obscure. **Margins** entire to wavy or with broad, shallow, rounded teeth. **Petioles** flat on top, 80% of blade length on lower leaves, shortening to 5% on the upper ones. **Inflorescence** tight clusters in a few upper leaf axils, the pedicels 1–5 mm. **Flowers** (summer) 0.4–0.8" (1–2 cm) long, the calyx 2-lipped, with long, pointed, hairy lobes. The corolla is pink-purple with 2 lips, the lower one much broader and 3-lobed.

HABITAT: Open woodlands, forest borders, clearings, fields, disturbed sites in woods; in heavy shade to full sun, but preferring dry soil. Native.

FOOD USE: Young **greens** in spring can be used as a slightly aromatic herb, sort of like a lame version of basil. **Conservation 1.**

COMMENTS: The taste is better than the aftertaste, which is bitter and not pleasant. This mint is barely good enough to include in this book, but since it is called "wild basil" and is extremely common, people often wonder and ask about it. **AKA** dog mint (as if dogs are really into bad basil), *Clinopodium vulgare*.

6 Oregano
Origanum vulgare ✦ *Lamiaceae* (Mint family)

QUICK CHECK: Clumped aromatic mint with untoothed leaves on short petioles; small reddish-purple flowers in dense terminal clusters at the ends of tri-forked branches. **ID difficulty 1.**

DESCRIPTION: Clump-forming perennial herb from tough, creeping surface stems with tiny leaves; these stems eventually turn erect and thicken. **Erect stems** 12–32" (30–80 cm) tall, purplish (especially near nodes), squared but with the corners often blunt, hairy (especially on shoots); hairs near the base point downward. The lower stems are often *twisted for 2 internodes* after turning erect. There are short branches in most axils, even near the base, but the form is taller than wide. **Leaves** paired, ovate to elliptic, 0.6–1.5" (15–38 mm) long, soft-hairy on both sides, the tips blunt, often downcurved (at least when young),

▲ The wild range of this plant is hard to discern because cultivated plants are frequently put into botanical records.

the margin entire or with a few scattered purple teeth. **Midvein** depressed above and protruding below. Secondary veins few, depressed. Petioles 10–20% of blade length (60–110% on young shoots). **Inflorescence** (summer) *branches in threes*, with a slightly thicker central stem and a pair of lateral branches at the 45° angle. Each branch terminates in a dense, round or pyramid shaped *cluster of purplish bracts* from which the flowers protrude. **Corolla** purple-red to pale pink and irregular, tubular with a *very narrowed base*, hairy, the end with 2 lips, the upper lip with a shallow notch at the tip, the lower lip strongly recurved and split into 3 lobes. **Calyx** regular, with triangular lobes. **LYDS** persistent and often wavy—the inflorescence form remains evident.

HABITAT: Dry, sunny, disturbed ground, mostly on limestone or dolomite. Roadsides, construction sites, gravel pits and quarries, old fields and pastures. Introduced.

FOOD USE: Dried or fresh **leaves** can be used as a seasoning.

COMMENTS: This is the domestic herb gone feral, and it is locally abundant in the right habitat.

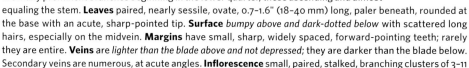

7 Dittany
Cunila origanoides • Lamiaceae (Mint family)

QUICK CHECK: Bush-like, branchy mint with wiry stems; leaves toothed and nearly sessile, the veins light and not depressed above. **ID difficulty 1.**

DESCRIPTION: Perennial quasi-shrub from a woody base. **Stems** one to several, in close proximity but not tightly clumped, erect to leaning or spreading, up to 24" (60 cm) tall and 2–3 mm thick, pithy, stiff and tough, purplish, squared, with scattered long, soft hairs. There are many prominent branches beginning in the lower quarter, these ascending and almost equaling the stem. **Leaves** paired, nearly sessile, ovate, 0.7–1.6" (18–40 mm) long, paler beneath, rounded at the base with an acute, sharp-pointed tip. **Surface** *bumpy above and dark-dotted below* with scattered long hairs, especially on the midvein. **Margins** have small, sharp, widely spaced, forward-pointing teeth; rarely they are entire. **Veins** are *lighter than the blade above and not depressed*; they are darker than the blade below. Secondary veins are numerous, at acute angles. **Inflorescence** small, paired, stalked, branching clusters of 3–11

from upper leaf axils and the stem tip; tiny linear bracts are mingled with the flowers. **Flowers** (mid summer to fall) 5 mm long, the corolla an elongated light purplish tube with 2 lips, the upper lip shallowly 2-lobed, the lower lip reflexed and deeply 3-lobed. The filaments *extend far beyond the lips.* The tubular, striped calyx has 5 regular, triangular lobes.

HABITAT: Dry, open forests, rocky barrens and outcrops, ledges, oak savannahs, sandy prairies, roadsides in wooded areas, abandoned fields and pastures, steep banks. Native. 🔥

FOOD USE: Use leaves fresh or dried for a tea or seasoning. The taste is reminiscent of oregano or bergamot. **Conservation 2.**

COMMENTS: This plant sometimes produces "frost flowers" in late autumn; as the roots push sap out of the broken vascular tissues, the sap freezes in thin sheets, curling around in layers to form erratic and beautiful formations. (Frostweed *Verbesina virginica* is more famous for these ice ribbon structures.) **AKA** stone mint, wild oregano.

8 Anise hyssop
Agastache foeniculum ◆ *Lamiaceae* (Mint family)

QUICK CHECK: Erect, unbranched mint with well-spaced, tough, glossy leaves, 2-lipped flowers, and a fennel-like aroma. **ID difficulty 1.**

DESCRIPTION: Perennial from short rhizomes. **Stems** single or in loose colonies, erect, 2–3.5' (60–110 cm) tall, 4-sided, hairless, purple and green, *each side channeled*, usually unbranched below the inflorescence. **Leaves** paired at *widely spaced nodes*, (often with tufts of smaller leaves in the axils, lanceolate to ovate, 2–3.5" (5–9 cm) long, stiff and almost leathery. Surface blue-green and somewhat glossy above; paler with small dots and very short, fine (almost invisible), appressed hairs below. **Midvein** and secondary veins are depressed above; secondary veins at a 25–35° angle. **Margins** have widely-spaced, broad, nipple-tipped teeth. **Inflorescence** a terminal spike to 7" (18 cm) long, sometimes interrupted near the base but *very densely packed* near the tip. **Flowers** (late summer) 4–6 mm long, the corolla 2-lipped and blue-purple, the lower lip broad and 2-lobed. Sexual parts *protrude far*—by about the length of the corolla. The calyx is green with a *symmetrical* 5-lobed tip.

▲ Widely planted and often feral outside the native range.

HABITAT: Dry fields, prairies, meadows, forest borders, pine and oak barrens. Likes full sun on well-drained soil, especially sand. Native (but often planted and persisting outside its range). 🔥

FOOD USE: Gather **leaves** at any time to use for tea; steep in hot water. May be used fresh or dried. Excellent mixed with other teas. The tender tips can be used as a seasoning. **Conservation 2.**

COMMENTS: This herb is one of our best wild teas, with a strong, distinct, and pleasant flavor that is reminiscent of anise or fennel, but better than either (as a drink, at least). In some circles the tea is highly regarded as a cold remedy.

9 Horehound

Marrubium vulgare ◆ Lamiaceae (Mint family)

QUICK CHECK: Extremely woolly, dark gray-green, clumped mint with a mild scent and short, blunt, well-spaced, deeply ruffled leaves; flowers tightly clustered in leaf axils. **ID difficulty 1.**

DESCRIPTION: Perennial with clumped stems. **Stems** 14–30" (36–76 cm) tall, leaning to upright, 3–5 mm thick, squared, concave or channeled on all sides, densely coated with white-gray wool, especially near the base; unbranched or with short, minor, ascending branches. **LYDS** prominent. **Leaves** paired, well-spaced, to 1.2" (3 cm) long in full sun but larger in shade, the blades broadly ovate to nearly round, about as wide as long, *densely coated with wool* (especially below), blunt-tipped, curled, *ruffled by extremely depressed veins above*, which protrude greatly below. Margins have large, blunt teeth. There are several prominent secondary veins from the base. **Petioles** woolly, broad and flat or slightly channeled, the lower petioles to 60% of the blade length, the upper ones reduced to sessile. **Inflorescence** (summer) dense axillary clusters of 8–30 flowers in the upper half of branches and stems, with naked stem sections separating them; the clusters spaced more closely toward the top. Beneath each cluster is a pair of *drooping leaves*. **Calyx** has 7–10 recurved needle-like teeth that persist after bloom, forming *hooks that attach it to clothing and fur*; the walls are *pleated by prominent veins*, and the tube is hairy inside. **Corolla** tubular and whitish, tiny, with 2 strongly diverging lips that are nearly equal in length, the upper one rising and nearly straight with a split tip, the lower downcurved with 3 lobes.

▲ Much more common west.

HABITAT: Dry, usually open, moderately disturbed places. Old homesites, meadows, roadsides, fields, vacant lots, open woods, prairie dog towns. Introduced.

FOOD USE: The **leaves** are steeped for tea or boiled as a flavoring for candies. They can also be chewed for their flavor.

COMMENTS: This mint has a bitter flavor that can be addictive. It is soothing to the throat and has long been used to treat cold symptoms.

10 **Catnip**
Nepeta cataria ✦ *Lamiaceae* (Mint family)

QUICK CHECK: Aromatic mint with tightly clumped, tall stems and blunt-tipped, corrugated, woolly leaves that are silvery beneath. **ID difficulty 1.**

DESCRIPTION: Perennial herb from a woody base with a peculiar minty-musky smell. **Stems** clumped, to 40" (1 m) tall, squared with 2 or all sides usually concave or channeled, almost evenly covered in short, dense, fine, soft hairs, much branched in full sun. **Leaves** paired, 0.8–3" (2–8 cm) long, ovate or triangular with heart-shaped bases, blunt-pointed with nipple tips, moderately soft-hairy above, *densely woolly and silvery beneath*. **Midvein**, veins, and veinlets are *deeply depressed above* and protruding below. **Margins** have large, blunt to rounded, dot-tipped, *often overlapping* teeth. **Petioles** 10% of blade length, hairy, channeled. **Inflorescence** terminal clusters, at first densely packed, later elongating and spike-like (some flowers are sessile and others on short pedicels), often branched into panicles, the flowers in small whorls. **Flowers** (summer) 8–12 mm long, irregular, tubular, the calyx curvy with regular lobes, the corolla 2-lipped, the lower lip bent *strongly downward and toothed or scalloped*, whitish with pink-purple spots; the sexual parts not or scarcely extending past the lips.

CONFUSING PLANTS: Yellow giant hyssop *Agastache nepetoides* (not dangerous and probably also edible) looks very similar but tends to be taller and have a less clumping habit; the leaves and internodes are longer. It is not similarly aromatic.

HABITAT: Partial sun on rich, disturbed soil. Open forests, forest edges, vacant lots, fence lines, along building foundations, thickets. Introduced.

FOOD USE: Tender new **leaves** can be nibbled or used as a seasoning, if one likes the potent flavor. Leaves of any age can be used to make an aromatic tea.

COMMENTS: This is the plant so adored by cats; it has no such intoxicating effect on humans. Catnip is easy to find around most human habitations and the smell makes it hard to forget. Catnip must be pretty resilient; I often see it growing along railroad tracks where all other vegetation has been killed off by herbicides. Don't be tempted to collect it there. **AKA** catmint.

11 Shiso
Perilla frutescens ✦ *Lamiaceae* (Mint family)

QUICK CHECK: Odd-smelling mint with large, broad, leaves with purple midveins, coarsely-toothed margins, and prominent arching secondary veins. **ID difficulty 1.**

DESCRIPTION: Annual emerging in early spring. **Stem** erect, single, straight, 6"–6' (15–180 cm) tall, square with rounded corners and 4 grooves (like stinging nettle stalks), usually evenly and symmetrically branched, starting near the base in full sun. The lowest branches of robust plants reach nearly as high as the main stalk. Stems of mature plants have short hairs on the ridges; seedlings are hairy all around the stems and petioles. **Leaves** paired, 2–6" (5–15 cm) long, broadly ovate to nearly rounded or heart-shaped. The upper surface is bumpy, sometimes reddish-purple (especially in full sun), sparsely to moderately hairy, more so on margins and veins. **Midvein** depressed, *purple* even on green leaves. Secondary veins are prominent, depressed, and arch toward the tip; veinlets are also lightly depressed. **Margins** have large, broad, sharp, forward-pointed teeth. **Petioles** 15–30% of blade length, narrowly channeled. **Inflorescence** numerous terminal and axillary racemes up to 6" (15 cm) long, the flowers mostly absent on the side facing the main stem, evenly spaced on pedicels 3–4 mm long. **Flowers** (mid-summer to fall) tubular, 3–4 mm long, the calyx nearly regular and densely covered with long, erect, needle-like hairs. The corolla is light purple with 4 lobes of similar length but the upper one is slightly broader and split in two. Each flower has a small, broad bract beneath it. After flowering the calyx enlarges to 6–7 mm long with 2 lower and 3 upper lobes, all pointed and upturned, the mature calyx holding 4 almost spherical smooth seeds, their light surface with dark reticulations.

HABITAT: Moist, rich, disturbed soil in shade or sun; yards, parks, pastures, barnyards, disturbed woodlots and meadows. Introduced. **I**

FOOD USE: The **greens** can be collected from spring through late summer, but they are tenderest in spring and early summer before flowering. They are used as a flavoring in many Asian cuisines—finely chopped raw, cooked, fermented, or infused in vinegars and sauces. The **seeds** are oil-rich but have a strong flavor; they are ground into a nutritive seasoning or pressed for an edible oil.

COMMENTS: Shiso is a little-known edible weed that is widespread and often abundant. It has been cultivated for thousands of years in Asia and is grown and sold commercially in this country for Asian cuisine. The flavor is strong and distinct and quite unlike our other mints. **AKA** beefsteak plant, perilla.

12 **Mint** 🍶 ☕ 📖 IWE-224
genus *Mentha* ✦ *Lamiaceae* (Mint family)

QUICK CHECK: Aromatic mints with tiny, nearly regular flowers in leaf axils. **ID difficulty 1.**

DESCRIPTION: Perennials forming colonies by a rhizome network, the aerial parts minty-aromatic. **Stems** squared, the faces concave, branched or unbranched, erect. **Leaves** alternate, toothed, ovate to elliptic, 0.7–3" (18–80 mm) long, blunt-tipped when young but pointed at maturity, sparsely to densely hairy, sessile or with short petioles. **Midvein** and secondary veins are deeply depressed above; the veinlets are depressed but less so, giving the leaves a slightly corrugated look. **Inflorescence** dense clusters in multiple leaf axils of the upper stem—sometimes these are normal-sized leaves, other times they are reduced. **Flowers**

▲ Collective range of mints.

(summer) 2–6 mm long, the calyx almost symmetrical with 5 triangular lobes. **Corolla** tubular, almost twice as long as the calyx, 2–4 mm across when open, purplish, 4 lobed (rarely 5), nearly regular in appearance but the upper petal is usually slightly larger. Stamens and styles protrude. **Seeds** small and brown, 2–4 per capsule.

FOOD USE: To use fresh mint **greens** in salads, smoothies, or as a nibble, pick the new shoots and tips in spring to early summer. Leaves can be picked any time and used fresh or dried for tea.

COMMENTS: North America is home to both native and introduced species of mint, and the introduced populations are often cultivated hybrids. Peppermint is a hybrid between spearmint *M. spicata* and *M. aquatica*. Both peppermint and spearmint are widespread as escapes from cultivation. While it is fun to learn to identify the species, it is not necessary, as all members of the genus *Mentha* can be used similarly. However, the flavor varies; most people prefer the flavor of peppermint and spearmint over our native wild mint. Just the three most common mints are covered here.

Field mint ✦
Mentha arvensis

This is the native mint that is widespread across eastern North America, growing primarily on moist sites in full to partial sun. It is most common in wet meadows, swamps, and wetland margins. The stems and leaves are somewhat to very soft-hairy, and the flowers are in the axils of normal-sized leaves rather than reduced bracts in terminal spikes. The flavor of wild mint can be like a cross between spearmint and catnip, but the aroma varies among different populations of this species. If you separate the Old-World species from the American, ours is *M. canadensis*. **Conservation 1.**

(Continued on the next page.)

12 **Mint** (continued)

Spearmint ◆ *M. spicata* and **Peppermint** ◆ *M. x piperata*

These mints have the flower whorls in the axils of reduced upper leaves, the whorls taken together making a stout terminal spike. Their stems and leaves are hairless to faintly hairy (especially on veins below). The differences between these two are subtle, but normally peppermint stems are purple, while spearmint stems are green. Peppermint has darker purple flowers and short petioles 12–15% of blade length, and the teeth are sharper and more prominent. Spearmint flowers are pale purple and the leaves are sessile.

▲ Spearmint.

▲ Peppermint shoots.

13 Tall woodmint
Blephilia hirsuta + *Lamiaceae* (Mint family)

QUICK CHECK: Tall mint with lanceolate, hairy leaves with a few teeth; stacked, rounded, packed clusters of flowers in progressively closer leaf axils at the apex. **ID difficulty 1.**

DESCRIPTION: Perennial spreading by short rhizomes and layering, usually growing in clumps, often with reduced, soft but *evergreen overwintering leaves* on short stems forming a ground-hugging mat. **Stems** 20–74" (50–185 cm) tall, erect but weak, often leaning on other vegetation, simple or with occasional major branches, squared with a shallow trough on each side, *densely covered with long, erect to downcurved hairs*, the internodes 4–8" (10–20 cm) long. **Leaves** 2.5–4" (6–10 cm) long, lanceolate or ovate, acute at the base, pointed at the tip, the margins with a few scattered, small teeth. **Surface** densely erect-hairy above, less so below; *secondary veins are deeply depressed above.* **Inflorescence** 1–5 densely-packed whorls stacked on top of each other to form a terminal spike 0.8–3" (2–8 cm) long; the lowermost whorls are often separated by a small space, but the others are touching. Underneath each whorl of flowers are 2 reduced leaves and a dense whorl of overlapping, elliptic to ovate, often purplish bracts 7–9 mm long (shorter than the flowers), with long hairs on the margins. **Flowers** (summer) 8–12 mm long, the *calyx almost symmetrical.* **Corolla** white with purple spots, highly irregular, the lower lip 3-lobed and bent down; 2 stamens are held close to the upper lip and extend beyond it at maturity.

HABITAT: Rich forests with moist soil, especially high parts of floodplains and lower slopes, growing best in sunny openings or on the margins of such forests. Native.

FOOD USE: Young **greens** in spring as an herb; through the growing season the mature leaves can be used for **tea.** A flush of new growth is produced in autumn after the tops die, available until severe cold. **Conservation 2.**

COMMENTS: This tall, elegant, and fragile species has a strong, pleasant scent closer to *Mentha* than any other non-Mentha species. The name *Blephilia* is Greek for "eyelash," in reference to the long hairs on the bracts. **AKA** hairy woodmint. There is a close relative, *B. ciliata,* usually called "downy woodmint." These names are too similar to be functional, so the two species have been frequently confused, even in the professional literature, with the qualities of one often attributed to the other. *B. ciliata* is much smaller, grows in dry limestone woodlands, and has little minty scent.

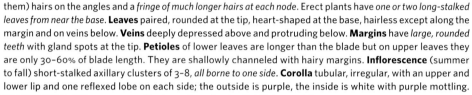

14 Creeping Charlie
Glechoma hederacea ✦ *Lamiaceae* (Mint family)

QUICK CHECK: Creeping plant with an odd musky smell forming mats over the ground; broad leaves have blunt teeth; purple flowers hang to one side of short erect stems. **ID difficulty 1.**

DESCRIPTION: Perennial spreading by rhizomes or rooting at stem nodes to form colonies. Rhizomes whitish, thinner than the erect stems. **Stems** may creep or stand erect up to 13" (33 cm); they are squared and hollow with very short (almost invisible, but you can feel them) hairs on the angles and a *fringe of much longer hairs at each node.* Erect plants have *one or two long-stalked leaves from near the base.* **Leaves** paired, rounded at the tip, heart-shaped at the base, hairless except along the margin and on veins below. **Veins** deeply depressed above and protruding below. **Margins** have *large, rounded teeth* with gland spots at the tip. **Petioles** of lower leaves are longer than the blade but on upper leaves they are only 30–60% of blade length. They are shallowly channeled with hairy margins. **Inflorescence** (summer to fall) short-stalked axillary clusters of 3–8, *all borne to one side.* **Corolla** tubular, irregular, with an upper and lower lip and one reflexed lobe on each side; the outside is purple, the inside is white with purple mottling. The lower lip extends slightly beyond the upper.

HABITAT: Lawns, forest edges, fields, brushy areas, from full sun to moderate shade. Prefers moist soil with moderate to high fertility. Introduced. **I**

FOOD USE: The **leaves** can be used as a flavoring in brewing beer or for tea.

COMMENTS: For millions of us, the smell of this plant when hit by a lawnmower is a familiar part of summer. **AKA** gill-over-the-ground, ground ivy, runaway-robin, jenny-run-up-the-hedge-and-around-back-of-the-duck-coop-then-slowly-through-the-orchard-to-the-rhubarb-and-back-in-just-a-month.

15 Horsemints
genus *Monarda* (in part) ✦ *Lamiaceae* (Mint family)

QUICK CHECK: Mints of dry, poor soil with leaves of varying size in opposing clusters; stacked whorls of spotted flowers with long divergent lips, above a whorl of showy bracts. **ID difficulty 1.**

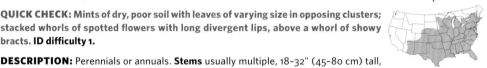

▲ Collective range.

DESCRIPTION: Perennials or annuals. **Stems** usually multiple, 18–32" (45–80 cm) tall, squared, with minute downcurved hairs, usually more at the nodes. **Leaves** usually *drooping and deeply folded* on mature plants, borne in pairs with an axillary cluster of 2 or more smaller leaves. This often takes the appearance of opposing *sets of 3*, with the middle leaf of each set much longer than the outer 2. **Blades** long-elliptic, pointed, tapered at both ends, with widely-spaced teeth, hairy on both sides. **Midvein** and secondary veins are depressed above and protruding below; secondary veins curve back toward the leaf tip. **Petioles** up to 30% of blade length (but upper leaves often sessile), ciliate on the margins and scarcely channeled. **Inflorescence** *multiple axillary whorls stacked along the upper stem,* sometimes widely separated, the associated leaves progressively decreasing in size. Underneath each whorl of flowers is a crowded, *overlapping whorl of many oval, entire, hairy-edged, sharp-tipped bracts* with multiple prominent veins from the base. These bracts are usually green on *M. pectinata*, but on our other species they are red to pink or whitish and *showier than the flowers.* **Flowers** (summer) 0.6–1.2" (15–30 mm) long with a tubular calyx separating into 5 nearly equal, narrow, pointed, hairy-edged lobes. **Corolla** tubular at first, the tubular portion about as long as the calyx; it diverges widely into two long, narrow, spotted lips. The upper lip arches; the lower is folded downward and 3-lobed at the tip. **Stamens** hidden beneath the upper lip.

HABITAT: Dry, poor, and typically sandy soil, usually in full sun; most common on roadsides, dry prairies, pine or oak barrens, and steep open slopes. Native.

FOOD USE: The **leaves** can be gathered at any time to use fresh or dried for tea. As a seasoning herb you want tender ones from spring or early summer. **Flowers** can be picked as a flavoring in late summer.

COMMENTS: These beautiful natives are a pleasant sight on summer roadsides, perfect to establish in a sandy front yard. There are 2 basic groups in the genus *Monarda*: those with single terminal flower clusters (#16, bergamots), and those with multiple stacked whorls below the terminal cluster (#15, horsemints). There are at least 4 species in the horsemint-monarda group; two of them are shown here.

Dotted horsemint *M. punctata* is a short-lived perennial with very showy whitish to pink bracts and yellowish flowers.

Lemon monarda *M. citriodora* is distinguished by having several small leaves of varying size, often asymmetrical, clustered in the leaf axils. The bracts are whitish to purple and the corolla ranges from white to red-purplish and is gland-dotted, hairy on the outside and in the throat. This species is only slightly more lemony than the others.

▲ (left) Dotted horsemint. (middle and right) Lemon monarda. ▲

16 Bergamot
genus *Monarda* (in part) ✦ *Lamiaceae* (Mint family)

QUICK CHECK: Aromatic mints with toothed leaves and dense, rounded, terminal clusters of tubular, purple to red flowers with long, thin, divergent lips. **ID difficulty 1.**

DESCRIPTION: Perennial herbs often growing in colonies from thin rhizomes, the form much taller than wide. **Stems** erect, 2–6' (60–180 cm) tall, unbranched or with ascending axillary branches, squared but the angles not sharp, hollow, soft-hairy, the sides flat and the internodes long. **Leaves** paired, 2–4" (5–10 cm) long, narrowly ovate to lanceolate, pointed, the margins entire or with scattered teeth, sometimes with a purplish halo when young. Surface hairy, more so below and along the midvein. (Continued on the next page.)

16 Bergamot (continued)

Midvein depressed above. Secondary veins 9–11 per side, 45° to the midvein, depressed above. Leaves sessile or on short, shallowly channeled petioles up to 25% of blade length. There is sometimes a tuft of hair below the petiole. Leaves are often covered with a white fungal infection later in the summer. **Inflorescence** (summer) a densely packed, convex terminal cluster 0.7–1.5" (18–38 mm) across (not stacked whorls), resembling a composite head; beneath it is a whorl of several elliptic to ovate, entire bracts, to 1.3" (33 mm) long. **Flowers** 0.8–1.6" (2–4 cm) long, narrow, whitish to pink, purple or bright scarlet. **Calyx** tubular, tipped with 5 narrow, pointed lobes almost equal in length. **Corolla** extends far beyond the calyx, a thin tube at the base gradually widening, then diverging at a broad angle into 2 *long and slender lips*, the upper one narrower and arching. The style is hidden beneath the downcurved edges of the upper lip; so are the stamens, but they protrude beyond it.

HABITAT: Well-drained soil in full to partial sun; occasionally in moister sites. Fields, roadsides, meadows, pastures, sparse woods, forest openings. All listed species are native, although some are planted outside of their native ranges. 🔥

FOOD USE: Gather **leaves** and dry them; they're best in early summer but can be used any time in teas, or dried and used as a seasoning similar to oregano. Tender growing **tops** in spring are best. **Flowers** can be used similarly; they're extremely potent. **Conservation 2.**

COMMENTS: This strongly and uniquely flavored mint is one of our most common. The flowers have the most potent minty-hot flavor that I have encountered in any North American plant. Although it is commonly claimed that bergamot is a flavoring in Earl Grey tea, this refers to a different and totally unrelated plant in the citrus family. There are several species in our region, and although the flavor of all varies slightly, they can be used similarly. A few common ones are pictured below. **AKA** bee-balm, Oswego tea.

Wild bergamot *M. fistulosa* is the most common species in our region, growing 2–4' (60–120 cm) tall and producing light purple flowers. It inhabits well-drained sunny fields and meadows. This species is highly variable and some taxonomists have divided it into several species.

Scarlet bee-balm *M. didyma* is our tallest species, and with its large scarlet flowers, probably our most striking. It is less aromatic than the others, and the milder flowers make a beautiful garnish. It is found in openings or sparse woodlands with rich, moist soil, especially in floodplains and valleys.

▲ (left) Scarlet bee balm. (middle and right) Wild bergamot. ▲

GROUP 32 BASAL LEAVES ABSENT, LEAVES PAIRED, STEMS SQUARE, NOT STRONGLY AROMATIC

This group contains several non-aromatic members of the mint family, as well as square-stemmed plants from several other families. The edible parts produced include many leafy greens and shoots as well as some tubers and rhizomes; one species produces edible seeds. Plants in group 32 have *decussate* leaves (the axis of each opposing pair is 90° to that of the adjacent pairs). Giant St. John's wort has stems that are very strongly squared when young but only faintly so when older, and so may key to group 33. Cup plant has basal leaves when young and is included in group 21, but since this is surprising based on its form, and the basal leaves disappear completely by flowering, it is included in this key as well.

TENTATIVE IDENTIFICATION KEY TO GROUP 32
The key is not your final answer!

Leaf simple.	
Leaf margins toothed, not bristled or lobed.	
or Leaves winged to the stem, the wings joined and enlarged to form a cup. Cup plant (p. 307).	
Leaves with distinct petioles.	
Leaves drooping, crowded, and overlapping above a conspicuously naked stem section.	1. Purple deadnettle
Leaves spreading to ascending, not crowded and overlapping, evenly spaced.	
Plants less than 20" tall at maturity, leaves blunt, teeth rounded.	3. Florida betony
or Plants more than 24" tall at maturity, leaves and teeth pointed.	
or Stem conspicuously enlarged below each node, flowers pink-purple and 2-lipped, all secondary veins pinnate, stinging hairs absent.	5. Hemp-nettle
Stem not enlarged below the node, flowers tiny and unshowy in drooping clusters, some major veins from the leaf base, stinging hairs present.	7. Stinging nettle
or Leaves mostly sessile or nearly sessile.	
Leaves drooping, crowded, and overlapping above a conspicuously naked stem section.	1. Purple deadnettle
Leaves not drooping, evenly spaced.	
Blade stiff-hairy with strongly depressed veinlets, flowers 2-lipped.	4. Woundwort
Blades hairless or soft hairy, veinlets scarcely depressed, flowers 4-lobed.	6. Bugleweed
or Leaf lobed, with large rounded teeth.	2. Henbit
or Leaf margins with tiny, bristle-tipped teeth.	8. Virginia meadow beauty
or Leaf entire.	
Stems erect and stiff, 3–6' (1–2 m) tall, more than 4 mm thick.	
Stems 4–7 mm thick, stem and leaves hairless, veins strongly offset by light color, flowers yellow.	9. Giant St. John's wort
or Stems 8–15 mm thick, stem and leaves at least faintly hairy, veins not strongly offset by light color, flowers purple.	10. Purple loosestrife
Stems creeping to weakly erect, to 30" (75 cm) long, 1–2 mm thick.	11. Stitchwort
Leaf compound.	
Leaflets ovate or lanceolate and unlobed; heads with white rays.	12. Romerillo
or Leaflets deeply lobed; heads with yellow rays, or no rays.	13. Spanish needles

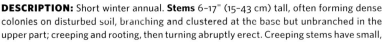

1 Purple deadnettle 2
Lamium purpureum + *Lamiaceae* (Mint family)

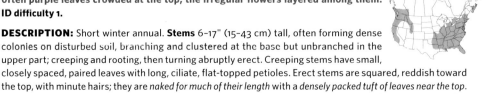

QUICK CHECK: Short, erect stems naked most of their length with a tuft of drooping, often purple leaves crowded at the top, the irregular flowers layered among them. **ID difficulty 1.**

DESCRIPTION: Short winter annual. **Stems** 6–17" (15–43 cm) tall, often forming dense colonies on disturbed soil, branching and clustered at the base but unbranched in the upper part; creeping and rooting, then turning abruptly erect. Creeping stems have small, closely spaced, paired leaves with long, ciliate, flat-topped petioles. Erect stems are squared, reddish toward the top, with minute hairs; they are *naked for much of their length* with a *densely packed tuft of leaves near the top.* **Leaves** (of erect stems) paired, up to 1.4" (36 mm) long, *largest at the bottom of the tuft and progressively smaller upward*, heart-shaped to ovate or triangular, crowded (especially at the beginning of flowering) and overlapping at the stem apex, drooping, the topmost often purplish. Surfaces densely covered with soft, nearly appressed hairs. **Midvein** and veins are *deeply depressed*, giving a highly corrugated texture. **Margins** have large, blunt to rounded teeth. **Petioles** channeled, hairy, on flowering stems decreasing upward from 25% to 5% of the blade length. **Winter growth** has decumbent stems, longer petioles, and green leaves. **Inflorescence** whorls of several from crowded leaf axils. **Flowers** (mostly late winter and early spring, but occasionally other times) tubular and irregular, 0.4–0.7" (10–18 mm) long. **Calyx** bristly, the lobes longer than the tube. **Corolla** about 3 times the calyx length, the upper lip hood-like and hairy, the lower lip *pinched together in the middle*, beyond which it *angles sharply downward* and splits into two lobes, each with a purple spot in the middle.

HABITAT: Moist, fertile soil in sunlit to partially shaded disturbed ground such as lawns, yards, parks, trailsides, orchards. Introduced.

FOOD USE: Gather the tender stems and **greens** by plucking or cutting in early spring—preferably before any flowers open. Their flavor is mild and the texture pleasant—good but not exceptional as a nibble, in salad, or as a potherb.

COMMENTS: Abundant in many urban and rural areas, these pretty little weeds are easy-to-locate springtime edibles for the backyard forager. Interestingly, the plant produces some self-pollinating flowers with smaller corollas that do not open.

2 Henbit 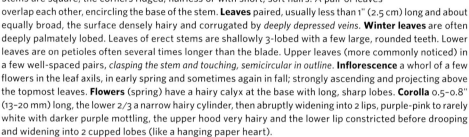 1
Lamium amplexicaule • Lamiaceae (Mint family)

QUICK CHECK: Short, unbranched mint with well separated pairs of broad, scalloped, clasping, ruffled leaves; flowers projecting above the upper leaves. **ID difficulty 2.**

DESCRIPTION: Short winter annual. **Stems** prostrate, twisted, rooting, and much-branched in winter, forming mats over the soil. In early spring these mats give rise to **erect stems** 4–12" (10–30 cm) tall which are rarely branched and have very long internodes near the base. Stems are square, the corners ridged, hairless or with short, soft hairs. A pair of leaves overlap each other, encircling the base of the stem. **Leaves** paired, usually less than 1" (2.5 cm) long and about equally broad, the surface densely hairy and corrugated by *deeply depressed veins*. **Winter leaves** are often deeply palmately lobed. Leaves of erect stems are shallowly 3-lobed with a few large, rounded teeth. Lower leaves are on petioles often several times longer than the blade. Upper leaves (more commonly noticed) in a few well-spaced pairs, *clasping the stem and touching, semicircular in outline.* **Inflorescence** a whorl of a few flowers in the leaf axils, in early spring and sometimes again in fall; strongly ascending and projecting above the topmost leaves. **Flowers** (spring) have a hairy calyx at the base with long, sharp lobes. **Corolla** 0.5–0.8" (13–20 mm) long, the lower 2/3 a narrow hairy cylinder, then abruptly widening into 2 lips, purple-pink to rarely white with darker purple mottling, the upper hood very hairy and the lower lip constricted before drooping and widening into 2 cupped lobes (like a hanging paper heart).

CONFUSING PLANTS: Creeping charlie (p. 528) is aromatic and has leaves that are bluntly toothed but not lobed; all of its leaves have petioles, and its flowers are not held erect.

HABITAT: Moist, rich soil in sun or light shade: lawns, parks, forest borders. Introduced.

FOOD USE: Collect tender young **leaves** and upper stems in early to mid spring, and use as a potherb or salad green.

COMMENTS: The flavor is not bitter or astringent; it's peculiar, with a faint aroma. Don't let that description trick you into thinking it's particularly exciting.

▲ Henbit blooming.

3 Florida betony ⊚ 3 🖎 2
Stachys floridana ✦ *Lamiaceae* (Mint family)

QUICK CHECK: Short, erect, colony-forming mint with lanceolate, blunt, round-toothed leaves; 2-lipped light pink flowers. **ID difficulty 2.**

DESCRIPTION: Perennial spreading by rhizomes to form colonies. **Rhizomes** thin and white, rooting at spaced nodes, producing blunt white **tubers** 0.7–1.2" (18–30 mm) long and 6–14 mm thick, *smooth but with a few deep transverse constrictions.* **Stems** often decumbent in winter, erect in spring, 8–20" (20–50 cm) tall and 2–4 mm thick, square, hollow, thin-walled, usually unbranched, the surface purplish or green, sparsely to moderately hairy—more so on the angles. **Leaves** paired, narrowly ovate to lanceolate with a blunt tip, truncate to heart-shaped at the base, 0.7–2.5" (18–65 mm) long, sparsely to moderately short-hairy on both sides. **Margins** often purple with broad, blunt, nipple-tipped teeth. **Midvein**, veins, and veinlets are depressed; secondary veins are few and arching. **Petioles** narrow, straight, hairy, shallowly channeled, uniform in width, at a nearly right angle to the stem, 60–90% of blade length on lower leaves, shortening greatly near the top. **Inflorescence** a terminal spike, the flowers in whorls of 4–9 in the axils of reduced, crowded leaf pairs. **Flowers** (mid to late spring) 9–11 mm long. **Corolla** 2-lipped, pale pink to nearly white with darker pink mottling. The upper lip is hood-like. The lower lip is 3-lobed with 3 broken stripes, the middle lobe much larger and rounded. **Stamens** 4–5, ascending under the upper lip but not surpassing it. **Calyx** bell-like, green, hairy, about 40% as long as the corolla, with 5 pointed lobes nearly equal in size. **Seeds** dark brown.

HABITAT: Disturbed sandy soil with ample sun: forest edges, disturbed open woods, roadsides, lawns, fields. Native.

FOOD USE: Collect **tubers** any time (but they are lowest in quality at peak green growth, when they are easiest to find). They are delicious raw or cooked and are reported to make good pickles. Young **shoots/greens**, collected in spring from plants before flowering, can be eaten raw or cooked. Lawn plants usually have lame little tubers. **Conservation 2/1.**

COMMENTS: This is a close relative of a cultivated vegetable, *Stachys affinis*, called "crosne" or "Chinese artichoke," which is probably not popular here because English speakers hate trying to pronounce its French name. Crosnes have similar tubers that are not quite as good as Florida betony, and can occasionally be found at high prices in grocery stores. The *haute*st *cuisine* is free and fun.

4 Woundwort 🦷3 🌡 2
Stachys palustris (species complex) ✦
Lamiaceae (Mint family)

QUICK CHECK: Hairy stem with sessile, hairy, blunt-toothed leaves with deeply depressed veins; pink flowers in spaced whorls subtended by a pair of leaves. **ID difficulty 2.**

DESCRIPTION: Perennial herb spreading by rhizome to form loose colonies. **Rhizomes** long and narrow with thinner and thicker sections; the enlarged portion is 3–9 mm thick (slightly thicker than the lower stems), unbranched, whitish, brittle, mostly smooth but with occasional roots and faintly constricted rings that are associated with tiny, triangular, scale-like leaves. **Stems** 14–40" (36–100 cm) tall and 3–7 mm thick, single, erect, squared, hollow with thin walls, the surface often purplish when young or near the base, densely hairy, especially on the angles, with erect, straight, stiff hairs. Plants are usually unbranched but sometimes much-branched from near the base on open, sunny shores. **Shoots** have narrower, blunt-pointed, nearly appressed leaves with tapered bases and fewer teeth. **Leaves** paired, mostly sessile but sometimes with broadly channeled petioles to 25% of blade length, widely-spaced, lanceolate to narrowly oblong, 1.5–3.5" (4–9 cm) long, the tip pointed and the base broad. The upper surface is uniformly and densely covered with stiff hairs. **Midvein**, veins, and veinlets are *strongly depressed above and protruding below*, making a highly corrugated surface. **Margins** have broad, blunt, sometimes downturned teeth, each with a small dark spot on the tip. **Inflorescence** spikes with whorls of 4–6 on the upper stem, separated by small gaps, evenly spaced at maturity, each whorl subtended by a pair of reduced leaves. **Flowers** (mid summer) 8–13 mm long, the corolla hairy, pink and white (whiter inside) mottled with darker purple spots, with two lips. The lower lip is longer and much broader with 3 lobes at the end; the upper lip is 2-lobed. **Calyx** of 4 nearly regular lobes, turning purple and then brown after flowering, holding 4 ovate black seeds about 1.5 mm long.

CONFUSING PLANTS: American germander *Teucrium canadense* is a mint of dry savannahs with dense, soft hairs on its surfaces, giving them a grayish look. The spike is uninterrupted, and the flowers lack an upper lip.

HABITAT: Moist open or semi-open sites. Floodplain forests, wet meadows, lake and pond edges, ditches. Native.

FOOD USE: Dig **rhizomes** from fall through spring; they are brittle and break easily. They are delicious raw or cooked. Tender **shoots** can also be eaten in spring, raw or cooked. **Conservation 3/2.**

COMMENTS: Woundwort is widespread and common and produces two good edible parts. Formerly

considered a single species, this group (species complex) shows multiple chromosome counts and has been divided by taxonomists into several similar species. Size and hairiness vary between populations, but the overall form of the group is recognizable. **AKA** hedge-nettle. Hyssop hedge-nettle *S. hyssopifolia* is generally too small to warrant collection; it grows in wet, sandy, acidic soil.

5 Hemp-nettle 🌿 3 🍃 1
Galeopsis tetrahit ◆ *Lamiaceae* (Mint family)

QUICK CHECK: Very stiff-hairy, non-aromatic mint with swellings below the nodes, toothed leaves, and spiny bracts when fruiting. **ID difficulty 2.**

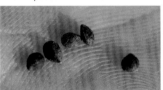

DESCRIPTION: Weedy annual. Many parts of the plant have *hairs of 2 distinct kinds*: long, stiff, and needle-like, and gland-tipped hairs about half as long. **Stems** 20-40" (50-100 cm) tall and 3-8 mm thick, erect, simple or branchy, taller than wide, densely covered in erect hairs, green, hollow, with a distinct *swelling below each node.* **Leaves** ovate, 1.5-4" (4-10 cm) long, the tips long-pointed but not particularly sharp, angled at the base, the surfaces densely to sparsely covered with leaning hair. **Midvein** deeply depressed above. Secondary veins 7-10 per side (a large number for the mint family), deeply depressed above, running nearly straight and unbroken to a notch between teeth; veinlets are depressed more lightly. **Margins** have broad, blunt teeth. **Petioles** deeply channeled, ranging from 60% of blade length on lower leaves to 20% on the upper stem. **Inflorescence** whorls of several sessile flowers in the axils of often reduced upper leaves. **Flowers** (mid summer) 8-11 mm long, the calyx with 5 long, *sharp lobes that stiffen into prickly spines after flowering.* **Corolla** much longer than the calyx, whitish to pink with darker pink or purple lines, the tip with a hairy hood covering the sexual parts and a 3-lobed lower lip. **Capsule** contains 4 dark brown seeds 2-3 mm long, each shaped somewhat like a plum pit.

CONFUSING PLANTS: Often mistaken for stinging nettle before flowering, but *Galeopsis* stems have sharper corners and the sides lack deep grooves, plus the hairs do not sting.

HABITAT: Disturbed soil, especially where moist, in full sun to moderate shade. Gardens, barnyards, roadsides. Introduced.

FOOD USE: Gather **seeds** in late summer as they darken and become loose in their capsules. Lean the plants over a container and strike or shake them with a gloved hand. Gather from still-green plants with *green* bracts—brown ones have already dropped their good seed. Look for *dark* seeds; light brown ones are empty. Sift out insects and trash, then use the seeds in baking or hot cereal. The young **greens** in spring have a mild flavor reminiscent of purple dead-nettle.

▼ *Galeopsis tetrahit* seeds in hand.

COMMENTS: This plant is not a nettle, nor a hemp. Its greens have often been eaten by confused foragers and are apparently safe but not particularly good. The seeds of hemp-nettle have been found in ancient European archaeological sites where they were apparently stored in large quantities as food. They are oily and have a delicious, nutty taste—in both form and flavor reminiscent of hemp seed. The similarity of the seeds appears to be the most likely explanation for the name, and hints at more widespread use in the past. There are some dubious reports of the toxicity of these seeds.

6 Bugleweed 🌿 2 📖 NG-393
genus *Lycopus* (in part) ✦ *Lamiaceae* (Mint family)

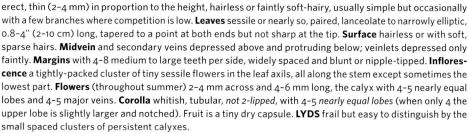

QUICK CHECK: Non-aromatic mints with coarsely toothed leaves and small clusters of tiny, nearly regular flowers in the leaf axils. **ID difficulty 3.**

DESCRIPTION: Perennial herbs without a strong scent, spreading by short rhizomes. **Tubers** 0.5-3" (13-80 mm) long, narrow, tapered at both ends, usually curved, some kinds regularly constricted, the surface otherwise mostly smooth and whitish or greenish, with a bud or compact shoot at the tip. **Stems** single to few, 10-40" (25-100 cm) tall, squared, erect, thin (2-4 mm) in proportion to the height, hairless or faintly soft-hairy, usually simple but occasionally with a few branches where competition is low. **Leaves** sessile or nearly so, paired, lanceolate to narrowly elliptic, 0.8-4" (2-10 cm) long, tapered to a point at both ends but not sharp at the tip. **Surface** hairless or with soft, sparse hairs. **Midvein** and secondary veins depressed above and protruding below; veinlets depressed only faintly. **Margins** with 4-8 medium to large teeth per side, widely spaced and blunt or nipple-tipped. **Inflorescence** a tightly-packed cluster of tiny sessile flowers in the leaf axils, all along the stem except sometimes the lowest part. **Flowers** (throughout summer) 2-4 mm across and 4-6 mm long, the calyx with 4-5 nearly equal lobes and 4-5 major veins. **Corolla** whitish, tubular, *not 2-lipped*, with 4-5 *nearly equal lobes* (when only 4 the upper lobe is slightly larger and notched). Fruit is a tiny dry capsule. **LYDS** frail but easy to distinguish by the small spaced clusters of persistent calyxes.

CONFUSING SPECIES: Not all members of this genus have tubers. *Lycopus americanus* is a very common species without tubers; it can be told apart by the elongated lobe-teeth on its leaves.

WARNING! Bugleweed often grows beside **water hemlock** (see p. 668 and p. 13), which is *deadly*. The plants do not look similar at all, except possibly for the small, single roots of water hemlock seedlings. Water hemlock roots have faint yellow lines inside plus a stronger scent; bugleweed tubers lack yellow lines inside and have a smoother and glossier surface.

a smoother and glossier surface.

HABITAT: Wet soil or shallow water, usually in moderate shade. Lakeshores, marshes, stream edges, springs, fens, ponds (often on mossy or mucky logs or stones). Native.

FOOD USE: Tubers are usually very close to the surface and close to the parent plant; you can often get them out easily with your fingers. Gather them from fall through early spring. They can be eaten raw or cooked. **Conservation 3.**

(Continued on the next page.)

◄▲ **Northern bugleweed** *L. uniflorus* is our most common species, found in cool, shady wetlands; it is small with small tubers.

537

6 Bugleweed (continued)

COMMENTS: Bugleweeds are mundane in appearance but the group is easily recognized. Almost any wetland in our region is likely to have a species present, and the tubers are easily incorporated into cooking. The biggest drawback is their small size. I have not eaten all of the species of bugleweed in our region, but I have eaten all of the common ones pictured here.

◀ **Western bugleweed** *L. asper* is a smaller species found in wetlands from the Great Plains westward. The stems are densely hairy, the leaves more closely spaced and ascending, and the tubers small.

◀▲ (left and above middle and right) **Taper-leaf bugleweed** *L. rubellus* is a taller species with widely spaced leaves and larger tubers, often found in shallow, rocky streams.

7 Stinging nettle 🖋 3 ☕ 📖 FH-170
Urtica dioica ✦ *Urticaceae* (Nettle family)

QUICK CHECK: Tall, erect, mostly unbranched herb with lanceolate, paired leaves, stinging hairs, tiny unshowy flowers, and four grooves in its stem. **ID difficulty 2.**

DESCRIPTION: Perennial herb forming colonies by thin, pale rhizomes. Above-ground parts are armed with stinging, needle-like hairs—more so in full sun or on richer soil. The plant has a musky odor, especially when young. **Stems** not clumped, erect, 3–10' (1–3 m) tall, *with blunt corners and 4 deep, narrow grooves*, mostly unbranched unless the plants are cut or toppled. (Branches are minor if present, sometimes producing greatly reduced leaves.) **Leaves** numerous, paired, evenly-spaced, nearly uniform in size, 3–6" (8–15 cm) long, broadly ovate to lanceolate, dark green and rough, the tips long-pointed to blunt. (The first leaves of shoots are broader and blunter than older leaves.)

Both surfaces have erect, *needle-like stinging hairs*, but these are more prominent on major veins and are smaller and sparser above. **Midvein** deeply depressed above and protruding below. There are 2–6 major secondary veins from the base, plus a few more arising distally on the midvein, also deeply depressed, giving a pleated appearance. Veinlets are depressed but less so. **Margins** have large, sharp teeth, often double-toothed. **Petioles** 40–80% of the blade length, grooved on top. **Stipules** narrow and tapered, 1 cm, straight-edged, minutely wavy. **Flowers** tiny, greenish, inconspicuous, clustered along short stems hanging from leaf axils from early to late summer.

CONFUSING PLANTS: Wood nettle (p. 609) has broader, alternate leaves; false nettle (p. 561) has no stinging hairs. Mint family members such as woundwort (p. 535) and hemp-nettle (p. 536) have sharp-cornered stems and pinnate secondary veins; they lack stingers and have larger, tubular flowers.

HABITAT: Rich, moist soil with high nitrogen in full to partial sun, especially where occasional disturbances occur. Most commonly in floodplains, ditches, barnyards, field edges, moist meadows, openings or trails in rich hardwood forests, and along waterways. Native.

FOOD USE: Gather tender **leafy tops** in spring, using gloves if desired to prevent getting stung. Briefly boiling or steaming destroys the capacity to sting. Use the cooked greens as you would spinach. The cooking water makes an excellent **tea** (or if salted, broth). Older leaves become tough but remain suitable for tea or broth. The young leaves are easy to dry for future use. A new flush of growth usually appears in autumn, but tends to be of lesser quality than the spring growth. **Conservation 2.**

COMMENTS: Common, widespread, and well-liked, this plant is often erroneously reported as not native. Nettle greens are extremely nutritious and high in protein. Because patches are highly productive, stinging nettles are difficult to overharvest. This incredibly useful plant also produces a strong fiber that has been employed for cordage and textiles for thousands of years. (Continued on the next page.)

7 Stinging nettle (continued)

Taxonomists have long debated whether they should split this plant into multiple species (in which case you will find our native stinging nettle designated *U. gracilis*) or lump all regional populations together under the name *U. dioica*. In any case, all members of this "species complex" are similarly edible. The oft-repeated warning about older leaves becoming unsafe for tea should be ignored.

Related edibles:

Ball-head nettle ✦ *Urtica chamaedryoides*

This is a native annual of disturbed, rich sites in forests or barnyards of the South, attaining heights of up to 2' (60 cm) on flimsy stems often supported by surrounding vegetation. It often has multiple stems or branches from the base, and the leaves are broadly ovate to nearly triangular. The flower clusters are nearly spherical. **AKA** heart-leaf nettle, weak nettle, dwarf nettle. The greens can be used like those of stinging nettle, but the growth is never as tender, rapid, or voluminous.

Dog nettle ✦ *Urtica urens*

An annual introduced from Europe, this plant is found in moist, disturbed, shaded soil. It is spottily distributed, mostly in the southern states. It has broad, closely-spaced leaves and rarely exceeds 20" (50 cm) in height, but is otherwise very similar to stinging nettle and can be used similarly. However, since it is an annual, the tender portion is smaller.

8 Virginia meadow beauty ⑭ 2 ⚕ 2
Rhexia virginica ✦ family *Melastomataceae*

QUICK CHECK: Paired, sessile leaves with 3 main veins and tiny teeth; stems squared with winged angles. **ID difficulty 1.**

DESCRIPTION: Perennial herb spreading by rhizome. **Tubers** tooth-like, tapering to a point at both ends, 0.6–1.0" (15–25 mm) long, firm and crisp, with a thin black skin and light grayish flesh. **Stems** erect, or creeping and rooting at the nodes before turning erect, sometimes with multiple branches from the base, delicate, to 30" (75 cm) tall and 3 mm thick, scarcely tapered, simple or with a few branches, *squared and winged on the angles*, the wings with long, gland-tipped hairs. Stems become rough with age. **Leaves** sessile, paired, 0.8–2.5" (2–6 cm) long, ovate to lanceolate, pointed at the tip, rounded at the base, surfaces *rough and bristly* with scattered long hairs. **Veins** mostly obscure, but there is *one prominent vein on each side of the midvein*, all three strongly depressed above and protruding below; the outer veins arise at the base and *arch back toward the midvein* to almost meet near the leaf tip. A faint vein is sometimes visible just inside the margin. **Margins** have widely spaced *tiny teeth with bristle-tips*. **Inflorescence** a terminal umbel-like or bifurcating cluster with a few to several flowers, the junctures with reduced leaves. **Flowers** (all summer) with a tubular green calyx 0.6–0.8" (15–20 mm) long, bulged at the base and flared into 4 triangular lobes at the tip. **Corolla** spreads 1–2" (2.5–5 cm) wide with 4 broad, very thin, pink to purple petals. The flowers are turned to the side and the *sexual parts, especially the long style, droop over the lower petal*. The yellow *anthers are long and banana-shaped or hooked, attached near the end* rather than the middle. **Fruit** is a persistent *vase-shaped capsule*.

HABITAT: Margins of moderately acidic wetlands on sand: ditches, ponds, wet meadows, and low spots in sandy woods. Full sun to moderate shade. Usually not in sphagnum bogs. Native.

FOOD USE: Tubers are crisp and slightly tangy, but tiny and hard to gather in quantity. Collect tender young **leaves** and growing tips in spring or early summer, before they get too tough and raspy. They have a tangy flavor and are best raw as a salad or nibble. **Conservation 3/2.**

COMMENTS: Occasionally common, this dainty herb is a pleasant nibble and rarely more—it does not often warrant collection in any volume. Other members of this genus are reported or presumed to be edible but I have not tried them.

9 Giant St. John's wort  2
Hypericum ascryon ✦ family *Hypericaceae*

QUICK CHECK: Tall, clumped, erect stems with thin, blunt, entire leaves; large, yellow, 5-petaled flowers. **ID difficulty 2.**

DESCRIPTION: Perennial herb from rhizomes. **Stems** clumped, 3-6' (1-2 m) tall and 4-7 mm thick, erect, straight, smooth, hairless, *somewhat squared*, branching but not near the base, the branches strongly ascending, the form always much taller than wide. **Shoots** purple-tinted with faint bloom, *definitely squared*, with overlapping, ascending leaves. **Leaves** paired, ovate to lanceolate, clasping, entire, very thin and soft, smooth, completely hairless, 2-4" (5-10 cm) long; the tips are tapered to a point, not acuminate. **Midvein** slightly depressed above and protruding below. There are usually 3 secondary veins per side, diverging at 45° to the midvein; these and veinlets are nearly flat above. All of the *veins stand out from light color.* **Inflorescence** a forking cluster of several flowers, only a few blooming at once. **Flowers** (mid summer) about 2" (5 cm) across, with 5 bright yellow petals at least twice as long as wide, above a calyx of 5 triangular sepals that partly overlap at the base. The flowers have 5 *styles and several dozen stamens.* As they age, *the petals roll up to one side.* **Fruit** is a *pyramidal or conical capsule* 0.6-1" (15-25 mm) long, held erect, green at first but eventually turning brown and woody, longer than wide, holding numerous tiny seeds, splitting open into 5 lobes at maturity. **LYDS** prominent, stiff and hard with reddish-brown papery bark.

HABITAT: Rich soil, moist but not swampy, in full to partial sun. Floodplains, beaver meadows, tallgrass prairies, oak savannahs, old fields and pastures, ditches, brushy areas, hardwood forest clearings. Native. 🔥

FOOD USE: Tender **shoots**, which appear in mid spring, can be eaten raw or cooked. I strip off the leaves and eat only the stems, because they taste much better. **Conservation 2.**

COMMENTS: This circumpolar species has the unique piney flavor characteristic of other St. John's worts, but milder. Although traditionally used as food in Asia, it probably contains some hypericin, which causes photosensitivity in some people; it may also be mildly psychoactive. Eat in moderation. Although widespread, this beautiful plant is often sparse—but colonies respond well to tending and seeding. **AKA** *Hypericum pyramidatum.*

10 Purple loosestrife 1 1
Lythrum salicaria ◆ *Lythraceae* (Loosestrife family)

QUICK CHECK: Tall, clumped, square-stemmed wetland plant with paired, sessile, entire leaves and showy spikes of purple flowers. **ID difficulty 2.**

DESCRIPTION: Perennial from a woody crown, spreading only short distances by root suckers. **Stems** clumped, to 6' (2 m) tall and 0.6" (15 mm) thick, straight, erect, squared with a tiny wing on the angles, hairless or with sparse, soft hairs, solid. The top half often has many strongly ascending branches, especially where the plants are not crowded, but the form remains taller than wide. **LYDS** prominent, stiff, light brownish-gray, often curving. **Leaves** sessile, usually paired but occasionally in whorls of 3, 1.3–4.5" (3.3–11 cm) long, ascending, lanceolate, soft-hairy to hairless, the bases rounded to heart-shaped, tapered to a sharp tip, the margins entire. **Midvein** and secondary veins are lightly depressed above. Leaves get progressively smaller toward the top. **Inflorescence** interrupted terminal spikes to 18" (46 cm) long, the flowers in small clumps in the axils of reduced leaves, those at the bottom of the spike blooming first. Lower inflorescence leaves are paired; upper ones are alternate. **Flowers** (July–September) 0.6–0.8" (15–20 mm) across with a green, hairy, tubular or bell-like calyx with 4–8 short, pointed, triangular lobes. There are 8–16 stamens and a single pistil. **Petals** 4–8 (usually 5–6), purple with a prominent darker vein in the center, wrinkled or ruffled, narrowed at the base and broad at the tip, more than twice as long as wide, spreading, not touching each other. **Fruit** a capsule 6 mm long with 2 chambers containing numerous tiny seeds.

HABITAT: Wetlands in full sun. Marshes, lake and pond margins, ditches, rocky riverbanks. Occasionally upland on disturbed soil. Introduced. **I**

FOOD USE: Young **shoots** and attached **leaves** can be eaten cooked as a potherb. The **flowers** can also be eaten as a garnish or used to impart color to infusions and confections.

COMMENTS: These greens are not all that good, but they have been recorded as a wild vegetable in Europe for a long time. Purple loosestrife is absolutely striking when it blooms in late summer and was once widely planted as an ornamental. Unfortunately it reproduces rapidly and is highly invasive; it has taken over vast wetland areas to the near exclusion of other plants. There have been intensive efforts to eradicate the plant from these habitats, including hand-pulling, chemical warfare, and the introduction of a beetle that feeds on it. Nevertheless it remains abundant in many areas.

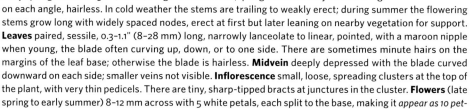

11 Stitchwort 🖋 3 📖 IWE-90
Stellaria graminea, S. longifolia ◆
Caryophyllaceae (Pink family)

QUICK CHECK: Mat-forming plant with sharply angled stems; narrow leaves extremely depressed in the center with downcurved margins; flowering stems tall and thread-like. **ID difficulty 1.**

DESCRIPTION: Perennial with a creeping, vegetative growth phase and an erect, flowering phase. The creeping phase forms dense mats with closely-spaced nodes in fall and early spring. **Stems** to 32" (80 cm) long and 1 mm thick, 4-angled with a very narrow wing on each angle, hairless. In cold weather the stems are trailing to weakly erect; during summer the flowering stems grow long with widely spaced nodes, erect at first but later leaning on nearby vegetation for support. **Leaves** paired, sessile, 0.3–1.1" (8–28 mm) long, narrowly lanceolate to linear, pointed, with a maroon nipple when young, the blade often curving up, down, or to one side. There are sometimes minute hairs on the margins of the leaf base; otherwise the blade is hairless. **Midvein** deeply depressed with the blade curved downward on each side; smaller veins not visible. **Inflorescence** small, loose, spreading clusters at the top of the plant, with very thin pedicels. There are tiny, sharp-tipped bracts at junctures in the cluster. **Flowers** (late spring to early summer) 8–12 mm across with 5 white petals, each split to the base, making it *appear as 10 petals at a glance.* The sharp-tipped green sepals have prominent ridges and are about as long as the petals.

HABITAT: Moist soil in full sun to partial shade. Lawns, fields, meadows, pastures, roadsides, shores, stream banks. *S. longifolia* is considered native; *S. graminea* might be native or introduced. **Conservation 1.**

FOOD USE: When spring mats first start to turn upright, grab small clumps and cut the tender **leafy tips** with scissors. They make a tasty nibble or salad ingredient. Older stems are very tough.

COMMENTS: Little known despite being incredibly common, this unobtrusive chickweed is excellent. However, it is small and quickly becomes tough by flowering. The listed species are nearly identical, and there are several additional native ones. **AKA** starwort.

12 Romerillo 🪶 2 ⚱
Bidens alba ✦ *Asteraceae* (Composite family)

QUICK CHECK: Low plant with wide-spreading branches; leaves mostly compound with 3–5 leaflets, flowers composite with a yellow center and white rays; seeds sticktight needles. **ID difficulty 1.**

DESCRIPTION: Annual, often spreading low and wide before standing erect, occasionally to 4' (1.2 m) tall when leaning on other vegetation, but usually much shorter, sometimes flowering at 4" (10 cm). **Stems** tough and stiff, to 6 mm thick, squarish or strongly angled, *deeply grooved above the petioles* (especially on young plants), convex on the non-petiole stem faces, solid with a pinhole hollow, the surface green when young, developing purple lines with age, bearing soft hair mostly on the angles. **Branches** profuse, usually widely angled near the base but less so above, with long internodes on upper branches. **Leaves** paired, the first ones simple but later leaves compound with 3 or 5 leaflets. **Petiole** 30–60% of blade length, much shorter on upper branches, deeply wing-channeled with hairs along the margins. **Leaflets** (especially terminal) may be deeply lobed; otherwise they are ovate to lanceolate with pointed tips. They are sessile, semi-sessile, or with a narrow, decurrent base. Blades are flat and thin with erect, soft, fine hairs on both sides, especially the veins. **Midvein** green, raised in a gentle valley above, protruding below; secondary veins several, broadly angled, flat to faintly raised above and slightly protruding below. **Margins** have moderately broad, sharp teeth with claw tips. **Inflorescence** dichotomously or ternately branched loose clusters, the branches long and straight, with simple leaves at the junctures. **Heads** 0.7–1.4" (18–35 mm) across, each with a ring of ovate bracts with maroon tips behind it. **Rays** usually 5–7, white with broad tips and maroon veins visible on the back. The rays are not symmetrically arranged and *it often appears as if one is missing*. **Disk** yellow with 2–3 dozen tiny florets. **Fruits** black and needle-like, 1 cm long, with 3–4 mm barbed prongs at the tip.

HABITAT: Disturbed soil in full to partial sunlight. Roadsides, urban lots, lawns, shores, sidewalks. Native.

FOOD USE: Tender young **leaves** have a peculiar but not unpleasant flavor, rather strong, and can be eaten raw or cooked. The **flowerheads** have a strong marigold-like flavor and are an excellent seasoning. **Conservation 1.**

COMMENTS: Like its close relative listed next, this is a common tropical weed across the world and is widely eaten as a potherb. It is available almost year-round in warmer locations near the Gulf Coast, and everyone in such locations has easy access to it. **AKA** beggar's ticks, Spanish needles, butterfly needles, *Bidens pilosa*.

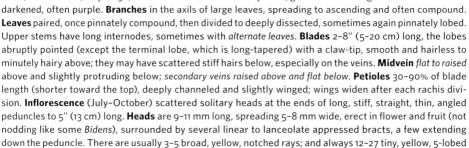

13 Spanish needles 2
Bidens bipinnata ◆ *Asteraceae* (Composite family)

QUICK CHECK: Square-stemmed erect herb with paired leaves that are twice pinnately divided; yellow flowerheads produce dark, 4-pronged, needle-like seeds. **ID difficulty 1.**

DESCRIPTION: Warm-weather annual, 1-5' (30-150 cm) tall; spreading and bushy at maturity in full sun, tall and lanky in competition. **Stem** square with finely grooved or ridged sides, to 1 cm thick, *very tough*, hairless or with scattered tiny hairs, green with the ridges darkened, often purple. **Branches** in the axils of large leaves, spreading to ascending and often compound. **Leaves** paired, once pinnately compound, then divided to deeply dissected, sometimes again pinnately lobed. Upper stems have long internodes, sometimes with *alternate leaves*. **Blades** 2-8" (5-20 cm) long, the lobes abruptly pointed (except the terminal lobe, which is long-tapered) with a claw-tip, smooth and hairless to minutely hairy above; they may have scattered stiff hairs below, especially on the veins. **Midvein** *flat to raised* above and slightly protruding below; *secondary veins raised above and flat below*. **Petioles** 30-90% of blade length (shorter toward the top), deeply channeled and slightly winged; wings widen after each rachis division. **Inflorescence** (July-October) scattered solitary heads at the ends of long, stiff, straight, thin, angled peduncles to 5" (13 cm) long. **Heads** are 9-11 mm long, spreading 5-8 mm wide, erect in flower and fruit (not nodding like some *Bidens*), surrounded by several linear to lanceolate appressed bracts, a few extending down the peduncle. There are usually 3-5 broad, yellow, notched rays; and always 12-27 tiny, yellow, 5-lobed disk florets. **Fruits** spread at maturity in an umbel-like or sunburst-like cluster, the achenes needle-like, dark brown, mottled, strongly ridged, 0.4-0.6" (10-15 mm) long, the tips with 4 barbed prongs 3-4 mm long, by which the seeds stick to fur and clothing.

HABITAT: Prefers moist to dry disturbed rich soil in semi-shade: Rocky wooded slopes, floodplain forests, stream banks, gardens, crop fields, pastures, orchards, urban woodlots. Native.

FOOD USE: Tender **greens** can be eaten raw or cooked from early summer to early fall. The **flowerheads** have a marigold-like flavor and can be used as a seasoning (though it is weaker than romerillo). **Conservation 1.**

COMMENTS: Spanish needles has tender young greens in mid to late summer when most other plants are old and tough, making it especially nice when you need a flavorful dash of green in a dish. This species is abundant and widespread in our region. It is also native to Southeast Asia and possibly elsewhere; it is now a cosmopolitan weed through most of the warm parts of the world, where it is commonly eaten. It has probably remained so little known in North American foraging circles because it was not widely eaten in Europe.

GROUP 33 BASAL LEAVES ABSENT, STEMS NOT SQUARE, LEAVES PAIRED, ENTIRE

A few distinct families of plants compose group 33. The edible parts produced are not very diverse, consisting almost entirely of greens, shoots, flowers, buds, and pods. The plants in this group are generally fairly easy for beginners to recognize, with the exception that milkweed shoots can easily be confused with those of dogbane.

TENTATIVE IDENTIFICATION KEY TO GROUP 33
The key is not your final answer!

Stems trailing, creeping, decumbent, or reclining; if erect, weakly and inconsistently so.
- Leaves thick and succulent.
  - Leaves broad and ovate, the members of the pair similar in size. — **1. Seabeach sandwort**
  - Leaves long and narrow, often mismatched in size.
    - Leaves green and somewhat glossy; coastal. — **2. Sea-purslane**
    - Leaves gray-green and dull; mostly inland. — **3. Western sea-purslane**
- Leaves thin and delicate.
  - Some stems with a line of fine hairs on one side only.
    - Flowers less than 8 mm across with petals shorter than sepals. — **4. Common chickweed**
    - Flowers more than 1 cm across, petals much longer than sepals. — **5. Star chickweed**
  - All stems either hairless or hairy all around (hairs never in a line).
    - Stems and leaves hairless or with very short, soft, woolly hair.
      - Leaves ovate, acute-pointed; petals longer than sepals. — **6. Water chickweed**
      - Leaves roundish, abruptly nipple-tipped; petals shorter than sepals. — **8. Drymary**
    - Stems and leaves densely covered with long, stiff hair. — **7. Mouse-ear chickweed**

Stems generally erect and self-supporting (although possibly toppling with age).
- Lower leaves paired, upper leaves alternate; surfaces sticky-hairy-smelly. — **9. Devil's claw**
- Lower leaves paired, upper leaves packed into whorls. Swedish bunchberry (p. 507).
- All leaves paired (except occasionally alternate near the flowers); not sticky-hairy-smelly.
  - Stems less than 4 mm thick; sap not milky.
    - Stems not branched, leaves faintly hairy, flowers blue. — **10. Woodland phlox**
    - Stems often branched, leaves densely hairy, flowers purple. — **11. Prairie phlox**
  - Stems more than 1 cm thick; sap milky.
    - Flowers in branchy clusters; pods needle-like. Dogbanes (poisonous, p. 675).
    - Flowers in umbels; pods pointed but not needle-like, more than 12 mm thick.
      - Stems densely covered with very fine, short, soft wool; leaves abruptly pointed.
        - Flower crown longer than the central structure; Crown and petals pinkish-purple.
          - Crown points not curved, clearly shorter than petals. — **12. Common milkweed**
          - Crown points curved, elongated, about equal to petals. — **13. Showy milkweed**
        - Flower crown equal to or shorter than the central structure, usually pale.
          - Crown points pressed against the central structure; pod smooth. — **14. Green milkweed**
          - Crown points not pressed against the central structure; pod densely woolly. — **15. Sand milkweed**
      - Stems very sparsely woolly; leaves with long-pointed tips. — **16. Poke milkweed**

1   Seabeach sandwort 🌿 2
Honckenya peploides ✦ *Caryophyllaceae* (Pink family)

QUICK CHECK: Mat-forming seashore herb with succulent stems and paired, succulent leaves; flowers with 5 white petals. **ID difficulty 1.**

DESCRIPTION: Perennial often forming large, dense mats over seashore rocks and beaches. **Non-flowering stems** are thick and succulent, to 6 mm thick and 14" (36 cm) tall, decumbent to leaning or prostrate—more erect in dense clumps. The surface is hairless, smooth, light (nearly white) in the shade but with purple tints in sunlight. Branches are uncommon; if present they are minor and and axillary. **Leaves** paired, spaced 1–2" (2.5–5 cm) on the lower stem but crowded near the tip. The blades are glossy, elliptic to obovate, succulent, clasping, to 1" (2.5 cm) long, abruptly pointed, *slightly cupped*, the margins entire. **Midvein** may be flat or slightly depressed or raised; *other veins are not evident*. **Flowering stems** thinner and creeping or decumbent, forking, with 2 *shallow grooves on opposite sides*; the grooves switch sides after each node. **Flowers** 10–12 mm across, with 5 broadly elliptic white, almost translucent petals, each well *separated on a long stalk*. A calyx of 5 triangular sepals spreads a bit beyond the petals. Stamens spread about as far as the petals.

HABITAT: Rocky, gravelly, or sandy ocean beaches. Native.

FOOD USE: The **leaves** and **stem tips** remain succulent and tender through the growing season and can be gathered all summer and eaten raw as a snack, in salads, or cooked as a vegetable. These are traditionally mixed with other vegetables and fermented for storage by peoples of the Far North.

COMMENTS: Non-flowering plants I have tried in several locations tasted like a non-tangy or slightly bland purslane. I have only seen it blooming once, in northern Newfoundland, and that plant tasted like slightly salty fish-flavored chickweed, which was pretty good once I got past the weirdness of it. Some botanists have split *Honckenya peploides* into 2 or more species, in which case the fishy flowering plant I ate from might have been *H. diffusa*. Interestingly, there were non-flowering, bland-tasting colonies a few feet away. I have not had sufficient experience with these plants to develop an opinion on the taxonomy.

2 Sea-purslane 3
Sesuvium portulacastrum ◆ family *Aizoaceae*

QUICK CHECK: Long, succulent, vine-like stems growing near beaches, with elliptic leaves in pairs of unequal size. **ID difficulty 1.**

DESCRIPTION: Perennial forming mats, all parts hairless, thick, and succulent. **Stems** creeping, to 8' (2.4 m) long, uniform in thickness, solid, roundish, layered in cross section with a tougher core, the surface smooth, hairless, brownish red to green. Where mixed with other vegetation the stems may stand weakly erect and reach 3' (1 m) off the ground. **Branches** occasional at about 45°, the tips often ascending a few inches. Internodes 3–5" (8–13 cm). **Leaves** paired, the node thickened with a darkened ring; one member of the pair notably larger than the other. Blades narrowly elliptic, pointed at both ends, entire, 0.8–1.7" (20–43 mm) long and 5–12 mm wide, flattish but succulent. **Midvein** faint; other veins obscure. **Petioles** 15–20% of blade length, sheathing the stem. **Flowers** single from leaf axils, 0.5–0.7" (13–18 mm) across, on pedicels 6–8 mm long, the petals triangular, not of identical width, light purple inside and green on the back. The stamens are numerous.

HABITAT: Seashores, salt marshes, mud flats; occasionally on beaches inland. Native.

FOOD USE: The tender **stem tips** and **leaves** are pleasantly salty and can be eaten raw or cooked year-round. Some overwintering leaves become enlarged and are especially good. **Conservation 2.**

COMMENTS: This seashore vegetable is a locally abundant, irresistible nibble. Annual sea-purslane *S. maritimum* is much less common, and I have not eaten it. It is a smaller plant with broader leaves and smaller white flowers.

◀ *Sesuvium portulacastrum* colony.

Related edible:
3 Western sea-purslane ◆ *Sesuvium verrucosum*

This species inhabits salt flats and basins at scattered locations inland. It is a smaller, more upright plant with smaller, more crowded leaves that are made gray by a bumpy-sparkly coating. The flowers are purple. This species is not quite as good to eat as its coastal cousin, but still makes a nice salty nibble.

CHICKWEED 📖 IWE-90
genus *Stellaria* (in part) ✦ *Caryophyllaceae* (Pink family)

QUICK GROUP ID: Low creeping or lax plants with non-tapered stems, paired entire leaves, and flowers with 5 white petals deeply cut to look like 10. **ID difficulty 2.**

DESCRIPTION: Perennial or annual herbs, often branched heavily at or near the base and sometimes rooting from nodes. They have *very different growth forms during flowering (hot) and non-flowering (cool) periods* and can look like entirely different plants: Cool weather plants have broader, larger, and more crowded leaves. **Stems** weakly erect, especially where crowded, often spreading or creeping to form mats, rarely more than 18" (46 cm) high, 1–3 mm thick, *nearly uniform in thickness along their length*, round, delicate, not becoming woody, branching dichotomously especially toward the tips. Several species have *hairs in a line on one side of the stem only.* **Leaves** paired, entire, ovate to lanceolate, thin and delicate. Upper leaves may be sessile while lower leaves may have petioles up to 100% of blade length. **Midveins** depressed, not distinctly offset by color. **Secondary veins** faintly evident, faintly depressed, 40–60° to the midvein, 2–3 arising on each side of it. **Inflorescence** a loose, spreading, cluster from branch tips or leaf axils, often *forking dichotomously.* **Flowers** 3–20 mm across with 5 narrow, triangular, green sepals and *5 white petals*, each *split to the base, giving the appearance of 10 narrow petals.* (Flowers occasionally lack petals.) **Fruit** a tiny oval capsule that splits open at maturity to release several brown seeds.

CONFUSING PLANTS: Scarlet pimpernel, *Anagallis arvensis* has a twisted, hairless stem with four unequal winged angles. All the leaves are sessile, the major secondary veins all arise at or near the base, and the blade is minutely dotted below. The flowers are red.

FOOD USE: Collect **leafy greens** from young stems that are still tender—not from flowering branches. These are most abundant during the cool periods of spring and fall. Use in salads, as a raw nibble, or cooked. The mild flavor reminds people of corn silk.

COMMENTS: Those chickweeds considered annuals sometimes stay green and half-alive under snow or through deep frost and continue growing the next season. There are numerous species of chickweed in our area; below I cover a few of the largest or most common.

4 Common chickweed ✦ *Stellaria media* 🌿 3

QUICK CHECK: Chickweed with broad, ovate leaves, hairy on only one side of stem.

DESCRIPTION: Annual, often forming dense, lush clumps in cool weather. **Stems** thin and rounded, to 32" (80 cm) long, some internodes with a dense row of *hairs on one side only*—the hairy side sometimes *switching between nodes.* **Leaves** hairless, triangular to ovate or broadly elliptic, 0.2–2" (5–50 mm) long, the upper nearly sessile, but the petioles longer toward the base of the plant. **Petioles** broadly U-channeled with hairy margins. **Flower** (most

of the year) tiny, in clusters of up to 7, the sepals 3–6 mm long and hairy, the *petals sometimes absent; if present shorter than the sepals* (1–4 mm). There are 3–5 stamens.

HABITAT: Disturbed, moist, shaded areas, such as along house foundations and woodland trails, in flower gardens, shady ditches, backyards, weedy areas. Considered introduced but possibly native.

COMMENTS: Common chickweed is especially prevalent in urban areas and is an excellent salad green. Lesser chickweed *S. pallida* is like a miniature version of common chickweed, but its flowers rarely have petals and most of them are self-pollinated and do not open. It is also possibly introduced.

5 Star chickweed ✦ *Stellaria pubera* 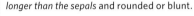 3

QUICK CHECK: Clump-forming chickweed with large, showy flowers; the upper leaves hairy.

DESCRIPTION: Perennial. **Stems** to 22" (56 cm) long, rounded, often maroon, sometimes numerous from the root crown giving a bushy appearance. **Flowering stems** have a row of hairs on one side only. **Leaves** ovate to lanceolate, *sessile* (or tapered to a short, narrow, petiole-like base) to 3.5" (9 cm) long, slightly hairy, especially on the margins of upper leaves. **Vegetative stems** are *erect and much larger*, with larger leaves, and resemble honeysuckle shoots; they usually have *hair all around*. **Flowers** *abundant and showy*, but only in spring, 11–14 mm across, the *petals much longer than the sepals* and rounded or blunt.

HABITAT: Hardwood forests, well-drained with moderate shade, especially oak-hickory. Native.

COMMENTS: Flowering stems quickly become tough, but very young or non-flowering stems are as good as those of common chickweed. **AKA** giant chickweed.

6 Water chickweed ✦ *Stellaria aquatica* ✐ 3

QUICK CHECK: Mat-forming chickweed with long stems and large, pointed leaves, the upper stems hairy all around, the petal lobes pointed. **ID difficulty 1.**

DESCRIPTION: Trailing or decumbent perennial herb with thin rhizomes. **Stems** rounded, up to 44" (112 cm) long. They may be hairless or *minutely hairy on all sides—often very densely toward the tips*. **Leaves** hairless (near the base) to densely soft-hairy (near the flowers), ovate, pointed. **Petioles** broadly channeled with *long hairs on their margins*, to 100% of blade length near the base; leaves near flower clusters are sessile. **Flowers** (summer to early fall) 9–13 mm across with usually 10 stamens, the petals greatly exceeding the sepals.

HABITAT: Rich moist soil in shade. Backyards, gardens, forest paths, woodland puddles, pond and brook edges. Introduced.

COMMENTS: This plant is similar to common chickweed but larger and more robust; the flavor is almost as good. In some regions water chickweed is much more abundant than common chickweed, and it is frequently collected by foragers who assume it is that species. **AKA** giant chickweed, *Myosoton aquaticum*.

7 Mouse-ear chickweed ✦ *Cerastium fontanum* ✐ 1

QUICK CHECK: Small chickweed with very hairy stems and broad, very hairy leaves with a bumpy surface.

DESCRIPTION: Perennial from a tough root, often forming mats. **Stems** multiple, creeping or decumbent, to 16" (40 cm) long and 2 mm thick, hollow, often branched, reddish or striped with reddish and green, evenly covered with long, erect, straight, moderately stiff hairs.

Leaves paired, 0.3-0.8" (8-20 mm) long, ovate to nearly round, the tips rounded to blunt but with a down-turned golden nipple, sessile, the midvein *strongly depressed* but *other veins obscure*, the *surface granular or bumpy and densely covered with long, stiff hairs*. Mostly evergreen. **Inflorescence** a small panicle at the stem tip. **Flowers** 8-12 mm across, the 5 petals almost as long as the 5 very hairy sepals. **Fruit** an elongated pod with many teeth at the tip where it splits open.

HABITAT: Repeatedly disturbed soils of all kinds in full to partial sun. Lawns, sidewalk cracks, beaches, roadsides. Usually considered introduced but probably native.

FOOD USE: The tenderest **young leaves** can be eaten raw or cooked, if you don't mind the dirt held by the hairs in the leaves.

COMMENTS: Extremely common, but never as tender or flavorful as common chickweed. There are numerous species in this genus, all safe but mediocre and barely worth eating. **AKA** C. *vulgatum*.

8 **Drymary** ✦ *Drymaria cordata* 2

QUICK CHECK: Limp or trialing chickweed-like plant with pairs of nearly sessile, nearly round leaves and bi-forking clusters of a few small, white flowers with 5 deeply cleft petals.

DESCRIPTION: Annual. **Stem** thin, 1-2 mm, very finely hairy (most visible on the growing tip), prostrate or lax, to 14" (36 cm) long, with a tuft of longer hair at the nodes. **Leaves** paired, entire, roundish with a slightly heart-shaped base, the tips rounded or very blunt-pointed but with a nipple or claw-like tip. Blades smooth but not glossy, hairless or with very fine, sparse hairs. Major **veins** flat to slightly raised above and protruding below, emanating at or near the base and rounding back toward the tip. **Petioles** shallowly channeled, 3-5% of blade length toward stem tips but much longer near the base. **Inflorescence** a repeatedly bi-forking cluster, the branches getting shorter with each fork; the flowers are crowded on thin pedicels. **Flowers** 4-6 mm across, with 5 triangular, pointed, cupped or boat-like sepals, the tip with a claw and the *margins white*. **Petals** 5, each split to the base (looks like 10), white, pointed, shorter than the sepals.

CONFUSING SPECIES: Thick-leaf drymary *Drymaria pachyphylla* (reportedly poisonous) is a relative found in Texas that has smaller, darker, thickened, crowded, succulent leaves and shorter stems that hug the ground. The petals are of varying lengths, and the longer ones exceed the sepals.

HABITAT: Lightly disturbed areas in partial shade, especially with moderately moist, rich soil. Yards, parks, orchards, pastures, open woodlots. Adventive or possibly native.

FOOD USE: Tender **leaves** are eaten raw or cooked.

COMMENTS: This chickweed relative looks the part, but its taste is more like carpetweed or common plantain. **AKA** tropical chickweed, whitesnow. As if there is another kind of snow.

9   Devil's claw 🖋 2 🌿
Proboscidea louisiana + family *Martyniaceae*

QUICK CHECK: Low, hairy, musky plant with large leaves (looks like a zuchini plant from afar), large irregular white flowers and large, hook-shaped pods. **ID difficulty 1.**

DESCRIPTION: Annual, at first erect but eventually spreading wider than tall, the surfaces densely covered with sticky, musky hairs giving the whole plant a *rather foul odor.* **Stems** robust, up to 1.3" (33 mm) thick, rounded, with a few major divergent branches. **Leaves** *paired near the base, alternate near the top.* **Blades** kidney to heart-shaped, up to 12" (30 cm) long and about as broad, heart-shaped at the base with the lobes curled upward, the tips blunt. **Margins** wavy but without teeth. **Veins** *palmate,* depressed above and protruding below. **Petioles** very thick, *rounded, hollow, unchanneled,* 120–160% of blade length. **Inflorescence** a stout, erect raceme 10–20" (25–50 cm) long, with a dozen or more flowers on pedicels 1–2" (2–5 cm) long. **Flowers** *hanging,* tubular, about 1.9" (48 mm) long, irregular. **Corolla** has 5 lobes; the upper 2 curled back, the lowest much larger and protruding, the stamens and pistils pressed against the top of the tube. The corolla is whitish with some purple outside; the inside has purple spots and a *streaked yellow runway on the bottom.* **Calyx** 5-lobed and irregular with the upper lobe distinctly longer, narrower, and more erect. Behind the calyx are 2 bracts, one on each side, *curled up like horns.* **Pods** 7–9" (18–23 cm) long, green at first, drooping, enlarged at the base with an elongated, pointed, hook-like tip. At maturity the fuzzy outer coating splits and falls away, leaving a dry structure with a net-like surface and a fringed ridge along the top, the hook splitting into 2. **Seeds** 7–9 mm long, broadly elliptic, wrinkly, dark, angled in cross section, oily.

▲ Rare in the eastern mapped range. Scattered outside mapped area.

HABITAT: Disturbed soil in full sun, especially where sandy: pastures, barnyards, waste areas, streamsides, washes, ditches. Native.

FOOD USE: Tender, **immature pods** can be cooked as a vegetable or made into pickles. You may want to rub them in water to wash and remove the sticky hairs; or parboil them, since the skins contain a bitter element. Ripe **seeds** can also be eaten raw or cooked, although I've only tried them once and don't have much of an opinion. **Conservation 2.**

COMMENTS: Although widespread in the Great Plains, this plant is more common to the southwest, where it is culturally important to many Native Americans. Devil's claw is sometimes cultivated for its fruit, which is used in making pickles. **AKA** ram's horn, unicorn plant.

10 Woodland phlox 🌿 3 🌸 3
Phlox divaricata ✦ family *Polemoniaceae*

QUICK CHECK: Short plant with thin, hairy stems and paired, entire leaves with no obvious secondary veins; flowers with a thin tube abruptly spreading into 5 blue petals. **ID difficulty 1.**

DESCRIPTION: Perennial herb from a thin, tough rhizome. **Stems** have an evergreen, semi-woody horizontal portion that overwinters; the tips grow erect in spring. Upright stems are long-hairy, solid, rounded, to 18" (46 cm) tall and 2–3 mm thick, flimsy, not branched, often in small clumps. **Leaves** paired, spreading to slightly ascending, the nodes *widely spaced*. Blades are lanceolate, entire, sessile, to 1.5" (4 cm) long, the margins hairy. The upper surface has scattered hairs; the underside is glossy and hairless except on the **midvein**, which is *deeply depressed above* and protruding below. *Other veins are obscure*, although if you look carefully you can see the secondary veins faintly raised. Each side of the blade is gently downcurved. **Inflorescence** (spring) a forking cluster at the apex, often with 3–4 pedicels at umbel-like junctures. Flower buds *long and pointed*, beak-like. **Sepals** 5, long and pointed, hairy, dark green-brown, in bud mostly not touching, the white of the immature corolla showing between the gaps and making the bud striped. **Corolla** blue, a *long, thin tube 2–3 mm wide abruptly widening* at a right angle into 5 lobes (petals), these narrow at the base with broad, rounded tips, spreading 1–1.3" (25–33 mm) wide. Sexual parts are mostly hidden in this tube. Petals form a *neatly twisted cone* just before opening.

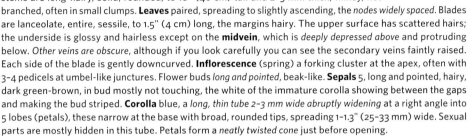

HABITAT: Hardwood forests where a little extra light hits the forest floor, especially floodplains, hilltops, forest edges, roadsides, young forests, savannahs. Native.

FOOD USE: Tender new **leaves** and tops can be eaten raw or cooked in spring—generally before blooming. You can also eat new flowers and buds on slightly older plants. **Conservation 2.**

COMMENTS: Easy to overlook before bloom, woodland phlox greens have a mild, pleasant flavor. Phlox flowers are more generally known as edible, but this species is the best I've tried. On most summer and fall-blooming species the greens are too tough and bitter. **AKA** blue phlox.

Related edible:
11 Prairie phlox ✦ *Phlox pilosa*

This is another small, spring-blooming species with tender greens. The stems are more densely hairy, reddish, and often branch. Leaves are narrower and longer, almost linear, and hairier; the midveins are depressed even more deeply, and the sides of the leaf scrolled downward very strongly. The flowers are purple. This plant grows in dry, open areas. **AKA** downy phlox. 🔥

MILKWEED (Not all species are edible!)   2   2   2   2
genus *Asclepias* (in part) ✦ family *Asclepiadaceae*   📖 FH-290

QUICK GROUP CHECK: Unbranched stems, milky sap, paired leaves on very short petioles; umbels of flowers with a 5-part crown; green tapered pods with parachuted seeds. ID difficulty 3/1.

DESCRIPTION: Perennials, mostly erect, spreading by rhizomes, exuding copious milky sap from wounds. **Stems** clumped or in loose colonies, unbranched, roundish to faintly 4-sided, solid, tapered little, 2–6' (60–180 cm) tall. **Leaves** alternate (occasionally whorled), entire, 3–9" (8–23 cm) long. **Midveins** prominent, offset by light color, flat to slightly depressed above. **Secondary veins** usually 10 or more per side, light in color, at broad angles (60–80° to midvein), flat to faintly depressed above, not reaching the margin. **Petioles** 2–8% of blade length. **Inflorescence** stalked umbels 1–4" (2.5–10 cm) wide from upper leaf axils, with numerous pedicels several times longer than the flowers, some flowers drooping in the edible species listed below. **Flowers** 6–15 mm wide, with a unique form: 5 elliptic, cupped petals are folded back along the pedicel, hiding the 5 calyx lobes, which are also reflexed. Pointed forward is a crown composed of 5 "hoods," each covering a "horn" curved in toward the center, where the sex organs are hidden in a complex structure. **Fruit** a green pod, *held erect*, narrowed to a pointed or acuminate tip, opening on one side to release extremely flattened, winged seeds attached to a silky parachute.

CONFUSING PLANTS: Various milkweed shoots are often confused with those of **common dogbane**, which are extremely bitter. This confusion accounts for the widespread belief that milkweed shoots are very bitter. (If you encounter bitter milkweed, *do not eat it*.) The stems of dogbane shoots are smooth, hairless, and covered with a faint bloom, while those of all the milkweeds listed here lack bloom and are minutely fuzzy. Dogbane leaves (in the shoot stage) get progressively smaller toward the top, while those of milkweed shoots get larger. Dogbane stems and young leaves are typically more reddish. Mature plants are easy to tell apart. (See **dogbanes**, p .675)

FOOD USE: All parts of milkweed should be boiled before consumption, although the multiple changes of boiling water urged by many authors are generally unnecessary. Young **shoots** (spring), tender **leafy tops** (early summer), **flower buds** (early to mid summer), and **immature pods** (mid to late summer) can all be used in soups or casseroles, or served alone as a vegetable. The young pods may be eaten whole, but with larger (but still immature) pods I like to remove the silk and use that by itself; it is mild and sweet and adds a melted cheese-like texture to casseroles.

WARNINGS: Some milkweeds are toxic. All species contain bitter cardiac glycosides, and in some species these are sufficiently concentrated to render the plants unsafe. I have listed 5 edible species below, but do not assume that unlisted species are similarly safe. Milkweeds should always be eaten well-boiled and in moderation. Gastric upset has been reported by some, even with the traditionally eaten species. The raw sap contains compounds that soften protein structures and these can make your fingertips sore from handling them—so it makes sense that they could irritate your intestines. Consume cautiously at first.

COMMENTS: Despite the above warnings, this is one of the best-known, most popular, and best-documented wild vegetables, providing several good products through much of the growing season. It is a traditional food for many Native Americans. Milkweeds also provide a highly insulative down-like fiber from the seed floss, and all the species have bast fibers in the bark that can be used to make cordage. You've all heard about milkweeds being important for monarch butterflies. The monarchs need more foragers planting, preserving, and caring for backyard milkweed patches. Regular picking of shoots improves these milkweed colonies for monarch habitat by extending the availability of meristematic growth later into the summer. All the listed species are native.

Common milkweed shoot at a good stage to eat. ▶

12 Common milkweed ✦ *Asclepias syriaca*

By far the most common species, inhabiting fields, roadsides, forest edges, and almost any other disturbed sunny area. The stems are erect, 3–6' (1–2 m) tall and 8–14 mm thick, not clumped, covered with very fine, soft hair. Shoots are thick-walled with a thin hollow. Leaves are 4–9" (10–23 cm) long, elliptic, thick, the tips obtusely pointed to rounded, midvein much lighter than the rest of the blade, the surface faintly velvety-hairy on all parts, especially the midvein below. Flowers are a mixture of pink, purple, and white. Pod is teardrop-shaped, 3–6" (8–15 cm) long, the surface covered with warts or soft spurs.

◄ The lower pods are too old; the middle and upper ones are still tender.

13 Showy milkweed ✦ *Asclepias speciosa*

The nearly identical western counterpart to common milkweed. The stems tend to grow more clumped, and the points in the flower's crown are narrower, more elongated, and curved at the tip.

14 Green milkweed ✦ *Asclepias viridiflora*

A species of sandy soil in dry prairies and pine or oak barrens. Its leaves range from narrowly elliptic to nearly linear; linear leaves are often folded along the midvein, while broader leaves may be very wavy. This species produces tight clusters of pale greenish flowers, the crowns never spreading from the central structure. Pods are long, narrow, and smooth. 🔥

▲ (left) Showy milkweed, *Asclepias speciosa*. (middle) Green milkweed, *Asclepias viridiflora*. (right) The blunt, wavy-leaved form of green milkweed hardly looks like the same species. ▲

15 Sand milkweed ◆ *Asclepias arenaria*

Grows in sandy soil on the southern Great Plains, and is especially abundant in the Sandhills region of Nebraska. This species has unbranched stems 20–32" (50–80 cm) long growing in small clumps; by maturity these stems often lean or fall over. The leaves are wavy, 3–5" (8–13 cm) long, densely soft-hairy, and the flowers are creamy. Pods are stout and short, shaped much like those of common milkweed but not bumpy.

16 Poke milkweed ◆ *Asclepias exaltata*

A tall species with loose flower clusters. Its leaves are narrower, thinner, and more pointed than those of most other species, and are sometimes borne in whorls of 3 or 4. The pods are much narrower. The stems of robust plants are clumped from a large root mass (like its namesake, poke, which its leaves also resemble). Poke milkweed is native to dry forests and savannahs, particularly oak and hickory. The flowers often exude a thick, sugary nectar which was reportedly collected by some Native Americans as a sweetener. **Note**: Poke milkweed is not the same as pokeweed! 🔥

GROUP 34 BASAL LEAVES ABSENT, STEMS NOT SQUARE, LEAVES PAIRED AND TOOTHED, LOBED, OR COMPOUND

The plants in group 34 produce edible greens, shoots, seeds, and underground storage organs. There are few dangerously toxic plants sharing their growth form, making this one of the safer groups for beginners to identify. A few species have grooves in the stem that can give the impression of the stem being squared. Jack-in-the-pulpit is problematic because the leaves are actually basal leaves extending up the stem on a sheath; but since they appear paired and diverge on the stem I have placed the plant in this group.

TENTATIVE IDENTIFICATION KEY TO GROUP 34
The key is not your final answer!

Leaves lanceolate, elliptic, or ovate—not lobed.	
Stem erect.	
Stem hairless or faintly hairy.	
Stem translucent; tiny flowers in spreading, branching, leafless clusters.	1. Clearweed
Stem opaque; tiny flowers in ascending spikes with miniature leaves.	2. False nettle
Stem densely hairy or roughened by sparse but stiff hairs.	
Plant less than 30" (75 cm) tall with soft hairs.	3. Quickweed
Plant more than 3' (90 cm) tall with stiff hairs.	
Flowers in large, showy, sunflower-like heads.	4. Jerusalem-artichoke
Flowers in spikes of many small, unshowy, nodding heads.	5. Sumpweed
Stem creeping, prostrate, or spreading.	7. Yerba de tago
Leaves lobed or triangular.	
Leaf usually deeply palmately 3–7 lobed (occasionally unlobed).	6. Giant ragweed
Leaf ruffled, with 8–11 pinnate lobes per side.	8. Swamp lousewort
Leaf very flat, thick, roughly triangular, broad and angled at the base.	9. Orache
Leaves compound, the leaflets entire.	10. Jack-in-the-pulpit

1 Clearweed  2 2
Pilea pumila + Urticaceae (Nettle family)

QUICK CHECK: Erect herb with a thick, succulent, translucent, hairless stem and paired leaves; flowers tiny, clustered, not showy. **ID difficulty 2.**

DESCRIPTION: Annual, highly variable in size. **Stem** 3–28" (8–70 cm) tall at maturity and 1–18 mm thick, hairless, succulent, solid, *translucent*, usually unbranched, proportionately *very thick, cross section with 2 opposing flat to slightly concave sides alternating with 2 convex sides.* **Leaves** paired, 0.6–5" (15–130 mm) long, broadly ovate, round to obtuse at the base. The tip is like an *elongated, narrow, blunt lobe.* **Blade** thin, smooth except for scattered long, erect hairs—on the upper surface these arise from a raised bump. **Major veins** *3 major ones from the base, very deeply depressed above* and protruding below, the outer 2 arching back toward the tip forming a "leaf within a leaf." Smaller lateral veins are numerous, at broad angles, depressed but not as deeply. **Margin** has large, long blunt teeth with nipple tips. *Stipules absent.* **Petioles** 60–110% of blade length, narrow, grooved, hairless. **Inflorescence** short, densely packed, branching, axillary and terminal clusters, the branches *spreading* (not drooping or ascending). **Flowers** tiny and inconspicuous, producing small, dark, ovate seeds.

HABITAT: Rich, moist soil subject to minor surface disturbance, in moderate to heavy shade. Native.

FOOD USE: The young **greens** can be gathered in spring or early summer and eaten raw or cooked, but are

better cooked. They are reminiscent of their relatives, the nettles, although not as good. The better part of clearweed is the succulent **stem**. Because these are held stiff by turgor pressure rather than cellulose and lignin fibers, they remain tender throughout the growing season. They make a delightfully crisp and juicy addition to salads, or a raw snack. **Conservation 2.**

COMMENTS: Clearweed plants are highly variable in size; the smaller ones are hardly worth the time, but large ones may have quite substantial stems. Not a well-known edible, but once you try it, you'll always keep your eye out for it.

RELATED EDIBLE: Lesser clearweed *Pilea fontana* is very similar but tends to be smaller and have less clear stems and less deeply depressed veins. It grows around mossy springs and swamps.

2 False nettle ✎ 2 ⏳ 2
Boehmeria cylindrica ⬧ *Urticaceae* (Nettle family)

QUICK CHECK: Erect, unbranched herb with a 4-grooved stem, lacking stingers; leaves with 3 main veins from the base; ascending axillary spikes of tiny greenish flowers. **ID difficulty 2.**

DESCRIPTION: Perennial herb from thin rhizomes, forming colonies. **Stems** often clumped, erect, unbranched, 24–52" (60–132 cm) tall and 4–6 mm thick, tapering below ground, hairless or faintly pubescent (especially when young), with 4 low ridges and 4 shallow grooves between them. Two of the ridges are narrower, running down from the petiole bases. Young stems are dark green to purple-brown and rough toward the base, solid. **Leaves** paired, 2–5" (5–13 cm) long, sometimes not perfectly opposing, oval or broadly ovate, rounded at the base and tapered to an acuminate tip. Blades have minute, stiff, leaning hair above, and longer hair on the protruding main veins below. **Prominent veins** 3 from the base, the outer 2 not strongly arching; all veins and veinlets are deeply depressed above. **Margins** serrated with large, sharp teeth. **Petioles** 20–60% of blade length, light in color (almost translucent), grooved on top but otherwise thick and nearly round; fine-hairy, especially on top and when young. **Stipules** elongated, small, leaning toward and often touching those of the opposing leaf. **Inflorescence** *ascending unbranched spikes* 0.4–4" (1–10 cm) long, paired from upper leaf axils; *they have a tiny leaf or leaves at or near the tip.* Female spikes are continuous; male spikes are interrupted. **Flowers** tiny, greenish, unshowy, and inconspicuous. **Fruits** flattened and disc-like with a bulge around the seed.

HABITAT: Moist semi-open soil; river floodplains, rich meadows, marsh and lake borders. Native.

FOOD USE: Gather **tender tops** and **shoots** in spring and use as a potherb. These can also be boiled for tea or broth throughout the growing season. **Conservation 2.**

COMMENTS: This usually overlooked species looks and tastes similar to stinging and wood nettles but is not quite as good. False nettle has very strong bast fibers. A close relative, ramie (*Boehmeria nivea*) is cultivated as a fiber crop in Asia (and also has edible greens). **AKA** bog hemp.

3   Quickweed   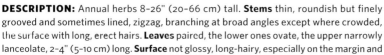 3   📖 IWE-315
genus *Galinsoga* ✦ *Asteraceae* (Composite family)

QUICK CHECK: Short, hairy, branched herb with ovate, toothed leaves and tiny flowerheads with 5 well-spaced, 3-lobed white rays. **ID difficulty 1.**

DESCRIPTION: Annual herbs 8–26" (20–66 cm) tall. **Stems** thin, roundish but finely grooved and sometimes lined, zigzag, branching at broad angles except where crowded, the surface with long, erect hairs. **Leaves** paired, the lower ones ovate, the upper narrowly lanceolate, 2–4" (5–10 cm) long. **Surface** not glossy, long-hairy, especially on the margin and main veins below. **Veins** deeply depressed above. *Two major veins arise at the base on each side of the midvein, these arching and nearly re-converging at the leaf tip.* **Margins** have coarse, dull, well-spaced, nipple-tipped teeth curling toward the tip; often these are little more than bumps on upper leaves. **Petiole** broadly channeled, 25–40% of blade length on lower leaves; the upper leaves are nearly sessile. **Inflorescence** a branching cluster of a few small heads at the branch tips, the peduncles long. **Heads** 5–7 mm wide, with ray and disk florets. The disk is greenish yellow, the florets 5-lobed and tiny. **Rays** white (rarely pink), almost as wide as long, *usually 5, spaced so as not to touch each other, 2- or 3-lobed.*

SPECIES: *G. quadriradiata* is the more common of the two very similar species. *G. parviflora* is smaller and less hairy, with narrower leaves that are scarcely toothed, and smaller rays.

HABITAT: Disturbed ground with moist soil, partial sun preferred. Gardens, lawn edges, lakeshores, barnyards, construction sites. Usually said to be non-native, but this is likely a native species that has increased its abundance and distribution due to human disturbance.

FOOD USE: Gather tender **leafy tops** before or at the beginning of flowering, most often from late spring through early summer. Look for clean plants, as the hairy surface readily holds dirt. They are edible raw and excellent in smoothies, but more commonly used as a potherb.

COMMENTS: The flavor is mild and young growth is tender, but some object to the hairiness. It is often said that this weed has invaded North America from Central and South America over the last few hundred years, but it may have been here all along. Quickweed is a key ingredient in the traditional Columbian soup *ajiaco*, along with corn, potatoes, and chicken. **AKA** guascas.

▲ *Galinsoga quadriradiata* flowers.

▲ *Galinsoga parviflora* flowering.

4 Jerusalem-artichoke 🍽 2 📖 NG-413
Helianthus tuberosus ✦ *Asteraceae* (Composite family)

QUICK CHECK: Tall, unbranched sunflower, rough all over from stiff hairs, the leaves toothed; disk and rays yellow. **ID difficulty 2.**

DESCRIPTION: Perennial sunflower 5–9' (1.5–2.7 m) tall and up to 0.8" (2 cm) thick, forming colonies by rhizome. **Tubers** elongated and gradually thickening, 2–6" (5–15 cm) long and 0.4–1.2" (1–3 cm) thick, light brown, tan, or reddish, with bulged buds and often an upturned tip. Occasionally they are knobby and clustered. **Stem** erect, green, round-ish, pithy-solid, with *stiff, erect hairs growing from pedestals*, giving it a *sandpapery feel*, unbranched except near the top, the form always much taller than wide. **Leaves** paired, but often alternate in the top quarter, especially on robust specimens; rarely whorled. Blades ovate, 3–7" (8–18 cm) long, with a long, sharp tip, the base obtusely rounded but then *decurrent along the petiole*. The surface is *roughened above with sand-like bumps*. **Midvein** flat to slightly depressed above in a broad valley. Secondary veins are lightly depressed above and protruding below. There are *2 major secondary veins near (but not at) the base* at 25–35°, fading before the midpoint of the blade; other secondary veins are much smaller and at broader angles. **Margins** have broad, shallow, forward-pointing, nipple-tipped teeth. **Petioles** less than 20% of blade length, flat to slightly channeled on top, *the non-winged portion very short*. **Inflorescence** (late summer through fall) loose, spreading clusters of 3–25, the heads 2.5–3.5" (6–9 cm) wide, with disk and ray florets *both yellow*, the rays long-elliptic, overlapping at the base, and spreading (not drooping). The disk is a semicircular mound. **Seeds** like sunflower seeds in miniature. Domesticated varieties, which often escape, are more robust, with larger, stouter, more numerous tubers clustered close to the base.

CONFUSING PLANTS: Wild sunflower (p. 603) is not colonial; it has more wide-spreading branches, broader leaves, and flowerheads that are dark in the center. It lacks tubers.

HABITAT: Naturally found in river floodplains in full to partial sunlight. It has spread to meadows, fencerows, and roadsides, especially in areas with rich, sandy soils. Native.

FOOD USE: Tubers of genetically wild plants are usually 4–24" (10–60 cm) from the parent plant on thin rhizomes, and 1–3" (2.5–8 cm) below the soil surface; you must dig a large area to get them. The tubers are best collected as late as possible—through the winter if the ground is not frozen, or early the following spring. They should be well-cooked before eating to avoid excessive flatulence. The tubers are good mashed like potatoes (although dissimilar in texture) or in soups and stews. Some cultivars are sweet enough to eat raw. **Conservation 2.**

COMMENTS: The tubers of this well-known wild edible are highly variable. Don't expect wild ones to look like the domestic cultivars. The tubers taste good but can cause serious and often uncomfortable gas in many individuals. This can be mitigated by a combination of very late harvest and prolonged cooking. **AKA** sunroot, sunchoke, fartichoke.

5 Sumpweed 🌾 2
Iva annua ✦ *Asteraceae* (Composite family)

QUICK CHECK: Tall, hairy herb with pointed leaves in pairs; crowded terminal spike of tiny, round flower/fruit clusters, each with an ascending bract curled over it. **ID difficulty 1.**

DESCRIPTION: Annual, 3–6' (1–2 m) tall, somewhat aromatic, the form much taller than wide. **Stems** single, erect, straight, to 0.6" (15 mm) thick, rounded, green or reddish (mostly in sun), solid near the base but hollow above, the surface roughened by bumps bearing stiff, curved hairs (but typically hairless near the base), unbranched where crowded but often branchy in the open. **Branches** thin, straight, simple, and strongly ascending. **Leaves** paired (reduced leaves near the inflorescence may be alternate), the blades 2–6" (5–15 cm) long, ovate to lanceolate, the bases acute or obtuse, the tips acuminate. There are scattered short hairs below and minute hairs above, with longer hairs on the margins and main veins. **Major veins** 3 from the base, slightly depressed above and protruding below. **Margins** have widely yet variably spaced teeth of variable size. **Petioles** 20–30% of blade length, narrowly channeled, the margins hairy. **Inflorescence** several crowded terminal and axillary spikes 2–9" (5–23 cm) long, uniform in thickness, held vertically or nearly so on long peduncles in the top third of the plant. **Heads** (late summer) evenly-spaced, bell-like, drooping, about 6 mm across, not showy, each head with 12–20 florets. There is *a curved, strongly ascending bract to the left of each head*, much longer than the head, broad-based with a *long acuminate tip*, a prominent midvein ridge, and a hairy margin. **Seed** (achene) slightly flattened, triangle to teardrop-shaped, 2–4 mm long, borne singly or in small groups, enclosed by 3–5 chaffy bracts, ripening to dark brown.

HABITAT: Partial shade to full sun in moist, disturbed soil. Crop fields, banks, ditches, river floodplains, construction sites, waste ground. Native.

FOOD USE: When mature in autumn the **seeds** can be stripped off by hand or beaten into a container. After drying, rub and winnow to remove the chaff. The seeds are very oily and can be used like sunflower seeds. There is a bitter substance on the exterior that is removed with the chaff—the kernels have a pleasant flavor. **Conservation 1.**

COMMENTS: Though little known and almost never collected today, this was once a staple food in the central US, extensively cultivated in prehistory. Domesticated forms with large seeds were developed but are now extinct, and efficient processing techniques have been lost. What we know of this plant's food use comes primarily from archaeology. **AKA** marsh-elder.

6 Giant ragweed 🌱 3 pith 2
Ambrosia trifida ✦ *Asteraceae* (Composite family)

QUICK CHECK: Towering, rough, straight-stemmed herb with deeply 3-lobed leaves.
ID difficulty 1.

DESCRIPTION: Very large annual, much taller than wide, occasionally branchy but most
often with only a few ascending, paired branches near the top. **Stem** straight, erect, 5–13'
(1.5–4 m) tall and 0.4–0.9" (10–23 mm) thick, roundish but somewhat ridged, covered with
stiff hairs, pithy in the center, with a bulged collar around the stem at each node. **Leaves** 3–10"
(8–25 cm) long, normally deeply 3-lobed but occasionally 5 or 7-lobed or unlobed (the uppermost commonly
unlobed), the tip acuminate, the base broad but then decurrent. The surface is rough above from stiff hairs.
There are 2 major secondary veins arising near (but not at) the base; **veins** and veinlets are depressed above.
Margins serrated. **Petioles** 25–45% of blade length, often with winged margins. **Inflorescence** male and female
separate on the same plants. The male heads are numerous, in crowded terminal racemes 4–14" (10–36 cm)
long, hanging bell-like at the end of short 90° pedicels, the bracts with a few black stripes, the florets yellowish to creamy. Female heads are fewer, *in clusters in the axils of small upper leaves* below the male flowers, not
showy. **Fruits** *spongy-woody, 9–11 mm long, with a narrow, blunt base and six prongs at the end—5 of the prongs
on the outside and shorter, the middle prong much longer.* Inside is the single, soft, edible kernel.

HABITAT: Rich disturbed soil in full sun. A common and often troublesome weed of high-quality farmland,
roadsides, ditches, and barnyards. Native; originally found in floodplains.

FOOD USE: In early fall, strip the ripe fruits off by hand, or lean the plants and beat with a stick into a clean
sled, then dry them. The **seeds** ripen while the plants are still green. They are soft, oily, and delicious—similar
to sunflower seeds, but I have not found a labor-efficient way to remove the corky husks. The **pith** can be eaten
out of the center of half-grown stalks. **Conservation 1.**

COMMENTS: This is one of our largest and most distinctive herbs. Its
pollen is a frequent cause of hay fever. Giant ragweed seeds were eaten
by prehistoric people in the Midwest and upper South, where it was commonly cultivated. Domestic strains with larger seeds and thinner husks were
developed, but these seem to have gone extinct before Europeans arrived in
North America. The techniques and technology used in processing ragweed
seeds have been lost.

7   Yerba de tago 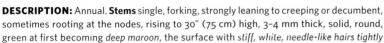 1
Eclipta prostrata ✦ *Asteraceae* (Composite family)

QUICK CHECK: Knee-high spreading plant with narrow, sessile leaves, stiff-haired maroon stems, and single, white, daisy-like flowers. **ID difficulty 1.**

DESCRIPTION: Annual. **Stems** single, forking, strongly leaning to creeping or decumbent, sometimes rooting at the nodes, rising to 30" (75 cm) high, 3-4 mm thick, solid, round, green at first becoming *deep maroon*, the surface with *stiff, white, needle-like hairs tightly appressed toward the tip.* **Leaves** paired, 1.2–3.9" (3–10 cm) long, lanceolate to narrowly elliptic, blunt-pointed, tapered to a narrow sessile base. Terminal leaves, especially in full sun, are often deeply folded along the midvein. The blade has scattered stiff hairs appressed toward the tip on both sides. New growth (such as you would eat) has glossier leaves that may not yet have developed hair. **Midvein** depressed above and protruding below. There is one secondary vein on each side arising close to the base and running at a low angle, forming a perimeter vein where the other secondary veins stop. These major veins may be slightly depressed, flat, or slightly raised; on small terminal leaves they are often obscure. **Margins** have *small, blunt, widely-spaced, forward-pointed, nipple-tipped teeth.* **Inflorescence** (summer to fall) composite heads in groups of 1–3 borne on peduncles 5–10 mm long directly from the axil of usually just *one leaf per pair.* **Heads** 6–8 mm across, surrounded by 8–10 triangular bracts of varying size, with a row of narrow white rays on the outside; the inside has tiny disk flowers with 5 white petals and yellow anthers.

HABITAT: Moist and often fertile disturbed ground in full sun; river floodplains, wetland edges, lawns, disturbed meadows and weedy areas. Much more common in the South. Native.

FOOD USE: Tender young **leaves** and **stem tips** can be used raw or cooked, but sparingly, as the flavor is strong. **Conservation 1.**

COMMENTS: This species is found around the world at lower latitudes and seems much better known outside the US. It doesn't even really have a common name in English. Besides being a well-known leafy green, it is traditionally used as a medicinal for several purposes, including reversing hair loss. Research has shown that an extract stimulates hair growth in mice. So make sure to plant some if your mice aren't hairy enough. **AKA** false daisy, bhringraj, *Eclipta alba.*

▼ Young greens for eating.

8 Swamp lousewort 1
Pedicularis lanceolata + family *Orobanchaceae*

QUICK CHECK: Hairy, erect plant of wetland margins with leaves that are deeply pinnately lobed and ruffled by extremely depressed veins. **ID difficulty 1.**

DESCRIPTION: Perennial. Stems clumped, 20–40" (50–100 cm) tall and 5–8 mm thick, solid with long, soft hairs curving toward the base, with *four grooves* running down the sides (two of them more prominent). There are ascending branches in the upper third. **Leaves** paired, 2–2.5" (5–6.5 cm) long, oblanceolate to lanceolate or long-elliptic, tapered to both ends, sessile or nearly so. Lower leaves are blunt-tipped; upper leaves are pointed. *Margins have 8–11 evenly spaced blunt lobes per side, cut about halfway to the midvein, the lobes close together, nearly touching, often slightly twisted, each with small blunt*

teeth or sub-lobes. Blades ruffly, with scattered long hairs on both sides. **Midvein** broad, whitish, strongly depressed above and protruding below, shallowly U-channeled with a faint, thin groove in the center; smaller veins are also strongly depressed. **Petiole** very short to absent, wing-channeled when present. **Inflorescence** erect, crowded, terminal spikes with bracts progressively smaller toward the top. **Flowers** (mid to late summer) 0.7–1" (18–25 mm) long, the base with a tubular, hairy calyx. The corolla is tubular and much longer, creamy to pale yellow, 2-lipped, the upper lip longer and curling over the lower. From the top the spike looks like a pinwheel, the flower tips curving clockwise.

HABITAT: Full sun or light shade in swamps, wet meadows, marsh edges, along ponds and lakes, mostly in rich soils. Native.

FOOD USE: In late spring and early summer the tender **leaves** can be eaten raw or cooked. **Conservation 2.**

COMMENTS: This tastes much like lousewort (p. 394) but not as good, and the stems are not nearly as tender. It blooms three months later and has no basal leaves. This

▲ Emerging spring plants.

species is partly parasitic and has the odd parasitic plant flavor.

WARNING: These parasitic plants are known to absorb chemicals from their host plants and should not be eaten when growing beside poisonous species.

◄ Early summer shoots.

9 Orache ✎ 3 🌿 2
genus *Atriplex* + family *Amaranthaceae*

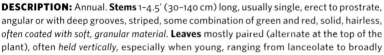

QUICK CHECK: Erect to creeping herb with unshowy flowers; leaves triangular and often with backward-pointed lobes; lower leaves paired, the upper alternate. **ID difficulty 1.**

DESCRIPTION: Annual. **Stems** 1–4.5' (30–140 cm) long, usually single, erect to prostrate, angular or with deep grooves, striped, some combination of green and red, solid, hairless, *often coated with soft, granular material.* **Leaves** mostly paired (alternate at the top of the plant), often *held vertically*, especially when young, ranging from lanceolate to broadly triangular—broad leaves generally have *two lobes jutting outward at the base.* **Surfaces** hairless, flat, sometimes with a granular coating. **Veins** not depressed and sometimes slightly protruding above; they protrude below. There are 2 major secondary veins arising at or near the base. **Margins** sometimes entire but usually wavy or with scattered, broad, dull teeth. **Petioles** 5–40% of blade length, channeled. **Inflorescence** a small spike growing from upper leaf axils. In the lower part of the spike a few flowers may be subtended by miniature leaves, but above that the spike is denser and leafless. **Flowers** unshowy, green, and very small, with 5 parts. Female flowers (and fruit) are subtended by 2 identical triangular or diamond-shaped fleshy bracts with teeth on the outer edges. These are pressed together and conceal the ripening seed.

CONFUSING PLANTS: Lambsquarters (p. 601) have all the leaves alternate and the seeds are not borne between triangular bracts.

HABITAT: Disturbed, sunny soil, especially where it is moist and salty. Coastal flats and estuary shores, seasonal wet spots, drainages, washes, pastures, crop fields, roadsides. Native, but some populations are weedy and introduced.

FOOD USE: Gather **leafy tops** while still tender from spring through midsummer and occasionally later. After the stems toughen, pluck individual leaves. Use in salads or as a potherb. In some cases you will probably want it mixed with other greens to dilute the saltiness, or boil it and drain off the water. Fruit can be stripped by hand in late summer or autumn, dried, and then rubbed and winnowed (see p. 27) to clean the seeds. These can then be used for porridge or flour like goosefoot or amaranth seeds, but I've only eaten a few palmfuls. **Conservation 1.**

COMMENTS: Orache is a superb leafy green—think of it as pre-salted lambsquarters or spinach. This plant is very sporadic in occurrence, but is most common in dry parts of the Great Plains and near the Coast. It also thrives along heavily salted highways. There are many edible species in this genus, but for this account I'm lumping them together. Pronounced OR-ITCH.

10 Jack-in-the-pulpit
Arisaema triphyllum ✦ *Araceae* (Arum family)

QUICK CHECK: Straight, erect, thick stem with a pair of compound leaves, each with 3 large, entire leaflets; single hooded flower producing a spike of red fruits. **ID difficulty 1.**

DESCRIPTION: Perennial from a corm, sometimes producing offset corms at its base or at the tips of thin rhizomes, forming dense colonies of smaller plants surrounding a parent. **Corm** stout, not fibrous, slightly wider than tall, with a single large bud at the top; the bottom half has numerous roots emanating from a wrinkly skin. **Stem** single, erect, stout, 8–20" (20–50 cm) tall and 0.3–0.8" (8–20 mm) thick, unbranched, solid. The surface is smooth and hairless with light bloom, mottled purple and green (either color can be predominant). The lower stem is covered with *long, tubular sheaths* that eventually give rise to petioles. **Shoot** (not edible, mentioned here only for comparison) thick, surrounded by a sheath fully encircling the stem that is split less than halfway to the base; *one leaflet points up, two down.* **Leaves** ternately compound with *all leaflets sessile.* Young plants consist of just a single leaf from the base; mature plants have 2 leaves at the top in a slightly offset pair, the petioles strongly ascending and rising far above the flower and stem. **Leaflets** ovate to elliptic and entire with pointed tips, to 12" (30 cm) long, the blades thin, hairless on both sides. **Veins** depressed and not set off by color. Secondary veins several on each side, broadly angled, *running straight* until just before the edge, where they join a wavy marginal vein. **Petiole** thick, round, smooth, not channeled. **Inflorescence** (early summer) single on a long, stout, smooth peduncle, a leaf-like structure wrapped into a tube before narrowing into a tapered, pointed hood that rises on one side and arches over the opening. Inside the tube stands a stout, round-tipped, club-like rachis (spadix) with numerous small, petal-less flowers on its hidden lower part. The hood (spathe) is usually striped in various mixtures of green, purple, and white. **Fruit** (fall) bright red berries, numerous, the sides flattened where they are packed together on the spadix, each pulpy berry containing 1–3 hard, roundish, whitish seeds.

HABITAT: Deciduous forests with rich soil of moderate moisture. Native.

FOOD USE: The **corms** can be gathered in the dormant season and used as a starchy food. **Conservation 3.**

WARNING! Corms contain calcium oxalate raphides (see p. 22) and cannot be eaten unless processed carefully.

COMMENTS: The common name "Indian turnip" seems to preserve some knowledge about this plant's former importance, yet detailed ethnographic information on its use is lacking. However, its content of raphides is no more formidable than other wild species that have been bred into major food crops (such as taro). JITP seems to be thriving in places where earthworms have eaten all the leaf litter, leaving bare soil. An inflorescence is usually exclusively male or female, but the plants switch genders from year to year based upon the amount of stored energy in the corm.

NOT
EDIBLE

▲ JITP berries (not edible).

GROUP 35 BASAL LEAVES ABSENT, LEAVES ALTERNATE AND ENTIRE

This is one of the largest and most diverse groups in the book. Most of these are leafy greens, but a few have edible seeds or root vegetables. A few plants with variable leaf margins that I have placed in other groups might occasionally key here, such as lambsquarters or ground cherry.

TENTATIVE IDENTIFICATION KEY TO GROUP 35
The key is not your final answer!

Leaf veins not visible or visible and not parallel (see botanical definition of parallel).	
Leaves needle-like or thread-like, less than 2 mm wide.	
or Leaves limp and thread-like.	1. Asparagus
Leaves stiff and needle-like.	2. Russian tumbleweed
Leaves succulent, greater than 2 mm wide.	
or Erect plant with linear leaves.	3. Sea-blite
Prostrate to decumbent plant with spoon-shaped leaves.	7. Purslane
Leaves not needle-like, not thread-like, not succulent.	
Secondary veins and veinlets invisible or nearly so.	
Sap milky. Harebell (p. 336).	
Sap not milky.	
or Plant spreading wider than tall; finely hairy ovate leaves.	8. Prairie tea
Plant taller than wide; hairless, very narrow leaves.	
Flowers blue; plants more than 20" (50 cm) tall.	9. Blue flax
Flowers yellow; plants less than 14" (36 cm) tall.	10. Stiff yellow flax
or Secondary veins indistinct; a discontinuous network of raised veinlets.	11. Horseweed
or Secondary veins visible, several major ones from the base.	12. Thoroughwax
or Secondary veins visible, pinnate or no more than 2 from the base.	
Leaves with a distinct petiole.	
Secondary veins depressed above.	
Stem jointed at each node.	
or Leaves ovate to elliptic; stem with a large hollow, joints not bulging.	13. Japanese knotweed
or Leaves lanceolate; stems almost solid, bulged near each joint.	14. Smartweeds
Stem not jointed at the nodes.	
Flowers showy, in racemes.	
or Stems widely branching, clumped, raceme drooping.	17. Poke
Stems not branching, colonial, raceme erect.	18. Fireweed
or Flowers unshowy, tiny.	
Flowers in small clusters mixed with leafy bracts; mature leaves minutely raspy and sticking to clothing.	19. American pellitory
Flowers in clusters with stiff chaffy bracts; mature leaves not raspy.	
Plants erect; some inflorescences terminal.	4. Amaranth
Plants creeping; all inflorescences axillary.	5. Creeping amaranth
Secondary veins not depressed above.	
Petioles less than 5% of blade length; secondary veins less than 30° to the midvein; flowers large and showy.	20. Bush morning glory
Petiole more than 20% of blade length; secondary veins greater than 50° to the midvein; flowers small and unshowy.	16. Willow-leaved dock
Leaves sessile.	
Leaves stiff-hairy on the margin.	11. Horseweed
Leaves soft-hairy on the margin; surfaces velvety from appressed hair.	6. Kochia
Leaves hairless.	
Stems clumped, leaning, straight, usually unbranched below the inflorescence.	21. Bastard toadflax
Stems single, erect, zigzag, branchy.	15. Erect knotweed
Leaf veins visible and parallel (see botanical definition of parallel).	See key next page.

(Continued on next page.)

(Continued from previous page.)

Leaf veins visible and parallel (see botanical definition of parallel).

Stem wrapped with a sheath below each leaf, hairy-fringed where sheath margins meet.

or

Stem lax or trailing, much branched, leaves <5" (13 cm).	22. Common dayflower
Stem erect and usually unbranched; leaves often >5" (13 cm).	23. Tall dayflower

Stem not wrapped in a sheath below each leaf.

Stem smooth, hairless, with bloom (occasionally hairy at the base); leaf margins hairless.

Stems usually branched; leaves strongly clasping or perfoliate.

or *or*

Leaf clasping, stem 2-5' (60-150 cm), fruit a red berry.	24. White twisted-stalk
Leaf perfoliate, stem less than 20" (50 cm), fruit a green capsule.	26. Large bellwort
Stems not branched; leaves sessile to almost clasping.	27. Smooth Solomon's seal

Stem hairy or ridged, without bloom; leaf margins hairy.

Stem ridged, not hairy; leaf margins with stiff, straight hairs.	28. False Solomon's seal
Stem with gland-tipped hairs; leaf margins with hooked hairs.	25. Rosy twisted-stalk
Stem and leaf with soft appressed hairs; leaf margins with soft hairs.	6. Kochia

1 **Asparagus** 3
Asparagus officinalis ◆ *Asparagaceae* (Asparagus family)

QUICK CHECK: Point-tipped, solid, hairless shoot with no unfurled leaves; mature plant branchy with thread-like leaves and round, red fruit. **ID difficulty 2.**

DESCRIPTION: Identical to cultivated asparagus: clumping perennial that spreads short distances by a stout rhizome, reaching 3–7' (1–2 m) tall. **Stem** straight, erect, solid, round-ish, smooth, hairless, green, tough, with numerous much smaller ascending branches;

these again branching freely to make a dense Christmas-tree like form. **LYDS** prominent, straw-colored. There is a *ridged, brown, triangular sheath 8–14 mm long with a hanging spur-like appendage and one major thread-like appendage at each major branch juncture*; even after falling off these leave conspicuous bumps on the stem. **Leaves** 6–20 mm long, extremely thin and *thread-like*, single or in *clumps of 2–3*. **Inflorescence** 1–2 flowers on long, drooping, pedicels from branch junctures and axils, each with a *bulged joint just past the middle*; many empty pedicels usually persist. **Flowers** 6–7 mm long, yellow-green, bell-like, with 6 tepals, the tips reflexed. **Fruit** a spherical red berry 5–7 mm, not edible.

CONFUSING PLANTS: Members of the genus *Baptisia* (p. 678) have clumped, spear-like shoots that are toxic. *Baptisia* shoots sometimes (but not always) lean and have broader embryonic leaves. The mature stems are very different in every feature.

HABITAT: Roadsides, old fields, meadows; in full sun on well-drained soil, especially loamy sand. Introduced.

FOOD USE: Gather young **shoots** by cutting or snapping off at the base; eat raw or cooked like cultivated asparagus.

COMMENTS: This plant looks and tastes like cultivated asparagus, but it's a little better and way more fun. It is among the most coveted and beloved of wild vegetables.

2 Russian tumbleweed 3
Salsola tragus + family *Amaranthaceae*

QUICK CHECK: Bushy, spreading herb with needle-like leaves with stiff, sharp tips. ID difficulty 1.

DESCRIPTION: Bushy, spreading, annual 1.5–3.5' (45–105 cm) tall and about as wide, breaking off at the base in late summer or autumn to form a tumbleweed. **Stems** erect, single, solid, to 0.6" (15 mm) thick, strongly tapered, with darkened and often purple-topped ridges and scattered, short, stiff hairs. **Branches** numerous, beginning at the base; lower branches longest, these spreading to weakly ascending and then sweeping up at the tips. The top of each branch juncture is purple. **Leaves** alternate, *tufted on short spurs, most of which point vertically*, needle-like, to 1 mm wide, bluish green, with scattered minute (nearly invisible) hairs. Leaves have a thin, colorless sheath at the base, especially the outer leaf in a tuft. In cross section the leaves are round with a tiny groove on the upper/inside surface. At first they are soft and fleshy, but upon maturing become stiff and painful to touch. **Inflorescence** mostly single in the axils of small modified leaves (with widened bases) at the ends of the branches; numerous such axillary flowers are evenly spaced at branch tips. **Flowers** tiny and unshowy, lacking petals, reddish in the center. **Fruits** dry with a thin, papery flesh and a single dark brown, elongated seed.

CONFUSING PLANTS: Sea-blite leaves do not become stiff and sharp.

HABITAT: Well-drained, disturbed soil in full sun; mostly crop fields, pastures, urban areas, railroads, roadsides, and upper sea beaches. Introduced.

FOOD USE: Pick young **stem tips** when tender and the leaves are soft in early summer. Boil or steam before eating.

COMMENTS: This is one of the common "tumbleweeds" of the Great Plains, and perhaps the best known. The young stems are surprisingly good, and like amaranth they soften to a remarkable degree when cooked. While less abundant farther east, it is still locally common. **AKA** Russian-thistle, *Salsola kali*.

3 Sea-blite 2
Suaeda spp. • family *Amaranthaceae*

QUICK CHECK: Shin to knee-high plant with small, narrow, pointed, thick, succulent leaves; flowers unshowy. **ID difficulty 1.**

DESCRIPTION: Annuals. **Stems** erect to decumbent, 8–34" (20–86 cm) tall and 2–7 mm thick, the surface hairless and glaucous, green with darker green or purplish lines when young, graying and becoming tough with age, not jointed, usually bushy with many ascending, often red-tipped branches. **Leaves** needle-like, densely packed on new branches, alternate (the lowest ones may be paired), 0.4–1.8" (10–46 mm) long, often curved, pointed but not stiff or needle-sharp, hairless and often glaucous, sessile but not clasping, thick and succulent. Leaf cross-section nearly flat to slightly channeled above, rounded below. Lower leaves wither and droop on older plants. **Inflorescence** many terminal spikes, the flowers sessile, solitary or in small clusters in the axils of broader, shorter leaves. **Flowers** tiny and irregular with a 5-lobed calyx and 5 light yellowish sepals, one or more of which is enlarged. The sepals persist after pollination and enclose the tiny, round, single-seeded fruit.

SPECIES: *S. linearis* is our tallest species, the stem usually erect and becoming rigid, almost woody with maturity. The sepals of the fruit are keeled on the back. It is native. *S. maritima* is shorter and more weakly erect; the sepals of the fruit are rounded on the back. This species has native and introduced populations, which have been divided by some into separate species. *S. depressa* has creeping stems—only the branches are erect. This species has also been subdivided by some taxonomists.

CONFUSING PLANTS: Russian tumbleweed is a plant of dry land that has stiff, sharp leaf tips.

HABITAT: Salty soil in full sun: upper edges of beaches where some organic matter is deposited, salt marshes, and tidal wetlands. *Suaeda depressa* is also found in salty inland basins.

FOOD USE: Gather tender **stem tips** and **leaves** from spring through mid summer. **Conservation 2.**

COMMENTS: These are unpleasantly over-salty when raw but make a nice vegetable after boiling and draining to reduce the saltiness, or when mixed with other vegetables.

4 **Amaranth** 🌿 3 🌱 3 📖 NG-215
Amaranthus spp. ◆ family *Amaranthaceae*

QUICK CHECK: Branching herbs with tapered, gently-ridged stems; alternate, entire leaves; spiky clusters of unshowy flowers. **ID difficulty 2.**

DESCRIPTION: Erect annuals to 7' (2.1 m) tall, often with major ascending branches. **Stems** robust, strongly tapered, green (sometimes with reddish stripes), solid, ridged but not sharply, usually with fine hair but some species hairless. **Leaves** alternate, 0.5–8" (1.3–20 cm) long, entire, thin, spoon-shaped to narrowly elliptic or lanceolate, the bases tapered or acuminate, the tips blunt to pointed. Surfaces hairless or hairy. **Midvein** depressed above ▲ Collective range. and protruding below; secondary veins likewise, 45–55° to the midvein, running almost to the margins intact before curving forward and becoming faint. **Petioles** range from very short to 100% of blade length, channeled. **Inflorescence** dense terminal and axillary clusters (spikes, racemes, or panicles), by maturity usually encompassing a large portion of the upper plant with few leaves, the leaves fewer and smaller (often absent) toward the tips. **Flowers** tiny, not showy, with 0–5 (usually 3–5) *chaffy and semi-dry* sepals that are green in the center and papery on the edges, often *stiff-prickly at maturity with a hardened spine-like tip.* Stamens 3–5. **Fruit** a thin-walled, bladder-like structure 2–3 mm long with 2–3 small beaks at the end, holding a *single seed.* **Seeds** somewhat flattened, the edges rounded or sharp, shaped like a deformed M&M, the surface smooth and hardened, brown to nearly black.

CONFUSING PLANTS: Eastern black nightshade (p. 606) leaves often have blunt teeth and usually have a coppery to purple sheen on their lower surface.

HABITAT: Disturbed, rich soil in full sun. Abundant in many human-made habitats, such as gardens, crop fields, compost heaps, and building sites. Also riverbanks, shores, wetlands, disturbed floodplains and washes. Native.

FOOD USE: Gather the **greens** and **young stems** whenever they are tender—mostly late spring and early summer. They can be eaten raw but are much better cooked, which softens them considerably. Harvest the

▶ (top left) Green Amaranth
A. hybridus is a common weed similar to redroot pigweed in general appearance but is smoother and hairless with narrower leaves and longer petioles. Flower clusters are more elongated with fewer branches. In my opinion it is somewhat better as a vegetable.

▶▶ (right) Redroot Pigweed
A. retroflexus is probably the most widespread species. It has broad leaves, hairy stems and leaves, and very spiky, bushy flowerheads. The upper root and lower stem are distinctly red.

▶ (bottom left) *A. powelli* and *A. palmeri* are very similar species that resemble slender versions of green amaranth. Their branches and stems are slimmer, the foliage is sparser, and the petioles are proportionately longer. The flower clusters differ in being long and narrow, rarely branching, and drooping or sagging rather than stiff and erect. Both of these species are widespread, locally abundant, and delicious.

seeds in fall to early winter by beating the ripe, dry seedheads over a tarp or tub. Dry, rub, and winnow (see p. 27). Amaranth grain from the wild tastes almost identical to that of the cultivated crop, but is much darker. It should be ground or soaked and long-boiled to break up the seedcoat and facilitate digestion before cooking into porridge or using the flour. **Conservation 1.**

COMMENTS: This is one of our most common and delicious wild greens—one of the first plants any forager should learn. We can these in large quantity for winter eating. Some of the better and most common amaranth species are listed here:

▶ (both photos) Water-hemp *Amaranthus tuberculatus* is a species of floodplains, mucky river margins, and very rich farmland. It has hairless stems and is tall and lanky. The leaves are on long petioles, and while the lower ones may be broadly elliptic, the upper ones are very narrow but still blunt at the tip. Inflorescences are long, narrow, and not drooping.

5   Creeping amaranth   🌿 2
Amaranthus blitoides ✛ family *Amaranthaceae*

QUICK CHECK: Creeping herb with thick stems and crowded, alternate, spoon-shaped leaves with whitish margins. **ID difficulty 2.**

DESCRIPTION: Creeping annual, sometimes forming mats; usually ground-hugging in full sun but stems may be weakly erect near the tip. **Stems** usually multiple from the base, up to 32" (80 cm) long, usually hairless but sometimes sparsely hairy, light reddish, solid, roundish in cross section but with a few faint grooves. **Branches** many and mostly short, but occasionally major; short flowering branches have very reduced leaves. **Leaves** alternate, spoon-shaped to elliptic with blunt tips (sometimes notched) and an acute or tapered bases, 0.3–1.8" (8–46 mm) long. The blade is hairless on both sides and sparkly above. **Midvein** and major veins depressed above and protruding below; secondary veins about 45° to the midvein, rarely branched, terminating before the margin; veinlets not evident. **Margins** entire, *traced in whitish.* **Petioles** flat, 30% of blade length, gradually widening into the blade. **Flowers** tiny and drab, in dense, spiny, axillary clusters that are usually shorter than the petiole.

HABITAT: Well-drained disturbed soil in full sun: prairie dog towns, sidewalk cracks, roadsides, pastures, urban lots, gardens. More common westward. Native.

FOOD USE: Gather **tender leafy tips** and eat them cooked. Because they are low to the ground, wash well. **Conservation 1.**

COMMENTS: This is one of the least desirable species of amaranth due to the small size and low-growing habit, but it's still not a bad green when lush and abundant. I separated it from the other amaranths because the form is so different. **AKA** prostrate pigweed, *A. graecizans.*

575

6 Kochia 🌿 2 🌿 2
Kochia scoparia ✦ family *Amaranthaceae*

QUICK CHECK: Densely branched, erect plants with striped stems; narrow, finely-hairy leaves; stemless flowers in the leaf axils. **ID difficulty 1.**

DESCRIPTION: Erect annual 2–6' tall, profusely branching at the base as well as above, forming a tumbleweed at maturity. **Stems** solid with smooth-topped ridges, green, striped with purple or darker green. *All parts have fine, soft hairs lying flat against the surface*—the least hair is on the stems, there is more on the branches, and more still on the leaves. **Branches** slightly ascending at first, the tips eventually sweeping upward. **Leaves** alternate, tufted on spur-like branches that are spreading or drooping; there is a *much longer leaf at the branch base.* **Blades** narrow-elliptic to long-lanceolate, tapered to both ends, 1–3" (2.5–8 cm) long, symmetrical, *soft and velvety* (especially when young) with *3 prominent veins, which remain separate from base to tip,* protruding and flat-bottomed below. **Margins** entire and hairy. Lower leaves have short petioles, but most upper leaves are sessile. **Inflorescence** a terminal spike interrupted by small, linear leaves (bracts) that have very long hair on the margins; bracts are several times longer than the flower or fruit and often lean over it but do not wrap tightly around it. **Flowers** inconspicuous, borne singly or in pairs in bract axils, flat-faced with 5 spreading, whitish-green, petal-like lobes with scurfy edges. **Fruit** has 5 thick lobes or wings and a very thin flesh over a seed shaped like a flattened coil 1 mm across. When the seed is mature, the tops have cottony tufts on each fruiting spike; these persist after the seed is removed. Mature, fruiting plants appear scarcely leafy and lose the stripes on the stems.

▲ Much more common westward.

HABITAT: Dry, sunny, disturbed soil. Roadsides, construction sites, banks, cropland. Introduced. East of the Great Plains it is mostly confined to highways and railroads.

FOOD USE: Gather young tender **leafy tops** from late spring through midsummer and use as a potherb. Ripe **seeds** can be stripped by hand, dried, rubbed, and winnowed, then used as a gruel, grain, or flour. The seeds should be soaked and rinsed before eating.

COMMENTS: It baffles me that an edible plant so widespread and common remains so obscure. At a glance this herb resembles a bushy, narrow-leaved lambsquarters, and it can be thought of similarly as food—although the leaves of kochia toughen more as they mature. **AKA** summer-cypress.

7 Purslane ✎ 3 🌿 2 📖 IWE-309
Portulaca oleracea + family *Portulacaceae*

QUICK CHECK: Trailing hairless plant with thick, succulent stems and blunt succulent leaves. **ID difficulty 1.**

DESCRIPTION: Prostrate, creeping annual, sometimes with the tips erect where vegetation is dense. **Stems** round, thick, succulent, hairless, reddish, branching repeatedly. **Leaves** thick and succulent, up to 0.8" (2 cm) long, obovate or spatulate, entire, the tips rounded, alternate but crowded toward the branch tips, the surface smooth with *veins invisible or scarcely evident*. **Petioles** 5–10% of blade length, flat above and rounded below. **Flowers** (throughout summer) open only in the morning; sessile and single, 5 mm across, flat with 5 broad, touching or overlapping yellow petals that are cleft or indented at the tip. **Fruit** a small, egg-shaped capsule containing several black seeds.

CONFUSING PLANTS: Various creeping spurges of the genus *Euphorbia* are similar in form but have stems and leaves that are thinner and not succulent. They may also have hairy stems, notched leaf tips, leaves with a dark central spot, and milky sap.

HABITAT: Disturbed sunny soil. Common weed of gardens, yards, flower beds, agricultural fields, road shoulders, riverbanks, construction sites. Does especially well on rich, sandy soil. Native.

FOOD USE: Gather **tender growth** and use raw or cooked. Stems and leaves remain succulent and tender much longer than most greens. Be cautious of dirt, as the plant is low-growing; however, being hairless, it washes easily. **Seeds** are very labor-intensive to use. Gather whole mature plants and hang in bundles to dry; seeds will ripen after plants are cut and can then be shaken onto a sheet. **Conservation 1.**

COMMENTS: The thick, crisp leaves and stems have a slightly tangy flavor and are delectable, although the

texture is somewhat mucilaginous. This plant has long been cultivated in parts of Asia for its leaves and sometimes seeds. Purslane is extremely high in iron. Because this plant uses CAM photosynthesis, it builds up acids in its tissues, which peak late on sunny mornings. This is when the leaves taste tangiest.

8 Prairie tea ☕
Croton monanthogyna ✦ Euphorbiaceae (Spurge family)

QUICK CHECK: Low, spreading, flat-topped herb with small, entire, blunt leaves of vary-ing size on very thin zigzag stems; flowers evenly distributed in leaf axils. **ID difficulty 2.**

DESCRIPTION: Annual with a single stem, *unbranched at first but soon branching widely,* the plant to 24" (60 cm) tall and spreading somewhat wider. Pleasantly but moderately aromatic. **Stem** *tough*, thin, rigid, solid, to 5 mm thick, strongly zigzag, the lower part dull green with a broken layer of brown cuticle on the outside, the upper part green or brown-ish with scattered clumps of tiny appressed hairs. **Leaves** alternate but *clustered near branch tips,* 0.4-0.9" (10-23 mm) long, ovate, entire, rounded or abrupt at the base and blunt-tipped, thin, gray-green, densely covered with very fine appressed hairs below, less densely above. **Veins** obscure except the midvein and 2 secondary veins arising near the base, and occasionally another pair near the tip; these are depressed above and protruding below. **Petioles** thin, 30-60% of blade length. **Inflorescence** small, short-stemmed clusters from leaf axils. **Flowers** tiny with a 5-lobed green calyx and zero (female) or 3-8 (male) white petals, the stamens extending beyond the petals. **Fruit** 3 mm long, green, egg-shaped except angled slightly, with 5 linear sepals about half the fruit length; a persistent style protrudes at the tip. Each contains a single seed; there is a white outer layer, a blackish seedshell, and whitish kernel.

HABITAT: Dry, open, sunny sites; fields, roadsides, vacant lots, brushy areas, lightly used pastures, edges of parking lots, dry prairies—especially where disturbed. Native.

FOOD USE: Gather **leaves** at any time during the growing season. Pour boiling water over fresh or dried leaves and steep for tea. **Conservation 2.**

COMMENTS: This is abundant in much of its range and does well in areas of heavy human use. It lines the expressways in the Dallas area, looking like miniature live-oak bonsai trees. The tea is easy to collect and pleasant to drink.

9 Blue flax 🌿 2
Linum perenne ✦ family Linaceae

QUICK CHECK: Clumped, knee-high, hairless herb with thin stems and numerous small, linear, sessile leaves and bright blue 5-petaled flowers. **ID difficulty 2.**

DESCRIPTION: Perennial with many stems from a tough woody base. **Stems** erect to leaning, round, tough, rigid, solid, smooth, hairless, 18-24" (46-60 cm) tall and 2-6 mm thick with fibrous outer bark. They have ascending branches occasionally near the base and often in the upper third—rarely between. **Leaves** alternate, *numerous,* very crowded on young stems, evenly distributed all the way up to the inflorescence, 0.4-1.4" (10-35 mm)

▲ Occasional out-side mapped area.

▼ Flax pods and ripe seeds.

long and 2–4 mm wide, sessile, overlapping, *appressed,* linear to narrowly elliptic, tapered at both ends, pointed, flat, hairless. The *midvein is scarcely evident, and other veins are invisible.* **Inflorescence** a branching panicle of multiple racemes, the pedicels 0.3–0.5" (8–13 mm) long, the buds egg-shaped. **Flowers** (early to mid summer) 0.7–0.9" (18–23 mm) across, opening in the morning and usually closing by afternoon. **Sepals** 5, oval, green, entire, 3 mm long, the tips blunt-pointed. **Petals** 5, very thin, pale to bright blue with darker radiating veins, narrow at the base and broad with a slight notch at the tip. **Pods** nearly spherical, very symmetrical, 5 mm long, ripening to straw color and splitting into 10 sharp-tipped sections. The pods contain up to 10 **seeds**, flattened and teardrop-shaped like domestic flax seeds, but darker brown to black and about 1/3 the size.

HABITAT: Well-drained, sunny, disturbed soil, especially where poor and sandy or gravelly. Roadsides, steep slopes, vacant lots, river banks, old fields, etc. Introduced and native.

FOOD USE: The **seeds** can be used like those of domestic flax. Strip ripe pods by hand from mid to late summer; dry pods need to be beaten and then winnowed to separate the chaff. Tender greens and flower buds are bitter and distasteful. **Conservation 1.**

COMMENTS: *Linum perenne* is the wild flax from which domestic flax *L. usitatissimum* was derived. The nearly identical native blue flax is sometimes separated as *L. lewisii,* but the differences are minor. Flaxes are some of our most attractive wildflowers. There are several other native flax species, some with yellow flowers, of unknown edibility. I have only tried the following:

Related edible:

10 Stiff yellow flax ✦ *Linum rigidum/berlandieri* 🌿 3 🌱 3 🌸 3

This native flax is sometimes divided into two similar species. It is an annual with stiff, erect stems that

only reaches 6–12" (15–30 cm) in height, found on dry prairies, roadsides, and disturbed fields. There are paired leaves near the stem base. The flowers bloom in spring and are arranged in a flat-topped cluster at the apex. The petals are yellow, sometimes (especially in *L. berlandieri*) coppery-orange at the base. I have not eaten the ripe seeds of stiff yellow flax, but the tender **tips**, **flowers**, and flower **buds** are excellent.

11 Horseweed
Conyza canadensis + *Asteraceae* (Composite family)

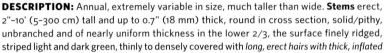

QUICK CHECK: Tall, columnar plant with long, narrow, crowded leaves; the upper third has numerous small ascending branches bearing small white flowerheads. **ID difficulty 2.**

DESCRIPTION: Annual, extremely variable in size, much taller than wide. **Stems** erect, 2"–10' (5–300 cm) tall and up to 0.7" (18 mm) thick, round in cross section, solid/pithy, unbranched and of nearly uniform thickness in the lower 2/3, the surface finely ridged, striped light and dark green, thinly to densely covered with *long, erect hairs with thick, inflated bases and thin, wispy tips.* The upper third of the plant has *numerous strongly ascending branches*, straight and simple, scarcely tapering, bearing flowerheads. **Leaves** alternate, sessile or with a short, winged petiole, numerous, crowded, ascending, lanceolate or oblanceolate to narrowly elliptic, tapered at the base and sharp-tipped, 2–7" (5–18 cm) long, hairy near the midvein or hairless, wilting from the bottom up before flowering. **Midvein** with a flat to slightly raised double ridge in a gentle valley above, and a dull keel below. **Secondary veins** few or often not evident, 10–20° to the midvein; the first pair from the base runs *close to the margin for half the leaf length.* There may appear to be an almost discontinuous random assortment of veinlets *raised on the upper surface.* **Margins** with sparse, stiff hairs, entire on upper leaves; lower leaves have a few scattered teeth—up to 4 per side. Leaves often have 1–2 tiny leaves in the axil, which may eventually erupt into branches. **Inflorescence** the entire upper third of the plant can be construed as a giant leafy panicle, or each branch as its own panicle, with heads in smaller sub-clusters. **Heads** 3–5 mm across, numerous but not crowded, cylindrical, not spreading open, containing disk and ray florets. Thread-thin white rays scarcely surpass the narrow, green bracts. **Seed** compressed, yellowish, and shiny, attached to a white to tan parachute.

CONFUSING PLANTS: Goldenrods have veins depressed above.

HABITAT: Disturbed, sunny, well-drained soil. Crop fields, roadsides, construction sites, and clearcuts—especially those sprayed with herbicide. Native.

FOOD USE: The new **leaves** and tender **stem tips** have a unique, hot, spicy flavor. This is a seasoning to be used sparingly. **Conservation 1.**

COMMENTS: Dense, nearly pure stands of horseweed after logging are a good indicator of herbicide use—the plant has lately been increasing greatly in abundance. It has been grown commercially as a flavoring for at least one soft drink—taste it and see if you can identify which one. The dried stems make excellent spindles for friction fires. **AKA** *Erigeron canadensis.*

12 Thoroughwax 🖋 1
Bupleurum rotundifolium ✦ Apiaceae (Carrot family)

▲ Sparsely
distributed.

QUICK CHECK: Smooth, hairless plant with forking stems, broad perfoliate leaves, and umbels of tiny yellow flowers with whorls of ovate bracts. **ID difficulty 2.**

DESCRIPTION: Low annual herb to 2' (60 cm) tall. **Stems** 2-3 mm thick at the base, rounded, smooth, hairless, solid, pale green (sometimes with reddish areas), Y-forking frequently by flowering, becoming very tough and wiry with age. **Leaves** *perfoliate* (the stems grow through them), close together on young stems and near the base but widely separated on branches. The blades are ovate (often broadly), 1-3" (2.5-8 cm) long, cupped, rounded at the base and blunt-pointed with a nipple tip. The surface is smooth and hairless on both sides. Margins are entire and *light in color.* **Veins** colorless (especially evident when held up to light). The midvein is slightly depressed above and protruding below; all other veins are flat on both sides. *All major veins radiate from the base,* curving, not branching until near the margins. **Inflorescence** (summer) several terminal, flat to slightly convex *compound umbels.* The first juncture, without bracts, has 5-9 rays 10-14 mm long. The second juncture is subtended by a *whorl of 5-6 unequal, ovate, sharp-pointed, entire, bristle-tipped bracts* extending well beyond the flowers and overlapping with those of adjacent umbels. The 5-10 flowers of each umbellet are tiny, nearly touching, yellow, on very short pedicels, with tiny petals almost indiscernible.

HABITAT: Disturbed, dry, sunny ground, especially where sandy or gravelly. Locally common but overall scarce, scattered, and unpredictable. Introduced.

FOOD USE: Young, tender **leafy tips** can be eaten raw or cooked in spring.

COMMENTS: The flavor is slightly aromatic and a tad bitter, but not unpleasant in moderation—it reminds me of eryngo. However, it can be stunning as a garnish. The inflorescence unmistakably puts it in the carrot family (*Apiacieae*) but the stems and leaves are quite unusual for that group. The name means "growing through" in reference to the perfoliate leaves. The genus name means "ox rib" in reference to the rib-like vein pattern.

13 Japanese knotweed $\quad$ 2 $\quad$ IWE-171
Reynoutria japonica + *Polygonaceae* (Buckwheat family)

QUICK CHECK: Very large, arching herbs with hollow, jointed stems and large, broad leaves; forming thickets. **ID difficulty 1.**

DESCRIPTION: Large, arching, cane-like perennial herb growing in dense colonies from a network of tough, dark, stout rhizomes. **Stems** 6-10' (2-3 m) long and 0.8-1.6" (2-4 cm) thick, arching, distinctly jointed at the nodes (which are darkened), hollow between the nodes, smooth with many fine grooves (and a larger groove above each petiole), hairless, often with bloom, green with purplish spots (may be mostly purple in the shoot stage). **LYDS** persistent and *prominent*. **Leaves** alternate, 4-10" (10-25 cm) long, ovate with heart-shaped or truncated bases and acuminate tips, hairless on top but sometimes faintly hairy below, with entire margins. **Midvein** and secondary veins are lightly depressed. **Petioles** 10-25%

▲ Composite range of Japanese and giant knotweeds.

of blade length, as deep as wide and slightly channeled; there is a thin, papery sheath where they attach to the stem, but this may disintegrate and fall off. **Inflorescence** dense, erect to ascending panicles at the stem tips, and smaller panicles from leaf axils; each panicle composed of many smaller racemes of 3-10 flowers. Pedicels thin and white, widening toward the flower. Flower buds 3-sided. **Flowers** (late summer) tiny with 4 white spreading petals. **Fruit** a 3-sided seed (achene) in a papery sheath.

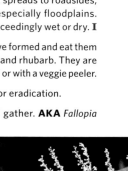

CONFUSING PLANT: Chameleon plant *Houttuynia cordata* (also edible but tastes totally different) has a *solid* and proportionately thinner stem that is reddish but not mottled, the nodes lightened. The petioles are deeply channeled; leaves are more acuminate and heart-shaped, and the young leaves are variegated. The plant is strongly scented.

HABITAT: An invasive escape from ornamental plantings that spreads to roadsides, old fields, abandoned home sites, orchards, woodlots, and especially floodplains. Likes full sun to partial shade on a wide range of soils, but not exceedingly wet or dry. **I**

FOOD USE: Gather tender **shoots** in spring before the leaves have formed and eat them raw or cooked. They are sour with a flavor reminiscent of dock and rhubarb. They are better after the skin has been peeled off, which you can do by hand or with a veggie peeler.

WARNING! Beware of herbicide. This plant is often sprayed for eradication.

COMMENTS: This plant is remarkably easy to identify and gather. **AKA** *Fallopia japonica, Polygonum cuspidatum.*

Related edible:
Giant knotweed +
Reynoutria sachalinensis

A larger plant with proportionately narrower leaves up to 16" (40 cm) long, drooping with more heart-shaped bases, and secondary veins that are more prominent and deeply depressed. The stem walls are thinner. Both species are used similarly, and hybrids occur. **I**

14 SMARTWEED
genus *Persicaria* ✦ *Polygonaceae* (Buckwheat family)

QUICK GROUP ID: Zigzag stems with a papery sheath above each enlarged node; leaves narrow and entire; tiny white to pink flowers in small spike-like clusters. **ID difficulty 1.**

DESCRIPTION: Annual or perennial herbs, erect to lax. **Stems** round, smooth or sometimes faintly ribbed but not angled, *bulged at the nodes*, zigzag, 1–7' (30–210 cm) long, up to 0.8" (2 cm) thick, usually branched. **Sheath** (these may wither with age) wrapped around the stem *above each node*, thin and papery, the base fused to the petiole, split down one side, the end unlobed but often with protruding bristles at the apex. **Leaves** alternate, mostly sessile or on short petioles, 1–9" (2.5–23 cm) long, entire, lanceolate to elliptic or ovate, the tips pointed. The leaves of several species may have a large dark zone (thumbprint) in the center. **Petioles** D-shaped, not channeled, flaring gradually into the blade. **Midveins** prominent, offset by light color, raised at the bottom of a gentle valley. **Secondary veins** numerous, prominent, and usually lightly depressed, 45–80° to the midvein. **Inflorescence** terminal on all species, also axillary on some; a spike or spike-like raceme, erect or drooping and *often resembling a catkin*, bearing numerous small flowers in mini-clusters, the pedicels very short, *neither the raceme or any individual flowers subtended by leafy bracts*.

▲ Composite range of smartweeds. The 4 species shown are each widely distributed through most of this range.

Flowers tiny, about 3 mm across, white or greenish or pink to red, often multiple colors on the same spike, with 4–5 hairless tepals that scarcely open on most species. After blooming the sepals close around the single developing seed (achene). **Seeds** dark, 2–3 mm long, broadly oval with a nipple-point, often slightly flattened.

FOOD USE: Tender young **leaves** and **stem tips** can be used raw but are better cooked. The **flowering spikes** make a fun but not delicious nibble. **Conservation 1.**

COMMENTS: In older classifications this group is part of the genus *Polygonum*, but today most botanists split the smartweeds into their own genus. All smartweeds are safe to eat as tender young greens—although some are *hot* and others more or less astringent. The name "smartweed" comes from the pain caused by the peppery components of some species after you touch them and then touch sensitive areas such as your eyes or lips. Highlighted below are a few of the best and most common species.

Dock-leaved smartweed ✦ *Persicaria lapathifolia* 2

Annual 2–7' (60–210 cm) tall with stems up to 0.8" (2 cm) thick, usually erect and spreading with major branches. **Leaves** large, narrowly lanceolate, 3–9" (8–23 cm) long, the blades smooth and usually hairless below; above they have sparse, stiff, leaning hairs mostly near the margin. When young the leaves usually have a large dark spot in the center, but this is often absent at flowering. **Sheath** has prominent, raised, darkened veins, but *no extending bristles*. **Inflorescence** 1–3" (2.5–8 cm) long, *arching or drooping*. **Flowers** tiny, white, greenish, or pinkish, the tepals not spreading and scarcely distinguishable. (Continued on the next page.)

▲ (left) Young leaves of dock-leaved smartweed. (middle and right) The flowers can also be pink. ▲

Dock-leaved smartweed (continued)

HABITAT: Disturbed, rich, moist soil in full to partial sun. Disturbed woods, barnyards and fields, floodplains, pond margins, roadsides, beaver lodges and dams. Native.

COMMENTS: This is the largest of our smartweeds. I think it has a good flavor and texture, although older leaves get astringent. This species can be separated from *P. maculosa* when young by the lack of bristles on its leaf sheath.

Lady's Thumb ✦ *Persicaria maculosa* 2

Medium-sized annual to 3.5' (1 m) tall, sometimes sprawling or semi-erect and rooting at the nodes. **Leaves** 1–6" (2.5–15 cm) long, narrowly lanceolate, usually with a dark "thumbprint" in the center. **Sheath** has a fringe of short bristles. **Flowers** white to pink, in short, dense, *erect* spikes to 2" (5 cm) long.

HABITAT: Disturbed, moist, rich soil in full sun to moderate shade. Grows in weedy situations such as yards, gardens, crop fields, vacant lots, disturbed woods, riverbanks, dried up puddles, washouts.

COMMENTS: This common weed makes a good vegetable and is often abundant in urban and agricultural landscapes.

◄ (left) Mature lady's thumb. (above) Young greens of lady's thumb. ▲

Pepper smartweed ✦ *Persicaria hydropiper*

Annual, leaning to spreading or weakly erect, the stems to 30" (75 cm) long. Lower branches are spreading; *upper branches are sometimes appressed to the stem by a sheath, only diverging after the first node.* **Leaves** 2–5" (5–13 cm) long, on petioles 3–5% of blade length, lanceolate, *often wavy, especially before flowering*, lacking the dark thumbprint. The sheath has bristles on the upper margin. The zigzag inflorescence branches often droop and are up to 7" (18 cm) long, with well-spaced flowers at each node, getting closer together toward the branch tips. **Flowers** white, often with a pink tip; the corolla does not spread. There is often one or a few flowers in a smaller upper leaf axil enclosed by a sheath—these flowers never open and presumably self-fertilize. There are sometimes tiny flower clusters near the plant's base. **Seed** single, shiny, enclosed in a green calyx that is *dotted with numerous tiny pits* (hard to see without magnification).

HABITAT: Sunny to partly shaded, rich, moist, disturbed soil: mucky depressions in floodplain woods, pond or lake margins, beaver dams and lodges, dried-up puddles, marshes (especially on muskrat lodges); also upland sites such as barnyards, backyards, weedy woodlots, construction sites, and gardens. Probably native.

FOOD USE: The **leaves** can be used as a hot seasoning; the effect is potent but delayed several seconds, and does not linger like capsaicin. They are best when young and tender; if gathered when tough they should be chopped fine. Most of the heat is lost by drying or canning. **Conservation 1.**

COMMENTS: This plant is very hot, and should be used in moderation. Cultivated varieties with milder flavor are grown in East Asia. This is the species for which the name "smartweed" was given; any gardeners who have touched their lips or eyes after pulling this out can attest to its potency. The chemical primarily responsible for this hotness is *warburganal*. **AKA** water pepper.

RELATED EDIBLES: The only other hot species I have identified in this genus is *Persicaria punctata*, a native which is very similar to the above species but has broader, flatter leaves and flowers that are usually not tinged pink; magnification reveals the seed (achene) to be smooth and glossier than that of *P. hydropiper*. The false water pepper *P. hydropiperoides* is not hot.

Water smartweed ⬩ *Persicaria amphibia* & *P. coccinea* 1 ⎮ 1

Two similar species share this common name; both of them spread by rhizome to form loose colonies on land or in the water. The form is variable in both species due to growing conditions—there are floating-leaved aquatic stems as well as erect terrestrial stems. The latter tend to have large leaves. Water smartweeds have showy red flowers densely packed into erect, usually solitary clusters 0.6–3.5" (1.5–9 cm) long.

HABITAT: Sunny or partially sunny shallow water, wetlands, and dry land near water, especially where the water level fluctuates dramatically. Most common along large rivers, pothole ponds, and marshes with no outlet. Native.

FOOD USE: The **shoots** and **young leaves**, especially those that are still scrolled, can be eaten raw or cooked as a potherb. With age they quickly become tough and very astringent. **Conservation 1.**

COMMENTS: This adaptable plant spreads great distances by rhizomes, and can survive fluctuating water levels by living in standing water or on dry ground. *P. coccinea* produces semi-woody tubers that don't taste bad if you have an extra set of teeth and a few hours for chewing.

◀ Water smartweed shoot (left) and flower (right).

15 Erect knotweed 🌿 1 🌱 2
Polygonum erectum + *Polygonaceae* (Buckwheat family)

QUICK CHECK: Calf to knee-high with entire, elliptic leaves of very different sizes; tough, jointed, green, zigzag stems and tiny flowers in the leaf axils. **ID difficulty 2.**

DESCRIPTION: Annual herb 9–28" (23–71 cm) tall, erect to erratically leaning or spreading. **Stems** flexible and tough but not brittle, specially adapted to spring back up unharmed after trampling, roundish, to 5 mm thick, zigzag, bright green, finely striated, jointed and bulged at the closely spaced nodes, strongly tapered between them. Sheaths at nodes are small, brown, papery, and cut into sharp-pointed sections. **Branches** at 45–70° angles, may be prominent and wide spreading in light competition, absent or few (but often long) where crowded. **Leaves** alternate, thin, entire, flat, elliptic, tapered to the base, nearly sessile, the tips acute and usually pointed but often blunt; the leaves are *extremely variable in size, 0.3–2.2" (8–56 mm) long—those on branches much smaller than those borne on the main stem.* **Veins** flat above, slightly protruding below; the secondary veins are 45° to the midvein. **Flowers** tiny, in small groups on short, thread-like pedicels from leaf axils, greenish and white with 5 spreading, triangular tepals. After pollination the tepals close over the fruit, which is a single, dry, triangular, brown seed (achene).

HABITAT: Moist, rich soil in full sun to semi-shade, in areas where taller plants are trampled but not mowed or herbicided. Mostly openings in river floodplains, forest edges, boat landing areas, bridges, trails, road edges, margins of dirt parking areas, poorly maintained parks, barnyards. Native.

FOOD USE: Tender young **leaves** are marginally edible, like those of other knotweeds. Ripe **seeds** (late autumn) can be winnowed, cracked, and cooked like buckwheat, to which it is related. **Conservation 3.**

COMMENTS: We don't really know the distribution of this plant because it has been so often misidentified by botanists, and because a similar species, *P. achoreum,* has sometimes been lumped with it. Prehistorically erect knotweed was grown as a seed crop in the lower Midwest and upper South; it was domesticated thousands of years ago, but those strains are now extinct. Once fairly common as a weed, this species has declined drastically over the last 70 years, probably due to the advent of riding lawnmowers, weedwackers, and herbicide. It thrived in areas moderately trodden by horses, but most such areas are mowed or sprayed now. Don't gather unless abundant; curate the conditions to maintain a colony.

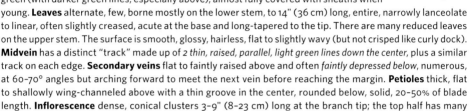

16 **Willow-leaved dock** 🖌 1 ┃ 2 🍃 2 📖 NG-226
Rumex triangulivalvis ✦ *Polygonaceae* (Buckwheat family)

QUICK CHECK: Multiple leaning stems with long, narrow, entire, glossy, hairless leaves, some of them over a foot long; unshowy flowers and dry triangular fruits. **ID difficulty 1.**

DESCRIPTION: Perennial herb from a taproot, the greenery dying back in late summer. **Stems** clumped, weakly erect, leaning, or spreading, to 5' (1.5 m) tall and 13 mm thick, solid, round but for one shallow trough in each internode, the surface smooth, hairless, light green (with darker green lines, especially above), almost fully covered with sheaths when young. **Leaves** alternate, few, borne mostly on the lower stem, to 14" (36 cm) long, entire, narrowly lanceolate to linear, often slightly creased, acute at the base and long-tapered to the tip. There are many reduced leaves on the upper stem. The surface is smooth, glossy, hairless, flat to slightly wavy (but not crisped like curly dock). **Midvein** has a distinct "track" made up of 2 *thin, raised, parallel, light green lines down the center*, plus a similar track on each edge. **Secondary veins** flat to faintly raised above and often *faintly depressed below*, numerous, at 60-70° angles but arching forward to meet the next vein before reaching the margin. **Petioles** thick, flat to shallowly wing-channeled above with a thin groove in the center, rounded below, solid, 20-50% of blade length. **Inflorescence** dense, conical clusters 3-9" (8-23 cm) long at the branch tip; the top half has many

such clusters. **Flowers** (spring) tiny, greenish, and unshowy. **Seeds** brown, 2-3 mm long, 3-sided, the edges sharp, enclosed by 3 triangular leafy structures 5-6 mm long with heart-shaped bases, each with a large kidney-shaped thingamajigger (tubercle) in the center.

HABITAT: Disturbed soil in full sun, especially where sandy and rich. Likes well-drained but periodically moist sites. Roadsides, steep slopes, field edges, vacant lots, river banks, ditches. Native.

FOOD USE: The young **leaves**, **stems**, and **petioles** can be eaten raw or cooked in spring or early summer, as long as they remain tender. **Conservation 2.**

COMMENTS: This good-tasting dock is unusual in not having a basal rosette; you might fail to notice this at a glance. In much of our area it is the only weedy dock that is native. **AKA** *Rumex mexicanus.*

17 **Poke** ┃ 3 🖌 3 📖 IWE-266
Phytolacca americana ✦ family *Phytolaccaceae*

QUICK CHECK: Thick, tapered, hairless, clumped shoots with entire, elliptic, alternate leaves; very large branchy herb with drooping racemes of squat purple berries in late summer. **ID difficulty 2.**

DESCRIPTION: Perennial from a fleshy taproot that may be very thick. **Stems** 3-10' (1-3 m) tall, in clumps of up to 40, hairless, smooth, glaucous, round, solid at first becoming pithy, up to 2" (5 cm) thick, red to purple at maturity but light green when young, erect to leaning, with prominent ascending branches in the upper half. **LYDS** prominent, light straw-colored, *the pith chambered and sometimes breaking into discs.* **Leaves** 3-12" (8-30 cm) long, alternate, lanceolate to narrowly ovate, hairless, entire, sometimes wavy-edged, acute at the base and tip, the tips blunt with a tiny indent where there is a *downturned tooth* about 2 mm long. New leaves are slightly ascending, but *older ones are descending to drooping.* **Midvein** slightly depressed above and protruding below. (Continued on the next page.)

17 Poke (continued)

Secondary veins broadly angled, slightly depressed above, dividing before reaching the margins. **Petioles** 8–15% of blade length, broadly channeled, the edges with a wing tapering from the leaf base. *From each node there are two faint wing-ridges, often purple tinted, running down the otherwise smooth stem to the next node below.* **Shoots** *taper strongly* and have *skin that peels in thin, translucent strips.* New leaves are *crinkled,* the upper ones pointing vertically. **Inflorescence** (summer into fall) a raceme 5–14" (13–36 cm) long, descending to drooping, usually curving, with 40–90 flowers on pedicels 5–12 mm long. **Flowers** white to light pinkish, 5 mm across, with 5 sepals (looking like petals), these broadly elliptic and spreading to reflexed, cupped with incurved tips. **Fruit** (late summer to fall) a purple-black berry containing several dark seeds, broader than long and flattened like a doughnut, 9–10 mm across, with usually 11 radiating sections (evident when the fruit is green), each section with a tiny protruding "whisker" at the tip. They are borne almost touching one another on a drooping raceme.

HABITAT: Young or open disturbed woods, logged areas, forest edges, fields, pastures, roadsides, fencerows, floodplain forests. Especially likes sandy soil. Native.

FOOD USE: Gather young **shoots** and their **leaves** in spring while still tender and meristematic. Leaves should be small, ruffled, clustered, and erect; stems should be robust, not fibrous, and green. Before eating, shoots and greens **must be boiled in two changes of water** for 10 minutes each. **Conservation 1.**

WARNING! Poke should not be eaten raw! Raw poke is toxic and will make you severely ill. Only young, tender, meristematic greens can be eaten.

COMMENTS: In much of our region this is our most commonly eaten and best-known wild vegetable. The stems are large, succulent, mild in flavor, easily collected, and prolific—but **they must be young and meristematic**. The berries are sometimes used in small amounts medicinally but I recommend against eating them. Although I have heard second-hand reports of them being used for pie, jelly, or juice, the absence of first-hand accounts despite extensive interviews is suspicious, and the taste of the berries is not good.

▲ The ideal stage for harvest.

18 Fireweed 🥄 1 ☕ pith 2
Epilobium angustifolium + family *Onagraceae*

QUICK CHECK: Tall, straight colonial plant with thin, unbranched stems; numerous nearly sessile, linear leaves and 4-part pink-purple flowers in a raceme. **ID difficulty 1.**

DESCRIPTION: Perennial forming colonies by rhizome. **Stems** erect, not clumped, 4–9' (1.2–2.7 m) tall and 5–13 mm thick, mostly unbranched, proportionately thin, straight, hairless or slightly woolly, the surface with faint bloom and gentle ridges (more prominent toward the top) running down from each node, the bark stringy. The inside is solid green flesh with a whitish center, *slimy and soft.* **Shoots** tapered, light green, sometimes with a faint purplish cast, vertically lined. Lowest **shoot leaves** tiny with prominent midveins protruding below, the margins with a few tiny, scattered, darkened bumps. **Leaves** alternate, crowded, narrow-lanceolate, tapered to the base, long-pointed, 2–7" (5–18 cm) long, pale and hairless below, hairless or nearly so above. There are tiny leaf clusters in each axil. **Midvein** very prominent and light-colored (sometimes purplish)—depressed and sometimes faintly hairy above, projecting and rounded below. **Secondary veins** slightly depressed above and protruding below, 75–80°, looping forward and linking just before hitting the margin. **Margins** curled downward, entire or with a few tiny, scattered tooth-like bumps. **Petiole** 1–3% of blade length. **Inflorescence** a raceme to 18" (46 cm) long, the lower part with flowers in the axils of leaves gradually decreasing in size, the pedicels 4–9 mm. **Flowers** (mid to late summer) very showy, a long purple tube flaring into 4 linear sepals behind 4 lighter pink-purple petals, broad-tipped and narrowed to a stalked base, *asymmetrical* as if a petal is missing. The filaments and style are *drooping and white,* the stigma 4-lobed. After blooming in late summer, the reddish stems of the inflorescence give the whole colony a purplish haze. **Fruit** a thin, almost needle-like capsule 1–2.5" (2.5–6.5 cm) long, ascending at maturity, with fine hairs, splitting open to release numerous seeds with silky parachutes.

CONFUSING PLANTS: Goldenrods have rough or fuzzy leaves with less prominent midveins, and secondary veins at sharper angles. Horseweed is conspicuously hairy.

HABITAT: Sunny, disturbed sites in forested regions; along trails and roads, riverbanks, clearings, landslides, forest edges. Often abundant after clearcutting or forest fires. Native. 🔥

FOOD USE: Gather young **shoots** while still tender, from 6–14" (15–36 cm) tall. Remove leafy tips and discard, then boil shoots to remove bitterness. Dried leaves make a good **tea**; properly fermented leaves make an excellent tea. **Pith** from young stalks can be broken out and eaten raw or cooked. **Conservation 2.**

COMMENTS: Although often mentioned in the wild food literature, the shoots of this plant are not much liked as a vegetable, as the leaves and skin are astringent. **AKA** *Chamaenerion platyphyllum.*

19 American pellitory 2
Parietaria pensylvanica ◆ *Urticaceae* **(Nettle family)**

QUICK CHECK: Small, light green, erect herb with thin, entire, alternate leaves; prominent clusters of bracts in each axil. **ID difficulty 2.**

DESCRIPTION: Small, delicate annual to 23" (58 cm) tall. **Stems** erect (sometimes trailing for an inch or so before turning erect), *very thin* (1–3 mm), often leaning onto nearby vegetation, light green or reddish to colorless, solid and succulent, *nearly clear*, with faint ridges and fine woolly hairs that become more prominent with age. Unbranched or occasionally with a few ascending branches near the base. **Leaves** alternate (but close together on young plants and thus appearing paired at a glance) 0.6–2.5" (15–64 mm) long, *entire, very thin*, ovate-lanceolate to oblong, with an angled base and tapering to a *blunt or rounded tip*. **Midvein** lightly depressed above. There are usually 2 depressed secondary veins per side, the lower one arising near but not at the base. **Surfaces** minutely bumpy and hairy, especially on top. Mature plants develop stiff-hairy leaves and often *cling to pants or shoes* as a means of seed dispersal. **Petioles** thin, hairy, faintly grooved, lacking stipules, 25–50% of blade length, often light red. **Inflorescence** small, sessile clusters of 3–5 nestled in the axils, each cluster with a few *entire, lanceolate bracts* at the base, forming an *involucre obscuring the flowers*. **Flowers** tiny, drab and greenish-white, with 4 parts.

CONFUSING PLANTS: Three-seeded mercury (genus *Acalyphya*) has toothed leaves and petioles almost as long as the blade. The bracts are single, broad, and lobed, while those of pellitory are multiple, narrow, and unlobed.

HABITAT: Seasonally moist but well-drained alkaline soil in partial to heavy shade. Masonry walls, limestone formations, trailsides, disturbed woods, especially where steep or beside large objects such as cliffs, boulders, buildings, and large stumps. Native.

FOOD USE: When young and tender the **whole plant** can be used raw or cooked; it has a cucumber flavor. **Conservation 2.**

COMMENTS: These mild-flavored greens are not well known by foragers but are widely available and good when young. The much larger and better known European pellitory *P. officinale* has not been documented in North America. In England it is sometimes called "pellitory against the wall." It has an affinity for calcium, which it finds in limestone, mortar, or concrete. Pellitory in the southwestern part of our area (especially Texas) is sometimes considered a separate species; it tends to be slightly tougher and much hairier. **AKA** cucumber weed. **Florida pellitory** *P. floridana* is a cool-weather winter edible confined to the Southeast, where it is locally prevalent as a yard weed on high-calcium sandy soils.

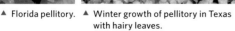

▲ Florida pellitory.   ▲ Winter growth of pellitory in Texas with hairy leaves.

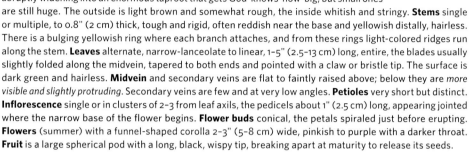

20 Bush morning glory   1
Ipomoea leptophylla ✦ family *Convolvulaceae*

QUICK CHECK: Large bushy herb with numerous spreading branches, dark narrow leaves, and large pink flowers. **ID difficulty 1.**

DESCRIPTION: Large, bushy, willow-like perennial herb to 4' (1.2 m) tall and 5' (1.5 m) wide, with spreading branches starting at the base and sweeping out then upward. **Root** (and underground stem) is at first narrow and vertical for 9–14" (23–36 cm) before abruptly widening into an enormous taproot that gets God-knows-how-big, but small ones are still huge. The outside is light brown and somewhat rough, the inside whitish and stringy. **Stems** single or multiple, to 0.8" (2 cm) thick, tough and rigid, often reddish near the base and yellowish distally, hairless. There is a bulging yellowish ring where each branch attaches, and from these rings light-colored ridges run along the stem. **Leaves** alternate, narrow-lanceolate to linear, 1–5" (2.5–13 cm) long, entire, the blades usually slightly folded along the midvein, tapered to both ends and pointed with a claw or bristle tip. The surface is dark green and hairless. **Midvein** and secondary veins are flat to faintly raised above; below they are *more visible and slightly protruding*. Secondary veins are few and at very low angles. **Petioles** very short but distinct. **Inflorescence** single or in clusters of 2–3 from leaf axils, the pedicels about 1" (2.5 cm) long, appearing jointed where the narrow base of the flower begins. **Flower buds** conical, the petals spiraled just before erupting. **Flowers** (summer) with a funnel-shaped corolla 2–3" (5–8 cm) wide, pinkish to purple with a darker throat. **Fruit** is a large spherical pod with a long, black, wispy tip, breaking apart at maturity to release its seeds.

HABITAT: Dry prairies in sandy soil; sensitive to grazing. Native.

FOOD USE: Dig up the **roots** at any time of year (but especially when the tops are dormant). Select the small plants; larger ones will be too big to dig out, and the roots will be excessively fibrous. Cleaned roots can

be sliced and eaten raw or cooked and have a mild, sweet flavor—but they are rather tough, and they are tough to dig up. **Conservation 3.**

COMMENTS: The size of these roots is legendary, and the legend isn't kidding. When young and tender, it's an okay vegetable. Look between the road and the barbed wire, which is often the only place the cows don't graze. Because the enormous roots store water, bush morning glory is sometimes an island of green in a late summer droughty landscape.

591

21 Bastard toadflax 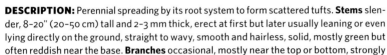 2
Comandra umbellata + family *Santalaceae*

QUICK CHECK: Clumped shin-high stems, the gray-green leaves entire, sessile, smooth, decreasing in size toward the tip; fruit shaped like a rose hip. **ID difficulty 1.**

DESCRIPTION: Perennial spreading by its root system to form scattered tufts. **Stems** slender, 8–20" (20–50 cm) tall and 2–3 mm thick, erect at first but later usually leaning or even lying directly on the ground, straight to wavy, smooth and hairless, solid, mostly green but often reddish near the base. **Branches** occasional, mostly near the top or bottom, strongly ascending. **Leaves** alternate, sessile or on very short petioles, *numerous and overlapping*, evenly distributed along the stem but *drastically decreasing in size* distally, *strongly ascending* with the tips often curled back toward the stem. **Blades** ovate to narrowly lanceolate, 0.3–1.9" (8–48 mm) long, acute at the base and rounded to blunt at the tip, light grayish green, smooth and hairless, slightly waxy. **Midvein** flat above and protruding below; other veins are faint, flat or nearly so on both sides; veinlets are more evident below. **Inflorescence** a terminal cluster (cyme) of 3–6, or, more commonly, several such cymes packed together into a crowded, flat-topped to convex cluster (not an umbel as the name suggests, but it kind of looks like one). **Flowers** (May–July) 4–6 mm wide when spread, with 5 (occasionally 4) triangular white sepal lobes (which look like petals) fused at the base, hairy inside. There is one stamen per lobe, the anthers dull yellow, and one pistil per flower. **Fruit** urnshaped with the calyx persisting at the tip, 4–7 mm long, turning from green to reddish to brown, ripening mid to late summer, with a thin green skin around a single nut-like seed 2–4 mm long.

HABITAT: Dry, sunny sites, especially on poor soil. Common in rocky glades, dry prairies and savannahs, sandy open woods, beaches, ridge tops, road banks. Native. 🔥

FOOD USE: The nut-like seeds make a tasty snack. They are larger in the western part of our area. **Conservation 1.**

COMMENTS: This is not one of the plants that hippies name their children after—neither the scientific name nor the common one. The nutlets are quite good—I just crunch up the shells as I eat them. Too bad they are so small. Bastard toadflax is a partially parasitic generalist that appears to be able to steal nutrients and moisture from the roots of virtually any plant that grows near it. At a glance it looks like flax, but even toads make their bedsheets from real linen. This plant is variable in form and has been divided by some botanists into several species.

22 Common dayflower 🖋 2
Commelina communis + family *Commelinaceae*

QUICK CHECK: Clasping, alternate leaves; flowers with 2 large blue petals above and one small white one below. **ID difficulty 1.**

DESCRIPTION: Annual, often forming dense mats. **Stems** single but often branching near the base, to 38" (1 m) long and 12" (30 cm) high, creeping to decumbent or weakly ascending, sometimes rooting at the nodes, smooth and mostly round but flattened on one side above each node, solid, zigzag. **Leaves** alternate, widely spaced, 2–5" (5–13 cm) long, entire, ovate to lanceolate, the base rounded and the tip pointed, *clasping with a veiny sheath constricted below each leaf.* Blades are slightly thick and succulent, sometimes hairy (more so at the point where they clasp the stem). **Veins** parallel, depressed scarcely if at all, except the midvein, which is depressed above and weakly keeled below. **Inflorescence** (mid to late summer) small clusters from the leaf axils, one blooming at a time, on short stems hidden mostly within *a large, deeply folded bract* 1–2" (2.5–5 cm) long. **Flowers** (summer to early fall) last for only one day, 11–13 mm across with two larger, broad, blue petals above, these narrowed to a stalked base, and one *much smaller whitish petal below.* There are several filaments of various lengths bearing yellow, *3-lobed flattened anthers* with a purplish spot in the center. **Fruit** a blunt, thick, slightly flattened capsule on a kinked, *umbilical-cord-like stalk,* the capsule milky inside when young, splitting into 2 parts at maturity to release 4 large seeds that are flattened on 1 or 2 sides.

HABITAT: Moist, rich soil in partial shade where the ground has been disturbed. Backyards, parks, forest edges, urban woodlots. Sporadic and unpredictable but often common. Introduced.

FOOD USE: Gather the tender terminal sections of **leaves** and **stems** and eat them raw or cooked. With a mild, cucumber-like flavor, they are a pleasant wild nibble or addition to salads. The **flowers** and immature **seedpods** can be eaten along with the greens.

COMMENTS: Pretty good, pretty common, pretty enough. Tender parts of all the dayflower species are edible.

RELATED EDIBLE: Climbing dayflower *C. diffusa* is another introduced species, frequent in disturbed moist soils of the Southeast, creeping and rooting at the nodes, the erect stems 10–12" (25–30 cm) tall and 3–5 mm thick, forming dense clumps in sunny areas. Its sharp-tipped leaves are deeply folded when young, reaching 1–2" (2.5–5 cm) long. They are sometimes raspy on top and the sheath suture is hairy. The flowers have 3 blue petals, the lower one almost as large as the upper two. One yellow anther is much larger than the others. The young greens are similarly edible.

Commelina diffusa greens. ▶

23 Tall dayflower 〜2 ⁣ 2 ⁣ 1
Commelina virginica ◆ family *Commelinaceae*

QUICK CHECK: Waist-high plant with erect zigzag stems in loose colonies, the leaves attached with sheaths; midvein very depressed, veins parallel. **ID difficulty 2.**

DESCRIPTION: Perennial herb spreading by rhizomes about 5 mm thick, forming loose colonies. **Stems** mostly erect, rounded, solid, hairless to slightly hairy, to 44" (112 cm) tall and 5–8 mm thick, zigzag between nodes spaced 2–5" (5–13 cm) apart, unbranched or with a few minor branches in the upper third. **Leaves** alternate, entire, several *concentrated near the top of the plant*, held about 90° to the stem, 5–8" (13–20 cm) long, flat, narrowly elliptic or long-lanceolate, tapered to a point, the tip drooping. **Blades** have fine, soft hairs below; above they are *roughened* by very short, stiff hairs. **Midvein** *very strongly depressed above*, protruding and often hairy below. **Veins** parallel, with several major ones protruding slightly *above and below*. Leaves are narrowed at the base to a short, winged **petiole** connecting to a *clasping sheath* 1–1.5" (2.5–4 cm) long. **Sheath** has prominent, protruding, darkened veins and is *hairy/bristly along the top*; it fully encircles the stem and is fused on the side opposite the leaf, where there is a *line of long yellowish to brown hairs*. Brown sheaths remain along the lower stem where dead leaves have withered. **Inflorescence** a crowded terminal cluster of several, a succession of *flowers emerging from a single folded bract* about 0.8" (2 cm) long, the bract margins fused in the lower third. **Flowers** 0.8" (2 cm) wide with three blue petals, one scarcely smaller than the other two. **Stamens** protruding and yellow, the anthers like mini yellow pompoms. **Fruit** a boat-shaped capsule 4–6 mm long, hidden in the folded bract and holding 4–5 boat-shaped seeds.

HABITAT: Moderate to light shade in rich, moist soil, especially where disturbed. Forms large colonies in floodplain forests and hardwood flats. Also found in swamps, ditches, wet forest edges, stream banks, low spots in woods. Native.

FOOD USE: All parts are edible raw or cooked: **Laterals** from summer to fall, **shoots** and **leafy tops** in late spring. **Conservation 3/2.**

COMMENTS: This, our largest dayflower, is abundant and easy to recognize by its form. It seems to replace wood nettle in southern floodplains. **AKA** Virginia dayflower.

▲ Young greens.　　▲ Mature plant with fruit.

Related edible:

Slender dayflower ◆ *Commelina erecta*

A native species of sandy, open areas that is usually knee-high or shorter. The lower petal is very pale and so small that at a glance it appears absent. The anthers are 4-lobed, sometimes shaped like a headless human body. The rhizomes are edible but too small to justify digging it up; you can nibble a few leaves from the stem tip in spring.

Commelina erecta. ▶

24 White twisted-stalk 3 3 1
Streptopus amplexifolius + *Liliaceae* (Lily family)

QUICK CHECK: Belly-high plant; stems smooth, glaucous, zigzag, and forked, with clasping leaves and white flowers. **ID difficulty 2.**

DESCRIPTION: Perennial to 44" (112 cm) tall, forming loose colonies by rhizome. **Stems** 0.2–0.6" (5–15 mm) thick, erect to leaning or arching, *smooth and glaucous* except near *the base, which is wrapped by a hairy sheath*. In the shoot stage, stem bases are pink with purple spots. Stems have a bifurcating branch pattern. **Leaves** alternate, clasping the stem at the base, generally appearing entire but they may have scattered minute teeth. The lowest leaves remain wrapped around the stem as a sheath. The blades are ovate to elliptic, 1.5–3.5" (4–9 cm) long, pointed and often acuminate at the tip, green above and pale gray below, hairless (including on the margins). **Veins** parallel, 3 major ones deeply depressed above and strongly protruding below; there are a few less deeply depressed veins; between these are many small ones essentially flat on both sides. **Inflorescence** single (or occasionally in pairs) from the leaf axils, on a long, very thin, and *distinctly twisted or kinked pedicel*. **Flower** (early summer) 7–9 mm across, drooping, bell-like with 6 long, narrow, white to pinkish tepals *strongly curled backward*, usually with a darker stripe down the center. **Fruit** (late summer) a soft, bright red, juicy berry, spherical to elliptic, 8–12 mm long, containing several seeds.

CONFUSING PLANTS: Rosy twisted stalk is much smaller on average, more leaning or arching, and has leaf margins with stiff, hooked hairs. False Solomon's seal has rough-hairy leaf margins and the stems do not fork. **False hellebore** (p. 674) is much more leafy when emerging.

HABITAT: Forests with rich, moist, rocky soil, especially openings near seeps and streams. Native.

FOOD USE: Tender **shoots** and **greens** in spring and early summer are excellent and mild, with less bitterness than most of its relatives, reminiscent of cucumber. They can be eaten raw or cooked. The **berries** make a nice nibble when they are ripe in late summer, but in quantity are reported to be laxative. **Conservation 3/1.**

COMMENTS: This species probably has the best greens among the many similar edible plants that have alternate leaves with parallel veins (the "Solomon's seal group"). In some regions, particularly in the southern part of its range, it has suffered greatly from overbrowsing by deer and should not be collected. However, it is widespread and common in many remote areas. **AKA** clasping twisted-stalk.

25 Rosy twisted-stalk 🌿 2 🍇 1
Streptopus lanceolatus + *Liliaceae* (Lily family)

QUICK CHECK: Shin-high plant with branching, zigzag, arching stem, alternate leaves with raspy hairs on the margin, and red berries. **ID difficulty 2.**

DESCRIPTION: Perennial from a short rhizome, spreading to form small colonies. **Stems** single to closely spaced and almost clumped, arching, zigzag, 12–26" (30–66 cm) tall and 3–5 mm thick, round with several *small wing-ridges*, solid. The surface is green (reddish at the base when young) with scattered, *stiff, gland-tipped hairs, mostly on the wings*, more so near the nodes and toward the tip. **Branches** simple if present, 2–4 on robust stems. **Leaves** alternate, sessile to slightly clasping (the lowest leaf strongly clasping, sheath-like, and later withering), ovate to elliptic, 1–2.5" (2.5–6.5 cm) long. **Veins** parallel, 2–3 major ones on each side of the middle, these *deeply depressed* above and

protruding below, giving the leaf a pleated look. **Margins** entire, *downcurved*, especially on older leaves, with *stiff, curved, forward-pointing hairs*. **Flowers** (spring) hang singly or occasionally in pairs from leaf axils, the thread-like pedicels curved but not kinked or twisted. Six petals form a bell 6–8 mm long, white to pink or purple with darker markings inside, the sharp ends spread outward and recurved. **Fruit** (late summer) a spherical, red, juicy, partly translucent berry 6 mm across, the skin smooth and glossy, containing 3–10 lopsided-ovoid whitish seeds that are tough but not crunchy.

CONFUSING SPECIES: White twisted-stalk is a more robust plant, told apart before flowering by its more clasping leaves and the lack of stiff hairs on leaf margins and stems. False Solomon's seal leaf margins have hairs that are stiff but not hooked or curved.

HABITAT: Forests where there is an accumulation of moist, slightly acidic organic matter in the soil, often near boulders or the base of tree trunks; conifer or mixed forests, especially with white birch or red oak. Native.

FOOD USE: Pick the **tender tips** of growing plants in spring and very early summer. The greens have a mild cucumber flavor—better raw, in my opinion. Unlike some plants in this section, you don't want to throw out the leaves; they're most of what you get. The cucumbery **berries** can be eaten raw in late summer. **Conservation 2/1.**

COMMENTS: The berries are really just a decorative nibble—nothing to be picked in quantity. Their faintly sweet cucumber-like flavor does not deliver on the high expectations levied by the fruit's brilliant color. The young greens of rosy twisted stalk are not quite as good as those of its larger cousin.

0 mm   1 cm

26 Large Bellwort 2 ✐ 1
Uvularia grandiflorum ✦ family *Colchicaceae*

QUICK CHECK: Thin stem with entire alternate leaves; yellow flowers drooping. **ID difficulty 2.**

DESCRIPTION: Perennial herb from a short rhizome. **Stem** 12–18" (30–46 cm) tall and 2–5 mm thick, solid, smooth, glaucous gray-green, arching, usually with a few major branches, the tips drooping when in bloom, stiffer in fruit. **Shoots** erect, the leaves wrapped into a tight spear. **Leaves** alternate, entire, long-elliptic, pointed, with the stem puncturing the blade near the base (perfoliate), hairless on the upper surface but the underside is dense with minute hairs. **Veins** parallel, a few major ones depressed above; otherwise the blade is smooth. There are multiple sheaths around the lower stem, separating from it and loose near the tip, but the sheath edges are fused in the lower part. When young, the leaves are *drooping and often spiraled*; older leaves are flatter and stiffer, showing the perfoliation more clearly. **Flowers** (spring) bell-like, dangling singly from leaf axils, with 6 yellow petals up to 1.8" (46 mm) long, usually spiraled, not spreading open. **Fruit** (early summer) a 3-sided green pod.

CONFUSING PLANTS: In the shoot stage this plant can be easily confused with Solomon's seal and false Solomon's seal, but these species are similarly edible.

HABITAT: Hardwood forests with rich soil. Native.

FOOD USE: Gather young **shoots** when leaves are still furled up and flowers have yet to emerge. They can be eaten raw but are better cooked, in which case they are just okay. The tender **greens** at the stem tips can also be eaten through early flowering. **Conservation 2.**

COMMENTS: The shoots are small and not very practical as a food source, but every now and then I grab a few to cook. I know one person who thinks the greens are great, but I'm not keen on them.

RELATED EDIBLES: At least 3 other, smaller species of bellwort are found in our region: *U. perfoliata, U. puberula,* and *U. sessifolia.* These can be eaten but are really too small to bother with.

27 Smooth Solomon's seal 🐛1 ❘ 3
Polygonatum biflorum ✦ *Asparagaceae* (Asparagus family)

QUICK CHECK: Arching unbranched herb with a smooth stem and flowers hanging in small clusters from leaf axils. **ID difficulty 2.**

DESCRIPTION: Perennial herb forming colonies by rhizome. **Rhizome** whitish, thick but irregular with transverse constrictions, moderately fibrous, showing prominent scars from previous years' stems. **Stem** single, unbranched, arching, 1–6' (30–180 cm) long and 0.2–0.8" (5–20 mm) thick, round, solid, smooth, hairless, bloom-covered. **Shoots** initially have the leaves rolled into a sharp tip pointing vertically. **Leaves** alternate, clasping, 1–6" (2.5–15 cm) long, elliptic, angled at the base and broadly pointed at the tip, the margins entire and *hairless*. Surfaces smooth and hairless on both sides, somewhat glaucous below. **Veins** parallel, very close together (1–3 mm), some of them very deeply depressed above. **Inflorescence** small *clusters of 2–10 hanging from leaf axils*, the peduncles to 2" (5 cm) long. **Flowers** (early to mid summer) whitish green, 0.5–0.9" (13–23 mm) long, tubular, the tip split into 6 lobes. **Fruit** a round berry 6–12 mm, the surface smooth and bloom-coated, the flesh green, containing a few large whitish seeds.

CONFUSING PLANTS: False Solomon's seal has rough-hairy leaf margins and flowers in a large terminal panicle.

HABITAT: Open woodlands, forest edges, and savannahs on well-drained, rich soil. Native. 🔥

FOOD USE: **Rhizomes** can be gathered all year but are best in the dormant season. They can be cooked as a vegetable or added to stews. Gather **shoots** in spring before the leaves unfurl. Discard leaves and cook the stems like asparagus. **Conservation 3/2.**

COMMENTS: These plants are sensitive to overharvest and should be used sparingly and only where thriving. The rhizomes of robust plants can be a large vegetable, but I find the flavor slightly disagreeable. Shoots are delicious, however—among the few wild vegetables that actually taste similar to asparagus. There is an abnormally large form that has been separated as *P. commutatum*, (giant Solomon's seal)—although some claim this is just a chromosome abnormality and not a real species. These large plants are the best ones to eat.

RELATED EDIBLE: Small Solomon's seal *Polygonatum pubescens* is much smaller and sometimes branches. It typically has only 1–2 flowers or fruits per leaf axil, and the leaves have faint pubescence on the more prominent veins of the undersurface. The shoots of this species are good but almost too small to bother with. The rhizomes are tiny and don't taste very good.

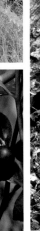

28 False Solomon's seal 1 2 1 NG-91
Maianthemum racemosum ◆ *Asparagaceae* (Asparagus family)

QUICK CHECK: Arching unbranched herb with entire alternate leaves and flowers in a large terminal panicle. **ID difficulty 3.**

DESCRIPTION: Colony-forming perennial from tough, yellowish, branching rhizomes 7–10 mm thick. **Stems** 18–44" (46–112 cm) long and 4–12 mm thick, solid, slightly ridged, faintly roughened, reddish-purple near the nodes, arching, zigzag, unbranched. **Shoots** erect with large reddish sheaths; shoot leaves pressed into a spear-like tip. **Leaves** alternate, broadly elliptic, entire, 3–6" (8–15 cm) long, angled at the base and pointed at the tip, often acuminate. Surface with short hairs above and denser, longer hairs below. **Veins** parallel, the major ones deeply depressed above and protruding below. Minor veins are *faintly incised* below. The leaf is somewhat pleated along the major veins. **Margins** entire with stiff hairs. Leaves are sessile or have an extremely short, usually maroon, petiole-like constriction at the base. **Inflorescence** a slightly Christmas-tree shaped terminal panicle of 30–400 flowers, 2–7" (5–18 cm) long, the branches in the form of racemes. Pedicels 1–2 mm long, white, right angled to the rachis. **Flowers** (late spring to early summer) 3 mm across with 6 tiny linear white tepals, the white stamens thicker and longer than the tepals. **Fruits** spherical, 3–5 mm, gold at first but soft and red when ripe, containing a single, round, light-colored seed with a darker "eye" spot.

CONFUSING PLANTS: Solomon's seals and bellworts have smooth leaves and smooth, unridged stems.

White twisted-stalk has forked stems. **False hellebore** (p. 674) has larger, broader leaves and never appears as an elongated, pointed, leafless shoot.

HABITAT: Moderately shaded forests of hardwoods or mixed conifers and hardwoods, on well-drained but rich soils. Especially common under oak and white pine. Native.

FOOD USE: Rhizomes can be dug all year. They were traditionally soaked in wood ash lye to denature their irritating quality, then boiled as a vegetable. Gather **shoots** in spring before the leaves unfurl; discard leaves and cook the stems. Collect ripe **berries** in fall and nibble them raw—they are very sweet but have a bitter aftertaste. **Conservation 3/2/1.**

COMMENTS: The best edible part of this common and widespread woodland plant is the shoot; the tough rhizome and bittersweet berries are only marginal. Gather the shoots sparingly from healthy populations. **AKA** Solomon's plume, spikenard, *Smilacina racemosa*. Starry Solomon's plume *Maianthemum stellatum* is a smaller but similar plant that grows in dense colonies in moist, sandy soil. The leaves are narrower, and the unripe fruit is attractively bicolored. The edible parts are of poor quality.

GROUP 36 BASAL LEAVES ABSENT, LEAVES ALTERNATE, TOOTHED

To use this key you may need to review the difference between clumped and colonial (see glossary). A few plants have bumps on the leaf margins that may be considered teeth, and these might key here or in group 35. I have included American bellflower in this key even though it has basal leaves because these wilt rather early in spring, and by flowering they are not evident.

TENTATIVE IDENTIFICATION KEY TO GROUP 36
The key is not your final answer!

Stems single, not appearing connected to other stems.
- Leaves hairless.
  - Stems opaque, solid, and ridged or winged; leaves with blunt to wavy teeth.
    - Plant taller than wide, the leaves often mealy-white below. — 1. Lambsquarters
    - Plant as wide or wider than tall, the leaves not mealy below. — 6. Black nightshade
  - Stems roundish, hollow, and transparent; leaves with needle-teeth. — 2. Jewelweed
- Leaves with hairs on one or more sides.
  - Plants distinctly taller than wide.
    - Leaves lanceolate, narrowly elliptic, or linear.
      - Leaf lanceolate, sap milky, flowers bluish-purple. American bellflower (p. 337).
      - Leaf narrowly elliptic to linear, sap not milky. Horseweed (p. 580).
    - Leaves broadly ovate or heart-shaped, mostly over 3" (8 cm) long.
      - Leaf and stem covered with short, stiff hairs; sandpapery feeling. — 3. Sunflower
      - Leaf and stem covered with short, soft hairs; velvety feeling. — 4. Velvetleaf
    - Leaves elliptic, less than 3" long. — 5. Prickly sida
  - Plants as wide or wider than tall.
    - Petals separated more than half their length, flowers in clusters, fruit not in a papery husk. — 6. Black nightshade
    - Petals fused to the tip, flowers single, fruit in a papery husk. — 7. Ground-cherry

Stems colonial, usually multiple but not clumped; connected by rhizomes.
- Leaves on long petioles, with stingers, the blade broadly ovate to heart-shaped. — 8. Wood nettle
- Leaves sessile or on petioles < 10% of blade length, lanceolate and tapered at the base, without stingers.
  - Leaves soft-woolly and silvery-white below. — 9. Serrated sage
  - Leaves roughened by minute hairs but not silvery. — 10. Common goldenrod
  - Leaves hairless on both sides. — 11. Ditch stonecrop

Stems usually clumped, the bases touching or nearly so.
- Leaves ovate to obovate, blunt-tipped, thick and fleshy-succulent. — 12. Orpine
- Leaves narrowly elliptic to lanceolate, sharp-tipped, not thick and succulent.
  - Sap not milky; leaves coated with very fine, soft, appressed hairs. — 13. Bigfruit evening-primrose
  - Sap milky, leaves hairless. — 14. Appalachian bellflower

1 Lambsquarters ⚘ 3 🌿 2 📖 FH-186
Chenopodium (in part) ✦ family *Amaranthaceae*

QUICK CHECK: Diamond-shaped leaves with a few large teeth, growing tips often covered with a light, powdery coating; clusters of small, unshowy flowers and dull fruits. **ID difficulty 1.**

DESCRIPTION: Branchy annual herb, the limbs ascending. **Stems** erect, 1–10' (30–300 cm) tall and up to 1.2" (3 cm) thick, solid, hairless, ridged, mostly green but sometimes red, especially near the nodes. **Leaves** alternate, 1–4" (2.5–10 cm) long, moderately thick and semi-succulent, lanceolate to triangular or diamond-shaped, sometimes broad and resembling the namesake goose's foot, the base broadly angled with straight edges, the blades flat. **Surface** dull bluish-green above but grayish-green below with a powdery coating that is often very prominent, especially on the tips of vigorously growing shoots. **Midvein** and secondary veins are slightly depressed above; veinlets mostly flat and obscure. **Margins** may be entire (especially on narrow leaves), wavy, or coarsely and irregularly toothed with large blunt teeth—but teeth usually appear only distal to the widest point. **Petioles** 40–80% of blade length, roundish with a small groove on top. **Inflorescence** dense and often very large branching clusters at the ends of stems and in upper leaf axils, spike-like with sessile flowers. **Flowers** tiny and unshowy. **Seeds** dark, roundish, semi-flat, 1–1.5 mm across, enclosed in a granular, usually adhering coat.

SPECIES: There are multiple common species that go by the name of lambsquarters, and few foragers distinguish them. There are native and non-native species.

HABITAT: Disturbed, sunny ground such as gardens, crop fields, construction sites, logged areas, steep sunny slopes, road shoulders, floodplains, and shores. Seeds can remain dormant for centuries and then germinate after disturbance.

FOOD USE: Gather tender **leafy tops** of young plants from spring through early autumn—most commonly in late spring through early summer. They can be eaten raw or cooked in any way you would use spinach. On older plants you can pluck individual leaves, which will remain tender while the stems toughen. In late summer and autumn, the fruiting heads can be gathered by hand-stripping or beating them into a container. After drying and rubbing off the chaff (see p. 27), the **seeds** should be soaked, rubbed, and drained to remove the saponins in the seedcoat. Then they can be cooked into a porridge or dried and ground into flour. **Conservation 1.**

COMMENTS: This is one of the best known and most commonly used wild plants in North America. It is related to spinach, tastes similar, and is exceptionally nutritious. Various species, including quinoa, have been domesticated for seed production. Separation and winnowing seeds of the wild plants is actually very labor-efficient if you have the appropriate equipment and technique. **AKA** goosefoot, fat hen, pigweed, wild spinach.

2 Jewelweed 🌿 1 🍃 2
genus *Impatiens* ✦ family *Balsaminaceae*

QUICK CHECK: Translucent, succulent, hollow stems and thin leaves with sparse, needle-like teeth; irregular, tubular, yellow or orange flowers. **ID difficulty 1.**

DESCRIPTION: Erect annuals 2-6' (60–180 cm) tall, branching only in the upper half. **Stem** smooth, hairless, hollow, roundish, *translucent*, succulent, thick in proportion to its height, bulged at branch junctures, often reddish at the base but light green above that. **Leaves** very thin and soft, 1–4" (2.5–10 cm) long, hairless, pale beneath, ovate to elliptic, the base broadly angled and the tip blunt with an extending claw. The first few sets of leaves on seedlings are paired; later leaves are alternate. **Midvein** purple to pale

▲ Composite range.

and slightly depressed above. Secondary veins are several, flat to faintly depressed above, arching toward the leaf tip and terminating near the notch between two teeth. **Margins** sparsely serrated with large, blunt teeth tipped with a downturned claw. There are 1–6 *tooth-like appendages* at the leaf base. **Cotyledon leaves** are very thick and succulent and persist for a few weeks. **Petioles** hairless, thin, elliptic to D-shaped in cross section—not channeled. Lower petioles are up to 120% of blade length; ascending they progressively shorten. When water falls onto the leaves it beads up into silvery droplets and rolls off—hence the name jewelweed. The plants often wilt severely in bright sunlight, only to absorb water and recover at night or in cloudy weather. **Inflorescence** spreading clusters of 2–4, the flowers *hanging on long, thin pedicels*. **Flowers** (mid to late summer) about 1" (2.5 cm) long, irregularly shaped, with one hood-like petal above and two hanging petals side by side. In the rear of the flower is an enlarged, cone-shaped, sac-like sepal, and on the narrow end of this cone is a spur that curls back toward the front (*I. capensis*) or downward (*I. pallida*). **Fruit** a green, 5-sided, somewhat banana-shaped capsule, under tension when ripe and exploding upon contact to expel the seeds. **Seeds** elliptic and dark, somewhat flattened, about 4 mm long.

SPECIES: Common jewelweed *I. capensis* has an orange flower mottled with dark reddish-brown. **Yellow jewelweed** *I. pallida* has light yellow flowers that are sometimes mottled with reddish. Both are widespread, common, and native.

HABITAT: Moist, rich, bare soil high in organic matter, most often in moderate shade. Shores and banks, especially where debris is piled; pond edges, low spots in woods, ravines, streamsides, seepage areas. Native.

FOOD USE: Cotyledon leaves of new seedlings can be nibbled raw or eaten cooked. Very young plants, generally 6–10" (15–25 cm) tall or less with the leaves still paired, make decent **greens** after boiling and discarding the water. The ripe **seeds**, in late summer, taste like slightly bitter walnuts but are hard to collect in volume. **Conservation 2/1.**

COMMENTS: Best known as a cure or preventive for poison ivy—the juice is rubbed on the affected area after exposure to prevent the rash from forming. I cannot vouch for its effectiveness, but many people swear by it. Jewelweed reduces its energy needs by producing very little cellulose and having very thin leaves, instead holding itself rigid with water pressure. This allows it to thrive in deep shade, but only where there is ample soil moisture. (Images continued on the next page.)

▲ Orange jewelweed shoots.

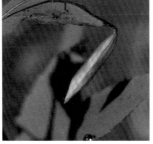

▲ Yellow jewelweed flowers.　　▲ Orange jewelweed pods.　　▲ Jewelweed seeds.

3 Sunflower 🌿 3 ✎ 1
Helianthus annuus ✦ *Asteraceae* (Composite family)

QUICK CHECK: Tall, stout plant with spreading branches and large, rough, heart-shaped leaves; sunflowers with yellow rays and dark disks. **ID difficulty 1.**

DESCRIPTION: Large, widely-branching annual. **Stems** coarse, stout, 2–7' (60–210 cm) tall and up to 1.2" (3 cm) thick, solid, aromatic, with a few large ascending branches. The surface is tacky, rough-hairy with hairs both long and short, purple and green mottled, with many small ridges and a few larger grooves. **Leaves** mostly alternate (lower ones paired), broadly triangular, ovate or heart-shaped, blunt-tipped, to 12" (30 cm) long and almost as broad. Blades rough-hairy, especially beneath and on veins, with 2 prominent, light-colored, arching secondary veins from the base. **Veins** faintly depressed above.

▲ Much more common in the western half of the range.

Margins irregularly large-toothed, wavy, or sometimes entire. **Petioles** 40–100% of blade length, channeled, rough-hairy. **Inflorescence** solitary, nodding composite heads, on peduncles 6–15" (15–38 cm) long, 3–23 per plant. **Heads** (mid summer to fall) 2–4.6" (5–12 cm) across, bearing numerous bracts with acuminate tips. The disk is brown, nearly flat to convex, 1–2" (2.5–5 cm) across. Ray florets are about 1" (2.5 cm) long and bright yellow. **Seeds** resemble those of domestic sunflowers but are smaller and narrower.

CONFUSING PLANTS: There are many other native sunflowers, but they tend to have narrower leaves, smaller heads, and/or yellow disks. The seeds of all are safe to eat.

HABITAT: Dry, sunny, disturbed ground, especially along highways, ravines, and river floodplains; most common in the Great Plains. Native.

FOOD USE: Gather seedheads in late summer as they ripen. You'll know they are ripe because the florets will fall off and the seeds, when vigorously rubbed, will detach from the receptacle. Once separated, dry the **seeds**, then rub them to loosen the hulls and winnow. **Flower buds** can also be eaten cooked. **Conservation 1.**

COMMENTS: This is the ancestor of the cultivated sunflower, which was domesticated long ago by Native Americans. The seeds of wild sunflowers taste as good as their cultivated relatives but are much smaller and therefore more labor-intensive to utilize. They are also often plagued by seed-eating insects.

4 Velvetleaf 🖐 1 ✐ 1 🌿 1 💧
Abutilon theophrasti ✦ *Malvaceae* (Mallow family)

QUICK CHECK: Tall plant with large, sparse, drooping, velvety, heart-shaped leaves on long petioles; yellow flowers and ridged, beaked, bowl-shaped brown capsules. ID difficulty 1.

DESCRIPTION: Large annual, the form taller than wide. **Stem** single, erect, 3–7' (90–210 cm) tall and up to 0.7" (18 mm) thick, rounded, solid, densely soft-hairy, zigzag, with fibrous bark that peels in thick strips when mature. **Branches** few, minor, slightly ascending. **Leaves** alternate, broadly heart-shaped with an acuminate tip, 3–8" (8–20 cm) long, drooping at a right angle to the petiole, folding up at night. Both surfaces are densely covered with short, soft hair (velvet). Beside the midvein are 4–6 major veins from the base. **Veins** and veinlets are depressed above and protruding below. **Margin** has widely and irregularly spaced small teeth. **Petiole** 70–100% of blade length, not channeled, straight. **Flowers** (late summer) single from upper leaf axils on pedicels about 1" (2.5 cm) long. **Sepals** 5, light green, broadly triangular, velvety. **Petals** 5, slightly longer than the sepals, spreading 0.6–0.8" (15–20 mm) across, orange-yellow, broad and flat or truncated at the tip. Sexual parts are yellow. **Fruit** roughly bowl-shaped, green at first turning dark gray-brown at maturity, the base rounded and the tip flat, 0.8" (2 cm) across, divided into 10–15 keeled sections, each with a hooked beak and containing several seeds. **Seeds** about 3 mm long, dark gray and rough, shaped like a lopsided kidney if you tried to press the ends together.

▲ Most abundant in the Corn Belt.

HABITAT: Disturbed rich soil in full sun. A weed of crop field, gardens, construction sites, etc. Introduced.

FOOD USE: The youngest **leaves** can be eaten cooked but are pretty lame; there is usually something better nearby. The tender **stem tips** can be peeled and eaten; they have an odd musky flavor. **Unripe seeds** can be taken out of the green pods and eaten raw. **Ripe seeds** can be soaked or briefly boiled, drained, and then ground up for a flour or gruel. They can also be pressed for **oil**.

COMMENTS: This plant is very easy to recognize and does not resemble much else. It is one of the less culinarily useful members of the mallow family. I helped make the oil once and it was oily. I liked it. The seeds can remain viable in the soil for decades. Velvetleaf has been grown for millennia as a bast fiber crop; its widespread introduction to North America was likely for this purpose, but such use has been mostly abandoned. Regarding natural toilet paper, velvetleaf is way, way up there.

Tender tip. ▶

5 Prickly sida 🌿 2 ☕
Sida spinosa ✦ *Malvaceae* (Mallow family)

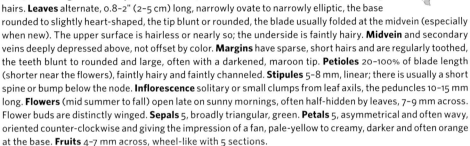

QUICK CHECK: Thin-stemmed plant with round-toothed leaves with deeply depressed major veins; half-hidden flowers with 5 yellowish petals oriented counter-clockwise. **ID difficulty 2.**

DESCRIPTION: Warm-weather annual. **Stems** 10–40" (25–100 cm) tall and 2–6 mm thick, branching occasionally, rounded, solid, the surface with clumps of soft, radiating hairs. **Leaves** alternate, 0.8–2" (2–5 cm) long, narrowly ovate to narrowly elliptic, the base rounded to slightly heart-shaped, the tip blunt or rounded, the blade usually folded at the midvein (especially when new). The upper surface is hairless or nearly so; the underside is faintly hairy. **Midvein** and secondary veins deeply depressed above, not offset by color. **Margins** have sparse, short hairs and are regularly toothed, the teeth blunt to rounded and large, often with a darkened, maroon tip. **Petioles** 20–100% of blade length (shorter near the flowers), faintly hairy and faintly channeled. **Stipules** 5–8 mm, linear; there is usually a short spine or bump below the node. **Inflorescence** solitary or small clumps from leaf axils, the peduncles 10–15 mm long. **Flowers** (mid summer to fall) open late on sunny mornings, often half-hidden by leaves, 7–9 mm across. Flower buds are distinctly winged. **Sepals** 5, broadly triangular, green. **Petals** 5, asymmetrical and often wavy, oriented counter-clockwise and giving the impression of a fan, pale-yellow to creamy, darker and often orange at the base. **Fruits** 4–7 mm across, wheel-like with 5 sections.

CONFUSING PLANTS: *Sida rhombifolia* is a relative that has broader leaves and lacks the spine below the node. I have not eaten it, but presume it safe to consume in small amounts, since it traditionally has numerous medicinal uses and is sold commercially as a therapeutic herb.

HABITAT: Rich, loose, disturbed soil in full sun: fields, roadsides, gardens, vacant lots, prairies. Native.

FOOD USE: The tender **leaves** of young plants make a nice green raw or cooked. Older leaves are sometimes used for **tea**.

WARNING: The plant contains ephedrine, a stimulant, so it should be consumed in moderation; avoid it if ephedrine is contraindicated for you. **Conservation 1.**

COMMENTS: In my limited sampling of this common weed I have enjoyed the young greens, but I cannot vouch for the edibility of other members of this genus. The plant is not prickly when young—the "spine" is an innocuous spur under the nodes. **AKA** Prickly fanpetals.

6 Black nightshade 🖊 3 🍇 3 📖 NG-375
Solanum nigrum (species complex) ᐟ
Solanaceae (Nightshade family)

QUICK CHECK: Widely branching stems with ridges from the nodes, leaves with a few blunt teeth, white flowers, and spherical, pea-sized black fruit in clusters. **ID difficulty 2.**

DESCRIPTION: Annual (rarely perennial in warm climates), wide-spreading and branchy, to 40" (1 m) tall and spreading up to 5' (1.5 m) wide, weakly erect, the branches often resting on the ground. **Stems** to 0.6" (15 mm) thick, solid, dull green, gently angled. **Shoots** often have a short, wing-like ridge extending down from each node, but these are less promi-nent on older stems. The surface ranges from hairless to moderately hairy; if present the hairs are leaning and tapered, and those on the ridges may be stout. **Leaves** alternate, 2–4" (5–10 cm) long, roughly ovate or diamond-shaped, the bases broad but often decurrent, the tips acutely angled and blunt. Blades hairless to moderately hairy, often with holes in them (from insects). **Midvein** slightly depressed. **Secondary veins** 4–5 per side, broadly angled, moderately depressed, as are the veinlets. **Margins** rarely entire or wavy, but most often irregularly and shallowly toothed, the tooth tips blunt or rounded. Often there are a few teeth between the base and the midpoint, but none distally. **Petioles** 20–60% of blade length, generally flat on top, but with a decurrent wing gradually tapering down from the blade; near the base the petiole usually has a light green center with a thin, dark green wing channel. **Inflorescence** an umbel or very short raceme (the rachis shorter than individual pedicels) containing 2–12 flowers, the peduncle and pedicels rounded, the pedicels variable in length and thickening before the fruit. **Flowers** (summer through fall) 8–11 mm across. **Calyx** green with 5 blunt triangular lobes much shorter than the petals. **Corolla** fused and greenish at the base with 5 reflexed, white, triangular lobes, each with a depressed central vein. Robust yellow stamens are pressed together in the center, mostly hiding the pistil. **Berries** spherical, 5–8 mm, green at first but ripening to dark purple-black, soft and juicy when ripe with numerous tiny, soft seeds.

SPECIES: This is a "species complex"—it was once considered a single species but closer observation has revealed multiple, distinct genetic groups within that population. Whether these segregates should be con-sidered species, subspecies, or (in some cases) chromosome abnormalities is debated. The black nightshades used to all be lumped under *Solanum nigrum*—but now more than two dozen very similar species are recognized worldwide, at least 4 of which are regularly found in our region. The leaves of our native plants often have a coppery sheen on the lower surface when young, the flower clusters are umbels, and the leaf and stem sur-faces are sparsely hairy to hairless. *S. nigrum* in the stricter sense is the European species, only occasionally established in North America. It is soft-hairy with slightly elongated flower/fruit clusters (racemes). All the species in our area are edible.

CONFUSING PLANTS: Garden tomatil-los are similar in form and may be easily confused before fruiting; their greens are

Tender young greens. ▶

bitter and probably should not be eaten. **Belladonna** *Atropa belladonna* has much larger, poisonous fruit, borne singly, with a very large calyx under the berry.

HABITAT: Weedy habitats: gardens, yards, building sites, agricultural fields, disturbed soil, rubbish piles. Also found in wilder landscapes along river banks and in hardwood forests after fires, logging, or windstorms. Native, although the European species is established in a few areas.

FOOD USE: Tender young **stem tips** and attached **leaves**, before the flowers open, make excellent greens but should be steamed or boiled; older leaves are bitter and mildly toxic. Ripe **fruit**, dark purple-black and juicy, is eaten out of hand or used in salads, salsa, pies, jams, burritos, and applesauce, from midsummer through fall. **Conservation 1.**

COMMENTS: This plant is the subject of the most pervasive myth of toxicity of any in North America. Both ignorance and racism have fed that myth. Doctors are not botanists—I have examined several documented poisonings from "*Solanum nigrum*" that were clearly and unambiguously misidentified *Atropa belladonna*. The two plants are easily distinguished. The ripe berries of the *S. nigrum* complex are enjoyed by hundreds of millions of people worldwide, and the greens are among the most commonly eaten leafy vegetables in the world. Nevertheless, many Europeans have asserted for centuries that this plant is poisonous, despite ample living proof that this is nonsense.

7 Ground-cherry 🍓 1-3
Physalis spp. ✦ *Solanaceae* (Nightshade family)

QUICK CHECK: Low plant with spreading branches, zigzag stems, and hanging, spherical fruit enclosed in a loose, 5-part, papery husk. **ID difficulty 1.**

DESCRIPTION: Perennials usually knee-high or shorter, spreading and widely branched, the limbs of large plants sometimes resting on the ground. **Stems** single, erect in the lower part before branching, ridged, often with small wings on the ridges, solid, usually hairy. **Leaves** alternate or in unequal, non-opposing pairs, 1-3" (2.5-8 cm) long, narrowly elliptic or lanceolate to ovate, with the base tapered to broadly angled, the tip tapered or acutely angled with a blunt tip. Blades may be hairless or hairy. **Veins** and veinlets are depressed above and protrude below. **Margins** most often have a few large, blunt teeth (lacking claws or nipples), but sometimes are wavy or entire. **Petioles** 20-40% of blade length, channeled. (Continued on the next page.)

▲ Collective range of genus *Physalis*.

◀ *Physalis longifolia.*

7 Ground-cherry (continued)

Flowers (mid to late summer) single, open toward the ground, hanging on long pedicels from leaf axils. **Calyx** 5 pointed, green, triangular lobes fused at the base. **Corolla** like a wide-spreading bell of five fused petals, looking like a sloppy pentagon from the end, yellow on most species. **Fruit** (late summer through fall) a tomato-like spherical berry 0.3 0.7" (8–18 mm) in diameter, enclosed in a 5-part, inflated, papery husk, the berry ripening dull yellow to orange, straw, or occasionally purple-black, often with a sticky surface. Inside are numerous tiny, soft seeds.

HABITAT: Open, sunny, dry ground, especially well-drained sand or gravel: prairies, savannahs, woodland openings, roadsides, meadows, fields, pastures, building sites, empty lots, dry streambanks, disturbed ground. Native.

FOOD USE: Gather papery husks from the plant or off the ground beneath it in late summer or fall. After removing the husks the ripe **fruit** can be eaten raw as a snack, added to salads or burritos, or made into jam, pie, or sauces. They can also be dried. Unripe fruit is usually bitter. **Conservation 1.**

COMMENTS: These delicious fruits are often produced sparingly, but when you can find enough, wonderful things can be made from them. The cultivated tomatillo is a member of the same genus.

SPECIES: There are numerous ground cherries native in our region; the four most common are pictured here. Of these, **clammy ground-cherry** *P. heterophylla* has the best-tasting and largest fruit. This species can be identified by its broad leaves and the fact that all parts are densely covered with soft but sticky, erect hairs. **Virginia ground-cherry** *P. virginiana* has narrower leaves and is less hairy; its fruit ripens to a deeper orange, and the stem end of the husk is deeply depressed. **Long-leaved ground-cherry** *P. longifolia* has few to no hairs. The leaves are really no narrower than those of Virginia ground-cherry, but the fruit husk is more rounded on top. A common species across the South is **cut-leaf ground-cherry** *P. angulata* (another misnomer, for this one has large teeth, but the leaves are not deeply cut). This annual has fruit that is not quite as good as the perennials mentioned above.

▲ *Physalis angulata.*   ▼ *Physalis virginiana.*

▲ (above and below) *Physalis heterophylla.* ▼

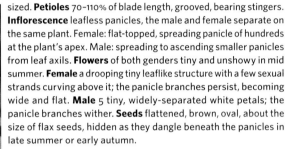

8 Wood nettle ⌇ 3 ✎ 3 ✿ 2 ▭ FH-177
Laportea canadensis ✦ *Urticaceae* (Nettle family)

QUICK CHECK: Broad, pointed, alternate leaves on long petioles concentrated near the top of erect stems armed with many long stingers; flowers unshowy. **ID difficulty 2.**

DESCRIPTION: Erect perennial spreading by rhizome, often forming extensive colonies. **Stems** 2-6' (60-180 cm) tall, solid, round below but with smooth-topped ridges in the upper part, green, zigzag (especially in the upper half), covered with erect stinging hairs, unbranched or branching minimally and only near the top. **Leaves** alternate, 6-14 per stalk, 2-8" (5-20 cm) long and almost as wide, heart-shaped or broadly ovate to nearly round with acuminate tips. Both sides have erect, stiff hairs and stingers—the latter especially along the veins. **Midvein** narrow, green, and depressed above. **Secondary veins** 5-6 per side, 2 major ones arising at the base, depressed above, as are the veinlets. **Margins** serrated, the teeth large and evenly spaced and

sized. **Petioles** 70-110% of blade length, grooved, bearing stingers. **Inflorescence** leafless panicles, the male and female separate on the same plant. Female: flat-topped, spreading panicle of hundreds at the plant's apex. Male: spreading to ascending smaller panicles from leaf axils. **Flowers** of both genders tiny and unshowy in mid summer. **Female** a drooping tiny leaflike structure with a few sexual strands curving above it; the panicle branches persist, becoming wide and flat. **Male** 5 tiny, widely-separated white petals; the panicle branches wither. **Seeds** flattened, brown, oval, about the size of flax seeds, hidden as they dangle beneath the panicles in late summer or early autumn.

CONFUSING PLANTS: Often confused with stinging nettle, for which I accept no excuse.

HABITAT: Rich, moist, but not permanently wet soil in full to partial shade, on sites where periodic disturbance leaves bare soil. Most abundant and largest in river floodplains; also in hardwood forests on steep slopes and along trails and dirt roads. Native.

FOOD USE: Harvest **shoots** in mid spring while the leaves have scarcely unfurled; eat cooked. A little later in the season collect the tender **leafy tops** and boil or steam as a potherb. By the time the leaves unfurl the stingers may be very potent, so wear gloves when collecting greens. Ripe **seeds** can be collected in autumn and cooked like flax seeds. **Conservation 2/1.**

COMMENTS: Not as well-known as stinging nettle (probably because it is absent from Europe), many people (including me)

consider wood nettle a better food plant. This is one of the best of all green vegetables. Not only does it have flax-like seeds, but the stem fibers are very similar and have been used like linen for making nets, ropes, and cloth.

▲ (top) Wood nettle flowering. (bottom left) Shoots. (bottom right) Inflorescence.

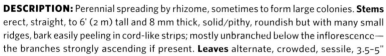

9 Serrated sage 🍶 ☕
Artemisia serrata ✦ *Asteraceae* (Composite family)

QUICK CHECK: Tall, unbranched plant with numerous long, pointed, sharply-toothed leaves that are silvery-white on the underside. **ID difficulty 1.**

DESCRIPTION: Perennial spreading by rhizome, sometimes to form large colonies. **Stems** erect, straight, to 6' (2 m) tall and 8 mm thick, solid/pithy, roundish but with many small ridges, bark easily peeling in cord-like strips; mostly unbranched below the inflorescence— the branches strongly ascending if present. **Leaves** alternate, crowded, sessile, 3.5-5" (9-13 cm) long, narrowly lanceolate or elliptic, tapered at the base and the pointed tip. Blades are flat except for downcurved margins. The upper surface is hairless and dark green; the lower surface is whitish gray from a covering of soft, matted hairs. There are numerous secondary **veins** about 45° to the midvein, these light in color, depressed on the upper surface, protruding below. **Margins** with long, sharp, widely-spaced, forward-pointing teeth. **Stipules** have 1-3 lanceolate lobes, becoming more prominent upward. **Inflorescence** branchy ascending panicles of hundreds of small heads on stems of various length, interspersed with reduced leaves. **Heads** 4-6 mm long and about 3 mm wide, mostly drooping, with gray-green bracts at the base. **Florets** few, lacking petals, a mixture of yellowish and reddish open florets with 3-5 pale yellow, thread-like sexual parts protruding.

HABITAT: Sunny openings in floodplains and river valleys, meadows, marsh edges, low savannahs, roadsides—especially on rich sandy soil. Native.

FOOD USE: The young **leafy tips** can be used as an herb or tea like mugwort. **Conservation 1.**

COMMENTS: This is a native alternative to mugwort, common in many areas where mugwort is absent; the flavor is very similar but slightly milder.

10 Common goldenrod 🥢 2 | 1 ☕
Solidago canadensis ◆ *Asteraceae* (Composite family)

QUICK CHECK: Colonies of tall, straight stems with numerous narrow, sessile, pointed leaves with a few scattered teeth; tiny yellow flowerheads in an elongated panicle. ID difficulty 2.

DESCRIPTION: Perennial forming clones by rhizome. **Stems** dense but not clumped, 4–6' (1.2–1.8 m) tall, 4–8 mm thick, round, nearly solid but with a pinhole hollow, erect, straight, the surface reddish and green, with scattered, short, erect hair (more on the upper stem). **Shoots** have crowded lower leaves that may appear basal for a short time after emerging. **Branches** many and strongly ascending, but small and only on the upper stalk. **Leaves** numerous, alternate, evenly spaced and overlapping along most of the stem, ascending, minutely hairy (more so above), 2–5" (5–13 cm) long, sessile, with a bump under each node. Blades are elongate-elliptic, tapered at the base and the pointed tip. **Major veins** depressed above, protruding below, and hairy on the underside. There are only two prominent secondary veins, diverging in the lower quarter of the leaf, running parallel to the midvein, and reconverging at the tip. **Margins** purplish and hairy with a few widely-spaced, sharp teeth with light-colored, needle-like tips; the lower 25–40% of the blade is toothless. Branches may have paired leaves. **Inflorescence** a panicle of numerous tiny composite heads (late summer to autumn) borne mostly on the upper sides of the branches, the florets yellow. **LYDS** persistent.

CONFUSING SPECIES: Giant goldenrod *Solidago gigantea* is another large, widespread goldenrod that looks strikingly similar at a glance; it differs in having smooth, glaucous stems. While not dangerous, giant goldenrod shoots are bitter and disappointing.

HABITAT: Well-drained to moist soil in full sun. Fields, pastures, roadsides, savannahs, floodplains, forest clearings. Native.

FOOD USE: Lateral shoots in summer are good raw or cooked. **Erect shoots** are better peeled or cooked with the leaves removed. Blanched shoots (do this by placing a piece of plywood over a colony in spring before they emerge) are whitish and very tender—much better than the green shoots. Leaves can be used for **tea**. **Conservation 1.**

COMMENTS: This abundant, beautiful, and well-known plant is allelopathic—producing chemicals that inhibit the growth of competing plants. This makes it a strong competitor, excellent at taking over abandoned farmland, where it often forms large, pure colonies. It is one of the most abundant plants in our region. People like to hate it because it is so common, but it didn't really do anything wrong. There are many goldenrods and all are safe to try, but this is one of the largest, most common, and best-tasting.

◀ (top left) *Solidago canadensis* lateral shoot.
   (bottom left) Shoot.

611

11 Ditch stonecrop  1
Penthorum sedoides ✦ family *Penthoraceae*

QUICK CHECK: Thigh-high plant of wet soil with ridged stems and thin, alternate, sharp-toothed leaves, and a cluster of one-sided racemes with star-like fruit. **ID difficulty 3.**

DESCRIPTION: Perennial spreading short distances by rhizome. **Stems** to 30" (75 cm) tall and 1 cm thick, erect, solid, ridged, the base nearly hairless but the upper part with scattered thin, gland-tipped hairs, especially on the angles. Stems often reddish at maturity but green when young. **Branches** ascending, borne occasionally near the base but mostly near the top. **Leaves** to 3.5" (9 cm) long, alternate, elliptic to lanceolate, thin, the base tapered, the tip sharp-pointed, the surface hairless, lighter and glossier below. Lower leaves are borne on **petioles** up to 10% of blade length; upper leaves are sessile. **Midvein** often pink with age; above it protrudes in a shallow depression. **Secondary veins** 55–70° to the midvein at first then curving toward the tip, slightly depressed, regularly spaced and prominent but dividing and becoming faint before reaching the margin. All veins protrude below. **Margins** have small, sharp, closely spaced, forward-pointing teeth of variable or alternating size. **Inflorescense** a branching terminal cluster of multiple ascending racemes, the flowers packed closely together on very short pedicels, mostly on one side of the curved rachis and oriented toward the center of the cluster. **Flowers** 3–6 mm across with 5 narrow, greenish, pointed, spreading sepals. Petals are usually absent; 5 white, bottle-shaped carpels (pistil bases) are prominent, surrounded by 10 white stamens. **Fruit** a star-like, 5-pointed, many-seeded capsule 5–7 mm across that turns red in autumn; each point ends with a nipple.

HABITAT: Muddy areas with disturbed soil, usually in full sun or light shade. Riverbanks, puddles on clay soil, ditches, gravel bars, marshes, pond edges. Native.

FOOD USE: The tender young **greens** can be collected in early summer and eaten raw or cooked. They are somewhat astringent and bitter—the flavor reminds me of brooklime. **Conservation 2.**

COMMENTS: This plant is remarkably beautiful when mature; when young it is nondescript, and thus rarely noticed until mid to late summer. It is recorded as a traditional Anishinaabe food, and I've eaten it, but it's not very exciting. Sources say the petals are "usually absent." I've never seen petals on this plant, but such phrasing suggests that they are sometimes present.

12 Orpine ⓘ 1 🌿 1
Hylotelephium telephium ◆ family *Crassulaceae*

QUICK CHECK: Shin-high, clumping succulent with unbranched stems and toothed leaves. **ID difficulty 1.**

DESCRIPTION: Perennial with tufted stems from a thick root system, forming dense colonies of erect or semi-erect plants 12–30" (30–75 cm) tall. All parts are hairless. **Roots** short, stout, strongly tapered, with many bulbous tuber-like attachments. **Stems** rounded, solid, succulent, often purplish, unbranched below the bottom quarter but with very crowded leaves near the top, naked in the bottom quarter but with very crowded leaves near the top. **LYDS** very stiff and tough, bumpy from numerous raised leaf scars. **Leaves** alternate, thick and fleshy, 1–3.5" (2.5–9 cm) long, elliptic to ovate or obovate and blunt at the tip. There is a waxy outer layer that can be rubbed and peeled from the fleshy inner leaf. **Midvein** and secondary veins are flat and obscure above. **Margins** toothed, but not near the base. Most leaves are sessile, but lower ones may have very short petioles. Stringy bark often remains attached to a plucked leaf. **Inflorescence** a tight, spreading, flat-topped to slightly convex, crowded, branching terminal cluster 2–7" (5–18 cm) across. **Flowers** 5–9 mm across with 5 pink to purple petals, ovate with an acuminate tip, the center broad with 5 large compartments (carpels). **Fruit** is a capsule, rarely formed.

HABITAT: Moderate shade to sun, usually found near old home sites or in meadows, disturbed woods, forest edges, and parks. Introduced.

FOOD USE: The fleshy **leaves** are edible raw or cooked, and are best early in the growing season—but in no case are they especially good. The **roots** are prolific and form a tangled mass under the colony. Harvested from fall through early spring, they can be eaten as a cooked vegetable, but they taste pretty bad. The young roots are also sometimes made into pickles.

COMMENTS: The name "live-forever" derives from the fact that severed plants remain green for a very long time, drawing upon the water stored in the succulent flesh. The plant is erratically distributed and infrequently encountered in most regions, but in specific localities it can be prolific. **AKA** live-forever, *Sedum purpureum, S. telephium*. A very similar native species, *Sedum telephioides*, has a limited distribution in dry, rocky terrain of the Appalachians.

◀ (far left) Orpine with young greens.

Related edible:
Roseroot ◆ *Sedum roseum*

This is a larger plant found on rocky, sunny slopes mostly near the coast in eastern Canada. The leaves are scarcely toothed, and the flowers are yellow. This species has edible young leaves and edible rose-scented roots. (I have not tried the roots.) Both parts are traditionally fermented and eaten by some northern peoples. This plant has long been used in traditional medicine, and unfortunately has been heavily harvested commercially in some areas. **AKA** *Rhodiola rosea*.

613

13 Bigfruit evening-primrose 🌿 2 🌸 2
Oenothera grandiflora ✦ family *Onagraceae*

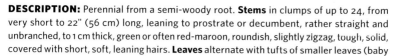

QUICK CHECK: Low plant with tough, spreading, simple stems, narrow leaves, large yellow flowers with long tubular bases, and pods with 4 broad wings. **ID difficulty 1.**

DESCRIPTION: Perennial from a semi-woody root. **Stems** in clumps of up to 24, from very short to 22" (56 cm) long, leaning to prostrate or decumbent, rather straight and unbranched, to 1 cm thick, green or often red-maroon, roundish, slightly zigzag, tough, solid, covered with short, soft, leaning hairs. **Leaves** alternate with tufts of smaller leaves (baby branches) in some axils. Blades are 2–4.5" (5–11 cm) long, narrowly lanceolate to narrowly elliptic, tapered to both ends, the tips pointed, often with a dark nipple. Both surfaces are faintly coated with soft, appressed hairs. **Midvein** light in color and faintly raised above. Secondary veins 2–4 per side, arching strongly forward, light in color, flat to raised above. **Margins** nearly entire but with a few scattered nipple-teeth. **Petioles** about 10% of blade length, but it is hard to say where the petiole ends and the blade begins. **Flowers** (spring to late summer) single from the leaf axils, opening in the afternoon and closing the next morning. The base is an enlarged ovary, narrowed to a long tube (false pedicel) of uniform thickness, 3–5.5" (8–14 cm) long and 5–6 mm thick, pale reddish and finely hairy. **Sepals** 4, pale yellow with maroon mottling, narrowly triangular, partially fused with bristle tips. **Petals** 4, yellow fading to dull orange, obtusely angled at the base, the tip broad with 2 shallow lobes; there is an acuminate point between the lobes. Petal midvein is deeply depressed. The filaments and style are yellow. The anthers are 11–14 mm long, linear, attached in the middle, and folded; the stigma is 4-pronged. **Pods** green, 1.5–2" (4–5 cm) long at maturity, with 4 broad, rounded wings up to 1" (2.5 cm) wide.

HABITAT: Dry prairies, mostly where steep and rocky on limestone. Also limestone road cuts and ledges. Native.

FOOD USE: Both **flowers** and **flower buds** are excellent raw or cooked, from spring to late summer. **Conservation 1.**

COMMENTS: This plant is remarkably distinct and easy to recognize. The flowers are probably the largest of any evening primrose in our region. This variable species has been divided into different subspecies or species based on regional variation. **AKA** *Oenothera missouriensis*, Missouri evening-primrose.

(right) Flower bud. (far right) Winged pods. ▶

14 Appalachian bellflower 🌿 2
Campanula divaricata ✦ family *Campanulaceae*

QUICK CHECK: Knee-high clumped herb with lax stems and milky sap, narrowly lanceolate leaves with sparse teeth, and drooping blue bell-like flowers on thin branches. **ID difficulty 2.**

DESCRIPTION: Perennial from a taproot. Sap milky. **Stems** 1-3' (30–90 cm) tall, multiple, slender, to 4 mm thick, erect to leaning, stiff, zigzag, solid, hairless, with fine wing ridges running down from the nodes, unbranched at first but branching at blooming in the upper half. **Branches** delicate, slightly ascending to spreading, the tips sometimes drooping. **Leaves** alternate, sessile (or the lower ones with a taper-winged petiole), 0.8–3" (2–8 cm) long, narrowly lanceolate, tapered at the base, the tip often curved and very long-tapered to a sharp point. **Surfaces** hairless on both sides but minutely granular above. **Midvein** flat or nearly so above, protruding slightly below. Secondary veins are faint, flat to faintly protruding above and below, soon breaking up. Veins are as dark or darker than the blade. **Margins** sparsely toothed, the teeth large or small, turned outward and nipple-tipped. **Inflorescence** a loose leafy panicle composing the top half of the plant, the leaves within it thin and small, the pedicels long, thin, and single or in small clusters from the axils. **Flowers** (June–October) blue, bell-shaped, hanging, 7–9 mm long. **Calyx** united, green, with 5 linear lobes spreading 90° to the pedicel. **Corolla** united for about 60% of its length, the 5 lobes then strongly recurving. **Style** prominent and blue, protruding by about the length of the bell, with a light-colored, gradually thickened tip. **Fruit** a top-shaped capsule with numerous tiny seeds.

CONFUSING PLANTS: A goldenrod with very similar form shares its habitat, but has more forward-pointed teeth on the leaves, and lacks milky sap.

HABITAT: Rocky slopes and outcroppings, usually in partial sun. Native.

FOOD USE: Tender **stem tips** make a nice mild green, raw or cooked, in spring. **Conservation 2.**

COMMENTS: Because this plant is rather slow-growing it never produces a large tender shoot. Although easy to identify in bloom, the young plants are rather non-descript. This species is sparsely distributed due to its specialized habitat, so collect it sparingly.

615

GROUP 37 BASAL LEAVES ABSENT, LEAVES ALTERNATE AND LOBED

This group contains several mallows, a few composites, a few members of the amaranth family, and some odds and ends. Many of them are physically very distinct at a glance. A few members might key into group 36 if one interprets their small lobes as large teeth.

TENTATIVE IDENTIFICATION KEY TO GROUP 37
The key is not your final answer!

Leaf entire and linear, or with 2-3 linear lobes.	
Blade usually hairless, <6 mm wide; plant <20" (50 cm) tall.	1. Tarragon
Blade densely soft-hairy, >1cm wide; plant >20" (50 cm) tall.	3. Downy paintbrush
Lobed leaves palmate, or elongated with 2 lobes near the base.	
Stem creeping or decumbent, less than 10" (25 cm) tall.	
Stem hairless, flowers not showy.	4. Common pennywort
Stem with long hairs, flowers orange-red.	8. Bristly mallow
Stem erect to leaning, more than 10" (25 cm) tall.	
All leaves deeply palmately lobed, most with 5 or more lobes.	
Covered with needle-like stingers growing from white pustules.	5. Bull-nettle
Covered with needle-like, non-stinging hairs; no white pustules.	6. Pineland hibiscus
Hairless, the lobes almost linear and toothless.	7. Scarlet hibiscus
Lobed leaves typically have 3 major lobes, not deeply cut.	
Lobed leaves all about as broad as long.	
Erect wetland plant with giant pink flowers 5-9" (13-23 cm) across.	9. Swamp rose mallow
Leaning woodland plant with twisted scarlet flowers that never open.	11. Turk's cap mallow
Leaning to sprawling weed with non-showy flowers and spiny fruit.	14. Cocklebur
Lobed leaves sometimes much longer than broad, with an elongated tip.	
Stem hairless or nearly so, flowers 4-5" (10-13 cm) across, stamens whitish.	10. Halberd-leaf rose mallow
Stem densely stiff-hairy, flowers 2" (5 cm) across, stamens yellow.	12. Seashore mallow
Stems densely soft-hairy, flowers 1" (2.5 cm) across, stamens maroon.	13. Marsh mallow
Leaves pinnately lobed, the blades clearly longer than wide with 2 or more lobes per side.	
Lobes compound, each lobed again; stems clumped.	2. Mugwort
Lobes simple; stems single or few.	
Blades hairless.	
Sprawling seashore plant with succulent leaves.	15. Sea rocket
Tumbleweed.	16. Tumble ringwing
Erect to leaning stems; leaves with numerous, erratic teeth.	17. Epazote
Erect stems; leaves with a few large teeth but no small ones.	18. Maple-leaved goosefoot
Blades hairy or velvety on one or both sides.	
Leaves less than 3" (8 cm) long with a few blunt teeth.	19. Showy evening primrose
Leaves more than 5" long with many sharp teeth.	
Margins spiny.	20. Canada thistle
Margins not spiny.	21. Burnweed

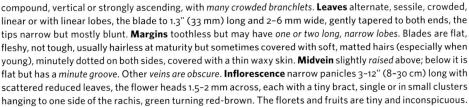

1 Tarragon
Artemisia dracunculus ◆ *Asteraceae* (Composite family)

QUICK CHECK: Clumped, erect, thin, waist-high stems, the leaves linear, some of them lobed; often aromatic; panicles of numerous tiny flower heads. **ID difficulty 2.**

DESCRIPTION: Perennial with several to many clumped stems; variably aromatic, sometimes strongly resembling cultivated tarragon. **Stems** erect to slightly leaning, to 5' (1.5 m) tall and 5-8 mm thick, solid, tough, the surface mostly reddish brown, usually hairless at maturity but sometimes soft-hairy, especially when young. **Branches** many and prominent, compound, vertical or strongly ascending, with *many crowded branchlets*. **Leaves** alternate, sessile, crowded, linear or with linear lobes, the blade to 1.3" (33 mm) long and 2-6 mm wide, gently tapered to both ends, the tips narrow but mostly blunt. **Margins** toothless but may have *one or two long, narrow lobes*. Blades are flat, fleshy, not tough, usually hairless at maturity but sometimes covered with soft, matted hairs (especially when young), minutely dotted on both sides, covered with a thin waxy skin. **Midvein** slightly *raised* above; below it is flat but has a *minute groove*. Other *veins are obscure*. **Inflorescence** narrow panicles 3-12" (8-30 cm) long with scattered reduced leaves, the flower heads 1.5-2 mm across, each with a tiny bract, single or in small clusters hanging to one side of the rachis, green turning red-brown. The florets and fruits are tiny and inconspicuous.

HABITAT: Dry prairies, especially on sandy or gravelly slopes. Native. 🔥

FOOD USE: Leaves can be used fresh or dried as a seasoning like domestic tarragon. **Conservation 2.**

COMMENTS: Few people know that the familiar seasoning tarragon is native to North America and is widespread in dry prairies. The wild plants have highly variable flavor; some are almost unscented, while others have a strong aroma resembling cultivated clones.

2 Mugwort
Artemisia vulgaris ◆ *Asteraceae* (Composite family)

QUICK CHECK: Tall, aromatic, clumped, grayish plant with doubly pinnately lobed leaves with silvery, woolly undersides. **ID difficulty 2.**

DESCRIPTION: Tall aromatic perennial from rhizomes, colonies *appearing grayish from a distance.* **Stems** 4–7' (1.2–2.1 m) tall and 4–9 mm thick, straight, stiff, solid/pithy, roundish but irregularly ridged, often reddish, *woolly,* especially on ridge tops. **LYDS** nearly woody, reddish-brown. **Branches** numerous but only in the upper third, small, strongly ascending. Mature plants often lean or arch due to the weight of the fruits. **Leaves** alternate, sessile or on short petioles, the blades 2–7" (5–18 cm) long and deeply pinnately lobed or divided (nearly to the midvein), the lobes wider toward the end, bearing large teeth or smaller lobes. Each of the larger divisions is again pinnately lobed, but more shallowly. There are often a few small lobes at the leaf base that curl back around the stem. Leaves are crowded on the lower stem in spring, almost appearing basal. Leaves get

▲ Rapidly expanding.

smaller, thinner, and simpler going up the stalk; upper leaves may be entire or have just a few elongated lobes. **Surface** nearly hairless on top, but coated with fine, dense, whitish wool on the underside. **Veins** prominent, depressed and light-colored above, darker and protruding below, running to lobe tips, which have a light-colored nipple. **Inflorescence** a panicle or panicles interspersed with smaller leaves and bearing hundreds of tiny composite flowerheads on short stalks. **Florets** (midsummer to fall) greenish yellow, bearing single-seeded fruits (achenes).

CONFUSING PLANTS: Common ragweed (*Ambrosia artemisifolia*) is a much shorter annual, not clump-ing, without crowded lower leaves in spring, and the leaves have longer, thinner, and more numerous lobes.

HABITAT: Sunny, well-drained, usu-ally coarse soil; roadsides, railroad banks, empty lots, fields. Introduced.

FOOD USE: The **leaves** can be used as a tea or in tea mixtures, fresh or dried. The youngest shoots and leaves can be eaten sparingly raw or cooked, more as a seasoning than a vegeta-ble. To find young shoots in spring, remember the location of colonies from the previous growing season, or look for the distinctive old stalks.

COMMENTS: This herb has a rich tradition of use both as a flavoring and a medicinal. Before the introduc-tion of hops to England, mugwort was often used to flavor beer, hence the name.

3 Downy paintbrush 🌿 2
Castilleja sessiflora • family *Orobanchaceae*

QUICK CHECK: Shin-high, gray-green, hairy plant of dry prairies packed with thin, pointed leaves and a spike of pale flowers layered with leaves. **ID difficulty 1.**

DESCRIPTION: Perennial. **Stems** clumped, erect to leaning, 8–20" (20–50 cm) tall, roundish but slightly ridged, usually not branching, *very densely covered with soft, curvy hairs.* **Shoots** with drooping tops. **LYDS** stiff, curvy, dark brown, with many attached 4-lobed capsules 11–13 mm long in the terminal third, these opening toward the inside with 2 recurved claw-like tips. **Leaves** alternate, clasping, 2–4" (5–10 cm) long, *densely soft-hairy on both sides,* folded along the midvein, pointed with a boat-tip. *Lower leaves are entire and linear; upper leaves usually have two long, forward-pointing lobes from just below the midpoint,* roughly equal in length to the main blade. Leaves have *one prominent vein on each side of the midvein,* light in color, deeply depressed above and protruding below. Mini branch tufts are hidden in leaf axils. **Inflorescence** (spring) could be described as a leafy spike, or as solitary flowers in the axils of each upper leaf. **Calyx** tube is light creamy yellow (or pink, especially in southwestern parts of its range, 1.5–2" (4–5 cm) long, curved outward, ridged lengthwise, with soft hairs on the ridges. **Corolla** tubular, about the same length, whitish, densely soft-hairy, *slit open near the end from which 3–4 claw-like lobes emerge* and a pistil protrudes; below that anthers with orange pollen peek out of the slot.

HABITAT: Dry prairies, especially around rock outcroppings on limestone soil. Native. 🔥

FOOD USE: Young **shoots** and **tender tips** can be eaten raw or cooked. **Conservation 2.**

COMMENTS: Being only partially parasitic, this plant has a mild version of the odd but pleasant "parasitic plant flavor" that is stronger in louseworts (genus *Pedicularis*). **Purple paintbrush** *C. purpurea* is a similar species of Texas and Oklahoma that normally has bright flowers.

WARNING: These parasitic plants are suspected of absorbing toxins from host plants and should not be eaten when growing beside poisonous species.

◄ *Castilleja sessiflora.*

▼ *Castilleja purpurea.*

4 Common pennywort  1
Hydrocotyle americana ✦ *Araliaceae* (Ginseng family)

QUICK CHECK: Low plant with palmate, shallow-lobed, smooth and shiny leaves with blunt teeth. **ID difficulty 1.**

DESCRIPTION: Creeping perennial herb to 9" (23 cm) tall, from a rhizome with a few constrictions. **Stems** light in color, smooth, round, 1–2 mm thick, hairless, not fibrous but turgid. **Leaves** few, alternate, 0.3–1.5" (8–38 mm) long, flat, thin, shiny, hairless, rounded in outline with 5–7 shallow palmate lobes, each of these with a few large, blunt, rounded teeth. **Major veins** *protrude above and are flat below*. **Petiole** 80–220% of blade length, round, smooth, attached at the edge of the blade (not peltate), with small stipules. **Inflorescence** a tiny, nearly ses-

sile umbel hidden under the leaves, with 3–7 flowers, each on a very short pedicel. **Flowers** about 2 mm across with 5 ovate, pointed, whitish petals. **Fruit** a tiny flat schizocarp breaking into 2 seeds.

HABITAT: Moist, shady, often disturbed sites associated with conifer forests, such as forest clearings, stream valleys, along dirt roads or trails, seepages, swamp margins. Native.

FOOD USE: Greens can be eaten raw or cooked, from spring through early autumn. **Conservation 2.**

COMMENTS: This mud-loving plant is low, tiny, and often hard to notice but sometimes abundant. See close relatives on pages 221 and 288.

5 Texas bull-nettle ⬡ 3 ⚘
Cnidoscolus texanum ✦ *Euphorbiaceae* (Spurge family)

QUICK CHECK: Large spreading plant with numerous stinging, white-based needle-hairs and deeply ruffled, palmately lobed leaves. **ID difficulty 1.**

DESCRIPTION: Robust perennial from an enormous root; sap milky. Petioles, leaves, peduncles, pedicels, calyx, fruit, and even the outside of the corolla are armed with stinging hairs! **Stems** stout, up to 1.3" (33 mm) thick, often multiple per plant, branching near the base at broad angles and spreading up to 7' (2 m) wide, the branches often resting on the ground. The surface is bright green with *elongated white dots* from which long, whitish, stinging hairs arise. **Leaves** alternate, ruffled (those near the inflorescence extremely so) and *deeply palmately lobed* with usually 5 major lobes, the lobe margins with erratic teeth or smaller lobes. Lower leaves are 5–9" (13–23 cm) long; the upper leaves are smaller.

▲ Texas bull-nettle (western range) and spurge-nettle (eastern range).

Veins are light in color. **Petiole** long, thick, rounded, unchanneled, about equal to the blade. **Inflorescence** *umbel or umbel-like, with usually 3–4 rays at the first juncture,* each terminating in a *tight cluster of nearly sessile flowers or fruit.* **Flowers** (mid to late summer) have a tube about 1" (2.5 cm) long spreading into 5 thick, white, blunt-tipped lobes about 1" (2.5 cm) long. Sexual parts are buried deep in the tube. **Fruit** an ellipsoid, green, 3-part capsule about 0.9" (23 mm) long, covered with stingers. Each capsule contains 3 **nuts** encased in a fleshy skin, each about 0.6" (15 mm) long and half as wide, rounded on the outside and flattened on the inside, the thin shell smooth and brown when ripe. Each nut looks like a beetle and has *a light fleshy appendage* (called a caruncle) that looks like the beetle's head attached at one end.

HABITAT: Sandy, sunny, well-drained sites, especially where disturbed. Roadsides, hillsides, dunes, and pastures. Native. 🔥

FOOD USE: Ripe **nuts** are delicious, available through late summer and fall. Collect them with tongs or very thick gloves and parch off the stingers before removing the husks. You have to take off 3 layers to get to the kernels. **Conservation 1.**

COMMENTS: The roots are reported to be edible but are enormous and hard to dig out, and I have not tried them. The nuts are delicious, and well protected. **AKA** great spurge-nettle.

WARNING: Causes serious, painful stings!

Related edible:

Spurge-nettle ◆ *Cnidoscolus stimulosus* 2 1

This plant lives in sandy soil and prefers full sun in similar habitats further east, especially near the coast. It is very similar but smaller in all respects. The nuts are likewise edible, but smaller and more difficult to get out. I've eaten the root of this species, which is okay when cooked. 🔥

6 Pineland hibiscus 🌿 2 🌾 3 🌸 2
Hibiscus aculeatus + *Malvaceae* (Mallow family)

QUICK CHECK: Plant of sandy areas with multiple leaning stems covered with dense needle-like hairs; leaves palmately lobed; flowers large and creamy with a dark red-brown center. **ID difficulty 1.**

DESCRIPTION: Perennial from a tough base. **Taproot** may be several inches long and a few inches thick, the skin thin, brown, and rather smooth; the inside is whitish and muci-laginous. **Stems** multiple, ascending to decumbent or nearly prostrate, to 40" (1 m) long and 13 mm thick, solid, with a few broadly spreading minor branches. The surface is green and *extremely rough* from numerous *needle-hairs in spreading clumps on bumps*. **Bark** very stringy. **Leaves** alternate, evenly distrib-uted along the stem, 1.5–5" (4–13 cm) long, palmately 3–7 lobed, the lobes wider toward the tip, sometimes cut almost to the base. **Surfaces** rough-hairy, the major veins raised in a gentle valley above and protruding below. **Margins** coarsely and irregularly toothed with some minor lobes, the teeth broadly pointed, with no bristle or nipple. *Teeth of newly expanding leaves form reddish glands, giving them a warty appearance.* **Petioles** 60–100% of blade length, rounded, solid, not channeled, covered with stiff hairs. **Stipules** linear, curved, entire, 1 mm wide and 7–10 mm long. **Flowers** (June–September) solitary from axils of small upper leaves, the pedicels 5–12 mm. **Corolla** 3.5–4.5" (9–11 cm) across, broadly funnel-shaped, the 5 separate petals overlapping to form a broad funnel, white at first, turning faintly yellowish with age, the broad tips wavy or ragged; the petal base inside the funnel is dark red. The column is deep red. **Calyx** 5 narrowly triangular lobes, 8–12 mm long (longer in fruit), sharp-tipped, strongly keeled with thickened margins, covered with long, stiff, gummy-based hairs. **Fruit** a capsule 0.7–0.8" (18–20 mm) long, contracted to a beak, covered with bristly hairs, containing many brown seeds 4 mm long.

HABITAT: Pine savannahs, forest edges, openings, or roadsides on sandy soil, especially near water and where the ground is sloped and occasionally disturbed. Native. 🔥

FOOD USE: The mild, mucilaginous **roots** are best when the tops are dormant; they should be cooked. Tender growing **stem tips** and **young leaves** are prickly-hairy with an intensely sour but pleasant flavor, reminiscent of red zinger hibiscus tea. The hairs are too prickly to eat these parts raw but they can be used in a smoothie, green sauce, or soup. The **flowers** are also mild and pleasant.

COMMENTS: This gor-geous species of longleaf pine savannahs has been reduced by habitat loss and fire suppression, and should be managed carefully where found. **AKA** comfort root.

Reddish glands on new growth. ▶

7 Scarlet hibiscus ✎ 3 ✿ 3 ❀ 3 ⬯
Hibiscus coccineus ✦ *Malvaceae* (Mallow family)

QUICK CHECK: Tall, clumped, smooth-stemmed plant of swamps with large, deeply-lobed, hemp-like leaves and enormous bright red flowers with 5 petals. **ID difficulty 1.**

DESCRIPTION: Perennial from a woody base. **Stems** usually several, to 8' (2.4 m) tall and 1" (2.5 cm) thick, erect, sometimes branched above but always much taller than wide, solid or with a tiny hollow, roundish, the surface smooth and hairless, green to maroon, bloom-covered. **LYDS** prominent, stiff and strong with stringy bark, dark brown, pithy with a small hollow. **Leaves** alternate, *hemp-like*, at a right angle to the petiole, deeply palmately cleft into usually 5 divisions, these *sometimes fully separated leaflets* but more often lobes with at least a narrow wing connecting them. **Divisions** very narrowly lanceolate with acuminate tips, to 7" (18 cm) long and 1.2" (3 cm) wide, usually folded along the midvein, drooping, the surfaces smooth and hairless. **Primary veins** raised in a shallow trough above, often purplish; they protrude below. Secondary veins 25–40° to the primary, widely separated, arching toward the tip, flat to faintly protruding on both sides. **Margins** have sparse erratic teeth and are often purplish; teeth lack claws, nipples, or bristles. **Petioles** about equal to blade length, strongly ascending, rounded with no grooves, solid, lacking stipules. **Flowers buds** sharp-pointed, forming ridges where the sepals meet; 10–14 *linear bracts curve around the bud.* **Flowers** borne singly on long pedicels from upper leaf axils, to 6" (15 cm) wide, deep scarlet with a white eye in the center. **Petals** 5, veiny, broad at the tip and narrowed at the base, not overlapping when fully open. **Sepals** 5, long-pointed, sharp-tipped, light green, showing through the gaps between petals. **Fruit** an egg-shaped, multi-sectioned, many-seeded, *ridged* pod about 1" (2.5 cm) long, green at first turning brown.

HABITAT: Swamps, marshes, and ditches in full sun to moderate shade. Native.

FOOD USE: In spring and early summer the **leafy stem tips** make excellent greens raw or cooked. The **flower buds** are a great vegetable; I have never had a chance to try the immature pods. **Flowers** are both delicious and beautiful. **Conservation 2.**

COMMENTS: The enormous scarlet flowers shine like a beacon from swamps on warm summer mornings. It is used often (but not nearly enough) as an ornamental. The greens are easy to gather in quantity due to the large size; be sure not to overdo it. This plant is often erroneously reported as "not edible" simply because it lacks the tangy flavor of some commercially cultivated hibiscuses. This is a strange conclusion because, actually, most vegetables don't taste like cranberries.

▲ Flower bud.   ▲ Tender tip.

8 Bristly mallow 3
Modiola caroliniana ✦ *Malvaceae* (Mallow family)

QUICK CHECK: Ground-hugging lawn plant with palmately lobed alternate leaves, tiny red flowers, and bristly round fruits. **ID difficulty 2.**

DESCRIPTION: Low, creeping, short-lived perennial. **Stems** to 40" (1 m) long, single or multiple (branched at the base), creeping, rooting from nodes, usually ground-hugging and rising slightly at the tips but sometimes clambering over other plants well above the ground, 2–5 mm thick, unbranched or branching sparsely above the base; rounded in cross section, solid, the surface with scattered long, erect hairs and glandular dots. **Leaves** alternate, 0.8–1.4" (20–36 mm) long, palmately 5–7 lobed, each lobe with smaller lobes or large teeth. Leaves near the flowers have the *lobes narrower and cut more deeply*, almost to the leaf center. The surface is often ruffled, with scattered long hairs and large, broad-pointed teeth. **Major veins** mostly from the base, *raised above* and slightly protruding below. **Petioles** shallowly channeled, hairy, 60–120% of blade length. **Stipules** entire, lanceolate to triangular, 2–3 mm. **Flowers** (spring through fall) 7–10 mm across, borne singly in leaf axils, with 5 scarlet petals, *opening for just a brief time in the morning*. The calyx is symmetrical with 5 triangular lobes, each with a prominent central vein and a *bristle tip*. **Fruit** a many-sectioned wheel about 9 mm across, ripening to chocolate brown, each section U-shaped with hairy margins, the tip with a fine bristle.

HABITAT: Disturbed, sunny ground such as lawns, sidewalk cracks, vacant lots, gardens. Native.

FOOD USE: Tender **leaves** and stem **tips** can be eaten raw or cooked—all year but especially from late winter to early summer. Leaves can be chopped and steeped for **tea. Conservation 1.**

COMMENTS: This mallow has a beautiful flower that is hard to get a glimpse of. The flavor of the greens is excellent, if you can find a clean handful—much better than the more well-known common mallow.

9 Swamp rose mallow 1 ❀ 2 ✎ 2 ◊ 3
Hibiscus moscheutos ◆ *Malvaceae* (Mallow family)

QUICK CHECK: Tall, clumped, wetland plant with 3-lobed leaves and giant pink flowers. **ID difficulty 1.**

DESCRIPTION: Perennial from a woody root crown. **Stems** clumped, 4-7' (1.2-2.1 m) tall, erect to slightly leaning, zigzag, unbranched or with a few branches in the upper half, solid and roundish, to 0.8" (2 cm) thick, the surface green with scattered clumps of short, stiff, curved hairs. **Leaves** alternate, 4-9" (10-23 cm) long, the base broad and the tip acuminate; terminal leaves are broadly ovate, while the lower and middle ones often have 3 shallow, sharp-tipped lobes. The blade is tough, dark, not glossy, *velvety on both sides* but more so below. There are 3-5 major **veins** from the base, offset by light color, protruding slightly in a gentle valley above, protruding strongly below. **Margins** have large, irregular, blunt teeth. **Petiole** 20-80% of blade length, often upturned, velvety, enlarged just before the blade, roughly triangular with a faint groove. **Flowers** (mid to late summer) single from upper axils, on velvety pedicels 1-1.7" (25-43 mm) long. **Flower buds** about 1" (2.5 cm) long and almost as wide, abruptly pointed, with 5 broad wings starting near the midpoint and 10-14 linear bracts about 0.9" (23 mm) long neatly arranged around it, curving inward but not touching the bud. **Calyx** green and symmetrical with 5 lobes joined at the base. **Petals** 5, large, blunt, 3-5" (8-13 cm) long, overlapping at the base, pink with darker veins, corrugated below from protruding veins. The central column is white, the tip divided into a 5-lobed stigma; sexual parts have yellow tips. **Pods** short and stout but pointed, breaking into sections upon drying to release the seeds.

HABITAT: Sunny, rich sites along waterways; marsh edges, riverbanks, floodplain openings, ditches, lake and pond shores. Native, but often planted as an ornamental.

▼ Young pods.

FOOD USE: Tender young **leaves** can be eaten in early summer—they are better cooked, but are always rather tough. **Flowers** and **flower buds** are edible in mid to late summer. Immature **pods** are somewhat like okra, and are the best part of the plant. You have to get them before they toughen, while they are less than full-size (pod sides should not yet touch the cup formed by the calyx). **Conservation 2.**

COMMENTS: This plant has one of the largest flowers native to our region. The immature pods are a tiny fraction of the biomass, but they are good food. Swamp rose mallow is worth planting for its beauty alone; the pods are a bonus. **Giant rose mallow** *H. grandiflorus* of the coastal Deep South is an even larger species with more deeply lobed leaves. It is similarly edible.

▲ Giant rose mallow leaves. **625**

Related edible:

10 Halberd-leaf rose mallow   🌿 2 🍃 2 ✾ 2 🌰 3
   Hibiscus laevis ✦ *Malvaceae* **(Mallow family)**

This species is similar but smaller in all respects, and in general is much more common. The stems are somewhat shorter and thinner, 3–5' (1–1.5 m) tall, with the surface smooth and hairless or nearly so. The leaves are much narrower, either triangular or with 2 prominent lobes near the base, and the surfaces are faintly hairy to hairless. The flowers are smaller, with white to pink petals and a deep red center. This species is more of a generalist than the swamp rose mallow, found in full to partial sun in swamps or at the margins of lakes, rivers, ditches, and ponds with muck or clay soil, and in wet meadows and around depressions in disturbed fields near waterways. **Flower buds**, **flowers**, and **immature pods** are all edible in mid to late summer. The young **greens** of rapidly growing stems in late spring and early summer are more tender and better eating than those of its larger cousin. **AKA** *Hibiscus militaris*, smooth rose mallow. **ID difficulty 1.**

Tender tip. ▶

11 Turk's cap mallow 🌿 1 ❀ 2 🐝 3
Malvaviscus arboreus ◆ *Malvaceae* (Mallow family)

QUICK CHECK: Tall, leaning plant with multiple stems, soft-hairy palmately lobed leaves, and scarlet flowers that are closed and twisted with a protruding style; squat red fruit. **ID difficulty 1.**

DESCRIPTION: Semi-woody perennial 3-8' (1-2.5 m) tall with multiple stems from the base, evergreen or nearly so, often in colonies. **Stems** round and solid, to 1 cm thick, mostly leaning, with short ascending branches concentrated in the upper part. **Bark** green, fibrous, peeling readily, densely covered with soft, fine, curved hairs. **Leaves** alternate, to 6" (15 cm) long and almost equally wide, thin, hairy on both sides with 3 shallow, palmate lobes. **Major veins** 3-5 from the base; these and the veinlets are modestly depressed above. **Margins** have large, irregular, blunt-pointed teeth. Upper leaves have small, linear stipules. **Petioles** 60-80% of blade length, straight, soft-hairy, elliptic in cross section, deeper than wide, not channeled, enlarged and upcurved toward the tip. **Inflorescence** terminal, small clusters of 2-3 or panicles interrupted by miniature leaves. **Flowers** scarlet, *the petals not opening, remaining wrapped tightly around the protruding column*. There are 4-5 thin, light green, hairy sepals fused more than halfway from the base, the lobes triangular with a prominent central vein. Outside the sepals are 7-8 entire, hairy, linear bracts, blunt-pointed and broadened near the tip. **Column** bright red, spiraled, protruding up to 1" (2.5 cm), the tip split into several parts. **Fruit** red, broad and flattened, 0.6" (15 mm) wide and 0.3" (8 mm) long, wheel-like with a star-shaped depression in the end, the flesh white. The fruit breaks into 5 sections, each with a large crunchy seed. Juice is clear to faintly reddish.

HABITAT: Open forests and forest borders, brushy areas; pine and oak savannahs, especially on limestone soils. Native. 🔥

FOOD USE: Young **leaves** are edible but mediocre as cooked greens. **Flowers** and **ripe fruits**, which are available for most of the growing season (but especially in late summer and fall) are delicious raw nibbles. **Conservation 1.**

COMMENTS: A large, gorgeous, charismatic mallow. The greens are hardly worth mentioning, but the flowers are good, and the fruit is delicious and unique. These are not for making jam or juice—just eat them. The flavor is mild and sweet, reminding me of raw figs and prickly pears, and the crunchy seeds are like little nuts inside. This fire-dependent species has become uncommon in the eastern part of its range, where fires and limestone are infrequent. Plant some!

12 Seashore mallow 🌿 1 🌿 1 🌸 1
Kosteletzkya pentacarpos ◆ *Malvaceae* (Mallow family)

QUICK CHECK: Chest-high seashore plant with grayish, rough-hairy stems and long-pointed leaves; large, showy, 5-petaled pink flowers with a thick, yellow central column. **ID difficulty 1.**

DESCRIPTION: Perennial. **Stems** clumped, erect to leaning, 2-5' (60-150 cm) tall, round, solid, mostly unbranched, covered with *radiating clumps of short, stiff hairs giving it a rough texture.* Bark is very stringy. **Leaves** alternate, 2.5-6" (6-15 cm) long, wide at the base with an elongated, tapered point, typically *drooping at a right angle to the petiole.* Lower leaves are heart-shaped; upward they become more elongated and triangular, bulged at the base or with 2 short *divergent lobes*—these longer in full sun. The surface is gray-green, roughened by stiff, clumped hairs. **Midvein** nearly flat above and slightly protruding below; secondary veins (several of which arise from the base) are nearly flat on both sides. **Petiole** 50-90% of blade length, not channeled or with a faint groove. **Inflorescence** a loose cluster at the apex or the tips of short upper branches, with reduced leaves. **Flowers** (early summer to fall) purple to light pink, 1.5-2.5" (4-6 cm) across. **Petals** 5, overlapping at the base, broad and wavy at the end, with many prominent veins. Numerous narrowly lanceolate or linear bracts are immediately behind the 5 triangular calyx lobes. The stigma column is thick, protruding 0.5-1.2" (13-30 cm), tapered, *yellow*, with short filaments along its length, the tip with 5 red stigmas. **Fruit** a 5-celled capsule, roundish and slightly flattened, the surface stiff-hairy, with one seed per cell.

HABITAT: Salt marshes and other wetlands near the coast, in full sun. Native.

FOOD USE: Tender **leafy tips**, **flowers**, and **flower buds** are edible from late spring through early autumn, but the surfaces of all parts have stiff hairs giving them a rough, granular texture that is especially unpleasant on the greens. Even the flower petals feel gritty. The buds are the best part, but they are tiny. **Conservation 2.**

COMMENTS: This plant is not nearly as good an edible as most of the other large mallows listed here. There are reports of the roots being used like those of marshmallow; I have not tried this myself. This plant is also found in Eurasia, where it is rare due to habitat loss. **AKA** saltmarsh mallow, and when the American populations are separated from the Eurasian, *Kosteletzkya virginica.*

13 Marsh mallow ![glyph] 2 ![glyph] 1 ![glyph] 2 ![glyph] 2
Althaea officinalis ◆ *Malvaceae* (Mallow family)

QUICK CHECK: Chest-high mallow of wetland margins with clumped, velvety stems, velvety leaves, and pale flowers about an inch across. **ID difficulty 1.**

DESCRIPTION: Perennial from a large, gently tapered, light-colored, semi-fibrous tap-root to 1.5" (4 cm) thick, the flesh whitish and very mucilaginous. **Stems** single or more often in clumps of a few, 2-7' (60-210 cm) tall and 0.2-0.7" (5-18 mm) thick, straight, erect at first but usually leaning at maturity, simple or branched sparsely and not widely, the form taller than wide. Cross section is round. The surface is *densely coated with short, soft, grayish hair* (as is almost every part of the plant). Bark is stringy. Shoots are purplish.

▲ Very rare in mapped area. Occasional elsewhere.

Leaves alternate, broadly ovate to triangular or shallowly 3-lobed (the center much longer than the side lobes), 2-4" (5-10 cm) long. The base is broadly notched or right-angled to the petiole. Lobes and tip are pointed. The surface is densely velvety-hairy, giving it a *dull gray-green* look. **Major veins** palmate and pinnate, depressed above, running straight to lobe tips; veinlets are faintly depressed. **Margins** coarsely and irregularly toothed. **Petioles** 20-50% of blade length, roughly D-shaped, not or faintly channeled, downy. **Stipules** linear, sharp-tipped, soon falling off. **Inflorescence** usually 2 short-stalked, tight clusters of 2-9 flowers from each upper leaf axil, each flower on a pedicel 4-10 mm. There are 6-9 narrowly lanceolate bracts just behind the 5 ovate sepals. **Flowers** (midsummer to early fall) pale pink to white, 1-1.2" (25-30 mm) across, the petals about as broad as long, broad at the tip and sometimes slightly notched. The column is pinkish, to 9 mm long, the anthers maroon. **Fruit** wheel-shaped, 8-10 mm across, composed of 15-20 sections (carpels), pale green drying to brown, velvety, the sepals wrapping around it.

HABITAT: Disturbed margins of wetlands, especially brackish marshes. Introduced.

FOOD USE: The large **root** can be cooked and used as a vegetable. **Shoots** can be eaten raw or cooked in late spring (I have not tried them). Young **greens** are rather tough and woolly, but edible. **Flowers** and new green **fruits** are available over a long season and are good raw or cooked. All parts are highly mucilaginous.

COMMENTS: Yes, this is the plant from which a fluffy white confection was made before they invented the fake marshmallow stuff you can buy today, which has nothing to do with the plant. I have never made real "marshmal-low," but I tried it once, and it's delicious. John Kallas has written extensively about the process. This plant is very rare in the wild in our region, but many people call certain other native mallows "marshmal-low," inflating the perception of its abundance. I have only encountered one wild popu-lation. Systematic botanical copying must have occurred, because North American floras report this species as way shorter than it actually is.

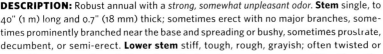

14 Cocklebur 🌿 2
Xanthium strumarium ✦ *Asteraceae* (Composite family)

QUICK CHECK: Thick-stemmed, leaning to spreading herb with thick, rough leaves and football-shaped burs covered with hooked hairs. **ID difficulty 1.**

DESCRIPTION: Robust annual with a *strong, somewhat unpleasant odor.* **Stem** single, to 40" (1 m) long and 0.7" (18 mm) thick; sometimes erect with no major branches, sometimes prominently branched near the base and spreading or bushy, sometimes prostrate, decumbent, or semi-erect. **Lower stem** stiff, tough, rough, grayish; often twisted or curved to repose on the soil. Stem above the base is green to maroon, stiff, with a pithy center; the surface has scattered, stiff, appressed hairs. Mid to **upper stem** obscurely angled with usually 5 somewhat flattened faces, which may have a small channel. Branches mostly at 60–80° angles. **Leaves** few and large, alternate, 3–7" (8–18 cm) long, about equally wide, usually with 3 major lobes, the side lobes blunt-tipped, the middle lobe with an elongated tip. The blade is moderately thick and sandpapery to the touch from stiff hairs; the surface is dull, lighter green and often yellowing, not glossy. Major veins protrude below but are *not depressed* above. **Margins** have erratic large teeth and small lobes. **Petioles** 60–80% of blade length, thick, tough, solid, with stiff appressed hairs, nearly rounded with a very small channel. **Inflorescence** (mid summer to fall) a dense raceme of composite heads from leaf axils, female at the base and male at the tip. Female heads are much larger and contain only 2 florets, but neither gender is showy. **Fruit** is a football-shaped bur about 0.9" (23 mm) long covered with hooked bristles and stiff hairs, the tip with 2 enlarged hooks curved inward like a beetle's pinchers. The flesh is very tough and leathery. Inside are two narrow, elongated, flattened kernels (flatter on one side), striated when dry.

HABITAT: Open, sunny, well-drained sites. Natural habitat is river floodplains, washes, and sandy shores; now also abundant in disturbed soil as a weed. Native.

FOOD USE: Gather ripe brown burs in late summer or fall. Allow them to dry, then clip the base end with a wire cutter and squeeze the **seed** out with pliers, or let it fall out. Eat like sunflower nuts. **Conservation 1.**

COMMENTS: These seeds were an important winter food source for the only parrot native to the eastern US, *Conuropsis carolinensis*, before it was hunted to extinction. Cocklebur kernels taste good but are laborious to extract.

15 Sea rocket 3
Cakile edentula + *Brassicaceae* (Mustard family)

QUICK CHECK: Widely branched mustard of beaches with small, succulent, sparsely-toothed leaves. **ID difficulty 1.**

DESCRIPTION: Succulent annual branching from the base, to 22" (56 cm) long, often spreading wider than tall or appearing to be toppled over. **Stems** hairless, succulent, solid, zigzag, proportionately thick, smooth with gentle ridges and valleys. **Branches** frequent, borne anywhere on the stem. **Leaves** alternate, *thick and fleshy*, 0.8-3" (2-8 cm) long, elliptic to spatulate in outline with a blunt-pointed tip, often cupped, the surface *glossy, hairless, and smooth*. **Midvein** nearly flat above, offset by light color; other veins obscure and flat. **Margins** sometimes entire but usually with erratic, variably sized, blunt teeth or waves and often lobes. **Petioles** of lower leaves 40-90% of blade length, *deeply U-channeled*, the edges sometimes inrolled; upper leaves are nearly sessile with a long-tapered base. **Inflorescence** a terminal raceme, with the pedicels thick and only diverging slightly from the rachis. **Flowers** 5-6 mm across, white to light purple, with 4 petals not at right angles to each other. **Fruit** a distinct pod 0.4-1" (1-2.5 cm) long shaped *like an ice-cream cone* held close to the rachis, with two one-seeded segments divided by a constriction; the thicker outer section detaches to be dispersed by waves, while the inner section remains attached.

RELATED EDIBLE: *C. maritima* is a close edible relative native to Europe, rarely established on our coast. The leaves are deeply pinnately lobed.

HABITAT: Ocean beaches and some parts of the Great Lakes, growing from the sand or gravel where there is often little other vegetation. Native.

FOOD USE: Gather tender **greens** and **stems** as a spicy vegetable, raw or cooked. Spring to early summer is best but individual leaves remain tender through the growing season. **Conservation 2.**

COMMENTS: The flavor is pungent and strong; on salty coasts it tastes slightly salty, but when growing inland (such as along the Great Lakes) it does not.

16 Tumble ringwing 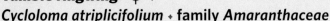 1
Cycloloma atriplicifolium ◆ family *Amaranthaceae*

QUICK CHECK: Low, stout, bushy tumbleweed growing on sand, with many tiny winged fruits, losing its leaves by fruiting. **ID difficulty 1.**

DESCRIPTION: Annual to 28" (70 cm) tall, erect to leaning but with many widely spreading branches from the base, curving upward to form a *bushy tumbleweed wider than tall.* **Stems** and branches are thick at the base in proportion to their length, tapering quickly; they are finely ridged and have small, soft hairs. **Leaves** alternate, 0.8–2.5" (2–6 cm) long, oblanceolate with a tapered base, ascending and often curling, flat, slightly succulent, hairless but often scurfy, the tips broadly angled with a sharp claw. **Midvein** flat to slightly raised above; other veins obscure. **Margins** wavy with a few large teeth and *small lobes at right angles,* these sharp-pointed with light-colored claw tips. **Petiole** to 15% of blade length; some leaves are sessile. **Inflorescence** numerous small, terminal, compound spikes, the flowers usually well-spaced, each with a single, tiny, lanceolate bract underneath. **Flowers** greenish, unshowy, tiny, with 5 tepals joined at the base. **Seeds** single, dark, round, slightly flattened, surrounded by an irregular, thin, *frilly wing radiating on all sides like a wheel.*

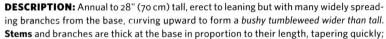

HABITAT: Well-drained sandy disturbed soil in full sun, such as riverbanks, sandy prairies, roadsides, and beaches. Highly associated with clammy-weed (p. 643). More common westward and along coasts and major river systems. Native.

FOOD USE: Cut dry plants in late summer, rub over a tub to collect **seeds.** Dry, rub, winnow, then use as a cooked grain. The chaff is highly aromatic and the seeds have an odd flavor. **Conservation 1.**

COMMENTS: We call this species "sand pile plant" because it covers every old heap of dredged sand along the upper Mississippi River. It is not a very practical food plant for the modern forager, but has served as a staple in the past. Sand sticking to the surface and getting into the seeds is a major problem.

17 Epazote
Chenopodium ambrosioides + family *Amaranthaceae*

QUICK CHECK: Knee to waist-high aromatic herb with many branches and small lanceolate leaves with small lobes; flowers tiny and unshowy. **ID difficulty 2.**

DESCRIPTION: Aromatic perennial from a stout taproot. **Stems** single, 2-4' (60-120 cm) tall, and 4-12 mm thick, solid, tough, almost woody, often curvy, the surface brown, splitting in strips, hairless, with many small ridges. **Branches** numerous and compound, often widely spreading from near the base on full-sun plants; smaller and strongly ascending where crowded or in shade. **Leaves** alternate, extremely variable in size, 0.5-3.5" (13-90 mm) long, mostly lanceolate, tapered to the base, the blades thin and hairless, the surface finely bumpy. **Midvein** offset by light color, slightly raised in a valley or depressed above. Secondary veins 5-9 per side, at broad angles, faintly depressed above and much protruding below, terminating in tooth tips. **Margins** have several *variably spaced and sized large teeth or small lobes* pointing toward the tip; the tapered base is toothless. **Petioles** 5-15% of blade length on lower leaves; upper leaves are nearly sessile. **Inflorescence** numerous spikes from the upper leaf axils, often discontinuous. **Flowers** tiny, unshowy, sessile; ripening to a dry fruit containing a single seed.

HABITAT: Sunny to semi-shaded sites in river floodplains, also disturbed forest edges, young woods, steep slopes, and crop field margins. Possibly introduced.

FOOD USE: The dried or fresh leaves are used as a **seasoning**, traditionally with beans in Mexican cuisine.

COMMENTS: This herb is easy to recognize by its aroma and is common in much of our area. The leaves have anti-worm compounds which are toxic in large doses. Epazote also reduces the flatulence caused by beans. **AKA** Mexican tea, *Dysphania ambrosioides.*

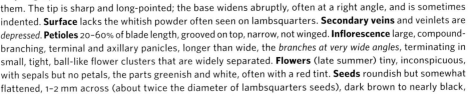

18 Maple-leaved goosefoot ✎ 3 🌿 2 📖 FH-186
Chenopodium hybridum + family *Amaranthaceae*

QUICK CHECK: Tall, musky-scented herb, the leaves with a few very large teeth or small lobes; flowers unshowy in large, sparse panicles; fruits tiny. **ID difficulty 2.**

DESCRIPTION: Branchy, erect annual with a strong musky scent, especially when young. **Stem** 2-7' (60-210 cm) tall, to 0.6" (15 mm) thick, *strongly ridged*, hairless, green, solid. **Leaves** alternate, 2-8" (5-20 cm) long, flat, ovate or triangular in outline with a few, often very large, prominent, sharp teeth or small lobes with broad, rounded sinuses between them. The tip is sharp and long-pointed; the base widens abruptly, often at a right angle, and is sometimes indented. **Surface** lacks the whitish powder often seen on lambsquarters. **Secondary veins** and veinlets are *depressed.* **Petioles** 20-60% of blade length, grooved on top, narrow, not winged. **Inflorescence** large, compound-branching, terminal and axillary panicles, longer than wide, the *branches at very wide angles*, terminating in small, tight, ball-like flower clusters that are widely separated. **Flowers** (late summer) tiny, inconspicuous, with sepals but no petals, the parts greenish and white, often with a red tint. **Seeds** roundish but somewhat flattened, 1-2 mm across (about twice the diameter of lambsquarters seeds), dark brown to nearly black, encased in a thin layer of greenish stuff.

CONFUSING PLANTS: When young, leaves resemble those of strawberry spinach (p. 350), a relative that is also edible—but young strawberry spinach has a rosette, while maple-leaf goosefoot never does.

HABITAT: Disturbed, well-drained soil in wooded areas: logged sites, roadsides, burns, blowdowns. Also a weed of yards, gardens, and empty lots. Most common in light shade. Native.

FOOD USE: Eat tender **leafy tips** raw or cooked; they can be collected from late spring through summer. Leaf blades remain palatable even as the stems toughen and mature. The musky scent goes away with cooking. The **seeds** are larger than those of other goosefoots and easier to clean and winnow. **Conservation 1.**

COMMENTS: This less-known relative of lambsquarters is equally good as a potherb and perhaps a better candidate for collecting seed. This species is native to North America and Eurasia. It pops up after disturbances in forest ecosystems. **AKA** *Chenopodium simplex, Chenopodium gigantospermum, Chenopodiastrum hybridum.*

19 Showy evening primrose 🌿 1 🌿 2 🌼 1
Oenothera speciosa ✦ *Onagraceae* (Evening primrose family)

QUICK CHECK: Low colonial plant of open areas, with erratically toothed gray-green leaves and large pinkish flowers in small clusters. **ID difficulty 1.**

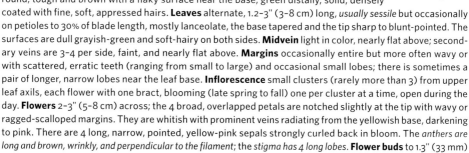

DESCRIPTION: Perennial spreading by rhizomes. **Stems** weakly erect to decumbent or sprawling with a few branches, 6–22" (15–56 cm) tall and 2–5 mm thick, slightly zigzag, round, tough and brown with a flaky surface near the base, green distally, solid, densely coated with fine, soft, appressed hairs. **Leaves** alternate, 1.2–3" (3–8 cm) long, *usually sessile* but occasionally on petioles to 30% of blade length, mostly lanceolate, the base tapered and the tip sharp to blunt-pointed. The surfaces are dull grayish-green and soft-hairy on both sides. **Midvein** light in color, nearly flat above; secondary veins are 3–4 per side, faint, and nearly flat above. **Margins** occasionally entire but more often wavy or with scattered, erratic teeth (ranging from small to large) and occasional small lobes; there is sometimes a pair of longer, narrow lobes near the leaf base. **Inflorescence** small clusters (rarely more than 3) from upper leaf axils, each flower with one bract, blooming (late spring to fall) one per cluster at a time, open during the day. **Flowers** 2–3" (5–8 cm) across; the 4 broad, overlapped petals are notched slightly at the tip with wavy or ragged-scalloped margins. They are whitish with prominent veins radiating from the yellowish base, darkening to pink. There are 4 long, narrow, pointed, yellow-pink sepals strongly curled back in bloom. The *anthers are long and brown, wrinkly, and perpendicular to the filament*; the *stigma has 4 long lobes*. **Flower buds** to 1.3" (33 mm)

long, tapered at the base and more gradually to a pointed tip, the outside covered with soft hairs. **Pod** has 4 large and 4 small wings and holds many small seeds.

HABITAT: Dry, often rocky, poor soil in full sun. Native, but widely planted as an ornamental. 🔥

FOOD USE: The tender **leafy stem tips, flower buds**, and **flowers** can all be eaten raw or cooked. They have a little bit of the irritating quality typical of the evening primrose genus, so are better cooked. The best time to get them is in spring and early summer, but good nibbles can be found from April through early autumn. **Conservation 1.**

RELATED EDIBLES: There are numerous members of the genus *Oenothera*. These are safe to try, and can be eaten to the extent that they are pleasant, but many are strong flavored or tough.

COMMENTS: One of the most commonly noted wildflowers of dry roadsides and meadows from Missouri south and west, blooming heavily in early summer but occasionally through autumn. The flowers grow preposterously large for such a small plant. Showy evening primrose is easy to spot, easy to identify, and abundant. **AKA** Mexican primrose, pinkladies.

20 Canada thistle   ⌇ 3 ▱ 3 ▭ FH-333
Cirsium arvense ✦ *Asteraceae* (Composite family)

QUICK CHECK: Colonial thistle with slender stems, shallowly lobed leaves without stiff hairs, and small (for a thistle) pink-purple heads. **ID difficulty 1.**

DESCRIPTION: Perennial spreading by rhizome to form colonies, the plants much taller than wide. **Root system** of thick, fleshy roots and rhizomes to 0.6" (15 mm) thick, vertical for 3–10" (8–25 cm), then turning horizontal to spread and send up new crowns. **Stems** single, 3–6' (1–2 m) tall, up to 0.8" (2 cm) thick, strongly grooved, erect, straight with little taper, hairless when young but becoming hairy, hollow, branching only in the upper third, the branches ascending. **Leaves** alternate, sessile, to 12" (30 cm) long, narrowly elliptic in outline, the margins lobed, usually shallowly, and extremely ruffled, with sharp spines. **Surface** usually hairless above, often covered with whitish wool below. **Midvein** prominently offset by light color, flat to faintly raised in a valley above; secondary veins are slightly depressed. **Inflorescence** a loose terminal panicle of 3–10 heads, with a reduced leaf at the base of each branch. **Heads** roundish to egg-shaped at first, elongated in bloom and constricted beneath the spreading florets, 0.5–0.8" (13–20 mm) across in bloom, covered with numerous layered ovate bracts tipped with a reddish zone. Plants are either male or female. **Florets** (mid to late summer) light purple to pink (rarely white), long and thin (hair-like), the male florets 0.4–0.6" (10–15 cm), the female 0.7–1" (18–25 cm). **Fruit** a brown seed attached to a tan parachute.

HABITAT: Fields, roadsides, pastures, meadows, stream banks, disturbed open areas in woodland. **I**

FOOD USE: Rhizome tips are unarmed, very tender, and delicious. If you put plywood over a thick Canada thistle colony in spring, rhizomes (or shoots) will crawl along beneath it looking for light. The youngest **shoots**, when still pushing through mulch, make an excellent vegetable. These will have developed thorns only on the very tip, which can be snipped off. **Green shoots** are good raw or cooked after being carefully peeled.

COMMENTS: This is one of the few thistles that spreads by rhizome. The edible parts are smaller than those of other thistles and small specimens are not worth your foraging attention.

Canada thistle shoot. ▶

21 Burnweed  1
Erechtites hieracifolia ✦ Asteraceae (Composite family)

QUICK CHECK: Tall plant with numerous ragged-edged leaves, strong scent, and composite flowerheads with florets mostly hidden by bracts. **ID difficulty 2.**

DESCRIPTION: Erect annual 1–8' (30–240 cm) tall. **Stems** to 0.7" (18 mm) thick, round, solid, the surface with many deep grooves, the ridges between them evenly spaced and sized, covered with soft, spreading hairs. **Shoot** tips have spider-web like hairs between clustered leaves. **Branches** numerous but small and strongly ascending, mostly in the upper half. **Leaves** alternate, 4–11" (10–28 cm) long, thin, sessile (almost clasping), elliptic to lanceolate in outline. Both surfaces have fine, sparse hairs—especially the midvein below. **Midvein** offset by whitish color above, depressed (especially distally). **Secondary veins** numerous, broadly angled, and depressed above; veinlets less so. **Margins** usually shallowly pinnately lobed with smaller teeth between and on the lobes, these angled but not curving forward, with nipple-tips. **Inflorescence** loosely branching terminal panicles somewhat longer than wide, the branches ridged, with numerous bracts, the smaller ones linear and entire. **Heads** (mid to late summer) tubular with a bulged base, 0.7" (18 mm) long, often drooping, the green bracts numerous and linear. **Ray florets** light yellow, barely extending past the bracts on the outside of the flower head—giving the impression, even at the peak of flowering, that the plant is just about to bloom. **Fruit** a small, dark seed attached to a parachute, borne in fluffy balls.

CONFUSING PLANTS: Wild lettuces have milky sap and basal leaves; the stem leaves are fewer, less ruffled, and less hairy.

HABITAT: Disturbed ground in forested ecosystems; often becoming temporarily abundant after fires, floods, construction, or logging. Also in urban and agricultural areas. Native.

FOOD USE: Gather young **leaves** and tender tops in early summer. Use sparingly in salads, boiled or steamed as a potherb, or fried. The flavor and scent are strong. **Conservation 1.**

COMMENTS: This plant is also known as "fireweed," and is sometimes confused with *Epilobium angustifolium* (the other fireweed, p. 589) simply because they share common names; they are not similar in appearance. Burnweed greens are traditionally eaten in eastern Asia, but their flavor is strong, unique, and not commonly liked by the uninitiated. This is one of our most abundant and ubiquitous weeds, and it is becoming more common because it thrives after herbicide application. **AKA** pilewort, fireweed.

GROUP 38   BASAL LEAVES ABSENT, LEAVES ALTERNATE AND COMPOUND OR DIVIDED

This group contains several legumes and a few species from a few other families. Numerous toxic or non-edible legumes will key into this group. A few other edible plants may key here late in the growing season after they have lost their basal leaves; check the bottom of the stem for leaf scars and find the corresponding group among plants with basal leaves.

TENTATIVE IDENTIFICATION KEY TO GROUP 38
The key is not your final answer!

Leaves palmately divided, each division deeply lobed.	
Stem covered with fine, soft, grayish hair; flowers bright orange-red.	1. Scarlet globe mallow
Stem covered with sparse needle-like hair; flowers pale yellow.	2. Flower-of-an-hour
Leaves once compound with discrete leaflets.	
Typical leaves with 3 leaflets.	
Terminal (middle) leaflet with a distinct petiolule.	
Stem unbranched, leaves densely packed almost into a whorl.	7. Point-leaf tick trefoil
Stem much branched, the leaves widely spaced.	8. Sweet clovers
Terminal (middle) leaflet sessile or nearly so.	
Leaflets shaped like a folded paper heart; corolla yellow.	3. Yellow wood sorrel
Leaflets ovate, lanceolate, or elliptic; corolla not yellow.	
Stem mostly hairless; corolla pink-purple.	4. Rocky Mountain beeplant
Stem covered with sticky-tipped hairs; corolla white.	5. Clammy weed
Leaves pinnately compound, many or all with more than 3 discrete leaflets.	
Leaves with 9 or fewer leaflets.	
Single-stemmed, delicate spring ephemeral less than 12" (30 cm) tall.	6. Hot mermaid
Stems tough, persistent, clumped; 1–4' (30–120 cm) tall.	9. Prairie clovers
Leaves with 9 or more leaflets.	
Stems single, erect, spreading by rhizome to form colonies.	10. American licorice
Stems clumped on a tough root crown, leaning or decumbent.	
Stems to 18" (46 cm) long; fruit plum-shaped and juicy.	11. Ground-plum milkvetch
Stems over 20" (50 cm) long; fruit a jointed, constricted pod.	12. Alpine sweetvetch
Leaves palmately compound with usually more than 3 leaflets.	
Stem more than 5' (150 cm) tall; leaflets toothed with strongly depressed veins.	13. Hemp
Stem less than 30" (75 cm) tall; leaflets entire with veins flat or nearly so.	
Stem erect and densely covered with long, erect hairs.	14. Prairie-turnip
Stem leaning and sparsely covered with leaning to appressed hairs.	15. Tall breadroot
Leaves 2–3 times compound.	
Stem with scattered hairs but no bristles.	16. Spikenard
Stem with scattered spines or bristles.	17. Bristly sarsaparilla

1 Scarlet globe mallow 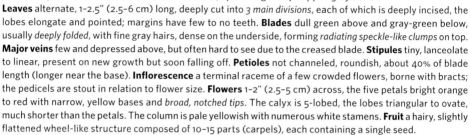 2
Sphaeralcea coccinea ✦ *Malvaceae* (Mallow family)

QUICK CHECK: Low gray-green plant with deeply cut, hairy leaves and bright orange-red flowers with 5 broad, shallowly notched petals. **ID difficulty 2.**

DESCRIPTION: Perennial forming colonies by a deep horizontal root system, up to 20" (50 cm) tall but often blooming when the plants are only 3-4" (8-10 cm). Vertical roots at the stem base are tough and woody. **Stems** leaning to erect, 1-4 mm thick, tough in the lower portions, round, covered with matted *clumps of fine grayish hair.*
Leaves alternate, 1-2.5" (2.5-6 cm) long, deeply cut into *3 main divisions*, each of which is deeply incised, the lobes elongate and pointed; margins have few to no teeth. **Blades** dull green above and gray-green below, usually *deeply folded*, with fine gray hairs, dense on the underside, forming *radiating speckle-like clumps* on top. **Major veins** few and depressed above, but often hard to see due to the creased blade. **Stipules** tiny, lanceolate to linear, present on new growth but soon falling off. **Petioles** not channeled, roundish, about 40% of blade length (longer near the base). **Inflorescence** a terminal raceme of a few crowded flowers, borne with bracts; the pedicels are stout in relation to flower size. **Flowers** 1-2" (2.5-5 cm) across, the five petals bright orange to red with narrow, yellow bases and *broad, notched tips*. The calyx is 5-lobed, the lobes triangular to ovate, much shorter than the petals. The column is pale yellowish with numerous white stamens. **Fruit** a hairy, slightly flattened wheel-like structure composed of 10-15 parts (carpels), each containing a single seed.

HABITAT: Dry prairies, especially on hills or where sandy. Native. 🔥

FOOD USE: Eat the tender **greens**, including buds and flowers, in summer, raw or cooked. **Conservation 2.**

COMMENTS: The edible parts of this absolutely beautiful flower are all good, and more tender than they look, although the plant's small stature and growing conditions mean that it is often dirty. **AKA** red false mallow, cowboy's delight.

2   Flower-of-an-hour   🌿 3   🌿 1
Hibiscus trionum + Malvaceae (Mallow family)

QUICK CHECK: Low herb with needle hairs and leaves divided into 3 blunt leaflets or lobes, large yellowish flowers with maroon centers, the bud with dark-edged ridges. **ID difficulty 1.**

▲ Most abundant in the corn belt.

DESCRIPTION: Annual, usually less than 16" (40 cm) tall, branching widely at right angles, the branches few but often long and prominent, those near the base often resting on the ground. The plant is sparsely hairy near the base but conspicuously so toward the inflorescences, the hairs needle-like and often arranged in clumps on raised bumps. **Stems** 2–4 mm thick, green, round, solid, with sparse, long, needle-like hairs. There is *a narrow row of small, dense hairs running on one or two sides of each node to the next node above*, except on the lower stems. **Leaves** deeply 3-lobed or ternately compound. If lobed, the major lobes are *narrowed near the base* with smaller, blunt sub-lobes. If compound, the leaflets are all sessile, 0.7–1.8" (18–46 cm) long. **Blades** hairless above except for the midvein, which has scattered needle-hairs; the underside is sparsely hairy. Few **veins** evident, these slightly depressed above and protruding below, light in color. **Margins** untoothed and usually darkened. **Petioles** 80–140% of blade length, straight, with scattered needle-hairs; there is a shallow channel lined with fine hairs. Stipules are tiny. **Flowers** (summer) single, opening briefly in the morning, about 1.3" (33 mm) across, the pedicels about 1" (2.5 cm) long. **Flower bud** *inflated with 5 wide wings with hairy purple-brown edges*; between these are 3–5 shorter dark ridges, and between the ridges the sepals are veiny and nearly transparent. **Calyx** of 5 triangular sepals fused at the base. Beneath the calyx is a whorl of numerous linear bracts 40% of its length, curving toward the tip but not touching the sepals. **Petals** 5, broad, veiny, separate, pale yellow but maroon at the base. The column and 5-lobed stigma are maroon, the anthers yellow-orange. After blooming the calyx closes to form a papery husk around the very hairy 5-part capsule, which contains numerous seeds that ripen to dark brown.

HABITAT: Disturbed rich soil in full sun; crop fields, gardens, yards, construction sites. Introduced.

FOOD USE: All the **tender new parts** are edible raw or cooked from midsummer to early fall. Ripe **seeds** can be used like poppy seeds from late summer to early fall.

COMMENTS: Common and widespread, this is one of our best tasting mallow greens, the only trouble being the annoying hairs, and the fact that they often catch dirt. This might have the prettiest flower of any common agricultural weed.

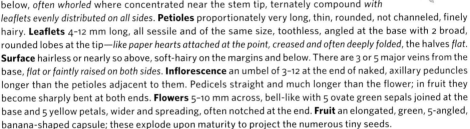

3 Yellow wood sorrel ✎ 3 ⬩ 2 ▭ NG-338
genus *Oxalis* (in part) ⬩ family *Oxalidaceae*

QUICK CHECK: Compound leaves with 3 identical heart-shaped leaflets connected at
the tip and folded or creased along the midvein; yellow flowers and banana-like pods.
ID difficulty 1.

DESCRIPTION: Small annuals. **Stems** single or clumped, 2–26" (5–56 cm) tall and 2–5 mm
thick, delicate, rounded, solid, soft-hairy, erect or spreading to bushy. **Leaves** alternate
below, *often whorled* where concentrated near the stem tip, ternately compound *with
leaflets evenly distributed on all sides.* **Petioles** proportionately very long, thin, rounded, not channeled, finely
hairy. **Leaflets** 4–12 mm long, all sessile and of the same size, toothless, angled at the base with 2 broad,
rounded lobes at the tip—*like paper hearts attached at the point, creased and often deeply folded,* the halves *flat.*
Surface hairless or nearly so above, soft-hairy on the margins and below. There are 3 or 5 major veins from the
base, *flat or faintly raised on both sides.* **Inflorescence** an umbel of 3–12 at the end of naked, axillary peduncles
longer than the petioles adjacent to them. Pedicels straight and much longer than the flower; in fruit they
become sharply bent at both ends. **Flowers** 5–10 mm across, bell-like with 5 ovate green sepals joined at the
base and 5 yellow petals, wider and spreading, often notched at the end. **Fruit** an elongated, green, 5-angled,
banana-shaped capsule; these explode upon maturity to project the numerous tiny seeds.

SPECIES: There are two common, widespread, annual, yellow-flowered wood sorrels. *O. stricta* is characteristic
of moist but well-drained soil in shade, such as yards, gardens, along house foundations, disturbed woods,
and moist fields. *O. dillenii* is smaller and thrives in drier soil and sunnier sites, such as sidewalk cracks and
lawns. Both are probably native.

FOOD USE: Gather **greens** and nibble any time of the growing season, or use them in soup or salad. It is
easiest to find tender growth in spring and early summer. The greens can be chopped in a blender and then
steeped in cold water to make a sour drink. The tiny banana-shaped **pods**, found from late summer onward,
make a fun snack. **Conservation 1.**

COMMENTS: This is one of our most commonly eaten wild greens. Children love its sour, lemony flavor and
teach each other to recognize it. They are high in oxalic acid. (Wood sorrels; children have much lower levels.)

4 Rocky mountain beeplant 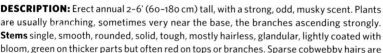 2 🌸 2 🌿 2
Cleome serrulata • family Cleomaceae

QUICK CHECK: Erect, musky herb with 3-part compound leaves, the leaflets sessile and entire; purple flowers and long, thin, hanging pods. **ID difficulty 1.**

DESCRIPTION: Erect annual 2-6' (60-180 cm) tall, with a strong, odd, musky scent. Plants are usually branching, sometimes very near the base, the branches ascending strongly. **Stems** single, smooth, rounded, solid, tough, mostly hairless, glandular, lightly coated with bloom, green on thicker parts but often red on tops or branches. Sparse cobwebby hairs are often found around the nodes on young growth. **Leaves** alternate, compound with three leaflets about equal in size borne on very short petiolules. **Leaflets** 0.8-2" (2-5 cm) long, elliptic to lanceolate, entire, tapered to a point on both ends, the tip with a hook or nipple. In full sun the leaflets are often *folded up along the midvein, with their tips oriented vertically.* **Surfaces** have sparse hairs, especially below. **Midveins** strongly depressed above and protruding below. **Secondary veins** numerous, 55° to the midvein, flat to faintly depressed above and protruding below. **Margins** usually have tiny teeth, but these are hard to notice. **Petioles** 70-100% of terminal leaflet length. **Inflorescence** dense terminal racemes to 10" (25 cm) long, the rachis sparsely hairy with 6-30 blooming flowers crowded in a short section, with numerous unopened buds at the tip. **Pedicels** thread-thin, about 0.8" (2 cm) long, each with a narrowly lanceolate bract at the base. Bracts persist after unfertilized flowers fall off, leaving the lower rachis crowded with tiny bracts. **Flowers** (summer) have 4 sepals fused to their midpoint, ending in small triangular lobes, and 4 pink to light purple petals about 1 cm long. Petals are similar in size but *asymmetrically arranged.* There are 6 *radiating stamens protruding* about twice the length of the petals. **Pod** thin, often slightly curved, 1-2.5" (2.5-6 cm) long, green, cylindrical, slightly constricted between the seeds, drooping. **Seeds** numerous, about 3 mm, slightly flattened, roundish with a slight coil.

HABITAT: Sunny, disturbed soils; steep slopes, washes, ravines, roadsides, construction sites, etc., especially where sandy. Native.

FOOD USE: The tender young **stems**, **leaves**, and **flowers** are used as a seasoning or vegetable. Raw, they are spicy-hot; cooking makes them milder. Leaflets remain tender long after the stems toughen. The ripe pods can be collected and dried, then broken up to release the **seeds**, which can be sifted or winnowed to remove the trash. The seeds can be ground and eaten or cooked as a porridge. **Conservation 2.**

COMMENTS: Like many culinary herbs, beeplant is often considered to have a disagreeable odor by those who don't use it. The smell is strong and unique, and the flavor is among the hottest of our wild edibles. Beeplant is strikingly beautiful and rightfully popular as an ornamental. There are numerous other common names.

5 Clammy weed 🌿 3 🌱 2
Polanisia dodecandra • family *Cleomaceae*

QUICK CHECK: Shin to thigh-high bushy herb of open, sandy areas, sticky and strong-smelling, with 3-part compound leaves, racemes, and elongated upright pods. **ID difficulty 1.**

DESCRIPTION: Annual, as wide as tall when growing in the open but taller than wide in competition. The whole plant has a strong green-pepper odor. **Stems** to 40" (1 m) tall and 0.8" (2 cm) thick, often leaning or falling over at maturity, solid, round, faintly and gently ridged, light green, covered with short, sticky, gland-tipped hairs, often branching heavily near the base, the branches spreading to weakly ascending at first, then turning more erect. Some branches are red-brown on the upper side. **Leaves** alternate, ternately compound; near the top is an occasional simple leaf, or one with 2 leaflets. (Bracts are simple.) **Petiole** 60–90% of terminal leaflet length, with a tiny groove on top. **Leaflets** sessile, thin, elliptic to oval, entire, 0.2–0.8" (5–20 mm) long, the tips blunt to pointed but not acuminate; the terminal leaflet is slightly larger. The surface has sparse, tiny hairs and glands. **Midvein** and secondary veins are depressed above; veinlets are flat. **Inflorescence** a raceme with many simple bracts; this could also be construed as individual flowers held erect on long, thin pedicels from the axils of simple upper leaves. **Flowers** (summer) about 5 mm long with 4 sharp-tipped, cupped, ovate, purple-brown sepals and 4 white petals scarcely exceeding the sepals; the petals are narrow at the base and broad at the *notched tip*. The *long-protruding stamens are purplish-red*. **Pods** green, 0.9–2" (23–50 mm) long, shaped like a pea pod, the walls thin and flexible, drying to light brown, containing 2 rows of roundish but slightly flattened brown seeds 2–3 mm in diameter. The pedicel is 45° to the stem but the pod is held vertically; both parts are sticky-hairy.

CONFUSING PLANTS: Rocky Mountain beeplant has drooping pods and thicker, darker leaves.

HABITAT: Open, sandy, disturbed sites; riverbanks, sandbars, roadsides, construction sites, sandpits. Likely to be found on any pile of sand near a major riverway, and strongly associated with tumble ringwing (p. 632). Native.

FOOD USE: The **tender tops** can be used raw or as a potherb, especially as a flavoring in stews. They are most available in early to mid summer. **Seeds** can be boiled and eaten, whole or ground. **Conservation 2.**

COMMENTS: For some reason this Indigenous culinary herb of the Southwest is little known as an edible. It is usually reported in the literature to have an unpleasant scent, but the smell reminds people of green bell peppers, and I think the flavor goes well with red meat in a stew or pot roast. Although sporadic in occurrence due to its specialized habitat needs, this plant is widespread and locally abundant.

6 Hot mermaid 🌿 3
Floerkia proserpinacoides ✦ family *Limnanthaceae*

QUICK CHECK: Tiny, flimsy, hairless plant forming carpets in spring; 3–5 part compound leaves; tiny, single 3-petal flowers on long pedicels. **ID difficulty 2.**

DESCRIPTION: Annual *spring ephemeral* 6–11" (15–28 cm) tall, often found in dense masses or carpets, the plants usually tangled. *All parts hairless.* **Stems** often branched at the base, light green, weakly erect, solid, hairless, 1–2 mm thick. **Leaves** alternate, 0.4–0.8" (1–2 cm) long, pinnately compound, one (rarely a few of them) borne at the base. Lower leaves have 3 leaflets; upper leaves have 5 or 7 leaflets, the terminal sometimes lobed or conjoined. **Leaflets** sessile, 5–11 mm, narrowly elliptic to oblanceolate, tapered to a point on both ends, the surface sparkly in the sun and flat, the margins entire. **Midvein** lightly incised. Faint secondary veins, almost parallel, arise near mid-leaflet; other veins are not evident. **Petioles** 3–4 times the blade length, thin with a narrow groove, those of the upper leaves with a small sheath at the base. **Flowers** few, 3 mm across, single on long pedicels to 1.3" (33 mm) from upper leaf axils, ascending but with the tip drooping. There are 3 triangular green sepals with prominent veins and 3 smaller, narrow, whitish petals set between them; the sepals get longer with fruiting. **Fruit** 1–3 bumpy greenish balls, ripening to brown and containing a single, proportionately large seed.

HABITAT: Moist to mucky, rich, frequently but lightly disturbed soil in shade: depressions in small floodplains (or the higher parts of large floodplains where floods aren't too intense), low spots in woods, pond and swamp margins, mucky seeps, shrub swamps. Native.

FOOD USE: The **greens** (all parts) are delicious raw and can also be eaten cooked. They have a fleeting heat with a fruity undertone and the green mildness of chickweed. This is the best leafy green you will ever put on a taco, or perhaps in your mouth in any form. Snip with scissors where the plants are crowded, leaving many to go to seed, and curate your patch. **Conservation 2.**

COMMENTS: This is said to be the only North American dicot herb with 3-petaled flowers. It also has the highest seed recruitment rate (25% of seeds became adults in one study) of any plant ever studied. I don't know what baffles me more: that such a magical dainty even exists, that almost nobody talks of it, or that it took me four decades to discover it. Just this one tiny green is worth this book's price. **AKA** false mermaid.

7 Point-leaf tick trefoil 🌿 3
Desmodium glutinosum ⁘ *Fabaceae* (Bean family)

QUICK CHECK: Erect, knee-high woodland plant with a whorl-like cluster of ternately compound leaves atop a naked stalk; D-shaped seeds connected in chains. **ID difficulty 1.**

DESCRIPTION: Herbaceous perennial. **Stems** single or few per crown, vertical, straight, stiff, solid, round, green, smooth with fine sparse hairs and stringy bark. The *stem is unbranched, naked for the lower 8–17" (20–43 cm), then has a whorl-like cluster of 5–9 alternate leaves densely packed into less than 2" (5 cm) of stem*—the uppermost appearing paired.
Leaves ternately compound with 3 leaflets, spreading to form a horizontal leafy layer. Side leaflets are on very short petiolules (3–6 mm); the terminal is much longer. **Rachis** naked for 40–70% of its length, green or maroon with an enlarged base, stiff, thin, sparsely soft-hairy with a shallow groove near the top of each side and a shallow channel on top; there is a small ridge running inside this channel. **Leaflets** thin, sparsely hairy, 2.5–4" (6–10 cm) long with entire but hairy margins and a *long acuminate tip*. Side leaflets are broadly ovate, lopsided with a broad base; terminal leaflets are much broader, often almost rounded. **Midvein** and secondary veins are lightly, often broadly, depressed; they protrude below. **Inflorescence** (midsummer) an elongated, erect panicle or raceme, to 28" (70 cm) long with a dominant, straight central rachis and a few minor side branches, the flowers in pairs or small clusters (occasionally single) spaced along the raceme, the pedicels 3–5 mm. **Flowers** tiny, the corolla 4–6 mm long, pea-like, the wings and banner cupped, pink outside and pale inside; calyx 2–3 mm. **Fruit** (late summer to fall) a short chain of 2–3 D-shaped, flattened segments (loments) which stick to clothing, connected at constricted points, the skin tightly enclosing one seed.

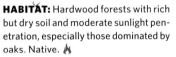

HABITAT: Hardwood forests with rich but dry soil and moderate sunlight penetration, especially those dominated by oaks. Native. 🔥

FOOD USE: Ripe **seeds** make an excellent cooked bean, but they are hard to collect in quantity. When I clean them off my clothing, I usually nibble them. I gather them by whipping the tops with an old t-shirt in late summer or early autumn. **Conservation 1.**

COMMENTS: The annoying half-moon seeds stick to your clothes when you hike in late summer. They have been frequently found in archaeological remains in our region but seem to have fallen out of favor with the arrival of more labor-efficient domesticated beans. It is hard to avoid nibbling a food that collects itself, but like other beans, these should be cooked if eaten in quantity.

RELATED EDIBLES: Other members of the genus presumably have usable seeds; I have tried several, all of which tasted nearly identical. Archaeologists have not specified the species recovered, but this one has the largest seeds and I commonly eat them. **AKA** *Hylodesmum glutinosum.*

8 Sweet clovers (white and yellow)
Melilotus albus and *M. officinalis* ♦ Fabaceae (Bean family)

QUICK CHECK: Tall and branchy, compound leaves with 3 leaflets, small yellow or white flowers in elongated, curving racemes. **ID difficulty 2.**

DESCRIPTION: Biennial or annual aromatic herbs 3-7' (90-210 cm) tall, with many ascending branches (including at the base), the form taller than wide and typically leaning. **Stems** 5-14 mm thick, zigzag, ridged, with a small hollow, hairless or with extremely fine hairs, the surface green (reddish at the base). **Leaves** alternate, ternately compound, the terminal one with a short stalk and the other 2 sessile. **Petioles** deeply channeled above, broadly keeled below, 70-90% of terminal leaflet length. **Stipules** small, fused and sheath-like at the base, then wispy and pointed. **Leaflets** 0.5-1.2" (13-30 mm) long, obovate to oblanceolate (wider toward the tip), the bases angled, the tips pointed to blunt or flat, the blades hairless. **Midvein** depressed above; secondary veins are numerous and flat to faintly raised above. **Margins** with *very*

▲ Composite range.

fine, widely spaced teeth. **Inflorescence** numerous thin, erect but curved racemes 2-8" (5-20 cm) long on peduncles 60-100% of the cluster's length. **Flowers** narrow and pea-like, drooping, 5-7 mm long, white or yellow, the banner longer than the other parts, folded only slightly back, keeled. **Pods** egg-shaped with 1-2 light brown seeds.

SPECIES: Yellow sweet clover blooms earlier and tends to be shorter, but otherwise these two species are nearly identical except for the flower color.

HABITAT: Dry, disturbed soil in full sun. Roadsides (usually right next to the gravel shoulder), railroad tracks, steep meadows, vacant lots, rubble heaps, dry fields. Introduced.

FOOD USE: Flowers and leaves can be used for **tea**, fresh or dried. The youngest **leaves** and **growing tips** can supposedly be used raw in salads or eaten as a cooked vegetable—they are very tender but also exceptionally bitter. I only consider them suitable as a seasoning. When dried, the leaves have a fragrance reminiscent of vanilla and have been widely used as a flavoring, as have the **seeds**.

COMMENTS: Yellow and white sweet clover can be used interchangeably as a flavoring. Literature often contains warnings that moldy sweet clover can produce coumarin, a potentially dangerous anti-coagulant. This means that if your sweet clover hay is moldy, don't eat it. I bet you weren't going to do that anyway.

9 Prairie clovers (white and purple) 🧍 1 🌿 2 ☕
Dalea candida, D. purpurea ✦ Fabaceae (Bean family)

QUICK CHECK: Slender and hairless with clumped stems and small pinnately compound leaves, the leaflets thin and entire; cylindrical head of tightly packed tiny flowers. **ID difficulty 2.**

DESCRIPTION: Perennials. **Root** 0.5–0.9" (13–23 mm) thick at the top, woody and branching but soon becoming thin, fleshy, and long-tapered, the skin smooth to slightly corrugated, yellow-brown to greenish. **Stems** multiple, clumped, 1–4' (30–120 cm) tall and 3–5 mm thick, erect to leaning or spreading, straight, thin, tough, roundish with small ridges, hairless but with a few scattered glands, simple or branching. **LYDS** often persistent. **Leaves** alternate, up to 3" (8 cm) long, pinnately compound with 3–9 leaflets, nearly sessile or on short petioles; the terminal leaflet is distinctly longer. The leaves are *sometimes borne in clumps*, with 1 or 2 smaller leaves beside a larger leaf in the center. **Leaflets** 0.3–0.8" (8–20 mm) long, linear, oblanceolate, or long-elliptic, entire, the tips often *blunt with a needle-like point*, sessile or with very short petiolules. Blades are deeply folded along the midvein, often appearing channeled, with small glands below making them sticky. **Inflorescence** erect terminal spikes 1–3" (2.5–8 cm) long borne singly and widely separated on long, naked, grooved peduncles,

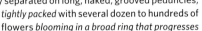

▲ White prairie clover.

▲ Purple prairie clover.

tightly packed with several dozen to hundreds of flowers *blooming in a broad ring that progresses from the bottom to the top*. **Flowers** 3–4 mm long with 5 elliptic petals, stalked at the base, of nearly the same size and form. Anthers on long filaments protrude well beyond the petals. **Seed** tiny, kidney-shaped, one per each tiny pod enclosed in the calyx.

SPECIES: White prairie clover *D. candida* has white flowers and the spike has numerous tiny, ascending, stiff bracts. The stems tend to lean and spread widely and have many small branches; the leaflets are broader and hairless. **Purple prairie clover** *D. purpurea* has purple flowers with a downcurved bract beneath the bud. The leaflets are much narrower and often have fine hairs on the margins. The branches tend to be fewer but larger. Other species in this genus may be similarly edible, but some are bitter and distasteful. These two are the only species I know to be foodworthy.

HABITAT: Dry, sunny open areas, especially rocky slopes; meadows, roadsides, prairies, open oak woods, savannahs. Preferred by cattle and thus heavily impacted by grazing. Native. 🔥

FOOD USE: Roots can be eaten as a vegetable when the top is dormant. The flavor is good, but they are quite tough. The tender **young leaves** can also be chopped fine and used as an herb. The aromatic leaves make a delicious **tea**, fresh or dried, at any age. **Conservation 3/2.**

COMMENTS: These marvelous and distinctive prairie plants should be propagated by anyone owning suitable habitat.

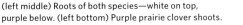

◄ (left middle) Roots of both species—white on top, purple below. (left bottom) Purple prairie clover shoots.

647

10 American licorice 🌿 2 🦋 1 🏺 ☕
Glycirrhiza lepidota • *Fabaceae* (Bean family)

QUICK CHECK: Erect, waist-high colonial herb with pinnately compound leaves and entire leaflets; irregular white flowers and burs in dense clusters. **ID difficulty 3.**

DESCRIPTION: Aromatic perennial forming loose colonies by a network of rhizomes. **Rhizomes** long, thin, hardly tapering, tough, almost woody, brown outside and whitish inside, running *very deep*, rarely thicker than 0.7" (18 mm). **Stems** 2–3.5' (0.6–1 m) tall, erect, single or in small clumps, usually simple but sometimes branching. The surface is faintly ridged and often dark reddish with scattered, *sticky, mostly stalkless, light-dotted glands* and few to no hairs. **Shoots** have ridges, scales, and sticky glands. **Leaves** alternate, pinnately compound, 7–12" (18–30 cm) long with 11–19 leaflets, each on a short, stout, petiolule; the terminal leaflet is largest. **Stipules** tiny and triangular. **Rachis** naked in the proximal 10% with a channel near the base, narrowing to a deep groove distally. **Leaflets** 1–2" (2.5–5 cm) long, paired, lanceolate with pointed or blunt tips and entire margins, typically angled upward to form a shallow V along the rachis; each leaflet is likewise folded along its midvein. Surfaces are *sticky and glandular*, especially the lower. **Midvein** strongly depressed above, protruding and often hairy beneath; secondary veins are several per side and slightly depressed. **Inflorescence** a *tightly packed, spike-like raceme* 1.2–2" (3–5 cm) long, from the axils of upper leaves on a peduncle about as long as the raceme. **Flowers** pea-like, about 0.5" (13 mm) long, the corolla whitish, the banner elongated and curled upward. **Fruit** a pod about 0.7" (18 mm) long, slightly curved, dark brown at maturity, *covered with numerous hooked bristles* that make it a *stick-tight bur*; inside are 3–5 bean-like seeds about 2 mm long.

▲ Rare east of the Mississippi River.

HABITAT: Sunny, moist, well-drained sites in full sun: ravines, slopes, and near watercourses in prairies and savannahs. Also roadsides, meadows, and forest edges. Native. 🔥.

FOOD USE: It is often reported that the **rhizomes** can be "eaten" raw or cooked. They are really too tough to eat and devoid of any substantial starchy portion, but they can be chewed or brewed into tea for their flavor—which is very strong, and quite unlike what most people expect. The **shoots** can be collected in late spring, at the height of 10–20" (25–50 cm), and eaten raw or cooked after peeling the bitter skin. They remind me of sumac shoots. **Flowers** can also be nibbled. **Conservation 2.**

COMMENTS: This is a close relative of licorice (*Glycirrhiza glabra*), which is found in Europe. The root was more widely chewed in the past. Since it has significant medicinal qualities, this should be done in moderation. Certain historical and ethnographic reports of this plant's use are in error due to its frequent confusion with related members of *Hedysarum, Astragalus*, or *Lupinus*, or with the unrelated licorice-tasting members of *Ozmorhiza*. This probably explains the reports of the rhizomes being cooked and eaten "like sweet potatoes."

Shoot. ▶

The same shoot after peeling. ▶

11 Ground-plum milkvetch 🔵 3
Astragalus crassicarpus ✦ *Fabaceae* (Bean family)

QUICK CHECK: Small, many-stemmed decumbent plant with finely compound leaves and plump, green, grape-sized fruit. **ID difficulty 2.**

DESCRIPTION: Perennial from a thick, tough root. **Stems** several to many *in a tuft*, up to 18" (46 cm) long, *weakly erect to leaning* in bloom but *lying on the ground when in fruit*, not branched, round, the surface with fine, soft hairs pressed toward the tip. **Leaves** alternate, once pinnately compound, to 4.5" (11 cm) long, the leaflets beginning close to the bottom of the rachis, widely spaced, often folded strongly upward. **Rachis** usually curved, grooved on top, covered with hairs appressed toward the tip. **Stipules** small and tapered to a sharp tip. **Leaflets** usually 9–21, on very short petiolules, the blades 0.4–0.9" (10–23 mm) long, thin, entire, lanceolate to long-elliptic, often strongly cupped or folded, sharp or blunt at the tip with a downturned claw. **Surfaces** with fine appressed hairs, the midvein and secondary veins faint and flat on both sides. **Inflorescence** dense racemes 1–3" (2.5-8 cm) long on peduncles 2–4" (5-10 cm) long from lower leaf axils, each raceme with 5–14 flowers. **Flowers** (spring) 5–8 mm long, the calyx tubular, reddish, with sharp triangular lobes of equal size, the lobes much shorter than the tube. **Corolla** light pinkish purple, irregular (pea-like), the banner longer than wide and *folded upward*, much larger than the narrow wings and keel. **Fruit** a *thick, juicy, plum-shaped pod* 0.6–0.9" (15–23 mm) long, green with a reddish tint on the upper side as it ripens, containing many small, round seeds that blacken as the pods dry.

CONFUSING PLANTS: Many other legumes, including several members of the genus *Astragalus*, are similar in appearance, but lack plump pods this large.

HABITAT: Dry prairies, grassy or rocky slopes, open sunny woods. Native. 🔥

FOOD USE: Gather **pods** when very young and eat raw as a snack. When slightly older just chew on them, suck the juice, and spit out the skin. Mature fruits get very tough. **Conservation 1.**

COMMENTS: This unique edible tastes like sweet peas and makes a pleasant snack. A very similar species, *A. bibullatus*, is confined to the cedar glades of central Tennessee and is disappearing primarily from fire suppression; its edibility is unknown to me, and it should never be collected due to its rarity.

12 Alpine sweetvetch 2
Hedysarum alpinum ✦ *Fabaceae* (Bean family)

QUICK CHECK: Multi-stemmed; pinnately compound leaves with numerous small, blunt leaflets, long one-sided racemes of pink flowers, pods constricted between the seeds. **ID difficulty 3.**

DESCRIPTION: Perennial. **Taproot** enlarged, often multi-crowned, to 1.2" (3 cm) thick, long-tapered, often crooked, the thin skin brown to black, readily peeling, flesh white and fibrous. Shoot buds in spring are pink and blunt. **Stems** clumped, leaning or spreading to weakly erect, hairless to minutely pubescent, pithy in the center (hollow at the base when young), finely ridged and often lightly striped, 20–32" (50–80 cm) tall and up to 1 cm thick, tough, branched at narrow angles and mostly in the upper half. **LYDS** persistent, reddish-brown, the bark fibrous. **Leaves** pinnately compound, 2.5–7" (6–18 cm) long, with 9–21 leaflets, paired or offset, starting very near the base and often angled upward. **Rachis** shallowly channeled, with minute appressed hairs. **Stipules** dry and brown, 4–22 mm long (much longer on lower leaves), fused on early growth, later *splitting and separating from the tip down, with a broad, sheathing base and a needle-like tip.* **Leaflets** 0.6–1.3" (15–33 mm) long, nearly sessile, elliptic to lanceolate, entire, the tips blunt or pointed (*not notched*), with *a small, sharp, downturned tooth*, the blade slightly folded along the midvein. The terminal leaflet is often downturned. **Surface** hairless or nearly so above but with soft, light, appressed hairs below. **Secondary veins** several per side, 45–55°, nearly flat above. **Inflorescence** racemes 3–11" (13–28 cm) long on a long peduncle from an upper leaf axil, the numerous flowers on pedicels 3–4 mm, oriented mostly to one side. **Flowers** drooping, 0.5–0.7" (13–18 mm) long, irregular (pea-like), pinkish to purple. The *keel is much longer than the banner and wings*, deeply folded and enclosing the sexual parts. The banner is 2-lobed at the top and curved upward, the wings strongly hooked. The calyx has 5 triangular, folded lobes. **Pods** (loments) flat, segmented, constricted and occasionally stalked between its 3–5 seeds.

CONFUSING PLANTS: *H. mackenzii* has smaller, tougher roots not worthy of eating; its flowers are larger and its leaves have obscure secondary veins.

HABITAT: Boreal forest openings, especially steep slopes and stream banks on limestone. Native.

FOOD USE: Gather **roots**, preferably when the plant is dormant. They are stringy but have a sweet pea-pod flavor; slice crosswise and cook well to counter the toughness. **Conservation 3.**

COMMENTS: There are few root vegetables in the Far North, so this one has been highly appreciated by subarctic foragers despite its modest sustenance value. Christopher McCandless collected and ate this plant during the summer of 1992 when he starved to death in Alaska. The author John Krakauer concocted several implausible scenarios in which this or a related plant supposedly poisoned McCandless, but provides no good evidence that such a thing took place. Chris clearly starved to death, and there is no reason to blame it on this or any other plant. **AKA** wild sweet pea.

▼ (top) *Hedysarum alpinum* roots.

13 Hemp 🌿 3
Cannabis sativa + *Cannabinaceae* (Hemp family)

QUICK CHECK: Tall, aromatic herb with palmately compound leaves with 5–9 narrow, pointed, toothed leaflets with strongly depressed secondary veins. **ID difficulty 1.**

DESCRIPTION: Weedy annual, aromatic, branching heavily in the open, but little if crowded. **Stem** straight, erect, prominent, reaching 5–16' (1.5–5 m) in height, up to 1" (2.5 cm) thick, roundish but with many gentle ridges, the bark fibrous, pithy-hollow between the nodes, the surface roughened by very short, stiff, appressed or leaning hairs. **Leaves** palmately compound with typically 5–9 leaflets, sparse and widely spaced, *paired along the lower stem* but alternate in the upper part. The uppermost leaves often have only 3 leaflets. **Leaflets** sessile, narrowly lanceolate to nearly linear, long-tapered at the base and the pointed tip. The upper surface is roughened by sparse, appressed, needle-like hairs; the underside has denser, softer, almost woolly hair. **Midvein** incised, as are the numerous secondary veins running at low angles; they protrude strongly below. Veinlets are flat and nearly invisible. **Margins** coarsely and evenly serrated with large, sharp, forward-pointing teeth with claw tips. **Stipules** long-lanceolate, to 12 mm, sharp-tipped, soon browning. **Petiole** about 60% of the longest leaflet, hairy, roundish with a deep, narrow groove. **Inflorescence** a large, crowded, spike-like raceme interspersed with leaves at the branch tips. **Flowers** small and unshowy, the female ripening to produce small, hard, oval **seeds** 2–3 mm long; enclosed in small bracts.

▲ Escaped cannabis may be found almost anywhere but hemp is often an abundant weed in the mapped area.

CONFUSING PLANTS: leaves of some cinquefoils (*Potentilla*) are commonly confused with young hemp, but they are usually soft-hairy and never produce tall stalks.

HABITAT: Roadsides, railroad tracks, pastures, and agricultural land with very rich soil. Introduced.

FOOD USE: Lean the tops of ripe plants (late summer or early fall) over a sled or wheel barrow and beat them with a stick to dislodge the **seeds**. Or cut mature tops and dry them before beating the seeds out. Rub and winnow (see p. 27) to separate the chaff. Seeds have an annoying shell that is hard to remove, but can be roasted, ground, and used in porridge, seed butter, or added to baked goods.

COMMENTS: Certain cultivated forms of this plant produce marijuana, and it is therefore illegal to gather or use in most areas, although wild forms have little THC. Despite attempts by the government to eradicate the plant, wild hemp is still very common in some areas, particularly the western Corn Belt. It is a highly preferred food by pheasants and doves. The seeds can be collected very fast and are highly nutritious.

14 Prairie-turnip   3   IWE-282
Pediomelum esculentum • *Fabaceae* (Bean family)

QUICK CHECK: Shin-high, bushy herb with very hairy stems; palmately compound leaves with 5 deeply folded, entire leaflets; flowers packed in a short raceme with hairy bracts. **ID difficulty 3.**

DESCRIPTION: Perennial herb with *a strong turpentine-like smell*, about as wide as tall, dying back by late spring to mid summer and *detaching as a tumbleweed*. **Roots** widen 2–6" (5–13 cm) underground into turnip-like or elongated enlargements 1–2.5" (2.5–6 cm) thick, with a tough, waxy, dark outer skin that separates readily, and a long, cord-like taproot below. **Stems** usually single but occasionally few, 6–16" (10–40 cm) tall, rigid, 2–4 mm thick, hollow, with a few gentle angles, *densely covered with long, straight, stiff, erect hairs*. **Branches** few or absent, mostly near the base, spread at wide angles. **Leaves** alternate but often borne very close together, palmately compound with 3–10 (usually 5) leaflets. **Petioles** 1–2 times the terminal leaflet length, weakly ascending, roundish with one or more small grooves, often twisted, hairy. **Stipules** lanceolate, whitish on the lower half and green toward the tip and edge. **Leaflets** elliptic, obovate, or oblanceolate, 0.7–2" (18–50 cm) long, *strongly folded along the midvein*, abruptly pointed at both ends, the margins entire with long hairs. **Surface** glossy and hairless or nearly so on top, the underside covered with whitish hairs pressed toward the tip. The midvein is light in color, depressed above and projecting below. **Secondary veins** many, 45° to the midvein, inconspicuous and flat above. **Inflorescence** a cylindrical, usually ascending, crowded, fluffy-looking raceme 1–2.8" (2.5–7 cm) long and 1" (2.5 cm) wide, borne on an up-curved, hairy, hollow, proportionately thick peduncle to 4" (10 cm) long. The raceme is tightly packed with ovate, hairy, ascending bracts, hiding the rachis and short pedicels. **Flowers** (late spring or early summer) ascending, the calyx with 5 sharp lobes, 2 of them smaller and conjoined to the midpoint, with a bulge on one side near the base. **Corolla** light blue-purple, pea-like with a *large, rounded banner*. **Pods** have a single bean-like seed 4–6 mm long and a long, thin, hairy, sharp beak.

CONFUSING PLANTS: Some lupines have similar leaves, but the fruits and roots differ. Many members of the genus *Pediomelum* (*Psoralea*) have smaller and tougher roots, which may also be bitter.

HABITAT: Dry prairies, sparse woodlands, lightly grazed lands, especially on slopes. Native.

FOOD USE: Dig **roots** whenever the tops are visible—best as the tops finish blooming and begin to ripen seeds, so they can be replanted with harvest. After peeling, the roots can be eaten raw or cooked, sliced or diced or ground into flour. They are easily stored by drying. **Conservation 3.**

COMMENTS: This is a fantastic staple food of the prairies and the harvest remains a vibrant tradition for many Indigenous people today. These roots are high in protein and starch. They are delicious and hearty, great in stews. **AKA** breadroot, tinpsila, *Psoralea esculenta*. The similar but stemless **small prairie-turnip** is covered on page 300.

15 Tall breadroot 1
Pediomelum cuspidatum + Fabaceae (Bean family)

QUICK CHECK: Leaning, lanky, hairy, knee-high plant; leaves palmately compound with 5 entire, shiny leaflets; bluish flowers in a tight cluster. **ID difficulty 3.**

DESCRIPTION: Perennial, the form lanky and longer than wide. **Taproot** enlarged and *elongated*, narrow at the top, tapering to both ends, widest in the middle, the enlarged portion 6–14" (15–36 cm) long, the surface brown and flaky outside with whitish flesh and a rind that readily peels. **Stems** one to few, 10–34" (25–86 cm) long and 3–6 mm thick, almost always strongly leaning or even lying on the ground, simple or branched, roundish but with faint grooves, *sparsely covered with curvy and leaning to appressed hairs*, usually maroon on the sunny side and green toward the ground. **Leaves** alternate, often widely spaced, palmately compound, most with 5 leaflets, all sessile. **Petioles** 40–70% of the longer leaflet length. **Stipules** linear, 7–11 mm long. **Leaflets** elliptic to obovate, 1–2.5" (2.5–6 cm) long, creased and often folded along the midvein, the bases acute and the tips acute to rounded with a claw. **Surface** semi-glossy and hairless or nearly so above; the underside has scattered, appressed hair. **Midvein** depressed above and protruding below; secondary veins are faint, nearly flat above and below. **Inflorescence** a densely packed, spike-like raceme 1.5–3.5" (4–9 cm) long with very short pedicels. **Flowers** (late spring to early summer) tubular, pea-like, 0.5–0.7" (13–18 mm) long, the *calyx lobes unequal (the lowest is longest) with long acuminate tips.* **Corolla** purple-blue and pea-like. **Pods** 6–7 mm long, enclosed in the *inflated, persistent calyx, which turns dull yellowish.*

HABITAT: Well-drained, rocky, short-grass or mixed prairies. Native.

FOOD USE: The **root** can be dug at any time but is best early or late in the growing season, or under old, dead stems. It is quite deep. The flesh is very bitter when raw, but this can be eliminated by slicing and then boiling and draining off the water, after which it is pretty good. **Conservation 3.**

COMMENTS: If you get past the initial bitterness, this root has a coconut-like aftertaste that grows on you. Books often call it "tall-bread scurf-pea," with the hyphens arranged just like that, which seems to suggest that it can be used to make "tall bread," which is perhaps an alternative to short-bread, which is pretty darn good with strawberries on top. Oh wait, that's cake. Forget it—I have no idea what that name means.

◀ Root; the stem end is on the right.

16 Spikenard ⌇ 3 🍇 1 🏺 ☕
Aralia racemosa ✦ *Araliaceae* (Ginseng family)

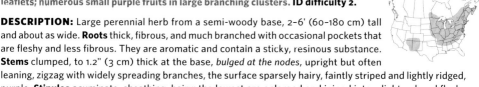

QUICK CHECK: Large, wide-spreading herb with doubly compound leaves and broad leaflets; numerous small purple fruits in large branching clusters. **ID difficulty 2.**

DESCRIPTION: Large perennial herb from a semi-woody base, 2–6' (60–180 cm) tall and about as wide. **Roots** thick, fibrous, and much branched with occasional pockets that are fleshy and less fibrous. They are aromatic and contain a sticky, resinous substance. **Stems** clumped, to 1.2" (3 cm) thick at the base, *bulged at the nodes*, upright but often leaning, zigzag with widely spreading branches, the surface sparsely hairy, faintly striped and lightly ridged, purple. **Stipules** acuminate, sheathing, hairy; the lowest are enlarged and joined into a light-colored fleshy sheath. **Shoots** erect, nearly straight, strongly tapered, leafy (not pointed) at the tip, *densely covered with soft, white, curving hairs*, purple-brown, solid and light green inside. Leaves of *shoots have long, thick, erect petioles, scarcely diverging from the stem*, which has its deepest groove on the side facing the petiole. Shoot leaves are densely hairy, folded, ruffled, and *very light green*. **Leaves** few in number but large and 2 or 3 times compound. **Petioles** roundish in cross section, *solid, not channeled*. After 3–11" (8–28 cm) the petiole divides ternately, each division pinnately compound with 3–7 leaflets. Rachis branches are channeled. **Leaflets** 2–6" (5–15 cm) long, the size highly variable on the same leaf, heart-shaped to broadly ovate, sessile or with short petiolules (much longer on the terminal leaflet). The surface is faintly downy and ruffled. **Veins** above are broadly depressed. **Margins** sharply, densely, and usually doubly serrated. Each *leaflet or rachis juncture has a light-colored enlargement often forming an X on the rachis*. **Inflorescence** an elongated panicle from a leaf axil, 4–26" (10–66 cm) long, finely pubescent, with many branches bearing numerous umbels of 14–18. **Flowers** (summer) tiny, greenish-white, with 5 petals. **Berries** spherical, 3 mm, dark purple, with 5 protruding bristles, a depressed end, and a single seed.

HABITAT: Rich, well-drained soil in hardwood forests, especially where rocky or gravelly, growing best in small openings with a bit of sun, such as trailsides and forest edges. Native. 🔥

FOOD USE: Roots were traditionally boiled for tea and used in root beer, along with sassafras. The thick **shoots** in spring make an excellent and interesting aromatic vegetable, raw or cooked. The ripe **berries** are sweet but also have a soapy flavor reminiscent of sarsaparilla (p. 290); they can be nibbled in moderation and have been used for wines, jellies, and liqueurs. **Conservation 3/2/1.**

COMMENTS: This striking, distinctive herb is one of our largest. I have seen individual berry clusters weighing over a pound. The flavor of the root is much stronger than that of its better-known cousin, sarsaparilla (*Aralia nudicaulis*). The shoots are a little-known exotic delicacy.

Aralia racemosa shoots. ▶

17 Bristly sarsaparilla 1
Aralia hispida ✦ *Araliaceae* (Ginseng family)

QUICK CHECK: Robust plant with a woody base and thick, prickly stems; toothed, folded, sessile leaflets; umbels of tiny flowers and berries. **ID difficulty 2.**

DESCRIPTION: Perennial herb, *woody at the base,* the woody portion usually a few inches but occasionally as much as 2' (60 cm) tall (in which case it would key as a shrub). **Stems** to 1" (2.5 cm) thick, single or multiple from the base, often branching close to the ground, all branches vertical. **Bark** of the woody portion gray-brown with *raised rings around the stem, erratic variations in thickness, and a few bristles.* **Herbaceous growth** very light green, 2–6' (60–180 cm) tall, the stems round and smooth but for scattered bristles. **Leaves** alternate, borne densely at the base of the herbaceous portion, widely spaced above this, 9–16" (23–46 cm) long and 2 or 3 times compound. **Petiole/rachis** bristly with a small sheath at the base, green to reddish, rounded, grooved only in the thinnest parts. After 3–7" (8–18 cm) the rachis splits 3 ways; 2 leaflets attach at this juncture; rachis junctures are enlarged. Rachis branches are pinnately compound with 5–9 leaflets, some of them clustered. **Leaflets** sessile, ovate, curved downward, folded along the midvein, 1.5–3.5" (4–9 cm) long, mostly hairless except along major veins below; the margins are coarsely and irregularly toothed with occasional lobes. **Veins** light green, depressed above and protruding below. **Inflorescence** a loosely branching terminal cluster of umbels (or a sloppy compound umbel), the peduncles 4–10" (10–25 cm) long, the branches naked except for scattered bracts. **Umbels** rounded with up to 90 straw-colored rays 1–1.5" (25–38 mm) long. **Flowers** (early summer) 3–5 mm across with 5 reflexed creamy petals with a prominent central vein and an incurved, pointed tip; there are 5 protruding stamens. The calyx is a light green cup with 5 teeth on the rim. **Berries** spherical, 3–4 mm across, ripening in late summer to purple-black.

HABITAT: Disturbed, sunny sites on poor sandy, gravelly, or rocky soil. Most common along roads and after burns or logging; also riverbanks and cliffs. Native. 🔥

FOOD USE: Tender **shoots** in late spring can be used as a vegetable after peeling, raw or cooked. The flavor is strong and almost spicy. **Conservation 2.**

COMMENTS: This unusual plant straddles the fence between an herb and a shrub. I list it here because the woody base is not immediately or always evident. The shoots are smaller than those of *A. spinosa* (p. 98) but the flavor is similar.

▲ *Aralia hispida* shoot.

POISONOUS AND CONFUSING PLANTS

As I mentioned in the "Poisonous Plants" section of the introduction (p. 21), you *do not* need to recognize any poisonous plant to identify an edible one. Nevertheless, studying the differences between an edible plant and a poisonous "look-alike" is a great confidence builder. Due to space considerations, I have limited this list to a small number of poisonous or frequently confused plants that are mentioned in one or more edible plant accounts. They are listed in the order of the groups to which they would belong, based on their physical form. These plants are not all highly toxic—some, like buckthorn and honeysuckle, are so common and frequently confused that I think all berry pickers should learn to recognize them. I also included the dermatitis triumvirate (poison ivy, poison oak, and poison sumac). *There are many poisonous plants, including deadly ones, not included here.* It would not be possible for me to predict or cover all potentially confusing species. But I must reiterate that *you can never recognize an edible plant by a process of elimination*—just because a plant *isn't* water hemlock does *not* mean you can assume it is some safe edible relative.

✦ Buckeye and horse-chestnut (Group 5) Poisonous. genus *Aesculus* ✦ family *Sapindaceae*

DESCRIPTION: Small to large trees or shrubs, the **crowns** spreading in full sun. **Bark** thin, silver-gray, typically with numerous lenticels and thin, neat plates, not peeling or shagging, but falling and *leaving a hewn look*. **Twigs** stout, smooth, with large terminal buds. **Leaves** paired, palmately compound with 5 leaflets, petioles 3-6" (8-15 cm) long. **Leaflets** 2-7" (5-18 cm) long, often hairy below, elliptic, acute at both ends, the tips acuminate, the margins finely serrated, on petiolules 5-10% of blade length. **Secondary veins** closely spaced, strongly depressed, straight, 45° to the midvein. **Inflorescence** a showy panicle 5-8" (13-20 cm) long at the branch tip. **Flowers** (late spring) numerous, tubular or narrowly bell-shaped, about 1" (2.5 cm) long with 4 petals, the stamens protruding on long filaments, the calyx tubular with 5 lobes. **Fruit** roundish, 1-3" (2.5-8 cm) in diameter, with a thick, yellowish-brown, leathery husk that may be smooth or studded with spikes (depending on species), splitting open into usually 3 unequal sections. **Nuts** 1-3 per fruit, *smooth, glossy, and brown with conspicuous "eye spots,"* usually somewhat flattened on one side.

▲ Composite range of Ohio and yellow buckeyes.

SPECIES: Ohio buckeye *A. glabra* is a medium-sized tree with pale yellow flowers and spiky husks enclosing a single nut. **Yellow buckeye** *A. flava* is a medium to large tree with yellow flowers and minutely roughened but not spiky husks. There are other native shrubby species. The European horse-chestnut *A. hippocastanum* is widely planted as an ornamental; it has broader leaves and spiky husks.

CONFUSING PLANTS: Actual chestnuts have simple leaves and husks with long, sharp spines. Nevertheless, they have been repeatedly confused by people who refuse to pay attention to details.

HABITAT: Hardwood forests with rich, moist soil—especially valleys, hillsides, and floodplains.

TOXICITY: The nuts contain a glucoside called aesculin, and other toxic compounds. Aesculin has therapeutic uses but in high doses causes gastric distress, and at very high doses brings on more serious nervous symptoms. Buckeye nuts have resulted in at least one documented death of a child who insisted on eating them raw.

COMMENTS: After undergoing a careful process of leaching to detoxify them, buckeye nuts were once an important food source for some Native Californians, and they are still eaten regularly in parts of rural Japan. These are different species than those native in our region, but I have successfully leached and eaten yellow buckeye nuts by these traditional methods. Nevertheless I would not be comfortable recommending them for general consumption until evidence of their traditional use is found, or tests of the concentration of the toxic compounds are performed, or at least until I am able to compare the finished and unfinished product from our species with those traditionally used. Interestingly, for years a farmer in my area mistakenly sold horse-chestnuts *Aesculus hippocastanum* to customers and local grocery stores, before I informed authorities of the problem. Buyers had been upset with the terrible flavor of their roasted "chestnuts,"

   Ohio buckeye flowers. ▶

but amazingly, no poisoning incidents were attributed to this egregious error—which is a testament to how well the body can usually recognize and avoid chemically unfit items offered as food.

▲ Yellow buckeye fruits.

▲ Opened to reveal the nuts.

✦ Invasive bush honeysuckles (Group 10) Inedible, frequently confused. *Lonicera tatarica, morrowii, x-bella,* and *maackii* ✦ Family *Caprifoliaceae*

DESCRIPTION: Dense, multi-stemmed, thicket-forming shrubs, the *trunks arching* with light gray-brown bark peeling in flaky strips. Shoots are straight and erect. Sapwood is green and aromatic. **Leaves** paired, on petioles about 5% of blade length, ovate to elliptic, hairless or downy. **Flowers** (late spring to early summer) paired, on short peduncles with a pair of reduced leaves. **Corolla** tubular or funnel-like at the base, the tube dividing into either 5 slightly unequal white to pinkish lobes (tatarica, morrowii, and x-bella), or 2 unequal lips (*maackii*), the larger with 3 shallow lobes, the smaller unlobed and recurved. **Fruit** paired; adjacent, touching, or conjoined; spherical or nearly so, juicy, the skin soft and translucent; red, orange, or yellow; containing multiple soft seeds.

Tatarian honeysuckle *Lonicera tatarica* has leaves that are hairless except on the margins, pink or white flowers, and orange to red, united berries. *L. morrowii* has leaves that are soft and hairy. The flowers are white or cream, the berries red or yellow and separate. These two species frequently hybridize, and the hybrid *L. x-bella* is more common than either parent in many areas. **Amur honeysuckle** *L. maackii* has hairy twigs thicker than those of our other honeysuckles. The leaves have a broad base and are tapered to a sharp point. The flowers are larger than those of the other species in this account and differ as described above; the peduncles are shorter. The berries are separate and deep red.

MISTAKEN FOR: Most frequently, autumnberry (p. 139), because the berries are red and they often grow in the same places. autumnberry berries are not in pairs, are elliptic, and have silvery scales.

HABITAT: Disturbed forests, forest edges, brushy areas, vacant lots, old fields. **I**

TOXICITY: Not dangerous in small quantities but not edible either.

COMMENTS: These are the wild berries I am most often asked to identify.

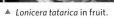

▲ *Lonicera tatarica* in fruit.

▲ Amur honeysuckle in fruit.

657

✦ Poison ivy, poison oak (Group 11) Irritant.
genus *Toxicodendron* (3 species) ✦
Anacardiaceae (Cashew family)

DESCRIPTION: Plants with variable form as creepers, shrubs, or vines. The bark is gray and smooth; twigs are sparse and moderately thick. When growing as vines, the stems attach to support trees by numerous *dark aerial roots*. **Leaves** alternate, *ternately compound*. **Petioles** long and straight, exceeding the length of any leaflet, faintly to moderately hairy. Side leaflets are almost sessile; the terminal leaflet is on a petiolule about 25% of blade length. **Leaflets** 2–6" (5–15 cm) long, ovate, rather thick and leathery for a deciduous leaf, *entire or with a few large, erratic teeth or lobes*. The upper surface is semi-glossy with sparse appressed hair; the underside is hairier. **Midvein** slightly depressed above. **Secondary veins** 7–11 per side, broadly angled, slightly depressed, rather straight. **Inflorescence** ascending or erect panicles or clumps of panicles 2–5" (5–13 cm) long, each with a dozen to several dozen flowers, the pedicels 4–7 mm. **Flowers** (early summer) 5–6 mm across, the corolla creamy with 5 blunt, roughly triangular, recurved lobes. **Fruit** almost spherical, 4–6 mm, dryish, ivory to pale yellow with a waxy rippled surface, often persisting into winter. I think there is one seed, but I didn't want to check.

SPECIES: Western poison ivy *T. rydbergii* is a creeper or low bush spreading by stolons with simple or few-branched stems, rarely more than thigh-high. **Common poison ivy** *T. radicans* may become a larger bush to 10' (3 m) tall that produces many branches—or it is a vine that climbs with aerial roots and sends out long, leafy branches. Both species of poison ivy have sharp-pointed leaves that may be entire or have large teeth or small lobes. **Eastern poison oak** *T. toxicarium* is a small bush growing to waist-high and forming colonies by rhizome. The leaves are blunt and usually lobed, sometimes quite oak-like.

MISTAKEN FOR: Nothing edible generally, but the resemblance to fragrant sumac (p. 658) is strong; if you rip the wrong leaf for a sniff, that could be bad. Note the longer terminal petiolule on poison ivy/oak.

HABITAT: Mostly well-drained (but sometimes seasonally wet), semi-sunny sites with a long-term history of disturbance, such as floodplains, savannahs, steep slopes, roadsides, forest edges, dry forests, brushy areas.

TOXICITY: Oils cause contact dermatitis in many, perhaps most individuals, although the reaction is allergic and thus variably severe.

COMMENTS: These are some of the most widespread, abundant, and ecologically versatile plants on our continent, and anyone who spends time outdoors should learn to identify them.

▶ (right) Poison ivy berries.
(far right) Poison ivy flowers.

▲ Poison oak leaves.

▲ Poison ivy leaves.

◆ **Poison sumac** (Group 11) Irritant.
Toxicodendron vernix ◆ *Anacardiaceae* (Cashew family)

DESCRIPTION: Tall shrub or small tree to 17' (5 m) tall and 6" (15 cm) thick, the trunks usually single or sometimes 2–3, crooked with sparse branches and thick, hairless twigs. **Bark** gray and nearly smooth, not flaky or peeling, rather thin with large transverse lenticels. **Leaves** alternate, 7–12" (18–30 cm) long, densely packed toward branch tips, pinnately compound with 7–15 leaflets. **Petiole/rachis** hairless, reddish, naked in the lower quarter; side leaflets are on very short petiolules. **Leaflets** 2.5–5" (6–13 cm) long, long-elliptic to obovate, entire, the base acute and the tip short-acuminate, hairless or nearly so and glossy above, pale and hairless below. There are sparse hairs around the margins. **Midvein** flat above; secondary veins 7–10 per side, broadly angled, flat above. **Inflorescence** ascending or spreading panicles 6–10" (15–25 cm) long, with several dozen flowers on very short pedicels. **Flowers** (early summer) male and female on different trees, 3–5 mm across with 5 whitish petals. **Fruit** roughly spherical, 4–5 mm, dryish, ivory to cream with a waxy, rippled surface, the clusters drooping when ripe in late summer.

MISTAKEN FOR: Nothing edible—just watch out for it.

HABITAT: Shrub swamps and bogs, pond and lake margin wetlands, in full to partial sun. Native.

TOXICITY: Causes severe dermatitis—like poison ivy, but the active principle seems to be much more abundant.

COMMENTS: I walk though poison ivy in shorts with little worry, but no way will I touch this plant willingly—I have had the rash twice, and that's enough for a lifetime. I have watched cardinals, robins, and cedar wax-wings devour the fruit.

✦ Common buckthorn (Group 11) Mildly toxic, often confused.
Rhamnus cathartica ✦ *Rhamnaceae* (Buckthorn family)

DESCRIPTION: Large shrub or small tree to 40' (12 m) tall and 8" (20 cm) thick, the trunks single or in small groups. **Bark** thin, dark gray, smooth, shiny, with raised transverse lenticels; on older trunks becoming *black and flaky*. Heartwood is deep red and urine-scented. **Twigs** green at first, minutely hairy to hairless, becoming gray with age; older twigs may bear spurs with numerous buds and scars. Branchlets often end in a *straight, sharp thorn*. **Leaves** paired (but the pairs are often offset and occasionally a few are alternate), 1–3" (2.5–8 cm) long, broadly ovate or broadly elliptic to nearly round, the tip

abruptly pointed or rounded with a nipple, the base rounded or broadly angled. The upper surface is hairless or nearly so, the underside sparsely hairy. Leaves persist green late into fall when nearby native shrubs are bare. **Midvein** depressed above; secondary veins 3–5 per side, 2 of which arise very near the base, depressed, arching toward the tip; veinlets are flat. **Margin** *serrated with very small, blunt, gland-tipped teeth.* **Petioles** hairy, channeled, 20–40% of blade length. **Inflorescence** single flowers or umbels of up to 5 attached directly to the twigs, on second-year growth near the base of new growth, the pedicels 3–8 mm long. **Flowers** (late spring to early summer) male and female on separate trees, 4–6 mm across with 4 triangular, yellow-green petals. **Fruit** blackish, spherical, 5–7 mm, maturing in late summer, juicy, containing 3–4 seeds.

MISTAKEN FOR: Black cherry (p. 101) or chokecherry (p. 161), but those have single-stone fruits in racemes.

HABITAT: Most soil types, but especially where rich and well-drained. Invades old fields and disturbed forests first, and does very well in the understory of oaks. **I**

TOXICITY: Moderate: a palmful will give you serious diarrhea.

COMMENTS: This is one of the most invasive shrubs in our region. I have seen many native forests where it has eliminated nearly every trace of native vegetation in the understory.

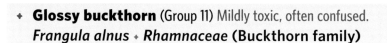

✦ **Glossy buckthorn** (Group 11) Mildly toxic, often confused.
Frangula alnus ✦ *Rhamnaceae* (Buckthorn family)

DESCRIPTION: Large shrub or small tree to 23' (7 m) tall and 4" (10 cm) thick, with one to several trunks. **Bark** gray, thin, smooth, with many whitish lenticels, not becoming scaly. **Twigs** brown and very finely hairy with *no thorns*. **Leaves** alternate, obovate to broadly elliptic, 1.5–3" (4–8 cm) long, *entire*, acute or obtuse at the base, the tip abruptly blunt-pointed or rounded. The upper surface is hairless and glossy; the underside is duller and usually finely hairy on the major veins. **Midvein** depressed above. Secondary veins 5–8 per side, none from the base, depressed above, running relatively straight then curving just before the margin. **Petiole** 20–30% of the blade length, hairy. **Inflorescence** umbels of 2–8 directly from first-year twigs, the pedicels 4–9 mm. **Flowers** (early to mid summer) bisexual, not showy, 3–5 mm across with 5 pale, triangular petals. **Fruit** a blackish spherical berry 6–10 mm, maturing in late summer, the surface smooth and glossy, the inside juicy, containing 2–3 seeds.

MISTAKEN FOR: Black cherry (p. 101) or chokecherry (p. 161), but those have single-stone fruits in racemes, and toothed leaves.

HABITAT: Moist soil in full sun to moderate shade. This invasive species seems to do best in hardwood and shrub swamps, but also fills in the gaps of conifer swamps and sometimes becomes common in uplands. **I**

TOXICITY: This fruit is not particularly toxic but it is going to give you diarrhea if you insist on eating a serving despite the bitterness.

COMMENTS: Despite the name, this bush has no thorns. It is much more elegant than common buckthorn. When leafless it resembles a chokecherry, but lacks the cherry scent when scratched. When in leaf and fruit there is no excuse for confusing it with chokecherry, but it still happens. **AKA** *Rhamnus frangula*.

✦ **Canada moonseed** (Group 13) Poisonous.
Menispermum canadense ✦ family *Menispermaceae*

DESCRIPTION: Woody vine spreading by rhizome to form colonies, growing *without tendrils*, often as several parallel vines wrapped around each other. **Stems** twining, to 30' (9 m) long, 0.2–0.8" (5–20 mm) thick with a white pithy center, smooth and greenish when young and slightly hairy; older bark turns brown. Branches few. **Leaves** alternate, 2–7" (5–18 cm) long and about equally wide or wider, heart-shaped or palmately lobed with 3–7 shallow, blunt lobes, the margins otherwise without teeth; heart-shaped at the base. **Surface** hairless or sparsely hairy above, hairier below. **Midvein** and 4 prominent secondary veins emanate from the base; these are offset by light color and raised in a narrow valley; veinlets are depressed. *Margins are downcurved.* **Inflorescence** a drooping axillary panicle of 15–50, the panicle stems thin and limp, *the naked portion longer than the branching portion.* **Petioles** about 100% of blade length, round, not channeled, enlarged and often curved at the base, sparsely hairy, *attached just barely inside the leaf margin.* **Flowers** (early summer, male and female in separate clusters on the same plant) 4–5 mm wide, off-white, with 4–8 petals and 4–8 sepals, the sepals larger. Stamens numerous in male flowers. **Fruit** (late summer to early fall) spherical, 6–12 mm, blue-black with a bloom, hairless, soft, containing multiple hard seeds shaped like a slightly flattened crescent moon.

MISTAKEN FOR: Any of the smaller species of wild grape (p. 188). Moonseed differs in having blunt leaf lobes and toothless margins. Moonseed vines lack tendrils and are never shaggy. Moonseed fruit clusters have proportionately longer stems that are much thinner and limp, and the seed shape differs.

HABITAT: Open forests with rich soil, floodplain forests, forest edges, fence lines; much the same habitat as wild grape and often growing together with it. Native.

TOXICITY: The fruit contains isoquinoline alkaloids, which have a paralyzing effect. Although widely reported as toxic I have found little information on the potency or case reports pertaining to this North American species.

▲ Moonseed vine growing on a grapevine.

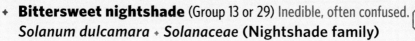
✦ **Bittersweet nightshade** (Group 13 or 29) Inedible, often confused. ☠
Solanum dulcamara ✦ *Solanaceae* **(Nightshade family)**

DESCRIPTION: Semi-woody vine (the bases woody but the tips dying back in winter), sprawling or twining to 13' (4 m) long. **Stems** to 1 cm thick, branched. Older bark is thin and light gray-brown; newer bark is green or purplish. **Leaves** alternate, 2–5" (5–13 cm) long, larger leaves usually with 2 or 4 deep lobes near the base, these lobes *asymmetrically ovate and constricted near the base*. The tip is blunt. **Secondary veins** are depressed, arching toward the tip and dividing or conjoining before reaching the margins. Margins lack teeth. **Petioles** winged, 40–60% of blade length. **Inflorescence** a *spreading cluster of 10–25* at the end of a thick, naked peduncle; cluster stems have a bulging ring where they branch. **Flowers** 12 mm long with 5 tiny sepals and 5 lanceolate, purple, reflexed petals. The **anthers** are bright yellow, pressed together into a central bullet-shaped ring around the protruding style. **Fruit** a shiny, *red, elliptic* berry with a delicate, translucent skin, 8–11 mm, maturing midsummer through fall, the inside juicy with numerous seeds.

MISTAKEN FOR: Nothing in particular but people like to eat bright red things. Some confuse it with the edible black nightshades (p. 606) just because of the name.

HABITAT: Full sun to moderate shade, especially on rich, moist soil. Brushy areas, streamsides, forest margins, old beaver dams, fences, other disturbed sites. Supposedly introduced but I question this assertion.

TOXICITY: This species is the cause of many asymptomatic calls to poison control centers. The ripe berries are widely believed to be dangerous but I know 5 people who have eaten them repeatedly with no ill effect. Nevertheless, I consider the berries inedible and implore you to avoid them—the taste is terrible. The leaves and green fruits are poisonous and contain a glycoside similar to atropine.

▲ These are robust leaves; smaller ones are often unlobed.

✦ **Iris** (Group 17) Poisonous.
genus *Iris* ✦ family *Iridaceae*

DESCRIPTION: Perennials spreading by thick, fleshy rhizomes to form colonies. **Rhizome** whitish and tough with a short distance between nodes, crooked, often highly variable in thickness over short distances, densely covered in roots. **Basal leaves** sword-like, to 44" (112 cm) long and 2" (5 cm) wide, the thicker ones spongy inside, the tips usually curved and sharp-pointed. *The cluster is flattened into one plane at the base, with each inner leaf inserted into slots in the side of outer leaves.* Margins are entire and veins parallel; a few veins are raised on each side. **Stem leaves** also sometimes present; if so, they are alternate, 2-ranked, deeply folded, slotted on the stem side, clasping and partly enclosing the stem. **Stems** erect, round, solid or with a spongy hollow, zigzag, smooth, on the larger species up to 38" (1 m) tall. **Flowers** single or in a small cluster, subtended by canoe-like bracts. They are radially symmetrical and up to 5" (13 cm) wide on some species, with 9 petal-like parts of 3 different kinds. The 3 sepals are broadest and lowest and often strongly recurved; the 3 petals are thinner and spreading to ascending; and 3 narrow, modified stigmas project between the sepals and petals. There are 3 hidden stamens. The most common irises, the blue flags, have purple sepals and petals with darker purple veins, and a hairy yellow zone at the base. **Fruit** a rather large capsule 1–3" (2.5–8 cm) long depending on species, with 3–6 often ribbed angles, containing numerous flattened seeds, each with a fleshy coating.

MISTAKEN FOR: Cattails (p. 205), bur-reed (p. 207), and calamus (p. 208).

HABITAT: Wetlands and wetland margins in full sun to moderate shade.

TOXICITY: There are numerous species in this genus, and many have been used medicinally. The roots are generally considered the strongest part. The toxins they contain have not been identified but are known to cause abdominal pain, nausea, vomiting, diarrhea, and fever. While dangerous in large quantities, iris roots are distasteful and therefore unlikely to be consumed. Documented human poisonings are rare to non-existent.

▲ (top left) Iris fruits. (bottom left) Note the flat cluster and slotted leaves.
(right) Blue flag iris, flowering.

◆ **Death camas** (Group 17) Highly poisonous.
genera Anticlea, Zigadenus, and *Toxicoscordion* ◆
family *Melanthiaceae*

DESCRIPTION: Perennial herbs from whitish bulbs. **Leaves** alternate, concentrated on the lower stem (few or none truly basal at blooming), the highest leaves attached about 5" from the ground. At each leaf's base a sheath fully encircles the stem. **Blades** linear, *deeply folded* all the way to the tip, hairless, pointed, 6–10" (15–25 cm) long and up to 8 mm wide. There are 2 small depressed parallel veins on each side

▼ (top) *Toxicoscordion venenosum* bulbs. (left bottom) *Toxicoscordion venenosum* in bloom. (right bottom) *Toxicoscordion nuttallii.*

▲ Composite range of several species in 3 genera.

of the midvein. **Stems** to 18" (46 cm) tall, solid, roundish, hairless, the *sap not slimy*. **Inflorescence** a *densely packed raceme*, the flowers touching, *each pedicel with a whitish bract at the base*. The bract is broad in the lower fifth then abruptly narrowing, needle-like, and slightly exceeds the pedicel length. **Flowers** 5–10 mm across with 6 petals, white to creamy yellow or greenish or faintly pink, the pistils usually creamy. **Fruit** cylindrical or stout 3-part capsules.

MISTAKEN FOR: Mostly onions (pp. 234–241) or camas (p. 262). •

HABITAT: Dry prairies, forest openings, rocky hillsides and outcroppings, beaches; likes full sun. Native.

TOXICITY: All parts contain toxic alkaloids that cause burning, watering, and numbness of the mouth, excessive thirst, headache, dizziness, nausea, nervous system and circulatory depression, respiratory trouble, and other big problems. Bulbs are generally the culprit, but severe human poisonings are rare because the unpleasant flavor and burning sensation usually prevent significant ingestion.

COMMENTS: This group contains several similar species that were once classified in a single genus which has now been split into three closely related genera. Because there are so many death camas species the description is a little loose.

665

✦ Star-of-Bethlehem (Group 17) Poisonous.
Ornithogalum umbellatum and *O. nutans* ✦
Asparagaceae (Asparagus family)

DESCRIPTION: Perennial spring ephemeral from a bulb, spreading by seed and offsets. **Leaves** all basal, linear, 5–16" (13–40 cm) long and 3–6 mm wide, soft and succulent, erect to lax, 1–6 per bulb but forming a carpet when the plants are densely clumped. The blade is not hollow; it is broadly U-shaped, with a *silvery-white stripe running down the center*, minutely ridged below, the *sap slimy*. Leaves begin to wither by flowering. **Inflorescence** a raceme of 3–12 on an erect peduncle, the pedicels often very long, each with a sharp, linear, membranous bract partially wrapped around the base. **Flowers** 1–2" (2.5–5 cm) across with 6 long-elliptic, pointed white petals, each with a green stripe on the underside. **Fruit** a 3-sided capsule. **Bulb** close to the surface, egg-shaped to nearly round, to 0.5" (mm) long, whitish with an adhering papery skin, *wrapped around green leaves which extend through the bulb center to the root crown below.*

MISTAKEN FOR: Onions (pp. 234–241) or false garlic (p. 259), but Star-of-Bethlehem can be distinguished by its lack of onion scent, its bulb wrapped around leaf bases, its slimy sap, the silvery leaf stripe, the green stripe on the back of the petals, the inflorescence not being an umbel, and (you shouldn't get this far) the bitter unoniony flavor.

TOXICITY: In the fresh state this species is moderately toxic, containing various glycosides that cause nausea, vomiting, and abdominal cramps. It is reported in some sources to be edible after processing the bulbs to eliminate toxins; I have not done this and have not found reliable first-hand reports.

✦ **Purple foxglove** (Group 23) Deadly.
Digitalis purpurea ✦ *Plantaginaceae* (Plantain family)

DESCRIPTION: **Rosette leaves** ovate, to 6" (15 cm) long, the surfaces *velvety from soft, erect hairs*. **Margins** have broad, shallow, rounded teeth with dotted tips, the dots dark at first but becoming light. **Veins** and veinlets are *deeply depressed above* and protruding below. **Petiole** winged, purple at the base, velvety, about 100% of blade length, shallowly channeled above, strongly keeled below. The leafy wing is 4–5 mm wide and *not jagged or tapering*. **Stem** single, rigid, hollow, *straight, erect, unbranched*, thick-walled, *round except for a ridge on one side* extending down from the nearest node (the lower stem may have 3 of these ridges), soft-hairy. **Stem leaves** alternate, the blade size and petiole length reducing progressively upward; uppermost leaves are sessile with a clasping base. **Inflorescence** a raceme up to 28" (70 cm) long from the axil of an entire, lanceolate bract 0.5–0.8" (13–20 mm) long, the pedicels 6–10 mm. **Flowers** drooping, tubular, purple with a lighter area inside that has dark purple spots, the 4 stamens and pistils pressed against the upper part of the tube, the large yellow anthers with purple dots. There are scattered long white hairs on the inside of the lower lip. The calyx has 5 unequal sepals.

MISTAKEN FOR: Most likely comfrey (p. 330).

HABITAT: Openings in forests, edges, weedy areas in rich moist soil. Introduced and rather rare in most of our region, but locally common.

TOXICITY: This plant contains glycosides with a powerful effect on cardiac muscle. Symptoms may include painful throat, nausea, vomiting, headache, diarrhea, irregular heartbeat, and convulsions. Several fatalities are recorded, mostly from medical overdoses.

COMMENTS: Other species in this genus are similarly poisonous. None are native to our area, and the introduced species are rare but locally established in large colonies where they have escaped from flower or herb gardens.

▲ Leaf and stem detail.

✦ Common water hemlock (Group 27) Deadly.
Cicuta maculata ✦ *Apiaceae* (Carrot family)

DESCRIPTION: Perennial herb 3–6' (1–2 m) tall, spreading only by seed. *All surfaces hairless* (a few tiny hairs can sometimes be found along the leaflet midveins). **Roots** radiate from the stem base, *enlarged and tuber-like*, constricted at both ends, stiff, to 5" (13 cm) long and 0.9" (23 mm) thick, not branching, skin pale to light brown, the inside whitish-yellow with yellow oily fluid visible in broken veins. (This yellow fluid is also seen at the stem base when broken.) **Basal leaves** 2–3 times compound, pinnate or ternate at the first two divisions, to 18" (32 cm) long. The leaflets are spaced, rarely overlapping or touching at maturity. Newly emerging basal leaves have the parts folded together but not tightly wrapped in an asparagus-like spear; the petioles do not have bulging rings below the first division. **Leaflets** 1–3.8" (2.5–10 cm) long, sessile or on short petiolules, lanceolate, the bases mostly abruptly broadening but terminal leaflets are usually tapered, the tips sharp-pointed but not acuminate, the blades often folded along the midvein. **Surfaces** *hairless*, the *midvein deeply depressed or etched above*. **Secondary veins** several per side, 45° to the midvein, depressed above, protruding below; *most run rather straight to terminate in a notch between teeth*. Veinlets slightly etched or flat above. **Margins** serrated with 4–6 teeth per inch, the teeth pointed forward with a claw tip. **Petiole** roundish, hollow and thin-walled, not channeled or with a very shallow, round-edged groove, the surface faintly ribbed and coated with a very light bloom. **Rachis** (after the first division) round, hollow, with a tiny groove on top, green except for purple zones where it branches. **Stem** erect, hollow, moderately stout, to 0.8" (2 cm) thick, smooth with a light bloom, *hairless*, not ridged but lined. **Stem leaf sheath** 1–2.5" (25–64 mm) long, smooth, strongly inrolled to make a petiole-like structure. **Inflorescence** a compound umbel 2–5" (5–13 cm) across with 15–30 primary rays. There are usually a few linear to lanceolate rays beneath the great umbels and umbellets, but they may be absent. **Flowers** (early to mid summer) white, 2–3 mm across with 5 strongly in-curved pet-als. **Fruit** oval to rounded, 2 mm long, ribbed, splitting in two when dry.

MISTAKEN FOR: *Oxypolis rigidior* (p. 424), *Sium suave* (p. 213), *Oenanthe javanica* (p. 443), *Berula erecta* (p. 216), mountain angelica (p. 449), American lovage (p. 441), purple angelica (p. 447). Eastern yampa (p. 464) does not have similar leaves or habitat, but the roots are the most similar of all edible carrot family plants. Has been confused with black elderberry (p. 163) when blooming. Roots of very small plants may look like those of bugleweeds (p. 537), which grow in similar habitat.

HABITAT: Low, wet, ground in full sun to partial shade. Pond edges, marshes, swamps, ditches, streamsides, wet meadows. This species usually grows near water but is not aquatic.

TOXICITY: A yellow alcohol known as cicutoxin is a powerful neurotoxin that causes convulsions, tremors, heart disturbances, low blood pressure, delirium, coma, and respiratory paralysis. This genus has caused many documented fatalities.

COMMENTS: The roots, shoots, stem bases, and possibly the seeds are exceedingly poisonous; the leaves are also toxic but less so. What makes this one of the most dangerous poisonous plants in the world is the toxicity of the roots combined with a large, inviting root-structure with a carroty scent that does not have a strong unpleasant flavor.

✦ Bulblet water hemlock (Group 15, 27, or 28) Deadly.
Cicuta bulbifera ✦ *Apiaceae* (Carrot family)

DESCRIPTION: Perennial 3–5' (90–150 cm) tall, from a small overwintering root. *Normally rooted at water level*—on the shoreline, floating wood, mats of vegetation, or emergent rocks or stumps—rather than in the bottom. Early rosettes have 1–3 leaves. **Basal leaves** 3–4 times compound, roughly triangular in outline. **Petioles** rounded and hollow, not spongy, lacking visible air channels in the walls, and *without transverse bands below the first division.* Rachises have a small groove on top. **Leaflets** very narrowly elliptic to linear, entire or with a few scattered large teeth or lobes, hairless on both sides. Secondary veins are not very conspicuous but end in a notch if there is one in the area. **Stem** single, round, erect, smooth, hollow, to 0.8" (2 cm) thick at the base, sometimes rooting at lower nodes, mostly green, coated with bloom, branching mostly in the upper half, the branches thin and delicate, with *tiny bulblets forming in the leaf axils* at maturity. **Stem leaves** widely spaced, sheathed at the base, similar to basal leaves but progressively smaller and on shorter petioles, becoming sessile. The leaflets of these upper leaves may be extremely narrow, almost thread-like. **Inflorescence** a flat-topped compound umbel 1–2" (2.5–5 cm) across with 5–8 primary rays. There are no bracts beneath the umbellets or great umbels, but there may be a small leaf under the great umbel. **Flowers** (mid to late summer) 2 mm across, white with 5 incurved petals, rarely setting seed. **Fruit** tiny, slightly flattened, ribbed.

MISTAKEN FOR: *Oxypolis rigidior* (p. 424), *Sium suave* (p. 213) or eastern yampa (p. 464).

HABITAT: Marshes and shores, beaver lodges and dams, and floating logs or mats of vegetation. More aquatic than common water hemlock, and likes more stable permanent water.

TOXICITY: I can find no documented poisonings from this species (probably because the root is comparatively small and does not look attractive as a vegetable) but it is presumed to have a similar chemical profile to the three other members of its genus, all of which are robustly documented as deadly.

COMMENTS: In extensive searching of the scientific literature I can find no research published on this plant specifically. It has a small overwintering root system and emerges and blooms later than common water hemlock. This species reproduces primarily by its tiny floating bulblets.

▲ Upper branch showing leaves and bulblets.

✦ Poison hemlock (Group 28) Deadly.
Conium maculatum ✦ *Apiaceae* (Carrot family)

DESCRIPTION: Very tall biennial herb, crushed parts with an *unpleasant smell*. All *sur-faces are hairless*. **Rosette** of a dozen or so basal leaves up to 32" (80 cm) long, the petiole about as long as the blade. **Leaves** 3–5 times compound/divided. The first 1–2 divisions are stalked; further divisions are stalked proximally but sessile distally. **Petioles** about equal to blade length and up to 0.9" (23 cm) thick, with many small ridges, hollow, deeper than wide, often roughly triangular with an *angled or ridged rather than channeled top*, the surface green and *bloom coated*, usually with purple blotches and lines. Thicker **rachis branches** are hollow and not channeled, but thinner distal ones have a *deep, narrow groove on top, the groove margins raised and sharp*, with an angled bottom. The petiole base abruptly widens to a short, broad **sheath** *which often ends in a projecting blunt lobe*. Ultimate leaflets are deeply and *symmetrically* pinnately lobed with large teeth or small sub-lobes, each *tipped with a whitish claw*. There are no hairs on the petiole, rachises, or blades. **Very small basal leaves** (with petioles less than 3 mm thick) *have solid petioles with a channeled top* and the bloom may be absent. **Leaflets/smallest divisions** are 0.5–1" (13–25 mm) long, lanceolate to ovate with and angled base and a pointed tip with a light-colored claw. Leaflets are pinnately lobed, the lobes occasionally with teeth, the teeth and lobes similarly claw-tipped. **Midvein** of each leaflet/division is *deeply depressed*, and the blade is usually folded along it; other veins are somewhat less depressed and end in claw-tips. **Stems** erect, single, 4–10' (1.2–3 m) tall and up to 0.9" (23 mm) thick, slightly zigzag, *hollow*, round and smooth in cross sec-tion, light green, usually mixed with *deep purple streaks and blotches*, the surface *completely hairless* and very *densely covered in white bloom*. The form is taller than wide with strongly ascending branches, often near the base on robust full-sun specimens. **Stem leaves** alternate, similar to the basal. **Inflorescence** (late spring to mid summer) numerous slightly convex compound umbels 2–5" (5–13 cm) across with 8–20 strongly ridged primary rays. **Umbellets** moderately spaced, but the 12–25 flowers within them are crowded. There is a whorl of bracts with long-pointed tips beneath the great umbels and umbellets. **Flowers** (late spring to early sum-mer) 3 mm across with 5 slightly unequal white petals, not touching each other, broad and in-curved to appear notched at the tip; the sexual parts are white or creamy. **Fruit** broadly oval, slightly flattened, with several wavy lengthwise ribs. **Seedlings** often appear very densely in autumn or winter. **(Continued on the next page.)**

◀ Stem showing heavy bloom.

✦ Poison hemlock (continued) (Group 28) Deadly.

MISTAKEN FOR: Wild carrot (p. 472), caraway (p. 462), hemlock parsley (p. 460), cow parsley (p. 469), hedge parsley (p. 470), American chervils (p. 474), eastern yampa (p. 464), harbinger of spring (p. 466).

HABITAT: Disturbed, well-drained but rich soil in full or partial sun: waste areas, fields, vacant lots, forest edges and openings, fence lines, floodplains, ditches; occasionally invades prairies. **I**

TOXICITY: Contains coniine and several related alkaloids, which depress the central nervous system, causing respiratory paralysis, heartbeat suppression, and convulsions. All parts are poisonous, and numerous documented deaths are known.

COMMENTS: This extremely poisonous plant is often very abundant and resembles several edible members of the carrot family. Most poisonings come from eating the root, but all parts are highly toxic, including the powder on the surface; one should wash hands after handling it and avoid handling large amounts.

✦ **Crown vetch** (Group 29) Poisonous.
Coronilla varia ✦ *Fabaceae* (Legume family)

DESCRIPTION: Herbaceous perennial vine often forming dense tangles or mounds over the ground. **Stems** 3–5 mm thick with many branches, hollow, rounded but with *numerous small, sharp ridges*, with sparse erect hairs. **Leaf** pinnately compound with 17–21 leaflets, 3–4 of these *crowded near the base of the rachis and almost wrapped back around the stem*; terminal leaflet present, *tendrils absent*. **Rachis** thin, shallowly channeled. **Leaflets** 11–14 mm long, ovate to lanceolate, the tip blunt with a nipple, the margins entire; on petiolules 5–8% of blade length. Midvein is depressed; other veins not evident. **Stipules** ovate, 4 mm, hidden by first leaflets. **Inflorescence** on a peduncle 3" (8 cm) long, from a leaf axil, ending in a tight umbel of 17–23 flowers, the pedicels 5–7 mm. **Flowers** (summer) have a narrow, pale, dark-pointed keel, curved upward just past the wings and almost meeting the banner tip. The banner is light purple, the wings pale.

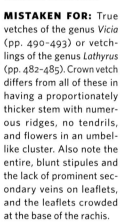

HABITAT: Roadsides, banks, meadows, fields, forest edges; moderate to full sun, rich soil with ample moisture. Introduced.

MISTAKEN FOR: True vetches of the genus *Vicia* (pp. 490–493) or vetchlings of the genus *Lathyrus* (pp. 482–485). Crown vetch differs from all of these in having a proportionately thicker stem with numerous ridges, no tendrils, and flowers in an umbel-like cluster. Also note the entire, blunt stipules and the lack of prominent secondary veins on leaflets, and the leaflets crowded at the base of the rachis.

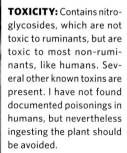

TOXICITY: Contains nitroglycosides, which are not toxic to ruminants, but are toxic to most non-ruminants, like humans. Several other known toxins are present. I have not found documented poisonings in humans, but nevertheless ingesting the plant should be avoided.

AKA *Securigera varia*.

✦ **False hellebore** (Group 35) Highly poisonous.
genus *Veratrum* ✦ family *Melanthiaceae*

DESCRIPTION: Large perennial herb from a thick, long-lived root system. **Stems** usually single but sometimes clumped, *erect, unbranched*, to 6' (2 m) tall and 1" (2.5 cm) thick, with leaves distributed evenly up its length. **Leaves** 6–12" (15–30 cm) long, alternate, broadly elliptic, *strongly ascending*, sessile, the base narrowed to a sheath that wraps around the stem. Blades are *conspicuously pleated* (folded accordion-like), the *veins parallel*. **Inflorescence** a single large *panicle at the apex*, oriented vertically, 12–24" (30–60 cm) long. **Panicle branches** in the form of a densely packed raceme, the rachis hairy, subtended by a *canoe-shaped bract*, the pedicels 1–5 mm. **Flowers** (June–August) 13 mm across with 6 yellow-green petals. These are broadly elliptic with a *blunt tip and a narrowed base*, not touching each other when open, their margins light-colored and *minutely fringed or broken*. The petals have darkened veins. **Fruit** an ellipsoid, 3-lobed capsule 0.5–1" (13–25 mm) long, splitting along sutures to release straw-colored, flat, winged, crooked-lanceolate seeds with a pointed tip.

MISTAKEN FOR: Possibly false Solomon's seal (p. 599) in the shoot stage. A few species are sometimes mistaken for ramps (p. 233), especially the small *V. parviflorum*.

HABITAT: Open woods and meadows with moist soil, especially rocky wet areas or near springs and seeps.

TOXICITY: High, but rarely deadly. Contains a staggering array of neurotoxic alkaloids that cause salivation, vomiting, abdominal pain, convulsions, and heart disturbances. There have been many serious poisonings, but the only fatal case I found was of two men in France who cooked and ate a large number of seeds from *V. album*, a European species.

▲ Newly emerging spring plants may appear to have basal leaves.

✦ **Dogbane** (Group 35) Poisonous.
genus *Apocynum* ✦ family *Apocynaceae*

DESCRIPTION: Perennial herbs 2–6' (0.6–2 m) tall, spreading by rhizome to form colonies. All parts exude milky sap. **Stems** single, erect, to 12 mm thick, smooth with a faint bloom, often reddish, hairless, round, unbranched in the lower half and much branched above. **Leaves** paired, entire, 2–4" (5–10 cm) long, elliptic to ovate, rounded at the base and abruptly pointed at the tip, hairless above or nearly so, usually with very fine hairs below. **Midvein** offset by light color; secondary veins several, 55–80° to the midvein, lightly depressed, intact nearly to the margins. **Petioles** 1–5% of blade length, or the lowest leaves sessile. **Flowers** (early to mid summer) bell-like, sweetly fragrant, 3–6 mm wide, in clusters of 6–40 at branch tips, the 5 petals white, often with pink lines, fused at the base. The calyx is symmetrical and 5-lobed. The pistils and stamens do not protrude; the 5 stamens lean in toward the center to form a cone over the pistil. **Fruit** a needle-like pod 3–7" (8–18 cm) long and 2–3 mm thick, often curved, containing tiny brown seeds attached to a silky parachute; often borne in pairs.

Common Dogbane *A. cannabinum* reaches 3–6' (1–2 m) tall, the branches and leaves ascending. It grows usually in rich, moist soil and forms dense colonies. The flowers are much smaller than those of spreading dogbane and white. The corolla lobes are straight or only slightly spreading, and the calyx is almost as long as the corolla tube. The leaf blades are elliptic and the shoot tapers minimally.

Spreading Dogbane *A. androsaemifolium* is 1–4' (30–120 cm) tall with drooping leaves and widely spreading branches. It grows in drier sites with poorer soil and forms sparser colonies than common dogbane. The flower clusters are smaller but the flowers are larger, white with pink stripes; the calyx is less than half the length of the tube, and the lobes are spread wide and recurved. The shoot tapers strongly and the leaf blades are ovate.

▼ (left top) Common dogbane blooming top.
(right top) Common dogbane shoot by dead stem.

MISTAKEN FOR: Milkweeds (pp. 556–558) when in the shoot stage. At maturity these plants are easy to differentiate because dogbanes branch. However, common dogbane shoots are very difficult to tell from those of some milkweeds, the best distinguishing feature being a dense felty coating of minute hairs on the leaves and stems of milkweed, and the presence of bloom on dogbane stems. Other distinguishing features are subtle. I have investigated several reports of "extremely bitter milkweed shoots" over the years and most of them turned out to be common dogbane. If you encounter bitter milkweed, don't eat it!

HABITAT: Roadsides, ditches, fields, open woodlands, forest margins, floodplain openings.

TOXICITY: Dogbanes contain several glycosides and have cardiac effects, but the strong unpleasant taste generally prevents consumption sufficient to cause serious poisoning. I have found no documented human cases.

▲ Spreading dogbane flowers.
◀ Common dogbane flowers.

675

✦ Baneberry, white and red (Group 38) Highly poisonous.
Actaea pachypoda, A. rubra ✦
Ranunculaceae (Buttercup family)

DESCRIPTION: Perennials to 40" (1 m) tall, from knobby rootstocks but rarely forming large colonies. **Stems** one or few, erect, smooth, bloom-coated, greenish or reddish (the latter especially near the base), *solid*, round, 4–8 mm thick, straight, unbranched and naked for half their length or more, bulged and darker where leaves are attached. The flowering stalk grows vertical, then abruptly zags to one side where it bears one leaf on a short, thick petiole, with the inflorescence rising vertically above that. **Leaves** few, alternate (basal leaves absent), 7–14" (18–36 cm) long, twice compound, spreading widely, ternate at the first division, typically with 9–21 leaflets. Rachises and rachis branches are 2–4 mm

▲ White and red, collective range.

thick, solid, deeper than wide, the top with a narrow, sharp-edged channel. Side leaflets may be sessile or on petiolules up to 30% of blade length. **Leaflets** 3–5" (8–13 cm) long, mostly ovate to lanceolate with acuminate tips, but terminal leaflets are often broader and deeply 3-lobed. Blades are flat and hairless above. **Midvein** deeply depressed above and protruding below, as are the 3–5 secondary veins per side; veinlets are flat above. **Margins** coarsely double-toothed, the teeth claw-tipped. **Inflorescence** a single *raceme* 1–3" (2.5-8 cm) long held above the leaves at the apex of a *long, naked stalk*, rather crowded with 16–45 white flowers. **Flowers** with 4–10 flimsy, widely spaced, white petals, narrow at the base; there are numerous

stamens, and a single stout pistil. Racemes elongate as fruit ripens, sometimes reaching 8" (20 cm). **Fruit** is an oblong to spherical shiny white or red berry 7–10 mm long with a *dark black tip* (more noticeable on white berries), each containing multiple, flattened, crescent or D-shaped dark brown seeds.

▲ *Actaea rubra* with white fruit.

SPECIES: Red baneberry *A. rubra* has flowers that are 6–7 mm wide with sharp-tipped petals. The stem and leaf rachises are sparsely soft-hairy, the leaf blades soft-hairy below, and the fruiting pedicels thin and green to brown. The fruit is normally red but often white. **White baneberry** *A. pachypoda* flowers are 3–4 mm wide with blunt or 2-lobed petals. All parts are hairless. Fruiting pedicels are bright red and bulged at both ends. The fruit is normally white, rarely red.

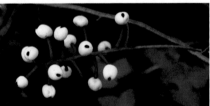

▲ *Actaea pachypoda* fruit.

MISTAKEN FOR: As a shoot, red baneberry especially can be mistaken for sarsaparilla (p. 290), and the two often grow together. The berries do not strongly resemble any edible kind.

HABITAT: Rich-soiled, well-drained deciduous forests; red baneberry also grows in mixed forests containing conifers.

TOXICITY: The important toxin(s) remain unidentified but ingestion causes gastric upset, dizziness, rapid but weak heartbeat, headache, and cognitive disturbances. I can find no recorded deaths from these species. All parts are presumed toxic, especially the roots and berries.

COMMENTS: This is probably the most poisonous fleshy berry in our region— which means that there is nothing in the real wild anything like the imaginary nightlock berries of *The Hunger Games*.

Actaea rubra shoot. ▲
Actaea rubra with red fruit. ▶

PLANTS NOT INCLUDED

Following is a short list of plants reported as edible in some other sources, and the reasons that I have left them out of this book.

Broomrape *Orobanche ludoviciana* (group 2): I've never found this plant, so I haven't eaten the shoots. If I ever get a chance to try broomrape myself, I'll tell you all about it.

Tamarack *Larix laricina* (group 4): The shoots and cambium can be eaten like those of spruce and balsam fir. They have not appealed to me enough to make me write about them.

White cedar *Thuja occidentalis* (group 4): The leaves are used to make an infusion that prevents people from dying of scurvy, and for this reason it is also called *arbor vitae* (tree of life). Not dying is popular, but this wouldn't be a popular drink on account of its taste.

Pear *Pyrus communis* and **Peach** *Prunus persica* (group 6): These sometimes go feral, but much less often than apples or sweet cherries, and I don't think of them as wild species.

Sweet gum *Liquidamabar styraciflua* (group 8): You can chew on the hardened gum. That's fun but it's not really food. My son calculated that he would need to chew 270 packs of his favorite chewing gum to get a day's calories. TMJ pain.

Sycamore *Platanus occidentalis* (group 8): You can tap these and boil the sap down to make syrup, which is actually delicious, but there's a reason it isn't done with any regularity. The sugar is too dilute to make it practical. You can say this about ironwood *Ostrya virginiana* too.

Coral bean *Erythrina herbacea* (group 12): The seeds of this vine-like shrub are extremely poisonous, but the tender young greens and flowers are reportedly edible after boiling and draining. I have not tried them yet.

Golden club *Orontium aquaticum* (group 15): Another arum family plant with raphides (see p. 22), this one might have been traditionally used as food, but the accounts are uncertain, and there's only so many times I'm going to burn my mouth with raphides to figure things out.

Sago pondweed *Potamogeton pectinatus* (group 15): This abundant aquatic species has edible tubers, and they taste good, but they are tiny and I have found no effective way of gathering them in meaningful amounts.

Water milfoil *Myriophyllum spicatum* and *M. sibiricum* (group 15): These aquatic plants reportedly have edible tubers but I have never found any such thing beneath them, nor do I know anyone who has eaten them. I hope to figure this out some day, because it sounds like a good food.

White water-lily, genus *Nymphaea* (group 15): This group is an enigma. There are several ethnographic reports of the rhizomes or tubers being used as food in North America and elsewhere. Important details of preparation or processing must be missing for our species, because I know a few people who have gotten sick from eating them. Meriwether Lewis reported an elaborate process by which Native Americans detoxified a plant that he *thought* was a water-lily, but he never actually saw the plant from which the roots were harvested. I have tried various species on numerous occasions at different times of year, and have found that rhizome slices can be transformed into a limp, bland, faintly disgusting spongy mass through repeated boiling and draining. I find the flower buds, also reported edible, to taste terrible. Not worth a whole page.

Wild calla *Calla palustris* (group 15): This plant, like other members of the arum family, has raphides in its flesh (see p. 22). It tastes pleasantly sweet-starchy moments before it begins burning your mouth. The rhizome could technically be rendered safe, but I think it's too small to bother with.

Star-of-Bethlehem *Ornithogalum umbellatum* (group 17): The bulbs are known to be toxic but can be rendered edible through processing. I have not done this, nor do I know anyone who has, and the small bulbs are low on my list of foods to experiment with. But someday I will. (See p. 666.)

Fairy slipper *Calypso bulbosa* (group 18): This orchid is generally rare in our region (it is much more common in the West) and is killed when the bulb is eaten. I have never tried it. This is one of several uncommon to rare orchids with edible USOs in the region covered by this guide that I have refrained from eating.

Pony's foot *Dichondra carolinensis* (group 18): This plant is very common in lawns of the South. I have eaten the leaves, but they are tiny, kind of tough, and just don't taste very good.

Rush skeletonweed *Chondrilla juncea* (group 19): This introduced dandelion relative is highly esteemed by foragers in Europe. Its range is restricted in our region mostly to Delaware, New Jersey, Michigan, and the High Plains-Mountain border region. I have not tried it.

Buckbean *Menyanthes trifoliata* (group 20): The starch from the root is reported as a starvation food in Europe. My experiments have not shed a favorable light on its culinary potential.

Common valerian *Valeriana officinale* (group 21): Francois Couplan lists the greens as edible. I used to live where it is as abundant, and through no number of compulsory ingestions could I "develop a taste" for it.

Edible valerian *Valeriana edulis* (group 21): This plant is much larger and more abundant in the Rockies, where the baked root was used as a food by Indigenous people. To my knowledge it was not used in our region, where it is smaller and uncommon in rocky prairies and fens.

Geranium (group 21): I don't think any members of this genus are dangerously toxic, and some are eaten occasionally, but I have not tried any that I thought were worth including.

Borage *Borago officinalis* (group 22): This plant is often reported in the foraging literature, but I have yet to find it growing wild. It is mostly a garden plant or a short-lived escape in backyards.

Elecampane *Inula helenium* (group 23): This plant begs the timeless childhood question: Is candy food? I guess my answer is no, because I know of no other culinary use for this strong-flavored elegant herb, and I left it out.

Canadian burnet *Sanguisorba canadensis* (group 26): I tried this a couple times and didn't like it; it's much more astringent than the cultivated salad burnet. But I might change my mind if I try it earlier in the spring.

Chamomile *Matricaria chamomilla* (group 28): This plant makes a nice tea but is almost never found wild in our area. Most reports of it are mistaken pineapple weed (p 458) or other relatives.

Potato bean *Apios priceana* (group 29): This is a close relative of hopniss (p. 489), and the relationship and names (also called "traveler's delight") suggest that it may be one of the most promising native food plants on our continent. It is also rare and fully protected in the wild. This vine has a single large tuber and yam-like ecology; it should be explored as an Indigenous food crop in ecoculture systems.

Wild yam *Dioscorea villosa* (group 29): The roots of this species are often reported as edible by people who have not tried it. Because it is in the same genus as the many edible tropical yams, it is easy to assume that it produces an edible root. Having dug up many of these over the decades I have never found anything but a tough, woody, relatively thin rhizome. The greens of some tropical yams are traditionally eaten, and I have eaten the young shoots of our native yam after boiling. I have also eaten the immature fruits raw or cooked. These practices should be considered tentative until we have direct ethnographic evidence or stronger experiential comparisons.

Blue vervain *Verbena hastata* (group 32): The seeds are reported as a traditional Indigenous food. I gathered and processed a batch; it was a lot of work and I did not like them at all.

Muster John Henry *Tagetes minuta* (group 34): I bet I would really like this seasoning, and with a name like that, who wouldn't want to try it? I tried to find this plant but have so far failed.

Maximilian sunflower *Helianthus maximiliani* (group 36): This plant is reported as having edible tubers. I have dug it up many times and have found no such thing, but I nibbled the lateral tips and they were good. Linda Black Elk (personal communication) tells me that she usually finds them without tubers, but she knows of one population that regularly produces edible tubers of reasonably good size. We are not aware of the conditions stimulating tuber production.

Alfalfa *Medicago sativa* (group 38): I have nibbled this plenty while putting up hay. It's not very exciting for direct human consumption and I rarely see it go feral.

Black medick *Medicago lupulina* (group 38): I have to admit, many times I have looked at the tiny seedheads of this plant and thought, "No way that's going to be worth my time to parch, rub, and winnow." I haven't.

Canada milkvetch *Astragalus canadensis* (group 38): The roots are reported as a traditional food for some Indigenous people; I have had no luck trying to use them.

False indigo (genus *Baptisia*) (group 38): The shoots of one species are reported as edible in an older source. I ate two raw and it was a very bad experience. I later heard a report of two people who were hospitalized after eating *Baptisia* shoots. Do not.

Hop clover *Trifolium aureum* (group 38): The greens and flowers are reported as edible. I have not tried this one, but considering the characteristics of clovers as human food I suspect I'm not missing much. I still hope to, though.

Tansy *Tanacetum vulgare* (group 38): Often reported as a culinary herb in European and older American sources, but questions have been raised about its safety. This plant thrives in my backyard but I have never found a way that I enjoy using it.

11 IMPORTANT PLANT FAMILIES FOR GATHERERS

As you learn plants you will begin to recognize patterns of form that repeat themselves in multiple species, and you will likely intuit that some of these similarities are based on genetic relationships. Following that taxonomic inkling will make learning plants much easier. Recognizing the family to which an unfamiliar plant belongs instantly narrows the identification possibilities. It also sets some parameters for its potential edibility or toxicity. Although there are numerous plant families, there are 11 important ones that I suggest gatherers make a conscious effort to learn early in their journey. These 11 include well over half of the edible species in this book (382 out of 700). Below I describe key characteristics of each of these families and provide representative photos to show you some of the patterns. After this is a list of the species in each family covered in this guide, with the plant numbers for your reference. The family descriptions that follow contain many generalizations; research individual species before using any plant. All of these families contain some toxic species. For a deeper exploration of plant families, I recommend Thomas Elpel's *Botany in a Day*.

Composite Family • *Asteraceae* (formerly *Compositae*)   68 edible plants covered

The *composites* are almost all herbaceous in our region. They typically have alternate leaves that are toothed or lobed, but there are many exceptions to this pattern. What all composites share is a structure with multiple small flowers (florets) packed together with their bases embedded in a spongy, pitted, disk-like structure (receptacle). This gives the impression of a single complex flower. Examples include dandelion, daisy, and sunflower. Petal-like florets (like the outer ones on a sunflower) are called *ray florets*. *Disk florets* are tubular with 5 tiny petals (like those in the center of a sunflower). Some composites have both ray and disk florets, others have only one kind. The composite structure is called a head (capitulum). Behind the head are many bracts. The fruit is a single seed (achene, cypsela), often with a hairy pappus attached. This enormous family has several distinct subfamilies, such as the dandelion group (which has milky sap and only ray florets) and the thistle group (large heads with numerous stiff bracts). The edible parts in this family include USOs, seeds, greens, and stems. There are few dangerously poisonous species.

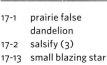   

17-1 prairie false dandelion	24-3 scorzonera	34-3 quickweed
17-2 salsify (3)	24-4–11 thistles (8)	34-4 jerusalem-artichoke
17-13 small blazing star	24-12 nipplewort	34-5 sumpweed
19-4 dandelion	24-13 Japanese hawksbeard	34-6 giant ragweed
19-5 potato dandelion	24-14 Carolina dandelion	34-7 yerba de tago
19-6 tuberous false dandelion	24-15 false dandelion	35-11 horseweed
19-7 hairy cat's ear	24-16 chicory	36-3 sunflower
19-8 fall dandelion	24-17–19 sow-thistles (3)	36-9 serrated sage
19-10 English daisy	24-20–27 wild lettuces (7)	36-10 common goldenrod
19-13 coltsfoot	25-2 sochan	37-1 tarragon
19-14 northern coltsfoot	25-15 compass plant	37-2 mugwort
21-3 common dwarf dandelion	25-17 ox-eye daisy	37-14 cocklebur
21-5 cup plant	28-1 pineapple weed	37-20 Canada thistle
22-14 seaside goldenrod	32-12 romerillo	37-21 burnweed
22-16–18 burdock (3)	32-13 Spanish needles	
22-19 New England aster		
23-17 prairie-dock		
23-18 bigleaf aster		
24-1 white lettuce		
24-2 Texas skeletonplant		

Carrot Family • *Apiaceae* (formerly *Umbelliferae*)   **48 edible plants covered**

This family contains many edible plants as well as the deadliest plants in our region (water hemlocks *Cicuta* and poison hemlock *Conium maculatum*). Because these highly toxic plants have a strong resemblance to one or more edible species, extreme caution is due when gathering certain members of the carrot family. Some members, however, are not hard to identify. Several species in this family have sap that can cause rashes and blisters (p. 22).

Plants in the carrot family tend to have deeply divided to multi-compound leaves. Most members have basal leaves. The stem leaves are alternate, with the petiole often sheath-like at the base. The herbage is often aromatic. The most distinctive feature is the inflorescence, which is a compound umbel (rarely a simple umbel). The flowers are small with 5 petals, often folded back in toward the center; there are 5 stamens and 2 styles. The fruit (schizocarp) is dry at maturity and often highly flavored; it splits into 2 equal halves, each with one seed. Members of the carrot and mustard families can have similar leaf shape and growth form. At maturity these families can easily be recognized by their very different flowering and fruiting parts. With young plants, the carrot family can be distinguished by the presence of jointed stems with rings at the nodes—mustards lack both of these features. The carrot family includes USOs, leafy greens, shoots, culinary herbs, and spices. The closely related ginseng family *Araliaceae* is sometimes lumped with it, and is included in this list.

15-3 water parsnip	27-5-8 angelica (4)
15-4 springwater parsnip	27-10 prairie parsnip
15-8 water pennywort	27-11 aniseroot
19-15 beach pennywort (2)	27-12 sweet cicely
19-16 coinleaf	28-2 fennel
20-1 wild sarsaparilla	28-3 hemlock parsley
20-3 yellow prairie biscuitroot	28-4 caraway
20-4 thread-leaf musineon	28-5 eastern yampa
20-5 small winged biscuitroot	28-6 harbinger of spring
20-6 large winged biscuitroot	28-7 broad-leaf musineon
23-14 rattlesnake master	28-8 white prairie biscuitroot
26-1 cow parsnip	28-9 cow parsley
26-2 giant hogweed	28-10 erect hedge parsley
26-3 mitsuba	28-11 wild carrot
26-4 sanicle (spp.)	28-12 southern wild chervil
26-5 Cherokee swamp potato	28-13 spreading chervil
26-6 parsnip	30-9 dwarf ginseng
26-7 burnet-saxifrage	30-10 ginseng
27-1 yellow pimpernel	35-12 thoroughwax
27-2 American lovage	37-4 common pennywort
27-3 Javan water celery	38-16 spikenard
27-4 sea lovage	38-17 bristly sarsaparilla

Legume Family • *Fabaceae* (formerly *Leguminosae*)   43 edible plants covered

This family includes trees, woody and herbaceous vines, and herbs. Most are perennials. Regardless of the size or growth form, leaves are usually compound with entire leaflets. Stipules are common and sometimes large. Typical legume flowers are not radially symmetrical. They have 5 united sepals forming a tube at the base. The corolla has a large, 2-lobed upper petal called a *banner*, a pair of side petals called *wings*, and 2 more petals at the bottom fused to form a *keel*. (A few woody members have very different corollas.) The fruit is a pod, usually elongated and containing multiple seeds. Legumes form a very important group of food plants that are often high in protein due to their ability to fix nitrogen. The edible parts include seeds, immature pods, leafy greens, and USOs. This family also includes many toxic members.

8-1	redbud
8-2	Kentucky coffeetree
8-3	honey mesquite
8-4	honeylocust
8-5–8	Robinia locusts (4)
12-6	leadplant
13-8	kudzu
13-9	wisteria (2)
20-2	white clover
20-11	small prairie-turnip
20-12	Nashville breadroot
26-14	red clover
26-14	alsike clover
29-2	everlasting pea
29-3	narrow-leaved vetchling
29-4	tuber vetchling
29-5	pale vetchling
29-6	marsh pea
29-7	veiny pea
29-8	beach pea
29-9	ground bean
29-10	wild bean
29-11	fuzzy bean
29-12	hopniss
29-13	common vetch
29-14	Carolina vetch
29-15	American vetch
29-16	hairy vetch
29-17	tufted vetch
38-7	point-leaf tick trefoil
38-8	sweet clovers (2)
38-9	prairie clovers (2)
38-10	American licorice
38-11	ground-plum milkvetch
38-12	alpine sweetvetch
38-14	prairie-turnip
38-15	tall breadroot

Mustard Family ᐧ *Brassicaceae* (formerly *Cruciferae*)   42 edible plants covered

Herbaceous in our region, these are mostly disturbance-dependent annuals but a few are long-lived perennials. Leaves are alternate and usually deeply lobed or divided. The inflorescence is a raceme. Flowers have 4 petals, often not at right angles to each other. There are 6 stamens, 2 of which are shorter than the others. The fruit is a small, dry capsule containing multiple small seeds. Mustards tend to have strong hot or pungent flavors, especially in their seeds. The edible parts are usually leafy greens, shoots, or flower buds. A few have edible roots, and the seeds of some species are used as a seasoning. Members of this family may be mildly toxic but none are highly dangerous.

15-2 watercress	25-28 tower mustard
21-12-15 toothworts (4)	25-29 field mustard
22-20 hoary alyssum	25-30 bastard cabbage
23-5 scurvy-grass	25-31 hill mustard
23-6 bulbous bittercress	25-32 black mustard
23-7 field pennycress	25-33 white mustard
23-8 garlic pennycress	25-34 hedge mustard
23-9 horseradish	25-35 tall hedge mustard
23-10 smooth rock cress	25-36 tumble mustard
23-11 dame's rocket	25-37 highway mustard
23-12 whitetop	25-38 French rocket
23-13 garlic mustard	25-39 charlock mustard
25-19 annual wall rocket	25-40 wild radish
25-20 marsh yellowcress	26-8 cuckoo flower
25-21 creeping yellowcress	26-9 shotweed
25-22 wintercress	26-10 Pennsylvania cress
25-23 southern wintercress	26-11 narrow-leaf bittercress
25-24 blue mustard	26-12 twin cress
25-25 shepherd's purse	28-14 western tansy mustard
25-26 field pepperweed	28-15 European tansy mustard
25-27 common pepperweed	37-15 sea rocket

Greater Lily Family • *Liliaceae*   **41 edible plants covered**

Taxonomists used to recognize a large lily family but lately have broken this up into several smaller families including *Agavoideae, Alliaceae, Amaryllidaceae, Asparagaceae, Ashphodeloideae, Colchicaceae, Hemerocallidoidea, Melanthiaceae, Nolinoideae,* and *Smilacaceae*—all of which have members covered in this guide. For our purposes we will lump them together and focus on their similarities. Plants in this super-family have the primary leaf veins botanically parallel, and the leaves are entire. Physical structure is simple—most stems are unbranched, but a few branch minimally. Flowers have 3 petals and 3 sepals, usually similar in form and color (in which case many elect to call them all *tepals*). The ovary has 3 carpels, and the fruit matures into a capsule or berry. Many of these species have edible greens, shoots, or USOs; a few have edible fruits. This group also has some very toxic plants, such as the death camasses and false hellebore (in *Melanthiaceae*).

13-4 greenbrier (5)	18-4 trout lily (3)
16-1 ramps (2)	18-5 bluebead lily
16-2 field garlic	29-18 carrion flower (spp.)
16-3 chives	30-1 trillium (3)
16-4 feral garlic	30-2 lilies (3)
16-5 American garlic	30-3 cucumber root
16-6-9 wild onion (4)	35-1 asparagus
17-4 day lily	35-24 white twisted-stalk
17-7 prairie star lily	35-25 rosy twisted-stalk
17-15 yucca (2)	35-26 large bellwort
17-16 false garlic	35-27 smooth Solomon's seal
17-18 grape hyacinth	35-28 false Solomon's seal
17-19 camas (2)	

Rose Family • *Rosaceae*

34 edible plants covered

This diverse family includes many herbaceous and woody plants that were formerly divided into subfamilies. The leaves are alternate and may be compound or simple, but in either case the leaves or leaflets are always toothed. Stipules are often present. The flowers have 5 sepals and 5 separate petals. The sexual parts appear crowded; there are numerous stamens and multiple styles. Fruits are highly variable, but when fleshy they are often edible. The vegetative parts tend to be high in tannin but low in other toxins. A few have edible shoots or leaves that are used for tea. One even produces a root vegetable.

3-3	purple-flowered raspberry	7-1	mountain-ash (spp.)
3-4	thimbleberry	7-5	black cherry
3-5	red raspberry	7-6	pin cherry
3-6	wineberry	7-7	feral cherries (2)
3-7	black raspberry	7-13	serviceberry (spp.)
3-8	blackberry (spp.)	7-14	hawthorn (spp.)
3-9	dewberry (spp.)	7-15	mayhaw
3-10	cloudberry	10-7	rose (spp.)
3-11	plumboy	10-16	red aronia
3-12	nagoonberry	11-6	chokecherry
6-1	rugosa rose	11-7	sandcherry
6-7	native crabapple (2)	11-14	black aronia
6-8	apple	20-7	silverweed
6-9	Eurasian crabapple	20-8-9	strawberry (2)
6-10	wild plums (4)	26-13	false strawberry
		26-17	chocolate root

Mint Family + *Lamiaceae* (formerly *Labiatae*)   33 edible plants covered

These plants are mostly herbaceous. They are characterized by square stems and simple paired leaves. The herbage is highly aromatic on over half the species. Flowers have a tubular calyx with usually 5 lobes, and a tubular corolla. On a few species the corolla has 4 or 5 nearly regular lobes, but more often it is highly irregular in shape with an upper and lower lip, the lips often kinked, twisted, folded, or lobed. Flowers tend to be in densely packed clusters. The fruit is typically a dry capsule releasing 4 seeds. Many mints are used as culinary herbs or flavorings. Others have edible greens, shoots, USOs, or seeds. There are few toxic members.

11-13	beautyberry
21-4	lyre-leaf sage
21-8	heal-all
31-1	calamint
31-2-3	mountain mint (4)
31-4	American pennyroyal
31-5	wild basil
31-6	oregano
31-7	dittany
31-8	anise hyssop
31-9	horehound
31-10	catnip
31-11	shiso
31-12	mints (3)
31-13	tall woodmint
31-14	creeping charlie
31-15	horsemints (2)
31-16	bergamot
31-16	scarlet bee balm
32-1	purple deadnettle
32-2	henbit
32-3	Florida betony
32-4	woundwort
32-5	hemp-nettle
32-6	bugleweeds (3)

Buckwheat Family • *Polygonaceae*   **20 edible plants covered**

The members in our region are herbaceous, many of them weedy. The leaves are alternate and entire. Stems are jointed with a papery sheath at each node (which may disappear with age). The flowers are tiny, numerous, and arranged in clusters on a branching inflorescence. They have 5–6 tepals and are not showy. The fruit is an achene containing one black or brown seed, often 3-sided but sometimes flattened. The plants are sour and astringent but generally free of strong toxins. The edible parts are usually leaves, stalks, and petioles; occasionally seeds.

18-7	mountain sorrel
22-1-2	sheep sorrel (2)
22-3	sorrel
22-5	alpine bistort
22-6-10	docks (5)
29-20	black bindweeds (2)
35-13	giant knotweeds (2)
35-14	smartweeds (4)
35-15	erect knotweed
35-16	willow-leaved dock

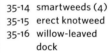

Heath Family • *Ericaceae*   *20 edible plants covered*

Mostly woody plants, the heath family includes a bunch of edible berries and a few teas. These shrubs have alternate leaves that are typically entire and often evergreen. They specialize in poor and acidic soil. The flowers have 5 sepals, and 5 fused petals that often form a vase- or bell-shaped corolla. The fruit is a fleshy berry or a dry capsule.

9-1	trailing arbutus	9-9	arctic bearberries (2)	11-20	lowbush blueberries (2)
9-3	creeping snowberry	11-1	deerberry	11-21	mayberry
9-4-5	cranberries (2)	11-16	black huckleberry	11-22	bilberry
9-6	lingonberry	11-17	dangleberry	12-12	Labrador tea
9-7	wintergreen	11-18	farkleberry	12-13	leatherleaf
9-8	bearberry	11-19	highbush blueberry		

Mallow Family • *Malvaceae*   **20 edible plants covered**

These are mostly herbs in our region. The leaves are alternate, palmately veined or with multiple major veins from the base, and usually lobed. The sap is slimy, the stems and petioles are solid, and the bark usually stringy. The flowers have 3–5 sepals, often with bracts just behind them, and 5 separate petals. The sexual parts are diagnostic—numerous stamens are fused together to form a column around the single pistil, which protrudes from the column's end. The fruit is often squat and composed of multiple units (carpels), shaped like a cheese wheel. Haven't you been handling cheese wheels recently? Anyway, this family has little toxicity concern, and produces many edible roots, greens, stalks, flowers, and fruits.

8-9	basswood	36-5 prickly sida	37-10 halberd-leaved rose mallow
25-4-5	poppy mallow (2)	37-6 pineland hibiscus	
25-6	common mallow	37-7 scarlet hibiscus	37-11 Turk's cap mallow
25-7	musk mallow	37-8 bristly mallow	37-12 seashore mallow
25-8	high mallow	37-9 swamp rose mallow	37-13 marsh mallow
25-9	glade mallow	37-9 giant rose mallow	38-1 scarlet globe mallow
36-4	velvetleaf		38-2 flour-of-an-hour

Amaranth Family + *Amaranthaceae*   **17 edible plants covered**

These are mostly weedy plants, many of them annuals. Stems are solid. Leaves are alternate, simple, and most often entire. The inflorescence is usually a branching cluster of numerous tiny flowers. Flowers lack petals and are not showy, although they may have colored bracts. There are 4–5 tiny sepals and the same number of stamens. The fruit is usually a one-seeded dry capsule or bladder-like structure. Many members have edible stems, greens, or seeds; few have serious toxicity concerns. The goosefoot family *Chenopodiaciae* is closely related and often lumped with the amaranth family, as it is here.

2-5	glasswort (spp.)	35-4	amaranth (4)
15-6	alligator weed	35-5	creeping amaranth
23-15	strawberry spinach	35-6	kochia
25-3	poverty weed	36-1	lambsquarters (spp.)
34-9	orache (spp.)	37-16	tumble ringwing
35-2	Russian tumbleweed	37-17	epazote
35-3	sea-blite	37-18	maple-leaved goosefoot

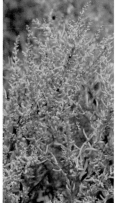

FINDING EDIBLE WILD PLANTS BY HABITAT AND SEASON

Although this book is designed to facilitate identifying a plant once it is found, all experienced gatherers sometimes **learn about a plant first, and then go looking for it**. This section suggests what plants to look for in eighteen of the major habitats within our region, and when to look for them. (Not all edible species or parts are listed.) Because natural communities change gradually based upon many variables, some locations will not fit perfectly into one of the described plant communities. Not every "dry deciduous forest" will be the same: One in Pennsylvania might be dominated by chestnut oak, another in Oklahoma by black hickory. No site will contain all the plants on the list, and some edible plants not listed will also be present. Nevertheless, this habitat guide gives you a good starting point.

After you have determined which habitat best represents your gathering location, peruse the list for suggestions of edible plants to look for. The plants are listed in the order in which they appear in the book, each plant with its group number for easy reference, so you can turn to its plant account, read more about it, and positively identify it. Beside the name you will find a produce icon indicating one or more edible parts. The season of availability is marked to the right of that. Edible parts with different seasons may be listed beneath the first entry.

Timing is an enormous part of successful foraging. Unfortunately, because plant phenology is so variable and local, it is impossible to provide a calendar that is fine-tuned over a broad area like this. You will have to learn what specific dates coincide with the phenological growth stages referenced in the chart below in your location. The seasons listed are generally for the middle section of the US, with a rough Chicago-New York line marking the north and Dallas-Atlanta marking the south. North of that, "spring" phenology might happen in early summer—and in the Far North, the growing season is so short that all things grow and ripen about the same time. In the Deep South, many of the "spring" edibles appear in the winter, and "summer" edibles in spring. By autumn, however, things are more normalized: whether you are in Minnesota or Alabama, acorns ripen in the fall (which means later in Alabama). The seasons listed are those traditionally recognized, and are not calendar-based. (The first day of winter is not December 21; winter is longer, and summer is shorter, toward the north.) For plants or habitats found only in the northern and southern extremities of our area, the listed seasons refer to those regions.

Regardless of the habitat, astute foragers learn to look for **fertility** and **disturbance**, because both of these factors tend to increase the abundance of edible plants. Disturbance is any event that kills plants, resulting in gaps or empty growing spaces where new plants can colonize. These rapidly growing pioneer plants are more likely to be edible.

Notes on the phenology chart: An empty square means the edible part is generally unavailable. (Parts that are invisible due to disappearance of the above-ground parts may be listed as unavailable.) A full green square means the part is available during this period (although not always the whole time—a plant that ripens in summer probably will not be ripe all summer). USOs may be listed in winter—but you can't get to them in areas that are frozen or snow-covered. When a box is half filled at an angle, this indicates that the edible part is available in the early (descending) or late (ascending) half of that season. When the filled area tapers over multiple seasons, this indicates a long but suboptimal period for collecting that part.

Dry Deciduous Forest and Woodland (Mostly Oak-Hickory)

These forests occupy hilly or sandy country over much of our region. Soils range from slightly acidic on sand to alkaline on limestone hills. These forests often have sparse canopies, and before European settlement they experienced frequent but light litter fires. On more fertile sites the fires were more severe, resulting in oak savannahs, which are almost gone today. With fire control, dry woodlands have been slowly losing their sun-loving species. These forests are excellent for nuts and fairly good to excellent for USOs and green vegetables.

Plant	spr	sum	fall	win
Rattlesnake fern 1-2				
Bracken fern 1-3				
American mulberry 3-2				
Bramble berries 3-7–9				
Walnut, Butternut 5-1–2				
Hickory nuts 5-3–10				
American hazel 5-15				
Acorns 5-18–23				
Persimmon 6-3				
American crabapples 6-7				
Wild plum 6-10				
Black cherry 7-5				
Sassafras 7-11				
Redbud 8-1				
Slippery elm 8-19				
Deerberry 11-1				
Black haw 11-4				
Gooseberry 11-9				
Black huckleberry 11-16				
Farkleberry 11-18				
Lowbush blueberry 11-20				
Sumacs 12-1–4				
Grapes 13-1				
Greenbriers 13-4				
American garlic 16-5				
Spiderwort 17-3				
False garlic 17-16				
Camas 17-20				

Plant	spr	sum	fall	win
Arrowhead violet 19-2				
Wild sarsaparilla 20-1				
Violet woodsorrel 20-10				
Mayapple 21-12				
Toothworts 21-14–17				
American bellflower 23-2				
Smooth rock cress 23-10				
Prenanthes 24-1				
Tall thistle 24-5				
Wild lettuces 24-20–27				
Lousewort 25-16				
Sanicles 26-4				
Purple phacelia 26-16				
Yellow pimpernel 27-1				
American lovage 27-2				
Hairy angelica 27-8				
Sweet cicely 27-12				
Red columbine 27-13				
Pale vetchling 29-5				
Ground bean 29-9				
Wild bean 29-10				
Carolina vetch 29-14				
Mints 31-3–7				
Bergamot 31-16				
Star chickweed 33-5				
Phloxes 33-10–11				
Poke milkweed 33-16				
Pellitory 35-19				
Smooth Solomon's seal 35-27				
False Solomon's seal 35-28				
Spikenard 38-16				

Mesic Forest (Rich Hardwoods)

These forests are dominated by trees such as sugar maple, white ash (formerly), buckeye, beech, hemlock, basswood, elms, and yellow birch. They are characterized by moister and often richer soils than dry forests as well as a denser canopy casting heavier shade. These forests, where spring ephemerals reach their peak of importance, provide excellent foraging for greens at that time; otherwise they provide a few nuts and fewer fruits.

Plant	spr	sum	fall	win
Rattlesnake fern 1-2	█			
Ostrich fern 1-6	█			
Lady fern 1-7	█			
American mulberry 3-2		█		
Walnut, butternut 5-1-2			█	█
Bitternut 5-5			█	█
Beech 5-11			█	█
Northern red oak 5-18			█	█
Pawpaw 6-5			█	
Redbud 8-1	█			
Basswood 8-9	█	█		
Maples 8-15-18	█			
Spicebush 10-13	█	█	█	
Hobblebush 11-5			█	
Gooseberry 11-9		█		
Ramps 16-1	█			
American garlic 16-5	█			
Wild ginger 18-3	█			
Trout lily 18-4	█			
Spring beauties 21-7-8	█			

Plant	spr	sum	fall	win
Toothworts 21-13-16	█			█
Virginia bluebells 22-11	█			█
Garlic mustard 23-13	█			█
Canada violet 23-19	█	█		
Nipplewort 24-12	█			█
Waterleafs 25-10-13	█	█		█
Mitsuba 26-3	█	█		
Sanicles 26-4	█			
Purple phacelia 26-16	█			█
Aniseroot 27-11	█			█
Harbinger of spring 28-6	█			█
Spreading chervil 28-13	█			█
Trilliums 30-1	█			
Woodland stonecrop 30-7	█	█		█
Dwarf ginseng 30-9	█			
Tall woodmint 31-13		█		
Clearweed 34-1		█	█	█
Large bellwort 35-26	█			█
Wood nettle 36-8	█	█		█

Northern Conifer and Boreal Forest

Poor or thin soils of the northern US and southern Canada support forests dominated by pine, spruce, and fir mixed with deciduous trees such as red oak, red maple, white birch, and aspen. Further north the tree diversity lessens to only 4–10 cold-hardy species. This boreal forest community is maintained by infrequent but severe fires. Recently burned (or logged) boreal forests, or sparse forest on the tundra border, tend to have very good berry picking. Disturbed or deciduous areas provide some vegetables. Older stands, especially of conifers, have few edible plants.

Plant	spr	sum	fall	win
Bracken fern 1-3	▨	▨		
Lady fern 1-7	▨			
Red raspberry 3-5		▨	▨	
Plumboy 3-11		▨		
Pine 4-1	▨			
Spruce 4-2	▨			
Canada yew 4-9		▨	▨	
Beaked hazelnut 5-14			▨	
Pin cherry 7-6		▨		
Serviceberry 7-13		▨		
White birch 8-11	▨			
Wintergreen 9-7	▨		▨	▨
Squashberry 10-6			▨	
Rose 10-7			▨	
Currants 10-14–15		▨		
Chokecherry 11-6			▨	
Gooseberries 11-9		▨		
Lowbush blueberry 11-20		▨		
Bluebead lily 18-5	▨			
Northern coltsfoot 19-14	▨			
Wild sarsaparilla 20-1				
Woodland strawberry 20-9		▨		
Northern bluebells 22-12	▨			
Harebell 23-1	▨			

Plant	spr	sum	fall	win
Strawberry spinach 23-15	▨			▨
Bigleaf aster 23-18	▨			
Canada violet 23-19	▨			
Prenanthes 24-1	▨		▨	
Wild lettuce 24-20		▨		
Lousewort 25-16				
Aniseroot 27-11			▨	▨
Pale vetchling 29-5				
Cucumber root 30-3				
Bunchberry 30-4			▨	
Dwarf ginseng 30-9				
Fireweed 35-18	▨			
Twisted stalks 35-24–25	▨			
False Solomon's seal 35-28	▨			
Alpine sweetvetch 38-12				

Southern Evergreen Forest (Pine-Oak)

These forests have developed mostly on poor soils of the southern states through the action of frequent fire. The poorest, sandy areas are dominated by pines and evergreen or semi-evergreen oaks, but on slightly better sites this community grades into dominance by deciduous trees. Many of these areas were formerly savannahs or sparse woodlands. With fire suppression the savannahs have become forest, and the forests are slowly converting to a greater dominance of deciduous trees. Southern pinelands are pretty good for wild fruits and nuts, and average to poor for vegetables—both much better where the canopies are sparse.

Plant	spr	sum	fall	win
Bracken fern 1-3	■		■	
Dwarf palmetto 1-10	■	■		
Blackberry 3-8		■		
Pine 4-1	■			
Mockernut 5-8			■	■
Acorns 5-16–23			■	■
Red bay 7-8	■	■	■	■
Sassafras 7-11	■	■	■	■
Yaupon 10-17	■	■	■	■
Black haws 11-4	■	■	■	■
Beautyberry 11-13			■	
Farkleberry 11-18		■		
Mayberry 11-21	■			
Winged sumac 12-1		■	■	
Grapes, muscadine 13-1–2			■	
Greenbriers 13-4	■	■		
Spiderworts 17-3	■			

Plant	spr	sum	fall	win
Yucca 17-14	■	■		
Arrowhead violet 19-2	■			■
Whorled pennywort 19-15	■	■	■	■
Coinleaf 19-16	■	■	■	■
Southern sheep sorrel 22-2	■			■
Japanese hawksbeard 24-13	■			■
Lousewort 25-16	■			■
Sanicles 26-4	■	■		
Hairy angelica 27-8	■	■		
Wild bean 29-10			■	
Carolina vetch 29-14	■	■		
Broad-leaved mountain mint 31-3		■	■	
Horsemint 31-15		■	■	
Pokeweed 35-17	■	■		
Pineland hibiscus 37-6		■	■	
Turk's cap mallow 37-11		■	■	

Floodplain

Floodplains are regularly inundated, especially during spring, but they also experience dry conditions. These complex ecosystems experience frequent disturbance and have a mosaic of young and old trees, sun and shade, high and low ground, with erratic erosion and deposition creating pockets of high fertility. Due to the disturbance and variety, riparian areas are the most productive foraging environments.

Plant	spr	sum	fall	win
Ostrich fern 1-6	▓			
Dwarf palmetto 1-10				
Mulberries 3-1–2			▓	
Pecan 5-3			▓	
Shellbark 5-7			▓	
Oaks 5-16–21			▓	
Persimmon 6-3			▓	
Pawpaw 6-5			▓	
Wild plums 6-10				
Hackberry, sugarberry 7-3–4				
Hawthorn 7-14				
Mayhaw 7-15	▓			
Kentucky coffeetree 8-2 (imm.)			▓	▓
Honeylocust 8-4			▓	
Silver maple 8-17	▓			
Boxelder 8-18	▓			
Highbush cranberry 10-5			▓	▓
Spicebush 10-13				
Black haws 11-4			▓	
Chokecherry 11-6		▓		
Black elder 11-8		▓		

Plant	spr	sum	fall	win
Gooseberry 11-9		▓		
Grapes 13-1			▓	
Greenbriers 13-4		▓		
Wisteria 13-9 flowers	▓			
Water parsnip 15-3	▓			
Ramps 16-1	▓			
American garlic 16-5	▓			
Spiderwort 17-3	▓			
Chufa 17-5			▓	
Trout lilies 18-4	▓			
Blue violet 19-1	▓			
Swamp saxifrage 19-11	▓			
Cup plant 21-5	▓			
Virginia spring beauty 21-7	▓			
Toothworts 21-13–16	▓			
Golden dock 22-7	▓			
American bellflower 23-2			▓	
Bulbous bittercress 23-6	▓			
Garlic mustard 23-13	▓			
Sochan 25-2	▓			
Virginia waterleaf 25-12	▓			
Wintercress 25-22	▓			
Cow parsnip 26-1	▓			
Mitsuba 26-3	▓			
Pennsylvania cress 26-10	▓			
Narrowleaf bittercress 26-11	▓			
Purple phacelia 26-16	▓			
Purple angelica 27-6	▓			

(Continued on the next page.)

Floodplain (continued)

Plant	spr	sum	fall	win
Aniseroot 27-11				
Harbinger of spring 28-6				
Native chervils 28-12–13				
Balloon vine 29-1				
Ground bean 29-9				
Fuzzy bean 29-11				
Hopniss 29-12				
American vetch 29-15				
Carrion flowers 29-18				
Melonette 29-25				
Hops 29-26				
Maypop 29-28				
Yellow passion flower 29-29				
Cucumber root 30-3				
Cleavers 30-8				
Tall woodmint 31-13				
Florida betony 32-2				
Woundwort 32-4				

Plant	spr	sum	fall	win
Bugleweeds 32-6				
Stinging nettle 32-7				
Giant St. John's wort 32-9				
Spanish needles 32-13				
Woodland phlox 33-10				
Clearweed 34-1				
False nettle 34-2				
Jerusalem-artichoke 34-4				
Yerba de tago 34-8				
Japanese knotweed 35-13				
Smartweeds 35-14				
Willow-leaved dock 35-16				
Tall dayflower 35-23				
Ground cherries 36-7				
Wood nettle 36-8				
Halberd-leaf rose mallow 37-10				
Epazote 37-17				
Hot mermaid 38-6				
American licorice 38-10				

Fields

These are open areas dominated by perennial and biennial herbaceous plants. They may be mowed occasionally, but not regularly like lawns. Unlike prairies, fields are created by humans eliminating natural plant communities, and the vegetation is usually composed of a mixture of native and introduced species. Field habitat most often develops on abandoned farmland, roadsides, and in vacant lots. These are good foraging areas for leafy greens and shoots in spring, and sometimes for root vegetables in autumn.

Plant	spr	sum	fall	win
Field horsetail 1-1				
Bracken fern 1-3				
Dewberry 3-9				
Field garlic 16-2				
Salsify 17-2				
Yucca 17-14				
False garlic 17-16				
Plantains 18-9–10				
Blue violet 19-1				
Dandelion 19-4				
White clover 20-2				
Common strawberry 20-8				
Bladder campion 21-10				
Sheep sorrel 22-1				
Sorrel 22-3				
Docks 22-6–9				
Comfrey 22-15				
Burdocks 22-16–18				
New England Aster 22-19				
Creeping bellflower 23-3				
Horseradish 23-9				
Dame's rocket 23-11				
White top 23-12				
Evening primrose 23-16				

Plant	spr	sum	fall	win
Thistles 24-4–11				
Chicory 24-16				
Perennial sow-thistle 24-19				
Wild lettuces 24-20–27				
Sochan 25-2				
Field pansy 25-14				
Ox-eye daisy 25-17				
Wintercress 25-22				
Cut-leaf evening primrose 25-18				
Tower mustard 25-28				
Black mustard 25-32				
Red clover 26-14				
Parsnip 26-6				
Caraway 28-4				
Cow parsley 28-9				
Wild carrot 28-11				

(Continued on the next page.)

Fields (continued)

Plant	spr	sum	fall	win
Balloon vine 29-1				
Everlasting pea 29-2				
Tuber vetchling 29-4				
Vetches 29-13–17				
Buffalo gourd 29-23				
Mints 31-2–15				
Bergamot 31-16				
Stinging nettle 32-7				
Stitchwort 32-11				
Milkweeds 33-12–13				
Jerusalem-artichoke 34-4				

Plant	spr	sum	fall	win
Asparagus 35-1				
Prairie tea 35-8				
Pokeweed 35-17				
Fireweed 35-18				
Ground cherry 36-7				
Common goldenrod 36-10				
Mugwort 37-2				
Bull nettle 37-5				
Showy evening primrose 37-19				
Canada thistle 37-20				

Yards and Lawns

These plants are short. They are more often perennials than annuals. These are some of our most accessible wild edibles, but are often mediocre in quality. For many, mowing reduces the quality. Beware of herbicide.

Plant	spr	sum	fall	win
Field garlic 16-2				
False garlic 17-16				
Grape hyacinth 17-18				
Plantains 18-9–10				
Blue violet 19-1				
Dandelion 19-4				
Tuberous false dandelion 19-6				
Hairy cat's ear 19-7				
English daisy 19-10				
Beach pennywort 19-15				
Coinleaf 19-16				
White clover 20-2				
Common dwarf dandelion 21-3				
Lyre-leaf sage 21-4				
Sheep sorrel 22-1				
Lesser celandine 22-10				
Scorzonera 24-3				

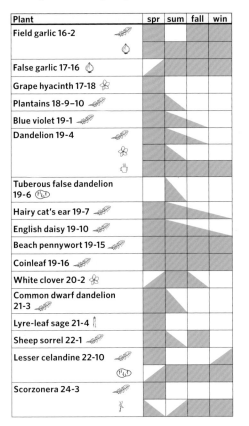

Plant	spr	sum	fall	win
Carolina dandelion 24-14				
Pansy 25-14				
Creeping yellowcress 25-21				
Shotweed 26-9				
Twin cress 26-12				
False strawberry 26-13				
Goutweed 27-9				
Pineapple weed 28-1				
Alfilaria 28-16				
Purple deadnettle 32-1				
Henbit 32-2				
Florida betony 32-3				
Stitchwort 32-11				
Drymary 33-8				
Bristly mallow 37-8				
Yellow woodsorrel 38-3				

Brushlands

These are young forests or transitory zones between field and forest. They can be found along roadsides, fence lines, abandoned fields and pastures, young forests, urban settings, and any other location where woody cover is in the process of regenerating. Brushy areas often have a mixture of native and introduced shrubs and vines along with young, mostly native trees. Oak savannahs and prairies in many areas have mostly turned into brushlands with the suppression of fire. Brushlands have many vegetables and are some of the best areas for picking wild fruits, but you must beware of herbicide spraying.

Plant	spr	sum	fall	win
Bracken fern 1-3				
Asian mulberry 3-1				
Bramble berries 3-3–9				
Hazelnuts 5-14–15				
Trifoliate orange 6-2				
Persimmons 6-3–4				
Crabapples 6-8–9				
Wild plums 6-10				
Devil's walking stick 7-2				
Black cherry 7-5				
Pin cherry 7-6				
Sweet cherry 7-7				
Cornelian-cherry 7-10				
Sassafras 7-11				
Serviceberry 7-13				
Hawthorn 7-14				
Redbud 8-1				
Robinia locusts 8-5–8				
Siberian elm 8-20				
Autumnberry 10-4				
Roses 10-7				
Agarita 10-8				
Barberry 10-11–12				
Yaupon 10-17				
Black haws 11-4				
Chokecherry 11-6				
Black elder 11-8				

Plant	spr	sum	fall	win
Gooseberry 11-9				
American black currant 11-11				
Sumacs 12-2–4				
Grapes 13-1–2				
Greenbriers 13-4				
Kudzu 13-8				
Wisteria 13-9				
Wild sarsaparilla 20-1				
Prenanthes 24-1				
Wild lettuces 24-20–27				
Musk mallow 25-7				
Yellow pimpernel 27-1				
Hairy angelica 27-8				
Wild bean 29-10				
Hopniss 29-12				
American vetch 29-15				
Air potato 29-19				
Melonette 29-25				
Hops 29-26				
Maypop 29-28				
Yellow passion flower 29-29				
Bergamot 31-16				
Giant St. John's wort 32-9				
Common milkweed 33-12				
Japanese knotweed 35-13				
Pokeweed 35-17				

Tallgrass Prairie

Tallgrass prairies are characterized by native, mostly perennial, herbaceous vegetation, although a few shrubs are commonly associated. Native tallgrass prairies once covered a large part of central North America but nearly all have been turned into cropland. Tallgrass prairie plants are found today in fields and meadows, in isolated pockets along river courses, on roadsides, and in moist valleys within shortgrass prairie regions. There is not a distinct line between tallgrass and shortgrass prairies—it is a gradual change based on moisture, temperature, and soil conditions. Restoration of tallgrass prairies is important, and foragers should be involved.

Plant	spr	sum	fall	win
Leadplant 12-6				
Large New Jersey tea 12-8				
Nodding onion 16-8				
Spiderwort 17-3				
Camas 17-20				
Shooting stars 18-8				
Blue violet 19-1				
Common strawberry 20-8				
Violet woodsorrel 20-10				
Cup plant 21-5				
New England aster 22-19				
Rattlesnake master 23-14				
Prairie-dock 23-17				
Thistles 24-4–11				

Plant	spr	sum	fall	win
Wild lettuces 24-20–27				
Compass plant 25-15				
Lousewort 25-16				
Parsnip 26-6				
Anise hyssop 31-8				
Bergamots 31-16				
Giant St. John's wort 32-9				
Common milkweed 33-12				
Prairie clovers 38-9				
American licorice 38-10				

Short and Mixed Grass Prairie

These are found primarily west of the tallgrass prairie, but also on open, dry or rocky south slopes further east. Although much has been converted to farmland, and most of the remainder is used as stock range, this habitat is much more intact than the tallgrass prairies because it tends to be less suitable for farming. Shortgrass prairies have many root vegetables; despite their lower biomass, they tend to be better foraging areas than tallgrass prairies.

Plant	spr	sum	fall	win
Prickly pears 2-2				
Silver buffaloberry 10-2				
Sand cherry 11-7				
Buffalo currant 11-10				
Leadplant 12-6				
Small New Jersey tea 12-9				
Textile and prairie onions 16-6–7				
Tall pink onion 16-9				
Prairie false dandelion 17-1				
Salsify 17-2				
Spiderworts 17-3				
Yucca 17-14				
Birdfoot violet 19-3				
Yellow prairie biscuitroot 20-3				
Winged biscuitroots 20-5–6				
Small prairie-turnip 20-11				
Texas skeletonplant 24-2				
Scarlet paintbrush 25-1				
Poppy mallows 25-4–5				

Plant	spr	sum	fall	win
White prairie biscuitroot 28-8				
Western tansy mustard 28-14				
Horsemint 31-15				
Prairie phlox 33-11				
Milkweeds 33-14–15				
Bastard toadflax 35-2				
Prairie tea 35-8				
Blue flax 35-9				
Stiff yellow flax 35-10				
Bush morning glory 35-20				
Ground cherries 36-7				
Bigfruit evening primrose 36-12				
Tarragon 37-1				
Downy paintbrush 37-3				
Scarlet globe mallow 38-1				
Rocky Mountain bee plant 38-4				
Clammyweed 38-5				
Prairie clovers 38-9				
Ground plum milkvetch 38-11				
Prairie-turnip 38-14				
Tall breadroot 38-15				

Disturbed Soil

This habitat includes human-made disturbances such as gardens, agricultural fields, construction sites, and road edges. It also refers to natural soil disturbances such as flood-scoured areas, exposed riverbanks, and tip-up mounds from fallen trees. The plants that pop up in these disturbed environments tend to be annuals or biennials and are often high-quality edibles. These areas are great for gathering leafy greens and sometimes seeds.

Plant	spr	sum	fall	win
Salsify 17-2				
Chufa 17-5				
Purple nutsedge 17-6				
Dandelion 19-4				
Coltsfoot 19-13				
Carpetweed 21-2				
Cornsalad 21-6				
Bladder campion 21-10				
Sheep sorrel 22-1				
Docks 22-6–10				
Pennycresses 23-7–8				
Scorzonera 24-3				
Thistles 24-4–11				
Nipplewort 24-12				
Japanese hawksbeard 24-13				
Chicory 24-16				
Sow-thistles 24-17–18				
Prickly lettuce 24-26				
Poverty weed 25-3				
Common mallow 25-6				
Ox-eye daisy 25-17				
Mustards (many) 25-19–40				
Wild carrot 28-11				
Southern chervil 28-12				
Tansy mustards 28-14–15				

Plant	spr	sum	fall	win
Cleavers 30-8				
Hemp-nettle 32-5				
Stinging nettle 32-7				
Romerillo 32-12				
Spanish needles 32-13				
Chickweeds 33-4–6				
Devil's claw 33-9				
Clearweed 34-1				
Quickweed 34-3				
Giant ragweed 34-7				
Yerba de tago 34-8				
Orache 34-10				
Russian tumbleweed 35-2				
Amaranths 35-4				
Kochia 35-6				
Purslane 35-7				
Prairie tea 35-8				
Horseweed 35-11				
Smartweeds 35-14				
Pokeweed 35-17				
Pellitory 35-19				
Common dayflower 35-22				
Lambsquarters 36-1				
Sunflower 36-3				
Velvetleaf 36-4				
Prickly sida 36-5				
Black nightshade 36-6				
Maple-leaved goosefoot 37-18				
Flower of an hour 38-2				
Clammy weed 38-5				

Seashores (Including Dunes and Saltmarsh)

This habitat primarily refers to seashores but similar plant communities also exist around the Great Lakes and a few of our other largest inland waters. Because of frequent disturbances, coastal habitats are fairly good for plant gathering, especially where fertility accumulates. Many of these plants are exclusive to coastal environments, but some salt-adapted plants are found inland in salty basins of semi-arid regions, or around mineral-rich springs.

Plant	spr	sum	fall	win
Glasswort 2-5				
Saltwort 4-5				
Rugosa rose 6-1				
Beach plum 6-10				
Christmas berry 10-10				
Sand cherry 11-7				
Bayberry 12-11				
Grapes 13-1				
Chive 16-3				
Seaside plantain 17-13				
Seaside arrow-grass 17-17				
Beach pennywort 19-15				
Coinleaf 19-16				
Seaside bluebells 22-13				
Seaside goldenrod 22-14				

Plant	spr	sum	fall	win
Scurvy-grass 23-5				
Sow thistles 24-17–19				
Sea lovage 27-4				
Seaside angelica 27-5				
Fennel 28-2				
Beach pea 29-8				
Seabeach sandwort 33-1				
Sea-purslane 33-2				
Orache 34-10				
Russian tumbleweed 35-2				
Sea blite 35-3				
Cocklebur 37-14				
Sea rocket 37-15				

Open water

These are plants that typically might have fish under or between them; they may be in ponds, rivers, or lakes. Because water levels fluctuate, it is not unusual to see most of these occasionally in mud flats or dried up shoreland. The diversity of plants in aquatic environments is low, but a large percentage of the species produce edible parts.

Plant	spr	sum	fall	win
Soft-stem bulrush 14-1				
Rice cutgrass 14-2				
Wild rice 14-3				
Cattail 14-5				
Great bur reed 14-6				
Calamus 14-7				

Plant	spr	sum	fall	win
American eelgrass 15-1				
Alligator weed 15-6				
Water chestnut 15-7				
Water pennywort 15-8				
Wapato 15-9				
Lotus 15-13				
Yellow pond-lily 15-14				
Water hyacinth 15-17				

Springs, Brooks, and Fens

These habitats are characterized by springwater, either free-flowing or seeping in the ground. Certain plants are especially adapted to these conditions, which tend to form isolated foraging hot spots.

Plant	spr	sum	fall	win
Watercress 15-2				
Springwater parsnip 15-4				
Brooklime 15-5				
Brook saxifrage 19-12				
Coinleaf 19-16				
Marsh-marigold 23-4				
Bulbous bittercress 23-6				
Cherokee swamp potato 26-5				
Cuckooflower 26-8				

Plant	spr	sum	fall	win
Pennsylvania cress 26-10				
Purple angelica 27-6				
Mountain angelica 27-7				
Hopniss 29-12				
Mint 31-12				
Bugleweed 32-6				
Common pennywort 37-19				
Hot mermaid 38-6				

Marsh

Marshes are characterized by full sun and wet soil with occasional but not permanent standing water. They differ from swamps in not being dominated by woody plants. Marshes may cover extensive basins, often associated with riverways, but also exist in a narrow band around open waterways. The diversity of these ecosystems is moderately low, but the biomass is high—freshwater marshes are the most productive ecosystems on Earth. A large portion of this biomass belongs to food plants.

Plant	spr	sum	fall	win
Sweet bulb-rush 14-4 (imm.)				
Cattail 14-5				
Great bur reed 14-6				
Calamus 14-7				
Water parsnip 15-3				
Wapato 15-9–10				
Water-plantain 15-11				

Plant	spr	sum	fall	win
Phragmites reed 17-8				
Seaside arrow-grass 17-17				
Coinleaf 19-16				
Pennsylvania cress 26-10				
Marsh pea 29-6				
Mint 31-12				
Woundwort 32-4				
Bugleweed 32-6				
Virginia meadow beauty 32-8				
False nettle 34-2				
Swamp lousewort 34-9				
Smartweed 35-14				
Swamp rose mallow 37-9				
Halberd-leaf rose mallow 37-10				

Swamp

These are wet areas dominated by trees and shrubs. Poorly drained swamps, especially in sandy soils, tend to become acidic. Only a specialized subset of plants can tolerate the extreme fluctuation of water levels in the floodplain swamps of large rivers. An opening in a swamp may have marsh-like vegetation, but generally the herbaceous plants are shade tolerant. Swamps tend to be moderately good but highly variable foraging areas.

Plant	spr	sum	fall	win
Red raspberry 3-5		■		
Plumboy 3-11		■		
Oaks 5-16–20			■	
Ogeche lime 6-6			■	
Red bay 7-8	■	■		
Mayhaw 7-15	■			
Highbush cranberry 10-5			■	■
Swamp rose 10-7		■		
Red currant 10-14		■		
Wild raisin 11-4			■	
Black elder 11-8		■		
Gooseberry 11-9		■		
American black currant 11-11		■		
Blue honeysuckle 11-12		■		
Dangleberry 11-17		■		
Highbush blueberry 11-19		■		
Swamp saxifrage 19-11	■	■		

Plant	spr	sum	fall	win
Marsh-marigold 23-4	■			
Bulbous bittercress 23-6	■			
Cherokee swamp potato 26-5			■	■
Chocolate root 26-17	■			
Purple angelica 27-6	■	■		
Mountain angelica 27-7	■	■		
Hopniss 29-12			■	■
Bunchberry 30-4		■		
Bugleweed 32-6			■	■
Swamp lousewort 34-9	■	■		
Jewelweed 36-2		■		
Common pennywort 37-4	■	■	■	■
Scarlet hibiscus 37-7		■		
Hot mermaid 38-6		■		

Bog

Bogs are highly acidic wetlands in which organic matter accumulates faster than it decomposes. They typically form in northern latitudes and on very nutrient-poor soils. Bog communities are highly specialized and many of the plants are rarely or never found in other habitats. Bogs have a few notable edibles but are generally low in edible biomass and diversity.

Plant	spr	sum	fall	win
Cloudberry 3-10		■		
Creeping snowberry 9-3		■	■	■
Bog cranberries 9-4			■	■
Aronias 10-16 and 11-14			■	
Wild raisin 11-4			■	
Blue honeysuckle 11-12		■		
Highbush blueberry 11-19		■		

Plant	spr	sum	fall	win
Lowbush blueberry 11-20		■		
Bilberry 11-22		■		
Sweet gale 12-10			■	■
Labrador tea 12-12	■	■	■	■
Leatherleaf 12-13	■			
Virginia meadow beauty 32-8		■		

Tundra

These open habitats develop in cold northern areas too windy for trees. The growing season is very short; spring, summer, and fall are contracted to a few weeks. Many of the berries persist from one year to the next under the snow and are available immediately upon snowmelt. On the tundra proper there isn't much plant food besides berries—but *there are tons of berries!* Additional edible species are found in wetlands, shores, and sheltered valleys or depressions in the tundra region.

Plant	spr	sum	fall	win
Cloudberry 3-10		▨	▨	
Nagoonberry 3-12		▨		
Crowberries 4-6	▨		▨	
Lingonberry 9-6	▨		▨	
Bearberry 9-8	▨		▨	
Alpine/ Arctic bearberry 9-9–10	▨	▨		
Bilberry 11-22		▨	▨	
Labrador tea 12-12		▨	▨	
Chive 16-3	▨	▨		
Mountain sorrel 18-7	▨	▨		
Wild strawberry 20-8		▨		
Alpine bistort 22-5	▨	▨	▨	
Swedish bunchberry 30-5		▨	▨	
Alpine sweetvetch 38-12	▨			

Urban Foraging

While urban areas have a lot of concrete, they also have a lot of fertility and disturbance, as well as a great variety of introduced edible landscape plants. Urban dwellers have access to a great diversity of edible plants within walking distance. Weeds of **disturbed soil** and **lawns** abound, while vacant lots and park hedges are full of **brushland** vegetation. Since wild birds and mammals (except squirrels) are much less common in cities, there is more fruit left for the human picker. The kinds and abundance of vegetation are about the same regardless of the size of the municipality—urban foraging in New York City is similar to that in a small town in rural New York.

ILLUSTRATED GLOSSARY

Abscission: The separation of two bonded parts at a pre-determined point (as when a deciduous leaf falls).

Achene: A single-seeded fruit that is dry when mature, lacks an adhering pulp or flesh, and does not open to release the seed. Most people just call this a seed (as does this guide), but technically it's a little bit more than a seed.

Acuminate: Tapering to a long, narrow, needle-like point. (F. 13, 14, 19)

Adventive: Native species that have expanded their ranges due to human-caused habitat changes. I consider these native in the areas to which they have expanded.

Aerial: In the air; plant parts growing above the ground or the water.

Alternate: Growing from opposite sides of a stalk at different points along its length (rather than at the same point as in opposite leaves). Not paired. (F. 4)

Appressed: Laying flat or nearly so against the surface from which it grows. Said mostly of hairs, spines, or leaves.

Areole: A depression on the surface of a cactus, from which spines grow.

Ascending: When said of branches, this means they are angled upward, somewhere between horizontal and vertical. (F. 36–37)

Auricle: An ear-like projection or lobe at the base of a leaf. (F. 3)

Awn: An elongated bristle, often found on the lemma of a grass seed.

Axil: The upper angle where a leaf or petiole joins a stem. (F. 4, 5)

Axillary: Found in or growing from the axil.

Banner: The uppermost petal of a typical legume flower. (F. 27)

Basal: Growing from the base of the plant, attached at or near ground level. (F. 3, 8)

Beak: A long, thin projection from a larger structure.

Berry hook: A pole or stick with a hook on the end, used to pull down and hold out-of-reach branches for fruit picking.

Biennial: A plant that normally has a two-year life cycle, spending the first year as a stalkless rosette storing energy, and using that energy to produce a flowering stalk the second year, after which the plant dies. Most biennials will spend multiple years as a rosette before flowering if the growing conditions are poor.

Blade: On a simple leaf, the thin, broad main body of the leaf designed for light collection (everything but the petiole). On a compound leaf, the entire portion of the leaf beyond the first leaflet or rachis division.

Blanch: To briefly boil a vegetable in order to destroy enzymes and kill individual cells; generally done before freezing. Also, to cover growing plants so as to keep light from them, making them grow lighter in color, more tender, and less strong in flavor.

Blickey: A berry-picking container that straps onto the waist, leaving both hands free.

Bloom: A thin waxy or powdery coating that can be rubbed off, often found on fruit and smooth stems, giving the surface a lighter hue. See *glaucous*.

Bog: A wetland in which organic matter accumulates and decomposes slowly, acidifying the water.

Boreal forest: Northern forests characterized by fir, spruce, aspen, white birch, and other northern plants.

Bract: A small, modified leaf found beneath or near a flower or flower cluster. (F. 33, 34)

Bulb: A modified bud, such as an onion, in which the leaves are enlarged and thickened to store energy. (F. 10)

Bundle scar: The smaller scars or marks within a leaf scar where vascular bundles had been attached.

Calcareous: Rich in calcium—usually said of limestone-derived soils or springwater.

Calyx: The sepals of a flower, collectively. These sometimes remain attached to mature fruit, at either the base or the end (never both). (F. 26, 35)

Cambium: The layer of dividing cells that lies between the wood and bark, and which produces both; often erroneously called "inner bark," it generally remains attached to the trunk when bark is peeled off.

Capsule: A fruit in the form of a container holding multiple seeds; usually these split open from the tip at maturity. A pod, but with a different connotation as to shape.

Carpel: One of the female units of a flower. (If the pistil has 1 carpel these are essentially the same thing, so "carpel" is most often used to refer to 1 sexual unit of a multi-carpel pistil.)

Chaff: The unwanted, inedible dried flower and fruit parts that are separated from a seed by rubbing and then removed by winnowing.

Chambered: Divided into compartments, often with hollow spaces, by transverse partitions; said of pith or hollow stalks.

Channeled: Having a groove or depression running its length; usually said of petioles. (F. 38, 39)

Ciliate: With long hairs on the margin.

Climax community: A plant community that persists indefinitely in the absence of significant environmental disturbances; the last stage in plant succession on a particular site.

Clone: A colony of genetically identical plants or stems that have propagated themselves through some form of vegetative reproduction; a clone is essentially one large plant with many stems.

Clumped: Having multiple stems tightly packed (adjacent or nearly so) on a root crown. (F. 37)

Colonial: Having multiple stems produced individually, variably spaced along a rhizome. (F. 37)

Colony: A group of many stems of the same genetic plant found growing together, spreading vegetatively. Contrast this to a population, in which many genetically different individuals inhabit an area.

Composite: A flower cluster that appears as one flower (such as dandelion) in which many tiny florets are clustered on a receptacle. Also, any plant of the Composite family *Asteraceae*, all of which share this characteristic. (F. 34)

Compound leaf: A leaf that consists of multiple leaflets connected, often by petioles (petiolules), to a central point or rachis. (F. 20–23)

Corm: The base of an upright stem, enlarged to store energy. (F. 11)

Corrugated: Having a rough surface texture formed by valleys, ridges, wrinkles, or folds. Finely corrugated is called *rugose*.

Cotyledon: Embryonic leaf inside of a seed; there are one or two. These emerge first upon germination, usually differing in shape from all subsequent leaves. Also called *seed-leaves*.

Cyme: A broad, flat-topped or convex branching cluster which is not an umbel. (F. 33)

Deciduous: Dying and falling away from the plant at the end of the growing season.

Decumbent: (Of stems) Lying along the ground at first, then sweeping upward toward the tip. (F. 37)

Decurrent: Extending down the stem from the point of attachment, usually said of leafy wings. **Dermatitis**: Rash or irritation of the skin.

Dicot: (Short for dicotyledon) One of the two major divisions within the angiosperms (typical flowering plants). Dicots generally have net-patterned veins, a main central root, and two seed-leaves (cotyledons) when germinating. Examples include maple, strawberry, dandelion, and clover.

Discrete: Clearly separated from other such structures; distinct. Usually said of leaflets.

Distal: Toward the tip or the end; away from the inside, base, or center. Contrast with *proximal*. (F. 1, 2)

Disturbance: An event that kills plants, creating a location in which new plants can grow.

Divided: (of leaves) Cut deeply and separated into smaller parts. I use divided rather than *compound* when the location, size, and shape of the divided parts is unpredictable or irregular, and when similar sections of blade may or may not be fully separated within the same leaf. (F. 18)

Double-toothed: Having large teeth with smaller teeth upon them. (F. 41)

Emergent: Growing out of (the water).

Entire: A leaf or leaflet with no divisions, lobes, or teeth. In this book, heart- or arrowhead-shaped leaves are considered entire. (F. 13–16)

Erect: For stems and branches I use this to mean more or less vertical. When I use "erect" to describe hair, I mean "perpendicular to the surface on which it is attached" regardless of gravity. Most botanists call this "spreading" but this use generates much confusion. (F. 36–37)

Fen: A wetland formed by springs or flowing groundwater.

Fiddlehead: The shoot of a fern, upon which the end parts are coiled or drooping rather than pointed. (F. 1)

Floret: One of the many tiny flowers in a composite cluster (F. 34); also, a grass flower.

Flower bud: A flower that is not ready to open; the bud that will later become a flower.

Frond: The leaf or above-ground stem of a fern. (F. 1)

Fruit leather: Thin sheets of dried fruit pulp.

Gland: An small, enlarged, and usually darkened structure that exudes a substance. (F. 41, 42)

Glaucous: Some botanists use this term to mean "bloom-coated" but I reserve it to mean, more specifically, a surface that is notably pale in color due to a coating of bloom.

Glochids: Tiny loose spines that readily detach.

Great umbel: The largest of the umbels in a compound umbel. (F. 31) (Compare to *umbellet*.)

Greens: The edible leaves or leafy portion of a plant.

Grooved: Having a small or narrow channel running its length. (F. 38, 39)

Hip: A mealy or pulpy fruit-like structure (technically not a fruit) surrounding the seeds of roses.

Incised: Appearing to be cut, with little to no space between lobes. (Said of leaves.)

Inflorescence: A flower or cluster of flowers and all that comes with it, such as stems and bracts; the whole flowering portion of the plant.

Internode: The space or distance along the stem between nodes (leaf attachment points). (F. 5)

Inulin: A non-digestible starch that can be broken down by prolonged cooking, found in many underground vegetables.

Involucre: A whorl, set, cluster, or ring of *bracts* beneath an inflorescence, flower, or fruit.

Irregular: A flower in which the members of a floral ring (petals or sepals) are not all of the same size and shape, or are not arranged with radial symmetry. (F. 27)

Jointed: With a transverse band on the stem where a leaf attaches, usually corresponding to an internal septum and sometimes a bulge. The stem angle usually changes at a joint.

Keel: The lowermost petal on typical legume flowers, between and below the *wings* (F. 27). Also, any linear ridge with a sharp or angled extremity, such as the underside of some leaf midribs. (F. 39)

Kernel: An edible seed, or the edible portion of a seed.

Lanceolate: Shaped like a lance head: much longer than wide, broadest near the base, tapering to a pointed tip. (F. 14)

Latex: A white, milky sap that dries as a rubbery substance, used to heal wounds.

Layering: Reproducing by rooting and producing new shoots where branch tips contact the soil.

Leach: To remove water-soluble compounds such as tannin through soaking material and then draining off the water.

Leaflet: One of the smaller leaves or blades within a compound leaf. (F. 20–23)

Leaf scar: The mark left on a stem or twig where a leaf or petiole was formerly attached. (F. 2)

Lenticel: A small corky spot on the bark of small trees and shrubs, used for gas exchange. (F. 2)

Linear: Long and narrow, shaped like a blade of grass. (F. 8)

Linnaean: Referring to Linnaeus, who devised the Latin binomial system often referred to as "scientific" names.

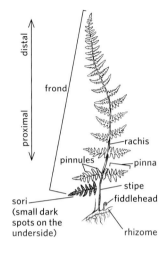

Figure 1
Pinnate fern frond

distal

proximal

frond

rachis

pinnules

pinna

stipe

sori
(small dark
spots on the
underside)

fiddlehead

rhizome

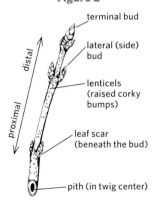

Figure 2

terminal bud

lateral (side)
bud

lenticels
(raised corky
bumps)

leaf scar
(beneath the bud)

pith (in twig center)

distal

proximal

Figure 3

sessile leaf

wing

clasping leaf

auricle

whorl

basal rosette

Figure 4

alternate leaves

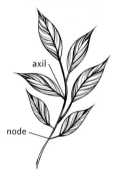

axil

node

Figure 5

paired/opposite leaves

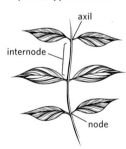

axil

internode

node

Figure 6

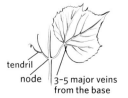

tendril

node | 3–5 major veins from the base

Lobe: An extension of a leaf blade, broadly attached rather than constricted or stalked at the base. (F. 17–19, 23)

Loment: A jointed legume pod, breaking up at maturity into one-seeded sections.

LYDS: Abbreviation for "last year's dead stalk."

Margin: The outer edge of a leaf. (F. 13–15, 19, 20)

Mesic: Refers to soils with a medium level of moisture, or the plant communities that develop on these soils. Mesic hardwood forests are usually dominated by trees such as maple, beech, basswood, elm, yellow birch, and ash.

Midrib: The enlarged main vein of a divided or lobed leaf. (F. 18)

Midvein: The main or central vein of a leaf or leaflet. (F. 17, 20)

Monocarpic: Flowering and fruiting only once, then dying.

Monocot: (Short for monocotyledon) One of the two main divisions within the angiosperms (typical flowering plants), having a single seed-leaf (cotyledon) when germinating. Examples include lilies and grasses.

Mucilage: A sticky or slimy substance, usually indicating the presence of dissolved starches.

Mucilaginous: Plants or plant parts containing mucilage, or which produce it when chewed.

Mucronate: With a short, abruptly sharp point (mucro). (F. 41)

Multi-compound: A compound leaf with a branched rachis bearing its leaflets, or a rachis bearing multiple compound or divided leafy units. (F. 23–24)

Muskeg: A bog with trees (black spruce, tamarack, cedar or pine) scattered or forming a sparse canopy.

Node: The point on a stem where one or more leaves are attached. (F. 4, 5, 21)

Nutmeat: The edible portion of a nut.

Oblanceolate: Lance-shaped, much longer than broad, but with the widest part nearer the tip.

Obovate: Egg-shaped; longer than broad with the widest part nearer the tip.

Obscure: Difficult to see; most often said of veins.

Offset: A small bulb produced beside a parent bulb (also called a *daughter bulb*).

Opposite: Growing from the same point along a stalk but on opposite sides of it; paired. (F. 5)

Ovate: Roughly egg-shaped; somewhat longer than broad, with the widest part nearer the base. (F. 13)

Palmate: (Of simple leaves) having four or more lobes spreading from a central blade area. (Of veins) having 3 or more nearly equal major veins spreading from a central point. (F. 19, 20)

Palmately compound: Having four or more leaflets radiate from the same point. (F. 20)

Panicle: A flower cluster with a compound branching pattern, the branches growing from an elongated central axis (like grapes). (F. 28)

Pappus: A tuft of feathery or hairy stuff attached to a seed to aid in wind dispersal; parachute.

Parallel: This normally has a specialized meaning in botany, referring to veins that run from the base to the tip of a leaf—arching and meeting at both points. (F. 16) Sometimes, however, veins are *literally parallel*, like you were taught in geometry (as in the veinlets of the arum family).

Parch: To heat and cook (a grain) to harden the kernel and make the chaff brittle.

Pedicel: The stem of an individual flower or fruit within a cluster. (F 29, 31–33)

Peduncle: The stem of an individual flower that is not in a cluster, or the stem of a flower cluster. (F. 28–34)

Perennial: Any plant that typically lives for more than two years.

Peltate: With the stalk attached to the underside of the leaf rather than the edge.

Perfoliate: With the stem appearing to grow through the leaf.

Petal: One of the innermost set of modified leaves of a flower, usually brightly colored. (F. 25, 26)

Petiole: The stem or stalk of a leaf. (F. 13, 15, 18, 21–24)

Petiolule: The stalk of a leaflet within a compound leaf. (F. 22)

Phenology: The timing, sequence, and co-occurrence of seasonal biological events.

Pinna: A primary division of a fern frond. (F. 1)

Pinnate: Feather-like; with leaflets, branches, or veins arranged in two rows along opposite sides of a midvein, midrib, or rachis. (F. 1, 22, 24)

Pinnule: The smallest division of a fern frond: a division of a *pinna*. (F. 1)

Pistil: The central female part of the flower, which receives the pollen. It is usually larger than the stamens (if both present). Composed of an ovary, stigma, and style. (F. 25)

Pith: The soft, spongy material found in the center of many stems. Usually not evident inside shoots. (F. 2)

Pod: A fruit containing multiple seeds that dries upon maturity and opens to release them. In this book I reject stricter definitions that are sometimes asserted, and often use **pod** in lieu of more specific pod types such as follicle, silique, legume, or capsule.

Polycarpic: Fruiting or flowering multiple times in its life; plants that do not die after flowering.

Potherb: A green eaten after boiling or steaming.

Prostrate: Laying flat against the ground.

Proximal: Toward the center or base; away from the tip. Contrast with *distal*. (F. 1, 2)

Pubescent: Covered with hairs.

Figure 7   **Figure 8**

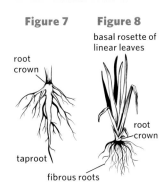

root
crown

basal rosette of linear leaves

root crown

taproot

fibrous roots

Figure 9

enlarged rhizome (rootstock)

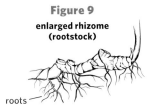

roots

Figure 10   **Figure 11**

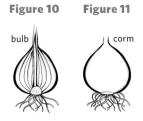

bulb

corm

Figure 12

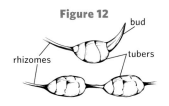

bud

tubers

rhizomes

Figure 13   **Figure 14**   **Figure 15**   **Figure 16**

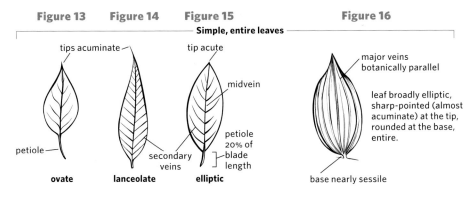

Simple, entire leaves

tips acuminate

tip acute

midvein

major veins botanically parallel

leaf broadly elliptic, sharp-pointed (almost acuminate) at the tip, rounded at the base, entire.

petiole

secondary veins

petiole 20% of blade length

ovate   **lanceolate**   **elliptic**

base nearly sessile

Figure 17

Pinnately lobed

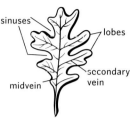

sinuses

lobes

secondary vein

midvein

Figure 18

Deeply lobed/divided

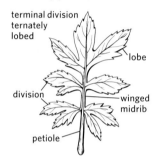

terminal division
ternately lobed

lobe

division

winged midrib

petiole

Figure 19

Palmately lobed with palmate primary veins

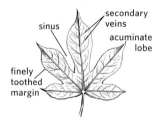

secondary veins

sinus

acuminate lobe

finely toothed margin

Figure 20

Palmately compound

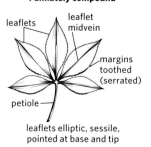

leaflets

leaflet midvein

margins toothed (serrated)

petiole

leaflets elliptic, sessile, pointed at base and tip

Puree: The pulp of fruit after the seeds, skins, and stems have been removed by straining.

Raceme: A cluster in which each flower or fruit is borne on a stem (pedicel) emanating directly from one elongated central stem (rachis). (F. 29)

Rachis: The primary stem of a compound leaf or flower cluster. There is a gray area whether or not this term should apply on a partly divided leaf; and another gray area regarding whether or not the portion proximal to the first division of a compound leaf is called a *rachis* or *petiole*. I consider both correct, but usually call it the *petiole* if its structure or angle is distinctly different from the portion distal to the first leaflet or division. (F. 22-24, 29, 30)

Radially symmetrical: (said mostly of flowers; also called *actinomorphic*) This means that there are multiple places you could cut it into two identical halves (as opposed to bilateral symmetry (*zygomorphic*), where you have 2 identical sides only if cut in a certain dimension). (F. 26)

Raphide: Needle-shaped crystals of calcium oxalate found in some plant tissues; these are often accompanied by irritating chemicals and can cause severe pain.

Ray: One of the strap-shaped florets of a composite flowerhead (F. 34). Also, one of the radiating stems of an umbel. (F. 31) In a compound umbel, the first set of rays are often called "primary rays."

Receptacle: Spongy disk-like structure of a composite flowerhead, into which the bases of the florets are embedded. (The thing left when you blow away dandelion fluff.) Also, similar structures on other plants, like the piece left behind when you pick a raspberry.

Reflexed: Curved or folded backwards.

Regular: (of flowers) With all members of each floral ring (petals and sepals) of the same size and shape and arranged in a radially symmetrical pattern. (F. 26)

Reticulated: Net-like, usually said of veinlets.

Rhizome: A horizontal stem of a perennial plant, found under or on the ground, usually thick and rooting at the nodes; it spreads the plant and stores energy. (F. 9, 12)

Rib: A pronounced vein in a leaf, or raised linear structures on other plant surfaces.

Root: The part of a plant which serves to anchor it and absorb water and dissolved nutrients. The root does not have leaves or buds. (F. 7-9)

Root crown: The transition area from root to stem. (F. 7,8)

Rootstock: A rhizome that is enlarged to store energy. (F. 9)

Rosette: A cluster of leaves radiating from a root crown, the base of a stem, or an underground stem portion terminating at the soil surface (as in many fire-adapted prairie plants). (F. 3, 8)

Sagittate: Arrow or arrowhead-shaped, with two sharp lobes at the base of the leaf.

Samara: A winged fruit, such as produced by maple, ash, and elm.

Scape: A flower stalk arising from the base and bearing no leaves.

Schizocarp: A dry fruit that breaks into single-seeded units (mericarps) when ripe, such as in *Apiaceae* and many members of *Malvaceae*.

Scurfy: Having small scales or flakes on the surface.

Secondary veins: Smaller but still prominent veins arising from the midvein. (F. 14, 15)

Sepal: One of the outer ring of modified leaves in a flower. Sepals may be green or they may be colored—in the latter case they may be hard to tell from petals. It is occasionally hard to tell a sepal from a *bract*, but bracts tend to be less uniform in size and shape. (F. 25, 26)

Serrated: With sharp teeth of somewhat uniform size.

Sessile: Attached directly, without a stalk or petiole. *Half-sessile* means the blade is inequilateral and touches the stem/rachis on one side of the midvein but not the other. (F. 3, 21, 30)

Shoot: Rapidly growing stem, like asparagus. Leaves may be present, but are not fully formed and comprise a small portion of the shoot's mass.

Simple: Not compound; a single-leaf unit. Also said of branches or inflorescences that do not branch further. (F. 13–17, 19)

Single: (of flowers or fruits) Borne on an individual stem directly from a branch; not in a cluster. (There may still be many single fruits near each other.)

Sinus: The space between two lobes of a leaf. (F. 17, 19)

Solid: Not hollow (said of stems and petioles).

Sorus: A tiny cluster of spore-producing organs (sporangia) on a fern. Plural *sori*. (F. 1)

Spike: An elongated, unbranched flower cluster in which the flowers are attached directly to a main stem without individual stems. (F. 30)

Sporangia: The spore-producing organ of a fern.

Sporophore: The spore-bearing structure on a fern, which bears *sori* (see *sorus*).

Spreading: For branches, this means growing in a horizontal plane. For stems, it means radiating from a central point in a horizontal to somewhat elevated position. For hairs on stems many botanists use it to mean "at a right angle to the stem" but I do not use it in this sense (I call this *erect hair*). I sometimes refer to "clumps of spreading hair," which means radiating from a central point (just as with stems); botanical manuals often call this by the ill-defined word "stellate." (F. 36, 37)

Spring ephemeral: A plant with a brief growing season in spring, the above-ground portion dying back in late spring or early summer.

Spur: A very short branch supporting a tuft of leaves and reproductive parts, which grows just a tiny bit each year.

Stamen: The male, pollen-bearing part of a flower. Usually multiple, consisting of a filament and anther. (F. 25)

Stigma: The enlarged tip of the pistil that receives the pollen. (F. 25)

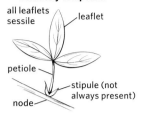

Figure 21
Ternately compound

all leaflets sessile
leaflet
petiole
stipule (not always present)
node

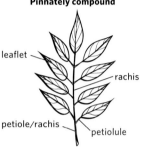

Figure 22
Pinnately compound

leaflet
rachis
petiole/rachis
petiolule

leaflets narrowly ovate to lanceolate

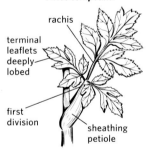

Figure 23
Twice compound

rachis
terminal leaflets deeply lobed
first division
sheathing petiole

Figure 24
Three-times pinnately compound

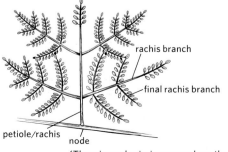

rachis branch
final rachis branch
petiole/rachis
node
(There is an abscission zone where the leaf falls off, which is how we know it's not a branch.)

Figure 25
Typical flower parts

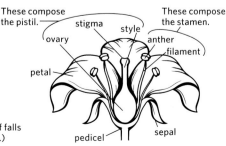

These compose the pistil.
stigma
style
These compose the stamen.
ovary
anther
filament
petal
sepal
pedicel

Figure 26

Regular flower (radially symmetrical) with 5 parts

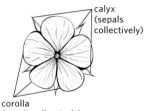

calyx (sepals collectively)

corolla (petals collectively)

Figure 27

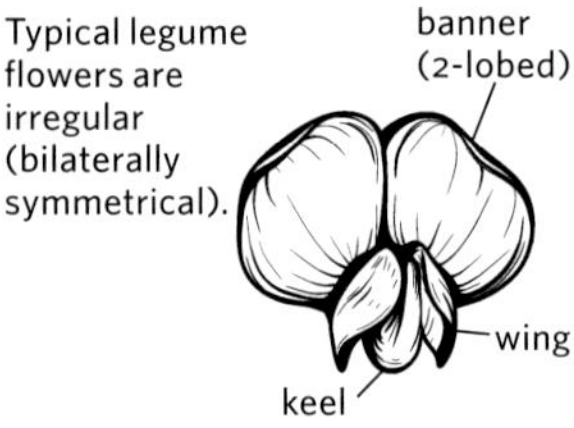

Typical legume flowers are irregular (bilaterally symmetrical).

banner (2-lobed)

wing

keel

Figure 28

Panicle

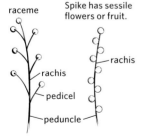

peduncle

Figure 29

raceme

Figure 30

Spike has sessile flowers or fruit.

rachis

rachis

pedicel

peduncle

Stipe: The stem of a fern frond. As if we don't already have enough words for stems. (F. 1)

Stipule: A leaf-like appendage at the base of a leaf or petiole, usually in pairs. (F. 21)

Stolon: Thin, horizontal stem that is not a storage organ, by which a plant spreads vegetatively; a runner.

Stone: A seed with a hard shell that is enclosed in a fruit; a pit.

Straining: The process of removing seeds, skins, stems, and other unwanted coarse material from fruit or berry pulp.

Style: The shaft connecting the stigma to the ovary in the pistil of a flower. (F. 25)

Sub-lobe: A lobe on a larger lobe.

Subtend: To be in a position just underneath. (F. 34)

Sucker: A shoot that arises from the root system of a woody plant, distant from the original stem.

Succulent: Thick, fleshy, and juicy.

Swamp: A wetland dominated by trees or shrubs.

Taproot: A primary, central root that grows downward rather than laterally or horizontally. (F. 7)

Taxonomic: Pertaining to the naming and classification of organisms.

Tendril: A modified leaf or branch that grasps or coils around other objects to support a vine. (F. 6)

Tepals: This is what you call sepals and petals when they can't be readily told apart.

Ternate: With 3 parts. (F. 18, 21)

Tip-up mound: The mound of dirt formed by the soil attached to an uprooted tree's roots.

Truncated: Suddenly terminating, appearing as if the end was cut off.

Tuber: An enlargement of a stem in which energy is stored; sometimes used for an enlarged portion of a root system. (F. 12)

Tumbleweed: A plant with a dense bushy form and stiff branches after dying, and that naturally detaches from the root, so that it is blown by the wind as a means of seed dispersal. Many species use this strategy.

Two-ranked: Arranged in only two opposing positions or rows rather than in right-angled sets, spiraling, or radiating in all directions. Said mostly of leaves.

Umbel: A flower cluster in which all of the pedicels (flower stalks) radiate from the same point. (F. 31-32)

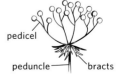

Two-ranked

Umbellet: The smallest umbels within a compound umbel. (F. 31)

Figure 31

Compound umbel

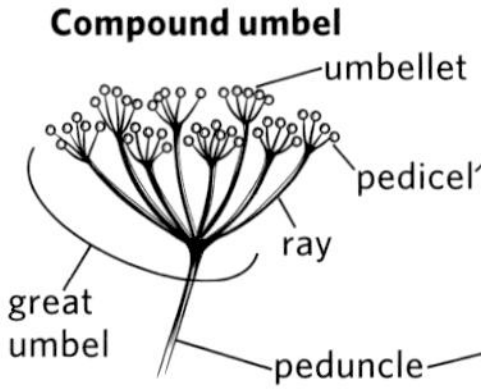

umbellet

pedicel

ray

great umbel

peduncle

Figure 32

Umbel

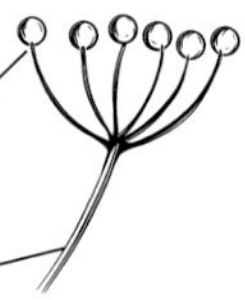

pedicel

peduncle

Figure 33

Cyme

pedicel

peduncle

bracts

USO: Abbreviation for "underground storage organ," a collective term for tubers, corms, taproots, rhizomes, bulbs, and other such things.

Vegetative: Any form of reproduction or propagation that does not involve seeds, such as spreading by tubers, suckers, or rhizomes. Also, the non-sexual portions of a plant.

Veinlets: The smallest visible veins of a leaf.

Whorl: Three or more leaves borne at the same level on a stalk, and distributed around it. (F. 3) (If they are all borne on one side they form a *tuft* or *fascicle*.

Wing: A thin, flat, usually leafy extension from a stalk, petiole, fruit, or other plant part (F. 3). Also, the two side petals on a typical legume flower (F. 27).

Wing-channel: I use this term to describe a channel formed by two wings raised on the sides of a petiole that is otherwise not channeled. (F. 39)

Winnow: To separate kernels or seeds from chaff using wind, air, or the different rates that different materials fall or travel through the air.

Winter annual: A plant with a life cycle completed in less than a year, germinating in late summer or fall, then flowering and dying the following spring.

Wool: Long, matted hair, lying on the surface rather than erect. (F. 42)

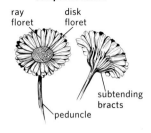

Figure 34

Composite heads

ray floret · disk floret

subtending bracts

peduncle

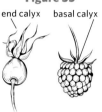

Figure 35

end calyx · basal calyx

Interpreting Descriptive Terms

Figure 36

Branch position

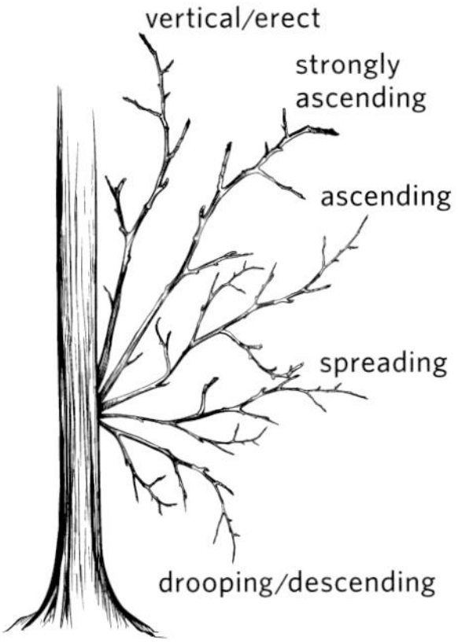

vertical/erect

strongly ascending

ascending

spreading

drooping/descending

Figure 37

Clumped stems

leaning/ascending · erect · leaning or ascending

spreading

decumbent

spreading

decumbent

creeping or prostrate

Colonial stems

erect

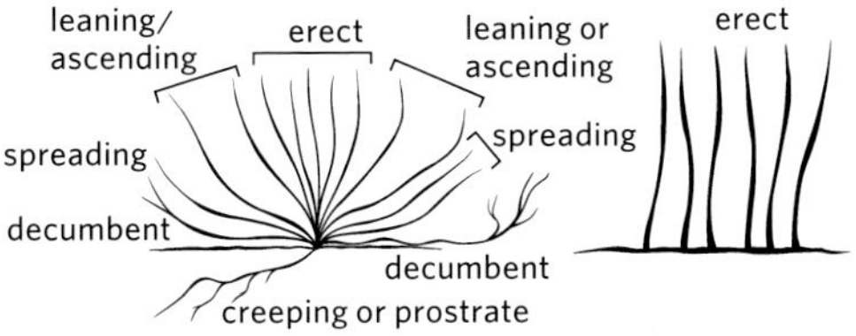

Figure 38

Stem cross sections

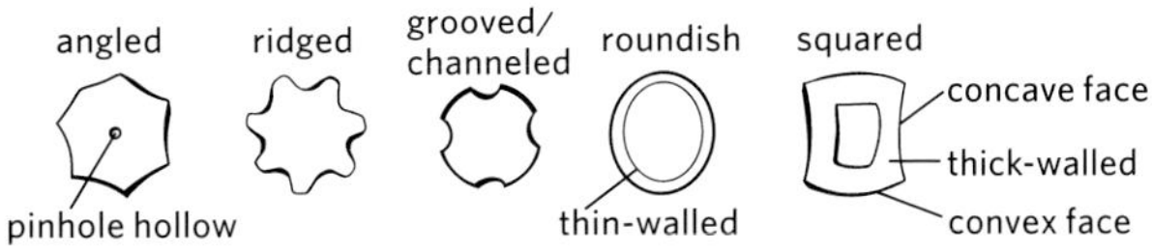

angled · ridged · grooved/channeled · roundish · squared

pinhole hollow

thin-walled

concave face

thick-walled

convex face

Figure 39

Petiole cross sections

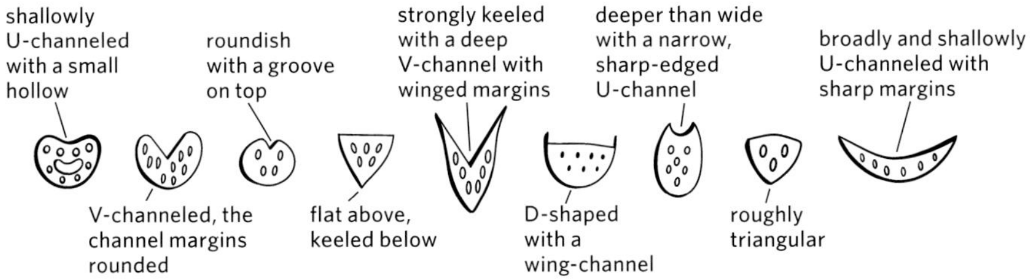

shallowly U-channeled with a small hollow

roundish with a groove on top

strongly keeled with a deep V-channel with winged margins

deeper than wide with a narrow, sharp-edged U-channel

broadly and shallowly U-channeled with sharp margins

V-channeled, the channel margins rounded

flat above, keeled below

D-shaped with a wing-channel

roughly triangular

Figure 40
Vein relief in cross section

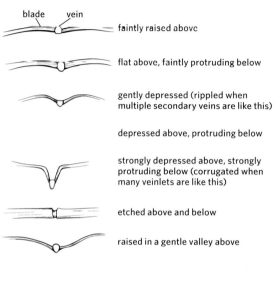

faintly raised above

flat above, faintly protruding below

gently depressed (rippled when multiple secondary veins are like this)

depressed above, protruding below

strongly depressed above, strongly protruding below (corrugated when many veinlets are like this)

etched above and below

raised in a gentle valley above

Figure 41
Leaf tooth form

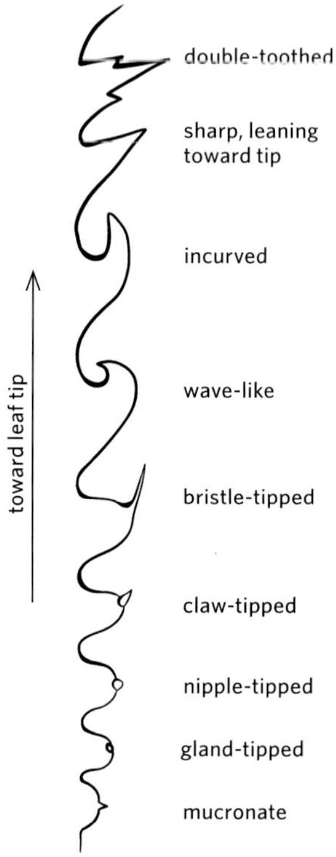

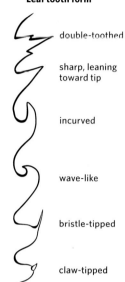

double-toothed

sharp, leaning toward tip

incurved

wave-like

bristle-tipped

claw-tipped

nipple-tipped

gland-tipped

mucronate

toward leaf tip

Figure 42
Hair arrangement

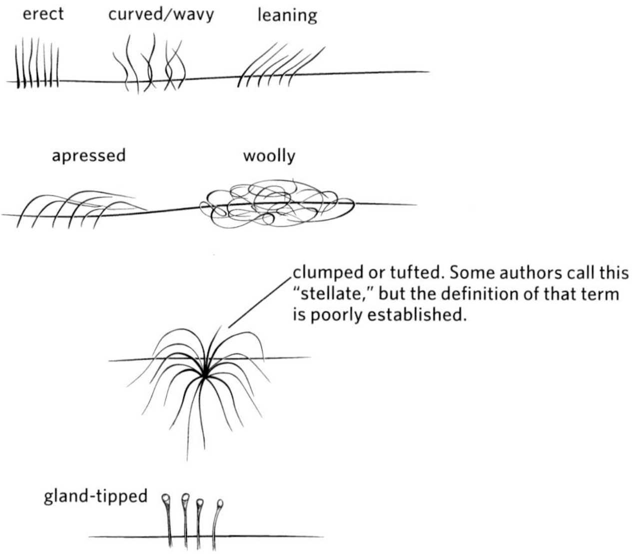

erect   curved/wavy   leaning

apressed   woolly

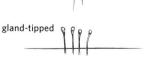

clumped or tufted. Some authors call this "stellate," but the definition of that term is poorly established.

gland-tipped

REFERENCES

There is no way that I could list, or even recall, all of the information sources I used in the 12 years over which I actively wrote this book—much less in the earlier decades I spent learning before I began the project. This list contains just a few of the resources that have proven most helpful in compiling this guide.

FLORAS comprehensively and systematically cover all of the plants known to occur in a region. All contain identification keys, and some contain technical descriptions of the plants.

Correll, Donovan and Marshall Johnston. *Manual of the Vascular Plants of Texas*. 1970. Texas Research Foundation.

Gleason, Henry and Arthur Cronquist. *Manual of the Vascular Plants of the Northeastern United States and Adjacent Canada* (2nd Edition). 1990. New York Botanical Garden Press.

Great Plains Flora Association (multi-author). *Great Plains Flora*. 1986. University Press of Kansas.

Kaul, Robert et al. *Flora of Nebraska*. 2012. University of Nebraska Press.

Weakley, Alan. *Flora of Virginia*. 2012. Botanical Research Institute of Texas.

Yatskievych, George. *Steyermark's Flora of Missouri* (3-volume set). (Revised and expanded; original by Julian Steyermark.) 1999, 2006, 2013. Missouri Botanical Garden Press.

WOODY PLANT REFERENCES

Barnes, Burton and Warren Wagner. *Michigan Trees* (revised ed.). 2004. Univ. of Michigan Press.

Godfrey, Robert. *Trees, Shrubs, and Woody Vines of Northern Florida and Adjacent Georgia and Alabama*. 1989. University of Georgia Press.

Nelson, Gil, Christopher Earle, et al. *Trees of Eastern North America*. 2014. Princeton University Press.

Smith, Welby. *Trees and Shrubs of Minnesota*. 2008. University of Minnesota Press.

Soper, James and Margaret Heimburger. *Shrubs of Ontario*. 1982. Royal Ontario Museum.

Vines, Robert. *Trees, Shrubs, and Woody Vines of the Southwest* (5th edition). 2004. Blackburn Press. (Covers the woody plants of Arkansas, Louisiana, Texas, Oklahoma, and New Mexico)

HERBACEOUS PLANT AND WILDFLOWER GUIDES: There are hundreds of regional wildflower guides, and it is a good idea to get a few pertaining to your area. Here are a few that I use often.

Chafin, Linda. *Field Guide to Wildflowers of Georgia and Surrounding States*. 2016. University of Georgia Press.

Cochrane, Theodore et al. *Prairie Plants of the University of Wisconsin-Madison Arboretum*. 2006. University of Wisconsin Press.

Cotterman, Laura et al. *Wildflowers of the Atlantic Southeast*. 2019. Timber Press.

Haddock, Michael et al. *Kansas Wildflowers and Weeds*. 2015. University Press of Kansas. (This is a hybrid flora, field guide, and encyclopedia.)

Horn, Dennis and Tavia Cathcart. *Wildflowers of Tennessee, the Ohio Valley, and the Southern Appalachians*, 3rd Edition. 2018. Partners Publishing.

Lapointe, Martine. *Plantes de milieux humides et de bord de mer du Québec et des Maritimes*. 2014. Michel Quintin. (Excellent book for northern coastal and wetland plants.)

Larson, Gary and James Johnson. *Plants of the Black Hills and Bear Lodge Mountains*. 1999. South Dakota State University Press.

Newcomb, Lawrence. *Newcomb's Wildflower Guide*. 1977. Little, Brown.

Porcher, Richard and Douglas Rayner. *A Guide to the Wildflowers of South Carolina*. 2001. University of South Carolina Press.

Royer, France and Richard Dickinson. *Weeds of the Northern US and Canada*. 2004. University of Alberta Press.

EDIBLE WILD PLANT BOOKS: There are hundreds of edible wild plant books. Most have highly repetitive coverage of the same few species; some contain significant inaccuracies. There are a few dozen that I consult regularly and from which I originally learned much of the material in this book.

Couplan, Francois. *The Encyclopedia of Edible Plants of North America*. 1998. Keats Publishing. (More of a list than an encyclopedia.)

Couplan, Francois. *Guide des plantes sauvages comestibles et toxiques*. 1994. Delachaux. (This French field guide was a major inspiration for the present book. About a third of the plants are found in our region.)

Elias, Thomas and Peter Dykeman. *Edible Wild Plants: A North American Field Guide to over 200 Natural Foods*. 1982. Outdoor Life Books.

Fernald, Merritt, and Alfred Kinsey. *Edible Wild Plants of Eastern North America*. 1943. Harper and Row. (This was the first attempt at a comprehensive guide for our region.)

Gibbons, Euell. *Stalking the Wild Asparagus* and *Stalking the Healthful Herbs*. 1962 and 1966. McKay. (These classic books are now published by Stackpole.)

Gibbons, Euell and Gordon Tucker. *Euell Gibbons' Handbook of Edible Wild Plants*. 1979. Unilaw.

Kallas, John. *Edible Wild Plants: Wild Foods from Dirt to Plate*. 2010. Gibbs Smith.

Kindscher, Kelly. *Edible Wild Plants of the Prairie: An Ethnobotanical Guide*. 1987. University Press of Kansas.

Koutsos, Theodoros. *Gathering Greens and Herbs from God's Garden*. 2020. Austin Macauley. (For southern Europe, but many of the species grow wild in our region.)

Medsger, Oliver Perry. *Edible Wild Plants*. 1939. MacMillan.

Peterson, Lee. *A Field Guide to Edible Wild Plants of Eastern and Central North America*. 1978. Houghton Mifflin. (A useful compendium despite some questionable information.)

Schofield, Janice. *Discovering Wild Plants: Alaska, Western Canada, the Northwest*. 1989. Alaska Northwest Books. (Many of our tundra, boreal, and northern seashore plants are the same.)

Tull, Delena. *Edible and Useful Plants of Texas and the Southwest*. 1987. University of Texas Press.

Turner, Nancy. *Food Plants of Interior First Peoples* and *Food Plants of Coastal First Peoples*. Royal BC Museum. (These pertain to the Pacific Northwest but many of the plants are found in our region.)

Vorderbruggen, Mark. *Foraging* (Idiot's Guides). 2015. Penguin, Random House.

ETHNOBOTANY: I consulted hundreds of ethnobotanical papers from around the world, and listing these is beyond the scope of a field guide. Shiu-ying Hu's *Food Plants of China* (Chinese University Press, 2005) was an important secondary source, as was Daniel Moerman's *Native American Ethnobotany* (Timber Press, 1998), which catalogs the plant uses listed in 206 ethnobotanical papers. A Google Scholar search can reveal additional sources.

INTERNET RESOURCES: Those I have found most helpful are listed below.

BONAP.org The Biota of North America Program has distribution maps compiled from herbarium records for every plant known to grow wild on our continent. To see the maps, click on NAPA and then select the genus of the plant you wish to research.

Eattheweeds.com Green Deane has a wealth of articles featuring a great array of wild edibles here.

Foragingtexas.com This site is run by foraging expert Mark Vorderbruggen and contains a detailed list of wild edibles found in Texas, along with photos, ID tips, and information on use.

Illinoiswildflowers.info This site covers several hundred of the common herbaceous plants in our region. The photos and descriptions are some of the most detailed and accurate anywhere.

Inaturalist.org Members can post photos, location, and other info regarding any organism observed anywhere in the world. This is a great way to research the distribution, habitat, and phenology of wild plants—but since the information is crowd-generated, the reports of certain species are highly inaccurate.

Minnesotawildflowers.info Has photos, description, habitat info, and a range map for almost every flowering plant occurring in the state.

PFAF.org This site lists a huge number of food plants from around the world, although the information associated with each one is limited.

REGULAR OLD BORING INDEX

The heading of each plant's account appears in the same form in the index (black walnut), as usually does the inverse form (walnut, black). Alternative names are sometimes listed. To reduce clutter, when multiple species in a taxonomic group are covered on one or a few consecutive pages, I sometimes index only the group name. Family names are indexed only when there is a generalized discussion of that family. Plant appearances in the keys, and some incidental mentions, are not indexed. Page numbers in **bold** refer to the location of a primary plant account. An asterisk * indicates a common name that is used for more than one species covered in this guide.

THE BEST INDEX (IN THE AUTHOR'S OPINION)

PHOTOGRAPHY AND ARTWORK CREDITS

I would like to express my sincere gratitude to each of the following photographers, who generously allowed use of their photographs, as listed below. They helped produced a better-quality book for every reader.

Jesse Akozbek: whorled stonecrop flowers, (p. 508)

Kim Calhoun: stalk of Carolina dandelion (p. 367, upper left)

Erica Davis: shoot of field pennycress (p. 343, upper right); rosette of whitetop (p. 347, lower right); rosette of scorzonera (p. 360, bottom center); rosette of blue lettuce (p. 375, upper left); rosette of poverty weed (p. 382, top); shoot of white twisted stalk (p. 595, center)

Gregg Davis: cane cholla fruit (p. 44, top center)

Louis Dutrieux: horseradish flowers (p. 344)

Jenn Dyson: glasswort in fall color (p. 45, right)

Todd Elliott: American mulberry fruit (p. 48, lower left); *Acorus calamus* leaf cross section (p. 209); Carolina dandelion flower (p. 367, upper right)

Adam Haritan: all three photos of cornelian cherry (p. 106); fox grape with fruit (p. 192, middle right); narrow-leaf bittercress rosette (p. 432, lower left)

Delaney Humphrey: prickly sida flowers (p. 605)

Jeffery Karafa: bearberry flowers (p. 133)

Jill Lipoti: giant hogweed flowering (p. 421, lower left)

Scott Matthewman: dwarf black haw (p. 159, lower right)

John Mcluckie: young field pepperweed plant (p. 404, bottom left)

Scott O'Donnell: lingonberry flowers (p. 131)

Eric Powell: saw palmetto fruit (p. 40)

Joshua Price: rosette of small prairie turnip (p. 300, bottom); author photo (p. 736)

Myrica Price: winnowing wild rice (p. 27)

Haijun Qiu: rosette of high mallow (p. 387, lower right)

Brooke Reutinger: flowers of Appalachian bellflower (p. 615)

Ryan Sealy: nagoonberry flower (p. 57)

Emily Summerbell: trifoliate orange flowers (p. 87)

Bob Whyte: Japanese honeysuckle berries (p. 196)

Steven Zoromski: wild parsnip rash (p. 23)

All line drawings by **Amy Schmidt** of Old Soul Tattoo Studio LLC (oldsoulamy@gmail.com)

OTHER BOOKS BY SAMUEL THAYER

Samuel Thayer's *Forager's Harvest* series revolutionized modern foraging information in North America by giving readers in-depth, detailed chapters on every plant. In these pages the author battles myths, clears up controversies, and reveals obscure but fabulous foods. His clear instructions share details and insights that only experience can bring to light. Crisp color photos and thorough descriptions make the plants accessible to beginners and seasoned gatherers alike. Deepen your foraging journey with these classic books!

— Order from foragersharvest.com or your favorite bookseller. —

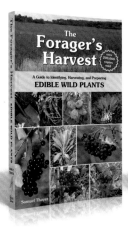 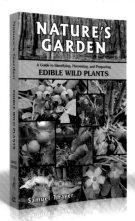 

The Forager's Harvest (2006)		Nature's Garden (2010)		Incredible Wild Edibles (2017)	
Basswood	Parsnip	Acorns	Hazelnuts	Black mustard	Maple
Black locust	Pin cherry	Amaranth	Honewort	Bladder	Miner's lettuce
Burdock	Serviceberry	American lotus	(mitsuba)	campion	Mint
Butternut	Sheep sorrel	Aronia	Jerusalem-	Blackberry	Mulberry
Carrion flower	Siberian elm	Autumnberry	artichoke	Dewberry	Pawpaw
Cattail	Spring beauty	Black cherry	Mayapple	Black raspberry	Persimmon
Chokecherry	Stinging nettle	Black	Maypop	Red raspberry	Poke
Common	Sumac	huckleberry	New Jersey tea	Thimbleberry	Prairie turnip
milkweed	Swamp	Black	Ox-eye daisy	Wineberry	Purple poppy
Evening	saxifrage	nightshade	Prenanthes	Salmonberry	mallow
primrose	Thistle	Blueberry /	Prickly pear	Nagoonberry	Purslane
Goosefoot /	Virginia	Huckleberry	Salsify	Cloudberry	Quickweed
Lambsquarters	waterleaf	Bugleweed	Sandcherry	Calamus	Rose
Ground bean	Wapato	Bunchberry	Solomon's seal	Caraway	Sassafras
Highbush	Wild grape	Chicory	Sow-thistle	Chickweed	Shepherd's
cranberry	Wild Leek	Cow parsnip	Toothwort	Chufa	purse
Hopniss	(Ramp)	Cranberry /	Trout lily	Creeping	Sochan
Marsh marigold	Wild rice	Lingonberry	Walnuts	bellflower	Strawberry
Nannyberry	Wood nettle	Dandelion	Wild carrot	Fennel	spinach
Ostrich fern		Dock	Wild lettuce	Wild Garlic	Sweetroot
		Elderberry	Wild plum	Gooseberry	Violet
		False Solomon's	Wild Strawberry	Hickory	Watercress
		seal	Wood sorrel	Hops	Water parsnip
		Garlic mustard		Japanese	Wild radish
		Hackberry /		knotweed	Wintercress
		Sugarberry		Kentucky	
				coffeetree	

ABOUT THE AUTHOR

SAMUEL THAYER has been avidly gathering and eating wild plants since early childhood. At the age of eighteen he purchased some cheap land in remote northern Wisconsin where he built a log cabin to pursue his homesteading dreams. A year later he led his first edible plant walks.

Today Sam is an award-winning author and internationally recognized authority on edible wild plants who speaks and teaches around the United States. He makes maple syrup and hickory nut oil, harvests wild rice, and runs a small organic orchard featuring apples and several native fruits and berries. He lives in rural northern Wisconsin with his wife and three children in an off-grid log home, where they manage their land for wildlife and edible native plants. He still likes to roam the woods in search of wolf tracks, wildflowers, and salamanders.